H O L M A N
I L L U S T R A T E D
P O C K E T
B I B L E
CONCORDANCE

P O C K E T R E F E R E N C E
E D I T I O N

HOLMAN
CHRISTIAN STANDARD BIBLE®

Holman Pocket Bible Concordance
© 2005 by Holman Bible Publishers
Nashville, Tennessee
All rights reserved

Based on the Holman Christian Standard Bible®
Copyright © 1999, 2000, 2002, 2003
Holman Bible Publishers

ISBN: 978-0-8054-9452-5

Dewey Decimal Classification: 220.3
Subject Heading: Bible—Dictionaries

Printed in China
6 7 8 9 10 11 12   20 19 18 17 16

INTRODUCTION TO THE
HOLMAN POCKET BIBLE CONCORDANCE

What is a concordance?

A concordance is a listing that allows you to find where words occur in a literary work—in this case, the Bible. Each listing will show a word, abbreviated, in the context of the words that come before and after. The context helps you recognize the passage. For example, here are some of the entries under WORLD:

yet the **w** did not recognize Him.	Jn 1:10
who takes away the sin of the **w**!	Jn 1:29
For God loved the **w** in this way:	Jn 3:16
His Son into the **w** that He might	Jn 3:17
this really is the Savior of the **w**.	Jn 4:42

The "**w**" is the abbreviation for "world." If you were using the concordance, you might recognize the third one as the one you were looking for. The concordance tells you that this phrase occurs in John 3:16.

There are three kinds of Bible concordances. An abridged concordance contains a selection of key words and a partial list of their occurrences. The intention is to have all the words that a student of the Bible might be expected to need in order to find key passages in the Bible. For example, an abridged concordance would include the word SHEPHERD and a reference to Psalm 23:1, "The LORD is my **s**." An abridged concordance might also include descriptions of people and places and a partial listing of where they appear in the Bible. The *Holman Pocket Bible Concordance* is an abridged concordance. Any concordance found in the back of a study Bible is also an abridged concordance.

A "complete" or "comprehensive" concordance includes all the words in the Bible with the exception of certain common words such as "the" and "and." Of the words that are included, all occurrences are listed. That is, in an HCSB comprehensive concordance under SHEPHERD all 73 occurrences would be listed. There would also be separate entries for SHEPHERDED, SHEPHERDESS, SHEPHERDING, SHEPHERD'S, and SHEPHERDS.

An "exhaustive" concordance is like a comprehensive concordance, except that it will connect each indexed word to the Hebrew, Aramaic, or Greek word from which it is derived. For example, in many exhaustive concordances the word "world" in John 3:16 is indexed to Greek word number 2889 in Strong's lexicon, which is included in the back of the concordance.

How the Holman Pocket Bible Concordance was created.

There are 718,394 words in the Holman Christian Standard Bible, made up from a vocabulary of about 10,600 different words and names. This concordance indexes 48,893 words, plus 1,084 paragraphs of biographical and geographical information, from a vocabulary of 6,241 different words and names. So this *Holman Pocket Bible Concordance* references nearly 60 percent of the words and names occurring in the Holman Christian Standard Bible.

We worked prayerfully to provide access to all the most familiar and theologically important passages of the Bible. Of course, every word of the Bible is important, but there are certain passages that readers and theologians turn to again and again for comfort, instruction, and "training in righteousness." We looked at those passages and considered what words you might think of when you look for them.

We also included other less familiar passages containing certain theologically important words so that you could use this concordance to conduct word studies. For example, under DIVORCE you can find the original teaching in Deuteronomy, the comment in Malachi, and Jesus' teachings in Matthew.

Some phrases are listed that you might find helpful, such as I AM and SON OF MAN. There are also biographical and geographical entries that give a brief explanation of the person or place followed by some annotated references. If there is more than one person or place with that name, there are separate numbered entries. For example, there are three persons named James: the Apostle, son of Zebedee; the Apostle, son of Alphaeus; and the brother of Jesus.

How to use a concordance.

One way that you may use a concordance is to find a passage; you know some of the words in it, but you can't quote it exactly and you don't know where it's found. Say, for example, that you are thinking of the passage that says something about our being representatives of Christ to the world, and that we are appealing to people to be reconciled to God. You would look it up under the significant words: "representative," "appeal," "reconcile." Note that you should expect to look under the root word "appeal" rather than the derived form "appealing," and that you need to look under the verb rather than the noun. Realize, too, that it would be unlikely that you could find the verse you're looking for under common words such as "Christ" or "people" or "God."

As it turns out, you wouldn't find it under "representative," but under APPEAL (v) you would find the phrase "God is a-ing through us" in 2 Corinthians 5:20, where it says, "Therefore, we are ambassadors for Christ; certain that God is appealing through us, we plead on Christ's behalf, 'Be reconciled to God.' "

The other way you might use this concordance is to do a word study. For example, after reading 2 Corinthians 5:20, you might want to know more about how the Bible uses the word "reconcile." You would find nine entries under RECONCILE, plus another four under RECONCILIATION. If you were to read all of those passages in context, you would learn something about reconciliation in the Bible.

And I pray this: that your love will keep on growing in knowledge and every kind of discernment, so that you can determine what really matters and can be pure and blameless in the day of Christ, filled with the fruit of righteousness that comes through Jesus Christ, to the glory and praise of God. (Philippians 1:9-11)

David K. Stabnow
January 2005

A

AARON

Levite, brother of Moses (Ex 4:14; 6:16-20). Spokesman for Moses (4:14-16; 7:1-2). Consecrated (Ex 29) and ordained (Lv 8) as priest (Ex 28:1; 1Ch 6:49; Heb 5:1-4; 7). Made golden calf (Ex 32). Died outside the promised land (Nm 20:1-12,22-29; 33:38-39).

ABADDON

Your faithfulness in **A**?	Ps 88:11
Sheol and **A** lie open before the LORD	Pr 15:11
his name in Hebrew is **A**,	Rv 9:11

ABANDON

because they **a-ed** the covenant	Dt 29:25
I will **a** them and hide My face	Dt 31:17
certainly not **a** the LORD	Jos 24:16
a-ed the LORD, ... who had brought	Jdg 2:12
the LORD has **a-ed** us	Jdg 6:13
LORD will not **a** His people,	1Sm 12:22
a-ing their tents, horses,	2Kg 7:7
a-ed all the commandments	2Kg 17:16
I will **a** the remnant	2Kg 21:14
but if you **a** Him, He will **a** you.	2Ch 15:2
For You will not **a** me to Sheol;	Ps 16:10
do not leave me or **a** me, God of my	Ps 27:9
or **a** His heritage,	Ps 94:14
to David, a promise He will not **a**:	Ps 132:11
Don't **a** wisdom,	Pr 4:6
I have **a-ed** My house;	Jr 12:7
all who **a** You will be put to shame.	Jr 17:13
a-ed the love (you had) at first.	Rv 2:4

ABBA

He said, "**A**, Father!	Mk 14:36
we cry out, "**A**, Father!"	Rm 8:15
crying, "**A**, Father!"	Gl 4:6

ABEDNEGO

Daniel's companion; originally called Azariah (Dn 1:7; 3:12-30).

ABEL

Shepherd, second son of Adam; brought acceptable sacrifice; was murdered (Gn 4:2-8; Mt 23:35; Heb 11:4).

ABHOR

LORD **a-s** a man of bloodshed	Ps 5:6
He **a-ed** His own inheritance.	Ps 106:40
I hate and **a** a falsehood,	Ps 119:163
to one **a-ed** by people,	Is 49:7
who **a** justice	Mc 3:9

ABHORRENT

shepherds are **a** to Egyptians.	Gn 46:34

ABHORRENTLY

ashamed when they acted so **a**?	Jr 6:15; 8:12

ABIATHAR

High Priest who was faithful to David (1Sm 22:20-23; 2Sm 15:24-29) but supported Adonijah instead of Solomon (1Kg 1:7) and was deposed (2:26-35).

ABIGAIL

Intelligent wife of the fool Nabal; pled for his life; married David after Nabal died (1Sm 25).

ABIHU

Priest (Ex 28:1), son of Aaron (6:23), died for offering unauthorized fire (Lv 10:1-2; Nm 26:60-61).

ABIJAH

1. Son of Samuel (1Sm 8:2).
2. Tragic son of King Jeroboam of Israel (1Kg 14:1,13).
3. Son of Rehoboam, King of Judah (2Ch 13). Also known as Abijam (1Kg 15:1-8).

ABILITY

filled him with ... **a** in every craft	Ex 31:3
my own **a** have gained this wealth	Dt 8:17
each according to his own **a**.	Mt 25:15
as the Spirit gave them **a**	Ac 2:4
according to his **a**, determined	Ac 11:29
according to their **a**	2Co 8:3

ABIMELECH

1. King of Gerar at the time of Abraham (Gn 20:1-18; 21:22-32).
2. King of Gerar at the time of Isaac (Gn 26:1-31).

3. Son of Gideon, tried to become king of Shechem (Jdg 9).

ABINADAB

1. David's brother (1Sm 17:13).

2. Saul's son (1Ch 9:39; 10:2).

3. Owner of the house where the ark resided (1Sm 7:1-2; 2Sm 6:3-4).

ABISHAG

Shunammite wife in David's old age (1 Kg 1:3,15; 2:17-22).

ABISHAI

David's nephew (1Ch 2:16) and leader among his warriors (11:20). Wanted to kill Saul (1Sm 26:8).

ABLAZE

Weren't our hearts a within us   Lk 24:32

ABLE

count the stars, if you are a	Gn 15:5
Moses chose a men	Ex 18:25
God is a to raise up children	Mt 3:9
Are you a to drink the cup	Mt 20:22
the Lord is a to make him stand.	Rm 14:4
a to instruct one another.	Rm 15:14
tempted beyond what you are a,	1Co 10:13
a to make every grace overflow	2Co 9:8
Now to Him who is a to do	Eph 3:20
persuaded that He is a to guard	2Tm 1:12
a to help those who are tested.	Heb 2:18
He is a to deal gently	Heb 5:2
He is always a to save	Heb 7:25
to Him who is a to protect you	Jd 24
a to open the scroll	Rv 5:3

ABNER

Saul's cousin and commander of his army (1Sm 14:50). At first supported Saul's son Ish-bosheth (2Sm 2:8-9) but defected to David (3:6-21). Killed by Joab and mourned by David (3:22-39).

ABNORMALLY

Last of all, as to one a born,   1Co 15:8

ABOLISH

They will a the daily sacrifice   Dn 11:31

ABOMINATION

committed all these a-s,   Lv 18:27

they have both committed an a.	Lv 20:13
all the a-s of the nations	1Kg 14:24
imitating the a-s of the nations	2Kg 16:3
imitating the a-s of the nations	2Kg 21:2
Milcom, the a of the Ammonites.	2Kg 23:13
there are seven a-s in his heart.	Pr 26:25
You will see even greater a-s.	Ezk 8:6
the a of desolation will be on a wing	Dn 9:27
and set up the a of desolation.	Dn 11:31
the a of desolation is set up,	Dn 12:11
see the a that causes desolation,	Mt 24:15
see the a that causes desolation	Mk 13:14

ABOUND

when their grain and new wine a.   Ps 4:7

ABOVE

the LORD is God in heaven a	Dt 4:39
A all, fear the LORD	1Sm 12:24
the name that is a every name,	Php 2:9
Set your minds on what is a,	Col 3:2
A all, {put on} love	Col 3:14

ABRAHAM

Born Abram son of Terah in Ur, Mesopotamia; married Sarai, then lived in Haran (Gn 11:31; Ac 7:2-4). Called to Canaan and given a promise of progeny and prosperity (Gn 12:1-3). Lied to Pharaoh in Egypt about Sarai (12:10-20). Separated from his nephew Lot (Gn 13). Rescued Lot (14:1-16) and was blessed by Melchizedek (14:17-20; Heb 7:1-10). God declared him righteous because of his faith (Gn 15:6; Rm 4:3,20-22; Gl 3:6; Jms 2:23).

Fathered Ishmael by Hagar (Gn 16). Name changed (17:5); circumcised (17:9-27; Rm 4:9-12). Visited by angels (Gn 18); promised a son with Sarah (18:9-14; cp. 17:15-19). Lied to Abimelech in Gerar about Sarah (Gn 20). Fathered Isaac (21:1-7). Sent Hagar away at Sarah's request (21:8-14). Tested by God concerning Isaac (Gn 22; Heb 11:17-19; Jms 2:21-24). Buried Sarah at Machpelah (Gn 23). Sent servant to find wife for Isaac (24:1-9). Died and was buried with Sarah (25:7-11).

God promised a covenant with Abraham, then made it and confirmed it (Gn 12:1-3; 13:14-17; 15; 17; 22:15-18). It was the basis of future blessings for many people (Ex 2:24; Lv 26:42; 2Kg 13:23; Ps 105:6-11; Ac 3:25).

ABRAM

Given name of Abraham before God changed it (Gn 11:26; 17:5).

ABSALOM

Son of David by Maacah (2Sm 3:3). Known for his looks and hair (14:25-26). Killed Amnon for raping Tamar and was banished by David (2Sm 13). Reinstated by David at Joab's insistence (2Sm 14). Rebelled, ousted David (2Sm 15–17). Killed by Joab (18:9-15) despite David's warning (18:5). Greatly mourned by David (18:33–19:4).

ABSENCE

| even more in my a, | Php 2:12 |

ABSENT

a in body but present in spirit,	1Co 5:3
but bold toward you when a.	2Co 10:1
I may be a in body, but	Col 2:5

ABSTAIN

he is to a from wine and beer.	Nm 6:3
a from food offered to idols,	Ac 15:29
a from sexual immorality,	1Th 4:3
a from fleshly desires	1Pt 2:11

ABSTINENCE

| demand a from foods that God created | 1Tm 4:3 |

ABUNDANCE

Seven years of great a	Gn 41:29
bearing spices, gold in great a,	1Kg 10:2
He gives food in a.	Jb 36:31
the a of the rich permits him no sleep	Ec 5:12
one's life is not in the a	Lk 12:15
have life and have it in a.	Jn 10:10
their a of joy ... overflowed	2Co 8:2
whether in a or in need.	Php 4:12
in full, and I have an a.	Php 4:18

ABUNDANTLY

| The LORD will make you prosper a | Dt 28:11; 30:9 |
| This Spirit He poured out on us a | Ti 3:6 |

ABUSED

| a her all night | Jdg 19:25 |

ABYSS

not to banish them to the a.	Lk 8:31
Who will go down into the a?	Rm 10:7
The key to the shaft of the a	Rv 9:1
beast that comes up out of the a	Rv 11:7
He threw him into the a,	Rv 20:3

ACCENT

| your a gives you away." | Mt 26:73 |

ACCEPT

He wouldn't have a-ed	Jdg 13:23
Naaman urged him to a it,	2Kg 5:16
Should we a only good from God	Jb 2:10
the LORD a-ed Job's {prayer}.	Jb 42:9
I will not a a bull	Ps 50:9
My son, if you a my words	Pr 2:1
A my instruction	Pr 8:10
they would not a discipline.	Jr 2:30
if you're willing to a it,	Mt 11:14
Not everyone can a this saying,	Mt 19:11
yet no one a-s His testimony.	Jn 3:32
This ... is hard! Who can a it?	Jn 6:60
a one another,	Rm 15:7
you will not a any other view.	Gl 5:10
a-ing one another	Eph 4:2; Col 3:13
a an accusation against an elder	1Tm 5:19
a him as you would me.	Phm 17
a-ed with joy the confiscation	Heb 10:34

ACCEPTABLE

the meditation of my heart be a	Ps 19:14
who fears Him ... is a to Him.	Ac 10:35
my service for Jerusalem may be a	Rm 15:31
Food will not make us a to God.	1Co 8:8
Look, now is the a time;	2Co 6:2
spiritual sacrifices a to God	1Pt 2:5

ACCEPTANCE

what will their a mean	Rm 11:15
and deserving of full a:	1Tm 1:15
trustworthy and deserves full a.	1Tm 4:9

ACCESS

| a by faith into this grace | Rm 5:2 |

we both have a by one Spirit — Eph 2:18
boldness, a, and confidence — Eph 3:12

ACCIDENTALLY
killed his neighbor a — Dt 4:42; 19:4

ACCOMPANY
prophesy a-ied by lyres, harps, — 1Ch 25:1
singing a-ied by cymbals, harps, — Neh 12:27
signs will a those who believe: — Mk 16:17

ACCOMPLISH
zeal of the LORD of Hosts will
  a this. — 2Kg 19:31
it will a what I please, — Is 55:11
I watch over My word to a it." — Jr 1:12
except what Christ has a-ed — Rm 15:18

ACCORDING
living creatures a to their kinds: — Gn 1:24
Repay them a to the work — Ps 28:4
not ... repaid us a to our offenses. — Ps 103:10
be done for you a to your faith! — Mt 9:29
be done to me a to your word. — Lk 1:38
each one a to his works: — Rm 2:6
who do not walk a to the flesh — Rm 8:4
zeal ... but not a to knowledge. — Rm 10:2
A to the grace given to us, — Rm 12:6
distributions of gifts from the
  Holy Spirit a to His will. — Heb 2:4
A to His great mercy, He has — 1Pt 1:3
ask anything a to His will, — 1Jn 5:14
were judged a to their works — Rv 20:12

ACCOUNT (n)
a king who wanted to settle a-s — Mt 18:23
to you on a of My name, — Jn 15:21
but sin is not charged to one's a — Rm 5:13
each of us will give an a — Rm 14:12
charge that to my a. — Phm 18
Him to whom we must give an a. — Heb 4:13
as those who will give an a, — Heb 13:17
They will give an a — 1Pt 4:5

ACCOUNT (v)
No a-ing was required — 2Kg 12:15
But no a-ing is to be required — 2Kg 22:7
a for every careless word — Mt 12:36

ACCOUNTABILITY
thinks: "There is no a, — Ps 10:4

ACCOUNTABLE
You can hold me personally a! — Gn 43:9
but I will hold the watchman a — Ezk 33:6

ACCUMULATE
will a teachers for themselves — 2Tm 4:3

ACCURATE
an a weight is His delight. — Pr 11:1
taught ... about Jesus a-ly, — Ac 18:25

ACCURSED
trained in greed. A children! — 2Pt 2:14

ACCUSATION
Who can bring an a — Rm 8:33
an a against an elder — 1Tm 5:19

ACCUSE
testifies against someone a-ing
  him of a crime, — Dt 19:16
He will not always a {us} — Ps 103:9
let an a-r stand at his right hand. — Ps 109:6
Don't a anyone without cause, — Pr 3:30
I will not a {you} forever, — Is 57:16
who had maliciously a-d Daniel — Dn 6:24
standing at his right side to a — Zch 3:1
in order to a Him — Mt 12:10; Mk 3:2
while He was being a-d — Mt 27:12
They began to a Him, — Lk 23:2
Your a-r is Moses, — Jn 5:45
thoughts either a or excuse — Rm 2:15
no opportunity to a us. — 1Tm 5:14
not a-d of wildness or rebellion. — Ti 1:6
so that when you are a-d, — 1Pt 3:16
the a-r of our brothers — Rv 12:10
the one who a-s them — Rv 12:10

ACHAIA
he wanted to cross over to A, — Ac 18:27
they are the firstfruits of A — 1Co 16:15

ACHAN
  Sinned at Jericho; stoned (Jos 7; 1Ch 2:7).

ACHIEVE
your plans will be a-d. — Pr 16:3
thought they had a-d their purpose; — Ac 27:13
Israel, ... has not a-d the law. — Rm 9:31

ACHISH
1. King of Gath before whom David
feigned madness (1Sm 21:10-15). Later, he
favored David (1Sm 27-29).

2. King of Gath to whom Shimei's slaves defected (1Kg 2:39).

ACHOR
called the Valley of A   Jos 7:26

ACHSAH
Caleb's daughter, given to his nephew Othniel for valor, and granted watered land (Jos 15:15-19; Jdg 1:12-15).

ACKNOWLEDGE
Then I a-d my sin to You	Ps 32:5
a that the Most High is ruler	Dn 4:25
I will also a him before My Father in heaven	Mt 10:32
the Son of Man will also a him	Lk 12:8
will a his name before My Father	Rv 3:5

ACQUAINTANCE
an object of dread to my a-s;   Ps 31:11

ACQUIRE
move about, and a property	Gn 34:10
he must not a many horses	Dt 17:16
He must not a many wives	Dt 17:17
you will also a Ruth	Ru 4:5
A wisdom	Pr 16:16
I a-d male and female servants	Ec 2:7
What you a, you cannot save,	Mc 6:14
deacons a a good standing	1Tm 3:13

ACQUIT
I know You will not a me.	Jb 9:28
A-ting the guilty and condemning the just	Pr 17:15

ACROSS
near the Jordan a from Jericho.	Nm 22:1
their inheritance a the Jordan	Nm 34:15
And it is not a the sea,	Dt 30:13

ACT (n)
an outstretched arm and great a-s	Ex 6:6
If a thief is caught in the a	Ex 22:2
she wasn't caught (in the a);	Nm 5:13
deeds and mighty a-s like Yours?	Dt 3:24
my guilty a-s are not hidden	Ps 69:5
all people of Your mighty a-s	Ps 145:12
Praise Him for His powerful a-s;	Ps 150:2
this woman was caught in the a	Jn 8:4
Males committed shameless a-s	Rm 1:27
linen represents the ... a-s of the	Rv 19:8

ACT (v)
Does He speak and not a,	Nm 23:19
He a-ed like a madman	1Sm 21:13
Why do you a this way?	1Kg 1:6
trust in Him, and He will a,	Ps 37:5
they refuse to a justly.	Pr 21:7
will bring every a to judgment,	Ec 12:14
I a, and who can reverse it?	Is 43:13
I a-ed for the sake of My name,	Ezk 20:9
not for your sake that I will a,	Ezk 36:22
these words of Mine and a-s	Mt 7:24
hears My words, and a-s	Lk 6:47
both to will and to a	Php 2:13
I had a-ed in unbelief,	1Tm 1:13
how people ought to a	1Tm 3:15
but a doer who a-s	Jms 1:25
a as those who will be judged	Jms 2:12
He was also given authority to a	Rv 13:5

ACTION
a-s are weighed by Him.	1Sm 2:3
get your minds ready for a,	1Pt 1:13

ACTIVE
You see that faith was a   Jms 2:22

ADAM
First man. Created by God (Gn 1:26-27; 2:7). Named animals (2:18-20). Given Eve (2:21-25). Failed to obey and was evicted (1:15-17; 3:6-24; Rm 5:14; 1Co 15:22). Died at 930 years (Gn 5:3-5).

ADD
You must not a anything	Dt 4:2
we have a-ed to all our sins	1Sm 12:19
I will a 15 years to your life.	2Kg 20:6
struggle a-s nothing to it.	Pr 10:22
no a-ing to it or taking from it.	Ec 3:14
by a-ing one thing to another	Ec 7:27
the LORD has a-ed misery	Jr 45:3
Can any of you a a single cubit	Mt 6:27
about 3,000 people were a-ed	Ac 2:41
Believers were a-ed to the Lord	Ac 5:14
numbers of people were a-ed	Ac 11:24
If anyone a-s to them,	Rv 22:18
God will a to him the plagues	Rv 22:18

ADDICTED
not a to wine,	1Tm 3:3; Ti 1:7
not a to much wine.	Ti 2:3

ADDITION
a to the offerings for ... Sabbaths, Lv 23:38
in a to whatever else Nm 6:21
in a to the regular burnt offering Nm 29:16

ADDRESS
he a-ed them in ... Hebrew Ac 21:40
that a-es you as sons: Heb 12:5
you a as Father the One who judges 1Pt 1:17

ADMINISTER
a-ing justice ... for all his people 2Sm 8:15
You have a-ed justice ... in Jacob. Ps 99:4
reign ... and a justice ... in the land. Jr 23:5
He will a justice and righteousness Jr 33:15
a-ed justice, obtained promises, Heb 11:33

ADMINISTRATION
the a of the mystery Eph 3:9
God's a that was given to me Col 1:25

ADMIRE
I a-d the dead, Ec 4:2

ADMONISHING
teaching and a one another Col 3:16

ADONIJAH
1. Son of David (2Sm 3:4). Conspired for the throne and was executed by Solomon (1Kg 1–2).
2. Levite teacher under Jehoshaphat (2Ch 17:8).
3. Postexilic leader (Neh 10:16).

ADOPT
He predestined us to be a-ed Eph 1:5

ADOPTION
but you received the Spirit of a, Rm 8:15
eagerly waiting for a, Rm 8:23
to them belong the a, Rm 9:4
that we might receive a as sons. Gl 4:5

ADORE
No wonder young women a you. Sg 1:3

ADORN
A yourself with majesty Jb 40:10
He a-s the humble with salvation. Ps 149:4
as a bride a-s herself Is 61:10
it was a-ed with beautiful stones Lk 21:5
a the teaching of God our Savior Ti 2:10

a-ed with gold, precious stones, Rv 17:4
a bride a-ed for her husband. Rv 21:2

ADORNMENT
life for you and a for your neck. Pr 3:22

ADULLAM
took refuge in the cave of A. 1Sm 22:1

ADULT
as an a he wrestled with God. Hs 12:3
be infants in evil and a in 1Co 14:20

ADULTERER
both the a and the adulteress Lv 20:10
a-'s eye watches for twilight, Jb 24:15
you associate with a-s. Ps 50:18
offspring of an a and a prostitute! Is 57:3
the land is full of a-s; Jr 23:10
idolaters, a-s, male prostitutes, 1Co 6:9
judge immoral people and a-s. Heb 13:4

ADULTERESS
both the adulterer and the a Lv 20:10
an a goes after {your} very life. Pr 6:26
This is the way of an a: she eats Pr 30:20
I will judge you the way a-es Ezk 16:38
they are a-es Ezk 23:45
loved by another man and is an a, Hs 3:1
A-es! Do you not know Jms 4:4

ADULTEROUS
You a wife, Ezk 16:32
An evil and a generation Mt 12:39; 16:4
this a and sinful generation, Mk 8:38

ADULTERY
Do not commit a. Ex 20:14; Dt 5:18
If a man commits a Lv 20:10
one who commits a lacks sense; Pr 6:32
committed a with stone and tree. Jr 3:9
woman worn out by a: Ezk 23:43
her a from between her breasts. Hs 2:2
already committed a with her Mt 5:28
marries a divorced ... commits a. Mt 5:32
marries another, commits a. Mt 19:9
do not commit a; do not steal; Mt 19:18
brought a woman caught in a, Jn 8:3
say, "You must not commit a"—
do you commit a? Rm 2:22
Do not commit a, Rm 13:9
who said, Do not commit a, also Jms 2:11

having eyes full of a   2Pt 2:14
those who commit a with her   Rv 2:22

ADVANCE (n)
I have told you in a.   Mt 24:25
told you everything in a.   Mk 13:23

ADVANCE (v)
will a, each man straight ahead.   Jos 6:5
those carrying the ark ... a-ed six   2Sm 6:13
kings assembled; they a-ed together.   Ps 48:4
I a-ed in Judaism   Gl 1:14

ADVANCEMENT
resulted in the a of the gospel,   Php 1:12
for your a and joy in the faith,   Php 1:25

ADVANTAGE
I realized that there is an a to
    wisdom over folly,   Ec 2:13
the a of wisdom   Ec 10:10
a that one man should die   Jn 11:50
So what a does the Jew have?   Rm 3:1
Did I take a of you   2Co 12:17
to be used for His own a.   Php 2:6

ADVANTAGEOUS
a that one man should die   Jn 18:14

ADVERSARY
I will take vengeance on My a-ies   Dt 32:41
You exalt me above my a-ies;   Ps 18:48
May my a-ies be disgraced   Ps 71:13
avenge Himself against His a-ies.   Jr 46:10
As you are going with your a to   Lk 12:58
wisdom that none of your a-ies   Lk 21:15
give the a no opportunity   1Tm 5:14
to consume the a-ies.   Heb 10:27
Your a the Devil is prowling   1Pt 5:8

ADVERSITY
life and prosperity, death and a.   Dt 30:15
only good from God and not a?   Jb 2:10
a-ies come to the ... righteous,   Ps 34:19
LORD will save him in a day of a.   Ps 41:1
but in the day of a, consider: Ec 7:14
both a and good come from   Lm 3:38

ADVICE
The a of Hushai the Archite   2Sm 17:14
rejected the elders' a   2Ch 10:13
not follow the a of the wicked,   Ps 1:1

good a and competence;   Pr 8:14
should have followed my a   Ac 27:21

ADVISERS
with many a they succeed.   Pr 15:22
Pharaoh's wisest a   Is 19:11
My a and my nobles sought me   Dn 4:36

ADVOCATE
my a is in the heights!   Jb 16:19
we have an a with the Father   1Jn 2:1

AFAR
He knows the haughty from a.   Ps 138:6

AFFAIRS
He set his a in order   2Sm 17:23
Put your a in order,   2Kg 20:1; Is 38:1

AFFECTION
limited by your own a-s.   2Co 6:12
with the a of Christ Jesus.   Php 1:8
if any a and mercy,   Php 2:1
godliness with brotherly a,
    and brotherly a with love.   2Pt 1:7

AFFLICT
Egyptians mistreated and a-ed us,   Dt 26:6
the Almighty has a-ed me?   Ru 1:21
Evildoers will not a them   2Sm 7:10
But I am a-ed and needy;   Ps 70:5
For I am a-ed all day long,   Ps 73:14
It was good for me to be a-ed   Ps 119:71
You have a-ed me fairly.   Ps 119:75
compassion on His a-ed ones.   Is 49:13
struck down by God, and a-ed.   Is 53:4
He was oppressed and a-ed,   Is 53:7
Though I have a-ed you, I will
    a you no longer.   Nah 1:12
all those who were a-ed,   Mt 4:24
If we are a-ed, it is for your   2Co 1:6
we were a-ed in every way: 2Co 7:5
you who are a-ed, along with us.   2Th 1:7
destitute, a-ed, and mistreated.   Heb 11:37

AFFLICTED (n)
open your hand to your a   Dt 15:11
He heard the outcry of the a   Jb 34:28
rescues the a by afflicting them;   Jb 36:15
not forget the cry of the a.   Ps 9:12
hope of the a will not perish   Ps 9:18
lurks in order to seize the a.   Ps 10:9

Do not forget the a. | Ps 10:12
The LORD helps the a | Ps 147:6

AFFLICTION

fruitful in the land of my a. | Gn 41:52
take notice of Your servant's a, | 1Sm 1:11
each man knowing his own a-s | 1Kg 8:38
LORD saw that the a of Israel | 2Kg 14:26
Consider my a and trouble, | Ps 25:18
Fools suffered a | Ps 107:17
This is my comfort in my a: | Ps 119:50
tested you in the furnace of a. | Is 48:10
LORD, look on my a, | Lm 1:9
He does not enjoy bringing a | Lm 3:33
When a or persecution comes | Mk 4:17
she was cured of her a. | Mk 5:29
a-s are waiting for me | Ac 20:23
we also rejoice in our a-s, | Rm 5:3
a produces endurance, | Rm 5:3
be patient in a; | Rm 12:12
comforts us in all our a, so that we | 2Co 1:4
momentary light a is producing | 2Co 4:17
during a severe testing by a, | 2Co 8:2

AFFORD

if he cannot a two turtledoves | Lv 5:11
if he is poor and cannot a {these} | Lv 14:21

AFRAID

I was a because I was naked, | Gn 3:10
not be a, Abram. I am your shield | Gn 15:1
he was a to look at God. | Ex 3:6
not a to speak against My servant | Nm 12:8
a of them, for the LORD ... fights for | Dt 3:22
Do not be a, alarmed, or terrified | Dt 20:3
Do not be a or discouraged, | Jos 1:9
I was a of the people, | 1Sm 15:24
How is it that you were not a | 2Sm 1:14
a to tell him the baby was dead | 2Sm 12:18
be a of the sword, | Jb 19:29
I am not a of the thousands | Ps 3:6
of whom should I be a? | Ps 27:1
we will not be a, though the earth | Ps 46:2
When I am a, I will trust in You. | Ps 56:3
I will not be a. What can man do | Ps 118:6
lie down, you will not be a; | Pr 3:24
She is not a for her household | Pr 31:21
they are a of heights | Ec 12:5
I will trust {Him} and not be a. | Is 12:2
do not be a, for I am your God. | Is 41:10

Do not be a of anyone, for I will be | Jr 1:8
no longer be a or dismayed, | Jr 23:4
Don't be a to serve the Chaldeans | Jr 40:9
Don't be a of their words | Ezk 2:6
with nothing to make {them} a. | Zph 3:13
don't be a to take Mary | Mt 1:20
It is I. Don't be a. | Mt 14:27; Mk 6:50
Jesus told them, "Do not be a. | Mt 28:10
Don't be a. Only believe. | Mk 5:36
they were a to ask Him. | Mk 9:32
they were a of Him, | Mk 11:18
they were a of the crowd | Mk 11:32; 12:12
Do not be a, Mary, | Lk 1:30
angel said to them, "Don't be a, | Lk 2:10
they were a of the people. | Lk 22:2
It is I. Don't be a! | Jn 6:20
they were a of the Jews, | Jn 9:22
But if you do wrong, be a, | Rm 13:4
so that the rest will also be a. | 1Tm 5:20
I will not be a. What can man do | Heb 13:6

AFTERNOON

until three in the a | Mt 27:45; Mk 15:33

AGABUS

Early church prophet (Ac 11:28; 21:10).

AGAG

Amalekite king spared by Saul, executed
by Samuel (1Sm 15).

AGAIN

man lies down never to rise a. | Jb 14:12
and they flow there a. | Ec 1:7
After three days I will rise a. | Mt 27:63
you must be born a. | Jn 3:7
My life so I may take it up a. | Jn 10:17

AGAINST

A You—You alone—I have sinned | Ps 51:4
Do not hold past sins a us; | Ps 79:8
who is not with Me is a Me, | Mt 12:30
whoever is not a us is for us. | Mk 9:40
If God is for us, who is a us? | Rm 8:31
A such things there is no law. | Gl 5:23

AGE

be buried at a ripe old a. | Gn 15:15
borne him a son in his old a. | Gn 21:7
I thought that a should speak | Jb 32:7
already existed in the a-s before | Ec 1:10
at the a for love. | Ezk 16:8

AGED

never existed in a-s past and never	Jl 2:2
in this a or in the one to come.	Mt 12:32
the worries of this a	Mt 13:22; Mk 4:19
to the end of the a.	Mt 28:20
the sons of this a are more astute	Lk 16:8
He's of a; ask him.	Jn 9:23
secret kept silent for long a-s,	Rm 16:25
Where is the debater of this a?	1Co 1:20
God predestined before the a-s	1Co 2:7
the god of this a has blinded	2Co 4:4
from this present evil a,	Gl 1:4
in the coming a-s He might display	Eph 2:7

AGED

a feast of a wine, choice meat,	Is 25:6

AGITATING

they came there too, a	Ac 17:13

AGONIZE

to a together with me	Rm 15:30

AGONY

a like that of a woman in labor,	Ps 48:6
a like a woman in labor.	Jr 22:23
I am in a in this flame!	Lk 16:24

AGREE

walk together without a-ing	Am 3:3
If two of you on earth a	Mt 18:19
you a with me on a denarius?	Mt 20:13
but the testimonies did not a.	Mk 14:56
since the Jews had already a-d	Jn 9:22
Why did you a to test the Spirit	Ac 5:9
Saul a-d with putting him to death.	Ac 8:1
the words of the prophets a	Ac 15:15
I a with the law that it is good	Rm 7:16
except when you a, for a time,	1Co 7:5
Euodia and ... Syntyche to a	Php 4:2
does not a with the sound teaching	1Tm 6:3

AGREEMENT

making a binding a in writing	Neh 9:38
entered into an a with a stranger,	Pr 6:1
who hates such a-s is protected.	Pr 11:15
One without sense enters an a	Pr 17:18
one of those who enter a-s,	Pr 22:26
we have made an a with Sheol;	Is 28:15
I took the purchase a	Jr 32:11
Be in a with one another.	Rm 12:16
a does Christ have with Belial?	2Co 6:15

in a with the decision of His will,	Eph 1:11
these three are in a.	1Jn 5:8

AGRIPPA

Herodian king who heard Paul's testimony (Ac 25–26).

AHAB

1. Son of Omri, king of Israel (1Kg 16:28–22:40). Married Jezebel and promoted baalism (16:31-33). Killed Naboth (21:1-14). Condemned by Elijah (18:18; 21:17-24) and other prophets (20:35-43; 22:19-28). Died in disguise in battle (22:29-40).

2. False prophet (Jr 29:21-22).

AHASUERUS

1. King of Persia, son of Darius and grandson of Cyrus. Greek name is Xerxes. Dismissed Vashti and married Esther (Est 1–2). Signed Haman's decree (Est 3) then was convinced by Esther to reverse it and hang Haman (Est 4–7) and allow the Jews to defend themselves (Est 8–9).

2. Father of Darius the Mede (Dn 9:1).

AHAZ

Idolatrous king of Judah (2Kg 16:2-4). Son of Jotham. Attacked by Aram and Israel (16:5-6; 2Ch 28:5-7). Refused Isaiah's advice and turned to Assyria for help (Is 7). Not buried among the kings (2Ch 28:27).

AHAZIAH

1. Son of Ahab; king of Israel (1Kg 22:40). Injured in a fall; condemned by Elijah for seeking Baal (2Kg 1:2-17).

2. Son of Jehoram; king of Judah (2Kg 8:25-27). Mortally wounded by Jehu while visiting King Joram of Israel (9:27).

AHEAD

the gift was sent on a of him	Gn 32:21
God sent me a of you	Gn 45:5
your fighting men will cross over	
... a of your brothers	Dt 3:18; Jos 1:14
each man straight a	Jos 6:5,20
ran a of Ahab	1Kg 18:46
shadow go a 10 steps or go back	2Kg 20:9
fix your gaze straight a.	Pr 4:25
who go straight a on their paths:	Pr 9:15
Everything lies a of them.	Ec 9:1

Each creature went
straight **a**. Ezk 1:9; 10:22
sending My messenger **a** of You; Mt 11:10
go **a** of Him to the other side, Mt 14:22
I will go **a** of you to Galilee. Mt 26:32
someone goes down **a** of me. Jn 5:7
he goes **a** of them. Jn 10:4
went on **a** and waited for us Ac 20:5
which God prepared **a** of time Eph 2:10
reaching forward to what is **a**, Php 3:13

AHIJAH
1. Priest at the time of Saul (1Sm 14:3-4,18).

2. Solomon's scribe (1Kg 4:3).

3. Prophet from Shiloh to Jeroboam (1Kg 11:29-39).

4. Issacharite, father of King Baasha of Israel (1Kg 15:27).

5. Son of Jerahmeel (1Ch 2:25).

6. Son of Ehud; official in Geba (1Ch 8:7).

7. One of David's 30 warriors (1Ch 11:36).

8. Signed Nehemiah's covenant (Neh 10:26).

AHIKAM
Son of Shaphan the scribe (1Kg 22:12), father of Gedaliah (Jr 40:5). Protected Jeremiah (26:24).

AHIMAAZ
1. Saul's father-in-law (1Sm 14:50).

2. Son of Zadok; worked for David as a spy (2Sm 15:26,36; 17:17-21; 18:19-33).

AHIMELECH
1. Priest of Nob who was killed by Saul for aiding David (1Sm 21–22).

2. One of David's warriors (1Sm 26:6).

AHITHOPHEL
David's counselor (2Sm 15:12); defected to Absalom (15:31); committed suicide when his advice was not taken (16:20–17:23).

AI
Bethel on the west and **A** on the Gn 12:8
they fled from the men of **A**. Jos 7:4
Joshua burned **A** Jos 8:28

AIJALON
moon, over the valley of **A**. Jos 10:12

A with its pasturelands, Jos 21:24
he was buried in **A** Jdg 12:12

AIM
without taking special **a** 1Kg 22:34

AIMLESSLY
do not run like one who runs **a**, 1Co 9:26

AIR
box like one who beats the **a**. 1Co 9:26
you will be speaking into the **a**. 1Co 14:9
meet the Lord in the **a**; 1Th 4:17
poured out his bowl into the **a**, Rv 16:17

ALABASTER
His legs are **a** pillars Sg 5:15
an **a** jar Mt 26:7; Mk 14:3

ALARM
In my **a** I had said, "I am cut off Ps 31:22
my **a** I said, "Everyone is a liar." Ps 116:11
sound the **a** on My holy mountain! Jl 2:1

ALARMED
See that you are not **a**, Mt 24:6
and rumors of wars, don't be **a**; Mk 13:7
wars and rebellions, don't be **a**. Lk 21:9

ALERT
be **a**, since you don't know Mt 24:42
whom the master will find **a** Lk 12:37
Be **a**, stand firm in the faith, 1Co 16:13
stay **a** in this, with all perseverance Eph 6:18
prayer; stay **a** in it Col 4:2
Be sober! Be on the **a**! 1Pt 5:8

ALEXANDER
Hymenaeus and **A** 1Tm 1:20
A the coppersmith 2Tm 4:14

ALIEN
I am a resident **a** among you. Gn 23:4
the land where you live as an **a**, Gn 28:4
if you no longer oppress the **a**, Jr 7:6
His descendants would be **a-s** Ac 7:6
I urge you as **a-s** 1Pt 2:11

ALIENATED
are **a** from Christ; Gl 5:4
you were once **a** and hostile Col 1:21

ALIVE
to keep them **a** with you. Gn 6:19
Is your father still **a**? Gn 43:7

They went down a into Sheol | Nm 16:33
but with all of us who are a | Dt 5:3
While the baby was a, | 2Sm 12:21
This is my son who is a, | 1Kg 3:23
let them go down to Sheol a, | Ps 55:15
Let's swallow them a, like Sheol, | Pr 1:12
to mute stone: Come a! | Hab 2:19
while this deceiver was still a, | Mt 27:63
when they heard that He was a | Mk 16:11
son of mine was dead and is a | Lk 15:24
He also presented Himself a | Ac 1:3
dead to sin, but a to God | Rm 6:11
as those who are a from the dead, | Rm 6:13
in Christ all will be made a. | 1Co 15:22
made us a with the Messiah | Eph 2:5
He made you a with Him | Col 2:13
Then we who are still a | 1Th 4:17
made a in the spiritual realm. | 1Pt 3:18
but look—I am a forever | Rv 1:18
have a reputation for being a, but | Rv 3:1

ALL

to put an end to a flesh, | Gn 6:13
with a your heart, with a your soul,
    and with a your strength. | Dt 6:5
search for Me with a your heart. | Jr 29:13
love the Lord ... with a your heart, | Lk 10:27
A have turned away, | Rm 3:12
a have sinned and fall short | Rm 3:23
He died to sin once for a; | Rm 6:10
We will not a fall asleep, but
    we will a be changed, | 1Co 15:51
the One who fills a things | Eph 1:23
I am able to do a things | Php 4:13
A Scripture is inspired by God | 2Tm 3:16
but a to come to repentance. | 2Pt 3:9

ALLEGIANCE

a to King Solomon. | 1Ch 29:24
every tongue will swear a. | Is 45:23
free from a to righteousness. | Rm 6:20

ALLEYS

into the streets and a of the city, | Lk 14:21

ALLIANCE

unified a to fight against Joshua | Jos 9:2
having no a with anyone. | Jdg 18:7
Solomon made an a with Pharaoh | 1Kg 3:1
he made an a with Ahab | 2Ch 18:1

formed an a with Ahaziah, | 2Ch 20:37
they will form an a, | Dn 11:6

ALLOTMENT

the a Pharaoh had given them; | Gn 47:22
Israel according to their a-s: | Jos 12:7

ALLOTTED

it will be a to you as an inheritance | Nm 34:2
took longer than the time a | 2Sm 20:5

ALLOW

must not a a sorceress to live. | Ex 22:18
will not a Your Faithful One to see | Ps 16:10
never a the righteous to be shaken. | Ps 55:22
does not a our feet to slip. | Ps 66:9
He will not a your foot to slip; | Ps 121:3
I will not a my eyes to sleep | Ps 132:4
God does not a him to enjoy them | Ec 6:2
I will a you to live in this place. | Jr 7:3
A it for now, | Mt 3:15
don't a those entering to go in. | Mt 23:13
would not a them to speak, | Lk 4:41
a Your Holy One to see decay. | Ac 2:27
a Your Holy One to see decay. | Ac 13:35
a-ed all the nations to go their own | Ac 14:16
Spirit of Jesus did not a them. | Ac 16:7
Am I a-ed to say something | Ac 21:37
Justice does not a him to live! | Ac 28:4
will not a you to be tempted | 1Co 10:13
time with you, if the Lord a-s. | 1Co 16:7
words ... man is not a-ed to speak. | 2Co 12:4
I do not a a woman to teach | 1Tm 2:12

ALLOWANCE

a regular a was given to him | 2Kg 25:30

ALMIGHTY

I am God A. | Gn 17:1
Isaac, and Jacob as God A, | Ex 6:3
who sees a vision from the A, | Nm 24:4
the A has made me very bitter. | Ru 1:20
discover the limits of the A? | Jb 11:7
when the A was still with me | Jb 29:5
the breath of the A gives me life. | Jb 33:4
dwells in the shadow of the A. | Ps 91:1
devastation from the A. | Jl 1:15
was, and who is coming, the A. | Rv 1:8
holy, holy, holy, Lord God, the A, | Rv 4:8
God, the A, has begun to reign! | Rv 19:6

ALMOND

cups shaped like a blossoms,   Ex 25:33
blossomed, and produced a-s!   Nm 17:8
the a tree blossoms,   Ec 12:5
I see a branch of a tree.   Jr 1:11

ALMOST

my feet a slipped;   Ps 73:2
Babylon's time is a up;   Is 13:22

ALOES

perfumed my bed with myrrh, a,   Pr 7:17
frankincense, myrrh and a,   Sg 4:14

ALONE

not good for the man to be a.   Gn 2:18
man does not live on bread a   Dt 8:3
See now that I a am He;   Dt 32:39
Why are you a   1Sm 21:1
If he's a, he bears good news.   2Sm 18:25
I a am left,   1Kg 19:10
You a are the LORD.   Neh 9:6
I a have escaped to tell you!   Jb 1:15
Against You—you a—   Ps 51:4
He a is my rock   Ps 62:2,6
Your righteousness, Yours a.   Ps 71:16
who a does wonders.   Ps 72:18
You a are God.   Ps 86:10
He a does great wonders.   Ps 136:4
They should be for you a   Pr 5:17
can one person a keep warm?   Ec 4:11
the LORD a will be exalted   Is 2:11
not even a gate bar; they live a.   Jr 49:31
she sits a, the city {once} crowded   Lm 1:1
a, looking at this great vision.   Dn 10:8
They live a in a scrubland,   Mc 7:14
Man must not live on bread a   Mt 4:4
to a remote place to be a.   Mt 14:13
Who can forgive sins but God a?   Mk 2:7
Leave us a!   Lk 4:34
will leave Me a. Yet I am not a,   Jn 16:32
no church ... except you a.   Php 4:15
by works and not by faith a.   Jms 2:24
Because You a are holy,   Rv 15:4

ALOOF

On the day you stood a,   Ob 11

ALOUD

read {it} a to the people.   Ex 24:7
Joshua read a all the words   Jos 8:34

I cry a to God, a to God,   Ps 77:1
read all these words a.   Jr 51:61

ALPHA

the A and the Omega,   Rv 1:8; 21:6; 22:13

ALREADY

You were a born;   Jb 38:21
It has a existed   Ec 1:10
will do what has a been done.   Ec 2:12
Whatever is, has a been, and
    whatever will be, a is.   Ec 3:15
the dead, who have a died,   Ec 4:2
God has a accepted your works.   Ec 9:7
has a committed adultery   Mt 5:28
surprised that He was a dead.   Mk 15:44
The door is a locked,   Lk 11:7
how I wish it were a set ablaze!   Lk 12:49
does not believe is a judged,   Jn 3:18
You are a clean   Jn 15:3
they saw that He was a dead.   Jn 19:33
A you are full! A you are rich!   1Co 4:8
I have a decided about him   1Co 5:3
Was anyone a circumcised   1Co 7:18
Not that I have a reached   Php 3:12
saying that the resurrection has a   2Tm 2:18
the true light is a shining.   1Jn 2:8
he is a in the world now.   1Jn 4:3

ALTAR

Noah built an a to the LORD.   Gn 8:20
Isaac and placed him on the a,   Gn 22:9
he built an a there, worshiped   Gn 26:25
he set up an a there   Gn 33:20
Jacob built an a there   Gn 35:7
Moses built an a   Ex 17:15
not go up to My a on steps,   Ex 20:26
construct the a of acacia wood.   Ex 27:1
an a for the burning of incense;   Ex 30:1
tear down their a-s,   Ex 34:13
Build me seven a-s here   Nm 23:1
tear down their a-s,   Dt 7:5
Build an a of stones there   Dt 27:5
Joshua built an a on Mount Ebal   Jos 8:30
impressive a there by the Jordan.   Jos 22:10
tear down their a-s.   Jdg 2:2
Gideon built an a to the LORD   Jdg 6:24
tear down the a of Baal   Jdg 6:25
people ... built an a there,   Jdg 21:4
he had built an a   1Sm 7:17

Saul built an **a** to the LORD;	1Sm 14:35
He built an **a** to the LORD	2Sm 24:25
take hold of the horns of the **a**.	1Kg 1:50
took hold of the horns of the **a**.	1Kg 2:28
on the **a** he had set up	1Kg 12:33
A, **a**, this is what the LORD says	1Kg 13:2
He set up an **a** for Baal	1Kg 16:32
he repaired the LORD's **a**	1Kg 18:30
built the **a** according to all the instructions King Ahaz sent	2Kg 16:11
built **a-s** to the ... heavenly host	2Kg 21:5
tore down the **a** at Bethel	2Kg 23:15
to build the **a** of Israel's God	Ezr 3:2
I will come to the **a** of God,	Ps 43:4
leave your gift ... in front of the **a**.	Mt 5:24
takes an oath by the **a**,	Mt 23:18
those who serve at the **a** share in the offerings of the **a**?	1Co 9:13
the gold **a** of incense	Heb 9:4
We have an **a** from which	Heb 13:10
when he offered Isaac ... on the **a**?	Jms 2:21
I saw under the **a** the souls	Rv 6:9
the four horns of the gold **a**	Rv 9:13

ALTOGETHER

reliable and **a** righteous.	Ps 19:9
righteous and a trustworthy.	Ps 119:138

ALWAYS

I keep the LORD in mind **a**.	Ps 16:8
my sin is **a** before me.	Ps 51:3
You **a** have the poor with you,	Mt 26:11
I am with you **a**,	Mt 28:20
the need for them to pray **a**	Lk 18:1
Rejoice in the Lord **a**.	Php 4:4
so we will **a** be with the Lord.	1Th 4:17
Rejoice **a**!	1Th 5:16
Cretans are **a** liars,	Ti 1:12
a be ready to give a defense	1Pt 3:15

AM see I AM

AMASA

David's nephew; commander of Absalom's army (2Sm 17:25). Reinstated by David (19:13). Killed by Joab (20:10).

AMAZED

He was **a** that there was no one	Is 59:16
I was **a** that no one assisted;	Is 63:5
Hearing this, Jesus was **a**	Mt 8:10
a and asked, "What kind of man	Mt 8:27
the crowds were **a**,	Mt 9:33
crowd was **a** when they saw	Mt 15:31
heard this, they were **a**.	Mt 22:22
governor was greatly **a**.	Mt 27:14
He was **a** at their unbelief.	Mk 6:6
they were astounded and **a**,	Ac 2:7
The whole earth was **a**	Rv 13:3

AMAZIAH

1. Son of Joash; king of Judah. Defeated Edom but adopted their gods (2Ch 25:11-14). Rejected God's rebuke, challenged King Jehoash of Israel, and was defeated (26:15-24). Killed by a conspiracy (26:27).

2. Priest; opposed Amos (Am 7:10-17).

AMBASSADOR

we are **a-s** for Christ;	2Co 5:20
For this I am an **a** in chains.	Eph 6:20

AMBITION

bitter envy and selfish **a**	Jms 3:14

AMBUSH

Set an **a** behind the city.	Jos 8:2
set up an **a** around Gibeah.	Jdg 20:29
Jeroboam had sent an **a**	2Ch 13:13
Let's set an **a** and kill someone.	Pr 1:11
prepare the **a**.	Jr 51:12
All of them wait in **a**	Mc 7:2
40 of them arranging to **a** him,	Ac 23:21

AMEN

all the people will reply, '**A**!'	Dt 27:15
all the people said, "**A**"	1Ch 16:36
The whole assembly said, "**A**,"	Neh 5:13
is filled with His glory. **A** and **a**.	Ps 72:19
LORD be praised forever. **A** and **a**.	Ps 89:52
Let all the people say, "**A**!"	Ps 106:48
God over all, blessed forever. **A**.	Rm 9:5
to Him be the glory forever! **A**.	Rm 16:27
will the uninformed ... say "**A**"	1Co 14:16
the "**A**" is also through Him	2Co 1:20
The **A**, the faithful and true	Rv 3:14
A! Come, Lord Jesus!	Rv 22:20

AMETHYST

an agate, and an **a**;	Ex 28:19; Ex 39:12
the twelfth **a**.	Rv 21:20

AMMINADAB

Judahite leader (Ru 4:19-20; 1Ch 2:10; Mt 1:14; Lk 3:33).

AMMON, AMMONITE

Founder and namesake of a Canaanite nation east of the Jordan; the people of that nation (Gn 19:38; Dt 2:19,37; 23:3; Jdg 11; 2Sm 10; 1Ch 19; Neh 2:10; Ezk 25:1-7).

AMNON

Oldest son of David (2Sm 3:2). Raped his sister Tamar; killed by Absalom (2Sm 13).

AMON

1. Governor of Samaria under Ahab (1Kg 22:26).
2. Son of Manasseh; king of Judah; killed by his servants (2Kg 21:18-26).

AMORITES

Canaanite nation (Gn 10:16; 15:16; Nm 13:29; Jos 10:5; 1Sm 7:14; Ezk 16:3).

AMOS

Prophet against moral decay in Israel under Jeroboam II (Am 5:24).

AMOZ

Father of Isaiah (Is 1:1).

AMRAM

1. Father of Moses (Ex 6:20).
2. Son of Kohath (Nm 3:19).
3. Son of Bani (Ezr 10:34).

ANAK, ANAKIM

Founder, nation of tall people (Dt 1:28; 2:10-11; 9:2).

ANANIAS

1. Lied about gift to the church at Jerusalem and died (Ac 5:1-6).
2. Disciple in Damascus who visited Paul (Ac 9:10-19).
3. High priest at Paul's arrest (Ac 23:1-5; 24:1).

ANATHOTH

Hometown of Abiathar and Jeremiah (1Kg 2:26; Jr 1:1).

ANCESTORS

gods your a worshiped	Jos 24:14
gathered to their a.	Jdg 2:10
from the day their a came out	2Kg 21:15
returned to the sins of their a	Jr 11:10
covenant I made with their a	Jr 31:32
zealous for the traditions of my a.	Gl 1:14
For by it our a were approved.	Heb 11:2

ANCHOR

casting off the a-s,	Ac 27:40
sure and firm a of the soul	Heb 6:19

ANCIENT

products of the a mountains	Dt 33:15
the a river, the river Kishon.	Jdg 5:21
{names} are from a records.	1Ch 4:22
Will you continue on the a path	Jb 22:15
Rise up, a doors!	Ps 24:7,9
I was formed before a times,	Pr 8:23
Don't move an a property line	Pr 22:28
Ask about the a paths:	Jr 6:16
the A of Days took His seat.	Dn 7:9
since a times, Moses	Ac 15:21
if He didn't spare the a world,	2Pt 2:5
seized the dragon, that a serpent	Rv 20:2

ANDREW

Apostle; fisherman; Peter's brother (Mt 4:18; 10:2; Mk 1:16,29; 3:18; 13:3; Lk 6:14; Jn 1:35-44; 6:8-9; 12:12; Ac 1:13).

ANGEL

two a-s entered Sodom	Gn 19:1
A of the LORD called to him	Gn 22:11
He will send His a before you,	Gn 24:7
a-s were going up and down	Gn 28:12
God's a-s met him.	Gn 32:1
A of the LORD appeared to him	Ex 3:2
going to send an A before you	Ex 23:20
A of the LORD took His stand	Nm 22:22
seen the A of the LORD face to face!	Jdg 6:22
The A of the LORD appeared	Jdg 13:3
wisdom of the A of God,	2Sm 14:20
is like the A of God,	2Sm 19:27
God sent an a to Jerusalem	1Ch 21:15
a of the LORD encamps around	Ps 34:7
People ate the bread of a-s.	Ps 78:25
He will give His a-s orders	Ps 91:11
Praise the LORD, {all} His a-s	Ps 103:20
the a of the LORD ... struck down	Is 37:36
A of His Presence saved them.	Is 63:9
He sent His a and rescued	Dn 3:28
My God sent His a and shut	Dn 6:22

Jacob struggled with the **A**	Hs 12:4	kindled because of My a	Dt 32:22
he did as the Lord's **a** had	Mt 1:24	LORD's a burned against Israel	Jdg 2:14
a of the Lord suddenly appeared	Mt 2:13	For a kills a fool,	Jb 5:2
a of the Lord suddenly appeared	Mt 2:19	God does not hold back His a;	Jb 9:13
He will give His a-s orders	Mt 4:6	His a may ignite at any moment.	Ps 2:12
is going to come with His a-s	Mt 16:27	do not rebuke me in Your a;	Ps 6:1
their a-s continually view	Mt 18:10	Rise up, LORD, in Your a;	Ps 7:6
are like a-s in heaven.	Mt 22:30	For His a lasts only a moment,	Ps 30:5
for the Devil and his a-s!	Mt 25:41	do not punish me in Your a	Ps 38:1
more than 12 legions of a-s?	Mt 26:53	Your a burn against the sheep	Ps 74:1
the a-s began to serve Him.	Mk 1:13	in a withheld His compassion?	Ps 77:9
neither the a-s in heaven nor	Mk 13:32	Will You prolong Your a	Ps 85:5
the a Gabriel was sent	Lk 1:26	we are consumed by Your a;	Ps 90:7
a said to them, "Don't be afraid	Lk 2:10	I swore in My a, 'They will not	Ps 95:11
When the a-s had left them	Lk 2:15	a fool is easily a-ed	Pr 14:16
acknowledge him before the a-s	Lk 12:8	A gentle answer turns away a,	Pr 15:1
joy in the presence of God's a-s	Lk 15:10	A fool gives full vent to his a,	Pr 29:11
the a-s of God ascending	Jn 1:51	a burns against His people.	Is 5:25
an a would go down into the pool	Jn 5:4	In all this, His a is not removed,	Is 9:12
a of the Lord opened the doors	Ac 5:19	Assyria, the rod of My a	Is 10:5
face was like the face of an a.	Ac 6:15	I will delay My a for the honor	
they said, "It's his a!"	Ac 12:15	of My name,	Is 48:9
or an a has spoken to him?	Ac 23:9	In a surge of a I hid My face	Is 54:8
nor a-s nor rulers,	Rm 8:38	provoke Me to a by the work of your	Jr 25:6
we will judge a-s?	1Co 6:3	When My a is spent	Ezk 5:13
because of the a-s.	1Co 11:10	I give you a king in My a	Hs 13:11
languages of men and of a-s,	1Co 13:1	compassionate, slow to a,	Jl 2:13
disguised as an a of light.	2Co 11:14	not hold on to His a forever,	Mc 7:18
even if we or an a from heaven	Gl 1:8	looking around at them with a	Mk 3:5
you received me as an a of God,	Gl 4:14	jealousy, outbursts of a, 2Co 12:20; Gl 5:20	
the worship of a-s,	Col 2:18	sun go down on your a,	Eph 4:26
seen by a-s,	1Tm 3:16	All bitterness, and wrath,	Eph 4:31
some have welcomed a-s as guests	Heb 13:2	fathers, don't stir up a	Eph 6:4
A-s desire to look into	1Pt 1:12	a, wrath, malice, slander,	Col 3:8
if God didn't spare the a-s	2Pt 2:4	So I swore in My a,	Heb 3:11
seven stars are the a-s	Rv 1:20	slow to speak, and slow to a,	Jms 1:19
To the a of the church in	Rv 2:2	the cup of His a.	Rv 14:10
acknowledge his name before ... a-s.	Rv 3:5	winepress of the fierce a of God,	Rv 19:15
I saw four a-s standing	Rv 7:1		
I saw the seven a-s	Rv 8:2	**ANGRY**	
Twelve a-s were at the gates;	Rv 21:12	the LORD was a with me	Dt 3:26

ANGER

		was a at Job because he had justified	Jb 32:2
until your brother's a subsides	Gn 27:44	the Son, or He will be a,	Ps 2:12
LORD's a burned against Moses,	Ex 4:14	Be a and do not sin;	Ps 4:4
My a will burn,	Ex 22:24	Will You be a forever?	Ps 79:5
alone, so that My a can burn	Ex 32:10	Will You be a with us forever?	Ps 85:5
gracious God, slow to a	Ex 34:6	accuse {us} or be a forever.	Ps 103:9
from their land in {His} a,	Dt 29:28	friends with an a man,	Pr 22:24
		An a man stirs up conflict,	Pr 29:22

Don't let your spirit rush to be a,   Ec 7:9
LORD, do not be terribly a   Is 64:9
I will not be a forever.   Jr 3:12
will be silent and no longer a.   Ezk 16:42
slow to become a,   Jnh 4:2
Is it right for you to be a?   Jnh 4:4
who is a with his brother   Mt 5:22
I will make you a by a nation   Rm 10:19
Be a and do not sin.   Eph 4:26

ANGUISH

you will bear children in a.   Gn 3:16
praying from the depth of my a   1Sm 1:16
I groan because of the a   Ps 38:8
courage melting away in a,   Ps 107:26
He will see {it} out of His a,   Is 53:11
My a, my a! I writhe in agony!   Jr 4:19
give them a heart filled with a.   Lm 3:65
in a, He prayed more fervently,   Lk 22:44
intense sorrow and continual a   Rm 9:2
out of an ... a-ed heart I wrote
   to you   2Co 2:4

ANIMAL

LORD God formed ... each wild a   Gn 2:19
I will require the life of every a   Gn 9:5
both man and a; it is Mine.   Ex 13:2
with an a must be put to death.   Ex 22:19
may eat all these {kinds} of land a-s.   Lv 11:2
with any a, defiling yourself   Lv 18:23
a, he must be put to death   Lv 20:15
I will remove dangerous a-s   Lv 26:6
both man and a; they are Mine;   Nm 3:13
is Mine, both man and a.   Nm 8:17
a-s will become too numerous   Dt 7:22
These are the a-s you may eat: Dt 14:4
he is like the a-s that perish.   Ps 49:12
every a of the forest is Mine,   Ps 50:10
cares about his a-'s health,   Pr 12:10
and the fate of a-s is the same.   Ec 3:19
the wild a-s to serve him.   Jr 27:6
as well as many a-s?   Jnh 4:11
stolen, lame, or sick a-s.   Mal 1:13
four-footed a-s and reptiles   Ac 10:12
humans, another for a-s,   1Co 15:39
these people, like irrational a-s   2Pt 2:12
by instinct, like unreasoning a-s   Jd 10

ANKLES

my a do not give way.   Ps 18:36
It came up to {my} a.   Ezk 47:3

ANNA

Prophetess who spoke of Jesus (Lk 2:36-
38).

ANNAS

High priest, along with his son-in-law Caiaphas, who sentenced Jesus (Lk 3:2; Jn
18:13,24) and threatened Peter and John
(Ac 4:6).

ANNIHILATE

a all the Jewish people   Est 3:13
fury to destroy and a many.   Dn 11:44

ANNOUNCE

a it in the streets of Ashkelon,   2Sm 1:20
I a them to you before they occur   Is 42:9
I a-d it to you before it occurred,   Is 48:5
I might a concerning a nation   Jr 18:7
A a sacred fast;   Jl 2:15
Don't a it in Gath,   Mc 1:10
Mary Magdalene went and a-d   Jn 20:18
who a-d beforehand the coming   Ac 7:52
feet of those who a the gospel   Rm 10:15
that have now been a-d to you   1Pt 1:12
will be completed, as He a-d   Rv 10:7

ANNUAL

to make the a sacrifice   1Sm 1:21
Bethlehem for an a sacrifice   1Sm 20:6
the three a appointed festivals: 2Ch 8:13

ANNULLED

the previous commandment is a   Heb 7:18

ANOINT

a, ordain, and consecrate them   Ex 28:41
A Aaron and his sons   Ex 30:30
a-ed the tabernacle   Lv 8:10
A him ruler over My people   1Sm 9:16
LORD sent me to a you as king   1Sm 15:1
The LORD a-ed you king   1Sm 15:17
A him, for he is the one   1Sm 16:12
a Jehu son of Nimshi as king   1Kg 19:16
You a my head with oil;   Ps 23:5
a-ed Me to bring good news   Is 61:1
to a the most holy place.   Dn 9:24
a-ed My body in advance   Mk 14:8
a-ed Me to preach good news   Lk 4:18

You didn't **a** My head with oil, Lk 7:46
a-ed Jesus' feet, Jn 12:3
against ... Jesus, whom You **a-ed**, Ac 4:27
pray over him after **a-ing** him Jms 5:14

ANOINTED (adj)
If the **a** priest sins, Lv 4:3
he will walk before My **a** one 1Sm 2:35
shield of Saul, no longer **a** 2Sm 1:21
Do not touch My **a** ones 1Ch 16:22
against the LORD and His **A** One: Ps 2:2
Do not touch My **a** ones, Ps 105:15
an **a** guardian cherub, Ezk 28:14
These are the two **a** ones, Zch 4:14

ANOINTED (n)
lift my hand against ... LORD's **a**. 1Sm 24:6
my hand against the LORD's **a**. 1Sm 26:11
He shows loyalty to His **a**, Ps 18:50
Cyrus, His **a**, Is 45:1

ANOINTING (n)
Their **a** will serve to inaugurate Ex 40:15
an **a** from the Holy One, 1Jn 2:20
His **a** teaches you 1Jn 2:27

ANOINTING (adj)
spices for the **a** oil Ex 25:6
This will be My holy **a** oil Ex 30:31
die, for the LORD's **a** oil is on you. Lv 10:7

ANOTHER
Let **a** praise you, and not your Pr 27:2
I will not give My glory to **a**. Is 48:11
He will give you **a** Counselor Jn 14:16
not that there is **a** {gospel}, Gl 1:7

ANSWER (n)
decide what **a** I should take 2Sm 24:13
decide what **a** I should take 1Ch 21:12
A gentle **a** turns away anger, Pr 15:1
a of the tongue is from the LORD Pr 16:1
who gives an **a** before he listens Pr 18:13
money is the **a** for everything. Ec 10:19
were astounded at ... His **a-s**. Lk 2:47
But Jesus did not give him an **a**. Jn 19:9

ANSWER (v)
He doesn't **a** me anymore, 1Sm 28:15
The God who **a-s** with fire, 1Kg 18:24
A me, LORD! **A** me 1Kg 18:37
He **a-ed** him with fire 1Ch 21:26
Will anyone **a** you? Jb 5:1

but You do not **a** me; Jb 30:20
these three men quit **a-ing** Job, Jb 32:1
Get ready to **a** Me like a man; Jb 38:3
a-s me from His holy mountain. Ps 3:4
a me, for I am poor and needy Ps 86:1
the LORD **a-ed** me {and put me} Ps 118:21
Don't **a** a fool according to Pr 26:4
A a fool according to Pr 26:5
Even before they call, I will **a**; Is 65:24
but He will not **a** them. Mc 3:4
My name, and I will **a** them. Zch 13:9
No one was able to **a** Him Mt 22:46
being accused ... He didn't **a**. Mt 27:12
But Jesus still did not **a** Mk 15:5
but Jesus did not **a** him. Lk 23:9
give an **a** to those who sent us. Jn 1:22
may know how you should **a** Col 4:6

ANT
Go to the **a**, you slacker! Pr 6:6
a-s are not a strong people, Pr 30:25

ANTICHRIST
heard, "**A** is coming," even now
  many **a-s** have come. 1Jn 2:18
He is the **a**, the one who denies 1Jn 2:22
spirit of the **a**; you have heard 1Jn 4:3
This is the deceiver and the **a**. 2Jn 7

ANTIOCH
first called Christians in **A**. Ac 11:26
reached **A** in Pisidia. Ac 13:14
when Cephas came to **A**, Gl 2:11

ANTIPAS
  Martyr of Pergamum (Rv 2:13).

ANTIQUITY
love ... they have existed from **a**. Ps 25:6
origin is from **a**, from eternity. Mc 5:2

ANXIETY
A in a man's heart weighs Pr 12:25
will eat their bread with **a** Ezk 12:19

ANXIOUS
he was **a** about the ark of God. 1Sm 4:13
don't be **a**. Lk 12:29
and I may be less **a**. Php 2:28

ANYTHING
Is **a** impossible for the LORD? Gn 18:14
Is **a** too difficult for Me? Jr 32:27

A more than this is from | Mt 5:37
A you ask the Father | Jn 16:23

APART
I am the LORD who sets you a. | Lv 20:8
regarding the things set a | Jos 7:1
the LORD has set a the faithful | Ps 4:3
a from Him not one thing was created | Jn 1:3
Set a for Me Barnabas and Saul | Ac 13:2
a from the law ... righteousness has | Rm 3:21
justified by faith a from works | Rm 3:28
a from the law sin is dead. | Rm 7:8
from my mother's womb set me a | Gl 1:15
a special instrument, set a, | 2Tm 2:21
set a the Messiah as Lord | 1Pt 3:15

APOLLOS
   Alexandrian Jew, became a Christian apologist after being instructed in doctrine by Priscilla and Aquila in Ephesus (Ac 18:24-28). Was popular like Paul and Peter (1Co 1:12) but not a rival (3:5-6,22; 4:6; 16:12; Ti 3:13).

APOLLYON
in Greek he has the name A. | Rv 9:11

APOLOGIZED
So they came and a to them, | Ac 16:39

APOSTASY
a-ies will reprimand you. | Jr 2:19
save them from all their a-ies | Ezk 37:23
I will heal their a; | Hs 14:4
unless the a comes first | 2Th 2:3

APOSTLE
the names of the 12 a-s: | Mt 10:2
12—He also named them a-s | Mk 3:14
send them prophets and a-s, | Lk 11:49
numbered with the 11 a-s. | Ac 1:26
signs were ... through the a-s. | Ac 2:43
laid them at the a-s' feet. | Ac 4:35
laid it at the a-s' feet. | Ac 5:2
laying on of the a-s' hands, | Ac 8:18
called as an a and singled out | Rm 1:1
I am an a to the Gentiles, | Rm 11:13
first a-s, second prophets, | 1Co 12:28
unworthy to be called an a, | 1Co 15:9
such people are false a-s, | 2Co 11:13
signs of an a were performed | 2Co 12:12
on the foundation of the a-s | Eph 2:20

some to be a-s, some prophets, | Eph 4:11
I was appointed a herald, an a | 1Tm 2:7
Jesus, the a and high priest | Heb 3:1
call themselves a-s and are not, | Rv 2:2
names of the Lamb's 12 a-s. | Rv 21:14

APOSTLESHIP
We have received grace and a | Rm 1:5
you are the seal of my a | 1Co 9:2
Peter in the a to the circumcised | Gl 2:8

APPALLED
Just as many were a at You | Is 52:14

APPAREL
gold, pearls, or expensive a, | 1Tm 2:9

APPEAL (n)
prayers and a-s, with loud cries | Heb 5:7
He has heard my a for mercy. | Ps 116:1

APPEAL (v)
I a to Caesar! | Ac 25:11
if he had not a-ed to Caesar. | Ac 26:32
I was compelled to a to Caesar; | Ac 28:19
God is a-ing through us, | 2Co 5:20
I a, instead, on the basis of love. | Phm 9

APPEAR
the LORD a-ed to Abram | Gn 12:7
the LORD a-ed to Abraham | Gn 18:1
LORD a-ed to him that night | Gn 26:24
God a-ed to Jacob again | Gn 35:9
I a-ed to Abraham, Isaac, | Ex 6:3
the LORD's glory a-ed. | Ex 16:10
the LORD a-ed to Solomon | 1Kg 3:5
a-ed to Solomon a second time | 1Kg 9:2
who had a-ed to him twice. | 1Kg 11:9
someone who a-ed to be a man. | Dn 8:15
It a-ed in a night and perished | Jnh 4:10
able to stand when He a-s? | Mal 3:2
sign of the Son of Man will a | Mt 24:30
and a-ed to many. | Mt 27:53
He a-ed first to Mary | Mk 16:9
Later, He a-ed to the Eleven | Mk 16:14
the third time Jesus a-ed | Jn 21:14
a-ing to them during 40 days | Ac 1:3
a-ed to our father Abraham | Ac 7:2
Philip a-ed in Azotus, | Ac 8:40
who a-ed to you on the road | Ac 9:17
He a-ed to over 500 brothers | 1Co 15:6
Last of all, ... also a-ed to me. | 1Co 15:8

all **a** before the judgment seat | 2Co 5:10
until the **a-ing** of our Lord | 1Tm 6:14
those who have loved His **a-ing.** | 2Tm 4:8
hope and the **a-ing** of the glory | Ti 2:13
goodness and love for man **a-ed** | Ti 3:4
He has **a-ed** one time, | Heb 9:26
will **a** a second time, | Heb 9:28
smoke that **a-s** for a little while, | Jms 4:14
when the chief Shepherd **a-s,** | 1Pt 5:4
when He **a-s,** we will be | 1Jn 3:2
A great sign **a-ed** in heaven: | Rv 12:1

APPEARANCE

The **a** of the LORD's glory | Ex 24:17
Do not look at his **a** | 1Sm 16:7
His **a** was so disfigured that | Is 52:14
no **a** that we should desire Him. | Is 53:2
examine **a** and the **a** of | Dn 1:13
His **a** is as sure as the dawn. | Hs 6:3
how to read the **a** of the sky, | Mt 16:3
His **a** was like lightning, | Mt 28:3
until the day of his public **a** | Lk 1:80
judging according to outward **a-s;** | Jn 7:24
take pride in the outward **a** | 2Co 5:12

APPEASE

I want to **a** Esau | Gn 32:20
He will not be **a-d** by anything | Pr 6:35

APPETITE

But now our **a** is gone; | Nm 11:6
treacherous ... have an **a** for violence | Pr 13:2
A worker's **a** works for him | Pr 16:26
if you have a big **a;** | Pr 23:2
yet the **a** is never satisfied. | Ec 6:7
bread will be for their **a-s** {alone}; | Hs 9:4
He enlarges his **a** like Sheol, | Hab 2:5
Lord Christ but their own **a-s,** | Rm 16:18

APPLAUD

to be **a-ed** by people. | Mt 6:2
but even **a** others who practice | Rm 1:32

APPLE

Guard me as the **a** of Your eye; | Ps 17:8
like golden **a-s** on a silver tray. | Pr 25:11

APPLY

a to both the native and | Ex 12:49
law **a-ies** to every man or woman | Est 4:11
a your mind to my knowledge. | Pr 22:17
A yourself to instruction | Pr 23:12

I **a-ied** my mind to seek | Ec 1:13
figs and **a** it to his infected skin, | Is 38:21
a-ied these things to myself | 1Co 4:6

APPOINT

These are the LORD's **a-ed** times, | Lv 23:4
Let's **a** a leader and go back | Nm 14:4
A a king from your brothers. | Dt 17:15
a a king to judge us | 1Sm 8:5
A king for them. | 1Sm 8:22
a-ed time that Samuel had set, | 1Sm 13:8
a-ed me the head of nations; | 2Sm 22:44
a-ed you ruler over My people | 1Kg 14:7
Moons, and the **a-ed** festivals | 2Ch 2:4
Jeroboam **a-ed** his own priests | 2Ch 11:15
a magistrates and judges | Ezr 7:25
I will **a** peace as your guard | Is 60:17
I **a-ed** you a prophet to the nations | Jr 1:5
abolished **a-ed** festivals | Lm 2:6
a-ed a sword for slaughter | Ezk 21:15
a over them a single shepherd | Ezk 34:23
will still come at the **a-ed** time. | Dn 11:35
A harvest is also **a-ed** for you, | Hs 6:11
the LORD **a-ed** a great fish | Jnh 1:17
the Lord GOD **a-ed** a plant, | Jnh 4:6
God **a-ed** a worm | Jnh 4:7
God **a-ed** a scorching east wind. | Jnh 4:8
vision is yet for the **a-ed** time; | Hab 2:3
He also **a-ed** 12 | Mk 3:14
the Lord **a-ed** 70 others, | Lk 10:1
who **a-ed** Me a judge | Lk 12:14
who has been **a-ed** Messiah | Ac 3:20
Who **a-ed** you a ruler | Ac 7:35
God did not **a** us to wrath, | 1Th 5:9
For this I was **a-ed** a herald, | 1Tm 2:7
I was **a-ed** a herald, apostle, | 2Tm 1:11
a elders in every town: | Ti 1:5
He has **a-ed** heir of all things | Heb 1:2
law **a-s** as high priests men | Heb 7:28
it is **a-ed** for people to die once | Heb 9:27

APPROACH

no ... person outside the lineage
of Aaron should **a** to offer | Nm 16:40
toward Esther, and she **a-ed** | Est 5:2
near and rapidly **a-ing.** | Zph 1:14
He **a-ed** Pilate and asked | Lk 23:52
let us **a** the throne of grace | Heb 4:16

APPROPRIATE

the righteous know what is a,	Pr 10:32
Excessive speech is not a	Pr 17:7
Luxury is not a for a fool	Pr 19:10
made everything a in its time.	Ec 3:11
awaken love until the a time.	Sg 2:7; 3:5; 8:4
a penalty for their perversion.	Rm 1:27

APPROVAL

appointed leaders, but without My a.	Hs 8:4
Father has set His seal of a on Him.	Jn 6:27

APPROVE

Lord does not a {of these things}.	Lm 3:36
was standing by and a-ing,	Ac 22:20
and a-d by men.	Rm 14:18
by what he a-s.	Rm 14:22
just as we have been a-d by God	1Th 2:4
to present yourself a-d to God,	2Tm 2:15
by it our ancestors were a-d.	Heb 11:2

AQUILA

Husband of Priscilla; tentmaker; Jewish Christian; teacher; co-worker with Paul (Ac 18:2,18,26; Rm 16:3; 1Co 16:19; 2Tm 4:19).

ARAB

the A-s brought him flocks:	2Ch 17:11
the Philistines and the A-s	2Ch 21:16
the A-s that live in Gur-baal,	2Ch 26:7
Geshem the A	Neh 2:19; 6:1
the A-s, Ammonites,	Neh 4:7
Cretans and A-s	Ac 2:11

ARABAH

in the A opposite Suph,	Dt 1:1
the Sea of the A (the Dead Sea)	Jos 3:16
along the route to the A,	2Kg 25:4
a dry land, a wilderness, an A.	Jr 50:12
and goes down to the A.	Ezk 47:8
Hamath to the Brook of the A.	Am 6:14

ARABIA

An oracle against A:	Is 21:13
A ... your business partners,	Ezk 27:21
instead I went to A	Gl 1:17
Now Hagar is Mount Sinai in A	Gl 4:25

ARABIAN

all the A kings	1Kg 10:15; 2Ch 9:14

ARAD

A country in the Negev (Nm 21:1; 33:40; Jos 12:14; Jdg 1:16).

ARAM

1. Son of Shem (Gn 10:22). The nation named for him, perennial enemy of Israel (Jdg 3:8; 2Sm 8:6; 1Kg 11:25; 20; 22; 2Kg 6:8-24; 8:12-13; 13:3,22; 16:7).

2. Grandson of Abraham's brother Nahor (Gn 22:21).

3. Ancestor of Jesus (Mt 1:3-4); also called Ram (Ru 4:19; Lk 3:33).

ARAMAIC

speak to your servants in A,	2Kg 18:26
The letter was written in A	Ezr 4:7
speak to your servants in A,	Is 36:11
spoke to the king (A begins here):	Dn 2:4

ARAMEAN

My father was a wandering A.	Dt 26:5
the A-s from Kir?	Am 9:7

ARARAT

on the mountains of A.	Gn 8:4
escaped to the land of A.	2Kg 19:37

ARAUNAH

Man whose threshing floor David bought (2Sm 24:15-25); also called Ornan (1Ch 21:15-28); threshing floor became site of the temple (1Ch 22:1; 2Ch 3:1).

ARCHANGEL

a shout, with the a-'s voice,	1Th 4:16
Michael the a,	Jd 9

ARCHER

the a-s caught up with him	1Sm 31:3
a-s who, using either ... hand	1Ch 12:2
The a-s shot King Josiah,	2Ch 35:23
His a-s surround me.	Jb 16:13
like an a who wounds everyone	Pr 26:10

ARCHITECT

whose a and builder is God.	Heb 11:10

AREOPAGUS

stood in the middle of the A	Ac 17:22

ARGUE

So they a-d before the king.	1Kg 3:22
a my case before God.	Jb 13:3

Let him who a-s with God give | Jb 40:2
let us a our case together. | Is 43:26
Woe ... who a-s with his Maker | Is 45:9
He will not a or shout, | Mt 12:19
began to a among themselves, | Mt 21:25
Pharisees ... to a with Him, | Mk 8:11
What were you a-ing about | Mk 9:33
began to a among themselves | Lk 22:23
don't a about doubtful issues. | Rm 14:1
if anyone wants to a | 1Co 11:16
without grumbling and a-ing, | Php 2:14

ARGUMENT

Hear now my a, | Jb 13:6
not one of you refuted his a-s. | Jb 32:12
has no a-s in his mouth. | Ps 38:14
Present your a-s, | Is 41:21
Then an a started among them | Lk 9:46
We demolish a-s | 2Co 10:4
deceive you with empty a-s, | Eph 5:6
deceive you with persuasive a-s. | Col 2:4
holy hands without anger or a. | 1Tm 2:8
sick interest in disputes and a-s | 1Tm 6:4

ARISE

A, LORD! Let Your enemies | Nm 10:35
No prophet has a-n again | Dt 34:10
A, LORD God, {come} to | 2Ch 6:41
God a-s. His enemies scatter, | Ps 68:1
A, God, defend Your cause! | Ps 74:22
A, my darling. Come away, | Sg 2:10
A, shine, for your light has come | Is 60:1
kings will a in Persia, | Dn 11:2
false prophets will a | Mt 24:24
no prophet a-s from Galilee. | Jn 7:52
priest like Melchizedek a-s, | Heb 7:15

ARK

Make ... an a of gofer wood. | Gn 6:14
entered the a | Gn 7:7
make an a of acacia wood, | Ex 25:10
Put the tablets ... into the a. | Ex 25:16
made the a of acacia wood, | Ex 37:1
waters ... cut off in front of the a | Jos 4:7
The a of God was captured, | 1Sm 4:11
Nothing was in the a except | 1Kg 8:9
a place there for the a, | 1Kg 8:21
reached out to hold the a, | 1Ch 13:9
to bring the a of the LORD | 1Ch 15:3
the a {that shows} Your strength. | Ps 132:8

the day Noah boarded the a. | Mt 24:38
a ... in which there was | Heb 9:4
built an a to deliver his family. | Heb 11:7
while an a was being prepared; | 1Pt 3:20
the a of His covenant appeared | Rv 11:19

ARM (n)

with an outstretched a | Ex 6:6
a strong hand and an outstretched a, | Dt 4:34
underneath are the everlasting a-s. | Dt 33:27
delivered the a that is weak! | Jb 26:2
Do you have an a like God's? | Jb 40:9
Break the a of the wicked | Ps 10:15
a-s can bend a bow of bronze. | Ps 18:34
a-s of the wicked will be broken | Ps 37:17
a did not bring them victory | Ps 44:3
holy a have won Him victory. | Ps 98:1
folding of the a-s to rest, | Pr 6:10; 24:33
her a-s are strong. | Pr 31:17
The fool folds his a-s | Ec 4:5
His a-s are rods of gold | Sg 5:14
as a seal on your a. | Sg 8:6
eats the flesh of his own a. | Is 9:20
gathers the lambs in His a-s | Is 40:11
a of the LORD been revealed to? | Is 53:1
its chest and a-s were silver, | Dn 2:32
taking them in My a-s, | Hs 11:3
taking them in His a-s, | Mk 10:16
who has the a of the Lord
   been revealed to? | Jn 12:38

ARM (v)

a yourselves also with the same | 1Pt 4:1

ARMAGEDON

place called in Hebrew A. | Rv 16:16

ARMED (adj)

a men crosses the Jordan | Nm 32:21
a troops go ahead of the ark | Jos 6:7
a strong man, fully a, guards | Lk 11:21

ARMOR

David ... had him put on a. | 1Sm 17:38
him who puts on his a boast | 1Kg 20:11
through the joints of his a. | 1Kg 22:34
penetrate his double layer of a? | Jb 41:13
put on the a of light. | Rm 13:12
Put on the full a of God | Eph 6:11
put the a of faith and love on | 1Th 5:8

ARMOR-BEARER

called his a and said to him,	Jdg 9:54
Jonathan and his a struck	1Sm 14:14
David became his a.	1Sm 16:21
Saul said to his a,	1Sm 31:4

ARMY

chariots and his a into the sea;	Ex 15:4
he must not go out with the a	Dt 24:5
commander of the LORD's a.	Jos 5:14
defied the a-ies of the	
living God.	1Sm 17:36
a great a, like an a of God.	1Ch 12:22
Uzziah had an a equipped for	2Ch 26:11
Though an a deploy against me,	Ps 27:3
king is not saved by a large a;	Ps 33:16
hurled Pharaoh and his a into	Ps 136:15
and a king at the head of his a.	Pr 30:31
as an a with banners	Sg 6:4,10
stood on their feet, a vast a.	Ezk 37:10
he will advance with a great a	Dn 11:13
like a mighty a deployed for war.	Jl 2:5
Jerusalem surrounded by a-ies,	Lk 21:20
put foreign a-ies to flight.	Heb 11:34
The a-ies that were in heaven	Rv 19:14
on the horse and against His a.	Rv 19:19

AROMA

LORD smelled the pleasing a,	Gn 8:21
It is a pleasing a, a fire offering	Ex 29:18
a fire offering of a pleasing a	Lv 1:9
and his a hasn't changed.	Jr 48:11

ARRAY

stars—all the a of heaven	Dt 4:19

ARREST

Herod had a-ed John,	Mt 14:3
looking for a way to a Him,	Mt 21:46
hold of Jesus, and a-ed Him.	Mt 26:50
when they a you	Mk 13:11
sent temple police to a Him.	Jn 7:32
report to so they could a Him.	Jn 11:57
they a-ed the apostles	Ac 5:18
he proceeded to a Peter too,	Ac 12:3

ARROGANCE

your a have reached My ears,	2Kg 19:28
A leads to nothing but strife,	Pr 13:10
his haughtiness, his pride, his a,	Is 16:6

gossip, a, and disorder.	2Co 12:20
you boast in your a.	Jms 4:16

ARROGANT

boast so proudly, or let a {words}	1Sm 2:3
he became strong, he grew a	2Ch 26:16
For I envied the a;	Ps 73:3
a people have attacked me;	Ps 86:14
anyone with ... an a heart.	Ps 101:5
The a constantly ridicule me,	Ps 119:51
I hate a pride, evil conduct,	Pr 8:13
an a spirit before a fall.	Pr 16:18
became a, he was deposed	Dn 5:20
God-haters, a, proud, boastful,	Rm 1:30
Do not be a, but be afraid.	Rm 11:20
not to be a or to set their hope	1Tm 6:17
a people! They do not tremble	2Pt 2:10
their mouths utter a words,	Jd 16

ARROGANTLY

it had a mouth that spoke a.	Dn 7:8

ARROW

I will shoot three a-s beside it	1Sm 20:20
Elisha said, "Take the a-s!"	2Kg 13:18
enter this city or shoot an a	2Kg 19:32
a-s of the Almighty have pierced	Jb 6:4
they put the a on the bowstring	Ps 11:2
shatters the bow's flaming a-s,	Ps 76:3
Your a-s flashed back and forth.	Ps 77:17
the a that flies by day,	Ps 91:5
a-s in the hand of a warrior	Ps 127:4
until an a pierces its liver,	Pr 7:23
a club, a sword, or a sharp a.	Pr 25:18
He made me like a sharpened a;	Is 49:2
Their tongues are deadly a-s	Jr 9:8
I shoot deadly a-s of famine	Ezk 5:16
he shakes the a-s,	Ezk 21:21
extinguish the flaming a-s	Eph 6:16

ARTAXERXES

King of Persia who allowed Ezra to rebuild the temple (Ezr 6:14; 7:1-26) and Nehemiah to rebuild the wall of Jerusalem (Neh 2:1-6).

ARTEMIS

Greek goddess (Ac 19:24-35).

ARTISTIC

to design a works	Ex 31:4; 35:32

ASA

Son of Abijam; king of Judah (1Kg 15:8). Instituted reforms (15:13). Rebuked for relying on Aram for military help and on doctors for healing rather than on the Lord (2Ch 16:1-12).

ASAHEL

David's nephew (1Ch 2:16); one of his warriors (11:26; 27:7). Killed by Abner (2Sm 2:18-32), avenged by Joab, his brother (3:22-39).

ASAPH

Levite musician appointed by David (1Ch 16:4-7,37; Ezr 2:41). Psalms 50, 73–83 are attributed to him.

ASCEND

their cry for help a-ed to God	Ex 2:23
Who may a the mountain	Ps 24:3
God a-s amid shouts of joy,	Ps 47:5
I will a to the heavens;	Is 14:13
they a-ed, the wheels a-ed	Ezk 10:17
angels of God a-ing and	Jn 1:51
No one has a-ed into heaven	Jn 3:13
observe the Son of Man a-ing	Jn 6:62
not yet a-ed to the Father.	Jn 20:17
it was not David who a-ed	Ac 2:34
same as the One who a-ed	Eph 4:10
Her smoke a-s forever and ever!	Rv 19:3

ASCENTS

song of a.	Pss 120–134

ASCETIC

insisting on a practices	Col 2:18
promoting a practices, humility,	Col 2:23

ASCRIBE

a to the LORD glory	
and strength.	1Ch 16:28; Ps 96:7
A power to God.	Ps 68:34

ASENATH

Wife of Joseph (Gn 41:45,50; 46:20).

ASHAMED

All my enemies will be a	Ps 6:10
Then I would not be a	Ps 119:6
Jacob will no longer be a	Is 29:22
Were they a	Jr 6:15; 8:12
Be a and humiliated	Ezk 36:32

is a of Me and of My words	Mk 8:38
I'm a to beg.	Lk 16:3
I am not a of the gospel	Rm 1:16
don't be a of the testimony	2Tm 1:8
was not a of my chains.	2Tm 1:16
who doesn't need to be a,	2Tm 2:15
so that the opponent will be a,	Ti 2:8
not a to call them brothers,	Heb 2:11
is not a to be called their God,	Heb 11:16
Christian, he should not be a,	1Pt 4:16
have boldness and not be a	1Jn 2:28

ASHDOD

Philistine city (Jos 13:3; 1Sm 5:1-8; Am 3:9; Zph 2:4).

ASHER

Jacob's eighth son, born of Zilpah (Gn 30:13; 35:26). The tribe's territory was in the northwest on the Phoenician coast (Jos 19:24-31). Also, a town (17:7).

ASHERAH

chop down their A poles.	Ex 34:13
cut down their A poles,	Dt 7:5
worshiped the Baals and the A-s.	Jdg 3:7
cut down the A pole beside it.	Jdg 6:25
and the 400 prophets of A	1Kg 18:19
A poles on every high hill	2Kg 17:10
cut down the A (poles).	2Kg 18:4
He made an A, as King Ahab	2Kg 21:3
weaving tapestries for A.	2Kg 23:7
cut down the A poles,	2Kg 23:14
an obscene image of A.	2Ch 15:16

ASHES

even though I am dust and a	Gn 18:27
remove the a of the burnt	Lv 6:10
gather up the cow's a	Nm 19:9
Tamar put a on her head	2Sm 13:19
the a spilled off the altar,	1Kg 13:5
put on sackcloth and a,	Est 4:1
he sat among the a.	Jb 2:8
repent in dust and a.	Jb 42:6
I eat a like bread	Ps 102:9
a crown of beauty instead of a,	Is 61:3
with fasting, sackcloth, and a.	Dn 9:3
put on sackcloth, and sat in a.	Jnh 3:6
in sackcloth and a long ago!	Mt 11:21
the a of a heifer	Heb 9:13
Sodom and Gomorrah to a	2Pt 2:6

ASHKELON
Philistine city (Jos 13:3; Jdg 1:18; 2Sm 1:20; Am 1:8; Zph 2:4).

ASHTAROTH
Canaanite capital of Bashan (Dt 1:4; Jos 13:31).

ASHTORETH
Sidonian goddess (Jdg 2:13; 10:6; 1Sm 7:4; 31:10; 1Kg 11:5; 2Kg 23:13).

ASIA
prevented from speaking ... in ... A.	Ac 16:6
province of A ... heard the word	Ac 19:10
first convert to Christ from A.	Rm 16:5
those in A have turned away	2Tm 1:15
churches in the province of A.	Rv 1:4

ASIDE
My lords, turn a	Gn 19:2
everything left over set a	Ex 16:23
set a a tenth of all the produce	Dt 14:22
Do not turn a to the right or	Dt 28:14
David; he did not turn a	2Ch 34:2
His way and not turned a.	Jb 23:11
Everyone has turned a;	Ps 53:3
turned a and have gone away.	Jr 5:23
set me a like an empty dish;	Jr 51:34
set a a donation to the LORD,	Ezk 45:1
Jesus took the 12 disciples a	Mt 20:17
set something a and save	1Co 16:2
let us lay a every weight	Heb 12:1

ASK
a me, 'What is His name	Ex 3:13
When your children a you,	Ex 12:26
a about the earlier days	Dt 4:32
When your son a-s you	Dt 6:20
your God a of you except to fear	Dt 10:12
when your children a you,	Jos 4:6
Did I a my lord for a son?	2Kg 4:28
Who can a Him,	Jb 9:12
A of Me, and I will make	Ps 2:8
not a for a whole burnt offering	Ps 40:6
Two things I a of You;	Pr 30:7
A for a sign from the LORD	Is 7:11
sought by those who did not a;	Is 65:1
when you a yourself: Why	Jr 13:22
you a: "How have You loved us?"	Mal 1:2
You a: "How do we rob You?"	Mal 3:8

Give to the one who a-s you,	Mt 5:42
you need before you a Him.	Mt 6:8
Keep a-ing, and it will be given	Mt 7:7
good things to those who a Him!	Mt 7:11
don't know what you're a-ing.	Mt 20:22
whatever you a for in prayer.	Mt 21:22
I will also a you one question,	Mt 21:24
sisters are outside a-ing for You.	Mk 3:32
What should I a for?	Mk 6:24
they were afraid to a Him.	Mk 9:32
you pray and a for—believe	Mk 11:24
Holy Spirit to those who a	Lk 11:13
A him; he's of age.	Jn 9:21
whatever You a from God,	Jn 11:22
Whatever you a in My name,	Jn 14:13
will a the Father, and He will give	Jn 14:16
a whatever you want	Jn 15:7
whatever you a the Father in My	Jn 15:16
In that day you will not a Me	Jn 16:23
A and you will receive,	Jn 16:24
In that day you will a in My name.	Jn 16:26
None of the disciples dared a	Jn 21:12
the Jews a for signs	1Co 1:22
should a their own husbands	1Co 14:35
beyond all that we a or think	Eph 3:20
lacks wisdom, he should a God,	Jms 1:5
But let him a in faith	Jms 1:6
because you do not a.	Jms 4:2
You a and don't receive because you a wrongly,	Jms 4:3
defense to anyone who a-s you	1Pt 3:15
a anything according to His will,	1Jn 5:14
He hears whatever we a,	1Jn 5:15

ASLEEP
The child is not dead but a.	Mk 5:39
as they were sailing He fell a.	Lk 8:23
Lazarus has fallen a,	Jn 11:11
saying this, he fell a.	Ac 7:60
many have fallen a.	1Co 11:30
who have fallen a in Christ	1Co 15:18
the firstfruits of those who have fallen a.	1Co 15:20
We will not all fall a,	1Co 15:51
concerning those who are a,	1Th 4:13
fallen a through Jesus.	1Th 4:14
no advantage over those who have fallen a.	1Th 4:15
whether we are awake or a,	1Th 5:10

ASPHALT

brick for stone and a for mortar.   Gn 11:3
coated it with a and pitch.   Ex 2:3

ASSASSINS

led 4,000 A into the desert?   Ac 21:38

ASSAY

an a-er ... so you may know
  and a their way of life.   Jr 6:27

ASSEMBLE

a the whole community   Lv 8:3
David a-d all Israel,   1Ch 13:5
the peoples are a-d.   Is 43:9
A on the mountains of Samaria   Am 3:9
to gather nations, to a kingdoms,   Zph 3:8
a-d together against Your holy
  Servant Jesus,   Ac 4:27
the apostles and the elders a-d   Ac 15:6
to a them for the battle   Rv 16:14

ASSEMBLY

sacred a on the first day and another
  sacred a on the seventh.   Ex 12:16
proclaim as sacred a-ies.   Lv 23:2
the a in front of the rock,   Nm 20:10
stands trial before the a.   Nm 35:12
this song to the entire a   Dt 31:30
before the entire a of Israel,   Jos 8:35
until he stands trial before the a   Jos 20:6
a solemn a for Baal.   2Kg 10:20
before the a of men, women,   Neh 8:2
praise the LORD in the a-ies.   Ps 26:12
Let them exalt Him in the a   Ps 107:32
in the a of the upright   Ps 111:1
His praise in the a of the godly.   Ps 149:1
a solemn a of treacherous people.   Jr 9:2
a sacred fast; proclaim an a.   Jl 2:15
stench of your solemn a-ies.   Am 5:21
the a was divided.   Ac 23:7
the a of the firstborn   Heb 12:23

ASSESSMENT

pay according to judicial a.   Ex 21:22

ASSIGN

Levites were a-ed to   1Ch 6:48
I have a-ed you 40 days,   Ezk 4:6
king a-ed them daily provisions   Dn 1:5
a him a place with the hypocrites.   Mt 24:51
a-ed four squads of four soldiers   Ac 12:4

the situation the Lord a-ed   1Co 7:17
{of ministry} that God has a-ed   2Co 10:13

ASSIST

their duty will be to a   1Ch 23:28
a her in whatever matter   Rm 16:2

ASSISTANCE

no one came to my a,   2Tm 4:16

ASSOCIATE

worthless or a with hypocrites.   Ps 26:4
you a with adulterers.   Ps 50:18
Don't a with those who drink   Pr 23:20
don't a with rebels,   Pr 24:21
Jews do not a with Samaritans.   Jn 4:9
he tried to a with the disciples,   Ac 9:26
to a with or visit a foreigner.   Ac 10:28
a with the humble.   Rm 12:16
not to a with sexually immoral   1Co 5:9
not to a with anyone who bears
  the name of brother   1Co 5:11
don't a with him,   2Th 3:14

ASSUME

a that I came to destroy the law   Mt 5:17
Don't a that I came to bring peace   Mt 10:34
they a-d they would get more,   Mt 20:10
A-ing He was in the traveling party,   Lk 2:44
a-ing you heard Him   Eph 4:21
by a-ing the form of a slave,   Php 2:7
a-ing that I will somehow reach   Php 3:11

ASSURANCE

Holy Spirit, and with much a.   1Th 1:5
true heart in full a of faith,   Heb 10:22

ASSURED

stand mature and fully a   Col 4:12

ASSYRIA

From that land he went to A   Gn 10:11
Pul king of A invaded   2Kg 15:19
Tiglath-pileser king of A came   2Kg 15:29
Shalmaneser king of A attacked   2Kg 17:3
The king of A deported the
  Israelites to A   2Kg 18:11
what the kings of A have done   2Kg 19:11
the king of A {is coming}.   Is 7:17
Woe to A, the rod of My anger   Is 10:5
just as I punished the king of A.   Jr 50:18
gather them from A.   Zch 10:10

ASTONISHED

crowds were a at His teaching.	Mt 7:28
were a and said, "How did this	Mt 13:54
they were a at His teaching.	Mt 22:33
were a. "Where did this man get	Mk 6:2
They were extremely a	Mk 7:37
disciples were a at His words.	Mk 10:24
parents saw Him, they were a,	Lk 2:48
all a at the greatness of God.	Lk 9:43

ASTOUNDED

observe—be utterly a!	Hab 1:5
all the crowds were a	Mt 12:23
all a and gave glory to God,	Mk 2:12
were a at His understanding	Lk 2:47
they were a and amazed,	Ac 2:7
he had a them with his sorceries	Ac 8:11
But all who heard him were a	Ac 9:21

ASTRAY

do not be led a to bow down	Dt 4:19
led a to bow down to other gods	Dt 30:17
he led Judah a.	2Ch 21:11
let a large ransom lead you a.	Jb 36:18
gone a and have acted wickedly	Ps 106:6
who rejects correction goes a.	Pr 10:17
Don't those who plan evil go a?	Pr 14:22
foolishness leads him a,	Pr 19:3
We all went a like sheep;	Is 53:6
led My people Israel a.	Jr 23:13
You have led your own selves a	Jr 42:20
their shepherds have led them a,	Jr 50:6
prophets who lead my people a,	Mc 3:5
let what is going a go a;	Zch 11:9
and one of them goes a,	Mt 18:12
lead a, if possible, the elect.	Mk 13:22
always go a in their hearts,	Heb 3:10
Don't be led a by various kinds	Heb 13:9
you were like sheep going a,	1Pt 2:25

ASTUTE

sons of this age are more a	Lk 16:8

ATHALIAH

Wife of Jehoram and mother of Ahaziah, kings of Judah; descendant of Omri (2Kg 8:26). Encouraged Baal worship (8:27). Killed heirs and ruled after her son's death (11:1-3). Jehoiada the priest executed her and crowned Josiah, the only surviving heir (11:4-20).

ATHENS

City in Greece (Ac 17; 1Th 3:1).

ATHLETE

if anyone competes as an a,	2Tm 2:5

ATONE

shekel ... to a for your lives.	Ex 30:15
sin offerings to a for Israel,	Neh 10:33
only You can a for our rebellions	Ps 65:3
He a-d for {their} guilt	Ps 78:38
Deliver us and a for our sins,	Ps 79:9
Wickedness is a-d for by loyalty	Pr 16:6
your sin is a-d for.	Is 6:7

ATONEMENT

eat those things by which a was	Ex 29:33
blood of the sin offering for a.	Ex 30:10
priest will make a on their behalf,	Lv 4:20
make a before the LORD	Lv 14:31
is the Day of A.	Lv 23:27
he ... made a for the Israelites.	Nm 25:13
there can be no a for the land	
because of the blood	Nm 35:33

ATTACK (n)

an a against these Philistines?	1Sm 23:2
Jews made a united a	Ac 18:12
The Jews also joined in the a,	Ac 24:9

ATTACK (v)

he may come and a me,	Gn 32:11
a-ed their army	Jdg 8:11
Whoever a-s the Jebusites must	2Sm 5:8
a them opposite the balsam	2Sm 5:23
I will a him while he is weak	2Sm 17:2
With You I can a a barrier,	2Sm 22:30
you must a every fortified city	2Kg 3:19
There are many who a me.	Ps 3:1
they have often a-ed me	Ps 129:1
Let's a some innocent person	Pr 1:11
a worm that a-ed the plant,	Jnh 4:7
when one stronger than he a-s	Lk 11:22

ATTEMPTED

a to establish their own righteousness,	Rm 10:3
When the Egyptians a to do this,	Heb 11:29

ATTEND

a the king and be his caregiver.	1Kg 1:2

ATTENDANT

became his personal a.	Gn 39:4
all his a-s left him.	Jdg 3:19
his a-s' service and their attire,	1Kg 10:5
Gehazi, the a of Elisha	2Kg 5:20
king's personal a-s suggested,	Est 2:2
gave it back to the a, and sat	Lk 4:20

ATTENTION

not pay a to deceptive words.	Ex 5:9
paid a to His people's need	Ru 1:6
paid a to Hannah's need,	1Sm 2:21
not respond, and did not pay a.	1Sm 4:20
to pay a {is better} than the fat	1Sm 15:22
pay so much a to him?	Jb 7:17
Pay a to the sound of my cry,	Ps 5:2
pay a to my cry;	Ps 17:1
Pay a to me and answer me.	Ps 55:2
hear my cry; pay a to my prayer.	Ps 61:1
He has paid a to ... my prayer.	Ps 66:19
The God of Jacob doesn't pay a.	Ps 94:7
pay a so that you may gain	Pr 4:1
My son, pay a to my words;	Pr 4:20
My son, pay a to my wisdom;	Pr 5:1
pay a to the words of the wise,	Pr 22:17
get rich; stop giving your a to it.	Pr 23:4
pay a to your herds,	Pr 27:23
Don't pay a to everything people	Ec 7:21
Listen, heavens, and pay a, earth,	Is 1:2
it burned him, but he paid no a.	Is 42:25
pay no a to things of old.	Is 43:18
pay a, earth and everyone in it!	Mc 1:2
no a to them, tell the church.	Mt 18:17
pay a to myths and endless	1Tm 1:4
give your a to public reading,	1Tm 4:13
not pay a to Jewish myths	Ti 1:14
more a to what we have heard	Heb 2:1
his a was on the reward.	Heb 11:26

ATTENTIVE

Your ears a to the prayer	2Ch 6:40
My ears a to prayer	2Ch 7:15
Your ears be a to hear	Neh 1:6
Your ears be a to my cry	Ps 130:2

ATTESTED

a by the Law and the Prophets	Rm 3:21

ATTIRE

attendants' service and their a,	1Kg 10:5
but you wear your royal a.	1Kg 22:30

ATTITUDE

from your father's face that his a	Gn 31:5
Render service with a good a,	Eph 6:7
Make your own a that of Christ	Php 2:5

ATTRIBUTES

His invisible a,	Rm 1:20

AUGUSTUS

Title for Emperor Octavian, who ruled when Jesus was born (Lk 2:1).

AUTHORITY

Confer some of your a on him	Nm 27:20
Who gave Him a over the earth?	Jb 34:13
I will put your a into his hand,	Is 22:21
was given a to rule.	Dn 7:6
like one who had a,	Mt 7:29
I too am a man under a,	Mt 8:9
Son of Man has a on earth	Mt 9:6
gave them a over unclean spirits	Mt 10:1
By what a are You doing	Mt 21:23
All a has been given to Me	Mt 28:18
with a and power, He commands	Lk 4:36
Fear Him who has a to throw	Lk 12:5
rulers and a-ies, don't worry	Lk 12:11
You gave Him a over all flesh;	Jn 17:2
You would have no a over Me	Jn 19:11
law has a over someone as long	Rm 7:1
submit to the governing a-ies,	Rm 13:1
there is no a except from God,	Rm 13:1
{a-ies} are God's public servants,	Rm 13:6
not have a over her own body,	1Co 7:4
{a symbol of} a on her head:	1Co 11:10
far above every ruler and a,	Eph 1:21
rulers and a-ies in the heavens	Eph 3:10
rulers, against the a-ies,	Eph 6:12
or dominions or rulers or a-ies	Col 1:16
head over every ruler and a.	Col 2:10
disarmed the rulers and a-ies	Col 2:15
all those who are in a,	1Tm 2:2
teach or to have a over a man;	1Tm 2:12
be submissive to rulers and a-ies,	Ti 3:1
a-ies, and powers subjected	1Pt 3:22
glory, majesty, power, and a	Jd 25
I will give him a over the nations	Rv 2:26
A was given to them	Rv 6:8
the a of His Messiah	Rv 12:10
because he gave a to the beast.	Rv 13:4

given **a** to act for 42 months. Rv 13:5
who were given **a** to judge. Rv 20:4

AVENGE

He will **a** the blood Dt 32:43
kept me from ... **a-ing** myself 1Sm 25:33
Don't say, "I will **a** this evil!" Pr 20:22
Should I not **a** Myself Jr 5:9
I will **a** the bloodshed of Jezreel Hs 1:4
a jealous and **a-ing** God; Nah 1:2
do not **a** yourselves; Rm 12:19
how long until You judge and **a** Rv 6:10

AVENGER

cities as a refuge from the **a**, Nm 35:12
a of blood himself is to kill Nm 35:19
a of blood finds him outside Nm 35:27
hand him over to the **a** of blood Dt 19:12
refuge from the **a** of blood. Jos 20:3
to silence the enemy and the **a**. Ps 8:2
an **a** that brings wrath Rm 13:4
Lord is an **a** of all these offenses 1Th 4:6

AVOID

A it; don't travel on it. Pr 4:15
he may **a** going down to Sheol. Pr 15:24
highway of the upright **a-s** evil; Pr 16:17
a someone with a big mouth. Pr 20:19
hates the light and **a-s** it, Jn 3:20
A them; Rm 16:17
only to **a** being persecuted Gl 6:12
a-ing irreverent, empty speech 1Tm 6:20
a irreverent, empty speech 2Tm 2:16
A these people! 2Tm 3:5
to **a** fighting, and to be kind, Ti 3:2
But **a** foolish debates, genealogies, Ti 3:9

AWAKE

Noah **awoke** from his drinking Gn 9:24
Jacob **awoke** from his sleep, Gn 28:16
A! **A**, Deborah! Jdg 5:12
when I **a**, I will be satisfied Ps 17:15
the Lord **awoke** as if from sleep, Ps 78:65
I am **a** through each watch Ps 119:148
or **a-n** love until Sg 2:7; 3:5; 8:4
A-n, north wind Sg 4:16
I sleep, but my heart is **a**. Sg 5:2
I **a-ned** you under the apricot tree. Sg 8:5
He **a-ns** {Me} each morning; Is 50:4
    He **a-ns** My ear to listen Is 50:4
a great nation will be **a-ned** Jr 6:22

in the dust of the earth will **a**, Dn 12:2
Couldn't you stay **a** one hour? Mk 14:37
we must stay **a** and be sober. 1Th 5:6
whether we are **a** or asleep, 1Th 5:10
I **a-n** your pure understanding 2Pt 3:1

AWARE

If I had been **a** of malice in my Ps 66:18
When Jesus became **a** of this, Mt 12:15
But Jesus, **a** of this, said Mt 26:10

AWAY

put **a** all the following: anger, Col 3:8

AWE

Serve the LORD with reverential **a**, Ps 2:11
of the world stand in **a** of Him. Ps 33:8
I tremble in **a** of You; Ps 119:120
so that people will be in **a** of Him. Ec 3:14
only He should be held in **a**. Is 8:13
stand in **a** of the God of Israel, Is 29:23
They will tremble with **a** Jr 33:9
will come with **a** to the LORD Hs 3:5
they will stand in **a** of You. Mc 7:17
I stand in **a** of Your deeds. Hab 3:2
stood in **a** of My name. Mal 2:5
Herod was in **a** of John Mk 6:20
they were filled with **a** and said, Lk 5:26
serve ... with reverence and **a**; Heb 12:28

AWE-INSPIRING

looked like the **a** Angel of God. Jdg 13:6
the great and **a** God who keeps Neh 1:5
great, mighty, and **a** God Neh 9:32
right hand show your **a** deeds. Ps 45:4
the LORD Most High is **a**, Ps 47:2
You answer us ... with **a** works, Ps 65:5
How **a** are Your works! Ps 66:3
His acts toward mankind are **a**. Ps 66:5
You are **a** in Your sanctuaries. Ps 68:35
more **a** than all who surround Ps 89:7
praise Your great and **a** name. Ps 99:3
a deeds at the Red Sea. Ps 106:22
His name is holy and **a**. Ps 111:9
the power of Your **a** works, Ps 145:6
a as an army with banners Sg 6:4,10
LORD—the great and **a** God Dn 9:4
great and **a** Day of the LORD Jl 2:31
I saw another great and **a** sign Rv 15:1
Great and **a** are Your works, Rv 15:3

AWESOME

What an **a** place this is!	Gn 28:17
the great, mighty, and a God,	Dt 10:17
glorious and a name—Yahweh,	Dt 28:58
a majesty surrounds Him.	Jb 37:22
a deeds that we did not expect,	Is 64:3
great and a Day of the LORD	Mal 4:5

AWL

pierce his ear with an **a**,	Ex 21:6
an a and pierce through his ear into	Dt 15:17

AX

Philistines to sharpen ... **a**-es,	1Sm 13:20
iron (a head) fell into the water,	2Kg 6:5
If the a is dull,	Ec 10:10
Does an a exalt itself	Is 10:15
the a is ready to strike	Mt 3:10; Lk 3:9

AZARIAH

1. Samuel's ancestor (1Ch 6:36).
2. Priest under Solomon (1Kg 4:2).
3. Solomon's official (1Kg 4:5).
4. Prophet (2Ch 15:1-8).
5. King of Judah, also called Uzziah (2Kg 15:1-7).
6. Priest who opposed Uzziah when he tried to burn incense (2Ch 26:16-21).
7. Opponent of Jeremiah (Jr 43:2).
8. Abednego's original name (Dn 1:7).

AZAZEL

the LORD and the other for **A**,	Lv 16:8

AZOTUS

Philip appeared in **A**,	Ac 8:40

B

BAAL

Israel aligned itself with **B** of Peor,	Nm 25:3
They worshiped the B-s	Jdg 2:11
tear down the altar of B	Jdg 6:25
Let B plead his case	Jdg 6:32
the 450 prophets of B	1Kg 18:19
But if B, follow him.	1Kg 18:21
knee that has not bowed to B	1Kg 19:18
The prophets prophesied by B	Jr 2:8

no longer call Me: My **B**.	Hs 2:16
who have not bowed down to B.	Rm 11:4

BAASHA

King of Israel (1Kg 15:16–16:7). Exterminated Jeroboam's family (15:29).

BABBLE

When you pray, don't **b**	Mt 6:7

BABY

don't let her be like a dead {**b**}	Nm 12:12
afraid to tell him the b was dead.	2Sm 12:18
Give the living b to the first	1Kg 3:27
bring a b to the point of birth	Is 66:9
the b leaped inside her,	Lk 1:41
you will find a b wrapped	Lk 2:12
b who was lying in the manger.	Lk 2:16
as b-ies in Christ.	1Co 3:1

BABYLON

Mesopotamian city; place of captivity (2Kg 24; Dn 1:1-6); symbol of wickedness (Rv 17:5).

Therefore its name is called **B**,	Gn 11:9
from a distant country, from B,	2Kg 20:14
Nebuchadnezzar king of B	2Kg 24:1
deported Jehoiachin to B.	2Kg 24:15
king of B, entered Jerusalem.	2Kg 25:8
Judah was exiled to B because	1Ch 9:1
Nebuchadnezzar ... bound him	
... to take him to B.	2Ch 36:6
went up from B to Jerusalem.	Ezr 1:11
Cyrus king of B, he issued	Ezr 5:13
By the rivers of B	Ps 137:1
oracle against B that Isaiah	Is 13:1
B has fallen, has fallen.	Is 21:9
serve the king of B for 70 years.	Jr 25:11
first year of Belshazzar king of B,	Dn 7:1
She who is in B, also chosen,	1Pt 5:13
It has fallen, B the Great	Rv 14:8

BACK (adv)

looked **b** and became a pillar	Gn 19:26
ahead 10 steps or go b 10 steps?	2Kg 20:9
plow and looks b is fit for	Lk 9:62

BACK (n)

beatings for the **b**-s of fools.	Pr 19:29
a rod for the b-s of fools.	Pr 26:3
have turned their b-s (on Him).	Is 1:4

gave My **b** to those who beat Me, Is 50:6
have turned their **b**-s to Me Jr 32:33

BACKBITING
a **b** tongue, angry looks. Pr 25:23

BACKWARDS
Eli fell **b** off the chair 1Sm 4:18

BAD
to Jacob, either good or **b**. Gn 31:24
brought a **b** report about them Gn 37:2
a **b** report about the land Nm 14:36
do something good or **b**, Is 41:23
basket contained very **b** figs, Jr 24:2
but a **b** tree produces **b** fruit. Mt 7:17
or done anything good or **b**, Rm 9:11
B company corrupts good 1Co 15:33
in the body, whether good or **b**. 2Co 5:10

BAG
in each man's sack was his **b** of Gn 42:35
two different weights in your **b**, Dt 25:13
David put his hand in the **b**, 1Sm 17:49
150 pounds of silver in two **b**-s 2Kg 5:23
weeping, carrying the **b** of seed, Ps 126:6
He took a **b** of money with him Pr 7:20
weights in the **b** are His concern. Pr 16:11
pack your **b**-s for exile Ezk 12:3
or **b**-s of deceptive weights? Mc 6:11
wages into a **b** with a hole in it. Hg 1:6

BAILIFF
the **b** throw you into prison. Lk 12:58

BAIT
if there is no **b** for it? Am 3:5

BAKE
b-d unleavened bread for them, Gn 19:3
b-d goods for Pharaoh, Gn 40:17
b-d the dough they had brought Ex 12:39
B what you want to **b**, Ex 16:23
a grain offering **b**-d in an oven, Lv 2:4
b it into 12 loaves; Lv 24:5
he kindles a fire and **b**-s bread; Is 44:15

BAKER
Egypt's cupbearer and his **b** Gn 40:1
but he hanged the chief **b**, Gn 40:22
perfumers, cooks, and **b**-s. 1Sm 8:13
each day from the **b**-'s street Jr 37:21
like an oven heated by a **b** Hs 7:4

BALAAM
Prophet hired by King Balak of Moab to curse Israel (Nm 22). His donkey talked (22:21-30; 2Pt 2:16). He blessed Israel (Nm 23–24; Jos 24:10; Neh 13:2). Executed for practicing divination (Nm 31:8; Jos 13:22; 2Pt 2:15; Jd 11; Rv 2:14).

BALAK
King of Moab who hired Balaam to curse Israel (Nm 22–24).

BALANCE
You are to have honest **b**-s, Lv 19:36
weigh me with an accurate **b**, Jb 31:6
On a **b** scale, they go up; Ps 62:9
b-s and scales are the LORD's; Pr 16:11
weighed the mountains in a **b** Is 40:12
You must have honest **b**-s, Ezk 45:10
you have been weighed in the **b** Dn 5:27

BALD
he is **b**, but he is clean. Lv 13:40
Priests may not make **b** spots Lv 21:5
or make a **b** spot on your head Dt 14:1
every head is **b** and every beard Jr 48:37
Every head was made **b** Ezk 29:18

BALDY
chanting, "Go up, **b**! 2Kg 2:23

BALM
Is there no **b** in Gilead? Jr 8:22
Go up to Gilead and get **b**, Jr 46:11

BALSAM
sound of marching in the
　　tops of the **b** trees, 2Sm 5:24; 1Ch 14:15
your perfume than any **b**. Sg 4:10

BAN
be **b**-ned from the synagogue. Jn 9:22
so they would not be **b**-ned Jn 12:42
will **b** you from the synagogues. Jn 16:2

BAND
b-s of the posts must be silver. Ex 27:10
they saw a marauding **b**, 2Kg 13:21
a **b** of deadly messengers. Ps 78:49
They **b** together against the life Ps 94:21
b of iron and bronze around it, Dn 4:15

BANDAGE
disguised himself with a **b** 1Kg 20:38

BANDIT
cleansed, **b-d**, or soothed with oil. Is 1:6
LORD **b-s** His people's injuries Is 30:26
Look, it has not been **b-d** Ezk 30:21
healed the sick, **b-d** the injured Ezk 34:4
and **b-d** his wounds, Lk 10:34

BANDIT
your need, like a **b**. Pr 6:11; 24:34

BANISH
plans so that the one **b-ed** from
    Him does not remain **b-ed**. 2Sm 14:14
b-ed the male shrine prostitutes 1Kg 15:12
until He had **b-ed** them 2Kg 17:20
He finally **b-ed** them 2Kg 24:20
Didn't you **b** the priests 2Ch 13:9
not **b** me from Your presence Ps 51:11
from all the lands where
    I have **b-ed** them, Jr 23:3
will **b** you, and you will perish. Jr 27:10
nations where I will **b** them. Ezk 4:13
not to **b** them to the abyss. Lk 8:31

BANK
put my money in the **b**? Lk 19:23

BANKERS
deposited my money with the **b**. Mt 25:27

BANKRUPT
weak and **b** elemental forces? Gl 4:9

BANNER
The LORD Is My **B**. Ex 17:15
camp under their respective **b-s** Nm 2:2
lift the **b** in the name of our God. Ps 20:5
as an army with **b-s** Sg 6:4,10
will lift up a **b** for the nations Is 11:12
or a **b** on a hill. Is 30:17
Raise a **b** for the peoples. Is 62:10

BANQUET
the king held a week-long **b** Est 1:5
He brought me to the **b** hall, Sg 2:4
invite everyone you find to the **b**. Mt 22:9
love the place of honor at **b-s**, Mt 23:6
Herod gave a **b** for his nobles, Mk 6:21
a **b**, invite those who are poor, Lk 14:13
not one ... will enjoy my **b**! Lk 14:24

BAPTISM
Sadducees coming to ... his **b**, Mt 3:7
Where did John's **b** come from? Mt 21:25
preaching a **b** of repentance Mk 1:4
with the **b** I am baptized with? Mk 10:38
Was John's **b** from heaven or Mk 11:30
baptized with John's **b**. Lk 7:29
I have a **b** to be baptized with, Lk 12:50
proclaimed a **b** of repentance Ac 13:24
he knew only John's **b**. Ac 18:25
John baptized with a **b** of Ac 19:4
we were buried with Him by **b** Rm 6:4
one Lord, one faith, one **b**, Eph 4:5
buried with Him in **b**, Col 2:12
B ... now saves you 1Pt 3:21

BAPTIST
In those days John the **B** came, Mt 3:1
no one greater than John the **B** Mt 11:11
Give me John the **B-'s** head Mt 14:8
Some say John the **B**; Mt 16:14
that He spoke ... about John the **B**. Mt 17:13
John the **B** sent us to ask You, Lk 7:20

BAPTIZE
I **b** you with water for Mt 3:11
He ... will **b** you with ... fire Mt 3:11
at the Jordan, to be **b-d** by him. Mt 3:13
I need to be **b-d** by You, Mt 3:14
b-ing them in the name of Mt 28:19
I have **b-d** you with water, but He
    will **b** you with the Holy Spirit. Mk 1:8
was **b-d** in the Jordan by John. Mk 1:9
to be **b-d** with the baptism I Mk 10:38
and is **b-d** will be saved, Mk 16:16
Tax collectors also ... to be **b-d**, Lk 3:12
Jesus also was **b-d**. Lk 3:21
they had been **b-d** with John's Lk 7:29
I have a baptism to be **b-d** with, Lk 12:50
were coming and being **b-d**, Jn 3:23
b-ing more disciples than John Jn 4:1
Jesus Himself was not **b-ing**, Jn 4:2
will be **b-d** with the Holy Spirit Ac 1:5
repent ... and be **b-d**, Ac 2:38
there's water! What would keep
    me from being **b-d**? Ac 8:36
Then he got up and was **b-d**. Ac 9:18
John **b-d** with water, but you will
    be **b-d** with the Holy Spirit. Ac 11:16
and her household were **b-d**, Ac 16:15
he and all his family were **b-d**. Ac 16:33
heard, believed and were **b-d**. Ac 18:8
what {baptism} were you **b-d**? Ac 19:3

b-d with a baptism of repentance — Ac 19:4
be b-d, and wash away your sins — Ac 22:16
who were b-d into Christ Jesus
    were b-d into His death? — Rm 6:3
were you b-d in Paul's name? — 1Co 1:13
I b-d none of you except — 1Co 1:14
I did, in fact, b the household — 1Co 1:16
Christ did not send me to b, but — 1Co 1:17
all were b-d into Moses — 1Co 10:2
we were all b-d by one Spirit — 1Co 12:13
are being b-d for the dead? — 1Co 15:29
as have been b-d into Christ — Gl 3:27

BAR

I broke the b-s of your yoke — Lv 26:13
a b of gold weighing 50 shekels, — Jos 7:21
installed its doors, bolts, and b-s. — Neh 3:3
put {its} b-s and doors in place, — Jb 38:10
cut through the iron b-s. — Ps 107:16
quarrels are like the b-s — Pr 18:19
cut the iron b-s in two. — Is 45:2
yoke b from ... Jeremiah — Jr 28:10
I break the b-s of their yoke — Ezk 34:27
without walls and without b-s — Ezk 38:11
earth with its prison b-s closed — Jnh 2:6
Fire will devour the b-s — Nah 3:13

BARABBAS

Insurrectionist released by Pilate instead of Jesus (Mt 27:16-26; Mk 15:7-15; Lk 23:18; Jn 18:40).

BARAK

Reluctantly joined Deborah to fight Canaanites (Jdg 4–5; 1Sm 12:11; Heb 11:32).

BARBARIAN

You subdue the uproar of b-s. — Is 25:5
You will no longer see the b-s, — Is 33:19
obligated both to Greeks and b-s, — Rm 1:14
b, Scythian, slave and free; — Col 3:11

BARBS

Death, where are your b? — Hs 13:14

BAREFOOT

he was walking b. — 2Sm 15:30
He leads priests away b — Jb 12:19
he did so, going naked and b — Is 20:2

BAR-JESUS

Elymas (Ac 13:6-8).

BARK (n)

peeled {the b}, exposing white — Gn 30:37

BARK (v)

mute dogs, they cannot b; — Is 56:10

BARLEY

a loaf of b bread came tumbling — Jdg 7:13
the beginning of the b harvest. — Ru 1:22
plot of ground full of b — 1Ch 11:13
silver and five bushels of b. — Hs 3:2
five b loaves and two fish — Jn 6:9
three quarts of b for a denarius — Rv 6:6

BARN

your b-s will be completely filled, — Pr 3:10
gather His wheat into the b. — Mt 3:12
sow or reap or gather into b-s, — Mt 6:26
but store the wheat in my b. — Mt 13:30
gather the wheat into His b, — Lk 3:17
I'll tear down my b-s and build — Lk 12:18
don't have a storeroom or a b; — Lk 12:24

BARNABAS

Levite from Cyprus, named Joseph (Ac 4:36). Introduced Paul to Jerusalem church (9:26-27). Worked with Paul, initially as leader in Antioch (11:19-30), then on a journey (Ac 13–14), then in Jerusalem (15:1-21). Separated from Paul over whether to bring John Mark with them again (15:36-41).

BARRACKS

to be taken into the b. — Ac 21:34
entered the b and reported it — Ac 23:16

BARREN

Sarai was b; she had no child. — Gn 11:30
Rachel was b. — Gn 29:31
No woman will miscarry or be b — Ex 23:26
in a b, howling wilderness; — Dt 32:10
Manoah; his wife was b — Jdg 13:2
b woman gives birth to seven, — 1Sm 2:5
Sheol; a b womb; earth, — Pr 30:16
Rejoice, b one, — Is 54:1
for her who was called b. — Lk 1:36
Blessed are the b, — Lk 23:29
Rejoice, O b woman — Gl 4:27

BARRIER

With You I can attack a b, — 2Sm 22:30
With You I can attack a b, — Ps 18:29
your iniquities have built b-s — Is 59:2

BARSABBAS
1. Apostle candidate (Ac 1:23).
2. Companion of Paul (Ac 15:22).

BARTHOLOMEW
Apostle (Mt 10:3; Mk 3:18; Lk 6:14; Ac 1:13), possibly also called Nathanael (Jn 1:43-51).

BARTIMAEUS
Blind man healed by Jesus (Mk 10:46).

BARUCH
1. Jeremiah's scribe (Jr 36).
2. Priest (Neh 3:20).
3. Father of Maaseiah, a settler (Neh 11:5).

BARZILLAI
Gileadite who helped David; David supported his sons (2Sm 17:27-29; 19:31-39; 1Kg 2:7).

BASE
stood at the **b** of the mountain,   Dt 4:11

BASED
b on the number of years since   Lv 25:15
death **b** on the testimony of one   Nm 35:30
not be **b** on men's wisdom   1Co 2:5
not **b** on a human point of view.   Gl 1:11
the law is not **b** on faith;   Gl 3:12
righteousness from God **b** on faith.   Php 3:9
empty deceit **b** on human tradition,
    b on the elemental forces of the
    world, and not **b** on Christ.   Col 2:8
b on the glorious gospel   1Tm 1:11
b on the testimony of two   Heb 10:28
b on what seemed good to them   Heb 12:10
B on the gift they have received   1Pt 4:10

BASEMATH
1. Wife of Esau (Gn 26:34).
2. Daughter of Solomon (1Kg 4:15).

BASHAN
went up the road to **B**,   Nm 21:33
the rest of Gilead and all **B**,   Dt 3:13
kingdom of Og king of **B**,   Jos 13:30
settled in the land from **B** to   1Ch 5:23
strong ones of **B** encircle me.   Ps 22:12

against all the oaks of **B**,   Is 2:13
you cows of **B**   Am 4:1
Let them graze in **B** and Gilead   Mc 7:14

BASIC
teach you again the **b** principles   Heb 5:12

BASIN
Make a bronze **b** for washing   Ex 30:18
he made 10 bronze **b-s**   1Kg 7:38
poured water into a **b** and began to   Jn 13:5

BASIS
appeal, instead, on the **b** of love.   Phm 9

BASKET
Three **b-s** ... were on my head   Gn 40:16
she got a papyrus **b** for him   Ex 2:3
put their heads in **b-s**,   2Kg 10:7
LORD showed me two **b-s** of figs   Jr 24:1
A **b** of summer fruit.   Am 8:1
a woman sitting inside the **b**.   Zch 5:7
a lamp and puts it under a **b**,   Mt 5:15
they picked up 12 **b-s** full   Mt 14:20
pieces—seven large **b-s** full.   Mt 15:37
how many **b-s** you collected?   Mt 16:9
lowered him in a large **b**   Ac 9:25
I was let down in a **b**   2Co 11:33

BAT
heron, the hoopoe, and the **b**.   Lv 11:19

BATCH
loaf from your first **b** of dough   Nm 15:20
loaf from our first **b** of dough   Neh 10:37
holy, so is the whole **b**.   Rm 11:16
yeast permeates the whole **b**   1Co 5:6
so that you may be a new **b**,   1Co 5:7

BATHE
and **b** with water; he is clean.   Lv 14:8
he saw a woman **b-ing**   2Sm 11:2
the prostitutes **b-d** [in it],   1Kg 22:38
when my feet were **b-d** in cream   Jb 29:6
One who has **b-d**,   Jn 13:10

BATHSHEBA
Wife of Uriah the Hittite. David committed adultery with her, then married her (2Sm 11). Solomon's mother (2Sm 12; 1Kg 1–2).

BATH-SHUA

1. Judah's wife (1Ch 2:3).
2. Another name for Bathsheba (1Ch 3:5).

BATTLE

man ran from the **b**	1Sm 4:12
and fight our **b-s**.	1Sm 8:20
the **b** is the LORD's.	1Sm 17:47
goes into **b** is to be the same	1Sm 30:24
again go out with us to **b**.	2Sm 21:17
another **b** with the Philistines	2Sm 21:18
killed because it was God's **b**.	1Ch 5:22
the **b** is not yours, but God's.	2Ch 20:15
to help us and to fight our **b-s**.	2Ch 32:8
in **b**, from the power of the sword	Jb 5:20
He smells the **b** from a distance	Jb 39:25
clothed me with strength for **b**;	Ps 18:39
the LORD, mighty in **b**.	Ps 24:8
who trains my hands for **b**	Ps 144:1
horse is prepared for ... **b**,	Pr 21:31
or the **b** to the strong,	Ec 9:11
You are My **b** club,	Jr 51:20
not in anger or in **b**.	Dn 11:20
roar of **b** will rise against	Hs 10:14
nations against Jerusalem for **b**.	Zch 14:2
our **b** is not against flesh and blood	Eph 6:12
like horses equipped for **b**.	Rv 9:7
the **b** of the great day of God,	Rv 16:14
Magog, to gather them for **b**.	Rv 20:8

BDELLIUM

b and onyx are also there.	Gn 2:12
appearance was like that of **b**.	Nm 11:7

BEACH

kneeling down on the **b** to pray,	Ac 21:5
sighted a bay with a **b**.	Ac 27:39

BEAM

shaft was like a weaver's **b**,	1Sm 17:7
spear was like a weaver's **b**.	2Sm 21:19
like a weaver's **b**,	1Ch 11:23
was like a weaver's **b**.	1Ch 20:5
Let a **b** be torn from his house	Ezr 6:11
the **b-s** of our house are cedars,	Sg 1:17

BEAR (n)

Whenever a lion or a **b** came	1Sm 17:34
a wild **b** robbed of her cubs.	2Sm 17:8
two female **b-s** came out	2Kg 2:24

He makes the stars: the **B**, Orion,	Jb 9:9
lead the **B** and her cubs?	Jb 38:32
to meet a **b** robbed of her cubs	Pr 17:12
The cow and the **b** will graze,	Is 11:7
We all growl like **b-s**	Is 59:11
He is a **b** waiting in ambush,	Lm 3:10
second one, that looked like a **b**.	Dn 7:5
I will attack them like a **b**	Hs 13:8
only to have a **b** confront him.	Am 5:19

BEAR (v)

b-ing fruit with seed in it,	Gn 1:11
you will **b** children in anguish.	Gn 3:16
punishment is too great to **b**!	Gn 4:13
wife Sarah will **b** you a son,	Gn 17:19
I myself **bore** the loss.	Gn 31:39
woman will **b** the consequences	Nm 5:31
man will **b** the consequences	Nm 9:13
will help you **b** the burden	Nm 11:17
You will **b** the consequences of your sins 40 years	Nm 14:34
B with me while I speak;	Jb 21:3
that **b-s** its fruit in season	Ps 1:3
a burden too heavy for me to **b**.	Ps 38:4
I could **b** it; it is not a foe	Ps 55:12
He **b-s** our burdens;	Ps 68:19
They will still **b** fruit in old age,	Ps 92:14
will **b** {you} up when you turn gray	Is 46:4
He Himself **bore** our sicknesses,	Is 53:4
yet He **bore** the sin of many	Is 53:12
Will He **b** a grudge forever?	Jr 3:5
good for a man to **b** the yoke while	Lm 3:27
we **b** their punishment.	Lm 5:7
You must also **b** your disgrace,	Ezk 16:52
you will **b** the consequences	Ezk 23:49
They **b** their disgrace	Ezk 32:24
Samaria will **b** her guilt	Hs 13:16
who **bore** the burden of the day	Mt 20:12
Elizabeth will **b** you a son,	Lk 1:13
womb that **bore** You ... blessed!	Lk 11:27
does not **b** his own cross	Lk 14:27
wombs that never **bore**,	Lk 23:29
but you can't **b** them now.	Jn 16:12
nor we have been able to **b**?	Ac 15:10
that we may **b** fruit for God.	Rm 7:4
b the weaknesses of those	Rm 15:1
who **b-s** the name of brother	1Co 5:11
so that you are able to **b** it.	1Co 10:13
b-s all things, believes all	1Co 13:7

BEARD (continued)

we will also **b** the image of	1Co 15:49
It is **b-ing** fruit and growing	Col 1:6
b-ing fruit in every good work	Col 1:10
offered once to **b** the sins of	Heb 9:28
He Himself **bore** our sins	1Pt 2:24
tree of life **b-ing** 12 kinds of fruit	Rv 22:2

BEARD

or mar the edge of your **b**.	Lv 19:27
shaved off half their **b-s**,	2Sm 10:4
Joab grabbed Amasa by the **b**	2Sm 20:9
in Jericho until your **b-s** grow	1Ch 19:5
on the **b**, running down Aaron's **b**,	Ps 133:2
to those who tore out My **b**.	Is 50:6

BEAST

no vicious **b** will go up on it;	Is 35:9
seed of man and the seed of **b**.	Jr 31:27
Four huge **b-s** came up	Dn 7:3
the foal of a **b** of burden.	Mt 21:5
b that comes up out of the abyss	Rv 11:7
a **b** coming up out of the sea.	Rv 13:1
whole earth ... followed the **b**.	Rv 13:3
calculate the number of the **b**,	Rv 13:18
who had the **mark of the b**	Rv 16:2
woman sitting on a scarlet **b**,	Rv 17:3
who accepted the mark of the **b**	Rv 19:20
who had not worshiped the **b**	Rv 20:4

BEAT

saw an Egyptian **b-ing** a Hebrew,	Ex 2:11
b the donkey with his stick.	Nm 22:27
were **b-en** down by their sin.	Ps 106:43
if you **b** him with a rod,	Pr 23:13
They **b** me, but I didn't know it	Pr 23:35
gave My back to those who **b** Me,	Is 50:6
will **b** their swords into plows,	Mc 4:3
b one, killed another,	Mt 21:35
they spit in His face and **b** Him;	Mt 26:67
to **b** Him, saying, "Prophesy!"	Mk 14:65
b the male and female slaves,	Lk 12:45
will be **b-en** lightly.	Lk 12:48
they stopped **b-ing** Paul.	Ac 21:32
or box like one who **b-s** the air.	1Co 9:26
Three times I was **b-en**	2Co 11:25
when you sin and are **b-en**?	1Pt 2:20

BEATING (n)

his mouth provokes a **b**.	Pr 18:6
and **b-s** for the backs of fools.	Pr 19:29
b-s cleanse the innermost parts.	Pr 20:30

Why do you want more **b-s**?	Is 1:5
by **b-s**, by imprisonments, by riots,	2Co 6:5
far worse **b-s**, near death	2Co 11:23

BEAUTIFIED

also **b** themselves in this way,	1Pt 3:5

BEAUTIFUL

daughters of man were **b**,	Gn 6:2
know what a **b** woman you are.	Gn 12:11
Now the girl was very **b**,	Gn 24:16
Rebekah, for she is a **b** woman.	Gn 26:7
but Rachel was shapely and **b**.	Gn 29:17
when she saw that he was **b**,	Ex 2:2
How **b** are your tents, Jacob,	Nm 24:5
He had **b** eyes	1Sm 16:12
woman was intelligent and **b**,	1Sm 25:3
bathing—a very **b** woman.	2Sm 11:2
had a **b** sister named Tamar,	2Sm 13:1
They searched for a **b** girl	1Kg 1:3
Let a search be made for **b** young	Est 2:2
No women as **b** as Job's	Jb 42:15
praise from the upright is **b**.	Ps 33:1
A **b** woman who rejects good	Pr 11:22
most **b** of women,	Sg 1:8
How **b** you are, my darling,	Sg 1:15; 4:1
You are absolutely **b**, my darling,	Sg 4:7
as **b** as the moon,	Sg 6:10
How **b** you are and how pleasant,	Sg 7:6
branch of the LORD will be **b**	Is 4:2
How **b** on the mountains are	Is 52:7
the most **b** of all lands.	Ezk 20:6
and toward the **b** land.	Dn 8:9
How lovely and **b** they will be!	Zch 9:17
which appear **b** on the outside,	Mt 23:27
used to sit and beg at the **B** Gate	Ac 3:10
they saw that the child was **b**,	Heb 11:23

BEAUTY

gazing on the **b** of the LORD	Ps 27:4
the king will desire your **b**.	Ps 45:11
Zion, the perfection of **b**,	Ps 50:2
holiness is the **b** of Your house	Ps 93:5
and **b** are in His sanctuary.	Ps 96:6
she will give you a crown of **b**.	Pr 4:9
Don't lust in your heart for her **b**	Pr 6:25
is deceptive and **b** is fleeting,	Pr 31:30
of Hosts will become a crown of **b**	Is 28:5
eyes will see the king in his **b**;	Is 33:17
a crown of **b** instead of ashes,	Is 61:3

called the perfection of **b**, Lm 2:15
you declared: I am perfect in **b**. Ezk 27:3
proud because of your **b**; Ezk 28:17
b should not consist of outward 1Pt 3:3

BECOMING

by **b** a curse for us, Gl 3:13
humbled Himself by **b** obedient Php 2:8

BED

bowed ... at the head of his **b**. Gn 47:31
His **b** was made of iron. Dt 3:11
king bowed in worship on his **b**. 1Kg 1:47
I say: My **b** will comfort me, Jb 7:13
and drench my **b** every night. Ps 6:6
on my **b**, I think of You, Ps 63:6
if I make my **b** in Sheol, Ps 139:8
How long will you stay in **b**, Pr 6:9
I've perfumed my **b** with myrrh, Pr 7:17
and a slacker, on his **b**. Pr 26:14
makes her own **b** coverings; Pr 31:22
Our **b** is lush with foliage; Sg 1:16
with only the corner of a **b** Am 3:12
They lie on **b-s** {inlaid with} ivory, Am 6:4
prepare evil {plans} on their **b-s**! Mc 2:1
lying in with a fever. Mt 8:14
under a basket or under a **b**? Mk 4:21
I have gone to **b**. I can't get up Lk 11:7
be in one **b**: one will be taken Lk 17:34
the marriage **b** kept undefiled, Heb 13:4

BEDCLOTHES

with **b**, he could not get warm. 1Kg 1:1

BEDROLL

pick up your **b** and walk! Jn 5:8

BEDROOM

into your palace, into your **b** Ex 8:3
Bring the meal to the **b**, 2Sm 13:10
words you speak in your **b**. 2Kg 6:12
even in your **b**, for a bird Ec 10:20
Let the bridegroom leave his **b**, Jl 2:16

BEE

chased you like a swarm of **b-s**. Dt 1:44
b-s with honey in the carcass. Jdg 14:8
They surrounded me like **b-s**; Ps 118:12
b that is in the land of Assyria Is 7:18

BEELZEBUL

the head of the house 'B,' Mt 10:25

if I drive out demons by **B**, Mt 12:27
said, "He has **B** in Him!" Mk 3:22

BEER

or **b** when you enter the tent Lv 10:9
he is to abstain from wine and **b**. Nm 6:3
Pour out the offering of **b** Nm 28:7
wine, **b**, or anything you desire. Dt 14:26
eat bread or drink wine or **b** Dt 29:6
I haven't had any wine or **b**; 1Sm 1:15
Wine is a mocker, **b** is a brawler, Pr 20:1
or for rulers {to desire} **b**. Pr 31:4
Give **b** to one who is dying, Pr 31:6
your **b** is diluted with water. Is 1:22
in the morning in pursuit of **b**, Is 5:11
who are fearless at mixing **b**, Is 5:22
b is bitter to those who drink it Is 24:9
They stumble because of **b**, Is 28:7
they stagger, but not with **b**. Is 29:9
let's guzzle {some} **b**; Is 56:12
preach to you about wine and **b**, Mc 2:11
will never drink wine or **b**. Lk 1:15

BEER-SHEBA

place was called **B** because Gn 21:31
Abraham settled in **B**. Gn 22:19
From there he went up to **B**, Gn 26:23
the city is **B** to this day. Gn 26:33
All the Israelites from Dan to **B** Jdg 20:1
throne of David ... from Dan to **B**. 2Sm 3:10
Dan to **B** and register the troops 2Sm 24:2
lived in safety from Dan to **B**, 1Kg 4:25
count Israel from **B** to Dan 1Ch 21:2
all Israel, from **B** to Dan, 2Ch 30:5

BEFORE

B the mountains were born, Ps 90:2
B a word is on my tongue, Ps 139:4
No god was formed **b** Me, Is 43:10
Even **b** they call, I will answer; Is 65:24
messenger ... clear the way **b** Me. Mal 3:1
Father knows ... **b** you ask Him. Mt 6:8
B the rooster crows, Mt 26:75
B the rooster crows twice, Mk 14:72
B the rooster crows today, Lk 22:61
B Philip called you, Jn 1:48
B Abraham was, I am. Jn 8:58
B his own Lord he stands or Rm 14:4
who for the joy that lay **b** Him Heb 12:2

BEFOREHAND

did not hate him **b**.	Jos 20:5
worry **b** what you will say.	Mk 13:11
objects of mercy ... He prepared **b**	Rm 9:23

BEG

At that time I **b-ged** the LORD:	Dt 3:23
to **b** Queen Esther for his life	Est 7:7
only **b** my judge for mercy.	Jb 9:15
or his children **b-ging** bread.	Ps 37:25
Little children **b** for bread,	Lm 4:4
b-ging him, 'Be patient with me	Mt 18:29
I **b** You, don't torment me!	Lk 8:28
I'm ashamed to **b**.	Lk 16:3
Isn't this the man who sat **b-ging**?	Jn 9:8
used to sit and **b** at the Beautiful	Ac 3:10
people **b-ged** him not to go up to Jerusalem	Ac 21:12
b-ged us ... for the privilege	2Co 8:4

BEGAN

people **b** to call on the name	Gn 4:26
before a single one of them **b**.	Ps 139:16
all that Jesus **b** to do and teach	Ac 1:1
in Christ Jesus before time **b**.	2Tm 1:9
promised before time **b**,	Ti 1:2

BEGGAR

Let his children wander as **b-s**,	Ps 109:10
a blind **b**, was sitting by	Mk 10:46
formerly had seen him as a **b**	Jn 9:8

BEGIN

he will **b** to save Israel from	Jdg 13:5
when these things **b** to take	Lk 21:28

BEGINNING

In the **b** God created the heavens	Gn 1:1
at the **b** of the barley harvest.	Ru 1:22
of the LORD is the **b** of wisdom;	Ps 111:10
of the LORD is the **b** of knowledge;	Pr 1:7
The LORD made me at the **b**	Pr 8:22
of the LORD is the **b** of wisdom,	Pr 9:10
of a matter is better than its **b**;	Ec 7:8
b of the words of his mouth	Ec 10:13
I declare the end from the **b**,	Is 46:10
This was the **b** of sin	Mc 1:13
it was not like that from the **b**.	Mt 19:8
are the **b** of birth pains.	Mt 24:8
The **b** of the gospel of Jesus	Mk 1:1
b with Moses and all the	Lk 24:27

all the nations, **b** at Jerusalem.	Lk 24:47
In the **b** was the Word,	Jn 1:1
He was a murderer from the **b**	Jn 8:44
After **b** with the Spirit, are you	Gl 3:3
He is the **b**, the firstborn	Col 1:18
having neither **b** of days nor end	Heb 7:3
What was from the **b**,	1Jn 1:1
the One who is from the **b**.	1Jn 2:13
as you have heard it from the **b**:	2Jn 6
Omega, the **B** and the End.	Rv 21:6

BEHALF

the priest will make atonement on their **b**,	Lv 4:20
pray to the LORD on your **b**.	1Sm 7:5
the dead on **b** of the living?	Is 8:19
to the Father on your **b**.	Jn 16:26
to perform on **b** of the beast,	Rv 13:14

BEHAVED

You **b** more wickedly than all	1Kg 14:9
you **b** more corruptly than	Ezk 16:47

BEHAVIOR

by whether his **b** is pure	Pr 20:11
women are to be reverent in **b**,	Ti 2:3
distressed by the unrestrained **b**	2Pt 2:7

BEHEADED

they **b** him, took his head,	2Sm 4:7
had John **b** in the prison.	Mt 14:10
John, the one I **b**, has	Mk 6:16
"I **b** John," Herod said,	Lk 9:9
souls of those who had been **b**	Rv 20:4

BEHEMOTH

Look at **B**, which I made	Jb 40:15
the river rages, **B** is unafraid;	Jb 40:23

BEHIND

the testimony there **b** the veil,	Ex 26:33
into the holy place **b** the veil	Lv 16:2
Set an ambush **b** the city.	Jos 8:2
those who were to remain **b**	1Sm 30:9
Leave inexperience **b**,	Pr 9:6
B your veil,	Sg 4:1,3; 6:7
thrown all my sins **b** Your back.	Is 38:17
leave a blessing **b** Him,	Jl 2:14
told Peter, "Get **b** Me, Satan!	Mt 16:23
said, "Get **b** Me, Satan,	Mk 8:33
boy Jesus stayed **b** in Jerusalem,	Lk 2:43

forgetting what is **b**	Php 3:13
inner sanctuary **b** the curtain.	Heb 6:19

BEING

the man became a living **b**.	Gn 2:7
destroyed every living **b**,	Jos 10:40
my whole **b** is shaken with terror.	Ps 6:3
He spoke, and it came into **b**;	Ps 33:9
praises with the whole of my **b**.	Ps 108:1
praise before the heavenly **b-s**.	Ps 138:1
goes down to one's innermost **b**.	Pr 18:8
My innermost **b** will cheer	Pr 23:16
goes down to one's innermost **b**.	Pr 26:22
did not resemble a human **b**	Is 52:14
and so they all came into **b**.	Is 66:2
Joseph, **b** a righteous man,	Mt 1:19
b in torment in Hades,	Lk 16:23
You—**b** a man—make Yourself	Jn 10:33
seen, **b** understood through	Rm 1:20
for every human **b** who does evil,	Rm 2:9
we are **b** put to death all day	Rm 8:36
Adam became a living **b**;	1Co 15:45
law no human **b** will be justified.	Gl 2:16
learned the secret {of **b** content}	Php 4:12

BEL

Babylonian god (Is 46:1; Jr 50:2; 51:44).

BELA

1. City near the Dead Sea (Gn 14:2,8).

2. King of Edom (Gn 36:32-33; 1Ch 1:43-44).

3. Son of Benjamin (Gn 46:21; Nm 26:38, 40; 1Ch 7:6-7; 8:1,3).

4. A Reubenite (1Ch 5:8).

BELIAL

A name meaning "worthless," used to refer to the devil or the antichrist (2Co 6:15).

BELIEF

and through **b** in the truth.	2Th 2:13

BELIEVE

Abram **b-d** the LORD,	Gn 15:6
What if they won't **b** me	Ex 4:1
b-d in Him and in His servant	Ex 14:31
You did not **b** or obey Him.	Dt 9:23
But I didn't **b** the reports until	1Kg 10:7

B in the LORD your God, and you will be established; **b** in His prophets, and you will succeed.	2Ch 20:20
they did not **b** God or rely on	Ps 78:22
did not **b** His wonderful works.	Ps 78:32
Then they **b-d** His promises	Ps 106:12
did not **b** His promise.	Ps 106:24
I **b-d**, even when I said,	Ps 116:10
The inexperienced **b** anything,	Pr 14:15
speaks graciously, don't **b** him,	Pr 26:25
one who **b-s** will be unshakable.	Is 28:16
so that you may know and **b** Me	Is 43:10
Who has **b-d** what we have heard?	Is 53:1
The men of Nineveh **b-d** in God.	Jnh 3:5
Do you **b** that I can do this?	Mt 9:28
of these little ones who **b** in Me	Mt 18:6
if you **b**, you will receive.	Mt 21:22
Then why didn't you **b** him?	Mt 21:25
prostitutes did **b** him, but you,	Mt 21:32
or, 'Over here!' do not **b** it!	Mt 24:23
Repent and **b** in the good news!	Mk 1:15
Don't be afraid. Only **b**.	Mk 5:36
is possible to the one who **b-s**.	Mk 9:23
I do **b**! Help my unbelief.	Mk 9:24
these little ones who **b** in Me	Mk 9:42
not doubt in his heart, but **b-s**	Mk 11:23
b that you have received them,	Mk 11:24
come down now from the cross, so that we may see and **b**.	Mk 15:32
Whoever **b-s** and is baptized will be saved, but whoever does not **b** will be condemned.	Mk 16:16
will accompany those who **b**:	Mk 16:17
that they may not **b** and be saved.	Lk 8:12
Don't be afraid. Only **b**,	Lk 8:50
they did not **b** the women.	Lk 24:11
slow you are to **b** in your hearts	Lk 24:25
so that all might **b** through him.	Jn 1:7
to those who **b** in His name,	Jn 1:12
Do you **b** {only} because I told you	Jn 1:50
And they **b-d** the Scripture	Jn 2:22
so that everyone who **b-s** in Him	Jn 3:16
who does not **b** is already judged, because he has not **b-d**	Jn 3:18
b-s in the Son has eternal life, but the one who refuses to **b**	Jn 3:36
and **b-s** Him who sent Me	Jn 5:24

you don't **b** the One He sent. — Jn 5:38
if you **b-d** Moses, you would **b** — Jn 5:46
you **b** in the One He has sent. — Jn 6:29
b-s in Me will ever be thirsty — Jn 6:35
seen Me, and yet you do not **b**. — Jn 6:36
who sees the Son and **b-s** in Him — Jn 6:40
Anyone who **b-s** has eternal life. — Jn 6:47
some among you who don't **b**. — Jn 6:64
who **b-s** in Me, as the Scripture — Jn 7:38
if you do not **b** that I am {He}, — Jn 8:24
I tell the truth, you do not **b** Me. — Jn 8:45
Do you **b** in the Son of Man? — Jn 9:35
I did tell you and you don't **b**, — Jn 10:25
you don't **b** Me, **b** the works. — Jn 10:38
And many **b-d** in Him there. — Jn 10:42
b-s in Me will never die — Jn 11:26
I **b** You are the Messiah, — Jn 11:27
in this way, everybody will **b** — Jn 11:48
b in the light — Jn 12:36
Lord, who has **b-d** our message? — Jn 12:38
who **b-s** in Me **b-s** not in Me, but — Jn 12:44
when it does happen you will **b** — Jn 13:19
B in God; **b** also in Me. — Jn 14:1
B Me that I am in the Father — Jn 14:11
b-s in Me will also do the works — Jn 14:12
when it does happen you may **b**. — Jn 14:29
have **b-d** that I came from God. — Jn 16:27
By this we **b** that You came — Jn 16:30
Do you now **b**? — Jn 16:31
They have **b-d** that You sent Me. — Jn 17:8
for those who **b** in Me through — Jn 17:20
world may **b** You sent Me. — Jn 17:21
entered the tomb, saw, and **b-d**. — Jn 20:8
seen Me, have **b-d**. Those who
   b without seeing are blessed. — Jn 20:29
written so that you may **b** — Jn 20:31
by **b-ing** you may have life — Jn 20:31
those who **b-d** were of one heart — Ac 4:32
b-d Philip, as he proclaimed — Ac 8:12
If you **b** with all your heart — Ac 8:37
who **b-s** in Him is justified — Ac 13:39
appointed to eternal life **b-d**. — Ac 13:48
B on the Lord Jesus, — Ac 16:31
heard, **b-d** and were baptized. — Ac 18:8
Holy Spirit when you **b-d**? — Ac 19:2
but others did not **b**. — Ac 28:24
salvation to everyone who **b-s**, — Rm 1:16
in Jesus Christ, to all who **b**, — Rm 3:22

Abraham **b-d** God, and it was — Rm 4:3
does not work, but **b-s** on Him — Rm 4:5
the father of all who **b** — Rm 4:11
who **b-s** on Him will not be put — Rm 9:33
end of the law for righteousness
   to everyone who **b-s**. — Rm 10:4
b in your heart that God raised — Rm 10:9
With the heart one **b-s**, — Rm 10:10
whom they have not **b-d**? And
   how can they **b** without — Rm 10:14
who has **b-d** our message? — Rm 10:16
nearer than when we first **b-d**. — Rm 13:11
with all joy and peace in **b-ing**, — Rm 15:13
b-s all things, hopes all things, — 1Co 13:7
unless you **b-d** to no purpose. — 1Co 15:2
I **b-d**, therefore I spoke, — 2Co 4:13
Just as Abraham **b-d** God, and it — Gl 3:6
promise ... given to those who **b**. — Gl 3:22
His power to us who **b**, — Eph 1:19
Since we **b** that Jesus died and — 1Th 4:14
that they will **b** what is false, — 2Th 2:11
b-d on in the world, taken up — 1Tm 3:16
especially of those who **b**. — 1Tm 4:10
I know whom I have **b-d** — 2Tm 1:12
we who have **b-d** enter the rest — Heb 4:3
must **b** that He exists — Heb 11:6
You **b** that God is one; ... The
   demons also **b** — Jms 2:19
Abraham **b-d** God, and it was — Jms 2:23
not seeing Him now, you **b** — 1Pt 1:8
who **b-s** in Him will never be put — 1Pt 2:6
this is His command: that we **b** — 1Jn 3:23
do not **b** every spirit, but test — 1Jn 4:1
Everyone who **b-s** that Jesus is the
   Messiah has been born of God, — 1Jn 5:1
he has not **b-d** in the testimony — 1Jn 5:10
destroyed those who did not **b**; — Jd 5

BELIEVER

all the **b-s** were together — Ac 2:44
circumcised **b-s** who had come — Ac 10:45
If you consider me a **b** — Ac 16:15
intended as a sign, not to **b-s** — 1Co 14:22
what does a **b** have in common — 2Co 6:15
an example to all the **b-s** — 1Th 1:7
example to the **b-s** in speech, — 1Tm 4:12
who through Him are **b-s** — 1Pt 1:21
love **b-s**, and be compassionate — 1Pt 3:8

BELLS

Put gold **b** between them	Ex 28:33
on the **b** of the horses.	Zch 14:20

BELLY

move on your **b** and eat dust	Gn 3:14
anything that moves on its **b**	Lv 11:42
in the **b** of Sheol; You heard	Jnh 2:2
For as Jonah was in the **b** of	Mt 12:40

BELONG

Don't interpretations **b** to God?	Gn 40:8
that **b-s** to your neighbor.	Ex 20:17
The firstborn male from every womb **b-s** to Me,	Ex 34:19
grain offering will **b** to Aaron	Lv 2:3
The rest will **b** to the priest,	Lv 5:13
It will **b** permanently to you	Lv 10:15
The Levites **b** to Me,	Nm 3:12
every firstborn **b-s** to Me.	Nm 3:13
of their gifts also **b-s** to you.	Nm 18:11
a holy people **b-ing** to the LORD	Dt 7:6
hidden things **b** to the LORD our God, but the revealed things **b**	Dt 29:29
and on earth **b-s** to You.	1Ch 29:11
our lands **b-s** to the Levites,	Neh 10:37
Wisdom and strength **b** to God;	Jb 12:13
Dominion and dread **b** to Him,	Jb 25:2
under heaven **b-s** to Me.	Jb 41:11
Salvation **b-s** to the LORD;	Ps 3:8
kingship **b-s** to the LORD;	Ps 22:28
its inhabitants, **b** to the LORD;	Ps 24:1
the leaders of the earth **b** to God;	Ps 47:9
strength **b-s** to God,	Ps 62:11
for all the nations **b** to You.	Ps 82:8
reflections of the heart **b** to man,	Pr 16:1
I **b** to my love, and his desire is	Sg 7:10
Look, every life **b-s** to Me.	Ezk 18:4
write on it: **B-ing** to Judah	Ezk 37:16
{to the LORD} will **b** to them.	Ezk 44:29
forgiveness **b** to the Lord our God	Dn 9:9
The silver and gold **b** to Me	Hg 2:8
kingdom of God **b-s** to such	Mk 10:14
found any who **b-ed** to the Way,	Ac 9:2
you may **b** to another—to Him	Rm 7:4
to them **b** the adoption, the glory	Rm 9:4
we live or die, we **b** to the Lord.	Rm 14:8
you **b** to Christ, and Christ to	1Co 3:23
I don't **b** to the body,	1Co 12:15
those who **b** to Christ Jesus	Gl 5:24

who **b** to the household of faith.	Gl 6:10
as if you still **b-ed** to the world?	Col 2:20
if they had **b-ed** to us, they would have remained with us.	1Jn 2:19
Salvation **b-s** to our God,	Rv 7:10
glory, and power **b** to our God,	Rv 19:1

BELOVED

The LORD's **b** rests securely	Dt 33:12
This is My **b** Son. I take delight	Mt 3:17
My **b** in whom My soul delights;	Mt 12:18
This is My **b** Son. I take delight	Mt 17:5
I will send my **b** son.	Lk 20:13
and she who is "Unloved," "**B**."	Rm 9:25
He favored us with in the **B**.	Eph 1:6
This is My **b** Son. I take delight	2Pt 1:17
of the saints, the **b** city.	Rv 20:9

BELOW

"You are from **b**," He told them,	Jn 8:23

BELSHAZZAR

King of Babylon (Dn 5; 7:1; 8:1).

BELT

his sword, his bow, and his **b**.	1Sm 18:4
a leather **b** around his waist.	2Kg 1:8
faithfulness ... a **b** around His waist.	Is 11:5
with a leather **b** around his waist,	Mt 3:4
took Paul's **b**, tied his own feet	Ac 21:11
with truth like a **b** around your	Eph 6:14

BELTESHAZZAR

Daniel's Babylonian name (Dn 1:7).

BENAIAH

Heroic warrior in charge of David's body-guard (2Sm 8:18; 20:23; 23:20-23). Loyal to Solomon (1Kg 1; 4:4); executed Adonijah, Joab, and Shimei (2:25-46).

BEND

my arms can **b** a bow of bronze.	2Sm 22:35; Ps 18:34

BENEFACTOR

she has been a **b** of many	Rm 16:2

BENEFICIAL

but godliness is **b** in every way,	1Tm 4:8

BENEFIT

didn't respond according to the **b** that had come to him.	2Ch 32:25

and do not forget all His **b**-s. Ps 103:2
are of no **b**, they are no help; Is 30:5
worthless idols of no **b** at all. Jr 16:19
they are of no **b** at all Jr 23:32
Whatever **b** you might have Mt 15:5
What will it **b** a man if he gains Mt 16:26
you have **b-ed** from their labor. Jn 4:38
It is for your **b** that I go away, Jn 16:7
circumcision **b-s** you if you Rm 2:25
what is the **b** of circumcision? Rm 3:1
for the **b** of my brothers, Rm 9:3
shared in their spiritual **b-s**, Rm 15:27
your **b**, so that you may learn 1Co 4:6
may become a partner in its **b-s**. 1Co 9:23
so you could have a double **b**, 2Co 1:15
Christ will not **b** you at all. Gl 5:2
the body has a limited **b**, 1Tm 4:8
message they heard did not **b** Heb 4:2

BEN-HADAD

1. King of Aram in Asa's time (1Kg 15:18-20; 2Ch 16:2-4).

2. King of Aram from Ahab's time (1Kg 20; 2Kg 6:24; 8:7-13).

3. King of Aram in Jehoash's time (2Kg 13:24-25).

BENJAMIN

Second son of Rachel, twelfth son of Jacob (Gn 35:17-18,24). Tribe with the smallest territory; Jerusalem may have originally been in it (Jos 18:16; Jdg 1:21). Nearly wiped out (Jdg 20–21). Saul and Paul were Benjaminites (1Sm 9:1; Rm 11:1; Php 3:5).

BENT

I **b** down to give them food. Hs 11:4
She was **b** over and could not Lk 13:11
their backs be **b** continually. Rm 11:10

BEREAVE

if they raise children, I will **b** Hs 9:12

BERNICE

Wife of Agrippa (Ac 25:13,23; 26:30).

BEROEA

sent Paul and Silas off to **B**. Ac 17:10

BERYL

b, an onyx, and a jasper. Ex 28:20; 39:13
was like the gleam of **b**, Ezk 1:16
wheels was like the gleam of **b**. Ezk 10:9

b, onyx, and jasper, Ezk 28:13
the eighth **b**, the ninth topaz, Rv 21:20

BESIDE

place it **b** the ark of the Dt 31:26
a tree planted **b** streams of water Ps 1:3
He leads me **b** quiet waters. Ps 23:2
I was a skilled craftsman **b** Him. Pr 8:30
I was **b** the Ulai Canal. Dn 8:2
the Lord standing **b** the altar, Am 9:1

BESIDES

not have other gods **b** Me. Ex 20:3; Dt 5:7
There is no one **b** You! 1Sm 2:2
and there is no God **b** You, 2Sm 7:22
who is God **b** the LORD? 2Sm 22:32
there is no one **b** You to help 2Ch 14:11
who is God **b** the LORD? Ps 18:31
no Savior exists **b** Me. Hs 13:4
I am, and there is no one **b** me. Zph 2:15

BESIEGE

marched up to **b** Samaria. 2Kg 6:24
his servants were **b-ing** it. 2Kg 24:11
when their enemies **b** them 2Ch 6:28
of Babylon was **b-ing** Jerusalem, Jr 32:2

BEST

the **b** of the land of Egypt, Gn 45:18
Bring the **b** of the firstfruits Ex 23:19
The **b** part of the tenth is to be Nm 18:29
He chose the **b** {part} for himself, Dt 33:21
oil, and wear your {b} clothes. Ru 3:3
spared ... the **b** of the sheep, 1Sm 15:9
gave ... of the **b** of the grain, 2Ch 31:5
don't recline at the **b** place, Lk 14:8
do my **b** to have a clear Ac 24:16

BETHANY

to **B**, and spent the night there. Mt 21:17
in **B** at the house of Simon, Mt 26:6
He led them out as far as **B**, Lk 24:50
in **B** ... where John was baptizing. Jn 1:28
Lazarus, from **B**, Jn 11:1
B was near Jerusalem Jn 11:18
came to **B** where Lazarus was, Jn 12:1

BETHEL

east of **B** and pitched his tent, Gn 12:8
and named the place **B**, Gn 28:19
circuit to **B**, Gilgal, and Mizpah 1Sm 7:16
He set up one in **B**, 1Kg 12:29

cried out against the altar at **B**, 1Kg 13:4
tore down the altar at **B** 2Kg 23:15
Do not seek **B** or go to Gilgal Am 5:5

BETHESDA

there is a pool, called **B** Jn 5:2

BETHLEHEM

Ephrathites from **B** in Judah. Ru 1:2
I am sending you to Jesse of **B** 1Sm 16:1
B Ephrathah, you are small Mc 5:2
After Jesus was born in **B** Mt 2:1
And you, **B**, in the land of Judah, Mt 2:6
city of David, which is called **B**, Lk 2:4
Let's go straight to **B** and see Lk 2:15

BETHSAIDA

Woe to you, **B**! For if Mt 11:21
withdrew privately to ... **B**. Lk 9:10
Philip was from **B**, the hometown of
Andrew and Peter. Jn 1:44

BETRAY

my servant {Ziba} **b**-ed me. 2Sm 19:26
When you have finished **b**-ing,
they will **b** you. Is 33:1
as a woman may **b** her lover, so
you have **b**-ed Me, Jr 3:20
Moreover, wine **b**-s; Hab 2:5
Brother will **b** brother to death, Mt 10:21
Son of Man is about to be **b**-ed Mt 17:22
take offense, **b** one another Mt 24:10
a good opportunity to **b** Him. Mt 26:16
One of you will **b** Me. Mt 26:21
brother will **b** brother to death, Mk 13:12
a good opportunity to **b** Him. Mk 14:11
One of you will **b** Me Mk 14:18
Son of Man is about to be **b**-ed Lk 9:44
will even be **b**-ed by parents, Lk 21:16
a good opportunity to **b** Him Lk 22:6
that man by whom He is **b**-ed! Lk 22:22
b-ing the Son of Man with a kiss Lk 22:48
into the hands ... to **b** Him. Jn 13:2
He knew who would **b** Him. Jn 13:11
One of you will **b** Me! Jn 13:21
who is the one that's going to **b** Jn 21:20
the night when He was **b**-ed, 1Co 11:23

BETRAYERS

One, whose **b** and murderers Ac 7:52

BETTER

is **b** to you than seven sons, Ru 4:15
Am I not **b** to you than 10 sons? 1Sm 1:8
b if the troops had eaten 1Sm 14:30
to obey is **b** than sacrifice, 1Sm 15:22
is **b** than Ahithophel's advice. 2Sm 17:14
rivers of Damascus, **b** than 2Kg 5:12
B the little that the righteous Ps 37:16
Your faithful love is **b** than life. Ps 63:3
B a day in Your courts Ps 84:10
b to take refuge in the LORD Ps 118:8
wisdom is **b** than precious stones, Pr 8:11
B a little with the fear of Pr 15:16
B a meal of vegetables where Pr 15:17
B a little with righteousness Pr 16:8
B to be lowly of spirit Pr 16:19
Patience is **b** than power, Pr 16:32
B a dry crust with peace Pr 17:1
B for a man to meet a bear Pr 17:12
B a poor man who walks in Pr 19:1
b to be a poor man than a perjurer. Pr 19:22
B to live on the corner of a roof Pr 21:9
B to live in a wilderness Pr 21:19
favor is **b** than silver and gold. Pr 22:1
A wise warrior is **b** than a strong Pr 24:5
b for him to say to you, "Come Pr 25:7
B to live on the corner of a roof Pr 25:24
B an open reprimand Pr 27:5
a friend is **b** than self-counsel. Pr 27:9
b a neighbor nearby Pr 27:10
B a poor man who lives with Pr 28:6
nothing **b** for man than to eat, Ec 2:24
B one handful with rest, Ec 4:6
Two are **b** than one Ec 4:9
B is a poor but wise youth Ec 4:13
B to draw near in obedience Ec 5:1
B that you do not vow Ec 5:5
a stillborn child is **b** off than he. Ec 6:3
B what the eyes see Ec 6:9
good name is **b** than fine perfume Ec 7:1
Grief is **b** than laughter, Ec 7:3
The end of a matter is **b** than Ec 7:8
nothing **b** for man under the sun Ec 8:15
a live dog is **b** than a dead lion. Ec 9:4
Wisdom is **b** than strength, Ec 9:16
Your love is much **b** than wine, Sg 4:10
they looked **b** and healthier Dn 1:15
then it was **b** for me than now. Hs 2:7

it is **b** for me to die than to live	Jnh 4:3
it is **b** that you lose one of your	Mt 5:29
b for him if a heavy millstone	Mt 18:6
b for you to enter life maimed	Mt 18:8
b for that man if he had not	Mt 26:24
Are we any **b**? Not at all!	Rm 3:9
it is **b** to marry than to burn	1Co 7:9
who does not marry will do **b**.	1Co 7:38
we are not **b** if we do eat.	1Co 8:8
I will show you an even **b** way.	1Co 12:31
be with Christ—which is far **b**	Php 1:23
we are confident of the **b** things	Heb 6:9
the guarantee of a **b** covenant.	Heb 7:22
a **b** covenant, which has been	
legally enacted on **b** promises.	Heb 8:6
{to be purified} with **b** sacrifices	Heb 9:23
Abel offered to God a **b** sacrifice	Heb 11:4
they now aspire to a **b** land	Heb 11:16
might gain a **b** resurrection,	Heb 11:35
it is **b** to suffer for doing good,	1Pt 3:17

BETWEEN

hostility **b** you and the woman,	
and **b** your seed and her seed.	Gn 3:15
torch ... **b** the divided animals.	Gn 15:17
the LORD judge **b** me and you.	Gn 16:5
and to discern **b** good and evil.	1Kg 3:9
angel ... standing **b** earth and	1Ch 21:16
arbitrate **b** a man and God	Jb 16:21
that no air can pass **b** them.	Jb 41:16
spending the night **b** my breasts.	Sg 1:13
passed **b** the pieces of the calf	Jr 34:19
and forth **b** the living creatures	Ezk 1:13
lifted me up **b** earth and heaven	Ezk 8:3
three ribs in its mouth **b** its teeth.	Dn 7:5
conspicuous horn **b** his eyes.	Dn 8:5
b the sea and the beautiful	Dn 11:45
things from **b** their teeth.	Zch 9:7
witness **b** you and the wife of	Mal 2:14
you murdered **b** the sanctuary	Mt 23:35
who perished **b** the altar and	Lk 11:51
distinction **b** Jew and Greek,	Rm 10:12
able to arbitrate **b** his brothers?	1Co 6:5
distinguishing **b** spirits,	1Co 12:10
what partnership is there **b**	2Co 6:14
one mediator **b** God and man,	1Tm 2:5

BEWARE

B of false prophets who come	Mt 7:15
b of the yeast of the Pharisees	Mt 16:6
B of the yeast of the Pharisees	Mk 8:15
B of the scribes, who want to	Mk 12:38
B of the scribes ... in long robes,	Lk 20:46

BEYOND

not too difficult or **b** your reach.	Dt 30:11
the arrows are **b** you!	1Sm 20:22
knowledge is **b** me.	Ps 139:6
Three things are **b** me; four	Pr 30:18
amassed wisdom far **b** all those	Ec 1:16
b these, my son, be warned:	Ec 12:12
Nothing **b** what is written.	1Co 4:6
tempted **b** what you are able,	1Co 10:13
according to their ability and **b**	2Co 8:3
gospel to the regions **b** you,	2Co 10:16
Judaism **b** many contemporaries	Gl 1:14
able to do above and **b** all	Eph 3:20
message is to be sound **b** reproach,	Ti 2:8
about Christ, but goes **b** it,	2Jn 9

BEZALEL
Tabernacle craftsman (Ex 31:2-5).

BIGGER

my barns and build **b** ones,	Lk 12:18

BILDAD
One of Job's friends (Jb 2:11).

BILHAH
Rachel's slave, mother of Dan and Naphtali (Gn 30:1-7).

BILLOWS

Your **b** have swept over me.	Ps 42:7
Your **b** swept over me.	Jnh 2:3

BIND

He **bound** his son Isaac	Gn 22:9
her vows are **b-ing**,	Nm 30:7
B them as a sign on your hand	Dt 6:8
b them as a sign on your hands,	Dt 11:18
bound him with bronze	Jdg 16:21
Your hands were not **bound**,	2Sm 3:34
For He crushes but also **b-s** up;	Jb 5:18
B the festival sacrifice	Ps 118:27
and **b-s** up their wounds.	Ps 147:3
Always **b** them to your heart;	Pr 6:21
is like **b-ing** a stone in a sling.	Pr 26:8
Who has **bound** up the waters	Pr 30:4
B up the testimony.	Is 8:16
bound, into the fire?	Dn 3:24
and He will **b** up our wounds.	Hs 6:1

whatever you **b** on earth is already
   bound in heaven,   Mt 16:19; 18:18
sanctuary is **bound** by his oath.   Mt 23:16
Satan has **bound** this woman   Lk 13:16
came out **bound** hand and foot   Jn 11:44
bound in my spirit, not knowing   Ac 20:22
ready not only to be **bound**,   Ac 21:13
married woman is legally **bound**   Rm 7:2
Are you **bound** to a wife?   1Co 7:27
A wife is **bound** as long as   1Co 7:39
with the peace that **b-s** {us}.   Eph 4:3
but God's message is not **bound**.   2Tm 2:9
through angels was legally **b-ing**,   Heb 2:2
and **bound** him for 1,000 years.   Rv 20:2

BIRD

created every winged **b** according   Gn 1:21
You may eat every clean **b**,   Dt 14:11
a **b-'s** nest with chicks or eggs,   Dt 22:6
b-s of the sky, and fish of the sea   Ps 8:8
I know every **b**   Ps 50:11
a net where any **b** can see it,   Pr 1:17
like a **b** darting into a snare   Pr 7:23
a **b** of the sky may carry   Ec 10:20
one rises at the sound of a **b**,   Ec 12:4
I call a **b** of prey from the east,   Is 46:11
food for the **b-s** of the sky   Jr 7:33; 34:20
B-s of every kind will nest   Ezk 17:23
in its branches the **b-s** of the air   Dn 4:21
Does a **b** land in a trap   Am 3:5
Look at the **b-s** of the sky: Mt 6:26
b-s of the sky have nests, but   Mt 8:20
the **b-s** came and ate them up.   Mt 13:4
b-s of the sky come and nest in   Mt 13:32
worth much more than the **b-s**?   Lk 12:24
another for **b-s**, and another   1Co 15:39
b-s were filled with their flesh.   Rv 19:21

BIRTH

Did I give them **b**   Nm 11:12
the Rock who gave you **b**;   Dt 32:18
I was given over to You at **b**;   Ps 22:10
liars err from **b**.   Ps 58:3
I have leaned on You from **b**;   Ps 71:6
a time to give **b** and a time to die;   Ec 3:2
death than the day of one's **b**.   Ec 7:1
we gave **b** to wind.   Is 26:18
you will give **b** to stubble.   Is 33:11
children come to the point of **b**,   Is 37:3
Maker who shaped you from **b**;   Is 44:2

carried along since **b**.   Is 46:3
to a stone: You gave **b** to me.   Jr 2:27
see whether a male can give **b**.   Jr 30:6
no **b**, no gestation, no conception   Hs 9:11
b of Jesus Christ came about   Mt 1:18
are the beginning of **b** pains.   Mt 24:8
she gave **b** to her firstborn Son,   Lk 2:7
gives **b** to sin, and when sin is fully
   grown, it gives **b** to death.   Jms 1:15
He gave us a new **b**   Jms 1:18
a new **b** into a living hope   1Pt 1:3
woman who was about to give **b**,   Rv 12:4

BIRTHDAY

Pharaoh's **b**, he gave a feast   Gn 40:20
Herod's **b** celebration came,   Mt 14:6
b, when Herod gave a banquet   Mk 6:21

BIRTHRIGHT

First sell me your **b**.   Gn 25:31
So Esau despised his **b**.   Gn 25:34
He took my **b**,   Gn 27:36
the **b** was given to Joseph.   1Ch 5:2
b in exchange for one meal.   Heb 12:16

BIT

and My **b** in your mouth;   2Kg 19:28
must be controlled with **b**   Ps 32:9
put **b-s** into the mouths of horses   Jms 3:3

BITE

anyone who is **bitten** looks at it,   Nm 21:8
In the end it **b-s** like a snake   Pr 23:32
If the snake **b-s** before it is   Ec 10:11
only to have a snake **b** him.   Am 5:19
command the sea serpent to **b**   Am 9:3
if you **b** and devour one another,   Gl 5:15

BITHYNIA

they tried to go into **B**, but   Ac 16:7
the provinces of ... Asia, and **B**,   1Pt 1:1

BITTER

and made their lives **b**   Ex 1:14
unleavened bread and **b** herbs.   Ex 12:8
water at Marah because it was **b**   Ex 15:23
the **b** water that brings a curse.   Nm 5:18
unleavened bread and **b** herbs;   Nm 9:11
Almighty has made me very **b**.   Ru 1:20
life to those whose existence is **b**,   Jb 3:20
Almighty who has made me **b**,   Jb 27:2
aim **b** words like arrows,   Ps 64:3

in the end she's as **b** as wormwood — Pr 5:4
to a hungry person, any **b** thing — Pr 27:7
wine to one whose life is **b**. — Pr 31:6
who substitute **b** for sweet — Is 5:20
beer is **b** to those who drink it. — Is 24:9
don't become **b** against them. — Col 3:19
pour out sweet and **b** water — Jms 3:11
But if you have envy — Jms 3:14
because they had been made **b**. — Rv 8:11
it will be **b** in your stomach, — Rv 10:9

BITTERNESS
the **b** of death has come. — 1Sm 15:32
The heart knows its own **b**, — Pr 14:10
and **b** to the one who bore him. — Pr 17:25
For I see you are poisoned by **b** — Ac 8:23
mouth is full of cursing and **b**. — Rm 3:14
All **b**, anger and wrath, — Eph 4:31
that no root of **b** springs up, — Heb 12:15

BLACK
daylight will turn **b** over them. — Mc 3:6
the second chariot **b** horses, — Zch 6:2
make a single hair white or **b**. — Mt 5:36
I looked, and there was a **b** horse. — Rv 6:5
the sun turned **b** like sackcloth — Rv 6:12

BLACKSMITH
No **b** could be found — 1Sm 13:19

BLAME (n)
without spot or **b** — 1Tm 6:14

BLAME (v)
Job did not sin or **b** God — Jb 1:22

BLAMELESS
Noah was a righteous man, **b** — Gn 6:9
You must be **b** before the LORD — Dt 18:13
b man You prove Yourself **b**; — 2Sm 22:26
The LORD watches over the **b** — Ps 37:18
You are **b** when You judge. — Ps 51:4
happy are those whose way is **b**, — Ps 119:1
with **b** conduct are His delight. — Pr 11:20
the **b** will inherit what is good. — Pr 28:10
b in the day of our Lord Jesus — 1Co 1:8
to be holy and **b** in His sight. — Eph 1:4
but holy and **b**. — Eph 5:27
pure and **b** in the day of Christ, — Php 1:10
so that you may be **b** and pure, — Php 2:15
in the law, **b**. — Php 3:6
faultless, and **b** before Him — Col 1:22

May He make your hearts **b** — 1Th 3:13
body be kept sound and **b** — 1Th 5:23
be tested first; if they prove **b**, — 1Tm 3:10
b, the husband of one wife, — Ti 1:6
b and with great joy, — Jd 24
they are **b**. — Rv 14:5

BLANKET
and thick darkness its **b**, — Jb 38:9

BLASPHEME
You must not **b** God — Ex 22:28
Whoever **b-s** the name of the
  LORD is to be put to death; — Lv 24:16
My name is continually **b-d** — Is 52:5
your fathers **b-d** Me — Ezk 20:27
He's **b-ing**! — Mt 9:3
He has **b-d**! — Mt 26:65
He's **b-ing**! Who can forgive sins — Mk 2:7
b-s against the Holy Spirit — Mk 3:29
who **b-s** against the Holy Spirit — Lk 12:10
say, 'You are **b-ing**' to the One — Jn 10:36
I often tried to make them **b** — Ac 26:11
God is **b-d** among the Gentiles — Rm 2:24
they may be taught not to **b**. — 1Tm 1:20
His teaching will not be **b-d**. — 1Tm 6:1
Don't they **b** the noble name — Jms 2:7
way of truth will be **b-d**. — 2Pt 2:2
b anything they don't understand — Jd 10
So they **b-d** the name of God — Rv 16:9

BLASPHEMER
one who was formerly a **b**, — 1Tm 1:13
b-s, disobedient to parents, — 2Tm 3:2

BLASPHEMOUS
We heard him speaking **b** words — Ac 6:11
and on his heads were **b** names. — Rv 13:1
was covered with **b** names, — Rv 17:3

BLASPHEMY
had committed terrible **b-ies**, — Neh 9:18
b against the Spirit will not — Mt 12:31
you've heard the **b**! — Mt 26:65
You have heard the **b**! — Mk 14:64
this man who speaks **b-ies**? — Lk 5:21
stoning You ... for **b**, — Jn 10:33
speak **b-ies** about things they
  don't understand, — 2Pt 2:12
to speak boasts and **b-ies**. — Rv 13:5

BLAZE

fire from the LORD **b**-d among	Nm 11:1
mountain was **b**-ing with fire.	Dt 5:23
in the morning it **b**-s like	Hs 7:6

BLAZING (adj)

into the furnace of **b** fire.	Dn 3:20
into the **b** furnace	Mt 13:42

BLEEDING

had suffered from **b** for 12 years	Mt 9:20

BLEMISH

he must present one without **b**	Lv 3:1
offered Himself without **b** to God,	Heb 9:14
a lamb without defect or **b**.	1Pt 1:19
They are blots and **b**-es,	2Pt 2:13
without spot or **b** before Him.	2Pt 3:14

BLENDED

Prepare expertly **b** incense	Ex 30:35
full of wine **b** with spices,	Ps 75:8

BLESS

God **b**-ed them, "Be fruitful,	Gn 1:22
God **b**-ed the seventh day	Gn 2:3
God **b**-ed Noah and his sons	Gn 9:1
I will **b** you,	Gn 12:2
I will **b** those who **b** you,	Gn 12:3
peoples on earth will be **b**-ed	Gn 12:3
I will **b** her; indeed,	Gn 17:16
b you and make your offspring	Gn 22:17
I will be with you and **b** you.	Gn 26:3
B me—me too, my father!	Gn 27:34
let You go unless You **b** me,	Gn 32:26
Jacob ... and He **b**-ed him.	Gn 35:9
the LORD **b**-ed the Sabbath day	Ex 20:11
I will come to you and **b** you	Ex 20:24
LORD **b** you and protect you;	Nm 6:24
since He has **b**-ed, I cannot	Nm 23:20
Don't curse them and don't **b**	Nm 23:25
who **b** you will be blessed,	Nm 24:9
He will love you, **b** you,	Dt 7:13
When the LORD your God **b**-es	Dt 15:6
the LORD **b**-ed Obed-edom	2Sm 6:11
The king ... **b**-ed the entire congregation of Israel	1Kg 8:14
If only You would **b** me,	1Ch 4:10
You, LORD, **b** the righteous one;	Ps 5:12
b Your possession,	Ps 28:9
b-es His people with peace.	Ps 29:11

God be gracious to us and **b** us;	Ps 67:1
they curse, You will **b**.	Ps 109:28
of the upright will be **b**-ed.	Ps 112:2
fears the LORD will be **b**-ed.	Ps 128:4
b you in the name of the LORD	Ps 129:8
the godly will **b** You.	Ps 145:10
b-es your children within you.	Ps 147:13
b-es the home of the righteous;	Pr 3:33
will not be **b**-ed ultimately.	Pr 20:21
A generous person will be **b**-ed,	Pr 22:9
b-es his neighbor with a loud	Pr 27:14
the nations will be **b**-ed by Him	Jr 4:2
from this day on I will **b** you.	Hg 2:19
took bread, **b**-ed and broke it,	Mt 26:26
He **b**-ed and broke the loaves.	Mk 6:41
hands on them and **b**-ed them.	Mk 10:16
b those who curse you,	Lk 6:28
He **b**-ed and broke them.	Lk 9:16
bread, **b**-ed and broke it,	Lk 24:30
He **b**-ed them.	Lk 24:50
families of the earth will be **b**-ed.	Ac 3:25
B those who persecute you; **b**	Rm 12:14
When we are reviled, we **b**;	1Co 4:12
All the nations will be **b**-ed in you.	Gl 3:8
has **b**-ed us with every spiritual	Eph 1:3
I will most certainly **b** you,	Heb 6:14
inferior is **b**-ed by the superior.	Heb 7:7
will be **b**-ed in what he does.	Jms 1:25
With it we **b** our Lord	Jms 3:9

BLESSED (adj)

said: Abram is **b** by God	Gn 14:19
who bless you will be **b**,	Nm 24:9
You will be **b** in the city and **b** in the country.	Dt 28:3
Jael is most **b** of women,	Jdg 5:24
May he be **b** by the LORD,	Ru 2:20
May you be **b** by the LORD,	Ps 115:15
B is he who comes in the name of the LORD.	Ps 118:26
Let your fountain be **b**,	Pr 5:18
sons rise up and call her **b**.	Pr 31:28
B is the man who trusts	Jr 17:7
B are the poor in spirit,	Mt 5:3
B are those who mourn,	Mt 5:4
B are the gentle,	Mt 5:5
B are those who hunger and	Mt 5:6
B are the merciful,	Mt 5:7
B are the pure in heart,	Mt 5:8

B are the peacemakers, Mt 5:9
B are those who are persecuted Mt 5:10
B are you when they insult you Mt 5:11
are b because they do see, Mt 13:16
Simon son of Jonah, you are b Mt 16:17
B is He who comes in the name Mt 21:9
until you say, B is He who Mt 23:39
B is He who comes in the name Mk 11:9
You are the most b of women, Lk 1:42
all generations will call me b, Lk 1:48
B are you who are poor, Lk 6:20
B are you who are hungry now, Lk 6:21
B are you who weep now, Lk 6:21
B are you when people hate you, Lk 6:22
see the things you see are b! Lk 10:23
one who nursed You are blessed! Lk 11:27
eat bread in the kingdom ... is b! Lk 14:15
Hosanna! B is He who comes Jn 12:13
you are b if you do them. Jn 13:17
who believe without seeing are b. Jn 20:29
more b to give than to receive. Ac 20:35
the Creator, who is b forever. Rm 1:25
who is God over all, b forever. Rm 9:5
B be the God and Father 2Co 1:3
The eternally b One, 2Co 11:31
B be the God and Father Eph 1:3
while we wait for the b hope Ti 2:13
B is a man who endures trials, Jms 1:12
we count as b those who Jms 5:11
B be the God and Father 1Pt 1:3
for righteousness, you are b. 1Pt 3:14
name of Christ, you are b, 1Pt 4:14
B is the one who reads and b Rv 1:3
B are the dead who die in Rv 14:13
B is the one who is alert and Rv 16:15
B are those invited to Rv 19:9
B is the one who keeps Rv 22:7
B are those who wash their Rv 22:14

BLESSING (n)

you will be a b. Gn 12:2
deceitfully and took your b. Gn 27:35
with b-s of the heavens above,
  b-s of the deep that lies below,
  and b-s of the breasts Gn 49:25
set before you a b and a curse: Dt 11:26
He turned the curse into a b Dt 23:5
these b-s will come and overtake Dt 28:2
life and death, b and curse. Dt 30:19

the b-s as well as the curses Jos 8:34
to pronounce b-s in His name 1Ch 23:13
God turned the curse into a b. Neh 13:2
rain will cover it with b-s. Ps 84:6
no delight in b—let it be far Ps 109:17
May the LORD's b be on you. Ps 129:8
B-s are on the head of the righteous, Pr 10:6
The LORD's b enriches, Pr 10:22
b will come to the one who sells Pr 11:26
faithful man will have many b-s, Pr 28:20
send down ... showers of b. Ezk 34:26
and I will curse your b-s. Mal 2:2
pour out a b for you Mal 3:10
The cup of b that we bless, 1Co 10:16
b of Abraham ... to the Gentiles Gl 3:14
blessed us with every spiritual b Eph 1:3
mouth come b and cursing. Jms 3:10
so that you can inherit a b. 1Pt 3:9
and honor and glory and b! Rv 5:12
B and honor and glory and Rv 5:13
B and glory and wisdom and Rv 7:12

BLIGHT

I struck you with b and mildew; Am 4:9
work of your hands—with b, Hg 2:17

BLIND (adj)

mute or deaf, seeing or b? Ex 4:11
no man who is b, lame, Lv 21:18
that is b, injured, maimed, Lv 22:22
one who leads a b person astray Dt 27:18
Who is b but My servant, Is 42:19
Israel's watchmen are b, Is 56:10
When you present a b (animal) Mal 1:8
Woe to you, b guides, Mt 23:16
a b beggar, was sitting Mk 10:46
invite those who are ... b. Lk 14:13
He saw a man b from birth. Jn 9:1
I was b, and now I can see! Jn 9:25
If you were b, ... you wouldn't Jn 9:41
who lacks these things is b 2Pt 1:9
are wretched, pitiful, poor, b, Rv 3:17

BLIND (n)

block in front of the b, Lv 19:14
the b and lame can repel you 2Sm 5:6
I was eyes to the b Jb 29:15
LORD opens {the eyes of} the b. Ps 146:8
the eyes of the b will be opened, Is 35:5
the b see, the lame walk, Mt 11:5

BLIND

if the **b** guide the **b**, both will	Mt 15:14
recovery of sight to the **b**,	Lk 4:18
Can the **b** guide the **b**?	Lk 6:39
bring in here the poor, ... **b**,	Lk 14:21
you are a guide for the **b**,	Rm 2:19

BLIND (v)

a bribe **b**-s the clear-sighted	Ex 23:8
not accept a bribe, for it **b**-s	Dt 16:19
king of Babylon **b**-ed Zedekiah,	2Kg 25:7
deafen their ears and **b** their eyes;	Is 6:10
He has **b**-ed their eyes	Jn 12:40
the god of this age has **b**-ed	2Co 4:4
the darkness has **b**-ed his eyes.	1Jn 2:11

BLINDFOLD

to **b** Him, and to beat Him,	Mk 14:65
After **b**-ing Him, they	Lk 22:64

BLINDNESS

will afflict you with madness, **b**,	Dt 28:28
strike this nation with **b**.	2Kg 6:18
horses of the nations with **b**.	Zch 12:4

BLOCK (n)

I will bow down to a **b** of wood.	Is 44:19
stumbling **b** before his face,	Ezk 14:4
became a sinful stumbling **b**	Ezk 44:12
decide not to put a stumbling **b**	Rm 14:13
Christ crucified, a stumbling **b**	1Co 1:23
a stumbling **b** to the weak.	1Co 8:9
Balak to place a stumbling **b**	Rv 2:14

BLOCK (v)

He has **b**-ed my way	Jb 19:8
I will **b** her way with thorns;	Hs 2:6
b the path of the needy.	Am 2:7

BLOOD

Your brother's **b** cries out to Me	Gn 4:10
Whoever sheds man's **b**, his **b** will	
be shed by man,	Gn 9:6
dipped the robe in its **b**.	Gn 37:31
You are a bridegroom of **b**	Ex 4:25
Nile ... will turn to **b**.	Ex 7:17
b and put it on the two doorposts	Ex 12:7
see the **b**, I will pass over you.	Ex 12:13
This is the **b** of the covenant	Ex 24:8
the priests are to present the **b**	Lv 1:5
must not eat any fat or any **b**.	Lv 3:17
life of a creature is in the **b**,	Lv 17:11
None of you ... may eat **b**.	Lv 17:12

judge ... the avenger of **b**	Nm 35:24
no atonement for the land because	
of the **b** that is shed on it,	Nm 35:33
but you must not eat the **b**;	Dt 12:16
avenge the **b** of His servants.	Dt 32:43
refuge from the avenger of **b**.	Jos 20:3
gray head down to Sheol with **b**.	1Kg 2:9
You have shed much **b**	1Ch 22:8
a man of war and have shed **b**.	1Ch 28:3
or drink the **b** of goats?	Ps 50:13
land became polluted with **b**.	Ps 106:38
hands that shed innocent **b**,	Pr 6:17
twisting a nose draws **b**,	Pr 30:33
I have no desire for the **b** of bulls,	Is 1:11
Your hands are covered with **b**.	Is 1:15
hold you responsible for his **b**.	Ezk 3:18
saw you lying in your **b**,	Ezk 16:6
rinsed off your **b**,	Ezk 16:9
ignored the warning, his **b** is on his	Ezk 33:5
hold you responsible for his **b**.	Ezk 33:8
you will eat flesh and drink **b**.	Ezk 39:17
moon to **b** before the great	Jl 2:31
Woe to the city of **b**,	Nah 3:1
flesh and **b** did not reveal this	Mt 16:17
from the **b** of righteous Abel	Mt 23:35
this is My **b** ... the covenant;	Mt 26:28
it is **b** money.	Mt 27:6
field has been called "**B** Field"	Mt 27:8
I am innocent of this man's **b**.	Mt 27:24
b be on us and on our children	Mt 27:25
This is My **b** ... the covenant,	Mk 14:24
sweat became like drops of **b**	Lk 22:44
who were born, not of **b**,	Jn 1:13
and drinks My **b** has eternal life,	Jn 6:54
b and water came out.	Jn 19:34
Hakeldama, that is, Field of **B**.	Ac 1:19
the moon to **b**, before the great	Ac 2:20
been strangled, and from **b**.	Ac 15:20
He purchased with His own **b**.	Ac 20:28
Their feet are swift to shed **b**;	Rm 3:15
through faith in His **b**,	Rm 3:25
declared righteous by His **b**,	Rm 5:9
is it not a sharing in the **b**?	1Co 10:16
the new covenant in My **b**.	1Co 11:25
flesh and **b** cannot inherit	1Co 15:50
redemption through His **b**,	Eph 1:7
brought near by the **b**	Eph 2:13
battle is not against flesh and **b**,	Eph 6:12

by making peace through the **b**   Col 1:20
not by the **b** of goats and calves,
   but by His own **b**,
   without ... **b** there is no
   forgiveness   Heb 9:22
is impossible for the **b** of bulls   Heb 10:4
to the point of shedding your **b**.   Heb 12:4
with the precious **b** of Christ,   1Pt 1:19
b of Jesus His Son cleanses us   1Jn 1:7
One who came by water and **b**;   1Jn 5:6
Spirit, the water, and the **b**   1Jn 5:8
set us free from our sins by His **b**,   Rv 1:5
You redeemed people ... by Your **b**   Rv 5:9
the entire moon became like **b**;   Rv 6:12
made them white in the **b**   Rv 7:14
a third of the sea became **b**,   Rv 8:8
conquered ... by the **b** of the Lamb   Rv 12:11
was drunk on the **b** of the saints   Rv 17:6
He wore a robe stained with **b**,   Rv 19:13

BLOODGUILT

b on your house if someone falls   Dt 22:8
b will be a fugitive until death.   Pr 28:17
Lᴏʀᴅ will leave his **b** on him   Hs 12:14
I will pardon their **b**,   Jl 3:21

BLOODSHED

no one is guilty of **b**.   Ex 22:2
avenger will not be guilty of **b**,   Nm 35:27
b defiles the land,   Nm 35:33
absolved of responsibility for **b**.   Dt 21:8
kept you from participating in **b**   1Sm 25:26
the Lᴏʀᴅ abhors a man of **b**   Ps 5:6
Save me from the guilt of **b**,   Ps 51:14
save me from men of **b**.   Ps 59:2
Woe to the city of **b**   Ezk 24:6,9
not hate **b**, it will pursue you.   Ezk 35:6
one act of **b** follows another.   Hs 4:2
who build Zion with **b**   Mc 3:10
who builds a city with **b**   Hab 2:12
{your} human **b** and violence   Hab 2:17

BLOODTHIRSTY

B men hate an honest person,   Pr 29:10

BLOOM (n)

our vineyards are in **b**.   Sg 2:15
if the pomegranates are in **b**.   Sg 7:12

BLOOM (v)

he **b**-s like a flower of the field   Ps 103:15
Israel will blossom and **b**   Is 27:6

BLOSSOM (n)

cups shaped like almond **b**-s,   Ex 25:33
carved ... flower **b**-s on them   1Kg 6:32
My love is a cluster of henna **b**-s   Sg 1:14
has budded, if the **b** has opened,   Sg 7:12
their **b**-s will blow away like dust,   Is 5:24

BLOSSOM (v)

sprouted, formed buds, **b**-ed,   Nm 17:8
b-s like a flower, then withers;   Jb 14:2
the almond tree **b**-s,   Ec 12:5
Jacob will take root. Israel will **b**   Is 27:6
the desert will rejoice and **b**   Is 35:1
he will **b** like the lily   Hs 14:5

BLOT (v)

b out the memory of Amalek   Ex 17:14
I will destroy them and **b** out   Dt 9:14
b out my rebellion.   Ps 51:1
b out all my guilt.   Ps 51:9

BLOTS (n)

They are **b** and blemishes,   2Pt 2:13

BLOW (n)

rod and with **b**-s from others.   2Sm 7:14
did things deserving of **b**-s   Lk 12:48

BLOW (v)

While the trumpets were **b**-ing,   Jos 6:9
like chaff that the wind **b**-s away.   Ps 1:4
smoke is **b**-n away, so You **b**
   {them} away.   Ps 68:2
south wind. **B** on my garden,   Sg 4:16
b a ram's horn among   Jr 51:27
b fire on them and melt them,   Ezk 22:20
B the horn in Zion; sound the   Jl 2:1
If a ram's horn is **b**-n in a city,   Am 3:6
blew and pounded that house.   Mt 7:25
The wind **b**-s where it pleases,   Jn 3:8
b-n around by every wind   Eph 4:14
seven trumpets prepared to **b** them.   Rv 8:6
seventh angel **blew** his trumpet,   Rv 11:15

BLUE

b, purple, and scarlet yarn   Ex 26:1,31,36
robe of the ephod entirely of **b**   Ex 28:31

BLURTS

mouth of fools **b** out foolishness. Pr 15:2
mouth of the wicked **b** out evil Pr 15:28

BOANERGES

Name given to James and John (Mk 3:17).

BOAST

Do not **b** so proudly, 1Sm 2:3
who puts on his armor **b** like 1Kg 20:11
I will **b** in the LORD; Ps 34:2
We **b** in God all day long; Ps 44:8
all who swear by Him will **b**, Ps 63:11
who **b** in idols, will be put to Ps 97:7
The man who **b-s** about a gift Pr 25:14
Don't **b** about tomorrow, Pr 27:1
you will **b** in the Holy One Is 41:16
the rich must not **b** in his riches. Jr 9:23
the one who **b-s** should **b** in this, Jr 9:24
rest in the law, and **b** in God, Rm 2:17
You who **b** in the law, Rm 2:23
I have reason to **b** in Christ Rm 15:17
no one can **b** in His presence. 1Co 1:29
one who **b-s** must **b** in the Lord. 1Co 1:31
why do you **b** as if you hadn't 1Co 4:7
will not **b** beyond measure, 2Co 10:13
who **b-s** must **b** in the Lord. 2Co 10:17
I will also **b**. 2Co 11:18
I will **b** about my weaknesses. 2Co 11:30
gladly **b** ... about my weaknesses, 2Co 12:9
b about anything except the cross Gl 6:14
so that no one can **b**. Eph 2:9
we ourselves **b** about you 2Th 1:4
{should **b**} in his humiliation, Jms 1:10
it **b-s** great things. Jms 3:5

BOASTFUL

b cannot stand in Your presence; Ps 5:5
God-haters, arrogant, proud, **b**, Rm 1:30
Love does not envy; is not **b**; 1Co 13:4
lovers of money, **b**, proud, 2Tm 3:2

BOASTING (n)

Where is **b**? It is excluded. Rm 3:27
you boast in your arrogance. All
such **b** is evil. Jms 4:16

BOASTS

to speak **b** and blasphemies. Rv 13:5

BOAT

by like **b-s** made of papyrus, Jb 9:26

they left the **b** and their father Mt 4:22
the **b** was being swamped Mt 8:24
climbing out of the **b**, Peter Mt 14:29
teaching the crowds from the **b**. Lk 5:3
filled both **b-s** so full that Lk 5:7
at once the **b** was at the shore Jn 6:21
knew there had been only one **b**. Jn 6:22
on the right side of the **b**, Jn 21:6

BOAZ

1. Husband of Ruth (Ru 4:13), kinsman redeemer (2:20; 3:1; 4:3-10,16-17). Ancestor of David (4:21-22; 1Ch 2:11-12) and Jesus (Mt 1:5; Lk 3:32).

2. Left pillar in temple (1Kg 7:21).

BOCHIM

they named that place **B** Jdg 2:5

BODY

one who comes from your own **b** Gn 15:4
He must not go near a dead **b** Nm 6:6
Anyone who touches a **b** Nm 19:13
and you hang his **b** on a tree, Dt 21:22
my **b** also rests securely. Ps 16:9
There is no soundness in my **b** Ps 38:3
my **b** faints for You in a land Ps 63:1
This will be healing for your **b** Pr 3:8
how to let my **b** enjoy life Ec 2:3
their **b-ies** will rise. Is 26:19
dead **b-ies**, thrown everywhere! Am 8:3
child of my **b** for my own sin? Mc 6:7
corpses, dead **b-ies** without end Nah 3:3
whole **b** to be thrown into hell. Mt 5:29
The eye is the lamp of the **b**. Mt 6:22
your **b**, what you will wear. Mt 6:25
Don't fear those who kill the **b** Mt 10:28
Take and eat it; this is My **b**. Mt 26:26
many **b-ies** of the saints Mt 27:52
did not find the **b** of the Lord Lk 24:3
the sanctuary of His **b**. Jn 2:21
that sin's dominion over the **b** Rm 6:6
let sin reign in your mortal **b**, Rm 6:12
rescue me from this **b** of death? Rm 7:24
present your **b-ies** as a living Rm 12:1
many are one in Christ Rm 12:5
absent in **b** but present in spirit, 1Co 5:3
b is not for sexual immorality 1Co 6:13
b-ies are the members of Christ? 1Co 6:15
know that your **b** is a sanctuary 1Co 6:19

over his own **b**, but his wife does 1Co 7:4
I discipline my **b** 1Co 9:27
a sharing in the **b** of Christ? 1Co 10:16
we who are many are one **b**, 1Co 10:17
This is My **b**, which is for you 1Co 11:24
b is one and has many parts, 1Co 12:12
I don't belong to the **b**, 1Co 12:15
If the whole **b** were an eye, 1Co 12:17
you are the **b** of Christ, 1Co 12:27
sown a natural **b**, raised a
spiritual **b**. 1Co 15:44
out of the **b** and at home with 2Co 5:8
Whether he was in the **b** or out
of the **b**, I don't know; 2Co 12:2
carry the marks of Jesus on my **b**. Gl 6:17
There is one **b** and one Spirit, Eph 4:4
to build up the **b** of Christ, Eph 4:12
their wives as their own **b-ies**. Eph 5:28
since we are members of His **b**. Eph 5:30
He will transform the **b** Php 3:21
He is also the head of the **b**, Col 1:18
I may be absent in **b**, but I am Col 2:5
spirit, soul, and **b** be kept sound 1Th 5:23
training of the **b** has a limited 1Tm 4:8
You prepared a **b** for Me. Heb 10:5
our **b-ies** washed in pure water Heb 10:22
bore our sins in His **b** on 1Pt 2:24
Devil in a debate about Moses' **b**, Jd 9
nations will view their **b-ies** Rv 11:9

BODILY
fullness of God's nature dwells **b**, Col 2:9

BOIL (n)
festering **b-s** on people Ex 9:9
When a **b** appears on the skin Lv 13:18
afflict you with the **b-s** of Egypt, Dt 28:27
infected Job with incurable **b-s** Jb 2:7

BOIL (v)
and **b** what you want to **b**, Ex 16:23
not **b** a ... goat in ... milk. Ex 23:19; Dt 14:21
not **b** a ... goat in ... milk. Ex 34:26
we **b-ed** my son and ate him, 2Kg 6:29
I see a **b-ing** pot, Jr 1:13

BOILED (adj)
won't accept **b** meat ... only raw. 1Sm 2:15

BOLD
A wicked man puts on a **b** face, Pr 21:29

the righteous are as **b** as a lion. Pr 28:1
but **b** toward you when absent. 2Co 10:1
Pray that I might be **b** enough Eph 6:20

BOLDLY
spoken **b** in the name of Jesus. Ac 9:27
spoke **b**, in reliance on the Lord, Ac 14:3
speak **b** in the synagogue, Ac 18:26
b say: The Lord is my helper; Heb 13:6

BOLDNESS
speak God's message with **b**. Ac 4:31
in whom we have **b**, access, Eph 3:12
make known with **b** Eph 6:19
great **b** in Christ to command Phm 8
approach the throne ... with **b**, Heb 4:16
have **b** to enter the sanctuary Heb 10:19

BOLT
He hurled lightning **b-s** 2Sm 22:15
installed its doors, **b-s**, and bars. Neh 3:3
Can you send out lightning **b-s**, Jb 38:35
myrrh on the handles of the **b**. Sg 5:5

BOND (n)
neither **b** nor free. 2Kg 14:26
You have loosened my **b-s**. Ps 116:16
into the **b** of the covenant. Ezk 20:37
love—the perfect **b** of unity. Col 3:14

BOND (v)
and **b-s** with his wife, Gn 2:24

BONDAGE
she be untied from this **b** Lk 13:16
set free from the **b** of corruption Rm 8:21

BONE
This one, at last, is **b** of my **b**, Gn 2:23
carry my **b-s** up from here. Gn 50:25
not break any of its **b-s**. Ex 12:46
Moses took the **b-s** of Joseph Ex 13:19
or break any of its **b-s**. Nm 9:12
the one who touched a **b**, Nm 19:18
Joseph's **b-s**, ... were buried Jos 24:32
Human **b-s** will be burned on 1Kg 13:2
he touched Elisha's **b-s**, 2Kg 13:21
he burned human **b-s** on 2Kg 23:20
wove me together with **b-s** Jb 10:11
my **b-s** burn with fever. Jb 30:30
my **b-s** are shaking, Ps 6:2
all my **b-s** are disjointed; Ps 22:14
I can count all my **b-s**; Ps 22:17

b-s; not one of them is broken. Ps 34:20
there is no health in my b-s Ps 38:3
b-s have crushed rejoice. Ps 51:8
My b-s were not hidden Ps 139:15
is like rottenness in his b-s. Pr 12:4
jealousy is rottenness to the b-s. Pr 14:30
good news strengthens the b-s. Pr 15:30
a gentle tongue can break a b. Pr 25:15
how b-s develop in the womb Ec 11:5
shut up in my b-s. Jr 20:9
valley; it was full of b-s. Ezk 37:1
can these b-s live? Ezk 37:3
Dry b-s, hear the word of the LORD Ezk 37:4
the b-s came together, b to b. Ezk 37:7
Rottenness entered my b-s; Hab 3:16
are full of dead men's b-s Mt 23:27
does not have flesh and b-s Lk 24:39
Not one of His b-s will be Jn 19:36

BOOK

erase me from the b You have Ex 32:32
this b of the law and place it Dt 31:26
b of instruction must not depart Jos 1:8
Joshua recorded these things in
  the b of the law of God; Jos 24:26
I have found the b of the law 2Kg 22:8
Ezra read out of the b of the
  law of God every day, Neh 8:18
be erased from the b of life Ps 69:28
days were written in Your b Ps 139:16
no end to the making of many b-s, Ec 12:12
and the b-s were opened. Dn 7:10
seal the b until the time of Dn 12:4
b of remembrance was written Mal 3:16
that are not written in this b. Jn 20:30
could contain the b-s that Jn 21:25
collected their b-s and burned Ac 19:19
whose names are in the b of life. Php 4:3
never erase his name from the b Rv 3:5
b-s were opened. Another b was
  opened, which is the b of life, Rv 20:12
written in the Lamb's b of life. Rv 21:27
Blessed is the one who keeps the
  prophetic words of this b. Rv 22:7
God will add to him the plagues
  that are written in this b. Rv 22:18

BOOTH

The Festival of B-s to the LORD Lv 23:34
live in b-s for seven days. Lv 23:42

celebrate the Festival of B-s Dt 16:13
celebrated the Festival of B-s Ezr 3:4
dwell in b-s during the festival Neh 8:14
restore the fallen b of David: Am 9:11
celebrate the Festival of B-s. Zch 14:16

BORDER

outside the b of the city of refuge Nm 35:26
Arabah and Jordan are also b-s Dt 3:17
the Jordan a b between us Jos 22:25
bless me, extend my b, 1Ch 4:10
You have expanded all the b-s Is 26:15
This is the b you will {use to}
  divide the land Ezk 47:13
The LORD is great, {even} beyond
  the b-s of Israel. Mal 1:5

BORN

cursed the day he was b. Jb 3:1
But mankind is b for trouble Jb 5:7
we were {b only} yesterday Jb 8:9
as a wild donkey is b a man! Jb 11:12
Man b of woman is short of days Jb 14:1
Were you the first person ever b, Jb 15:7
can one b of woman be pure? Jb 25:4
You were already b; Jb 38:21
tell a people yet to be b about Ps 22:31
I was guilty {when I} was b; Ps 51:5
Before the mountains were b, Ps 90:2
brother is b for a difficult time. Pr 17:17
slaves who were b in my house. Ec 2:7
a child will be b for us, Is 9:6
LORD called me before I was b. Is 49:1
Can a land be b in one day, Is 66:8
I set you apart before you were b. Jr 1:5
be the day on which I was b. Jr 20:14
despised on the day you were b. Ezk 16:5
who has been b King of the Jews Mt 2:2
Among those b of women no Mt 11:11
if he had not been b. Mt 26:24
was b for you in the city of David. Lk 2:11
who were b, not of blood, Jn 1:13
Unless someone is b again, Jn 3:3
you must be b again. Jn 3:7
that he was b blind? Jn 9:2
You were b entirely in sin, Jn 9:34
I was b for this, Jn 18:37
But I myself was b a citizen, Ac 22:28
though they had not been b yet Rm 9:11
as to one abnormally b, 1Co 15:8

b of a woman, **b** under the law, Gl 4:4
was **b** according to the flesh Gl 4:23
since you have been **b** again 1Pt 1:23
who loves has been **b** of God 1Jn 4:7
b of God conquers the world. 1Jn 5:4
has been **b** of God does not sin, 1Jn 5:18

BORNE

just as we have **b** the image of
the man made of dust, 1Co 15:49

BORROW

When a man **b-s** {an animal} Ex 22:14
You will lend to many nations,
but you will not **b**. Dt 28:12
Go and **b** empty containers 2Kg 4:3
Oh, my master, it was **b-ed**! 2Kg 6:5
wicked **b-s** and does not repay, Ps 37:21
the **b-er** is a slave to the lender. Pr 22:7
one who wants to **b** from you. Mt 5:42

BOTHER

David's conscience **b-ed** him 1Sm 24:5
Don't **b** me! The door is Lk 11:7

BOTTLE

Put my tears in Your **b**. Ps 56:8

BOTTOM

was split in two from top to **b**; Mt 27:51
split in two from top to **b**. Mk 15:38

BOUNDARY

Put a **b** around the mountain Ex 19:23
move your neighbor's **b** marker, Dt 19:14
He set the **b-ies** of the peoples Dt 32:8
The wicked displace **b** markers. Jb 24:2
b between light and darkness. Jb 26:10
when I determined its **b-ies** Jb 38:10
The **b** lines have fallen for me
in pleasant places; Ps 16:6
set all the **b-ies** of the earth; Ps 74:17
You set a **b** they cannot cross; Ps 104:9
set the sand as the **b** of the sea, Jr 5:22
like those who move **b** markers; Hs 5:10
that day {your} **b** will be extended Mc 7:11
the **b-ies** of where they live, Ac 17:26

BOUNDING

like a deer **b** toward a trap Pr 7:22
b over the hills. Sg 2:8

BOUNTIFUL

with the **b** harvest from the sun Dt 33:14

BOUNTY

given her out of his royal **b**. 1Kg 10:13
Your sins have withheld {My} **b** Jr 5:25

BOW (n)

placed My **b** in the clouds, Gn 9:13
Yet his **b** remained steady, Gn 49:24
b-s of the warriors are broken, 1Sm 2:4
be taught {The Song of} the B. 2Sm 1:18
arms can bend a **b** of bronze. 2Sm 22:35
a man drew his **b** without 1Kg 22:34
Take a **b** and arrows. 2Kg 13:15
He has strung His **b** Ps 7:12
the wicked string the **b**; Ps 11:2
arms can bend a **b** of bronze. Ps 18:34
I do not trust in my **b**, Ps 44:6
He shatters **b-s** and cuts spears Ps 46:9
became warped like a faulty **b**. Ps 78:57
bent their tongues {like} their **b-s**; Jr 9:3
I will break the **b** of Israel Hs 1:5
they are like a faulty **b**. Hs 7:16
I will bend Judah {as My **b**}; Zch 9:13

BOW (v)

May ... nations **b** down to you. Gn 27:29
and **b-ed** down to my sheaf. Gn 37:7
11 stars were **b-ing** down to me. Gn 37:9
His brothers came and **b-ed** Gn 42:6
worship them or **b** down to them. Jos 23:7
king **b-ed** in worship on his bed 1Kg 1:47
knee that has not **b-ed** to Baal 1Kg 19:18
do not **b** down to them; 2Kg 17:35
Mordecai was not **b-ing** down Est 3:5
nations will **b** down before You, Ps 22:27
let all kings **b** down to him, Ps 72:11
Come, let us worship and **b** down; Ps 95:6
b down to the work of their hands Is 2:8
will **b** down to a block of wood. Is 44:19
Every knee will **b** to Me, Is 45:23
when I come to **b** before God Mc 6:6
coastlands of the nations will **b** Zph 2:11
who have not **b-ed** down to Baal. Rm 11:4
every knee will **b** to Me, Rm 14:11
For this reason I **b** my knees Eph 3:14
of Jesus every knee should **b** Php 2:10

BOWL

Jerusalem ... as one wipes a **b** 2Kg 21:13

buries his hand in the **b**; Pr 19:24; 26:15
the golden **b** is broken, Ec 12:6
Your navel is a rounded **b**; Sg 7:2
fill **b-s** of mixed wine for Destiny Is 65:11
one who dipped his hand with
  Me in the **b** Mt 26:23
the seven **b-s** of God's wrath Rv 16:1
the seven **b-s** filled with Rv 21:9

BOWLFUL
They drink wine by the **b** Am 6:6

BOWSHOT
nearby, about a **b** away, Gn 21:16

BOWSTRINGS
tie me up with seven fresh **b** Jdg 16:7

BOX (n)
the **b** {containing} the gold mice 1Sm 6:11

BOX (v)
the wilderness has **b-ed** them in. Ex 14:3
or **b** like one who beats the air. 1Co 9:26

BOY
sent her and the **b** away. Gn 21:14
they let the **b-s** live. Ex 1:17
pleaded with God for the **b**. 2Sm 12:16
Cut the living **b** in two 1Kg 3:25
enter the city, the **b** will die. 1Kg 14:12
let this **b-'s** life return to him! 1Kg 17:21
some small **b-s** came out 2Kg 2:23
he discovered the **b** lying dead 2Kg 4:32
they bartered a **b** for a prostitute Jl 3:3
b grew up and became strong, Lk 2:40
b here who has five barley loaves Jn 6:9

BOZRAH
  Edomite city (Gn 36:33; 1Ch 1:44;
Is 34:6; 63:1; Jr 49:13,22; Am 1:12).

BRACELETS
and the **b** on her wrists. Gn 24:47
jingling their ankle **b**, Is 3:16
putting **b** on your wrists Ezk 16:11

BRAG
Israel might **b**: 'I did it myself.' Jdg 7:2
Don't **b** about yourself Pr 25:6
he has something to **b** about Rm 4:2
b about you to the Macedonians: 2Co 9:2
are not **b-ging** beyond measure 2Co 10:15
don't **b** and lie in defiance of Jms 3:14

BRAMBLE
said to the **b**, 'Come and reign Jdg 9:14

BRANCH
mule went under the ... **b-es** 2Sm 18:9
his **b-es** above wither away. Jb 18:16
b of the LORD will be beautiful Is 4:2
a **b** from his roots will bear fruit. Is 11:1
raise up a righteous **B** of David. Jr 23:5
I will cause a **B** of righteousness
  to sprout up for David Jr 33:15
putting the **b** to their nose? Ezk 8:17
strong **b-es**, {fit} for the scepters Ezk 19:11
birds of the air lived in its **b-es**, Dn 4:12
about to bring My servant, the **B**. Zch 3:8
a man whose name is **B**; Zch 6:12
come and nest in its **b-es**. Mt 13:32
Every **b** in Me that does not produce Jn 15:2
I am the vine; you are the **b-es**. Jn 15:5
root is holy, so are the **b-es**. Rm 11:16
a wild olive **b**, were grafted in Rm 11:17

BRAWLER
Wine is a mocker, beer is a **b**, Pr 20:1

BRAZENLY
kisses him; she **b** says to him, Pr 7:13

BRAZIER
scroll was consumed ... in the **b**. Jr 36:23

BREACH
stood before Him in the **b** Ps 106:23
will go through **b-es** in the wall, Am 4:3

BREAD
eat **b** by the sweat of your brow Gn 3:19
unleavened **b** and bitter herbs. Ex 12:8
unleavened **b** for seven days. Ex 12:15
{Festival of} Unleavened **B** Ex 12:17
b of the Presence on the table Ex 25:30
b is to be set out before the LORD
  every Sabbath day Lv 24:8
man does not live on **b** alone Dt 8:3
loaf of barley **b** came tumbling Jdg 7:13
gave him the consecrated {**b**}, 1Sm 21:6
You provided **b** from heaven Neh 9:15
or his children begging **b**. Ps 37:25
I trusted, one who ate my **b**, Ps 41:9
with **b** from heaven. Ps 105:40
prostitute's fee is only a loaf of **b**, Pr 6:26
b {eaten} secretly is tasty! Pr 9:17

b on the surface of the waters, Ec 11:1
Ephraim is unturned **b**, Hs 7:8
will be like the **b** of mourners; Hs 9:4
not a famine of **b** or a thirst Am 8:11
Those who eat your **b** will set a
   trap for you. Ob 7
tell these stones to become **b**. Mt 4:3
Man must not live on **b** alone Mt 4:4
Give us today our daily **b**. Mt 6:11
if his son asks him for **b**, Mt 7:9
took **b**, blessed and broke it, Mt 26:26
one who is dipping {**b**} with Me Mk 14:20
eat **b** in the kingdom of God! Lk 14:15
He gave them **b** from heaven Jn 6:31
I am the **b** of life, Jn 6:35
one who eats My **b** has Jn 13:18
breaking of **b**, and to prayers. Ac 2:42
the Lord Jesus took **b**, 1Co 11:23
For as often as you eat this **b** 1Co 11:26

BREADTH
what is the **b** and width, Eph 3:18

BREAK see also BROKEN (adj)
you may not **b** any of its bones. Ex 12:46
is caught in the act of **b**-ing in, Ex 22:2
first tablets, which you **broke**. Ex 34:1
I will **b** down your strong pride. Lv 26:19
or **b** any of its bones. Nm 9:12
he must not **b** his word; Nm 30:2
I will never **b** My covenant Jdg 2:1
trumpets and **broke** the pitchers Jdg 7:19
bows of the warriors are **broken**, 1Sm 2:4
b your treaty with Baasha 1Kg 15:19
Jerusalem's wall has been **broken** Neh 1:3
will **b** them with a rod of iron; Ps 2:9
You **b** the teeth of the wicked. Ps 3:7
bones; not one of them is **broken**. Ps 34:20
they have **broken** Your law. Ps 119:126
a devious tongue **b**-s the spirit. Pr 15:4
stop the dispute before it **b**-s out. Pr 17:14
a gentle tongue can **b** a bone. Pr 25:15
three strands is not easily **broken**. Ec 4:12
who **b**-s through a wall may be Ec 10:8
the golden bowl is **broken**, Ec 12:6
Before the day **b**-s and the
   shadows flee, Sg 2:17; 4:6
He will not **b** a bruised reed, Is 42:3
long ago I **broke** your yoke; Jr 2:20
took the yoke ... and **broke** it. Jr 28:10

I will **b** his yoke from your neck Jr 30:8
the city was **broken** into. Jr 39:2
I will **b** the bow of Israel Hs 1:5
where thieves **b** in and steal. Mt 6:19
He will not **b** a bruised reed, Mt 12:20
He **broke** the loaves and gave Mt 14:19
Your disciples **b** the tradition Mt 15:2
bread, blessed and **broke** it, Mt 26:26
waves were **b**-ing over the boat, Mk 4:37
She **broke** the jar and poured it Mk 14:3
He was made known to them in
   the **b**-ing of the bread. Lk 24:35
not only was He **b**-ing the
   Sabbath, Jn 5:18
the Scripture cannot be **broken** Jn 10:35
they did not **b** His legs Jn 19:33
of His bones will be **broken**. Jn 19:36
broke bread from house to house Ac 2:46
severe persecution **broke** out Ac 8:1
weeping and **b**-ing my heart? Ac 21:13
do you dishonor God by **b**-ing Rm 2:23
Branches were **broken** off so that Rm 11:19
gave thanks, **broke** it, 1Co 11:24
is guilty of {**b**-ing it} all. Jms 2:10
to open the scroll and **b** its seals? Rv 5:2
war **broke** out in heaven: Rv 12:7

BREAKERS
b and Your billows have swept Ps 42:7
waters—the mighty **b** of the sea Ps 93:4
b and Your billows swept over me Jnh 2:3

BREAKFAST
have **b**," Jesus told them. Jn 21:12

BREAST
infant is snatched from the **b**; Jb 24:9
secure while at my mother's **b**. Ps 22:9
let her **b**-s always satisfy you; Pr 5:19
the night between my **b**-s. Sg 1:13
Your **b**-s are like two fawns, Sg 4:5; 7:3
your **b**-s are clusters {of fruit}. Sg 7:7
adultery from between her **b**-s. Hs 2:2

BREASTPLATE
righteousness like a **b**, Is 59:17
they had chests like iron **b**-s; Rv 9:9

BREATH
breathed the **b** of life into Gn 2:7
it took her **b** away. 1Kg 10:5

Remember that my life is {but} a **b**.   Jb 7:7
my days are a **b**.   Jb 7:16
He doesn't let me catch my **b**   Jb 9:18
My **b** is offensive to my wife,   Jb 19:17
as long as my **b** is still in me   Jb 27:3
blast of the **b** of Your nostrils.   Ps 18:15
You take away their **b**, they die   Ps 104:29
there is no **b** in their mouths.   Ps 135:17
Man is like a **b**;   Ps 144:4
are a lie; there is no **b** in them.   Jr 10:14
the **b** entered them,   Ezk 37:10
yet there is no **b** in it at all.   Hab 2:19
gives everyone life and **b**   Ac 17:25
with the **b** of His mouth   2Th 2:8
b of life from God entered them   Rv 11:11

BREATHE

b-d the breath of life into   Gn 2:7
Let everything that **b-s** praise   Ps 150:6
b into these slain so that they   Ezk 37:9
a loud cry and **b-d** His last.   Mk 15:37
He **b-d** on them and said,   Jn 20:22
Saul, still **b-ing** threats   Ac 9:1

BREED

would **b** in front of the branches.   Gn 30:41
Mesha of Moab was a sheep **b-er**.   2Kg 3:4

BRIBE

trustworthy, and hating **b-s**.   Ex 18:21
not take a **b**, for a **b** blinds   Ex 23:8
no partiality and taking no **b**.   Dt 10:17
Do not accept a **b**, for it blinds   Dt 16:19
have I taken a **b** to overlook   1Sm 12:3
the one who hates **b-s** will live.   Pr 15:27
A **b** seems like a magic stone   Pr 17:8
a **b** destroys the mind.   Ec 7:7
love graft and chase after **b-s**.   Is 1:23
who acquit the guilty for a **b**   Is 5:23
oppress the righteous, take a **b**,   Am 5:12
leaders issue rulings for a **b**,   Mc 3:11
and the judge demand a **b**;   Mc 7:3

BRICK

They had **b** for stone   Gn 11:3
require the same quota of **b-s**   Ex 5:8
burning incense on **b-s**,   Is 65:3
take a **b**, set it in front of you   Ezk 4:1

BRIDE

When a man takes a **b**,   Dt 24:5

my sister, my **b**   Sg 4:9,10,12; 5:1
b adorns herself with her jewels   Is 61:10
rejoices over {his} **b**, so your God   Is 62:5
I will remove ... the voices of the
   bridegroom and the **b**,   Jr 7:34
the **b** her honeymoon chamber.   Jl 2:16
He who has the **b** is the groom.   Jn 3:29
the **b**, the wife of the Lamb.   Rv 21:9
Spirit and the **b** say, "Come!"   Rv 22:17

BRIDEGROOM

You are a **b** of blood to me!   Ex 4:25
as a **b** wears a turban   Is 61:10
as a **b** rejoices over {his} bride,   Is 62:5
I will remove ... the voices of the
   b and the bride,   Jr 7:34
Let the **b** leave his bedroom,   Jl 2:16

BRIDLE

must be controlled with bit and **b**,   Ps 32:9
a **b** for the donkey, and a rod   Pr 26:3
a **b** on the jaws of the peoples   Is 30:28
up to the horses' **b-s**   Rv 14:20

BRIEF

I deserted you for a **b** moment,   Is 54:7

BRIEFLY

as I have **b** written above.   Eph 3:3
I have written **b**,   1Pt 5:12

BRIGHT

B eyes cheer the heart;   Pr 15:30
wise will shine like the **b**   Dn 12:3
suddenly a **b** cloud covered   Mt 17:5
dressed in clean, **b** linen,   Rv 15:6
the **B** Morning Star.   Rv 22:16

BRIGHTER

shining **b** and **b**   Pr 4:18

BRIGHTLY

light of the righteous shines **b**,   Pr 13:9

BRIGHTNESS

the **b** of the moon will not shine   Is 60:19
with the **b** of the LORD's glory.   Ezk 10:4
even gloom without any **b** in it?   Am 5:20
I couldn't see because of the **b**   Ac 22:11
with the **b** of His coming.   2Th 2:8

BRILLIANCE

I did not come with **b** of speech   1Co 2:1

BRIMSTONE

fire, and **b** on him,   Ezk 38:22

BRING

brought each to the man to see	Gn 2:19
b into the ark two of every	Gn 6:19
LORD who **brought** you from Ur	Gn 15:7
b my gray hairs down to Sheol	Gn 44:29
to **b** about the present result	Gn 50:20
I will **b** you to the land	Ex 6:8
b you every important case	Ex 18:22
the bitter water that **b-s** a curse.	Nm 5:18
B out the men who came to you	Jos 2:3
I **brought** you out of Egypt	Jdg 2:1
LORD **b-s** death and gives life;	1Sm 2:6
Saul told Ahijah, "**B** the ark	1Sm 14:18
who plays well and **b** him	1Sm 16:17
Why did you **b** him to me?	1Sm 21:14
Can I **b** him back again?	2Sm 12:23
b me water ... from the well at	2Sm 23:15
in order to **b** the ark	1Kg 8:1
king of Babylon also **brought** captive into Babylon	2Kg 24:16
Then let us **b** back the ark	1Ch 13:3
to **b** the ark of the LORD	1Ch 15:3
brought him to Babylon	2Ch 36:10
They are to be **brought** to the temple in Jerusalem,	Ezr 6:5
b out the constellations	Jb 38:32
kings will **b** tribute to You.	Ps 68:29
b an offering and enter	Ps 96:8
b-s the wind from His storehouses.	Ps 135:7
I was **brought** forth when	Pr 8:24
wise son **b-s** joy to his father,	Pr 10:1; 15:20
don't know what a day might **b**.	Pr 27:1
will **b** every act to judgment,	Ec 12:14
Oh, that the king would **b** me to	Sg 1:4
brought me to the banquet hall,	Sg 2:4
B water for the thirsty.	Is 21:14
I **brought** you from the ends of	Is 41:9
B My sons from far away,	Is 43:6
I have spoken; so I will also **b** it	Is 46:11
who **b-s** news of good things,	Is 52:7
anointed Me to **b** good news	Is 61:1
Will I **b** a baby to the point of birth and not	Is 66:9
I am about to **b** a nation from far	Jr 5:15
I will **b** them back to this city.	Jr 34:22
about to **b** a sword against you,	Ezk 6:3

will **b** you into your own land.	Ezk 36:24
they **brought** in the gold vessels	Dn 5:3
from there I will **b** them down.	Am 9:2
Didn't I **b** Israel from the land of	Am 9:7
from there I will **b** you down.	Ob 4
What should I **b** before the LORD	Mc 6:6
the feet of one **b-ing** good news	Nah 1:15
At that time I will **b** you back,	Zph 3:20
I will **b** them {back} to live in	Zch 8:8
B the full 10 percent into	Mal 3:10
they **brought** to Him all those	Mt 4:24
be **brought** before governors	Mt 10:18
I did not come to **b** peace, but	Mt 10:34
who **b-s** out of his storeroom	Mt 13:52
brought to Him all who were sick.	Mt 14:35
came to Him **b-ing** a paralytic,	Mk 2:3
were **b-ing** little children	Mk 10:13
I came to **b** fire on the earth,	Lk 12:49
b in here the poor, maimed,	Lk 14:21
b here these enemies of mine,	Lk 19:27
and he **brought** {Simon} to Jesus.	Jn 1:42
not of this fold; I must **b** them	Jn 10:16
Did you **b** Me offerings	Ac 7:42
Who can **b** an accusation	Rm 8:33
more will their full number **b**!	Rm 11:12
have been **brought** near	Eph 2:13
b them up in the training and	Eph 6:4
brought nothing into the world,	1Tm 6:7
When you come, **b** the cloak	2Tm 4:13
know what tomorrow will **b**	Jms 4:14

BRITTLE

I kept silent, my bones became **b**	Ps 32:3
part of the kingdom ... will be **b**.	Dn 2:42

BROAD

I will do this ... in **b** daylight.	2Sm 12:12
is **b** that leads to destruction,	Mt 7:13
middle of the **b** street {of the city}.	Rv 22:2

BROKEN (adj) *see also* BREAK

sacrifice pleasing to God is a **b** spirit. God, You will not despise a **b** and humbled heart.	Ps 51:17
a **b** spirit dries up the bones.	Pr 17:22
who can survive a **b** spirit?	Pr 18:14

BROKENHEARTED

The LORD is near the **b**;	Ps 34:18
He heals the **b** and binds up	Ps 147:3
He has sent Me to heal the **b**,	Is 61:1

BROKENNESS
they have treated My people's b superficially,	Jr 6:14
They have treated superficially the b of My dear people,	Jr 8:11

BRONZE
all kinds of b and iron tools.	Gn 4:22
works in gold, silver, and b,	Ex 31:4
So Moses made a b snake	Nm 21:9
The sky above you will be b,	Dt 28:23
my arms can bend a bow of b.	2Sm 22:35
whose appearance was like b,	Ezk 40:3
its stomach and thighs were b,	Dn 2:32
a third kingdom, of b,	Dn 2:39

BROOD
And here you, a b of sinners,	Nm 32:14
gather {her b} under her shadow.	Is 34:15
B of vipers! Who warned you	Mt 3:7
B of vipers!	Mt 12:34
Snakes! B of vipers!	Mt 23:33
B of vipers! Who warned you	Lk 3:7

BROOM
He sat down under a b tree	1Kg 19:4

BROTHER
Am I my b-'s guardian?	Gn 4:9
lowest of slaves to his b-s.	Gn 9:25
His b-s were jealous of him,	Gn 37:11
When b-s ... and one of them dies without a son,	Dt 25:5
I have become a b to jackals	Jb 30:29
pleasant it is when b-s can live	Ps 133:1
who stirs up trouble among b-s.	Pr 6:19
a b is born for a difficult time.	Pr 17:17
offended b is {harder to reach}	Pr 18:19
friend who stays closer than a b.	Pr 18:24
the b-s of a poor man hate him;	Pr 19:7
better a neighbor nearby than a b far away.	Pr 27:10
be reconciled with your b,	Mt 5:24
if you greet only your b-s,	Mt 5:47
B will betray b to death,	Mt 10:21
mother and b-s were standing	Mt 12:46
If your b sins against you,	Mt 18:15
forgive his b from his heart.	Mt 18:35
for one of the least of these b-s	Mt 25:40
Whoever does the will of God is My b and sister and mother.	Mk 3:35

It is not lawful for you to have your b-'s wife!	Mk 6:18
no one who has left house, b-s	Mk 10:29
b of yours was dead and is alive	Lk 15:32
not even His b-s believed in Him.	Jn 7:5
here, my b wouldn't have died.	Jn 11:21
the firstborn among many b-s.	Rm 8:29
benefit of my b-s, my countrymen	Rm 9:3
b goes to law against b,	1Co 6:6
if food causes my b to fall,	1Co 8:13
the other apostles, the Lord's b-s,	1Co 9:5
my b Titus,	2Co 2:13
James, the Lord's b.	Gl 1:19
Epaphroditus—my b,	Php 2:25
and Timothy our b:	Col 1:1
Tychicus, a loved b,	Col 4:7
Onesimus, a faithful and loved b,	Col 4:9
keep away from every b who	2Th 3:6
but warn him as a b.	2Th 3:15
not ashamed to call them b-s,	Heb 2:11
to be like His b-s in every way,	Heb 2:17
each his b, saying, 'Know	Heb 8:11
for sincere love of the b-s,	1Pt 1:22
by your b-s in the world.	1Pt 5:9
Silvanus, whom I consider ... b,	1Pt 5:12
the one who hates his b is in the darkness,	1Jn 2:11
life because we love our b-s.	1Jn 3:14
lay down our lives for our b-s.	1Jn 3:16
Jude ... a b of James:	Jd 1

BROTHERHOOD
and broke a treaty of b.	Am 1:9
Love the b. Fear God.	1Pt 2:17

BROTHER-IN-LAW
Perform your duty as her b	Gn 38:8
Her b is to take her as his wife,	Dt 25:5

BROTHERLY
Let b love continue.	Heb 13:1
godliness with b affection, and b affection with love.	2Pt 1:7

BROW
eat bread by the sweat of your b	Gn 3:19

BRUISE
b for b, wound for wound.	Ex 21:25

BRUISED (adj)
He will not break a b reed,	Is 42:3; Mt 12:20

BUCKET

nations are like a drop in a **b**;	Is 40:15
You don't even have a **b**,	Jn 4:11

BUD

soon as it **b**-ded, its blossoms	Gn 40:10
let's see if the vine has **b**-ded,	Sg 7:12
Though the fig tree does not **b**	Hab 3:17
Aaron's rod that **b**-ded,	Heb 9:4

BUILD

Noah **built** an altar to the LORD	Gn 8:20
let us **b** ourselves a city	Gn 11:4
They **built** Pithom and Rameses	Ex 1:11
cities that you did not **b**,	Dt 6:10
He will **b** a house for My name,	2Sm 7:13
Solomon {began to} **b** the temple	1Kg 6:1
So he **built** it in seven years.	1Kg 6:38
You are not the one to **b** Me a	1Ch 17:4
He will **b** a house for Me,	1Ch 17:12
began to **b** the LORD's temple	2Ch 3:1
appointed me to **b** Him a house	Ezr 1:2
heard ... exiles were **b**-ing a temple	Ezr 4:1
if a fox climbed up what they are **b**-ing,	Neh 4:3
Unless the LORD **b**-s a house,	Ps 127:1
Wisdom has **built** her house;	Pr 9:1
wise woman **b**-s her house,	Pr 14:1
A house is **built** by wisdom,	Pr 24:3
I **built** houses and planted vineyards	Ec 2:4
to tear down and a time to **b**;	Ec 3:3
He **built** a tower in the middle of it	Is 5:2
B it up, **b** it up, prepare the way	Is 57:14
B it up, **b** up the highway;	Is 62:10
B houses and live {in them}.	Jr 29:5
Isn't the time near to **b** houses?	Ezk 11:3
b houses, and plant vineyards.	Ezk 28:26
I have **built** by my vast power	Dn 4:30
who **b**-s a city with bloodshed	Hab 2:12
b houses but never live in them	Zph 1:13
who **built** his house on the rock.	Mt 7:24
on this rock I will **b** My church,	Mt 16:18
and **built** a watchtower.	Mt 21:33
barns and **b** bigger ones,	Lk 12:18
which is able to **b** you up	Ac 20:32
his good, in order to **b** him up.	Rm 15:2
b-ing on someone else's foundation,	Rm 15:20
be careful how he **b**-s on it,	1Co 3:10
pride, but love **b**-s up.	1Co 8:1

but not everything **b**-s up.	1Co 10:23
Lord gave for **b**-ing you up	2Co 10:8
built on the foundation of the apostles and prophets,	Eph 2:20
are being **built** together	Eph 2:22
to **b** up the body of Christ,	Eph 4:12
rooted and **built** up in Him	Col 2:7
and **b** each other up	1Th 5:11
being **built** into a spiritual house	1Pt 2:5

BUILDING (n)

the **b** that faced the temple	Ezk 41:12
Do you see these great **b**-s?	Mk 13:2
You are God's field, God's **b**.	1Co 3:9
we have a **b** from God,	2Co 5:1
b is being fitted together in Him	Eph 2:21

BUILDER

Solomon's **b**-s and Hiram's **b**-s,	1Kg 5:18
the **b**-s had laid the foundation	Ezr 3:10
The stone that the **b**-s rejected	Ps 118:22
its **b**-s labor over it in vain;	Ps 127:1
The stone that the **b**-s rejected	Mt 21:42
The stone despised by you **b**-s,	Ac 4:11
as a skilled master **b**	1Co 3:10
whose architect and **b** is God.	Heb 11:10
The stone that the **b**-s rejected	1Pt 2:7

BULL

their hands on the **b**-'s head.	Ex 29:10
unblemished **b** as a sin offering	Lv 4:3
1,000 **b**-s, 1,000 rams,	1Ch 29:21
Many **b**-s surround me;	Ps 22:12
I will not accept a **b** from	Ps 50:9
Do I eat the flesh of **b**-s	Ps 50:13
no desire for the blood of **b**-s,	Is 1:11
give a **b** from the herd as a sin offering	Ezk 43:19
b and purify the sanctuary.	Ezk 45:18
impossible for the blood of **b**-s	Heb 10:4

BULLY

not a **b** but gentle,	1Tm 3:3
not a **b**, not greedy for money,	Ti 1:7

BUNDLES

gather {grain} among the **b**,	Ru 2:15

BURDEN (n)

bear the **b** of the people,	Nm 11:17
you'll be a **b** to me,	2Sm 15:33
they are a **b** too heavy for me	Ps 38:4

Cast your **b** on the LORD,	Ps 55:22
Day after day He bears our **b-s**;	Ps 68:19
relieved his shoulder from the **b**;	Ps 81:6
stone is heavy and sand, a **b**,	Pr 27:3
They have become a **b** to Me;	Is 1:14
What is the **b** of the LORD?	Jr 23:33
no longer refer to the **b** of the LORD	Jr 23:36
yoke is easy and My **b** is light.	Mt 11:30
the foal of a beast of **b**.	Mt 21:5
You load people with **b-s**	Lk 11:46
no greater **b** on you than these	Ac 15:28
Carry one another's **b-s**;	Gl 6:2
would not be a **b** to any of you.	2Th 3:8
Now His commands are not a **b**,	1Jn 5:3

BURDEN (v)

Although my father **b-ed** you	1Kg 12:11
have **b-ed** Me with your sins;	Is 43:24
you who are weary and **b-ed**,	Mt 11:28
I did not **b** anyone,	2Co 11:9
I will not **b** you,	2Co 12:14
that we would not **b** any of you,	1Th 2:9
the church should not be **b-ed**,	1Tm 5:16
idle women **b-ed** down with sins,	2Tm 3:6

BURIAL

Give me a **b** site among you	Gn 23:4
does not even have a proper **b**,	Ec 6:3
she has prepared Me for **b**.	Mt 26:12
according to the **b** custom	Jn 19:40

BURN

Why isn't the bush **b-ing** up?	Ex 3:3
b for **b**, bruise for bruise,	Ex 21:25
the lamp **b-ing** continually.	Ex 27:20
calf they had made, **b-ed** {it} up,	Ex 32:20
b-ing on the altar continually;	Lv 6:13
Both he and they must be **b-ed**	Lv 20:14
she must be **b-ed** up.	Lv 21:9
they **b-ed** all the cities where the Midianites lived,	Nm 31:10
Then the LORD's anger will **b**	Dt 7:4
They **b-ed** up the city	Jos 6:24
Joshua **b-ed** Ai	Jos 8:28
Then he **b-ed** down Hazor.	Jos 11:11
Israel did not **b** any of the cities	Jos 11:13
sanctuary to **b** incense	2Ch 26:16
and his clothes not be **b-ed**?	Pr 6:27
He **b-s** half of it in a fire,	Is 44:16
to **b** their sons and daughters	Jr 7:31

becomes a fire **b-ing** in my heart,	Jr 20:9
king not to **b** the scroll,	Jr 36:25
b incense to the queen of heaven	Jr 44:17
the chaff He will **b** up with fire	Mt 3:12
into the fire, and they are **b-ed**.	Jn 15:6
collected their books and **b-ed**	Ac 19:19
If anyone's work is **b-ed** up,	1Co 3:15
better to marry than to **b**	1Co 7:9
if I give my body to be **b-ed**,	1Co 13:3
are **b-ed** outside the camp.	Heb 13:11
the elements will **b**	2Pt 3:10
a third of the earth was **b-ed** up,	Rv 8:7
the smoke from her **b-ing**	Rv 18:18
lake of fire that **b-s** with sulfur.	Rv 19:20

BURNING (adj)

who appeared in the {**b**} bush	Dt 33:16
turned from His **b** anger.	Jos 7:26
my loins are full of **b** pain,	Ps 38:7
the day of His **b** anger.	Is 13:13
b anger will not turn back	Jr 30:24
in My **b** zeal I speak against	Ezk 36:5
the day and the **b** heat!	Mt 20:12

BURNT

If his gift is a **b** offering	Lv 1:3

BURST

the watery depths **b** open,	Gn 7:11
Like a **b-ing** flood, the LORD has **b** out against my enemies.	2Sm 5:20
about to **b** like new wineskins.	Jb 32:19
the skins **b**, the wine spills out,	Mt 9:17
the wine will **b** the skins,	Mk 2:22
the new wine will **b** the skins,	Lk 5:37
falling headfirst, he **b** open	Ac 1:18

BURY

be **b-ied** at a ripe old age.	Gn 15:15
so that I can **b** my dead.	Gn 23:4
B me with my fathers	Gn 49:29
b-ied him in the cave	Gn 50:13
Joseph's bones ... were **b-ied**	Jos 24:32
and there I will be **b-ied**.	Ru 1:17
no one will **b** her.	2Kg 9:10
did not **b** him in the tombs	2Ch 24:25
The slacker **b-ies** his hand in the bowl;	Pr 19:24; 26:15
first let me go **b** my father.	Mt 8:21
let the dead **b** their own dead.	Mt 8:22

BUSH

is like treasure, **b-ied** in a field,	Mt 13:44
devout men **b-ied** Stephen	Ac 8:2
were **b-ied** with Him by baptism	Rm 6:4
was **b-ied**, that He was raised	1Co 15:4
b-ied with Him in baptism,	Col 2:12

BUSH

the boy under one of the **b-es**.	Gn 21:15
the **b** was on fire but was not	Ex 3:2
who appeared in the {burning} **b**.	Dt 33:16
passage about the burning **b**,	Mk 12:26
in the flame of a burning **b**.	Ac 7:30

BUSHELS

I bought her for ... five **b** of barley.	Hs 3:2

BUSINESS

of Kedar were your **b** partners,	Ezk 27:21
went about the king's **b**.	Dn 8:27
What is your **b** and where	Jnh 1:8
Engage in **b** until I come back.	Lk 19:13
our **b** may be discredited,	Ac 19:27
to mind your own **b**,	1Th 4:11
and do **b** and make a profit.	Jms 4:13
sailors, and all who do **b** by sea,	Rv 18:17

BUSY

while your servant was **b** here	1Kg 20:40
each of you is **b** with his own	Hg 1:9

BUSYBODIES

are also gossips and **b**,	1Tm 5:13

BUTTER

churning of milk produces **b**,	Pr 30:33
he will be eating **b** and honey.	Is 7:15

BUY

B us and our land	Gn 47:19
b from them on the Sabbath	Neh 10:31
B—and do not sell—truth,	Pr 23:23
She evaluates a field and **b-s** it;	Pr 31:16
b wine and milk without money	Is 55:1
So I **bought** the field in Anathoth	Jr 32:9
I **bought** her for 15 shekels of silver	Hs 3:2
We can **b** the poor with silver	Am 8:6
sells everything he has and **b-s**	Mt 13:44
sold everything ... and **bought** it.	Mt 13:46
drove out all those **b-ing** and	Mt 21:12
I have **bought** a field, and I must	Lk 14:18
eating, drinking, **b-ing**, selling,	Lk 17:28
I **bought** this citizenship for	Ac 22:28
for you were **bought** at a price;	1Co 6:20

You were **bought** at a price;	1Co 7:23
denying the Master who **bought**	2Pt 2:1
b from Me gold refined	Rv 3:18
no one can **b** or sell unless	Rv 13:17
no one **b-s** their merchandise	Rv 18:11

BUYER

it's worthless!" the **b** says,	Pr 20:14
Let the **b** not rejoice	Ezk 7:12

C

∽

CAESAR

1. Name implying Rome's authority in Palestine (Mt 22:17-21; Mk 12:14-17; Lk 20:22-25; 23:2; Jn 19:12,15; Ac 17:7).

2. Augustus (Lk 2:1).

3. Tiberius (Lk 3:1).

4. Claudius (Ac 11:28; 18:2).

5. Nero (Ac 25:8-12,21; 26:32; 27:24; 28:19; Php 4:22).

CAESAREA

came to the region of **C** Philippi,	Mt 16:13
a man in **C** named Cornelius,	Ac 10:1
Paul should be kept at **C**,	Ac 25:4

CAIAPHAS

High priest, along with his father-in-law Annas, who sentenced Jesus (Mt 26:3; Lk 3:2; Jn 18:13). Spoke prophetically (Jn 11:49-52). Threatened Peter and John (Ac 4:6).

CAIN

Firstborn of Adam and Eve; crop farmer; murdered his brother; God marked and banished him (Gn 4:1-25; Heb 11:4; 1Jn 3:12; Jd 11).

CALAMITY

He will rescue you from six **c-ies**;	Jb 5:19
will laugh at your **c**.	Pr 1:26
c will strike him suddenly;	Pr 6:15
the day of their **c** is coming on them,	Jr 46:21
your brother in the day of his **c**;	Ob 12
Isn't the LORD among us? No **c**	
will overtake us.	Mc 3:11

CALCULATE

first sit down and c the cost | Lk 14:28
c the number of the beast, | Rv 13:18

CALEB

Judahite who scouted Canaan and, along with Joshua, recommended invasion (Nm 13:30–14:38). Entered the promised land (Dt 1:36); received Hebron (Jos 14:13).

CALF

got a tender, choice c. | Gn 18:7
made it into an image of a c. | Ex 32:4
take their c-ves away and pen them | 1Sm 6:7
Then he made two gold c-ves, | 1Kg 12:28
He makes Lebanon skip like a c, | Ps 29:6
The c, the young lion, | Is 11:6
The c of Samaria will be smashed | Hs 8:6
men who sacrifice kiss the c-ves. | Hs 13:2
playfully jump like c-ves | Mal 4:2
bring the fattened c and slaughter | Lk 15:23
not by the blood of goats and c-ves | Heb 9:12
second living creature was like a c; | Rv 4:7

CALL

to see what he would c it. | Gn 2:19
people began to c on the name | Gn 4:26
I c heaven and earth as witnesses | Dt 4:26
the LORD c-ed Samuel, | 1Sm 3:4
I c-ed to the LORD in my distress; | 2Sm 22:7
c on the name of your god, and I
will c on the name of Yahweh. | 1Kg 18:24
thanks to the LORD; c on His name | 1Ch 16:8
people who are c-ed by My name | 2Ch 7:14
Answer me when I c, God, | Ps 4:1
LORD, hear my voice when I c; | Ps 27:7
I c to You; my rock, do not be deaf | Ps 28:1
Deep c-s to deep in the roar | Ps 42:7
C on Me in a day of trouble; | Ps 50:15
I c to You from the ends of the earth | Ps 61:2
blessed by him and c him blessed. | Ps 72:17
faithful love to all who c on You. | Ps 86:5
I c on You in the day of my distress, | Ps 86:7
thanks to the LORD, c on His name; | Ps 105:1
is near all who c out to Him, | Ps 145:18
they will c me, but I won't answer; | Pr 1:28
Doesn't Wisdom c out? | Pr 8:1
Her sons rise up and c her blessed. | Pr 31:28
Woe to those who c evil good | Is 5:20
I have c-ed you by your name; | Is 43:1

c to Him while He is near. | Is 55:6
Even before they c, I will answer; | Is 65:24
everyone who c-s on the name of | Jl 2:32
Get up! C to your god. | Jnh 1:6
I didn't come to c the righteous, | Mt 9:13
will be c-ed a house of prayer. | Mt 21:13
as for you, do not be c-ed 'Rabbi,' | Mt 23:8
you will c His name JESUS. | Lk 1:31
all generations will c me blessed, | Lk 1:48
Why do you c Me 'Lord, Lord,' | Lk 6:46
Go c your husband, | Jn 4:16
He c-s his own sheep by name | Jn 10:3
You c Me Teacher and Lord. | Jn 13:13
I do not c you slaves anymore, | Jn 15:15
whoever c-s on the name of | Ac 2:21
wash away your sins by c-ing on
   His name. | Ac 22:16
those He c-ed, He also justified; | Rm 8:30
Lord of all is rich to all who c | Rm 10:12
everyone who c-s on the name of | Rm 10:13
how can they c on Him in whom | Rm 10:14
God has c-ed you to peace. | 1Co 7:15
you are c-ed to freedom, brothers; | Gl 5:13
God's heavenly c in Christ Jesus. | Php 3:14
God has not c-ed us to impurity, | 1Th 4:7
He who c-s you is faithful, | 1Th 5:24
One who c-ed you out of darkness | 1Pt 2:9
that we should be c-ed God's
   children. | 1Jn 3:1

CALLED (n)

To those who are the c, | Jd 1

CALLING (n)

the c of solemn assemblies | Is 1:13
God's ... and c are irrevocable. | Rm 11:29
Brothers, consider your c: | 1Co 1:26
walk worthy of the c you have | Eph 4:1
called us with a holy c, | 2Tm 1:9
confirm your c and election, | 2Pt 1:10

CALM (adj)

The c words of the wise are heeded | Ec 9:17
keep c and not do anything rash. | Ac 19:36

CALM (n)

c and quiet with no one to frighten | Jr 30:10
And there was a great c. | Mt 8:26

CALM (v)

I have c-ed and quieted myself | Ps 131:2

a man slow to anger c-s strife. Pr 15:18
do to you to c this sea that's Jnh 1:11

CAMEL
she got down from her c Gn 24:64
{You are} a swift young c Jr 2:23
John himself had a c-hair garment Mt 3:4
easier for a c to go through the eye Mt 19:24
gnat, yet gulp down a c! Mt 23:24

CAMP (n)
Jacob said, "This is God's c." Gn 32:2
There is a sound of war in the c. Ex 32:17
he will bring the bull outside the c Lv 4:21
the sin offering ... must be brought
    outside the c Lv 16:27
outside the c and slaughtered Nm 19:3
ark of the LORD had entered the c, 1Sm 4:6
asleep in the inner circle of the c 1Sm 26:7
The c was intact, and they had fled 2Kg 7:7
the dance of the two c-s? Sg 6:13
are burned outside the c. Heb 13:11
go to Him outside the c, Heb 13:13

CAMP (v)
they c-ed there by the waters. Ex 15:27
c-ed there in front of the mountain. Ex 19:2
c around the tent of meeting Nm 2:2
would c at the LORD's command Nm 9:20
the Israelites c-ed at Gilgal Jos 5:10
are c-ing in the open field. 2Sm 11:11

CANA
a wedding took place in C of Galilee. Jn 2:1

CANAAN
  Son of Ham, his descendants, and the land
they populated (Gn 9:18-27; 10:15-19). God
promised the land to Abraham (12:4-7;
17:8; Ex 6:4; 1Ch 16:15-18).

CANAANITE
commanded Jacob not to marry a C Gn 28:6
drive out the C-s, Amorites, Hittites, Ex 33:2
dispossess before you the C-s, Jos 3:10
You can also drive out the C-s, Jos 17:18
so the C-s lived among them Jdg 1:30
But they settled among the C-s, Jdg 3:5
give the land of the C-s, Hittites, Neh 9:8
a C woman from that region came Mt 15:22

CANAL
and Egypt's c-s will be parched. Is 19:6

among the exiles by the Chebar C, Ezk 1:1
I was beside the Ulai C. Dn 8:2

CANCEL
But if her husband c-s them Nm 30:12
every seven years you must c debts. Dt 15:1
Do we then c the law Rm 3:31

CANOPY
made darkness a c around Him, 2Sm 22:12
spreading out the sky like a c, Ps 104:2

CAPABLE
A c wife is her husband's crown, Pr 12:4
Who can find a c wife? Pr 31:10

CAPER
and the c berry has no effect; Ec 12:5

CAPERNAUM
went to live in C by the sea, Mt 4:13
C, will you be exalted to heaven? Mt 11:23
that took place in C, do here Lk 4:23
teaching in the synagogue in C. Jn 6:59

CAPHTOR
the Philistines from C, Am 9:7

CAPITAL
I had not committed a c offense. Ac 28:18

CAPITALS
made two c of cast bronze 1Kg 7:16
Strike the c of the pillars Am 9:1

CAPPADOCIA
those who live in ... C, Ac 2:9
the provinces of Pontus, Galatia, C, 1Pt 1:1

CAPSTONE
he will bring out the c Zch 4:7

CAPTAIN
Potiphar, ... the c of the guard, Gn 39:1
King Ahaziah sent a c of 50 2Kg 1:9
the c and the owner of the ship Ac 27:11

CAPTIVATE
or let her c you with her eyelashes. Pr 6:25
eyes away from me, for they c me. Sg 6:5

CAPTIVE
the king of Babylon took him {c} 2Kg 24:12
took many c-s to Damascus. 2Ch 28:5
the LORD restores His c people, Ps 14:7
to the heights, taking away c-s; Ps 68:18

a king could be held c in your tresses. Sg 7:5
to proclaim liberty to the c-s, Is 61:1
to proclaim freedom to the c-s Lk 4:18
taking every thought c 2Co 10:5
Be careful that no one takes you c Col 2:8
c-s of various passions and pleasures, Ti 3:3

CAPTIVITY

returned to Jerusalem from the c, Ezr 3:8
those {destined} for c, to c. Jr 15:2
you will go into c. ... to Babylon. Jr 20:6
they will go into exile, into c. Ezk 12:11
When I return My people from c, Hs 6:11
into c, from there I will command Am 9:4
took prisoners into c; He gave gifts Eph 4:8
destined for c, into c he goes. Rv 13:10

CAPTORS

pitied before all their c. Ps 106:46
for our c there asked us for songs, Ps 137:3
They will make captives of their c Is 14:2

CAPTURE

They c-d all their possessions, Gn 34:29
At that time we c-d all his cities Dt 2:34
The ark of God was c-d, 1Sm 4:11
He c-d Agag king of Amalek 1Sm 15:8
Can anyone c him Jb 40:24
c-d my heart with one glance Sg 4:9
they have dug a pit to c me Jr 18:22
growl from its lair unless it has c-d Am 3:4
if someone c-s you, 2Co 11:20

CARAVAN

and there was a c of Ishmaelites Gn 37:25
c-s of Tema look {for these streams}. Jb 6:19
you c-s of Dedanites. Is 21:13

CARCASS

who touches its c will be unclean Lv 11:39
You are not to eat any c; Dt 14:21
honey from the lion's c. Jdg 14:9
the c is, there the vultures Mt 24:28

CARE (n)

Put him in my c, Gn 42:37
When I am filled with c-s, Ps 94:19
the sheep under His c. Ps 95:7
come, and I will take c of you. Jr 40:4
I was sick and you took c of Me; Mt 25:36
to an inn, and took c of him. Lk 10:34
on me: my c for all the churches. 2Co 11:28

you have renewed your c for me. Php 4:10
how will he take c of God's
church? 1Tm 3:5
casting all your c upon Him, 1Pt 5:7

CARE (v)

a land the LORD your God c-s for. Dt 11:12
None of you c-s about me 1Sm 22:8
the LORD c-s for me. Ps 27:10
Happy is one who c-s for the poor; Ps 41:1
no one c-s about me. Ps 142:4
what is man, that You c for him, Ps 144:3
you will be called C-d For, Is 62:12
No one c-d {enough} about you Ezk 16:5
Should I not c about the great city Jnh 4:11
c-s for those who take refuge in Him Nah 1:7
but provides and c-s for it, Eph 5:29
genuinely c about your interests; Php 2:20
son of man, that You c for him? Heb 2:6
because He c-s about you. 1Pt 5:7

CAREFUL

be c not to forget the LORD Dt 6:12
Be c to obey all these things Dt 12:28
Now please be c not to drink wine Jdg 13:4
c not to practice your righteousness Mt 6:1
each one must be c how he builds 1Co 3:10
But be c that this right of yours 1Co 8:9
c attention, then, to how you walk Eph 5:15

CAREFULLY

listen to Me and c keep My
covenant Ex 19:5
c follow every command I am giving Dt 8:1
c observe everything written in it. Jos 1:8
you will succeed if you c follow 1Ch 22:13

CARELESS

a fool is easily angered and is c. Pr 14:16
to account for every c word Mt 12:36

CARESSING

surprised to see Isaac c his wife Gn 26:8

CARMEL

Saul went to C 1Sm 15:12
servants came to Abigail at C, 1Sm 25:40
gathered the prophets at
Mount C. 1Kg 18:20
Elisha went to Mount C, 2Kg 2:25
Your head crowns you like Mount C, Sg 7:5

CARMI

Son of Reuben (Gn 46:9; Nm 26:6).

CAROUSING

not in c and drunkenness;	Rm 13:13
envy, drunkenness, c,	Gl 5:21
evil desires, drunkenness, orgies, c,	1Pt 4:3

CARPENTER

c-s, and stonemasons,	2Sm 5:11
{give it} to the c-s, builders,	2Kg 22:6
Isn't this the c-'s son?	Mt 13:55
Isn't this the c, the son of Mary,	Mk 6:3

CARRIERS

| became woodcutters and water c | Jos 9:21 |

CARRY

c my bones up from here.	Gn 50:25
I c-ied you on eagles' wings	Ex 19:4
Kohathites will come and c them,	Nm 4:15
God c-ied you as a man c-ies his son	Dt 1:31
the tribe of Levi to c the ark	Dt 10:8
c on the name of the dead brother,	Dt 25:6
c-ied out the LORD's instructions.	1Sm 15:13
Spirit of the LORD may c you off	1Kg 18:12
and c-ied the bronze to Babylon.	2Kg 25:13
No one but the Levites may c	1Ch 15:2
shepherd them, and c them forever.	Ps 28:9
he will take nothing ... that he can c	Ec 5:15
sentence ... is not c-ied out quickly,	Ec 8:11
bird of the sky may c the message,	Ec 10:20
lambs in His arms and c-ies {them}	Is 40:11
and He c-ied our pains;	Is 53:4
He will c their iniquities.	Is 53:11
be c-ied because they cannot walk.	Jr 10:5
not c a load ... on the Sabbath day	Jr 17:22
I will c {them} off,	Hs 5:14
He Himself ... c-ied our diseases.	Mt 8:17
heavy loads that are hard to c	Mt 23:4
forced this man to c His cross.	Mt 27:32
Don't c a money-bag, traveling bag,	Lk 10:4
c you where you don't want to go	Jn 21:18
Spirit of the Lord c-ied Philip away,	Ac 8:39
c the death of Jesus in our body,	2Co 4:10
will not c out the desire of the flesh.	Gl 5:16
C one another's burdens;	Gl 6:2
person will have to c his own load.	Gl 6:5
I c the marks of Jesus on my body	Gl 6:17
will c it on to completion	Php 1:6

CART

new c and two milk cows	1Sm 6:7
the ark of God on a new c	2Sm 6:3
he made 10 bronze water c-s.	1Kg 7:27

CARVED (adj)

and burn up their c images.	Dt 7:5
who makes a c idol or cast image,	Dt 27:15
Manasseh set up the c image	2Kg 21:7
All who serve c images,	Ps 97:7

CARVED (v)

paneling inside the temple was c	1Kg 6:18
she has c out her seven pillars.	Pr 9:1
c with cherubim and palm trees.	Ezk 41:18

CASE

bring you every important c	Ex 18:22
If a c is too difficult for you	Dt 17:8
Let Baal plead his c	Jdg 6:32
argue my c before God.	Jb 13:3
I would plead my c before Him	Jb 23:4
The first to state his c seems right	Pr 18:17
the LORD will take up their c	Pr 22:23
He will take up their c against you.	Pr 23:11
"Submit your c," says the LORD.	Is 41:21
let us argue our c together.	Is 43:26
He took up the c of the poor	Jr 22:16
brings a c against the nations.	Jr 25:31
LORD has a c against the inhabitants	Hs 4:1
the LORD has a c against His people,	Mc 6:2
When Lysias ... comes down, I will decide your c.	Ac 24:22

CAST (adj)

Do not make c images of gods	Ex 34:17
his c images are a lie;	Jr 10:14; 51:17
{only} a c image, a teacher of lies.	Hab 2:18

CAST (v)

c spells, consult a medium or	Dt 18:11
Joshua c lots for them at Shiloh	Jos 18:10
the king had them c in clay molds.	1Kg 7:46
He c the Pur (that is, the lot)	Est 9:24
would c {lots} for a fatherless child	Jb 6:27
they c lots for my clothing.	Ps 22:18
C your burden on the LORD,	Ps 55:22
The lot is c into the lap,	Pr 16:33
{C-ing} the lot ends quarrels	Pr 18:18
have ... c Me behind your back,	Ezk 23:35
They c lots for My people;	Jl 3:3

foreigners ... c lots for Jerusalem,   Ob 11
You will c all our sins into   Mc 7:19
divided His clothes by c-ing lots   Mt 27:35
divided His clothes, c-ing lots   Mk 15:24
who comes to Me I will never c out.   Jn 6:37
they c lots for My clothing.   Jn 19:24
c-ing all your care upon Him,   1Pt 5:7
c their crowns before the throne,   Rv 4:10

CASTRATED
might also get themselves c!   Gl 5:12

CATCH
saw a ram **caught** by its horns   Gn 22:13
If a thief is **caught** in the act   Ex 22:2
your sin will c up with you.   Nm 32:23
c a wife for yourself   Jdg 21:21
Absalom's head was **caught** fast   2Sm 18:9
lizard can be **caught** in your hands,   Pr 30:28
like fish **caught** in a cruel net,   Ec 9:12
C the foxes for us—the little foxes   Sg 2:15
They set a trap; they c men.   Jr 5:26
he will be **caught** in My snare.   Ezk 12:13
all night long and **caught** nothing!   Lk 5:5
now on you will be c-ing people!   Lk 5:10
brought a woman **caught** in adultery,   Jn 8:3
He c-es the wise in their craftiness   1Co 3:19
caught up into the third heaven   2Co 12:2
be **caught** up together with them   1Th 4:17
her child was **caught** up to God   Rv 12:5

CATTLE
an unblemished male from the c,   Lv 22:19
what is this sound of sheep and c   1Sm 15:14
Why are we regarded as c, as stupid   Jb 18:3
is Mine, the c on a thousand hills.   Ps 50:10
the fat of well-fed c; I have no desire   Is 1:11
You will feed on grass like c   Dn 4:25
and no c in the stalls,   Hab 3:17

CAUSE (n)
may You ... uphold their c.   1Kg 8:45
For You have upheld my just c;   Ps 9:4
LORD, hear a just c;   Ps 17:1
they dug a pit for me without c.   Ps 35:7
Those who hate me without c   Ps 69:4
have persecuted me without c,   Ps 119:161
upholds the just c of the poor,   Ps 140:12
Don't accuse anyone without c,   Pr 3:30
against your neighbor without c.   Pr 24:28
defend the c of the oppressed   Pr 31:9

Plead the widow's c.   Is 1:17
You defend my c, Lord;   Lm 3:58

CAUSE (v)
so that I will not c any pain.   1Ch 4:10
and c-s grass to grow on the hills.   Ps 147:8
Even if He c-s suffering,   Lm 3:32
c you to follow My statutes   Ezk 36:27
If your right eye c-s you to sin,   Mt 5:29
He c-s His sun to rise on the evil   Mt 5:45
whoever c-s the downfall of one of   Mt 18:6
And if your eye c-s your downfall,   Mt 18:9
c one of these little ones to stumble   Lk 17:2
Spirit He has c-d to live in us yearns   Jms 4:5

CAVALRY
the chariot cities, the c cities,   1Kg 9:19
to ask the king for infantry and c   Ezr 8:22
walls will shake from the noise
of c, wagons, and chariots.   Ezk 26:10

CAVE
give me the c of Machpelah   Gn 23:9
buried him in the c of Machpelah   Gn 25:9
Open the mouth of the c, and
bring those five kings   Jos 10:22
took refuge in the c of Adullam.   1Sm 22:1
Then Saul left the c and went on   1Sm 24:7
hid them, 50 men to a c,   1Kg 18:4
stood at the entrance of the c.   1Kg 19:13
hid in the c-s and among the rocks   Rv 6:15

CEASE
and day and night will not c.   Gn 8:22
there will never c to be poor people   Dt 15:11
the manna c-d.   Jos 5:12
not sin ... by c-ing to pray for you   1Sm 12:23
Why should the work c while
I leave   Neh 6:3
He makes wars c   Ps 46:9
who grind c because they are few,   Ec 12:3
highways are deserted; travel
has c-d.   Is 33:8
then also Israel's descendants will
c to be a nation before Me   Jr 31:36
got into the boat, the wind c-d.   Mt 14:32
otherwise grace c-s to be grace.   Rm 11:6
as for languages, they will c;   1Co 13:8

CEDAR
live bird together with the c wood,   Lv 14:6

priest is to take c wood, hyssop, Nm 19:6
I am living in a c house while 2Sm 7:2
command that c-s from Lebanon be 1Kg 5:6
The c paneling inside the temple 1Kg 6:18
LORD shatters the c-s of Lebanon. Ps 29:5
and grow like a c tree in Lebanon. Ps 92:12
c-s of Lebanon that He planted. Ps 104:16
fire will consume your c-s. Zch 11:1

CELEBRATE

c it throughout your generations Ex 12:14
c it as a festival to the LORD Lv 23:41
c the Passover to the LORD Dt 16:1
c the Festival of Weeks Dt 16:10
c the Festival of Booths for seven Dt 16:13
King David dancing and c-ing, 1Ch 15:29
Let Israel c its Maker; Ps 149:2
Let the godly c in triumphal glory; Ps 149:5
C His deeds among the peoples. Is 12:4
you are to c the Passover, Ezk 45:21
and to c the Festival of Booths. Zch 14:16
c and send gifts to one another, Rv 11:10

CELEBRATIONS

I will put an end to all her c: Hs 2:11

CELESTIAL

the c powers will be shaken. Mt 24:29

CENSUS

When you take a c of the Israelites Ex 30:12
Take a c of the entire Nm 1:2; 26:2
he had taken a c of the troops. 2Sm 24:10
against Israel a c of this {c}, 1Ch 27:24
Solomon took a c of all the foreign 2Ch 2:17
rose up in the days of the c Ac 5:37

CENT

until you have paid the last c. Lk 12:59

CENTER

who live at the c of the world. Ezk 38:12

CENTURION

a c came to Him, pleading with Him Mt 8:5
When the c saw what happened, Lk 23:47
in Caesarea named Cornelius, a c Ac 10:1
Taking along soldiers and c-s, Ac 21:32
c-s and said, "Take this young man Ac 23:17
the c paid attention to the captain Ac 27:11

CEPHAS

Aramaic for "Rock"; Peter (Jn 1:42; 1Co 1:12; 3:22; 9:5; 15:5; Gl 1:18; 2:9,11,14).

CERTAIN

the dream is true, and its
interpretation c. Dn 2:45
eat with the Gentiles before c men Gl 2:12
command c people not to teach 1Tm 1:3
He specifies a c day—today Heb 4:7

CERTAINTY

so that you may know the c Lk 1:4
all the house of Israel know with c Ac 2:36

CERTIFICATE

he may write her a divorce c, Dt 24:1
He erased the c of debt, Col 2:14

CHAFF

and make hills like c. Is 41:15
were shattered and became like c Dn 2:35
like c blown from a threshing floor, Hs 13:3
But the c He will burn up with fire Mt 3:12

CHAIN

gold c-s across the ... sanctuary 1Kg 6:21
decorated with palm trees and c-s. 2Ch 3:5
Can you fasten the c-s of Jb 38:31
Let us tear off their c-s Ps 2:3
and broke their c-s apart. Ps 107:14
and a {gold} c around your neck. Pr 1:9
the c-s fell off his wrists. Ac 12:7
and everyone's c-s came loose. Ac 16:26
as I am—except for these c-s. Ac 26:29
For this I am an ambassador in c-s. Eph 6:20
was not ashamed of my c-s. 2Tm 1:16
to be kept in c-s of darkness 2Pt 2:4
a great c in his hand. Rv 20:1

CHALDEA

Another name for the Babylonian empire (Jr 51:24; Ezk 12:13; 23:15).

CHALDEAN

Inhabitants of Chaldea (Gn 11:28). Known as sages or magicians (Dn 2:2; 4:7). Took Judah into exile (2Kg 25; 2Ch 36:17-19; Ezr 5:12; Jr 32).

CHAMBER

The windstorm comes from its c, Jb 37:9
a groom coming from the bridal c; Ps 19:5

In {her c}, the royal daughter is   Ps 45:13
descending to the c-s of death.   Pr 7:27
the king would bring me to his c-s.   Sg 1:4
and the bride her honeymoon c.   Jl 2:16
builds His upper c-s in the heavens   Am 9:6

CHAMPION

a c named Goliath, from Gath,   1Sm 17:4
and a c of widows is God   Ps 68:5

CHANCE

something that happened to us by c.   1Sm 6:9
time and c happen to all of them.   Ec 9:11

CHANGE (n)

each of the brothers c-s of clothes,   Gn 45:22
silver and two c-s of clothes.   2Kg 5:22
when there is a c of the priesthood,
    there must be a c of law as well.   Heb 7:12

CHANGE (v)

c-d my wages 10 times.   Gn 31:7
Purify yourselves and c your clothes   Gn 35:2
The people will c their minds   Ex 13:17
c Your mind about this disaster   Ex 32:12
or a son of man who c-s His mind.   Nm 23:19
since He has blessed, I cannot c it.   Nm 23:20
God c-d his heart,   1Sm 10:9
does not lie or c His mind,   1Sm 15:29
Jehoiachin c-d his prison clothes,   2Kg 25:29
will not ... c what My lips have said   Ps 89:34
You will c them like a garment,   Ps 102:26
if you really c your ways   Jr 7:5
Can the Cushite c his skin,   Jr 13:23
it is irrevocable and cannot be c-d.   Dn 6:8
Because I, Yahweh, have not c-d,   Mal 3:6
but we will all be c-d,   1Co 15:51
and want to c the gospel of Christ.   Gl 1:7
and they will be c-d like a robe.   Heb 1:12
and He will not c His mind,   Heb 7:21

CHANGERS

He overturned the money c' tables   Mt 21:12
He overturned the money c' tables   Mk 11:15
poured out the money c' coins   Jn 2:15

CHANNEL

Who cuts a c for the flooding rain   Jb 38:25
A king's heart is a water c   Pr 21:1

CHANTED

Jeremiah c a dirge over Josiah,   2Ch 35:25

CHAOS

all Jerusalem was in c.   Ac 21:31

CHARACTER

you are a woman of noble c.   Ru 3:11
c, and proven c produces hope.   Rm 5:4
so I may know your proven c,   2Co 2:9
But you know his proven c,   Php 2:22

CHARCOAL

the temple police had made a c fire,   Jn 18:18
they saw a c fire there, with fish   Jn 21:9

CHARGE (n)

Joseph was in c of the country;   Gn 42:6
keep the LORD's c   Lv 8:35
LORD brings {this} c against the elders   Is 3:14
they could find no c or corruption,   Dn 6:4
has put in c of his household,   Mt 24:45
didn't answer him on even one c,   Mt 27:14
Above His head they put up the c   Mt 27:37
that they could find a c against Him.   Lk 6:7
He was in c of the money-bag   Jn 12:6
What c do you bring against   Jn 18:29
bring c-s against one another.   Ac 19:38
the gospel and offer it free of c,   1Co 9:18
gospel of God to you free of c?   2Co 11:7

CHARGE (v)

you must not c him interest.   Ex 22:25
Do not c your brother interest   Dt 23:19
let us stop c-ing this interest.   Neh 5:10
man the LORD does not c with sin,   Ps 32:2
I saw the ram c-ing to the west,   Dn 8:4
will be c-d to you, from the blood   Mt 23:35
Lord, do not c them with this sin!   Ac 7:60
whom the Lord will never c with sin!   Rm 4:8
sin is not c-d to one's account when   Rm 5:13
I solemnly c you, before God   1Tm 5:21
before Christ Jesus ... I c you   1Tm 6:13
c-ing them before God not to fight   2Tm 2:14
I solemnly c you: 2Tm 4:1
c that to my account.   Phm 18

CHARIOT

had Joseph ride in his second c,   Gn 41:43
came back and covered the c-s   Ex 14:28
even though they have iron c-s   Jos 17:18
because those people had iron c-s.   Jdg 1:19
because Jabin had 900 iron c-s,   Jdg 4:3
against Israel: 3,000 c-s,   1Sm 13:5

the c cities, the cavalry cities, 1Kg 9:19
Solomon accumulated 1,400 c-s 1Kg 10:26
tell Ahab, 'Get {your c} ready 1Kg 18:44
flowed into the bottom of the c. 1Kg 22:35
a c of fire with horses of fire 2Kg 2:11
when the man got down from his c 2Kg 5:26
covered with horses and c-s of fire 2Kg 6:17
hear the sound of c-s, horses, 2Kg 7:6
the c-s and horsemen of Israel! 2Kg 13:14
A c could be imported from Egypt 2Ch 1:17
Some take pride in a c, Ps 20:7
God's c-s are tens of thousands, Ps 68:17
making the clouds His c, Ps 104:3
They trust in the number of c-s Is 31:1
Their sound is like the sound of c-s, Jl 2:5
c-s dash madly through the streets; Nah 2:4
saw four c-s coming Zch 6:1
I will cut off the c from Ephraim Zch 9:10
told Philip, "Go and join that c." Ac 8:29
the sound of c-s with many horses Rv 9:9

CHARIOTEERS
David killed 700 of their c 2Sm 10:18
David killed 7,000 of their c 1Ch 19:18

CHARITABLE
He did many c deeds for the Jewish Ac 10:2

CHARITY
But give to c what is within, Lk 11:41
doing good works and acts of c. Ac 9:36
your acts of c have come up Ac 10:4

CHARM
C is deceptive and beauty is Pr 31:30

CHARMED
If the snake bites before it is c, Ec 10:11
poisonous vipers that cannot be c. Jr 8:17

CHASE
He c-d Abner and did not turn 2Sm 2:19
whoever c-s fantasies lacks sense. Pr 12:11
whoever c-s fantasies will have
  his fill of poverty Pr 28:19
I will draw a sword {to c} after them. Ezk 5:2
Ephraim c-s the wind Hs 12:1

CHASM
a great c has been fixed between us Lk 16:26

CHEAT
c-ed me and changed my wages Gn 31:7

do not c one another. Lv 25:14
We can ... c with dishonest scales. Am 8:5
Why not rather be c-ed? 1Co 6:7

CHEBAR
among the exiles by the C Canal, Ezk 1:1

CHEDORLAOMER
King of Elam; one of the kings who attacked Sodom and Gomorrah. Abram rescued Lot from him (Gn 14:1-17).

CHEEK
You strike all my enemies on the c; Ps 3:7
My c-s to those who tore out My Is 50:6
Let him offer {his} c to the one Lm 3:30
striking the judge of Israel on the c Mc 5:1
If anyone slaps you on your right c, Mt 5:39
If anyone hits you on the c, Lk 6:29

CHEER
my wine that c-s both God
  and man, Jdg 9:13
a good word c-s it up. Pr 12:25
Bright eyes c the heart; Pr 15:30
then who will c me other than 2Co 2:2

CHEERFUL
God with joy and a c heart, Dt 28:47
a c heart has a continual feast. Pr 15:15
drink your wine with a c heart, Ec 9:7
God loves a c giver. 2Co 9:7
Is anyone c? He should sing Jms 5:13

CHEERFULNESS
showing mercy, with c. Rm 12:8

CHEMOSH
Moab's god (Jdg 11:24; 1Kg 11:7,33).

CHERETHITES
Tribe among the Philistines whom David employed as bodyguards (1Sm 30:14; 2Sm 8:18; 15:18; 20:7,23; 1Kg 1:38,44; 1Ch 18:17; Ezk 25:16; Zph 2:5).

CHERISH
C her, and she will exalt you; Pr 4:8

CHERITH
Elijah ... lived by the Wadi C 1Kg 17:5

CHERUB
Make one c at one end and Ex 25:19
He rode on a c and flew, 2Sm 22:11

The first c-'s height was 15 feet   1Kg 6:26
the first face was that of a c,   Ezk 10:14
You were an anointed guardian c,   Ezk 28:14

CHERUBIM

He stationed c with a flaming,   Gn 3:24
Make two c of gold;   Ex 25:18
from between the two c.   Nm 7:89
who dwells {between}
    the c.   1Sm 4:4; 2Sm 6:2
he made two c 15 feet high   1Kg 6:23
beneath the wings of the c.   1Kg 8:6
who is enthroned {above} the c,   2Kg 19:15
You who sit enthroned {on} the c,   Ps 80:1
He is enthroned above the c.   Ps 99:1
there were four wheels beside
    the c,   Ezk 10:9
The c of glory were above it   Heb 9:5

CHEST

Jehoiada the priest took a c,   2Kg 12:9
brought the tax, and put it in
    the c   2Ch 24:10
righteousness like armor on your c,   Eph 6:14
armor of faith and love on our c-s,   1Th 5:8

CHICKS

a bird's nest with c or eggs,   Dt 22:6
as a hen gathers her c   Mt 23:37; Lk 13:34

CHIEF

These are the c-s of Esau's sons: Gn 36:15
the c cupbearer and the c baker,   Gn 40:2
the c-s of David's warriors   1Ch 11:10
appointed him c of the diviners,   Dn 5:11
rejected by the elders, the c priests,   Mk 8:31
when the c Shepherd appears,   1Pt 5:4

CHILD see also CHILDREN

Can a c be born to a
    hundred-year-old man?   Gn 17:17
quieted myself like a little weaned c   Ps 131:2
For a c will be born for us,   Is 9:6
and a c will lead them.   Is 11:6
Can a woman forget her nursing c,   Is 49:15
When Israel was a c, I loved him,   Hs 11:1
Then He called a c to Him   Mt 18:2
whoever humbles himself like this c   Mt 18:4
does not welcome the kingdom of
    God like a little c will
    never enter   Lk 18:17

When I was a c, I spoke like a c,   1Co 13:11
who loves the parent also loves his c.   1Jn 5:1
give birth he might devour her c.   Rv 12:4

CHILDBEARING

Sarah had passed the age of c.   Gn 18:11
But she will be saved through c,   1Tm 2:15

CHILDHOOD

from c you have known the sacred   2Tm 3:15

CHILDISH

a man, I put aside c things.   1Co 13:11
don't be c in your thinking,   1Co 14:20

CHILDLESS

I am c and the heir of my house is   Gn 15:2
they will bear their guilt and die c.   Lv 20:20
but Hannah was c.   1Sm 1:2
your sword has made women c, so
    your mother will be c   1Sm 15:33
Record this man as c,   Jr 22:30

CHILDREN

you will bear c in anguish.   Gn 3:16
When your c ask you,   Ex 12:26
punishing the c for the fathers' sin,   Ex 20:5
Teach them to your c   Dt 4:9
Repeat them to your c.   Dt 6:7
Teach them to your c,   Dt 11:19
Fathers are not to be put to death for
    {their} c or c for {their} fathers; Dt 24:16
In the future, when your c ask you,   Jos 4:6
c have come to the point of birth,   2Kg 19:3
my own c find me repulsive.   Jb 19:17
a stronghold from the mouths of c   Ps 8:2
or his c begging bread.   Ps 37:25
from the LORD, c, a reward.   Ps 127:3
the c of the forsaken one will be
    more than the c of the married   Is 54:1
Rachel weeping for her c, refusing to
    be comforted for her c because   Jr 31:15
and the c-'s teeth are set on edge.   Jr 31:29
Little c beg for bread, but no one   Lm 4:4
and the c-'s teeth are set on edge   Ezk 18:2
and {have} c of promiscuity,   Hs 1:2
fathers to {their} c and the hearts
    of c to their fathers.   Mal 4:6
the male c in and around Bethlehem   Mt 2:16
Rachel weeping for her c;   Mt 2:18
c for Abraham from these stones!   Mt 3:9

how to give good gifts to your c,   Mt 7:11
like c sitting in the marketplaces   Mt 11:16
are converted and become like c,   Mt 18:3
from the mouths of c and   Mt 21:16
the c to be satisfied first, because it
     isn't right to take the c-'s bread   Mk 7:27
Let the little c come to Me.   Mk 10:14
C will rise up against parents   Mk 13:12
to turn the hearts of fathers to their c   Lk 1:17
wisdom is vindicated by all her c.   Lk 7:35
gave them the right to be c of God,   Jn 1:12
If you were Abraham's c,   Jn 8:39
promise is for you and for your c,   Ac 2:39
testifies ... that we are God's c,   Rm 8:16
not the c by physical descent who are
     God's c, but the c of the promise   Rm 9:8
Otherwise your c would be
     unclean   1Co 7:14
For c are not obligated to save up
     for their parents, but parents for
     their c.   2Co 12:14
not c of the slave but of the free   Gl 4:31
we will no longer be little c,   Eph 4:14
Walk as c of light   Eph 5:8
C, obey your parents in the Lord,   Eph 6:1
fathers, don't stir up anger in your c,   Eph 6:4
C, obey your parents in everything,   Col 3:20
Fathers, do not exasperate your c,   Col 3:21
managing their c and their own   1Tm 3:12
that we should be called God's c.   1Jn 3:1
This is how God's c—and the
     Devil's c—are made evident.   1Jn 3:10
To the elect lady and her c,   2Jn 1

CHILION

One of Naomi's sons (Ru 1:2,4; 4:9).

CHINNERETH

Another name for the Sea of Galilee (Nm 34:11; Jos 13:27) and a city there (Jos 19:35).

CHISEL

use your c on it, you will defile it   Ex 20:25
no hammer, c, or any iron tool   1Kg 6:7

CHOICE

There were 700 c men   Jdg 20:16
I am offering you three (c-s).   2Sm 24:12
struck down Israel's c young men.   Ps 78:31

gossip's words are like c food   Pr 18:8; 26:22
Mary has made the right c,   Lk 10:42

CHOICEST

to his garden and eat its c fruits.   Sg 4:16

CHOKE

thorns came up and c-d them.   Mt 13:7
the seduction of wealth c the word,   Mt 13:22
started c-ing him, and said, 'Pay   Mt 18:28

CHOOSE   see also CHOSEN (adj)

Lot chose the entire Jordan Valley   Gn 13:11
He will let the one He c-s come   Nm 16:5
He chose their descendants   Dt 4:37
Lord ... chose you, not because   Dt 7:7
the place the Lord your God c-s   Dt 12:5
C life so that you   Dt 30:19
c for yourselves today the one   Jos 24:15
the one the Lord has chosen?   1Sm 10:24
Lord hasn't chosen this one   1Sm 16:8
who chose me over your father   2Sm 6:21
David, whom I chose   1Kg 11:34
I have chosen Jerusalem ... and I
     have chosen David   2Ch 6:6
God who chose Abram and
     brought   Neh 9:7
show him the way he should c.   Ps 25:12
He chose David His servant   Ps 78:70
I have chosen the way of truth;   Ps 119:30
the Lord has chosen Zion;   Ps 132:13
Lord has chosen Jacob for Himself   Ps 135:4
didn't c to fear the Lord,   Pr 1:29
He directs it wherever He c-s.   Pr 21:1
A good name is to be chosen over   Pr 22:1
reject what is bad and c what is good,   Is 7:15
will c Israel again.   Is 14:1
servant, Jacob, whom I have chosen,   Is 41:8
I chose you before I formed you   Jr 1:5
The Lord has rejected the two
     families He had chosen.   Jr 33:24
On the day I chose Israel,   Ezk 20:5
are invited, but few are chosen.   Mt 22:14
and He chose 12 of them   Lk 6:13
You did not c Me, but I chose you.   Jn 15:16
a remnant chosen by grace.   Rm 11:5
He chose us in Him, before the   Eph 1:4
I don't know which one I should c.   Php 1:22
Didn't God c the poor in this world   Jms 2:5

CHOP

c down their Asherah poles.   Ex 34:13
c-ped down their Asherah poles.   2Ch 14:3
c-ped down all the incense altars   2Ch 34:7
above the one who c-s with it?   Is 10:15
and c off its branches;   Dn 4:14

CHORAZIN

Woe to you, C!   Mt 11:21; Lk 10:13

CHOSEN (adj)

You are God's c one among us.   Gn 23:6
{this is} My C One; I delight in Him.   Is 42:1
This is My Son, the C One;   Lk 9:35
God's c ones, holy and loved,   Col 3:12
a c and valuable cornerstone,   1Pt 2:6
you are a c race, a royal priesthood,   1Pt 2:9

CHRIST *see also* MESSIAH

The birth of Jesus C came about   Mt 1:18
Messiah is coming (who is called C)   Jn 4:25
through faith in Jesus C, to all   Rm 3:22
at the appointed moment, C died   Rm 5:6
we were still sinners C died for us!   Rm 5:8
life through the one man, Jesus C.   Rm 5:17
if we died with C, we believe that   Rm 6:8
no condemnation now exists for
    those in C Jesus,   Rm 8:1
does not have the Spirit of C, he
    does not belong to Him   Rm 8:9
heirs of God and co-heirs with C   Rm 8:17
can separate us from the love of C?   Rm 8:35
For C is the end of the law   Rm 10:4
who are many are one body in C   Rm 12:5
But put on the Lord Jesus C,   Rm 13:14
C died and came to life for this: Rm 14:9
but we preach C crucified,   1Co 1:23
except Jesus C and Him crucified.   1Co 2:2
any other foundation than what has
    been laid—that is, Jesus C.   1Co 3:11
C our Passover has been sacrificed.   1Co 5:7
one Lord, Jesus C, through whom   1Co 8:6
and that rock was C.   1Co 10:4
imitators of me, as I also am of C.   1Co 11:1
C is the head of every man,   1Co 11:3
you are the body of C,   1Co 12:27
C died for our sins according to   1Co 15:3
if C has not been raised, then   1Co 15:14
also in C all will be made alive.   1Co 15:22
victory through our Lord Jesus C!   1Co 15:57

Jesus C as Lord, and ourselves as   2Co 4:5
before the judgment seat of C,   2Co 5:10
For C-'s love compels us,   2Co 5:14
in C, there is a new creation;   2Co 5:17
What agreement does C have with
    Belial?   2Co 6:15
to present a pure virgin to C.   2Co 11:2
that C-'s power may reside in me.   2Co 12:9
justified by faith in C and not by   Gl 2:16
I no longer live, but C lives in me.   Gl 2:20
C has redeemed us from the curse   Gl 3:13
C has liberated us into freedom.   Gl 5:1
except the cross of our Lord Jesus C,   Gl 6:14
every spiritual blessing in the
    heavens, in C;   Eph 1:3
C Jesus Himself as the cornerstone   Eph 2:20
into Him who is the head—C.   Eph 4:15
as also C is head of the church.   Eph 5:23
just as also C loved the church   Eph 5:25
living is C and dying is gain.   Php 1:21
manner worthy of the gospel of C.   Php 1:27
confess that Jesus C is Lord,   Php 2:11
considered to be a loss because of C.   Php 3:7
through faith in C—the righteousness
    from God   Php 3:9
His riches in glory in C Jesus.   Php 4:19
what is lacking in C-'s afflictions   Col 1:24
this mystery, which is C in you,   Col 1:27
present everyone mature in C.   Col 1:28
as you have received C Jesus the
    Lord, walk in Him,   Col 2:6
C is all and in all.   Col 3:11
the dead in C will rise first.   1Th 4:16
the coming of our Lord Jesus C   2Th 2:1
C ... came into the world to save   1Tm 1:15
one mediator between God and
    man, a man, C Jesus,   1Tm 2:5
as a good soldier of C Jesus.   2Tm 2:3
salvation, which is in C Jesus,   2Tm 2:10
our great God and Savior, Jesus C.   Ti 2:13
But C was faithful as a Son   Heb 3:6
offering of the body of Jesus C   Heb 10:10
Jesus C is the same yesterday,   Heb 13:8
but with the precious blood of C,   1Pt 1:19
C also suffered for you,   1Pt 2:21
C also suffered for sins once for all,   1Pt 3:18
ridiculed for the name of C,   1Pt 4:14
coming of our Lord Jesus C;   2Pt 1:16

advocate with the Father—Jesus C | 1Jn 2:1
Jesus C—He is the One who came | 1Jn 5:6
confess the coming of Jesus C
   in the flesh. | 2Jn 7
through Jesus C our Lord, be glory, | Jd 25

CHRISTIAN

were first called C-s in Antioch. | Ac 11:26
persuade me to become a C | Ac 26:28
is sanctified by the C husband. | 1Co 7:14
if {anyone suffers} as a C, | 1Pt 4:16

CHURCH

on this rock I will build My c, | Mt 16:18
no attention to them, tell the c. | Mt 18:17
persecution broke out against the c | Ac 8:1
prayer was being made ... by the c. | Ac 12:5
appointed elders in every c | Ac 14:23
elders, with the whole c, decided | Ac 15:22
traveled ... strengthening the c-es. | Ac 15:41
as overseers, to shepherd the c | Ac 20:28
but so do all the Gentile c-es. | Rm 16:4
the c that meets in their home. | Rm 16:5
what I command in all the c-es. | 1Co 7:17
when you come together as a c | 1Co 11:18
God has placed these in the c: | 1Co 12:28
he who prophesies builds up the c. | 1Co 14:4
should keep silent in the c | 1Co 14:28
As in all the c-es of the saints, | 1Co 14:33
should be silent in the c-es, | 1Co 14:34
for a woman to speak in the c | 1Co 14:35
the c that meets in their home. | 1Co 16:19
who is praised throughout the c-es | 2Co 8:18
messengers of the c-es, the glory | 2Co 8:23
on me: my care for all the c-es. | 2Co 11:28
be made known through the c | Eph 3:10
to Him be glory in the c | Eph 3:21
as also Christ is head of the c. | Eph 5:23
as to zeal, persecuting the c; | Php 3:6
the head of the body, the c; | Col 1:18
to Nympha and the c in her house. | Col 4:15
how will he take care of God's c? | 1Tm 3:5
which is the c of the living God, | 1Tm 3:15
to the c that meets in your house. | Phm 2
are the angels of the seven c-es, | Rv 1:20
To the angel of the c in Ephesus | Rv 2:1

CHURNING

the c of milk produces butter, | Pr 30:33

CILICIA

He traveled through Syria and C, | Ac 15:41
Jewish man, born in Tarsus of C, | Ac 22:3
I went to the regions of Syria and C. | Gl 1:21

CIRCLE

as He walks on the c of the sky. | Jb 22:14
I will camp in a c around you; | Is 29:3
enthroned above the c of the earth; | Is 40:22

CIRCUIT

he would go on a c to Bethel, | 1Sm 7:16
going around the villages in a c, | Mk 6:6

CIRCUMCISE

your males must be c-d. | Gn 17:10
Abraham c-d him, | Gn 21:4
condition: if all your males are c-d | Gn 34:15
must be c-d on the eighth day. | Lv 12:3
Therefore, c your hearts | Dt 10:16
God will c your heart | Dt 30:6
c the Israelite men again. | Jos 5:2
C yourselves to the LORD; | Jr 4:4
they came to c the child | Lk 1:59
you c a man on the Sabbath. | Jn 7:22
Unless you are c-d according to | Ac 15:1
Not while he was c-d, | Rm 4:10
already c-d when he was called? | 1Co 7:18
Peter in the apostleship to the c-d | Gl 2:8
if you get c-d, Christ will not benefit | Gl 5:2
even the c-d don't keep the law | Gl 6;13
by those called "the c-d," | Eph 2:11
c-d the eighth day; | Php 3:5

CIRCUMCISION

she said, "You are a bridegroom of
   blood," referring to the c. | Ex 4:26
c benefits you if you observe
   the law, | Rm 2:25
and c is of the heart | Rm 2:29
C does not matter | 1Co 7:19
he feared those from the c party. | Gl 2:12
in Christ Jesus neither c nor | Gl 5:6
if I still preach c, why am I still | Gl 5:11
c and uncircumcision mean nothing; | Gl 6:15
we are the c, the ones who serve | Php 3:3
with a c not done with hands, | Col 2:11
there is not Greek and Jew, c and | Col 3:11

CIRCUMSTANCES

learned to be content in whatever c | Php 4:11

CISTERN

brother of humble c should boast in   Jms 1:9
what c the Spirit of Christ within   1Pt 1:11

CISTERN

may drink water from his own c   2Kg 18:31
Drink water from your own c,   Pr 5:15
dug c-s for themselves, cracked c-s   Jr 2:13
Jeremiah had been put into the c.   Jr 38:7

CITADELS

note its ramparts; tour its c   Ps 48:13
it will consume the c of Jerusalem   Jr 17:27
it will devour Ben-hadad's c.   Jr 49:27
and it will consume their c.   Hs 8:14
it will consume Ben-hadad's c.   Am 1:4
Proclaim on the c in Ashdod   Am 3:9

CITIZEN

Paul and Silas were Roman c-s.   Ac 16:38
realized Paul was a Roman c   Ac 22:29
I learned that he is a Roman c.   Ac 23:27
but fellow c-s with the saints,   Eph 2:19

CITIZENSHIP

I bought this c for a large amount   Ac 22:28
excluded from the c of Israel,   Eph 2:12
but our c is in heaven,   Php 3:20

CITY

Lot lived in the c-ies of the valley   Gn 13:12
Levitical c-ies are their possession   Lv 25:33
give c-ies ... for the Levites   Nm 35:2
will include six c-ies of refuge,   Nm 35:6
designate c-ies to serve as
  c-ies of refuge   Nm 35:11
Moses set apart three c-ies across the   Dt 4:41
beautiful c-ies that you did not build,   Dt 6:10
set apart three c-ies for yourselves   Dt 19:2
Israel did not burn any of the c-ies
  that stood on their mounds   Jos 11:13
Select your c-ies of refuge,   Jos 20:2
gave the Levites these c-ies   Jos 21:3
and c-ies you did not build,   Jos 24:13
which he named the c of David.   2Sm 5:9
the storage c-ies ... the chariot c-ies,
  the cavalry c-ies,   1Kg 9:19
is the c of the great King.   Ps 48:2
Glorious things are said about
  you, c of God.   Ps 87:3
unless the LORD watches over a c,   Ps 127:1
wealth is his fortified c;   Pr 10:15; 18:11

the righteous thrive, a c rejoices,   Pr 11:10
her works praise her at the c gates.   Pr 31:31
he delivered the c by his wisdom.   Ec 9:15
One of the c-ies will be called
  the C of the Sun.   Is 19:18
Say to the c-ies of Judah,
  "Here is your God!"   Is 40:9
Jerusalem, the Holy C!   Is 52:1
will call you the C of the LORD,   Is 60:14
gods are as numerous as your c-ies,   Jr 2:28
she sits alone, the c {once} crowded   Lm 1:1
c-ies will be inhabited and   Ezk 36:10
Seventy weeks are decreed about
  your people and your holy c   Dn 9:24
If a disaster occurs in a c, hasn't the   Am 3:6
rain on one c but no rain on another.   Am 4:7
Nineveh was an extremely large c,   Jnh 3:3
will be called the Faithful C,   Zch 8:3
c situated on a hill cannot be hidden.   Mt 5:14
or by Jerusalem, because it is
  the c of the great King.   Mt 5:35
to the c of David, which is called
  Bethlehem,   Lk 2:4
born for you in the c of David.   Lk 2:11
Those inside the c must leave it,   Lk 21:21
I have many people in this c.   Ac 18:10
in the c, dangers in the open   2Co 11:26
he was looking forward to the c   Heb 11:10
we do not have an enduring c;   Heb 13:14
we will travel to such and such a c   Jms 4:13
saw the Holy C, new Jerusalem,   Rv 21:2

CLAIM (n)

your c-s are good and right, but   2Sm 15:3
we have a greater {c} to David   2Sm 19:43
who has died is freed from sin's c-s.   Rm 6:7

CLAIM (v)

that day the forest c-ed more
  people than the sword.   2Sm 18:8
rose up, c-ing to be somebody,   Ac 5:36
while c-ing to be somebody great.   Ac 8:9
C-ing to be wise, they became fools   Rm 1:22
c-ing access to a visionary realm   Col 2:18
synagogue of Satan, who c to be Jews   Rv 3:9

CLAN

Israelite community by their c-s   Nm 1:2
by lot according to your c-s.   Nm 33:54
come forward c by c.   Jos 7:14

isn't my c the least important
of all the c-s 1Sm 9:21
by your tribes and c-s. 1Sm 10:19
you out of all the c-s of the earth; Am 3:2
small among the c-s of Judah; Mc 5:2

CLANGING
a sounding gong or a c cymbal. 1Co 13:1

CLAP
C your hands, all you peoples; Ps 47:1
Let the rivers c their hands; Ps 98:8
trees of the field will c {their} Is 55:12

CLASHING
praise Him with c cymbals. Ps 150:5

CLASPS
make 50 gold c and join the curtains Ex 26:6

CLAUDIA
Roman Christian (2Tm 4:21).

CLAUDIUS
1. Roman emperor (Ac 11:28); expelled
Jews from Rome (18:2).
2. Roman commander who protected Paul
(Ac 23:26).

CLAY
those who dwell in c houses, Jb 4:19
You formed me like c. Jb 10:9
pinched off from {a piece of} c. Jb 33:6
changed as c is by a seal; Jb 38:14
strength is dried up like baked c; Ps 22:15
out of the muddy c, and set my feet Ps 40:2
Does c say to the one forming it: Is 45:9
we are the c, and You are our potter; Is 64:8
jar that he was making from the c Jr 18:4
Just like c in the potter's hand, Jr 18:6
they are regarded as c jars, Lm 4:2
partly iron and partly fired c. Dn 2:33
has the potter no right over His c, Rm 9:21
Now we have this treasure in c jars, 2Co 4:7

CLEAN
of all the c animals, and two Gn 7:2
every kind of c animal and every Gn 8:20
a clear conscience and c hands. Gn 20:5
Everyone who is c may eat any Lv 7:19
in any ceremonially c place, Lv 10:14
between the unclean and the c, Lv 11:47
priest is to pronounce him c; Lv 13:6

and you will be c from all your Lv 16:30
must distinguish the c animal Lv 20:25
Every c person in your house may Nm 18:13
through fire, and it will be c. Nm 31:23
both the c and the unclean may Dt 12:22
You may eat every c bird, Dt 14:11
be restored and you will be c. 2Kg 5:10
whose hands are c will grow Jb 17:9
The one who has c hands and a Ps 24:4
with hyssop, and I will be c; Ps 51:7
create a c heart for me and Ps 51:10
between the c and the unclean. Ezk 22:26
sprinkle c water on you, and
you will be c. Ezk 36:25
You can make me c. Mt 8:2
You c the outside of the cup and Mt 23:25
He made all foods c. Mk 7:19
then everything is c for you. Lk 11:41
You are c, but not all of you. Jn 13:10
You are already c because of the Jn 15:3
God has made c, you must not Ac 10:15
Everything is c, but it is wrong Rm 14:20
sprinkled {c} from an evil Heb 10:22

CLEANNESS
according to the c of my hands. 2Sm 22:21

CLEANSE
for you on this day to c you, Lv 16:30
So he c-d Judah and Jerusalem. 2Ch 34:5
C me from my hidden faults. Ps 19:12
my guilt, and c me from my sin. Ps 51:2
I am c-d from my sin Pr 20:9
and beatings c the innermost Pr 20:30
Wash yourselves. C yourselves. Is 1:16
I will c you from all your Ezk 36:25
refiner's fire and like c-ing lye. Mal 3:2
Moses prescribed for your c-ing, Mk 1:44
Jesus said, "Were not 10 c-d? Lk 17:17
us and them, c-ing their hearts Ac 15:9
c-ing her in the washing of water Eph 5:26
to c for Himself a special people Ti 2:14
C your hands, sinners, and Jms 4:8
forgotten the c-ing from his past sins 2Pt 1:9
Jesus His Son c-s us from all sin 1Jn 1:7
to c us from all unrighteousness 1Jn 1:9

CLEAR (adj)
best to have a c conscience Ac 24:16
exposed by the light is made c, Eph 5:13

the faith with a c conscience. 1Tm 3:9
I serve with a c conscience as 2Tm 1:3
keep a c head about everything, 2Tm 4:5
that we have a c conscience, Heb 13:18
keeping your conscience c, 1Pt 3:16
was pure gold like c glass. Rv 21:18

CLEAR (v)

of the blameless c-s his path, Pr 11:5
the highway; c away the stones Is 62:10
and he will c the way before Me Mal 3:1
and He will c His threshing Mt 3:12

CLEARLY

Write c all the words of this Dt 27:8
will speak c and fluently. Is 32:4
you will see c to take the speck Mt 7:5
and he began to speak c. Mk 7:35
nature, have been c seen, being Rm 1:20
purpose even more c to the heirs Heb 6:17

CLEFTS

My dove, in the c of the rock Sg 2:14
who live in the c of the rock, Jr 49:16
you who live in c of the rock in Ob 3

CLEMENT

along with C and the rest of my Php 4:3

CLEOPAS

The one named C answered Him, Lk 24:18

CLEVER

They devise c schemes against Ps 83:3
and c in their own sight. Is 5:21
not with c words, so that 1Co 1:17

CLEVERLY

did not follow c contrived myths 2Pt 1:16

CLIFF

your nest is set in the c-s. Nm 24:21
shattering c-s before the LORD 1Kg 19:11
It lives on a c where it spends Jb 39:28
the c-s are a refuge for hyraxes. Ps 104:18
be thrown off the sides of a c, Ps 141:6
they make their homes in the c-s; Pr 30:26
Live in the c-s, residents of Moab Jr 48:28
to hurl Him over the c. Lk 4:29

CLIMB

in his hand, he c-ed Mount Sinai Ex 34:4
even if a fox c-ed up what they are Neh 4:3
I will c the palm tree and take Sg 7:8

and he who c-s from the pit will Jr 48:44
they c into the houses; Jl 2:9
he c-ed up a sycamore tree to see Lk 19:4
by the door but c-s in some other Jn 10:1

CLING

will make pestilence c to you Dt 28:21
diseases ... will c to you. Dt 28:60
but Ruth clung to her. Ru 1:14
my flesh c to my bones; Jb 19:20
I will c to my righteousness Jb 27:6
our bodies c to the ground. Ps 44:25
as underwear c-s to one's waist, Jr 13:11
infant's tongue c-s to the roof of Lm 4:4
Those who c to worthless idols Jnh 2:8
"Don't c to Me," Jesus told her Jn 20:17
Detest evil; c to what is good. Rm 12:9

CLOAK

Put your hand inside your c. Ex 4:6
neighbor's c as collateral, Ex 22:26
a beautiful c from Babylon, Jos 7:21
Spread your c over me, for you Ru 3:9
will wear their shame like a c. Ps 109:29
has bound up the waters in a c? Pr 30:4
You have a c—you be our Is 3:6
Wrap your c around you, Ac 12:8
bring the c I left in Troas with 2Tm 4:13
You will roll them up like a c, Heb 1:12

CLOSE (adj)

this town is c enough for me Gn 19:20
The man is a c relative. Ru 2:20
there is a redeemer c-r than I Ru 3:12
my c friends have forgotten me. Jb 19:14
We used to have c fellowship; Ps 55:14
Israelites, the people c to Him. Ps 148:14

CLOSE (adv)

So Jacob came c-r to his father Gn 27:22
"Do not come c-r," He said. Ex 3:5
Why did you get so c to the wall? 2Sm 11:21
who stays c-r than a brother. Pr 18:24
because he came c to death for Php 2:30

CLOSE (v)

ribs and c-d the flesh at that place. Gn 2:21
floodgates of the sky were c-d, Gn 8:2
The earth c-d over them, Nm 16:33
He will c the sky, and there Dt 11:17
and Eglon's fat c-d in over it, Jdg 3:22

If I c the sky so there is no   2Ch 7:13
the gaps were being c-d,   Neh 4:7
of evildoers has c-d in on me;   Ps 22:16
one's eyes do not c in sleep day   Ec 8:16
what he opens, no one can c;   Is 22:22
This gate will remain c-d.   Ezk 44:2
But their minds were c-d.   2Co 3:14
who opens and no one will c,   Rv 3:7
the power to c the sky so that   Rv 11:6
will never c because it will   Rv 21:25

CLOTH

spread a solid blue c on top,   Nm 4:6
wrapped in a c behind the ephod   1Sm 21:9
of unshrunk c on an old garment   Mk 2:21
left the linen c behind and ran   Mk 14:52
Him snugly in c and laid Him   Lk 2:7
he saw only the linen c-s.   Lk 24:12
he saw the linen c-s lying there,   Jn 20:5
dealer in purple c from the city   Ac 16:14

CLOTHE

He c-d them.   Gn 3:21
C Aaron with the holy garments,   Ex 40:13
the feeble are c-d with strength.   1Sm 2:4
You have c-d me with strength   2Sm 22:40
You c-d me with skin and flesh,   Jb 10:11
c yourself with honor and glory.   Jb 40:10
He c-s me with strength   Ps 18:32
and c-d me with gladness   Ps 30:11
over me be c-d with shame   Ps 35:26
The pastures are c-d with flocks,   Ps 65:13
You will c Yourself with their   Ps 76:10
You are c-d with majesty and   Ps 104:1
I will c its priests with salvation,   Ps 132:16
I will c his enemies with shame,   Ps 132:18
in her household are doubly c-d.   Pr 31:21
man among them, c-d in linen,   Ezk 9:2
I c-d you in embroidered cloth   Ezk 16:10
they c-d Daniel in purple,   Dn 5:29
He will be c-d in splendor and   Zch 6:13
If that's how God c-s the grass of   Mt 6:30
I was naked and you c-d Me;   Mt 25:36
we are poorly c-d, roughly treated   1Co 4:11
mortal is c-d with immortality,   1Co 15:54
not want to be unclothed but c-d,   2Co 5:4
all of you c yourselves with humility   1Pt 5:5
a woman c-d with the sun, with the   Rv 12:1

CLOTHES

smelled his c, he blessed him   Gn 27:27
remove the c she was wearing
   when she was taken prisoner,   Dt 21:13
your c ... did not wear out;   Dt 29:5
anointed himself, changed his c,   2Sm 12:20
a time to accept money and c,   2Kg 5:26
because you have torn your c   2Kg 22:19
changed his prison c,   2Kg 25:29
Their c did not wear out,   Neh 9:21
fire and his c not be burned?   Pr 6:27
and splendid c instead of despair.   Is 61:3
Tear your hearts, not just your c,   Jl 2:13
Joshua was dressed with filthy c   Zch 3:3
And why do you worry about c?   Mt 6:28
who wear soft c are in kings'   Mt 11:8
get in here without wedding c?   Mt 22:12
divided His c by casting lots   Mt 27:35
stood by them in dazzling c.   Lk 24:4
shook out his c and told them,   Ac 18:6
in fine c, and a poor man dressed
   in dirty c also comes in.   Jms 2:2
is without c and lacks daily   Jms 2:15
of gold ornaments or fine c;   1Pt 3:3
who have not defiled their c,   Rv 3:4
white c so that you may be dressed   Rv 3:18

CLOTHING

LORD God made c out of skins   Gn 3:21
must not reduce the food, c,   Ex 21:10
Your c did not wear out, and   Dt 8:4
A woman is not to wear male c,   Dt 22:5
and they cast lots for my c.   Ps 22:18
all of them will wear out like c.   Ps 102:26
her c is fine linen and purple.   Pr 31:22
Strength and honor are her c,   Pr 31:25
and the body more than c?   Mt 6:25
come to you in sheep's c   Mt 7:15
they cast lots for My c.   Jn 19:24
anyone's silver or gold or c.   Ac 20:33
dress themselves in modest c,   1Tm 2:9
But if we have food and c,   1Tm 6:8
They will all wear out like c;   Heb 1:11

CLOUD

I have placed My bow in the c-s,   Gn 9:13
a pillar of c to lead them   Ex 13:21
a thick c on the mountain,   Ex 19:16
the mountain, the c covered it.   Ex 24:15
He called to Moses from the c.   Ex 24:16

The c covered the tent of	Ex 40:34
appear in the c above the mercy seat.	Lv 16:2
the c covered the tabernacle,	Nm 9:15
the c filled the LORD's temple,	1Kg 8:10
a c as small as a man's hand	1Kg 18:44
He enfolds the waters in His c-s,	
yet the c-s do not burst	Jb 26:8
when I made the c-s its garment	Jb 38:9
a dark c beneath His feet.	Ps 18:9
faithfulness reaches to the c-s.	Ps 57:10
C-s and thick darkness surround	Ps 97:2
spoke to them in a pillar of c;	Ps 99:7
making the c-s His chariot,	Ps 104:3
He spread a c as a covering	Ps 105:39
faithfulness reaches the c-s.	Ps 108:4
who covers the sky with c-s,	Ps 147:8
and the c-s dripped with dew.	Pr 3:20
looks at the c-s will not reap.	Ec 11:4
and the c-s return after the rain	Ec 12:2
the LORD rides on a swift c	Is 19:1
You have covered Yourself with a c	Lm 3:44
temple was filled with the c,	Ezk 10:4
Its top was among the c-s.	Ezk 31:3
coming with the c-s of heaven.	Dn 7:13
a day of c-s and dense overcast,	Jl 2:2
a day of c-s and blackness,	Zph 1:15
a bright c covered them, and a	
voice from the c said:	Mt 17:5
coming on the c-s of heaven with	Mt 24:30
coming on the c-s of heaven.	Mt 26:64
coming in c-s with great power	Mk 13:26
of Man coming in a c with power	Lk 21:27
a c received Him out of their sight.	Ac 1:9
fathers were all under the c,	1Co 10:1
in the c-s to meet the Lord in the	1Th 4:17
have such a large c of witnesses	Heb 12:1
are waterless c-s carried along	Jd 12
He is coming with the c-s,	Rv 1:7
They went up to heaven in a c,	Rv 11:12
Son of Man was seated on the c,	Rv 14:14

CLOUDLESS

the sun rises on a c morning,	2Sm 23:4

CLUB

went down to him with a c,	2Sm 23:21
his neighbor is like a c,	Pr 25:18
You are My battle c, My weapons	Jr 51:20
you come out with swords and c,	Mt 26:55

CLUSTER

with a single c of grapes,	Nm 13:23
breasts be like c-s of grapes,	Sg 7:8

COALS

c-s were set ablaze by it.	2Sm 22:9
His breath sets c-s ablaze,	Jb 41:21
will rain burning c-s and sulfur	Ps 11:6
a man walk on c-s without	Pr 6:28
you will heap c-s on his head,	Pr 25:22
a glowing c that he had taken	Is 6:6
be heaping fiery c-s on his head.	Rm 12:20

COARSE

And c and foolish talking	Eph 5:4

COAST

along the c of the Mediterranean Sea	Jos 9:1

COAT

He wore cursing like his c	Ps 109:18
let him have your c as well.	Mt 5:40

COBRA

the deadly poison of c-s.	Dt 32:33
turns into c-s' venom inside him.	Jb 20:14
tread on the lion and the c;	Ps 91:13
will play beside the c-'s pit,	Is 11:8

COFFIN

and placed him in a c in Egypt.	Gn 50:26
came up and touched the open c,	Lk 7:14

CO-HEIR

will not be a c with my son	Gn 21:10
heirs of God and c-s with Christ	Rm 8:17
the Gentiles are c-s, members of	Eph 3:6
Isaac and Jacob, c-s of the same	Heb 11:9
them honor as c-s of the grace of	1Pt 3:7

COIN

open its mouth you'll find a c.	Mt 17:27
Show Me the c used for the tax.	Mt 22:19
if she loses one c,	Lk 15:8
widow dropping in two tiny c-s.	Lk 21:2

COLD

seedtime and harvest, c and heat,	Gn 8:22
Who can withstand His c?	Ps 147:17
taking off clothing on a c day,	Pr 25:20
is like c water to a parched throat.	Pr 25:25
just a cup of c water to one	Mt 10:42
the love of many will grow c.	Mt 24:12

without food, c, and lacking   2Co 11:27
that you are neither c nor hot.   Rv 3:15

COLLAPSED
a great shout, and the wall c.   Jos 6:20
It c on the young people so that   Jb 1:19
pounded that house, and it c.   Mt 7:27

COLLATERAL
your neighbor's cloak as c,   Ex 22:26
and take the widow's ox as c.   Jb 24:3
get c if it is for foreigners.   Pr 20:16; 27:13
altar on garments taken as c,   Am 2:8

COLLEAGUES
the rest of his c wrote to King   Ezr 4:7

COLLECT
Moses c-ed the redemption money   Nm 3:49
Levites are to c the one-tenth   Neh 10:37
He will c the scattered of Judah   Is 11:12
she c-ed the wages of a prostitute,   Mc 1:7
I will c the remnant of Israel.   Mc 2:12
Don't c for yourselves treasures   Mt 6:19
Then they c-ed the leftover pieces   Mt 15:37
pieces of bread did you c?   Mk 8:19
Don't c any more than what you   Lk 3:13
I would have c-ed it with interest!   Lk 19:23
C the leftovers so that nothing   Jn 6:12
practiced magic c-ed their books   Ac 19:19
this lineage c-ed tithes from   Heb 7:6

COLLECTION
let your c (of idols) deliver you!   Is 57:13
Now about the c for the saints: 1Co 16:1

COLLECTOR
send out a tax c for the glory   Dn 11:20
even the tax c-s do the same?   Mt 5:46
many tax c-s and sinners came   Mt 9:10
Thomas and Matthew the tax c;   Mt 10:3
a friend of tax c-s and sinners!   Mt 11:19
let him be like ... a tax c to you.   Mt 18:17
Tax c-s and prostitutes are entering   Mt 21:31
Tax c-s also came to be baptized,   Lk 3:12
out and saw a tax c named Levi   Lk 5:27
the tax c-s, heard this, they   Lk 7:29
a Pharisee and the other a tax c.   Lk 18:10
chief tax c, and he was rich.   Lk 19:2

COLONNADE
temple complex in Solomon's C.   Jn 10:23

in what is called Solomon's C.   Ac 3:11
would all meet in Solomon's C.   Ac 5:12

COLORS
made a robe of many c for him.   Gn 37:3
the robe of many c that he had   Gn 37:23
robe of many c to their father   Gn 37:32

COLOSSAL
watching, a c statue appeared   Dn 2:31

COLT
c of his donkey to the choice vine   Gn 49:11
on a donkey, on a c, the foal of   Zch 9:9
a donkey, even on a c, the foal   Mt 21:5
sitting on a donkey's c.   Jn 12:15

COLUMN
But when the c of smoke began to   Jdg 20:40
were sharp c-s of rock on both   1Sm 14:4
to silver rods on marble c-s.   Est 1:6
the wilderness like c-s of smoke,   Sg 3:6
blood, fire, and c-s of smoke.   Jl 2:30

COMB
than honey dripping from the c.   Ps 19:10

COME
Blessed is he who c-s in the name   Ps 118:26
If they say—"C with us!   Pr 1:11
Your kingdom will be   Mt 6:10
to another, 'C!' and he c-s   Mt 8:9
Are You the One who is to c,   Mt 11:3
Blessed is He who c-s in the name   Mt 21:9
Father gives Me will c to Me,   Jn 6:37
No one c-s to the Father except   Jn 14:6
who is, who was, and who is c-ing;   Rv 1:4
Spirit and the bride say, "C!   Rv 22:17
one who is thirsty should c.   Rv 22:17
Amen! C, Lord Jesus!   Rv 22:20

COMFORT (n)
Your c brings me joy.   Ps 94:19
This is my c in my affliction: Ps 119:50
There is no one to offer her c,   Lm 1:2
and offer empty c.   Zch 10:2
through the c we ourselves receive
    from God.   2Co 1:4
it is for your c and salvation;   2Co 1:6

COMFORT (v)
Then David c-ed his wife
    Bathsheba   2Sm 12:24

his relatives came to c him. 1Ch 7:22
rod and Your staff—they c me. Ps 23:4
LORD, have helped and c-ed me. Ps 86:17
May Your faithful love c me, Ps 119:76
they have no one to c them. Ec 4:1
"C, c My people," says your God. Is 40:1
For the LORD has c-ed His people, Is 49:13
For the LORD will c Zion; Is 51:3
I—I am the One who c-s you. Is 51:12
to c all who mourn, Is 61:2
As a mother c-s her son, so I will c
   you, and you will be c-ed Is 66:13
refusing to be c-ed for her Jr 31:15
the LORD will once more c Zion Zch 1:17
mourn, because they will be c-ed. Mt 5:4
able to c those who are in any kind
   of affliction, through the c we 2Co 1:4
forgive and c him instead; 2Co 2:7
c the discouraged, 1Th 5:14

COMFORTERS
You are all miserable c. Jb 16:2
I waited ... for c, but found no one. Ps 69:20

COMING
can endure the day of His c? Mal 3:2
what is sign of Your c and of the Mt 24:3
so will be the c of the Son of Man. Mt 24:27
firstfruits; afterward, at His c, 1Co 15:23
still alive at the Lord's c 1Th 4:15
Now concerning the c of our Lord 2Th 2:1
be patient until the Lord's c. Jms 5:7
because the Lord's c is near. Jms 5:8
Where is the promise of His c? 2Pt 3:4
be ashamed before Him at His c. 1Jn 2:28
confess the c of Jesus Christ 2Jn 7

COMMAND (n)
because you have obeyed My c. Gn 22:18
Keep this c permanently Ex 12:24
who love Me and keep My c-s. Ex 20:6
These are the c-s the LORD gave Lv 27:34
They camped at the LORD's c, and
   they set out at the LORD's c. Nm 9:23
These are the c-s and ordinances Nm 36:13
rebelling against the c of the LORD Dt 1:26
who love Me and keep My c-s. Dt 5:10
who love Him and keep His c-s. Dt 7:9
if you obey the c-s of the LORD Dt 11:27
turn from this c to the right or Dt 17:20

This c that I give you today is Dt 30:11
disobeyed the c of the LORD. 1Kg 13:26
these years except by my c! 1Kg 17:1
the king's c was detestable to 1Ch 21:6
according to the king's c. 2Ch 35:10
do His word, obedient to His c. Ps 103:20
when I think about all Your c-s. Ps 119:6
in Your c-s, which I love. Ps 119:47
for I rely on Your c-s. Ps 119:66
All Your c-s are true; Ps 119:86
but Your c-s are my delight. Ps 119:143
that executes His c, Ps 148:8
but let your heart keep my c-s; Pr 3:1
Keep my c-s and live; Pr 7:2
A wise heart accepts c-s, but foolish Pr 10:8
who respects a c will be rewarded. Pr 13:13
Keep the king's c. Ec 8:2
fear God and keep His c-s, Ec 12:13
having soldiers under my c. Mt 8:9
teaching as doctrines the c-s of men. Mt 15:9
Disregarding the c of God, Mk 7:8
one who has My c-s and keeps them Jn 14:21
If you keep My c-s you will remain Jn 15:10
This is My c: love one another Jn 15:12
as a concession, not as a c. 1Co 7:6
I have no c from the Lord, 1Co 7:25
I write to you is the Lord's c. 1Co 14:37
I am not saying this as a c. 2Co 8:8
they are human c-s and doctrines. Col 2:22
I am not writing you a new c, 1Jn 2:7
Now this is His c: that we 1Jn 3:23
who keeps His c-s remains in Him, 1Jn 3:24
And we have this c from Him: 1Jn 4:21
love for God is: to keep His c-s. 1Jn 5:3
Now His c-s are not a burden, 2Jn 6
This is the c as you have heard

COMMAND (v)
the tree about which I c-ed you, Gn 3:17
everything that God had c-ed him. Gn 6:22
so that he will c his children Gn 18:19
You must say whatever I c you; Ex 7:2
Observe what I c you today. Ex 34:11
just as the LORD had c-ed Moses. Ex 39:1
not add anything to what I c you Dt 4:2
c-ing you today to love the LORD Dt 30:16
so that you may c your children Dt 32:46
Haven't I c-ed you: be strong and Jos 1:9
you have c-ed us we will do, Jos 1:16

He c-ed, and it came into existence   Ps 33:9
for He c-ed, and they were created.   Ps 148:5
or c them concerning burnt offering   Jr 7:22
in the fire, a thing I did not c;   Jr 7:31
nor did I c them or speak to them.   Jr 14:14
there I will c the sword to kill   Am 9:4
as the Lord's angel had c-ed him.   Mt 1:24
everything I have c-ed you.   Mt 28:20
He c-s even the unclean spirits,   Mk 1:27
as the Father c-ed Me, so I do.   Jn 14:31
friends if you do what I c you.   Jn 15:14
He c-ed us to preach to the people   Ac 10:42
And he c-ed them to be baptized in   Ac 10:48
this is what the Lord has c-ed us: Ac 13:47
God now c-s all people everywhere   Ac 17:30
I c you by the Jesus whom Paul   Ac 19:13
c-ed that those who preach   1Co 9:14
you, this is what we c-ed you: 2Th 3:10
C and teach these things.   1Tm 4:11
love one another as He c-ed us.   1Jn 3:23

COMMANDER

I have now come as c of the LORD's   Jos 5:14
name of the c of his army was   1Sm 14:50
a leader and c for the peoples,   Is 55:4
that you may eat ... the flesh of c-s   Rv 19:18

COMMANDMENT

the covenant—the Ten C-s.   Ex 34:28
follow the Ten C-s, which He wrote   Dt 4:13
the Ten C-s that He had spoken to   Dt 10:4
did not keep the c-s of the LORD   2Kg 17:19
the c of the LORD is radiant,   Ps 19:8
I love Your c-s more than gold,   Ps 119:127
for all Your c-s are righteous.   Ps 119:172
For a c is a lamp, teaching is a light   Pr 6:23
who love Him and keep His c-s   Dn 9:4
least of these c-s and teaches   Mt 5:19
the greatest and most important c.   Mt 22:38
Prophets depend on these two c-s.   Mt 22:40
I give you a new c: Jn 13:34
love Me, you will keep My c-s.   Jn 14:15
the c is holy and just and good.   Rm 7:12
but keeping God's c-s does.   1Co 7:19
is the first c with a promise   Eph 6:2
myths and the c-s of men who   Ti 1:14
who keep the c-s of God and   Rv 14:12

COMMEMORATE

of Israel would c the daughter   Jdg 11:40

COMMEND

So I c-ed enjoyment, because there   Ec 8:15
I c to you our sister Phoebe,   Rm 16:1
beginning to c ourselves again   2Co 3:1
not the one c-ing himself who is
   approved, but the one the
   Lord c-s.   2Co 10:18

COMMENDABLE

whatever is c—if there is any   Php 4:8

COMMISSION

and c him in their sight.   Nm 27:19
But c Joshua and encourage and   Dt 3:28
Call Joshua ... that I may c him.   Dt 31:14
The LORD c-ed Joshua son of Nun,   Dt 31:23

COMMIT

Do not c adultery.   Ex 20:14; Dt 5:18
You have c-ted a great sin.   Ex 32:30
is to confess the sin he has c-ted.   Nm 5:7
you have c-ted all this evil,   1Sm 12:20
Jonathan c-ted himself to David,   1Sm 18:1
and caused them to c great sin.   2Kg 17:21
and c-ted them into the care of   2Ch 12:10
C your way to the LORD;   Ps 37:5
If only my ways were c-ted to   Ps 119:5
one who c-s adultery lacks sense;   Pr 6:32
C your activities to the LORD   Pr 16:3
My people have c-ted a double evil: Jr 2:13
c-ting the same abominations   Ezk 18:24
it was said, Do not c adultery.   Mt 5:27
c-ted adultery with her in his heart.   Mt 5:28
causes her to c adultery.   Mt 5:32
a divorced woman c-s adultery.   Mt 5:32
Is a gift {c-ted to the temple}   Mt 15:5
and marries another, c-s adultery.   Mt 19:9
do not murder; do not c adultery;   Mt 19:18
Everyone who c-s sin is a slave of   Jn 8:34
they c-ted them to the Lord   Ac 14:23
And now I c you to God   Ac 20:32
Males c-ted shameless acts with   Rm 1:27
over the sins previously c-ted.   Rm 3:25
You shall not c adultery,   Rm 13:9
He has c-ted the message ... to us.   2Co 5:19
c to faithful men who will be   2Tm 2:2
of the people c-ted in ignorance.   Heb 9:7
said, Do not c adultery, also said,   Jms 2:11
and if he has c-ted sins, he will be   Jms 5:15

He did not c sin, and no deceit   1Pt 2:22
but c-ted Himself to the One who   1Pt 2:23

COMMON

between the holy and the c,   Lv 10:10
made silver as c in Jerusalem as   1Kg 10:27
of God, what do we have in c?   1Kg 17:18
Israel, "We have nothing in c.   2Kg 3:13
and the poor have this in c: Pr 22:2
the oppressor have this in c: Pr 29:13
between the holy and the c,   Ezk 22:26
separate the holy from the c.   Ezk 42:20
between the holy and the c,   Ezk 44:23
and had everything in c.   Ac 2:44
they held everything in c.   Ac 4:32
made clean, you must not call c.   Ac 10:15
except what is c to humanity.   1Co 10:13
believer have in c with an   2Co 6:15
have flesh and blood in c,   Heb 2:14

COMMUNITY

the c assembled at the entrance   Lv 8:4
have the whole c stone him.   Lv 24:14
the entire c is to gather before   Nm 10:3
entire Israelite c assembled at   Jos 22:12
and the c assembled as one body   Jdg 20:1
not be in the c of the righteous   Ps 1:5

COMPANION

and a c of ostriches.   Jb 30:29
is my peer, my c and good friend   Ps 55:13
who abandons the c of her youth   Pr 2:17
but a c of fools will suffer harm.   Pr 13:20
a c of gluttons humiliates his father. Pr 28:7
is a c to a man who destroys.   Pr 28:24
falls, his c can lift him up;   Ec 4:10
Paul and his c-s set sail from   Ac 13:13
who were Paul's traveling c-s.   Ac 19:29
have become c-s of the Messiah   Heb 3:14
became with the Holy Spirit,   Heb 6:4

COMPANY

He keeps c with evildoers and   Jb 34:8
enjoyed your c for a while.   Rm 15:24
Bad c corrupts good morals.   1Co 15:33

COMPARE

none can c with You.   Ps 40:5
nothing you desire c-s with her.   Pr 3:15
nothing desirable can c with it.   Pr 8:11
I c you, my darling, to a mare   Sg 1:9

Who will you c God with?   Is 40:18
To what should I c this generation?   Mt 11:16
kingdom of heaven may be c-d to   Mt 13:24
What can I c the kingdom of God   Lk 13:20
are not worth c-ing with the glory   Rm 8:18
c-ing themselves to themselves,   2Co 10:12

COMPASS

and outlines it with a c.   Is 44:13

COMPASSION

I will have c on whom I have c.   Ex 33:19
and have c on His servants   Dt 32:36
for He had c on His people and   2Ch 36:15
because of Your great c.   Neh 9:19
do not withhold Your c from me;   Ps 40:11
according to Your abundant c,   Ps 51:1
Has He in anger withheld His c?   Ps 77:9
will arise and have c on Zion,   Ps 102:13
you with faithful love and c.   Ps 103:4
As a father has c on his children,   Ps 103:13
Your c-s are many, LORD;   Ps 119:156
His c {rests} on all He has made   Ps 145:9
or lack c for the child of her   Is 49:15
take you back with great c.   Is 54:7
once again have c on them and   Jr 12:15
I am tired of showing c.   Jr 15:6
C and forgiveness belong to the   Dn 9:9
Name her No C, for I will no   Hs 1:6
and I will have c on No C;   Hs 2:23
My c is stirred!   Hs 11:8
C is hidden from My eyes.   Hs 13:14
He will again have c on us;   Mc 7:19
shepherds have no c for them.   Zch 11:5
I will have c on them as a man
   has c on his son   Mal 3:17
crowds, He felt c for them   Mt 9:36
a huge crowd, felt c for them   Mt 14:14
and said, "I have c on the crowd   Mt 15:32
saw her, He had c on her and said   Lk 7:13
saw him and was filled with c.   Lk 15:20
I will have c on whom I have c.   Rm 9:15
put on heartfelt c, kindness   Col 3:12

COMPASSIONATE

I will listen because I am c.   Ex 22:27
Yahweh is a c and gracious God,   Ex 34:6
the LORD your God is a c God.   Dt 4:31
gracious and c, slow to anger   Neh 9:17
The LORD is c and gracious,   Ps 103:8

The LORD is gracious and c, Ps 145:8
is gracious and c, slow to anger Jl 2:13
You are a merciful and c God, Jnh 4:2
And be kind and c to one another Eph 4:32
Lord is very c and merciful. Jms 5:11
believers, and be c and humble, 1Pt 3:8

COMPELS

and my spirit c me {to speak}. Jb 32:18
Christ's love c us, since we 2Co 5:14

COMPENSATION

slave go free in c for his eye. Ex 21:26
owner of the pit must give c; Ex 21:34
He is to pay full c, add a fifth Nm 5:7
The money from the c offering 2Kg 12:16

COMPETE

how can you c with horses? Jr 12:5
and their c-ing thoughts either Rm 2:15
Now everyone who c-s exercises 1Co 9:25
if anyone c-s as an athlete, 2Tm 2:5
unless he c-s according to the rules. 2Tm 2:5

COMPETENCE

I possess good advice and c; Pr 8:14
but our c is from God. 2Co 3:5

COMPETENT

not that we are c in ourselves 2Co 3:5
He has made us c to be ministers 2Co 3:6

COMPLACENCY

the c of fools will destroy them. Pr 1:32

COMPLACENT

Stand up, you c women; Is 32:9

COMPLAIN

But Abraham c-ed to Abimelech Gn 21:25
So the people c-ed to Moses: Ex 17:2
the people began c-ing openly
  before Nm 11:1
All the Israelites c-ed about Moses Nm 14:2
I will c in the bitterness of my Jb 7:11
I c and groan morning, noon, and Ps 55:17
God, hear my voice when I c. Ps 64:1
scribes were c-ing to His disciples Lk 5:30
them, "Stop c-ing among yourselves. Jn 6:43
Nor should we c as some of them 1Co 10:10
do not c about one another, Jms 5:9
to one another without c-ing. 1Pt 4:9

COMPLAINT

He has heard your c-s about Him. Ex 16:7
the Israelites' c-s that they make Nm 14:27
I will express my c and speak Jb 10:1
Today also my c is bitter. Jb 23:2
I pour out my c before Him; Ps 142:2
Who has c-s? Who has wounds Pr 23:29
what I should reply about my c. Hab 2:1
there arose a c by the Ac 6:1
anyone has a c against another Col 3:13

COMPLETE (adj)

a Sabbath of c rest to the LORD Ex 35:2
must be a Sabbath of c rest, Lv 23:3
to count seven c weeks starting Lv 23:15
70 years for Babylon are c, Jr 29:10
Zion, your punishment is c; Lm 4:22
So this joy of mine is c. Jn 3:29
in you and your joy may be c. Jn 15:11
that your joy may be c. Jn 16:24
sanctification c in the fear of 2Co 7:1
once your obedience is c. 2Co 10:6
to be made c by the flesh? Gl 3:3
that the man of God may be c, 2Tm 3:17
that you may be mature and c, Jms 1:4
so that our joy may be c. 1Jn 1:4
face so that our joy may be c. 2Jn 12

COMPLETE (v)

God c-d His work that He had done Gn 2:2
C this week {of wedding Gn 29:27
the temple was c-d in every detail 1Kg 6:38
So he c-d the temple. 1Kg 9:25
The wall was c-d in 52 days, Neh 6:15
C your outdoor work, and prepare Pr 24:27
When the 70 years are c-d, Jr 25:12
until the time of wrath is c-d, Dn 11:36
the eight days were c-d for His Lk 2:21
see if he has enough to c it? Lk 14:28
by c-ing the work You gave Me Jn 17:4
they may have My joy c-d in them. Jn 17:13
he should also c this grace to 2Co 8:6
and I am c-ing in my flesh what is Col 1:24
and to c what is lacking 1Th 3:10
God's hidden plan will be c-d, Rv 10:7
When the 1,000 years are c-d, Rv 20:7

COMPLETELY

spirit and has followed Me c, Nm 14:24
they did not follow Me c, Nm 32:11

because he followed the LORD c.	Dt 1:36
you must c destroy them.	Dt 7:2
They c destroyed everything in	Jos 6:21
but never drove them out c.	Jdg 1:28
and I c destroyed the Amalekites	1Sm 15:20
heart was not c with the LORD	1Kg 11:4
in the LORD's sight but not c.	2Ch 25:2
unless You have c rejected us	Lm 5:22
his feet, but he is c clean.	Jn 13:10
Himself sanctify you c.	1Th 5:23
set your hope c on the grace to	1Pt 1:13

COMPLETION

carry it on to c until the day	Php 1:6

COMPREHEND

great things that we cannot c.	Jb 37:5
Have you c-ed the extent of the	Jb 38:18
may be able to c with all the	Eph 3:18

COMPRESSES

the one who c his lips brings	Pr 16:30

COMPULSION

who is under no c, but has	1Co 7:37
overseeing out of c but freely,	1Pt 5:2

CONCEAL

but it is c-ed from her husband,	Nm 5:13
Who is this who c-s {My} counsel	Jb 42:3
For He will c me in His shelter	Ps 27:5
You c them in a shelter from the	Ps 31:20
You and did not c my iniquity.	Ps 32:5
I did not c Your constant love	Ps 40:10
mouth of the wicked c-s violence.	Pr 10:6
A shrewd person c-s knowledge,	Pr 12:23
Whoever c-s an offense promotes	Pr 17:9
the glory of God to c a matter	Pr 25:2
an open reprimand than c-ed love.	Pr 27:5
who c-s his sins will not prosper,	Pr 28:13
They do not c it. Woe to them	Is 3:9
They are not c-ed from Me,	Jr 16:17
For nothing is c-ed that won't be	Lk 8:17
it was c-ed from them so that they	Lk 9:45
use your freedom as a way to c evil.	1Pt 2:16

CONCEIT (n)

Do nothing out of rivalry or c,	Php 2:3

CONCEITED (adj)

So that you will not be c,	Rm 11:25
is not boastful; is not c;	1Co 13:4
must not become c, provoking	Gl 5:26

or he might become c and fall	1Tm 3:6
he is c, understanding nothing	1Tm 6:4
reckless, c, lovers of pleasure	2Tm 3:4

CONCEIVE

and she c-d and gave birth to Cain	Gn 4:1
and his wife Rebekah c-d.	Gn 25:21
Leah c-d, gave birth to a son, and	Gn 29:32
Bilhah c-d and bore Jacob a son.	Gn 30:5
Did I c all these people?	Nm 11:12
but you will c and give birth to	Jdg 13:3
the LORD enabled her to c,	Ru 4:13
Hannah c-d and gave birth to a son	1Sm 1:20
The woman c-d and sent word to	2Sm 11:5
They c trouble and give birth to	Jb 15:35
pregnant with evil, c-s trouble, and	Ps 7:14
was sinful when my mother c-d me.	Ps 51:5
chamber of the one who c-d me.	Sg 3:4
The virgin will c, have a son	Is 7:14
You will c chaff; you will give	Is 33:11
they c trouble and give birth to	Is 59:4
what has been c-d in her is by the	Mt 1:20
wife Elizabeth c-d and kept	Lk 1:24
You will c and give birth to a	Lk 1:31
received power to c offspring,	Heb 11:11
desire has c-d, it gives birth	Jms 1:15

CONCEPTION

no birth, no gestation, no c.	Hs 9:11

CONCERN (n)

test me and know my c-s.	Ps 139:23
weights in the bag are His c.	Pr 16:11
Then I had c for My holy name,	Ezk 36:21
not thinking about God's c-s,	Mt 16:23
I want you to be without c-s.	1Co 7:32
have the same c for each other.	1Co 12:25

CONCERN (v)

master does not c himself with	Gn 39:8

CONCERNED (adj)

Do not be c about the boy	Gn 21:12
stopped being c about the	1Sm 10:2
married man is c about	1Co 7:33
Is God really c with oxen?	1Co 9:9

CONCERNING

give His angels orders c you	Mt 4:6
them the things c Himself in all	Lk 24:27
brothers, c those who are asleep	1Th 4:13
C this salvation, the prophets	1Pt 1:10

CONCESSION

I say this as a c, not as a — 1Co 7:6

CONCLUSION

been heard, the c of the matter — Ec 12:13

CONCUBINE

with his father's c Bilhah, — Gn 35:22
Bethlehem in Judah as his c. — Jdg 19:1
Now Saul had a c whose name was — 2Sm 3:7
he left behind 10 c-s to take care — 2Sm 15:16
He had 700 wives ... and 300 c-s, — 1Kg 11:3
eunuch in charge of the c-s. — Est 2:14
myself, and many c-s, the delights — Ec 2:8
wives, and c-s drank from them. — Dn 5:3

CONDEMN

the innocent and c the guilty. — Dt 25:1
my own mouth would c me; — Jb 9:20
Your own mouth c-s you, not I; — Jb 15:6
c the mighty Righteous One? — Jb 34:17
to set free those c-ed to die, — Ps 102:20
save him from those who would c — Ps 109:31
the guilty and c-ing the just — Pr 17:15
who is he who will c Me? — Is 50:9
by your words you will be c-ed. — Mt 12:37
this generation and c it, because — Mt 12:41
and they will c Him to death. — Mt 20:18
can you escape being c-ed to hell? — Mt 23:33
And they all c-ed Him — Mk 14:64
does not believe will be c-ed. — Mk 16:16
Do not c, and you will not be c-ed. — Lk 6:37
"Neither do I c you," said Jesus — Jn 8:11
you c yourself, since you, — Rm 2:1
He c-ed sin in the flesh by sending — Rm 8:3
Who is the one who c-s? — Rm 8:34
who does not c himself by what — Rm 14:22
doubts stands c-ed if he eats, — Rm 14:23
may not be c-ed with the world. — 1Co 11:32
to his face because he stood c-ed. — Gl 2:11
because if our hearts c us, — 1Jn 3:20

CONDEMNATION

Their c is deserved! — Rm 3:8
as through one trespass there is c
  for everyone, — Rm 5:18
no c now exists for those in — Rm 8:1
if the ministry of c had glory, — 2Co 3:9
fall into the c of the Devil. — 1Tm 3:6
Their c, {pronounced} long ago — 2Pt 2:3

CONDITION

be one people only on this c: — Gn 34:22
Know well the c of your flock, — Pr 27:23
that man's last c is worse than — Mt 12:45

CONDUCT (n)

shameful c is pleasure for a fool, — Pr 10:23
will get what their c deserves, — Pr 14:14
A guilty man's c is crooked, — Pr 21:8
them according to their own c, — Ezk 7:27
rulers are not a terror to good c, — Rm 13:3
in speech, in c, in love, in — 1Tm 4:12
works by good c with wisdom's — Jms 3:13
are to be holy in all your c; — 1Pt 1:15
be in holy c and godliness — 2Pt 3:11

CONDUCT (v)

knows how to c himself before — Ec 6:8
that we have c-ed ourselves in the — 2Co 1:12
blamelessly we c-ed ourselves with — 1Th 2:10
you are to c yourselves in — 1Pt 1:17
C yourselves honorably among the — 1Pt 2:12

CONFER

C some of your authority on him — Nm 27:20
You c majesty and splendor on — Ps 21:5

CONFESS

he is to c he has committed that — Lv 5:5
the live goat and c over it all — Lv 16:21
But if they will c their sin — Lv 26:40
person is to c the sin he has — Nm 5:7
Ezra prayed and c-ed, weeping — Ezr 10:1
I c the sins we have committed — Neh 1:6
they stood and c-ed their sins — Neh 9:2
I will c my transgressions to — Ps 32:5
So I c my guilt; I am anxious — Ps 38:18
but whoever c-es and
  renounces them — Pr 28:13
c-ing my sin and the sin of my — Dn 9:20
Jordan River as they c-ed their sins. — Mt 3:6
that if anyone c-ed Him as Messiah — Jn 9:22
Pharisees they did not c Him, — Jn 12:42
But I c this to you: — Ac 24:14
if you c with your mouth, "Jesus — Rm 10:9
tongue should c that Jesus — Php 2:11
c your sins to one another and — Jms 5:16
If we c our sins, He is faithful — 1Jn 1:9
he who c-es the Son has the Father — 1Jn 2:23
Every spirit who c-es that Jesus — 1Jn 4:2

who does not c Jesus is not	1Jn 4:3
Whoever c-es that Jesus is the Son	1Jn 4:15

CONFESSION

make a c to the LORD God	Ezr 10:11
obedience to the c of the gospel	2Co 9:13
have made a good c before many	1Tm 6:12
and high priest of our c;	Heb 3:1
let us hold fast to the c.	Heb 4:14
us hold on to the c of our hope	Heb 10:23

CONFIDENCE

intimidated and lost their c,	Neh 6:16
Lord GOD, my c from my youth.	Ps 71:5
will be your c and will keep	Pr 3:26
but the trustworthy keeps a c.	Pr 11:13
so that your c may be in the	Pr 22:19
strength will lie in quiet c.	Is 30:15
What are you basing your c on?	Is 36:4
whose c indeed is the LORD.	Jr 17:7
have this kind of c toward God	2Co 3:4
I have great c in you;	2Co 7:4
In the Lord I have c in you that you	Gl 5:10
and c through faith in Him.	Eph 3:12
your c may grow in Christ Jesus	Php 1:26
and do not put c in the flesh	Php 3:3
We have c in the Lord about you	2Th 3:4
courage and the c of our hope.	Heb 3:6
So don't throw away your c,	Heb 10:35
Now this is the c we have before	1Jn 5:14

CONFIDENT

My heart is c, God	Ps 57:7; 108:1
his heart is c, trusting in the	Ps 112:7
But you were c in your beauty	Ezk 16:15
If anyone is c that he belongs	2Co 10:7
Since I am c of your obedience,	Phm 21
we are c of the better things	Heb 6:9

CONFINED

the prison where Joseph was c.	Gn 40:3
They will be c to a dungeon;	Is 24:22
he was still c in the guard's courtyard,	Jr 33:1
we were c under the law	Gl 3:23

CONFIRM

I c My covenant with you that	Gn 9:11
I will c My covenant with him as	Gn 17:19
and I will c the oath that I	Gn 26:3
and c My covenant with you.	Lv 26:9
in order to c His covenant He	Dt 8:18

May the LORD c your word.	1Sm 1:23
please c what You promised to	1Kg 8:26
and his house be c-ed forever,	1Ch 17:23
and c-ed to Jacob as a decree and	Ps 105:10
C what You said to Your servant	Ps 119:38
who c-s the message of His servant	Is 44:26
to you and will c My promise	Jr 29:10
working with them and c-ing the word	Mk 16:20
to c the promises to the fathers	Rm 15:8
about Christ was c-ed among you,	1Co 1:6
He will also c you to the end,	1Co 1:8
Lord and was c-ed to us by those	Heb 2:3
every effort to c your calling	2Pt 1:10
the prophetic word strongly c-ed.	2Pt 1:19

CONFISCATION

with joy the c of your	Heb 10:34

CONFLICT

Hatred stirs up c-s, but love	Pr 10:12
A hot-tempered man stirs up c,	Pr 15:18
A contrary man spreads c,	Pr 16:28
To start a c is to release a flood;	Pr 17:14
Drive out a mocker, and c goes too;	Pr 22:10
Who has sorrow? Who has c-s?	Pr 23:29
without a gossip, c dies down.	Pr 26:20
A greedy person provokes c,	Pr 28:25
an angry man stirs up c,	Pr 29:22
true and was about a great c.	Dn 10:1

CONFORMED

predestined to be c to the image	Rm 8:29
Do not be c to this age, but be	Rm 12:2
being c to His death,	Php 3:10
do not be c to the desires of	1Pt 1:14

CONFOUND

be disgraced and c-ed	Ps 40:14; 70:2; 71:13
confuse and c their speech,	Ps 55:9
who c-s the wise	Is 44:25

CONFRONT

going out to c the Philistine,	1Sm 17:55
the snares of death c-ed me.	2Sm 22:6
King Josiah went to c him,	2Kg 23:29
days of suffering c me.	Jb 30:27
Let us c each other.	Is 50:8
their wickedness has c-ed Me.	Jnh 1:2

CONFUSE

down there and c their language	Gn 11:7

c and confound their speech,   Ps 55:9
of beer, they are c-d by wine.   Is 28:7

CONFUSION

and throw into c all the nations   Ex 23:27
throw them into great c until   Dt 7:23
blindness, and mental c,   Dt 28:28
threw them into c before Israel.   Jos 10:10
against each other in great c!   1Sm 14:20
the city of Susa was in c.   Est 3:15
wander in c since they have   Jl 1:18
So the city was filled with c;   Ac 19:29

CONGEALED

The watery depths c in the heart   Ex 15:8

CONGREGATION

front of the entire c of Israel   1Kg 8:22
presence of the king and the c,   2Ch 29:23
I will praise You in the c.   Ps 22:22
I will praise You in the great c;   Ps 35:18
sing hymns to You in the c.   Heb 2:12

CONNECTED

Solomon's fame c with the name   1Kg 10:1
so closely c they cannot be   Jb 41:17
better things c with salvation.   Heb 6:9

CONQUER

because we can certainly c it!   Nm 13:30
The wise c a city of warriors   Pr 21:22
I have c-ed the world.   Jn 16:33
Do not be c-ed by evil, but c evil   Rm 12:21
who by faith c-ed kingdoms   Heb 11:33
and you have c-ed them, because the   1Jn 4:4
been born of God c-s the world.   1Jn 5:4
victory that has c-ed the world: 1Jn 5:4
he went out as a victor to c.   Rv 6:2
They c-ed him by the blood of the   Rv 12:11
the Lamb will c them because he   Rv 17:14

CONSCIENCE

with a clear c and clean hands.   Gn 20:5
David's c bothered him because   1Sm 24:5
David's c troubled him after he   2Sm 24:10
My c will not accuse {me} as   Jb 27:6
at night my c instructs me.   Ps 16:7
a clear c toward God and men.   Ac 24:16
Their c-s testify in support of   Rm 2:15
my c is testifying to me with   Rm 9:1
but also because of your c.   Rm 13:5
their c, being weak, is defiled.   1Co 8:7

and wound their weak c,   1Co 8:12
no questions for c' sake,   1Co 10:25
judged by another person's c?   1Co 10:29
testimony of our c that we have   2Co 1:12
to every person's c by an open   2Co 4:2
open to your c-s as well.   2Co 5:11
a good c, and a sincere faith.   1Tm 1:5
of the faith with a clear c.   1Tm 3:9
of liars whose c-s are seared.   1Tm 4:2
their mind and c are defiled.   Ti 1:15
perfect the worshiper's c.   Heb 9:9
cleanse our c-s from dead works to   Heb 9:14
sprinkled {clean} from an evil c   Heb 10:22
that we have a clear c,   Heb 13:18
keeping your c clear, so that   1Pt 3:16
pledge of a good c toward God   1Pt 3:21

CONSCIOUS

For I am c of my rebellion,   Ps 51:3

CONSECRATE

C every firstborn male to Me,   Ex 13:2
offerings that the Israelites c   Ex 28:38
c them to serve Me as priests.   Ex 29:1
c it along with all its furnishings   Ex 40:9
he c-d Aaron and his garments,   Lv 8:30
C yourselves and be holy, for I   Lv 20:7
When a man c-s his house as holy   Lv 27:14
I c-d every firstborn in Israel to   Nm 3:13
a Nazirite vow, to c himself to   Nm 6:2
he anointed and c-d these things,   Nm 7:1
best part of the tenth is to be c-d.   Nm 18:29
Joshua told the people, "C yourselves   Jos 3:5
I personally c the silver to   Jdg 17:3
I have c-d this temple you have   1Kg 9:3
C a solemn assembly for Baal.   2Kg 10:20
Solomon c-d the middle of the   2Ch 7:7
chosen and c-d this temple   2Ch 7:16
C yourselves now and c the temple   2Ch 29:5
I have c-d My King on Zion,   Ps 2:6
but you must c the Sabbath day,   Jr 17:22
He has c-d His guests.   Zph 1:7

CONSECRATED (adj)

However, there is c bread, but   1Sm 21:4
men's bodies are c even on   1Sm 21:5
father's c gifts and his own c   1Kg 15:15
items that ... Ahaziah—had c,   2Kg 12:18
along with his own c items   2Ch 26:18
only the c priests,   2Ch 26:18

CONSECRATION

for the c of the anointing oil Lv 21:12
the time of his vow of c. Nm 6:5

CONSEQUENCES

bringing the c of the fathers' Ex 34:7
he bears the c of his guilt. Lv 5:17
he will bear the c of his sin. Lv 24:15
bringing the c of the fathers' Nm 14:18
must bear the c of your Ezk 16:58; 23:35

CONSIDER

Now c that this nation is Your Ex 33:13
Now c carefully what you
  must do 1Sm 25:17
Have you c-ed My servant Job? Jb 1:8
Have you c-ed My servant Job? Jb 2:3
Stop and c God's wonders. Jb 37:14
LORD; c my sighing. Ps 5:1
C me and answer, LORD, my God. Ps 13:3
C my affliction and trouble, Ps 25:18
C my enemies; they are numerous Ps 25:19
He c-s all their works. Ps 33:15
I c days of old, years long past Ps 77:5
c the LORD's acts of faithful love. Ps 107:43
C my affliction and rescue me, Ps 119:153
if You c-ed sins, Lord, who Ps 130:3
She doesn't c the path of life; Pr 5:6
Even a fool is c-ed wise when he Pr 17:28
but the upright man c-s his way. Pr 21:29
He who weighs hearts c it? Pr 24:12
C the work of God; for who can Ec 7:13
but in the day of adversity, c: Ec 7:14
and who c-ed His fate? Is 53:8
C the ravens: they don't sow or Lk 12:24
C how the wildflowers grow: Lk 12:27
And now, Lord, c their threats Ac 4:29
He c-ed his own body to be already Rm 4:19
you too c yourselves dead to sin Rm 6:11
For I c that the sufferings of Rm 8:18
Brothers, c your calling: 1Co 1:26
but in humility c others as more Php 2:3
did not c equality with God as Php 2:6
I also c everything to be a loss Php 3:8
I do not c myself to have taken Php 3:13
leaders should be c-ed worthy of 1Tm 5:17
So if you c me a partner, accept Phm 17
she c-ed that the One who had Heb 11:11
C it a great joy, my brothers Jms 1:2

CONSIDERABLE

C in every way. Rm 3:2

CONSIDERATION

he has no c for his neighbor. Pr 21:10
out of c for the one who told 1Co 10:28

CONSIGN

Isn't mankind c-ed to forced labor Jb 7:1
c your gold to the dust, Jb 22:24
c them to terror and plunder, Ezk 23:46
they have all been c-ed to death, Ezk 31:14

CONSIST

should not c of outward things 1Pt 3:3

CONSISTENT

produce fruit c with repentance Mt 3:8
must speak what is c with sound Ti 2:1

CONSOLATION

Are God's c-s not enough for you, Jb 15:11
A cup of c won't be given him Jr 16:7
looking forward to Israel's c, Lk 2:25
encouragement, and c. 1Co 14:3
Christ, if any c of love, if any Php 2:1

CONSOLE

brother Esau is c-ing himself by Gn 27:42
sent his emissaries to c Hanun 2Sm 10:2
refused to be c-d, because they Mt 2:18

CONSORTS

but one who c with prostitutes Pr 29:3

CONSPICUOUS

The goat had a c horn between Dn 8:5

CONSPIRACY

So the c grew strong, and the 2Sm 15:12
discovered a c by Hoshea 2Kg 17:4
The c of her prophets within her Ezk 22:25
the Jews formed a c and bound Ac 23:12

CONSPIRE

all of you have c-d against me! 1Sm 22:8
He c-d with Joab son of Zeruiah 1Kg 1:7
It was I who c-d against my master 2Kg 9:14
Joash's servants c-d against him 2Kg 12:20
But they c-d against him and 2Ch 24:21
and the rulers c together Ps 2:2
they c against Your treasured Ps 83:3
For they have c-d with one mind; Ps 83:5
Amos has c-d against you Am 7:10

they c-d to arrest Jesus | Mt 26:4
the Jews c-d to kill him, | Ac 9:23

CONSTANT
God's faithful love is c. | Ps 52:1
You are in c dread all day long | Is 51:13

CONSTANTLY
They c tested God and provoked | Ps 78:41
My life is c in danger, yet I do | Ps 119:109
witness that I c mention you, | Rm 1:9
remembering you c in our prayers | 1Th 1:2
Pray c. | 1Th 5:17
when I c remember you in my | 2Tm 1:3

CONSTELLATIONS
moon, c, and the whole heavenly | 2Kg 23:5
bring out the c in their season | Jb 38:32
its c will not give their light. | Is 13:10

CONSTRUCT
You are to c the tabernacle | Ex 26:1
You are to c the altar of | Ex 27:1
c a siege wall, build a ramp, | Ezk 4:2

CONSTRUCTION
Leave the c of this house of God | Ezr 6:7
myself to the c of the wall, | Neh 5:16

CONSULT
who wanted to c the LORD would | Ex 33:7
turn to mediums or c spiritists, | Lv 19:31
c a medium or a familiar spirit | Dt 18:11
Saul said, "C a spirit for me. | 1Sm 28:8
Rehoboam c-ed with the elders | 1Kg 12:6
even c-ed a medium for guidance | 1Ch 10:13
a priest who could c the Urim | Ezr 2:63
he will not c the wise. | Pr 15:12
shouldn't a people c their God? | Is 8:19
Who did He c with? | Is 40:14
I will not be c-ed by you. | Ezk 20:3,31
My people c their wooden {idols}, | Hs 4:12
not immediately c with anyone. | Gl 1:16

CONSUME
bush was on fire but was not c-d. | Ex 3:2
Fire ... c-d the burnt offering | Lv 9:24
so I may c them instantly. | Nm 16:21
the LORD your God is a c-ing fire, | Dt 4:24
This great fire will c us | Dt 5:25
over ahead of you as a c-ing fire; | Dt 9:3
up from the rock and c-d the meat | Jdg 6:21
the bramble and the cedars | Jdg 9:15

fire fell and c-d the burnt offering | 1Kg 18:38
and c you and your 50 | 2Kg 1:10,12
c My people as they c bread; | Ps 14:4; 53:4
zeal for Your house has c-d me, | Ps 69:9
For we are c-d by Your anger; | Ps 90:7
his arms and c-s his own flesh. | Ec 4:5
but the lips of a fool c him. | Ec 10:12
His tongue is like a c-ing fire. | Is 30:27
entire scroll was c-d by the fire | Jr 36:23
of fiery flames c-ing stubble, | Jl 2:5
it will c its citadels. | Am 1:7
earth will be c-d by the fire | Zph 1:18; 3:8
and how it c-s Me until it is | Lk 12:50
Zeal for Your house will c Me. | Jn 2:17
or you will be c-d by one another | Gl 5:15
for our God is a c-ing fire. | Heb 12:29

CONTAIN
every tree whose fruit c-s seed. | Gn 1:29
heaven, cannot c You, much less | 1Kg 8:27
highest heaven cannot c Him? | 2Ch 2:6
itself could c the books that | Jn 21:25

CONTAINER
borrow empty c-s from everyone | 2Kg 4:3
to her son, "Bring me another c. | 2Kg 4:6

CONTEMPLATE
but I c Your decrees. | Ps 119:95

CONTEMPORARIES
beyond many c among my people, | Gl 1:14

CONTEMPT
the LORD's offering with c. | 1Sm 2:17
He pours out c on nobles | Jb 12:21
the righteous with pride and c. | Ps 31:18
He pours c on nobles | Ps 107:40
we've had more than enough c. | Ps 123:3
Whoever shows c for his neighbor | Pr 11:12
one who has c for instruction | Pr 13:13
some to shame and eternal c. | Dn 12:2
things and be treated with c? | Mk 9:12
treated Him with c, mocked Him | Lk 23:11
of God and holding Him up to c. | Heb 6:6

CONTEND
tested Him at Massah and c-ed with
   him at the waters of Meribah. | Dt 33:8
Will the one who c-s with the | Jb 40:2
will c with the one who c-s with you | Is 49:25
who will c with Me? | Is 50:8

Yet, I wish to c with You: Jr 12:1
women who have c-ed for the gospel   Php 4:3
exhort you to c for the faith   Jd 3

CONTENT
If only we had been c to remain   Jos 7:7
are still not c with riches.   Ec 4:8
have learned to be c in whatever   Php 4:11
we will be c with these.   1Tm 6:8

CONTENTMENT
godliness with c is a great gain   1Tm 6:6

CONTINUAL
a cheerful heart has a c feast.   Pr 15:15

CONTINUALLY
to keep the lamp burning c.   Ex 27:20
be kept burning on the altar c;   Lv 6:13
prayer be offered for him c,   Ps 72:15
Your house, who praise You c.   Ps 84:4
and My name is c blasphemed all   Is 52:5
their angels c view the face of   Mt 18:10
All these were c united in   Ac 1:14
and their backs be bent c.   Rm 11:10
Him let us c offer up to God   Heb 13:15

CONTINUE
God will not c to drive these   Jos 23:13
If I c to live, treat me with   1Sm 20:14
so that it will c before You   2Sm 7:29
were not able to c ministering,   1Kg 8:11
the people c-d sacrificing and   2Kg 12:3
So we c-d the work, while half of   Neh 4:21
May he c while the sun endures,   Ps 72:5
The scepter will not c.   Ezk 21:13
If you c in My word,   Jn 8:31
they c-d teaching and proclaiming   Ac 5:42
persuading them to c in the grace   Ac 13:43
encouraging them to c in the faith,   Ac 14:22
Should we c in sin in order that   Rm 6:1
if she c-s in faith, love   1Tm 2:15
c-s night and day in her petitions   1Tm 5:5
c in what you have learned   2Tm 3:14
they did not c in My covenant,   Heb 8:9
Let brotherly love c.   Heb 13:1
all things c as they have been   2Pt 3:4

CONTRADICT
will be able to resist or c.   Lk 21:15
and to refute those who c it.   Ti 1:9

CONTRADICTIONS
empty speech and c from the   1Tm 6:20

CONTRARY
A c man spreads conflict, and a   Pr 16:28
On the c, if anyone slaps you on   Mt 5:39
On the c, whoever is greatest   Lk 22:26
are all acting c to Caesar's   Ac 17:7
to worship God c to the law!   Ac 18:13
and pitfalls c to the doctrine   Rm 16:17
a gospel c to what you received,   Gl 1:9
law therefore c to God's promises?   Gl 3:21
whatever else is c to the sound   1Tm 1:10

CONTRIBUTION
offering as a c to the LORD.   Lv 7:14
is not to eat from the holy c-s.   Lv 22:12
are to offer a c to the LORD   Nm 15:19
in charge of the c-s brought to Me.   Nm 18:8
your tenths and personal c-s,   Dt 12:6
the c for the house of our God   Ezr 8:25
the supplies, c-s, firstfruits   Neh 12:44
along with the c-s for the priests   Neh 13:5
{who demands} "c-s" demolishes it.   Pr 29:4
of 10 percent and the c-s.   Mal 3:8
to make a c to the poor among   Rm 15:26

CONTRIVED
we did not follow cleverly c myths   2Pt 1:16

CONTROL (n)
the people were out of c,   Ex 32:25
Spirit of the LORD took c of him,   Jdg 14:6,19
Spirit of the LORD took c of him,   Jdg 15:14
Spirit of God took c of him,   1Sm 10:10
Spirit of God suddenly took c of   1Sm 11:6
Spirit of the LORD took c of David   1Sm 16:13
spirit from God took c of Saul,   1Sm 18:10
the Spirit took c of Amasai,   1Ch 12:18
Spirit of God took c of Zechariah   2Ch 24:20
but has c over his own will   1Co 7:37
are under the c of the prophets   1Co 14:32
having his children under c   1Tm 3:4

CONTROL (v)
that must be c-led with bit and   Ps 32:9
but the one who c-s his lips is wise. Pr 10:19
man who does not c his temper is   Pr 25:28
The one who c-s her c-s the wind   Pr 27:16
hand and who c-s the whole course   Dn 5:23

in one body, c your hearts. | Col 3:15
is also able to c his whole body | Jms 3:2

CONVENED
The court was c, and the books | Dn 7:10

CONVENIENT
persist in it whether c or not; | 2Tm 4:2

CONVERSION
in detail the c of the Gentiles, | Ac 15:3

CONVERT
the first c to Christ from Asia. | Rm 16:5
must not be a new c, or he might | 1Tm 3:6

CONVERTED
foreigner who has c to the LORD | Is 56:3
unless you are c and become like | Mt 18:3
understand ... and be c | Jn 12:40; Ac 28:27

CONVICT
with those who c the guilty, | Pr 24:25
Who among you can c Me of sin? | Jn 8:46
He will c the world about sin, | Jn 16:8
he is c-ed by all and is judged by | 1Co 14:24
c them of all their their ungodly deeds | Jd 15

CONVICTION
same understanding and the same c | 1Co 1:10

CONVINCE
will c our hearts in His presence. | 1Jn 3:19

CONVINCED
they are c that John was a prophet. | Lk 20:6
fully c that what He had promised | Rm 4:21
must be fully c in his own mind | Rm 14:5
And I am c in the Lord that I | Php 2:24
and that I am c is in you also. | 2Tm 1:5

CONVINCING (adj)
alive to them by many c proofs, | Ac 1:3

CONVULSE
And the unclean spirit c-ed him, | Mk 1:26
shrieking and c-ing him violently. | Mk 9:26

CONVULSIONS
throws him into c until he foams | Lk 9:39

COOK
Once when Jacob was c-ing a stew, | Gn 25:29
You are to c and eat {it} in the | Dt 16:7
women have c-ed their own
　children | Lm 4:10

COOL
one who keeps a c head is a man | Pr 17:27
in water and c my tongue, | Lk 16:24

COPIED
Joshua c the law of Moses, | Jos 8:32

COPING
from foundation to c and from | 1Kg 7:9

COPPER
whose hills you will mine c. | Dt 8:9
and c is smelted from ore. | Jb 28:2
All of them are c, tin, iron | Ezk 22:18
it becomes hot and its c glows. | Ezk 24:11
gold, silver, or c for your | Mt 10:9

COPPERSMITH
blacksmiths and c-s to repair the | 2Ch 24:12
Alexander the c did great harm | 2Tm 4:14

COPY
write a c of this instruction | Dt 17:18
A c of the document was to be | Est 8:13
with the sealed c and this open c | Jr 32:14
These serve as a c and shadow of | Heb 8:5
c-ies of the things in the heavens | Heb 9:23

CORBAN
have received from me is C | Mk 7:11

CORD
signet ring, your c, and the staff | Gn 38:18
tie this scarlet c to the window | Jos 2:18
he measured them off with a c. | 2Sm 8:2
trapped by the c-s of affliction, | Jb 36:8
A c of three strands is not | Ec 4:12
before the silver c is snapped, | Ec 12:6
Your lips are like a scarlet c, | Sg 4:3
drag wickedness with c-s of deceit | Is 5:18
all my tent c-s are snapped. | Jr 10:20
them with human c-s, with ropes | Hs 11:4
After making a whip out of c-s, | Jn 2:15

CORIANDER
It resembled c seed, was white | Ex 16:31
The manna resembled c seed, | Nm 11:7

CORINTH
from Athens and went to C, | Ac 18:1
Apollos was in C, Paul traveled | Ac 19:1
God's church at C, to those who | 1Co 1:2
To God's church at C, with all | 2Co 1:1
Erastus has remained at C; | 2Tm 4:20

CORINTHIANS

and many of the C, when they | Ac 18:8

CORMORANT

owl, the c, the long-eared | Lv 11:17
desert owl, the osprey, the c, | Dt 14:17

CORNELIUS

Centurion; Christian (Ac 10).

CORNER

cord on the tassel at {each} c. | Nm 15:38
cut off the c of Saul's robe. | 1Sm 24:4
struck the four c-s of the house. | Jb 1:19
she lurks at every c. | Pr 7:12
on the c of a roof than | Pr 21:9; 25:24
from the four c-s of the earth. | Is 11:12
called you from its farthest c-s. | Is 41:9
from the four c-s of the heavens, | Jr 49:36
come on the four c-s of the land. | Ezk 7:2
with {only} the c of a bed or | Am 3:12
on the street c-s to be seen by people. | Mt 6:5
to the earth by its four c-s. | Ac 10:11
since this was not done in a c! | Ac 26:26
at the four c-s of the earth, | Rv 7:1; 20:8

CORNERSTONE

Or who laid its c | Jb 38:6
rejected has become the c. | Ps 118:22
a precious c, a sure foundation; | Is 28:16
No one will be able to retrieve a c | Jr 51:26
From them will come the c, | Zch 10:4
builders rejected has become the c. | Mt 21:42
this has become the c | Mk 12:10; Lk 20:17
This Jesus ... has become the c. | Ac 4:11
Christ Jesus Himself as the c. | Eph 2:20
in Zion, a chosen and valuable c, | 1Pt 2:6
this One has become the c, | 1Pt 2:7

CORPSE

who is defiled because of a c. | Nm 5:2
he sinned because of the c. | Nm 6:11
Your c-s will fall in this | Nm 14:29
not to leave his c on the tree | Dt 21:23
Your c-s will be food for all the | Dt 28:26
the lion standing beside the c. | 1Kg 13:28
Their c-s will become food for the | Jr 16:4
heaps of slain, mounds of c-s, | Nah 3:3
The boy became like a c, | Mk 9:26
he gave the c to Joseph. | Mk 15:45
Where the c is, there also | Lk 17:37

CORRECT

See how happy the man is God c-s; | Jb 5:17
The one who c-s a mocker will | Pr 9:7
mocker doesn't love one who c-s | Pr 15:12
Seek justice. C the oppressor | Is 1:17
C your ways and your deeds, | Jr 7:3
for rebuking, for c-ing, for training | 2Tm 3:16
rebuke, c, and encourage | 2Tm 4:2

CORRECTION

and did not accept my c, | Pr 1:25
and how my heart despised c. | Pr 5:12
one who rejects c goes astray. | Pr 10:17
but one who hates c is stupid. | Pr 12:1
person who heeds c is sensible. | Pr 15:5
the one who hates c will die. | Pr 15:10
listens to c acquires good sense. | Pr 15:32
Don't withhold c from a youth; | Pr 23:13
A wise c to a receptive ear is | Pr 25:12
A rod of c imparts wisdom, | Pr 29:15
certainly fear Me and accept c. | Zph 3:7

CORRECTLY

he could not pronounce it c, | Jdg 12:6
prophesied c about you when he | Mt 15:7
You have c said that He is One, | Mk 12:32
You have judged c, | Lk 7:43
You've answered c, | Lk 10:28
You have c said, 'I don't have | Jn 4:17
The Holy Spirit c spoke through | Ac 28:25
c teaching the word of truth. | 2Tm 2:15

CORRESPONDS

Hagar ... c to the present Jerusalem; | Gl 4:25
Baptism, which c to this, now saves | 1Pt 3:21

CORRODED

your silver and gold are c, | Jms 5:3

CORRUPT (adj)

the earth was c in God's sight, | Gn 6:11
one who is revolting and c, | Jb 15:16
They are c; | Ps 14:1; 53:1
all alike have become c. | Ps 14:3
all of them are c. | Jr 6:28
Be saved from this c generation! | Ac 2:40
men who are c in mind, | 2Tm 3:8

CORRUPT (v)

splendor you c-ed your wisdom. | Ezk 28:17
They have deeply c-ed themselves as | Hs 9:9
Bad company c-s good morals. | 1Co 15:33

the old man that is c-ed | Eph 4:22
prostitute who c-ed the earth with | Rv 19:2

CORRUPTIBLE
Because this c must be clothed | 1Co 15:53

CORRUPTION
they could find no charge or c, | Dn 6:4
set free from the bondage of c | Rm 8:21
Sown in c, raised in | 1Co 15:42
flesh will reap c from the flesh | Gl 6:8
escaping the c that is in the | 2Pt 1:4
themselves are slaves of c, | 2Pt 2:19

COSMETICS
perfumes and c for {another} six | Est 2:12

COST
sinned at the c of their own lives, | Nm 16:38
{at the c of} his firstborn | Jos 6:26
offerings that c {me} nothing. | 2Sm 24:24
request at the c of his life. | 1Kg 2:23
At the c of Abiram his firstborn | 1Kg 16:34
offerings that c {me} nothing. | 1Ch 21:24
The c is to be paid from the | Ezr 6:4
keeps his word whatever the c, | Ps 15:4
know it will c him his life. | Pr 7:23
without money and without c! | Is 55:1
calculate the c to see if he has | Lk 14:28

COUCH
falling on the c where Esther | Est 7:8
sprawled out on their c-es, | Am 6:4

COUNCIL
May I never enter their c; | Gn 49:6
feared in the c of the holy ones | Ps 89:7
praise Him in the c of the elders. | Ps 107:32
who has stood in the c of the LORD | Jr 23:18
Festus conferred with his c, | Ac 25:12
on of hands by the c of elders. | 1Tm 4:14

COUNSEL (n)
but did not seek the LORD's c. | Jos 9:14
please turn the c of Ahithophel | 2Sm 15:31
used to say, 'Seek c in Abel,' | 2Sm 20:18
c and understanding are His. | Jb 12:13
The c of the wicked is far from me! | Jb 21:16
obscures {My} c with ignorant | Jb 38:2
The secret c of the LORD is for | Ps 25:14
with My eye on you, I will give c. | Ps 32:8
frustrates the c of the nations | Ps 33:10
The c of the LORD stands forever | Ps 33:11

and would not wait for His c. | Ps 106:13
despised the c of the Most High | Ps 107:11
neglected all my c and did not | Pr 1:25
whoever listens to c is wise. | Pr 12:15
Plans fail when there is no c, | Pr 15:22
Listen to c and receive | Pr 19:20
Finalize plans through c, and wage | Pr 20:18
and no c {will prevail} against | Pr 21:30
LORD, or who gave Him His c? | Is 40:13
let them take c together. | Is 45:21
or c from the wise, | Jr 18:18
the One great in c and mighty in | Jr 32:19
Has c perished from the prudent | Jr 49:7
will be ashamed of its c. | Hs 10:6
revealing His c to His servants | Am 3:7

COUNSEL (v)
will praise the LORD who c-s me | Ps 16:7

COUNSELOR
Ahithophel was the king's c. | 1Ch 27:33
king and his c-s have willingly | Ezr 7:15
The king and his c-s approved the | Est 1:21
the kings and c-s of the earth, | Jb 3:14
He leads c-s away barefoot and | Jb 12:17
but with many c-s there is | Pr 11:14
victory comes with many c-s. | Pr 24:6
He will be named Wonderful C, | Is 9:6
you another C to be with you | Jn 14:16
But the C, the Holy Spirit—the | Jn 14:26
When the C comes, the One I | Jn 15:26
go away the C will not come to | Jn 16:7
Or who has been His c? | Rm 11:34

COUNT
so that if one could c the dust | Gn 13:16
c the stars, if you are able to c them. | Gn 15:5
this will be c-ed as righteousness | Dt 24:13
c {the people of} Israel and | 2Sm 24:1
temple and c the money found | 2Kg 12:10
incited David to c {the people | 1Ch 21:1
I can c all my bones; | Ps 22:17
we are c-ed as sheep to be | Ps 44:22
I am c-ed among those going down | Ps 88:4
and let his prayer be c-ed as sin. | Ps 109:7
If I c-ed them, they would | Ps 139:18
He c-s the number of the stars; | Ps 147:4
what is lacking cannot be c-ed. | Ec 1:15
and was c-ed among the rebels; | Is 53:12
hosts of heaven cannot be c-ed; | Jr 33:22

of the earth are c-ed as nothing,	Dn 4:35
of your head have all been c-ed.	Mt 10:30
And He was c-ed among outlaws.	Mk 15:28
that they were c-ed worthy to be	Ac 5:41
we are c-ed as sheep to be	Rm 8:36
not c-ing their trespasses against	2Co 5:19
May it not be c-ed against them.	2Tm 4:16

COUNTLESS

How c are Your works, LORD!	Ps 104:24
even if you offer c prayers,	Is 1:15
Their number was c thousands,	Rv 5:11

COUNTRY

in the city and blessed in the c.	Dt 28:3
in the city and cursed in the c.	Dt 28:16
heard in my own c about your	1Kg 10:6
and gather you from all the c-ies,	Ezk 36:24
while I was still in my own c?	Jnh 4:2
and traveled to a distant c,	Lk 15:13
who are in the c must not enter	Lk 21:21
has no honor in his own c.	Jn 4:44
would be aliens in a foreign c,	Ac 7:6
in the city, dangers in the open c,	2Co 11:26

COUNTRYMEN

not be exalted above his c,	Dt 17:20
is charging his c interest.	Neh 5:7
brothers, my c by physical descent.	Rm 9:3

COUNTRYSIDE

into the open c outside the city	Lv 14:53
surrounding c and villages to	Mk 6:36
disciples went to the Judean c,	Jn 3:22

COURAGE

and everyone's c failed because	Jos 2:11
has found the c to pray this	2Sm 7:27
he took c and removed the	2Ch 15:8
their c melting away in anguish	Ps 107:26
Have c, son, your sins	Mt 9:2
"Have c, daughter," He said.	Mt 9:22
Have c! It is I. Don't be afraid.	Mt 14:27
stood by him and said, "Have c!	Ac 23:11
take c, men, because I believe God	Ac 27:25
we hold on to the c and the	Heb 3:6

COURAGEOUS

Be c. Bring back some fruit	Nm 13:20
Be strong and c; don't be	Dt 31:6
Be strong and c, for you will go	Jos 1:6
Be strong and c, for the LORD	Jos 10:25

be strong and c, for though Saul	2Sm 2:7
Be strong and c!	2Sm 13:28
Be strong and c, and do the work	1Ch 28:20
Be strong and c!	2Ch 32:7
be c and let your heart be strong.	Ps 27:14
Be strong and c, all you who put	Ps 31:24
Be c! I have conquered the world.	Jn 16:33

COURIERS

So the c went throughout Israel	2Ch 30:6
were sent by c to each of the	Est 3:13

COURSE

of the Jordan resumed their c,	Jos 4:18
like an athlete running a c.	Ps 19:5
The c of my life is in Your	Ps 31:15
keep your mind on the right c.	Pr 23:19
has stayed his c like a horse	Jr 8:6
and they do not change their c.	Jl 2:7
I may finish my c and the	Ac 20:24
sets the c of life on fire,	Jms 3:6

COURT

If one wanted to take Him to c,	Jb 9:3
a day in Your c-s than a thousand	Ps 84:10
an offering and enter His c-s.	Ps 96:8
and His c-s with praise.	Ps 100:4
in the c-s of the LORD's house	Ps 116:19
in the c-s of the house of our God	Ps 135:2
Don't take a matter to c hastily.	Pr 25:8
If a wise man goes to c with a fool,	Pr 29:9
{this} trampling of My c-s?	Is 1:12
Take Me to c; let us argue our	Is 43:26
The c was convened, and the books	Dn 7:10
the c-s are in session,	Ac 19:38
you and drag you into the c-s?	Jms 2:6

COURTYARD

make the c for the tabernacle.	Ex 27:9
He had a well in his c,	2Sm 17:18
Stand in the c of the LORD's	Jr 26:2
confined in the guard's c,	Jr 33:1
was confined in the guard's c:	Jr 39:15
Peter was sitting outside in the c.	Mt 26:69
led Him away into the c	Mk 15:16
Jesus into the high priest's c.	Jn 18:15

COUSIN

His uncle or c may redeem him,	Lv 25:49
married c-s on their father's side	Nm 36:11

guardian of his c Hadassah	Est 2:7
Mark, Barnabas' c	Col 4:10

COVENANT

I will establish My c with you,	Gn 6:18
I am confirming My c with you	Gn 9:9
is the sign of the c I am making	Gn 9:12
the LORD made a c with Abram,	Gn 15:18
My c will be in your flesh	Gn 17:13
the two of them made a c.	Gn 21:27
Let us make a c with you:	Gn 26:28
remembered His c with Abraham,	Ex 2:24
carefully keep My c,	Ex 19:5
must not make a c with them	Ex 23:32
then took the c scroll and read	Ex 24:7
generations as a perpetual c.	Ex 31:16
Look, I am making a c.	Ex 34:10
and confirm My c with you.	Lv 26:9
will remember My c with Jacob.	Lv 26:42
with the ark of the LORD's c	Nm 10:33
I grant him My c of peace.	Nm 25:12
our God made a c with us at	Dt 5:2
Joshua made a c for the people	Jos 24:25
will never break My c with you.	Jdg 2:1
not to make a c with the people	Jdg 2:2
has violated My c that I made	Jdg 2:20
Jonathan made a c with David	1Sm 18:3
Jonathan made a c with the house	1Sm 20:16
King David made a c with them at	2Sm 5:3
keeping the gracious c with Your	1Kg 8:23
because of His c with Abraham,	2Kg 13:23
They rejected ... His c	2Kg 17:15
book of the c that had been found	2Kg 23:2
Remember His c forever	1Ch 16:15
forever by a c of salt?	2Ch 13:5
Let us ... make a c before our God	Ezr 10:3
His gracious c with those who	Neh 1:5
the c of the priesthood	Neh 13:29
I have made a c with my eyes.	Jb 31:1
and He reveals His c to them.	Ps 25:14
and to take My c on your lips?	Ps 50:16
they were unfaithful to His c.	Ps 78:37
I have made a c with My chosen	Ps 89:3
I will not violate My c or change	Ps 89:34
who keep His c, who remember to	Ps 103:18
He forever remembers His c,	Ps 105:8
He remembers His c forever.	Ps 111:5

and broken the everlasting c.	Is 24:5
I make you a c for the people	Is 42:6
make an everlasting c with them.	Is 61:8
Obey the words of this c	Jr 11:6
Judah broke My c	Jr 11:10
I will make a new c with	Jr 31:31
If you can break My c with the day	Jr 33:20
an everlasting c that will never	Jr 50:5
I will establish an everlasting c	Ezk 16:60
heart will be set against the holy c;	Dn 11:28
He makes a c with Assyria,	Hs 12:1
because of the blood of your c,	Zch 9:11
partner and your wife by c.	Mal 2:14
Messenger of the c you desire	Mal 3:1
and remembered His holy c	Lk 1:72
This cup is the new c	Lk 22:20
You are the sons ... of the c	Ac 3:25
gave him the c of circumcision	Ac 7:8
the adoption, the glory, the c-s,	Rm 9:4
this will be My c with them,	Rm 11:27
This cup is the new c in My blood	1Co 11:25
to be ministers of a new c,	2Co 3:6
at the reading of the old c,	2Co 3:14
does not revoke a c that was	Gl 3:17
the women represent the two c-s.	Gl 4:24
to the c-s of the promise,	Eph 2:12
the guarantee of a better c.	Heb 7:22
He is the mediator of a better c,	Heb 8:6
not like the c that I made with	Heb 8:9
He is the mediator of a new c,	Heb 9:15
first c was inaugurated with blood.	Heb 9:18
the blood of the c that God has	Heb 9:20
the blood of the everlasting c,	Heb 13:20
the ark of His c appeared in His	Rv 11:19

COVER (n)

For it is his only c-ing;	Ex 22:27
Make a c-ing for the tent from ram skins ... and a c-ing of manatee skins	Ex 26:14
wife took the c, placed it over	2Sm 17:19
formed a c above the ark	2Ch 5:8
He spread a cloud as a c-ing	Ps 105:39
I've spread c-ing-s on my bed	Pr 7:16
sees danger and takes c,	Pr 22:3
She makes her own bed c-ing-s;	Pr 31:22
Then a lead c was lifted, and	Zch 5:7
hair is given to her as a c-ing.	1Co 11:15

COVER (v)

darkness c-ed the surface of the	Gn 1:2

and c it with pitch inside and | Gn 6:14
water c-ed the earth. | Gn 7:6
they c-ed their father's nakedness | Gn 9:23
our brother and c up his blood? | Gn 37:26
the rock and c you with My hand | Ex 33:22
its blood and c it with dirt. | Lv 17:13
c them with ... manatee skin | Nm 4:8
Although they c-ed him with | 1Kg 1:1
Do not c their guilt | Neh 4:5
and You would c over my iniquity | Jb 14:17
hide me under the c of His tent; | Ps 27:5
is forgiven, whose sin is c-ed! | Ps 32:1
shame has c-ed my face | Ps 44:15; 69:7
violence c-s them like a garment. | Ps 73:6
C their faces with shame so that | Ps 83:16
You c-ed all their sin. | Ps 85:2
He will c you with His feathers | Ps 91:4
His majesty c-s heaven and earth. | Ps 148:13
but love c-s all offenses. | Pr 10:12
Your hands are c-ed with blood. | Is 1:15
with two he c-ed his face, with two | Is 6:2
c-ed you in the shadow of My hand, | Is 51:16
cannot c themselves with their works. | Is 59:6
For look, darkness c-s the earth | Is 60:2
let our disgrace c us. | Jr 3:25
You have c-ed Yourself in anger | Lm 3:43
and two wings c-ing its body. | Ezk 1:11
say to the mountains, "C us!" | Hs 10:8
must be c-ed with sackcloth, | Jnh 3:8
as the waters c the sea. | Hab 2:14
His splendor c-s the heavens, | Hab 3:3
you c the LORD's altar with tears, | Mal 2:13
he c-s his garment with injustice | Mal 2:16
there is nothing c-ed that won't be | Mt 10:26
and to the hills, 'C us!' | Lk 23:30
forgiven and whose sins are c-ed! | Rm 4:7
if a woman's head is not c-ed, | 1Co 11:6
man, in fact, should not c his head | 1Co 11:7
and c a multitude of sins. | Jms 5:20
since love c-s a multitude of sins | 1Pt 4:8

COVET

Do not c your neighbor's | Ex 20:17
No one will c your land when you | Ex 34:24
or c your neighbor's house, | Dt 5:21
shekels, I c-ed them and took them. | Jos 7:21
They c fields and seize them; | Mc 2:2
I have not c-ed anyone's silver | Ac 20:33
what it is to c if the law had not | Rm 7:7

you shall not steal, you shall not c, | Rm 13:9
You murder and c and cannot | Jms 4:2

COVETING

produced in me c of every kind. | Rm 7:8

COW

seven other c-s, sickly and thin | Gn 41:3
red c that has ... never been yoked. | Nm 19:2
get a c that has not been yoked | Dt 21:3
hadn't plowed with my young c, | Jdg 14:18
Hitch the c-s to the cart, but | 1Sm 6:7
The c and the bear will graze, | Is 11:7
Egypt is a beautiful young c, | Jr 46:20
as obstinate as a stubborn c. | Hs 4:16
young c that loves to thresh, | Hs 10:11
you c-s of Bashan who are on the | Am 4:1

COWARDS

But the c, unbelievers, vile, | Rv 21:8

CO-WORKERS

For we are God's c. | 1Co 3:9
that we can be c with the truth | 3Jn 8

COZBI

Midianite woman slain to end a plague (Nm 25:15,18).

CRACKED

c cisterns that cannot hold | Jr 2:13
The ground is c since no rain | Jr 14:4

CRAFT

and ability in every c | Ex 31:3
and ability in every kind of c | Ex 35:31

CRAFTINESS

He traps the wise in their c | Jb 5:13
He catches the wise in their c | 1Co 3:19

CRAFTS

He alone c their hearts; | Ps 33:15

CRAFTSMAN

I have placed wisdom within every skilled c | Ex 31:6
carved idol ... the work of a c, | Dt 27:15
all the c-men and metal smiths. | 2Kg 24:14
Valley of C-men | 1Ch 4:14; Neh 11:35
I was a skilled c beside Him. | Pr 8:30
for a skilled c to set up an idol | Is 40:20
I have created the c | Is 54:16
a goldsmith, the work of a c. | Jr 10:9

a c made it, and it, and it is not God. Hs 8:6
all of them the work of c-men. Hs 13:2
the LORD showed me four c-men. Zch 1:20
business for the c-men. Ac 19:24
no c ... will ever be found in you Rv 18:22

CRAFTY
He frustrates the schemes of the c Jb 5:12

CRAG
its stronghold is on a rocky c. Jb 39:28
snow ... ever leave the highland c-s? Jr 18:14

CRAVE
people who had c-d {the meat}. Nm 11:34
for He gave them what they c-d. Ps 78:29
denies the wicked what they c. Pr 10:3
The slacker c-s, yet has nothing Pr 13:4
by c-ing it, some have wandered 1Tm 6:10
The fruit you c-d has left you. Rv 18:14

CRAVING (n)
people among them had a strong c Nm 11:4
a slacker's c will kill him Pr 21:25
over in the c-s of their hearts Rm 1:24
come from the c-s that are at war Jms 4:1

CRAWL
creatures that c on the ground Gn 1:25
creature that c-s on the ground. Lv 11:44

CRAZY
the man is c," Achish said 1Sm 21:14
Why did this c person come 2Kg 9:11
He has a demon and He's c! Jn 10:20
"You're c!" they told her. Ac 12:15

CREAM
when my feet were bathed in c Jb 29:6

CREATE
In the beginning God c-d the heavens Gn 1:1
God c-d man in His own image; Gn 1:27
On the day that God c-d man, Gn 5:1
You c-d the heavens, Neh 9:6
c a clean heart for me Ps 51:10
North and south—You c-d them. Ps 89:12
a newly c-d people will praise Ps 102:18
send Your breath, they are c-d, Ps 104:30
You who c-d my inward parts Ps 139:13
He commanded, and they were c-d. Ps 148:5
the One who c-d it long ago. Is 22:11
Look up and see: who c-d these? Is 40:26

who c-d the heavens and stretched Is 42:5
everyone called by My name and
  c-d for My glory. Is 43:7
I form light and c darkness, Is 45:7
I, the LORD, have c-d it. Is 45:8
the earth, and c-d man on it. Is 45:12
He did not c it to be empty, Is 45:18
For I will c a new heaven and Is 65:17
For the LORD c-s something new Jr 31:22
forms the mountains, c-s the wind Am 4:13
Didn't one God c us? Mal 2:10
He who c-d them in the beginning Mt 19:4
the world, which God c-d, Mk 13:19
All things were c-d through Him, Jn 1:3
the world was c-d through Him, Jn 1:10
served something c-d instead Rm 1:25
nor any other c-d thing will have Rm 8:39
man was not c-d for woman, 1Co 11:9
c-d in Christ Jesus for good works Eph 2:10
c in Himself one new man from Eph 2:15
in God who c-d all things. Eph 3:9
c d according to God's likeness in Eph 4:24
by Him everything was c-d, Col 1:16
things have been c-d through Him Col 1:16
For Adam was c-d first, then Eve. 1Tm 2:13
everything c-d by God is good, 1Tm 4:4
the universe was c-d by the word Heb 11:3
can be shaken—that is, c-d things Heb 12:27
You have c-d all things,
  and because of Your will
  they ... were c-d. Rv 4:11
who c-d heaven and what is in it, Rv 10:6

CREATION
He rested from His work of c. Gn 2:3
me at the beginning of His c, Pr 8:22
the beginning of c God made them Mk 10:6
the gospel to the whole c. Mk 16:15
From the c of the world His Rm 1:20
For the c eagerly waits with Rm 8:19
For the c was subjected to Rm 8:20
is in Christ, there is a new c; 2Co 5:17
{what matters} instead is a new c. Gl 6:15
For we are His c—created in Eph 2:10
the firstborn over all c; Col 1:15
gospel has been proclaimed in all c Col 1:23
been since the beginning of c. 2Pt 3:4

CREATOR
God Most High, C of heaven and Gn 14:22

Isn't He your Father and C?	Dt 32:6
So remember your C in the days	Ec 12:1
God, the C of the whole earth.	Is 40:28
Holy One, the C of Israel,	Is 43:15
God is the C of the heavens.	Is 45:18
created instead of the C,	Rm 1:25
to the image of his C.	Col 3:10
themselves to a faithful C.	1Pt 4:19

CREATURE

and every living c that moves	Gn 1:21
the man called a living c,	Gn 2:19
Every living c will be food for	Gn 9:3
life of every c is its blood,	Lv 17:14
may eat every clean flying c.	Dt 14:20
the c-s of the field are Mine	Ps 50:11
the earth is full of Your c-s.	Ps 104:24
He gives food to every c.	Ps 136:25
a winged c may report the matter.	Ec 10:20
four living c-s came from it.	Ezk 1:5
the living c-s I had seen	Ezk 10:15
No c is hidden from Him,	Heb 4:13
be the firstfruits of His c-s.	Jms 1:18
For every c—animal or bird	Jms 3:7
c-s of instinct born to be caught	2Pt 2:12
four living c-s covered with eyes	Rv 4:6
the four living c-s gave the seven	Rv 15:7

CREDIT (n)

what c is that to you?	Lk 6:32
what c is there if you endure	1Pt 2:20

CREDIT (v)

He c-ed it to him as righteousness.	Gn 15:6
It will not be c-ed to the one who	Lv 7:18
They c-ed tens of thousands to	1Sm 18:8
It was c-ed to him as righteousness	Ps 106:31
it was c-ed to him for righteousness.	Rm 4:3
to whom God c-s righteousness	Rm 4:6
It will be c-ed to us who believe	Rm 4:24
it was c-ed to him for righteousness,	Gl 3:6
it was c-ed to him for righteousness	Jms 2:23

CREDITOR

Every c is to cancel what he has	Dt 15:2
Now the c is coming to take my	2Kg 4:1
Let a c seize all he has;	Ps 109:11
Or who were My c-s that I sold you	Is 50:1

CRETANS

C and Arabs—we hear them	Ac 2:11
prophets said, C are always	Ti 1:12

CRETE

Island in the Mediterranean Sea. Paul assigned Titus as supervisor there (Ti 1:5) and moored there on his way to Rome (Ac 27).

CREVICE

put you in the c of the rock	Ex 33:22
the rock, in the c-s of the cliff	Sg 2:14
rocks and the c-s in the cliffs,	Is 2:21

CRIME

What is my c?" he said to Laban	Gn 31:36
would be a c deserving punishment.	Jb 31:11
C and trouble are within it;	Ps 55:10
They devise c-s	Ps 64:6
sinner commits c a hundred times	Ec 8:12
is filled with c-s of bloodshed,	Ezk 7:23
not committed a c against you	Dn 6:22
punishing Damascus for three c-s,	Am 1:3
For I know your c-s are many and	Am 5:12
and God has remembered her c-s.	Rv 18:5

CRIMINAL

against a c act is not carried out	Ec 8:11
as if I were a c, to capture Me	Mt 26:55
Then two c-s were crucified with	Mt 27:38
and clubs as if I were a c?	Lk 22:52
man weren't a c, we wouldn't	Jn 18:30
point of being bound like a c;	2Tm 2:9

CRIMSON

hyssop, and c yarn,	Nm 19:6
with purple, c, and blue yarn.	2Ch 2:7
though they are as red as c,	Is 1:18
from Edom in c-stained garments	Is 63:1

CRIPPLED

had a son whose feet were c.	2Sm 4:4

CRISPUS

A leader of the synagogue in Corinth whom Paul baptized (Ac 18:8; 1Co 1:14).

CRITICIZE

Miriam and Aaron c-d Moses	Nm 12:1
not eat must not c one who does,	Rm 14:3
Who are you to c another's servant?	Rm 14:4
why do you c your brother?	Rm 14:10
all generously and without c-ing,	Jms 1:5

Don't c one another, brothers. Jms 4:11
who c-s a brother ... c-s the law Jms 4:11

CROOKED

a devious and c generation. Dt 32:5
with the c You prove 2Sm 22:27; Ps 18:26
those who turn aside to c ways, Ps 125:5
A guilty man's conduct is c, Pr 21:8
snares on the path of the c; Pr 22:5
What is c cannot be straightened Ec 1:15
out what He has made c? Ec 7:13
They have made their roads c; Is 59:8
He has made my paths c. Lm 3:9
the c will become straight, Lk 3:5
faultless in a c and perverted Php 2:15

CROP

a c sufficient for three years. Lv 25:21
they ate from the c-s of the land Jos 5:12
He gave their c-s to the caterpillar Ps 78:46
and our land will yield its c-s. Ps 85:12
and {provides} c-s for man to Ps 104:14
though the olive c fails and the Hab 3:17
rain and c-s in the field Zch 10:1
good ground, and produced a c; Mt 13:8
have anywhere to store my c-s? Lk 12:17
it dies, it produces a large c. Jn 12:24
do so in hope of sharing the c. 1Co 9:10
first to get a share of the c-s. 2Tm 2:6

CROSS (n)

doesn't take up his c and follow Mt 10:38
take up his c, and follow Me. Mt 16:24
forced this man to carry His c. Mt 27:32
come down from the c! Mt 27:40
take up his c daily, and follow Lk 9:23
bear his own c and come after Lk 14:27
those from there c over to us. Lk 16:26
Carrying His own c, He went out Jn 19:17
Standing by the c of Jesus were Jn 19:25
so that the c of Christ will not 1Co 1:17
message of the c is foolishness 1Co 1:18
offense of the c has been Gl 5:11
persecuted for the c of Christ. Gl 6:12
except the c of our Lord Jesus Gl 6:14
reconcile both ... through the c Eph 2:16
death—even to death on a c. Php 2:8
as enemies of the c of Christ. Php 3:18
through the blood of His c Col 1:20
the way by nailing it to the c. Col 2:14
joy that lay before Him endured a c Heb 12:2

CROSS (v)

I c-ed over this Jordan with my Gn 32:10
and c-ing his hands, put Gn 48:14
Don't make us c the Jordan. Nm 32:5
for you will not c this Jordan. Dt 3:27
Today you are about to c the Jordan Dt 9:1
your God will c over ahead of you Dt 9:3
broke camp to c the Jordan, Jos 3:14
while all Israel c-ed on dry ground Jos 3:17
said, "Let me c over," the Jdg 12:5
let's c over to the garrison of 1Sm 14:6
the two of them c-ed over on dry 2Kg 2:8
they will c the river {of death} Jb 36:12
set a boundary they cannot c; Ps 104:9
C over to Tarshish; Is 23:6
barrier that it cannot c? Jr 5:22
C over to Calneh and see; Am 6:2
C over to Macedonia and help us Ac 16:9
he wanted to c over to Achaia, Ac 18:27

CROSSBREED

You must not c two different Lv 19:19

CROSS-EXAMINE

until another comes and c-s him. Pr 18:17
fiercely and to c Him about many Lk 11:53

CROSSROADS

road, at the c, she takes her Pr 8:2

CROUCH

sin is c-ing at the door. Gn 4:7
he c-es; he lies down like a lion Gn 49:9
He c-es, he lies down like a lion Nm 24:9
They c down to give birth to Jb 39:3
nothing to do} except c among Is 10:4
Bel c-es; Nebo cowers. Is 46:1

CROW

the rooster c-s, you will deny Me Mt 26:34
Immediately a rooster c-ed. Mt 26:74
or at the c-ing of the rooster Mk 13:35
before the rooster c-s twice, Mk 14:30
and a rooster c-ed. Mk 14:68
rooster will not c today until Lk 22:34
still speaking, a rooster c-ed. Lk 22:60
rooster will not c until Jn 13:38
Immediately a rooster c-ed. Jn 18:27

CROWD

ethnically diverse c also went Ex 12:38
not follow a c in wrongdoing. Ex 23:2

I hate a c of evildoers,	Ps 26:5
walked with the c into the house	Ps 55:14
Large c-s followed Him	Mt 4:25
he feared the c, since they	Mt 14:5
He saw a huge c, felt compassion	Mt 14:14
Send the c-s away so they can go	Mt 14:15
I have compassion on the c,	Mt 15:32
a large c followed Him.	Mt 20:29
The c told them to keep quiet,	Mt 20:31
afraid of the c, because	Mt 21:26
they feared the c-s, because they	Mt 21:46
persuaded the c-s to ask for	Mt 27:20
him to Jesus because of the c,	Mk 2:4
Him in the c and touched His	Mk 5:27
while He dismissed the c.	Mk 6:45
Summoning the c again, He told	Mk 7:14
into the house away from the c,	Mk 7:17
stirred up the c so that he	Mk 15:11
through the c and went on His	Lk 4:30
was a large c of tax collectors	Lk 5:29
Who do the c-s say that I am?	Lk 9:18
spoke, and the c-s were amazed.	Lk 11:14
a c of many thousands came	Lk 12:1
was not able because of the c,	Lk 19:3
them when the c was not present	Lk 22:6
stirred up the c and the city	Ac 17:8

CROWDED

the city (once) c with people!	Lm 1:1

CROWN (n)

on the c of the prince of his	Gn 49:26
He took the c from the head of	2Sm 12:30
king's son, put the c on him,	2Kg 11:12
placed the royal c on her head	Est 2:17
You place a c of pure gold on	Ps 21:3
completely dishonored his c.	Ps 89:39
she will give you a c of beauty.	Pr 4:9
wife is her husband's c,	Pr 12:4
The c of the wise is their	Pr 14:24
Gray hair is a glorious c;	Pr 16:31
are the c of the elderly,	Pr 17:6
not even a c lasts for all time	Pr 27:24
to the majestic c of Ephraim's	Is 28:1
to give them a c of beauty	Is 61:3
The c has fallen from our head.	Lm 5:16
they are like jewels in a c,	Zch 9:16
twisted together a c of thorns,	Mt 27:29
twisted together a c of thorns,	Mk 15:17
twisted together a c of thorns,	Jn 19:2

came out wearing the c of thorns	Jn 19:5
it to receive a perishable c,	1Co 9:25
my joy and c, stand firm	Php 4:1
or c of boasting in the presence	1Th 2:19
for me the c of righteousness,	2Tm 4:8
receive the c of life that He	Jms 1:12
the unfading c of glory.	1Pt 5:4
I will give you the c of life.	Rv 2:10
so that no one takes your c.	Rv 3:11
cast their c-s before the throne,	Rv 4:10
a c was given to him, and he	Rv 6:2
and a c of 12 stars on her head	Rv 12:1
with a gold c on His head	Rv 14:14
on His head were many c-s.	Rv 19:12

CROWN (v)

than God and c-ed him with glory	Ps 8:5
He c-s you with faithful love	Ps 103:4
sensible are c-ed with knowledge.	Pr 14:18
Your head c-s you like Mount	Sg 7:5
he is not c-ed unless he competes	2Tm 2:5
You c-ed him with glory and honor	Heb 2:7

CRUCIBLE

A c is for silver and a smelter	Pr 17:3
Silver is (tested) in a c,	Pr 27:21

CRUCIFY see also RECRUCIFYING

to be mocked, flogged, and c-ied,	Mt 20:19
Some of them you will kill and c,	Mt 23:34
will be handed over to be c-ied.	Mt 26:2
But they kept shouting, "C Him!"	Mt 27:23
and led Him away to c Him.	Mt 27:31
two criminals were c-ied with Him,	Mt 27:38
looking for Jesus who was c-ied.	Mt 28:5
be c-ied, and rise on the third day	Lk 24:7
Take Him and c Him yourselves,	Jn 19:6
to them, "Should I c your king?	Jn 19:15
they c-ied Him and two others	Jn 19:18
Jesus, whom you c-ied, both Lord	Ac 2:36
you c-ied and whom God raised	Ac 4:10
our old self was c-ied with Him in	Rm 6:6
Was it Paul who was c-ied for you?	1Co 1:13
we preach Christ c-ied,	
a stumbling	1Co 1:23
except Jesus Christ and Him c-ied.	1Co 2:2
would not have c-ied the Lord of	1Co 2:8
In fact, He was c-ied in weakness	2Co 13:4
I have been c-ied with Christ;	Gl 2:19
was vividly portrayed as c-ied?	Gl 3:1

CRUDE

Jesus have c-ied the flesh with	Gl 5:24
the world has been c-ied to me,	Gl 6:14
where also their Lord was c-ied.	Rv 11:8

CRUDE

or c joking are not suitable,	Eph 5:4

CRUEL

and your years to someone c;	Pr 5:9
but a c man brings disaster on	Pr 11:17
merciful acts of the wicked are c.	Pr 12:10
like fish caught in a c net,	Ec 9:12
are c and show no mercy.	Jr 6:23; 50:42
have become c like ostriches	Lm 4:3

CRUMBS

the dogs eat the c that fall	Mt 15:27
the table eat the children's c.	Mk 7:28

CRUSH

For He c-es but also binds up;	Jb 5:18
that a foot may c them	Jb 39:15
I c them, and they cannot get up	Ps 18:38
the bones You have c rejoice.	Ps 51:8
Surely God c-es the heads of His	Ps 68:21
the poor, and c the oppressor.	Ps 72:4
You c the heads of Leviathan;	Ps 74:14
You c Rahab like one who is	Ps 89:10
LORD, they c Your people;	Ps 94:5
He will c kings on the day of	Ps 110:5
and don't c the oppressed at the	Pr 22:22
lying tongue hates those it c-es,	Pr 26:28
Why do you c My people and grind	Is 3:15
c because of our iniquities;	Is 53:5
the LORD was pleased to c Him,	Is 53:10
It will c and smash all the others.	Dn 2:40
and c all their bones.	Dn 6:24
the poor and c the needy,	Am 4:1
will soon c Satan under your feet.	Rm 16:20

CRUSHED (adj)

rash, scabs, or a c testicle.	Lv 21:20
He saves those c in spirit.	Ps 34:18
I am faint and severely c;	Ps 38:8
in every way but not c;	2Co 4:8

CRUST

Better a dry c with peace than a	Pr 17:1

CRY (n)

for their c has come to Me.	1Sm 9:16
and my c for help {reached} His	2Sm 22:7
may hear the c and the prayer	1Kg 8:28
attention to the sound of my c,	Ps 5:2
attention to my c; listen to my	Ps 17:1
His ears are open to their c for help.	Ps 34:15
and listen to my c for help;	Ps 39:12
turned to me and heard my c for help	Ps 40:1
God, hear my c; pay attention to	Ps 61:1
heart and flesh c out for the	Ps 84:2
I c out before You day and night	Ps 88:1
He heard their c, He took note	Ps 106:44
Let my c reach You, LORD;	Ps 119:169
be attentive to my c for help.	Ps 130:2
He hears their c for help and	Ps 145:19
his ears to the c of the poor	Pr 21:13
Do not ignore my c for relief.	Lm 3:56

CRY (v)

Your brother's blood c-ies out to Me	Gn 4:10
difficult labor, and they c-ied out;	Ex 2:23
Moses c-ied out to the LORD for help	Ex 8:12
Why are you c-ing out to Me?	Ex 14:15
they will no doubt c to Me,	Ex 22:23
because you c-ied before the LORD	Nm 11:18
When we c-ied out to the LORD,	Nm 20:16
she did not c out in the city	Dt 22:24
The Israelites c-ied out to the LORD	Jdg 3:9
Israelites c-ied out to	Jdg 3:15; 4:3; 6:6
so they c-ied out to the LORD,	Jdg 10:10
Hannah, why are you c-ing?	1Sm 1:8
Don't stop c-ing out to the LORD	1Sm 7:8
so they c-ied out to the LORD.	2Ch 13:14
poor man who c-ied out for help,	Jb 29:12
I c aloud to the LORD, and He	Ps 3:4
and I c-ied to my God for help.	Ps 18:6
They c for help, but there is no	Ps 18:41
My God, I c by day, but You do	Ps 22:2
They c-ied to You and were set free	Ps 22:5
when he c-ied to Him for help	Ps 22:24
LORD my God, I c-ied to You for help	Ps 30:2
when I c-ied to You for help	Ps 31:22
This poor man c-ied, and the LORD	Ps 34:6
Then they c-ied out to	Ps 107:6,13,19,28
I c aloud to the LORD; I plead	Ps 142:1
She c-ies out above the commotion;	Pr 1:21
the main entrance, she c-ies out:	Pr 8:3
A voice of one c-ing out:	Is 40:3
A voice was saying, "C out!"	Is 40:6
He will not c out or shout or	Is 42:2
C out loudly, don't hold back!	Is 58:1

and each c-ied out to his god. | Jnh 1:5
I c-ied out for help in the belly of | Jnh 2:2
Then they will c out to the LORD | Mc 3:4
or c out to You about violence | Hab 1:2
the stones will c out from the wall, | Hab 2:11
A voice of one c-ing out in the | Mt 3:3
Jesus c-ied out with a loud | Mt 27:46
on her and said, "Don't c." | Lk 7:13
He said, "Stop c-ing, for she is not | Lk 8:52
His elect who c out to Him day | Lk 18:7
silent, the stones would c out! | Lk 19:40
I am a voice of one c-ing out in | Jn 1:23
Woman, why are you c-ing? | Jn 20:13
he c-ied out in the Sanhedrin, | Ac 23:6
who reaped your fields c-ies out, | Jms 5:4
I c-ied and c-ied because no one | Rv 5:4

CRYING (n)
I am weary from my c; | Ps 69:3
My eyes are worn out from c. | Ps 88:9
grief, c, and pain will exist no | Rv 21:4

CRYPTIC
her forehead a c name was | Rv 17:5

CRYSTAL
a gleam like awe-inspiring c, | Ezk 1:22
a sea of glass, similar to c. | Rv 4:6
a jasper stone, bright as c. | Rv 21:11
water, sparkling like c, flowing | Rv 22:1

CUBIT
you add a single c to his height | Mt 6:27
any of you add a c to his height | Lk 12:25

CUBS
a wild bear robbed of her c. | 2Sm 17:8
robbed of her c than a fool in | Pr 17:12

CUD
hooves and that chews the c. | Lv 11:3
not chew the c are unclean for | Lv 11:26
divided in two and chews the c. | Dt 14:6

CULT
Where is the c prostitute who | Gn 38:21
No Israelite ... is to be a c prostitute | Dt 23:17

CULTIVATE
flock, but Cain c-d the land. | Gn 4:2
will plant and c vineyards but | Dt 28:39
useful to those it is c-d for, | Heb 6:7

CULTIVATED (adj)
grafted into a c olive tree, | Rm 11:24

CUMIN
mint, dill, and c, yet you have | Mt 23:23

CUNNING
was the most c of all the wild | Gn 3:1
serpent deceived Eve by his c, | 2Co 11:3
by human c with cleverness in | Eph 4:14

CUP
and the c was found in | Gn 44:12
food and drank from his c; | 2Sm 12:3
drinking c-s were gold, | 1Kg 10:21
head with oil; my c overflows. | Ps 23:5
For there is a c in the LORD's | Ps 75:8
I will take the c of salvation | Ps 116:13
it gleams in the c and goes down | Pr 23:31
who have drunk the c of His fury | Is 51:17
A c of consolation won't be | Jr 16:7
Take this c of the wine of | Jr 25:15
not deserve to drink the c must | Jr 49:12
Yet the c will pass to you as | Lm 4:21
You will drink your sister's c, | Ezk 23:32
gives just a c of cold water to | Mt 10:42
to drink the c that I am about | Mt 20:22
clean the inside of the c, | Mt 23:26
Then He took a c, and after | Mt 26:27
let this c pass from Me. | Mt 26:39
This c is the new covenant | Lk 22:20
cannot drink the c of the Lord and
the c of demons. | 1Co 10:21
This c is the new covenant in | 1Co 11:25
full strength in the c of His anger. | Rv 14:10
She had a gold c in her hand | Rv 17:4
In the c in which she mixed, | Rv 18:6

CUPBEARER
king of Egypt's c and his baker | Gn 40:1
attire, his c-s, and the burnt | 1Kg 10:5
I was the king's c. | Neh 1:11

CURDLE
and c me like cheese? | Jb 10:10

CURE (n)
Your pain has no c! | Jr 30:15

CURE (v)
he would c him of his skin disease. | 2Kg 5:3
But he cannot c you or heal your | Hs 5:13
word, and my servant will be c-d. | Mt 8:8

turn back—and I would c them. Mt 13:15
that moment her daughter was c-d. Mt 15:28
and c-d those who needed healing. Lk 9:11
doing good and c-ing all who were Ac 10:38
diseases also came and were c-d. Ac 28:9

CURRENT

seas, and the c overcame me. Jnh 2:3
world in its c form is passing 1Co 7:31

CURSE (n)

and I will bring a c rather than Gn 27:12
bitter water that brings a c. Nm 5:18
is to write these c-s on a scroll Nm 5:23
come and put a c on these people Nm 22:6
before you a blessing and a c: Dt 11:26
and the c at Mount Ebal. Dt 11:29
hung (on a tree) is under God's c. Dt 21:23
all these c-s will come Dt 28:15
life and death, blessing and c. Dt 30:19
blessings as well as the c-s Jos 8:34
C-ing, deceit, and violence fill his Ps 10:7
They utter c-s and lies. Ps 59:12
He loved c-ing—let it fall on him Ps 109:17
He wore c-ing like his coat—let it Ps 109:18
an undeserved c goes nowhere. Pr 26:2
eyes away will receive many c-s. Pr 28:27
he hears the c but will not Pr 29:24
name behind as a c for My chosen Is 65:15
land mourns because of the c, Jr 23:10
an object of scorn and c-ing Jr 25:18
an object of c-ing and insult among Jr 44:8
and strike the land with a c. Mal 4:6
and bound themselves under a c: Ac 23:12
is full of c-ing and bitterness. Rm 3:14
preached to you, a c be on him! Gl 1:8
works of the law are under a c, Gl 3:10
redeemed us from the c of the law
by becoming a c for us, Gl 3:13
mouth come blessing and c-ing. Jms 3:10
there will no longer be any c. Rv 22:3

CURSE (v)

will never again c the ground Gn 8:21
I will c those who treat you Gn 12:3
Those who c you will be c-d, Gn 27:29
Whoever c-s his father or his Ex 21:17
You must not c the deaf or put a Lv 19:14
If anyone c-s his father or Lv 20:9
If anyone c-s his God, he will Lv 24:15

and those you c are c-d. Nm 22:6
"C Meroz," says the Angel of the Jdg 5:23
the LORD told him, 'C David!' 2Sm 16:10
Naboth has c-d God and king! 1Kg 21:13
he will surely c You to Your Jb 1:11
C God and die! Jb 2:9
and c-d the day he was born. Jb 3:1
one who is greedy c-s and despises Ps 10:3
mouths, but they c inwardly. Ps 62:4
Though they c, You will bless. Ps 109:28
People will c anyone who hoards Pr 11:26
Whoever c-s his father or mother Pr 20:20
a generation that c-s its father Pr 30:11
may hear your servant c-ing you; Ec 7:21
Do not c the king even in your Ec 10:20
people the LORD has c-d forever. Mal 1:4
and I will c your blessings. Mal 2:2
he started to c and to swear Mt 26:74
fig tree that You c-d is withered. Mk 11:21
bless those who c you, pray for Lk 6:28
persecute you; bless and do not c. Rm 12:14
and with it we c men who are Jms 3:9

CURSED (adj)

The ground is c because of you. Gn 3:17
Canaan will be c. Gn 9:25
'C is the one who Dt 27:16
You will be c in the city
and c in the country Dt 28:16
a wife to a Benjaminite is c. Jdg 21:18
C is the man who eats food 1Sm 14:24
care of this c woman and bury 2Kg 9:34
C be the day on which I was born Jr 20:14
C is the one who does the LORD's
business deceitfully, Jr 48:10
Depart from Me, you who are c, Mt 25:41
that I myself were c and cut off Rm 9:3
no one speaking by the Spirit of
God says, "Jesus is c," 1Co 12:3
C is everyone who does not Gl 3:10
C is everyone who is hung on a Gl 3:13
is worthless and about to be c, Heb 6:8

CURTAIN

tabernacle itself with 10 c-s. Ex 26:1
lovely like the c-s of Solomon. Sg 1:5
let your tent c-s be stretched out Is 54:2
the c of the sanctuary was split Mt 27:51
inner sanctuary behind the c, Heb 6:19
inaugurated for us, through the c Heb 10:20

CUSH

1. Ancient land (Gn 2:13).

2. Son of Ham, and the region his descendants settled south of Egypt (Gn 10:6; Est 1:1; Ezk 29:10).

3. Benjaminite (Ps 7).

CUSHITE

criticized Moses because of the C	Nm 12:1
Zerah the C came against them	2Ch 14:9
Can the C change his skin,	Jr 13:23
are you not like the C-s to Me?	Am 9:7

CUSTOM

You must not follow their c-s.	Lv 18:3
Now it became a c in Israel	Jdg 11:39
do not know the c of the God of	2Kg 17:26
confirmed these c-s of Purim,	Est 9:32
it was Pilate's c to release for	Mk 15:6
according to the c of the	Lk 1:9
You have a c that I release one	Jn 18:39
to the burial c of the Jews.	Jn 19:40
and change the c-s that Moses	Ac 6:14
and are promoting c-s that are not	Ac 16:21
all the Jewish c-s and	Ac 26:3
or the c-s of our forefathers,	Ac 28:17
we have no other c, nor do the	1Co 11:16

CUT (adj)

is being built with c stones,	Ezr 5:8
we will rebuild with c stones;	Is 9:10

CUT (v)

C two stone tablets like the	Ex 34:1
he must c the contaminated	Lv 13:56
You are not to c off the hair at	Lv 19:27
You must not c his hair	Nm 6:5
c down their Asherah poles,	Dt 7:5
c down the carved images of	Dt 12:3
you are to c off her hand.	Dt 25:12
the Jordan's waters were c off.	Jos 4:7
You must never c his hair,	Jdg 13:5
his concubine, c her into 12	Jdg 19:29
up and secretly c off the corner	1Sm 24:4
C the living boy in two and	1Kg 3:25
and c themselves with knives and	1Kg 18:28
Who c-s a channel for the flooding	Jb 38:25
May the LORD c off all flattering lips	Ps 12:3
I am c off from Your sight.	Ps 31:22
He has c the ropes of the wicked	Ps 129:4

of the wicked are c short.	Pr 10:27
perverse tongue will be c out.	Pr 10:31
by a fool's hand c-s off his own feet	Pr 26:6
So the LORD c off Israel's head	Is 9:14
We have c a deal with Death,	Is 28:15
He c-s me off from the loom.	Is 38:12
the rock from which you were c,	Is 51:1
would c the scroll with	Jr 36:23
C down the tree and chop off its	Dn 4:14
Messiah will be c off and will	Dn 9:26
tree that doesn't produce good fruit will be c down	Mt 3:10
right hand causes you to sin, c it off	Mt 5:30
good fruit is c down and thrown	Mt 7:19
causes your downfall, c it off	Mt 18:8
He will c him to pieces and	Mt 24:51
the mountains and c-ing himself with	Mk 5:5
haven't found any. C it down!	Lk 13:7
slave, and c off his right ear.	Jn 18:10
man whose ear Peter had c off,	Jn 18:26
will be completely c off from	Ac 3:23
were cursed and c off from the	Rm 9:3
you too will be c off.	Rm 11:22
have her hair c off or her head	1Co 11:6

CYCLES

and the wind returns in its c.	Ec 1:6

CYMBAL

tambourines, sistrums, and c-s.	2Sm 6:5
harps, lyres, and c-s.	1Ch 15:16
by lyres, harps, and c-s.	1Ch 25:1
in the LORD's temple with c-s,	2Ch 29:25
Asaph, holding c-s, took their	Ezr 3:10
and singing accompanied by c-s,	Neh 12:27
Praise Him with resounding c-s;	Ps 150:5
sounding gong or a clanging c.	1Co 13:1

CYPRESS

the cedar and c timber.	1Kg 5:8
cedars, its choice c trees.	2Kg 19:23
send me cedar, c, and algum logs	2Ch 2:8
cedars, and our rafters are c-es.	Sg 1:17
I will put c trees in the desert	Is 41:19
Wail, c, for the cedar has	Zch 11:2

CYPRIOT

A person from Cyprus (Ac 4:36; 11:20; 21:16).

CYPRUS

Mediterranean island (Is 23:1,12; Jr 2:10; Ezk 27:6; Ac 11:19; 13:4; 15:39; 21:3; 27:4).

CYRENE

North African city (Ac 2:10; 6:9; 11:20; 13:1), home of Simon who carried Jesus' cross (Mt 27:32; Mk 15:21; Lk 23:26).

CYRUS

King of Persia; used by God (Is 44:28; 45:1); permitted the exiles to return and rebuild the temple (2Ch 36:22–Ezr 1:8; 3:7; 4:3-5; 5:13–6:14).

DAGON

Philistine god (Jdg 16:23; 1Sm 5:2-7; 1Ch 10:10).

DAILY

incense, the **d** grain offering	Nm 4:16
you are not to do any **d** work.	Nm 28:18
it removed His **d** sacrifice and	Dn 8:11
will abolish the **d** sacrifice and	Dn 11:31
Give us today our **d** bread.	Mt 6:11
up his cross **d**, and follow Me.	Lk 9:23
Give us each day our **d** bread.	Lk 11:3
in the **d** distribution.	Ac 6:1
and were increased in number **d**.	Ac 16:5
the Scriptures **d** to see if these	Ac 17:11
But encourage each other **d**,	Heb 3:13
clothes and lacks **d** food,	Jms 2:15

DAMARIS

a woman named **D**,	Ac 17:34

DAMASCUS

far as Hobah to the north of **D**.	Gn 14:15
king of Aram who lived in **D**,	1Kg 15:18
and took many captives to **D**.	2Ch 28:5
The head of Aram is **D**, the head	Is 7:8
An oracle against **D**:	Is 17:1
D was also your trading partner	Ezk 27:18
send you into exile beyond **D**.	Am 5:27

he traveled and was nearing **D**,	Ac 9:3
As I was traveling and near **D**,	Ac 22:6
traveling to **D** with authority	Ac 26:12
to Arabia and came back to **D**.	Gl 1:17

DAN

Son of Jacob and Bilhah (Gn 30:4-6; 35:25). Tribe; unable to conquer allotted land west of Jerusalem and up the coast to Joppa; took land in the far north (Jos 19:40-48; Jdg 18). City (Jdg 18:29).

DANCE (n)

her with tambourines and **d**-ing.	Ex 15:20
and saw the calf and the **d**-ing,	Ex 32:19
come out to perform the **d**-s,	Jdg 21:21
sing about him during their **d**-s:	1Sm 21:11
did their lame **d** around the	1Kg 18:26
You turned my lament into **d**-ing;	Ps 30:11
praise His name with **d**-ing	Ps 149:3
Praise Him with tambourine and **d**;	Ps 150:4
again and go forth in joyful **d**-ing.	Jr 31:4
our **d**-ing has turned to mourning.	Lm 5:15
house, he heard music and **d**-ing.	Lk 15:25

DANCE (v)

David was **d**-ing with all his might	2Sm 6:14
I was **d**-ing before the LORD who	2Sm 6:21
saw King David **d**-ing	1Ch 15:29
time to mourn and a time to **d**;	Ec 3:4
flute for you, but you didn't **d**;	Mt 11:17
Herodias' daughter **d**-d before them	Mt 14:6

DANCERS

needed from the **d** they caught.	Jdg 21:23

DANGER

I fear [no] **d**, for You are with	Ps 23:4
If I walk in the thick of **d**,	Ps 138:7
and be free from the fear of **d**.	Pr 1:33
person sees **d** and takes cover,	Pr 22:3
sensible see **d** and take cover;	Pr 27:12
or nakedness or **d** or sword?	Rm 8:35
Why are we in **d** every hour?	1Co 15:30
d-s in the city, **d**-s in the open	2Co 11:26

DANIEL

1. Son of David (1Ch 3:1).

2. Priest (Ezr 8:2; Neh 10:6).

3. Famous wise man (Ezk 14:14,20; 28:3).

4. Prophet during the exile in Babylon. Called Belteshazzar (Dn 1:7); refused to eat the king's food (1:8-20); interpreted the king's dreams (Dn 3; 4) and the writing on the wall (Dn 5); thrown in the lion's den (Dn 6). Received visions (Dn 7–12).

DAPPLED

| the fourth chariot **d** horses | Zch 6:3 |

DARE

day no one **d-d** to question Him	Mt 22:46
And no one **d-d** to question Him	Mk 12:34
And they no longer **d-d** to ask Him	Lk 20:40
of the disciples **d-d** ask Him,	Jn 21:12
someone might even **d** to die.	Rm 5:7
did not **d** bring an abusive	Jd 9

DARIUS

1. The Mede, who conquered Babylon (Dn 5:31).

2. Darius I of Persia allowed the rebuilding of the temple (Ezr 4:5; 5–6; Hg 1:1; Zch 1:1).

3. Darius II of Persia (Neh 12:22).

DARK

got up while it was still **d**.	Ru 3:14
the darkness is not **d** to You.	Ps 139:12
not stare at me because I am **d**,	Sg 1:6
sun will be **d** when it rises,	Is 13:10
and moon grow **d**, and the stars	Jl 2:10
The sun and moon will grow **d**,	Jl 3:15
I tell you in the **d**, speak in	Mt 10:27
have said in the **d** will be heard	Lk 12:3
early, while it was still **d**.	Jn 20:1

DARKENED

The sun will be **d**, and the moon	Mt 24:29
their senseless minds were **d**.	Rm 1:21
their eyes be **d** so they cannot	Rm 11:10
They are **d** in their	Eph 4:18
so that a third of them were **d**.	Rv 8:12

DARKEST

| when I go through the **d** valley, | Ps 23:4 |

DARKNESS

separated the light from the **d**.	Gn 1:4
there will be **d** over the land	Ex 10:21
He made **d** a canopy around Him,	2Sm 22:12
the LORD illuminates my **d**.	2Sm 22:29
even the light is like the **d**.	Jb 10:22

d is my {only} friend.	Ps 88:18
even the **d** is not dark to You.	Ps 139:12
his lamp will go out in deep **d**.	Pr 20:20
walking in **d** have seen a great	Is 9:2
I will turn **d** to light in front	Is 42:16
I form light and create **d**,	Is 45:7
your light will shine in the **d**,	Is 58:10
d covers the earth, and total **d** the	Is 60:2
a day of **d** and gloom, a day of	Jl 2:2
be turned to **d** and the moon to	Jl 2:31
It will be **d** and not light.	Am 5:18
a day of **d** and gloom,	Zph 1:15
who live in **d** have seen a great	Mt 4:16
if the light within you is **d**—how deep is that **d**!	Mt 6:23
be thrown into the outer **d**.	Mt 8:12
shines in the **d**, yet the **d** did not	Jn 1:5
and people loved **d** rather than	Jn 3:19
walk in the **d** but will have	Jn 8:12
light so that **d** doesn't overtake	Jn 12:35
in Me would not remain in **d**.	Jn 12:46
The sun will be turned to **d**,	Ac 2:20
they may turn from **d** to light	Ac 26:18
a light to those in **d**,	Rm 2:19
the deeds of **d** and put on the	Rm 13:12
what is hidden in **d** and reveal	1Co 4:5
"Light shall shine out of **d**"	2Co 4:6
fellowship does light have with **d**?	2Co 6:14
you were once **d**, but now	Eph 5:8
the world powers of this **d**,	Eph 6:12
the domain of **d** and transferred	Col 1:13
We're not of the night or of **d**.	1Th 5:5
called you out of **d** into His	1Pt 2:9
is absolutely no **d** in Him.	1Jn 1:5
and walk in **d**, we are lying	1Jn 1:6
but hates his brother is in the **d**	1Jn 2:9

DARLING

| How beautiful you are, my **d**. | Sg 1:15; 4:1 |

DARTS

| throws flaming **d** and deadly | Pr 26:18 |

DASH

You will **d** their little ones to	2Kg 8:12
all of them were **d-ed** to pieces.	2Ch 25:12
little ones and **d-es** them against	Ps 137:9
little ones will be **d-ed** to pieces,	Hs 13:16
children were also **d-ed** to pieces	Nah 3:10

DATHAN

Rebelled against Moses and Aaron (Nm 16; Dt 11:6; Ps 106:17).

DAUGHTER

sons of God came to the **d-s** of man,	Gn 6:4
both of Lot's **d-s** became pregnant	Gn 19:36
Now Laban had two **d-s:**	Gn 29:16
Leah bore a **d** and named her	Gn 30:21
a man sells his **d** as a slave,	Ex 21:7
The **d-s** of Zelophehad approached;	Nm 27:1
Do not give your **d-s** to their sons or take their **d-s** for your sons,	Dt 7:3
there was his **d**, coming out	Jdg 11:34
died having no sons, only **d-s.**	1Ch 23:22
Solomon brought the **d** of Pharaoh	2Ch 8:11
had seven sons and three **d-s.**	Jb 42:13
within the gates of **D** Zion.	Ps 9:14
Kings' **d-s** are among your honored	Ps 45:9
D Babylon, doomed to destruction	Ps 137:8
The leech has two **d-s:**	Pr 30:15
and all the **d s** of song grow faint	Ec 12:4
D Zion is abandoned like a	Is 1:8
without a throne, **D** Chaldea!	Is 47:1
I will destroy **D** Zion.	Jr 6:2
for the virgin **d** of my people	Jr 14:17
and get balm, Virgin **D** Egypt!	Jr 46:11
Like mother, like **d.**	Ezk 16:44
sons and your **d-s** will prophesy,	Jl 2:28
a **d** opposes her mother,	Mc 7:6
Rejoice greatly, **D** Zion!	Zch 9:9
a **d** against her mother,	Mt 10:35
loves son or **d** more than Me is	Mt 10:37
Herodias' **d** danced before them	Mt 14:6
mother against **d**, **d** against mother	Lk 12:53
this woman, a **d** of Abraham, for	Lk 13:16
Jesus said, "**D-s** of Jerusalem, do	Lk 23:28
Fear no more, **D** Zion;	Jn 12:15
sons and your **d-s** will prophesy,	Ac 2:17
had four virgin **d-s** who prophesied	Ac 21:9
you will be sons and **d-s** to Me,	2Co 6:18

DAVID

Youngest son of Jesse, anointed king by Samuel (Ru 4:17-22; 1Sm 16:1-13). Sought God's heart (1Sm 13:14; Ac 13:22). Killed Goliath (1Sm 17). Covenant of friendship with Jonathan (18:1-4; 19–20; 23:16-18). Spared Saul's life (1Sm 24; 26). Anointed king of Judah (2Sm 2:1-11) and Israel (5:1-4).

Conquered Jerusalem (5:6-9) and brought the ark there (2Sm 6). Was promised by God that He would keep his descendant on the throne (2Sm 7). Prepared for building the temple (1Ch 22–29). Psalmist, musician (Ps 23:1), and prophet (Mt 22:43; Ac 1:16; 4:25).

Committed adultery with Bathsheba and murdered Uriah, then was confronted by Nathan (2Sm 11–12). Family and political troubles followed: Amnon, Tamar, and Absalom (2Sm 13–18); Sheba (2Sm 20); punished for military census (2Sm 24; 1Ch 21); Adonijah and Solomon (1Kg 1–2).

Named Solomon as successor (1Kg 1:29-30). Died (2Sm 23:1-7; 1Kg 2:10-12). Ancestor of Jesus (Mt 1:1,6); Jesus is heir to his throne forever (Mt 12:23; 21:9; Mk 11:10; Lk 1:32; Rv 22:16).

DAWN (n)

or assigned the **d** its place,	Jb 38:12
righteousness shine like the **d,**	Ps 37:6
I will wake up the **d.**	Ps 57:8; 108:2
I rise before **d** and cry out for	Ps 119:147
is this who shines like the **d**	Sg 6:10
light will appear like the **d,**	Is 58:8
appearance is as sure as the **d.**	Hs 6:3
like the **d** spreading over the	Jl 2:2
who makes the **d** out of darkness	Am 4:13
the **D** from on high will visit us	Lk 1:78

DAWN (v)

help her when the morning **d-s.**	Ps 46:5
Light **d-s** for the righteous,	Ps 97:11
of darkness, a light has **d-ed.**	Is 9:2
of death, light has **d-ed.**	Mt 4:16
first day of the week was **d-ing,**	Mt 28:1
until the day **d-s** and the morning	2Pt 1:19

DAY

God called the light "**d,**"	Gn 1:5
festivals and for **d-s** and years.	Gn 1:14
By the seventh **d**, God completed	Gn 2:2
the earth 40 **d-s** and 40 nights,	Gn 7:4
and **d** and night will not cease.	Gn 8:22
to labor six **d-s** and do all your	Ex 20:9
the seventh **d** is a Sabbath to	Ex 20:10
for it is a **D** of Atonement	Lv 23:28
are to recite it **d** and night,	Jos 1:8

and cursed the **d** he was born.	Jb 3:1	Each **d** has enough trouble of its	Mt 6:34
Since man's **d-s** are determined and	Jb 14:5	and on the third **d** He will be	Mt 17:23
for the **d** of warfare and battle	Jb 38:23	Unless those **d-s** were limited,	Mt 24:22
he meditates on it **d** and night.	Ps 1:2	that **d** and hour no one	Mt 24:36
D after **d** they pour out speech	Ps 19:2	know either the **d** or the hour.	Mt 25:13
length of **d-s** forever and ever.	Ps 21:4	'After three **d-s** I will rise again.'	Mt 27:63
pursue me all the **d-s** of my life,	Ps 23:6	He was in the wilderness 40 **d-s**,	Mk 1:13
the LORD all the **d-s** of my life,	Ps 27:4	concerning that **d** or hour no one	Mk 13:32
Call on Me in a **d** of trouble;	Ps 50:15	until that **d** when I drink it	Mk 14:25
righteous flourish in his **d-s**,	Ps 72:7	Give us each **d** our daily bread.	Lk 11:3
He made their **d-s** end in futility	Ps 78:33	who cry out to Him **d** and night?	Lk 18:7
Better a **d** in Your courts than a	Ps 84:10	and rise on the third **d**'?	Lk 24:7
Teach us to number our **d-s**	Ps 90:12	will raise him up on the last **d**.	Jn 6:40
His salvation from **d** to **d**.	Ps 96:2	Him who sent Me while it is **d**.	Jn 9:4
For my **d-s** vanish like smoke,	Ps 102:3	Aren't there 12 hours in a **d**?	Jn 11:9
As for man, his **d-s** are like grass	Ps 103:15	will judge him on the last **d**.	Jn 12:48
This is the **d** the LORD has made	Ps 118:24	He has set a **d** on which He is	Ac 17:31
It is my meditation all **d** long.	Ps 119:97	considers one **d** to be above	Rm 14:5
sun will not strike you by **d**,	Ps 121:6	blameless in the **d** of our Lord	1Co 1:8
The night shines like the **d**;	Ps 139:12	for the **d** will disclose it,	1Co 3:13
all {my} **d-s** were written in Your	Ps 139:16	be saved in the **D** of the Lord.	1Co 5:5
I remember the **d-s** of old;	Ps 143:5	on the third **d** according to	1Co 15:4
know what a **d** might bring.	Pr 27:1	Jesus our Lord: I die every **d**!	1Co 15:31
d of one's death than the **d** of one's	Ec 7:1	is being renewed **d** by **d**.	2Co 4:16
were the former **d-s** better than	Ec 7:10	now is the **d** of salvation.	2Co 6:2
him remember the **d-s** of darkness,	Ec 11:8	a night and a **d** in the depths	2Co 11:25
Creator in the **d-s** of your youth:	Ec 12:1	you observe {special} **d-s**, months,	Gl 4:10
In the last **d-s** the mountain of	Is 2:2	time, because the **d-s** are evil.	Eph 5:16
For the **d** of the LORD is near.	Is 13:6	until the **d** of Christ Jesus.	Php 1:6
He will prolong His **d-s**,	Is 53:10	circumcised the eighth **d**;	Php 3:5
Can a land be born in one **d**,	Is 66:8	well that the **D** of the Lord will	1Th 5:2
break My covenant with the **d**	Jr 33:20	sons of light and sons of the **d**.	1Th 5:5
That **d** belongs to the Lord, the		But since we are of the **d**,	1Th 5:8
GOD of Hosts, a **d** of vengeance	Jr 46:10	that the **D** of the Lord has	2Th 2:2
On the **d** I cleanse you from all	Ezk 36:33	entrusted to me until that **d**.	2Tm 1:12
For the **D** of the LORD is near	Jl 1:15	times will come in the last **d-s**.	2Tm 3:1
a **d** of darkness and gloom,	Jl 2:2	In these last **d-s**, He has spoken	Heb 1:2
the **D** of the LORD is terrible	Jl 2:11	spoken later about another **d**.	Heb 4:8
pour out My Spirit ... in those **d-s**.	Jl 2:29	priest stands **d** after **d** ministering	Heb 10:11
keep silent ... for the **d-s** are evil.	Am 5:13	hearts for the **d** of slaughter.	Jms 5:5
who long for the **D** of the LORD!	Am 5:18	God in a **d** of visitation.	1Pt 2:12
For the **D** of the LORD is near,	Ob 15	and to see good **d-s** must keep his	1Pt 3:10
In the last **d-s** the mountain of	Mc 4:1	until the **d** dawns and the	2Pt 1:19
A **d** of the LORD is coming when	Zch 14:1	come in the last **d-s** to scoff,	2Pt 3:3
On that **d** living water will flow	Zch 14:8	kept until the **d** of judgment	2Pt 3:7
can endure the **d** of His coming?	Mal 3:2	one **d** is like 1,000 years,	2Pt 3:8
For indeed, the **d** is coming	Mal 4:1	But the **D** of the Lord will come	2Pt 3:10
had fasted 40 **d-s** and 40 nights,	Mt 4:2	confidence in the **d** of judgment;	1Jn 4:17

in the Spirit on the Lord's **d**,   Rv 1:10
D and night they never stop,   Rv 4:8
they will prophesy for 1,260 **d-s**,   Rv 11:3
battle of the great **d** of God,   Rv 16:14
plagues will come in one **d**   Rv 18:8
be tormented **d** and night forever   Rv 20:10

DAYBREAK

man wrestled with him until **d**.   Gn 32:24
At **d**, LORD, You hear my voice;   Ps 5:3
When **d** came, Jesus stood on the   Jn 21:4

DAYLIGHT

all Israel and in broad **d**.   2Sm 12:12
like infants who never see **d**?   Jb 3:16
and the **d** will turn black over   Mc 3:6
stern and prayed for **d** to come.   Ac 27:29
walk with decency, as in the **d**:   Rm 13:13

DAYTIME

a pleasure to carouse in the **d**.   2Pt 2:13

DAZZLING

and His clothes became **d**   Mk 9:3
and His clothes became **d** white.   Lk 9:29
men stood by them in **d** clothes.   Lk 24:4
then a man in a **d** robe stood   Ac 10:30

DEACONS

including the overseers and **d**.   Php 1:1
D, likewise, should be   1Tm 3:8
who have served well as **d** acquire   1Tm 3:13

DEAD

must not go near a **d** body during   Nm 6:6
between the **d** and the living,   Nm 16:48
your head on behalf of the **d**,   Dt 14:1
spirit, or inquire of the **d**.   Dt 18:11
have shown to the **d** and to me.   Ru 1:8
gone from memory like a **d** person   Ps 31:12
Do You work wonders for the **d**?   Ps 88:10
It is not the **d** who praise the   Ps 115:17
in darkness like those long **d**.   Ps 143:3
So I admired the **d**, who have   Ec 4:2
a live dog is better than a **d** lion.   Ec 9:4
but the **d** don't know anything.   Ec 9:5
Your **d** will live; their bodies   Is 26:19
Do not weep for the **d**;   Jr 22:10
and let the **d** bury their own **d**.   Mt 8:22
the deaf hear, the **d** are raised   Mt 11:5
He is not the God of the **d**,   Mt 22:32
inside are full of **d** men's bones   Mt 23:27

'He has been raised from the **d**.   Mt 28:7
and fled, leaving him half **d**.   Lk 10:30
son of mine was **d** and is alive   Lk 15:24
looking for the living among the **d**? Lk 24:5
when the **d** will hear the voice   Jn 5:25
that He must rise from the **d**.   Jn 20:9
whom God raised from the **d**;   Ac 3:15
Judge of the living and the **d**.   Ac 10:42
of the resurrection of the **d**!   Ac 23:6
consider yourselves **d** to sin,   Rm 6:11
apart from the law sin is **d**.   Rm 7:8
mean but life from the **d**?   Rm 11:15
over both the **d** and the living.   Rm 14:9
if in fact the **d** are not raised   1Co 15:15
are being baptized for the **d**?   1Co 15:29
you were **d** in your trespasses   Eph 2:1
though we were **d** in trespasses.   Eph 2:5
the firstborn from the **d**,   Col 1:18
when you were **d** in trespasses   Col 2:13
and the **d** in Christ will rise   1Th 4:16
is **d** even while she lives.   1Tm 5:6
risen from the **d**, descended from   2Tm 2:8
to judge the living and the **d**,   2Tm 4:1
of repentance from **d** works,   Heb 6:1
received their **d** raised to life   Heb 11:35
also faith without works is **d**.   Jms 2:26
to judge the living and the **d**,   1Pt 4:5
the firstborn from the **d** and   Rv 1:5
I was **d**, but look—I am alive   Rv 1:18
for being alive, but you are **d**.   Rv 3:1
Blessed are the **d** who die in the   Rv 14:13
and the **d** were judged according   Rv 20:12
and Hades gave up their **d**;   Rv 20:13

DEAD SEA

The end of the Jordan River, forming the southeastern border of Canaan (Nm 34:3; Jos 15:5); also called the Sea of the Arabah (Dt 3:17; Jos 3:16; 12:3; 2Kg 14:25) and the Eastern Sea (Ezk 47:18; Zch 14:8).

DEADLY

they should drink anything **d**,   Mk 16:18
evil, full of **d** poison.   Jms 3:8

DEADNESS

and the **d** of Sarah's womb,   Rm 4:19

DEAF

makes him mute or **d**, seeing or   Ex 4:11
You must not curse the **d** or   Lv 19:14

On that day the **d** will hear the	Is 29:18	the day of one's **d** than the day	Ec 7:1
the ears of the **d** unstopped.	Is 35:5	For love is as strong as **d**;	Sg 8:6
Listen, you **d**! Look, you blind	Is 42:18	He will destroy **d** forever.	Is 25:8
and are **d**, yet have ears.	Is 43:8	We have cut a deal with **D**,	Is 28:15
and their ears will become **d**.	Mc 7:16	**D** cannot praise You	Is 38:18
the **d** hear, the dead are raised,	Mt 11:5	and with a rich man at His **d**,	Is 53:9
He even makes **d** people hear,	Mk 7:37	He submitted Himself to **d**,	Is 53:12
You mute and **d** spirit, I command	Mk 9:25	Those {destined} for **d**, to **d**;	Jr 15:2

DEAFEN

d their ears and blind their	Is 6:10	pleasure in the **d** of the wicked?	Ezk 18:23
		take no pleasure in anyone's **d**.	Ezk 18:32

DEAL (n)

We have cut a **d** with Death,	Is 28:15	**D**, where are your barbs?	Hs 13:14
		and like **D** he is never satisfied	Hab 2:5

DEAL (v)

Let us **d** shrewdly with them;	Ex 1:10	will betray brother to **d**,	Mt 10:21
He has not **d-t** with us as our sins	Ps 103:10	or mother must be put to **d**.	Mt 15:4
God is **d-ing** with you as sons.	Heb 12:7	will not taste **d** until they see	Mt 16:28
		in sorrow—to the point of **d**.	Mt 26:38

DEAR

the slain of my **d** people.	Jr 9:1	darkness and the shadow of **d**,	Lk 1:79
destruction of my **d** people,	Lm 2:11; 3:48	but has passed from **d** to life.	Jn 5:24
to warn you as my **d** children.	1Co 4:14	he will never see **d**—ever!	Jn 8:51
because you had become **d** to us.	1Th 2:8	what kind of **d** He was about to	Jn 12:33
		what sort of **d** He was going to	Jn 18:32

DEARLY

as **d** loved children.	Eph 5:1	by what kind of **d** he would	Jn 21:19
		in this way **d** spread to all men	Rm 5:12

DEATH

Let me die the **d** of the upright	Nm 23:10	**d** reigned from Adam to Moses,	Rm 5:14
have set before you life and **d**,	Dt 30:19	Jesus were baptized into His **d**?	Rm 6:3
I bring **d** and I give life;	Dt 32:39	**D** no longer rules over Him.	Rm 6:9
if anything but **d** separates you	Ru 1:17	For the wages of sin is **d**,	Rm 6:23
For the waves of **d** engulfed me;	2Sm 22:5	of us and bore fruit for **d**.	Rm 7:5
There's **d** in the pot,	2Kg 4:40	for life resulted in **d** for me.	Rm 7:10
who wait for **d**, but it does not	Jb 3:21	was producing **d** in me through	Rm 7:13
Abaddon and **D** say, "We have	Jb 28:22	rescue me from this body of **d**?	Rm 7:24
is no remembrance of You in **d**;	Ps 6:5	from the law of sin and of **d**.	Rm 8:2
otherwise, I will sleep in **d**,	Ps 13:3	put to **d** the deeds of the body,	Rm 8:13
You put me into the dust of **d**.	Ps 22:15	that neither **d** nor life,	Rm 8:38
terrors of **d** sweep over me.	Ps 55:4	the Lord's **d** until He comes.	1Co 11:26
For You delivered me from **d**,	Ps 56:13	For since **d** came through a man,	1Co 15:21
The ropes of **d** were wrapped	Ps 116:3	last enemy He abolishes is **d**.	1Co 15:26
The **d** of His faithful ones is	Ps 116:15	**D** has been swallowed up in	1Co 15:54
Her feet go down to **d**;	Pr 5:5	O **D**, where is your victory?	1Co 15:55
all who hate me love **d**.	Pr 8:36	Now the sting of **d** is sin,	1Co 15:56
righteousness rescues from **d**.	Pr 10:2; 11:4	are a scent of **d** leading to **d**,	2Co 2:16
but its end is the way to **d**.	Pr 14:12	carry the **d** of Jesus in our	2Co 4:10
in the end it is the way of **d**.	Pr 16:25	but worldly grief produces **d**.	2Co 7:10
Life and **d** are in the power of	Pr 18:21	obedient to the point of **d**—even	
Rescue those being taken off to **d**,	Pr 24:11	to **d** on a cross.	Php 2:8
		being conformed to His **d**,	Php 3:10
		put to **d** whatever in you is	Col 3:5
		has abolished **d** and has brought	2Tm 1:10

DEBATE

He might taste **d** for everyone	Heb 2:9
through His **d** He might the one	
holding the power of **d**	Heb 2:14
grown, it gives birth to **d**.	Jms 1:15
passed from **d** to life because	1Jn 3:14
There is sin that brings **d**.	1Jn 5:16
I hold the keys of **d** and Hades.	Rv 1:18
faithful until **d**, and I will	Rv 2:10
The horseman on it was named **D**,	Rv 6:8
The second **d** has no power over	Rv 20:6
D and Hades were thrown into the	Rv 20:14
D will exist no longer;	Rv 21:4

DEBATE

After there had been much **d**,	Ac 15:7
Where is the **d-r** of this age?	1Co 1:20
But avoid foolish **d-s**, genealogies	Ti 3:9
the Devil in a **d** about Moses'	Jd 9

DEBAUCHERY

shame of your **d** will be exposed	Ezk 23:29
desires and **d**, people who have	2Pt 2:18

DEBIR

1. City in Judah (Jos 10:38; 11:21; 12:13; 15:15,49; 21:15; Jdg 1:11; 1Ch 6:58).
2. City in northern Judah (Jos 15:7).
3. City in Gad (Jos 13:26), also called Lodebar (2Sm 9:4-5; 17:27; Am 6:13).

DEBORAH

1. Rebekah's nurse (Gn 35:8).
2. Prophet and judge (Jdg 4–5).

DEBT

seven years you must cancel **d-s**.	Dt 15:1
Go sell the oil and pay your **d**;	2Kg 4:7
year and will cancel every **d**.	Neh 10:31
forgive us our **d-s**, as we also	Mt 6:12
he had been sold to pay the **d**.	Mt 18:25
forgive everyone in **d** to us.	Lk 11:4
He erased the certificate of **d**,	Col 2:14

DEBTORS

as we also have forgiven our **d**.	Mt 6:12
A creditor had two **d**.	Lk 7:41

DECAPOLIS

A group of Greek cities (Mt 4:25; Mk 5:20; 7:31).

DECAY

allow Your Holy One to see **d**.	Ac 2:27
His flesh did not experience **d**.	Ac 2:31
not allow Your Holy One to see **d**.	Ac 13:35
buried with his fathers, and **d-ed**.	Ac 13:36

DECEASED

the wife of the **d** man, to perpetuate	Ru 4:5

DECEIT

d, and violence fill his mouth;	Ps 10:7
and in whose spirit is no **d**!	Ps 32:2
D is in the hearts of those who	Pr 12:20
speech and harbors **d** within.	Pr 26:24
so their houses are full of **d**.	Jr 5:27
the house of Israel, with **d**.	Hs 11:12
greed, evil actions, **d**, lewdness	Mk 7:22
Israelite; no **d** is in him.	Jn 1:47
disputes, **d**, and malice.	Rm 1:29
and empty **d** based on human	Col 2:8
wickedness, all **d**, hypocrisy	1Pt 2:1
and no **d** was found in His mouth;	1Pt 2:22

DECEITFUL

but contrive **d** schemes against	Ps 35:20
but one who utters lies is **d**.	Pr 14:25
falsehood and **d** words far from	Pr 30:8
heart is more **d** than anything	Jr 17:9
a **d** tongue will not be found in	Zph 3:13
false apostles, **d** workers	2Co 11:13
paying attention to **d** spirits	1Tm 4:1

DECEITFULLY

and who has not sworn **d**.	Ps 24:4
violence and had not spoken **d**.	Is 53:9
made with him, he will act **d**.	Dn 11:23

DECEIVE

serpent. He **d-d** me, and I ate.	Gn 3:13
Why have you **d-d** me?	Gn 29:25
And Jacob **d-d** Laban the Aramean,	Gn 31:20
offends the LORD by **d-ing**	Lv 6:2
Why did you us by telling us	Jos 9:22
Didn't I say, 'Do not **d** me?	2Kg 4:28
'Don't let Hezekiah **d** you;	2Kg 18:29
you **d** Him as you would **d** a man?	Jb 13:9
An honest witness does not **d**,	Pr 14:5
so is the man who **d-s** his neighbor	Pr 26:19
(His) **d-d** mind has led him astray	Is 44:20
You have certainly **d-d** this people	Jr 4:10
You **d-d** me, LORD, and I was **d-d**.	Jr 20:7
if the prophet is **d-d** and speaks	Ezk 14:9
presumptuous heart has **d-d** you,	Ob 3

Watch out that no one d-s you.	Mk 13:5
I am He,' and they will d many.	Mk 13:6
the contrary, He's d-ing the people.	Jn 7:12
they d with their tongues.	Rm 3:13
flattering words they d the hearts	Rm 16:18
No one should d himself.	1Co 3:18
Do not be d-d: no sexually	1Co 6:9
Don't be d-d: God is not mocked	Gl 6:7
Let no one d you with empty	Eph 5:6
Adam was not d-d, but the woman	1Tm 2:14
worse, d-ing and being d-d.	2Tm 3:13
Don't be d-d, my dearly loved	Jms 1:16
not hearers only, d-ing yourselves.	Jms 1:22
his tongue but d-ing his heart,	Jms 1:26
have no sin," we are d-ing ourselves	1Jn 1:8
those who are trying to d you.	1Jn 2:26
children, let no one d you!	1Jn 3:7
the one who d-s the whole world.	Rv 12:9
nations were d-d by your sorcery	Rv 18:23

DECEIVER

The deceived and the d are His.	Jb 12:16
while this d was still alive	Mt 27:63
as d-s yet true;	2Co 6:8
idle talkers and d-s, especially	Ti 1:10
Many d-s have gone out into the	2Jn 7
This is the d and the antichrist	2Jn 7

DECENCY

Let us walk with d, as in the	Rm 13:13
clothing, with d and good sense	1Tm 2:9

DECENTLY

must be done d and in order.	1Co 14:40

DECEPTION

their womb prepares d.	Jb 15:35
Then the last d will be worse	Mt 27:64
in their d-s as they feast with	2Pt 2:13

DECEPTIVE

Charm is d and beauty is	Pr 31:30
will exploit you with d words.	2Pt 2:3

DECEPTIVELY

You must not act d or lie to one	Lv 19:11

DECIDE

think it over and d what answer	2Sm 24:13
you rather than to God, you d;	Ac 4:19
I have already d-d about him who	1Co 5:3
and has d-d in his heart to keep	1Co 7:37
do as he has d-d in his heart	2Co 9:7

DECISION

embroidered breastpiece for d-s.	Ex 28:15
but its every d is from the LORD	Pr 16:33
multitudes in the valley of d!	Jl 3:14
For My d is to gather nations,	Zph 3:8
it was the Holy Spirit's d	Ac 15:28
with the d of His will,	Eph 1:11

DECLARE

the seventh day and d-d it holy,	Gn 2:3
the Sabbath day and d-d it holy.	Ex 20:11
D the greatness of our God!	Dt 32:3
D His glory among the nations,	1Ch 16:24
I will d the LORD's decree:	Ps 2:7
The heavens d the glory of God,	Ps 19:1
my mouth will d Your praise.	Ps 51:15
to d Your faithful love in the	Ps 92:2
D His glory among the nations,	Ps 96:3
Now I d new events;	Is 42:9
I will d things kept secret from	Mt 13:35
what is Mine and d it to you.	Jn 16:14
languages and d-ing the greatness of God,	Ac 10:46
of the law will be d-d righteous.	Rm 2:13
be righteous and d righteous the	Rm 3:26
we have been d-d righteous by	Rm 5:1
and heard we also d to you,	1Jn 1:3

DECREASE

the waters had d-d significantly.	Gn 8:3
does not let their livestock d.	Ps 107:38
He must increase, but I must d.	Jn 3:30

DECREE

These are the d-s, statutes, and	Dt 4:45
he issued a d to rebuild this	Ezr 5:13
I will declare the LORD's d:	Ps 2:7
Happy are those who keep His d-s	Ps 119:2
but the LORD's d will prevail.	Pr 19:21
This word is by d of the observers;	Dn 4:17
Then he issued a d in Nineveh:	Jnh 3:7
In those days a d went out from	Lk 2:1
acting contrary to Caesar's d-s,	Ac 17:7

DECREED

Seventy weeks are d-d	Dn 9:24

DEDICATE

Remember to d the Sabbath day:	Ex 20:8
Be careful to d the Sabbath day	Dt 5:12
built a new house and not d-d it?	Dt 20:5

the Israelites **d-d** the LORD's | 1Kg 8:63
King David also **d-d** these to the | 1Ch 18:11
They **d-d** part of the plunder from | 1Ch 26:27
They **d-d** it and installed its | Neh 3:1
for anyone to **d** something rashly | Pr 20:25
is permanently **d-d** {to the LORD} | Ezk 44:29
male will be **d-d** to the Lord | Lk 2:23

DEDICATION

offering for the **d** of the altar. | Nm 7:11
for the **d** of the altar lasted | 2Ch 7:9
Temple **D** and the Passover | Ezr 6:15
At the **d** of the wall of | Neh 12:27
to attend the **d** of the statue | Dn 3:2
the Festival of **D** took place | Jn 10:22

DEED

can perform **d-s** and mighty acts | Dt 3:24
proclaim His **d-s** among
   the peoples | 1Ch 16:8
of our evil **d-s** and terrible guilt | Ezr 9:13
a person {according to} his **d-s,** | Jb 34:11
proclaim His **d-s** among the peoples | Ps 9:11
according to the evil of their **d-s.** | Ps 28:4
proclaim His **d-s** among | Ps 105:1
themselves by their **d-s.** | Ps 106:39
Celebrate His **d-s** among the | Is 12:4
repay according to {their} **d-s:** | Is 59:18
Repay her according to her **d-s;** | Jr 50:29
and repay them for their **d-s.** | Hs 4:9
LORD, I stand in awe of Your **d-s.** | Hab 3:2
wisdom is vindicated by her **d-s.** | Mt 11:19
because their **d-s** were evil. | Jn 3:19
put to death the **d-s** of the body, | Rm 8:13
let us discard the **d-s** of darkness | Rm 13:12
whatever you do, in word or in **d,** | Col 3:17
that your good **d** might not be | Phm 14
or speech, but in **d** and truth; | 1Jn 3:18

DEEP

God caused a **d** sleep to come | Gn 2:21
when **d** sleep descends on men, | Jb 4:13
{They are} **d-er** than Sheol | Jb 11:8
Your judgments, like the **d-est** sea. | Ps 36:6
D calls to **d** in the roar of | Ps 42:7
You teach me wisdom **d** within. | Ps 51:6
I have come into **d** waters, | Ps 69:2
His wonderful works in the **d.** | Ps 107:24
rescue me from **d** water, and set | Ps 144:7
of a man's mouth are **d** waters, | Pr 18:4

Laziness induces **d** sleep, | Pr 19:15
in a man's heart is **d** water; | Pr 20:5
lamp will go out in **d** darkness. | Pr 20:20
is high and the earth is **d,** | Pr 25:3
is beyond {reach} and very **d.** | Ec 7:24
He reveals the **d** and hidden | Dn 2:22
The **d** roars with its voice and | Hab 3:10
Put out into **d** water and let | Lk 5:4
a bucket, and the well is **d.** | Jn 4:11
water flow from **d** within him. | Jn 7:38
even the **d** things of God. | 1Co 2:10
of joy and their **d** poverty | 2Co 8:2
known the **d** things of Satan | Rv 2:24

DEEPLY

I am **d** depressed; therefore I | Ps 42:6
let's drink **d** of lovemaking | Pr 7:18
But sighing **d** in His spirit, | Mk 8:12
in His spirit and **d** moved. | Jn 11:33

DEER

like the feet of a **d** and sets me | Ps 18:33
As a **d** longs for streams of | Ps 42:1
like a **d** bounding toward a trap | Pr 7:22
the lame will leap like a **d,** | Is 35:6
makes my feet like those of a **d** | Hab 3:19

DEFEAT (n)

already a total **d** for you that | 1Co 6:7

DEFEAT (v)

you will be **d-ed** by your enemies | Nm 14:42
may be able to **d** them and drive | Nm 22:6
Israel was **d-ed** by the Philistines | 1Sm 4:2
David **d-ed** the Philistines | 2Sm 8:1
enslaved to whatever **d-s** them. | 2Pt 2:19

DEFECT

No man who has any **d** is to come | Lv 21:18
present anything that has a **d,** | Lv 22:20
men without any physical **d,** | Dn 1:4
like that of a lamb without **d** | 1Pt 1:19

DEFECTED

d to David | 1Ch 12:8,19

DEFECTIVE

but sacrifices a **d** {animal} to | Mal 1:14

DEFEND

I will **d** this city for My sake | 2Kg 20:6
to assemble and **d** themselves, | Est 8:11
I will still **d** my ways before | Jb 13:15

Arise, God, **d** Your cause!	Ps 74:22
D my cause, and redeem me;	Ps 119:154
and **d** the cause of the oppressed	Pr 31:9
D the rights of the fatherless.	Is 1:17
I will **d** this city and rescue it	Is 37:35
The LORD of Hosts will **d** them.	Zch 9:15
how you should **d** yourselves or	Lk 12:11
we were **d-ing** ourselves to you	2Co 12:19

DEFENSE

argument, and listen to my **d**.	Jb 13:6
and rise to my **d**, to my cause	Ps 35:23
prepare your **d** ahead of time,	Lk 21:14
My **d** to those who examine me is	1Co 9:3
for the **d** of the gospel;	Php 1:16
At my first **d**, no one came to my	2Tm 4:16
ready to give a **d** to anyone who	1Pt 3:15

DEFER

are truthful and **d** to no one,	Mk 12:14

DEFILE

that Shechem had **d-d** his daughter	Gn 34:5
father's bed and you **d-d** it	Gn 49:4
You must not **d** yourselves	Lv 11:44
If you **d** the land, it will vomit	Lv 18:28
goes astray and **d-s** herself	Nm 5:29
d-ing his consecrated head of hair,	Nm 6:9
Do not **d** the land where you are	Nm 35:33
You must not **d** the land the LORD	Dt 21:23
his sons are **d-ing** the sanctuary,	1Sm 3:13
because Reuben **d-d** his father's	1Ch 5:1
your hands are **d-d** with blood,	Is 59:3
will no longer **d** My holy name	Ezk 20:39
they **d-d** it with their conduct	Ezk 36:17
that he would not **d** himself with	Dn 1:8
touches ... does it become **d-d**?	Hg 2:13
out of the mouth, this **d-s** a man.	Mt 15:11
These are the things that **d** a man,	Mt 15:20
they would be **d-d** and unable to	Jn 18:28
conscience, being weak, is **d-d**.	1Co 8:7
mind and conscience are **d-d**.	Ti 1:15
these dreamers likewise **d** their flesh,	Jd 8
the garment **d-d** by the flesh.	Jd 23
who have not **d-d** their clothes,	Rv 3:4

DEFORMED

facially disfigured, or **d**;	Lv 21:18
the **d** restored, the lame walking,	Mt 15:31

DEFRAUD

do not **d**;	Mk 10:19
d his brother in this matter,	1Th 4:6

DEFY

for he has **d-ied** the armies of the	1Sm 17:36
Queen Vashti has **d-ied** not only the	Est 1:16
did they not **d** His commands?	Ps 105:28
against the LORD, **d-ing** His glorious	Is 3:8

DEGENERATE

then could you turn into a **d**,	Jr 2:21

DEGRADING

them over to **d** passions.	Rm 1:26

DEITIES

seems to be a preacher of foreign **d**	Ac 17:18

DELAY

Moses **d-ed** in coming down	Ex 32:1
of the sky and **d-ed** its setting	Jos 10:13
How long will you **d** going out	Jos 18:3
my deliverer; my God, do not **d**.	Ps 40:17
my deliverer; LORD, do not **d**.	Ps 70:5
D-ed hope makes the heart sick,	Pr 13:12
vow to God, don't **d** fulfilling it	Ec 5:4
and My salvation will not **d**.	Is 46:13
Though it **d-s**, wait for it,	Hab 2:3
in his heart, 'My master is **d-ed**,'	Mt 24:48
if I should be **d-ed**,	1Tm 3:15
Coming One will come and not **d**.	Heb 10:37
Lord does not **d** His promise, as some understand **d**,	2Pt 3:9

DELEGATION

he sends a **d** and asks for terms	Lk 14:32

DELIBERATELY

For if we **d** sin after receiving	Heb 10:26

DELICACY

Do not let me feast on their **d-ies**.	Ps 141:4
and at our doors is every **d**	Sg 7:13
who used to eat **d-ies** are destitute	Lm 4:5

DELICATE

Leah had **d** eyes, but Rachel was	Gn 29:17
{Though she is} beautiful and **d**,	Jr 6:2

DELICIOUS

make me the **d** food that I love	Gn 27:4

DELIGHT (n)

my lord is old, will I have **d**?	Gn 18:12

his **d** is in the LORD's Ps 1:2
noble ones in whom is all my **d**. Ps 16:3
Take **d** in the LORD, and He will Ps 37:4
Your instruction is my **d**. Ps 119:77,174
I was His **d** every day, Pr 8:30
an accurate weight is His **d**. Pr 11:1
but faithful people are His **d**. Pr 12:22
prayer of the upright is His **d**. Pr 15:8
Righteous lips are a king's **d**, Pr 16:13
he will also give you **d**. Pr 29:17
many concubines, the **d**-s of men. Ec 2:8
{my} love, with such **d**-s! Sg 7:6
His **d** will be in the fear of the Is 11:3
Chosen One; I **d** in Him. I have Is 42:1
if you call the Sabbath a **d**, Is 58:13
words became a **d** to me and the Jr 15:16
to take the **d** of your eyes away Ezk 24:16
beloved Son. I take **d** in Him! Mt 3:17
Son. I take **d** in Him. Listen to Him! Mt 17:5
beloved Son. I take **d** in Him! 2Pt 1:17

DELIGHT (v)

say, 'I do not **d** in you,' then 2Sm 15:26
who **d** to revere Your name. Neh 1:11
Then you will **d** in the Almighty Jb 22:26
Will he **d** in the Almighty? Jb 27:10
not a God who **d**-s in wickedness; Ps 5:4
rescued me because He **d**-ed in me. Ps 18:19
Who is the man who **d**-s in life, Ps 34:12
I will **d** in His deliverance. Ps 35:9
You do not **d** in sacrifice and Ps 40:6
I **d** to do Your will, my God; Ps 40:8
Then You will **d** in righteous Ps 51:19
just as a father, the son he **d**-s in. Pr 3:12
d-ing in the human race. Pr 8:31
because He does not **d** in fools. Ec 5:4
I **d** to sit in his shade, Sg 2:3
they **d** in the nearness of God. Is 58:2
for the LORD **d**-s in you, and your Is 62:4
and chose what I didn't **d** in. Is 66:4
for I **d** in these things. Jr 9:24
because He **d**-s in faithful love. Mc 7:18
He will **d** in you with shouts of Zph 3:17
My beloved in whom My soul **d**-s; Mt 12:18
You did not **d** in whole burnt Heb 10:6
d-ing in their deceptions as they 2Pt 2:13

DELIGHTFUL

good for food and **d** to look at, Gn 3:6
to His name, for it is **d**. Ps 135:3

your love is more **d** than wine. Sg 1:2
my love. How **d**! Our bed is lush Sg 1:16
How **d** your love is, Sg 4:10

DELILAH

Philistine woman who betrayed Samson (Jdg 16:4-22).

DELIVER

The LORD will **d** them over to you Dt 31:5
Lord, how can I **d** Israel? Jdg 6:15
that can't profit or **d** you; 1Sm 12:21
and He will **d** you from the hand 2Kg 17:39
Certainly the LORD will **d** us! 2Kg 18:30
and You will hear and **d**. 2Ch 20:9
no one who can **d** from Your hand Jb 10:7
let the LORD **d** him, since He Ps 22:8
to **d** them from death and to keep Ps 33:19
answered me and **d**-ed me from all my Ps 34:4
d-s them from all their troubles. Ps 34:17
the LORD **d**-s him from them all. Ps 34:19
The LORD helps and **d**-s them; Ps 37:40
D me from all my transgressions Ps 39:8
For You **d**-ed me from death, Ps 56:13
D us and atone for our sins, Ps 79:9
and You **d** my life from the depths Ps 86:13
devoted to Me, I will **d** him; Ps 91:14
d me because of the goodness of Ps 109:21
d me from lying lips and a Ps 120:2
and he **d**-ed the city by his wisdom Ec 9:15
Or do I have no power to **d**? Is 50:2
collection {of idols} **d** you! Is 57:13
or a nation be **d**-ed in an instant? Is 66:8
I will be with you to **d** you. Jr 1:8
will certainly **d** you so that you Jr 39:18
god who is able to **d** like this. Dn 3:29
He rescues and **d**-s; Dn 6:27
I will not **d** them by bow, sword Hs 1:7
but **d** us from the evil one. Mt 6:13
endures to the end will be **d**-ed. Mt 10:22
He was **d**-ed up according to Ac 2:23
Therefore God **d**-ed them over in the Rm 1:24
He was **d**-ed up for our trespasses Rm 4:25
just as I **d**-ed them to you. 1Co 11:2
He has **d**-ed us from such a terrible 2Co 1:10
our hope in Him that He will **d** us 2Co 1:10
and I have **d**-ed them to Satan, 1Tm 1:20
built an ark to **d** his family. Heb 11:7
faith that was **d**-ed to the saints once Jd 3

DELIVERANCE

to keep you alive by a great **d**.   Gn 45:7
LORD has provided **d** in Israel.   1Sm 11:13
but will grant them a little **d**.   2Ch 12:7
d will come to the Jewish people
   from another place,   Est 4:14
heart will rejoice in Your **d**.   Ps 13:5
so far from my **d**   Ps 22:1
me with joyful shouts of **d**.   Ps 32:7
and assure me: "I am your **d**."   Ps 35:3
Oh, that Israel's **d** would come   Ps 53:6
many counselors there is **d**.   Pr 11:14
wait quietly for **d** from the LORD.   Lm 3:26
will lead to my **d** through your   Php 1:19

DELIVERER

the LORD raised up ... a **d** to save   Jdg 3:9
Benjaminite, as a **d** for them.   Jdg 3:15
my fortress, and my **d**,   2Sm 22:2; Ps 18:2
gave Israel a **d**, and they   2Kg 13:5
compassion You gave them **d-s**,   Neh 9:27
You are my help and my **d**;   Ps 40:17; 70:5
my stronghold and my **d**.   Ps 144:2

DELUGE

I am bringing a **d**   Gn 6:17
The **d** continued 40 days on the   Gn 7:17
two years after the **d**.   Gn 11:10

DELUSION

Look, all of them are a **d**;   Is 41:29
them a strong **d** so that they   2Th 2:11

DEMAND

woman's husband **d-s** from him,   Ex 21:22
the LORD see and **d** an account.   2Ch 24:22
You will not **d** an account.   Ps 10:13
adulterous generation **d-s** a sign,   Mt 12:39
does this generation **d** a sign?   Mk 8:12
were **d-ing** of Him a sign   Lk 11:16
night your life is **d-ed** of you.   Lk 12:20
do what the law **d-s**,   Rm 2:14

DEMAS

   Paul's co-worker (Col 4:14; Phm 24);
deserted Paul (2Tm 4:10).

DEMETRIUS

   1. Ephesian silversmith; incited a riot
against Paul (Ac 19:23-41).
   2. A good Christian (3Jn 12).

DEMOLISH

and **d** all their high places.   Nm 33:52
to destroy and **d**, to build and   Jr 1:10
I will rebuild and not **d** you,   Jr 42:10
They may build, but I will **d**.   Mal 1:4
'I will **d** this sanctuary made by   Mk 14:58
We **d** arguments   2Co 10:4

DEMOLITION

for the **d** of strongholds.   2Co 10:4

DEMON

sacrificed to **d-s**, not God,   Dt 32:17
their sons and daughters to **d-s**.   Ps 106:37
drive out **d-s** in Your name   Mt 7:22
When the **d** had been driven out,   Mt 9:33
He drives out **d-s** by the ruler of   Mt 9:34
skin diseases, drive out **d-s**.   Mt 10:8
and they say, 'He has a **d**!'   Mt 11:18
if I drive out **d-s** by Beelzebul,   Mt 12:27
rebuked the **d**, and it came out   Mt 17:18
diseases and drove out many **d-s**.   Mk 1:34
not permit the **d-s** to speak,   Mk 1:34
have authority to drive out **d-s**.   Mk 3:15
The **d-s** begged Him, "Send us to   Mk 5:12
they were driving out many **d-s**,   Mk 6:13
Him to drive the **d** out of her   Mk 7:26
of whom He had driven seven **d-s**.   Mk 16:9
My name they will drive out **d-s**;   Mk 16:17
the **d** came out of him without   Lk 4:35
be driven by the **d** into deserted   Lk 8:29
because many **d-s** had entered him.   Lk 8:30
and authority over all the **d-s**,   Lk 9:1
the **d** knocked him down and threw   Lk 9:42
driving out **d-s** in Your name,   Lk 9:49
even the **d-s** submit to us in Your   Lk 10:17
driving out a **d** that was mute.   Lk 11:14
I'm driving out **d-s** and performing   Lk 13:32
You have a **d**!   Jn 7:20
You're a Samaritan and have a **d**?   Jn 8:48
Now we know You have a **d**.   Jn 8:52
Can a **d** open the eyes of the   Jn 10:21
sacrifice to **d-s** and not to God.   1Co 10:20
I do not want you to be partners
   with **d-s**!   1Co 10:20
of the Lord and the cup of **d-s**.   1Co 10:21
spirits and the teachings of **d-s**,   1Tm 4:1
The **d-s** also believe—and they   Jms 2:19
stop worshiping **d-s** and idols of   Rv 9:20

are spirits of **d-s** performing   Rv 16:14
has become a dwelling for **d-s,**   Rv 18:2

DEMONIC
but is earthly, sensual, **d.**   Jms 3:15

DEMON-POSSESSED
brought ... the **d,** the epileptics,   Mt 4:24
brought to Him many who were **d.**   Mt 8:16
two **d** men met Him as they came   Mt 8:28
a **d** man who was unable to speak   Mt 9:32
Then a **d** man who was blind and   Mt 12:22
who had been **d** by the legion,   Mk 5:15
how the **d** man was delivered.   Lk 8:36

DEMONSTRATE
And I will **d** My holiness through   Ezk 20:41
when I **d** My holiness through   Ezk 36:23
d-ing through the Scriptures that   Ac 18:28
to **d** His righteousness   Rm 3:25,26
He **d-ed** [this power] in
   the Messiah   Eph 1:20
might **d** the utmost patience   1Tm 1:16

DEMONSTRATION
but with a **d** of the Spirit and   1Co 2:4

DEN
lairs and stay in their **d-s.**   Jb 37:8
back and lie down in their **d-s.**   Ps 104:22
put his hand into a snake's **d.**   Is 11:8
become a **d** of robbers in your   Jr 7:11
threw him into the lions' **d.**   Dn 6:16
Foxes have **d-s** and birds of the   Mt 8:20
are making it a **d** of thieves!   Mt 21:13

DENARIUS
workers on one **d** for the day,   Mt 20:2
Show Me a **d.** Whose image and   Lk 20:24
Two hundred **d-i** worth of bread   Jn 6:7
A quart of wheat for a **d,**   Rv 6:6

DENOUNCE
come, **d** Israel!   Nm 23:7
let's **d** him and pay no attention   Jr 18:18
those who **d** your Christian life   1Pt 3:16

DENSE
Israel or a land of **d** darkness?   Jr 2:31
a day of clouds and **d** overcast,   Jl 2:2

DENY
Sarah **d-ied** it. "I did not laugh   Gn 18:15

You must not **d** justice to the   Ex 23:6
so that you will not **d** your God.   Jos 24:27
for I would have **d-ied** God above.   Jb 31:28
might have too much and **d** You,   Pr 30:9
eyes desired, I did not **d** them.   Ec 2:10
day for a person to **d** himself,   Is 58:5
d-ing justice to a man in the   Lm 3:35
But whoever **d-ies** Me before men,
   I will also **d** him before My   Mt 10:33
he must **d** himself, take up   Mt 16:24
you will **d** Me three times!   Mt 26:34
And again he **d-ied** it with an oath,   Mt 26:72
men will be **d-ied** before the angels   Lk 12:9
But you **d-ied** the Holy and
   Righteous   Ac 3:14
he has **d-ied** the faith and is worse   1Tm 5:8
if we **d** Him, He will also **d** us;   2Tm 2:12
for He cannot **d** Himself.   2Tm 2:13
of religion but **d-ing** its power.   2Tm 3:5
but they **d** Him by their works.   Ti 1:16
instructing us to **d** godlessness   Ti 2:12
d-ing the Master who bought them,   2Pt 2:1
who **d-ies** that Jesus is the Messiah?   1Jn 2:22
who **d-ies** the Father and the Son.   1Jn 2:22
No one who **d-ies** the Son can have   1Jn 2:23
and **d-ing** our only Master   Jd 4
and did not **d** your faith in Me   Rv 2:13
and have not **d-ied** My name, look, I   Rv 3:8

DEPART
scepter will not **d** from Judah,   Gn 49:10
must not **d** from your mouth;   Jos 1:8
The glory has **d-ed** from Israel,   1Sm 4:21
D from me, all evildoers, for   Ps 6:8
Do **d-ed** spirits rise up to praise   Ps 88:10
know that the **d-ed** spirits are   Pr 9:18
evil will never **d** from his house   Pr 17:13
the assembly of the **d-ed** spirits.   Pr 21:16
is old he will not **d** from it.   Pr 22:6
d-ed spirits do not rise up.   Is 26:14
D from Me, you lawbreakers!   Mt 7:23
on the left, '**D** from Me, you who   Mt 25:41
the desire to **d** and be with   Php 1:23
times some will **d** from the faith   1Tm 4:1

DEPARTURE
that after my **d** savage wolves   Ac 20:29
and the time for my **d** is close.   2Tm 4:6

DEPEND

you d-ed on the king of Aram and have not d-ed on the LORD	2Ch 16:7
those who d on His faithful love	Ps 33:18
for help and who d on horses!	Is 31:1
and the Prophets d on these two	Mt 22:40
then it does not d on human will	Rm 9:16

DEPENDENT

the mind {that is} d {on You},	Is 26:3
and not be d on anyone.	1Th 4:12

DEPLOY

Though an army d against me,	Ps 27:3
like a mighty army d-ed for war.	Jl 2:5

DEPORT

He d-ed the Israelites to Assyria	2Kg 17:6
Then he d-ed all Jerusalem	2Kg 24:14
So I will d you beyond Babylon!	Ac 7:43

DEPOSED

he was d from his royal throne	Dn 5:20

DEPOSIT (n)

his neighbor in regard to a d,	Lv 6:2

DEPOSIT (v)

having d-ed the scroll in the	Jr 36:20
you should have d-ed my money	Mt 25:27
collect what you didn't d and reap	Lk 19:21

DEPRAVED

among men whose minds are d	1Tm 6:5

DEPRESSED

Why am I so d? Why this turmoil	Ps 42:5,11
I am deeply d; therefore I	Ps 42:6
Why am I so d? Why this turmoil	Ps 43:5
and have become d.	Lm 3:20

DEPRIVE

yet God has d-d me of justice.	Jb 34:5
and d-ing myself from good?	Ec 4:8
and to d the afflicted ... of justice,	Is 10:2
d the righteous of justice.	Is 29:21
I am d-d of the rest of my years.	Is 38:10
and d the poor of justice at the	Am 5:12
Do not d one another—except	1Co 7:5
for anyone to d me of my boast!	1Co 9:15
depraved and d-d of the truth,	1Tm 6:5

DEPTH

sank to the d-s like a stone.	Ex 15:5

walked in the d-s of the oceans?	Jb 38:16
The d-s of the sea became visible	Ps 18:15
sinking down to the d-s,	Ps 107:26
Out of the d-s I call to You,	Ps 130:1
the watery d-s overcame me;	Jnh 2:5
our sins into the d-s of the sea.	Mc 7:19
drowned in the d-s of the sea!	Mt 18:6
nor height, nor d, nor any other	Rm 8:39
the d of the riches both of the	Rm 11:33
and a day in the d-s of the sea.	2Co 11:25
and width, height and d,	Eph 3:18

DEPUTY

Solomon had 12 d-ies for all Israel	1Kg 4:7
king in Edom; a d served as king	1Kg 22:47

DERBE

City in Galatia; Paul visited twice (Ac 14:6,20; 16:1); Gaius's hometown (20:4).

DERISION

He drinks d like water.	Jb 34:7
for me constant disgrace and d.	Jr 20:8

DESCEND

and kings will d from you.	Gn 35:11
Then the LORD d-ed in the cloud	Nm 11:25
the Spirit d-ing from heaven like	Jn 1:32
ascending and d-ing on the Son of	Jn 1:51
the One who d-ed from heaven	Jn 3:13
all who are d-ed from Israel are	Rm 9:6
except that He d-ed to the lower	Eph 4:9
The One who d-ed is the same as	Eph 4:10
Himself will d from heaven with	1Th 4:16
from the dead, d-ed from David	2Tm 2:8

DESCENDANT

the land to your d-s after you.	Gn 35:12
will raise up after you your d,	2Sm 7:12
to David and his d-s forever by a	2Ch 13:5
All you d-s of Jacob, honor Him!	Ps 22:23
and his d-s will inherit the land	Ps 25:13
set one of your d-s on your throne	Ps 132:11
Spirit on your d-s and My blessing	Is 44:3
None of his d-s will succeed in	Jr 22:30
"We are d-s of Abraham," they	Jn 8:33
one of his d-s on his throne.	Ac 2:30
who was a d of David according	Rm 1:3
So will your d-s be.	Rm 4:18
because they are Abraham's d-s.	Rm 9:7

DESCENT

my countrymen by physical **d**.	Rm 9:3
concerning physical **d** but based	Heb 7:16

DESCRIBE

and **d-ed** it by towns in a document	Jos 18:9
son of man, **d** the temple to	Ezk 43:10
eyewitnesses **d-ed** to them what	Mk 5:16
Who will **d** His generation?	Ac 8:33

DESECRATE

If you keep from **d-ing** the Sabbath,	Is 58:13
I am about to **d** My sanctuary,	Ezk 24:21
will rise up and **d** the temple	Dn 11:31
He even tried to **d** the temple,	Ac 24:6

DESERT (n)

him to the creatures of the **d**.	Ps 74:14
and grieved Him in the **d**.	Ps 78:40
flowed like a stream in the **d**.	Ps 105:41
and tested God in the **d**.	Ps 106:14
would make them fall in the **d**.	Ps 106:26
He turns a **d** into a pool of	Ps 107:35
the **d** will rejoice and blossom	Is 35:1
highway for our God in the **d**.	Is 40:3
rivers in the **d**, to give drink	Is 43:20
when He led them through the **d-s**;	Is 48:21
and in the **d** for 40 years.	Ac 7:36
He put up with them in the **d**;	Ac 13:18
they were struck down in the **d**.	1Co 10:5
whose bodies fell in the **d**?	Heb 3:17
They wandered in **d-s**, mountains	Heb 11:38

DESERT (v)

You will no longer be called **D-ed**,	Is 62:4
shepherd who **d-s** the flock!	Zch 11:17
the disciples **d-ed** Him and ran away	Mt 26:56
withdrew to **d-ed** places and prayed	Lk 5:16
this man who had **d-ed** them in	Ac 15:38
assistance, but everyone **d-ed** me.	2Tm 4:16

DESERTERS

the **d** who had defected to the	2Kg 25:11

DESERVE

the man who did this **d-s** to die!	2Sm 12:5
give them back what they **d**.	Ps 28:4
has not dealt with us as our sins **d**	Ps 103:10
will get what their conduct **d-s**,	Pr 14:14
wicked ... get what ... righteous **d**.	Ec 8:14
He has done nothing to **d** death.	Lk 23:15

back what we **d** for the things we	Lk 23:41
not done anything **d-ing** of death,	Ac 25:25
practice such things **d** to die	Rm 1:32
Their condemnation is **d-ed**!	Rm 3:8
and **d-ing** of full acceptance:	1Tm 1:15
and **d-s** full acceptance.	1Tm 4:9

DESIGN

the **d** of the tabernacle	Ex 25:9
to execute any **d** that may be	2Ch 2:14
Reveal the **d** of the temple	Ezk 43:11

DESIGNATE

d cities to serve as cities of	Nm 35:11
who were **d-ed** for this judgment	Jd 4

DESIGNED

not heard? I **d** it long ago;	2Kg 19:25

DESIRABLE

and that it was **d** for obtaining	Gn 3:6
They are more **d** than gold	Ps 19:10
and nothing **d** can compare with	Pr 8:11
He is absolutely **d**.	Sg 5:16

DESIRE (n)

Your **d** will be for your husband	Gn 3:16
Its **d** is for you, but you must	Gn 4:7
salvation and {my} every **d**?	2Sm 23:5
d of my father David to build	1Kg 8:17
keep this **d** forever in the	1Ch 29:18
have heard the **d** of the humble;	Ps 10:17
You have given him his heart's **d**	Ps 21:2
will give you your heart's **d-s**.	Ps 37:4
my every **d** is known to You;	Ps 38:9
The **d** of the wicked will come to	Ps 112:10
not grant the **d-s** of the wicked;	Ps 140:8
satisfy the **d** of every living	Ps 145:16
He fulfills the **d-s** of those who	Ps 145:19
are trapped by their own **d-s**.	Pr 11:6
d of the righteous {turns out} well,	Pr 11:23
but fulfilled **d** is a tree of	Pr 13:12
D fulfilled is sweet to the	Pr 13:19
the eyes see than wandering **d**.	Ec 6:9
my love, and his **d** is for me.	Sg 7:10
I have no **d** for the blood of	Is 1:11
Our **d** is for Your name and	Is 26:8
the wind in the heat of her **d**.	Jr 2:24
and the **d** of your heart.	Ezk 24:21
man communicates his evil **d**,	Mc 7:3
and the **d-s** for other things enter	Mk 4:19

to carry out your father's d-s.	Jn 8:44
body, so that you obey its d-s.	Rm 6:12
For the d to do what is good is	Rm 7:18
my heart's d and prayer to God	Rm 10:1
plans to satisfy the fleshly d-s.	Rm 13:14
to marry than to burn with d.	1Co 7:9
carry out the d of the flesh.	Gl 5:16
flesh with its passions and d-s.	Gl 5:24
among them in our fleshly d-s,	Eph 2:3
I have the d to depart and be	Php 1:23
lust, evil d, and greed, which	Col 3:5
not with lustful d-s, like the	1Th 4:5
drawn away from Christ by d,	1Tm 5:11
and many foolish and harmful d-s,	1Tm 6:9
but according to their own d-s,	2Tm 4:3
and enticed by his own evil d-s.	Jms 1:14
Then after d has conceived,	Jms 1:15
it on your d-s for pleasure.	Jms 4:3
from fleshly d-s that war against	1Pt 2:11
for human d-s, but for God's	1Pt 4:2
the polluting d-s of the flesh	2Pt 2:10
by fleshly d-s and debauchery,	2Pt 2:18
to their own ungodly d-s.	Jd 18

DESIRE (v)

Do not d your neighbor's wife or	Dt 5:21
who does all Israel d but you	1Sm 9:20
He does what He d-s.	Jb 23:13
it is what I d: to dwell	Ps 27:4
Surely You d integrity in the	Ps 51:6
And I d nothing on earth but You	Ps 73:25
nothing you d compares with her	Pr 3:15
don't d his choice food,	Pr 23:3
evil men or d to be with them,	Pr 24:1
that my eyes d-d, I did not deny	Ec 2:10
of all he d-s for himself,	Ec 6:2
that we should d Him.	Is 53:2
For I d loyalty and not	Hs 6:6
I d mercy and not sacrifice	Mt 9:13; 12:7
whom the Son d-s to reveal Him.	Mt 11:27
I have fervently d-d to eat this	Lk 22:15
I d those You have given Me to	Jn 17:24
d-ing to display His wrath and to	Rm 9:22
But d the greater gifts.	1Co 12:31
and d spiritual gifts,	1Co 14:1
there was eagerness to d it,	2Co 8:11
For the flesh d-s what is against	Gl 5:17
we greatly d-d and made every	1Th 2:17
an overseer, he d-s a noble work.	1Tm 3:1
You did not d or delight in	Heb 10:8

You d and do not have.	Jms 4:2
Angels d to look into these	1Pt 1:12
d the unadulterated spiritual	1Pt 2:2
earnestly d the coming	2Pt 3:12
Whoever d-s should take the living	Rv 22:17

DESOLATE

the land would become d,	Ex 23:29
Sabbaths by lying d without the	Lv 26:43
wandered in the d wilderness,	Ps 107:4
your land will not be called D;	Is 62:4
The d land will be cultivated	Ezk 36:34
your house is left to you d.	Mt 23:38
Let his dwelling become d;	Ac 1:20
the children of the d are many,	Gl 4:27

DESOLATION

would become a d and a curse,	2Kg 22:19
the days of the d until 70 years	2Ch 36:21
and you will become a d.	Ezk 35:4
of years for the d of Jerusalem	Dn 9:2
abomination of d will be on a	Dn 9:27
set up the abomination of d.	Dn 11:31
the abomination of d is set up,	Dn 12:11
D, decimation, devastation!	Nah 2:10
a day of destruction and d,	Zph 1:15
the abomination that causes d,	Mt 24:15
that causes d standing where it	Mk 13:14
that its d has come near.	Lk 21:20

DESPAIR (n)

broken my heart, and I am in d.	Ps 69:20
he will gnash his teeth in d.	Ps 112:10
myself over to d concerning all	Ec 2:20
splendid clothes instead of d.	Is 61:3
we are perplexed but not in d;	2Co 4:8

DESPAIRED (v)

so that we even d of life.	2Co 1:8

DESPAIRING (adj)

a d man's words are	Jb 6:26

DESPERATE

every man who was d, in debt,	1Sm 22:2
and are d like a wild bear	2Sm 17:8

DESPERATELY

while he flees d from its grasp	Jb 27:22

DESPICABLE

and his public speaking is d.	2Co 10:10
for every unclean and d beast.	Rv 18:2

DESPISE

So Esau **d-d** his birthright.   Gn 25:34
statutes and **d** My ordinances,   Lv 26:15
long will these people **d** Me?   Nm 14:11
Do not **d** an Egyptian,   Dt 23:7
but those who **d** Me will be   1Sm 2:30
and she **d-d** him in her heart.   2Sm 6:16
because you **d-d** Me and took   2Sm 12:10
my own clothes **d** me!   Jb 9:31
All of my best friends **d** me,   Jb 19:19
Why has the wicked **d-d** God?   Ps 10:13
scorned by men and **d-d** by people. Ps 22:6
You will not **d** a broken and   Ps 51:17
commands and **d-d** the counsel   Ps 107:11
fools **d** wisdom and instruction.   Pr 1:7
Do not **d** the LORD's instruction   Pr 3:11
and how my heart **d-d** correction.   Pr 5:12
People don't **d** the thief if he   Pr 6:30
The one who **d-s** his neighbor sins Pr 14:21
A fool **d-s** his father's   Pr 15:5
but a foolish one **d-s** his mother.   Pr 15:20
ignores instruction **d-s** himself,   Pr 15:32
don't **d** your mother when she   Pr 23:22
wisdom of the poor man is **d-d,**   Ec 9:16
I **d** {your} incense   Is 1:13
and they have **d-d** the word of the   Is 5:24
He was **d-d** and rejected by men,   Is 53:3
My son, the sword **d-s** every tree. Ezk 21:10
You **d** My holy things and profane   Ezk 22:8
I hate, I **d** your feasts!   Am 5:21
you priests, who **d** My name.   Mal 1:6
How have we **d-d** Your name?   Mal 1:6
devoted to one and **d** the other.   Mt 6:24
is The stone **d-d** by you builders,   Ac 4:11
Or do you **d** the riches of His   Rm 2:4
God has chosen ... **d-d** things   1Co 1:28
you did not **d** or reject me.   Gl 4:14
Don't **d** prophecies,   1Th 5:20
No one should **d** your youth;   1Tm 4:12
a cross and **d-d** the shame,   Heb 12:2
of the flesh and **d** authority   2Pt 2:10
defile their flesh, **d** authority   Jd 8

DESPITE

not trust in Me **d** all the signs   Nm 14:11
D all this, they kept sinning   Ps 78:32

DESTINE

he is **d-d** for the sword.   Jb 15:22
I will **d** you for the sword,   Is 65:12

{**d-d**} for death, to death;   Jr 15:2; 43:11
I will **d** you for bloodshed,   Ezk 35:6
this child is **d-d** to cause the   Lk 2:34
He was **d-d** before the foundation   1Pt 1:20
they were **d-d** for this.   1Pt 2:8
If anyone is **d-d** for captivity,   Rv 13:10

DESTINY

Such is the **d** of all who forget   Jb 8:13
Then I understood their **d.**   Ps 73:17
fill bowls of mixed wine for **D,**   Is 65:11
Their **d** will be according to   2Co 11:15

DESTITUTE

If your brother becomes **d** and sells Lv 25:25
of the oppressed and the **d.**   Ps 82:3
the prayer of the **d** and will not   Ps 102:17
A **d** leader who oppresses the   Pr 28:3
in goatskins, **d,** afflicted   Heb 11:37

DESTROY

the earth to **d** all flesh under   Gn 6:17
Will you **d** the whole city for   Gn 18:28
you must completely **d** them.   Dt 7:2
because He was about to **d** you.   Dt 9:19
He set out to **d** ... the Jews,   Est 3:6
He **d-s** both the blameless and the   Jb 9:22
You now turn around and **d** me?   Jb 10:8
Even after my skin has been **d-ed,**   Jb 19:26
Do not **d** me along with sinners,   Ps 26:9
He said He would have **d-ed** them   Ps 106:23
D it! **D** it down to its foundations! Ps 137:7
complacency of fools will **d** them.   Pr 1:32
whoever does so **d-s** himself,   Pr 6:32
foolish lips will be **d-ed.**   Pr 10:8,10
of the treacherous **d-s** them.   Pr 11:3
is a companion to a man who **d-s.**   Pr 28:24
with prostitutes **d-s** his wealth.   Pr 29:3
efforts on those who **d** kings.   Pr 31:3
a bribe **d-s** the mind.   Ec 7:7
Why should you **d** yourself?   Ec 7:16
but one sinner can **d** much good.   Ec 9:18
No one will harm or **d** on My entire   Is 11:9
He will **d** death forever.   Is 25:8
sign that will not be **d-ed.**   Is 55:13
and tear down, to **d** and demolish,   Jr 1:10
uproot, tear down, and **d** {it}.   Jr 18:7
the shepherds who **d** and scatter   Jr 23:1
His kingdom will never be **d-ed,**   Dn 6:26
He will **d** the powerful along   Dn 8:24

My people are **d-ed** for lack of | Hs 4:6
has left, the **d-ing** locust has eaten | Jl 1:4
did not come to **d** but to fulfill. | Mt 5:17
moth and rust **d** and where | Mt 6:19
who is able to **d** both soul and | Mt 10:28
Have You come to **d** us? | Mk 1:24
looking for a way to **d** Him. | Mk 11:18
to save life or to **d** it? | Lk 6:9
D this sanctuary, and I will raise it | Jn 2:19
to steal and to kill and to **d**. | Jn 10:10
say that Jesus ... will **d** this place | Ac 6:14
May your silver be **d-ed** with you, | Ac 8:20
I will **d** the wisdom of the wise | 1Co 1:19
we are struck down but not **d-ed**. | 2Co 4:9
our outer person is being **d-ed**, | 2Co 4:16
if our earthly house, a tent, is **d-ed**, | 2Co 5:1
the faith he once tried to **d**. | Gl 1:23
to what is **d-ed** by being used up | Col 2:22
Lord Jesus will **d** him with the | 2Th 2:8
who draw back and are **d-ed**, | Heb 10:39
who is able to save and to **d**. | Jms 4:12
things are to be **d-ed** in this way, | 2Pt 3:11
to **d** the Devil's works. | 1Jn 3:8
to **d** those who **d** the earth. | Rv 11:18

DESTROYER

not let the **d** enter your houses | Ex 12:23
Is that you, you **d** of Israel? | 1Kg 18:17
did, and were killed by the **d**. | 1Co 10:10
so that the **d** of the firstborn | Heb 11:28

DESTRUCTION

is to be set apart for **d**. | Ex 22:20
set apart to the LORD for **d**. | Jos 6:17
they have been set apart for **d**. | Jos 7:12
what was devoted to **d**. | 1Ch 2:7
to see the **d** of my relatives | Est 8:6
the torrents of **d** terrified me. | Ps 18:4
your tongue devises **d**, | Ps 52:2
mouth of the fool hastens **d**. | Pr 10:14
poverty of the poor is their **d**. | Pr 10:15
but **d** awaits the malicious. | Pr 10:29
Pride comes before **d**, | Pr 16:18
for their **d** will come suddenly; | Pr 24:22
D has been decreed; | Is 10:22
He will set them apart for **d**, | Is 34:2
road is broad that leads to **d**, | Mt 7:13
against itself is headed for **d**, | Mt 12:25
And the **d** of that house was | Lk 6:49
except the son of **d**, so that the | Jn 17:12

objects of wrath ready for **d**? | Rm 9:22
Satan for the **d** of the flesh, | 1Co 5:5
Their end is **d**; their god is | Php 3:19
then sudden **d** comes on them, | 1Th 5:3
the penalty of everlasting **d**, | 2Th 1:9
is revealed, the son of **d**. | 2Th 2:3
plunge people into ruin and **d**. | 1Tm 6:9
bring swift **d** on themselves. | 2Pt 2:1
twist them to their own **d**, | 2Pt 3:16
up from the abyss and go to **d**. | Rv 17:8

DESTRUCTIVE

taking refuge in his **d** behavior. | Ps 52:7
pays attention to a **d** tongue. | Pr 17:4
secretly bring in **d** heresies, | 2Pt 2:1

DETERMINE

to **d** when something is unclean | Lv 14:57
that Ruth was **d-d** to go with her, | Ru 1:18
his father was **d-d** to kill David. | 1Sm 20:33
Now **d** in your mind and heart to | 1Ch 22:19
Israel who had **d-d** in their hearts | 2Ch 11:16
did not **d** in his heart to seek | 2Ch 12:14
had not yet **d-d** in their hearts | 2Ch 20:33
Ezra had **d-d** in his heart to | Ezr 7:10
Since man's days are **d-d** and | Jb 14:5
when I **d-d** its boundaries and put | Jb 38:10
I have **d-d** that my mouth will not | Ps 17:3
but the LORD **d-s** his steps. | Pr 16:9
man's steps are **d-d** by the LORD, | Pr 20:24
no one who walks **d-s** his own steps. | Jr 10:23
will go away as it has been **d-d**, | Lk 22:22
up according to God's **d-d** plan and | Ac 2:23
earth and has **d-d** their appointed | Ac 17:26
For I **d-d** to know nothing among | 1Co 2:2
so that you can **d** what really | Php 1:10
the spirits to **d** if they are | 1Jn 4:1

DETEST

and we **d** this wretched food! | Nm 21:5
he has not despised or **d-ed** the
    torment of the afflicted. | Ps 22:24
and **d** those who rebel against | Ps 139:21
The LORD **d-s** the way of the wicked | Pr 15:9
The LORD **d-s** the plans of an evil | Pr 15:26
You who **d** idols, do you rob | Rm 2:22
D evil; cling to what is good. | Rm 12:9
hateful, **d-ing** one another. | Ti 3:3

DETESTABLE

But these are to be **d** to you: | Lv 11:10

a man as with a woman; it is **d**.   Lv 18:22
not imitate the **d** customs of   Dt 18:9
king's command was **d** to him.   1Ch 21:6
imitating the **d** practices of the   2Ch 28:3
peoples whose **d** practices are   Ezr 9:1
and wickedness is **d** to my lips.   Pr 8:7
Lying lips are **d** to the LORD,   Pr 12:22
a proud heart is **d** to the LORD;   Pr 16:5
sacrifice of a wicked person is **d**   Pr 21:27
the law—even his prayer is **d**.   Pr 28:9
They are **d**, disobedient, and   Ti 1:16

DEVASTATE
The famine will **d** the land.   Gn 41:30
He will **d** and subdue them before   Dt 9:3
You have **d-d** me!   Jdg 11:35
head and beard, and sat down **d-d**.   Ezr 9:3
You have **d-d** my entire family.   Jb 16:7
Their cities lie **d-d**, without a   Zph 3:6
We have been **d-d**, but we will   Mal 1:4

DEVASTATION
three months of **d** by your foes   1Ch 21:12
who brings **d** on the earth.   Ps 46:8
A fool's mouth is his **d**,   Pr 18:7
with a cup of **d** and desolation,   Ezk 23:33
Desolation, decimation, **d**!   Nah 2:10

DEVIANT
rise up with **d** doctrines to lure   Ac 20:30

DEVIATE
that they were **d-ing** from the truth   Gl 2:14
Some have **d-ed** from these and   1Tm 1:6
people have **d-ed** from the faith.   1Tm 6:21
They have **d-ed** from the truth,   2Tm 2:18

DEVIL
to be tempted by the **D**.   Mt 4:1
enemy who sowed them is the **D**.   Mt 13:39
for the **D** and his angels!   Mt 25:41
40 days to be tempted by the **D**.   Lk 4:2
Then the **D** comes and takes away   Lk 8:12
Yet one of you is the **D**!   Jn 6:70
You are of your father the **D**,   Jn 8:44
the **D** had already put it into   Jn 13:2
under the tyranny of the **D**,   Ac 10:38
You son of the **D**, full of all   Ac 13:10
don't give the **D** an opportunity   Eph 4:27
against the tactics of the **D**.   Eph 6:11
into the condemnation of the **D**.   1Tm 3:6

senses and escape the **D-'s** trap,   2Tm 2:26
of death—that is, the **D**—   Heb 2:14
But resist the **D**, and he will   Jms 4:7
adversary the **D** is prowling   1Pt 5:8
who commits sin is of the **D**,
   for the **D** has sinned from
   the beginning.   1Jn 3:8
purpose: to destroy the **D-'s** works.   1Jn 3:8
with the **D** in a debate about   Jd 9
the **D** is about to throw some of   Rv 2:10
who is called the **D** and Satan,   Rv 12:9
for the **D** has come down to you   Rv 12:12
serpent who is the **D** and Satan,   Rv 20:2
The **D** who deceived them was   Rv 20:10

DEVIOUS
A **d** heart will be far from me;   Ps 101:4
crooked, and whose ways are **d**.   Pr 2:15
for the **d** are detestable to the   Pr 3:32
but a **d** tongue breaks the spirit   Pr 15:4

DEVISE
plan Haman had **d-d** against the   Est 9:25
caught in the schemes they have **d-d**.   Ps 10:2
D a plan; It will fall.   Is 8:10

DEVOTE
They **d-d** themselves to do ... evil   2Kg 17:17
they **d-d** themselves to the
   apostles' teaching,   Ac 2:42
they **d-d** themselves {to meeting}   Ac 2:46
But we will **d** ourselves to   Ac 6:4
to **d** yourselves to prayer.   1Co 7:5
have **d-d** themselves to serving   1Co 16:15
D yourselves to prayer;   Col 4:2
d-d herself to every good work   1Tm 5:10
d themselves to good works   Ti 3:8,14

DEVOTED (adj)
The LORD was **d** to you and chose   Dt 7:7
those who are **d** to worthless idols,   Ps 31:6
Because he is lovingly **d** to Me,   Ps 91:14
be **d** to one and despise the other.   Mt 6:24
so that you may be **d** to the Lord   1Co 7:35

DEVOTION
abandoned their **d** to the LORD.   Hs 4:10
complete and pure **d** to Christ.   2Co 11:3

DEVOUR
A vicious animal has **d-ed** him.   Gn 37:33
Must the sword **d** forever?   2Sm 2:26

because the sword d-s all alike. 2Sm 11:25
you will be d-ed by the sword. Is 1:20
a garment; a moth will d them. Is 50:9
own sword has d-ed your prophets Jr 2:30
It will d the whole earth, Dn 7:23
You d widows' houses Mt 23:14
if someone d-s you, if someone 2Co 11:20
if you bite and d one another, Gl 5:15
looking for anyone he can d. 1Pt 5:8
birth he might d her child. Rv 12:4

DEVOURER

I will rebuke the d for you, Mal 3:11

DEVOURING (adj)

D fire precedes Him, and a storm Ps 50:3
What the d locust has left, Jl 1:4

DEVOUT

This man was righteous and d, Lk 2:25
d men from every nation under Ac 2:5
But d men buried Stephen and Ac 8:2
He was a d man and feared God Ac 10:2
servants and a d soldier, Ac 10:7
of the Jews and d proselytes Ac 13:43
a d man according to the law, Ac 22:12

DEW

May God give you—from the d Gn 27:28
When the layer of d evaporated, Ex 16:14
When the d fell on the camp at Nm 11:9
rain and my word settle like d, Dt 32:2
even his skies drip with d. Dt 33:28
If d is only on the fleece, Jdg 6:37
the d of Your youth belongs to Ps 110:3
favor is like d on the grass. Pr 19:12
like the early d that vanishes Hs 6:4; 13:3
I will be like the d to Israel; Hs 14:5

DIADEM

the holy d, out of pure gold, Ex 39:30
gold, the holy d, on the front Lv 8:9
of beauty and a d of splendor to Is 28:5
and a royal d in the palm of Is 62:3
and on his heads were seven d-s. Rv 12:3
On his horns were 10 d-s, Rv 13:1

DIAMOND

a sapphire, and a d; Ex 28:18; 39:11
With a d point it is engraved on Jr 17:1
made your forehead like a d, Ezk 3:9
topaz, and d, beryl, onyx Ezk 28:13

DIBON

Capital city of Moab (Nm 21:30; 32:3,34;
Jos 13:9,17; Is 15:2,9; Jr 48:18,22).

DICTATION

At Jeremiah's d, Baruch wrote on Jr 36:4
at Jeremiah's d in the fourth Jr 45:1

DIE

from it, you will certainly d. Gn 2:17
You will not d," the serpent said Gn 3:4
everything on dry land d-d. Gn 7:22
male in the land of Egypt will d, Ex 11:5
If only we had d-d by the LORD's Ex 16:3
Where you d, I will d, and there I Ru 1:17
Uriah the Hittite also d-d. 2Sm 11:17
away your sin; you will not d. 2Sm 12:13
On the seventh day the baby d-d. 2Sm 12:18
Saul d-d for his unfaithfulness 1Ch 10:13
each one will d for his own sin. 2Ch 25:4
When a man d-s, will he come back Jb 14:14
one can see that wise men d; Ps 49:10
set free those condemned to d, Ps 102:20
I will not d, but I will live Ps 118:17
will d because there is no
instruction, Pr 5:23
but fools d for lack of sense. Pr 10:21
When the wicked d-s, his Pr 11:7
have a refuge when they d. Pr 14:32
who hates correction will d. Pr 15:10
him with a rod, he will not d. Pr 23:13
Give beer to one who is dying, Pr 31:6
a time to give birth and a time to d; Ec 3:2
who have already d-d, more than Ec 4:2
Why should you d before your Ec 7:17
living know that they will d, Ec 9:5
In the year that King Uzziah d-d, Is 6:1
and drink, for tomorrow we d! Is 22:13
for their maggots will never d, Is 66:24
each will d for his own wrongdoing. Jr 31:30
he will d for his iniquity, Ezk 3:19; 33:9
who sins is the one who will d. Ezk 18:4
better for me to d than to live. Jnh 4:3,8
My Holy One, You will not d. Hab 1:12
Even if I have to d with You, Mt 26:35
where Their worm does not d, Mk 9:44
the poor man d-d and was carried Lk 16:22
all seven d-d and left no children Lk 20:31
For they cannot d anymore, Lk 20:36
anyone may eat of it and not d. Jn 6:50

your fathers ate—and they d-d.   Jn 6:58
and you will d in your sin.   Jn 8:21
in Me, even if he d-s, will live.   Jn 11:25
believes in Me will never d   Jn 11:26
one man should d for the people   Jn 11:50
Jesus was going to d for the nation,   Jn 11:51
wheat falls into the ground and d-s,   Jn 12:24
one man should d for the people   Jn 18:14
that this disciple would not d.   Jn 21:23
moment, Christ d-d for the ungodly   Rm 5:6
rarely will someone d for a just   Rm 5:7
still sinners Christ d-d for us!   Rm 5:8
How can we who d-d to sin still   Rm 6:2
Now if we d-d with Christ, we   Rm 6:8
if her husband d-s, she is free   Rm 7:3
the flesh, you are going to d.   Rm 8:13
and no one d-s to himself.   Rm 14:7
and if we d, we d to the Lord.   Rm 14:8
Christ d-d and came to life for this: Rm 14:9
that one for whom Christ d-d.   Rm 14:15
if her husband d-s, she is free to   1Co 7:39
the brother for whom Christ d-d,   1Co 8:11
that Christ d-d for our sins   1Co 15:3
For just as in Adam all d,   1Co 15:22
Jesus our Lord: I d every day!   1Co 15:31
and drink, for tomorrow we d.   1Co 15:32
not come to life unless it d-s.   1Co 15:36
if One d-d for all, then all d-d.   2Co 5:14
as **dying** and look—we live;   2Co 6:9
the law I have d-d to the law,   Gl 2:19
then Christ d-d for nothing.   Gl 2:21
living is Christ and **dying** is gain.   Php 1:21
If you d-d with Christ to the   Col 2:20
For you have d-d, and your life is   Col 3:3
that Jesus d-d and rose again,   1Th 4:14
who d-d for us, so that whether we   1Th 5:10
For if we have d-d with Him,   2Tm 2:11
for people to d once   Heb 9:27
These all d-d in faith without   Heb 11:13
when he was **dying**, blessed each   Heb 11:21
so that, having d-d to sins, we   1Pt 2:24
are the dead who d in the Lord   Rv 14:13

DIFFERENCE

not explain the d between the   Ezk 22:26
They must teach My people the d
  between the holy and   Ezk 44:23
really were makes no d to me;   Gl 2:6

DIFFERENT

Caleb has a d spirit and has   Nm 14:24
not have two d weights in your   Dt 25:13
be transformed into a d person.   1Sm 10:6
beasts came up from the sea, each d   Dn 7:3
began to speak in d languages,   Ac 2:4
But I see a d law in the parts   Rm 7:23
given to us, we have d gifts: Rm 12:6
Now there are d gifts, but the   1Co 12:4
to another, d kinds of languages   1Co 12:10
a d spirit, ... or a d gospel,   2Co 11:4
{and are turning} to a d gospel   Gl 1:6
prophets at d times and in d ways.   Heb 1:1

DIFFERENTLY

if you think d about anything,   Php 3:15

DIFFERING

must not have two d dry measures   Dt 25:14
D weights and varying measures   Pr 20:10
D weights are detestable to the   Pr 20:23

DIFFERS

for star d from star in splendor   1Co 15:41

DIFFICULT

If a case is too d for you   Dt 17:8
to test him with d questions.   1Kg 10:1
to Jerusalem is too d for you.   1Kg 12:28
too great or too d for me.   Ps 131:1
how d Your thoughts are for me   Ps 139:17
a brother is born for a d time.   Pr 17:17
If you do nothing in a d time,   Pr 24:10
Is anything too d for Me?   Jr 32:27
unintelligible speech or d language   Ezk 3:5
is the gate and d the road that   Mt 7:14
d times will come in the last days.   2Tm 3:1

DIFFICULTY

man who also had a speech d,   Mk 7:32
that whether easily or with d,   Ac 26:29
the righteous is saved with d,   1Pt 4:18

DIG

my witness that I dug this well.   Gn 21:30
Isaac's slaves dug in the valley   Gn 26:19
wells dug that you did not d,   Dt 6:11
d a hole with it and cover up your   Dt 23:13
He dug a pit and hollowed it out,   Ps 7:15
they dug a pit for me without   Ps 35:7
They dug a pit ahead of me,   Ps 57:6
until a pit is dug for the wicked   Ps 94:13

arrogant have **dug** pits for me;   Ps 119:85
The one who **d-s** a pit will fall   Pr 26:27
The one who **d-s** a pit may fall   Ec 10:8
So I **dug** through the wall,   Ezk 8:8
the evening I **dug** through the wall   Ezk 12:7
If they **d** down to Sheol, from   Am 9:2
fence around it, **dug** a winepress   Mt 21:33
talent went off, **dug** a hole in the   Mt 25:18
who **dug** deep and laid the   Lk 6:48
I'm not strong enough to **d**;   Lk 16:3

DIGNITARIES
Her **d** were brighter than snow,   Lm 4:7

DIGNITY
life in all godliness and **d**.   1Tm 2:2
under control with all **d**.   1Tm 3:4
integrity and **d** in your teaching   Ti 2:7

DILIGENCE
leading, with **d**;   Rm 12:8
Do not lack **d**;   Rm 12:11
your **d** for us might be made plain   2Co 7:12
in all **d**, and in your love   2Co 8:7
demonstrate the same **d** for the   Heb 6:11

DILIGENT
So be very **d** to love the LORD   Jos 23:11
but **d** hands bring riches.   Pr 10:4
The **d** hand will rule, but   Pr 12:24
but the **d** is fully satisfied.   Pr 13:4
plans of the **d** certainly lead to profit,   Pr 21:5
tested ... and found **d**   2Co 8:22
Be **d** to present yourself   2Tm 2:15

DILIGENTLY
be on your guard and **d** watch   Dt 4:9
that Your precepts be **d** kept.   Ps 119:4
loves him disciplines him **d**.   Pr 13:24
d keeping the unity of the   Eph 4:3

DILL
tenth of mint, **d**, and cumin, yet   Mt 23:23

DINAH
Daughter of Jacob and Leah (Gn 30:21). Raped by Shechem; avenged by Simeon and Levi (Gn 34).

DINE
you sit down to **d** with a ruler,   Pr 23:1
asked Him to **d** with him.   Lk 11:37

DINNER
Look, I've prepared my **d**;   Mt 22:4
When you give a lunch or a **d**,   Lk 14:12
in to him and have **d** with him,   Rv 3:20

DIONYSIUS
Aristocratic Athenian convert (Ac 17:34).

DIOTREPHES
Selfish opponent of John (3Jn 9).

DIP
and **d-ped** the robe in its blood.   Gn 37:31
d it in the blood that is in the   Ex 12:22
The priest is to **d** his finger in   Lv 4:6
and he **d-ped** his finger in the blood   Lv 9:9
and **d** them all into the blood of   Lv 14:6
some bread and **d** it in the   Ru 2:14
Naaman went down and **d-ped**   2Kg 5:14
one who **d-ped** his hand with Me   Mt 26:23
the one who is **d-ping** {bread}   Mk 14:20
send Lazarus to **d** the tip of his   Lk 16:24
of bread to after I have **d-ped** it.   Jn 13:26

DIRECT
He **d-s** it wherever He chooses.   Pr 21:1
Who has **d-ed** the Spirit of the LORD   Is 40:13
our Lord Jesus, **d** our way to you   1Th 3:11
May the Lord **d** your hearts to   2Th 3:5
the will of the pilot **d-s**.   Jms 3:4

DIRECTLY
speak with him **d**, openly, and   Nm 12:8
He spoke **d** to my father David,   1Kg 8:15
able to look **d** at Moses' face   2Co 3:7

DISABLED
who had been **d** by a spirit for   Lk 13:11
a good deed done to a **d** man   Ac 4:9

DISAGREEMENT
such a sharp **d** that they parted   Ac 15:39

DISAPPEAR
until you **d** from this good land   Jos 23:13
As water **d-s** from the sea and a   Jb 14:11
the loyal have **d-ed** from the human   Ps 12:1
but He **d-ed** from their sight.   Lk 24:31
is old and aging is about to **d**.   Heb 8:13
fled, and the mountains **d-ed**.   Rv 16:20

DISAPPOINT
hope does not **d**, because God's   Rm 5:5

DISARM

on nobles and d-s the strong.   Jb 12:21
He d-ed the rulers and authorities   Col 2:15

DISASTER

change Your mind about this d   Ex 32:12
He considers no d for Jacob;   Nm 23:21
did not know that d was about to   Jdg 20:34
to bring d on the house   1Kg 14:10
good about me, but only d.   1Kg 22:8
This d is from the LORD.   2Kg 6:33
No d {overcomes} the righteous,   Pr 12:21
the wicked for the day of d.   Pr 16:4
who rejoices over d will not go   Pr 17:5
I make success and create d;   Is 45:7
about to bring d on these people   Jr 6:19
will not bring the d on it I had   Jr 18:8
prophesied war, d, and plague   Jr 28:8
welfare, not for d, to give you   Jr 29:11
D after d will come,   Ezk 7:26
all this d has come on us,   Dn 9:13
and He relents from sending d.   Jl 2:13
If a d occurs in a city, hasn't   Am 3:6
D will never overtake or   Am 9:10
in the day of their d.   Ob 13
who relents from {sending} d.   Jnh 4:2

DISCARD

Don't d me in my old age: Ps 71:9
so let us d the deeds of   Rm 13:12

DISCERN

Can I d what is pleasant and   2Sm 19:35
people and to d between good   1Kg 3:9
so that you may d what is the   Rm 12:2
d-ing what is pleasing to the Lord.   Eph 5:10

DISCERNING (adj)

and a d man will obtain guidance   Pr 1:5
A d mind seeks knowledge, but   Pr 15:14
with a wise heart is called d,   Pr 16:21
d, when he seals his lips.   Pr 17:28
rebuke the d, and he gains   Pr 19:25
A d son keeps the law, but a   Pr 28:7
or riches to the d, or favor to   Ec 9:11

DISCERNMENT

Blessed is your d, and blessed   1Sm 25:33
but you asked d for yourself to   1Kg 3:11
Teach me good judgment and d,   Ps 119:66
man who has d sees through him   Pr 28:11

People without d are doomed.   Hs 4:14
knowledge and every kind of d,   Php 1:9

DISCHARGE

be clean from her d of blood.   Lv 12:7
anyone who has a d, whether male   Lv 15:33
a skin disease or a d is to eat   Lv 22:4
anyone who has a {bodily} d,   Nm 5:2

DISCIPLE

Seal ... instruction among my d-s.   Is 8:16
He sat down, His d-s came to Him.   Mt 5:1
Then John's d-s came to Him,   Mt 9:14
but Your d-s do not fast?   Mt 9:14
Summoning His 12 d-s, He gave   Mt 10:1
A d is not above his teacher,   Mt 10:24
little ones because he is a d   Mt 10:42
giving orders to His 12 d-s,   Mt 11:1
Your d-s are doing what is not   Mt 12:2
Why do Your d-s break the   Mt 15:2
Then all the d-s deserted Him   Mt 26:56
Then go quickly and tell His d-s,   Mt 28:7
'His d-s came during the night and   Mt 28:13
and make d-s of all nations,   Mt 28:19
Now John's d-s and the Pharisees   Mk 2:18
explain everything to His own d-s.   Mk 4:34
to eat the Passover with My d-s?   Mk 14:14
He summoned His d-s, and He chose   Lk 6:13
just as John also taught his d-s.   Lk 11:1
come after Me cannot be My d.   Lk 14:27
his possessions cannot be My d.   Lk 14:33
and His d-s believed in Him.   Jn 2:11
many of His d-s turned back and no   Jn 6:66
My word, you really are My d-s.   Jn 8:31
don't want to become His d-s too,   Jn 9:27
to wash His d-s' feet and to dry   Jn 13:5
will know that you are My d-s,   Jn 13:35
fruit and prove to be My d-s.   Jn 15:8
and the d He loved   Jn 19:26
the d-s were {gathered together}   Jn 20:19
others of His d-s were together.   Jn 21:2
the d, the one Jesus loved,   Jn 21:7
and saw the d Jesus loved   Jn 21:20
number of the d-s was multiplying   Ac 6:1
did not believe he was a d.   Ac 9:26
and the d-s were first called   Ac 11:26
that town and made many d-s,   Ac 14:21
strengthening all the d-s.   Ac 18:23
to Ephesus. He found some d-s   Ac 19:1
sent for the d-s, encouraged them   Ac 20:1
we found some d-s and stayed there   Ac 21:4

DISCIPLINE (n)

or saw the **d** of the LORD your	Dt 11:2
not reject the **d** of the Almighty	Jb 5:17
and do not loathe His **d**;	Pr 3:11
D is harsh for the one who	Pr 15:10
the rod of **d** will drive it away	Pr 22:15
they would not accept **d**.	Jr 2:30
not take the Lord's **d** lightly,	Heb 12:5
No **d** seems enjoyable at the time	Heb 12:11

DISCIPLINE (v)

proceed to **d** you seven times	Lv 26:18
d-ing you just as a man **d**-s his son.	Dt 8:5
I will **d** him with a human rod	2Sm 7:14
my father **d**-d you with whips,	1Kg 12:11
do not **d** me in Your wrath.	Ps 6:1
Your anger or **d** me in Your wrath	Ps 38:1
You **d** a man with punishment for	Ps 39:11
happy is the man You **d** and teach	Ps 94:12
for the LORD **d**-s the one He loves	Pr 3:12
who loves him **d**-s him diligently.	Pr 13:24
D your son while there is hope;	Pr 19:18
D your son, and he will give you	Pr 29:17
A servant cannot be **d**-d by words;	Pr 29:19
I will **d** you justly, but I will	Jr 30:11
been **d**-d like an untrained calf.	Jr 31:18
I **d** my body and bring it under	1Co 9:27
judged, we are **d**-d by the Lord,	1Co 11:32
for the Lord **d**-s the one He loves	Heb 12:6
there whom a father does not **d**?	Heb 12:7
For they **d**-d us for a short time	Heb 12:10
many as I love, I rebuke and **d**.	Rv 3:19

DISCLOSE

confessing and **d**-ing their practices	Ac 19:18
obvious, for the day will **d** it,	1Co 3:13
not yet been **d**-d while the first	Heb 9:8
and the works on it will be **d**-d.	2Pt 3:10

DISCONTENTED

in debt, or **d** rallied around him	1Sm 22:2

DISCOURAGED

they **d** the Israelites from	Nm 32:9
Do not be afraid or **d**.	Dt 1:21; 31:8
Do not be afraid or **d**.	Jos 1:9; 10:25
Don't be afraid or **d**	1Ch 22:13; 28:20
Do not be afraid or **d**.	2Ch 20:17
Don't be afraid or **d** before the king	2Ch 32:7
in the land **d** the people of Judah	Ezr 4:4
They will become **d** in the work,	Neh 6:9

He will not grow weak or be **d** until	Is 42:4
pray always and not become **d**:	Lk 18:1
so they won't become **d**.	Col 3:21
comfort the **d**, help the weak	1Th 5:14

DISCOVER

David and his men had been **d**-ed.	1Sm 22:6
or **d** the limits of the Almighty?	Jb 11:7
{too much} to **d** and hate his sin.	Ps 36:2
and the knowledge of God.	Pr 2:5
cannot **d** the work God has done	Ec 3:11
and very deep. Who can **d** it?	Ec 7:24
this I have **d**-ed, by adding one	Ec 7:27
is unable to **d** the work that is done	Ec 8:17
the woman saw that she was **d**-ed,	Lk 8:47

DISCREDIT

in order that they could **d** me.	Neh 6:13

DISCRETION

knowledge and **d** to a young man	Pr 1:4
D will watch over you, and	Pr 2:11
competence and **d**.	Pr 3:21
may maintain **d** and your lips	Pr 5:2
and have knowledge and **d**.	Pr 8:12
Daniel responded with tact and **d**	Dn 2:14

DISCRIMINATED

haven't you **d** among yourselves	Jms 2:4

DISCUSS

"Come, let us **d** this," says the	Is 1:18
And they **d**-ed among themselves,	Mt 16:7
d-ing what "rising from the dead"	Mk 9:10
they were **d**-ing everything that	Lk 24:14

DISCUSSION

and engaged in **d** with the Jews.	Ac 18:19
conducting **d**-s every day in the	Ac 19:9
turned aside to fruitless **d**.	1Tm 1:6

DISEASE

his hand was **d**-d, like snow.	Ex 4:6
of his body, it is a skin **d**.	Lv 13:3
law regarding skin **d** and mildew.	Lv 14:57
who is afflicted with a skin **d**,	Nm 5:2
Miriam's {skin} ... became **d**-d,	Nm 12:10
all the terrible **d**-s of Egypt that	Dt 7:15
warrior, but he had a skin **d**.	2Kg 5:1
Four men with skin **d**-s were at the	2Kg 7:3
Yet even in his **d** he didn't seek	2Ch 16:12
a skin **d** broke out on his	2Ch 26:19
King Uzziah was **d**-d to the time	2Ch 26:21

He heals all your **d-s.**	Ps 103:3
and healing every **d** and sickness	Mt 4:23
with a serious skin **d** came up and	Mt 8:2
weaknesses and carried our **d-s.**	Mt 8:17
and healing every **d** and every	Mt 9:35
cleanse those with skin **d-s,**	Mt 10:8
those with skin **d-s** are healed,	Mt 11:5
a man who had a serious skin **d,**	Mt 26:6
Simon who had a serious skin **d,**	Mk 14:3
demons, and {power} to heal **d-s.**	Lk 9:1
to the sick, and the **d-s** left them	Ac 19:12

DISFIGURED

lame, facially **d,** or deformed;	Lv 21:18
was so **d** that He did not	Is 52:14

DISGRACE

uncircumcised man is a **d** to us.	Gn 34:14
sexual relations, it is a **d.**	Lv 20:17
I have rolled away the **d** of Egypt	Jos 5:9
and would use my **d** as evidence	Jb 19:5
My **d** is before me all day long,	Ps 44:15
and his **d** will never be removed	Pr 6:33
When pride comes, **d** follows,	Pr 11:2
Poverty and **d** {come to} those	Pr 13:18
but sin is a **d** to any people.	Pr 14:34
and along with dishonor, **d.**	Pr 18:3
is foolishness and **d** for him.	Pr 18:13
himself is a **d** to his mother.	Pr 29:15
Take away our **d.**	Is 4:1
will bear your **d** and be ashamed	Ezk 16:54
They bear their **d** with those who	Ezk 32:24
not wanting to **d** her publicly,	Mt 1:19
take away my **d** among the people.	Lk 1:25
has long hair it is a **d** to him,	1Co 11:14
not fall into **d** and the Devil's	1Tm 3:7
the camp, bearing His **d.**	Heb 13:13

DISGRACED

those who despise Me will be **d.**	1Sm 2:30
trusted in You and were not **d.**	Ps 22:5
Do not let me be **d;**	Ps 25:2
let me never be **d.**	Ps 31:1
They will not be **d** in times of	Ps 37:19
and let those who hate us be **d.**	Ps 44:7
authorities and **d** them publicly;	Col 2:15

DISGRACEFUL

who sleeps during harvest is **d.**	Pr 10:5
but his anger falls on a **d** one.	Pr 14:35
will rule over a **d** son and share	Pr 17:2

his mother is a **d** and shameful	Pr 19:26
But if it is **d** for a woman to	1Co 11:6
for it is **d** for a woman to speak	1Co 14:35

DISGUISE

Saul **d-d** himself by putting on	1Sm 28:8
to his wife, "Go **d** yourself,	1Kg 14:2
He **d-d** himself with a bandage	1Kg 20:38
king of Israel **d-d** himself	1Kg 22:30
Josiah ... **d-d** himself.	2Ch 35:22
hateful person **d-s** himself with	Pr 26:24
d-ing themselves as apostles of	2Co 11:13
Satan himself is **d-d** as an angel	2Co 11:14

DISGUSTED

I am **d** with my life.	Jb 10:1

DISH

set me aside like an empty **d;**	Jr 51:34
the outside of the cup and **d,**	Mt 23:25

DISHONEST

they turned toward **d** gain,	1Sm 8:3
D scales are detestable to the	Pr 11:1
and **d** scales are unfair.	Pr 20:23
your iniquities in your **d** trade.	Ezk 28:18
to extort with **d** scales in his	Hs 12:7
price and cheat with **d** scales.	Am 8:5
by teaching for **d** gain what they	Ti 1:11

DISHONESTLY

paths of all who pursue gain **d;**	Pr 1:19
Don't let your mouth speak **d,**	Pr 4:24
who goes around speaking **d,**	Pr 6:12
one who profits **d** troubles his	Pr 15:27

DISHONOR (n)

not right for us to witness his **d,**	Ezr 4:14
but He holds up fools to **d.**	Pr 3:35
He will get a beating and **d,**	Pr 6:33
mocker will bring **d** on himself;	Pr 9:7
and along with **d,** disgrace.	Pr 18:3
for honor and another for **d?**	Rm 9:21
sown in **d,** raised in glory;	1Co 15:43
glory and **d,** through slander	2Co 6:8

DISHONOR (v)

Cursed is ... who **d-s** his father	Dt 27:16
if they **d** My statutes and do not	Ps 89:31
Better to be **d-ed,** yet have a	Pr 12:9
I honor My Father and you **d** Me.	Jn 8:49
counted worthy to be **d-ed** on behalf	Ac 5:41
do you **d** God by breaking the law	Rm 2:23

distinguished, but we are **d-ed**! 1Co 4:10
her head uncovered **d-s** her head, 1Co 11:5
Yet you **d-ed** that poor man. Jms 2:6

DISLOCATED
wrestled and **d** his hip socket. Gn 32:25

DISLOYAL
The **d** will get what their Pr 14:14

DISMAL
to a lamp shining in a **d** place, 2Pt 1:19

DISMAYED
boast will be **d** and ashamed. Is 20:5
to hear, too **d** to see. Is 21:3
will no longer be afraid or **d**, Jr 23:4
and do not be **d**, Israel, for I Jr 30:10

DISMISS
You **d** any thought of the evil Am 6:3
Then He **d-ed** the crowds
 and went Mt 13:36
while He **d-ed** the crowds. Mt 14:22
After **d-ing** the crowds, He got into Mt 15:39
You can **d** Your slave in peace, Lk 2:29

DISOBEDIENCE
through one man's **d**
 the many were Rm 5:19
received mercy through their **d**, Rm 11:30
we are ready to punish any **d**, 2Co 10:6
d received a just punishment, Heb 2:2
did not enter because of **d**, Heb 4:6
into the same pattern of **d**. Heb 4:11

DISOBEDIENT
But they were **d** and rebelled Neh 9:26
and the **d** to the understanding Lk 1:17
I was not **d** to the heavenly Ac 26:19
inventors of evil, **d** to parents, Rm 1:30
out My hands to a **d** and defiant Rm 10:21
spirit now working in the **d**. Eph 2:2
God's wrath is coming on the **d**. Eph 5:6
God's wrath comes on the **d**, Col 3:6
proud, blasphemers, **d** to parents, 2Tm 3:2
are detestable, **d**, and Ti 1:16
were once foolish, **d**, deceived Ti 3:3
in the past were **d**, when God 1Pt 3:20

DISOBEY
self-seeking and **d** the truth, Rm 2:8
you once **d-ed** God, but now have Rm 11:30

His rest," if not those who **d-ed**? Heb 3:18
They stumble by **d-ing** the message; 1Pt 2:8
be for those who **d** the gospel of 1Pt 4:17

DISORDER
is not a God of **d** but of peace. 1Co 14:33
gossip, arrogance, and **d**. 2Co 12:20
there is **d** and every kind of Jms 3:16

DISPERSE
I will **d** them throughout Jacob Gn 49:7
to {the place} where light is **d-d**? Jb 38:24
and would **d** their descendants Ps 106:27
and gather the **d-d** of Israel; Is 11:12
who gathers the **d-d** of Israel: Is 56:8
am the LORD when I **d** them
 among Ezk 12:15
that I would **d** them among the Ezk 20:23
I will **d** you among the nations Ezk 22:15
I **d-d** them among the nations, Ezk 36:19
where You have **d-d** them because Dn 9:7
supplicants, My **d-d** people, will Zph 3:10

DISPERSION
to go to the **D** among the Greeks Jn 7:35
To the 12 tribes in the **D**. Jms 1:1
of the **D** in the provinces 1Pt 1:1

DISPLAY
D the wonders of Your faithful Ps 17:7
but a fool **d-s** his stupidity. Pr 13:16
and I will **d** My glory within you Ezk 28:22
I will **d** My glory among the Ezk 39:21
I will **d** wonders in the heavens Jl 2:30
He **d-ed** His glory, and His Jn 2:11
God's works might be **d-ed** in him. Jn 9:3
I will **d** wonders in the heaven Ac 2:19
so that I may **d** My power in you Rm 9:17
desiring to **d** His wrath and to Rm 9:22
I think God has **d-ed** us, 1Co 4:9
always puts us on **d** in Christ, 2Co 2:14
ages He might **d** the immeasurable Eph 2:7

DISPLEASE
If she is **d-ing** to her master, Ex 21:8
but she becomes **d-ing** to him Dt 24:1
Jonah was greatly **d-d** and became Jnh 4:1

DISPLEASURE
You will know My **d**. Nm 14:34
and abandon Your **d** with us. Ps 85:4
A fool's **d** is known at once, Pr 12:16

DISPOSAL

was sold, wasn't it at your d?   Ac 5:4

DISPOSSESS

He will certainly d before you   Jos 3:10
nations the LORD had d-ed before   1Kg 14:24
the justice of all who are d-ed.   Pr 31:8
Israel will d their dispossessors,   Jr 49:2
Jacob will d those who d-ed them.   Ob 17
when they d-ed the nations   Ac 7:45

DISPUTE (n)

they have a d, it comes to me   Ex 18:16
Whoever has a d should go to   Ex 24:14
If there is a d between men,   Dt 25:1
stop the d before it breaks out   Pr 17:14
for a man to resolve a d,   Pr 20:3
He will settle d-s among the   Is 2:4
LORD also has a d with Judah.   Hs 12:2
He will settle d-s among many   Mc 4:3
Then a d also arose among them   Lk 22:24
What is this d that you're   Lk 24:17
Then a d arose between John's   Jn 3:25
a d broke out between the   Ac 23:7
envy, murder, d-s, deceit, and   Rm 1:29
sick interest in d-s and arguments   1Tm 6:4
reject foolish and ignorant d-s,   2Tm 2:23
quarrels, and d-s about the law   Ti 3:9
a confirming oath ends every d.   Heb 6:16

DISPUTE (v)

cases d-d at your gates   Dt 17:8
But let no one d; let no one   Hs 4:4
when he was d-ing with the Devil in   Jd 9

DISQUALIFY

others, I myself will not be d-ied.   1Co 9:27
Let no one d you, insisting on   Col 2:18

DISREGARD

D-ing the command of God, you   Mk 7:8
they d-ed the righteousness   Rm 10:3
Let no one d you.   Ti 2:15
in My covenant, I d-ed them," says   Heb 8:9
If anyone d-s Moses' law, he dies   Heb 10:28

DISSENSIONS

those who cause d and pitfalls   Rm 16:17
selfish ambitions, d, factions,   Gl 5:20

DISSIPATION

them into the same flood of d   1Pt 4:4

DISSOLVE

Your deal with Death will be d-d,   Is 28:18
All the heavenly bodies will d.   Is 34:4
elements will burn and be d-d,   2Pt 3:10
will be on fire and be d-d,   2Pt 3:12

DISTANCE

his sister stood at a d in order to see   Ex 2:4
will view the land from a d,   Dt 32:52
and keep their d from me;   Jb 30:10
its eyes penetrate the d.   Jb 39:29
and my relatives stand at a d.   Ps 38:11
friends keep their d from him!   Pr 19:7
also women looking on from a d.   Mk 15:40
Peter was following at a d.   Lk 22:54
but they saw them from a d,   Heb 11:13

DISTANT

We have come from a d land.   Jos 9:6
Good news from a d land is like   Pr 25:25
remember Me in the d lands;   Zch 10:9
and traveled to a d country,   Lk 15:13

DISTILL

they d the rain into its mist,   Jb 36:27

DISTINCTION

I will make a d between My   Ex 8:23
the LORD makes a d between Egypt   Ex 11:7
They make no d between the holy   Ezk 22:26
He made no d between us and them   Ac 15:9
believe, since there is no d.   Rm 3:22
for there is no d between Jew   Rm 10:12
don't make a d in the notes,   1Co 14:7

DISTINGUISH

You must d between the holy and   Lv 10:10
in order to d between the   Lv 11:47
you must d the clean animal   Lv 20:25
The people could not d the sound   Ezr 3:13
Daniel d-ed himself above the   Dn 6:3
who cannot d between their right   Jnh 4:11
to another, d-ing between spirits   1Co 12:10
been trained to d between good   Heb 5:14

DISTINGUISHED (adj)

holy God is d by righteousness.   Is 5:16
because a more d person than you   Lk 14:8
You are d, but we are dishonored   1Co 4:10

DISTINGUISHING (adj)

will be a d mark for you;   Ex 12:13

DISTORT

My clothing is **d-ed** with great   Jb 30:18

a rich man who **d-s** right and wrong   Pr 28:6

in deceit or **d-ing** God's message,   2Co 4:2

DISTRACTED

But Martha was **d** by her many   Lk 10:40

DISTRACTION

devoted to the Lord without **d**.   1Co 7:35

DISTRESS

Jacob was greatly afraid and **d-ed**;   Gn 32:7

who answered me in my day of **d**.   Gn 35:3

When you are in **d** and all these   Dt 4:30

I called to the LORD in my **d**;   2Sm 22:7

me in the day of my **d**,   2Sm 22:19

When he was in **d**, he sought the   2Ch 33:12

their time of **d**, they cried out   Neh 9:27

and constant **d** in his bones,   Jb 33:19

from the jaws of **d** to a spacious   Jb 36:16

exertion keep {you} from **d**?   Jb 36:19

The **d-es** of my heart increase;   Ps 25:17

their refuge in a time of **d**.   Ps 37:39

called out in **d**, and I rescued   Ps 81:7

call on You in the day of my **d**,   Ps 86:7

He rescued them from their **d**.   Ps 107:6

I called to the LORD in **d**;   Ps 118:5

In my **d** I called to the LORD,   Ps 120:1

done under the sun was **d-ing** to me.   Ec 2:17

gloom of the **d-ed** land will not be   Is 9:1

D has seized us—pain like a   Jr 6:24

LORD, see how I am in **d**.   Lm 1:20

spirit was deeply **d-ed** within me,   Dn 7:15

be a time of **d** such as never has   Dn 12:1

survivors in the day of **d**.   Ob 14

I called to the LORD in my **d**,   Jnh 2:2

a day of trouble and **d**, a day of   Zph 1:15

And they were deeply **d-ed**.   Mt 17:23

they were deeply **d-ed** and
went and   Mt 18:31

Deeply **d-ed**, each one began
to say   Mt 26:22

to be sorrowful and deeply **d-ed**.   Mt 26:37

will be great **d** in the land   Lk 21:23

affliction and **d** for every human   Rm 2:9

good because of the present **d**:   1Co 7:26

widows in their **d** and to keep   Jms 1:27

DISTRIBUTE

the men who are to **d** the land as   Nm 34:17

d the land as an inheritance   Jos 13:6

had finished **d-ing** the land   Jos 19:49

He **d-s** freely to the poor;   Ps 112:9

you have and **d** it to the poor,   Lk 18:22

property and **d-d** the proceeds to   Ac 2:45

This was then **d-d** to each person   Ac 4:35

as God has **d-d** a measure of faith   Rm 12:3

d-ing to each one as He wills.   1Co 12:11

DISTRIBUTION

overlooked in the daily **d**.   Ac 6:1

and **d-s** {of gifts} from the Holy   Heb 2:4

DISTRICT

of Keilah, made repairs for his **d**.   Neh 3:17

DISTURB

Why have you **d-ed** me
by bringing   1Sm 28:15

live there and not be **d-ed** again.   2Sm 7:10

Don't let anyone **d** his bones.   2Kg 23:18

and day so that no one **d-s** it.   Is 27:3

he was deeply **d-ed**, and all   Mt 2:3

those who are **d-ing** you might also   Gl 5:12

DISTURBANCE

I saw a big **d**, but I don't know   2Sm 18:29

was a major **d** about the Way.   Ac 19:23

DITCH

'Dig **d** after **d** in this wadi.   2Kg 3:16

DIVERSE

An ethnically **d** crowd also went   Ex 12:38

DIVERSIONS

No **d** were brought to him, and he   Dn 6:18

DIVIDE

his days the earth was **d-d**;   Gn 10:25

your hand over the sea, and **d** it   Ex 14:16

animal with **d-d** hooves and that   Lv 11:3

So they finished **d-ing** up the land.   Jos 19:51

the earth was **d-d** during his   1Ch 1:19

You **d-d** the sea before them,   Neh 9:11

They **d-d** my garments among   Ps 22:18

who stays at home **d-s** the spoil.   Ps 68:12

You **d-d** the sea with Your strength   Ps 74:13

He **d-d** the Red Sea His love is   Ps 136:13

humble than to **d** plunder with   Pr 16:19

whose land is **d-d** by rivers.   Is 18:2

be **d-d** into two kingdoms.   Ezk 37:22

kingdom has been **d-d** and given to   Dn 5:28

be broken up and **d-d** to the four	Dn 11:4
your land will be **d-d** up with a	Am 7:17
Every kingdom **d-d** against itself	Mt 12:25
Satan, he is **d-d** against himself	Mt 12:26
Him they **d-d** His clothes	Mt 27:35
my brother to **d** the inheritance	Lk 12:13
They will be **d-d**, father against	Lk 12:53
flames of fire that were **d-d**,	Ac 2:3
the people of the city were **d-d**,	Ac 14:4
Is Christ **d-d**? Was it Paul who was	1Co 1:13
tore down the **d-ing** wall of	Eph 2:14
as far as to **d** soul,	Heb 4:12

DIVINATION

drinks from and uses for **d**?	Gn 44:5
not to practice **d** or sorcery.	Lv 19:26
practice **d**, tell fortunes,	Dt 18:10
rebellion is like the sin of **d**,	1Sm 15:23
and practiced **d** and interpreted	2Kg 17:17
vision, worthless **d**, the deceit	Jr 14:14
and speak a lying **d** when you	Ezk 13:7
grow dark for you—without **d**.	Mc 3:6
prophets practice **d** for money.	Mc 3:11

DIVINE

So a **d** fire came down from	2Kg 1:12
His place in the **d** assembly;	Ps 82:1
think that the **d** nature is like	Ac 17:29
His eternal power and **d** nature,	Rm 1:20
For His **d** power has given us	2Pt 1:3
you may share in the **d** nature,	2Pt 1:4

DIVINER-PRIESTS

than all the **d** and mediums in	Dn 1:20
gave orders to summon the **d**,	Dn 2:2
When the **d**, mediums, Chaldeans	Dn 4:7

DIVINERS

to fortune-tellers and **d**,	Dt 18:14
from the direction of the **D'** Oak.	Jdg 9:37
Philistines summoned ... the **d**	1Sm 6:2
prophets and makes fools of **d**;	Is 44:25
and your **d** deceive you,	Jr 29:8
appointed him chief of the **d**,	Dn 5:11
ashamed and the **d** disappointed.	Mc 3:7
and the **d** see illusions;	Zch 10:2

DIVISION

d-s of the descendants of Aaron	1Ch 24:1
No, I tell you, but rather **d**!	Lk 12:51
So a **d** occurred among the crowd	Jn 7:43

And there was a **d** among them.	Jn 9:16
Again a **d** took place among the	Jn 10:19
that there be no **d-s** among you,	1Co 1:10
church there are **d-s** among you,	1Co 11:18
would be no **d** in the body,	1Co 12:25
people create **d-s** and are merely	Jd 19

DIVISIVE

Reject a **d** person after a first	Ti 3:10

DIVORCE

he cannot **d** her as long as he	Dt 22:19
may write her a **d** certificate,	Dt 24:1
Where is your mother's **d** certificate	Is 50:1
If a man **d-s** his wife and she	Jr 3:1
given her a certificate of **d**.	Jr 3:8
If he hates and **d-s** {his wife},	Mal 2:16
decided to **d** her secretly.	Mt 1:19
must give her a written notice of **d**.	Mt 5:31
for a man to **d** his wife on any	Mt 19:3
permitted you to **d** your wives	Mt 19:8
whoever **d-s** his wife, except for	Mt 19:9

DIVORCED (adj)

not to marry a widow, a **d** woman,	Lv 21:14
daughter becomes widowed or **d**,	Lv 22:13
to marry a widow or a **d** woman,	Ezk 44:22
marries a **d** woman commits	Mt 5:32

DO see also DOER, DOES, DONE

want others to **d** for you, **d** also	Mt 7:12
only what He sees the Father **d-ing**.	Jn 5:19
Sirs, what must I **d** to be saved?	Ac 16:30
I **d** not **d** the good that I want to **d**,	Rm 7:19
whatever you **d**, **d** everything for	1Co 10:31
But one thing I **d**: forgetting what	Php 3:13
able to **d** all things through Him	Php 4:13
whatever you **d**, in word or	
in deed, **d** everything	
in the name	Col 3:17
knows to **d** good and doesn't **d** it,	Jms 4:17

DOCTOR

you are all worthless **d-s**.	Jb 13:4
who are well don't need a **d**,	Mt 9:12
had endured much under many **d-s**.	Mk 5:26
proverb to Me: '**D**, heal yourself	Lk 4:23

DOCTRINE

teaching as **d-s** the commands of	Mt 15:9
rise up with deviant **d-s** to lure	Ac 20:30
contrary to the **d** you have	Rm 16:17

they are human commands and d-s.   Col 2:22
people not to teach other d   1Tm 1:3
teaches other d and does not   1Tm 6:3
they will not tolerate sound d,   2Tm 4:3

DOCUMENT

on a sealed d   Neh 9:38
A copy of the d was to be issued   Est 8:13
like the words of a sealed d.   Is 29:11
So King Darius signed the d.   Dn 6:9

DOE

A loving d, a graceful fawn   Pr 5:19

DOEG

Edomite, chief of Saul's shepherds; executed the priests of Nob (1Sm 21:1-7; 22:9-
22).

DOER

but the d-s of the law will be   Rm 2:13
But be d-s of the word and not   Jms 1:22
you are not a d of the law but a   Jms 4:11

DOES

oppose Him? He d what He desires   Jb 23:13
is in heaven and d whatever He   Ps 115:3
The LORD d whatever He pleases   Ps 135:6
He d what He wants with the   Dn 4:35
the one who d the will of My   Mt 7:21
'Do this!' and he d it.   Mt 8:9

DOG

the field; throw it to the d-s.   Ex 22:31
water with his tongue like a d.   Jdg 7:5
Am I a d that you come against   1Sm 17:43
after? A dead d? A flea?   1Sm 24:14
Am I a d-'s head who belongs to   2Sm 3:8
an interest in a dead d like me?   2Sm 9:8
should this dead d curse my lord   2Sm 16:9
in the city, the d-s will eat, and 1Kg 14:11
The d-s will eat Jezebel in the   1Kg 21:23
servant, a mere d, do this   2Kg 8:13
For d-s have surrounded me;   Ps 22:16
life from the power of the d.   Ps 22:20
snarling like d-s and prowling   Ps 59:6
As a d returns to its vomit,   Pr 26:11
one who grabs a d by the ears.   Pr 26:17
since a live d is better than a   Ec 9:4
of them are mute d-s, they cannot Is 56:10
a lamb, one breaks a d-'s neck;   Is 66:3
Don't give what is holy to d-s or Mt 7:6

bread and throw it to the d-s.   Mk 7:27
even the d-s under the table eat   Mk 7:28
but instead the d-s would come and Lk 16:21
Watch out for "d-s," watch out for Php 3:2
A d returns to its own vomit,   2Pt 2:22
Outside are the d-s, the sorcerers Rv 22:15

DOMAIN

flesh like ours under sin's d,   Rm 8:3
the ruler of the atmospheric d,   Eph 2:2
us from the d of darkness   Col 1:13

DOMINATE

husband, yet he will d you.   Gn 3:16
don't let sin d me.   Ps 119:133
rulers of the Gentiles d them,   Mt 20:25
if someone d-s you, or if   2Co 11:20

DOMINION

light to have d over the day   Gn 1:16
D and dread belong to Him,   Jb 25:2
The d will be vast, and its   Is 9:7
His d is an everlasting d,   Dn 4:34; 7:14
His d will extend from sea to   Zch 9:10
and the d of darkness.   Lk 22:53
in order that sin's d over the body Rm 6:6
power and d, and every title   Eph 1:21
whether thrones or d-s or rulers   Col 1:16
To Him be the d forever.   1Pt 5:11
the glory and d forever and ever   Rv 1:6
and glory and d to the One   Rv 5:13

DONATE

And if I d all my goods to feed   1Co 13:3

DONATION

must set aside a d to the LORD,   Ezk 45:1
This holy d will be set apart   Ezk 48:10

DONE

What will be d for the man who   1Sm 17:26
"What have I d now?" protested   1Sm 17:29
What should be d for the man   Est 6:6
says, "I've d nothing wrong."   Pr 30:20
what has been d is what will be d; Ec 1:9
or say to Him, "What have You d?" Dn 4:35
Your will be d on earth as it is   Mt 6:10
to him, 'Well d, good and   Mt 25:21
not My will, but Yours, be d.   Lk 22:42
been born yet or d anything good   Rm 9:11
the throne, saying, "It is d!   Rv 16:17

And He said to me, "It is **d**! Rv 21:6
according to what he has **d**. Rv 22:12

DONKEY

ties his **d** to a vine, and the colt Gn 49:11
slave, his ox or **d**, or anything Ex 20:17
the LORD opened the **d-**'s mouth, Nm 22:28
who ride on white **d-s**, who sit on Jdg 5:10
30 sons who rode on 30 young **d-s**. Jdg 10:4
30 grandsons, who rode on 70 **d-s**. Jdg 12:14
the jawbone of a **d** I have killed Jdg 15:16
One day the **d-s** of Saul's father 1Sm 9:3
Does a wild **d** bray over fresh Jb 6:5
soon as a wild **d** is born a man! Jb 11:12
Who set the wild **d** free? Jb 39:5
the wild **d-s** quench their thirst. Ps 104:11
bridle for the **d**, and a rod for Pr 26:3
and the **d** its master's Is 1:3
riders on **d-s**, riders on camels Is 21:7
Wild **d-s** stand on the barren Jr 14:6
riding on a **d**, on a colt, the foal of Zch 9:9
you will find a **d** tied there, Mt 21:2
mounted on a **d**, even on a colt Mt 21:5
untie his ox or **d** from the Lk 13:15
found a young **d** and sat on it, Jn 12:14
a speechless **d** spoke with a 2Pt 2:16

DOOM

and their **d** is coming quickly. Dt 32:35
their **d** would last forever. Ps 81:15
D has come on you, Ezk 7:7

DOOMED

without discernment are **d**. Hs 4:14

DOOR

sin is crouching at the **d**. Gn 4:7
locking the **d-s** of the upstairs Jdg 3:23
out of the **d-s** of my house to greet Jdg 11:31
slept at the **d** of the palace 2Sm 11:9
the sea behind **d-s** when it burst Jb 38:8
Rise up, ancient **d-s**! Then the King Ps 24:7
and opened the **d-s** of heaven. Ps 78:23
rather be at the **d** of the house Ps 84:10
keep watch at the **d** of my lips. Ps 141:3
watching at my **d-s** every day, Pr 8:34
A gift opens **d-s** for a man and Pr 18:16
A **d** turns on its hinge, and a Pr 26:14
and the **d-s** at the street are shut Ec 12:4
If she is a **d**, we will enclose Sg 8:9
and close your **d-s** behind you. Is 26:20

you would shut the {temple} **d-s**, Mal 1:10
room, shut your **d**, and pray to Mt 6:6
and the **d** will be opened to you Mt 7:7
that He is near—at the **d**! Mt 24:33
banquet, and the **d** was shut. Mt 25:10
The **d** is already locked, and my Lk 11:7
to enter through the narrow **d**, Lk 13:24
I am the **d**. If anyone enters by Jn 10:9
Even though the **d-s** were locked, Jn 20:26
He had opened the **d** of faith to Ac 14:27
because a wide **d** for effective 1Co 16:9
a **d** was opened to me by the Lord 2Co 2:12
that God may open a **d** to us for Col 3:3
the judge stands at the **d**! Jms 5:9
you an open **d** that no one Is Rv 3:8
I stand at the **d** and knock. Rv 3:20
there in heaven was an open **d**. Rv 4:1

DOORKEEPER

{the money} the **d-s** have collected 2Kg 22:4
commanded the **d** to be alert. Mk 13:34
The **d** opens it for him, and the Jn 10:3

DOORPOST

blood and put it on the two **d-s** Ex 12:7
Write them on the **d-s** of your house Dt 6:9
a chair by the **d** of the LORD's 1Sm 1:9
and apply {it} to the temple **d-s**, Ezk 45:19

DORCAS

Disciple; restored to life (Ac 9:36-42).

DOTHAN

City where Joseph was sold (Gn 37:17)
and where Elisha stayed (2Kg 6:13).

DOUBLE (adj)

by giving him a **d** portion of Dt 21:17
But he gave a **d** portion to Hannah, 1Sm 1:5
let there be a **d** portion of your 2Kg 2:9
people have committed a **d** evil: Jr 2:13
so you could have a **d** benefit, 2Co 1:15

DOUBLE (n)

thief, if caught, must repay **d**. Ex 22:7
the LORD's hand **d** for all her Is 40:2
repay them **d** for their guilt Jr 16:18
that I will restore **d** to you. Zch 9:12

DOUBLE (v)

d-d his {previous} possessions. Jb 42:10
and **d** it according to her works Rv 18:6

DOUBLE-EDGED

made himself a **d** sword 18 inches Jdg 3:16
and as sharp as a **d** sword. Pr 5:4

DOUBLE-MINDED

I hate the **d**, but I love Your Ps 119:113
purify your hearts, **d** people! Jms 4:8

DOUBLY

in her household are **d** clothed. Pr 31:21

DOUBT (n)

life will hang in **d** before you. Dt 28:66
No **d** you will quote this Lk 4:23
And why do **d-s** arise in your Lk 24:38
them with no **d-s** at all, Ac 10:20
Without a **d**, the inferior is Heb 7:7

DOUBT (v)

of little faith, why did you **d**? Mt 14:31
If you have faith and do not **d**, Mt 21:21
they worshiped, but some **d-ed**. Mt 28:17
whoever **d-s** stands condemned Rm 14:23
let him ask in faith without **d-ing**. Jms 1:6
Have mercy on some who **d**; Jd 22

DOUBTER

For the **d** is like the surging Jms 1:6

DOUBTFUL

but don't argue about **d** issues. Rm 14:1

DOUBTLESS

There are **d** many different kinds 1Co 14:10

DOUGH

took their **d** before it was leavened, Ex 12:34
from the first batch of your **d**. Nm 15:21
first batch of **d** to the priests Neh 10:37
first batch of **d** to the priest Ezk 44:30
permeates the whole batch of **d**? 1Co 5:6
leavens the whole lump of **d**. Gl 5:9

DOVE

he sent out a **d** to see whether Gn 8:8
If only I had wings like a **d**! Ps 55:6
beautiful! Your eyes are **d-s**. Sg 1:15
my darling, my **d**, my perfect one Sg 5:2
I moan like a **d**. My eyes grow Is 38:14
like bears and moan like **d-s**. Is 59:11
like a silly, senseless **d**; Hs 7:11
moan like the sound of **d-s**, Nah 2:7
Spirit of God descending like a **d** Mt 3:16
serpents and as harmless as **d-s**. Mt 10:16

the chairs of those selling **d-s**. Mt 21:12
descending to Him like a **d**. Mk 1:10
a physical appearance like a **d**. Lk 3:22
from heaven like a **d**, Jn 1:32

DOWNCAST

Cain was furious, and he was **d**. Gn 4:5

DOWNFALL

Ahaziah's **d** was from God, 2Ch 22:7
they were the **d** of him and of 2Ch 28:23
Before his **d** a man's heart is proud, Pr 18:12
Her **d** was astonishing; Lm 1:9
causes the **d** of one of these Mt 18:6
And if your eye causes your **d**, Mt 18:9

DOWNPOUR

a **d** of water sweeps by. Hab 3:10

DOWNWARD

again take root **d** and bear fruit 2Kg 19:30
of animals goes **d** to the earth? Ec 3:21
again take root **d** and bear fruit Is 37:31

DOWRY

gave it as a **d** to his daughter 1Kg 9:16

DRAFTED

King Solomon **d** forced laborers 1Kg 5:13

DRAG

Do not **d** me away with the wicked Ps 28:3
D the wicked away like sheep to Jr 12:3
the dogs to **d** away, and Jr 15:3
little lambs will be **d-ged** away; Jr 50:45
Then he won't **d** you before the Lk 12:58
after house, **d** off men and women Ac 8:3
they **d-ged** him out of the city, Ac 14:19
Paul and Silas and **d-ged** them into Ac 16:19
d-ged him out of the
   temple complex Ac 21:30
and **d** you into the courts? Jms 2:6

DRAGNET

them in their **d**, and gather them Hab 1:15

DRAGON

a great fiery red **d** having seven Rv 12:3
And the **d** stood in front of the Rv 12:4
angels fought against the **d**. Rv 12:7
the river that the **d** had spewed Rv 12:16
worshiped the **d** because he gave Rv 13:4
He seized the **d**, that ancient serpent Rv 20:2

DRAINING

will drink, **d** it to the dregs.   Ps 75:8

DRAW

the women went out to **d** water.   Gn 24:11
I **drew** him out of the water.   Ex 2:10
the path with a **d-n** sword in His   Nm 22:23
of him with a **d-n** sword in His   Jos 5:13
But a man **drew** his bow without   1Kg 22:34
The wicked have **d-n** the sword   Ps 37:14
but they are **d-n** swords.   Ps 55:21
D near to me and redeem me;   Ps 69:18
a man of understanding **d-s** it up.   Pr 20:5
and twisting a nose **d-s** blood,   Pr 30:33
Better to **d** near in obedience   Ec 5:1
You will joyfully **d** water from   Is 12:3
Now **d** some out and take it to   Jn 2:8
of Samaria came to **d** water.   Jn 4:7
the Father who sent Me **d-s** him,   Jn 6:44
earth I will **d** all (people) to   Jn 12:32
who had a sword, **drew** it, struck   Jn 18:10
they are **d-n** away from Christ   1Tm 5:11
through which we **d** near to God.   Heb 7:19
let us **d** near with a true heart   Heb 10:22
as you see the day **d-ing** near.   Heb 10:25
But we are not those who **d** back   Heb 10:39
when he is **d-n** away and enticed   Jms 1:14
D near to God, and He will **d** near   Jms 4:8

DREAD (n)

begin to put the fear and **d** of you   Dt 2:25
You will be in **d** night and day,   Dt 28:66
land and that **d** of you has   Jos 2:9
I am an object of **d** to my   Ps 31:11
There is no **d** of God before his   Ps 36:1
for **d** of Israel had fallen on   Ps 105:38

DREAD (v)

came to **d** the Israelites.   Ex 1:12
and what I **d-ed** has happened to me   Jb 3:25
What the wicked **d-s** will come   Pr 10:24
two kings you **d** will be   Is 7:16
will bring on them what they **d**,   Is 66:4

DREADFUL

the Day of the LORD is terrible and **d**   Jl 2:11

DREAM (n)

Joseph had a **d**.   Gn 37:5
cupbearer told his **d** to Joseph: Gn 40:9
years later Pharaoh had a **d**:   Gn 41:1

I speak with him in a **d**.   Nm 12:6
telling his friend {about} a **d**.   Jdg 7:13
LORD did not answer him in **d-s** or   1Sm 28:6
to Solomon in a **d** at night.   1Kg 3:5
fly away like a **d** and never be   Jb 20:8
Like one waking from a **d**, Lord,   Ps 73:20
For many **d-s** bring futility,   Ec 5:7
will then be like a **d**, a vision   Is 29:7
said: I had a **d**! I had a **d**!   Jr 23:25
Daniel also understood ... **d-s**   Dn 1:17
Nebuchadnezzar had **d-s**   Dn 2:1
I had a **d**, and it frightened me   Dn 4:5
and the ability to interpret **d-s**,   Dn 5:12
Daniel had a **d** with visions in   Dn 7:1
your old men will have **d-s**, and   Jl 2:28
appeared to him in a **d**,   Mt 1:20
appeared to Joseph in a **d**,   Mt 2:13
terribly in a **d** because of Him!   Mt 27:19
and your old men will dream **d-s**.   Ac 2:17

DREAM (v)

he **d-ed**: A stairway was set on   Gn 28:12
we were like those who **d**.   Ps 126:1
hungry one who **d-s** he is eating,   Is 29:8
they **d**, lie down, and love to   Is 56:10

DREAMER

Here comes that **d**!   Gn 37:19
That prophet or **d** must be put to   Dt 13:5
these **d-s** likewise defile their flesh,   Jd 8

DREGS

drink, draining it to the **d**.   Ps 75:8
drunk the goblet to the **d**   Is 51:17
settled (like wine) on its **d**.   Jr 48:11

DRENCH

with my tears I ... **d** my bed   Ps 6:6
For my head is **d-ed** with dew,   Sg 5:2
I **d** Heshbon ... with my tears.   Is 16:9
like cattle and be **d-ed** with dew   Dn 4:25

DRESS

of the temple with **d-ed** stones.   1Kg 5:17
and there was a man **d-ed** in linen,   Dn 10:5
a fast and **d-ed** in sackcloth   Jnh 3:5
Now Joshua was **d-ed** with filthy   Zch 3:3
A man **d-ed** in soft clothes?   Mt 11:8
who was not **d-ed** for a wedding.   Mt 22:11
sitting there, **d-ed** and in his   Mk 5:15
man who would **d** in purple and   Lk 16:19

the women are to **d** themselves in | 1Tm 2:9
a gold ring, **d-ed** in fine clothes | Jms 2:2
that you may be **d-ed** and your | Rv 3:18

DRIFT

so that we will not **d** away. | Heb 2:1

DRINK (n)

The **d** offering is to be a quart | Nm 28:7
and mingle my **d-s** with tears | Ps 102:9
I'll look for another {**d**}. | Pr 23:35
"Give Me a **d**," Jesus said to her | Jn 4:7
poured out as a **d**
    offering | Php 2:17; 2Tm 4:6

DRINK (v)

He **drank** some of the wine, | Gn 9:21
they got their father to **d** wine | Gn 19:33
What are we going to **d**? | Ex 15:24
saw Him, and they ate and **drank**. | Ex 24:11
people sat down to eat and **d**, | Ex 32:6
sons are not to **d** wine or beer | Lv 10:9
was in Tirzah **d-ing** himself drunk | 1Kg 16:9
and he **drank** from the wadi. | 1Kg 17:6
flesh of bulls or **d** the blood of | Ps 50:13
they gave me vinegar to **d**. | Ps 69:21
D water from your own cistern, | Pr 5:15
let's **d** deeply of lovemaking | Pr 7:18
his own feet and **d-s** violence. | Pr 26:6
not for kings to **d** wine or for | Pr 31:4
Let him **d** so that he can forget | Pr 31:7
to eat, **d**, and | Ec 2:24; 5:18; 8:15
and **d** your wine with a cheerful | Ec 9:7
D, be intoxicated with love! | Sg 5:1
those who are heroes at **d-ing** wine, | Is 5:22
eat and **d**, for tomorrow we die! | Is 22:13
who have **drunk** the cup of His fury | Is 51:17
and in dread **d** water by measure | Ezk 4:16
You will **d** your sister's cup, | Ezk 23:32
and concubines **drank** from them. | Dn 5:3
Bring us something to **d**. | Am 4:1
another city to **d** water but were | Am 4:8
You **d** but never have enough to | Hg 1:6
will eat or what you will **d**; | Mt 6:25
Son of Man came eating and **d-ing**, | Mt 11:19
to **d** the cup that I am about to **d**? | Mt 20:22
flood they were eating and **d-ing**, | Mt 24:38
and you gave Me something to **d**; | Mt 25:35
that day when I **d** it in a new way | Mt 26:29
Him wine mixed with gall to **d**. | Mt 27:34

cup of water to **d** because of My | Mk 9:41
and so they all **drank** from it. | Mk 14:23
if they should **d** anything deadly | Mk 16:18
Why do you eat and **d** with tax | Lk 5:30
no one, after **d-ing** old wine, wants | Lk 5:39
eat, **d**, and enjoy yourself. | Lk 12:19
went on eating, **d-ing**, marrying | Lk 17:27
after people have **drunk** freely, | Jn 2:10
But whoever **d-s** from the water | Jn 4:14
Unless you ... **d** His blood, | Jn 6:53
he should come to Me and **d**! | Jn 7:37
Am I not to **d** the cup the Father | Jn 18:11
who ate and **drank** with Him after | Ac 10:41
give him something to **d**. | Rm 12:20
of God is not eating and **d-ing**, | Rm 14:17
all **drank** the same spiritual **d** | 1Co 10:4
you eat or **d**, or whatever you | 1Co 10:31
Do this, as often as you **d** it, | 1Co 11:25
all made to **d** of one Spirit. | 1Co 12:13
eat and **d**, for tomorrow we die. | 1Co 15:32
Don't continue **d-ing** only water, | 1Tm 5:23
ground that has **drunk** the rain that | Heb 6:7
all nations **d** the wine of her | Rv 14:8
he will also **d** the wine of God's | Rv 14:10
nations have **drunk** the wine of her | Rv 18:3

DRIP

than honey **d-ping** from the comb. | Ps 19:10
lips of the forbidden woman **d** honey | Pr 5:3
an endless **d-ping** | Pr 19:13; 27:15
Your lips **d** {sweetness like} | Sg 4:11
My hands **d-ped** with myrrh, | Sg 5:5
lips are lilies, **d-ping** with flowing | Sg 5:13
mountains will **d** with sweet wine | Jl 3:18
mountains will **d** with sweet wine | Am 9:13

DRIVE

He **drove** man out, | Gn 3:24
arrived and **drove** them away, | Ex 2:17
and made them **d** with difficulty | Ex 14:25
I will **d** them out little by little | Ex 23:30
you must **d** out all the | Nm 33:52
did not **d** them out completely. | Jos 17:13
The LORD **drove** out before us all | Jos 24:18
they could not **d** out the people | Jdg 1:19
I will not **d** out these people | Jdg 2:3
angel of the LORD **d-ing** them away. | Ps 35:5
wish me harm be **d-n** back | Ps 40:14; 70:2
You **drove** out the nations and | Ps 80:8
D out a mocker, and conflict | Pr 22:10

discipline will **d** it away from Pr 22:15
the peg that was **d-n** into a firm Is 22:25
I will **d** you from My presence, Jr 7:15
I will **d** them from My house Hs 9:15
d out demons in Your name, Mt 7:22
drove out all those buying and Mt 21:12
Immediately the Spirit **drove** Him Mk 1:12
we saw someone **d-ing** out demons Mk 9:38
He **drove** everyone out of the temple Jn 2:15
perfect love **d-s** out fear, 1Jn 4:18

DRIVEN (adj)
the surging sea, **d** and tossed Jms 1:6

DRIVING (adj)
a **d** rain that leaves no food. Pr 28:3

DRIVING (n)
the **d** is like that of Jehu 2Kg 9:20

DROP (n)
nations are like a **d** in a bucket; Is 40:15
became like **d-s** of blood falling Lk 22:44

DROP (v)
Didn't a woman **d** an upper 2Sm 11:21
a letter in the law to **d** out. Lk 16:17

DROSS
on earth as if they were **d**; Ps 119:119
Your silver has become **d**, Is 1:22
will burn away your **d** completely; Is 1:25
Israel has become **d** to Me. Ezk 22:18

DROUGHT
a land of **d** and darkness, Jr 2:6
to Jeremiah concerning the d Jr 14:1
in a year of **d** or cease Jr 17:8
have summoned a **d** on the fields Hg 1:11

DROWNED
officers were **d** in the Red Sea. Ex 15:4
neck and he were **d** in the depths Mt 18:6
bank into the sea and **d** there. Mk 5:13

DRUNK (adj)
wine, became **d**, and uncovered Gn 9:21
make My arrows **d** with blood Dt 32:42
Eli thought she was **d** 1Sm 1:13
was in a good mood and very **d**, 1Sm 25:36
and David got him **d**. 2Sm 11:13
drinking himself **d** in the house 1Kg 16:9
were getting **d** in the tents. 1Kg 20:16
They are **d**, but not with wine; Is 29:9

I made them **d** with My wrath Is 63:6
Drink, get **d**, and vomit. Jr 25:27
hand making the whole earth **d**. Jr 51:7
I will make them **d** so that they Jr 51:39
never have enough to become **d**. Hg 1:6
For these people are not **d**, Ac 2:15
is hungry while another is **d**! 1Co 11:21
And don't get **d** with wine, Eph 5:18
and those who get **d** are **d** at night. 1Th 5:7
the earth became **d** on the wine Rv 17:2
the woman was **d** on the blood Rv 17:6

DRUNKARD
He's a glutton and a **d**. Dt 21:20
and **d-s** make up songs about me. Ps 69:12
For the **d** and the glutton will Pr 23:21
brandished by the hand of a **d**. Pr 26:9
staggers like a **d** and sways like Is 24:20
Wake up, you **d-s**, and weep; Jl 1:5
a glutton and a **d**, a friend of Mt 11:19
a reviler, a **d** or a swindler. 1Co 5:11
greedy people, **d-s**, revilers, or 1Co 6:10

DRUNKEN
and staggered like **d** men, Ps 107:27

DRUNKENNESS
for strength and not for **d**. Ec 10:17
be filled with **d** and grief, Ezk 23:33
from carousing, **d**, and worries Lk 21:34
not in carousing and **d**; Rm 13:13
envy, **d**, carousing, and anything Gl 5:21
evil desires, **d**, orgies 1Pt 4:3

DRUSILLA
Wife of Felix (Ac 24:24).

DRY (adj)
and let the **d** land appear. Gn 1:9
go through the sea on **d** ground. Ex 14:16
Israel crossed on **d** ground Jos 3:17
bread was **d** and crumbly. Jos 9:5
the fleece was **d**, and dew was Jdg 6:40
oil jug will not run **d** until 1Kg 17:14
crossed over on **d** ground. 2Kg 2:8
for You in a land that is **d**, Ps 63:1
d land into springs of water. Ps 107:35
Better a **d** crust with peace than Pr 17:1
like a root out of **d** ground. Is 53:2
whose waters never run **d**. Is 58:11
her sea and make her fountain run **d**. Jr 51:36

in a **d** and thirsty land — Ezk 19:13
D bones, hear the word of — Ezk 37:4
He makes all the rivers run **d**. — Nah 1:4
what will happen when it is **d**? — Lk 23:31

DRY (v)

the surface of the ground was **d-ing**. — Gn 8:13
how the LORD **d-ied** up the waters — Jos 2:10
My strength is **d-ied** up like baked — Ps 22:15
You **d-ied** up ever-flowing rivers. — Ps 74:15
by evening it withers and **d-ies** up. — Ps 90:6
a broken spirit **d-ies** up the bones. — Pr 17:22
I **d** up the sea by My rebuke; — Is 50:2
Wasn't it You who **d-ied** up the sea, — Is 51:10
the new wine is **d-ied** up; — Jl 1:10
heat and **d-ies** up the grass; — Jms 1:11

DUE

the LORD the glory **d** His name; — Ps 29:2
proclaim all the praise **d** Him? — Ps 106:2
give them their food in **d** time. — Ps 145:15
He may exalt you in **d** time, — 1Pt 5:6

DULL

If the axe is **d**, and one does — Ec 10:10
D these people's minds; — Is 6:10

DUMB

you were led to **d** idols—being — 1Co 12:2

DUNG

and its **d** outside the camp; — Ex 29:14
hide, flesh, and **d** burned up. — Lv 16:27
sweeps away **d** until it is all — 1Kg 14:10
cup of dove's **d** {sold for} five — 2Kg 6:25
repaired the **D** Gate. — Neh 3:14
you {use} cow **d** instead of human — Ezk 4:15

DUNGEON

they should put me in the **d**. — Gn 40:15
the prisoner who was in the **d**, — Ex 12:29
bring out prisoners from the **d**, — Is 42:7
a cell in the **d** and stayed there — Jr 37:16

DURING

His disciples came **d** the night — Mt 28:13
remember that **d** your life you — Lk 16:25
If anyone walks **d** the day, — Jn 11:9

DUST

man out of the **d** from the ground — Gn 2:7
belly and eat **d** all the days — Gn 3:14
you are **d**, and you will return to **d**. — Gn 3:19

offspring like the **d** of the earth, — Gn 13:16
even though I am **d** and ashes — Gn 18:27
All the **d** of the earth became — Ex 8:17
take some of the **d** from the — Nm 5:17
Who has counted the **d** of Jacob — Nm 23:10
the poor from the **d** and lifts — 1Sm 2:8
you up from the **d** and made you — 1Kg 16:2
Will You now return me to **d**? — Jb 10:9
and repent in **d** and ashes. — Jb 42:6
them like **d** before the wind; — Ps 18:42
You put me into the **d** of death. — Ps 22:15
go down to the **d** will kneel — Ps 22:29
Pit? Will the **d** praise You? Will — Ps 30:9
him and his enemies lick the **d**. — Ps 72:9
You return mankind to the **d**, — Ps 90:3
remembering that we are **d**. — Ps 103:14
they die and return to the **d**. — Ps 104:29
all come from **d**, and all return to **d**. — Ec 3:20
as a speck of **d** on the scales; — Is 40:15
who sleep in the **d** of the earth — Dn 12:2
will lick the **d** like a snake; — Mc 7:17
shake the **d** off your feet when — Mt 10:14
you even the **d** of your town that — Lk 10:11
But shaking the **d** off their feet — Ac 13:51
The first man was ... made of **d**; — 1Co 15:47
They threw **d** on their heads and — Rv 18:19

DUTY

Perform your **d** as her brother-in-law — Gn 38:8
army or be liable for any **d**. — Dt 24:5
perform the **d** of a brother-in-law — Dt 25:5
who come on **d** on the Sabbath — 2Kg 11:5
we've only done our **d**. — Lk 17:10
his marital **d** to his wife, — 1Co 7:3

DWARF

or who is a hunchback or a **d**, — Lv 21:20

DWELL

so that I might **d** among them. — Ex 29:46
God chooses to have His name **d**. — Dt 16:6
who **d-s** {between} the cherubim. — 2Sm 6:2
where I chose to have My name **d**. — Neh 1:9
LORD, who can **d** in Your tent? — Ps 15:1
and I will **d** in the house of the — Ps 23:6
I love the house where You **d**, — Ps 26:8
d in the land and live securely — Ps 37:3
d-s in the shadow of the Almighty. — Ps 91:1
he will **d** on the heights; — Is 33:16
and Israel will **d** securely. — Jr 23:6

and I will **d** among them forever   Ezk 43:9
and light **d**-s with Him.   Dn 2:22
I am coming to **d** among you   Zch 2:10
High does not **d** in sanctuaries   Ac 7:48
I will **d** among them and walk   2Co 6:16
the Messiah may **d** in your hearts   Eph 3:17
any praise—**d** on these things   Php 4:8
all His fullness **d** in Him,   Col 1:19
of God's nature **d**-s bodily,   Col 2:9
the Messiah **d** richly among you   Col 3:16
d-ing in unapproachable light,   1Tm 6:16

DWELLING

to put His name for His **d**.   Dt 12:5
a place for Your **d** forever.   1Kg 8:13
hear in Your **d** place in heaven   1Kg 8:30
How lovely is Your **d** place,   Ps 84:1
My **d** place will be with them;   Ezk 37:27
may welcome you into eternal **d**-s.   Lk 16:9
house are many **d** places;   Jn 14:2
might provide a **d** place for the   Ac 7:46
being built together for God's **d**   Eph 2:22
God's **d** is with men,   Rv 21:3

DWINDLE

Wealth obtained by fraud will **d**,   Pr 13:11

DYED

ram skins **d** red and manatee   Ex 35:7
of his warriors are **d** red;   Nah 2:3

DYNASTY

establish a lasting **d** for him,   1Sm 2:35
to make a lasting **d** for my lord   1Sm 25:28
and made me a **d** as He promised   1Kg 2:24
you a lasting **d** just as I built   1Kg 11:38
but to the **d** I am fighting.   2Ch 35:21

DYSENTERY

bed suffering from fever and **d**.   Ac 28:8

E

EAGER

feet **e** to run to evil,   Pr 6:18
my brothers, be **e** to prophesy   1Co 14:39

I am very **e** to send him so that   Php 2:28
special people, **e** to do good   Ti 2:14

EAGERLY

For the creation **e** waits with   Rm 8:19
spiritual gift as you **e** wait for   1Co 1:7
by the Spirit we **e** wait for the   Gl 5:5
which we also **e** wait for a   Php 3:20
not for the money but **e**;   1Pt 5:2

EAGERNESS

the message with **e** and examined   Ac 17:11
For if the **e** is there, it is   2Co 8:12

EAGLE

I carried you on **e**-s' wings and   Ex 19:4
to swoop down on you like an **e**,   Dt 28:49
nest like an **e** and hovers over   Dt 32:11
swifter than **e**-s, stronger than   2Sm 1:23
like an **e** swooping down on   Jb 9:26
youth is renewed like the **e**.   Ps 103:5
and flies like an **e** to the sky.   Pr 23:5
the way of an **e** in the sky,   Pr 30:19
they will soar on wings like **e**-s;   Is 40:31
His horses are swifter than **e**-s.   Jr 4:13
elevate your nest like the **e**,   Jr 49:16
the left, and the face of an **e**.   Ezk 1:10
and the fourth that of an **e**.   Ezk 10:14
A great **e** with great wings,   Ezk 17:3
like a lion but had **e**-'s wings.   Dn 7:4
creature was like a flying **e**.   Rv 4:7
given two wings of a great **e**,   Rv 12:14

EAR

must pierce his **e** with an awl,   Ex 21:6
through his **e** into the door,   Dt 15:17
eyes to see, or **e**-s to hear.   Dt 29:4
Doesn't the **e** test words   Jb 12:11; 34:3
and His **e**-s are open to their cry   Ps 34:15
One who shaped the **e** not hear,   Ps 94:9
They have **e**-s, but cannot hear   Ps 115:6
and the **e** of the wise seeks it.   Pr 18:15
The hearing **e** and the seeing eye   Pr 20:12
one who shuts his **e**-s to the cry   Pr 21:13
one who grabs a dog by the **e**-s.   Pr 26:17
otherwise they ... hear with their **e**-s,   Is 6:10
and the **e**-s of the deaf unstopped   Is 35:5
He awakens My **e** to listen like   Is 50:4
They have **e**-s, but they don't hear   Jr 5:21
and **e**-s to hear but do not hear,   Ezk 12:2
a piece of an **e** from the lion's   Am 3:12

Anyone who has e-s should listen!   Mt 11:15
their e-s are hard of hearing,   Mt 13:15
Immediately his e-s were opened,   Mk 7:35
touching his e, He healed him.   Lk 22:51
slave, and cut off his right e.   Jn 18:10
uncircumcised hearts and e-s!   Ac 7:51
stopped their e-s, and rushed   Ac 7:57
has seen and no e has heard,   1Co 2:9
And if the e should say   1Co 12:16
His e-s are open to their request.   1Pt 3:12
who has an e should listen to   Rv 2:7
If anyone has an e, he should   Rv 13:9

EARLOBE

and put it on Aaron's right e,   Ex 29:20
put {it} on Aaron's right e,   Lv 8:23
on the right e of the one to be   Lv 14:25

EARLY

in season, the e and late rains   Dt 11:14
vain you get up e and stay up   Ps 127:2
a loud voice e in the morning,   Pr 27:14
the rain, both e and late, in   Jr 5:24
Very e in the morning, while it   Mk 1:35
Very e in the morning, on the   Mk 16:2
the week, very e in the morning   Lk 24:1
Magdalene came to the tomb e,   Jn 20:1
it receives the e and the late   Jms 5:7

EARN

but whoever e-s it through labor   Pr 13:11
them to work, and e-ed five more.   Mt 25:16
your mina has e-ed 10 more minas.   Lk 19:16
the gospel should e their living   1Co 9:14

EARNESTLY

was being made e to God for him   Ac 12:5
as we pray e night and day to   1Th 3:10
yet he prayed e that it would   Jms 5:17
love one another e from a pure   1Pt 1:22
you wait for and e desire the   2Pt 3:12

EARNINGS

plants a vineyard with her e.   Pr 31:16

EARRING

brooches, e-s, rings, necklaces   Ex 35:22
rings, e-s, and necklaces   Nm 31:50
enemy had gold e-s because they   Jdg 8:24
him a qesitah, and a gold e.   Jb 42:11

EARTH

God created the heavens and the e.   Gn 1:1

Now the e was corrupt in God's   Gn 6:11
and multiply and fill the e.   Gn 9:1
Judge of all the e do what is just?   Gn 18:25
may know the e is the LORD's.   Ex 9:29
although all the e is Mine,   Ex 19:5
e below or the waters under the e.   Ex 20:4
as the whole e is filled with   Nm 14:21
The e opened its mouth and   Nm 16:32
and e as witnesses   Dt 4:26; 30:19; 31:28
now going the way of all the e,   Jos 23:14
will judge the ends of the e.   1Sm 2:10
going the way of all of the e.   1Kg 2:2
But will God indeed live on e?   1Kg 8:27
Sing to the LORD, all the e.   1Ch 16:23
He is coming to judge the e.   1Ch 16:33
the e and all that is on it,   Neh 9:6
He hangs the e on nothing.   Jb 26:7
you when I established the e?   Jb 38:4
kings of the e take their stand   Ps 2:2
has gone out to all the e,   Ps 19:4
The e and everything in it,   Ps 24:1
for God is King of all the e.   Ps 47:7
is the joy of the whole e.   Ps 48:2
Your glory be over the whole e.   Ps 57:5,11
whole e is filled with His glory.   Ps 72:19
I desire nothing on e but You.   Ps 73:25
Before You gave birth to the e   Ps 90:2
sing to the LORD, all the e.   Ps 96:1
He is coming to judge the e.   Ps 96:13
LORD reigns! Let the e rejoice;   Ps 97:1
Shout to the LORD, all the e;   Ps 98:4
as the heavens are above the e,   Ps 103:11
Your glory be over the whole e,   Ps 108:5
majesty covers heaven and e.   Ps 148:13
The LORD founded the e by wisdom   Pr 3:19
beginning, before the e began.   Pr 8:23
is high and the e is deep,   Pr 25:3
The e trembles under three   Pr 30:21
but the e remains forever.   Ec 1:4
is in heaven and you are on e,   Ec 5:2
His glory fills the whole e.   Is 6:3
a curse has consumed the e,   Is 24:6
enthroned above the circle of the e; Is 40:22
has established justice on e.   Is 42:4
salvation to the ends of the e.   Is 49:6
the e will wear out like a garment,   Is 51:6
all the ends of the e will see   Is 52:10
is called the God of all the e.   Is 54:5

For as heaven is higher than **e**,	Is 55:9
there without saturating the **e**,	Is 55:10
a new heaven and a new **e**;	Is 65:17
My throne, and **e** is My footstool	Is 66:1
as the new heavens and the new **e**,	Is 66:22
E, **e**, **e**, hear the word of the Lord!	Jr 22:29
not fill the heavens and the **e**?	Jr 23:24
the joy of the whole **e**?	Lm 2:15
lifted me up between **e** and heaven	Ezk 8:3
and the **e** shone with His glory.	Ezk 43:2
The **e** will respond to the grain	Hs 2:22
e will be filled with the knowledge	Hab 2:14
let everyone on **e** be silent in	Hab 2:20
The whole **e** will be consumed by	Zph 1:18
they will inherit the **e**.	Mt 5:5
Until heaven and **e** pass away,	Mt 5:18
or by the **e**, because it is His	Mt 5:35
will be done on **e** as it is in	Mt 6:10
for yourselves treasures on **e**,	Mt 6:19
authority on **e** to forgive sins	Mt 9:6
I came to bring peace on the **e**.	Mt 10:34
you bind on **e** is already bound	Mt 18:18
Heaven and **e** will pass away,	Mt 24:35
given to Me in heaven and on **e**.	Mt 28:18
and peace on **e** to people He	Lk 2:14
I came to bring fire on the **e**,	Lk 12:49
will He find that faith on **e**?	Lk 18:8
one who is from the **e** is earthly	Jn 3:31
up from the **e** I will draw all	Jn 12:32
I have glorified You on the **e** by	Jn 17:4
and to the ends of the **e**.	Ac 1:8
My throne, and **e** My footstool.	Ac 7:49
may be proclaimed in all the **e**.	Rm 9:17
has gone out to all the **e**,	Rm 10:18
the **e** is the Lord's, and all	1Co 10:26
The first man was from the **e**	1Co 15:47
in heaven and on **e** and under	
the **e**	Php 2:10
whether things on **e** or things in	Col 1:20
established the **e**, and the	Heb 1:10
voice shook the **e** at that time,	Heb 12:26
wait for new heavens and a new **e**,	2Pt 3:13
all the families of the **e** will mourn	Rv 1:7
in heaven or on **e** or under the	Rv 5:3
Don't harm the **e** or the sea or	Rv 7:3
was thrown to **e**, and his angels	Rv 12:9
the **e** opened its mouth and	Rv 12:16
beast coming up out of the **e**;	Rv 13:11
swung His sickle over the **e**,	Rv 14:16
bowls of God's wrath on the **e**.	Rv 16:1
E and heaven fled from His	Rv 20:11
I saw a new heaven and a new **e**,	Rv 21:1

EARTHEN
are like glaze on an **e** vessel.	Pr 26:23

EARTHENWARE
but also those of wood and **e**,	2Tm 2:20

EARTHLY
is **e** and speaks in **e** terms.	Jn 3:31
heavenly bodies and **e** bodies,	1Co 15:40
we know that if our **e** house,	2Co 5:1
They are focused on **e** things,	Php 3:19
During His **e** life, He offered	Heb 5:7
and an **e** sanctuary.	Heb 9:1
above, but is **e**, sensual	Jms 3:15

EARTHQUAKE
but the Lord was not in the **e**.	1Kg 19:11
with thunder, **e**, and loud noise	Is 29:6
Israel, two years before the **e**.	Am 1:1
you fled from the **e** in the days	Zch 14:5
be famines and **e**-s in various	Mt 24:7
Suddenly there was a violent **e**,	Mt 28:2
was such a violent **e** that the	Ac 16:26
A violent **e** occurred;	Rv 6:12
people were killed in the **e**.	Rv 11:13
And a severe **e** occurred like no	Rv 16:18

EASE
I was at **e**, but He shattered me	Jb 16:12
are always at **e**, and they	Ps 73:12
do the treacherous live at **e**?	Jr 12:1
go up against a nation at **e**,	Jr 49:31
who are at **e** in Zion and	Am 6:1
with the nations that are at **e**,	Zch 1:15

EASES
I was like one who **e** the yoke	Hs 11:4

EASIER
For which is **e**: to say, 'Your	Mt 9:5
it is **e** for a camel to go	Mt 19:24
But it is **e** for heaven and earth	Lk 16:17

EASILY
three strands is not **e** broken.	Ec 4:12
me to become a Christian so **e**?	Ac 26:28
the sin that so **e** ensnares us,	Heb 12:1

EAST

planted a garden in Eden, in the e,	Gn 2:8
in the land of Nod, e of Eden.	Gn 4:16
the LORD sent an e wind	Ex 10:13
He made the e wind blow in the	Ps 78:26
As far as the e is from the west	Ps 103:12
bring your descendants from the e,	Is 43:5
people of the e as a possession	Ezk 25:4
reports from the e and the north	Dn 11:44
sea and roam from north to e,	Am 8:12
appointed a scorching e wind.	Jnh 4:8
which faces Jerusalem on the e.	Zch 14:4
wise men from the e arrived	Mt 2:1
His star in the e and have come	Mt 2:2
many will come from e and west,	Mt 8:11
comes from the e and flashes as	Mt 24:27
angel rise up from the e,	Rv 7:2
way for the kings from the e.	Rv 16:12

EASTERN

and the e peoples came and	Jdg 6:3
If I live at the e horizon	Ps 139:9
a student of e kings.	Is 19:11

EASTWARD

Then Lot journeyed e, and they	Gn 13:11

EASY

This is e in the LORD's sight.	2Kg 3:18
It's e for the shadow to	2Kg 20:10
They have an e time until they	Ps 73:4
For My yoke is e and My burden	Mt 11:30
Take it e; eat, drink	Lk 12:19

EAT

You are free to e from any tree	Gn 2:16
she took some of its fruit and ate it;	Gn 3:6
and you will e the plants of the	Gn 3:18
you must not e meat with ... blood	Gn 9:4
thin cows ate the healthy,	Gn 41:4
Here is how you must e it:	Ex 12:11
Israelites ate manna for 40 years,	Ex 16:35
must not e any fat or any blood.	Lv 3:17
You may e all these ... animals.	Lv 11:2
You are not to e ... blood	Lv 19:26
It is to be e-en on the same day.	Lv 22:30
people ate and bowed in worship	Nm 25:2
But don't e the blood, since the	Dt 12:23
ate from the produce of the land,	Jos 5:12
he ate the honey,	1Sm 14:27
ate meat with the blood	1Sm 14:32
household ate for many days.	1Kg 17:15
we boiled my son and ate him,	2Kg 6:29
Job's sons and daughters were e-ing	Jb 1:13
humble will e and be satisfied;	Ps 22:26
People ate the bread of angels.	Ps 78:25
e-ing food earned by hard work;	Ps 127:2
and bread {e-en} secretly is tasty!	Pr 9:17
A righteous man e-s until he is	Pr 13:25
"E and drink," he says to you	Pr 23:7
give him food to e, and if he is	Pr 25:21
she e-s and wipes her mouth and	Pr 30:20
nothing better for man than to e,	Ec 2:24
he e-s in darkness all his days,	Ec 5:17
man under the sun except to e,	Ec 8:15
e your bread with pleasure,	Ec 9:7
one e-s the flesh of his own arm.	Is 9:20
the lion will e straw like an ox	Is 11:7
hungry one who dreams he is e-ing,	Is 29:8
year you will e what grows on	Is 37:30
without money, come, buy, and e!	Is 55:1
the lion will e straw like the	Is 65:25
e-ing meat from pigs, vermin,	Is 66:17
words were found, and I ate them	Jr 15:16
E this scroll, then go and speak	Ezk 3:1
He ate grass like cattle,	Dn 4:33
years that the swarming locust ate,	Jl 2:25
who e your bread will set a trap	Ob 7
You e the flesh of my people	Mc 3:3
worry, saying, 'What will we e?	Mt 6:31
of Man came e-ing and drinking,	Mt 11:19
they ate the sacred bread,	Mt 12:4
You give them something to e.	Mt 14:16
Everyone ate and was filled.	Mt 14:20
don't wash their hands when they e!	Mt 15:2
They all ate and were filled.	Mt 15:37
flood they were e-ing and drinking,	Mt 24:38
and you gave Me something to e;	Mt 25:35
and said, "Take and e it;	Mt 26:26
saw that He was e-ing with sinners	Mk 2:16
May no one ever e fruit from you	Mk 11:14
e the things set before you.	Lk 10:8
e, drink, and enjoy yourself.	Lk 12:19
who will e bread in the kingdom	Lk 14:15
sinners and e-s with them!	Lk 15:2
I will not e it again until it	Lk 22:16
and ate in their presence.	Lk 24:43
I have food to e that you don't know	Jn 4:32

because you **ate** the loaves | Jn 6:26
anyone **e-s** of this bread he will live | Jn 6:51
Anyone who **e-s** My flesh and drinks | Jn 6:54
Get up, Peter; kill and **e**! | Ac 10:13
not to **e** or drink until they kill him | Ac 23:21
believes he may **e** anything, | Rm 14:2
One who **e-s** must not look
  down on | Rm 14:3
Whoever **e-s**, **e-s** to the Lord | Rm 14:6
of God is not **e-ing** and drinking, | Rm 14:17
cause stumbling by what he **e-s**. | Rm 14:20
is a noble thing not to **e** meat, | Rm 14:21
because his **e-ing** is not from faith | Rm 14:23
Do not even **e** with such a person | 1Co 5:11
About **e-ing** food offered to idols, | 1Co 8:4
I will never again **e** meat, | 1Co 8:13
all **ate** the same spiritual food, | 1Co 10:3
E everything that is sold in the | 1Co 10:25
whether you **e** or drink, or | 1Co 10:31
For as often as you **e** this bread | 1Co 11:26
e-s and drinks judgment | 1Co 11:29
not raised, Let us **e** and drink, | 1Co 15:32
For he used to **e** with the | Gl 2:12
work, he should not **e**. | 2Th 3:10
do not have a right to **e**. | Heb 13:10
and will **e** your flesh like fire. | Jms 5:3
He said to me, "Take and **e** it; | Rv 10:9

EATER
Out of the **e** came something to | Jdg 14:14

EBAL
and the curse at Mount **E**. | Dt 11:29
will stand on Mount **E** to deliver | Dt 27:13
and half in front of Mount **E**, | Jos 8:33

EBB
all our days **e** away under Your | Ps 90:9

EBED-MELECH
Cushite court official (Jr 38:7–39:16).

EBENEZER
He named it **E**, explaining, "The | 1Sm 7:12

EBER
  1. Descendant of Shem; ancestor of Abraham (Gn 11:10-26).
  2. Descendant of Gad (1Ch 5:13).
  3. Son of Elpaal (1Ch 8:12).
  4. Son of Shashak (1Ch 8:22).
  5. Priest (Neh 12:20).

EBONY
tusks and **e** as your payment | Ezk 27:15

ECBATANA
fortress of **E** in the province | Ezr 6:2

ECHOES
For their cry **e** throughout the | Is 15:8

ECLIPSE
May an **e** of the sun terrify it. | Jb 3:5

EDEN
LORD God planted a garden in **E**, | Gn 2:8
make her wilderness like **E**, | Is 51:3
You were in **E**, the garden of God | Ezk 28:13
become like the garden of **E**. | Ezk 36:35
them is like the Garden of **E**, | Jl 2:3

EDGE
reap to the very **e** of your field | Lv 19:9
shave the **e** of their beards, | Lv 21:5
children's teeth are set on **e**. | Jr 31:29
children's teeth are set on **e**? | Ezk 18:2

EDICT
delivered the king's **e-s** | Ezr 8:36
command and **e** became public | Est 2:8
enforce an **e** that for 30 days | Dn 6:7
they didn't fear the king's **e**. | Heb 11:23

EDIFICATION
speaks to people for **e**, | 1Co 14:3
All things must be done for **e**. | 1Co 14:26

EDOM
Is why he was {also} named **E**. | Gn 25:30
land of Seir, the country of **E**. | Gn 32:3
records of Esau (that is, **E**). | Gn 36:1
E refused to allow Israel to | Nm 20:21
great slaughter in the land of **E**. | Is 34:6
Who is this coming from **E** in | Is 63:1
About **E**, this is what the LORD | Jr 49:7
Because **E** acted vengefully | Ezk 25:12
from punishing **E** for three | Am 1:11
the Lord GOD has said about **E**: | Ob 1
Though **E** says: "We have been | Mal 1:4

EDOMITE
records of Esau, father of the **E-s** | Gn 36:9
Do not despise an **E**, because he is | Dt 23:7
{what} the **E-s** said that day at | Ps 137:7

EDREI

whole army to do battle at E.	Nm 21:33
Bashan as far as Salecah and E,	Dt 3:10
who reigned in Ashtaroth and E;	Jos 13:12

EDUCATED

So Moses was e in all the wisdom	Ac 7:22
and e according to the strict	Ac 22:3

EFFECT

law went into e on the	Est 9:1
reaches him will have no e,	Jb 41:26
and the caper berry has no e;	Ec 12:5
the e of righteousness will be	Is 32:17

EFFECTIVE

a wide door for e ministry has	1Co 16:9
may become e through knowing	Phm 6
is living and e and sharper than	Heb 4:12

EFFECTIVELY

also works e in you believers	1Th 2:13

EFFORT

drinks, and enjoys all his e-s.	Ec 3:13
have a good reward for their e-s.	Ec 4:9
Make every e to enter through	Lk 13:24
not depend on human will or e,	Rm 9:16
but I make every e to take hold	Php 3:12
Make every e to come to me soon	2Tm 4:9
Make every e to come before	2Tm 4:21
make every e to come to me in	Ti 3:12
then make every e to enter that	Heb 4:11
make every e to supplement your	2Pt 1:5
make every e to be found in	2Pt 3:14

EGG

a bird's nest with chicks or e-s,	Dt 22:6
Is there flavor in an e white?	Jb 6:6
She abandons her e-s on the ground	Jb 39:14
he asks for an e, will give him	Lk 11:12

EGLON

1. City in Judah (Jos 10).
2. King of Moab (Jdg 3).

EGYPT

Abram went down to E to live	Gn 12:10
sold Joseph in E to Potiphar,	Gn 37:36
went down to buy grain from E.	Gn 42:3
children with him went to E.	Gn 46:6
the Israelites, out of E.	Ex 3:10
lived in E was 430 years.	Ex 12:40
you out of the land of E,	Ex 20:2
foreigners in the land of E;	Lv 19:34
that you were slaves in E;	Dt 16:12
back to E to acquire many horses	Dt 17:16
God who brought you out of E,	Neh 9:18
Ambassadors will come from E;	Ps 68:31
His miraculous signs in E	Ps 78:43
An oracle against E:	Is 19:1
Woe to those who go down to E for	Is 31:1
Judah: 'Don't go to E.'	Jr 42:19
About E and the army of Pharaoh	Jr 46:2
king of E and prophesy against him	Ezk 29:2
out of E I called My son.	Hs 11:1
E will become desolate, and Edom	Jl 3:19
Out of E I called My Son.	Mt 2:15
called, prophetically, Sodom and E,	Rv 11:8

EGYPTIAN

He saw an E beating a Hebrew,	Ex 2:11
E-s will know that I am the LORD	Ex 7:5
E-s will know that I am the LORD	Ex 14:4,18
Why should the E-s say, 'He	Ex 32:12
The E-s will hear about it,	Nm 14:13
not despise an E, because you	Dt 23:7

EHUD

Benjaminite judge (Jdg 3:12-30).

EIGHT

at e days old is to be circumcised.	Gn 17:12
his son Isaac was e days old,	Gn 21:4
Jesse had e sons,	1Sm 17:12
Josiah was e years old when he	2Kg 22:1
When the e days were completed	Lk 2:21
About e days after these words,	Lk 9:28
After e days His disciples were	Jn 20:26
had been bedridden for e years.	Ac 9:33
a few—that is, e people—were	1Pt 3:20

EIGHTH

be circumcised on the e day.	Lv 12:3
When you sow in the e year,	Lv 25:22
the child on the e day,	Lk 1:59
circumcised him on the e day;	Ac 7:8
circumcised the e day;	Php 3:5

EIGHTY

or, if we are strong, e years.	Ps 90:10

EITHER

using e their right or left hand	1Ch 12:2
But better than e of them is the	Ec 4:3

For if **e** falls, his companion   Ec 4:10
e by heaven, because it is God's   Mt 5:34
since **e** he will hate one and   Mt 6:24
e by heaven or by earth or with   Jms 5:12

EKRON
Judah captured ... E   Jdg 1:18
then sent the ark of God to E,   1Sm 5:10
Gaza, Ashkelon, Gath, and E.   1Sm 6:17
also turn My hand against E,   Am 1:8

ELABORATE
not with **e** hairstyles, gold   1Tm 2:9
things {like} **e** hairstyles   1Pt 3:3

ELAH
1. Edomite (Gn 36:41).
2. Valley where David fought Goliath
(1Sm 17:2,19; 21:9).
3. Son of Baasha; king of Israel (1Kg 16:6-
14).
4. Father of Hoshea (2Kg 15:30; 17:1).
5. Son of Caleb (1Ch 4:15).
6. Son of Uzzi (1Ch 9:8).

ELAM
1. Son of Shem (Gn 10:22).
2. Son of Shashak (1Ch 8:24).
3. Korahite Levite (1Ch 26:3).
4. Head of returning family (Ezr 2:7).
5. Head of returning people (Ezr 2:31).
6. Leader of returning people (Neh
10:14).
7. Priest (Neh 12:42).
8. Region of Babylon (Gn 14:1,9; Ezr 4:9;
Is 11:11; Jr 49:34-39; Ezk 32:24-25; Dn
8:2; Ac 2:9).

ELDAD
E and Medad are prophesying in Nm 11:27

ELDER
assemble the **e**-s of Israel and   Ex 3:16
and 70 of Israel's **e**-s, and bow in   Ex 24:1
placed {the Spirit} on the 70 **e**-s.   Nm 11:25
lifetimes of the **e**-s who outlived   Jos 24:31
Rehoboam rejected the **e**-s'
  advice   2Ch 10:13
and instructing his **e**-s.   Ps 105:22
Him in the council of the **e**-s.   Ps 107:32
more than the **e**-s because I obey Ps 119:100
sits among the **e**-s of the land.   Pr 31:23

against the **e**-s and leaders of His   Is 3:14
The head is the **e**, the honored one; Is 9:15
The **e**-s have left the city gate,   Lm 5:14
priests and counsel from the **e**-s.   Ezk 7:26
break the tradition of the **e**-s?   Mt 15:2
suffer many things from the **e**-s,   Mt 16:21
e-s of the people plotted against   Mt 27:1
accused by the chief priests and **e**-s Mt 27:12
assembled with the **e**-s and agreed Mt 28:12
and be rejected by the **e**-s,   Mk 8:31
and the **e**-s came and asked Him, Mk 11:27
had appointed **e**-s in every church Ac 14:23
apostles and the **e**-s assembled to Ac 15:6
called for the **e**-s of the church.   Ac 20:17
of hands by the council of **e**-s.   1Tm 4:14
The **e**-s who are good leaders   1Tm 5:17
accusation against an **e** unless   1Tm 5:19
to appoint **e**-s in every town: Ti 1:5
call for the **e**-s of the church,   Jms 5:14
as a fellow **e** ... I exhort the **e**-s   1Pt 5:1
men, be subject to the **e**-s.   1Pt 5:5
The E: To the elect lady and her   2Jn 1
The E: To my dear friend Gaius   3Jn 1
thrones sat 24 **e**-s dressed in   Rv 4:4
The 24 **e**-s, who were seated
  before   Rv 11:16
Then the 24 **e**-s and the four   Rv 19:4

ELDERLY
rise in the presence of the **e**   Lv 19:32
Wisdom is found with the **e**,   Jb 12:12
are the crown of the **e**,   Pr 17:6

ELEAZAR
1. Son of Aaron; high priest (Ex 6:23; Nm
20:25-28). Helped Joshua distribute land
(Jos 14:1).
2. Son of Abinadab (1Sm 7:1).
3. Son of Dodo; one of David's warriors
(2Sm 23:9-10).
4. Son of Mahli (1Ch 23:21-22).
5. Son of Phinehas (Ezr 8:33).
6. Son of Parosh (Ezr 10:25).
7. Priest (Neh 12:42).
8. Son of Eliud; ancestor of Jesus (Mt
1:15).

ELECT
be limited because of the **e**.   Mt 24:22
if possible, even the **e**.   Mt 24:24

will gather His e from the four | Mt 24:31
justice to His e who cry out to | Lk 18:7
an accusation against God's e? | Rm 8:33
but the e did find it. | Rm 11:7
Christ Jesus and the e angels, | 1Tm 5:21
I endure all things for the e: | 2Tm 2:10
faith of God's e and the | Ti 1:1
To the e lady and her children, | 2Jn 1
of your e sister send you | 2Jn 13
are called and e and faithful. | Rv 17:14

ELECTION

according to e might stand, | Rm 9:11
but regarding e, they are loved | Rm 11:28
knowing your e, brothers loved | 1Th 1:4
to confirm your calling and e, | 2Pt 1:10

ELEMENTAL

slavery under the e forces of | Gl 4:3
the weak and bankrupt e forces? | Gl 4:9
based on the e forces of the | Col 2:8
Christ to the e forces of this | Col 2:20

ELEMENTARY

leaving the e message about the | Heb 6:1

ELEMENTS

the e will burn and be dissolved | 2Pt 3:10

ELEVEN see also 11

appeared to the E themselves as | Mk 16:14
things to the E and to all the | Lk 24:9
They found the E and those with | Lk 24:33
But Peter stood up with the E, | Ac 2:14

ELHANAN

and E son of Jaare-oregim the | 2Sm 21:19
and E son of Jair killed Lahmi | 1Ch 20:5

ELI

High priest at Samuel's birth (1Sm 1–4). Blessed Hannah (1:17; 2:20). Failed to discipline his sons (2:12-17,22-36). Died when the ark was captured (4:11-18).

ELÍ

E, E, lemá sabachtháni? | Mt 27:46

ELIAB

1. Zebulunite leader (Nm 1:9).
2. Father of Dathan and Abiram (Nm 16:1).

3. David's oldest brother (1Sm 16:6; 17:13,28; 1Ch 2:13; 2Ch 11:18).
4. Levite (1Ch 6:27).
5. Levite musician (1Ch 15:18,20: 16:5).
6. Gadite leader (1Ch 12:9).

ELIAKIM

1. Son of Hilkiah; Hezekiah's administrator (2Kg 18:18; Is 22:20; 36:3).
2. Son of Josiah; king of Judah. Called Jehoiakim (2Kg 23:34; 2Ch 36:4).
3. Priest (Neh 12:41).
4. Ancestor of Jesus (Mt 1:13).
5. Ancestor of Jesus (Lk 3:30).

ELIASHIB

1. High priest at the time of Nehemiah (Neh 3:1,20; 12:10; 13:28).
2. Priest at the time of Nehemiah; abetted Tobiah (Neh 13:4-9).
3. Name of three who divorced foreign wives (Ezr 10:24,27,36).

ELIEZER

1. Abraham's servant (Gn 15:2).
2. Son of Moses (Ex 18:4; 1Ch 23:15).
3. Son of Becher (1Ch 7:8).
4. Priest (1Ch 15:24).
5. Son of Zichri (1Ch 27:16).
6. Prophet to Jehoshaphat (2Ch 20:37).
7. Leader under Ezra (Ezr 8:16).
8. Name of three of the men who had married foreign women (Ezr 10:18,23,31).
9. Ancestor of Jesus (Lk 3:29).

ELIHU

1. Son of Tohu; ancestor of Elkanah (1Sm 1:1).
2. Manassite captain who defected to David (1Ch 12:20).
3. Gatekeeper; descendant of Obed-edom (1Ch 26:7).
4. Judah's chief officer (1Ch 27:18).
5. One of Job's friends (Jb 32–36).

ELIJAH

Prophet against Ahab and Ahaziah. Predicted famine (1Kg 17:1; Jms 5:17). Fed by ravens (1Kg 17:2-7); fed by widow (17:8-16; Lk 4:26); raised widow's son (1Kg 17:17-

24). Defeated prophets of Baal (18:19-40). Fled Jezebel (19:1-3). Chose Elisha to succeed him (19:16,19-21); taken up into heaven (2Kg 2:1-12).

Forerunner to the Messiah, embodied in John the Baptist (Mal 4:5; Mt 11:14; 17:10-13; Lk 1:17). Appeared with Jesus (Mt 17:3-4).

ELIM

| they came to E, where there were | Ex 15:27 |
| water and 70 date palms at E, | Nm 33:9 |

ELIMELECH

Naomi's husband (Ru 1:2-3).

ELIMINATE

I will e all of Jeroboam's males	1Kg 14:10
I will e all of Ahab's males,	1Kg 21:21
transgressors will all be e-d;	Ps 37:38
I am about to e from this place	Jr 16:9
into the stomach and is e-d?	Mt 15:17

ELIPHAZ

1. Son of Esau (Gn 36:4,10-16).
2. One of Job's friends (Jb 2:11).

ELISHA

Prophet; successor to Elijah (1Kg 19:16-21; 2Kg 2:1-18). Made bad water good (2:19-22); called bear to punish boys (2:23-24); provided water for army (3:13-22). Provided miraculous supply of oil for widow (4:1-7); granted son to barren woman and restored him to life (4:8-37). Healed Naaman and punished Gehazi (5:1-27). Made axe head float (6:5-7). Blinded Syrian army (6:8–7:20). A man was revived by touching his dead bones (13:20-21). Made Hazael king of Syria (8:7-15) and Jehu king of Israel (9:1-13).

ELIZABETH

Mother of John the Baptist; Mary's relative (Lk 1).

ELKANAH

Father of Samuel; husband of Hannah (1Sm 1:1).

ELOI

| voice, "E, E, lemá sabachtháni | Mk 15:34 |

ELON

1. Son of Zebulun (Gn 46:14; Nm 26:26).
2. Judge (Jdg 12:11).

ELOQUENT

I have never been e—either in	Ex 4:10
a warrior, e, handsome, and	1Sm 16:18
an e man who was powerful in the	Ac 18:24

ELUDED

| struck the wall, David e Saul | 1Sm 19:10 |
| seize Him, yet He e their grasp. | Jn 10:39 |

ELYMAS

| But E, the sorcerer, which is | Ac 13:8 |

EMACIATED

| from fasting, and my body is e. | Ps 109:24 |

EMBALMED

| So they e Israel. | Gn 50:2 |
| They e him and placed him in a | Gn 50:26 |

EMBANKMENT

| will build an e against you, | Lk 19:43 |

EMBARRASSED

| about you, I have not been e; | 2Co 7:14 |

EMBARRASSMENT

| urged him to the point of e, | 2Kg 2:17 |

EMBEDDED

| are like firmly e nails. | Ec 12:11 |

EMBER

| extinguish my one remaining e | 2Sm 14:7 |

EMBOLDENED

| we were e by our God to speak | 1Th 2:2 |

EMBRACE

righteousness and peace will e.	Ps 85:10
if you e her, she will honor you	Pr 4:8
Can a man e fire and his clothes	Pr 6:27
a time to e and a time to avoid a-ing	Ec 3:5
and his right hand e-s me.	Sg 2:6; 8:3

EMBROIDERED

to make a screen e with blue,	Ex 26:36
finely spun linen e with gold,	Ex 28:6
her clothing e with gold.	Ps 45:13
I clothed you in e cloth and	Ezk 16:10

EMERALD

| row of carnelian, topaz, and e; | Ex 28:17 |
| sapphire, turquoise and e. | Ezk 28:13 |

that looked like an **e** surrounded — Rv 4:3
third chalcedony, the fourth **e**, — Rv 21:19

EMERGE
I will **e** as pure gold. — Jb 23:10

EMINENT
and none of the **e** among them. — Ezk 7:11

EMISSARIES
David sent his **e** to console — 2Sm 10:2

EMISSION
When a man has an **e** of semen, — Lv 15:16
of a bodily **e** during the night, — Dt 23:10

EMMAUS
on their way to a village called **E**, — Lk 24:13

EMPEROR
he himself appealed to the **E**, — Ac 25:25
whether to the **E** as the supreme — 1Pt 2:13
Fear God. Honor the **E**. — 1Pt 2:17

EMPOWERED
until you are **e** from on high. — Lk 24:49

EMPTY (adj)
The pit was **e**; — Gn 37:24
one hand and an **e** pitcher with — Jdg 7:16
the LORD has brought me back **e**. — Ru 1:21
because your seat will be **e**. — 1Sm 20:18
The flour jar did not become **e**, — 1Kg 17:16
Go and borrow **e** containers from — 2Kg 4:3
answer with **e** counsel or fill — Jb 15:2
The wicked man earns an **e** wage, — Pr 11:18
mouth will not return to Me **e**, — Is 55:11
They trust in **e** and worthless words; — Is 59:4
set me aside like an **e** dish; — Jr 51:34
relate **e** dreams and offer **e** comfort. — Zch 10:2
and sent the rich away **e**. — Lk 1:53
faith is made **e** and the promise — Rm 4:14
the matter would not prove **e**, — 2Co 9:3
deceive you with **e** arguments, — Eph 5:6
philosophy and **e** deceit based on — Col 2:8
These promote **e** speculations — 1Tm 1:4
e speech and contradictions from — 1Tm 6:20
irreverent, **e** speech, for this — 2Tm 2:16
redeemed from your **e** way of life — 1Pt 1:18
bombastic, **e** words, they seduce — 2Pt 2:18

EMPTY (v)
As they began **e-ing** their sacks, — Gn 42:35
Will they therefore **e** their net — Hab 1:17

cross of Christ will not be **e-ied** — 1Co 1:17
He **e-ied** Himself by assuming — Php 2:7

EMPTY-HANDED
you would have sent me off **e**. — Gn 31:42
No one is to appear before Me **e**. — Ex 23:15
is to appear before the LORD **e**. — Dt 16:16
go back to your mother-in-law **e**. — Ru 3:17
beat him and sent him away **e**. — Lk 20:10

ENABLE
and **e-d** you to live in freedom. — Lv 26:13
for he will **e** Israel to inherit — Dt 1:38
for the LORD **e-d** them to rejoice — 2Ch 20:27
the power that **e-s** Him to subject — Php 3:21
who has **e-d** you to share in the — Col 1:12

ENCAMPS
of the LORD **e** around those who — Ps 34:7

ENCIRCLE
completely **e-ing** the reservoir. — 1Kg 7:24
strong ones of Bashan **e** me. — Ps 22:12
You have **e-d** me; You have placed — Ps 139:5
who **e** yourselves with firebrands — Is 50:11

ENCLOSED
Who **e** the sea behind doors when — Jb 38:8

ENCOUNTER
not knowing what I will **e** there, — Ac 20:22

ENCOURAGE
commission Joshua and **e** — Dt 3:28
e-d him in {his faith in} God, — 1Sm 23:16
to be mutually **e-d** by each other's — Rm 1:12
learn and everyone may be **e-d**. — 1Co 14:31
we **e-d**, comforted, and implored — 1Th 2:12·
strengthen and **e** you concerning — 1Th 3:2
Therefore **e** one another with — 1Th 4:18
Therefore **e** one another and — 1Th 5:11
Teach and **e** these things. — 1Tm 6:2
and **e** with great patience and — 2Tm 4:2
that they may **e** the young women — Ti 2:4
But **e** each other daily, while it — Heb 3:13
e-ing you and testifying that this — 1Pt 5:12

ENCOURAGEMENT
which is translated Son of **E**, — Ac 4:36
they rejoiced because of its **e**. — Ac 15:31
through the **e** of the Scriptures — Rm 15:4
may the God of endurance and **e** — Rm 15:5
edification, **e**, and consolation — 1Co 14:3

I am filled with **e**; 2Co 7:4
then there is any **e** in Christ, Php 2:1
given us eternal **e** and good hope 2Th 2:16

END (n)

to put an **e** to all flesh, Gn 6:13
will judge the **e**-s of the earth. 1Sm 2:10
family, from beginning to **e**. 1Sm 3:12
filled it from **e** to **e** with their Ezr 9:11
they come to an **e** without hope. Jb 7:6
miner puts an **e** to the darkness Jb 28:3
He looks to the **e**-s of the earth Jb 28:24
and the **e**-s of the earth Your Ps 2:8
of the wicked come to an **e**, Ps 7:9
words to the **e**-s of the inhabited Ps 19:4
All the **e**-s of the earth will Ps 22:27
reveal to me the **e** of my life Ps 39:4
reaches to the **e**-s of the earth; Ps 48:10
They come to an **e**, swept away by Ps 73:19
all the **e**-s of the earth have seen Ps 98:3
In the **e** he will look in triumph Ps 112:8
Your statutes to the very **e**. Ps 119:112
in the ashes's as bitter as Pr 5:4
but its **e** is the way to death. Pr 14:12
but in the **e** it is the way of Pr 16:25
In the **e** it bites like a snake Pr 23:32
established all the **e**-s of the earth? Pr 30:4
though there is no **e** to all his Ec 4:8
The **e** of a matter is better than Ec 7:8
there is no **e** to the making of Ec 12:12
brought you from the **e**-s of the earth Is 41:9
I declare the **e** from the Is 46:10
all the **e**-s of the earth will see Is 52:10
rise from the **e**-s of the earth. Jr 10:13
cannot see what our **e** will be. Jr 12:4
Our **e** drew near; our time ran out.
   Our **e** had come! Lm 4:18
An **e**! The **e** has come on the four Ezk 7:2
{extends} to the **e**-s of the earth. Dn 4:22
and His dominion has no **e**. Dn 6:26
refers to the time of the **e**. Dn 8:17
for still the **e** will come at the Dn 11:27
sealed until the time of the **e**. Dn 12:9
The **e** has come for My people Am 8:2
will extend to the **e**-s of the earth. Mc 5:4
endures to the **e** will be delivered. Mt 10:22
came from the **e**-s of the earth to Mt 12:42
harvest is the **e** of the age, Mt 13:39
must take place, but the **e** is not yet. Mt 24:6

endures to the **e** will be delivered. Mt 24:13
from one **e** of the sky to the Mt 24:31
always, to the **e** of the age. Mt 28:20
and His kingdom will have no **e**. Lk 1:33
He loved them to the **e**. Jn 13:1
and to the **e**-s of the earth. Ac 1:8
salvation to the **e**-s of the earth. Ac 13:47
and the **e** is eternal life! Rm 6:22
Christ is the **e** of the law for Rm 10:4
words to the **e**-s of the inhabited Rm 10:18
will also confirm you to the **e**, 1Co 1:8
on whom the **e**-s of the ages have 1Co 10:11
the partial will come to an **e**. 1Co 13:10
Then comes the **e**, when
   He hands 1Co 15:24
Their **e** is destruction; Php 3:19
if we hold firmly until the **e** Heb 3:14
one time, at the **e** of the ages, Heb 9:26
revealed at the **e** of the times 1Pt 1:20
Now the **e** of all things is near 1Pt 4:7
In the **e** time there will be Jd 18
who keeps My works to the **e**: Rv 2:26
Omega, the Beginning and the **E**. Rv 21:6
Last, the Beginning and the **E**. Rv 22:13

END (v)

border **e**-ed at the Mediterranean Jos 15:4
made their days **e** in futility, Ps 78:33
and Your years will never **e**. Ps 102:27
be sad, and joy may **e** in grief. Pr 14:13
{Casting} the lot **e**-s quarrels and Pr 18:18
its prosperity will never **e**. Is 9:7
summer has **e**-ed, but we have not Jr 8:20
for His mercies never **e**. Lm 3:22
Love never **e**-s. But as for 1Co 13:8
oath **e**-s every dispute. Heb 6:16

ENDLESS

but **e** talk leads only to poverty Pr 14:23
nagging is an **e** dripping. Pr 19:13
An **e** dripping on a rainy day and Pr 27:15
to myths and **e** genealogies. 1Tm 1:4

ENDLESSLY

But the evening drags on **e**, Jb 7:4

ENDOR

is a woman at **E** who is a medium. 1Sm 28:7

ENDORSING

shuts his eyes to avoid **e** evil Is 33:15

ENDOWED

He has not e her with Jb 39:17

ENDURANCE

By your e gain your lives. Lk 21:19
that affliction produces e, Rm 5:3
that through our e and through Rm 15:4
may the God of e and Rm 15:5
the e of the same sufferings that we 2Co 1:6
for all e and patience, Col 1:11
about your e and faith in all 2Th 1:4
faith, love, e, and gentleness. 1Tm 6:11
faith, patience, love, and e, 2Tm 3:10
sound in faith, love, and e. Ti 2:2
For you need e, so that after Heb 10:36
and run with e the race that Heb 12:1
the testing of your faith produces e. Jms 1:3
heard of Job's e and have seen Jms 5:11
self-control with e, e with godliness 2Pt 1:6
Here is the e of the saints, Rv 14:12

ENDURE

As long as the earth e-s, seedtime Gn 8:22
you will be able to e, Ex 18:23
Your dwelling place is e-ing; Nm 24:21
but now your reign will not e. 1Sm 13:14
and kingdom will e before Me 2Sm 7:16
His faithful love e-s forever. 1Ch 16:34
of the LORD is pure, e-ing forever; Ps 19:9
For I have e-d insults because of Ps 69:7
he continue while the sun e-s, Ps 72:5
May his name e forever; Ps 72:17
My covenant with him will e. Ps 89:28
His faithfulness e-s through all Ps 100:5
glory of the LORD e forever; Ps 104:31
his righteousness e-s forever. Ps 112:3
LORD's faithfulness e-s forever. Ps 117:2
His faithful love e-s forever. Ps 118:1
Truthful lips e forever, but Pr 12:19
so will ... your name e. Is 66:22
Your throne e-s from generation to Lm 5:19
Will your courage e Ezk 22:14
because you have e-d the insults Ezk 36:6
but will itself e forever. Dn 2:44
and his strength will not e. Dn 11:6
and dreadful—who can e it? Jl 2:11
But who can e the day of His Mal 3:2
the one who e-s to the end will Mt 10:22
had e-d much under many doctors. Mk 5:26
on to it and by e-ing, bear fruit. Lk 8:15

e-d with much patience objects of Rm 9:22
we are persecuted, we e it; 1Co 4:12
hopes all things, e-s all things. 1Co 13:7
His righteousness e-s forever. 2Co 9:9
This is why I e all things for 2Tm 2:10
if we e, we will also reign with 2Tm 2:12
What persecutions I e-d! 2Tm 3:11
have a better and
  e-ing possession. Heb 10:34
that lay before Him e-d a cross Heb 12:2
Him who e-d such hostility Heb 12:3
E it as discipline: God is Heb 12:7
here we do not have
  an e-ing city; Heb 13:14
Blessed is a man who e-s trials, Jms 1:12
the living and e-ing word of God. 1Pt 1:23
the word of the Lord e-s forever. 1Pt 1:25
is there if you e when you sin 1Pt 2:20
you have kept My command to e, Rv 3:10

ENEMY

has handed over your e-ies to you. Gn 14:20
come across your e-'s stray ox or Ex 23:4
an e to your e-ies and a foe to Ex 23:22
Let Your e-ies be scattered, Nm 10:35
I brought you to curse my e-ies, Nm 23:11
he was not his e and wasn't Nm 35:23
to be defeated before your e-ies. Dt 28:25
Are You for us or for our e-ies? Jos 5:13
could no longer resist their e-ies. Jdg 2:14
Saul was David's e from then on 1Sm 18:29
a man finds his e, does he let 1Sm 24:19
has handed your e over to you. 1Sm 26:8
give you rest from all your e-ies. 2Sm 7:11
You love your e-ies and hate those 2Sm 19:6
and I was saved from my e-ies. 2Sm 22:4
He frees me from my e-ies. 2Sm 22:49
LORD put his e-ies under his feet. 1Kg 5:3
as an e against Solomon 1Kg 11:14,23
and hand them over to their
  e-ies. 2Kg 21:14
When all our e-ies heard this, Neh 6:16
Haman, the e of the Jews. Est 8:1
the Jews got rid of their e-ies. Est 9:22
and consider me Your e? Jb 13:24
He regards me as his e. Jb 33:10
strike all my e-ies on the cheek; Ps 3:7
to silence the e and the avenger Ps 8:2
How long will my e dominate me? Ps 13:2

and I was saved from my **e-ies**. Ps 18:3
me in the presence of my **e-ies**; Ps 23:5
do not let my **e-ies** gloat over me. Ps 25:2
not allowed my **e-ies** to triumph over Ps 30:1
because of the **e-**'s oppression? Ps 42:9; 43:2
it is not an **e** who insults me Ps 55:12
Deliver me from my **e-ies**, my God; Ps 59:1
tower in the face of the **e**. Ps 61:3
life from the terror of the **e**. Ps 64:1
God arises. His **e-ies** scatter, Ps 68:1
For my **e-ies** talk about me, and Ps 71:10
scattered Your **e-ies** with Your Ps 89:10
I make Your **e-ies** Your footstool. Ps 110:1
makes even than my **e-ies**, Ps 119:98
with {their} **e-ies** at the city gate Ps 127:5
my life from the anger of my **e-ies**. Ps 138:7
I consider them my **e-ies**. Ps 139:22
For the **e** has pursued me Ps 143:3
makes even his **e-ies** to be at peace Pr 16:7
Don't gloat when your **e** falls, Pr 24:17
If your **e** is hungry, give him Pr 25:21
kisses of an **e** are excessive. Pr 27:6
He became their **e** {and} fought Is 63:10
struck you like an **e** would, Jr 30:14
The Lord is like an **e**; Lm 2:5
a person's **e-ies** are the people in Mc 7:6
Do not rejoice over me, my **e**! Mc 7:8
love your **e-ies** and pray for those Mt 5:44
and a man's **e-ies** will be the Mt 10:36
e who sowed them is the Devil. Mt 13:39
I put Your **e-ies** under Your feet Mt 22:44
rescued from our **e-ies'** clutches, Lk 1:74
over all the power of the **e**; Lk 10:19
But bring here these **e-ies** of mine, Lk 19:27
I make Your **e-ies** Your footstool. Lk 20:43
I make Your **e-ies** Your footstool. Ac 2:35
e of all righteousness! Ac 13:10
if, while we were **e-ies**, we were Rm 5:10
they are **e-ies** for your advantage, Rm 11:28
But If your **e** is hungry, feed him. Rm 12:20
puts all His **e-ies** under His feet 1Co 15:25
The last **e** He abolishes is death 1Co 15:26
now become your **e** by telling you Gl 4:16
that many live as **e-ies** of the cross Php 3:18
Yet don't treat him as an **e**, 2Th 3:15
I make Your **e-ies** Your footstool? Heb 1:13
waiting until His **e-ies** are made Heb 10:13
world's friend becomes God's **e**. Jms 4:4
mouths and consumes their **e-ies**; Rv 11:5

ENERGY

could devote their **e** to the law 2Ch 31:4
Don't spend your **e** on women or Pr 31:3

ENGAGED

Has any man become **e** to a woman Dt 20:7
encounters the **e** woman in the Dt 22:25
I was **e** to her for the price of 2Sm 3:14
Mary had been **e** to Joseph, Mt 1:18
to a virgin **e** to a man named Lk 1:27
who was **e** to him and was pregnant. Lk 2:5

EN-GEDI

stayed in the strongholds of **E**. 1Sm 23:29

ENGRAVE

onyx stones and **e** on them the
names of Israel's sons Ex 28:9
stone must be **e-d** like a seal, Ex 28:21
God's writing, **e-d** on the tablets Ex 32:16
I will **e** an inscription on it Zch 3:9

ENGRAVING

is skilled in **e** to work with 2Ch 2:7

ENGULFED

For the waves of death **e** me; 2Sm 22:5
the waters would have **e** us; Ps 124:4
The waters **e** me up to the neck; Jnh 2:5

ENJOY

to eat, drink, and to **e** his work. Ec 2:24
for a person to **e** his activities Ec 3:22
a stranger will **e** them. Ec 6:2
E life with the wife you love Ec 9:9
were willing to **e** his light. Jn 5:35
provides us with all things to **e**. 1Tm 6:17

ENJOYABLE

No discipline seems **e** at the time, Heb 12:11

ENJOYMENT

So I commended **e**, because there Ec 8:15

ENLARGE

LORD your God **e-s** your territory Dt 19:8
He **e-s** nations, then leads them Jb 12:23
He **e-s** his appetite like Sheol, Hab 2:5
They **e** their phylacteries and Mt 23:5
area {of ministry} will be ... **e-d**, 2Co 10:15

ENLIGHTENED

eyes of your heart may be **e** Eph 1:18
those who were once **e**, Heb 6:4

after you had been **e**,
  you endured   Heb 10:32

ENLISTED

strong or brave man, he **e** him.   1Sm 14:52

ENOCH

1. Son of Cain (Gn 4:17).

2. Father of Methuselah (Gn 5:18-21);
prophet (Jd 14); walked with God, and God
took him (Gn 5:22-24; Heb 11:5).

ENOSH

Son of Seth (Gn 4:26; 5:6-11).

ENOUGH

E, withdraw your hand now!   2Sm 24:16
four never say, "E!":   Pr 30:15
I have had **e** of burnt offerings   Is 1:11
but never have **e** to be satisfied   Hg 1:6
E! The time has come.   Mk 14:41
see if he has **e** to complete it?   Lk 14:28
hands have more than **e** food,   Lk 15:17
two swords." "E of that!" He   Lk 22:38
the Father, and that's **e** for us.   Jn 14:8

ENRAGE

For jealousy **e-s** a husband, and he   Pr 6:34
Being greatly **e-d** at them, I even   Ac 26:11

ENRICH

The LORD's blessing **e-es**, and   Pr 10:22
A generous person will be **e-ed**,   Pr 11:25
You are the kings of the earth   Ezk 27:33
as you are **e-ed** in every way for   2Co 9:11
as poor yet **e-ing** many;   2Co 6:10

ENSLAVE

they will be **e-d** and oppressed 400 Gn 15:13
we have never been **e-d** to anyone.   Jn 8:33
we may no longer be **e-d** to sin,   Rm 6:6
from sin and become **e-d** to God,   Rm 6:22
put up with it if someone **e-s** you,   2Co 11:20
Christ Jesus, in order to **e** us.   Gl 2:4
want to be **e-d** to them all over again? Gl 4:9
since people are **e-d** to whatever   2Pt 2:19

ENSNARE

let the net that he hid **e** him;   Ps 35:8
e-d by the words of your mouth.   Pr 6:2
Will you **e** the lives of My   Ezk 13:18
the sin that so easily **e-s** us,   Heb 12:1

ENTANGLE

The ropes of Sheol **e-d** me;   2Sm 22:6
he is **e-d** in the ropes of his own   Pr 5:22
learn his ways and **e** yourself in   Pr 22:25
soldier gets **e-d** in the concerns   2Tm 2:4
they are again **e-d** in these things   2Pt 2:20

ENTER

said to Noah, "E the ark,   Gn 7:1
was unable to **e** the tent of   Ex 40:35
he will not **e** the land I have   Nm 20:24
no one leaving or **e-ing**.   Jos 6:1
anger, 'They will not **e** My rest.'   Ps 95:11
an offering and **e** His courts.   Ps 96:8
E His gates with thanksgiving   Ps 100:4
is inexperienced, **e** here!   Pr 9:4
He will **e** into peace   Is 57:2
the Spirit **e-ed** me and set me on my   Ezk 2:2
you will never **e** the kingdom of   Mt 5:20
E through the narrow gate.   Mt 7:13
'Lord, Lord!' will **e** the kingdom   Mt 7:21
had come out, they **e-ed** the pigs.   Mt 8:32
How can someone **e**
  a strong man's   Mt 12:29
better for you to **e** life maimed   Mt 18:8
for a rich person to **e** the kingdom   Mt 19:23
prostitutes are **e-ing** the kingdom   Mt 21:31
you don't allow those **e-ing** to go   Mt 23:13
like a little child will never **e** it.   Mk 10:15
When they **e-ed** the tomb, they saw   Mk 16:5
Whatever house you **e**, stay there   Lk 9:4
afraid as they **e-ed** the cloud.   Lk 9:34
When you **e** any town, and they   Lk 10:8
Make every effort to **e** through the   Lk 13:24
As you **e** it, you will find a   Lk 19:30
Then Satan **e-ed** Judas, called   Lk 22:3
Can he **e** his mother's womb a   Jn 3:4
he cannot **e** the kingdom of God.   Jn 3:5
doesn't **e** the sheep pen by the door, Jn 10:1
If anyone **e-s** by Me, he will be   Jn 10:9
piece of bread, Satan **e-ed** him.   Jn 13:27
He **e-ed** the tomb and saw the linen   Jn 20:6
just as sin **e-ed** the world through   Rm 5:12
anger, "They will not **e** My rest."   Heb 3:11
we who have believed **e** the rest   Heb 4:3
person who has **e-ed** His rest has   Heb 4:10
that **e-s** the inner sanctuary   Heb 6:19
Jesus has **e-ed** there on our behalf   Heb 6:20
priest alone **e-s** the second room,   Heb 9:7

He e-ed the holy of holies once for Heb 9:12
have boldness to e the sanctuary   Heb 10:19
and no one could e the sanctuary   Rv 15:8
Nothing profane will ever e it: Rv 21:27

ENTERTAIN
Bring Samson here to e us.   Jdg 16:25
never e-ed the thought Jr 7:31; 19:5; 32:35

ENTHRONED
who is e {above} the cherubim,   2Kg 19:15
The One e in heaven laughs;   Ps 2:4
But the LORD sits e forever;   Ps 9:7
e on the praises of Israel.   Ps 22:3
the LORD sits e, King forever.   Ps 29:10
God, the One e from long ago   Ps 55:19
May he sit e before God forever   Ps 61:7
You who sit e [on] the cherubim   Ps 80:1
He is e above the cherubim.   Ps 99:1
But You, LORD, are e forever;   Ps 102:12
our God—the One e on high,   Ps 113:5
to You, the One e in heaven.   Ps 123:1
who is e above the cherubim,   Is 37:16
God is e above the circle of the   Is 40:22
You, LORD, are e forever;   Lm 5:19

ENTHUSIASTIC
They are e about you, but not   Gl 4:17

ENTHUSIASTICALLY
you do, do it e, as something   Col 3:23

ENTICE
'Who will e Ahab to march up   1Kg 22:20
son, if sinners e you, don't be   Pr 1:10
drawn away and e-d by his
   own evil   Jms 1:14

ENTIRE
is obligated to keep the e law.   Gl 5:3
For the e law is fulfilled in   Gl 5:14
For whoever keeps the e law,   Jms 2:10

ENTRAILS
all the fat that covers the e,   Ex 29:13
the fat surrounding the e,   Lv 3:3

ENTREAT
when we are slandered, we e.   1Co 4:13

ENTRUST
Into Your hand I e my spirit;   Ps 31:5
Where is the flock e-ed to you,   Jr 13:20
All things have been e-ed to Me by Mt 11:27

one who has been e-ed with more.   Lk 12:48
into Your hands I e My spirit.   Lk 23:46
would not e Himself to them,   Jn 2:24
they were e-ed with the spoken   Rm 3:2
I am e-ed with a stewardship.   1Co 9:17
I had been e-ed with the gospel   Gl 2:7
by God to be e-ed with the gospel, 1Th 2:4
guard what has been e-ed to you,   1Tm 6:20
what has been e-ed to me
   until that   2Tm 1:12
that good thing e-ed to you.   2Tm 1:14
e themselves to a faithful Creator. 1Pt 4:19

ENVELOPED
Spirit of the LORD e Gideon,   Jdg 6:34
LORD is robed, e in strength.   Ps 93:1

ENVIOUS
the Philistines were e of him.   Gn 26:14
the camp they were e of Moses   Ps 106:16

ENVOY
Hiram of Tyre sent e-s to David;   2Sm 5:11
had sent e-s to So king of Egypt   2Kg 17:4
you sent your e-s far away and   Is 57:9
an e has been sent among the   Ob 1

ENVY (n)
Why gaze with e, you mountain   Ps 68:16
and their e have already disappeared, Ec 9:6
handed Him over because of e.   Mt 27:18
They are full of e, murder   Rm 1:29
since there is e and strife   1Co 3:3
e, drunkenness, carousing, and   Gl 5:21
preach Christ out of e and strife,   Php 1:15
From these come e, quarreling   1Tm 6:4
in malice and e, hateful   Ti 3:3
For where e and selfish ambition   Jms 3:16
hypocrisy, e, and all slander.   1Pt 2:1

ENVY (v)
do not e those who do wrong.   Ps 37:1
For I e-ied the arrogant;   Ps 73:3
Don't e a violent man or choose   Pr 3:31
Don't e evil men or desire to be   Pr 24:1
and don't e the wicked.   Pr 24:19
Love does not e; is not boastful   1Co 13:4
provoking one another, e-ing one   Gl 5:26

EPAPHRAS
   Colossian Christian (Col 1:7; 3:12);
imprisoned in Rome (Phm 23).

EPAPHRODITUS
Messenger between Paul and Philippi (Php 2:25; 4:18).

EPHAH
Two quarts are a tenth of an **e**.   Ex 16:36

EPHESIANS
Great is Artemis of the **E**!   Ac 19:28

EPHESUS
City in Asia Minor visited by Paul (Ac 18:19; 19:1; 1Co 16:8; Eph 1:1; Rv 2:1).

Paul spoke of fighting "animals" there (1Co 15:32); he stationed Timothy and Tychicus there (1Tm 1:3; 2Tm 4:12).

EPHOD
on the **e** and breastpiece	Ex 25:7
are to make the **e** of finely spun	Ex 28:6
Bezalel made the **e** of gold,	Ex 39:2
and put the **e** on him.	Lv 8:7
Gideon made an **e** from all this	Jdg 8:27
he made an **e** and household idols,	Jdg 17:5
presence and wore a linen **e**.	1Sm 2:18
was wearing an **e**,	1Sm 14:3
in a cloth behind the **e**.	1Sm 21:9
killed 85 men who wore	
linen **e-s**	1Sm 22:18
the priest, "Bring the **e**."	1Sm 23:9
of Ahimelech, "Bring me the **e**."	1Sm 30:7
David also wore a linen **e**.	1Ch 15:27
and without **e** or household idols	Hs 3:4

EPHPHATHA
and said to him, "**E**!"   Mk 7:34

EPHRAIM
Son of Joseph (Gn 41:52); tribe with territory north and west of Bethel (Gn 48; Jos 14:4; 16:4-5); designation for Israel (Is 11:13; Jr 7:15; Ezk 37:16; Hs 5:13).

EPHRATH
and was buried on the way to **E**   Gn 35:19

EPHRATHAH
you be powerful in **E** and famous	Ru 4:11
We heard of {the ark} in **E**;	Ps 132:6
Bethlehem **E**, you are small among	Mc 5:2

EPHRATHITE
They were **E-s** from Bethlehem in	Ru 1:2
the son of the **E** from Bethlehem	1Sm 17:12

EPHRON
ask **E** son of Zohar on my behalf	Gn 23:8
purchased from **E** the Hittite as	Gn 49:30

EPICUREAN
some of the **E** and Stoic   Ac 17:18

EPILEPTICS
the **e**, and the paralytics   Mt 4:24

EQUAL
compare Me to, or who is My **e**?	Is 40:25
you compare Me or make Me **e** to?	Is 46:5
you made them **e** to us who bore	Mt 20:12
making Himself **e** with God.	Jn 5:18

EQUALITY
for your need, that there may be **e**.	2Co 8:14
did not consider **e** with God as	Php 2:6

EQUIP
be complete, **e-ped** for every good	2Tm 3:17
e you with all that is good to	Heb 13:21

EQUIPMENT
and all the **e** for the service of	Ex 39:40
or the **e** for his chariots	1Sm 8:12
made all the **e** in the LORD's	1Kg 7:48
Take the **e** of a foolish shepherd.	Zch 11:15

ER
Judah's son (Gn 38:1-7; 46:12; 1Ch 2:3).

ERASE
against Me I will **e** from My book.	Ex 32:33
their sin be **e-d** from Your sight	Neh 4:5
and don't **e** the good deeds I	Neh 13:14
You have **e-d** their name forever	Ps 9:5
to **e** all memory of them from the	Ps 34:16
Let them be **e-d** from the book of	Ps 69:28
I will **e** the names of the idols	Zch 13:2
He **e-d** the certificate of debt,	Col 2:14
and I will never **e** his name from	Rv 3:5

ERASTUS
Corinthian Christian (Ac 19:22; Rm 16:23; 2Tm 4:20).

ERR
liars **e** from birth.   Ps 58:3

ERROR
behalf for the **e** he has	Lv 5:18
an **e** proceeding from the	Ec 10:5
didn't come from **e** or impurity	1Th 2:3

from the **e** of his way will   Jms 5:20
from those who live in **e**.   2Pt 2:18
led away by the **e** of the immoral   2Pt 3:17
to the **e** of Balaam for   Jd 11

ESAR-HADDON

King of Assyria (2Kg 19:37; Ezr 4:2;
Is 37:38).

ESAU

Son of Isaac; elder twin of Jacob (Gn 25:24-
26); rejected by God (Mal 1:2-3; Rm 9:13);
sold birthright (Gn 25:30-34; Heb 12:16);
tricked out of blessing (Gn 27:1-30; Heb
11:20); reconciled with Jacob (Gn 33:4-16).
Progenitor of Edomites in Seir (Dt 2:4-29).

ESCALATES

is ongoing, and conflict **e**.   Hab 1:3

ESCAPE (n)

Their way of **e** will be cut off,   Jb 11:20
and **e** from death belongs to the   Ps 68:20
there is no **e** from them.   Jl 2:3
E will fail the swift, the   Am 2:14
will be like an **e** through fire.   1Co 3:15
will also provide a way of **e**,   1Co 10:13

ESCAPE (v)

when he has **e**-d from his master to   Dt 23:15
Do not let even one of them **e**.   1Kg 18:40
whoever **e**-s the sword of Jehu.   1Kg 19:17
don't let anyone **e** from the city to   2Kg 9:15
and I alone have **e**-d to tell you!   Jb 1:15
I have **e**-d by the skin of my teeth   Jb 19:20
E to the mountain like a bird!   Ps 11:1
Will they **e** in spite of such sin   Ps 56:7
We have **e**-d like a bird from the   Ps 124:7
can I go to **e** Your Spirit?   Ps 139:7
the righteous **e**-s from trouble.   Pr 12:13
one who utters lies will not **e**.   Pr 19:5
Now, how will we **e**?   Is 20:6
one who does such things **e**?   Ezk 17:15
How can you **e** being condemned   Mt 23:33
strength to **e** all these things   Lk 21:36
he thought the prisoners had **e**-d.   Ac 16:27
that you will **e** God's judgment?   Rm 2:3
and they will not **e**.   1Th 5:3
and **e** the Devil's trap   2Tm 2:26
how will we **e** if we neglect such   Heb 2:3

if they did not **e** when they   Heb 12:25
e-ing the corruption that is in the   2Pt 1:4
having **e**-d the world's impurity   2Pt 2:20

ESPECIALLY

The altar will become **e** holy;   Ex 29:37
It is **e** holy, like the sin   Lv 6:17
of the mountain will be **e** holy.   Ezk 43:12
e for those who belong to the   Gl 6:10
of everyone, **e** of those who   1Tm 4:10

ESTABLISH

But I will **e** My covenant with   Gn 6:18
I will **e** My covenant between Me   Gn 17:2
LORD will **e** you as His holy people,   Dt 28:9
I will **e** a lasting dynasty for   1Sm 2:35
and I will **e** his kingdom.   2Sm 7:12
I will **e** your royal throne over   1Kg 9:5
I will **e** My name forever in   2Kg 21:7
The world is firmly **e**-d;   1Ch 16:30
I will **e** his kingdom forever if   1Ch 28:7
enough to **e** them forever,   2Ch 9:8
were you when I **e**-ed the earth?   Jb 38:4
e-ed a stronghold from the mouths of   Ps 8:2
and **e**-ed it on the rivers.   Ps 24:2
man's steps are **e**-ed by the LORD,   Ps 37:23
God will **e** it forever.   Ps 48:8
You **e** the mountains by Your   Ps 65:6
He **e**-ed a testimony in Jacob and   Ps 78:5
'I will **e** your offspring forever   Ps 89:4
I will **e** his line forever,   Ps 89:29
e for us the work of our hands   Ps 90:17
throne has been **e**-ed from the   Ps 93:2
The world is firmly **e**-ed;   Ps 96:10
The LORD has **e**-ed His throne in   Ps 103:19
and all your ways will be **e**-ed.   Pr 4:26
the mountains and hills were **e**-ed,   Pr 8:25
and it is **e**-ed by understanding;   Pr 24:3
his throne will be **e**-ed forever.   Pr 29:14
throne will be **e**-ed by faithful   Is 16:5
and His power **e**-es His rule.   Is 40:10
e-ed the world by His wisdom,   Jr 10:12
I will **e** an everlasting covenant   Ezk 16:60
He removes kings and **e**-es kings.   Dn 2:21
witnesses every fact may be **e**-ed.   Mt 18:16
and was **e**-ed as the powerful Son of   Rm 1:4
God and attempted to **e** their own   Rm 10:3
rooted and firmly **e**-ed in love,   Eph 3:17
up in Him and **e**-ed in the faith,   Col 2:7
away the first to **e** the second.   Heb 10:9

restore, e, strengthen 1Pt 5:10
them and are e-ed in the truth you 2Pt 1:12

ESTABLISHMENT
defense and e of the gospel. Php 1:7

ESTATE
have given Haman's e to Esther, Est 8:7
squandered his e in foolish Lk 15:13

ESTEEM
and to e them very highly 1Th 5:13

ESTHER
Persian name of Hadassah, Mordecai's cousin (Est 2:7). Chosen queen of Persia (2:16-18); interceded at great risk to foil a plot to exterminate the Jews (Est 3–9).

ESTIMATION
Do not be wise in your own e. Rm 12:16

ETERNAL
this land as an e possession Gn 48:4
bounty of the e hills Gn 49:26; Dt 33:15
the E One of Israel does not lie 1Sm 15:29
the LORD's e love for Israel 1Kg 10:9
right hand are e pleasures. Ps 16:11
is good, and His love is e; Ps 100:5
for He is good. His love is e. Ps 136:1
LORD, Your love is e; Ps 138:8
man is headed to his e home, Ec 12:5
Mighty God, E Father, Prince Is 9:6
His kingdom is an e kingdom, Dn 4:3
awake, some to e life, and some Dn 12:2
and be thrown into the e fire. Mt 18:8
must I do to have e life? Mt 19:16
more and will inherit e life? Mt 19:29
into the e fire prepared for the Mt 25:41
will go away into e punishment,
   but the righteous into e life. Mt 25:46
but is guilty of an e sin Mk 3:29
and e life in the age to come. Mk 10:30
welcome you into e dwellings. Lk 16:9
in Him will have e life. Jn 3:15
not perish but have e life. Jn 3:16
believes in the Son has e life, Jn 3:36
springing up within him for e life. Jn 4:14
and gathering fruit for e life, Jn 4:36
who sent Me has e life and will Jn 5:24
think you have e life in them, Jn 5:39
in Him may have e life, Jn 6:40

Anyone who believes has e life. Jn 6:47
You have the words of e life. Jn 6:68
I give them e life, and they Jn 10:28
that His command is e life. Jn 12:50
so He may give e life to all You Jn 17:2
This is e life: that they may Jn 17:3
appointed to e life believed. Ac 13:48
His e power and divine nature, Rm 1:20
e life to those who by patiently Rm 2:7
resulting in e life through Rm 5:21
and the end is e life! Rm 6:22
gift of God is e life in Christ Rm 6:23
incomparable e weight of glory. 2Co 4:17
but what is unseen is e. 2Co 4:18
with hands, e in the heavens. 2Co 5:1
believe in Him for e life. 1Tm 1:16
Now to the King e, immortal 1Tm 1:17
take hold of e life, to which 1Tm 6:12
in the hope of e life that God, Ti 1:2
heirs with the hope of e life. Ti 3:7
the source of e salvation to all Heb 5:9
of the dead, and e judgment. Heb 6:2
having obtained e redemption. Heb 9:12
who through the e Spirit offered Heb 9:14
promise of the e inheritance, Heb 9:15
you to His e glory in Christ 1Pt 5:10
to you the e life that was with 1Jn 1:2
He Himself made to us: e life. 1Jn 2:25
no murderer has e life residing 1Jn 3:15
has given us e life, and this 1Jn 5:11
may know that you have e life. 1Jn 5:13
He is the true God and e life. 1Jn 5:20
with e chains in darkness for Jd 6
the punishment of e fire. Jd 7
Lord Jesus Christ for e life. Jd 21
having the e gospel to announce Rv 14:6

ETERNALLY
they will be e destroyed. Ps 92:7
The e blessed One, the God and 2Co 11:31

ETERNITY
be praised ... from e to e. 1Ch 29:10
from e to e, You are God. Ps 90:2
the beginning; You are from e. Ps 93:2
from e to e the LORD's faithful Ps 103:17
has also put e in their hearts Ec 3:11
both now and to the day of e. 2Pt 3:18

ETHIOPIAN see also CUSH, CUSHITE
There was an E man, a eunuch Ac 8:27

ETHNIC

| not reveal her e background | Est 2:10 |
| There is one e group, scattered | Est 3:8 |

ETHNICALLY

| An e diverse crowd also went up | Ex 12:38 |

EUNICE

Timothy's mother (2Tm 1:5).

EUNUCH

they will become e-s in the palace	2Kg 20:18
the king's e in charge of the	Est 2:14
and the e should not say, "Look	Is 56:3
For the e-s who keep My Sabbaths	Is 56:4
For there are e-s who were born	Mt 19:12
The e replied to Philip, "I ask	Ac 8:34

EUPHRATES

And the fourth river is the E.	Gn 2:14
brook of Egypt to the E River:	Gn 15:18
the wilderness to the E River.	Ex 23:31
Lebanon and from the E River to	Dt 11:24
Lebanon to the great E River	Jos 1:4
worshiped beyond the E River,	Jos 24:15
everything west of the E	1Kg 4:24
to sea and from the E to the ends	Ps 72:8
defeated at Carchemish on the E	Jr 46:2
his bowl on the great river E,	Rv 16:12

EUTYCHUS

| a young man named E was sitting | Ac 20:9 |

EVALUATE

but the LORD e-s the motives.	Pr 21:2
She e-s a field and buys it;	Pr 31:16
it since it is e-d spiritually.	1Co 2:14
himself cannot be e-d by anyone.	1Co 2:15
In fact, I don't even e myself.	1Co 4:3
The One who e-s me is the Lord.	1Co 4:4
we were properly e-ing ourselves,	1Co 11:31
speak, and the others should e.	1Co 14:29

EVANGELIST

the house of Philip the e,	Ac 21:8
prophets, some e-s, some pastors	Eph 4:11
the work of an e, fulfill your	2Tm 4:5

EVANGELIZE

e-ing many villages of the	Ac 8:25
he was e-ing all the towns until he	Ac 8:40
And there they kept e-ing.	Ac 14:7
After they had e-d that town and	Ac 14:21

| God had called us to e them. | Ac 16:10 |
| to e where Christ has not been | Rm 15:20 |

EVE

First woman; wife of Adam (Gn 3:20; 4:1-2,25). Gave in to temptation (3:1; 2Co 11:3; 1Tm 2:13-14).

EVENING

E came, and then morning:	Gn 1:5
at the time of the e breeze,	Gn 3:8
But the e drags on endlessly,	Jb 7:4
and to his labor until e.	Ps 104:23
and at e do not let your hand	Ec 11:6
but there will be light at e.	Zch 14:7

EVENTS

the turn of e came from the LORD	1Kg 12:15
All these e are the beginning of	Mt 24:8
You know the e that took place	Ac 10:37

EVERLASTING

remember the e covenant between	Gn 9:16
as an e covenant to be your God	Gn 17:7
worshiped the LORD, the E God.	Gn 21:33
and underneath are the e arms.	Dt 33:27
be praised from e to e.	1Ch 16:36
LORD your God from e to e.	Neh 9:5
be praised from e to e,	Ps 41:13
and to Israel as an e covenant:	Ps 105:10
is an e righteousness,	Ps 119:142
lead me in the e way.	Ps 139:24
Your kingdom is an e kingdom;	Ps 145:13
in Yah, the LORD, is an e rock!	Is 26:4
Yahweh is the e God, the Creator	Is 40:28
the LORD with an e salvation;	Is 45:17
compassion on you with e love,	Is 54:8
I will make an e covenant with	Is 55:3
the LORD as an e sign that will	Is 55:13
the LORD will be your e light,	Is 60:19
have loved you with an e love;	Jr 31:3
it will be an e covenant with	Ezk 37:26
His dominion is an e dominion,	Dn 4:34
to bring in e righteousness,	Dn 9:24
the penalty of e destruction,	2Th 1:9
the blood of the e covenant,	Heb 13:20

EVERY

He wiped out e living thing that	Gn 7:23
and e firstborn {male} in the land	Ex 11:5
alone but on e word that comes	Dt 8:3

but its **e** decision is from the	Pr 16:33
E word of God is pure;	Pr 30:5
and a time for **e** activity under	Ec 3:1
God will bring **e** act to judgment	Ec 12:14
against **e** high tower, against	Is 2:15
E knee will bow to Me, **e** tongue	Is 45:23
Therefore **e** tree that doesn't	Mt 3:10
alone but on **e** word that comes	Mt 4:4
E tree that doesn't produce good	Mt 7:19
E kingdom divided against	Mt 12:25
will be forgiven **e** sin and	Mt 12:31
to account for **e** careless word	Mt 12:36
E branch in Me that does not	Jn 15:2
but in **e** nation the person who	Ac 10:35
so that **e** mouth may be shut and	Rm 3:19
in me coveting of **e** kind.	Rm 7:8
else considers **e** day to be the	Rm 14:5
e knee will bow to Me, and **e**	Rm 14:11
E sin a person can commit is	1Co 6:18
taking **e** thought captive to the	2Co 10:5
blessed us with **e** spiritual	Eph 1:3
from whom **e** family in heaven and	Eph 3:15
the name that is above **e** name,	Php 2:9
name of Jesus **e** knee should bow	Php 2:10
Stay away from **e** form of evil.	1Th 5:22
is beneficial in **e** way,	1Tm 4:8
equipped for **e** good work.	2Tm 3:17
be like His brothers in **e** way,	Heb 2:17
let us lay aside **e** weight and	Heb 12:1
Submit to **e** human institution	1Pt 2:13
do not believe **e** spirit, but	1Jn 4:1
the clouds, and **e** eye will see	Rv 1:7
from **e** tribe and language and	Rv 5:9
a vast multitude from **e** nation,	Rv 7:9
will wipe away **e** tear from	Rv 7:17; 21:4

EVERYONE

e who is angry with his brother	Mt 5:22
e who looks at a woman to lust	Mt 5:28
For **e** who asks receives, and the	Mt 7:8
Not **e** who says to Me, 'Lord	Mt 7:21
So it is with **e** born of the Spirit.	Jn 3:8
so that **e** who believes in Him	Jn 3:15,16
E the Father gives Me will come	Jn 6:37
E who is of the truth listens to	Jn 18:37
to **e** who believes.	Rm 10:4
For **e** who calls on the name of	Rm 10:13
who wants **e** to be saved and to	1Tm 2:4
but **e** deserted me.	2Tm 4:16

He might taste death for **e**	Heb 2:9
Honor **e**. Love the brotherhood	1Pt 2:17
E who has been born of God does	1Jn 3:9
E who believes that Jesus is the	1Jn 5:1

EVERYTHING

You put **e** under his feet:	Ps 8:6
The earth and **e** in it, the world	Ps 24:1
the world and **e** in it is Mine.	Ps 50:12
the seas and **e** that moves in	Ps 69:34
Let **e** that breathes praise the	Ps 150:6
has prepared **e** for His purpose	Pr 16:4
There is an occasion for **e**,	Ec 3:1
goes and sells **e** he has and buys	Mt 13:44
is coming and will restore **e**,	Mt 17:11
we have left **e** and followed You	Mt 19:27
them to observe **e** I have	Mt 28:20
comes, He will explain **e** to us.	Jn 4:25
E the Father has is Mine.	Jn 16:15
not also with Him grant us **e**?	Rm 8:32
E is clean, but it is wrong for	Rm 14:20
and **e** that is not from faith is	Rm 14:23
E is permissible	1Co 6:12; 10:23
you do, do **e** for God's glory.	1Co 10:31
For He has put **e** under His feet	1Co 15:27
not continue doing **e** written in	Gl 3:10
And He put **e** under His feet and	Eph 1:22
Do **e** without grumbling and	Php 2:14
because by Him **e** was created,	Col 1:16
For **e** created by God is good,	1Tm 4:4
and subjected **e** under his feet.	Heb 2:8
has given us **e** required for life	2Pt 1:3
I am making **e** new.	Rv 21:5

EVERYWHERE

The eyes of the LORD are **e**,	Pr 15:3
all people **e** to repent,	Ac 17:30

EVIDENT

about God is **e** among them,	Rm 1:19
your progress may be **e** to all.	1Tm 4:15
sins are **e**, going before	1Tm 5:24
Now it is **e** that our Lord came	Heb 7:14
Devil's children—are made **e**.	1Jn 3:10

EVIL

of the knowledge of good and **e**.	Gn 2:9
be like God, knowing good and **e**.	Gn 3:5
was nothing but **e** all the time,	Gn 6:5
inclination is **e** from his youth	Gn 8:21
Why have you repaid **e** for good?	Gn 44:4

You planned **e** against me;	Gn 50:20
the people are {intent} on **e**.	Ex 32:22
You must purge the **e** from you.	Dt 13:5
did what was **e** in the LORD's	Jdg 2:11
and an **e** spirit from the LORD	1Sm 16:14
was plotting **e** against him,	1Sm 23:9
yet he paid me back **e** for good.	1Sm 25:21
to discern between good and **e**.	1Kg 3:9
that rebellious and **e** city,	Ezr 4:12
feared God and turned away from **e**.	Jb 1:1
when I hoped for good, **e** came;	Jb 30:26
e cannot lodge with You.	Ps 5:4
Turn away from **e** and do what is	Ps 34:14
E brings death to the sinner,	Ps 34:21
They repay me **e** for good, making	Ps 35:12
not good and does not reject **e**.	Ps 36:4
Turn away from **e** and do what is	Ps 37:27
he stores up **e** in his heart;	Ps 41:6
and done this **e** in Your sight.	Ps 51:4
You love **e** instead of good,	Ps 52:3
thoughts are against me for **e**.	Ps 56:5
You who love the LORD, hate **e**!	Ps 97:10
They repay me **e** for good, and	Ps 109:5
feet from every **e** path to follow	Ps 119:101
the LORD and turn away from **e**.	Pr 3:7
feet eager to run to **e**,	Pr 6:18
To fear the LORD is to hate **e**.	Pr 8:13
but fools hate to turn from **e**.	Pr 13:19
The **e** bow before those who are	Pr 14:19
of the upright avoids **e**;	Pr 16:17
returns **e** for good, **e** will never	Pr 17:13
Don't envy **e** men or desire to be	Pr 24:1
For the **e** have no future;	Pr 24:20
with good, not **e**, all the days	Pr 31:12
lives long in spite of his **e**.	Ec 7:15
hearts of people are full of **e**,	Ec 9:3
hidden thing, whether good or **e**.	Ec 12:14
who call **e** good and good **e**,	Is 5:20
his eyes to avoid endorsing **e**	Is 33:15
away from the presence of **e**.	Is 57:1
feet run after **e**, and they rush	Is 59:7
have committed a double **e**:	Jr 2:13
whose hearts are bent on **e**,	Dn 11:27
a time, for the days are **e**.	Am 5:13
Hate **e** and love good; establish	Am 5:15
Each must turn from his **e** ways	Jnh 3:8
eyes are too pure to look on **e**,	Hab 1:13
Turn from your **e** ways and	Zch 1:4

do not plot **e** in your hearts	Zch 7:10; 8:17
sun to rise on the **e** and the good,	Mt 5:45
but deliver us from the **e** one.	Mt 6:13
then, who are **e**, know how to	Mt 7:11
Why are you thinking **e** things	Mt 9:4
an **e** man produces **e** things from	Mt 12:35
An **e** and adulterous generation	Mt 12:39
separate the **e** people from the	Mt 13:49
The one who speaks **e** of father	Mt 15:4
from the heart come **e** thoughts,	Mt 15:19
An **e** and adulterous generation	Mt 16:4
Sabbath to do good or to do **e**,	Mk 3:4
because their deeds were **e**.	Jn 3:19
protect them from the **e** one.	Jn 17:15
must not speak **e** of a ruler of	Ac 23:5
inventors of **e**, disobedient to	Rm 1:30
Let us do **e** so that good may	Rm 3:8
want to do good, **e** is with me.	Rm 7:21
Detest **e**; cling to what is	Rm 12:9
Do not repay anyone **e** for **e**.	Rm 12:17
conquered by **e**, but	
conquer **e** with	Rm 12:21
yet innocent about what is **e**.	Rm 16:19
be infants in **e** and adult in	1Co 14:20
us from this present **e** age,	Gl 1:4
because the days are **e**.	Eph 5:16
be able to resist in the **e** day,	Eph 6:13
flaming arrows of the **e** one.	Eph 6:16
no one repays **e** for **e** to anyone,	1Th 5:15
Stay away from every form of **e**.	1Th 5:22
is a root of all kinds of **e**,	1Tm 6:10
won't be in any of you an **e**,	Heb 3:12
distinguish between good and **e**.	Heb 5:14
For God is not tempted by **e**,	Jms 1:13
is a restless **e**, full of deadly	Jms 3:8
freedom as a way to conceal **e**.	1Pt 2:16
not paying back **e** for **e** or insult for	1Pt 3:9
his tongue from **e** and his lips	1Pt 3:10
Lord is against those who do **e**.	1Pt 3:12
had victory over the **e** one.	1Jn 2:13
and the **e** one does not touch him	1Jn 5:18
to him shares in his **e** works.	2Jn 11
do not imitate what is **e**, but what is	3Jn 11
one who does **e** has not seen God	3Jn 11
and that you cannot tolerate **e**.	Rv 2:2

EVILDOER

LORD repay the **e** according to	2Sm 3:39
E-s will not afflict them as they	2Sm 7:10

Will e-s never understand?	Ps 14:4; 53:4
a gang of e-s has closed in on me	Ps 22:16
Do not be agitated by e-s;	Ps 37:1
For e-s will be destroyed, but	Ps 37:9
brood of e-s, depraved children!	Is 1:4
The offspring of e-s will never be	Is 14:20
I tell you, don't resist an e.	Mt 5:39
a thief, an e, or as a meddler.	1Pt 4:15

EVIL-MERODACH
King of Babylon (2Kg 25:27; Jr 52:31).

EWE
had set apart seven e lambs	Gn 21:28
an unblemished year-old e lamb,	Lv 14:10
one small e lamb that he had	2Sm 12:3
from tending e-s to be shepherd	Ps 78:71
are like a flock of e-s coming up	Sg 6:6

EXACT (adj)
as well as the e amount of money	Est 4:7
asked them the e time the star	Mt 2:7
the e expression of His nature,	Heb 1:3

EXACT (v)
He e-ed the silver and the gold	2Kg 23:35
on the poor and e a grain tax	Am 5:11

EXACTLY
So David did e as the LORD	2Sm 5:25
order was written e as Haman	Est 3:12
was written e as Mordecai	Est 8:9
e as he comes, so he will go.	Ec 5:16

EXALT
father's God, and I will e Him.	Ex 15:2
Why then do you e yourselves	Nm 16:3
I will begin to e you in the	Jos 3:7
that day the LORD e-ed Joshua in	Jos 4:14
He humbles and He e-s.	1Sm 2:7
the rock of my salvation, is e-ed.	2Sm 22:47
You e me above my adversaries;	2Sm 22:49
indeed built an e-ed temple for You	1Kg 8:13
and You are e-ed as head over all.	1Ch 29:11
The LORD highly e-ed Solomon in	1Ch 29:25
and may it be e-ed above all	Neh 9:5
since He judges the e-ed ones?	Jb 21:22
shows Himself e-ed by His power.	Jb 36:22
God is e-ed beyond our knowledge;	Jb 36:26
reach Him—He is e-ed in power!	Jb 37:23
is worthless is e-ed by the human	Ps 12:8
The God of my salvation is e-ed.	Ps 18:46

Be e-ed, LORD, in Your strength;	Ps 21:13
I will e You, LORD, because You	Ps 30:1
let us e His name together.	Ps 34:3
I will e You among many people.	Ps 35:18
know that I am God, e-ed among	
the nations, e-ed on the earth.	Ps 46:10
be e-ed above the heavens;	Ps 57:5,11
should not e themselves.	Ps 66:7
brings down one and e-s another.	Ps 75:7
by Your favor our horn is e-ed.	Ps 89:17
But You, LORD, are e-ed forever.	Ps 92:8
You are e-ed above all the gods.	Ps 97:9
He is e-ed above all the peoples.	Ps 99:2
E the LORD our God; bow in	Ps 99:5,9
Let them e Him in the assembly	Ps 107:32
be e-ed above the heavens;	Ps 108:5
The LORD is e-ed above all the	Ps 113:4
{You are} my God; I will e You.	Ps 118:28
if I do not e Jerusalem as my	Ps 137:6
I e You, my God the King, and	Ps 145:1
for His name alone is e-ed.	Ps 148:13
her, and she will e you;	Pr 4:8
Righteousness e-s a nation, but	Pr 14:34
alone will be e-ed on that day.	Is 2:11,17
Declare that His name is e-ed.	Is 12:4
I will e You. I will praise Your name,	Is 25:1
The LORD is e-ed, for He dwells on	Is 33:5
e the lowly and bring down the	Ezk 21:26
will never again e itself over	Ezk 29:15
He will e and magnify himself	Dn 11:36
will you be e-ed to heaven?	Mt 11:23
humbles himself will be e-ed.	Mt 23:12
their thrones and e-ed the lowly.	Lk 1:52
He has been e to the right hand	Ac 2:33
God e-ed this man to His right hand	Ac 5:31
myself so that you might be e-ed,	2Co 11:7
God also highly e-ed Him and gave	Php 2:9
He opposes and e-s himself above	2Th 2:4
the Lord, and He will e you.	Jms 4:10
so that He may e you in due time	1Pt 5:6

EXALTATION
E does not come from the east,	Ps 75:6
Let the e of God be in their	Ps 149:6
should boast in his e;	Jms 1:9

EXAMINE
We found this. E it. Is it your	Gn 37:32
And she added, "E them.	Gn 38:25
The priest will e the infection on	Lv 13:3

EXAMPLE 163 EXCUSE

The One who e-s the thoughts and	Ps 7:9
The LORD e-s the righteous and the	Ps 11:5
e my heart and mind.	Ps 26:2
I, the LORD, e the mind, I test	Jr 17:10
search out and e our ways,	Lm 3:40
and e-d the Scriptures daily to see	Ac 17:11
that he be e-d with the scourge,	Ac 22:24
So a man should e himself;	1Co 11:28
in the faith. E yourselves. Or	2Co 13:5
person should e his own work,	Gl 6:4
rather God, who e-s our hearts.	1Th 2:4
am the One who e-s minds and	Rv 2:23

EXAMPLE

your sons do not follow your e.	1Sm 8:5
and followed the e of Jeroboam	1Kg 15:34
given you an e that you also	Jn 13:15
these things became e-s for us,	1Co 10:6
things happened to them as e-s,	1Co 10:11
to the e you have in us.	Php 3:17
ourselves an e to you so that	2Th 3:9
should be an e to the believers	1Tm 4:12
Set an e of good works yourself	Tt 2:7
leaving you an e, so that you	1Pt 2:21
you, but being e-s to the flock.	1Pt 5:3
making them an e to those who	2Pt 2:6
and serve as an e by undergoing	Jd 7

EXASPERATE

Fathers, do not e your children	Col 3:21

EXCEED

prosperity far e the report I heard.	1Kg 10:7

EXCEEDINGLY

LORD must be e great and famous	1Ch 22:5

EXCEL

seek to e in building up the	1Co 14:12
always e-ling in the Lord's work,	1Co 15:58
Now as you e in everything	2Co 8:7
you may e in every good work.	2Co 9:8

EXCELLENCE

is any moral e and if there is	Php 4:8

EXCELLENT

One person dies in e health,	Jb 21:23

EXCEPT

e in a case of sexual immorality	Mt 5:32
one knows the Son e the Father,	Mt 11:27
will be given to it e the sign	Mt 12:39

without honor e in his hometown	Mt 13:57
divorces his wife, e for sexual	Mt 19:9
into heaven e the One who	Jn 3:13
seen the Father e the One who is	Jn 6:46
to the Father e through Me.	Jn 14:6
"Jesus is Lord," e by the Holy	1Co 12:3

EXCESS

of all moral filth and evil e,	Jms 1:21

EXCESSIVE

E speech is not appropriate on a	Pr 17:7
wealth through e interest	Pr 28:8
may be overwhelmed by e grief.	2Co 2:7

EXCESSIVELY

Don't be e righteous, and don't	Ec 7:16

EXCHANGE

he owns in e for his life.	Jb 2:4
a man give in e for his life?	Mt 16:26

EXCHANGED

Gold cannot be e for it, and	Jb 28:15
They e their glory for the image	Ps 106:20
Has a nation (ever) e its gods?	Jr 2:11
My people have e their Glory	Jr 2:11
and e the glory of the immortal	Rm 1:23
They e the truth of God for a	Rm 1:25
their females e natural sexual	Rm 1:26

EXCLUDE

and would be e-d from	
the assembly	Ezr 10:8
who hate and e you because of Me	Is 66:5
when they e you, insult you,	Lk 6:22
boasting? It is e-d. By what kind	Rm 3:27
e-d from the citizenship of Israel	Eph 2:12
e-d from the life of God,	Eph 4:18

EXCREMENT

with it and cover up your e.	Dt 23:13
eat their own e and drink their	2Kg 18:27
to eat their e and drink their	Is 36:12
dried human e in their sight.	Ezk 4:12

EXCUSE (n)

they all began to make e-s.	Lk 14:18
they have no e for their sin.	Jn 15:22
As a result, people are without e.	Rm 1:20
of you who judges is without e.	Rm 2:1

EXCUSE (v)

either accuse or e them	Rm 2:15

EXECUTE

He e-s justice for the fatherless	Dt 10:18
and to e any design that	2Ch 2:14
He has e-d justice, striking down	Ps 9:16
The LORD e-s acts of righteousness	Ps 103:6
When will You e judgment on my	Ps 119:84
e-ing justice for the exploited	Ps 146:7
wind that e-s His command,	Ps 148:8
Justice e-d is a joy to the	Pr 21:15
the LORD will e judgment on all	Is 66:16
for the Lord will e His sentence	Rm 9:28
to e judgment on all, and to	Jd 15

EXEMPT

man's father e from paying taxes	1Sm 17:25

EXERCISE

high position e power over them	Mt 20:25
who competes e-s self-control	1Co 9:25

EXHAUST

Esau came in from the field, e-ed.	Gn 25:29
they were too e-ed to cross the	1Sm 30:10
Their might is e-ed; they have	Jr 51:30
I will e My wrath on them.	Ezk 6:12

EXHAUSTION

While he was sleeping from e,	Jdg 4:21

EXHORT

and e-ed them at length	Ac 20:2
we command and e such people,	2Th 3:12
older man, but e him as a father	1Tm 5:1
to write and e you to contend	Jd 3

EXHORTATION

with many other e-s, he proclaimed	Lk 3:18
if exhorting, in e;	Rm 12:8
reading, e, and teaching.	1Tm 4:13
forgotten the e that addresses	Heb 12:5
you to receive this word of e,	Heb 13:22

EXILE

and an e from your homeland.	2Sm 15:19
went into e from its land.	2Kg 25:21
the returned e-s were building	Ezr 4:1
The e-s observed the Passover on	Ezr 6:19
that had returned from e.	Neh 1:2
been taken into e from Jerusalem	Est 2:6
of Jerusalem went into e.	Jr 1:3
I was among the e-s by the Chebar	Ezk 1:1
Israel went into e on account of	Ezk 39:23

send you into e beyond Damascus.	Am 5:27
David until the e to Babylon,	Mt 1:17

EXILED

So Israel has been e-d to Assyria	2Kg 17:23
He gathers Israel's e-d people.	Ps 147:2

EXIST

{since} God does not e.	Ps 10:4
in his heart, "God does not e.	Ps 14:1; 53:1
It has already e-ed in the ages	Ec 1:10
and you will no longer e.	Ezk 26:21
and no Savior e-s besides Me.	Hs 13:4
me, because He e-ed before me.	Jn 1:15
with You before the world e,	Jn 17:5
in Him we live and move and e,	Ac 17:28
into existence that do not e.	Rm 4:17
condemnation now e-s for those in	Rm 8:1
who, e-ing in the form of God,	Php 2:6
and through whom all things e,	Heb 2:10
believe that He e-s and rewards	Heb 11:6
and the earth e out of water	2Pt 3:5
Your will they e and were	Rv 4:11

EXISTENCE

life to those whose e is bitter,	Jb 3:20
commanded, and it came into e.	Ps 33:9
things into e that do not exist	Rm 4:17

EXODUS

the days of your e from the land	Mc 7:15
mentioned the e of the sons of	Heb 11:22

EXORCISTS

itinerant Jewish e attempted to	Ac 19:13

EXPANSE

Let there be an e between the	Gn 1:6
be lights in the e of the sky to	Gn 1:14
God, and watery e-s are frozen.	Jb 37:10
The shape of an e, with a gleam	Ezk 1:22
there above the e over the heads	Ezk 10:1

EXPECT

I never e-ed to see your face	Gn 48:11
or should we e someone else?	Mt 11:3
coming at an hour you do not e.	Mt 24:44
and lend, e-ing nothing in return.	Lk 6:35
more will be e-ed of the one who	Lk 12:48
e-ing to get something from them.	Ac 3:5
e-ing the mercy of our Lord Jesus	Jd 21

EXPECTANTLY

my case to You and watch e.	Ps 5:3
the LORD and wait e for Him;	Ps 37:7

EXPECTATION

Men listened to me with e,	Jb 29:21
e of the wicked comes to nothing.	Pr 10:28
wicked dies, his e comes to nothing,	Pr 11:7
My eager e and hope is that I	Php 1:20
but a terrifying e of judgment,	Heb 10:27

EXPELS

and e them from the church.	3Jn 10

EXPENSE

ever goes to war at his own e?	1Co 9:7

EXPENSIVE

jar of very e fragrant oil.	Mt 26:7
gold, pearls, or e apparel,	1Tm 2:9

EXPERIENCE

and who had e-d all the works the	Jos 24:31
Samuel had not yet e-d the LORD,	1Sm 3:7
and e good in all the labor one	Ec 5:18
will not e anything harmful	Ec 8:5
and others e-d mockings and	Heb 11:36

EXPERT

an e in matters of the LORD's	Ezr 7:11
Woe also to you e-s in the law!	Lk 11:46
you are an e in all the Jewish	Ac 26:3
the understanding of the e-s.	1Co 1:19

EXPLAIN

were unable to e the riddle.	Jdg 14:14
difficult for Solomon to e to her.	2Ch 9:2
e-ed the law to the people as they	Neh 8:7
all this to heart and e-ed it all:	Ec 9:1
interpret dreams, e riddles, and	Dn 5:12
E the parable of the weeds	Mt 13:36
E this parable to us.	Mt 15:15
He would e everything to His own	Mk 4:34
on the road and e-ing the Scriptures	Lk 24:32
He will e everything to us.	Jn 4:25
e-ing and showing that the Messiah	Ac 17:3
e-ed the way of God to him more	Ac 18:26
e-ing spiritual things to spiritual	1Co 2:13
difficult to e, since you have	Heb 5:11

EXPLANATION

to another to find out the e,	Ec 7:27
He gave me this e:	Dn 9:22

EXPLICITLY

Now the Spirit e says that in	1Tm 4:1

EXPLOIT

You must not e a foreign	Ex 22:21
for the e-ed and giving food	Ps 146:7
Don't e or brutalize the alien,	Jr 22:3
greed they will e you with	2Pt 2:3

EXPLOITS

Such were the e of the three	2Sm 23:17

EXPLORE

through and e-d is an extremely	Nm 14:7
to seek and e through wisdom	Ec 1:13
I e-d with my mind how to let my	Ec 2:3
to know, e, and seek wisdom	Ec 7:25
weighed, e-d, and arranged many	Ec 12:9

EXPORTED

they e them to all the kings of	1Kg 10:29

EXPOSE

your nakedness is not e-d on it,	Ex 20:26
He e-d himself today in the sight	2Sm 6:20
and your shame will be e-d.	Is 47:3
will get drunk and e yourself.	Lm 4:21
and will e your sins.	Lm 4:22
all around and e your nakedness	Ezk 16:37
They e-d her nakedness, seized her	Ezk 23:10
Now I will e her shame in the	Hs 2:10
so that his deeds may not be e-d.	Jn 3:20
darkness, but instead, e them.	Eph 5:11
Everything e-d by the light is	Eph 5:13
you were publicly e-d to taunts	Heb 10:33
shameful nakedness not be e-d,	Rv 3:18

EXPOUNDED

dawn to dusk he e and witnessed	Ac 28:23

EXPRESSION

and the e on his face changed	Dn 3:19
in the law the full e of knowledge	Rm 2:20
the exact e of His nature,	Heb 1:3

EXTEND

the angel e-ed his hand toward	2Sm 24:16
would bless me, e my border,	1Ch 4:10
He has e-ed grace to us in the	Ezr 9:9

king e-ed the golden scepter   Est 5:2, 8:4
She e-s her hands to the spinning   Pr 31:19
and she e-s her hands to the needy   Pr 31:20
continued to e faithful love to   Jr 31:3
for her judgment e-s to the sky   Jr 51:9
His greatness will e to the ends   Mc 5:4
{your} boundary will be e-ed.   Mc 7:11
dominion will e from sea to sea   Zch 9:10

EXTENSION
but an e of life was granted to   Dn 7:12

EXTENT
comprehended the e of the earth?   Jb 38:18
and save to the e that he prospers,   1Co 16:2

EXTERMINATE
you until He has e-d you from the   Dt 28:21
Joshua proceeded to e the Anakim   Jos 11:21
and plotted to e us so we would   2Sm 21:5
So Zimri e-d the entire house of   1Kg 16:12

EXTERNAL
come as a man in His e form,   Php 2:7

EXTINGUISH
They would e my one remaining   2Sm 14:7
You must not e the lamp of   2Sm 21:17
My days are e-ed.   Jb 17:1
the light of the wicked is e-ed;   Jb 18:5
they were e-ed like a fire among   Ps 118:12
the lamp of the wicked is e-ed.   Pr 13:9
Mighty waters cannot e love;   Sg 8:7
they are e-ed, quenched like a wick   Is 43:17
of Jerusalem and not be e-ed.   Jr 17:27
It will not be e-ed.   Ezk 20:48
will be able to e the flaming   Eph 6:16

EXTORT
loves to e with dishonest   Hs 12:7
And if I have e-ed anything from   Lk 19:8

EXTORTION
the practice of e turns a wise   Ec 7:7
and committing e and oppression   Jr 22:17
have practiced e and committed   Ezk 22:29
ready as a gift and not an e.   2Co 9:5

EXTRA
or an e shirt, sandals   Mt 10:10

EXTRAORDINARY
{This} e knowledge is beyond me   Ps 139:6
was found to have an e spirit,   Dn 5:12

people showed us e kindness,   Ac 28:2
so that this e power may be from   2Co 4:7
because of the e revelations.   2Co 12:7

EXTREME
I hate them with e hatred;   Ps 139:22
because of your e evil.   Hs 10:15
I persecuted God's church to
    an e degree   Gl 1:13

EXTREMELY
and their sin is e serious.   Gn 18:20
and explored is an e good land.   Nm 14:7
small, yet they are e wise: Pr 30:24
see that you are e religious in   Ac 17:22

EXULT
and all that is in them e.   1Ch 16:32
and everything in them e.   Ps 96:12
My warriors, who e in My triumph   Is 13:3
in the LORD, I e in my God;   Is 61:10

EYE
you eat it your e-s will be opened   Gn 3:5
God opened her e-s, and she saw a   Gn 21:19
had delicate e-s, but Rachel was   Gn 29:17
His e-s are darker than wine,   Gn 49:12
e for e, tooth for tooth,   Ex 21:24; Lv 24:20
and you can serve as our e-s.   Nm 10:31
the LORD opened Balaam's e-s,   Nm 22:31
of the man whose e-s are opened,   Nm 24:3
will become thorns in your e-s   Nm 33:55
Your own e-s have seen everything   Dt 3:21
seems right in his own e-s.   Dt 12:8
for it blinds the e-s of the wise   Dt 16:19
e for e, tooth for tooth   Dt 19:21
to understand, e-s to see, or ears   Dt 29:4
guarded him as the pupil of His e.   Dt 32:10
and thorns in your e-s,   Jos 23:13
Your own e-s saw what I did to   Jos 24:7
him and gouged out his e-s.   Jdg 16:21
had beautiful e-s and a healthy,   1Sm 16:12
May Your e-s be open to Your   1Kg 8:52
My e-s and My heart will be there   1Kg 9:3
I came and saw with my own e-s.   1Kg 10:7
to mouth, e to e, hand to hand,   2Kg 4:34
open his e-s and let him see   2Kg 6:17
she painted her e-s, adorned her   2Kg 9:30
For the e-s of the LORD range   2Ch 16:9
us new life and light to our e-s.   Ezr 9:8
let Your e-s be open and Your ears   Neh 1:6

My **e** will never again see	Jb 7:7	that is pure in its own **e-s**,	Pr 30:12
My **e-s** have grown dim from grief,	Jb 17:7	As for the **e** that ridicules a father	Pr 30:17
I was **e-s** to the blind and feet to	Jb 29:15	The **e** is not satisfied by seeing	Ec 1:8
have made a covenant with my **e-s**.	Jb 31:1	The wise man has **e-s** in his head,	Ec 2:14
but now my **e-s** have seen You.	Jb 42:5	Better what the **e-s** see than	Ec 6:9
My **e-s** are swollen from grief;	Ps 6:7	Your **e-s** are doves.	Sg 1:15; 4:1
his **e-s** are on the lookout for the	Ps 10:8	with one glance of your **e-s**,	Sg 4:9
is in heaven. His **e-s** watch; He	Ps 11:4	your **e-s** like pools in Heshbon	Sg 7:4
Guard me as the apple of Your **e**;	Ps 17:8	and haughty **e-s** are humbled.	Is 5:15
radiant, making the **e-s** light up.	Ps 19:8	{and} because my **e-s** have seen the	Is 6:5
My **e-s** are always on the LORD,	Ps 25:15	they might see with their **e-s** and	Is 6:10
my **e-s** are worn out from angry	Ps 31:9	judge by what He sees with His **e-s**,	Is 11:3
with My **e** on you, I will give	Ps 32:8	the **e-s** of the blind will see.	Is 29:18
Now the **e** of the LORD is on	Ps 33:18	the **e-s** of the blind will be opened,	Is 35:5
The **e-s** of the LORD are on the	Ps 34:15	to open blind **e-s**, to bring out	Is 42:7
My **e-s** fail, looking for my God.	Ps 69:3	who are blind, yet have **e-s**,	Is 43:8
My **e-s** are worn out from crying.	Ps 88:9	has shut their **e-s** so they cannot	Is 44:18
One who formed the **e** not see?	Ps 94:9	for every **e** will see when the	Is 52:8
e-s, but cannot see	Ps 115:5; 135:16	no **e** has seen any God except You	Is 64:4
it is wonderful in our **e-s**.	Ps 118:23	don't Your **e-s** {look for} faithfulness?	Jr 5:3
Open my **e-s** so that I may see	Ps 119:18	They have **e-s**, but they don't see	Jr 5:21
I raise my **e-s** toward the	Ps 121:1	my **e-s** a fountain of tears,	Jr 9:1
I lift my **e-s** to You, the One	Ps 123:1	My **e-s** will overflow with tears,	Jr 13:17
not proud; my **e-s** are not haughty	Ps 131:1	I will keep My **e-s** on them for	Jr 24:6
not allow my **e-s** to sleep or my	Ps 132:4	My **e-s** are worn out from weeping,	Lm 2:11
But my **e-s** {look} to You, Lord	Ps 141:8	were full of **e-s** all around.	Ezk 1:18; 10:12
All **e-s** look to You, and You give	Ps 145:15	They have **e-s** to see but do not	Ezk 12:2
Let your **e-s** look forward;	Pr 4:25	look with your **e-s**, listen with	Ezk 40:4
sleep to your **e-s** or slumber to	Pr 6:4	There were **e-s** in this horn like a	Dn 7:8
arrogant **e-s**, a lying tongue	Pr 6:17	conspicuous horn between his **e-s**.	Dn 8:5
you would the pupil of your **e**.	Pr 7:2	his **e-s** like flaming torches,	Dn 10:6
sly wink of the **e** causes grief,	Pr 10:10	Compassion is hidden from My **e-s**.	Hs 13:14
way is right in his own **e-s**,	Pr 12:15	the **e-s** of the Lord GOD are on the	Am 9:8
The **e-s** of the LORD are everywhere	Pr 15:3	and let us feast our **e-s** on Zion.	Mc 4:11
Bright **e-s** cheer the heart;	Pr 15:30	{Your} **e-s** are too pure to look on	Hab 1:13
who narrows his **e-s** is planning	Pr 16:30	you touches the pupil of His **e**.	Zch 2:8
but a fool's **e-s** roam to the ends	Pr 17:24	These seven **e-s** of the LORD,	Zch 4:10
hearing ear and the seeing **e**	Pr 20:12	Your own **e-s** will see this, and	Mal 1:5
haughty **e-s** and an arrogant heart	Pr 21:4	If your right **e** causes you to	Mt 5:29
The LORD's **e-s** keep watch over	Pr 22:12	An **e** for an **e** and a tooth for	Mt 5:38
As soon as your **e-s** fly to it,	Pr 23:5	The **e** is the lamp of the body.	Mt 6:22
Who has red **e-s**?	Pr 23:29	the speck in your brother's **e** but	Mt 7:3
Your **e-s** will see strange things,	Pr 23:33	And their **e-s** were opened.	Mt 9:30
he'll become wise in his own **e-s**.	Pr 26:5	see with their **e-s** and hear with	Mt 13:15
In his own **e-s**, a slacker is wiser	Pr 26:16	But your **e-s** are blessed because	Mt 13:16
rich man is wise in his own **e-s**,	Pr 28:11	And if your **e** causes your	Mt 18:9
who turns his **e-s** away will	Pr 28:27	go through the **e** of a needle	Mt 19:24
gives light to the **e-s** of both.	Pr 29:13	they said to Him, "open our **e-s**!"	Mt 20:33

Lord and is wonderful in our e-s? Mt 21:42
could not keep their e-s open. Mt 26:43
For my e-s have seen Your Lk 2:30
would not even raise his e-s to Lk 18:13
now it is hidden from your e-s. Lk 19:42
Then their e-s were opened, and Lk 24:31
Open your e-s and look at the fields, Jn 4:35
and spread the mud on his e-s. Jn 9:6
has blinded their e-s and hardened Jn 12:40
see with their e-s and hear with Ac 28:27
e-s that cannot see and ears that Rm 11:8
What no e has seen and no ear 1Co 2:9
I'm not an e, I don't belong to 1Co 12:16
twinkling of an e, at the last 1Co 15:52
before whose e-s Jesus Christ was Gl 3:1
torn out your e-s and given them Gl 4:15
{I pray} that the e-s of your heart Eph 1:18
keeping our e-s on Jesus, Heb 12:2
is very valuable in God's e-s. 1Pt 3:4
because the e-s of the Lord are on 1Pt 3:12
having e-s full of adultery and 2Pt 2:14
what we have seen with our e-s, 1Jn 1:1
the lust of the e-s, and the pride 1Jn 2:16
clouds, and every e will see Him Rv 1:7
His e-s like a fiery flame, Rv 1:14
ointment to spread on your e-s so Rv 3:18
covered with e-s in front and in Rv 4:6
He had seven horns and seven e-s, Rv 5:6
away every tear from
their e-s. Rv 7:17; 21:4

EYELASHES
or let her captivate you with her e. Pr 6:25

EYELIDS
eyes to sleep or my e to slumber Ps 132:4
your eyes or slumber to your e. Pr 6:4

EYESIGHT
Now Jacob's e was poor because Gn 48:10
Eli, whose e was failing 1Sm 3:2

EYEWITNESSES
original e ... handed them down to us Lk 1:2
we were e of His majesty. 2Pt 1:16

EZEKIEL
Hebrew prophet at the time of the exile, writing from Babylon (Ezk 1:1; 2Kg 24:14-16). Wrote about the fall of Jerusalem (Ezk 33:21) and the ultimate restoration of the city and temple (Ezk 40–48).

EZEL
and stay beside the rock E. 1Sm 20:19

EZION-GEBER
Edomite city on the route of the exodus (Nm 33:35-36; Dt 2:8); used as a seaport (1Kg 9:26; 22:48; 2Ch 8:17; 20:36).

EZRA
Priest and teacher of the law; leader of the returning exiles, sent by King Artaxerxes of Persia to reestablish worship in the temple (Ezr 7–8). Nehemiah's colleague (Neh 8:2,6; 12:31-37). Made priests stop intermarriage with foreigners (Ezr 9–10).

F

FABRIC
If a f is contaminated with mildew Lv 13:47
and purple f from the coasts Ezk 27:7
fine f-s of linen, purple, silk Rv 18:12

FACE
I have seen God f to f, Gn 32:30
the LORD spoke with Moses f to f, Ex 33:11
cannot see My f, for no one can Ex 33:20
back, but My f will not be seen. Ex 33:23
Moses, the skin of his f shone! Ex 34:30
he put a veil over his f. Ex 34:33
LORD make His f shine on you, Nm 6:25
I will hide My f from them; Dt 32:20
whom the LORD knew f to f. Dt 34:10
the Angel of the LORD f to f! Jdg 6:22
he wrapped his f in his mantle 1Kg 19:13
place my staff on the boy's f. 2Kg 4:29
turned his f to the wall 2Kg 20:2
seek His f always. 1Ch 16:11
pray and seek My f, and turn 2Ch 7:14
not turn {His} f away from you 2Ch 30:9
will surely curse You to Your f. Jb 1:11; 2:5
and lift up your f to God. Jb 22:26
The upright will see His f. Ps 11:7
will You hide Your f from me? Ps 13:1
He did not hide His f from him, Ps 22:24
who seek the f of the God of Ps 24:6

LORD, I will seek Your f. Ps 27:8
Do not hide Your f from me; Ps 27:9
their f-s will never be ashamed. Ps 34:5
Turn Your f away from my sins Ps 51:9
Don't hide Your f from Your Ps 69:17
Cover their f-s with shame so that Ps 83:16
Why do You hide Your f from me? Ps 88:14
Do not hide Your f from me in my Ps 102:2
seek His f always. Ps 105:4
Don't hide Your f from me, Ps 143:7
heart makes a f cheerful, Pr 15:13
As the water reflects the f, Pr 27:19
A man's wisdom brightens his f, Ec 8:1
let me see your f, let me hear Sg 2:14
and grind the f-s of the poor? Is 3:15
I have set My f like flint, Is 50:7
of anger I hid My f from you for Is 54:8
Him hide {His} f from you so Is 59:2
backs to Me and not their f-s. Jr 32:33
had four f-s and four wings. Ezk 1:6
made your f as hard as their f-s Ezk 3:8
no longer hide My f from them, Ezk 39:29
Each cherub had two f-s: Ezk 41:18
all f-s turn pale. Jl 2:6
He will hide His f from them at Mc 3:4
animal waste over your f-s, Mal 2:3
make their f-s unattractive so Mt 6:16
oil on your head, and wash your f, Mt 6:17
and His f shone like the sun. Mt 17:2
view the f of My Father Mt 18:10
spit in His f and beat Him; Mt 26:67
appearance of His f changed, Lk 9:29
his f was like the f of an angel. Ac 6:15
a mirror, but then f to f. 1Co 13:12
at Moses' f because of the glory 2Co 3:7
a veil over his f so that the 2Co 3:13
with unveiled f-s, are reflecting 2Co 3:18
glory in the f of Jesus Christ. 2Co 4:6
if someone hits you in the f. 2Co 11:20
I opposed him to his f Gl 2:11
return and see you f to f. 1Th 2:17
at his own f in a mirror; Jms 1:23
But the f of the Lord is against 1Pt 3:12
you and talk f to f so that our joy 2Jn 12
and we will talk f to f. 3Jn 14
and His f was shining like the sun Rv 1:16
creature had a f like a man; Rv 4:7
their f-s were like men's f-s; Rv 9:7

His f was like the sun, his legs Rv 10:1
fell on their f-s and worshiped Rv 11:16
will see His f, and His name Rv 22:4

FACECLOTHS
so that even f or work aprons Ac 19:12

FACEDOWN
they fell f and were terrified. Mt 17:6
He fell f and prayed, "My Mt 26:39
He fell f at His feet, thanking Lk 17:16

FACING
their wings and f each other. Ex 37:9
12 oxen, three f north, f west, 1Kg 7:25

FACT
A f must be established by the Dt 19:15
witnesses every f may be Mt 18:16

FACTIONS
must, indeed, be f among you, 1Co 11:19
ambitions, dissensions, f, Gl 5:20

FADE
they will f away like smoke. Ps 37:20
the light of my eyes has f-d. Ps 38:10
I f away like a lengthening Ps 109:23
and your hope will never f. Pr 23:18; 24:18
while the sound of the mill f-s; Ec 12:4
and to the f-ing flower of its Is 28:1
the flowers f, but the word of Is 40:8
As my life was f-ing away, Jnh 2:7
from his face—a f-ing {glory}— 2Co 3:7

FAIL
not one promise has f-ed. Jos 23:14
because they f-ed to drive them out Jdg 1:32
you will never f to have a man 1Kg 2:4
You will never f to have a man 1Kg 8:25
Not one of all the good promises
 ... has f-ed. 1Kg 8:56
the sight of the wicked will f. Jb 11:20
my strength has f-ed because of Ps 31:10
My eyes f, looking for my God. Ps 69:3
as my strength f-s, do not abandon Ps 71:9
My flesh and my heart may f, Ps 73:26
their spirits f-ed within them. Ps 107:5
LORD; my spirit f-s. Don't hide Ps 143:7
Plans f when there is no counsel Pr 15:22
Devise a plan; it will f. Is 8:10
I will without f save you from Jr 30:10
David will never f to have a man Jr 33:17

for without f I will save you   Jr 46:27
and their fruit will not f.   Ezk 47:12
and the new wine will f them.   Hs 9:2
dried up; and the olive oil f-s.   Jl 1:10
Escape will f the swift, the   Am 2:14
the olive crop f-s and the fields   Hab 3:17
you that your faith may not f.   Lk 22:32
as though the word of God has f-ed.   Rm 9:6
is in you?—unless you f the test.   2Co 13:5

FAILURE
and their f riches for the   Rm 11:12

FAINT (adj)
the daughters of song grow f.   Ec 12:4

FAINT (v)
God has made my heart f;   Jb 23:16
my body f-s for You in a land that   Ps 63:1
Youths may f and grow weary,   Is 40:30
they will walk and not f.   Is 40:31
and infants f in the streets   Lm 2:11
People will f from fear and   Lk 21:26
f when you are reproved by Him;   Heb 12:5

FAINTHEARTED
Do not be f. Do not be afraid   Dt 20:3
be afraid or f because of these   Is 7:4
Say to the f: "Be strong; do not   Is 35:4

FAIR
said to the king, "The sentence is f; 1Kg 2:38
say: The Lord's way isn't f.   Ezk 18:25; 33:17
to a place called F Havens near   Ac 27:8
with what is right and f,   Col 4:1

FAIRLY
Do you judge people f?   Ps 58:1
He judges the peoples f.   Ps 96:10
righteously and the peoples f.   Ps 98:9
that You have afflicted me f.   Ps 119:75

FAIRNESS
judgment on the peoples with f.   Ps 9:8
the peoples with f and lead the   Ps 67:4
You have established f;   Ps 99:4
who judges the poor with f   Pr 29:14
in peace and f and turned many   Mal 2:6

FAITH
you broke f with Me among   Dt 32:51
If you do not stand firm in your f,   Is 7:9
righteous one will live by his f.   Hab 2:4

more for you—you of little f?   Mt 6:30
in Israel with so great a f!   Mt 8:10
you fearful, you of little f?   Mt 8:26
Seeing their f, Jesus told the   Mt 9:2
Your f has made you well.   Mt 9:22
for you according to your f!   Mt 9:29
You of little f, why did you   Mt 14:31
Woman, your f is great.   Mt 15:28
Jesus said, "You of little f!   Mt 16:8
If you have f the size of a mustard   Mt 17:20
If you have f and do not doubt,   Mt 21:21
law—justice, mercy, and f.   Mt 23:23
Do you still have no f?   Mk 4:40
Your f has healed you.   Mk 10:52
to them, "Have f in God.   Mk 11:22
woman, "Your f has saved you.   Lk 7:50
to the Lord, "Increase our f.   Lk 17:5
will He find that f on earth?   Lk 18:8
you that your f may not fail.   Lk 22:32
So the f that comes through Him   Ac 3:16
a man full of f and the Holy   Ac 6:5
became obedient to the f.   Ac 6:7
of the Holy Spirit and of f   Ac 11:24
that he had f to be healed,   Ac 14:9
the door of f to the Gentiles.   Ac 14:27
cleansing their hearts by f.   Ac 15:9
churches were strengthened in the f   Ac 16:5
who are sanctified by f in Me.   Ac 26:18
the obedience of f among all the   Rm 1:5
the news of your f is being   Rm 1:8
encouraged by each other's f,   Rm 1:12
is revealed from f to f,   Rm 1:17
The righteous will live by f.   Rm 1:17
through f in His blood,   Rm 3:25
is justified by f apart from   Rm 3:28
his f is credited for righteousness.   Rm 4:5
F was credited to Abraham for   Rm 4:9
righteousness that comes by f.   Rm 4:13
f is made empty and the promise   Rm 4:14
without weakening in the f.   Rm 4:19
been declared righteous by f,   Rm 5:1
they did not pursue it by f,   Rm 9:32
that comes from f speaks like   Rm 10:6
So f comes from what is heard,   Rm 10:17
unbelief, but you stand by f.   Rm 11:20
a measure of f to each one.   Rm 12:3
according to the standard of f;   Rm 12:6
Accept anyone who is weak in f,   Rm 14:1

Do you have f? Keep it to	Rm 14:22
everything that is not from f is sin.	Rm 14:23
the obedience of f among all	Rm 16:26
so that your f might not be	1Co 1:17
if I have all f, so that I can	1Co 13:2
three remain: f, hope, and love.	1Co 13:13
foundation, and so is your f.	1Co 15:14
stand firm in the f, be brave	1Co 16:13
for we walk by f, not by sight	2Co 5:7
hope that as your f increases,	2Co 10:15
{to see} if you are in the f.	2Co 13:5
preaches the f he once tried to	Gl 1:23
the law but by f in Jesus Christ	Gl 2:16
I live by f in the Son of God,	Gl 2:20
the law or by hearing with f?	Gl 3:2,5
those who have f are Abraham's sons.	Gl 3:7
the righteous will live by f.	Gl 3:11
But the law is not based on f;	Gl 3:12
promise of the Spirit through f.	Gl 3:14
Before this f came, we were	Gl 3:23
But since that f has come,	Gl 3:25
matters is f working through love.	Gl 5:6
patience, kindness, goodness, f,	Gl 5:22
belong to the household of f.	Gl 6:10
grace you are saved through f,	Eph 2:8
one Lord, one f, one baptism,	Eph 4:5
reach unity in the f and in the	Eph 4:13
situation take the shield of f,	Eph 6:16
advancement and joy in the f,	Php 1:25
righteousness from God based on f.	Php 3:9
strength of your f in Christ.	Col 2:5
Him and established in the f,	Col 2:7
your work of f, labor of love	1Th 1:3
what is lacking in your f?	1Th 3:10
the armor of f and love on our	1Th 5:8
for goodness and the work of f,	2Th 1:11
evil men, for not all have f.	2Th 3:2
my true child in the f.	1Tm 1:2
plan, which operates by f.	1Tm 1:4
the shipwreck of their f.	1Tm 1:19
she continues in f, love, and	1Tm 2:15
mystery of the f with a clear	1Tm 3:9
boldness in the f that is in	1Tm 3:13
some will depart from the f,	1Tm 4:1
in love, in f, in purity.	1Tm 4:12
has denied the f and is worse	1Tm 5:8
godliness, f, love, endurance	1Tm 6:11
Fight the good fight for the f;	1Tm 6:12
have deviated from the f.	1Tm 6:21
are overturning the f of some.	2Tm 2:18
instruct you for salvation through f	2Tm 3:15
finished the race, I have kept the f.	2Tm 4:7
my true child in our common f.	Ti 1:4
that they may be sound in the f	Ti 1:13
in the f may become effective	Phm 6
with those who heard it in f	Heb 4:2
from dead works, f in God,	Heb 6:1
through f and perseverance	Heb 6:12
heart in full assurance of f,	Heb 10:22
righteous one will live by f;	Heb 10:38
Now f is the reality of what is	Heb 11:1
By f we understand that the	Heb 11:3
By f Abel offered to God a	Heb 11:4
By f, Enoch was taken away so	Heb 11:5
Now without f it is impossible	Heb 11:6
By f Noah, after being warned	Heb 11:7
By f Abraham, when he was called	Heb 11:8
By f even Sarah herself, when	Heb 11:11
all died in f without having	Heb 11:13
By f Abraham, when he	
was tested	Heb 11:17
By f Isaac blessed Jacob and	Heb 11:20
By f Jacob, when he was dying	Heb 11:21
By f Joseph, as he was nearing	Heb 11:22
By f Moses, when he had	
grown up	Heb 11:24
By f Rahab the prostitute	Heb 11:31
source and perfecter of our f,	Heb 12:2
imitate their f.	Heb 13:7
testing of your f produces	Jms 1:3
let him ask in f without	Jms 1:6
says he has f, but does not have	Jms 2:14
f, if it doesn't have works, is dead	Jms 2:17
Show me your f without works,	Jms 2:18
by works and not by f alone.	Jms 2:24
so also f without works is dead	Jms 2:26
The prayer of f will save the	Jms 5:15
the genuineness of your f	1Pt 1:7
receiving the goal of your f,	1Pt 1:9
firm in the f, knowing that	1Pt 5:9
have obtained a f of equal	2Pt 1:1
supplement your f with goodness,	2Pt 1:5
has conquered the world: our f.	1Jn 5:4
contend for the f that was delivered	Jd 3
in your most holy f and praying	Jd 20
and did not deny your f in Me,	Rv 2:13

and the f of the saints.   Rv 13:10
of God and the f in Jesus.   Rv 14:12

FAITHFUL *see also* FAITHFUL LOVE
he is f in all My household.   Nm 12:7
the f God who keeps His gracious   Dt 7:9
A f God, without prejudice,   Dt 32:4
With the f You prove Yourself f;   2Sm 22:26
You found his heart f in Your sight,   Neh 9:8
set apart the f for Himself;   Ps 4:3
for no f one remains;   Ps 12:1
not allow Your **F** One to see the   Ps 16:10
With the f You prove Yourself f;   Ps 18:25
Love the LORD, all His f ones.   Ps 31:23
will not abandon His f ones.   Ps 37:28
My f God will come to meet me;   Ps 59:10
whose spirit was not f to God.   Ps 78:8
Protect my life, for I am f.   Ps 86:2
My eyes {favor} the f of the land   Ps 101:6
death of His f ones is valuable   Ps 116:15
The LORD is f in all His words   Ps 145:13
He remains f forever,   Ps 146:6
but f people are His delight.   Pr 12:22
A f man will have many blessings   Pr 28:20
the LORD, who is f, the Holy One   Is 49:7
be a true and f witness against   Jr 42:5
with El and is f to holy ones.   Hs 11:12
Jerusalem will be called the **F** City, Zch 8:3
Who then is a f and sensible   Mt 24:45
Well done, good and f slave!   Mt 25:21
You were f over a few things;   Mt 25:21
Whoever is f in very little is also f   Lk 16:10
if you have not been f with what   Lk 16:12
grant you the f covenant   Ac 13:34
God is f; by Him you were called   1Co 1:9
that each one be found f.   1Co 4:2
my beloved and f child in the   1Co 4:17
God is f and He will not allow   1Co 10:13
As God is f, our message to you   2Co 1:18
loved brother and f servant in   Eph 6:21
To the saints and f brothers in   Col 1:2
with Onesimus, a f and loved   Col 4:9
He who calls you is f, who also   1Th 5:24
But the Lord is f; He will   2Th 3:3
because He considered me f,   1Tm 1:12
self-controlled, f in everything.   1Tm 3:11
commit to f men who will be able   2Tm 2:2
He remains f, for He cannot deny   2Tm 2:13
a merciful and f high priest   Heb 2:17

He was f to the One who   Heb 3:2
But Christ was f as a Son over   Heb 3:6
for He who promised is f.   Heb 10:23
the One who had promised was f.   Heb 11:11
entrust themselves to a f Creator.   1Pt 4:19
He is f and righteous to forgive   1Jn 1:9
Jesus Christ, the f witness, the   Rv 1:5
Be f until death, and I will   Rv 2:10
The Amen, the f and true   Rv 3:14
Its rider is called F and True,   Rv 19:11
These words are f and true.   Rv 22:6

FAITHFUL LOVE
will deal with me in f.   Gn 47:29
but showing f to a thousand   Ex 20:6
and rich in f and truth,   Ex 34:6
to anger and rich in f,   Nm 14:18
but showing f to a thousand   Dt 5:10
the LORD show f to you as   Ru 1:8
don't ever withdraw your f from   1Sm 20:15
But My f will never leave   2Sm 7:15
His f endures forever.   1Ch 16:34
take away My f from him as   1Ch 17:13
His f endures forever;   2Ch 5:13
for His f endures forever.   2Ch 7:3
for His f endures forever.   2Ch 20:21
His f to Israel endures   Ezr 3:11
to anger and rich in f,   Neh 9:17
save me because of Your f.   Ps 6:4
I have trusted in Your f;   Ps 13:5
goodness and f will pursue   Ps 23:6
in keeping with Your f,   Ps 25:7
save me by Your f.   Ps 31:16
those who depend on His f   Ps 33:18
Your f {reaches} to heaven   Ps 36:5
Spread Your f over those   Ps 36:10
we contemplate Your f.   Ps 48:9
God, according to Your f;   Ps 51:1
God's f is constant.   Ps 52:1
For Your f is as high as   Ps 57:10
proclaim Your f in the   Ps 59:16
because Your f is better   Ps 63:3
or turned His f from me.   Ps 66:20
Has His f ceased forever?   Ps 77:8
Show us Your f, LORD, and   Ps 85:7
abundant in f to all who   Ps 86:5
and abundant in f and truth   Ps 86:15
Will Your f be declared in   Ps 88:11
will sing about the LORD's f forever;   Ps 89:1

f and truth go before You. Ps 89:14
not withdraw My f from him Ps 89:33
to declare Your f in the morning Ps 92:2
I will sing of f and Ps 101:1
He crowns you with f and Ps 103:4
so great is His f toward those Ps 103:11
His f endures forever. Ps 106:1; 107:1
give thanks to the LORD for His f Ps 107:8
For Your f is higher than Ps 108:4
For great is His f to us; Ps 117:2
His f endures forever. Ps 118:1
the earth is filled with Your f; Ps 119:64
May Your f comfort me, Ps 119:76
in accordance with Your f, Ps 119:88
In keeping with Your f, Ps 119:149
give me life, according to Your f. Ps 119:159
experience Your f in the morning, Ps 143:8
He is my f and my fortress Ps 144:2
those who put their hope in His f. Ps 147:11
who pursues ... f will find life, Pr 21:21
will be established by f. Is 16:5
the abundance of His f. Is 63:7
LORD, showing f, justice Jr 9:24
I have continued to extend f to you. Jr 31:3
You show f to thousands but Jr 32:18
His f endures forever as Jr 33:11
the LORD's f we do not perish, Lm 3:22
according to His abundant, f. Lm 3:32
no f, and no knowledge of God in Hs 4:1
Sow righteousness ... and reap f; Hs 10:12
slow to anger, rich in f, Jl 2:13
worthless idols forsake f, Jnh 2:8
slow to become angry, rich in f, Jnh 4:2
because He delights in f. Mc 7:18
Show f and compassion to Zch 7:9

FAITHFULLY

If you ... f observe My commands, Lv 26:3
Now if you f obey the LORD your Dt 28:1
if you have acted f and honestly Jdg 9:16
and worship Him f with all your 1Sm 12:24
Deal f with your servant, for 1Sm 20:8
careful to walk f before Me with 1Kg 2:4
things were brought f. 2Ch 31:12
You have acted f, while we have Neh 9:33
walked before You f and Is 38:3
I will f reward them and make an Is 61:8

FAITHFULNESS

kindness and f from my master. Gn 24:27

kindness and f You have shown Gn 32:10
show kindness and f to you when Jos 2:14
special kindness and f to you, 2Sm 2:6
LORD show you kindness and f. 2Sm 15:20
to heaven, Your f to the skies. Ps 36:5
about Your f and salvation; Ps 40:10
Your f reaches to the clouds. Ps 57:10
I will praise You for Your f, Ps 71:22
proclaim Your f to all generations. Ps 89:1
establish Your f in the heavens. Ps 89:2
Your f surrounds You. Ps 89:8
You swore to David in Your f? Ps 89:49
His f will be a protective shield. Ps 91:4
morning and Your f at night, Ps 92:2
f endures through all generations. Ps 100:5
Your f reaches the clouds. Ps 108:4
the LORD's f endures forever. Ps 117:2
Your f is for all generations; Ps 119:90
In Your f listen to my plea, Ps 143:1
let loyalty and f leave you. Pr 3:3
is atoned for by loyalty and f, Pr 16:6
Loyalty and f deliver a king; Pr 20:28
and f will be a belt Is 11:5
long ago, with perfect f. Is 25:1
will make Your f known to Is 38:19
great is Your f! Lm 3:23
justly, to love f, and to walk Mc 6:8
their unbelief cancel God's f? Rm 3:3

FAITHLESS

Return, you f children Jr 3:14,22
here and there, f daughter? Jr 31:22
flowing valley, you f daughter? Jr 49:4
If we are f, He remains faithful, 2Tm 2:13

FALL

an ox or a donkey f-s into it, Ex 21:33
Let my teaching f like rain and Dt 32:2
that dread of you has f-en on us, Jos 2:9
took his sword and fell on it. 1Sm 31:4
How the mighty have f-en! 2Sm 1:19
don't let me f into human hands. 2Sm 24:14
Yahweh's fire fell and consumed 1Kg 18:38
let them f by their own schemes Ps 5:10
but fell into the hole he had made Ps 7:15
lines have f-en for me in pleasant Ps 16:6
and my enemies stumbled and fell. Ps 27:2
Though he f-s, he will not be Ps 37:24
I am about to f, and my pain is Ps 38:17
of me, but they fell into it! Ps 57:6

who insult You have **f-en** on me.   Ps 69:9
Though a thousand f at your side   Ps 91:7
dread of Israel had **f-en** on them.   Ps 105:38
cursing—let it f on him;   Ps 109:17
pushed me hard to make me f,   Ps 118:13
Let the wicked f into their own   Ps 141:10
The LORD helps all who f;   Ps 145:14
wicked person will f because of his   Pr 11:5
Without guidance, people f, but   Pr 11:14
trusting in his riches will f,   Pr 11:28
an arrogant spirit before a f.   Pr 16:18
a righteous man **f-s** seven times,   Pr 24:16
Don't gloat when your enemy **f-s**,   Pr 24:17
who digs a pit will f into it,   Pr 26:27
evil way will f into his own pit   Pr 28:10
and wrong will suddenly f.   Pr 28:18
For if either **f-s**, his companion   Ec 4:10
who digs a pit may f into it,   Ec 10:8
whether a tree **f-s** to the south or   Ec 11:3
they will f and be broken;   Is 8:15
how you have **f-en** from
  the heavens   Is 14:12
Babylon has **f-en**, has **f-en**.   Is 21:9
stumble and the helped will f;   Is 31:3
and young men stumble and f,   Is 40:30
so that it will not f over.   Is 41:7
Do {people} f and not get up   Jr 8:4
Human corpses will f like manure   Jr 9:22
F down and never get up again,   Jr 25:27
you will f and become shattered   Jr 25:34
stumble and f with no one to pick   Jr 50:32
Suddenly Babylon **fell** and was   Jr 51:8
Babylon must f {because of} the   Jr 51:49
The crown has **f-en** from our head.   Lm 5:16
with you will f on the mountains   Ezk 39:4
f down and worship the statue I   Dn 3:15
of the host f to the earth,   Dn 8:10
will stumble, f, and be no more   Dn 11:19
and to the hills, "F on us!"   Hs 10:8
She has **f-en**; Virgin Israel will   Am 5:2
they will f, never to rise   Am 8:14
Though I have **f-en**, I will stand up   Mc 7:8
if You will f down and worship   Mt 4:9
The rain **fell**, the rivers rose, and   Mt 7:25
not one of them **f-s** to the ground   Mt 10:29
some seeds **fell** along the path,   Mt 13:4
stars will be **f-ing** from the sky,   Mt 13:25
blind, both will f into a pit.   Mt 15:14

the crumbs that f from their   Mt 15:27
Whoever **f-s** on this stone will be   Mt 21:44
the stars will f from the sky,   Mt 24:29
all became drowsy and **fell** asleep.   Mt 25:5
he saw Jesus, he **fell** at His feet   Mk 5:22
to cause the f and rise of many   Lk 2:34
they were sailing He **fell** asleep.   Lk 8:23
I watched Satan f from heaven   Lk 10:18
house divided against itself **f-s**.   Lk 11:17
tower in Siloam **fell** on and killed   Lk 13:4
whose son or ox **f-s** into a well,   Lk 14:5
filled with what **fell** from the rich   Lk 16:21
They will f by the edge of the   Lk 21:24
drops of blood **f-ing** to the ground.   Lk 22:44
say to the mountains, 'F on us!'   Lk 23:30
she **fell** at His feet and told Him,   Jn 11:32
grain of wheat **f-s** into the ground   Jn 12:24
back and **fell** to the ground.   Jn 18:6
and the lot **fell** to Matthias.   Ac 1:26
shadow might f on some of them   Ac 5:15
And saying this, he **fell** asleep.   Ac 7:60
like scales **fell** from his eyes,   Ac 9:18
Then the chains **fell** off his wrists   Ac 12:7
David's tent, which has **f-en** down.   Ac 15:16
the image that **fell** from heaven?   Ac 19:35
by sleep he **fell** down from the   Ac 20:9
have sinned and f short of the   Rm 3:23
have they stumbled so as to f?   Rm 11:11
his own Lord he stands or **f-s**.   Rm 14:4
who insult You have **f-en** on Me.   Rm 15:3
if food causes my brother to f,   1Co 8:13
must be careful not to f!   1Co 10:12
but some have **f-en** asleep.   1Co 15:6
We will not all f asleep, but we   1Co 15:51
you have **f-en** from grace!   Gl 5:4
over those who have **f-en** asleep.   1Th 4:15
become conceited and f into the   1Tm 3:6
to be rich f into temptation   1Tm 6:9
whose bodies **fell** in the desert?   Heb 3:17
and who have **f-en** away, because, to   Heb 6:6
thing to f into the hands   Heb 10:31
its flower **f-s** off, and its   Jms 1:11
that you won't f under judgment   Jms 5:12
then how far you have **f-en**;   Rv 2:5
and the 24 elders **fell** down before   Rv 5:8
the stars of heaven **fell** to the earth Rv 6:13
rocks, "F on us and hide us from   Rv 6:16
a great star ... **fell** from heaven.   Rv 8:10

a star that had **f-en** from heaven to Rv 9:1
f-en, Babylon the Great has **f-en**, Rv 14:8
five have **f-en**, one is, the other Rv 17:10
f-en, Babylon the Great has **f-en**! Rv 18:2
living creatures **fell** down and Rv 19:4
Then I **fell** at his feet to worship Rv 19:10
I **fell** down to worship at the feet Rv 22:8

FALLEN (adj)

f-en with his face to the ground 1Sm 5:3
are slain, **f-en** by the sword. Ezk 32:22
restore the **f-en** booth of David: Am 9:11

FALSE

Do not give **f** testimony against Ex 20:16
You must not spread a **f** report. Ex 23:1
not set his mind on what is **f**, Ps 24:4
for **f** witnesses rise up against Ps 27:12
The horse is a **f** hope for safety Ps 33:17
therefore I hate every **f** way. Ps 119:104
precepts and hate every **f** way. Ps 119:128
witness who gives **f** testimony, Pr 6:19
right, but a **f** witness, deceit. Pr 12:17
f witness will not go unpunished, Pr 19:5,9
prophesying to you a **f** vision, Jr 14:14
They see **f** visions and speak Ezk 13:6
Beware of **f** prophets who come Mt 7:15
do not bear **f** witness; Mt 19:18
Many **f** prophets will rise up and Mt 24:11
F messiahs and **f** prophets will Mt 24:24
were looking for **f** testimony Mt 26:59
a Jewish **f** prophet named Ac 13:6
found to be **f** witnesses about 1Co 15:15
For such people are **f** apostles, 2Co 11:13
and dangers among **f** brothers; 2Co 11:26
because of **f** brothers smuggled Gl 2:4
whether out of **f** motives or true Php 1:18
they will believe what is **f**, 2Th 2:11
there will be **f** teachers among you. 2Pt 2:1
because many **f** prophets have 1Jn 4:1
the mouth of the **f** prophet. Rv 16:13
beast and the **f** prophet are, Rv 20:10

FALSEHOOD

If I have walked in **f** or Jb 31:5
I hate and abhor **f**, {but} I love Ps 119:163
Keep **f** and deceitful words far Pr 30:8
we have made **f** our refuge and Is 28:15
forgotten Me and trusted in **F**. Jr 13:25
the idols speak **f**, and the Zch 10:2

FALSELY

or swears **f** about any of the Lv 6:3
must not swear **f** by My name, Lv 19:12
Your enemies swear {by You} **f**. Ps 139:20
the LORD lives," they are swearing **f**. Jr 5:2
are prophesying **f** in My name; Jr 27:15
one who swears **f** by My name. Zch 5:4
against those who swear **f**; Mal 3:5
f say every kind of evil against you Mt 5:11
that **f** bears that name 1Tm 6:20

FALTER

his steps do not **f**. Ps 37:31
a rotten tooth or a **f-ing** foot. Pr 25:19

FAME

heard of Your **f** will declare, Nm 14:15
and his **f** spread throughout the Jos 6:27
For we have heard of His **f**, Jos 9:9
of Sheba heard about Solomon's **f** 1Kg 10:1
Then David's **f** spread throughout 1Ch 14:17
So his **f** spread even to distant 2Ch 26:15
and his **f** spread throughout the Est 9:4
Your **f** {endures} to all Ps 102:12
not heard of My **f** or seen My Is 66:19
might be My people for My **f**, Jr 13:11
the earth receive praise and **f**. Zph 3:19
His **f** then spread throughout the Mk 1:28

FAMILIAR

consult a medium or a **f** spirit, Dt 18:11

FAMILY

the **f** records of ... Adam. Gn 5:1
the **f** records of Noah. Gn 6:9
the **f** records of Noah's sons, Gn 10:1
the **f** records of Shem. Gn 11:10
the **f** records of Terah. Gn 11:27
the **f** records of ... Ishmael, Gn 25:12
the **f** records of Isaac Gn 25:19
the **f** records of Esau Gn 36:1
the **f** records of Jacob. Gn 37:2
against that man and his **f**, Lv 20:5
If a man has no **f** redeemer, Lv 25:26
according to their **f** records by Nm 1:20
the **f** records of Aaron and Moses Nm 3:1
and rejoice with your **f**. Dt 14:26
you and your **f** are to eat it Dt 15:20
also show kindness to my **f**, Jos 2:12
As for me and my **f**, we will Jos 24:15
my **f** is the weakest in Manasseh Jdg 6:15

He is one of our f redeemers.   Ru 2:20
but you and all your father's f?   1Sm 9:20
Each man had his f with him,   1Sm 27:3
be against me and my father's f.   2Sm 24:17
These are their f records: 1Ch 1:29
All the f-ies of the nations will   Ps 22:27
the LORD, you f-ies of the peoples   Ps 96:7
makes their f-ies {multiply} like   Ps 107:41
be God of all the f-ies of Israel,   Jr 31:1
the two f-ies He had chosen.   Jr 33:24
will mourn, every f by itself: Zch 12:12
When His f heard this, they set   Mk 3:21
the house and f line of David,   Lk 2:4
in your seed all the f-ies of the earth   Ac 3:25
and Joseph's f became known to   Ac 7:13
he and all his f were baptized.   Ac 16:33
Show f affection to one another   Rm 12:10
from whom every f in heaven and   Eph 3:15
toward their own f first and to   1Tm 5:4
built an ark to deliver his f.   Heb 11:7
And all the f-ies of the earth will   Rv 1:7

FAMINE

There was a f in the land,   Gn 12:10
There was another f in the land   Gn 26:1
seven years of f will take place   Gn 41:30
Now the f in the land was severe   Gn 43:1
Canaan were exhausted by the f.   Gn 47:13
there was a f in the land.   Ru 1:1
The f was severe in Samaria.   1Kg 18:2
has announced a seven-year f,   2Kg 8:1
month the f was so severe   2Kg 25:3
In f He will redeem you from   Jb 5:20
and to keep them alive in f.   Ps 33:19
and destruction, f and sword.   Is 51:19
by sword, f, and plague.   Jr 14:12
{destined} for f, to f;   Jr 15:2
die by the sword, f, and plague   Jr 21:9
will send f and dangerous animals   Ezk 5:17
by the sword, f, and plague.   Ezk 6:11
and will not bring f on you.   Ezk 36:29
not a f of bread or a thirst for   Am 8:11
There will be f-s and earthquakes   Mt 24:7
a severe f struck that country,   Lk 15:14
Then a f came over all of Egypt   Ac 7:11
would be a severe f throughout   Ac 11:28
or persecution or f or nakedness   Rm 8:35
by the sword, by f, by plague   Rv 6:8
in one day—death, and grief, and f.   Rv 18:8

FAMISHED

and withheld food from the f,   Jb 22:7
When they are f, they will   Is 8:21
If I send them home f, they will   Mk 8:3

FAMOUS

powerful men of old, the f men.   Gn 6:4
May his name be f in Israel.   Ru 4:14
So his name became very f.   1Sm 18:30
it was the most f high place.   1Kg 3:4
King Ahasuerus, f among the Jews   Est 10:3
I will make you f and   Zph 3:20

FANGS

I shattered the f of the unjust   Jb 29:17

FANTASIES

whoever chases f lacks sense.   Pr 12:11
whoever chases f will have his   Pr 28:19

FAR

them, "You have gone too f!   Nm 16:3
of the wicked is f from me!   Jb 21:16
may come this f, but no farther   Jb 38:11
But You, LORD, don't be f away.   Ps 22:19
Lord, do not be f from me.   Ps 35:22
my God, do not be f from me.   Ps 38:21
God, do not be f from me;   Ps 71:12
Those f from You will certainly   Ps 73:27
As f as the east is from the   Ps 103:12
let it be f from him.   Ps 109:17
Salvation is f from the wicked   Ps 119:155
my thoughts from f away.   Ps 139:2
The LORD is f from the wicked,   Pr 15:29
nearby than a brother f away.   Pr 27:10
bringing her food from f away.   Pr 31:14
yet their hearts are f from Me,   Is 29:13
Bring My sons from f away,   Is 43:6
peace to the one who is f or near,   Is 57:19
Therefore justice is f from us,   Is 59:9
a nation from f away against you   Jr 5:15
and not a God who is f away?   Jr 23:23
People who are f off will come   Zch 6:15
but their heart is f from Me.   Mt 15:8
You are not f from the kingdom   Mk 12:34
though He is not f from each one   Ac 17:27
f above every ruler and   Eph 1:21
you who were f away have been   Eph 2:13
to you who were f away and peace   Eph 2:17

FARE

He paid the f and went down into | Jnh 1:3

FARMER

The f-s are ashamed;	Jr 14:4
Be ashamed, you f-s, wail, you	Jl 1:11
The f will be called on to mourn	Am 5:16
it to tenant f-s and went away.	Mt 21:33
hardworking f who ought to be	2Tm 2:6
See how the f waits for the	Jms 5:7

FARTHER

| He went a little f, fell to the | Mk 14:35 |
| impression that He was going f. | Lk 24:28 |

FAST (adv)

| He held f to the LORD and did | 2Kg 18:6 |
| let us hold f to the confession | Heb 4:14 |

FAST (n)

Proclaim a f and seat Naboth at	1Kg 21:9
do as you please on the day of your f,	Is 58:3
Will the f I choose be like this:	Is 58:5
Announce a sacred f;	Jl 1:14; 2:15
They proclaimed a f and dressed	Jnh 3:5
Since the F was already over,	Ac 27:9

FAST (v)

tree in Jabesh and f-ed seven days.	1Sm 31:13
baby was alive, you f-ed	2Sm 12:21
sackcloth over his body, and f-ed.	1Kg 21:27
So we f-ed and pleaded with our God	Ezr 8:23
in Susa and f for me.	Est 4:16
Why have we f-ed, but You have not	Is 58:3
You f {with} contention and	Is 58:4
If they f, I will not hear their	Jr 14:12
70 years, did you really f for Me?	Zch 7:5
After He had f-ed 40 days and 40	Mt 4:2
Whenever you f, don't be	Mt 6:16
but Your disciples do not f?	Mt 9:14
guests cannot f while the groom	Mk 2:19
I f twice a week; I give a tenth	Lk 18:12
after they had f-ed, prayed, and	Ac 13:3

FASTEN

Can you f the chains of the	Jb 38:31
He f-s it with nails so that it	Is 41:7
It is f-ed with hammer and nails,	Jr 10:4

FASTING

I mourned ... f and praying | Neh 1:4

practices of f and lamentation	Est 9:31
I humbled myself with f,	Ps 35:13
My knees are weak from f,	Ps 109:24
temple of the LORD on a day of f.	Jr 36:6
palace and spent the night f.	Dn 6:18
all your heart, with f, weeping	Jl 2:12
so their f is obvious to people	Mt 6:16
come out except by prayer and f.	Mt 17:21
night and day with f-s and prayers.	Lk 2:37
ministering to the Lord and f,	Ac 13:2

FAT

Take the f from the ram,	Ex 29:22
all the f that is on the	Lv 3:3
must not eat any f or any blood.	Lv 3:17
who was an extremely f man.	Jdg 3:17
and Eglon's f closed in over it	Jdg 3:22
Even before the f was burned,	1Sm 2:15
{is better} than the f of rams.	1Sm 15:22
You eat the f, wear the wool	Ezk 34:3

FATAL

| but his f wound was healed. | Rv 13:3 |
| beast, whose f wound was healed | Rv 13:12 |

FATE

If these people ... suffer the f of all	Nm 16:29
the west are appalled at his f,	Jb 18:20
knew that one f comes to them	Ec 2:14
the f of people and the f of animals	Ec 3:19
there is one f for the righteous	Ec 9:2
there is one f for everyone.	Ec 9:3
and who considered His f?	Is 53:8

FATHER

a man leaves his f and mother	Gn 2:24
he was the f of all who play the	Gn 4:21
saw his f naked and told his two	Gn 9:22
go to your f-s in peace and be	Gn 15:15
become the f of many nations	Gn 17:4
became pregnant by their f.	Gn 19:36
who took me from my f-'s house	Gn 24:7
Bless me—me too, my f!	Gn 27:38
listened to his f and mother and	Gn 28:7
the land of your f-s and to your	Gn 31:3
God of my f Abraham and God of	Gn 32:9
Esau, f of the Edomites	Gn 36:9
saw that their f loved him more	Gn 37:4
'Is your f still alive?	Gn 43:7
I am Joseph! Is my f still living?	Gn 45:3
He has made me a f to Pharaoh,	Gn 45:8

And bring my f here quickly.	Gn 45:13
I am God, the God of your f.	Gn 46:3
Bury me with my f-s in the cave in	Gn 49:29
Now let me go and bury my f.	Gn 50:5
I am the God of your f,	Ex 3:6
The God of your f-s has sent me to	Ex 3:13
He swore to your f-s that He would	Ex 13:5
my f-'s God, and I will exalt Him.	Ex 15:2
the children for the f-s' sin,	Ex 20:5
Honor your f and your mother so	Ex 20:12
strikes his f or his mother must	Ex 21:15
curses his f or his mother must	Ex 21:17
If anyone curses his f or mother,	Lv 20:9
and her f hears about her vow	Nm 30:4
land I swore to give your f-s,	Dt 1:35
for the f-s' sin to the third	Dt 5:9
Honor your f and your mother,	Dt 5:16
you and your f-s had not known,	Dt 8:3
does not obey his f or mother	Dt 21:18
F-s are not to be put to death for	Dt 24:16
My f was a wandering Aramean.	Dt 26:5
Isn't He your F and Creator?	Dt 32:6
gods your f-s worshiped beyond	Jos 24:15
God of their f-s, who had brought	Jdg 2:12
not tell his f or mother what	Jdg 14:6
and be my f and priest,	Jdg 17:10
and be a f and a priest to us.	Jdg 18:19
you left your f and mother,	Ru 2:11
asked, "And who is their f?"	1Sm 10:12
However, he did not tell his f.	1Sm 14:1
I will be a f to him, and he	2Sm 7:14
rested with his f-s and was buried	1Kg 2:10
not be put to death because of f-s;	2Kg 14:6
be My son, and I will be his f.	1Ch 22:10
be My son, and I will be his f.	1Ch 28:6
Praise the LORD God of our f-s,	Ezr 7:27
say to the Pit: You are my f,	Jb 17:14
I was a f to the needy,	Jb 29:16
Does the rain have a f?	Jb 38:28
today I have become Your F.	Ps 2:7
Our f-s trusted in You;	Ps 22:4
Even if my f and mother abandon	Ps 27:10
a sojourner like all my f-s.	Ps 39:12
A f of the fatherless and a	Ps 68:5
He commanded our f-s to teach to	Ps 78:5
You are my F, my God, the rock	Ps 89:26
As a f has compassion on his	Ps 103:13
Both we and our f-s have sinned;	Ps 106:6
Listen, my son, to your f-'s instruction	Pr 1:8
{my} sons, to a f-'s discipline,	Pr 4:1
My son, keep your f-'s command,	Pr 6:20
A wise son brings joy to his f,	Pr 10:1
wise son {hears his} f's instruction,	Pr 13:1
despises his f-'s instruction,	Pr 15:5
A wise son brings joy to his f,	Pr 15:20
the pride of sons is their f-s.	Pr 17:6
the f of a fool has no joy.	Pr 17:21
A foolish son is grief to his f	Pr 17:25
A foolish son is his f-'s ruin,	Pr 19:13
curses his f or mother	Pr 20:20
Listen to your f who gave you	Pr 23:22
The f of a righteous son will	Pr 23:24
Let your f and mother have joy,	Pr 23:25
of gluttons humiliates his f.	Pr 28:7
one who robs his f or mother and	Pr 28:24
wisdom brings joy to his f,	Pr 29:3
that curses its f and does not	Pr 30:11
Eternal F, Prince of Peace.	Is 9:6
because of the iniquity of their f-s.	Is 14:21
Yet LORD, You are our F;	Is 64:8
say to a tree: You are my f,	Jr 2:27
call Me, my F, and never turn	Jr 3:19
I am Israel's F, and Ephraim is	Jr 31:9
The f-s have eaten sour grapes,	Jr 31:29
Your f was an Amorite and your	Ezk 16:3
The f-s eat sour grapes, and the	Ezk 18:2
not die for his f-'s iniquity.	Ezk 18:17
the abominations of their f-s.	Ezk 20:4
and the injustices of our f-s,	Dn 9:16
A man and his f have sexual	Am 2:7
a son considers his f a fool,	Mc 7:6
when your f-s provoked Me	Zch 8:14
But if I am a f, where is My honor?	Mal 1:6
Don't all of us have one F?	Mal 2:10
he will turn the hearts of f-s to	Mal 4:6
We have Abraham as our f.	Mt 3:9
be sons of your F in heaven.	Mt 5:45
reward from your F in heaven.	Mt 6:1
And your F who sees in secret	Mt 6:4
because your F knows the things	Mt 6:8
Our F in heaven, Your name be	Mt 6:9
your heavenly F will forgive you	Mt 6:14
your heavenly F knows that you	Mt 6:32
more will your F in heaven give	Mt 7:11
one who does the will of My F	Mt 7:21
first let me go bury my f.	Mt 8:21

acknowledge him before My **F**	Mt 10:32
to turn a man against his **f**,	Mt 10:35
who loves **f** or mother more	Mt 10:37
knows the **F** except the Son	Mt 11:27
does the will of My **F** in heaven,	Mt 12:50
Honor your **f** and your mother;	Mt 15:4
speaks evil of **f** or mother must	Mt 15:4
'Whoever tells his **f** or mother,	Mt 15:5
the face of My **F** in heaven.	Mt 18:10
will leave his **f** and mother and	Mt 19:5
honor your **f** and your mother;	Mt 19:19
brothers or sisters, **f** or mother	Mt 19:29
Do not call anyone on earth your **f**,	Mt 23:9
you have one **F**, who is in heaven	Mt 23:9
had lived in the days of our **f-s**,	Mt 23:30
nor the Son—except the **F** only.	Mt 24:36
you who are blessed by My **F**,	Mt 25:34
a new way in My **F-**'s kingdom	Mt 26:29
prayed, "My **F**! If it is possible,	Mt 26:39
the name of the **F** and of the Son	Mt 28:19
glory of His **F** with the holy angels.	Mk 8:38
Abba, **F**! All things are possible	Mk 14:36
the hearts of **f-s** to their	Lk 1:17
Him the throne of His **f** David.	Lk 1:32
him Zechariah, after his **f**.	Lk 1:59
His **f** and mother were amazed at	Lk 2:33
that I had to be in my **F-**'s house?	Lk 2:49
I praise You, **F**, Lord of heaven	Lk 10:21
What **f** among you, if his son asks	Lk 11:11
the heavenly **F** give the Holy	Lk 11:13
and your **f-s** killed them.	Lk 11:47
said to him, '**F**, I have sinned	Lk 15:21
F, if You are willing, take	Lk 22:42
Jesus said, "**F**, forgive them	Lk 23:34
One and Only Son from the **F**,	Jn 1:14
Stop turning my **F**'s house into	Jn 2:16
The **F** loves the Son and has	Jn 3:35
Our **f-s** worshiped on this mountain	Jn 4:20
will worship the **F** in spirit and	Jn 4:23
to them, "My **F** is still working	Jn 5:17
was even calling God His own **F**,	Jn 5:18
only what He sees the **F** doing.	Jn 5:19
For the **F** loves the Son and	Jn 5:20
not honor the **F** who sent Him.	Jn 5:23
I will accuse you to the **F**.	Jn 5:45
Our **f-s** ate the manna in the	Jn 6:31
Everyone the **F** gives Me will	Jn 6:37

unless the **F** who sent Me	
draws him,	Jn 6:44
is from God. He has seen the **F**.	Jn 6:46
and the **F** who sent Me testifies	Jn 8:18
Me, you would also know My **F**.	Jn 8:19
But just as the **F** taught Me,	Jn 8:28
"Our **f** is Abraham!" they replied	Jn 8:39
said. "We have one **F**—God."	Jn 8:41
You are of your **f** the Devil,	Jn 8:44
is a liar and the **f** of liars.	Jn 8:44
snatch them out of the **F-**'s hand.	Jn 10:29
The **F** and I are one.	Jn 10:30
the **F** is in Me and I in the **F**.	Jn 10:38
eyes and said, "**F**, I thank You	Jn 11:41
F, glorify Your name!	Jn 12:28
In My **F-**'s house are many dwelling	Jn 14:2
comes to the **F** except through	Jn 14:6
show us the **F**, and that's enough	Jn 14:8
who has seen Me has seen the **F**.	Jn 14:9
I am in the **F** and the **F** is in Me?	Jn 14:10
because I am going to the **F**.	Jn 14:12
I will ask the **F**, and He will	Jn 14:16
loves Me will be loved by My **F**.	Jn 14:21
because the **F** is greater than I	Jn 14:28
and My **F** is the vineyard keeper	Jn 15:1
My **F** is glorified by this:	Jn 15:8
As the **F** has loved me, I have	Jn 15:9
you ask the **F** in My name,	Jn 15:16
Everything the **F** has is Mine.	Jn 16:15
you ask the **F** in My name,	Jn 16:23
For the **F** Himself loves you,	Jn 16:27
I came from the **F** and have come	Jn 16:28
F, the hour has come.	Jn 17:1
have not yet ascended to the **F**.	Jn 20:17
As the **F** has sent Me, I also	Jn 20:21
but to wait for the **F-**'s promise.	Ac 1:4
today I have become Your **F**.	Ac 13:33
to make him the **f** of all who	Rm 4:11
he became the **f** of many nations	Rm 4:18
by whom we cry out, "Abba, **F**!"	Rm 8:15
the God and **F** of our Lord Jesus	Rm 15:6
confirm the promises to the **f-s**,	Rm 15:8
but you can't have many **f-s**.	1Co 4:15
man is living with his **f-**'s wife.	1Co 5:1
that our **f-s** were all under the	1Co 10:1
the **F** of mercies and the God of	2Co 1:3
I will be a **F** to you, and you	2Co 6:18
until the time set by his **f**.	Gl 4:2

our hearts, crying, "Abba, F!"   Gl 4:6
access by one Spirit to the F.   Eph 2:18
I bow my knees before the F   Eph 3:14
one God and F of all, who is   Eph 4:6
a man will leave his f and mother   Eph 5:31
Honor your f and mother—which   Eph 6:2
And f-s, don't stir up anger in   Eph 6:4
to the glory of God the F.   Php 2:11
to our God and F be glory   Php 4:20
F-s, do not exasperate your   Col 3:21
like a f with his own children,   1Th 2:11
but exhort him as a f,   1Tm 5:1
spoke to the f-s by the prophets   Heb 1:1
I will be His F, and He will be   Heb 1:5
where your f-s tested Me,   Heb 3:9
without f, mother, or genealogy   Heb 7:3
son is there whom a f does not   Heb 12:7
we had natural f-s discipline us,   Heb 12:9
even more to the F of spirits   Heb 12:9
down from the F of lights;   Jms 1:17
With it we bless our Lord and F,   Jms 3:9
if you address as F the One who   1Pt 1:17
have an advocate with the F   1Jn 2:1
writing to you, f-s, because you   1Jn 2:13
you have come to know the F.   1Jn 2:14
love for the F is not in him.   1Jn 2:15
is not from the F, but is from   1Jn 2:16
a love the F has given us,   1Jn 3:1
that the F has sent the Son   1Jn 4:14
the Son of the F, in truth and   2Jn 3
acknowledge his name before My F   Rv 3:5

FATHERED
Who f the drops of dew?   Jb 38:28
Abraham f Isaac, Isaac f Jacob,   Mt 1:2
Now I have f you in Christ Jesus   1Co 4:15
whom I f while in chains   Phm 10

FATHERLESS
not mistreat any widow or f child.   Ex 22:22
will be widows and your children f.   Ex 22:24
He executes justice for the f and   Dt 10:18
left for the foreign resident, the f,   Dt 24:19
I rescued ... the f child who had no   Jb 29:12
ever cast my vote against a f child   Jb 31:21
You are a helper of the f.   Ps 10:14
doing justice for the f   Ps 10:18
A father of the f and a champion   Ps 68:5
Let his children be f   Ps 109:9
and helps the f and the widow,   Ps 146:9

don't encroach on the fields of the f   Pr 23:10
Defend the rights of the f.   Is 1:17
not defend the rights of the f,   Is 1:23
and they can plunder the f.   Is 10:2
The f and widow are oppressed in   Ezk 22:7
For the f receives compassion in   Hs 14:3
not oppress the widow or the f,   Zch 7:10
who oppress the widow and the f,   Mal 3:5

FATHOM
Can you f the depths of God or   Jb 11:7

FATLING
and the f will be together,   Is 11:6

FATNESS
Their eyes bulge out from f;   Ps 73:7

FATTENED
my oxen and f cattle have been   Mt 22:4
Then bring the f calf and   Lk 15:23
You have f your hearts for the   Jms 5:5

FAULT
Today I remember my f-s.   Gn 41:9
I've found no f with him.   1Sm 29:3
Cleanse me from my hidden f-s.   Ps 19:12
For no f of mine, they run and   Ps 59:4
Why then does He still find f?   Rm 9:19

FAULTLESS
who are f in a crooked   Php 2:15
first {covenant} had been f,   Heb 8:7

FAVOR (n)
Noah ... found f in the eyes of   Gn 6:8
Joseph found f in his master's   Gn 39:4
gave the people f in the sight   Ex 11:3
if I have indeed found f in Your   Ex 33:13
LORD look with f on you and give   Nm 6:26
She won more f and approval from   Est 2:17
Look on us with f, LORD.   Ps 4:6
him with f like a shield.   Ps 5:12
moment, but His f, a lifetime.   Ps 30:5
I sought f from my Lord: Ps 30:8
look {on us} with f, and we will be   Ps 80:3
You showed f to Your land;   Ps 85:1
Let the f of the Lord our God be   Ps 90:17
when You show f to Your people.   Ps 106:4
have sought Your f with all my   Ps 119:58
Show us f, LORD, show us f,   Ps 123:3
you will find f and high regard   Pr 3:4
and obtains f from the LORD,   Pr 8:35

good obtain f from the LORD,	Pr 12:2
Good sense wins f, but the way	Pr 13:15
his f is like a cloud with	Pr 16:15
and obtains f from the LORD.	Pr 18:22
but his f is like dew on the	Pr 19:12
f is better than silver and gold	Pr 22:1
the year of the LORD's f,	Is 61:2
scattered your f-s to strangers	Jr 3:13
They found f in the wilderness	Jr 31:2
your sexual f-s on everyone who	Ezk 16:15
offered her sexual f-s to them;	Ezk 23:7
granted Daniel f and compassion	Dn 1:9
my staff called F and cut it in	Zch 11:10
for you have found f with God.	Lk 1:30
and in f with God and with	Lk 2:52
God and having f with all the	Ac 2:47
He gave him f and wisdom in the	Ac 7:10
wanting to do a f for the Jews,	Ac 25:9
trying to win the f of people,	Gl 1:10
For it {brings} f if, because of	1Pt 2:19

FAVOR (v)

and f the plans of the wicked?	Jb 10:3
God ... does not f the rich over the	Jb 34:19
My eyes f the faithful of the land	Ps 101:6
will f those who abandon the holy	Dn 11:30
peace on earth to people He f-s!	Lk 2:14
grace that He f-ed us with in the	Eph 1:6

FAVORABLY

be like theirs, and speak f.	1Kg 22:13
Remember me f, my God, for all	Neh 5:19
does not look f on any who are	Jb 37:24
I will look f on this kind of	Is 66:2

FAVORITE

David ... the f singer of Israel:	2Sm 23:1
his soul {despises his} f food.	Jb 33:20
she is the f of her mother,	Sg 6:9

FAVORITISM

Do not show f to a poor person	Ex 23:3
he is not to show f to the son	Dt 21:16
that God doesn't show f,	Ac 10:34
There is no f with God.	Rm 2:11
God does not show f}—those	Gl 2:6
and there is no f with Him.	Eph 6:9
he has done, and there is no f.	Col 3:25
doing nothing out of f.	1Tm 5:21
Jesus Christ without showing f.	Jms 2:1

if you show f, you commit sin	Jms 2:9
without f and hypocrisy.	Jms 3:17

FAWN

loving doe, a graceful f—let her	Pr 5:19
Your breasts are like two f,	Sg 4:5; 7:3

FEAR (n)

absolutely no f of God in this	Gn 20:11
God of Abraham, the F of Isaac,	Gn 31:42
God will put f and dread of you	Dt 11:25
abandons the f of the Almighty	Jb 6:14
He laughs at f, since he is	Jb 39:22
earth—a creature devoid of f!	Jb 41:33
The f of the LORD is pure,	Ps 19:9
and delivered me from all my f-s.	Ps 34:4
teach you the f of the LORD.	Ps 34:11
matches the f that is due You.	Ps 90:11
f of the LORD is the beginning	Ps 111:10
The f of the LORD is the beginning	Pr 1:7
understand the f of the LORD	Pr 2:5
The f of the LORD is the beginning	Pr 9:10
The f of the LORD prolongs life	Pr 10:27
The f of the LORD is a fountain	Pr 14:27
Better a little with the f of the LORD	Pr 15:16
from evil by the f of the LORD.	Pr 16:6
The f of the LORD leads to life	Pr 19:23
result of humility is f of the LORD,	Pr 22:4
The f of man is a snare, but the	Pr 29:25
a Spirit of ... the f of the LORD.	Is 11:2
delight will be in the f of the LORD.	Is 11:3
and to have no f of Me.	Jr 2:19
and I will put f of Me in their	Jr 32:40
the tomb with f and great joy,	Mt 28:8
to serve Him without f	Lk 1:74
Then f came over everyone,	Lk 7:16
faint from f and expectation	Lk 21:26
because of the f of the Jews	Jn 19:38
There is no f of God before	Rm 3:18
of slavery to fall back into f,	Rm 8:15
in weakness, in f, and in much	1Co 2:3
one another in the f of Christ.	Eph 5:21
masters with f and trembling,	Eph 6:5
salvation with f and trembling.	Php 2:12
their lives by the f of death.	Heb 2:15
There is no f in love; instead,	
perfect love drives out f,	1Jn 4:18

FEAR (v)

For now I know that you f God,	Gn 22:12

said to them, "I f God—do this   Gn 42:18
midwives ... f-ed God and did not   Ex 1:17
the people f-ed the LORD and   Ex 14:31
may learn to f Me all the days   Dt 4:10
F the LORD your God, worship Him   Dt 6:13
You are to f the LORD your God   Dt 10:20
and learn to f the LORD your God   Dt 31:12
Do not f the gods of the   Jdg 6:10
David f-ed the LORD that day and   2Sm 6:9
Obadiah ... greatly f-ed the LORD   1Kg 18:3
they did not f the LORD.   2Kg 17:25
They f-ed the LORD, but they also   2Kg 17:33
Do not f other gods; do not bow   2Kg 17:35
He is f-ed above all gods.   1Ch 16:25
faithful man who f-ed God more   Neh 7:2
who f-ed God and turned away from   Jb 1:1
f-s God and turns away from   Jb 1:8; 2:3
Does Job f God for nothing?   Jb 1:9
For the thing I f-ed has overtaken   Jb 3:25
because I greatly f-ed the crowds,   Jb 31:34
Therefore, men f Him. He does   Jb 37:24
You who f the LORD, praise Him!   Ps 22:23
darkest valley, I f {no} danger, for   Ps 23:4
is the person who f-s the LORD?   Ps 25:12
LORD is for those who f Him,   Ps 25:14
my salvation—whom should I f?   Ps 27:1
stored up for those who f You,   Ps 31:19
encamps around those who f Him,   Ps 34:7
F the LORD, you His saints, for   Ps 34:9
I will not f. What can man do   Ps 56:4,11
listen, all who f God, and I will tell   Ps 66:16
ends of the earth will f Him.   Ps 67:7
And You—You are to be f-ed.   Ps 76:7
is very near those who f Him,   Ps 85:9
God is greatly f-ed in the council   Ps 89:7
You will not f the terror of the   Ps 91:5
He is f-ed above all gods.   Ps 96:4
love toward those who f Him.   Ps 103:11
Let those who f the LORD say,   Ps 118:4
I am a friend to all who f You,   Ps 119:63
my heart f-s {only} Your word   Ps 119:161
is everyone who f-s the LORD,   Ps 128:1
the desires of those who f Him;   Ps 145:19
LORD values those who f Him,   Ps 147:11
Don't f sudden danger or the   Pr 3:25
To f the LORD is to hate evil.   Pr 8:13
with integrity f-s the LORD,   Pr 14:2
My son, f the LORD, as well as   Pr 24:21

but a woman who f-s the LORD will   Pr 31:30
so for the one who f-s an oath.   Ec 9:2
f God and keep His commands,   Ec 12:13
Do not f what they f;   Is 8:12
Only He should be f-ed;   Is 8:13
do not f! Here is your God;   Is 35:4
Do not f, for I am with you;   Is 41:10
Do not f, for I have redeemed you;   Is 43:1
Do not f, for I am with you;   Is 43:5
do not f disgrace by men,   Is 51:7
Do you not f Me?   Jr 5:22
Who should not f You, King of   Jr 10:7
A lion has roared; who will not f?   Am 3:8
Do not f; Zion, do not let   Zph 3:16
So the people f-ed the LORD.   Hg 1:12
My name will be f-ed among the   Mal 1:14
They do not f Me," says the LORD   Mal 3:5
those who f-ed the LORD spoke   Mal 3:16
But for you who f My name,   Mal 4:2
f Him who is able to destroy both   Mt 10:28
to kill him, he f-ed the crowd   Mt 14:5
arrest Him, they f-ed the crowds   Mt 21:46
mercy is ... on those who f Him.   Lk 1:50
I will show you the One to f: Lk 12:5
town who didn't f God or respect   Lk 18:2
Don't you even f God, since you   Lk 23:40
Him because they f-ed the Jews.   Jn 7:13
F no more, Daughter Zion;   Jn 12:15
devout man and f-ed God along with   Ac 10:2
the person who f-s Him and does   Ac 10:35
and you who f God, listen!   Ac 13:16
because he f-ed those from the   Gl 2:12
wholeheartedly, f-ing the Lord.   Col 3:22
let us f so that none of you   Heb 4:1
F God. Honor the Emperor.   1Pt 2:17
Do not f what they f   1Pt 3:14
So the one who f-s has not reached   1Jn 4:18
F God and give Him glory,   Rv 14:7

FEARFUL

Why are you f, you of little   Mt 8:26
They were f and amazed, asking   Lk 8:25
must not be troubled or f.   Jn 14:27
I am f for you, that perhaps my   Gl 4:11

FEARFULNESS

has not given us a spirit of f,   2Tm 1:7

FEARLESS

wine, who are f at mixing beer,   Is 5:22

FEARLESSLY

even more to speak the message f.   Php 1:14

FEAST (n)

He prepared a f and baked	Gn 19:3
Samson prepared a f there,	Jdg 14:10
for we have come on a f day.	1Sm 25:8
he prepared a great f for them.	2Kg 6:23
celebrated the f for seven days	Neh 8:18
full moon, on the day of our f.	Ps 81:3
heart has a continual f.	Pr 15:15
A f is prepared for laughter,	Ec 10:19
At their f-s they have lyre,	Is 5:12
held a great f for 1,000 of his	Dn 5:1
an end to her celebrations: her f-s,	Hs 2:11
on the day of the LORD's f?	Hs 9:5
I hate, I despise your f-s!	Am 5:21
I will turn your f-s into mourning	Am 8:10
and let's celebrate with a f,	Lk 15:23
us observe the f, not with old	1Co 5:8
to the marriage f of the Lamb!	Rv 19:9

FEAST (v)

Let's f on each other's love!	Pr 7:18
your princes f in the morning.	Ec 10:16
They f with you, nurturing only	Jd 12

FEASTING (n)

than a house full of f with strife.	Pr 17:1
than to go to a house of f,	Ec 7:2
Let their f become a snare and a	Rm 11:9

FEATHERS

He will cover you with His f;	Ps 91:4
like eagles' {f} and his nails	Dn 4:33

FEE

a prostitute's f is only a loaf	Pr 6:26

FEEBLE

but the f are clothed with	1Sm 2:4

FEED

He fed you in the wilderness with	Dt 8:16
in prison and f him only bread	1Kg 22:27
You fed them the bread of tears	Ps 80:5
But He would f Israel with the	Ps 81:16
lips of the righteous f many,	Pr 10:21
mouth of fools f-s on foolishness	Pr 15:14
f me with the food I need.	Pr 30:8
he f-s among the lilies.	Sg 2:16; 6:3
to f in the gardens and gather	Sg 6:2
He f-s on ashes.	Is 44:20

will stand and f your flocks,	Is 61:5
and the lamb will f together,	Is 65:25
and f all those who are weak.	Jr 31:25
and He fed me the scroll.	Ezk 3:2
shepherds f themselves rather than	Ezk 34:8
he was fed grass like cattle,	Dn 5:21
They f on the sin of My people;	Hs 4:8
your heavenly Father f-s them.	Mt 6:26
we see You hungry and f You,	Mt 25:37
a barn; yet God f-s them.	Lk 12:24
so the one who f-s on Me will live	Jn 6:57
"F My lambs," He told him.	Jn 21:15
"F My sheep," Jesus said.	Jn 21:17
If your enemy is hungry, f him.	Rm 12:20
I fed you milk, not solid food	1Co 3:2
all my goods to f the poor,	1Co 13:3

FEEDING

the night by your f trough?	Jb 39:9
no oxen, the f trough is empty,	Pr 14:4
and the donkey its master's f trough,	Is 1:3
and laid Him in a f trough	Lk 2:7
who was lying in the f trough.	Lk 2:16

FEEL

They have hands, but cannot f,	Ps 115:7
They struck me, but I f no pain!	Pr 23:35
and to those who f secure on the	Am 6:1

FEELINGS

sharing the same f, focusing on one   Php 2:2

FELIX

Roman governor (Ac 23:24–25:14).

FELLOW

one of his f slaves who owed him	Mt 18:28
starts to beat his f slaves,	Mt 24:49
my f countrymen and f prisoners.	Rm 16:7
but f citizens with the saints,	Eph 2:19
brother, co-worker, and f soldier,	Php 2:25
and a f slave in the Lord,	Col 4:7
my f prisoner in Christ Jesus,	Phm 23
as a f elder and witness to the	1Pt 5:1
I am a f slave with you and your	Rv 19:10
I am a f slave with you, your	Rv 22:9

FELLOWSHIP

burnt offerings and f offerings,	Ex 20:24
his offering is a f sacrifice,	Lv 3:1
this is the law of the f sacrifice	Lv 7:11
thanksgiving sacrifice of f.	Lv 7:13

When you offer a f sacrifice to — Lv 19:5
a man presents a f sacrifice to — Lv 22:21
grain, drink, or f offerings. — Nm 29:39
Solomon offered a sacrifice of f — 1Kg 8:63
We used to have close f; — Ps 55:14
I've made f offerings; — Pr 7:14
will not be present in the f of My — Ezk 13:9
no regard for your f offerings — Am 5:22
teaching, to f, to the breaking — Ac 2:42
called into f with His Son, — 1Co 1:9
Or what f does light have with — 2Co 6:14
and the f of the Holy Spirit be — 2Co 13:13
the right hand of f to me and — Gl 2:9
if any f with the Spirit — Php 2:1
and the f of His sufferings, — Php 3:10
you may have f along with us; and
   indeed our f is with the Father — 1Jn 1:3
we say, "We have f with Him," — 1Jn 1:6
we have f with one another, — 1Jn 1:7

FEMALE

He created them male and f. — Gn 1:27
if she gives birth to a f child, — Lv 12:5
if the person is a f, your valuation — Lv 27:4
I acquired male and f servants and — Ec 2:7
new ... a f will shelter a man. — Jr 31:22
beginning made them male and f, — Mt 19:4
For even their f-s exchanged — Rm 1:26
left ... sexual intercourse with f-s — Rm 1:27
slave or free, male or f; — Gl 3:28

FENCE

wall or a tottering stone f? — Ps 62:3
vineyard, put a f around it, dug — Mt 21:33

FERTILE

Is the land f or unproductive? — Nm 13:20
They captured ... f land — Neh 9:25
I brought you to a f land to eat its — Jr 2:7
seed and put it in a f field; — Ezk 17:5

FERTILIZE

until I dig around it and f it. — Lk 13:8

FERVENT

and being f in spirit, he spoke — Ac 18:25
be f in spirit; serve the Lord. — Rm 12:11

FERVENTLY

I have f desired to eat this — Lk 22:15
He prayed more f, and His sweat — Lk 22:44

FESTERING

and it became f boils on man and — Ex 9:10
Egypt, tumors, a f rash, and — Dt 28:27
are foul and f because of my — Ps 38:5

FESTIVAL

celebrate it as a f to the LORD. — Ex 12:14
Celebrate a f in My honor three — Ex 23:14
Observe the F of Unleavened — Ex 34:18
Observe the F of Weeks with the — Ex 34:22
The F of Unleavened Bread to the — Lv 23:6
The F of Booths to the LORD — Lv 23:34
it as a f to the LORD seven — Lv 23:41
your appointed f-s, and the — Nm 10:10
the LORD at your {F of} Weeks; — Nm 28:26
a seven-day f for the LORD. — Nm 29:12
to celebrate the F of Weeks to — Dt 16:10
to celebrate the F of Booths for — Dt 16:13
hold a seven-day f for the LORD — Dt 16:15
and appointed f-s, they are to do — 1Ch 23:31
the three annual appointed f-s: — 2Ch 8:13
observed the F of Unleavened — 2Ch 30:21
celebrated the F of Booths as — Ezr 3:4
observed the F of Unleavened — Ezr 6:22
cannot stand iniquity with a f. — Is 1:13
that on the night of a holy f, — Is 30:29
At the f-s and appointed times, — Ezk 46:11
to celebrate during the F of Booths. — Zch 14:16
"Not during the f," they said — Mk 14:2
At the f it was Pilate's custom — Mk 15:6
Jerusalem for the Passover F. — Lk 2:41
Passover, a Jewish f, was near. — Jn 6:4
When the f was already half over — Jn 7:14
most important day of the f, — Jn 7:37
Then the F of Dedication took — Jn 10:22
the Passover F, Jesus knew that — Jn 13:1
the matter of a f or a new moon — Col 2:16

FESTIVE

leading the f procession to the — Ps 42:4
f oil instead of mourning, — Is 61:3
of angels in f gathering, — Heb 12:22

FESTUS

Roman governor (Ac 24:27–26:32).

FETTERS

had broken the yoke and torn off the f. — Jr 5:5

FEUDS

me from the f among my people; — 2Sm 22:44

FEVER

disease and f that will cause   Lv 26:16
wasting disease, f, inflammation   Dt 28:22
off, and my bones burn with f.   Jb 30:30
was lying in bed with a f,   Mk 1:30
The f left her, and she began to   Mk 1:31
in the morning the f left him,   Jn 4:52
suffering from f and dysentery.   Ac 28:8

FEW

My years have been f and hard,   Gn 47:9
are strong or weak, f or many.   Nm 13:18
saving, whether by many or by f.   1Sm 14:6
Do not get just a f.   2Kg 4:3
were f in number, very f indeed   Ps 105:12
Let his days be f; let another   Ps 109:8
so let your words be f.   Ec 5:2
grind cease because they are f,   Ec 12:3
leads to life, and f find it.   Mt 7:14
but the workers are f.   Mt 9:37
they said, "and a f small fish."   Mt 15:34
are invited, but f are chosen.   Mt 22:14
were faithful over a f things;   Mt 25:21
are there f being saved?   Lk 13:23
in it, a f—that is, eight   1Pt 3:20
But I have a f things against   Rv 2:14

FEWEST

you were the f of all peoples.   Dt 7:7

FIELD

So Ephron's f at Machpelah near   Gn 23:17
let me go into the f-s and gather   Ru 2:2
your servants set my f on fire?   2Sm 14:31
there was a f full of lentils.   2Sm 23:11
tax on our f-s and vineyards.   Neh 5:4
earth and sends water to the f-s.   Jb 5:10
creatures of the f are Mine.   Ps 50:11
cities like the grass of the f.   Ps 72:16
creatures of the f feed on it.   Ps 80:13
Let the f-s and everything in them   Ps 96:12
blooms like a flower of the f;   Ps 103:15
f of the poor yields abundant food,   Pr 13:23
don't encroach on the f-s of the   Pr 23:10
I went by the f of a slacker and   Pr 24:30
She evaluates a f and buys it;   Pr 31:16
my love, let's go to the f;   Sg 7:11
house and join f to f until there is   Is 5:8
is like the flower of the f.   Is 40:6
animals of the f will honor Me,   Is 43:20

trees of the f will clap   Is 55:12
Buy my f in Anathoth for yourself,   Jr 32:7
One f received rain while a f   Am 4:7
Zion will be plowed like a f,   Mc 3:12
fails and the f-s produce no food   Hab 3:17
how the wildflowers of the f grow: Mt 6:28
God clothes the grass of the f,   Mt 6:30
f is the world; and the good seed   Mt 13:38
is like treasure, buried in a f,   Mt 13:44
or f-s because of My name will   Mt 19:29
a man in the f must not go back   Mt 24:18
Then two men will be in the f: Mt 24:40
bought the potter's f with it   Mt 27:7
out in the f-s and keeping watch   Lk 2:8
which is in the f today and is   Lk 12:28
I have bought a f, and I must go   Lk 14:18
your eyes and look at the f-s,   Jn 4:35
this man acquired a f with his   Ac 1:18
You are God's f, God's building   1Co 3:9
away like a flower of the f.   Jms 1:10

FIERCE

afraid of the f anger the LORD   Dt 9:19
for the LORD's f wrath is on you   2Ch 28:11
to avert the f anger of our God   Ezr 10:14
and a covert bribe, f rage.   Pr 21:14
fiery flames—the f-est of all.   Sg 8:6
So My f wrath poured forth and   Jr 44:6
A f windstorm arose, and the   Mk 4:37
a f wind called the "northeaster   Ac 27:14
large and driven by f winds,   Jms 3:4
of the f anger of God,   Rv 19:15

FIERY

make them {burn} like a f furnace   Ps 21:9
Love's flames are f flames   Sg 8:6
on all flesh with His f sword,   Is 66:16
you walked among the f stones.   Ezk 28:14
will be heaping f coals on his   Rm 12:20
when the f ordeal arises among   1Pt 4:12
His eyes like a f flame,   Rv 1:14
went out, a f red one, and its   Rv 6:4
was a great f red dragon having   Rv 12:3
His eyes were like a f flame,   Rv 19:12

FIFTH

and then morning: the f day.   Gn 1:23
and bore Jacob a f son.   Gn 30:17
he must add a f to the valuation   Lv 27:13
When He opened the f seal,   Rv 6:9

The f angel blew his trumpet,   Rv 9:1
The f poured out his bowl on the   Rv 16:10

FIFTIES
captains of 50 with their f,   2Kg 1:14

FIFTIETH
The f year will be your Jubilee   Lv 25:11

FIG
so they sewed f leaves together   Gn 3:7
some pressed f-s and two clusters   1Sm 30:12
own vine and his own f tree.   1Kg 4:25
own vine and his own f tree,   2Kg 18:31
Bring a lump of pressed f-s.   2Kg 20:7
Whoever tends a f tree will eat   Pr 27:18
The f tree ripens its f-s;   Sg 2:13
be like a ripe f before the   Is 28:4
the vine, no f-s on the f tree   Jr 8:13
LORD showed me two baskets of f-s   Jr 24:1
and the f tree is withered;   Jl 1:12
and I took care of sycamore f-s.   Am 7:14
Though the f tree does not bud   Hab 3:17
under {his} vine and f tree.   Zch 3:10
thornbushes or f-s from thistles?   Mt 7:16
At once the f tree withered.   Mt 21:19
this parable from the f tree: Mt 24:32
F-s aren't gathered from thornbushes   Lk 6:44
A man had a f tree that was   Lk 13:6
when you were under the f tree,   Jn 1:48
Can a f tree produce olives,   Jms 3:12
the earth as a f tree drops its   Rv 6:13

FIGHT (n)
When men get in a f, and hit a   Ex 21:22
Fight the good f for the faith;   1Tm 6:12
I have fought the good f, I have   2Tm 4:7
the wars and the f-s among you?   Jms 4:1

FIGHT (v)
saw two Hebrews f-ing.   Ex 2:13
The LORD will f for you;   Ex 14:14
fought against Moses and Aaron;   Nm 26:9
goes before you will f for you,   Dt 1:30
If two men are f-ing   Dt 25:11
God of Israel, fought for Israel.   Jos 10:42
LORD your God was f-ing for you,   Jos 23:10
The stars fought from the heavens;   Jdg 5:20
Now be men and f!   1Sm 4:9
before us, and f our battles.   1Sm 8:20
will go and f this Philistine!   1Sm 17:32

for me and f the LORD's battles   1Sm 18:17
because he f-s the LORD's   1Sm 25:28
were f-ing in the field with no   2Sm 14:6
don't f against the LORD God of   2Ch 13:12
Our God will f for us!   Neh 4:20
LORD; f those who f me.   Ps 35:1
you fought against the LORD.   Jr 50:24
My servants would f, so that I   Jn 18:36
be found f-ing against God.   Ac 5:39
If I fought wild animals   1Co 15:32
F the good fight for the faith;   1Tm 6:12
God not to f about words;   2Tm 2:14
I have fought the good fight, I have   2Tm 4:7
angels fought against the dragon   Rv 12:7

FIGHTING (adj)
But your f men must cross over   Jos 1:14

FIGHTING (n)
Stop {your f}—and know that I   Ps 46:10
to avoid f, and to be kind,   Ti 3:2

FIGURE
in the shape of any f: Dt 4:16
had a beautiful f and was   Est 2:7
when she saw male f-s carved on   Ezk 23:14
no longer speak to you in f-s,   Jn 16:25

FILIGREE
Fashion gold f settings   Ex 28:13
cords to the two f settings and   Ex 28:25

FILL (n)
will have his f of poverty.   Pr 28:19
will drink its f of their blood   Jr 46:10

FILL (v)
Be fruitful, multiply, f the earth,   Gn 1:28
the earth was f-ed with violence.   Gn 6:11
and multiply and f the earth.   Gn 9:1
that the land was f-ed with them.   Ex 1:7
of the LORD f-ed the tabernacle.   Ex 40:34
whole earth is f-ed with
  the LORD's   Nm 14:21
glory of the LORD f-ed the temple.   1Kg 8:11
F four water pots with water   1Kg 18:33
They ate, were f-ed, became   Neh 9:25
He will yet f your mouth with   Jb 8:21
f my mouth with arguments.   Jb 23:4
Can you f his hide with harpoons   Jb 41:7
They are f-ed from the abundance of   Ps 36:8
God's stream is f-ed with water,   Ps 65:9

whole earth is **f-ed** with His glory   Ps 72:19
it took root and **f-ed** the land.   Ps 80:9
mouth wide, and I will **f** it.   Ps 81:10
sea and all that **f-s** it   Ps 96:11; 98:7
earth is **f-ed** with Your faithful   Ps 119:64
barns will be completely **f-ed**,   Pr 3:10
is **f-ed** with the product of his lips. Pr 18:20
the rooms are **f-ed** with every   Pr 24:4
all his days are **f-ed** with grief,   Ec 2:23
and His robe **f-ed** the temple.   Is 6:1
His glory **f-s** the whole earth.   Is 6:3
streams will **f** your entire land   Is 8:8
Do I not **f** the heavens and the   Jr 23:24
the city is **f-ed** with violence.   Ezk 7:23
and the cloud **f-ed** the inner court   Ezk 10:3
I will **f** you with people, with   Ezk 36:10
glory of the Lord **f-ed** the temple.   Ezk 43:5
mountain and **f-ed** the whole earth.   Dn 2:35
I am **f-ed** with power by the Spirit   Mc 3:8
the earth will be **f-ed** with the   Hab 2:14
and I will **f** this house with glory,   Hg 2:7
because they will be **f-ed**.   Mt 5:6
Everyone ate and was **f-ed**.   Mt 14:20
They all ate and were **f-ed**.   Mt 15:37
F up, then, the measure of your   Mt 23:32
He will be **f-ed** with the Holy   Lk 1:15
Elizabeth was **f-ed** with the Holy   Lk 1:41
valley will be **f-ed**, and every   Lk 3:5
so that my house may be **f-ed**.   Lk 14:23
"**F** the jars with water," Jesus   Jn 2:7
them and **f-ed** 12 baskets with   Jn 6:13
you ate the loaves and were **f-ed**.   Jn 6:26
house was **f-ed** with the fragrance   Jn 12:3
and it **f-ed** the whole house where   Ac 2:2
they were all **f-ed** with the Holy   Ac 2:4
You will **f** me with gladness in   Ac 2:28
Then Peter was **f-ed** with the Holy   Ac 4:8
they were all **f-ed** with the Holy   Ac 4:31
why has Satan **f-ed** your heart to   Ac 5:3
you have **f-ed** Jerusalem with your   Ac 5:28
But Stephen, **f-ed** by the Holy   Ac 7:55
sight and be **f-ed** with the Holy   Ac 9:17
called Paul—**f-ed** with the Holy   Ac 13:9
are **f-ed** with all unrighteousness,   Rm 1:29
the God of hope **f** you with all   Rm 15:13
f-ed with all knowledge,   Rm 15:14
who **f-s** all things in every way.   Eph 1:23
so you may be **f-ed** with all the   Eph 3:19

that He might **f** all things.   Eph 4:10
but be **f-ed** with the Spirit   Eph 5:18
f-ed with the fruit of   Php 1:11
and you have been **f-ed** by Him,   Col 2:10

FILTH

yet is not washed from its **f**.   Pr 30:12
washed away the **f** of the   Is 4:4
cloths, and call them **f**.   Is 30:22
like the **f** of all things.   1Co 4:13
all things and consider them **f**,   Php 3:8
of all moral **f** and evil excess,   Jms 1:21
removal of the **f** of the flesh,   1Pt 3:21

FILTHY

will seem like something **f**.   Ezk 7:19
was dressed with **f** clothes as he   Zch 3:3
and **f** language from your mouth.   Col 3:8
let the **f** go on being made **f**;   Rv 22:11

FINAL

The **f** glory of this house will   Hg 2:9

FINALIZE

F plans through counsel, and   Pr 20:18

FINALLY

F, he sent his son to them.   Mt 21:37
F, the woman died too.   Lk 20:32
F, my brothers, rejoice in the   Php 3:1

FIND

no helper was **found** who was like   Gn 2:20
Noah ... **found** favor in   Gn 6:8
If at Sodom I **f** 50 righteous   Gn 18:26
Can we **f** anyone like this,   Gn 41:38
you will **f** {Him} when you seek   Dt 4:29
F me someone who plays well   1Sm 16:17
F me a woman who is a medium,   1Sm 28:7
I have **found** the book of the law   2Kg 22:8
He will be **found** by you, but if   1Ch 28:9
sought Him, He was **found**   2Ch 15:4
I will not **f** a wise man among you.   Jb 17:10
If only I knew how to **f** Him,   Jb 23:3
But where can wisdom be **found**,   Jb 28:12
at a time that You may be **found**.   Ps 32:6
I have **found** David My servant;   Ps 89:20
like one who **f-s** vast treasure.   Ps 119:162
until I **f** a place for the Lord,   Ps 132:5
search for me, but won't **f** me.   Pr 1:28
are life to those who **f** them,   Pr 4:22
those who search for me **f** me.   Pr 8:17

For the one who f-s me f-s life   Pr 8:35
those who plan good f loyalty   Pr 14:22
who f-s a wife f-s a good thing   Pr 18:22
but who can f a trustworthy man   Pr 20:6
If you f it, you will have a   Pr 24:14
Who can f a capable wife?   Pr 31:10
I have **found** one {true} man   Ec 7:28
Whatever your hands f to do,   Ec 9:10
after many days you may f it.   Ec 11:1
if you f my love, tell him that   Sg 5:8
the LORD while He may be **found**;   Is 55:6
I was **found** by those who did not   Is 65:1
Then take it and f rest for yourselves.   Jr 6:16
will seek Me and f Me when you   Jr 29:13
I will be **found** by you   Jr 29:14
in the balance and **found** deficient.   Dn 5:27
or corruption was **found** in him.   Dn 6:4
Keep searching, and you will f.   Mt 7:7
leads to life, and few f it.   Mt 7:14
I have not **found** anyone in Israel   Mt 10:39
life because of Me will f it.   Mt 10:39
and you will f rest for   Mt 11:29
arrives, it f-s {the house} vacant,   Mt 12:44
treasure … that a man **found**   Mt 13:44
life because of Me will f it.   Mt 16:25
open its mouth you'll f a coin.   Mt 17:27
And if he f-s it, I assure you: Mt 18:13
whose master f-s him working   Mt 24:46
and **found** them sleeping.   Mt 26:40
for you have **found** favor with God.   Lk 1:30
you will f a baby wrapped snugly   Lk 2:12
found Him in the temple complex   Lk 2:46
Keep searching, and you will f.   Lk 11:9
I have **found** my lost sheep!   Lk 15:6
search carefully until she f-s it?   Lk 15:8
He was lost and is **found**!   Lk 15:24
will He f that faith on earth?   Lk 18:8
They found the stone rolled away   Lk 24:2
the tomb and **found** it just as the   Lk 24:24
We have **found** the Messiah!   Jn 1:41
Philip **found** Nathanael and told him   Jn 1:45
for Me, but you will not f Me;   Jn 7:34
in and go out and f pasture.   Jn 10:9
they might reach out and f Him,   Ac 17:27
Why then does He still f fault?   Rm 9:19
was **found** by those who were not   Rm 10:20
Israel did not f what it was   Rm 11:7
that each one be **found** faithful.   1Co 4:2

and be **found** in Him, not having a   Php 3:9
and f grace to help us   Heb 4:16
no deceit was **found** in His mouth;   1Pt 2:22
no one was **found** worthy to open   Rv 5:4
seek death and will not f it;   Rv 9:6
And anyone not **found** written in   Rv 20:15

FINE

purple, and scarlet yarn; and f linen.   Ex 28:5
gift must consist of f flour.   Lv 2:1
not good to f an innocent person   Pr 17:26
her clothing is f linen and   Pr 31:22
Your mouth is like f wine   Sg 7:9
wrapped it in clean, f linen,   Mt 27:59
ring, dressed in f clothes,   Jms 2:2
of gold ornaments or f clothes;   1Pt 3:3
His feet like f bronze fired in   Rv 1:15
For the f linen represents the   Rv 19:8

FINED

hit her must be f as the woman's   Ex 21:22

FINGER

"This is the f of God," the   Ex 8:19
inscribed by the f of God.   Ex 31:18
tablets, inscribed by God's f.   Dt 9:10
with six f-s on each hand   2Sm 21:20
'My little f is thicker than my   1Kg 12:10
the work of Your f-s, the moon and   Ps 8:3
and gestures with his f-s,   Pr 6:13
Tie them to your f-s; write them   Pr 7:3
to what their f-s have made.   Is 2:8
the f-s of a man's hand appeared   Dn 5:5
aren't willing to lift a f to move   Mt 23:4
out demons by the f of God,   Lk 11:20
the tip of his f in water and   Lk 16:24
put my f into the mark of the nails,   Jn 20:25

FINISH

So Moses f-ed the work.   Ex 40:33
When Solomon f-ed building the   1Kg 9:1
Will they ever f it?   Neh 4:2
it consumes Me until it is f-ed!   Lk 12:50
the foundation and cannot f it,   Lk 14:29
who sent Me and to f His work,   Jn 4:34
He said, "It is f-ed!"   Jn 19:30
so that I may f my course and   Ac 20:24
But now f the task as well,   2Co 8:11
I have f-ed the race, I have kept   2Tm 4:7
His works have been f-ed since the   Heb 4:3
in the flesh has f-ed with sin   1Pt 4:1

FIRE

he took the f and the … knife,	Gn 22:6
the bush was on f but was not	Ex 3:2
and the pillar of f by night	Ex 13:22
When a f gets out of control,	Ex 22:6
pleasing aroma, a f offering	Ex 29:18
I threw it into the f, out came	Ex 32:24
a f offering of a pleasing aroma	Lv 1:9
the f of the altar is kept burning	Lv 6:9
F came out from the LORD and	Lv 9:24
unauthorized f before the LORD,	Lv 10:1
pass through {the f} to Molech.	Lv 18:21
unauthorized f before the LORD	Nm 3:4
and the f from the LORD blazed	Nm 11:1
LORD spoke to you from the f.	Dt 4:12
LORD your God is a consuming f,	Dt 4:24
your servants set my field on f?	2Sm 14:31
consuming f {came} from His	2Sm 22:9
The God who answers with f,	1Kg 18:24
but the LORD was not in the f.	1Kg 19:12
Then f came down from heaven	2Kg 1:10
a chariot of f with horses of f	2Kg 2:11
and chariots of f all around	2Kg 6:17
as I mused, a f burned.	Ps 39:3
Devouring f precedes Him,	Ps 50:3
we went through f and water,	Ps 66:12
then f broke out against Jacob,	Ps 78:21
jealousy keep burning like f?	Ps 79:5
F goes before Him and burns up	Ps 97:3
flames of f His servants.	Ps 104:4
a man embrace f and his clothes	Pr 6:27
Without wood, f goes out;	Pr 26:20
burns like a f that consumes	Is 9:18
tongue is like a consuming f.	Is 30:27
when you walk through the f,	Is 43:2
their f will never go out,	Is 66:24
or My anger will flare up like f	Jr 21:12
Is not My word like f	Jr 23:29
consumed by the f in the brazier	Jr 36:23
great cloud with f flashing back	Ezk 1:4
to be His waist down was f,	Ezk 8:2
thrown into the furnace of blazing f.	Dn 3:21
A river of f was flowing, coming	Dn 7:10
calling for a judgment by f.	Am 7:4
will be a wall of f around it,	Zch 2:5
stick snatched from the f?	Zch 3:2
He will be like a refiner's f	Mal 3:2
cut down and thrown into the f.	Mt 3:10
you with the Holy Spirit and f.	Mt 3:11
burn up with f that never goes out.	Mt 3:12
cut down and thrown into the f.	Mt 7:19
often falls into the f	Mt 17:15
be thrown into the eternal f.	Mt 18:8
into the eternal f prepared for	Mt 25:41
and the f is not quenched.	Mk 9:44
everyone will be salted with f.	Mk 9:49
us to call down f from heaven to	Lk 9:54
I came to bring f on the earth,	Lk 12:49
they saw a charcoal f there,	Jn 21:9
like flames of f that were	Ac 2:3
he shook the creature off into the f	Ac 28:5
the f will test the quality of	1Co 3:13
with flaming f on those who	2Th 1:8
for our God is a consuming f.	Heb 12:29
And the tongue is a f.	Jms 3:6
will be on f and be dissolved,	2Pt 3:12
the punishment of eternal f.	Jd 7
by snatching {them} from the f;	Jd 23
filled it with f from the altar	Rv 8:5
f comes from their mouths and	Rv 11:5
Then f came down from heaven and	Rv 20:9
second death, the lake of f.	Rv 20:14
that burns with f and sulfur,	Rv 21:8

FIREBRANDS

two smoldering stubs of f,	Is 7:4

FIREPAN

and f-s must be of pure gold.	Ex 25:38
basins, meat forks, and f-s;	Ex 27:3
and Abihu each took his own f,	Lv 10:1
take a f full of fiery coals	Lv 16:12
Each of you is to take his f,	Nm 16:17
basins, ladles, and f-s;	1Kg 7:50
took away the f-s and the	2Kg 25:15

FIRM

Stand f and see the LORD's	Ex 14:13
currents stood f like a dam.	Ex 15:8
but we rise and stand f.	Ps 20:8
the earth, and it stands f.	Ps 119:90
If you do not stand f in your faith,	Is 7:9
he who stands f in his heart	1Co 7:37
Be alert, stand f in the faith	1Co 16:13
And our hope for you is f,	2Co 1:7
Therefore stand f and don't	Gl 5:1
are standing f in one spirit,	Php 1:27
stand f in the Lord	Php 4:1

if you stand **f** in the Lord. 1Th 3:8
stand **f** and hold to the 2Th 2:15
solid foundation stands **f**, 2Tm 2:19
like a sure and **f** anchor of the Heb 6:19
Resist him, **f** in the faith 1Pt 5:9

FIRMLY

covenant stood **f** on dry ground Jos 3:17
The world is **f** established; 1Ch 16:30
The world is **f** established; Ps 93:1; 96:10
it is **f** fixed in heaven. Ps 119:89
are like **f** embedded nails. Ec 12:11
and hold **f** to My covenant, Is 56:4
being rooted and **f** established Eph 3:17
Hold **f** the message of life. Php 2:16
have learned and **f** believed, 2Tm 3:14
if we hold **f** until the end Heb 3:14

FIRST

and then morning: the **f** day. Gn 1:5
it is the **f** month of your year. Ex 12:2
marital rights of the **f** wife. Ex 21:10
of all who come **f** from the womb, Nm 8:16
The fat must be burned **f**; 1Sm 2:16
it was the **f** time he had built 1Sm 14:35
The **f** woman said, "No, your 1Kg 3:22
Joab son of Zeruiah went up **f**, 1Ch 11:6
who had seen the **f** temple, Ezr 3:12
and with the **f** produce of your Pr 3:9
The **f** to state his case seems Pr 18:17
I, the LORD, am the **f**, and with the Is 41:4
Your **f** father sinned, and your Is 43:27
I am the **f** and I am the last. Is 44:6
I am the **f**, I am also the last. Is 48:12
F go and be reconciled with your Mt 5:24
But seek **f** the kingdom of God Mt 6:33
F take the log out of your eye, Mt 7:5
f let me go bury my father. Mt 8:21
unless he **f** ties up the strong Mt 12:29
say that Elijah must come **f**? Mt 17:10
f will be last, and the last **f**. Mt 19:30
last will be **f**, and the **f** last. Mt 20:16
wants to be **f** among you must be Mt 20:27
father's will?" "The **f**," they said. Mt 21:31
The **f** got married and died. Mt 22:25
F clean the inside of the cup, Mt 23:26
as the **f** day of the week was Mt 28:1
f the blade, then the head, and then Mk 4:28
the children to be satisfied **f**, Mk 7:27
good news must **f** be proclaimed Mk 13:10

He appeared **f** to Mary Magdalene Mk 16:9
f let me go bury my father. Lk 9:59
doesn't **f** sit down and calculate Lk 14:28
But **f** He must suffer many things Lk 17:25
He **f** found his own brother Simon Jn 1:41
performed this **f** sign in Cana Jn 2:11
should be the **f** to throw a stone Jn 8:7
who had reached the tomb **f**, Jn 20:8
were **f** called Christians in Antioch. Ac 11:26
message be spoken to you **f**. Ac 13:46
who believes, **f** to the Jew, and Rm 1:16
who does evil, **f** to the Jew, and Rm 2:9
Or who has ever **f** given to Him, Rm 11:35
nearer than when we **f** believed. Rm 13:11
f apostles, second prophets 1Co 12:28
The **f** man Adam became a living 1Co 15:45
which is the **f** commandment with Eph 6:2
the dead in Christ will rise **f**. 1Th 4:16
the apostasy comes **f** and the man 2Th 2:3
F of all, then, I urge that 1Tm 2:1
Adam was created **f**, then Eve. 1Tm 2:13
religion toward their own family **f** 1Tm 5:4
person after a **f** and second Ti 3:10
For if that **f** {covenant} had Heb 8:7
wisdom from above is **f** pure, Jms 3:17
is worse for them than the **f**. 2Pt 2:20
We love because He **f** loved us. 1Jn 4:19
loves to have **f** place among them 3Jn 9
I am the **F** and the Last, Rv 1:17
abandoned the love {you had} at **f**. Rv 2:4
The **f** {angel} blew his trumpet, Rv 8:7
This is the **f** resurrection. Rv 20:5
for the **f** heaven and the **f** earth had Rv 21:1

FIRSTBORN

his father, "I am Esau, your **f**. Gn 27:19
Israel is My **f** son. Ex 4:22
LORD struck every **f** {male} in Ex 12:29
Consecrate every **f** male to Me, Ex 13:2
Give Me the **f** of your sons. Ex 22:29
The **f** male from every womb Ex 34:19
because every **f** belongs to Me. Nm 3:13
For every **f** among the Israelites Nm 8:17
must not redeem the **f** of an ox, Nm 18:17
your God every **f** male produced Dt 15:19
the unloved wife has the **f** son, Dt 21:15
foundation {at the cost of} his **f**; Jos 6:26
At the cost of Abiram his **f**, 1Kg 16:34
He struck all the **f** in Egypt, Ps 78:51

I will also make him My f,   Ps 89:27
Should I give my f for my   Mc 6:7
for Him as one weeps for a f.   Zch 12:10
she gave birth to her f Son,   Lk 2:7
Every f male will be dedicated   Lk 2:23
He would be the f among many   Rm 8:29
God, the f over all creation   Col 1:15
beginning, the f from the dead   Col 1:18
brings His f into the world,   Heb 1:6
assembly of the f whose names   Heb 12:23
the f from the dead and the   Rv 1:5

FIRSTFRUITS

and the f of my virility,   Gn 49:3
with the f of your produce   Ex 23:16
of Weeks with the f of the wheat   Ex 34:22
offering of f to the LORD,   Lv 2:14
The f of all that is in their   Nm 18:13
On the day of f, you are to   Nm 28:26
give him the f of your grain,   Dt 18:4
for he is the f of his virility   Dt 21:17
{We will} bring the f of our land   Neh 10:35
who have the Spirit as the f   Rm 8:23
Now if the f offered up are holy   Rm 11:16
the f of those who have fallen   1Co 15:20
Christ, the f; afterward, at His   1Co 15:23
they are the f of Achaia and   1Co 16:15
we would be the f of His   Jms 1:18
human race as the f for God and   Rv 14:4

FISH (n)

will rule the f of the sea,   Gn 1:26
The f in the Nile died, and the   Ex 7:21
and f of the sea passing through   Ps 8:8
like f caught in a cruel net,   Ec 9:12
their f rot because of lack of   Is 50:2
Jonah was in the f three days   Jnh 1:17
mankind like the f of the sea,   Hab 1:14
he asks for a f, will give him   Mt 7:10
belly of the great f three days   Mt 12:40
It collected every kind {of f},   Mt 13:47
have five loaves and two f here,   Mt 14:17
the seven loaves and the f,   Mt 15:36
the first f that comes up.   Mt 17:27
caught a great number of f,   Lk 5:6
Him a piece of a broiled f,   Lk 24:42
full of large f—153 of them.   Jn 21:11
for birds, and another for f.   1Co 15:39
bird, reptile or f—is tamed   Jms 3:7

FISH (v)

I will make you f for people!   Mt 4:19

FISHING (adj)

burn incense to their f net,   Hab 1:16

FISHING (n)

"I'm going f," Simon Peter said   Jn 21:3

FISHERMEN

Then the f will mourn.   Is 19:8
I am about to send for many f   Jr 16:16
the sea, since they were f.   Mk 1:16

FISHHOOKS

every last {one} of you with f.   Am 4:2

FIT

looks back is f for the kingdom   Lk 9:62

FITTED

is being f together in Him   Eph 2:21
f and knit together by every   Eph 4:16

FITTING

husbands, as is f in the Lord.   Col 3:18
For it was f, in bringing many   Heb 2:10

FIVE

the whole city for lack of f?   Gn 18:28
So the f Amorite kings   Jos 10:5
When the f Philistine rulers   1Sm 6:16
hand and chose f smooth stones   1Sm 17:40
we only have f loaves and two   Mt 14:17
F of them were foolish and f were   Mt 25:2
To one he gave f talents;   Mt 25:15
Aren't f sparrows sold for two   Lk 12:6
f in one household will be   Lk 12:52
'I have bought f yoke of oxen,   Lk 14:19
For you've had f husbands,   Jn 4:18
rather speak f words with my   1Co 14:19
to torment {them} for f months;   Rv 9:5

FIX

Who f-ed its dimensions?   Jb 38:5
f your gaze straight ahead.   Pr 4:25
I will f My eyes on them for   Am 9:4
great chasm has been f-ed between   Lk 16:26

FIXED (adj)

and his gaze was f because he   1Sm 4:15
his gaze was f due to his age.   1Kg 14:4
it is firmly f in heaven.   Ps 119:89

FLAG

If this f order departs from My	Jr 31:36
establish the f order of heaven	Jr 33:25

FLAG

given a signal f to those who	Ps 60:4
a signal f for the distant	Is 5:26
Lift up a signal f toward Zion.	Jr 4:6
Raise a signal f in the land;	Jr 51:27

FLAME

to him in a f of fire within	Ex 3:2
of the LORD went up in its f.	Jdg 13:20
of the LORD flashes f-s of fire.	Ps 29:7
His messengers, f-s of fire His	Ps 104:4
f-s consumed the wicked.	Ps 106:18
Love's f-s are fiery f-s	Sg 8:6
as dry grass shrivels in the f,	Is 5:24
a fire, and its Holy One, a f.	Is 10:17
and a f of consuming fire.	Is 29:6
and the f will not burn you.	Is 43:2
and behind them a f devours.	Jl 2:3
because I am in agony in this f!	Lk 16:24
like f-s of fire that were divided	Ac 2:3
in the f of a burning bush.	Ac 7:30
and His servants a fiery f;	Heb 1:7
His eyes like a fiery f,	Rv 1:14
His eyes were like a fiery f,	Rv 19:12

FLAMING

cherubim with a f, whirling sword	Gn 3:24
who throws f darts and deadly	Pr 26:18
her salvation like a f torch.	Is 62:1
his eyes like f torches, his	Dn 10:6
to extinguish the f arrows of	Eph 6:16
vengeance with f fire on those	2Th 1:8

FLASH (n)

from heaven like a lightning f.	Lk 10:18
tthe throne came f-es of lightning,	Rv 4:5

FLASH (v)

Your arrows f-ed back and forth.	Ps 77:17
cloud with fire f-ing back and forth	Ezk 1:4
from the east and f-es as far as	Mt 24:27
he lightning f-es from horizon to	Lk 17:24
heaven suddenly f-ed around him.	Ac 9:3

FLASHING (adj)

horseman, f sword, shining	Nah 3:3

FLASK

Samuel took the f of oil, poured	1Sm 10:1
take this f of oil with you,	2Kg 9:1

oil in their f-s with their lamps	Mt 25:4
an alabaster f of fragrant oil	Lk 7:37

FLATTER

they f with their tongues.	Ps 5:9
than one who f-s with his tongue.	Pr 28:23
A man who f-s his neighbor spreads	Pr 29:5
f-ing people for their own advantage	Jd 16

FLATTERING (adj)

they speak with f lips and	Ps 12:2
LORD cut off all f lips and	Ps 12:3
from the f tongue of a stranger	Pr 6:24
a stranger with her f talk.	Pr 7:5
and a f mouth causes ruin.	Pr 26:28
Tell us f things.	Is 30:10
false vision or f divination	Ezk 12:24
smooth talk and f words they	Rm 16:18
For we never used f speech,	1Th 2:5

FLATTERY

With f he will corrupt those who	Dn 11:32

FLAVOR

Is there f in an egg white?	Jb 6:6
if the salt should lose its f,	Mk 9:50

FLAW

he did not have a single f.	2Sm 14:25
clay became f-ed in the potter's	Jr 18:4

FLAX

and the f was budding,	Ex 9:31
wool and f and works with	Pr 31:13
who work with f will be dismayed	Is 19:9

FLEA

chasing after? A dead dog? A f?	1Sm 24:14
has come out to search for a f,	1Sm 26:20

FLEE

F at once to my brother Laban in	Gn 27:43
Why did you secretly f from me,	Gn 31:27
But Moses fled from Pharaoh and	Ex 2:15
and you will f even though no	Lv 26:17
who hate You f from Your	Nm 10:35
who kills someone may f there;	Nm 35:6
can f to these cities	Dt 19:3
direction but f from you in	Dt 28:7
one direction but f from them in	Dt 28:25
but they fled from the men of Ai.	Jos 7:4
or accidentally may f there.	Jos 20:3
left his chariot and fled on foot.	Jdg 4:15
So David fled and escaped and	1Sm 19:18

he **f-s** like a shadow and does not	Jb 14:2
who hate Him **f** from His presence	Ps 68:1
At Your rebuke the waters **fled;**	Ps 104:7
sea looked and **fled;** the Jordan	Ps 114:3
Where can I **f** from Your presence	Ps 139:7
The wicked **f** when no one is	Pr 28:1
day breaks and the shadows **f,**	Sg 2:17; 4:6
your rulers have **fled** together,	Is 22:3
at the threat of five you will **f,**	Is 30:17
and sorrow and sighing will **f.**	Is 35:10
Every city **f-s** at the sound of the	Jr 4:29
like a man who **f-s** from a lion	Am 5:19
Jonah got up to **f** to Tarshish	Jnh 1:3
knew he was **f-ing** from the LORD's	Jnh 1:10
You will **f** as you **fled** from the	Zch 14:5
and His mother, **f** to Egypt,	Mt 2:13
warned you to **f** from the coming	Mt 3:7
the men who tended them **fled.**	Mt 8:33
in Judea must **f** to the mountains	Mt 24:16
F from sexual immorality!	1Co 6:18
dear friends, **f** from idolatry.	1Co 10:14
F from youthful passions, and	2Tm 2:22
we who have **fled** for refuge might	Heb 6:18
Devil, and he will **f** from you.	Jms 4:7
The woman **fled** into the wilderness	Rv 12:6
Earth and heaven **fled** from His	Rv 20:11

FLEECE

If dew is only on the **f,**	Jdg 6:37
warming himself with the **f** from	Jb 31:20

FLEET

put together a **f** of ships at	1Kg 9:26

FLEETING

is deceptive and beauty is **f,**	Pr 31:30
all the days of your **f** life,	Ec 9:9
and the prime of life are **f.**	Ec 11:10

FLESH

of my bone, and **f** of my **f;**	Gn 2:23
wife, and they become one **f.**	Gn 2:24
decided to put an end to all **f,**	Gn 6:13
God of the spirits of all **f,**	Nm 16:22
that I am your own **f** and blood.	Jdg 9:2
we are, your own **f** and blood.	2Sm 5:1
my brothers, my **f** and blood.	2Sm 19:12
yet I will see God in my **f.**	Jb 19:26
Do I eat the **f** of bulls or drink	Ps 50:13
that they were {only} **f,**	Ps 78:39
my heart and **f** cry out for the	Ps 84:2

my **f** sticks to my bones.	Ps 102:5
and consumes his own **f.**	Ec 4:5
one eats the **f** of his own arm.	Is 9:20
and give them a heart of **f,**	Ezk 11:19
and give you a heart of **f.**	Ezk 36:26
f grew, and skin covered them,	Ezk 37:8
You will eat the **f** of mighty men	Ezk 39:18
You eat the **f** of my people after	Mc 3:3
f and blood did not reveal this	Mt 16:17
and the two will become one **f?**	Mt 19:5
is willing, but the **f** is weak.	Mt 26:41
ghost does not have **f** and bones	Lk 24:39
will of the **f,** or of the will	Jn 1:13
The Word became **f** and took up	Jn 1:14
Whatever is born of the **f** is **f,**	Jn 3:6
the life of the world is My **f.**	Jn 6:51
you eat the **f** of the Son of Man	Jn 6:53
because My **f** is real food and My	Jn 6:55
one who eats My **f** and drinks My	Jn 6:56
The **f** doesn't help at all.	Jn 6:63
gave Him authority over all **f;**	Jn 17:2
His **f** did not experience decay.	Ac 2:31
of David according to the **f**	Rm 1:3
For no **f** will be justified in	Rm 3:20
forefather according to the **f,**	Rm 4:1
For when we were in the **f,**	Rm 7:5
lives in me, that is, in my **f.**	Rm 7:18
God, but with my **f,** to the law	Rm 7:25
condemned sin in the **f** by sending	
His own Son in **f** like ours	Rm 8:3
the mind-set of the **f** is death,	Rm 8:6
are not in the **f,** but in the Spirit,	Rm 8:9
if you live according to the **f,**	Rm 8:13
for the destruction of the **f,**	1Co 5:5
The two will become one **f.**	1Co 6:16
there is one **f** for humans,	1Co 15:39
f and blood cannot inherit the	1Co 15:50
tablets that are hearts of **f.**	2Co 3:3
we are walking in the **f,**	2Co 10:3
a thorn in the **f** was given to me	2Co 12:7
The life I now live in the **f,**	Gl 2:20
carry out the desire of the **f.**	Gl 5:16
the works of the **f** are obvious:	Gl 5:19
crucified the **f** with its	Gl 5:24
one who sows to his **f** will reap	Gl 6:8
reap corruption from the **f,**	Gl 6:8
showing in the **f** are the ones	Gl 6:12
in order to boast about your **f.**	Gl 6:13

done by hand in the f.   Eph 2:11
no one ever hates his own f,   Eph 5:29
and the two will become one f. Eph 5:31
is not against f and blood,   Eph 6:12
not put confidence in the f   Php 3:3
He was manifested in the f,   1Tm 3:16
the curtain (that is, His f); Heb 10:20
For All f is like grass,   1Pt 1:24
since Christ suffered in the f, 1Pt 4:1
the lust of the f, the lust of   1Jn 2:16
Christ has come in the f is from God. 1Jn 4:2
likewise defile their f,   Jd 8
birds were filled with their f. Rv 19:21

FLESHLY

plans to satisfy the f desires. Rm 13:14
because you are still f.   1Co 3:3
not by f wisdom but by God's 2Co 1:12
of our warfare are not f,   2Co 10:4
among them in our f desires, Eph 2:3
any value against f indulgence. Col 2:23
to abstain from f desires that 1Pt 2:11
to death in the f realm but made 1Pt 3:18
judged by men in the f realm, 1Pt 4:6

FLIGHT

leaf will put them to f,   Lv 26:36
or two put ten thousand to f, Dt 32:30
and put foreign armies to f. Heb 11:34

FLINT

Zipporah took a f, cut off her Ex 4:25
Make f knives and circumcise Jos 5:2
I have set My face like f,   Is 50:7

FLINTLIKE

out of the f rock for you.   Dt 8:15
the rock and oil from f rock, Dt 32:13

FLOAT

and made the iron f.   2Kg 6:6

FLOCK

Abel became a shepherd of a f, Gn 4:2
Take even your f-s and your herds Ex 12:32
pastures are clothed with f-s, Ps 65:13
You led Your people like a f Ps 77:20
them like a f in the wilderness Ps 78:52
who guides Joseph like a f; Ps 80:1
well the condition of your f, Pr 27:23
follow the tracks of the f,   Sg 1:8
are like a f of newly shorn   Sg 4:2

are like a f of ewes coming   Sg 6:6
protects His f like a shepherd Is 40:11
His Holy Spirit among the f? Is 63:11
You have scattered My f,   Jr 23:2
I will gather the remnant of My f Jr 23:3
as a shepherd {guards} his f, Jr 31:10
but you do not tend the f. Ezk 34:3
I will rescue My f from   Ezk 34:10
My f, the human f of My pasture, Ezk 34:31
following the f and said to me, Am 7:15
a young lion among f-s of sheep, Mc 5:8
the f intended for slaughter. Zch 11:4
shepherd who deserts the f! Zch 11:17
sheep of the f will be scattered. Mt 26:31
watch at night over their f. Lk 2:8
Don't be afraid, little f,   Lk 12:32
will be one f, one shepherd. Jn 10:16
yourselves and for all the f, Ac 20:28
among you, not sparing the f. Ac 20:29
does not drink the milk from the f? 1Co 9:7
shepherd God's f among you, 1Pt 5:2

FLOCKING

of the Jordan were f to him, Mt 3:5
of Jerusalem were f to him, Mk 1:5
and people were f to Him from Lk 8:4
and everyone is f to Him.   Jn 3:26

FLOGGED

He may be f with 40 lashes, Dt 25:3
to be mocked, f, and crucified Mt 20:19
having Jesus f, he handed Him Mt 27:26
and you will be f in the   Mk 13:9
took Jesus and had Him f.   Jn 19:1
in the apostles and had them f, Ac 5:40

FLOOD

lived 350 years after the f. Gn 9:28
The f-s covered them;   Ex 15:5
Terrors overtake him like a f; Jb 27:20
LORD sat enthroned at the f; Ps 29:10
and a f sweeps over me.   Ps 69:2
the f-s have lifted up their voice Ps 93:3
a conflict is to release a f; Pr 17:14
and anger is a f, but who can Pr 27:4
would never f the earth again Is 54:9
The end will come with a f, Dn 9:26
They didn't know until the f came Mt 24:39
When the f came, the river Lk 6:48
when He brought a f on the world 2Pt 2:5

FLOODED

my sins have f over my head;   Ps 38:4
when it was f by water.   2Pt 3:6

FLOODGATES

the f of the sky were opened,   Gn 7:11
depths and the f of the sky were   Gn 8:2
will not open the f of heaven   Mal 3:10

FLOODWATERS

f on the earth to destroy all   Gn 6:17
When great f come, they will not   Ps 32:6
Don't let the f sweep over me or   Ps 69:15

FLOOR

the threshing f of Atad,   Gn 50:10
Go down to the threshing f,   Ru 3:3
came to Nacon's threshing f,   2Sm 6:6
at the threshing f of Araunah   2Sm 24:16
the temple f with gold in both   1Kg 6:30
at the threshing f of Ornan the   1Ch 21:15
on the threshing f of Ornan the   2Ch 3:1
will clear His threshing f and gather   Mt 3:12
here on the f by my footstool   Jms 2:3

FLOUR

of fine f and make bread.   Gn 18:6
gift must consist of fine f.   Lv 2:1
The f jar will not become empty   1Kg 17:14
what sprouts fails to yield f.   Hs 8:7
50 pounds of f until it spread   Mt 13:33

FLOURISH

and his branch will not f.   Jb 15:32
But I am like a f-ing olive tree in   Ps 52:8
the righteous f in his days,   Ps 72:7
The trees of the LORD f,   Ps 104:16
righteous will f like foliage.   Pr 11:28
they are destroyed, the righteous f.   Pr 28:28
When the righteous f, the people   Pr 29:2
and you will f like grass;   Is 66:14
LORD named you a f-ing olive tree,   Jr 11:16
says: Will it f? Will he not   Ezk 17:9
So the preaching about God f-ed,   Ac 6:7
the people f-ed and multiplied in   Ac 7:17
God's message f-ed and multiplied.   Ac 12:24
Lord's message f-ed and prevailed.   Ac 19:20
your faith is f-ing, and the love   2Th 1:3

FLOW

which f-s to the east of Assyria.   Gn 2:14
a land f-ing with milk and honey   Ex 3:8

Indeed it is f-ing with milk and   Nm 13:27
grace f-s from your lips.   Ps 45:2
and made water f down like   Ps 78:16
it f-ed like a stream in the desert   Ps 105:41
His winds, and the waters f.   Ps 147:18
your springs f in the streets,   Pr 5:16
All the streams f to the sea,   Ec 1:7
well of f-ing water streaming from   Sg 4:15
f-ing smoothly for my love gliding   Sg 7:9
make peace f to her like a river,   Is 66:12
my eyes f with tears.   Lm 1:16
and the hills will f with milk.   Jl 3:18
But let justice f like water,   Am 5:24
living water will f out from   Zch 14:8
Instantly her f of blood ceased   Mk 5:29
streams of living water f from   Jn 7:38
f-ing from the throne of God   Rv 22:1

FLOWER

like a f, then withers;   Jb 14:2
blooms like a f of the field;   Ps 103:15
to the fading f of its beautiful   Is 28:1
is like the f of the field.   Is 40:6
withers, the f-s fade, but the word   Is 40:8
its f falls off, and its   Jms 1:11
withers, and the f drops off,   1Pt 1:24

FLUNG

but you have f Me behind your   1Kg 14:9

FLUTE

who play the lyre and the f.   Gn 4:21
tambourines, f-s, and lyres.   1Sm 10:5
playing f-s and rejoicing with   1Kg 1:40
praise Him with f and strings.   Ps 150:4
My heart moans like f-s for Moab,   Jr 48:36
of the horn, f, zither, lyre   Dn 3:5
He saw the f players and a crowd   Mt 9:23
We played the f for you, but you   Mt 11:17
is played on the f or harp be   1Co 14:7

FLUTISTS

musicians, f, and trumpeters   Rv 18:22

FLY (n)

send swarms of f-ies against you,   Ex 8:21
sent among them swarms of f-ies,   Ps 78:45
Dead f-ies make a perfumer's oil   Ec 10:1
will whistle to the f that is at   Is 7:18

FLY (v)

and let birds f above the earth   Gn 1:20

He rode on a cherub and **flew**,	2Sm 22:11
as surely as sparks f upward.	Jb 5:7
My days f by faster than a	Jb 9:25
He will f away like a dream and	Jb 20:8
I would f away and find rest.	Ps 55:6
pass quickly and we f away.	Ps 90:10
the arrow that f-ies by day,	Ps 91:5
for itself and f-ies like an eagle	Pr 23:5
and with two he **flew.**	Is 6:2
glory will f away like a bird:	Hs 9:11
at the flash of Your f-ing arrows,	Hab 3:11
"I see a f-ing scroll," I replied	Zch 5:2
heard an eagle, f-ing in mid-heaven,	Rv 8:13
another angel f-ing in mid-heaven,	Rv 14:6

FOAL

on a colt, the f of a donkey.	Zch 9:9
the f of a beast of burden.	Mt 21:5

FOAM

though its waters roar and f and	Ps 46:3
disappear like f on the surface	Hs 10:7
him down, and he f-s at the mouth	Mk 9:18
f-ing up their shameful deeds;	Jd 13

FOCUS

Wisdom is the f of the	Pr 17:24
So we do not f on what is seen,	2Co 4:18
same feelings, f-ing on one goal.	Php 2:2
They are f-ed on earthly things,	Php 3:19

FOE

and a f to your f-s.	Ex 23:22
LORD, how my f-s increase!	Ps 3:1
my f-s and my enemies stumbled	Ps 27:2
iniquity of my f-s surrounds me.	Ps 49:5
it is not a f who rises up	Ps 55:12
Give us aid against the f,	Ps 60:11
God, how long will the f mock?	Ps 74:10
He redeemed them from the f,	Ps 78:42
I will crush his f-s before him	Ps 89:23
from the hand of the f	Ps 107:2
will look in triumph on his f-s.	Ps 112:8
persecutors and f-s are many.	Ps 119:157
and rescued us from our f-s.	Ps 136:24
lightning and scatter the f;	Ps 144:6

FOLD (n)

I also shook the f-s of my robe	Neh 5:13
in the f of His {garment}.	Is 40:11

for shepherds and f-s for sheep.	Zph 2:6
sheep that are not of this f;	Jn 10:16

FOLD (v)

The fool f-s his arms and consumes	Ec 4:5
but was f-ed up in a separate place	Jn 20:7

FOLDING (n)

little f of the arms to rest,	Pr 6:10; 24:33

FOLIAGE

Our bed is lush with f;	Sg 1:16
grass is withered, the f is gone	Is 15:6

FOLLOW

unwilling to f me to this land	Gn 24:5
whether or not they will f	Ex 16:4
You must not f a crowd in	Ex 23:2
If you turn back from f-ing Him,	Nm 32:15
He commanded you to f the Ten	Dt 4:13
Do not f other gods, the gods of	Dt 6:14
leave you or go back and not f you.	Ru 1:16
sons do not f your example.	1Sm 8:5
and from f-ing the sheep to be	2Sm 7:8
did not completely f the LORD.	1Kg 11:6
as if f-ing the sin of Jeroboam	1Kg 16:31
If Yahweh is God, f Him.	1Kg 18:21
put anyone who f-s her to death	2Kg 11:15
Israel away from f-ing the LORD	2Kg 17:21
man who does not f the advice	Ps 1:1
his wealth will not f him down.	Ps 49:17
the upright in heart will f it.	Ps 94:15
He f-s her impulsively like an ox	Pr 7:22
When pride comes, disgrace f-s,	Pr 11:2
how you f-ed Me in the wilderness,	Jr 2:2
Stop f-ing other gods to serve them	Jr 35:15
one act of bloodshed f-s another.	Hs 4:2
LORD took me from f-ing the flock	Am 7:15
and pestilence f-s in His steps.	Hab 3:5
F Me, ... and I will make you	Mt 4:19
they left their nets and f-ed Him.	Mt 4:20
I will f You wherever You go!	Mt 8:19
Jesus told him, "F Me, and let	Mt 8:22
and He said to him, "F Me!"	Mt 9:9
his cross and f Me is not worthy	Mt 10:38
Huge crowds f-ed Him,	Mt 12:15
take up his cross, and f Me.	Mt 16:24
in heaven. Then come, f Me.	Mt 19:21
left everything and f-ed You.	Mt 19:27
women who had f-ed Jesus from	Mt 27:55
large crowd was f-ing and pressing	Mk 5:24

Peter f-ed Him at a distance,   Mk 14:54
him because he does not f us.   Lk 9:49
I will f You wherever You go!   Lk 9:57
I will f You, Lord, but first   Lk 9:61
Don't f or run after them.   Lk 17:23
Anyone who f-s Me will never walk   Jn 8:12
The sheep f him because they   Jn 10:4
I know them, and they f Me.   Jn 10:27
anyone serves Me, he must f Me.   Jn 12:26
I am going you cannot f Me now,   Jn 13:36
that to you? As for you, f Me.   Jn 21:22
As she f-ed Paul and us she cried   Ac 16:17
to those who f in the footsteps   Rm 4:12
a spiritual rock that f-ed them,   1Co 10:4
It f-s that speaking in other   1Co 14:22
good teaching that you have f-ed.   1Tm 4:6
{the sins} of others f them.   1Tm 5:24
But you have f-ed my teaching,   2Tm 3:10
and the glories that would f.   1Pt 1:11
that you should f in His steps.   1Pt 2:21
For we did not f cleverly   2Pt 1:16
astray and have f-ed the path of   2Pt 2:15
was amazed and f-ed the beast.   Rv 13:3
These are the ones who f the Lamb   Rv 14:4
labors, for their works f them!   Rv 14:13

FOLLOWING (adj)
The f Sabbath almost the whole   Ac 13:44

FOLLOWING (n)
the census and attracted a f.   Ac 5:37

FOLLOWER
he said to Korah and all his f-s,   Nm 16:5
protect the way of His loyal f-s.   Pr 2:8
If anyone wants to be My f,   Mk 8:34

FOLLY
not deal with you as your f deserves. Jb 42:8
The woman F is rowdy;   Pr 9:13
but f is the instruction of fools.   Pr 16:22
and knowledge, madness and f;   Ec 1:17
an advantage to wisdom over f,   Ec 2:13
so a little f outweighs wisdom   Ec 10:1

FOOD
every green plant for f.   Gn 1:30
saw that the tree was good for f   Gn 3:6
Every living creature will be f   Gn 9:3
offerings ... the f of their God.   Lv 21:6
LORD ... providing them f.   Ru 1:6

He gives f in abundance.   Jb 36:31
tears have been my f day and night,   Ps 42:3
You satisfy me as with rich f;   Ps 63:5
able to provide f in the wilderness?   Ps 78:19
producing f from the earth,   Ps 104:14
He gives f to every creature.   Ps 136:25
and giving f to the hungry.   Ps 146:7
than to act important but have no f.   Pr 12:9
works his land will have plenty of f, Pr 12:11
of the poor yields abundant f,   Pr 13:23
F gained by fraud is sweet to a   Pr 20:17
he shares his f with the poor.   Pr 22:9
don't desire his choice f, for that f
  is deceptive.   Pr 23:3
enemy is hungry, give him f   Pr 25:21
feed me with the f I need.   Pr 30:8
store up their f in the summer;   Pr 30:25
and provides f for her household   Pr 31:15
spend money on what is not f,   Is 55:2
not defile himself with the king's f   Dn 1:8
I didn't eat any rich f,   Dn 10:3
that there may be f in My house.   Mal 3:10
and his f was locusts and wild   Mt 3:4
Isn't life more than f   Mt 6:25
the worker is worthy of his f.   Mt 10:10
to give them f at the proper   Mt 24:45
As a result, He made all f-s clean.   Mk 7:19
the one who has f must do the   Lk 3:11
had gone into town to buy f.   Jn 4:8
I have f to eat that you don't   Jn 4:32
My f is to do the will of Him   Jn 4:34
Don't work for the f that perishes   Jn 6:27
flesh is real f and My blood is   Jn 6:55
They ate their f with gladness   Ac 2:46
abstain from f offered to idols   Ac 15:29
down God's work because of f.   Rm 14:20
milk, not solid f, because you   1Co 3:2
F-s for the stomach and   1Co 6:13
About f offered to idols: 1Co 8:1
F will not make us acceptable to   1Co 8:8
if f causes my brother to fall,   1Co 8:13
all ate the same spiritual f,   1Co 10:3
often without f, cold,   2Co 11:27
judge you in regard to f and drink   Col 2:16
demand abstinence from f-s   1Tm 4:3
But if we have f and clothing,   1Tm 6:8
You need milk, not solid f.   Heb 5:12

and only deal with f, drink, Heb 9:10
clothes and lacks daily f, Jms 2:15

FOOL

Should Abner die as a f dies? 2Sm 3:33
The f says in his heart, "God Ps 14:1; 53:1
a f does not understand this: Ps 92:6
F-s, when will you be wise? Ps 94:8
f-s despise wisdom and instruction Pr 1:7
complacency of f-s will destroy Pr 1:32
whoever spreads slander is a f. Pr 10:18
but f-s die for lack of sense. Pr 10:21
shameful conduct is pleasure for a f, Pr 10:23
A f-'s way is right in his own eyes, Pr 12:15
A f-'s displeasure is known at once, Pr 12:16
but f-s hate to turn from evil. Pr 13:19
stupidity of f-s deceives [them]. Pr 14:8
F-s mock at making restitution, Pr 14:9
A f despises his father's instruction, Pr 15:5
her cubs than a f in his foolishness. Pr 17:12
the father of a f has no joy. Pr 17:21
Even a f is considered wise when Pr 17:28
f does not delight in understanding, Pr 18:2
any f can get himself into a quarrel. Pr 20:3
Wisdom is inaccessible to a f; Pr 24:7
honor is inappropriate for a f. Pr 26:1
Don't answer a f according to Pr 26:4
Answer a f according to his Pr 26:5
more hope for a f than for him. Pr 26:12
who trusts in himself is a f, Pr 28:26
more hope for a f than for him. Pr 29:20
wise man dies just like the f? Ec 2:16
The f folds his arms and Ec 4:5
He does not delight in f-s. Ec 5:4
the wise man have over the f? Ec 6:8
Yet he multiplies words. Ec 10:14
and makes f-s of diviners; Is 44:25
they have played the f. Jr 5:4
The prophet is a f, Hs 9:7
whoever says to his brother, 'F!' Mt 5:22
Blind f-s! For which is greater Mt 23:17
But God said to him, 'You f! Lk 12:20
to be wise, they became f-s Rm 1:22
We are f-s for Christ, but you are 1Co 4:10
put up with f-s since you are so 2Co 11:19
I have become a f; you forced it 2Co 12:11

FOOLED

responded to them: "Are you f too? Jn 7:47

FOOLISH

you f and senseless people? Dt 32:6
said to Saul, "You have been f. 1Sm 13:13
I've been very f, please take 2Sm 24:10
You speak as a f woman speaks, Jb 2:10
but a f son, heartache to his mother. Pr 10:1
f lips will be destroyed. Pr 10:8,10
but a f one tears it down Pr 14:1
A f son is grief to his father Pr 17:25
but a f man consumes them. Pr 21:20
A f scheme is sin, Pr 24:9
the f keep going and are Pr 27:12
wicked, and don't be f. Ec 7:17
They are f children, Jr 4:22
you f and senseless people. Jr 5:21
the equipment of a f shepherd. Zch 11:15
like a f man who built his house on Mt 7:26
of them were f and five were Mt 25:2
God made the world's wisdom f? 1Co 1:20
has chosen the world's f things 1Co 1:27
he must become f so that he can 1Co 3:18
f Galatians! Who has hypnotized you Gl 3:1
And coarse and f talking or Eph 5:4
So don't be f, but understand Eph 5:17
But reject f and ignorant 2Tm 2:23
we too were once f, disobedient Ti 3:3
But avoid f debates, genealogies Ti 3:9
F man! Are you willing to learn Jms 2:20

FOOLISHLY

A quick-tempered man acts f, Pr 14:17
I am talking f—I also dare: 2Co 11:21

FOOLISHNESS

counsel of Ahithophel into f! 2Sm 15:31
and festering because of my f. Ps 38:5
You know my f, and my guilty Ps 69:5
but the f of fools produces f. Pr 14:24
her cubs than a fool in his f. Pr 17:12
A man's own f leads him astray, Pr 19:3
F is tangled up in the heart of Pr 22:15
a fool according to his f, Pr 26:4,5
not separate his f from him. Pr 27:22
For a fool speaks f and his mind Is 32:6
blasphemy, pride, and f. Mk 7:22
the message of the cross is f, 1Co 1:18
because God's f is wiser than 1Co 1:25
Spirit, because it is f to him; 1Co 2:14
of this world is f with God, 1Co 3:19
put up with a little f from me. 2Co 11:1

FOOT

Take your sandals off your **feet**,	Ex 3:5
on the big toe of his right f.	Lv 14:14
and your **feet** did not swell these	Dt 8:4
all the land where you set f,	Dt 11:25
In time their f will slip,	Dt 32:35
the sole of your f treads,	Jos 1:3
their **feet** touched the water	Jos 3:15
Remove the sandals from your **feet**,	Jos 5:15
where you have set f will be an	Jos 14:9
uncovered his **feet**, and lay down.	Ru 3:7
son who is lame in both **feet**.	2Sm 9:3
to your house and wash your **feet**.	2Sm 11:8
the sole of his f to the top of	2Sm 14:25
had not taken care of his **feet**,	2Sm 19:24
hand and six toes on each f	2Sm 21:20
He makes my **feet** like ... deer	2Sm 22:34
they fall beneath my **feet**.	2Sm 22:39
developed a disease in his **feet**.	1Kg 15:23
to the blind and **feet** to the lame.	Jb 29:15
You put everything under his **feet**:	Ps 8:6
they pierced my hands and my **feet**.	Ps 22:16
My f stands on level ground;	Ps 26:12
You have set my **feet** in a spacious	Ps 31:8
and set my **feet** on a rock,	Ps 40:2
and nations under our **feet**.	Ps 47:3
does not allow our **feet** to slip.	Ps 66:9
as for me, my **feet** almost slipped;	Ps 73:2
strike your f against a stone.	Ps 91:12
from tears, my **feet** from stumbling	Ps 116:8
I have kept my **feet** from every	Ps 119:101
is a lamp for my **feet** and a light	Ps 119:105
will not allow your f to slip;	Ps 121:3
their **feet** run toward trouble	Pr 1:16
your f will not stumble.	Pr 3:23
Her **feet** go down to death;	Pr 5:5
signals with his **feet**, and gestures	Pr 6:13
feet eager to run to evil,	Pr 6:18
her **feet** do not stay at home.	Pr 7:11
cuts off his own **feet**	Pr 26:6
How beautiful are your sandaled **feet**,	Sg 7:1
From the sole of the f even to	Is 1:6
with two he covered his **feet**,	Is 6:2
remove the sandals from your **feet**,	Is 20:2
on the mountains are the **feet** of	Is 52:7
up the waters with your **feet**,	Ezk 32:2
its **feet** were partly iron and	Dn 2:33
feet like the gleam of polished	Dn 10:6
are the dust beneath His **feet**.	Nah 1:3
the **feet** of one bringing good news	Nah 1:15
He makes my **feet** like	Hab 3:19
On that day His **feet** will stand on	Zch 14:4
strike your f against a stone	Mt 4:6
dust off your **feet** when you leave	Mt 10:14
f causes your downfall, cut it off	Mt 18:8
him up hand and f, and throw him	Mt 22:13
put Your enemies under Your **feet**	Mt 22:44
to wash His **feet** with her tears.	Lk 7:38
sitting at Jesus' **feet**, dressed and	Lk 8:35
showed them His hands and **feet**.	Lk 24:40
anointed Jesus' **feet**, and wiped	Jn 12:3
began to wash His disciples' **feet**	Jn 13:5
ought to wash one another's **feet**.	Jn 13:14
and at once his **feet** and ankles	Ac 3:7
laid them at the apostles' **feet**.	Ac 4:35
Take the sandals off your **feet**,	Ac 7:33
man without strength in his **feet**,	Ac 14:8
belt, tied his own **feet** and hands	Ac 21:11
Their **feet** are swift to shed blood	Rm 3:15
welcome are the **feet** of those who	Rm 10:15
soon crush Satan under your **feet**.	Rm 16:20
If the f should say, "Because	1Co 12:15
all His enemies under His **feet**.	1Co 15:25
under His **feet** and appointed Him	Eph 1:22
and your **feet** sandaled with	Eph 6:15
everything under his **feet**.	Heb 2:8
make straight paths for your **feet**,	Heb 12:13
His **feet** like fine bronze fired in	Rv 1:15
I fell at his **feet** to worship him,	Rv 19:10

FOOTPRINTS

but Your f were unseen.	Ps 77:19

FOOTSTEPS

follow in the f of the faith our	Rm 4:12
same spirit and in the same f?	2Co 12:18

FOOTSTOOL

and as a f for our God.	1Ch 28:2
bow in worship at His f.	Ps 99:5
I make Your enemies Your f.	Ps 110:1
and earth is My f.	Is 66:1
abandoned His f in the day of	Lm 2:1
the earth, because it is His f;	Mt 5:35
I make Your enemies Your f.	Lk 20:43
I make Your enemies Your f.	Ac 2:35
is My throne, and earth My f.	Ac 7:49
I make Your enemies Your f?	Heb 1:13

His enemies are made His **f**.   Heb 10:13
Sit here on the floor by my **f**,   Jms 2:3

FORBID

shape of anything He has **f-den** you.   Dt 4:23
You know it's **f-den** for a Jewish   Ac 10:28
do not **f** speaking in {other}   1Co 14:39
They **f** marriage and demand   1Tm 4:3

FORBIDDEN (adj)

you are to consider the fruit **f**.   Lv 19:23
will rescue you from a **f** woman,   Pr 2:16
the lips of the **f** woman drip   Pr 5:3
with a **f** woman or embrace   Pr 5:20
will keep you from a **f** woman,   Pr 7:5
mouth of the **f** woman is a deep   Pr 22:14
and a **f** woman is a narrow well;   Pr 23:27

FORCE (n)

in front of the Israelite **f-s**,   Ex 14:19
All these kings joined **f-s**;   Jos 11:5
I'll use **f** against you.   Neh 13:21
violent have been seizing it by **f**.   Mt 11:12
and the **f-s** of Hades will not   Mt 16:18
Don't take money from anyone by **f**   Lk 3:14
take Him by **f** to make Him king,   Jn 6:15
the elemental **f-s** of the world.   Gl 4:3
weak and bankrupt elemental **f-s**?   Gl 4:9
against the spiritual **f-s** of evil   Eph 6:12
the elemental **f-s** of the world,   Col 2:8,20
it is never in **f** while the   Heb 9:17

FORCE (v)

So I **f-d** myself to offer the burnt   1Sm 13:12
I **f-d** them to take an oath   Neh 13:25
And if anyone **f-s** you to go one   Mt 5:41
They **f-d** this man to carry His   Mt 27:32
become a fool; you **f-d** it on me.   2Co 12:11

FORCED (adj)

oppress them with **f** labor.   Ex 1:11
will become **f** laborers for you   Dt 20:11
Canaanites ... are **f** laborers.   Jos 16:10
the Canaanites serve as **f** labor   Jdg 1:28
Adoram was in charge of **f** labor;   2Sm 20:24
Solomon drafted **f** laborers from   1Kg 5:13
Solomon imposed **f** labor on them;   1Kg 9:21
consigned to **f** labor on earth?   Jb 7:1
laziness will lead to **f** labor.   Pr 12:24
men will be put to **f** labor.   Is 31:8

FORD

and crossed the **f** of Jabbok.   Gn 32:22
captured the **f-s** of the Jordan   Jdg 12:5
Don't spend the night at the ... **f**   2Sm 17:16
The **f-s** have been seized, the   Jr 51:32

FOREFATHER

brought your **f-s** up from the land   1Sm 12:6
soil that He gave to their **f-s**.   1Kg 14:15
Let his **f-s'** guilt be remembered   Ps 109:14
that God made with your **f-s**,   Ac 3:25
I am the God of your **f-s**   Ac 7:32
neither our **f-s** nor we have been   Ac 15:10
our **f** according to the flesh,   Rm 4:1
The **f-s** are theirs, and from them   Rm 9:5
a clear conscience as my **f-s** did,   2Tm 1:3
still within his **f** when Melchizedek   Heb 7:10

FOREHEAD

and as a reminder on your **f**,   Ex 13:9
It is always to be on his **f**,   Ex 28:38
let them be a symbol on your **f**.   Dt 6:8
hit the Philistine on his **f**.   1Sm 17:49
your **f** as hard as their **f-s**.   Ezk 3:8
a mark on the **f-s** of the men who   Ezk 9:4
slaves of our God on their **f-s**.   Rv 7:3
not have God's seal on their **f-s**.   Rv 9:4
on his right hand or on his **f**,   Rv 13:16
name written on their **f-s**.   Rv 14:1
a mark on his **f** or on his hand,   Rv 14:9
On her **f** a cryptic name was   Rv 17:5
mark on their **f-s** or their hands.   Rv 20:4
His name will be on their **f-s**.   Rv 22:4

FOREIGN

Get rid of the **f** gods that are   Gn 35:2
become a stranger in a **f** land.   Ex 2:22
the same law for the **f** resident   Lv 24:22
whether native or **f** resident,   Nm 15:30
and loves the **f** resident,   Dt 10:18
not deny justice to a **f** resident   Dt 24:17
get rid of the **f** gods that are   Jos 24:23
loved many **f** women in addition   1Kg 11:1
and I drank **f** waters.   2Kg 19:24
marrying **f** women   Ezr 10:2
must not bow down to a **f** god.   Ps 81:9
people who spoke a **f** language   Ps 114:1
sing the LORD's song on **f** soil?   Ps 137:4
speech and in a **f** language.   Is 28:11
and the **f** resident is exploited   Ezk 22:7

seems to be a preacher of f deities   Ac 17:18
and put f armies to flight.   Heb 11:34

FOREIGNER

This one came here as a f,   Gn 19:9
Abraham lived as a f in the land   Gn 21:34
the Passover: no f may eat it.   Ex 12:43
feels to be a f because you were f-s   Ex 23:9
you are only f-s and temporary   Lv 25:23
must love the f, since you were f-s   Dt 10:19
or you may sell it to a f.   Dt 14:21
are not to set a f over you,   Dt 17:15
You may charge a f interest,   Dt 23:20
notice me, although I am a f?   Ru 2:10
Even for the f who is not of   1Kg 8:41
For we are f-s and sojourners   1Ch 29:15
I am a f in their sight.   Jb 19:15
F-s submit to me grudgingly;   Ps 18:44
For I am a f residing with You,   Ps 39:12
Jacob lived as a f in the land   Ps 105:23
set me free from the grasp of f-s   Ps 144:7
The LORD protects f-s and helps   Ps 146:9
get collateral if it is for f-s.   Pr 20:16; 27:13
They are in league with f-s.   Is 2:6
F-s will build up your walls,   Is 60:10
to strangers, our houses to f-s.   Lm 5:2
No f, uncircumcised in heart   Ezk 44:9
while f-s entered his gate   Ob 11
who deny {justice to} the f.   Mal 3:5
as a burial place for f-s.   Mt 27:7
give glory to God except this f?   Lk 17:18
and the f-s residing there   Ac 17:21
the speaker will be a f to me.   1Co 14:11
by the lips of f-s, I will speak   1Co 14:21
are no longer f-s and strangers,   Eph 2:19
he stayed as a f in the land   Heb 11:9
that they were f-s and temporary   Heb 11:13

FOREKNEW

For those He f He also   Rm 8:29
rejected His people whom He f.   Rm 11:2

FOREKNOWLEDGE

to God's determined plan and f,   Ac 2:23
according to the f of God the   1Pt 1:2

FORERUNNER

entered there on our behalf as a f,   Heb 6:20

FORESAW

the Scripture f that God would   Gl 3:8

FORESKIN

circumcise the flesh of your f   Gn 17:11
100 Philistine f-s,   1Sm 18:25
for the price of 100 Philistine f-s.   2Sm 3:14
remove the f of your hearts,   Jr 4:4

FOREST

It is a f; clear it   Jos 17:18
and that day the f claimed more   2Sm 18:8
House of the F of Lebanon.   1Kg 7:2; 10:17
every animal of the f is Mine,   Ps 50:10
trees of the f will shout for   Ps 96:12
how large a f a small fire   Jms 3:5

FORETOLD

and f the good news to Abraham,   Gl 3:8
the words f by the apostles   Jd 17

FOREVER

tree of life, and eat, and live f.   Gn 3:22
will not remain with mankind f,   Gn 6:3
This is My name f;   Ex 3:15
The LORD will reign f and ever!   Ex 15:18
and they will inherit {it} f.   Ex 32:13
to us and our children f,   Dt 29:29
house would walk before Me f,   1Sm 2:30
your throne will be established f.   2Sm 7:16
Your name will be exalted f,   2Sm 7:26
to David and his descendants f.   2Sm 22:51
to put My name there f;   1Kg 9:3
and to minister before Him f.   1Ch 15:2
Remember His covenant f   1Ch 16:15
His faithful love endures f.   1Ch 16:34
His faithful love endures f   2Ch 5:13; 7:3
establish My name f in this temple 2Ch 33:7
I give up! I will not live f.   Jb 7:16
But the LORD sits enthroned f;   Ps 9:7
afflicted will not perish f.   Ps 9:18
us from this generation f.   Ps 12:7
to David and his descendants f.   Ps 18:50
the LORD is pure, enduring f;   Ps 19:9
LORD sits enthroned, King f.   Ps 29:10
Get up! Don't reject us f!   Ps 44:23
Your throne, God, is f and ever;   Ps 45:6
that he may live f and not see   Ps 49:9
Why have You rejected {us} f,   Ps 74:1
Will You be angry f?   Ps 79:5
Will You be angry with us f?   Ps 85:5
and will honor Your name f.   Ps 86:12
But You, LORD, are exalted f.   Ps 92:8

F, You are a priest like   Ps 110:4
His faithful love endures f.   Ps 118:1
Your decrees are righteous f.   Ps 119:144
cannot be shaken; it remains f.   Ps 125:1
This is My resting place f;   Ps 132:14
praise Your name f and ever.   Ps 145:1
He remains faithful f,   Ps 146:6
Truthful lips endure f, but a lying   Pr 12:19
for wealth is not f;   Pr 27:24
comes, but the earth remains f.   Ec 1:4
that all God does will last f;   Ec 3:14
the word of our God remains f.   Is 40:8
But My salvation will last f,   Is 51:6
and Exalted One who lives f,   Is 57:15
I will not be angry f.   Jr 3:12
to be a nation before Me f.   Jr 31:36
fall asleep f and never wake   Jr 51:39
Lord will not reject {us} f.   Lm 3:31
set My sanctuary among them f.   Ezk 37:26
and I will dwell among them f.   Ezk 43:9
like the stars f and ever.   Dn 12:3
will take you to be My wife f.   Hs 2:19
But Judah will be inhabited f,   Jl 3:20
of Yahweh our God f and ever.   Mc 4:5
over the house of Jacob f,   Lk 1:33
Abraham and his descendants f.   Lk 1:55
of this bread he will live f.   Jn 6:51
that the Messiah will remain f.   Jn 12:34
Counselor to be with you f.   Jn 14:16
His righteousness endures f.   2Co 9:9
whom be the glory f and ever.   Gl 1:5
to all generations, f and ever.   Eph 3:21
and Father be glory f and ever.   Php 4:20
throne, O God, is f and ever   Heb 1:8
You are a priest f in the order   Heb 5:6
a "high priest f in the order   Heb 6:20
You are a priest f in the order   Heb 7:17
Son, who has been perfected f.   Heb 7:28
one sacrifice for sins f,   Heb 10:12
same yesterday, today, and f.   Heb 13:8
the word of the Lord endures f.   1Pt 1:25
who does God's will remains f.   1Jn 2:17
before all time, now, and f.   Jd 25
I am alive f and ever, and I   Rv 1:18
and to the Lamb, f and ever!   Rv 5:13
and He will reign f and ever!   Rv 11:15
And they will reign f and ever.   Rv 22:5

FOREVERMORE
appointed the blessing—life f.   Ps 133:3

FOREWARNED
you have been f, be on your guard,   2Pt 3:17

FORFEITS
whole world, yet loses or f himself?   Lk 9:25

FORGET
did not remember Joseph; he f-got   Gn 40:23
has made me f all my hardship   Gn 41:51
Be careful not to f the covenant   Dt 4:23
be careful not to f the LORD who   Dt 6:12
you f-got the God who brought you   Dt 32:18
they f-got the LORD their God and   Jdg 3:7
the destiny of all who f God;   Jb 8:13
all the nations that f God.   Ps 9:17
oppressed will not ... be f-gotten;   Ps 9:18
Do not f the afflicted.   Ps 10:12
long will You continually f me?   Ps 13:1
Why have You f-gotten me?   Ps 42:9
If we had f-gotten the name   Ps 44:20
otherwise, my people will f.   Ps 59:11
Has God f-gotten to be gracious?   Ps 77:9
in God and not f God's works,   Ps 78:7
They f-got what He had done,   Ps 78:11
and do not f all His benefits.   Ps 103:2
They soon f-got His works   Ps 106:13
for I do not f Your commands.   Ps 119:176
If I f you, Jerusalem, may my
   right hand f {its skill}.   Ps 137:5
of her youth and f-s the covenant   Pr 2:17
My son, don't f my teaching, but   Pr 3:1
don't f or turn away from the   Pr 4:5
will drink, f what is decreed   Pr 31:5
so that he can f his poverty   Pr 31:7
the memory of them is f-gotten.   Ec 9:5
The Lord has f-gotten me!   Is 49:14
Can a woman f her nursing child   Is 49:15
Even if these f, yet I will not f you.   Is 49:15
For you will f the shame of your   Is 54:4
Can a young woman f her jewelry   Jr 2:32
Yet My people have f-gotten Me.   Jr 18:15
My people to f My name as their   Jr 23:27
I have f-gotten what happiness is.   Lm 3:17
Israel has f-gotten his Maker   Hs 8:14
Yet not one of them is f-gotten   Lk 12:6
f-ting what is behind and reaching   Php 3:13
He will not f your work and   Heb 6:10

you have f-gotten the exhortation　Heb 12:5
and right away f-s what kind of　Jms 1:24
has f-gotten the cleansing from his　2Pt 1:9

FORGETFUL

and is not a f hearer but a doer　Jms 1:25

FORGIVE

please f the transgression of　Gn 50:17
Please f my sin once more and　Ex 10:17
if You would only f their sin.　Ex 32:32
f-ing wrongdoing, rebellion, and　Ex 34:7
their behalf, and they will be f-n.　Lv 4:20
f-ing wrongdoing and rebellion.　Nm 14:18
May You hear and f.　1Kg 8:30
and the Lord would not f.　2Kg 24:4
f their sin, and heal their land.　2Ch 7:14
But You are a f-ing God, gracious　Neh 9:17
one whose transgression is f-n,　Ps 32:1
kind and ready to f, abundant in　Ps 86:5
He f-s all your sin; He heals all　Ps 103:3
our God, for He will freely f.　Is 55:7
For I will f their wrongdoing　Jr 31:34
and I will f all the wrongs they　Jr 33:8
Then I will f their wrongdoing　Jr 36:3
Lord, hear! Lord, f!　Dn 9:19
F all (our) sin and accept what　Hs 14:2
I said, "Lord God, please f!　Am 7:2
And f us our debts, as we also
　have f-n our debtors.　Mt 6:12
if you f people ... Father will f you　Mt 6:14
against the Spirit will not be f-n.　Mt 12:31
sin against me and I f him?　Mt 18:21
and f-gave him the loan.　Mt 18:27
I f-gave you all that debt because　Mt 18:32
Son, your sins are f-n.　Mk 2:5
Who can f sins but God alone?　Mk 2:7
authority on earth to f sins,　Mk 2:10
against anyone, f him, so that　Mk 11:25
F, and you will be f-n.　Lk 6:37
I suppose the one he f-gave more.　Lk 7:43
But the one who is f-n little,　Lk 7:47
Who is this man who even f-s sins?　Lk 7:49
and if he repents, f him.　Lk 17:3
Father, f them, because　Lk 23:34
If you f the sins of any, they
　are f-n them;　Jn 20:23
of your heart may be f-n you.　Ac 8:22
whose lawless acts are f-n and　Rm 4:7
now you should f and comfort him　2Co 2:7

Now to whom you f anything,　2Co 2:10
what I have f-n, if I have f-n　2Co 2:10
f-ing one another, just as God
　also f-gave you in Christ.　Eph 4:32
and f-gave us all our trespasses.　Col 2:13
and f-ing one another　Col 3:13
Just as the Lord has f-n you,　Col 3:13
committed sins, he will be f-n.　Jms 5:15
and righteous to f us our sins　1Jn 1:9
sins have been f-n on account of　1Jn 2:12

FORGIVENESS

You there is f, so that You may　Ps 130:4
Compassion and f belong to the　Dn 9:9
shed for many for the f of sins.　Mt 26:28
baptism of repentance for the f of　Mk 1:4
against the Holy Spirit never has f,　Mk 3:29
through the f of their sins.　Lk 1:77
repentance for f of sins would be　Lk 24:47
to Israel, and f of sins.　Ac 5:31
in Him will receive f of sins.　Ac 10:43
f of sins is being proclaimed　Ac 13:38
they may receive f of sins and a　Ac 26:18
through His blood, the f of our　Eph 1:7
have redemption, the f of sins.　Col 1:14
shedding of blood there is no f.　Heb 9:22

FORK

basins, meat f-s, and firepans;　Ex 27:3
whatever the meat f brought up.　1Sm 2:14
signpost at the f in the road to　Ezk 21:19

FORM (n)

he sees the f of the Lord.　Nm 12:8
words, but didn't see a f;　Dt 4:12
He had no f or splendor that we　Is 53:2
He appeared in a different f to　Mk 16:12
and you haven't seen His f.　Jn 5:37
in its current f is passing away　1Co 7:31
existing in the f of God, did not　Php 2:6
by assuming the f of a slave,　Php 2:7
Stay away from every f of evil.　1Th 5:22
holding to the f of religion but　2Tm 3:5
not the actual f of those　Heb 10:1

FORM (v)

Then the Lord God f-ed the man out　Gn 2:7
that You f-ed me like clay.　Jb 10:9
the One who f-ed the eye not see?　Ps 94:9
His hands f-ed the dry land.　Ps 95:5
Your hands made me and f-ed me;　Ps 119:73

when I was **f-ed** in the depths of   Ps 139:15
I was **f-ed** before ancient times,   Pr 8:23
How can what is **f-ed** say about
   the one who **f-ed** it,   Is 29:16
and the One who **f-ed** you, Israel   Is 43:1
No god was **f-ed** before Me, and   Is 43:10
Redeemer who **f-ed** you from   Is 44:24
I **f** light and create darkness,   Is 45:7
Does clay say to the one **f-ing** it;   Is 45:9
He **f-ed** the earth and made it;   Is 45:18
No weapon **f-ed** against you will   Is 54:17
you before I **f-ed** you in the womb;   Jr 1:5
He is the One who **f-ed** all   Jr 10:16; 51:19
the One who **f-s** the mountains,   Am 4:13
and **f-ed** the spirit of man within   Zch 12:1
Will what is **f-ed** say to the
   one who **f-ed** it,   Rm 9:20
you until Christ is **f-ed** in you.   Gl 4:19

FORMATION
man in battle **f** before the LORD   Nm 32:29
over in battle **f** ahead of your   Dt 3:18
over in battle **f** ahead of your   Jos 1:14
went in battle **f** in front   Jos 4:12
and shouted to the battle **f-s:**   1Sm 17:8

FORMER
the **f** acts of Your faithful love   Ps 89:49
Why were the **f** days better than   Ec 7:10
I will go back to my **f** husband,   Hs 2:7
saw this house in its **f** glory?   Hg 2:3
heard about my **f** way of life   Gl 1:13
took off your **f** way of life,   Eph 4:22
the desires of your **f** ignorance   1Pt 1:14

FORMERLY
He who **f** persecuted us now   Gl 1:23
one who was **f** a blasphemer,   1Tm 1:13
and those who **f** received the   Heb 4:6

FORMLESS
Now the earth was **f** and empty,   Gn 1:2
Your eyes saw me when I was **f**;   Ps 139:16
earth, and it was **f** and empty.   Jr 4:23

FORMULA
for yourselves using its **f.**   Ex 30:37

FORSAKE
He will not leave you or **f** you.   Dt 31:6
I will not leave you or **f** you.   Jos 1:5
who has not **f-n** his kindness to   Ru 2:20

but if you **f** Him, He will reject   1Ch 28:9
leave you or **f** you until all   1Ch 28:20
my God, why have You **f-n** me?   Ps 22:1
If his sons **f** My instruction and   Ps 89:30
The LORD will not **f** His people   Ps 94:14
and I will not **f** them.   Is 42:16
idols **f** faithful love,   Jnh 2:8
My God, why have You **f-n** Me?   Mt 27:46
My God, why have You **f-n** Me?   Mk 15:34
will never leave you or **f** you.   Heb 13:5

FORSAKEN (adj)
children of the **f** one will be   Is 54:1

FORTH
The earth brought **f** vegetation: Gn 1:12
I was brought **f** before the   Pr 8:25
the earth brings **f** its growth,   Is 61:11
will put **f** your branches and   Ezk 36:8
Break **f** and shout, you who are   Gl 4:27

FORTIFICATION
come trembling from their **f.**   Ps 18:45
Make their **f** desolate;   Ps 69:25
Man the **f-s!** Watch the road!   Nah 2:1

FORTIFIED
and the cities are large and **f.**   Nm 13:28
are large, **f** to the heavens.   Dt 1:28
large cities **f** to the heavens.   Dt 9:1
Jericho was strongly **f** because   Jos 6:1
and he **f** cities in Judah.   2Ch 11:5
Asa built **f** cities in Judah.   2Ch 14:6
man's wealth is his **f** city;   Pr 10:15; 18:11
{harder to reach} than a **f** city,   Pr 18:19
are {now} **f** and inhabited.   Ezk 36:35

FORTRESS
The LORD is my rock, my **f,**   2Sm 22:2
royal throne in the **f** at Susa,   Est 1:2
The LORD is my rock, my **f,**   Ps 18:2
a mountain **f** to save me.   Ps 31:2
for You are my rock and **f.**   Ps 71:3
refuge and my **f,** my God, in whom   Ps 91:2
prosperity within your **f-es.**   Ps 122:7
I was in the **f** city of Susa,   Dn 8:2

FORTUNATE
see her and declare her **f;**   Sg 6:9
nations will consider you **f,**   Mal 3:12

FORTUNATUS
of Stephanas, **F,** and Achaicus   1Co 16:17

FORTUNE

Then Leah said, "What good f!"	Gn 30:11
tell f-s, interpret omens	Dt 18:10
then He will restore your f-s,	Dt 30:3
LORD restored the f-s of Zion,	Ps 126:1
Restore our f-s, LORD, like	Ps 126:4
Making a f through a lying	Pr 21:6
who prepare a table for F and	Is 65:11
will restore the f-s of My people	Jr 30:3
restore their f-s, they will once	Jr 31:23
I will restore the f-s of Judah	Jr 33:7
will restore the f-s of Jacob and	Ezk 39:25
when I restore the f-s of Judah	Jl 3:1
will restore the f-s of My people	Am 9:14
to them and restore their f-s.	Zph 2:7

FORTUNE-TELLER

Though these nations ... listen to f-s	Dt 18:14
you will not have any more f-s.	Mc 5:12

FORTUNE-TELLING

profit for her owners by f.	Ac 16:16

FORWARD

control of David from that day f.	1Sm 16:13
started f to attack him,	1Sm 17:48
Let your eyes look f;	Pr 4:25
They went backward and not f.	Jr 7:24
himself looking f to the kingdom	Mk 15:43
who were looking f to the	Lk 2:38
and reaching f to what is ahead	Php 3:13
he was looking f to the city	Heb 11:10

FOSTER

Kings will be your f fathers,	Is 49:23

FOUL

My wounds are f and festering	Ps 38:5

FOUND see also FIND

the day it was f-ed until now.	Ex 9:18
everything in it—You f-ed them.	Ps 89:11
The LORD f-ed the earth by wisdom	Pr 3:19
and f-s a town with injustice!	Hab 2:12

FOUNDATION

He will lay its f {at the cost of}	Jos 6:26
the f-s of the world were exposed	2Sm 22:16
The f of the LORD's temple was	1Kg 6:37
he laid its f, and at the cost	1Kg 16:34
even though the f of the LORD's	Ezr 3:6
What supports its f-s?	Jb 38:6
When the f-s are destroyed, what	Ps 11:3

for He laid its f on the seas	Ps 24:2
His f is on the holy mountains.	Ps 87:1
justice are the f of Your throne	Ps 89:14
are the f of His throne.	Ps 97:2
established the earth on its f-s;	Ps 104:5
He laid out the f-s of the earth.	Pr 8:29
precious cornerstone, a sure f;	Is 28:16
restore the f-s laid long ago;	Is 58:12
I sank to the f-s of the mountains	Jnh 2:6
from the day the f of the LORD's	Hg 2:18
because its f was on the rock.	Mt 7:25
secret from the f of the world.	Mt 13:35
you from the f of the world.	Mt 25:34
shed since the f of the world	Lk 11:50
he has laid the f and cannot	Lk 14:29
loved Me before the world's f.	Jn 17:24
that the f-s of the jail were	Ac 16:26
building on someone else's f,	Rm 15:20
master builder I have laid a f,	1Co 3:10
lay any other f than what has	1Co 3:11
builds on the f with gold,	1Co 3:12
our preaching is without f,	1Co 15:14
before the f of the world,	Eph 1:4
built on the f of the apostles	Eph 2:20
the pillar and f of the truth.	1Tm 3:15
God's solid f stands firm,	2Tm 2:19
laying again the f of repentance	Heb 6:1
looking ... to the city that has f-s,	Heb 11:10
destined before the f of the world,	1Pt 1:20
written from the f of the world	Rv 13:8
of life from the f of the world	Rv 17:8
city wall had 12 f-s, and on them	Rv 21:14

FOUNTAIN

for with You is life's f.	Ps 36:9
the LORD from the f of Israel.	Ps 68:26
Let your f be blessed, and take	Pr 5:18
when the f-s of the ocean gushed	Pr 8:28
instruction is a f of life,	Pr 13:14
of the LORD is a f of life,	Pr 14:27
Insight is a f of life for its	Pr 16:22
a flowing river, a f of wisdom.	Pr 18:4
abandoned Me, the f of living water,	Jr 2:13
water, my eyes a f of tears, I	Jr 9:1
On that day a f will be opened	Zch 13:1

FOUR

became the source of f rivers.	Gn 2:10
that walk on all f-s are to be	Lv 11:20
and struck the f corners of the	Jb 1:19

never satisfied; f never say | Pr 30:15
are beyond me; f I can't | Pr 30:18
it cannot bear up under f: | Pr 30:21
F things on earth are small, | Pr 30:24
even f are stately in their walk | Pr 30:29
The form of f living creatures | Ezk 1:5
Each one had f faces: | Ezk 10:14
I see f men, not tied, walking | Dn 3:25
F huge beasts came up from | Dn 7:3
F conspicuous horns came up | Dn 8:8
for three crimes, even f, | Am 1:3
and saw f chariots coming | Zch 6:1
His elect from the f winds, | Mt 24:31
I'll pay back f times as much! | Lk 19:8
'There are still f more months, | Jn 4:35
been in the tomb f days. | Jn 11:17
to the earth by its f corners. | Ac 10:11
the throne were f living creatures | Rv 4:6
f angels standing at the f corners | Rv 7:1

FOUR-FOOTED

All the f animals that walk on | Lv 11:27
In it were all the f animals | Ac 10:12
mortal man, birds, f animals, | Rm 1:23

FOURTH

to the third and f generation. | Ex 34:7
to them over a f of the earth, | Rv 6:8

FOWL

birds, every f, and everything | Gn 7:14

FOWLER

like a bird from a f-'s trap. | Pr 6:5

FOX

he went out and caught 300 f-es. | Jdg 15:4
even if a f climbed up what they | Neh 4:3
Catch the f-es for us—the little f-es | Sg 2:15
F-es have dens and birds of the | Mt 8:20
Jesus told him, "F-es have dens | Lk 9:58
Go tell that f, 'Look! | Lk 13:32

FRAGRANCE

The f of your perfume is | Sg 1:3
vines give off their f. | Sg 2:13
The f of your garments is like | Sg 4:11
and the f of your breath like | Sg 7:8
his f, like {the forest of} Lebanon. | Hs 14:6
filled with the f of the oil. | Jn 12:3
we are the f of Christ among | 2Co 2:15

FRAGRANT

must burn f incense on it; | Ex 30:7
with the f smoke of rams; | Ps 66:15
from every f powder of the | Sg 3:6
jar of very expensive f oil. | Mt 26:7
and expensive f oil of nard. | Mk 14:3
an alabaster flask of f oil | Lk 7:37
Mary took a pound of f oil | Jn 12:3
sacrificial and f offering to God. | Eph 5:2
what you provided—a f offering, | Php 4:18
all kinds of f wood products; | Rv 18:12

FRAME

a three-inch f all around it | Ex 25:25
put {them} on the carrying f. | Nm 4:10
were three rows of window f-s, | 1Kg 7:4
the carts: They had f-s; | 1Kg 7:28
Ahaz cut off the f-s of the | 2Kg 16:17

FRANKINCENSE

spices and pure f are to be in | Ex 30:34
olive oil on it, put f on it, | Lv 2:1
not put olive oil or f on it, | Lv 5:11
of myrrh and the hill of f. | Sg 4:6
carry gold and f and proclaim | Is 60:6
gold, f, and myrrh. | Mt 2:11
spice, incense, myrrh, and f; | Rv 18:13

FRAUD

obtained by f will dwindle, | Pr 13:11
Food gained by f is sweet to a | Pr 20:17
full of all deceit and all f, | Ac 13:10

FREE (adj)

You are f to eat from any tree | Gn 2:16
is a doe set f that bears | Gn 49:21
seventh year he is to leave as a f | Ex 21:2
must set him f in the seventh | Dt 15:12
slave is set f from his master | Jb 3:19
cried to You and were set f; | Ps 22:5
to set f those condemned to die | Ps 102:20
Set me f and rescue me from the | Ps 144:11
to set the oppressed f, and to tear off | Is 58:6
You have received f of charge; | Mt 10:8
"Then the sons are f," Jesus told | Mt 17:26
blind, to set f the oppressed, | Lk 4:18
you are f of your disability. | Lk 13:12
and the truth will set you f. | Jn 8:32
if the Son sets you f, you really
 will be f. | Jn 8:36
you were f from allegiance to | Rm 6:20

dies, she is f from that law.	Rm 7:3
Jesus has set you f from the law	Rm 8:2
you can become f, by all means	1Co 7:21
she is f to be married to anyone	1Co 7:39
Am I not f? Am I not an apostle?	1Co 9:1
and offer it f of charge,	1Co 9:18
of God to you f of charge?	2Co 11:7
slave or f, male or female;	Gl 3:28
and the other by a f woman.	Gl 4:22
does, slave or f, he will receive	Eph 6:8
Scythian, slave and f;	Col 3:11
life should be f from the love	Heb 13:5
{live} as f people, but don't	1Pt 2:16
and has set us f from our sins	Rv 1:5
rich and poor, f and slave	Rv 13:16

FREE (v)

He f-s me from my enemies.	2Sm 22:49
You f-d me from affliction;	Ps 4:1
F me from prison so that I can	Ps 142:7
who f-s His servant David from	Ps 144:10
The LORD f-s prisoners.	Ps 146:7
who has died is f-d from sin's	Rm 6:7
and f those who were held in	Heb 2:15

FREEDMAN

as a slave is the Lord's f.	1Co 7:22

FREEDOM

and proclaim f in the land	Lv 25:10
and enabled you to live in f.	Lv 26:13
to proclaim ... f to the prisoners;	Is 61:1
to proclaim f to the captives	Lk 4:18
the glorious f of God's children	Rm 8:21
For why is my f judged by	1Co 10:29
Spirit of the Lord is, there is f.	2Co 3:17
Christ has liberated us into f.	Gl 5:1
don't use this f as an opportunity	Gl 5:13
will be judged by the law of f.	Jms 2:12
but don't use your f as a way to	1Pt 2:16

FREELY

He distributes f to the poor;	Ps 112:9
person gives f, yet gains more	Pr 11:24
our God, for He will f forgive.	Is 55:7
I will f love them, for My anger	Hs 14:4
are justified f by His grace	Rm 3:24
what has been f given to us by	1Co 2:12
out of compulsion but f,	1Pt 5:2

FREEWILL

brought a f offering to the LORD	Ex 35:29
fulfill a vow or as a f offering	Lv 22:21
vow offerings and f offerings,	Dt 12:6
that was given as a f offering.	Ezr 1:6
sacrifice a f offering to You	Ps 54:6
proclaim your f offerings,	Am 4:5

FRESH

then took branches of f poplar,	Gn 30:37
birds be slaughtered over f water	Lv 14:5
juice or eat f grapes or raisins	Nm 6:3
He found a f jawbone of a donkey	Jdg 15:15
tie me up with seven f bowstrings	Jdg 16:7
Since the water will become f,	Ezk 47:9
put new wine into f wineskins,	Mt 9:17
saltwater spring yield f water.	Jms 3:12

FRIEND

as a man speaks with his f.	Ex 33:11
the Archite was the king's f.	1Ch 27:33
descendants of Abraham Your f.	2Ch 20:7
Now when Job's three f-s—Eliphaz	Jb 2:11
My f-s scoff at me as I weep	Jb 16:20
All of my best f-s despise me,	Jb 19:19
as if for my f or brother;	Ps 35:14
My loved ones and f-s stand back	Ps 38:11
Even my f in whom I trusted,	Ps 41:9
When you see a thief, you make f-s	Ps 50:18
darkness is my {only} f.	Ps 88:18
but He is a f to the upright.	Pr 3:32
and a gossip separates f-s.	Pr 16:28
gossips about it separates f-s.	Pr 17:9
A f loves at all times,	Pr 17:17
but there is a f who stays closer	Pr 18:24
Wealth attracts many f-s, but a poor	Pr 19:4
everyone is a f of one who gives	Pr 19:6
Don't make f-s with an angry man,	Pr 22:24
wounds of a f are trustworthy	Pr 27:6
sweetness of a f is better than	Pr 27:9
Don't abandon your f or	Pr 27:10
to a man's jealousy of his f.	Ec 4:4
are rebels, f-s of thieves.	Is 1:23
brother and each against his f,	Is 19:2
descendant of Abraham, My f	Is 41:8
Each one betrays his f;	Jr 9:5
Do not rely on a f; don't trust	Mc 7:5
received in the house of my f-s.	Zch 13:6
a f of tax collectors and	Mt 11:19
He said, "F, your sins are forgiven	Lk 5:20

anything because he is his f,   Lk 11:8
make f-s for yourselves by means   Lk 16:9
day Herod and Pilate became f-s.   Lk 23:12
But the groom's f, who stands by   Jn 3:29
Our f Lazarus has fallen asleep   Jn 11:11
lay down his life for his f-s.   Jn 15:13
You are My f-s if you do what I   Jn 15:14
I have called you f-s, because   Jn 15:15
you are not Caesar's f.   Jn 19:12
any of his f-s from serving him.   Ac 24:23
Greet my dear f   Rm 16:5
our dear f and co-worker,   Phm 1
and he was called God's f.   Jms 2:23
be the world's f becomes God's   Jms 4:4
To my dear f Gaius, whom I love   3Jn 1
The f-s send you greetings.   3Jn 14

FRIENDLY
who speak in f ways   Ps 28:3
they do not speak in f ways,   Ps 35:20

FRIENDSHIP
seek peace or f with them as   Dt 23:6
youth when God's f rested on my   Jb 29:4
not know that f with the world   Jms 4:4

FRIGHTEN
lie down with nothing to f {you}.   Lv 26:6
then You f me with dreams,   Jb 7:14
quiet with no one to f him.   Jr 30:10; 46:27
and no one will f {them}.   Ezk 34:28
I had a dream, and it f-ed me;   Dn 4:5
with no one to f {him}.   Mc 4:4
with nothing to f them away?   Nah 2:11
not being f-ed in any way by your   Php 1:28
do good and aren't f-ed by anything 1Pt 3:6

FRINGES
are but the f of His ways;   Jb 26:14

FROGS
The Nile will swarm with f;   Ex 8:3
and f, which devastated them.   Ps 78:45
Their land was overrun with f,   Ps 105:30
unclean spirits like f   Rv 16:13

FRONDS
take ... palm f, boughs of leafy   Lv 23:40

FRONT
moved from in f of them and   Ex 14:19
inscribed f and back.   Ex 32:15
the LORD passed in f of him   Ex 34:6

before the LORD in f of the veil   Lv 4:6
was written on the f and back;   Ezk 2:10
they are right in f of My face.   Hs 7:2
A fire destroys in f of them,   Jl 2:3
violence are right in f of me.   Hab 1:3
gift there in f of the altar.   Mt 5:24
righteousness in f of people,   Mt 6:1
the f seats in the synagogues,   Mt 23:6
You love the f seat in the   Lk 11:43
Then those in f told him to keep   Lk 18:39
I told Cephas in f of everyone,   Gl 2:14
with eyes in f and in back.   Rv 4:6
gold altar in f of the throne.   Rv 8:3
dragon stood in f of the woman   Rv 12:4

FROST
as fine as f on the ground.   Ex 16:14
gave birth to the f of heaven   Jb 38:29
He scatters f like ashes;   Ps 147:16

FROZEN
and watery expanses are f.   Jb 37:10
of the watery depths is f?   Jb 38:30

FRUIT
f trees ... bearing f with seed in it,   Gn 1:11
took some of its f and ate {it};   Gn 3:6
to consider the f forbidden.   Lv 19:23
Bring back some f from the land.   Nm 13:20
that bears its f in season   Ps 1:3
My f is better than solid gold,   Pr 8:19
The f of the righteous is a tree   Pr 11:30
From the f of his mouth a man's   Pr 18:20
who love it will eat its f.   Pr 18:21
and his f is sweet to my taste.   Sg 2:3
garden and eat its choicest f-s.   Sg 4:16
tree and take hold of its f.   Sg 7:8
will eat the f of their deeds.   Is 3:10
and their f will not fail.   Ezk 47:12
you have eaten the f of lies.   Hs 10:13
your f comes from Me.   Hs 14:8
I destroyed his f above and his   Am 2:9
this: A basket of summer f.   Am 8:1
and there is no f on the vines,   Hab 3:17
the vine will yield its f,   Zch 8:12
produce f consistent with   Mt 3:8
recognize them by their f.   Mt 7:16
but a bad tree produces bad f.   Mt 7:17
doesn't produce good f is cut down Mt 7:19
for a tree is known by its f.   Mt 12:33

who does bear f and yields: Mt 13:23
May no f ever come from you   Mt 21:19
to a nation producing its f.   Mt 21:43
not drink of this f of the vine   Mt 26:29
that does not produce f He removes,   Jn 15:2
that produces f so that it will
    produce more f.   Jn 15:2
and I in him produces much f,   Jn 15:5
go out and produce f and that
    your f should remain,   Jn 15:16
And what f was produced then   Rm 6:21
that we may bear f for God.   Rm 7:4
But the f of the Spirit is love, joy,   Gl 5:22
for the f of the light {results} in   Eph 5:9
but I seek the f that is   Php 4:17
bearing f in every good work   Col 1:10
it yields the f of peace and   Heb 12:11
the f of our lips that confess   Heb 13:15
full of mercy and good f-s,   Jms 3:17
And the f of righteousness is   Jms 3:18
and the land produced its f.   Jms 5:18
tree of life bearing 12 kinds of f,   Rv 22:2

FRUITFUL

blessed them, "Be f, multiply,   Gn 1:22
Be f and multiply and fill the   Gn 9:1
I will make you f and numerous;   Gn 48:4
Joseph is a f vine, a f vine beside   Gn 49:22
But the Israelites were f,   Ex 1:7
make you f and multiply you,   Lv 26:9
LORD made His people very f;   Ps 105:24
will be like a f vine within   Ps 128:3
rain from heaven and f seasons,   Ac 14:17
I might have a f ministry among   Rm 1:13
this means f work for me;   Php 1:22

FRUITLESS

don't participate in the f works of   Eph 5:11
and turned aside to f discussion.   1Tm 1:6
f, twice dead, pulled out   Jd 12

FRUSTRATE

against them to f their plans   Ezr 4:5
He f-s the schemes of the crafty   Jb 5:12
The LORD f-s the counsel of the   Ps 33:10
but He f-s the ways of the wicked   Ps 146:9

FUEL

people are like f for the fire.   Is 9:19
I have given to the fire as f,   Ezk 15:6
You will be f for the fire.   Ezk 21:32

FUGITIVE

will be a f until death.   Pr 28:17
with no one to gather up the f-s.   Jr 49:5
a f from Jerusalem came to me   Ezk 33:21
none of their f-s will escape.   Am 9:1
crossroads to cut off their f-s,   Ob 14

FULFILL

to f a vow or as a freewill offering   Lv 22:21
or promise and not f?   Nm 23:19
does not come true or is not f-ed,   Dt 18:22
Everything was f-ed.   Jos 21:45
I will f My promise to you,   1Kg 6:12
LORD has f-ed what He promised   1Kg 8:20
until 70 years were f-ed.   2Ch 36:21
May the LORD f all your requests   Ps 20:5
I will f my vows before those   Ps 22:25
f-ing my vows day by day.   Ps 61:8
I will f my vows to the LORD   Ps 116:14,18
He f-s the desires of those who   Ps 145:19
today I've f-ed my vows.   Pr 7:14
but f-ed desire is a tree of life.   Pr 13:12
Desire f-ed is sweet to the taste,   Pr 13:19
F what you vow.   Ec 5:4
when I will f the good promises   Jr 33:14
I will f what I have vowed.   Jnh 2:9
Judah; f your vows.   Nah 1:15
took place to f what was spoken   Mt 1:22
through the prophet might be f-ed: Mt 2:15
Jeremiah the prophet was f-ed: Mt 2:17
Nazareth to f what was spoken   Mt 2:23
to f all righteousness.   Mt 3:15
This was to f what was spoken   Mt 4:14
not come to destroy but to f.   Mt 5:17
the prophet Isaiah might be f-ed: Mt 8:17
the prophet Isaiah might be f-ed: Mt 12:17
Isaiah's prophecy is f-ed in them,   Mt 13:14
through the prophet might be f-ed: Mt 13:35
through the prophet might be f-ed: Mt 21:4
Scriptures be f-ed that say it must   Mt 26:54
the prophet Jeremiah was f-ed: Mt 27:9
The time is f-ed, and the kingdom   Mk 1:15
But the Scriptures must be f-ed.   Mk 14:49
to her by the Lord will be f-ed!   Lk 1:45
this Scripture has been f-ed.   Lk 4:21
times of the Gentiles are f-ed.   Lk 21:24
until it is f-ed in the kingdom   Lk 22:16
is written must be f-ed in Me: Lk 22:37
and the Psalms must be f-ed.   Lk 24:44

But this was to f the word of	Jn 12:38
But the Scripture must be f-ed:	Jn 13:18
so that the Scripture may be f-ed.	Jn 17:12
This was to f the words He had	Jn 18:9
{They did this} to f the Scripture	Jn 19:24
that the Scripture might be f-ed,	Jn 19:28
had to be f-ed that the Holy	Ac 1:16
When they had f-ed all	Ac 13:29
but who f-s the law, will judge	Rm 2:27
loves another has f-ed the law.	Rm 13:8
husband should f his marital	1Co 7:3
entire law is f-ed in one statement	Gl 5:14
way you will f the law of Christ	Gl 6:2
f my joy by thinking the same	Php 2:2
f every desire for goodness and	2Th 1:11
an evangelist, f your ministry.	2Tm 4:5
the Scripture was f-ed that says,	Jms 2:23

FULFILLMENT

as well as the f of every vision	Ezk 12:23
about Me is coming to its f.	Lk 22:37
therefore, is the f of the law.	Rm 13:10
of the days of f	Eph 1:10

FULL

not yet reached its f measure.	Gn 15:16
his people, old and f of days.	Gn 35:29
houses f of every good thing	Dt 6:11
you eat and are f, you will	Dt 8:10
I left f, but the LORD has	Ru 1:21
I insist on paying the f price,	1Ch 21:24
David was old and f of days,	1Ch 23:1
short of days and f of trouble.	Jb 14:1
For I am f of words, and my	Jb 32:18
Job died, old and f of days.	Jb 42:17
earth is f of the LORD's unfailing	Ps 33:5
of the land are f of violence.	Ps 74:20
new moon and during the f moon,	Ps 81:3
Our storehouses will be f,	Ps 144:13
than a house f of feasting with	Pr 17:1
A person who is f tramples on a	Pr 27:7
sea, yet the sea is never f.	Ec 1:7
land will be as f of the knowledge	Is 11:9
four rims were f of eyes all	Ezk 1:18
the valley; it was f of bones.	Ezk 37:1
floors will be f of grain,	Jl 2:24
the earth is f of His praise.	Hab 3:3
Bring the f 10 percent into the	Mal 3:10
whole body will be f of light.	Mt 6:22

but inside are f of dead men's	Mt 23:27
to you who are f now, because	Lk 6:25
from the Father, f of grace and	Jn 1:14
men ... f of the Spirit and wisdom,	Ac 6:3
Stephen, f of grace and power	Ac 6:8
f of the Holy Spirit and of	Ac 11:24
that the city was f of idols.	Ac 17:16
more will their f number bring!	Rm 11:12
to Israel until the f number of	Rm 11:25
Already you are f!	1Co 4:8
Put on the f armor of God so	Eph 6:11
have received everything in f,	Php 4:18
and deserving of f acceptance:	1Tm 1:15
and deserves f acceptance.	1Tm 4:9
a true heart in f assurance of	Heb 10:22
for one another at f strength,	1Pt 4:8
but you may receive a f reward.	2Jn 8
which is mixed f strength in the	Rv 14:10

FULLNESS

grace after grace from His f,	Jn 1:16
come in the f of the blessing	Rm 15:29
the f of the One who fills all	Eph 1:23
filled with all the f of God.	Eph 3:19
stature measured by Christ's f.	Eph 4:13
have} all His f dwell in Him,	Col 1:19
Him the entire f of God's nature	Col 2:9

FULLY

This will happen when you f obey	Zch 6:15
My time has not yet f come.	Jn 7:8
because he was f convinced that	Rm 4:21
one must be f convinced in his	Rm 14:5
I have f proclaimed the good	Rm 15:19
I will know f, as I am f known.	1Co 13:12
or am already f mature,	Php 3:12
I am f supplied, having received	Php 4:18
worthy of the Lord, f pleasing	Col 1:10
to make God's message f known,	Col 1:25
might be f made through me,	2Tm 4:17
when sin is f grown, it gives	Jms 1:15

FUN

Hebrew man to us to make f of us.	Gn 39:14
our enemies make f of us.	Ps 80:6
innocent person just for f!	Pr 1:11
will begin to make f of him,	Lk 14:29

FUNCTION

parts do not have the same f,	Rm 12:4

FUR

grab it by its **f**, strike it down   1Sm 17:35

FURIOUS

Cain was **f**, and he was downcast.	Gn 4:5
Saul was **f** and resented this	1Sm 18:8
rebuilding the wall, he became **f**.	Neh 4:1
The king became **f** and his anger	Est 1:12
the LORD heard and became **f**;	Ps 78:21
in anger, wrath, and **f** rebukes.	Ezk 5:15
displeased and became **f**.	Jnh 4:1
the dragon was **f** with the woman	Rv 12:17

FURLOUGH

there is no **f** in battle,   Ec 8:8

FURNACE

out of Egypt's iron **f** to be a people	Dt 4:20
out of the middle of an iron **f**.	1Kg 8:51
silver refined in an earthen **f**,	Ps 12:6
like a fiery **f** when you appear;	Ps 21:9
and my bones burn like a **f**.	Ps 102:3
tested you in the **f** of affliction.	Is 48:10
of Egypt, out of the iron **f**.	Jr 11:4
thrown into a **f** of blazing fire.	Dn 3:6
burning like a **f**, when all the	Mal 4:1
and thrown into the **f** tomorrow,	Mt 6:30
throw them into the blazing **f**	Mt 13:42
like fine bronze fired in a **f**,	Rv 1:15
smoke from a great **f** so that the sun	Rv 9:2

FURNISHED

room upstairs, **f** and ready.	Mk 14:15
you a large, **f** room upstairs.	Lk 22:12

FURNISHINGS

the design of all its **f**.	Ex 25:9
to take care of all the **f** of the tent	Nm 3:8
consecrated it and all its **f**,	Nm 7:1
sprinkle the tent, all the **f**,	Nm 19:18
Others were put in charge of the **f**	1Ch 9:29

FURNITURE

any **f** he sits on will be unclean.   Lv 15:4

FURROWS

soaking its **f** and leveling its	Ps 65:10
they made their **f** long.	Ps 129:3

FURY

f, indignation, and calamity	Ps 78:49
A king's **f** is a messenger of death,	Pr 16:14
the rod of his **f** will be destroyed.	Pr 22:8

F is cruel, and anger is a flood,	Pr 27:4
who have drunk the cup of His **f**	Is 51:17
f to His enemies, retribution to	Is 59:18
My anger and **f** were poured out	Jr 42:18
it was uprooted in **f**, thrown to	Ezk 19:12
blow the fire of My **f** on you.	Ezk 21:31
will pour out My **f** on them like	Hs 5:10
vent the full **f** of My anger;	Hs 11:9
and the **f** of a fire about to	Heb 10:27
come down to you with great **f**,	Rv 12:12

FUTILE

you offer me such **f** comfort?	Jb 21:34
Everything is **f**.	Ec 1:2
But it turned out to be **f**.	Ec 2:1
to myself that this is also **f**.	Ec 2:15
This too is **f** and a great wrong	Ec 2:21
animals, for everything is **f**.	Ec 3:19
This too is **f** and a pursuit of	Ec 4:4
with income. This too is **f**.	Ec 5:10
This is **f** and a sickening	Ec 6:2
few days of his **f** life that he	Ec 6:12
of the fool. This too is **f**.	Ec 7:6
In my **f** life I have seen	Ec 7:15
they did so. This too is **f**.	Ec 8:10
All that comes is **f**.	Ec 11:8
the Teacher. "Everything is **f**."	Ec 12:8
and the peoples plot **f** things?	Ac 4:25
of the wise, that they are **f**.	1Co 3:20

FUTILITY

made to inherit months of **f**,	Jb 7:3
He made their days end in **f**,	Ps 78:33
"Absolute **f**," says the Teacher.	Ec 1:2
Again, I saw **f** under the sun:	Ec 4:7
dreams bring **f**, also many words	Ec 5:7
For he comes in **f** and he goes in	Ec 6:4
many words, they increase **f**.	Ec 6:11
There is a **f** that is done on the	Ec 8:14
"Absolute **f**," says the Teacher.	Ec 12:8
my strength for nothing and **f**;	Is 49:4
creation was subjected to **f**	Rm 8:20
in the **f** of their thoughts.	Eph 4:17

FUTURE

In the **f**, when your son asks	Ex 13:14
your son asks you in the **f**,	Dt 6:20
In the **f**, when your children ask	Jos 4:6
You hold my **f**.	Ps 16:5
the man of peace will have a **f**.	Ps 37:37

but must tell a **f** generation the   Ps 78:4
For then you will have a **f**,   Pr 23:18
For the evil have no **f**;   Pr 24:20
the outcome. Or tell us the **f**.   Is 41:22
to give you a **f** and a hope.   Jr 29:11
There is hope for your **f**   Jr 31:17
what will happen in the **f**.   Dn 2:29
refers to many days {in the **f**}.   Dn 8:26
in the **f** you will see the Son of   Mt 26:64
you are not sowing the **f** body,   1Co 15:37
In the **f**, there is reserved for   2Tm 4:8

G

GAAL
G son of Ebed came with his   Jdg 9:26

GAASH
of Ephraim north of Mount **G**.   Jos 24:30
Hurai from the wadis of **G**,   1Ch 11:32

GABBATHA
Pavement (but in Hebrew **G**).   Jn 19:13

GABRIEL
Angel who explained Daniel's visions (Dn 8:16; 9:21) and announced John's and Jesus' births (Lk 1:19,26).

GAD
1. Son of Jacob by Zilpah (Gn 30:9-11). Tribe with Transjordan territory north of the Dead Sea (Nm 32; Dt 3:16-17; Jos 18:7).
2. Seer at time of David (1Sm 22:5; 2Sm 24:11-19; 1Ch 21:9-19; 29:29; 2Ch 29:25).

GADARENES
to the region of the **G**,   Mt 8:28

GAIN (n)
they turned toward dishonest **g**,   1Sm 8:3
What **g** is there in my death,   Ps 30:9
decrees and not to material **g**.   Ps 119:36
all who pursue **g** dishonestly;   Pr 1:19
Ill-gotten **g-s** do not profit   Pr 10:2
who hates unjust **g** prolongs his   Pr 28:16
who refuses **g** from extortion,   Is 33:15
every last one for his own **g**.   Is 56:11

except your own unjust **g**,   Jr 22:17
in order to get unjust **g**.   Ezk 22:27
their hearts pursue unjust **g**.   Ezk 33:31
living is Christ and dying is **g**.   Php 1:21
everything that was a **g** to me,   Php 3:7
is a way to material **g**.   1Tm 6:5
with contentment is a great **g**.   1Tm 6:6
by teaching for dishonest **g**   Ti 1:11

GAIN (v)
God gives you the power to **g** wealth   Dt 8:18
For **g-ing** wisdom and being   Pr 1:2
gives freely, yet **g-s** more;   Pr 11:24
discerning, and he **g-s** knowledge.   Pr 19:25
Food **g-ed** by fraud is sweet to a   Pr 20:17
An inheritance **g-ed** prematurely   Pr 20:21
What does a man **g** for all his   Ec 1:3
nothing to be **g-ed** under the sun.   Ec 2:11
does the worker **g** from his   Ec 3:9
What does he **g** who struggles for   Ec 5:16
confused will **g** understanding   Is 29:24
everyone is **g-ing** profit unjustly.   Jr 6:13
who unjustly **g-s** wealth for his   Hab 2:9
What have we **g-ed** by keeping   Mal 3:14
a man if he **g-s** the whole world   Mt 16:26
benefit a man to **g** the whole world   Mk 8:36
benefited if he **g-s** the whole world   Lk 9:25
By your endurance **g** your lives.   Lk 21:19
do not have love, I **g** nothing.   1Co 13:3
in the Lord have **g-ed** confidence   Php 1:14
filth, so that I may **g** Christ   Php 3:8
so that they might **g** a better   Heb 11:35

GAIUS
1. Macedonian (Ac 19:29).
2. Paul's companion (Ac 20:4).
3. Corinthian believer (1Co 1:14; Rm 16:23).
4. John's friend (3Jn 1).

GALATIA
Roman region of Asia Minor (Ac 16:16; 18:23; 1Co 16:1; Gl 1:2; 2Tm 4:10; 1Pt 1:1).

GALILEAN
You were with Jesus the **G** too.   Mt 26:69
reported to Him about the **G-s**   Lk 13:1
he asked if the man was a **G**.   Lk 23:6
the **G-s** welcomed Him because they   Jn 4:45
all these who are speaking **G-s**?   Ac 2:7

GALILEE

1. Region in northern Palestine (Jos 20:7; 21:32; 1Kg 9:11); where Jesus lived (Mt 2:22; 3:13; 21:11) and ministered (Is 9:1; Mt 4:12,15,23); where He appeared after the resurrection (Mt 26:32; Ac 1:11).

2. Sea along the Jordan (Mt 4:18; 15:29).

GALL

| they gave me g for my food, | Ps 69:21 |
| Him wine mixed with g to drink. | Mt 27:34 |

GALLIO

| While G was proconsul of Achaia | Ac 18:12 |

GALLONS

| Each contained 20 or 30 g. | Jn 2:6 |

GALLOP

the g-ing, g-ing of his stallions.	Jdg 5:22
and they g like war horses.	Jl 2:4
g-ing horse and jolting chariot!	Nah 3:2

GALLOWS

both men were hanged on the g.	Est 2:23
he had the g constructed.	Est 5:14
Haman on the g he had prepared	Est 7:10
10 sons be hung on the g.	Est 9:13

GAMALIEL

1. Leader of Manassites (Nm 2:20).
2. Pharisee (Ac 5:34); Paul's teacher (22:3).

GAME

| hunt some g for me. | Gn 27:3 |
| A lazy man doesn't roast his g, | Pr 12:27 |

GANG

a g of evildoers has closed in	Ps 22:16
a g of ruthless men seeks my	Ps 86:14
a thief breaks in; a g pillages outside.	Hs 7:1

GANGRENE

| their word will spread like g, | 2Tm 2:17 |

GAP

had made this g in the tribes	Jdg 21:15
and that the g-s were being closed	Neh 4:7
and that no g was left in it	Neh 6:1
and stand in the g before Me on	Ezk 22:30
I will repair its g-s, restore its	Am 9:11

GARBAGE

lifts the needy from the g pile.	1Sm 2:8
lifts the needy from the g pile	Ps 113:7
We are ... like the world's g,	1Co 4:13

GARDEN

LORD God planted a g in Eden,	Gn 2:8
I made g-s and parks for myself	Ec 2:5
my bride, {you are} a locked g	Sg 4:12
My love has gone down to his g,	Sg 6:2
desert like the g of the LORD.	Is 51:3
like a watered g and like a	Is 58:11
Plant g-s and eat their produce.	Jr 29:5,28
will be like an irrigated g,	Jr 31:12
as if {it were} a g {booth},	Lm 2:6
You were in Eden, the g of God.	Ezk 28:13
in God's g could not rival	Ezk 31:8
has become like the g of Eden.	Ezk 36:35
of them is like the G of Eden,	Jl 2:3
make g-s and eat their produce.	Am 9:14
Kidron Valley, where there was a g,	Jn 18:1
A new tomb was in the g;	Jn 19:41

GARDENER

| Supposing He was the g, she | Jn 20:15 |

GARLAND

they will be a g of grace on	Pr 1:9
will place a g of grace on your	Pr 4:9
brought oxen and g-s to the gates.	Ac 14:13

GARLIC

| melons, leeks, onions, and g. | Nm 11:5 |

GARMENT

But leaving his g in her hand,	Gn 39:12
clothed him with fine linen g-s,	Gn 41:42
to make Aaron's g-s	Ex 28:3
the holy g-s for Aaron the priest	Ex 35:19
Clothe Aaron with the holy g-s,	Ex 40:13
he consecrated Aaron and his g-s,	Lv 8:30
is not to put on a woman's g,	Dt 22:5
take a widow's g as security.	Dt 24:17
30 linen g-s and 30 changes	Jdg 14:12
530 priestly g-s to the treasury	Neh 7:70
rotten, like a moth-eaten g.	Jb 13:28
the clouds its g and thick	Jb 38:9
out like {the folds of} a g.	Jb 38:14
They divided my g-s among	Ps 22:18
violence covers them like a g.	Ps 73:6
You will change them like a g,	Ps 102:26
the deep as if it were a g;	Ps 104:6
Take his g, for he has put up	Pr 20:16; 27:13

She makes and sells linen g-s; Pr 31:24
the bloodied g-s of war will be Is 9:5
earth will wear out like a g, Is 51:6
He put on g-s of vengeance Is 59:17
clothed me with the g-s of salvation Is 61:10
crimson-stained g-s from Bozrah Is 63:1
acts are like a polluted g; Is 64:6
every altar on g-s taken as Am 2:8
clothed him in g-s while the Angel Zch 3:5
he covers his g with injustice, Mal 2:16
a camel-hair g with a leather Mt 3:4
patches an old g with unshrunk Mt 9:16
he tied his outer g around him Jn 21:7
hating even the g defiled by the Jd 23

GARRISON

has attacked the Philistine g, 1Sm 13:4
Now a Philistine g took control 1Sm 13:23
Then he placed g-s in Aram of 2Sm 8:6
a Philistine g was at Bethlehem 2Sm 23:14
of Judah and set g-s in the land 2Ch 17:2

GASHED

they g themselves at the Jr 5:7
torn ... garments, and g themselves, Jr 41:5

GASHES

are not to make g on your bodies Lv 19:28
or make g on their bodies. Lv 21:5

GATE

Lot was sitting at Sodom's g. Gn 19:1
possess the g-s of their enemies. Gn 24:60
This is the g of heaven. Gn 28:17
foreigner who is within your g-s. Ex 20:10
your house and on your g-s. Dt 6:9
to the city elders at the g. Dt 22:15
will set up its g-s {at the cost of} Jos 6:26
Boaz went to the g Ru 4:1
began rebuilding the Sheep g. Neh 3:1
go down to the g-s of Sheol; Jb 17:16
When I went out to the city g Jb 29:7
saw that I had support in the city g, Jb 31:21
seen the g-s of death's shadow? Jb 38:17
Lift me up from the g-s of death, Ps 9:13
Lift up your heads, you g-s! Ps 24:7
at the city g talk about me, Ps 69:12
LORD loves the g-s of Zion more Ps 87:2
Enter His g-s with thanksgiving Ps 100:4
and came near the g-s of death. Ps 107:18
Open the g-s of righteousness for Ps 118:19

This is the g of the LORD; Ps 118:20
with {their} enemies at the city g. Ps 127:5
crush the oppressed at the g, Pr 22:22
not open his mouth at the g. Pr 24:7
husband is known at the city g-s, Pr 31:23
works praise her at the city g-s. Pr 31:31
Wail, you g-s! Cry out, Is 14:31
I must go to the g-s of Sheol; Is 38:10
Go out, go out through the g-s; Is 62:10
establish justice in the g. Am 5:15
Enter through the narrow g. Mt 7:13
For the g is wide and the road Mt 7:13
at the temple g called Beautiful Ac 3:2
her joy she did not open the g, Ac 12:14
also suffered outside the g, Heb 13:12
a massive high wall, with 12 g-s. Rv 21:12
The 12 g-s are 12 pearls; Rv 21:21
Each day its g-s will never close Rv 21:25
may enter the city by the g-s. Rv 22:14

GATEKEEPERS

men went and called to the city's g 2Kg 7:10
chosen to be g at the thresholds 1Ch 9:22
were to be g for the ark. 1Ch 15:23
the divisions of the g: 1Ch 26:1
The g' descendants {included}: Ezr 2:42
Levites, singers, g, and temple Neh 10:28

GATEPOSTS

city gate along with the two g, Jdg 16:3

GATEWAY

people trampled him in the g. 2Kg 7:17

GATH

Philistine city (Jos 11:22; 1Sm 6:17); hometown of Goliath (17:4) and other giants (2Sm 21:22). David took refuge there (1Sm 21:10; 27:3). David, Rehoboam, and Uzziah each defeated the city (1Ch 18:1; 2Ch 11:5-12; 26:6). Any good news announced in Gath would be bad news for Israel (2Sm 1:20; Mc 1:10). Amos said Israel was no better than Gath (Am 6:2).

GATHER

and he was g-ed to his people. Gn 25:8
They must go and g straw for Ex 5:7
and g enough for that day. Ex 16:4
the person who g-ed a lot had no Ex 16:18
they found a man g-ing wood on Nm 15:32

Will you let me g fallen grain | Ru 2:7
I am g-ing a couple of sticks in | 1Kg 17:12
He g-s the waters of the sea into | Ps 33:7
G My faithful ones to Me, | Ps 50:5
and has g-ed them from the lands | Ps 107:3
He g-s Israel's exiled people. | Ps 147:2
it g-s its food during harvest. | Pr 6:8
The son who g-s during summer is | Pr 10:5
the task of g-ing and accumulating | Ec 2:26
and a time to g stones; | Ec 3:5
in the gardens and g lilies. | Sg 6:2
and g the dispersed of Israel; | Is 11:12
He g-s the lambs in His arms and | Is 40:11
I have come to g all nations and | Is 66:18
I will g them from remote | Jr 31:8
I will g you from the peoples | Ezk 11:17
and g you from all the countries, | Ezk 36:24
He g-s all the nations to himself | Hab 2:5
I will g all the nations against | Zch 14:2
and g His wheat into the barn, | Mt 3:12
sow or reap or g into barns, | Mt 6:26
who does not g with Me scatters | Mt 12:30
G the weeds first and tie them | Mt 13:30
and g-ed the good (fish) into | Mt 13:48
or three are g-ed together in My | Mt 18:20
I wanted to g your children
 together, as a hen g-s
 her chicks | Mt 23:37
and they will g His elect from | Mt 24:31
and g where I haven't scattered, | Mt 25:26
nations will be g-ed before Him, | Mt 25:32
and g-ing fruit for eternal life, | Jn 4:36
they arrived and g-ed the church | Ac 14:27
As Paul g-ed a bundle of brushwood | Ac 28:3
The person who g-ed much did not | 2Co 8:15
Christ and our being g-ed to Him: | 2Th 2:1
toward earth and g-ed the grapes | Rv 14:19

GATHERING (n)

and He called the g of the water | Gn 1:10
a g of water and thick clouds. | 2Sm 22:12
a reason for this disorderly g. | Ac 19:40

GAZA

Philistine city (Gn 10:19; Jos 15:47; Jdg 1:18; 16:21; 1Sm 6:17); prophesied against (Jr 47:5; Am 1:6; Zph 2:4; Zch 9:5).

GAZE (n)

his g was fixed because he | 1Sm 4:15

his g was fixed due to his age. | 1Kg 14:4
Turn Your angry g from me so | Ps 39:13
fix your g straight ahead. | Pr 4:25

GAZE (v)

g-ing on the beauty of the LORD | Ps 27:4
He g-s on all the inhabitants of | Ps 33:14
So I g on You in the sanctuary | Ps 63:2
Why g with envy, you mountain | Ps 68:16
the LORD g-d out from heaven to | Ps 102:19
Don't g at wine when it is red, | Pr 23:31
dark, for the sun has g-d on me. | Sg 1:6
g-ing through the windows, | Sg 2:9
they were g-ing into heaven | Ac 1:10
the Holy Spirit, g-d into heaven. | Ac 7:55

GAZELLE

Escape like a g from a hunter, | Pr 6:5
I charge you, by the g-s | Sg 2:7; 3:5
love is like a g or a young stag | Sg 2:9
two fawns, twins of a g | Sg 4:5; 7:3
and be like a g or a young stag | Sg 8:14
Like wandering g-s and like sheep | Is 13:14

GEBA

G—12 cities, with their villages; | Jos 18:24
G with its pasturelands, | Jos 21:17
were staying in G of Benjamin, | 1Sm 13:16
King Asa built G of Benjamin | 1Kg 15:22

GECKO

the g, the monitor lizard, | Lv 11:30

GEDALIAH

Governor of Judah (2Kg 25:22-25; Jr 40–41).

GEHAZI

Elisha's attendant (2Kg 4:11-37; 5:20-27; 8:4-5).

GEM CUTTER

as a g engraves a seal. | Ex 28:11; 39:6
skill to do all the work of a g; | Ex 35:35
tribe of Dan, a g, a designer, | Ex 38:23

GENEALOGICAL

I found the g record of those | Neh 7:5
searched for their entries in the g | Neh 7:64

GENEALOGY

Now this is the g of Perez: | Ru 4:18
Israel was registered in the g-ies | 1Ch 9:1
to myths and endless g-ies. | 1Tm 1:4

foolish debates, g-ies, quarrels	Ti 3:9
without father, mother, or g,	Heb 7:3

GENERATION

righteous before Me in this g.	Gn 7:1
a covenant for all future g-s:	Gn 9:12
In the fourth g they will return	Gn 15:16
Throughout your g-s, every male	Gn 17:12
Israelites throughout their g-s.	Ex 12:42
to the third and fourth g.	Ex 34:7
until the whole g that had done	Nm 32:13
None ... in this evil g will see the	Dt 1:35
for a thousand g-s with those who	Dt 7:9
g rose up who did not know	Jdg 2:10
This was to teach the future g-s	Jdg 3:2
protect us from this g forever.	Ps 12:7
the next g will be told about	Ps 22:30
His heart from g to g.	Ps 33:11
to be remembered for all g-s;	Ps 45:17
Your power to {another} g,	Ps 71:18
must tell a future g the praises	Ps 78:4
a stubborn and rebellious g,	Ps 78:8
Your faithfulness to all g-s.	Ps 89:1
been our refuge in every g.	Ps 90:1
I was disgusted with that g;	Ps 95:10
endures through all g-s.	Ps 100:5
Your fame {endures} to all g-s.	Ps 102:12
the g of the upright will be	Ps 112:2
Your faithfulness is for all g-s;	Ps 119:90
One g will declare Your works to	Ps 145:4
Your rule is for all g-s.	Ps 145:13
There is a g that	Pr 30:11
A g goes and a g comes,	Ec 1:4
desolate, from g to g;	Is 34:10
and My salvation for all g-s.	Is 51:8
{Evil} g, pay attention to the	Jr 2:31
endures from g to g.	Lm 5:19
is from g to g.	Dn 4:3,34
and their children the next g.	Jl 1:3
Abraham to David were 14 g-s;	Mt 1:17
To what should I compare this g?	Mt 11:16
adulterous g demands a sign,	Mt 12:39
adulterous g wants a sign,	Mt 16:4
unbelieving and rebellious g!	Mt 17:17
things will come on this g!	Mt 23:36
This g will certainly not pass	Mt 24:34
from now on all g-s will call me	Lk 1:48
mercy is from g to g on those who	Lk 1:50
this g will be held responsible	Lk 11:51

Be saved from this corrupt g!	Ac 2:40
Who will describe His g?	Ac 8:33
In past g-s He allowed all the	Ac 14:16
people in other g-s as it is now	Eph 3:5
in a crooked and perverted g,	Php 2:15
for ages and g-s but now revealed	Col 1:26
provoked with this g and said,	Heb 3:10

GENEROSITY

giving, with g;	Rm 12:8
into the wealth of their g.	2Co 8:2
in every way for all g,	2Co 9:11

GENEROUS

He is always g, always lending	Ps 37:26
A g person will be enriched,	Pr 11:25
A g person will be blessed,	Pr 22:9
and a g blessing will come to	Pr 24:25
Are you jealous because I'm g?	Mt 20:15
in advance the g gift you	2Co 9:5
to be g, willing to share,	1Tm 6:18
Every g act and every perfect	Jms 1:17

GENEROUSLY

be able to give as g as this?	1Ch 29:14
because He has treated me g.	Ps 13:6
a man who lends g and conducts	Ps 112:5
me because You deal g with me.	Ps 142:7
who sows g will also reap g.	2Co 9:6
who gives to all g and without	Jms 1:5

GENITALS

out her hand and grabs his g,	Dt 25:11

GENNESARET

1. Sea of Galilee (Lk 5:1).
2. Region of Palestine (Mt 14:34; Mk 6:53).

GENTILE

uncleanness of the G-s of the land	Ezr 6:21
the power of the G kingdoms.	Hg 2:22
the Jordan, Galilee of the G-s!	Mt 4:15
Don't even the G-s do the same?	Mt 5:47
they will hand Him over to the G-s	Mt 20:19
rulers of the G-s dominate them,	Mt 20:25
a light for revelation to the G-s	Lk 2:32
For the G world eagerly seeks	Lk 12:30
trampled by the G-s until the	
times of the G-s are fulfilled.	Lk 21:24
Why did the G-s rage,	Ac 4:25
to carry My name before G-s,	Ac 9:15

been poured out on the **G**-s also.   Ac 10:45
resulting in life to even the **G**-s!   Ac 11:18
we now turn to the **G**-s!   Ac 13:46
When the **G**-s heard this,   Ac 13:48
the door of faith to the **G**-s.   Ac 14:27
take from the **G**-s a people for His   Ac 15:14
From now on I will go to the **G**-s.   Ac 18:6
and deliver him into **G** hands.   Ac 21:11
will send you far away to the **G**-s.   Ac 22:21
to our people and to the **G**-s.   Ac 26:23
of God has been sent to the **G**-s;   Ac 28:28
So, when **G**-s, who do not have the   Rm 2:14
God is blasphemed among the **G**-s   Rm 2:24
both Jews and **G**-s are all under   Rm 3:9
Is He not also for **G**-s?   Rm 3:29
G-s, who did not pursue   Rm 9:30
their failure riches for the **G**-s,   Rm 11:12
that I am an apostle to the **G**-s,   Rm 11:13
full number of the **G**-s has come   Rm 11:25
and so that **G**-s may glorify God   Rm 15:9
in Him the **G**-s will hope.   Rm 15:12
For if the **G**-s have shared in   Rm 15:27
but so do all the **G** churches.   Rm 16:4
Jews and foolishness to the **G**-s.   1Co 1:23
not even condoned among the **G**-s   1Co 5:1
I could preach Him among the **G**-s,   Gl 1:16
he used to eat with the **G**-s before   Gl 2:12
If you ... live like a **G** ... how can you
    compel **G**-s to live like Jews?   Gl 2:14
would justify the **G**-s by faith and   Gl 3:8
time you were **G**-s in the flesh   Eph 2:11
the **G**-s are co-heirs, members of   Eph 3:6
no longer walk as the **G**-s walk,   Eph 4:17
make known to those among the
    G-s the glorious wealth   Col 1:27
like the **G**-s who don't know God.   1Th 4:5
a teacher of the **G**-s in faith and   1Tm 2:7
preached among the **G**-s, believed   1Tm 3:16
honorably among the **G**-s,   1Pt 2:12

GENTLE

like **g** rain on new grass and   Dt 32:2
A **g** answer turns away anger,   Pr 15:1
a **g** tongue can break a bone.   Pr 25:15
Blessed are the **g**, because they   Mt 5:5
because I am **g** and humble in   Mt 11:29
is coming to you, **g**, and mounted   Mt 21:5
such a person with a **g** spirit,   Gl 6:1
instead we were **g** among you,   1Th 2:7

not a bully but **g**, not   1Tm 3:3
but must be **g** to everyone,   2Tm 2:24
peace-loving, **g**, compliant, full   Jms 3:17
to the good and **g** but also to   1Pt 2:18
quality of a **g** and quiet spirit   1Pt 3:4

GENTLENESS

or in love and a spirit of **g**?   1Co 4:21
appeal to you by the **g** ... of Christ   2Co 10:1
goodness, faith, **g**, self-control.   Gl 5:23
humility and **g**, with patience   Eph 4:2
humility, **g**, and patience,   Col 3:12
faith, love, endurance, and **g**.   1Tm 6:11
his opponents with **g**.   2Tm 2:25
always showing **g** to all people.   Ti 3:2
good conduct with wisdom's **g**.   Jms 3:13
do this with **g** and respect,   1Pt 3:16

GENTLY

Treat the young man Absalom **g**   2Sm 18:5
He **g** leads those that are   Is 40:11
is able to deal **g** with those who   Heb 5:2

GENUINE

and my prayer was **g**.   Ps 35:13
G righteousness {leads} to life   Pr 11:19
that John was a **g** prophet.   Mk 11:32
will trust you with what is **g**?   Lk 16:11

GENUINELY

who will **g** care about your   Php 2:20
widows who are **g** widows.   1Tm 5:3

GENUINENESS

am testing the **g** of your love.   2Co 8:8
so that the **g** of your faith   1Pt 1:7

GERAHS

shekel (20 **g** to the shekel).   Ex 30:13
shekel, 20 **g** to the shekel.   Lv 27:25
shekel—20 **g** to the shekel.   Nm 3:47
shekel, which is 20 **g**.   Nm 18:16
The shekel will weigh 20 **g**.   Ezk 45:12

GERAR

   Philistine town (Gn 10:19; 20:1-2; 26; 2Ch 14:13-14).

GERASENE

to the region of the **G**-s.   Mk 5:1
sailed to the region of the **G**-s,   Lk 8:26
people of the **G** region asked Him   Lk 8:37

GERIZIM

Mountain, opposite Ebal, near Shechem (Dt 11:29; 27:12; Jos 8:33; Jdg 9:7).

GERSHOM

1. Son of Moses (Ex 2:22; 8:3).
2. Son of Levi (1Ch 6:1).
3. Descendant of Phinehas (Ezr 8:2).

GERSHON

Oldest son of Levi, also spelled "Gershom" (Gn 46:11; Ex 6:16-17; Nm 3:17-25; 4:22-41; 7:7; 10:17; 26:57; Jos 21:6,27,33; 1Ch 26:21; 29:8,12).

GESHUR

City-state of Aram not conquered by Israel (Dt 3:14; Jos 12:5; 13:2,11,13; 1Ch 2:23); hometown of Absalom's mother (2Sm 3:3; 13:38).

GESTATION

| no birth, no g, no conception. | Hs 9:11 |

GESTURES

| his feet, and g with his fingers | Pr 6:13 |

GET

G rid of the gods your ancestors	Jos 24:14
told his father, "G her for me,	Jdg 14:3
"G up," he told her. "Let's go."	Jdg 19:28
Now he's g-ing away.	2Sm 3:24
G up! Don't reject us forever!	Ps 44:23
In vain you g up early and stay	Ps 127:2
G wisdom, g understanding;	Pr 4:5
whatever else you g, g understanding.	Pr 4:7
what does a man g with all his	Ec 2:22
G up! Go to the great city of	Jnh 1:2; 3:2
They've got their reward!	Mt 6:2,5,16
He told the paralytic, "G up,	Mt 9:6
told Peter, "G behind Me, Satan	Mt 16:23
what time he got better.	Jn 4:52
got to the tomb first.	Jn 20:4
G up, sleeper, and rise up from	Eph 5:14
And don't g drunk with wine,	Eph 5:18

GETHSEMANE

| with them to a place called G, | Mt 26:36 |
| they came to a place named G, | Mk 14:32 |

GEZER

Canaanite city-state, defeated by Joshua but not dispossessed (Jos 10:33; 16:10; Jdg 1:29); given as a dowry to Solomon (1Kg 9:16).

GHOST

will seek idols, g-s, spirits of	Is 19:3
"It's a g!" they said,	Mt 14:26
they thought it was a g and cried	Mk 6:49
thought they were seeing a g.	Lk 24:37
because a g does not have flesh	Lk 24:39

GIANT

descendants of the g	2Sm 21:16,18
descended from the g	2Sm 21:20,22
a descendant of the g-s,	1Ch 20:4
descended from the g.	1Ch 20:6
descendants of the g	1Ch 20:8

GIBEAH

go in and spend the night in G.	Jdg 19:15
Citizens of G ganged up on me	Jdg 20:5
Hand over the perverted men in G	Jdg 20:13
Saul also went to his home in G,	1Sm 10:26
Blow the horn in G, the trumpet	Hs 5:8
corrupted ... as in the days of G.	Hs 9:9

GIBEON

inhabitants of G heard what	Jos 9:3
Sun, stand still over G,	Jos 10:12
G the LORD appeared to Solomon	1Kg 3:5
Jeiel fathered G and lived in G.	1Ch 9:35

GIBEONITES

| So the G became woodcutters | Jos 9:21 |
| Saul ... when he killed the G. | 2Sm 21:1 |

GIDEON

Judge (Jdg 6–8; Heb 11:32). The fleece (Jdg 6:36-40). God reduced his army (7:2-8).

GIFT

God has given me a good g,	Gn 30:20
So the g was sent on ahead of	Gn 32:21
in addition to ... your g-s,	Lv 23:38
work of the priesthood as a g,	Nm 18:7
of their g-s also belongs to you.	Nm 18:11
and a g from the king followed	2Sm 11:8
will seek your favor with g-s.	Ps 45:12
You received g-s from people,	Ps 68:18
or be persuaded by lavish g-s.	Pr 6:35
A g opens doors for a man and	Pr 18:16
is a friend of one who gives g-s.	Pr 19:6

A secret g soothes anger, and a	Pr 21:14
boasts about a g that does not	Pr 25:14
It is also the g of God whenever	Ec 3:13
his labor. This is a g of God,	Ec 5:19
the nations as a g to the LORD	Is 66:20
presented Him with g-s: gold,	Mt 2:11
leave your g there in front of	Mt 5:24
to give good g-s to your children,	Mt 7:11
might have received from me is a g	Mt 15:5
an oath by the g that is on it	Mt 23:18
from me is *Corban*" (that is, a g	Mk 7:11
stones and g-s dedicated to God,	Lk 21:5
If you knew the g of God,	Jn 4:10
will receive the g of the Holy	Ac 2:38
thought the g of God could be	Ac 8:20
because the g of the Holy Spirit	Ac 10:45
them the same g that He also	Ac 11:17
some spiritual g to strengthen	Rm 1:11
pay is not considered as a g,	Rm 4:4
But the g is not like the	Rm 5:15
grace and the g of righteousness	Rm 5:17
but the g of God is eternal life	Rm 6:23
God's gracious g-s and calling are	Rm 11:29
we have different g-s:	Rm 12:6
any spiritual g as you eagerly	1Co 1:7
each has his own g from God,	1Co 7:7
Now there are different g-s,	1Co 12:4
But desire the greater g-s.	1Co 12:31
If I have [the g of] prophecy,	1Co 13:2
and desire spiritual g-s,	1Co 14:1
your gracious g to Jerusalem.	1Co 16:3
behalf for the g that came to us	2Co 1:11
to God for His indescribable g.	2Co 9:15
yourselves; it is God's g	Eph 2:8
He gave g-s to people.	Eph 4:8
Not that I seek the g, but I seek	Php 4:17
not neglect the g that is in you	1Tm 4:14
keep ablaze the g of God that is	2Tm 1:6
to offer both g-s and sacrifices	Heb 5:1
who tasted the heavenly g,	Heb 6:4
to offer g-s and sacrifices;	Heb 8:3
because God approved his g-s,	Heb 11:4
every perfect g is from above,	Jms 1:17
Based on the g they have	1Pt 4:10
and send g-s to one another,	Rv 11:10
spring of living water as a g.	Rv 21:6
take the living water as a g.	Rv 22:17

GIHON

name of the second river is G,	Gn 2:13
have anointed him king in G.	1Kg 1:45
water of ... G and channeled it	2Ch 32:30

GILBOA

found Saul ... dead on Mount G.	1Sm 31:8
Mountains of G, let no dew or	2Sm 1:21

GILEAD

Region east of the Jordan and north of Moab, allotted to Reuben, Gad, and half of Manasseh (Nm 32:40; Dt 3:12-13; Jos 13:8-31; 17:1-6).

G remained beyond the Jordan.	Jdg 5:17
The elders of G said to Jephthah,	Jdg 11:10
G is Mine,	Ps 60:7; 108:8
goats streaming down Mount G.	Sg 4:1
Is there no balm in G?	Jr 8:22
G is a city of evildoers	Hs 6:8
they threshed G with iron	Am 1:3

GILGAL

opposite G, near the oaks	Dt 11:30
Joshua set up in G the 12 stones	Jos 4:20
has been called G to this day.	Jos 5:9
circuit to Bethel, G, and Mizpah	1Sm 7:16
go ahead of me to G.	1Sm 10:8
summoned to join Saul at G.	1Sm 13:4
Elisha were traveling from G,	2Kg 2:1
They sacrifice bulls in G;	Hs 12:11
for G will certainly go into exile,	Am 5:5

GIRGASHITES

Canaanite tribe dispossessed by Israel (Gn 10:16; 15:21; Dt 7:1; Jos 3:10; 24:11; 1Ch 1:14; Neh 9:8).

GIRL

Now the g was very beautiful,	Gn 24:16
The g was of unsurpassed beauty	1Kg 1:4
of Israel a young g who served	2Kg 5:2
and a serving g when she ousts	Pr 30:23
and sold a g for wine to drink.	Jl 3:3
by the hand, and the g got up.	Mt 9:25
Little g, I say to you, get up!	Mk 5:41
platter, and gave it to the g.	Mk 6:28
Then the slave g who was the	Jn 18:17

GITTITE

and the G-s—600 men	
who came	2Sm 15:18
killed Goliath the G.	2Sm 21:19

GIVE

I have g-n you every seed-bearing	Gn 1:29
The man gave names to all the	Gn 2:20
she also gave {some} to her husband	Gn 3:6
The woman You gave to be with me—	
she gave me {some fruit}	Gn 3:12
I will g this land to your offspring.	Gn 12:7
and gave her to her husband Abram	Gn 16:3
Abraham gave everything he owned	Gn 25:5
the land God gave to Abraham.	Gn 28:4
So Rachel gave her slave Bilhah to	Gn 30:4
Zilpah and gave her to Jacob as	Gn 30:9
He gave him the two tablets of the	Ex 31:18
favor on you and g you peace.	Nm 6:26
So they gave a negative report to	Nm 13:32
our God gave everything to us	Dt 2:36
words that I am g-ing you today are	Dt 6:6
the LORD gave me the two stone	Dt 9:10
possess the land I have g-n you	Dt 9:23
the Rock who gave you birth;	Dt 32:18
I have g-n you every place where	Jos 1:3
Joshua then gave it as an	Jos 11:23
The LORD gave them rest on every	Jos 21:44
this good land He has g-n you.	Jos 23:16
I gave you a land you did not labor	Jos 24:13
So Caleb gave her both the upper	Jdg 1:15
and his wife was g-n to one of the	Jdg 14:20
so I gave her to one of the men	Jdg 15:2
I will g him to the LORD all the	1Sm 1:11
Jonathan gave his equipment to	1Sm 20:40
Saul gave his daughter Michal,	1Sm 25:44
I gave your master's house to you	2Sm 12:8
the advice Ahithophel gave	2Sm 16:23
Ask. What should I g you?	1Kg 3:5
God gave Solomon wisdom,	1Kg 4:29
He has g-n David a wise son to be	1Kg 5:7
land that You gave Your people	1Kg 8:36
He has g-n rest to His people	1Kg 8:56
queen of Sheba gave to King	1Kg 10:10
G thanks to the LORD, for He is	1Ch 16:34
of the king's work gave willingly.	1Ch 29:6
because the LORD gave him rest.	2Ch 14:6
possession that You gave us as an	2Ch 20:11
the Israelites gave liberally of	2Ch 31:5

they gave it to the carpenters and	2Ch 34:11
what they could g, they gave	Ezr 2:69
offerings g-n by the people	Ezr 7:16
family leaders gave to the project	Neh 7:70
translating and g-ing the meaning	Neh 8:8
in the land You gave our ancestors	Neh 9:36
you ask will be g-n to you.	Est 5:6; 7:2; 9:12
The LORD g-s, and the LORD takes	Jb 1:21
A man will g up everything he	Jb 2:4
or gave the mind understanding?	Jb 38:36
May He g you what your heart	Ps 20:4
I was g-n over to You at birth;	Ps 22:10
Do not g me over to the will of	Ps 27:12
g the LORD glory and strength.	Ps 29:1
The LORD g-s His people strength;	Ps 29:11
He will g you your heart's desires.	Ps 37:4
righteous is gracious and g-ing.	Ps 37:21
a sacrifice, or I would g it;	Ps 51:16
We g thanks to You, God;	Ps 75:1
He gave them grain from heaven.	Ps 78:24
So I gave them over to their	Ps 81:12
The LORD g-s grace and glory;	Ps 84:11
G me an undivided mind to fear	Ps 86:11
For He will g His angels orders	Ps 91:11
G thanks to Him and praise His	Ps 100:4
G thanks to the LORD, for He is	Ps 106:1
He gave them what they	
asked for,	Ps 106:15
Let them g thanks to the LORD	Ps 107:8
the earth He has g-n to the human	Ps 115:16
light and g-s understanding	Ps 119:130
G praise, you servants of the	Ps 135:1
G thanks to the God of gods.	Ps 136:2
gave their land as an inheritance,	Ps 136:21
For the LORD g-s wisdom;	Pr 2:6
Come back later. I'll g it tomorrow	Pr 3:28
but g-s grace to the humble.	Pr 3:34
for I am g-ing you good instruction.	Pr 4:2
One person g-s freely, yet gains	Pr 11:24
the righteous g and don't hold	Pr 21:26
My son, g me your heart, and let	Pr 23:26
if he is thirsty, g him water	Pr 25:21
G-ing honor to a fool is like	Pr 26:8
The one who g-s to the poor will	Pr 28:27
G me neither poverty nor wealth	Pr 30:8
leech has two daughters: G, G.	Pr 30:15
G beer to one who is dying,	Pr 31:6
G her the reward of her labor,	Pr 31:31

God g-s a man riches, wealth, and | Ec 6:2
days that God g-s him under the | Ec 8:15
which has been g-n to you under | Ec 9:9
spirit returns to God who **gave** it. | Ec 12:7
a man were to **g** all his wealth | Sg 8:7
be born for us, a son will be g-n to us, | Is 9:6
Who **gave** Him understanding | Is 40:14
He g-s strength to the weary and | Is 40:29
I will not **g** My glory to another | Is 42:8
gave My back to those who beat Me | Is 50:6
I will **g** you a new heart and | Ezk 36:26
the land that I **gave** your fathers; | Ezk 36:28
God **gave** these four young men | Dn 1:17
because You have g-n me wisdom | Dn 2:23
of heaven has g-n you sovereignty | Dn 2:37
He g-s it to anyone He wants | Dn 4:17
been divided and g-n to the Medes | Dn 5:28
it is I who **gave** her the grain, | Hs 2:8
How can I **g** you up, Ephraim? | Hs 11:8
He will **g** His angels orders | Mt 4:6
G to the one who asks you, | Mt 5:42
so that your g-ing may be in secret. | Mt 6:4
G us today our daily bread. | Mt 6:11
Don't **g** what is holy to dogs or | Mt 7:6
Keep asking, and it will be g-n | Mt 7:7
for bread, will **g** him a stone? | Mt 7:9
know how to **g** good gifts to your | Mt 7:11
gave them authority over unclean | Mt 10:1
free of charge; **g** free of charge, | Mt 10:8
whoever g-s just a cup of cold | Mt 10:42
and I will **g** you rest. | Mt 11:28
no sign will be g-n to it except | Mt 12:39
but it has not been g-n to them. | Mt 13:11
what will a man **g** in exchange for | Mt 16:26
belongings and **g** to the poor, | Mt 19:21
to **g** His life—a ransom for many. | Mt 20:28
Who **gave** You this authority? | Mt 21:23
away from you and g-n to a nation | Mt 21:43
g back to Caesar the things that | Mt 22:21
marry nor are g-n in marriage but | Mt 22:30
marrying and g-ing in marriage, | Mt 24:38
to **g** them food at the proper | Mt 24:45
who has, more will be g-n, | Mt 25:29
hungry and you **gave** Me | Mt 25:35
g-ing thanks, He **gave** it to them | Mt 26:27
loud voice and **gave** up His spirit. | Mt 27:50
All authority has been g-n to Me | Mt 28:18
to the one who has, it will be g-n, | Mk 4:25

You **g** them something to eat, | Mk 6:37
right or left is not Mine to **g**; | Mk 10:40
they all **gave** out of their surplus, | Mk 12:44
Lord God will **g** Him the throne | Lk 1:32
Then she **gave** birth to her | Lk 2:7
G, and it will be g-n to you; | Lk 6:38
Much will be required of everyone
who has been g-n much. | Lk 12:48
g me the share of the estate I | Lk 15:12
'**G** me justice against my | Lk 18:3
they saw it, **gave** praise to God. | Lk 18:43
is My body, which is g-n for you. | Lk 22:19
He **gave** them the right to be | Jn 1:12
the law was g-n through Moses, | Jn 1:17
He **gave** His One and Only Son, | Jn 3:16
thing unless it's g-n to him from | Jn 3:27
"**G** Me a drink," Jesus said to | Jn 4:7
and after g-ing thanks He | Jn 6:11
the Father g-s Me will come to Me | Jn 6:37
lose none of those He has g-n Me | Jn 6:39
Spirit is the One who g-s life. | Jn 6:63
and told him, "**G** glory to God. | Jn 9:24
I **g** them eternal life, | Jn 10:28
Father, who has g-n them to Me, is | Jn 10:29
the Father had g-n everything into | Jn 13:3
I **g** you a new commandment: | Jn 13:34
not **g** to you as the world g-s. | Jn 14:27
the work You **gave** Me to do. | Jn 17:4
men You **gave** Me from the world. | Jn 17:6
I have g-n them the glory You
have g-n Me. | Jn 17:22
not lost one of those You have g-n | Jn 18:9
He **gave** up His spirit. | Jn 19:30
as the Spirit **gave** them ability | Ac 2:4
but what I have, I **g** to you: | Ac 3:6
Holy Spirit was g-n through the | Ac 8:18
since He Himself g-s everyone life | Ac 17:25
blessed to **g** than to receive. | Ac 20:35
Holy Spirit who was g-n to us. | Rm 5:5
God **gave** them a spirit of stupor, | Rm 11:8
Or who has ever first g-n to Him, | Rm 11:35
g-ing, with generosity; | Rm 12:8
each of us will **g** an account of | Rm 14:12
has been freely g-n to us by God. | 1Co 2:12
watered, but God **gave** the growth. | 1Co 3:6
G no offense to the Jews or the | 1Co 10:32
gave thanks, broke it, and said | 1Co 11:24

who g-s us the victory
   through our   1Co 15:57
sealed us and g-n us the Spirit as   2Co 1:22
they **gave** themselves especially to   2Co 8:5
who **gave** Himself for our sins to   Gl 1:4
loved me and **gave** Himself for me.   Gl 2:20
Now grace was **g-n** to each one of   Eph 4:7
He **gave** gifts to people   Eph 4:8
He personally **gave** some to be   Eph 4:11
and don't **g** the Devil an   Eph 4:27
loved us and **gave** Himself for us,   Eph 5:2
g-ing thanks always   Eph 5:20
church and **gave** Himself for her   Eph 5:25
message may be **g-n** to me when I   Eph 6:19
I **g** thanks to my God for every   Php 1:3
exalted Him and **gave** Him the name   Php 2:9
the matter of **g-ing** and receiving   Php 4:15
G thanks in everything, for this   1Th 5:18
gave Himself—a ransom for all   1Tm 2:6
g your attention to public   1Tm 4:13
For God has not **g-n** us a spirit of   2Tm 1:7
gave Himself for us to redeem us   Ti 2:14
ask God, who **g-s** to all generously   Jms 1:5
and it will be **g-n** to him.   Jms 1:5
but **g-s** grace to the humble.   Jms 4:6
from the dead and **gave** Him glory,   1Pt 1:21
be ready to **g** a defense to   1Pt 3:15
They will **g** an account to the   1Pt 4:5
but **g-s** grace to the humble.   1Pt 5:5
divine power has **g-n** us everything   2Pt 1:3
love the Father has **g-n** us,   1Jn 3:1
God has **g-n** us eternal life,   1Jn 5:11
that God **gave** Him to show His   Rv 1:1
I will **g** the victor the right to   Rv 2:7
and I will **g** you the crown of   Rv 2:10
white robe was **g-n** to each of them   Rv 6:11
asked him to **g** me the little scroll. Rv 10:9
The dragon **gave** him his power,   Rv 13:2
to be **g-n** a mark on his right hand   Rv 13:16
Fear God and **g** Him glory,   Rv 14:7
creatures **gave** the seven angels   Rv 15:7
Then the sea **gave** up its dead,   Rv 20:13
I will **g** to the thirsty from the   Rv 21:6

GIVER

for God loves a cheerful **g**.   2Co 9:7

GLAD

Let the heavens be **g** and   1Ch 16:31
my heart is **g**, and my spirit   Ps 16:9

rejoice and be **g** in Your   Ps 31:7
Be **g** in the LORD and rejoice,   Ps 32:11
the humble will hear and be **g**.   Ps 34:2
rejoice and be **g** in You;   Ps 40:16; 70:4
Let the heavens be **g** and   Ps 96:11
many coasts and islands be **g**.   Ps 97:1
wine that makes man's heart **g**   Ps 104:15
let us rejoice and be **g** in it.   Ps 118:24
face is sad, a heart may be **g**.   Ec 7:3
let your heart be **g** in the days   Ec 11:9
will rejoice and be **g** for you;   Sg 1:4
rejoice and be **g** in His salvation.   Is 25:9
and the dry land will be **g**;   Is 35:1
shout for joy from a **g** heart,   Is 65:14
children will see it and be **g**;   Zch 10:7
Be **g** and rejoice, because your   Mt 5:12
heart was **g**, and my tongue rejoiced. Ac 2:26
saw the grace of God, he was **g**,   Ac 11:23
Let us be **g**, rejoice, and give   Rv 19:7

GLADLY

For you **g** put up with fools   2Co 11:19

GLADNESS

and clothed me with **g**,   Ps 30:11
Let me hear joy and **g**;   Ps 51:8
Serve the LORD with **g**;   Ps 100:2
Joy and **g** will overtake   Is 35:10; 51:11
a sound of joy and **g**, the voice   Jr 33:11
will rejoice over you with **g**.   Zph 3:17
their food with **g** and simplicity   Ac 2:46

GLANCE

heart with one **g** of your eyes,   Sg 4:9

GLASS

Gold and **g** do not compare with   Jb 28:17
was something like a sea of **g**,   Rv 4:6
like a sea of **g** mixed with fire   Rv 15:2
city was pure gold like clear **g**.   Rv 21:18

GLAZE

heart are like **g** on an earthen   Pr 26:23

GLEAM

there was a **g** like amber.   Ezk 1:4
like the **g** of polished bronze   Ezk 1:7
was like the **g** of beryl,   Ezk 1:16
bright, like the **g** of amber.   Ezk 8:2
wheels was like the **g** of beryl.   Ezk 10:9
and feet like the **g** of polished   Dn 10:6

GLEAMS

when it **g** in the cup and goes	Pr 23:31

GLEAN

you must not **g** what is left.	Dt 24:21
saw what she had **g-ed**.	Ru 2:18
in the field and **g** the vineyards	Jb 24:6

GLEANING (n)

or gather the **g-s** of your harvest	Lv 19:9
or gather the **g-s** of your harvest	Lv 23:22
Is not the **g** of Ephraim better	Jdg 8:2
wouldn't they leave some **g-s**?	Jr 49:9

GLEE

I stumbled, they gathered in **g**;	Ps 35:15

GLOAT

not let my enemies **g** over me.	Ps 25:2
how long will the wicked **g**?	Ps 94:3
after he is on his way, he **g-s**.	Pr 20:14
Don't **g** when your enemy falls,	Pr 24:17
Do not **g** over your brother in	Ob 12
on the earth will **g** over them	Rv 11:10

GLOOM

May darkness and **g** reclaim it,	Jb 3:5
go to a land of darkness and **g**,	Jb 10:21
Others sat in darkness and **g**	Ps 107:10
the **g** of the distressed land	Is 9:1
brings darkest **g** and makes thick	Jr 13:16
a day of darkness and **g**,	Jl 2:2
even **g** without any brightness in	Am 5:20
a day of darkness and **g**,	Zph 1:15
to darkness, **g**, and storm,	Heb 12:18
The **g** of darkness has been	2Pt 2:17

GLORIFY

My lips will **g** You because Your	Ps 63:3
G Him, all peoples!	Ps 117:1
and **g-ies** Himself through Israel.	Is 44:23
I will be **g-ied** in him.	Is 49:3
and I will **g** My dwelling place.	Is 60:13
so that I may be **g-ied**.	Is 60:21
the LORD be **g-ied**, so that we can	Is 66:5
honored and **g-ied** Him who lives	Dn 4:34
But you have not **g-ied** the God	Dn 5:23
g-ing and praising God for all they	Lk 2:20
and went home **g-ing** God.	Lk 5:25
and they **g-ied** God,	Lk 7:16
restored and began to **g** God.	Lk 13:13
began to follow Him, **g-ing** God.	Lk 18:43

Jesus had not yet been **g-ied**.	Jn 7:39
He is the One who **g-ies** Me.	Jn 8:54
when Jesus was **g-ied**, then they	Jn 12:16
for the Son of Man to be **g-ied**.	Jn 12:23
Father, **g** Your name!	Jn 12:28
I have **g-ied** it, and I will **g** it again!	Jn 12:28
the Son of Man is **g-ied**, and	
God is **g-ied** in Him.	Jn 13:31
My Father is **g-ied** by this:	Jn 15:8
G Your Son so that the Son may **g**	Jn 17:1
I have **g-ied** You on the earth by	Jn 17:4
g Me in Your presence with that	Jn 17:5
kind of death he would **g** God.	Jn 21:19
our fathers, has **g-ied** His Servant	Ac 3:13
they did not **g** Him as God or	Rm 1:21
we may also be **g-ied** with Him.	Rm 8:17
those He justified, He also **g-ied**.	Rm 8:30
Gentiles may **g** God for His mercy	Rm 15:9
therefore **g** God in your body.	1Co 6:20
they will **g** God for your obedience	2Co 9:13
And they **g-ied** God because of me.	Gl 1:24
He comes to be **g-ied** by His saints	2Th 1:10
g God in a day of visitation.	1Pt 2:12
God may be **g-ied** through Jesus	1Pt 4:11
but should **g** God with that name	1Pt 4:16
will not fear and **g** Your name?	Rv 15:4

GLORIOUS

Your right hand is **g** in power.	Ex 15:6
Who is like You, **g** in holiness	Ex 15:11
Praise Your **g** name, and may it	Neh 9:5
the royal daughter is all **g**,	Ps 45:13
make His praise **g**.	Ps 66:2
May His **g** name be praised	Ps 72:19
G things are said about you,	Ps 87:3
speak of Your **g** splendor and	Ps 145:5
Gray hair is a **g** crown;	Pr 16:31
LORD will be beautiful and **g**,	Is 4:2
His resting place will be **g**.	Is 11:10
LORD, for He has done **g** things.	Is 12:5
{His} instruction and make it **g**.	Is 42:21
Son of Man sits on His **g** throne,	Mt 19:28
into the **g** freedom of God's	Rm 8:21
ministry of the Spirit not be more **g**?	2Co 3:8
if what was fading away was **g**,	2Co 3:11
praise of His **g** grace that He	Eph 1:6
what are the **g** riches of His	Eph 1:18
the likeness of His **g** body,	Php 3:21
according to His **g** might,	Col 1:11

Gentiles the **g** wealth of this — Col 1:27
based on the **g** gospel of the — 1Tm 1:11
faith in our **g** Lord Jesus Christ — Jms 2:1
when they blaspheme the **g** ones; — 2Pt 2:10
and blaspheme **g** beings. — Jd 8

GLORY

when I receive **g** through Pharaoh — Ex 14:18
g of the LORD settled on ... Sinai, — Ex 24:16
Please, let me see Your **g**. — Ex 33:18
and when My **g** passes by, I will — Ex 33:22
g of the LORD filled the tabernacle. — Ex 40:34
I will reveal My **g** before all — Lv 10:3
earth is filled with the LORD's **g**, — Nm 14:21
The **g** has departed from Israel, — 1Sm 4:21
the **g** of the LORD filled the temple. — 1Kg 8:11
Declare His **g** among the nations — 1Ch 16:24
to the LORD **g** and strength. — 1Ch 16:28
power and the **g** and the splendor — 1Ch 29:11
my **g**, and the One who lifts — Ps 3:3
crowned him with **g** and honor. — Ps 8:5
heavens declare the **g** of God, — Ps 19:1
Then the King of **g** will come in. — Ps 24:7
Who is this King of **g**? — Ps 24:8
the place where Your **g** resides. — Ps 26:8
give the LORD **g** and strength. — Ps 29:1
In His temple all cry, "**G**!" — Ps 29:9
let Your **g** be above the whole — Ps 57:5
Sing the **g** of His name; — Ps 66:2
the whole earth is filled with His **g**. — Ps 72:19
Declare His **g** among the nations — Ps 96:3
ascribe to the LORD **g** and strength. — Ps 96:7
all the peoples see His **g**. — Ps 97:6
He will appear in His **g**. — Ps 102:16
exchanged their **g** for the image — Ps 106:20
let Your **g** be over the whole — Ps 108:5
nations, His **g** above the heavens. — Ps 113:4
not to us, but to Your name give **g** — Ps 115:1
for the LORD's **g** is great. — Ps 138:5
speak of the **g** of Your kingdom — Ps 145:11
The **g** of young men is their — Pr 20:29
It is the **g** of God to conceal a — Pr 25:2
much honey, or to seek **g** after **g**. — Pr 25:27
His **g** fills the whole earth. — Is 6:3
He will (display His) **g** — Is 24:23
And the **g** of the LORD will appear, — Is 40:5
will not give My **g** to another, — Is 42:8; 48:11
the **g** of the LORD shines over you. — Is 60:1
they will come and see My **g**. — Is 66:18

exchanged their **G** for useless — Jr 2:11
and **g** before all the nations of — Jr 33:9
Then the **g** of the LORD rose from — Ezk 10:4
The **g** of the LORD rose up from — Ezk 11:23
I will display My **g** within you. — Ezk 28:22
Who are you like in **g** — Ezk 31:18
will display My **g** among the — Ezk 39:21
and the earth shone with His **g**. — Ezk 43:2
the **g** of the LORD filled — Ezk 43:5; 44:4
throne and his **g** was taken from — Dn 5:20
the knowledge of the LORD's **g**, — Hab 2:14
The final **g** of this house will — Hg 2:9
and I will be the **g** within it. — Zch 2:5
the power and the **g** forever. — Mt 6:13
and gave **g** to God who had — Mt 9:8
And they gave **g** to the God of — Mt 15:31
angels in the **g** of His Father, — Mt 16:27
heaven with power and great **g**. — Mt 24:30
the Son of Man comes in His **g**, — Mt 25:31
and at Your left in Your **g**. — Mk 10:37
and the **g** of the Lord shone — Lk 2:9
G to God in the highest heaven, — Lk 2:14
Gentiles and **g** to Your people — Lk 2:32
We observed His **g**, the **g** as the
  One and Only Son — Jn 1:14
He displayed His **g**, and His — Jn 2:11
I do not accept **g** from men, — Jn 5:41
for himself seeks his own **g**. — Jn 7:18
I do not seek My **g**; the One who — Jn 8:50
and told him, "Give **g** to God. — Jn 9:24
death but is for the **g** of God, — Jn 11:4
with that **g** I had with You — Jn 17:5
will see My **g**, which You have — Jn 17:24
The God of **g** appeared to our — Ac 7:2
he did not give the **g** to God, — Ac 12:23
exchanged the **g** of the immortal — Rm 1:23
doing good seek for **g**, — Rm 2:7
and fall short of the **g** of God. — Rm 3:23
in his faith and gave **g** to God, — Rm 4:20
not worth comparing with the **g** — Rm 8:18
adoption, the **g**, the covenants — Rm 9:4
the riches of His **g** on objects — Rm 9:23
To Him be the **g** forever. — Rm 11:36
to Him be the **g** forever! — Rm 16:27
have crucified the Lord of **g**. — 1Co 2:8
do everything for God's **g**. — 1Co 10:31
but woman is man's **g**. — 1Co 11:7
has long hair, it is her **g**? — 1Co 11:15

sown in dishonor, raised in g; 1Co 15:43
because of the **g** that surpasses 2Co 3:10
the gospel of the **g** of Christ, 2Co 4:4
incomparable eternal weight of **g**. 2Co 4:17
to whom be the **g** forever and Gl 1:5
to the praise of His **g**. Eph 1:14
to Him be **g** in the church and in Eph 3:21
to the **g** of God the Father. Php 2:11
their **g** is in their shame. Php 3:19
His riches in **g** in Christ Jesus Php 4:19
Christ in you, the hope of **g**. Col 1:27
will be revealed with Him in **g**. Col 3:4
For you are our **g** and joy! 1Th 2:20
be honor and **g** forever and ever 1Tm 1:17
on in the world, taken up in **g**. 1Tm 3:16
To Him be the **g** forever and ever 2Tm 4:18
He is the radiance of His **g**, Heb 1:3
crowned him with **g** and honor Heb 2:7
in bringing many sons to **g**, Heb 2:10
to whom be **g** forever and ever. Heb 13:21
and the **g-ies** that would follow 1Pt 1:11
and all its **g** like a flower of 1Pt 1:24
Him belong the **g** and the power 1Pt 4:11
the Spirit of **g** and of God rests 1Pt 4:14
the unfading crown of **g**. 1Pt 5:4
to His eternal **g** in Christ Jesus 1Pt 5:10
us by His own **g** and goodness. 2Pt 1:3
to Him from the Majestic **G**: 2Pt 1:17
To Him be the **g** both now and to 2Pt 3:18
stand in the presence of His **g**, Jd 24
our Lord, be **g**, majesty, power Jd 25
to Him be the **g** and dominion Rv 1:6
worthy to receive **g** and honor Rv 4:11
and honor and **g** and blessing! Rv 5:12
smoke from God's **g** and from His Rv 15:8
Salvation, **g**, and power belong Rv 19:1
because God's **g** illuminates it, Rv 21:23

GLUTTON
He's a **g** and a drunkard. Dt 21:20
and the **g** will become poor Pr 23:21
a companion of **g-s** humiliates his Pr 28:7
they say, 'Look, a **g** and a drunkard Mt 11:19
always liars, evil beasts, lazy **g-s**. Ti 1:12

GNASH
He **g-es** His teeth at me. Jb 16:9
they **g-ed** their teeth at me. Ps 35:16
and **g-es** his teeth at him. Ps 37:12
he will **g** his teeth in despair. Ps 112:10

They hiss and **g** {their} teeth, Lm 2:16
will be weeping and **g-ing** of teeth.
Mt 8:12; 13:42, 50; 22:13;
24:51; 25:30; Lk 13:28
and **g-ed** their teeth at him. Ac 7:54

GNAT
and it will become **g-s** throughout Ex 8:16
g-s throughout their country. Ps 105:31
strain out a **g**, yet gulp down Mt 23:24

GNAWED
and hunger, they **g** the dry land Jb 30:3
People **g** their tongues from pain Rv 16:10

GO
not let You **g** unless You bless Gn 32:26
Let My people **g**, Ex 5:1
your God who **g-es** before you will Dt 1:30
God is with you wherever you **g**. Jos 1:9
For wherever you **g**, I will **g**, Ru 1:16
look for me, but I will be **gone**. Jb 7:8
Their message has **gone** out to all Ps 19:4
and show you the way to **g**; Ps 32:8
passed by and noticed he was **gone**; Ps 37:36
for me, where I can always **g**. Ps 71:3
we have **gone** astray and have Ps 106:6
Let us **g** to the house of the Ps 122:1
and it will **g** well for you. Ps 128:2
Let us **g** to His dwelling place; Ps 132:7
Where can I **g** to escape Your Ps 139:7
If I **g** up to heaven, You are Ps 139:8
to me the way I should **g**, Ps 143:8
G to the ant, you slacker! Pr 6:6
keep **g-ing** and are punished. Pr 22:3; 27:12
about the way he should **g**; Pr 22:6
but it will **g** well with those Pr 24:25
Who has **gone** up to heaven and Pr 30:4
her lamp never **g-es** out at night. Pr 31:18
said to myself, "**G** ahead, I will Ec 2:1
All are **g-ing** to the same place; Ec 3:20
as he comes, so he will **g**. Ec 5:16
better to **g** to a house of mourning Ec 7:2
it will **g** well with God-fearing Ec 8:12
after that they **g** to the dead. Ec 9:3
not let him **g** until I brought Sg 3:4
instruction will **g** out of Zion Is 2:3
the LORD is **g-ing** before you, Is 52:12
We all **went** astray like sheep; Is 53:6

where they **went**, they profaned
My holy name,   Ezk 36:20
Jonah got up and **went** to Nineveh   Jnh 3:1
I am **g-ing** to send   Mal 3:1; 4:5
forces you to **g** one mile, **g**   Mt 5:41
I say to this one, '**G**!' and he **g-es**;   Mt 8:9
will follow You wherever You **g**!   Mt 8:19
It's not what **g-es** into the mouth   Mt 15:11
We are **g-ing** up to Jerusalem.   Mt 20:18
you don't **g** in, and you don't allow   Mt 23:13
just like a man **g-ing** on a journey.   Mt 25:14
Judas ... **went** to the chief priests   Mt 26:14
Son of Man will **g** just as it is   Mt 26:24
G-ing a little farther, He fell   Mt 26:39
He is **g-ing** ahead of you to Galilee   Mt 28:7
G, therefore, and make disciples   Mt 28:19
they **went** away ... by themselves   Mk 6:32
went away to the mountain to pray.   Mk 6:46
G into all the world and preach   Mk 16:15
it comes from or where it is **g-ing**.   Jn 3:8
disciples had **gone** into town to buy   Jn 4:8
to the festival, then He also **went** up,   Jn 7:10
I come from or where I'm **g-ing**.   Jn 8:14
Where I'm **g-ing**, you cannot come.   Jn 8:21
the world has **gone** after Him!   Jn 12:19
Where I am **g-ing** you cannot come,   Jn 13:33
I am **g-ing** away to prepare a place   Jn 14:2
we don't know where You're **g-ing**.   Jn 14:5
because I am **g-ing** to the Father.   Jn 14:12
that I am **g-ing** to the Father,   Jn 14:28
asks Me, 'Where are You **g-ing**?'   Jn 16:5
because I am **g-ing** to the Father   Jn 16:10
looking for Me, let these men **g**.   Jn 18:8
you where you don't want to **g**.   Jn 21:18
Who will **g** up to heaven?   Rm 10:6
Their voice has **gone** out to all   Rm 10:18
brother **g-es** to law against brother   1Co 6:6
that it may **g** well with you and   Eph 6:3
as I see how things **g** with me.   Php 2:23
not knowing where he was **g-ing**.   Heb 11:8
Let us then **g** to Him outside the   Heb 13:13
and doesn't know where he's **g-ing**,   1Jn 2:11
went out from us, but they did not   1Jn 2:19

GOADS

sayings of the wise are like **g**,   Ec 12:11
for you to kick against the **g**.   Ac 26:14

GOAL

feelings, focusing on one **g**.   Php 2:2

I pursue as my **g** the prize   Php 3:14
Now the **g** of our instruction is   1Tm 1:5
receiving the **g** of your faith,   1Pt 1:9

GOAT

a young **g**, and dipped   Gn 37:31
fine linen and **g** hair;   Ex 25:4
the **g** chosen by lot   Lv 16:9,10
put them on the **g-'s** head and send   Lv 16:21
year-old female **g** as a sin offering   Nm 15:27
placed some **g-s'** hair on its head,   1Sm 19:13
bulls or drink the blood of **g-s**?   Ps 50:13
rooster, a **g**, and a king at   Pr 30:31
a flock of **g-s** streaming down   Sg 4:1; 6:5
blood of bulls, lambs, or male **g-s**.   Is 1:11
leopard will lie down with the **g**.   Is 11:6
The **g** had a conspicuous horn   Dn 8:5
The shaggy **g** represents the king   Dn 8:21
separates the sheep from the **g-s**.   Mt 25:32
For if the blood of **g-s** and bulls   Heb 9:13
of bulls and **g-s** to take away sins.   Heb 10:4
like sackcloth made of **g** hair;   Rv 6:12

GOATSKINS

She put the **g** on his hands and   Gn 27:16
in sheepskins, in **g**, destitute   Heb 11:37

GOBLET

have drunk the **g** to the dregs   Is 51:17
that **g**, the cup of My fury.   Is 51:22

GOD

In the beginning **G** created the   Gn 1:1
you will be like **G**, knowing good   Gn 3:5
walked with **G**, and he was not   Gn 5:24
the sons of **G** saw that the   Gn 6:2
Noah walked with **G**.   Gn 6:9
covenant between **G** and every   Gn 9:16
he was a priest to **G** Most High.   Gn 14:18
The **G** Who Sees, for she said   Gn 16:13
saying, "I am **G** Almighty.   Gn 17:1
and I will be their **G**.   Gn 17:8
G was with the boy, and he grew   Gn 21:20
the LORD, the Everlasting **G**.   Gn 21:33
G Himself will provide the lamb   Gn 22:8
G of heaven and **G** of earth,   Gn 24:3
LORD, **G** of my master Abraham   Gn 24:12
the **G** of your father Abraham
and the **G** of Isaac.   Gn 28:13
none other than the house of **G**.   Gn 28:17
If **G** will be with me and watch   Gn 28:20

then the LORD will be my **G**.	Gn 28:21
I am the **G** of Bethel, where you	Gn 31:13
but why have you stolen my **g-s**?	Gn 31:30
Jacob said, "This is **G**-'s camp.	Gn 32:2
called it "**G**, the **G** of Israel."	Gn 33:20
I am **G** Almighty.	Gn 35:11
Your **G** and the **G** of your father	Gn 43:23
I am **G**, the **G** of your father.	Gn 46:3
G Almighty appeared to me at	Gn 48:3
but **G** will be with you and will	Gn 48:21
Am I in the place of **G**?	Gn 50:19
G planned it for good to bring	Gn 50:20
So **G** heard their groaning,	Ex 2:24
to Horeb, the mountain of **G**.	Ex 3:1
I am the **G** of your father, the **G** of	
Abraham, the **G** of Isaac, and	
the **G** of Jacob.	Ex 3:6
he was afraid to look at **G**.	Ex 3:6
G replied to Moses, "I AM	Ex 3:14
Yahweh, the **G** of your fathers	Ex 3:15
G of Abraham, the **G** of Isaac,	Ex 3:15
The LORD, the **G** of the Hebrews,	Ex 3:18
and you will serve as **G** to him.	Ex 4:16
the LORD, the **G** of Israel, says:	Ex 5:1
and Jacob as **G** Almighty,	Ex 6:3
people, and I will be your **G**.	Ex 6:7
made you like **G** to Pharaoh,	Ex 7:1
against all the **g-s** of Egypt.	Ex 12:12
This is my **G**, and I will praise Him,	Ex 15:2
who is like You among the **g-s**?	Ex 15:11
the LORD is greater than all **g-s**,	Ex 18:11
some advice, and **G** be with you.	Ex 18:19
out of the camp to meet **G**,	Ex 19:17
I am the LORD your **G**,	Ex 20:2
Do not have other **g-s** besides Me.	Ex 20:3
I, the LORD your **G**, am a jealous **G**,	Ex 20:5
must not bow down to their **g-s**	Ex 23:24
the Israelites and be their **G**.	Ex 29:45
this is your **G**, who brought you	Ex 32:4
'Make us a **g** who will go before	Ex 32:23
a compassionate and gracious **G**,	Ex 34:6
by nature, is a jealous **G**.	Ex 34:14
I, the LORD your **G**, am holy.	Lv 19:2
walk among you and be your **G**,	Lv 26:12
the message **G** puts in my mouth	Nm 22:38
G is not a man who lies, or a	Nm 23:19
The LORD their **G** is with them,	Nm 23:21
for what **g** is there in heaven or	Dt 3:24

has a **g** near to it as the LORD our **G**	Dt 4:7
G is a consuming fire, a jealous **G**.	Dt 4:24
your **G** is a compassionate **G**.	Dt 4:31
the LORD is **G** in heaven above	Dt 4:39
Do not have other **g-s** besides Me.	Dt 5:7
I, the LORD your **G**, am a jealous **G**,	Dt 5:9
the voice of the living **G** speaking	Dt 5:26
The LORD our **G**, the LORD is One.	Dt 6:4
Love the LORD your **G** with all your	Dt 6:5
Do not follow other **g-s** of	Dt 6:14
G, who is among you, is a jealous **G**	Dt 6:15
Yahweh your **G** is **G**, the faithful **G**	Dt 7:9
G, a great and awesome **G**, is among	Dt 7:21
serve the LORD your **G** with all	Dt 10:12
the LORD your **G** is the **G** of **g-s**	Dt 10:17
A faithful **G**, without prejudice	Dt 32:4
there is no **G** but Me.	Dt 32:39
blessing that Moses, the man of **G**,	Dt 33:1
The **G** of old is {your} dwelling	Dt 33:27
for the LORD your **G** is with you	Jos 1:9
the LORD, the **G** of Israel, says	Jos 7:13
loyal to the LORD my **G**.	Jos 14:8
love the LORD your **G**, walk in all	Jos 22:5
The LORD is the **G** of **g-s**!	Jos 22:22
between us that the LORD is **G**.	Jos 22:34
Get rid of the **g-s** your ancestors	Jos 24:14
the LORD, because He is our **G**,	Jos 24:18
He is a holy **G**. He is a jealous **G**;	Jos 24:19
went after other **g-s** from the	Jdg 2:12
Israel chose new **g-s**, then war	Jdg 5:8
If he is a **g**, let him plead his	Jdg 6:31
because we have seen **G**!	Jdg 13:22
and your **G** will be my **G**.	Ru 1:16
there is no rock like our **G**.	1Sm 2:2
the LORD is a **G** of knowledge,	1Sm 2:3
The **g-s** have entered their camp!	1Sm 4:7
require because **G** is with you.	1Sm 10:7
and terror from **G** spread.	1Sm 14:15
But **G** did not answer him that	1Sm 14:37
evil spirit from **G** is tormenting	1Sm 16:15
defy the armies of the living **G**?	1Sm 17:26
Then he cursed David by his **g-s**.	1Sm 17:43
will know that Israel has a **G**,	1Sm 17:46
saying, 'Go and worship	
other **g-s**.	1Sm 26:19
strength in the LORD his **G**.	1Sm 30:6
"As **G** lives," Joab replied, "if	2Sm 2:27
LORD **G** of Hosts was with him.	2Sm 5:10

and there is no G besides You, 2Sm 7:22
You, LORD, have become their G. 2Sm 7:24
Lord G, You are G; 2Sm 7:28
my G, my mountain where I seek 2Sm 22:3
I called to my G. 2Sm 22:7
G—His way is perfect; 2Sm 22:31
who is G besides the LORD? And
   who is a rock? Only our G. 2Sm 22:32
G is my strong refuge; 2Sm 22:33
G of Israel, there is no G like You 1Kg 8:23
But will G indeed live on earth 1Kg 8:27
Chemosh, the g of Moab, 1Kg 11:33
here is your G who brought you 1Kg 12:28
A man of G came from Judah to 1Kg 13:1
As the LORD G of Israel lives, 1Kg 17:1
As the LORD your G lives, 1Kg 17:12
Elijah, "Man of G, what do we 1Kg 17:18
If Yahweh is G, follow Him. 1Kg 18:21
G who answers with fire, He is G 1Kg 18:24
Shout loudly, for he's a g! 1Kg 18:27
are G and that You have turned 1Kg 18:37
and said, "Yahweh, He is G! 1Kg 18:39
May the g-s punish me and do so 1Kg 19:2
for the LORD G of Hosts, 1Kg 19:10
Their g-s are g-s of the hill 1Kg 20:23
The LORD is a g of the mountains 1Kg 20:28
Is it because there is no G in Israel 2Kg 1:3
I am a man of G, may fire come 2Kg 1:10
asked, "Am I G, 2Kg 5:7
sinned against the LORD their G 2Kg 17:7
they had worshiped other g-s. 2Kg 17:7
custom of the G of the land. 2Kg 17:26
Where are the g-s of Hamath and 2Kg 18:34
And G granted his request. 1Ch 4:10
great army, like an army of G. 1Ch 12:22
Save us, G of our salvation; 1Ch 16:35
and musical instruments of G. 1Ch 16:42
your heart, for G is with you. 1Ch 17:2
know the G of your father, 1Ch 28:9
the LORD G, my G, is with you. 1Ch 28:20
I know, my G, that You test the 1Ch 29:17
The LORD his G was with him and 2Ch 1:1
our G is greater than any of the g-s. 2Ch 2:5
David, the man of G 2Ch 8:14
the turn of events came from G, 2Ch 10:15
as for us, the LORD is our G. 2Ch 13:10
the LORD his G was with him. 2Ch 15:9
I will say whatever my G says. 2Ch 18:13

the G who is in heaven, 2Ch 20:6
Are You not our G who drove out 2Ch 20:7
the battle is not yours, but G-'s. 2Ch 20:15
Ahaziah's downfall was from G, 2Ch 22:7
for G has the power to help or 2Ch 25:8
For the LORD your G is gracious 2Ch 30:9
The LORD, the G of heaven, has 2Ch 36:23
the G who is in Jerusalem. Ezr 1:3
house of the great G in the province Ezr 5:8
angered the G of heaven, Ezr 5:12
My G, I am ashamed and Ezr 9:6
LORD G of heaven, the great and
   awe-inspiring G who keeps His Neh 1:5
But You are a forgiving G, Neh 9:17
This is your G who brought you Neh 9:18
a gracious and compassionate G. Neh 9:31
Does Job fear G for nothing? Jb 1:9
only good from G and not Jb 2:10
yet I will see G in my flesh. Jb 19:26
a person be justified before G? Jb 25:4
since G is greater than man. Jb 33:12
For G speaks time and again, Jb 33:14
Yes, G is mighty, but He Jb 36:5
For You are not a G who delights Ps 5:4
You made him a little less than G Ps 8:5
thinks: ... G does not exist. Ps 10:4
says in his heart, "G does not exist." Ps 14:1
for G is with those who are Ps 14:5
my deliverer, my G, my mountain Ps 18:2
who is G besides the LORD? And
   who is a rock? Only our G. Ps 18:31
The heavens declare the glory of G, Ps 19:1
My G, my G, why have You Ps 22:1
You have been my G from Ps 22:10
I say, "You are my G." Ps 31:14
the nation whose G is the LORD Ps 33:12
I thirst for G, the living G. Ps 42:2
say to me, "Where is your G?" Ps 42:3
to G, my greatest joy. Ps 43:4
G is our refuge and strength, Ps 46:1
G is within her; she will not be Ps 46:5
the G of Jacob is our stronghold Ps 46:7
and know that I am G, Ps 46:10
for G is King of all the earth. Ps 47:7
This G, our G forever and ever Ps 48:14
G, the LORD G speaks; Ps 50:1
I am G, your G. Ps 50:7
Be gracious to me, G, according to Ps 51:1

G, create a clean heart for me   Ps 51:10
G, You will not despise a broken   Ps 51:17
says in his heart, "G does not exist." Ps 53:1
They have no regard for G.   Ps 54:3
with the crowd into the house of G.   Ps 55:14
whose word I praise, in G I trust;   Ps 56:4
This I know: G is for me.   Ps 56:9
I call to G Most High,   Ps 57:2
LORD G of Hosts, G of Israel, rise   Ps 59:5
G, You are my G; I eagerly seek   Ps 63:1
G, our G, blesses us.   Ps 67:6
G arises. His enemies scatter,   Ps 68:1
poured down {rain} before G,
   the G of Sinai, before G,
   the G of Israel.   Ps 68:8
Our G is a G of salvation,   Ps 68:20
continually say, "G is great!"   Ps 70:4
G is known in Judah;   Ps 76:1
What g is great like G?   Ps 77:13
Is G able to provide food in   Ps 78:19
nations ask, "Where is their G?"   Ps 79:10
not be a strange g among you;   Ps 81:9
He judges among the g-s: Ps 82:1
I said, "You are g-s; you are all   Ps 82:6
flesh cry out for the living G.   Ps 84:2
is no one like You among the g-s,   Ps 86:8
You alone are G.   Ps 86:10
are said about you, city of G.   Ps 87:3
from eternity to eternity, You are G.   Ps 90:2
G of vengeance—G of vengeance   Ps 94:1
For the LORD is a great G,   Ps 95:3
For He is our G, and we are the   Ps 95:7
He is feared above all g-s.   Ps 96:4
For all the g-s of the peoples are   Ps 96:5
are exalted above all the g-s.   Ps 97:9
for the LORD our G is holy.   Ps 99:9
Acknowledge that the LORD is G.   Ps 100:3
With G we will perform valiantly   Ps 108:13
Who is like the LORD our G   Ps 113:5
nations say, "Where is their G?"   Ps 115:2
You are my G, and I will give   Ps 118:28
our Lord is greater than all g-s.   Ps 135:5
Give thanks to the G of g-s.   Ps 136:2
Give thanks to the G of heaven!   Ps 136:26
Search me, G, and know
   my heart;   Ps 139:23
say to the LORD, "You are my G."   Ps 140:6
do Your will, for You are my G.   Ps 143:10

the people whose G is the LORD.   Ps 144:15
I exalt You, my G the King,   Ps 145:1
in the sight of G and man.   Pr 3:4
It is the glory of G to conceal   Pr 25:2
Every word of G is pure;   Pr 30:5
G is in heaven and you are on   Ec 5:2
G has made the one as well as   Ec 7:14
fear G and keep His commands,   Ec 12:13
Wonderful Counselor, Mighty G,   Is 9:6
Indeed, G is my salvation.   Is 12:2
LORD, You are my G; I will exalt   Is 25:1
it will be said, "Look, this is our G; Is 25:9
You are G—You alone   Is 37:16
have thrown their g-s into the fire;
   for they were not g-s but made   Is 37:19
of Judah, "Here is your G!"   Is 40:9
Yahweh is the everlasting G,   Is 40:28
not be afraid, for I am your G.   Is 41:10
we will know that you are g-s.   Is 41:23
No g was formed before Me,   Is 43:10
There is no G but Me.   Is 44:6
Let these g-s declare the coming   Is 44:7
makes it into a g and worships it;   Is 44:15
it, "Save me, for you are my g."   Is 44:17
G is indeed with you,
   and there is no other;
   there is no other G.   Is 45:14
G is the Creator of the heavens   Is 45:18
and pray to a g who cannot save   Is 45:20
says to Zion, "Your G reigns!"   Is 52:7
struck down by G, and afflicted   Is 53:4
so your G will rejoice over you.   Is 62:5
nation {ever} exchanged its g-s?   Jr 2:11
and then I will be your G,   Jr 7:23
But the LORD is the true G;   Jr 10:10
Can one make g-s for himself?   Jr 16:20
Am I a G who is only near   Jr 23:23
I will be their G because they   Jr 24:7
people, and I will be your G.   Jr 30:22
I will be their G, and they will   Jr 31:33
I am the LORD, the G of all flesh.   Jr 32:27
to other g-s to provoke Me to anger.   Jr 32:29
the LORD is a G of retribution;   Jr 51:56
opened and I saw visions of G.   Ezk 1:1
people, and I will be their G.   Ezk 11:20
I am the LORD your G.   Ezk 20:5
proud, and you have said: I am a g;   Ezk 28:2
Yet you are a man and not a g,   Ezk 28:2

know that I am the LORD their **G**.	Ezk 28:26	the Son of the living **G**!	Mt 16:16
people, and I will be your **G**.	Ezk 36:28	not thinking about **G**-'s concerns,	Mt 16:23
people, and I will be their **G**.	Ezk 37:23	Therefore what **G** has joined	Mt 19:6
In visions of **G** He took me to	Ezk 40:2	but with **G** all things are possible.	Mt 19:26
The **G** of heaven has given you	Dn 2:37	teach truthfully the way of **G**.	Mt 22:16
The great **G** has told the king	Dn 2:45	and to **G** the things that are **G**-'s.	Mt 22:21
Your **G** is indeed **G** of **g-s**,	Dn 2:47	Scriptures or the power of **G**.	Mt 22:29
If the **G** we serve exists, then	Dn 3:17	I am the **G** of Abraham and the **G**	Mt 22:32
looks like a son of the **g-s**.	Dn 3:25	He is not the **G** of the dead,	Mt 22:32
worship any **g** except their own **G**.	Dn 3:28	the Lord your **G** with all your	Mt 22:37
the spirit of the holy **g-s** is in him	Dn 4:8	If You are the Son of **G**, come	Mt 27:40
petitions any **g** or man except	Dn 6:7	has put His trust in **G**; let **G** rescue	Mt 27:43
He is the living **G**, and He endures	Dn 6:26	that is, "My **G**, My **G**, why have	Mt 27:46
awe-inspiring **G** who keeps His	Dn 9:4	of Jesus Christ, the Son of **G**.	Mk 1:1
say ... things against the **G** of **g-s**.	Dn 11:36	Who can forgive sins but **G** alone?	Mk 2:7
and I will not be your **G**.	Hs 1:9	Jesus, Son of the Most High **G**?	Mk 5:7
he will say: {You are} My **G**.	Hs 2:23	**G** made them male and female.	Mk 10:6
no knowledge of **G** in the land!	Hs 4:1	No one is good but One—**G**.	Mk 10:18
My **G**, we know You!	Hs 8:2	to them, "Have faith in **G**.	Mk 11:22
craftsman made it, and it is not **G**.	Hs 8:6	Lord our **G**, The Lord is One.	Mk 12:29
For I am **G** and not man, the Holy	Hs 11:9	not far from the kingdom of **G**.	Mk 12:34
But you must return to your **G**.	Hs 12:6	sat down at the right hand of **G**.	Mk 16:19
I have been the LORD your **G**	Hs 12:9; 13:4	you have found favor with **G**.	Lk 1:30
you know no **G** but Me,	Hs 13:4	has rejoiced in **G** my Savior,	Lk 1:47
and return to the LORD your **G**.	Jl 2:13	Glory to **G** in the highest heaven	Lk 2:14
the peoples, 'Where is their **G**?'	Jl 2:17	kingdom of **G** has come near you.	Lk 10:9
Israel, prepare to meet your **G**!	Am 4:12	Are You, then, the Son of **G**?	Lk 22:70
and say, "As your **g** lives, Dan,"	Am 8:14	was with **G**, and the Word was **G**.	Jn 1:1
Call to your **g**. Maybe this **g** will	Jnh 1:6	No one has ever seen **G**.	Jn 1:18
Yahweh, the **G** of the heavens	Jnh 1:9	is the Lamb of **G**, who takes away	Jn 1:29
a merciful and compassionate **G**,	Jnh 4:2	You do unless **G** were with him.	Jn 3:2
and to walk humbly with your **G**.	Mc 6:8	For **G** loved the world in this way:	Jn 3:16
Who is a **G** like You, removing	Mc 7:18	has affirmed that **G** is true.	Jn 3:33
is a jealous and avenging **G**;	Nah 1:2	**G** is spirit, and those who worship	Jn 4:24
their strength is their **g**.	Hab 1:11	was even calling **G** His own Father,	
rejoice in the **G** of my salvation!	Hab 3:18	making Himself equal with **G**.	Jn 5:18
have heard that **G** is with you.	Zch 8:23	This is the work of **G**:	Jn 6:29
For I am the LORD their **G**,	Zch 10:6	that You are the Holy One of **G**!	Jn 6:69
house of David will be like **G**,	Zch 12:8	If **G** were your Father, you would	Jn 8:42
Then the LORD my **G** will come	Zch 14:5	If this man were not from **G**,	Jn 9:33
Didn't one **G** create us?	Mal 2:10	being a man—make Yourself **G**.	Jn 10:33
or "Where is the **G** of justice?"	Mal 2:17	I said, you are **g-s**?	Jn 10:34
Will a man rob **G**?	Mal 3:8	but is for the glory of **G**,	Jn 11:4
is translated "**G** is with us."	Mt 1:23	was from **G**, and ... going back to **G**.	Jn 13:3
Spirit of **G** descending like a dove	Mt 3:16	Believe in **G**; believe also in Me.	Jn 14:1
that comes from the mouth of **G**.	Mt 4:4	Father—to My **G** and your **G**.	Jn 20:17
because they will see **G**.	Mt 5:8	to Him, "My Lord and my **G**!"	Jn 20:28
cannot be slaves of **G** and of money.	Mt 6:24	**G** raised Him up, ending the	Ac 2:24

exalted to the right hand of **G**	Ac 2:33
G has made this Jesus, whom you	Ac 2:36
The **G** of Abraham, Isaac, and Jacob,	
the **G** of our fathers	Ac 3:13
and whom **G** raised from dead	Ac 4:10
listen to you rather than to **G**,	Ac 4:19
have not lied to men but to **G**!	Ac 5:4
We must obey **G** rather than men	Ac 5:29
The **G** of our fathers raised up	Ac 5:30
G exalted this man to His right	Ac 5:31
but if it is of **G**, you will not	Ac 5:39
Make us **g-s** who will go before us	Ac 7:40
Jesus Christ is the Son of **G**.	Ac 8:37
What **G** has made clean,	Ac 10:15
G doesn't show favoritism,	Ac 10:34
G raised up this man on the	Ac 10:40
So **G** has granted repentance	Ac 11:18
the voice of a **g** and not of a man!	Ac 12:22
The **g-s** have come down to us in	Ac 14:11
TO AN UNKNOWN **G**	Ac 17:23
G now commands all people	Ac 17:30
back to you again, if **G** wills.	Ac 18:21
way of **G** to him more accurately.	Ac 18:26
g-s made by hand are not **g-s**!	Ac 19:26
to you the whole plan of **G**.	Ac 20:27
I commit you to **G** and to the	Ac 20:32
G has graciously given you all	Ac 27:24
and said he was a **g**.	Ac 28:6
in it **G-'s** righteousness is revealed	Rm 1:17
though they knew **G**, they did not	Rm 1:21
This is why **G** delivered them	Rm 1:26
is not from men but from **G**.	Rm 2:29
G must be true, but everyone is	Rm 3:4
there is no one who seeks **G**.	Rm 3:11
fall short of the glory of **G**.	Rm 3:23
there is one **G** who will justify	Rm 3:30
Abraham believed **G**, and it was	Rm 4:3
of the man to whom **G** credits	Rm 4:6
But **G** proves His own love for us	Rm 5:8
the gift of **G** is eternal life	Rm 6:23
limited by the flesh, **G** did.	Rm 8:3
flesh are unable to please **G**.	Rm 8:8
that we are **G-'s** children,	Rm 8:16
If **G** is for us, who is against	Rm 8:31
G is the One who justifies.	Rm 8:33
from the love of **G** that is in	Rm 8:39
Messiah, who is **G** over all	Rm 9:5
effort, but on **G** who shows mercy.	Rm 9:16

And what if **G**, desiring to	Rm 9:22
that exist are instituted by **G**.	Rm 13:1
because **G** has accepted him.	Rm 14:3
an account of himself to **G**.	Rm 14:12
The **G** of peace be with all of	Rm 15:33
the only wise **G**, through Jesus	Rm 16:27
G is faithful; by Him you were	1Co 1:9
of **G** except the Spirit of **G**.	1Co 2:11
watered, but **G** gave the growth.	1Co 3:6
and that "there is no **G** but one."	1Co 8:4
even if there are so-called **g-s**,	1Co 8:5
G is faithful and He will not	1Co 10:13
to demons and not to **G**.	1Co 10:20
do everything for **G-'s** glory.	1Co 10:31
and **G** is the head of Christ.	1Co 11:3
nor do the churches of **G**.	1Co 11:16
And **G** has placed these in the	1Co 12:28
not speaking to men but to **G**,	1Co 14:2
proclaiming, "**G** is really among	1Co 14:25
since **G** is not a **G** of disorder	1Co 14:33
by **G-'s** grace I am what I am,	1Co 15:10
testified about **G** that He raised	1Co 15:15
so that **G** may be all in all.	1Co 15:28
But thanks be to **G**, who gives us	1Co 15:57
of Christ Jesus by **G-'s** will,	2Co 1:1
not trust in ourselves, but in **G**	2Co 1:9
in Christ, as from **G** and before **G**.	2Co 2:17
but our competence is from **G**.	2Co 3:5
the **g** of this age has blinded	2Co 4:4
may be from **G** and not from us.	2Co 4:7
G was reconciling the world to	2Co 5:19
Be reconciled to **G**.	2Co 5:20
the righteousness of **G** in Him.	2Co 5:21
the sanctuary of the living **G**,	2Co 6:16
I will be their **G**, and they will be	2Co 6:16
for **G** loves a cheerful giver.	2Co 9:7
G is able to make every grace	2Co 9:8
Thanks be to **G** for His	2Co 9:15
body, I don't know; **G** knows.	2Co 12:2
and the **G** of love and peace will	2Co 13:11
win the favor of people, or **G**?	Gl 1:10
I'm not lying. **G** is my witness.	Gl 1:20
that I might live to **G**.	Gl 2:19
just one person, but **G** is one.	Gl 3:20
of the time came, **G** sent His Son,	Gl 4:4
that by nature are not **g-s**.	Gl 4:8
Don't be deceived: **G** is not mocked.	Gl 6:7
which **G** prepared ahead of time	Eph 2:10

and without G in the world.	Eph 2:12
one G and Father of all, who is	Eph 4:6
be imitators of G, as dearly	Eph 5:1
full armor of G so that you can	Eph 6:11
and this is from G.	Php 1:28
who, existing in the form of G,	Php 2:6
For it is G who is working in	Php 2:13
their g is their stomach;	Php 3:19
requests be made known to G.	Php 4:6
And my G will supply all your	Php 4:19
For G was pleased {to have} all	Col 1:19
G wanted to make known to those	Col 1:27
fullness of G-'s nature dwells	Col 2:9
faith in the working of G,	Col 2:12
hidden with the Messiah in G.	Col 3:3
not to please men, but rather G,	1Th 2:4
message about G that you heard	1Th 2:13
For G has not called us to impurity,	1Th 4:7
For G did not appoint us to wrath,	1Th 5:9
our G will consider you worthy	2Th 1:11
himself above every so-called g	2Th 2:4
publicizing that he himself is G.	2Th 2:4
For this reason G sends them a	2Th 2:11
one G and one mediator between G	1Tm 2:5
is the church of the living G,	1Tm 3:15
foods that G created to be received	1Tm 4:3
put our hope in the living G,	1Tm 4:10
parents, for this pleases G.	1Tm 5:4
you, man of G, run from these	1Tm 6:11
For G has not given us a spirit	2Tm 1:7
present yourself approved to G,	2Tm 2:15
rather than lovers of G,	2Tm 3:4
is inspired by G and is	2Tm 3:16
the man of G may be complete	2Tm 3:17
the teaching of G our Savior	Ti 2:10
our great G and Savior, Jesus	Ti 2:13
man appeared from G our Savior,	Ti 3:4
Long ago G spoke to the fathers	Heb 1:1
is why G, Your G, has anointed	Heb 1:9
G also testified by signs and	Heb 2:4
One who built everything is G.	Heb 3:4
For the word of G is living and	Heb 4:12
Jesus the Son of G—let us hold	Heb 4:14
For G is not unjust; He will not	Heb 6:10
it is impossible for G to lie,	Heb 6:18
I will be their G, and they will	Heb 8:10
into the hands of the living G!	Heb 10:31
faith it is impossible to please G,	Heb 11:6

Therefore G is not ashamed	
to be called their G,	Heb 11:16
for our G is a consuming fire.	Heb 12:29
offer up to G a sacrifice of praise,	Heb 13:15
say, "I am being tempted by G."	Jms 1:13
For G is not tempted by evil,	Jms 1:13
You believe that G is one;	Jms 2:19
and he was called G-'s friend.	Jms 2:23
world's friend becomes G-'s enemy.	Jms 4:4
Draw near to G, and He will draw	Jms 4:8
but now you are G-'s people;	1Pt 2:10
{should be} like the oracles of G;	1Pt 4:11
because G resists the proud,	1Pt 5:5
Now the G of all grace, who	1Pt 5:10
Holy Spirit, men spoke from G.	2Pt 1:21
the coming of the day of G,	2Pt 3:12
G is light, and there is	1Jn 1:5
G is greater than our hearts and	1Jn 3:20
come in the flesh is from G.	1Jn 4:2
does not know G, because G is love.	1Jn 4:8
G sent His One and Only Son into	1Jn 4:9
not that we loved G, but that He	1Jn 4:10
No one has ever seen G.	1Jn 4:12
G is love, and the one who	1Jn 4:16
the Messiah has been born of G,	1Jn 5:1
we love G and obey His commands.	1Jn 5:2
For this is what love for G is:	1Jn 5:3
that Jesus is the Son of G?	1Jn 5:5
G has given us eternal life,	1Jn 5:11
He is the true G and eternal	1Jn 5:20
goes beyond it, does not have G.	2Jn 9
The one who does good is of G;	3Jn 11
keep yourselves in the love of G,	Jd 21
to the only G our Savior,	Jd 25
pillar in the sanctuary of My G,	Rv 3:12
holy, holy, Lord G, the Almighty,	Rv 4:8
and G will wipe away every tear	Rv 7:17
gave glory to the G of heaven.	Rv 11:13
For G has put it into their hearts	Rv 17:17
because our Lord G, the Almighty	Rv 19:6
name is called the Word of G.	Rv 19:13
for the great supper of G,	Rv 19:17
G-'s dwelling is with men,	Rv 21:3
I will be his G, and he will be My	Rv 21:7
the Lord G will give them light.	Rv 22:5
G will add to him the plagues	Rv 22:18

GODDESS

Ashtoreth, the g of the Sidonians,	1Kg 11:5

Ashtoreth, the **g** of the	1Kg 11:33
temple of the great **g** Artemis	Ac 19:27
or blasphemers of our **g**.	Ac 19:37

GOD-FEARING

from all the people able men, **G**,	Ex 18:21
it will go well with **G** people,	Ec 8:12
but if anyone is **G** and does His will,	Jn 9:31
centurion, an upright and **G** man,	Ac 10:22
a great number of **G** Greeks,	Ac 17:4

GOD-GIVEN

with **G** sincerity and purity,	2Co 1:12

GOD-HATERS

slanderers, **G**, arrogant, proud	Rm 1:30

GODLESS

the hope of the **g** will perish.	Jb 8:13
happiness of the **g** has lasted only	Jb 20:5
With **g** mockery they gnashed	Ps 35:16
set anything **g** before my eyes.	Ps 101:3
send him against a **g** nation;	Is 10:6

GODLESSNESS

heaven against all **g** and	Rm 1:18
He will turn away **g** from Jacob.	Rm 11:26
an even greater measure of **g**.	2Tm 2:16
to deny **g** and worldly lusts	Ti 2:12

GODLINESS

own power or **g** we had made him	Ac 3:12
life in all **g** and dignity.	1Tm 2:2
the mystery of **g** is great:	1Tm 3:16
Rather, train yourself in **g**,	1Tm 4:7
but **g** is beneficial in every way	1Tm 4:8
the teaching that promotes **g**,	1Tm 6:3
who imagine that **g** is a way to	1Tm 6:5
But **g** with contentment is a	1Tm 6:6
righteousness, **g**, faith, love	1Tm 6:11
of the truth that leads to **g**,	Ti 1:1
required for life and **g**,	2Pt 1:3
endurance, endurance with **g**,	2Pt 1:6
should be in holy conduct and **g**	2Pt 3:11

GODLY

the flesh of Your **g** ones to the	Ps 79:2
protects the lives of His **g** ones;	Ps 97:10
in the assembly of the **g**.	Ps 149:1
honor is for all His **g** people.	Ps 149:9
G people have vanished from the	Mc 7:2
does the One seek? A **g** offspring.	Mal 2:15
For **g** grief produces a	2Co 7:10

over you with a **g** jealousy,	2Co 11:2
want to live a **g** life in Christ	2Tm 3:12
and **g** way in the present age,	Ti 2:12
how to rescue the **g** from trials	2Pt 2:9

GOFER

Make yourself an ark of **g** wood.	Gn 6:14

GOG

his son **G**, his son Shimei,	1Ch 5:4
I am against you, **G**, chief prince	Ezk 38:3
the day when **G** comes against	Ezk 38:18
G and Magog, to gather them	Rv 20:8

GOLAN

G, the city of refuge for the	Jos 21:27
G in Bashan and its pasturelands,	1Ch 6:71

GOLD

G from that land is pure;	Gn 2:12
Make a mercy seat of pure **g**,	Ex 25:17
Make two cherubim of **g**;	Ex 25:18
made for themselves a god of **g**.	Ex 32:31
must not acquire ... silver and **g**	Dt 17:17
and a bar of **g** weighing 50	Jos 7:21
Five **g** tumors and five **g** mice	1Sm 6:4
he overlaid it with pure **g**.	1Kg 6:20
that carried **g** from Ophir	1Kg 10:11
Solomon's drinking cups were **g**,	1Kg 10:21
Then he made two **g** calves,	1Kg 12:28
and consign your **g** to the dust,	Jb 22:24
tested me, I will emerge as pure **g**.	Jb 23:10
G cannot be exchanged for it,	Jb 28:15
If I placed my confidence in **g**	Jb 31:24
They are more desirable than **g**	Ps 19:10
more than **g**, even the purest **g**,	Ps 119:127
knowledge rather than pure **g**.	Pr 8:10
is like a **g** ring in a pig's	Pr 11:22
how much better it is than **g**!	Pr 16:16
is better than silver and **g**.	Pr 22:1
set on pedestals of pure **g**.	Sg 5:15
I will bring **g** instead of bronze	Is 60:17
head of the statue was pure **g**,	Dn 2:32
Nebuchadnezzar made a **g** statue,	Dn 3:1
The silver and **g** belong to Me	Hg 2:8
and test them as **g** is tested.	Zch 13:9
refine them like **g** and silver.	Mal 3:3
g, frankincense, and myrrh.	Mt 2:11
who takes an oath by the **g**	Mt 23:16
I have neither silver nor **g**,	Ac 3:6
not coveted anyone's silver or **g**	Ac 20:33

on the foundation with **g**,	1Co 3:12
not with elaborate hairstyles, **g**,	1Tm 2:9
your meeting wearing a **g** ring,	Jms 2:2
your silver and **g** are corroded,	Jms 5:3
valuable than **g**, which perishes	1Pt 1:7
perishable things, like silver or **g**,	1Pt 1:18
you to buy from Me **g** refined in	Rv 3:18
city was pure **g** like clear glass	Rv 21:18
street of the city was pure **g**,	Rv 21:21

GOLDEN

the **g** calves that were in Bethel	2Kg 10:29
is like **g** apples on a silver tray.	Pr 25:11
and the **g** bowl is broken	Ec 12:6

GOLDSMITH

they hire a **g** and he makes it	Is 46:6

GOLGOTHA

they came to a place called **G**	Mt 27:33
brought Jesus to the place called **G**	Mk 15:22
which in Hebrew is called **G**.	Jn 19:17

GOLIATH

Philistine giant from Gath killed by David (1Sm 17).

GOMER

1. Son of Japheth (Gn 10:2; 1Ch 1:5).
2. Hosea's wife (Hs 1:3,8).

GOMORRAH

City on the plain, near Sodom where Lot settled (Gn 10:19; 13:10; 14:11-12); destroyed by God (Gn 18:20; 19:24).

Came to symbolize debauchery (Dt 32:32; Jr 23:14; Mt 10:15; 2Pt 2:6; Jd 7) and the resulting devastation (Dt 29:23; Is 1:9; 13:19; Jr 49:18; 50:40; Am 4:11; Zph 2:9; Rm 9:29).

GONG

I am a sounding **g** or a clanging	1Co 13:1

GOOD

And God saw that it was **g**.	Gn 1:10
He had made, and it was very **g**.	Gn 1:31
tree of the knowledge of **g** and evil.	Gn 2:9
It is not **g** for the man to be	Gn 2:18
be like God, knowing **g** and evil.	Gn 3:5
God planned it for **g** to bring about	Gn 50:20
has promised **g** things to Israel.	Nm 10:29
We really had it **g** in Egypt.	Nm 11:18

the land they live in **g** or bad?	Nm 13:19
is an extremely **g** land.	Nm 14:7
Do what is right and **g** in the Lord's	Dt 6:18
None of the **g** promises the Lord	Jos 21:45
If he's alone, he bears **g** news.	2Sm 18:25
he never prophesies **g** about me,	1Kg 22:8
Lord that you have spoken is **g**,	2Kg 20:19
thanks to the Lord, for He is **g**;	1Ch 16:34
to seek **g** for his people	Est 10:3
we accept only **g** from God and	Jb 2:10
Who can show us anything **g**?	Ps 4:6
There is no one who does **g**.	Ps 14:1
The Lord is **g** and upright;	Ps 25:8
Taste and see that the Lord is **g**.	Ps 34:8
repay me evil for **g**, making me	Ps 35:12
Trust in the Lord and do what is **g**;	Ps 37:3
There is no one who does **g**.	Ps 53:1
for Your faithful love is **g**;	Ps 69:16
God is indeed **g** to Israel,	Ps 73:1
withhold the **g** from those who	Ps 84:11
It is **g** to praise the Lord,	Ps 92:1
For the Lord is **g**, and His love	Ps 100:5
to the Lord, for He is **g**;	Ps 106:1; 107:1
G will come to a man who lends	Ps 112:5
You are **g**, and You do what is **g**;	Ps 119:68
It was **g** for me to be afflicted	Ps 119:71
Do what is **g**, Lord, to the **g**,	Ps 125:4
How **g** and pleasant it is when	Ps 133:1
The Lord is **g** to everyone;	Ps 145:9
How **g** it is to sing to our God,	Ps 147:1
don't withhold **g** from the one to	Pr 3:27
I am giving you **g** instruction.	Pr 4:2
for what is **g** finds favor,	Pr 11:27
The **g** obtain favor from the Lord	Pr 12:2
a man will enjoy **g** things,	Pr 13:2
observing the wicked and the **g**.	Pr 15:3
If anyone returns evil for **g**,	Pr 17:13
A joyful heart is **g** medicine,	Pr 17:22
a wife finds a **g** thing and	Pr 18:22
A **g** name is to be chosen over	Pr 22:1
She rewards him with **g**, not evil,	Pr 31:12
pleasure and enjoy what is **g**.	Ec 2:1
rejoice and enjoy the **g** life.	Ec 3:12
and depriving myself from **g**?	Ec 4:8
is what I have seen to be **g**:	Ec 5:18
A **g** name is better than fine	Ec 7:1
It is **g** that you grasp the one	Ec 7:18
As it is for the **g**, so it is for	Ec 9:2

Learn to do what is g.	Is 1:17
who call evil g and g evil,	Is 5:20
Zion, herald of g news, go up	Is 40:9
Indeed, do {something} g or bad,	Is 41:23
who brings news of g things,	Is 52:7
has anointed Me to bring g news to	Is 61:1
not know how to do what is g.	Jr 4:22
not bring the g I had said I	Jr 18:10
basket {contained} very g figs,	Jr 24:2
for their g and for {the g of} their	Jr 32:39
rejoice over them to do what is g	Jr 32:41
fulfill the g promises that I	Jr 33:14
The LORD is g to those who wait	Lm 3:25
both adversity and g come from	Lm 3:38
Because you said: G! about My	Ezk 25:3
will tend them with g pasture,	Ezk 34:14
Israel has rejected what is g;	Hs 8:3
Seek g and not evil so that you	Am 5:14
you men what is g and what it is	Mc 6:8
the feet of one bringing g news	Nah 1:15
to rise on the evil and the g,	Mt 5:45
every g tree produces g fruit,	Mt 7:17
lawful to do g on the Sabbath.	Mt 12:12
A g man produces g things from	Mt 12:35
Still others fell on g ground,	Mt 13:8
didn't you sow g seed in your	Mt 13:27
Lord, it's g for us to be here	Mt 17:4
what g must I do to have eternal	Mt 19:16
Well done, g and faithful slave!	Mt 25:21
Salt is g, but if the salt	Mk 9:50
and asked Him, "G Teacher, what	Mk 10:17
Why do you call Me g? ...	
No one is g but One—God.	Mk 10:18
proclaim to you g news of great joy	Lk 2:10
anointed Me to preach g news to	Lk 4:18
do g to those who hate you,	Lk 6:27
Can anything g come out of	Jn 1:46
Some were saying, "He's a g man."	Jn 7:12
I am the g shepherd.	Jn 10:11
how He went about doing g and	Ac 10:38
for he was a g man,	Ac 11:24
a witness, since He did g:	Ac 14:17
and peace for everyone who does g,	Rm 2:10
do evil so that g may come"?	Rm 3:8
there is no one who does g,	Rm 3:12
though for a g person perhaps	Rm 5:7
commandment is holy and ... g.	Rm 7:12
I want to do g, evil is with me	Rm 7:21

together for the g of those who	Rm 8:28
yet or done anything g or bad,	Rm 9:11
announce the gospel of g things!	Rm 10:15
discern what is the g, pleasing,	Rm 12:2
Detest evil; cling to what is g.	Rm 12:9
by evil, but conquer evil with g.	Rm 12:21
is God's servant to you for g.	Rm 13:4
No one should seek his own {g},	1Co 10:24
Bad company corrupts g morals.	1Co 15:33
you may excel in every g work.	2Co 9:8
always g to be enthusiastic about g	Gl 4:18
must not get tired of doing g,	Gl 6:9
we must work for the g of all,	Gl 6:10
to His g pleasure that He	Eph 1:9
in Christ Jesus for g works,	Eph 2:10
who started a g work in you will	Php 1:6
bearing fruit in every g work	Col 1:10
Hold on to what is g.	1Th 5:21
Now we know that the law is g,	1Tm 1:8
This is g, and it pleases God	1Tm 2:3
everything created by God is g,	1Tm 4:4
Fight the g fight for the faith	1Tm 6:12
do g, to be rich in g works,	1Tm 6:18
prepared for every g work.	2Tm 2:21
equipped for every g work.	2Tm 3:17
I have fought the g fight,	2Tm 4:7
loving what is g, sensible,	Ti 1:8
tasted God's g word and the	Heb 6:5
a shadow of the g things to come	Heb 10:1
based on what seemed g to them,	Heb 12:10
What g is it, my brothers, if	Jms 2:14
who knows to do g and doesn't do	Jms 4:17
have tasted that the Lord is g.	1Pt 2:3
better to suffer for doing g,	1Pt 3:17

GOOD-BYE

but first me go and say g to	Lk 9:61
not say g to all his possessions	Lk 14:33
said g to the brothers and	Ac 18:18
but said g and stated, "I'll	Ac 18:21
after saying g, departed to go	Ac 20:1
we said g to one another.	Ac 21:6
but I said g to them and left	2Co 2:13

GOODNESS

cause all My g to pass in front	Ex 33:19
Only g and faithful love will	Ps 23:6
remember me because of Your g,	Ps 25:7
great is Your g that You have	Ps 31:19
You crown the year with Your g;	Ps 65:11

Show me a sign of Your g;   Ps 86:17
He satisfies you with g;   Ps 103:5
and all its g is like the flower   Is 40:6
will be satisfied with My g.   Jr 31:14
patience, kindness, g, faith,   Gl 5:22
the light {results} in all g,   Eph 5:9
us by His own glory and g.   2Pt 1:3
supplement your faith with g, g with 2Pt 1:5

GOODS

his relative Lot and his g,   Gn 14:16
to barter for your g.   Ezk 27:9
himself with g taken in pledge.   Hab 2:6
You have many g stored up for   Lk 12:19
I donate all my g to feed the   1Co 13:3
must share his g with the   Gl 6:6
has this world's g and sees his   1Jn 3:17

GORE

When an ox g-s a man or a woman   Ex 21:28
he g-s all the peoples with them   Dt 33:17
'You will g the Arameans with   1Kg 22:11

GOSHEN

1. Region of Egypt where Israel settled
(Gn 45:10; 46:28-34); the best part of the
land (47:6,27); excluded from plagues (Ex
8:22; 9:26).

2. City and region of Judah (Jos 10:41;
11:16; 15:51).

GOSPEL

Wherever this g is proclaimed in   Mt 26:13
beginning of the g of Jesus Christ   Mk 1:1
of Me and the g will save it.   Mk 8:35
fields because of Me and the g,   Mk 10:29
and preach the g to the whole   Mk 16:15
testify to the g of God's grace   Ac 20:24
For I am not ashamed of the g,   Rm 1:16
But all did not obey the g.   Rm 10:16
to preach the g—not with clever   1Co 1:17
earn their living by the g.   1Co 9:14
to me if I do not preach the g!   1Co 9:16
if, in fact, our g is veiled,   2Co 4:3
or a different g, which you had not 2Co 11:4
{and are turning} to a different g   Gl 1:6
entrusted with the g for the   Gl 2:7
the word of truth, the g   Eph 1:13
readiness for the g of peace.   Eph 6:15
life in a manner worthy of the g   Php 1:27
the hope of the g that you heard   Col 1:23

on the glorious g of the blessed   1Tm 1:11
from David, according to my g.   2Tm 2:8
was preached as the g to you.   1Pt 1:25
having the eternal g to announce   Rv 14:6

GOSSIP

I have heard the g of many;   Ps 31:13
A g goes around revealing a   Pr 11:13
and a g separates friends.   Pr 16:28
whoever g-s ... separates friends.   Pr 17:9
A g-'s words are like choice   Pr 18:8; 26:22
without a g, conflict dies down.   Pr 26:20
of people's g and slander,   Ezk 36:3
deceit, and malice. They are g-s,   Rm 1:29
ambitions, slander, g, arrogance, 2Co 12:20
but are also g-s and busybodies,   1Tm 5:13

GOUGE

that I g out everyone's right   1Sm 11:2
g it out and throw it away.   Mt 5:29; 18:9
causes your downfall, g it out.   Mk 9:47

GOURDS

as many wild g as his garment   2Kg 4:39

GOVERNING

while Quirinius was g Syria.   Lk 2:2
submit to the g authorities,   Rm 13:1

GOVERNMENT

and the g will be on His shoulders.   Is 9:6
g is God's servant   Rm 13:4

GOVERNOR

Bring it to your g!   Mal 1:8
brought before g-s and kings   Mt 10:18
so that the g was greatly amazed   Mt 27:14
stand before g-s and kings because Mk 13:9
Pontius Pilate was g of Judea,   Lk 3:1
before kings and g-s because of My Lk 21:12
who appointed him g over Egypt   Ac 7:10
To the most excellent g Felix: Ac 23:26
or to g-s as those sent out by him 1Pt 2:14

GRAB

I would g it by its fur   1Sm 17:35
right hand Joab g-bed Amasa
   by the   2Sm 20:9
is like one who g-s a dog by the   Pr 26:17
He g-bed him, started choking him Mt 18:28

GRACE

promised this g to Your servant   2Sm 7:28

g has come from the LORD our God | Ezr 9:8
g flows from your lips. | Ps 45:2
The LORD gives g and glory; | Ps 84:11
be a garland of g on your head | Pr 1:9; 4:9
but gives g to the humble. | Pr 3:34
by shouts of: G, g to it! | Zch 4:7
pour out a spirit of g and prayer | Zch 12:10
and God's g was on Him. | Lk 2:40
full of g and truth. | Jn 1:14
received g after g from His fullness. | Jn 1:16
g and truth came through Jesus | Jn 1:17
and great g was on all of them. | Ac 4:33
saved through the g of the Lord | Ac 15:11
to the gospel of God's g. | Ac 20:24
freely by His g through the | Rm 3:24
that it may be according to g, | Rm 4:16
the many by the g of the one man | Rm 5:15
the overflow of g and the gift | Rm 5:17
when sin multiplied, g multiplied | Rm 5:20
in order that g may multiply? | Rm 6:1
are not under law but under g. | Rm 6:14
if by g, then it is not by works; |
    otherwise g ceases to be g. | Rm 11:6
But by God's g I am what I am, | 1Co 15:10
Don't receive God's g in vain. | 2Co 6:1
For you know the g of our Lord | 2Co 8:9
to make every g overflow to you | 2Co 9:8
My g is sufficient for you, | 2Co 12:9
The g of the Lord Jesus Christ, | 2Co 13:13
do not set aside the g of God; | Gl 2:21
you have fallen from g! | Gl 5:4
to the riches of His g | Eph 1:7
By g you are saved! | Eph 2:5
immeasurable riches of His g in | Eph 2:7
For by g you are saved through | Eph 2:8
administration of God's g that He | Eph 3:2
Now g was given to each one of | Eph 4:7
are all partners with me in g, | Php 1:7
and good hope by g, | 2Th 2:16
be strong in the g that is in | 2Tm 2:1
For the g of God has appeared, | Ti 2:11
having been justified by His g, | Ti 3:7
The g of the Lord Jesus Christ | Phm 25
that by God's g He might taste | Heb 2:9
the throne of g with boldness, | Heb 4:16
find g to help us at the proper time. | Heb 4:16
and insulted the Spirit of g? | Heb 10:29
shaken, let us hold on to g. | Heb 12:28

But He gives greater g. | Jms 4:6
but gives g to the humble. | Jms 4:6
prophesied about the g that would | 1Pt 1:10
as co-heirs of the g of life, | 1Pt 3:7
but gives g to the humble. | 1Pt 5:5
that this is the true g of God. | 1Pt 5:12
But grow in the g and knowledge | 2Pt 3:18
turning the g of our God into | Jd 4
The g of the Lord Jesus be with | Rv 22:21

GRACEFUL

A loving doe, a g fawn—let her | Pr 5:19

GRACIOUS

May God be g to you, my son. | Gn 43:29
I will be g to whom I will be g, | Ex 33:19
is a compassionate and g God, | Ex 34:6
shine on you, and be g to you; | Nm 6:25
our God is g to all who seek Him, | Ezr 8:22
for You are a g ... God. | Neh 9:31
and to be g to him and say, | Jb 33:24
be g to me and hear my prayer. | Ps 4:1
Be g to me, LORD, for I am weak | Ps 6:2
Be g to me, LORD; consider my | Ps 9:13
Turn to me and be g to me, | Ps 25:16
redeem me and be g to me. | Ps 26:11
be g to me and answer me. | Ps 27:7
LORD, listen and be g to me; | Ps 30:10
Be g to me, LORD, because I am | Ps 31:9
the righteous is g and giving. | Ps 37:21
I said, "LORD, be g to me; | Ps 41:4
be g to me and raise me up; | Ps 41:10
Be g to me, God, according to | Ps 51:1
Be g to me, God, for man | Ps 56:1
Be g to me, God, be g to me, for I | Ps 57:1
May God be g to us and bless us | Ps 67:1
Has God forgotten to be g? | Ps 77:9
Be g to me, Lord, for I call to | Ps 86:3
are a compassionate and g God, | Ps 86:15
Turn to me and be g to me. | Ps 86:16
He is g, compassionate, and | Ps 112:4
be g to me according to Your | Ps 119:58
Turn to me and be g to me, | Ps 119:132
May Your g Spirit lead me on | Ps 143:10
A g woman gains honor, but | Pr 11:16
loves a pure heart and g lips | Pr 22:11
the mouth of a wise man are g, | Ec 10:12
LORD, be g to us! We wait for | Is 33:2
will be g to the remnant of | Am 5:15
amazed by the g words that came | Lk 4:22

GRACIOUSLY (cont.)

For He is **g** to the ungrateful — Lk 6:35
since God's **g** gifts and calling — Rm 11:29
Your speech should always be **g**, — Col 4:6

GRACIOUSLY

children God has **g** given your — Gn 33:5
When he speaks **g**, don't believe — Pr 26:25
God has **g** given you all those — Ac 27:24

GRACIOUSNESS

gentleness and **g** of Christ — 2Co 10:1
Let your **g** be known to everyone — Php 4:5

GRAFT (n)

They all love **g** and chase after — Is 1:23

GRAFT (v)

wild olive branch, were **g-ed** in — Rm 11:17
broken off so that I might be **g-ed** — Rm 11:19
God has the power to **g** them in — Rm 11:23
against nature were **g-ed** into a — Rm 11:24

GRAIN

went down to buy **g** from Egypt. — Gn 42:3
When someone presents a **g** offering — Lv 2:1
an ox while it treads out **g**. — Dt 25:4
have when their **g** and new wine — Ps 4:7
providing {people} with **g**. — Ps 65:9
be plenty of **g** in the land; — Ps 72:16
He gave them **g** from heaven. — Ps 78:24
will curse anyone who hoards **g**, — Pr 11:26
a land of **g** and new wine — Is 36:17
what is straw {compared} to **g**? — Jr 23:28
I will summon the **g** and make it — Ezk 36:29
it is I who gave her the **g**, — Hs 2:8
G will make the young men — Zch 9:17
pick and eat some heads of **g**. — Mt 12:1
way picking some heads of **g**. — Mk 2:23
then the ripe **g** on the head. — Mk 4:28
and store all my **g** and my goods — Lk 12:18
will be grinding **g** together: — Lk 17:35
Unless a **g** of wheat falls into — Jn 12:24
ox while it treads out the **g**. — 1Co 9:9
an ox that is threshing **g**, — 1Tm 5:18

GRAINFIELDS

through the **g** on the Sabbath. — Mt 12:1

GRAINS

would outnumber the **g** of sand; — Ps 139:18
as innumerable as the **g** of sand — Heb 11:12

GRANDCHILDREN

the children and **g** to the third — Ex 34:7
His righteousness toward the **g** — Ps 103:17
leaves an inheritance to his **g**, — Pr 13:22
G are the crown of the elderly, — Pr 17:6
with their children and **g**, — Ezk 37:25
if any widow has children or **g**, — 1Tm 5:4

GRANDDAUGHTER

daughters and **g-s**, indeed all his — Gn 46:7
was Athaliah, **g** of Israel's King — 2Kg 8:26

GRANDMOTHER

removed his **g** Maacah from — 1Kg 15:13
first lived in your **g** Lois, — 2Tm 1:5

GRANDSON

you may tell your son and **g** how — Ex 10:2
commands I am giving you, your
  son, and your **g**, — Dt 6:2
40 sons and 30 **g-s**, who rode on — Jdg 12:14
your master's **g** will have food — 2Sm 9:10

GRANT

And God **g-ed** his request. — 1Ch 4:10
He **g-ed** their request because they — 1Ch 5:20
g me wisdom and knowledge so — 2Ch 1:10
but will **g** them a little deliverance. — 2Ch 12:7
of God has been **g-ed** to you, — Mk 4:11
Will not God **g** justice to His — Lk 18:7
And He has **g-ed** Him the right to — Jn 5:27
to Me unless it is **g-ed** to him by — Jn 6:65
So God has **g-ed** repentance — Ac 11:18
also with Him **g** us everything? — Rm 8:32
grace of God **g-ed** to the churches — 2Co 8:1
may **g** you, according to the riches — Eph 3:16
God will **g** them repentance — 2Tm 2:25

GRAPE

his robes in the blood of **g-s**. — Gn 49:11
not drink any **g** juice or eat — Nm 6:3
with a single cluster of **g-s**, — Nm 13:23
drank wine from the finest **g-s**. — Dt 32:14
Their **g-s** are poisonous; — Dt 32:32
breasts be like clusters of **g-s**, — Sg 7:8
He expected it to yield good **g-s**, but — Is 5:2
a gleaning after a **g** harvest. — Is 24:13
There will be no **g-s** on the vine, — Jr 8:13
The fathers have eaten sour **g-s**, — Jr 31:29
fathers eat sour **g-s**, and the — Ezk 18:2
Are **g-s** gathered from thornbushes — Mt 7:16

When the g harvest drew near, Mt 21:34
because its g-s have ripened. Rv 14:18

GRAPEVINE

eat anything produced by the g, Nm 6:4
said to the g, "Come and reign Jdg 9:12
The g is dried up, and the fig Jl 1:12
sit under his g and under his Mc 4:4
or a g {produce} figs? Jms 3:12

GRASP

kingdom was firmly in his g, 2Kg 14:5
from the g of the unjust and Ps 71:4
free from the g of foreigners Ps 144:7
and g-s oil with his right hand. Pr 27:16
mind has thoroughly g-ed wisdom Ec 1:16
with wine and how to g folly Ec 2:3
good that you g the one and do Ec 7:18
so that they could not g it, Lk 9:45
they did not g what was said. Lk 18:34
Him, yet He eluded their g. Jn 10:39
me from Herod's g and from all Ac 12:11

GRASS

glisten of rain on sprouting g. 2Sm 23:4
tender g, ... blasted by ... wind. 2Kg 19:26
descendants like the g of the earth. Jb 5:25
Does a wild donkey bray over fresh g Jb 6:5
and cause the g to sprout? Jb 38:27
He eats g like an ox. Jb 40:15
rain that falls on the cut g, Ps 72:6
cities like the g of the field. Ps 72:16
They are like g that grows in Ps 90:5
is afflicted, withered like g; Ps 102:4
As for man, his days are like g Ps 103:15
them be like g on the rooftops Ps 129:6
his favor is like dew on the g. Pr 19:12
the g is withered, the foliage Is 15:6
All humanity is g, and all its Is 40:6
The g withers, the flowers fade Is 40:7
You will feed on g like cattle Dn 4:25
God clothes the g of the field, Mt 6:30
crowds to sit down on the g. Mt 14:19
heat and dries up the g; Jms 1:11
All flesh is like g, and all its 1Pt 1:24
The g withers, and the flower 1Pt 1:24

GRASSHOPPER

and the various kinds of g. Lv 11:22
To ourselves we seemed like g-s, Nm 13:33
the g loses its spring, Ec 12:5

its inhabitants are like g-s. Is 40:22

GRATE

Construct a g for it of bronze Ex 27:4
for the altar a g of bronze mesh Ex 38:4

GRATING

the pillars had g-s of latticework 1Kg 7:17
encircled by a g and 2Kg 25:17

GRATITUDE

glorify Him as God or show g. Rm 1:21
with g in your hearts to God. Col 3:16
be received with g by those who 1Tm 4:3

GRAVE

it is the marker at Rachel's g Gn 35:20
Is it because there are no g-s in Ex 14:11
bone, or a g, will be unclean Nm 19:16
this day knows where his g is. Dt 34:6
are glad when they reach the g? Jb 3:22
approach the g in full vigor, Jb 5:26
carried from the womb to the g. Jb 10:19
their throat is an open g; Ps 5:9
Their g-s are their eternal homes Ps 49:11
love be declared in the g, Ps 88:11
They made His g with the wicked Is 53:9
my mother might have been my g, Jr 20:17
her g-s are all around her. Ezk 32:22
open your g-s and bring you up Ezk 37:12
I will prepare your g, Nah 1:14
You are like unmarked g-s; Lk 11:44
who are in the g-s will hear His Jn 5:28
Their throat is an open g; Rm 3:13

GRAVEL

his mouth is full of g. Pr 20:17
my teeth on g and made me cower Lm 3:16

GRAY

will bring my g hairs down to Gn 42:38
do not let his g head descend to 1Kg 2:6
when I am old and g, God, do not Ps 71:18
G hair is a glorious crown; Pr 16:31
splendor of old men is g hair. Pr 20:29
bear {you} up when you turn g. Is 46:4
his hair is streaked with g, Hs 7:9

GRAY-HAIRED

the infant and the g man. Dt 32:25
Both the g and the elderly are Jb 15:10

GRAZE

The cow and the bear will g,	Is 11:7
return them to their g-ing land.	Jr 23:3
will once more be a g-ing land	Jr 33:12

GREAT

God made the two g lights	Gn 1:16
My punishment is too g to bear!	Gn 4:13
will make you into a g nation,	Gn 12:2
I will make your name g,	Gn 12:2
I will make you into a g nation.	Ex 32:10
people has committed a g sin;	Ex 32:31
the g, mighty, and awesome God,	Dt 10:17
the people gave a g shout,	Jos 6:20
has driven out g and powerful	Jos 23:9
to judge this g people of Yours?	1Kg 3:9
they will hear of Your g name,	1Kg 8:42
caused them to commit g sin.	2Kg 17:21
For the LORD is g and is highly	1Ch 16:25
because His mercies are very g,	1Ch 21:13
that I am building will be g,	2Ch 2:5
I am doing a g work and cannot	Neh 6:3
Ezra blessed the LORD, the g God,	Neh 8:6
He does g and unsearchable	Jb 5:9
makes nations g, then destroys	Jb 12:23
there is g reward in keeping	Ps 19:11
praise in the g congregation	Ps 22:25
forgive my sin, for it is g.	Ps 25:11
How g is Your goodness that You	Ps 31:19
continually say, The LORD is g!	Ps 40:16
The LORD is g and is highly	Ps 48:1
continually say, "God is g!"	Ps 70:4
You who have done g things;	Ps 71:19
His name is g in Israel.	Ps 76:1
What god is g like God?	Ps 77:13
LORD is a g God, a g King above all	Ps 95:3
For the LORD is g and is highly	Ps 96:4
The LORD is g in Zion;	Ps 99:2
so g is His faithful love toward	Ps 103:11
LORD my God, You are very g;	Ps 104:1
For g is His faithful love to us	Ps 117:2
LORD has done g things for them.	Ps 126:2
with things too g or too	Ps 131:1
He alone does g wonders.	Ps 136:4
Yahweh is g and is highly	Ps 145:3
and brings him before the g.	Pr 18:16
stand in the place of the g;	Pr 25:6
too is futile and a g wrong.	Ec 2:21
You are g; Your name is g in power.	Jr 10:6

g is Your faithfulness!	Lm 3:23
the holiness of My g name,	Ezk 36:23
not Babylon the G that I have	Dn 4:30
whatever he wanted and became g.	Dn 8:4
the g and awe-inspiring God who	Dn 9:4
and the g houses will come to an	Am 3:15
The g Day of the LORD is near,	Zph 1:14
My name will be g among the	Mal 1:11
before the g and awesome Day	Mal 4:5
darkness have seen a g light,	Mt 4:16
your reward is g in heaven.	Mt 5:12
will be called g in the kingdom	Mt 5:19
it is the city of the g King.	Mt 5:35
her, "Woman, your faith is g.	Mt 15:28
wants to become g among you	Mt 20:26
heaven with power and g glory.	Mt 24:30
He will be g and will be called	Lk 1:32
good news of g joy that will be	Lk 2:10
before the g and remarkable day	Ac 2:20
claiming to be somebody g.	Ac 8:9
is called the G Power of God!	Ac 8:10
G is Artemis of the Ephesians!	Ac 19:28
because of His g love that He	Eph 2:4
the mystery of godliness is g:	1Tm 3:16
with contentment is a g gain.	1Tm 6:6
glory of our g God and Savior,	Ti 2:13
we neglect such a g salvation?	Heb 2:3
we have a g high priest who	Heb 4:14
since we have a g high priest	Heb 10:21
the g Shepherd of the sheep	Heb 13:20
it boasts g things.	Jms 3:5
Look at how g a love the Father	1Jn 3:1
out of the g tribulation.	Rv 7:14
There was a g fiery red dragon	Rv 12:3
Babylon the G has fallen, who	Rv 14:8
G and awe-inspiring are Your	Rv 15:3
the battle of the g day of God,	Rv 16:14
BABYLON THE G	Rv 17:5
Then I saw a g white throne and	Rv 20:11
the dead, the g and the small	Rv 20:12

GREATER

the LORD is g than all gods,	Ex 18:11
nations g and stronger than you	Dt 4:38
since God is g than man.	Jb 33:12
our Lord is g than all gods.	Ps 135:5
house will be g than the first,	Hg 2:9
least in the kingdom of heaven is g	Mt 11:11

something g than the temple is here! | Mt 12:6
something g than Jonah is here! | Mt 12:41
something g than Solomon is here | Mt 12:42
other commandment g than these. | Mk 12:31
You will see g things than this. | Jn 1:50
You aren't g than our father | Jn 4:12
A slave is not g than his master | Jn 13:16
he will do even g works than | Jn 14:12
No one has g love than this, | Jn 15:13
Me over to you has the g sin. | Jn 19:11
and to g and g lawlessness, | Rm 6:19
we clothe these with g honor, | 1Co 12:23
But desire the g gifts. | 1Co 12:31
prophesies is g than the person | 1Co 14:5
since He had no one g to swear | Heb 6:13
the Messiah to be g wealth than | Heb 11:26
But He gives g grace. | Jms 4:6
God is g than our hearts and | 1Jn 3:20
the One who is in you is g than the | 1Jn 4:4
testimony is g, because it is | 1Jn 5:9
I have no g joy than this: | 3Jn 4

GREATEST

altar of God, to God, my g joy. | Ps 43:4
g of the kings of the earth. | Ps 89:27
exalt Jerusalem as my g joy! | Ps 137:6
from the g of them to the least | Jnh 3:5
Who is g in the kingdom | Mt 18:1
commandment in the law is the g? | Mt 22:36
g among you will be your servant. | Mt 23:11
who would be the g of them. | Lk 9:46
whoever is g among you must | Lk 22:26
But the g of these is love. | 1Co 13:13

GREATLY

belong to God; He is g exalted. | Ps 47:9
and lifted up and g exalted. | Is 52:13
Rejoice g, Daughter Zion! | Zch 9:9

GREATNESS

Proclaim with me the LORD's g; | Ps 34:3
His g is unsearchable. | Ps 145:3
and I will declare Your g. | Ps 145:6
praise Him for His abundant g. | Ps 150:2
and declaring the g of God. | Ac 10:46
immeasurable g of His power | Eph 1:19

GREECE

goat represents the king of G, | Dn 8:21
the prince of G will come. | Dn 10:20

Zion, against your sons, G. | Zch 9:13
them at length, he came to G | Ac 20:2

GREED

inside they are full of g | Mt 23:25
be on guard against all g | Lk 12:15
evil, g, and wickedness, | Rm 1:29
impurity or g should not even | Eph 5:3
evil desire, and g, which is | Col 3:5
and with hearts trained in g. | 2Pt 2:14

GREEDY

the one who is g curses and | Ps 10:3
A g man is in a hurry for wealth | Pr 28:22
A g person provokes conflict, | Pr 28:25
thieves, g people, drunkards | 1Co 6:10
immoral or impure or g person, | Eph 5:5
not quarrelsome, not g | 1Tm 3:3
not a bully, not g for money, | Ti 1:7

GREEK

You sold the people ... to the G-s | Jl 3:6
the woman was G, | Mk 7:26
among the G-s and teach the G-s, | Jn 7:35
written in Hebrew, Latin, and G. | Jn 19:20
of both Jews and G-s believed. | Ac 14:1
woman, but his father was a G. | Ac 16:1
the prominent G women as well as | Ac 17:12
He replied, "Do you know G? | Ac 21:37
to the Jew, and also to the G. | Rm 1:16
distinction between Jew and G, | Rm 10:12
signs and the G-s seek wisdom, | 1Co 1:22
though he was a G, was compelled | Gl 2:3
is no Jew or G, slave or free | Gl 3:28
Here there is not G and Jew, | Col 3:11
and in G he has the name | Rv 9:11

GREEN

every g plant for food. | Gn 1:30
hill and under every g tree. | 2Kg 17:10
lets me lie down in g pastures; | Ps 23:2
and there was a pale g horse. | Rv 6:8

GREET

and if a man g-s you, don't answer | 2Kg 4:29
And if you g only your brothers | Mt 5:47
G a household when you enter it | Mt 10:12
don't g anyone along the road. | Lk 10:4
G also the church that meets in | Rm 16:5
G one another with a holy kiss. | 1Co 16:20
G one another with a holy kiss. | 2Co 13:12

GREETING (continued)

G all the brothers with a holy	1Th 5:26
G one another with a kiss of	1Pt 5:14
G the friends by name.	3Jn 14

GREETING

When Elizabeth heard Mary's g,	Lk 1:41
who love g-s in the marketplaces	Lk 20:46

GRIEF

people were overcome with g.	Nm 14:39
If only my g could be weighed	Jb 6:2
My eyes are swollen from g;	Ps 6:7
have seen trouble and g,	Ps 10:14
I am weary from g; strengthen me	Ps 119:28
and joy may end in g.	Pr 14:13
A foolish son is g to his father	Pr 17:25
knowledge increases, g increases.	Ec 1:18
all his days are filled with g,	Ec 2:23
G is better than laughter,	Ec 7:3
be overwhelmed by excessive g.	2Co 2:7
because your g led to repentance.	2Co 7:9
For godly g produces a	2Co 7:10
not have one g on top of another	Php 2:27
this with joy and not with g,	Heb 13:17
g, crying, and pain will exist no	Rv 21:4

GRIEVE

and He was g-d in His heart.	Gn 6:6
since today is holy. Do not g.	Neh 8:11
my soul not g-d for the needy?	Jb 30:25
and g-d Him in the desert.	Ps 78:40
rebelled, and g-d His Holy Spirit.	Is 63:10
the land g-s;	Jl 1:10
Peter was g-d that He asked him	Jn 21:17
as g-ing yet always rejoicing;	2Co 6:10
For although I g-d you with my	2Co 7:8
And don't g God's Holy Spirit,	Eph 4:30
you will not g like the rest,	1Th 4:13

GRIND

he was forced to g grain in the	Jdg 16:21
Though you g a fool in a mortar	Pr 27:22
the women who g cease because	Ec 12:3
falls, it will g him to powder!	Mt 21:44
women will be g-ing at the mill:	Mt 24:41

GRIP

Fear and trembling g me;	Ps 55:5
they were g-ped by great fear.	Lk 8:37

GROAN

The Israelites g-ed because of	Ex 2:23
whenever they g-ed	Jdg 2:18
the city, men g; the mortally	Jb 24:12
Let the g-s of the prisoners reach	Ps 79:11
when the wicked rule, people g.	Pr 29:2
we also g within ourselves,	Rm 8:23
we who are in this tent g,	2Co 5:4

GROANING

God heard their g,	Ex 2:24
I am weary from my g;	Ps 6:6
and the g of the poor,	Ps 12:5
and from my words of g?	Ps 22:1
Because of the sound of my g,	Ps 102:5
I am worn out with g and	Jr 45:3
the whole creation has been g	Rm 8:22
intercedes for us with unspoken g-s.	Rm 8:26

GROOM

sad while the g is with them?	Mt 9:15
Since the g was delayed, they	Mt 25:5
He called the g	Jn 2:9
He who has the bride is the g.	Jn 3:29
But the g-'s friend, who stands by	Jn 3:29
the voice of a g and bride will	Rv 18:23

GROPE

noon you will g as a blind man	Dt 28:29
and they g at noon as if it were	Jb 5:14
They g around in darkness	Jb 12:25
We g along a wall like the blind	Is 59:10

GROUND

the man out of the dust from the g	Gn 2:7
The g is cursed because of you.	Gn 3:17
he released his semen on the g	Gn 38:9
you are standing is holy g.	Ex 3:5
went through the sea on dry g,	Ex 14:22
all Israel crossed on dry g	Jos 3:17
crossed over on dry g.	2Kg 2:8
My foot stands on level g;	Ps 26:12
our bodies cling to the g.	Ps 44:25
Spirit lead me on level g.	Ps 143:10
he returns to the g;	Ps 146:4
that of a spirit from the g;	Is 29:4
the uneven g will become smooth	Is 40:4
and rough places into level g.	Is 42:16
and streams on the dry g;	Is 44:3
and like a root out of dry g.	Is 53:2
Break up the unplowed g;	Jr 4:3
break up your untilled g.	Hs 10:12
them falls to the g without your	Mt 10:29

Others fell on rocky **g,** Mt 13:5
writing on the **g** with His finger Jn 8:6
falls into the **g** and dies, Jn 12:24
you are standing is holy **g.** Ac 7:33

GROUNDED
you remain **g** and steadfast Col 1:23

GROUNDS
to divorce his wife on any **g?** Mt 19:3
I find no **g** for charging this Lk 23:4
they found no **g** for the death Ac 13:28
thinks he has **g** for confidence Php 3:4

GROUP
or join a **g** of mockers! Ps 1:1
sit down in **g-s** of about 50 each Lk 9:14
who made both **g-s** one and tore Eph 2:14

GROVES
and olive **g** that you did not Dt 6:11
and olive **g** you did not plant. Jos 24:13

GROW
house until my son Shelah **g-s** up. Gn 38:11
after Moses had **g-n** up, Ex 2:11
not to reap what **g-s** by itself Lv 25:5
the boy Samuel **grew** up in the 1Sm 2:21
with David **g-ing** stronger and 2Sm 3:1
men who had **g-n** up with him 1Kg 12:8
you will eat what **g-s** on its own, 2Kg 19:29
David steadily **grew** more 1Ch 11:9
g like a cedar tree in Lebanon. Ps 92:12
causes grass to **g** for the livestock Ps 104:14
I will make a horn **g** for David; Ps 132:17
causes grass to **g** on the hills. Ps 147:8
a shoot will **g** from the stump Is 11:1
He never **g-s** faint or weary; Is 40:28
they will run and not **g** weary; Is 40:31
and the rain makes it **g.** Is 44:14
He **grew** up before Him like a young Is 53:2
and they will no longer **g** weak Jr 31:12
You **grew** up and matured Ezk 16:7
make flesh **g** on you, and Ezk 37:6
trees providing food will **g** along Ezk 47:12
horn emerged and **grew** extensively Dn 8:9
The sun and moon will **g** dark, Jl 3:15
not labor over and did not **g.** Jnh 4:10
the wildflowers of the field **g:** Mt 6:28
people's heart has **g-n** callous; Mt 13:15
the love of many will **g** cold. Mt 24:12

comes up and **g-s** taller than all Mk 4:32
The child **grew** up and became Lk 1:80
boy **grew** up and became strong, Lk 2:40
people's heart has **g-n** callous, Ac 28:27
in Him and is **g-ing** into a holy Eph 2:21
let us **g** in every way into Him Eph 4:15
will keep on **g-ing** in knowledge Php 1:9
bearing fruit and **g-ing** all over Col 1:6
g-ing in the knowledge of God. Col 1:10
when he had **g-n** up,
refused to be Heb 11:24
sin is fully **g-n,** it gives birth Jms 1:15
But **g** in the grace and knowledge 2Pt 3:18

GROWL
they **g** if they are not satisfied Ps 59:15
We all **g** like bears and Is 59:11

GROWTH
with showers and bless its **g,** Ps 65:10
is removed and new **g** appears and Pr 27:25
but only God who gives the **g.** 1Co 3:7
promotes the **g** of the body Eph 4:16
develops with **g** from God. Col 2:19

GRUDGE
Esau held a **g** against Jacob Gn 27:41
or bear a **g** against members Lv 19:18
So Herodias held a **g** against him Mk 6:19

GRUDGINGLY
Foreigners submit to me **g;** 2Sm 22:45

GRUMBLE
community **g-d** against Moses Ex 16:2
You **g-d** in your tents and said, Dt 1:27
whole community **g-d** against the Jos 9:18
They **g-d** in their tents and did Ps 106:25
without **g-ing** and arguing, Php 2:14

GRUMBLERS
people are discontented **g,** Jd 16

GUARANTEE (n)
also become the **g** of a better Heb 7:22

GUARANTEE (v)
who **g-s** to us the fixed weeks of Jr 5:24
to **g** it to all the descendants Rm 4:16
He **g-d** it with an oath Heb 6:17

GUARD (n)
that You keep me under **g?** Jb 7:12
Lord, set up a **g** for my mouth; Ps 141:3

The **g-s** who go about the city　Sg 3:3; 5:7
God of Israel is your rear **g**.　Is 52:12
peace as your **g** and　Is 60:17
you will be their **g**.　Ezk 38:7
The **g-s** were so shaken from fear　Mt 28:4
But you, be on your **g**!　Mk 13:9
Him and take Him away under **g**.　Mk 14:44
Be on your **g** against the yeast　Lk 12:1
Be on your **g**, so that your　Lk 21:34
be on your **g**, so that you are　2Pt 3:17

GUARD (v)

sword to **g** the way to the tree　Gn 3:24
g-ed him as the pupil of His eye.　Dt 32:10
He **g-s** the steps of His faithful　1Sm 2:9
G me as the apple of Your eye;　Ps 17:8
G me and deliver me; do not let　Ps 25:20
I will **g** my ways so that I may not　Ps 39:1
and truth will always **g** me.　Ps 40:11
love and truth to **g** him.　Ps 61:7
The LORD **g-s** the inexperienced;　Ps 116:6
The LORD **g-s** all those who love　Ps 145:20
and understanding will **g** you,　Pr 2:11
G your heart above all else,　Pr 4:23
The one who **g-s** his mouth protects　Pr 13:3
Righteousness **g-s** people of　Pr 13:6
The one who **g-s** his mouth and　Pr 21:23
the one who **g-s** himself stays far　Pr 22:5
with him, who were **g-ing** Jesus,　Mt 27:54
I **g-ed** them and not one of them is　Jn 17:12
and I **g-ed** the clothes of those who　Ac 22:20
with the soldier who **g-ed** him.　Ac 28:16
will **g** your hearts and your minds　Php 4:7
strengthen and **g** you from the　2Th 3:3
g what has been entrusted to you　1Tm 6:20
able to **g** what has been entrusted　2Tm 1:12
Little children, **g** yourselves　1Jn 5:21

GUARDIAN

Am I my brother's **g**?　Gn 4:9
and to the **g-s** of Ahab's sons,　2Kg 10:1
the day when the **g-s** of the house　Ec 12:3
You were an anointed **g** cherub,　Ezk 28:14
law, then, was our **g** until Christ,　Gl 3:24
we are no longer under a **g**,　Gl 3:25
he is under **g-s** and stewards until　Gl 4:2
shepherd and **g** of your souls.　1Pt 2:25

GUEST

sinners came as **g-s** to eat with　Mt 9:10

Can the wedding **g-s** be sad while　Mt 9:15
the king came in to view the **g-s**,　Mt 22:11
also prepare a **g** room for me,　Phm 22
angels as **g-s** without knowing it　Heb 13:2

GUIDANCE

Without **g**, people fall,　Pr 11:14
and wage war with sound **g**.　Pr 20:18
should wage war with sound **g**　Pr 24:6

GUIDE (n)

Woe to you, blind **g-s**, who say　Mt 23:16
Blind **g-s**! You strain out a gnat　Mt 23:24
who became a **g** to those who　Ac 1:16
that you are a **g** for the blind,　Rm 2:19

GUIDE (v)

You will **g** {them} to Your holy　Ex 15:13
G me in Your truth and teach me　Ps 25:5
You **g** me with Your counsel,　Ps 73:24
g-d them like a flock　Ps 78:52
who **g-d** Joseph like a flock;　Ps 80:1
Then He **g-d** them to the harbor　Ps 107:30
and there, they will **g** you;　Pr 6:22
of the upright **g-s** them,　Pr 11:3
The lamp that **g-s** the wicked　Pr 21:4
my mind still **g-ing** me with wisdom　Ec 2:3
compassionate One will **g** them,　Is 49:10
And if the blind **g** the blind,　Mt 15:14
G-d by the Spirit, he entered the　Lk 2:27
He will **g** you into all the truth　Jn 16:13
can I ... unless someone **g-s** me?　Ac 8:31
they are **g-d** by a very small　Jms 3:4

GUILT

You must not bring **g** on the land　Dt 24:4
take away Your servant's **g**.　2Sm 24:10
our **g** is as high as the heavens.　Ezr 9:6
by hiding my **g** in my heart,　Jb 31:33
I am clean and have no **g**.　Jb 33:9
You took away the **g** of my sin.　Ps 32:5
So I confess my **g**;　Ps 38:18
Wash away my **g**, and cleanse me　Ps 51:2
my sins and blot out all my **g**.　Ps 51:9
me from the **g** of bloodshed,　Ps 51:14
Add **g** to their **g**;　Ps 69:27
He atoned for {their} **g**　Ps 78:38
You took away Your people's **g**;　Ps 85:2
Let his forefathers' **g** be　Ps 109:14
their **g** is not hidden from My sight.　Jr 16:17
land is full of **g** against the Holy One　Jr 51:5

now they must bear their g.   Hs 10:2
I have removed your g from you,   Zch 3:4

GUILTY

I will not justify the g.   Ex 23:7
not leave {the g} unpunished,   Nm 14:18
a murderer who is g of killing   Nm 35:31
and condemn the g.   Dt 25:1
I was g {when I} was born;   Ps 51:5
and my g acts are not hidden   Ps 69:5
Acquitting the g and condemning   Pr 17:15
show partiality to the g by perverting   Pr 18:5
A g man's conduct is crooked,   Pr 21:8
says to the g, "You are innocent   Pr 24:24
with those who convict the g,   Pr 24:25
who acquit the g for a bribe and   Is 5:23
You are g of the blood you have   Ezk 22:4
but is g of an eternal sin"   Mk 3:29
will be g of sin against the body   1Co 11:27
is g of {breaking it} all.   Jms 2:10

GULLIBLE

she is g and knows nothing.   Pr 9:13
The g inherit foolishness,   Pr 14:18

GULP

will drink and g down and be as   Ob 16
out a gnat, yet g down a camel!   Mt 23:24

GUSHED

the rock and water g out;   Ps 78:20
opened a rock, and water g out;   Ps 105:41
fountains of the ocean g forth,   Pr 8:28
the rock, and water g out.   Is 48:21

HABAKKUK

Prophet in Judah before the exile (Hab 1:1).

HABIT

the ox was in the h of goring,   Ex 21:29

HABITUALLY

from our meetings, as some h do,   Heb 10:25

HABOR

Mespotamian river (2Kg 17:6; 18:11; 1Ch 5:26).

HACKED

Then he h Agag to pieces before   1Sm 15:33
it You who h Rahab to pieces,   Is 51:9

HADAD

1. Son of Ishmael (Gn 25:15).
2. Son of Bedad; king of Edom (Gn 36:35).
3. Son of Baal-hanan; king of Edom (1Ch 1:50). Also called Hadar (Gn 36:39).
4. Edomite enemy of Solomon (1Kg 11:14-25).

HADADEZER

Syrian king defeated by David (2Sm 8; 10; 1Ch 18).

HADASSAH

Esther's Hebrew name (Est 2:7).

HADES

You will go down to H.   Mt 11:23
and the forces of H will not   Mt 16:18
And being in torment in H,   Lk 16:23
will not leave my soul in H,   Ac 2:27
I hold the keys of death and H.   Rv 1:18
and H was following after him.   Rv 6:8
Death and H were thrown into the   Rv 20:14

HAGAR

Sarah's slave; mother of Ishmael (Gn 16; Gl 4:21-31). Sent away by Sarah (Gn 16:5-9; 21:9-21).

HAGGAI

Prophet after the exile, who encouraged rebuilding the temple (Ezr 5:1; 6:14; Hg 1–2).

HAGGITH

Wife of David; mother of Adonijah (2Sm 3:4; 1Kg 1:5,11; 2:13; 1Ch 3:2).

HAGRITE

Nomadic tribe defeated by Reuben (1Ch 5; Ps 83:6).

HAIL

I will rain down the worst h that   Ex 9:18
you seen the storehouses of h,   Jb 38:22
onward with h and blazing coals.   Ps 18:12
He gave them h for rain, and   Ps 105:32
H will sweep away the false   Is 28:17
mildew, and h, but you didn't   Hg 2:17
and mocked Him: "H, King of the   Mt 27:29

and **h** and fire, mixed with blood,   Rv 8:7
for the plague of **h** because that   Rv 16:21

HAILSTONES

LORD threw large **h** on them from   Jos 10:11
He throws His **h** like crumbs.   Ps 147:17
I will send **h** plunging down,   Ezk 13:11
Enormous **h**, each weighing about   Rv 16:21

HAIR

bring my gray **h-s** down to Sheol   Gn 42:38
Do not let your **h** hang loose   Lv 10:6
If the **h** in the infection has   Lv 13:3
not to cut off the **h** at the sides   Lv 19:27
is to let the **h** of his head grow   Nm 6:5
But his **h** began to grow back   Jdg 16:22
a stone at a **h** and not miss.   Jdg 20:16
not a **h** of his head will fall to   1Sm 14:45
would weigh the **h** from his head   2Sm 14:26
not a single **h** of his will fall   1Kg 1:52
are more than the **h-s** of my head,   Ps 40:12
Gray **h** is a glorious crown;   Pr 16:31
splendor of old men is gray **h**.   Pr 20:29
Your **h** is like a flock of goats   Sg 4:1; 6:5
His **h** is wavy and black as a   Sg 5:11
who clip the **h** on their temples   Jr 9:26
pair of scales and divide the **h**.   Ezk 5:1
were formed and your **h** grew,   Ezk 16:7
until his **h** grew like eagles'   Dn 4:33
make a single **h** white or black.   Mt 5:36
But even the **h-s** of your head have   Mt 10:30
My feet and wiped them with her **h**.   Lk 7:44
but not a **h** of your head will be   Lk 21:18
and wiped His feet with her **h**,   Jn 11:2
since not a **h** will be lost from   Ac 27:34
covered, her **h** should be cut off.   1Co 11:6
but that if a woman has long **h**,   1Co 11:15
His head and **h** were white like   Rv 1:14
they had **h** like women's **h**;   Rv 9:8

HAIRSTYLES

with elaborate **h**, gold, pearls,   1Tm 2:9
elaborate **h** and the wearing   1Pt 3:3

HAIRY

my brother Esau is a **h** man,   Gn 27:11
A **h** man with a leather belt   2Kg 1:8

HAKELDAMA

that field is called **H**,   Ac 1:19

HALF

This **h** shekel is a contribution   Ex 30:13
and **h** the tribe of Manasseh left   Jos 22:9
shaved off **h** their beards,   2Sm 10:4
boy in two and give **h** to one and   1Kg 3:25
Indeed, I was not even told **h**.   1Kg 10:7
h the people followed Tibni   1Kg 16:21
h of my men did the work while   Neh 4:16
want, even to **h** the kingdom   Est 5:3
will not live out **h** their days.   Ps 55:23
He burns **h** of it in a fire,   Is 44:16
a time, times, and **h** a time.   Dn 7:25
H the city will go into exile,   Zch 14:2
Mount of Olives will be split in **h**   Zch 14:4
give you, up to **h** my kingdom.   Mk 6:23
and fled, leaving him **h** dead.   Lk 10:30
I'll give **h** of my possessions to   Lk 19:8
in heaven for about **h** an hour.   Rv 8:1
for three and a **h** days and not   Rv 11:9
a time, times, and **h** a time.   Rv 12:14

HALL

He brought me to the banquet **h**,   Sg 2:4
he brought me into the great **h**   Ezk 41:1
in the lecture **h** of Tyrannus.   Ac 19:9

HALLELUJAH

My soul, praise the LORD! **H!**   Ps 104:35
H! I will praise the LORD with   Ps 111:1
H! Happy is the man who fears   Ps 112:1
H! Give praise, servants of the   Ps 113:1
H! Praise the name of the LORD   Ps 135:1
H! My soul, praise the LORD.   Ps 146:1
H! How good it is to sing to our   Ps 147:1
H! Praise the LORD from the   Ps 148:1
H! Sing to the LORD a new song   Ps 149:1
H! Praise God in His sanctuary   Ps 150:1
breathes praise the LORD. **H!**   Ps 150:6
multitude in heaven, saying: **H!**   Rv 19:1
they said: **H!** Her smoke ascends   Rv 19:3
on the throne, saying: Amen! **H!**   Rv 19:4
H—because our Lord God,   Rv 19:6

HAM

Son of Noah (Gn 5:32; 9:18-27). Ancestor of Cushites, Egyptians, and Canaanites (Gn 9:18-27; 10:6; Pss 78:51; 105:23,27; 106:22).

HAMAN

Nobleman of Persia at the time of Esther (Est 3:1-2); enemy of Jews (3:3-15). Hanged on his own gallows (7:9-10).

HAMATH

City-state on the northern border of Israel (Nm 34:8; Jos 13:5; 1Kg 8:65; 2Kg 14:25,28; 2Ch 8:4; Ezk 47:15-17,20).

HAMMER

cut at the quarry so that no **h**,	1Kg 6:7
How the **h** of the whole earth is	Jr 50:23

HAMMERED

She **h** the peg into his temple	Jdg 4:21
Then she **h** Sisera—she crushed	Jdg 5:26

HAMOR

Father of Shechem; sold land to Jacob (Gn 33:18-20; Jos 24:32; Ac 7:16); killed by Simeon and Levi for the rape of Dinah (Gn 34).

HAMSTRING

and on a whim they **h** oxen.	Gn 49:6
You are to **h** their horses and	Jos 11:6
and he hamstrung all the horses	2Sm 8:4

HANANIAH

1. Son of Zerubbabel (1Ch 3:19).
2. Benjaminite leader (1Ch 8:24).
3. Musician (1Ch 25:4,23).
4. Leader in Uzziah's army (2Ch 26:11).
5. Perfumer; helped repair wall (Neh 3:8).
6. Helped repair wall (Neh 3:30).
7. Commander in Jerusalem (Neh 7:2).
8. False prophet; opposed Jeremiah (Jr 28).
9. Shadrach's original name (Dn 1:6).

HAND (n)

His **h** will be against everyone,	Gn 16:12
Place your **h** under my thigh,	Gn 24:2
but the **h-s** are the **h-s** of Esau.	Gn 27:22
one of them put out his **h**,	Gn 38:28
and crossing his **h-s**, put his left	Gn 48:14
Put your **h** inside your cloak.	Ex 4:6
Your right **h** is glorious in	Ex 15:6
Aaron and Hur supported his **h-s**,	Ex 17:12
tooth for tooth, **h** for **h**,	Ex 21:24
lay their **h-s** on the bull's head.	Ex 29:10
rock and cover you with My **h**	Ex 33:22
are to lay their **h-s** on the bull's head	Lv 4:15

will lay both his **h-s** on the head	Lv 16:21
Israelites lay their **h-s** on them.	Nm 8:10
a sign on your **h** and let them be	Dt 6:8
out of Egypt with a strong **h**.	Dt 6:21
and irrigated by **h** as in a	Dt 11:10
open your **h** to your afflicted	Dt 15:11
you are to cut off her **h**.	Dt 25:12
Moses had laid his **h-s** on him.	Dt 34:9
we are in your **h-s**. Do to us	Jos 9:25
took his life in his **h-s** when he	1Sm 19:5
won't lift my **h** against my lord	1Sm 24:10
I will never lift my **h** against	1Sm 26:11
I took my life in my **h-s** and did	1Sm 28:21
to the cleanness of my **h-s**.	2Sm 22:21
He trains my **h-s** for war;	2Sm 22:35
don't let me fall into human **h-s**.	2Sm 24:14
spread out his **h-s** toward heaven.	1Kg 8:22
and the king's **h** was restored	1Kg 13:6
a cloud as small as a man's **h**	1Kg 18:44
to pour water on Elijah's **h-s**,	2Kg 3:11
will wave his **h** over the spot	2Kg 5:11
either their right or left **h**,	1Ch 12:2
The gracious **h** of his God was on	Ezr 7:9
spread out my **h-s** to the LORD my	Ezr 9:5
worked with one **h** and held a	Neh 4:17
strikes, but His **h** also heal.	Jb 5:18
and cleanse my **h-s** with lye,	Jb 9:30
Your **h-s** shaped me and formed me.	Jb 10:8
every living thing is in His **h**,	Jb 12:10
for God's **h** has struck me.	Jb 19:21
I place my **h** over my mouth.	Jb 40:4
if there is injustice on my **h-s**,	Ps 7:3
Because He is at my right **h**,	Ps 16:8
cleanness of my **h-s** in His sight.	Ps 18:24
He trains my **h-s** for war;	Ps 18:34
Your right **h** upholds me, and	Ps 18:35
they pierced my **h-s** and my feet.	Ps 22:16
who has clean **h-s** and a pure heart	Ps 24:4
Into Your **h** I entrust my spirit	Ps 31:5
and night Your **h** was heavy on me	Ps 32:4
because the LORD holds his **h**.	Ps 37:24
Clap your **h-s**, all you peoples;	Ps 47:1
Your name, I will lift up my **h-s**.	Ps 63:4
Your right **h** holds on to me.	Ps 63:8
Let Your **h** be with the man at	Ps 80:17
establish the work of our **h-s**!	Ps 90:17
ten thousand at your right **h**,	Ps 91:7
His **h-s** formed the dry land.	Ps 95:5

Let the rivers clap their **h-s**;   Ps 98:8
heavens are the work of Your **h-s**.   Ps 102:25
when You open Your **h**, they are   Ps 104:28
Sit at My right **h** until I make   Ps 110:1
They have **h-s**, but cannot feel,   Ps 115:7
Lift up your **h-s** in the holy place   Ps 134:2
may my right **h** forget {its skill}.   Ps 137:5
Your right **h** will save me.   Ps 138:7
even there Your **h** will lead me;   Ps 139:10
reflect on the work of Your **h-s**.   Ps 143:5
You open Your **h** and satisfy the   Ps 145:16
Long life is in her right **h**;   Pr 3:16
Idle **h-s** make one poor, but   Pr 10:4
tears it down with her own **h-s**.   Pr 14:1
buries his **h** in the bowl;   Pr 19:24
water channel in the LORD's **h**:   Pr 21:1
Her **h-s** reach out to the poor,   Pr 31:20
Whatever your **h-s** find to do,   Ec 9:10
evening do not let your **h** rest,   Ec 11:6
His left **h** is under my head,   Sg 2:6; 8:3
and His **h** is still raised   Is 5:25
the waters in the hollow of his **h**   Is 40:12
hid me in the shadow of His **h**.   Is 49:2
you on the palms of My **h-s**;   Is 49:16
of the field will clap {their} **h-s**   Is 55:12
the LORD's **h** is not too short to save,   Is 59:1
spread out My **h-s** all day long to   Is 65:2
My **h** made all these things,   Is 66:2
like clay in the potter's **h**,   Jr 18:6
and the LORD's **h** was on me   Ezk 3:14
appeared to be a **h** and took me   Ezk 8:3
and clap {your} **h-s** together.   Ezk 21:14
man's **h** appeared and began writing   Dn 5:5
be shattered, not by human **h-s**.   Dn 8:25
a **h** touched me and raised me to   Dn 10:10
winnowing shovel is in His **h**,   Mt 3:12
if your right **h** causes you to   Mt 5:30
let your left **h** know what your right   Mt 6:3
a man who had a paralyzed **h**.   Mt 12:10
be betrayed into the **h-s** of men.   Mt 17:22
If your **h** or your foot causes   Mt 18:8
Sit at My right **h** until I put   Mt 22:44
one who dipped his **h** with Me in   Mt 26:23
betrayed into the **h-s** of sinners.   Mt 26:45
at the right **h** of the Power   Mt 26:64
washed his **h-s** in front of the   Mt 27:24
Jesus to lay His **h** on him.   Mk 7:32
build another not made by **h-s**.   Mk 14:58

they will lay **h-s** on the sick,   Mk 16:18
one who puts his **h** to the plow   Lk 9:62
father's hired **h-s** have more than   Lk 15:17
into Your **h-s** I entrust My spirit.   Lk 23:46
He showed them His **h-s** and feet.   Lk 24:40
given all things into His **h-s**.   Jn 3:35
will snatch them out of My **h**.   Jn 10:28
feet, but also my **h-s** and my head.   Jn 13:9
and put my **h** into His side,   Jn 20:25
stretch out your **h-s** and someone   Jn 21:18
to my Lord, 'Sit at My right **h**   Ac 2:34
do whatever Your **h** and Your plan   Ac 4:28
standing at the right **h** of God!   Ac 7:56
laying on of the apostles' **h-s**,   Ac 8:18
is He served by human **h-s**,   Ac 17:25
also is at the right **h** of God   Rm 8:34
day long I have spread out My **h-s**   Rm 10:21
Because I'm not a **h**, I don't   1Co 12:15
This greeting is in my own **h**   1Co 16:21
a house not made with **h-s**, eternal   2Co 5:1
gave the right **h** of fellowship   Gl 2:9
do honest work with his own **h-s**,   Eph 4:28
a circumcision not done with **h-s**,   Col 2:11
seated at the right **h** of God.   Col 3:1
This greeting is in my own **h**   Col 4:18
and to work with your own **h-s**,   1Th 4:11
This greeting is in my own **h**   2Th 3:17
lifting up holy **h-s** without anger   1Tm 2:8
laying on of **h-s** by the council   1Tm 4:14
too quick to lay **h-s** on anyone,   1Tm 5:22
through the laying on of my **h-s**.   2Tm 1:6
Paul, write this with my own **h**:   Phm 19
Sit at My right **h** until I make   Heb 1:13
laying on of **h-s**, the resurrection   Heb 6:2
at the right **h** of the throne   Heb 8:1
tabernacle not made with **h-s**   Heb 9:11
sat down at the right **h** of God.   Heb 10:12
to fall into the **h-s** of the living   Heb 10:31
Cleanse your **h-s**, sinners, and   Jms 4:8
In His right **h** He had seven stars;   Rv 1:16
mark on his right **h** or on his   Rv 13:16

HAND (v)

for I have **h-ed** him over to you   Nm 21:34
for I have **h-ed** them over to you.   Jos 10:8
but I **h-ed** them over to you.   Jos 24:8
He **h-ed** them over to marauders   Jdg 2:14
He did not **h** them over to Joshua.   Jdg 2:23
the LORD **h-ed** you over to me   1Sm 24:10

and **h**-ed them over to plunderers 2Kg 17:20
and have not **h**-ed me over to Ps 31:8
He **h**-ed them over to the nations; Ps 106:41
ones will be **h**-ed over to him for Dn 7:25
because they **h**-ed over a whole Am 1:9
and do not **h** over their survivors Ob 14
will **h** you over to the sanhedrins Mt 10:17
be **h**-ed over to the chief priests Mt 20:18
will be **h**-ed over to be crucified. Mt 26:2
he **h**-ed Him over to be crucified. Mt 27:26
tradition that you have **h**-ed down. Mk 7:13
wouldn't have **h**-ed Him over Jn 18:30
h-ed Me over to you has the greater Jn 19:11
whom you **h**-ed over and denied Ac 3:13
when He **h**-s over the kingdom to 1Co 15:24

HANDFUL

Better one **h** with rest, than two Ec 4:6

HANDIWORK

Assyria My **h**, and Israel My Is 19:25

HANDLE

Don't **h**, don't taste, don't Col 2:21

HANDSOME

Joseph was well-built and **h**. Gn 39:6
just a youth, healthy and **h**. 1Sm 17:42
You are the most **h** of men; Ps 45:2
How **h** you are, my love. Sg 1:16

HANG

and **h** you on a tree. Gn 40:19
anyone hung {on a tree} is under Dt 21:23
affairs in order and **h**-ed himself. 2Sm 17:23
Absalom **h**-ing in an oak tree! 2Sm 18:10
They **h**-ed Haman on the gallows he Est 7:10
He **h**-s the earth on nothing. Jb 26:7
There we hung up our lyres on the Ps 137:2
is like lame legs that **h** limp. Pr 26:7
They will **h** on him the whole Is 22:24
millstone were hung around his Mt 18:6
Then he went and **h**-ed himself. Mt 27:5
murdered by **h**-ing Him on a tree. Ac 5:30
is everyone who is hung on a tree. Gl 3:13

HANNAH

Wife of Elkanah; mother of Samuel (1Sm 1–2).

HANUN

So **H** took David's emissaries, 2Sm 10:4

HAPPEN

If anything **h**-s to him Gn 42:38
She **h**-ed to be in the portion of Ru 2:3
All this has **h**-ed to us, but we Ps 44:17
What **h**-s to the fool will also Ec 2:15
Yet no one knows what will **h**, Ec 8:7
time and chance **h** to all of them Ec 9:11
come and tell us what will **h**. Is 41:22
Who is there who speaks and it **h**-s, Lm 3:37
All this **h**-ed to King Dn 4:28
concerning this. "It will not **h**," Am 7:3
when will these things **h**? Mt 24:3
But all this has **h**-ed so that the Mt 26:56
when you see these things **h**-ing, Mk 13:29
Bethlehem and see what has **h**-ed, Lk 2:15
the things that **h**-ed there in these Lk 24:18
telling you now before it **h**-s, so that Jn 13:19
when it does **h** you will believe
told you now before it **h**-s, so that Jn 14:29
when it does **h** you may believe.
Now these things **h**-ed to them as 1Co 10:11

HAPPIER

But she is **h** if she remains as 1Co 7:40

HAPPINESS

but does not experience **h**, Ec 6:6
and {bring} **h** out of grief. Jr 31:13
I have forgotten what **h** is. Lm 3:17

HAPPY

I am **h** that the women call me **h**, Gn 30:13
How **h** are these servants of yours, 1Kg 10:8
See how **h** the man is God corrects; Jb 5:17
How **h** is the man who does not Ps 1:1
who take refuge in Him are **h**. Ps 2:12
How **h** is the one whose Ps 32:1
How **h** is the man the LORD does Ps 32:2
H is the nation whose God is the Ps 33:12
How **h** is the man who takes Ps 34:8
How **h** is the man who has put his Ps 40:4
H is one who cares for the poor Ps 41:1
How **h** are those who reside in Ps 84:4
H are the people whose strength Ps 84:5
h is the person who trusts in Ps 84:12
H is the man who fears the LORD Ps 112:1
How **h** are those whose way is Ps 119:1
H are those who keep His decrees Ps 119:2
H is the man who has filled his Ps 127:5
How **h** is everyone who fears the Ps 128:1

You will be **h,** and it will go | Ps 128:2
H is he who takes your little ones | Ps 137:9
H are the people whose God is | Ps 144:15
H is the one whose help is the | Ps 146:5
H is a man who finds wisdom and | Pr 3:13
Anyone who listens to me is **h,** | Pr 8:34
kindness to the poor will be **h.** | Pr 14:21
trusts in the LORD will be **h.** | Pr 16:20
H is the one who is always | Pr 28:14
who keeps the law will be **h.** | Pr 29:18
wine makes life **h,** | Ec 10:19
H are all who wait patiently for | Is 30:18
How **h** those whose lawless acts | Rm 4:7
How **h** the man whom the Lord will | Rm 4:8

HARAN

Brother of Abraham; father of Lot (Gn 11:26-27).

HARASS

they will **h** you in the land | Nm 33:55
we did not **h** them, and | 1Sm 25:7
boys came out of the city and **h-ed** | 2Kg 2:23
tears (at me), and He **h-es** me. | Jb 16:9
You **h** me with Your strong hand. | Jb 30:21
on me and **h** me in anger. | Ps 55:3
and Judah will not **h** Ephraim. | Is 11:13

HARBOR

guided them to the **h** they longed | Ps 107:30

HARD

His heart is as **h** as a rock, | Jb 41:24
eating food earned by **h** work; | Ps 127:2
There is profit in all **h** work, | Pr 14:23
your face as **h** as their faces | Ezk 3:8
It will be **h** for a rich person | Mt 19:23
loads that are **h** to carry and | Mt 23:4
how **h** it is to enter the kingdom | Mk 10:24
This teaching is **h!** Who can accept | Jn 6:60
It is **h** for you to kick against | Ac 26:14
that are **h** to understand. | 2Pt 3:16

HARDEN

But I will **h** his heart so that | Ex 4:21
But I will **h** Pharaoh's heart and | Ex 7:3
But Pharaoh **h-ed** his heart | Ex 8:32
But the LORD **h-ed** Pharaoh's heart | Ex 9:12
I will **h** Pharaoh's heart so that | Ex 14:4
LORD's intention to **h** their hearts, | Jos 11:20
Why **h** your hearts as the Egyptians | 1Sm 6:6

when the dust **h-s** like cast metal | Jb 38:38
They have become **h-ed;** | Ps 17:10
Do not **h** your hearts as at Meribah, | Ps 95:8
but one who **h-s** his heart falls | Pr 28:14
Instead, their hearts were **h-ed.** | Mk 6:52
Is your heart **h-ed?** | Mk 8:17
their eyes and **h-ed** their hearts, | Jn 12:40
some became **h-ed** and would not | Ac 19:9
and He **h-s** whom He wills. | Rm 9:18
elect did find it. The rest were **h-ed,** | Rm 11:7
a partial **h-ing** has come to Israel | Rm 11:25
do not **h** your hearts as in the | Heb 3:8
none of you is **h-ed** by sin's | Heb 3:13
voice, do not **h** your hearts. | Heb 4:7

HARDER

brother is (**h** to reach) than | Pr 18:19
made their faces **h** than rock, | Jr 5:3
like a diamond, **h** than flint. | Ezk 3:9

HARDHEADED

of Israel is **h** and hardhearted. | Ezk 3:7

HARDHEARTED

you must not be **h** or tightfisted | Dt 15:7
Listen to me, you **h,** far removed | Is 46:12
children are obstinate and **h.** | Ezk 2:4
of Israel is hardheaded and **h.** | Ezk 3:7

HARDNESS

because of the **h** of your hearts | Mt 19:8
sorrow at the **h** of their hearts | Mk 3:5
their unbelief and **h** of heart, | Mk 16:14
of your **h** and unrepentant | Rm 2:5
because of the **h** of their hearts | Eph 4:18

HARDSHIP

forget all my **h** in my father's | Gn 41:51
You know all the **h-s** that have | Nm 20:14
unleavened bread ... the bread of **h** | Dt 16:3
heard our cry, and saw our misery, **h** | Dt 26:7
H-s assault me, wave after wave. | Jb 10:17
have made Your people suffer **h;** | Ps 60:3
David and all the **h-s** he endured, | Ps 132:1
by **h,** by pressures, | 2Co 6:4
by sharing with me in my **h.** | Php 4:14
you remember our labor and **h,** | 1Th 2:9
endure **h,** do the work | 2Tm 4:5

HARDWORKING

It is the **h** farmer who ought to | 2Tm 2:6

HARE

the **h**, though it chews the cud — Lv 11:6
the camel, the **h**, and the hyrax — Dt 14:7

HAREM

beautiful young virgins to the **h** — Est 2:3
her from the **h** to the palace. — Est 2:13
return to a second **h** under the — Est 2:14

HARM (n)

keep me from **h**, so that I will not — 1Ch 4:10
who plan to **h** me be turned back — Ps 35:4
agitated—it can only bring **h**. — Ps 37:8
no **h** will come to you; — Ps 91:10
will protect you from all **h**; — Ps 121:7
Don't plan any **h** against your — Pr 3:29
of fools will suffer **h**. — Pr 13:20
kept by Its owner to his **h**. — Ec 5:13
over another to his **h**. — Ec 8:9
won't happen. **H** won't come to us; — Jr 5:12
not fear them for they can do no **h** — Jr 10:5
Then I will do you no **h**. — Jr 25:6
fulfill My words for **h** and not for — Jr 39:16
doing such great **h** to yourselves? — Jr 44:7
on them for **h** and not for good — Am 9:4
how much **h** he has done to Your — Ac 9:13
coppersmith did great **h** to me. — 2Tm 4:14
to their own **h**, they are recrucifying — Heb 6:6

HARM (v)

Look, David intends to **h** you'? — 1Sm 24:9
anointed ones or **h** My prophets. — 1Ch 16:22
But they were planning to **h** me. — Neh 6:2
those who intended to **h** them. — Est 9:2
anointed ones, or **h** My prophets. — Ps 105:15
who sins against me **h-s** himself; — Pr 8:36
with many friends may be **h-ed**, — Pr 18:24
No one will **h** or destroy on My — Is 11:9
deadly, it will never **h** them; — Mk 16:18
nothing will ever **h** you. — Lk 10:19
voice, "Don't **h** yourself — Ac 16:28
And who will **h** you if you are — 1Pt 3:13
but do not **h** the olive oil and — Rv 6:6
Don't **h** the earth or the sea or — Rv 7:3

HARMFUL

will not experience anything **h**, — Ec 8:5
and many foolish and **h** desires, — 1Tm 6:9

HARMLESS

as serpents and as **h** as doves. — Mt 10:16

HARNESS

"**H**!" Joram shouted, — 2Kg 9:21
wild ox by its **h** to the furrow? — Jb 39:10
and **h** your tongue for deceit. — Ps 50:19
I will **h** Ephraim; Judah will plow; — Hs 10:11

HARP

who knows how to play the **h**. — 1Sm 16:16
musical instruments—**h-s**, lyres, — 1Ch 15:16
prophesy accompanied by ... **h-s**, — 1Ch 25:1
h-s, and lyres for the service — 1Ch 25:6
Levites ... with cymbals, **h-s**, — 2Ch 29:25
music to Him with a ten-stringed **h**. — Ps 33:2
h-s bring you joy. — Ps 45:8
Wake up, **h** and lyre! — Ps 57:8; 108:2
I will sing to You with a **h**, — Ps 71:22
on a ten-stringed **h** for You — Ps 144:9
praise Him with **h** and lyre. — Ps 150:3
zither, lyre, **h**, drum, and every — Dn 3:5
not listen to the music of your **h-s**. — Am 5:23
to the sound of the **h** and invent — Am 6:5
the flute or **h** be recognized? — 1Co 14:7
Each one had a **h** and gold bowls — Rv 5:8
sea of glass with **h-s** from God. — Rv 15:2

HARPOONS

Can you fill his hide with **h** — Jb 41:7

HARSH

was **h** and evil in (his) dealings — 1Sm 25:3
Your father made our yoke **h**. — 1Kg 12:4
but a **h** word stirs up wrath. — Pr 15:1
Discipline is **h** for the one who — Pr 15:10
affliction and **h** slavery; — Lm 1:3
Your words against Me are **h**, — Mal 3:13
and of all the **h** things ungodly — Jd 15

HARSHER

will receive a **h** punishment. — Mt 23:14

HARSHLY

strangers and spoke **h** to them. — Gn 42:7
the king answered the people **h**. — 1Kg 12:13
treats her young **h**, — Jb 39:16

HARVEST

earth endures, seedtime and **h**, — Gn 8:22
observe the Festival of **H** with — Ex 23:16
the firstfruits of the wheat **h**, — Ex 34:22
When you reap the **h** in your field, — Dt 24:19
the beginning of the barley **h**. — Ru 1:22
Isn't the wheat **h** today? — 1Sm 12:17

The earth has produced its **h**;   Ps 67:6
with the first produce of your entire **h**;   Pr 3:9
it gathers its food during **h**.   Pr 6:8
sleeps during **h** is disgraceful.   Pr 10:5
an abundant **h** {comes} through   Pr 14:4
h time he looks, and there is nothing. Pr 20:4
coolness of snow on a **h** day;   Pr 25:13
snow in summer and rain at **h**,   Pr 26:1
they rejoice at **h** time and   Is 9:3
like a rain cloud in **h** heat.   Is 18:4
consume your **h** and your food.   Jr 5:17
H has passed, summer has ended   Jr 8:20
while her **h** time will come.   Jr 51:33
A **h** is also appointed for you,   Hs 6:11
sickle because the **h** is ripe.   Jl 3:13
were still three months until **h**.   Am 4:7
The **h** is abundant, but the workers   Mt 9:37
pray to the Lord of the **h** to send   Mt 9:38
The **h** is the end of the age,   Mt 13:39
h drew near, he sent his slaves   Mt 21:34
fields, for they are ready for **h**.   Jn 4:35
and increase the **h** of your   2Co 9:10
since the **h** of the earth is ripe   Rv 14:15

HARVESTED
have sown wheat but **h** thorns.   Jr 12:13
have planted much but **h** little.   Hg 1:6

HARVESTERS
the outcry of the **h** has reached   Jms 5:4

HASN'T
The LORD **h** chosen this one   1Sm 16:8
in a city, **h** the LORD done it   Am 3:6

HASTENS
of the fool **h** destruction.   Pr 10:14

HASTILY
and the one who acts **h** sins.   Pr 19:2
Don't take a matter to court **h**.   Pr 25:8

HASTY
Do not be **h** to speak,   Ec 5:2

HATE
brothers, they **h-d** him even more.   Gn 37:5
{generations} of those who **h** Me,   Ex 20:5
You must not **h** your brother in   Lv 19:17
without previously **h-ing** him: Dt 19:4
You **h** me and don't love me!   Jdg 14:16
Amnon **h-d** Tamar with such   2Sm 13:15
but I **h** him because he never   1Kg 22:8

You **h** all evildoers.   Ps 5:5
I **h** a crowd of evildoers,   Ps 26:5
let those who **h** me without cause   Ps 35:19
love righteousness and **h** wickedness Ps 45:7
You **h** instruction and turn your   Ps 50:17
Those who **h** the LORD would   Ps 81:15
You who love the LORD, **h** evil!   Ps 97:10
I **h** the doing of transgression;   Ps 101:3
therefore I **h** every false way.   Ps 119:104
don't I **h** those who **h** You,   Ps 139:21
fools **h** knowledge?   Pr 1:22
Because they **h-d** knowledge,   Pr 1:29
Six things the LORD **h-s**;   Pr 6:16
To fear the LORD is to **h** evil.   Pr 8:13
The righteous **h** lying, but the   Pr 13:5
will not use the rod **h-s** his son,   Pr 13:24
and a man who schemes is **h-d**.   Pr 14:17
A poor man is **h-d** even by his   Pr 14:20
the one who **h-s** correction will   Pr 15:10
A lying tongue **h-s** those it   Pr 26:28
I **h-d** life because the work that   Ec 2:17
a time to love and a time to **h**;   Ec 3:8
I **h** robbery and injustice;   Is 61:8
H evil and love good;   Am 5:15
I **h**, I despise your feasts!   Am 5:21
You **h** good and love evil.   Mc 3:2
I loved Jacob, but I **h-d** Esau.   Mal 1:3
If he **h-s** and divorces   Mal 2:16
your neighbor and **h** your enemy.   Mt 5:43
either he will **h** one and love   Mt 6:24
You will be **h-d** by everyone   Mt 10:22
You will be **h-d** by all nations   Mt 24:9
one another and **h** one another.   Mt 24:10
are you when people **h** you,   Lk 6:22
do good to those who **h** you,   Lk 6:27
Me and does not **h** his own father   Lk 14:26
wicked things **h-s** the light   Jn 3:20
world cannot **h** you, but it does **h** Me Jn 7:7
and the one who **h-s** his life   Jn 12:25
If the world **h-s** you, understand   Jn 15:18
it **h-d** Me before it **h-d** you.   Jn 15:18
who **h-s** Me also **h-s** My Father. Jn 15:23
have seen and **h-d** both Me and My   Jn 15:24
They **h-d** Me for no reason.   Jn 15:25
The world **h-d** them because they   Jn 17:14
want to do, but I do what I **h**.   Rm 7:15
have loved, but Esau I have **h-d**.   Rm 9:13
no one ever **h-s** his own flesh,   Eph 5:29

and h-d lawlessness; | Heb 1:9
the light but h-s his brother is | 1Jn 2:9
brothers, if the world h-s you. | 1Jn 3:13
"I love God," yet h-s his brother, | 1Jn 4:20
h-ing even the garment defiled by | Jd 23
you h the practices of the Nicolaitans, | Rv 2:6
the beast, will h the prostitute | Rv 17:16

HATEFUL

me with h words and attack | Ps 109:3
A h person disguises himself | Pr 26:24
and envy, h, detesting one | Ti 3:3

HATRED

and h for my love. | Ps 109:5
I hate them with extreme h; | Ps 139:22
H stirs up conflicts, but love | Pr 10:12
who conceals h has lying lips, | Pr 10:18
than a fattened calf with h. | Pr 15:17
sorcery, h-s, strife, jealousy | Gl 5:20

HAUGHTY

surveys everything that is h; | Jb 41:34
You humble those with h eyes. | Ps 18:27
my eyes are not h. | Ps 131:1
but He knows the h from afar. | Ps 138:6
h eyes and an arrogant heart | Pr 21:4
arrogance, pride, and h heart. | Jr 48:29

HAUNT

a h for every unclean spirit, | Rv 18:2

HAVENS

called Fair H near the city | Ac 27:8

HAVILAH

the entire land of the H, | Gn 2:11
Seba, H, Sabtah, Raamah, and | Gn 10:7
they settled from H to Shur, | Gn 25:18
Ophir, H, and Jobab. | 1Ch 1:23

HAVING

H loved His own who were in the | Jn 13:1
H been buried with Him in | Col 2:12

HAVOC

Wherever he turned, he
caused h. | 1Sm 14:47
the destroyer to work h. | Is 54:16

HAY

stones, wood, h, or straw, | 1Co 3:12

HAZAEL

King of Syria (1Kg 19:15-17; 2Kg 8–13; Am 1:4).

HAZOR

Canaanite city (Jos 11:1-13; 19:36; Jdg 4:2,17).

HEAD

will strike your h, and you will | Gn 3:15
Seven h-s of grain, full and good | Gn 41:5
bowed ... at the h of his bed. | Gn 47:31
his right hand on Ephraim's h, | Gn 48:17
their hands on the bull's h. | Ex 29:10
lay their hands on the ram's h. | Ex 29:15
lay their hands on the bull's h | Lv 4:15
you may pluck h-s of grain with | Dt 23:25
make you the h and not the tail | Dt 28:13
he stood a h taller than anyone | 1Sm 10:23
took Goliath's h and brought it | 1Sm 17:54
His h will be thrown over the | 2Sm 20:21
to his father, "My h! My h!" | 2Kg 4:19
all 70, put their h-s in baskets | 2Kg 10:7
and the One who lifts up my h. | Ps 3:3
comes back on his own h, | Ps 7:16
You anoint my h with oil; | Ps 23:5
Lift up your h-s, you gates! | Ps 24:7
more than the hairs of my h, | Ps 40:12
You let men ride over our h-s; | Ps 66:12
He will lift up His h. | Ps 110:7
you will heap coals on his h, | Pr 25:22
The wise man has eyes in his h, | Ec 2:14
His left hand is under my h, | Sg 2:6; 8:3
For my h is drenched with dew, | Sg 5:2
His h is purest gold. | Sg 5:11
Your h crowns you like Mount | Sg 7:5
the h of Ephraim is Samaria, | Is 7:9
cut off Israel's h and tail, | Is 9:14
a helmet of salvation on His h; | Is 59:17
every h is bald and every beard | Jr 48:37
actions down on their own h-s. | Ezk 9:10
Every h was made bald and every | Ezk 29:18
his blood will be on his own h. | Ezk 33:4
The h of the statue was pure gold, | Dn 2:32
It had four h-s and was given | Dn 7:6
was wrapped around my h. | Jnh 2:5
should you swear by your h, | Mt 5:36
put oil on your h, and wash your | Mt 6:17
Man has no place to lay His h. | Mt 8:20
hairs of your h have all been | Mt 10:30

pick and eat some **h**-s of grain. Mt 12:1
His **h** was brought on a platter Mt 14:11
first the blade, then the **h**, Mk 4:28
not a hair of your **h** will be lost. Lk 21:18
but also my hands and my **h**. Jn 13:9
crown of thorns, put it on His **h**, Jn 19:2
bowing His **h**, He gave up His Jn 19:30
had been on His **h** was not lying Jn 20:7
heaping fiery coals on his **h**. Rm 12:20
Christ is the **h** of every man, the
   man is the **h** of the woman, 1Co 11:3
her **h** uncovered dishonors her **h**, 1Co 11:5
nor again the **h** to the feet, 1Co 12:21
Him as **h** over everything Eph 1:22
husband is **h** of the wife as also Eph 5:23
He is also the **h** of the body, Col 1:18
keep a clear **h** about everything 2Tm 4:5
His **h** and hair were white like Rv 1:14
having seven **h**-s and 10 horns, Rv 12:3
gold crown on His **h** and a sharp Rv 14:14
and on His **h** were many crowns. Rv 19:12

HEADFIRST
and falling **h**, he burst open in Ac 1:18

HEAL
For I am the LORD who **h**-s you. Ex 15:26
and I give life; I wound and I **h**. Dt 32:39
I have **h**-ed this water. 2Kg 2:21
their sin, and **h** their land. 2Ch 7:14
strikes, but His hands also **h**. Jb 5:18
h me, LORD, for my bones are Ps 6:2
h me, for I have sinned against You. Ps 41:4
He **h**-s all your diseases. Ps 103:3
He sent His word and **h**-ed them; Ps 107:20
He **h**-s the brokenhearted
   and binds Ps 147:3
The tongue that **h**-s is a tree of Pr 15:4
a time to kill and a time to **h**; Ec 3:3
mind, turn back, and be **h**-ed. Is 6:10
and **h**-s the wounds He inflicted. Is 30:26
and we are **h**-ed by His wounds. Is 53:5
has sent Me to **h** the brokenhearted, Is 61:1
I will **h** your unfaithfulness. Jr 3:22
H me, LORD, and I will be **h**-ed; Jr 17:14
vast as the sea. Who can **h** you? Lm 2:13
torn {us}, and He will **h** us; Hs 6:1
they never knew that I **h**-ed them. Hs 11:3
I will **h** their apostasy; Hs 14:4
the paralytics. And He **h**-ed them. Mt 4:24

and **h**-ed all who were sick, Mt 8:16
H the sick, raise the dead Mt 10:8
it lawful to **h** on the Sabbath? Mt 12:10
and He **h**-ed them all. Mt 12:15
at His feet, and He **h**-ed them. Mt 15:30
Your faith has **h**-ed you. Mk 10:52
Doctor, **h** yourself. Lk 4:23
Lord's power to **h** was in Him. Lk 5:17
see if He would **h** on the Sabbath Lk 6:7
And touching his ear, He **h**-ed him. Lk 22:51
converted, and I would **h** them. Jn 12:40
and they were all **h**-ed. Ac 5:16
Aeneas, Jesus Christ **h**-s you. Ac 9:34
seeing that he had faith to be **h**-ed, Ac 14:9
converted—and I would **h** them. Ac 28:27
be dislocated, but **h**-ed instead. Heb 12:13
so that you may be **h**-ed. Jms 5:16
His wounding you have been **h**-ed. 1Pt 2:24
but his fatal wound was **h**-ed. Rv 13:3

HEALING
This will be **h** for your body and Pr 3:8
tongue of the wise {brings} **h**. Pr 12:18
strike us with no hope of **h** for us? Jr 14:19
there is no **h** for you. Jr 46:11
will rise with **h** in its wings, Mal 4:2
gifts of **h** by the one Spirit, 1Co 12:9
Do all have gifts of **h**? 1Co 12:30
the tree are for **h** the nations, Rv 22:2

HEALTH
One person dies in excellent **h**, Jb 21:23
there is no **h** in my bones Ps 38:3
and **h** to one's whole body. Pr 4:22
to the taste and **h** to the body. Pr 16:24
I will bring you **h** and will heal Jr 30:17
in every way and be in good **h**, 3Jn 2

HEALTHIER
looked better and **h** than all the Dn 1:15

HEALTHY
still **h** as they go down to the Pr 1:12
The **h** don't need a doctor, Lk 5:31
is standing here before you **h**. Ac 4:10

HEAP (n)
the waters of the sea into a **h**; Ps 33:7

HEAP (v)
for you will **h** coals on his head Pr 25:22
you will be **h**-ing fiery coals Rm 12:20

HEAR

he said, "I **h-d** You in the garden,	Gn 3:10
God **h-d** the voice of the boy,	Gn 21:17
So God **h-d** their groaning,	Ex 2:24
I will certainly **h** their cry.	Ex 22:23
Has a people ever **h-d** God's voice	Dt 4:33
we have **h-d** how the LORD dried	Jos 2:10
sound of sheep and cattle I **h**?	1Sm 15:14
may You **h** in heaven and forgive	1Kg 8:34
then I will **h** from heaven,	2Ch 7:14
Will God **h** his cry when distress	Jb 27:9
I had **h-d** rumors about You, but	Jb 42:5
be gracious to me and **h** my prayer.	Ps 4:1
The LORD has **h-d** my plea for help	Ps 6:9
soon as they **h**, they obey me.	Ps 18:44
and the LORD **h-s**, and delivers	Ps 34:17
to me and **h-d** my cry for help	Ps 40:1
Let me **h** joy and gladness;	Ps 51:8
and night, and He **h-s** my voice.	Ps 55:17
God, **h** my cry; pay attention to	Ps 61:1
to You, the One who **h-s** prayer.	Ps 65:2
the sound of His praise be **h-d**.	Ps 66:8
One who shaped the ear not **h**,	Ps 94:9
Today, if you **h** His voice:	Ps 95:7
Zion **h-s** and is glad,	Ps 97:8
have ears, but cannot **h**	Ps 115:6; 135:17
LORD, **h** my prayer.	Ps 143:1
He **h-s** their cry for help and	Ps 145:19
but a poor man **h-s** no threat.	Pr 13:8
He **h-s** the prayer of the righteous.	Pr 15:29
When all has been **h-d**,	Ec 12:13
for your voice—let me **h** you!	Sg 8:13
see their eyes and **h** with their ears,	Is 6:10
that day the deaf will **h** the words	Is 29:18
are far off, **h** what I have done	Is 33:13
Let the earth **h**, and all that	Is 34:1
Have you not **h-d**? Has it not been	Is 40:21
His ear is not too deaf to **h**.	Is 59:1
ancient times no one has **h-d**,	Is 64:4
I spoke and you did not **h**;	Is 65:12
are still speaking, I will **h**.	Is 65:24
Who has **h-d** of such a thing?	Is 66:8
have ears, but they don't **h**.	Jr 5:21
A voice was **h-d** in Ramah, a lament	Jr 31:15
and ears to **h** but do not **h**,	Ezk 12:2
When you **h** a word from My	Ezk 33:7
Dry bones, **h** the word of the LORD	Ezk 37:4
I have **h-d** about you that you can	Dn 5:16

Lord, **h**! Lord, forgive!	Dn 9:19
belly of Sheol; You **h-d** my voice.	Jnh 2:2
A voice was **h-d** in Ramah, weeping	Mt 2:18
You have **h-d** that it was said	Mt 5:21
they'll be **h-d** for their many	Mt 6:7
everyone who **h-s** these words of	Mt 7:24
the deaf **h**, the dead are raised,	Mt 11:5
and **h-ing** they do not listen or	Mt 13:13
their eyes and **h** with their ears	Mt 13:15
longed … to **h** the things you **h**	Mt 13:17
You are going to **h** of wars and	Mt 24:6
who has ears to **h** should listen!	Mk 4:9
Pay attention to what you **h**.	Mk 4:24
do you have ears, and not **h**?	Mk 8:18
When Elizabeth **h-d** Mary's greeting	Lk 1:41
and **h-ing** they may not understand.	Lk 8:10
where it pleases, and you **h** its sound,	Jn 3:8
Anyone who **h-s** My word and	Jn 5:24
in the graves will **h** His voice	Jn 5:28
You have not **h-d** His voice at any	Jn 5:37
My sheep **h** My voice,	Jn 10:27
I know that You always **h** Me,	Jn 11:42
If anyone **h-s** My words and doesn't	Jn 12:47
I have **h-d** from My Father.	Jn 15:15
He will speak whatever He **h-s**.	Jn 16:13
we **h** them speaking in our own	Ac 2:11
those who **h-d** the message believed,	Ac 4:4
When the Gentiles **h-d** this, they	Ac 13:48
we haven't even **h-d** that there is	Ac 19:2
their eyes and **h** with their ears	Ac 28:27
And how can they **h** without a	Rm 10:14
So faith comes from what is **h-d**,	Rm 10:17
see and ears that cannot **h**,	Rm 11:8
who have not **h-d** will understand.	Rm 15:21
eye has seen and no ear has **h-d**,	1Co 2:9
He **h-d** inexpressible words,	2Co 12:4
not even be **h-d** of among you,	Eph 5:3
because you **h-d** that he was sick.	Php 2:26
received and **h-d** and seen in me,	Php 4:9
for we have **h-d** of your faith in	Col 1:4
that you have **h-d** from me,	2Tm 1:13
And what you have **h-d** from me in	2Tm 2:2
an itch to **h** something new.	2Tm 4:3
and all the Gentiles might **h**.	2Tm 4:17
attention to what we have **h-d**,	Heb 2:1
Today, if you **h** His voice,	Heb 3:7
and He was **h-d** because of His	Heb 5:7
everyone must be quick to **h**,	Jms 1:19

have seen and **h-d** we also declare   1Jn 1:3

according to His will, He **h-s** us.   1Jn 5:14

are those who **h** the words of   Rv 1:3

If anyone **h-s** My voice and opens   Rv 3:20

not able to see, **h**, or walk.   Rv 9:20

will never be **h-d** in you again;   Rv 18:22

I, John, am the one who **h-d** and   Rv 22:8

HEARERS

For the **h** of the law are not   Rm 2:13

save both yourself and your **h**.   1Tm 4:16

and leads to the ruin of the **h**.   2Tm 2:14

of the word and not **h** only,   Jms 1:22

HEARING (adj)

The **h** ear and the seeing eye   Pr 20:12

HEARING (n)

or the ear filled with **h**.   Ec 1:8

but of **h** the words of the LORD.   Am 8:11

will give you a **h** whenever your   Ac 23:35

an eye, where would the **h** be?   1Co 12:17

works of the law or by **h** with faith?   Gl 3:2

HEART

and He was grieved in His **h**.   Gn 6:6

I will harden his **h** so that he   Ex 4:21

Pharaoh's **h** hardened, and he   Ex 7:13

But Pharaoh's **h** was hardened,   Ex 9:7

the LORD hardened Pharaoh's **h**,   Ex 10:20

everyone whose **h** stirs him {to   Ex 25:2

Everyone whose **h** was moved and   Ex 35:21

women whose **h-s** were moved   Ex 35:26

person in whose **h** the LORD had   Ex 36:2

not hate your brother in your **h**.   Lv 19:17

when you seek Him with all your **h**   Dt 4:29

they had such a **h** to fear Me and   Dt 5:29

LORD your God with all your **h**,   Dt 6:5

you today are to be in your **h**.   Dt 6:6

circumcise your **h-s** and don't be   Dt 10:16

these words of Mine on your **h-s**   Dt 11:18

don't have a stingy **h** when you   Dt 15:10

God with joy and a cheerful **h**,   Dt 28:47

will circumcise your **h** and the **h-s**   Dt 30:6

in your mouth and in your **h**,   Dt 30:14

Take to **h** all these words I am   Dt 32:46

with all your **h** and all your   Jos 22:5

My **h** rejoices in the LORD;   1Sm 2:1

God changed his **h**, and all the   1Sm 10:9

but the LORD sees the **h**.   1Sm 16:7

and she despised him in her **h**.   2Sm 6:16

Me with their whole mind and **h**,   1Kg 2:4

you a wise and understanding **h**,   1Kg 3:12

May He incline our **h-s** toward   1Kg 8:58

My eyes and My **h** will be there   1Kg 9:3

700 wives ... turned his **h** away   1Kg 11:3

but Asa's **h** was completely with   1Kg 15:14

You have turned their **h-s** back.   1Kg 18:37

because your **h** was tender and   2Kg 22:19

his mind and with all his **h**,   2Kg 23:3

the LORD searches every **h** and   1Ch 28:9

whose **h-s** are completely His.   2Ch 16:9

Ezra had determined in his **h** to   Ezr 7:10

You found his **h** faithful in Your   Neh 9:8

place His sayings in your **h**.   Jb 22:22

God has made my **h** faint;   Jb 23:16

If ... my **h** has followed my eyes,   Jb 31:7

My **h** pounds at this and leaps   Jb 37:1

reflect in your **h** and be still.   Ps 4:4

The fool says in his **h**, "God   Ps 14:1; 53:1

meditation of my **h** be acceptable   Ps 19:14

my **h** is like wax, melting within   Ps 22:14

has clean hands and a pure **h**,   Ps 24:4

for joy, all you upright in **h**.   Ps 32:11

He alone crafts their **h-s**;   Ps 33:15

will give you your **h-'s** desires.   Ps 37:4

My **h** is moved by a noble theme   Ps 45:1

create a clean **h** for me and   Ps 51:10

despise a broken and humbled **h**.   Ps 51:17

My **h** is confident, God, my **h** is   Ps 57:7

been aware of malice in my **h**,   Ps 66:18

God is the strength of my **h**,   Ps 73:26

my **h** and flesh cry out for the   Ps 84:2

harden your **h-s** as at Meribah,   Ps 95:8

haughty eyes or an arrogant **h**.   Ps 101:5

let the **h-s** of those who seek the   Ps 105:3

have sought You with all my **h**;   Ps 119:10

Your word in my **h** so that I may   Ps 119:11

LORD, my **h** is not proud;   Ps 131:1

give You thanks with all my **h**;   Ps 138:1

Search me, God, and know my **h**;   Ps 139:23

Trust in the LORD with all your **h**,   Pr 3:5

Guard your **h** above all else,   Pr 4:23

them on the tablet of your **h**.   Pr 7:3

Delayed hope makes the **h** sick,   Pr 13:12

how much more, human **h-s**.   Pr 15:11

A joyful **h** makes a face cheerful   Pr 15:13

Bright eyes cheer the **h**;   Pr 15:30

reflections of the **h** belong to man,   Pr 16:1

A man's **h** plans his way, but the   Pr 16:9
but the LORD is a tester of **h-s**.   Pr 17:3
A joyful **h** is good medicine,   Pr 17:22
Many plans are in a man's **h**,   Pr 19:21
A king's **h** is a water channel in   Pr 21:1
He who weighs **h-s** consider it?   Pr 24:12
Singing songs to a troubled **h** is like   Pr 25:20
so the **h** reflects the person.   Pr 27:19
also put eternity in their **h-s**,   Ec 3:11
a face is sad, a **h** may be glad.   Ec 7:3
and a wise **h** knows the right time   Ec 8:5
captured my **h** with one glance   Sg 4:9
Set me as a seal on your **h**,   Sg 8:6
and the whole **h** is sick.   Is 1:5
yet their **h-s** are far from Me,   Is 29:13
and revive the **h** of the oppressed.   Is 57:15
remove the foreskin of your **h-s**,   Jr 4:4
of Israel is uncircumcised in **h**.   Jr 9:26
who tests **h** and mind,   Jr 11:20
The **h** is more deceitful than   Jr 17:9
will give them a **h** to know Me,   Jr 24:7
search for Me with all your **h**,   Jr 29:13
them and write it on their **h-s**.   Jr 31:33
My **h** is poured out in grief   Lm 2:11
will remove their **h** of stone   Ezk 11:19
a new **h** and a new spirit   Ezk 18:31
I will give you a new **h**   Ezk 36:26
I will remove your **h** of stone
  and give you a **h** of flesh.   Ezk 36:26
uncircumcised in both **h** and flesh,   Ezk 44:7
he will turn the **h-s** of fathers to   Mal 4:6
Blessed are the pure in **h**,   Mt 5:8
adultery with her in his **h**.   Mt 5:28
there your **h** will be also.   Mt 6:21
I am gentle and humble in **h**,   Mt 11:29
from the overflow of the **h**.   Mt 12:34
this people's **h** has grown   Mt 13:15
but their **h** is far from Me.   Mt 15:8
For from the **h** come evil   Mt 15:19
forgive his brother from his **h**.   Mt 18:35
Lord your God with all your **h**,   Mt 22:37
out of people's **h-s**, come evil   Mk 7:21
and does not doubt in his **h**,   Mk 11:23
to turn the **h-s** of fathers to   Lk 1:17
kept all these things in her **h**.   Lk 2:51
word with an honest and good **h**,   Lk 8:15
others, but God knows your **h-s**.   Lk 16:15
Weren't our **h-s** ablaze within us   Lk 24:32

Your **h** must not be troubled.   Jn 14:1
You, Lord, know the **h-s** of all;   Ac 1:24
they were pierced to the **h** and said   Ac 2:37
were of one **h** and soul,   Ac 4:32
Satan filled your **h** to lie to   Ac 5:3
because your **h** is not right   Ac 8:21
cleansing their **h-s** by faith.   Ac 15:9
the law is written on their **h-s**.   Rm 2:15
and circumcision is of the **h**   Rm 2:29
who searches the **h-s** knows the   Rm 8:27
believe in your **h** that God raised   Rm 10:9
With the **h** one believes   Rm 10:10
has never come into a man's **h**,   1Co 2:9
reveal the intentions of the **h-s**.   1Co 4:5
secrets of his **h** will be revealed,   1Co 14:25
on tablets that are **h-s** of flesh.   2Co 3:3
has shone in our **h-s** to give the   2Co 4:6
do as he has decided in his **h**   2Co 9:7
Spirit of His Son into our **h-s**,   Gl 4:6
the eyes of your **h** may be   Eph 1:18
dwell in your **h-s** through faith.   Eph 3:17
music to the Lord in your **h**,   Eph 5:19
do God's will from your **h**.   Eph 6:6
will guard your **h-s** and your minds   Php 4:7
let the peace ... control your **h-s**.   Col 3:15
rather God, who examines our **h-s**.   1Th 2:4
is love from a pure **h**,   1Tm 1:5
call on the Lord from a pure **h**.   2Tm 2:22
do not harden your **h-s** as in the   Heb 3:8
I will put My laws on their **h-s**,   Heb 10:16
let us draw near with a true **h**   Heb 10:22
and purify your **h-s**, double-minded   Jms 4:8
earnestly from a pure **h**,   1Pt 1:22
morning star arises in your **h-s**.   2Pt 1:19
God is greater than our **h-s**   1Jn 3:20
One who examines minds and **h-s**,   Rv 2:23

HEARTACHE
a foolish son, **h** to his mother.   Pr 10:1

HEARTFELT
and loved, put on **h** compassion   Col 3:12

HEAT (n)
seedtime and harvest, cold and **h**,   Gn 8:22
from the rain, a shade from the **h**.   Is 25:4
scorching **h** ... will not strike them;   Is 49:10
elements will melt with the **h**.   2Pt 3:12

HEAT (v)
gave orders to **h** the furnace   Dn 3:19

HEAVEN

God created the **h-s** and the earth. Gn 1:1
Most High, Creator of **h** and earth, Gn 14:19
LORD called to him from **h** Gn 22:11
ground with its top reaching **h**, Gn 28:12
This is the gate of **h**. Gn 28:17
with blessings of the **h-s** above, Gn 49:25
to rain bread from **h** for you. Ex 16:4
shape of anything in the **h-s** above Ex 20:4
I call **h** and earth as witnesses Dt 4:26
He let you hear His voice from **h** Dt 4:36
LORD is God in **h** above and on Dt 4:39
h-s, indeed the highest **h-s**, belong Dt 10:14
Who will go up to **h**, get it for us Dt 30:12
God is God in **h** above and on Jos 2:11
The LORD thundered from **h**; 2Sm 22:14
h, the highest **h**, cannot contain 1Kg 8:27
may You hear in **h** and forgive 1Kg 8:34
may fire come down from **h** 2Kg 1:10
Elijah up to **h** in a whirlwind. 2Kg 2:1
LORD were to make windows in **h**, 2Kg 7:2
standing between earth and **h**, 1Ch 21:16
will hear from **h**, forgive their 2Ch 7:14
our guilt is as high as the **h-s**. Ezr 9:6
You created the **h-s**, the highest Neh 9:6
up until the **h-s** are no more; Jb 14:12
Even now my witness is in **h**, Jb 16:19
Isn't God as high as the **h-s**? Jb 22:12
Do you know the laws of **h**? Jb 38:33
The One enthroned in **h** laughs; Ps 2:4
When I observe Your **h-s**, the work Ps 8:3
the LORD's throne is in **h**. Ps 11:4
looks down from **h** on the human Ps 14:2
The **h-s** declare the glory of God, Ps 19:1
The **h-s** were made by the word of Ps 33:6
faithful love (reaches) to **h**, Ps 36:5
The **h-s** proclaim His righteousness Ps 50:6
God, be exalted above the **h-s**; Ps 57:5
love is as high as the **h-s**; Ps 57:10
Let **h** and earth praise Him, Ps 69:34
Whom do I have in **h** but You? Ps 73:25
and opened the doors of **h**. Ps 78:23
Your faithfulness in the **h-s**. Ps 89:2
The **h-s** are Yours; the earth also Ps 89:11
idols, but the LORD made the **h-s**. Ps 96:5
Let the **h-s** be glad and the earth Ps 96:11
The **h-s** proclaim His righteousness Ps 97:6
h-s are the work of Your hands. Ps 102:25

For as high as the **h-s** are above Ps 103:11
established His throne in **h**, Ps 103:19
them with **bread** from **h**. Ps 105:40
love is higher than the **h-s**; Ps 108:4
nations, His glory above the **h-s**. Ps 113:4
Our God is in **h** and does Ps 115:3
LORD, the Maker of **h** and earth. Ps 115:15
The **h-s** are the LORD's, but the Ps 115:16
it is firmly fixed in **h**. Ps 119:89
Give thanks to the God of **h**! Ps 136:26
If I go up to **h**, You are there; Ps 139:8
Praise Him, highest **h-s**, Ps 148:4
Praise Him in His mighty **h-s**. Ps 150:1
established the **h-s** by understanding. Pr 3:19
there when He established the **h-s**, Pr 8:27
As the **h** is high and the earth Pr 25:3
has gone up to **h** and come down? Pr 30:4
time for every activity under **h**: Ec 3:1
God is in **h** and you are on earth, Ec 5:2
how you have fallen from the **h-s**! Is 14:12
For as **h** is higher than earth, Is 55:9
create a new **h** and a new earth; Is 65:17
H is My throne, and earth is My Is 66:1
The gods that did not make the **h-s** Jr 10:11
burn incense to the queen of **h** Jr 44:17
I will cover the **h-s** and darken Ezk 32:7
there is a God in **h** who reveals Dn 2:28
you acknowledge that **H** rules. Dn 4:26
and glorify the King of **h**, Dn 4:37
coming with the clouds of **h**. Dn 7:13
I will display wonders in the **h-s** and Jl 2:30
if they climb up to **h**, from there I Am 9:2
open the floodgates of **h** and pour Mal 3:10
the kingdom of **h** has come near! Mt 3:2
The **h-s** suddenly opened for Him, Mt 3:16
And there came a voice from **h**: Mt 3:17
your reward is great in **h**. Mt 5:12
Until **h** and earth pass away, Mt 5:18
either by **h**, because it is God's Mt 5:34
Our Father in **h**, Your name be Mt 6:9
be done on earth as it is in **h**. Mt 6:10
for yourselves treasures in **h**, Mt 6:20
will you be exalted to **h**? Mt 11:23
Him to show them a sign from **h**. Mt 16:1
on earth is already bound in **h**, Mt 16:19
you will have treasure in **h**. Mt 19:21
but are like angels in **h**. Mt 22:30
on the clouds of **h** with power Mt 24:30

H and earth will pass away,	Mt 24:35
and coming on the clouds of h.	Mt 26:64
given to Me in h and on earth.	Mt 28:18
Him a sign from h to test Him.	Mk 8:11
baptism from h or from men?	Mk 11:30
taken up into h and sat down at	Mk 16:19
I watched Satan fall from h like a	Lk 10:18
that your names are written in h.	Lk 10:20
be more joy in h over one sinner	Lk 15:7
sinned against h and in your	Lk 15:18
Peace in h and glory in	Lk 19:38
and great signs from h.	Lk 21:11
them and was carried up into h.	Lk 24:51
You will see h opened and the	Jn 1:51
No one has ascended into h except	Jn 3:13
gives you the real bread from h.	Jn 6:32
For I have come down from h,	Jn 6:38
Then a voice came from h:	Jn 12:28
will come in the same way you have seen Him going into h.	Ac 1:11
name under h given to people	Ac 4:12
H is My throne, and earth My	Ac 7:49
I see the h-s opened and the Son	Ac 7:56
saw h opened and ... a large sheet	Ac 10:11
of the image that fell from h?	Ac 19:35
is revealed from h against all	Rm 1:18
Who will go up to h?	Rm 10:6
the second man is from h.	1Co 15:47
with hands, eternal in the h-s.	2Co 5:1
to put on our house from h,	2Co 5:2
into the third h 14 years ago.	2Co 12:2
an angel from h should preach to	Gl 1:8
spiritual blessing in the h-s,	Eph 1:3
both things in h and things on	Eph 1:10
at His right hand in the h-s	Eph 1:20
seated us with Him in the h-s,	Eph 2:6
and authorities in the h-s.	Eph 3:10
family in h and on earth is	Eph 3:15
ascended far above all the h-s,	Eph 4:10
forces of evil in the h-s.	Eph 6:12
those who are in h and on earth	Php 2:10
but our citizenship is in h,	Php 3:20
the hope reserved for you in h,	Col 1:5
and to wait for His Son from h,	1Th 1:10
Lord Jesus from h with His	2Th 1:7
and the h-s are the works of Your	Heb 1:10
who has passed through the h-s	Heb 4:14

Messiah did not enter a sanctuary ... but into h itself,	Heb 9:24
do not swear, either by h or by	Jms 5:12
unfading, kept in h for you,	1Pt 1:4
Now that He has gone into h,	1Pt 3:22
that {day} the h-s will pass away	2Pt 3:10
wait for new h-s and a new earth	2Pt 3:13
and there in h was an open door	Rv 4:1
was silence in h for about half	Rv 8:1
A great sign appeared in h:	Rv 12:1
Then I saw h opened, and there	Rv 19:11
I saw a new h and a new earth	Rv 21:1

HEAVENLY

the whole h host was standing	1Kg 22:19
They worshiped the whole h host	2Kg 17:16
Asherah, and the whole h host.	2Kg 23:4
and the h host worships You.	Neh 9:6
All the h bodies will dissolve.	Is 34:4
sun, the moon, and the whole h host,	Jr 8:2
burned incense to the whole h host	Jr 19:13
It grew as high as the h host,	Dn 8:10
on the rooftops to the h host;	Zph 1:5
as your h Father is perfect.	Mt 5:48
your h Father will forgive you as well.	Mt 6:14
yet your h Father feeds them.	Mt 6:26
and your h Father knows that you	Mt 6:32
a multitude of the h host with	Lk 2:13
much more will the h Father give	Lk 11:13
There are h bodies and earthly	1Co 15:40
like the h man, so are those who	1Co 15:48
bear the image of the h man.	1Co 15:49
by God's h call in Christ	Php 3:14
me safely into His h kingdom.	2Tm 4:18
and companions in a h calling,	Heb 3:1
who tasted the h gift,	Heb 6:4
and shadow of the h things,	Heb 8:5
to a better land—a h one.	Heb 11:16
living God (the h Jerusalem), to	Heb 12:22

HEAVILY

wrath weighs h on me;	Ps 88:7
and it weighs h on humanity:	Ec 6:1

HEAVY

Moses' hands grew h, they took a	Ex 17:12
your bag, one h and one light.	Dt 25:13
and since he was old and h,	1Sm 4:18
Your father made our yoke h,	1Kg 12:10

burden on the people was so **h**.   Neh 5:18
night Your hand was **h** on me;   Ps 32:4
a burden too **h** for me to bear.   Ps 38:4
A stone is **h** and sand, a burden   Pr 27:3
man's troubles are **h** on him.   Ec 8:6
make Jerusalem a **h** stone for all   Zch 12:3
They tie up **h** loads that are   Mt 23:4

HEBER
Jael, the wife of **H** the Kenite   Jdg 4:17

HEBREW
came and told Abram the **H**,   Gn 14:13
brought a **H** man to us to make   Gn 39:14
from the land of the **H-s**,   Gn 40:15
Now a young **H**, a slave of the   Gn 41:12
Egyptians could not eat with **H-s**,   Gn 43:32
Egypt said to the **H** midwives,   Ex 1:15
born to the **H-s** into the Nile,   Ex 1:22
This is one of the **H** boys.   Ex 2:6
woman from the **H-s** to nurse the   Ex 2:7
He saw an Egyptian beating a **H**,   Ex 2:11
out and saw two **H-s** fighting.   Ex 2:13
The LORD, the God of the **H-s**,   Ex 3:18
the God of the **H-s**, has sent me to   Ex 7:16
LORD, the God of the **H-s**, says: Ex 9:1
When you buy a **H** slave, he is to   Ex 21:2
If your fellow **H**, a man or woman   Dt 15:12
this loud shout in the **H-s'** camp?   1Sm 4:6
land saying, "Let the **H-s** hear!"   1Sm 13:3
the **H-s** are coming out of the   1Sm 14:11
What are these **H-s** {doing here}?   1Sm 29:3
in **H** within earshot of the people   2Kg 18:26
peoples but could not speak **H**.   Neh 13:24
male and female **H** slaves and no   Jr 34:9
He answered them, "I am a **H**.   Jnh 1:9
Bethesda in **H**, which has five   Jn 5:2
Pavement (but in **H** Gabbatha).   Jn 19:13
which in **H** is called Golgotha).   Jn 19:17
was written in **H**, Latin, and   Jn 19:20
she said to Him in **H**, "Rabbouni!"   Jn 20:16
in the **H** language   Ac 21:40; 22:2; 26:14
Are they **H-s**? So am I.   2Co 11:22
of Benjamin, a **H** born of **H-s**;   Php 3:5
his name in **H** is Abaddon,   Rv 9:11
place called in **H** Armagedon.   Rv 16:16

HEBRON
1. City in Judah south of Jerusalem, also called Kiriath-arba; Abraham lived there, and Sarah died there (Gn 13:18; 23:2,19); visited by spies (Nm 13:22); conquered by Joshua (Jos 10); a city of refuge (20:7). David reigned over Judah from there (2Sm 2:11), and Absalom rebelled there (15:10).

2. A Levite (Ex 6:18).

3. A Calebite (1Ch 2:42).

HEDGE
You placed a **h** around him,   Jb 1:10
is worse than a **h** of thorns.   Mc 7:4

HEDGED
path is hidden, whom God has **h** in?   Jb 3:23

HEDGEHOG
owl and the **h** will possess it,   Is 34:11

HEEDS
person who **h** correction is sensible. Pr 15:5

HEEL
and you will strike his **h**.   Gn 3:15
Esau's **h** with his hand.   Gn 25:26
A trap catches {him} by the **h**;   Jb 18:9
has lifted up his **h** against me.   Ps 41:9
he grasped his brother's **h**,   Hs 12:3
has raised his **h** against Me.   Jn 13:18

HEIGHT
of Israel lies slain on your **h-s**.   2Sm 1:19
and sets me securely on the **h-s**.   2Sm 22:34
At the **h** of his success distress   Jb 20:22
and sets me securely on the **h-s**.   Ps 18:33
You ascended to the **h-s**, taking   Ps 68:18
built His sanctuary like the **h-s**,   Ps 78:69
praise Him in the **h-s**.   Ps 148:1
At the **h-s** overlooking the road,   Pr 8:2
fool is appointed to great **h-s**,   Ec 10:6
shout for joy on the **h-s** of Zion;   Jr 31:12
it was conspicuous for its **h**   Ezk 19:11
cedar became greater in **h** than all   Ezk 31:5
The ancient **h-s** have become our   Ezk 36:2
the earth, and its **h** was great.   Dn 4:10
his **h** was like the cedars,   Am 2:9
the rock in your home on the **h-s**,   Ob 3
me to walk on mountain **h-s**!   Hab 3:19
cubit to his **h** by worrying?   Mt 6:27
nor **h**, nor depth, nor any other   Rm 8:39

breadth and width, **h** and depth, | Eph 3:18
length, width, and **h** are equal. | Rv 21:16

HEIR

born in my house will be my **h**. | Gn 15:3
We will destroy the **h**! | 2Sm 14:7
to annihilate all the royal **h-s**. | 2Kg 11:1
h-s to My mountains from Judah | Is 65:9
Is he without an **h**? Why then has | Jr 49:1
This is the **h**. Come, let's kill him | Mt 21:38
If those who are of the law are **h-s**, | Rm 4:14
if children, also **h-s—h-s** of God | Rm 8:17
h-s according to the promise. | Gl 3:29
as long as the **h** is a child, | Gl 4:1
a son, then an **h** through God. | Gl 4:7
the Gentiles are co-**h-s**, members of | Eph 3:6
we may become **h-s** with the hope of | Ti 3:7
He has appointed **h** of all things | Heb 1:2
clearly to the **h-s** of the promise | Heb 6:17
world and became an **h** of the | Heb 11:7
Isaac and Jacob, co-**h-s** of the same | Heb 11:9
in faith and **h-s** of the kingdom | Jms 2:5
them honor as co-**h-s** of the grace of | 1Pt 3:7

HELL   see also HADES, HELLFIRE, SHEOL

whole body to be thrown into **h**. | Mt 5:29
to destroy both soul and body in **h**. | Mt 10:28
twice as fit for **h** as you are! | Mt 23:15
escape being condemned to **h**? | Mt 23:33
to have two hands and go to **h** | Mk 9:43
authority to throw {people} into **h** | Lk 12:5
and is set on fire by **h**. | Jms 3:6

HELLENISTIC

complaint by the **H** Jews against | Ac 6:1
and debated with the **H** Jews, | Ac 9:29

HELLENISTS

and began speaking to the **H**, | Ac 11:20

HELLFIRE

will be subject to **h**. | Mt 5:22
two eyes and be thrown into **h**! | Mt 18:9

HELMET

wore a bronze **h** and bronze scale | 1Sm 17:5
put a bronze **h** on David's head | 1Sm 17:38
and Ephraim is My **h**; | Ps 60:7; 108:8
and a **h** of salvation on His head; | Is 59:17
Take the **h** of salvation, | Eph 6:17
put on a **h** of the hope of salvation. | 1Th 5:8

HELP (n)

a male child with the LORD's **h**. | Gn 4:1
There is no **h** for him in God. | Ps 3:2
and I cried to my God for **h**. | Ps 18:6
They cry for **h**, but there is no | Ps 18:41
when he cried to Him for **h**. | Ps 22:24
You have been my **h**; do not leave | Ps 27:9
I cried to You for **h**, and You healed | Ps 30:2
He is our **h** and shield. | Ps 33:20
You are my **h** and my deliverer; | Ps 40:17
for human **h** is worthless. | Ps 60:11
You are my **h** and my deliverer; | Ps 70:5
I have granted **h** to a warrior; | Ps 89:19
If the LORD had not been my **h**, | Ps 94:17
let my cry for **h** come before You | Ps 102:1
He is their **h** and shield. | Ps 115:9
Where will my **h** come from? | Ps 121:1
Our **h** is in the name of the LORD | Ps 124:8
is the one whose **h** is the God of | Ps 146:5
I cried out for **h** in the belly | Jnh 2:2
gifts of healing, **h-ing**, managing, | 1Co 12:28

HELP (v)

The LORD has **h-ed** us to this point | 1Sm 7:12
cried out and the LORD **h-ed** him. | 2Ch 18:31
Since I cannot **h** myself, | Jb 6:13
The LORD **h-s** and delivers them; | Ps 37:40
God of our salvation, **h** us | Ps 79:9
me fall, but the LORD **h-ed** me. | Ps 118:13
H me understand Your instruction | Ps 119:34
The LORD **h-s** all who fall; | Ps 145:14
The LORD **h-s** the afflicted but | Ps 147:6
Let no one **h** him. | Pr 28:17
I will **h** you; I will hold on to you | Is 41:10
Him, and said, "Lord, **h** me!" | Mt 15:25
or in prison, and not **h** You? | Mt 25:44
I do believe! **H** my unbelief. | Mk 9:24
He has **h-ed** His servant Israel, | Lk 1:54
The flesh doesn't **h** at all. | Jn 6:63
over to Macedonia and **h** us! | Ac 16:9
necessary to **h** the weak and to | Ac 20:35
also joins to **h** in our weakness | Rm 8:26
the discouraged, **h** the weak, | 1Th 5:14
washed the saints' feet, **h-ed** the | 1Tm 5:10
He is able to **h** those who are | Heb 2:18
find grace to **h** us at the proper | Heb 4:16
But the earth **h-ed** the woman; | Rv 12:16

HELPER

I will make a **h** who is like him. | Gn 2:18

You are a **h** of the fatherless. Ps 10:14
gracious to me; LORD, be my **h**. Ps 30:10
a **h** who is always found in times Ps 46:1
God is my **h**; the Lord is the Ps 54:4
With the LORD for me as my **h**, Ps 118:7
Lord is my **h**; I will not be afraid. Heb 13:6

HELPFUL
but not everything is **h**. 1Co 6:12
but not everything is **h**. 1Co 10:23
to boast; it is not **h**, but I will 2Co 12:1

HELPLESS
are on the lookout for the **h**. Ps 10:8
The **h** entrusts himself to You; Ps 10:14
I was **h**, and He saved me. Ps 116:6
A wicked ruler over a **h** people Pr 28:15
For while we were still **h**, Rm 5:6

HEMAN
H the singer, son of Joel, son 1Ch 6:33
The singers **H**, Asaph, and Ethan 1Ch 15:19
sons of Asaph, **H**, and Jeduthun 1Ch 25:1
Levitical singers of Asaph, of **H**, 2Ch 5:12
A Maskil of **H** the Ezrahite. Ps 88 title

HEN
as a **h** gathers her chicks under Mt 23:37

HENNA
is a cluster of **h** blossoms to me Sg 1:14
choicest fruits, **h** with nard Sg 4:13
the night among the **h** blossoms. Sg 7:11

HERALD
Zion, **h** of good news, go up Is 40:9
are the feet of the **h**, who proclaims Is 52:7
and **h** to meet **h**, to announce to Jr 51:31
For this I was appointed a **h**, 1Tm 2:7
this {gospel} I was appointed a **h**, 2Tm 1:11

HERB
unleavened bread and bitter **h-s**. Ex 12:8
unleavened bread and bitter **h-s**; Nm 9:11
field to gather **h-s** and found a 2Kg 4:39
of mint, rue, and every kind of **h**, Lk 11:42

HERD
Abraham ran to the **h** and got Gn 18:7
is a burnt offering from the **h**, Lv 1:3
Every tenth animal from the **h** Lv 27:32
firstborn of your **h-s** and flocks. Dt 12:6
and pay attention to your **h-s**, Pr 27:23

I also owned many **h-s** of cattle Ec 2:7
man or beast, **h** or flock, is to Jnh 3:7
send us into the **h** of pigs. Mt 8:31

HERDSMAN
quarreling between the **h-men** Gn 13:7
h-men of Gerar quarreled with Gn 26:20
rather, I was a **h**, and I took Am 7:14

HERE
"**H** I am," he answered. Gn 22:1
Abraham!" He replied, "**H** I am." Gn 22:11
And he answered, "**H** I am." Gn 27:1
'Jacob!' and I said: **H** I am. Gn 31:11
And Jacob replied, "**H** I am." Gn 46:2
"**H** I am," he answered. Ex 3:4
ran to Eli and said, "**H** I am; 1Sm 3:5
H I am. Bring charges against me 1Sm 12:3
H I am, your servant, to wash 1Sm 25:41
then **h** I am—He can do with me 2Sm 15:26
Isn't there a prophet of Yahweh **h** 1Kg 22:7
I said: **H** I am. Send me. Is 6:8
cities of Judah, "**H** is your God!" Is 40:9
that I am He who says: **H** I am. Is 52:6
I said, **H** I am, **h** I am, to a nation Is 65:1
or, 'Over **h**!' do not believe it! Mt 24:23
He is not **h**! For He has been Mt 28:6
if You had been **h**, my brother Jn 11:32
said to them, "**H** is the man!" Jn 19:5
"Ananias!" "**H** I am, Lord!" Ac 9:10
H I am with the children God gave Heb 2:13
you say, "Sit **h** in a good place," Jms 2:3

HERESIES
bring in destructive **h**, 2Pt 2:1

HERITAGE
You have given a **h** to those who Ps 61:5
His people or abandon His **h**, Ps 94:14
nation, and boast about Your **h**. Ps 106:5
Your decrees as a **h** forever; Ps 119:111
Sons are indeed a **h** from the LORD, Ps 127:3
This is the **h** of the LORD's Is 54:17

HERMES
and Paul, **H**, because he was Ac 14:12

HERMON
Arnon Valley as far as Mount **H**, Dt 3:8
Lebanon at the foot of Mount **H**. Jos 11:17
of Jordan and the peaks of **H**, Ps 42:6

Tabor and H shout for joy at   Ps 89:12
It is like the dew of H falling   Ps 133:3

HERO
saw that their h was dead,   1Sm 17:51
Why brag about evil, you h!   Ps 52:1
the h and warrior, the judge and   Is 3:2
those who are h-es at drinking wine   Is 5:22

HEROD
1. The Great; King in Judea at the time of Jesus' birth; executed male babies (Mt 2).

2. Archelaus; son of 1. (Mt 2:22).

3. Philip; son of 1. (Mk 6:17).

4. Antipas; son of 1.; tetrarch of Galilee; arrested and executed John the Baptist (Mt 14:1-12).

5. Agrippa I; grandson of 1.; persecuted the church; died when he didn't give glory to God (Ac 12).

6. Agrippa II; son of 5. (Ac 25:13). Heard Paul's defense (25:22–26:32).

HERODIANS
disciples to Him, with the H.   Mt 22:16
with the H against Him,   Mk 3:6
and the H to Him to trap   Mk 12:13

HERODIAS
Wife of Herod Antipas, formerly of Herod Philip; requested head of John the Baptist (Mt 14:3-11; Mk 6:17-28; Lk 3:19).

HERSELF
So she laughed to h: Gn 18:12
Hannah was speaking to h,   1Sm 1:13

HESHBON
including H and all its villages   Nm 21:25
Reubenites rebuilt H, Elealeh   Nm 32:37
H and Elealeh cry out;   Is 15:4

HESITANT
I am slow and h in speech.   Ex 4:10

HESITATE
But he h-ed, so because of the   Gn 19:16
How long will you h between two   1Kg 18:21
not h-ing to keep Your commands.   Ps 119:60

HETH
Son of Canaan and progenitor of the Hittites (1Ch 1:13).

HEZEKIAH
Son of Ahaz; king of Judah (2Kg 18–20; 2Ch 29-32; Is 36–39). Reformer (2Kg 18:4; 2Ch 29–31). Healed of fatal illness (2Kg 20:1-11); showed treasuries to Babylonians (20:12-19).

HEZRON
1. Son of Reuben (Gn 46:9; Nm 26:6).

2. Grandson of Judah (Gn 46:12; Nm 26:21; Ru 4:19; Mt 1:3).

3. City on the south border of Judah (Jos 15:3).

HIDDEN (adj)
The h things belong to the LORD   Dt 29:29
may bring to light what is h.   Jb 28:11
Cleanse me from my h faults.   Ps 19:12
search for it like h treasure,   Pr 2:4
reveals the deep and h things;   Dn 2:22
and nothing h that won't be made   Mt 10:26
we speak God's h wisdom in a   1Co 2:7
of the mystery h for ages in God   Eph 3:9
the mystery h for ages and   Col 1:26
the h person of the heart   1Pt 3:4
the victor some of the h manna.   Rv 2:17
then God's h plan will be   Rv 10:7

HIDE (n)
But the h of the bull and all   Lv 4:11
Can you fill his h with harpoons   Jb 41:7

HIDE (v)
they hid themselves from the LORD   Gn 3:8
Should I h from Abraham what I   Gn 18:17
she hid him for three months.   Ex 2:2
dead and hid him in the sand.   Ex 2:12
Moses hid his face because he   Ex 3:6
abandon them and h My face   Dt 31:17
because she hid the men we sent.   Jos 6:17
So David hid in the field.   1Sm 20:24
and nothing is h-den from
    the king   2Sm 18:13
h yourself at the Wadi Cherith   1Kg 17:3
I hid 100 of the prophets of the   1Kg 18:13
and the LORD has h-den it
    from me.   2Kg 4:27
she hid Joash from Athaliah so   2Ch 22:11
by h-ing my guilt in my heart,   Jb 31:33
He h-s His face and will never see   Ps 10:11
How long will You h Your face   Ps 13:1

h me in the shadow of Your wings	Ps 17:8
He will h me under the cover of	Ps 27:5
when You hid Your face,	Ps 30:7
You h them in the protection of	Ps 31:20
I did not h Your righteousness	Ps 40:10
guilty acts are not h-den from You.	Ps 69:5
Will You h Yourself forever?	Ps 89:46
Surely the darkness will h me,	Ps 139:11
to power, people h themselves.	Pr 28:12
power, people h, but when they	Pr 28:28
My way is h-den from the LORD,	Is 40:27
You are a God who h-s Himself,	Is 45:15
hid me in the shadow of His hand.	Is 49:2
hid My face from you for a moment,	Is 54:8
You have h-den Your face from us	Is 64:7
River and h it in a rocky	Jr 13:4
I hid My face from them and	Ezk 39:23
I will no longer h My face from	Ezk 39:29
Compassion is h-den from My	Hs 13:14
If they h themselves on the top of	Am 9:3
This is where His power is h-den.	Hab 3:4
situated on a hill cannot be h-den.	Mt 5:14
and went off and hid your talent	Mt 25:25
This saying was h-den from them,	Lk 18:34
but now it is h-den from your eyes.	Lk 19:42
But Jesus was h-den and went out	Jn 8:59
then went away and hid from them.	Jn 12:36
to light what is h-den in darkness	1Co 4:5
of wisdom and knowledge are h-den.	Col 2:3
your life is h-den with the Messiah	Col 3:3
No creature is h-den from Him,	Heb 4:13
and free person hid in the caves	Rv 6:15
Fall on us and h us from the	Rv 6:16

HIDING (adj)

He made darkness His h place,	Ps 18:11
You are my h place;	Ps 32:7

HIGH see also HIGH PLACE,
HIGH PRIEST, MOST HIGH

reached down from on h and took	2Sm 22:17
of the man raised on h,	2Sm 23:1
on every h hill and under	2Kg 17:10
our guilt is as h as the heavens	Ezr 9:6
command and make its nest on h?	Jb 39:27
He will set me h on a rock.	Ps 27:5
On h, He summons heaven and	Ps 50:4
love is as h as the heavens;	Ps 57:10
to a rock that is h above me,	Ps 61:2

Your right hand is lifted h.	Ps 89:13
the LORD on h is majestic.	Ps 93:4
For as h as the heavens are	Ps 103:11
Reach down from on h; rescue me	Ps 144:7
it is like a h wall.	Pr 18:11
As the heaven is h and the earth is	Pr 25:3
seated on a h and lofty throne	Is 6:1
is exalted, for He dwells on h;	Is 33:5
your bed on a h and lofty	Is 57:7
I live in a h and holy place,	Is 57:15
On every h hill and under every	Jr 2:20
house to place his nest on h,	Hab 2:9
took Him to a very h mountain	Mt 4:8
and led them up on a h mountain	Mt 17:1
and the men of h position	Mt 20:25
you are empowered from on h.	Lk 24:49
religious women of h standing	Ac 13:50
He ascended on h, He took	Eph 4:8
right hand of the Majesty on h.	Heb 1:3

HIGH PLACE

and demolish all their h-s.	Nm 33:52
Samuel ... on his way to the h.	1Sm 9:14
prophets coming down from the h	1Sm 10:5
people were sacrificing on the h-s,	1Kg 3:2
Solomon built a h for Chemosh,	1Kg 11:7
priests for the h-s he had set up.	1Kg 12:32
h-s were not taken away	1Kg 15:14; 22:43
h-s were not taken	2Kg 12:3; 14:4; 15:4,35
They built h-s in all their towns	2Kg 17:9
He removed the h-s and	2Kg 18:4
He rebuilt the h-s that his	2Kg 21:3
He tore down the h-s of the	2Kg 23:8
LORD at the h in Gibeon	1Ch 16:39
They enraged Him with their h-s	Ps 78:58
plunder because of the sin of your h-s	Jr 17:3
They have built h-s to Baal	Jr 19:5
I will destroy your h-s.	Ezk 6:3
made colorful h-s for yourself,	Ezk 16:16
What is this h you are going to?	Ezk 20:29
The h-s of Aven, the sin of Israel,	Hs 10:8
the h of Judah? Isn't it Jerusalem?	Mc 1:5

HIGH PRIEST

of refuge until the death of the h.	Nm 35:28
Hilkiah the h ... found the book	2Kg 22:8
Eliashib the h and his fellow priests	Neh 3:1
h, had become a son-in-law to	Neh 13:28
Joshua son of Jehozadak, the h:	Hg 1:1

led Him away to Caiaphas the h,   Mt 26:57
during the **h-hood** of Annas and   Lk 3:2
but being **h** that year he prophesied   Jn 11:51
struck the **h-'s** slave, and cut off   Jn 18:10
this the way you answer the **h**?   Jn 18:22
Saul ... went to the **h**   Ac 9:1
Do you dare revile God's **h**?   Ac 23:4
become a merciful and faithful **h**   Heb 2:17
since we have a great **h** who has   Heb 4:14
we do not have a **h** who is unable   Heb 4:15
declared by God a **h** "in the order   Heb 5:10
become a "**h** forever in the order of   Heb 6:20
this is the kind of **h** we need: Heb 7:26
we have this kind of **h**,   Heb 8:1
the **h** alone enters the second room,   Heb 9:7
since we have a great **h** over   Heb 10:21

HIGHER

{They are} **h** than the heavens   Jb 11:8
love is **h** than the heavens   Ps 108:4
so My ways are **h** than your ways   Is 55:9
say to you, 'Friend, move up **h.**'   Lk 14:10
So He became **h** in rank than the   Heb 1:4

HIGHEST

indeed the **h** heavens, belong to   Dt 10:14
the **h** heaven, cannot contain   1Kg 8:27
Hosanna in the **h** heaven!   Mt 21:9
Glory to God in the **h** heaven,   Lk 2:14
and glory in the **h** heaven!   Lk 19:38

HIGHLIGHTS

if our unrighteousness **h** God's   Rm 3:5

HIGHLY

the LORD, for He is **h** exalted;   Ex 15:1
great and is **h** praised   Pss 48:1; 96:4; 145:3
of himself more **h** than he should   Rm 12:3
reason God also **h** exalted Him   Php 2:9

HIGH-MINDED

and every **h** thing that is raised   2Co 10:5

HIGHWAY

We will travel the King's **H;**   Nm 20:17
the path of the upright is a **h.**   Pr 15:19
there will be a **h** from Egypt to   Is 19:23
make a straight **h** for our God in   Is 40:3
and My **h-s** will be raised up.   Is 49:11
Build it up, build up the **h;**   Is 62:10
Go out into the **h-s** and lanes and   Lk 14:23

HILKIAH

1. Merarite Levite (1Ch 6:45).
2. Levite in David's time (1Ch 26:11).
3. Father of Eliakim (2Kg 18:18-37).
4. Father of Jeremiah (Jr 1:1).
5. Father of Gemariah (Jr 29:3).
6. High priest in Josiah's time who found the book of the law (2Kg 22:4–23:24).
7. Exile who stood with Ezra (Neh 8:4).
8. Priest who returned with Zerubbabel (Neh 12:7).

HILL

the bounty of the eternal **h-s.**   Gn 49:26
and from whose **h-s** you will mine   Dt 8:9
will come to the **H** of God where   1Sm 10:5
on every high **h** and under every   1Kg 14:23
gods are gods of the **h** country.   1Kg 20:23
on every high **h** and under every   2Kg 17:10
you brought forth before the **h-s**?   Jb 15:7
the cattle on a thousand **h-s.**   Ps 50:10
mountains and all **h-s,**   Ps 148:9
mountains and **h-s** were established   Pr 8:25
myrrh and the **h** of frankincense   Sg 4:6
Zion, the **h** of Jerusalem.   Is 10:32
mountain and **h** will be leveled;   Is 40:4
and to the **h-s,** "Fall on us!"   Hs 10:8
and the **h** of the temple mount   Mc 3:12
fortified **h** of Daughter Zion,   Mc 4:8
situated on a **h** cannot be hidden   Mt 5:14
mountain and **h** will be made low   Lk 3:5
and to the **h-s,** 'Cover us!'   Lk 23:30

HINDER

and **h** meditation before Him.   Jb 15:4
your steps will not be **h-ed;**   Pr 4:12
you **h-ed** those who were going in.   Lk 11:52
how could I possibly **h** God?   Ac 11:17
so that we will not **h** the gospel   1Co 9:12
h-ing us from speaking to   1Th 2:16
and again—but Satan **h-ed** us.   1Th 2:18
your prayers will not be **h-ed.**   1Pt 3:7

HINDRANCE

full boldness and without **h.**   Ac 28:31

HINGE

turns on its **h,** and a slacker   Pr 26:14

HINNOM

Valley of **H** to the southern Jebusite   Jos 15:8

Topheth ... in the Valley of H,   2Kg 23:10
of H and burned his children in   2Ch 28:3
through the fire in the Valley of H.   2Ch 33:6
Beer-sheba to the Valley of H.   Neh 11:30
of H in order to burn their sons   Jr 7:31

HIP

struck Jacob's h as they   Gn 32:25
off their clothes in half at the h-s,   2Sm 10:4

HIRAM

1. King of Tyre; helped David build his
palace and Solomon build the temple (2Sm
5:11; 2Kg 5). Manned Solomon's fleet (1Kg
9:27).

2. Craftsman; helped build the temple and
its furnishings (1Kg 7:13-14); also called
Huram (2Ch 4:11) or Huram-abi (2:13;
4:16).

HIRE

for I have h-d you with my son's   Gn 30:16
who are full h themselves out   1Sm 2:5
they h 20,000 foot soldiers from   2Sm 10:6
38 tons of silver to h chariots   1Ch 19:6
h-s a fool, or who h-s those passing   Pr 26:10
they h a goldsmith and he makes   Is 46:6
though they h (lovers) among   Hs 8:10
the morning to h workers for his   Mt 20:1

HIRED (adj)

Let him stay with you as a h hand   Lv 25:40
Do not oppress a h hand   Dt 24:14
will use a razor h from beyond   Is 7:20
of my father's h hands have more   Lk 15:17
he is a h man and doesn't care   Jn 10:13

HISS

will be appalled and will h.   1Kg 9:8
horror, and h-ing, as you see with   2Ch 29:8
Egypt will h like a slithering   Jr 46:22
They h and shake their heads at   Lm 2:15
They h and gnash (their) teeth,   Lm 2:16
among the peoples h at you;   Ezk 27:36

HISTORIAN

Jehoshaphat ... was court h;   2Sm 8:16
Asaph, the court h, came out to   2Kg 18:18

HISTORICAL

the H Record of Israel's Kings.   1Kg 14:19
in the H Record of Judah's Kings.   1Kg 14:29
in the H Record of King David.   1Ch 27:24

in the Book of the H Records   Neh 12:23
The h record of Jesus Christ,   Mt 1:1

HIT

when you h the rock, water will   Ex 17:6
and h a pregnant woman so that   Ex 21:22
If anyone h-s you on the cheek,   Lk 6:29
Prophesy! Who h You?   Lk 22:64
but if rightly, why do you h Me?   Jn 18:23
or if someone h-s you in the face   2Co 11:20

HITCH

H the cows to the cart, but take   1Sm 6:7

HITTITES

Ancient people of the promised land (Gn
10:15-18; 15:20; Jos 1:4); Abraham lived
among them (Gn 23); Esau married them
(26:34; 27:46; 36:2). Formerly lived in the
hill country (Nm 13:29; Jos 9:1; 11:3; 12:8);
dispossessed by Israel (Ex 23:23; Dt 7:1;
20:17; Jos 3:10); some remained (Jdg 1:6;
3:5; 1Kg 9:20-21); fought alongside Israel
(1Sm 26:6; 2Sm 23:39; 2Kg 7:6); intermar-
ried (2Sm 11:24-27; 1Kg 11:1).

HIVITE

Ancient people of the promised land (Gn
10:15-18; 34:2; Jos 9:7; 11:3,19; Jdg 3:3),
dispossessed by Israel (Ex 23:23; Dt 7:1;
20:17; Jos 3:10) except for those in Gibeon
(9:7; 11:19).

HOLD

I will h them accountable for   Ex 32:34
the first day you are to h a sacred   Lv 23:7
I will h accountable whoever   Dt 18:19
you're wearing and h it out.   Ru 3:15
ark of God and took h of it,   2Sm 6:6
It held 11,000 gallons.   1Kg 7:26
He held fast to the LORD and did   2Kg 18:6
strengthened his h on his kingdom.   2Ch 1:1
one hand and held a weapon with   Neh 4:17
You h my future.   Ps 16:5
from on high and took h of me;   Ps 18:16
because the LORD h-s his hand.   Ps 37:24
Your right hand h-s on to me.   Ps 63:8
You h my right hand.   Ps 73:23
Why do You h back Your hand?   Ps 74:11
Do not h past sins against us;   Ps 79:8
right hand will h on to me.   Ps 139:10

but He h-s up fools to dishonor.	Pr 3:35
Your heart must h on to my words	Pr 4:4
H on to instruction; don't let	Pr 4:13
give and don't h back.	Pr 21:26
but a wise man h-s it in check.	Pr 29:11
and her hands h the spindle.	Pr 31:19
I **held** on to him and would not let	Sg 3:4
tree and take h of its fruit.	Sg 7:8
I will h on to you with My	Is 41:10
LORD your God, h your right hand	Is 41:13
and I will h you by your hand.	Is 42:6
do not h back; lengthen your ropes,	Is 54:2
and h firmly to My covenant,	Is 56:4
cisterns that cannot h water.	Jr 2:13
I am tired of h-ing it back.	Jr 6:11
I become tired of h-ing it in,	Jr 20:9
I will h you responsible	Ezk 3:18; 33:8
no one who can h back His hand	Dn 4:35
h on to it and by enduring,	Lk 8:15
we have died to what **held** us,	Rm 7:6
if you h to the message I	1Co 15:2
H firmly the message of life.	Php 2:16
with all joy and h men like him	Php 2:29
make every effort to take h of it	Php 3:12
by Him all things h together.	Col 1:17
nourished and **held** together by its	Col 2:19
test all things. H on to what is	1Th 5:21
h-ing the mystery of the faith	1Tm 3:9
take h of eternal life, to which	1Tm 6:12
H on to the pattern of sound	2Tm 1:13
h-ing to the form of religion but	2Tm 3:5
h-ing to the faithful message as	Ti 1:9
let us h fast to the confession	Heb 4:14
He h-s His priesthood permanently	Heb 7:24
Let us h on to the confession of	Heb 10:23
and earth are **held** in store for	2Pt 3:7
and I h the keys of death and	Rv 1:18
The One who h-s the seven stars	Rv 2:1
H on to what you have, so that	Rv 3:11

HOLE

wages into a bag with a h in it.	Hg 1:6

HOLIDAY

There was a celebration and a h.	Est 8:17
It is a h when they send gifts	Est 9:19
and their mourning into a h.	Est 9:22

HOLIES

was called "the holy of h."	Heb 9:3

entered the holy of h once for all,	Heb 9:12
into the holy of h by the high	Heb 13:11

HOLIEST

the h part of the fire offerings	Lv 2:3,10
for it is the h portion for him	Lv 24:9
A portion of the h offerings	Nm 18:9

HOLINESS

Who is like You, glorious in h,	Ex 15:11
and He showed His h to them.	Nm 20:13
in the splendor of {His} h;	1Ch 16:29
praise the splendor of {His} h.	2Ch 20:21
in the splendor of {His} h.	Ps 29:2; 96:9
I have sworn an oath by My h;	Ps 89:35
h is the beauty of Your house	Ps 93:5
I demonstrate My h through you	Ezk 36:23
Lord GOD has sworn by His h:	Am 4:2
according to the Spirit of h.	Rm 1:4
blameless in h before our God	1Th 3:13
love, and h, with good sense	1Tm 2:15
so that we can share His h.	Heb 12:10
h without it no one will see	Heb 12:14

HOLLOW

the waters in the h of his hand	Is 40:12
18 feet, was h—four fingers thick	Jr 52:21
Wail, you residents of the H,	Zph 1:11

HOLY *see also* HOLY PLACE,
  HOLY SPIRIT

seventh day and declared it h,	Gn 2:3
you are standing is h ground.	Ex 3:5
complete rest, a h Sabbath to	Ex 16:23
of priests and My h nation.	Ex 19:6
Sabbath day and declared it h.	Ex 20:11
altar will become especially h;	Ex 29:37
it will be h anointing oil.	Ex 30:25
on a seal: H TO THE LORD.	Ex 39:30
between the h and the common,	Lv 10:10
and be h because I am h.	Lv 11:44
Consecrate yourselves and be h,	Lv 20:7
h to Me because I, the LORD, am h,	Lv 20:26
for the priest is h to his God.	Lv 21:7
You must not profane My h name;	Lv 22:32
the entire community is h,	Nm 16:3
For you are a h people	Dt 7:6
came with ten thousand h ones,	Dt 33:2
where you are standing is h.	Jos 5:15
is no one h like the LORD.	1Sm 2:2
Put the h ark in the temple	2Ch 35:3

so that the **h** people has become	Ezr 9:2
Be still, since today is is **h**.	Neh 8:11
in Jerusalem, the **h** city,	Neh 11:1
Which of the **h** ones will you	Jb 5:1
on Zion, My **h** mountain.	Ps 2:6
The LORD is in His **h** temple;	Ps 11:4
can live on Your **h** mountain?	Ps 15:1
But You are **h**, enthroned on the	Ps 22:3
God is seated on His **h** throne.	Ps 47:8
city of our God. His **h** mountain,	Ps 48:1
God, Your way is **h**.	Ps 77:13
He brought them to His **h** land,	Ps 78:54
in the assembly of the **h** ones.	Ps 89:5
He is **h**.	Ps 99:3
within me, praise His **h** name.	Ps 103:1
praise His **h** name forever	Ps 145:21
H, h, h is the LORD of Hosts;	Is 6:3
the LORD, the **H** One of Israel.	Is 10:20
on My entire **h** mountain,	Is 11:9
who is My equal?" asks the **H** One.	Is 40:25
Redeemer is the **H** One of Israel.	Is 41:14
lives forever, whose name is **H**	Is 57:15
will be called the **H** People,	Is 62:12
a **h** portion of the land,	Ezk 45:1
spirit of the **h** gods is in him	Dn 4:8
Then I heard a **h** one speaking,	Dn 8:13
the **H** One among you;	Hs 11:9
Prepare for **h** war;	Jl 3:9
the LORD is in His **h** temple;	Hab 2:20
other food, does it become **h**?	Hg 2:12
{the words} **H** TO THE LORD	Zch 14:20
Your name be honored as **h**.	Mt 6:9
Don't give what is **h** to dogs	Mt 7:6
entered the **h** city, and appeared	Mt 27:53
who You are—the **H** One of God!	Mk 1:24
he was a righteous and **h** man.	Mk 6:20
Therefore the **h** One to be born	Lk 1:35
that You are the **H** One of God!	Jn 6:69
or allow Your **H** One to see decay	Ac 2:27
against Your **h** Servant Jesus,	Ac 4:27
you are standing is **h** ground.	Ac 7:33
not allow Your **H** One to see	Ac 13:35
prophets in the **H** Scriptures	Rm 1:2
So then, the law is **h**, and the	Rm 7:12
And if the root is **h**, so are the	Rm 11:16
living sacrifice, **h** and pleasing to	Rm 12:1
one another with a **h** kiss.	Rm 16:16
sanctuary is **h**, and that is what you	1Co 3:17

that she may be **h** both in body	1Co 7:34
to be **h** and blameless in His sight.	Eph 1:4
to present you **h**, faultless	Col 1:22
lifting up **h** hands without anger	1Tm 2:8
and called us with a **h** calling,	2Tm 1:9
righteous, **h**, self-controlled,	Ti 1:8
you also are to be **h** in all your	1Pt 1:15
is written, Be **h**, because I am **h**.	1Pt 1:16
house for a **h** priesthood to	1Pt 2:5
priesthood, a **h** nation, a people	1Pt 2:9
you should be in **h** conduct and	2Pt 3:11
an anointing from the **H** One,	1Jn 2:20
with thousands of His **h** ones	Jd 14
The **H** One, the True One, the	Rv 3:7
H, h, h, Lord God, the Almighty,	Rv 4:8
You alone are **h**, because all	Rv 15:4
I also saw the **H** City, new	Rv 21:2
and let the **h** go on being made **h**.	Rv 22:11

HOLY PLACE

between the **h** and the most **h**.	Ex 26:33
It must be eaten in a **h**,	Lv 6:26
enter the {most} **h** in this way:	Lv 16:3
who are to eat it in a **h**,	Lv 24:9
inner sanctuary, the most **h**.	1Kg 6:16
Then he made the most **h**;	2Ch 3:8
to the most **h**, beneath the wings	2Ch 5:7
give us a stake in His **h**.	Ezr 9:8
Who may stand in His **h**?	Ps 24:3
up your hands in the **h**,	Ps 134:2
came and went from the **h**,	Ec 8:10
I live in a high and **h**,	Is 57:15
This is the most **h**.	Ezk 41:4
and to anoint the most **h**.	Dn 9:24
standing in the **h**" {let the reader	Mt 24:15
against this **h** and the law	Ac 6:13
and has profaned this **h**.	Ac 21:28
first room, which is called "the **h**,"	Heb 9:2

HOLY SPIRIT

Third person of the Trinity, through whom God acts, reveals His will, empowers individuals, and discloses His presence.

or take Your **H** from me	Ps 51:11
and grieved His **H**.	Is 63:10
was pregnant by the **H**.	Mt 1:18
baptize you with the **H** and fire.	Mt 3:11
speaks against the **H**, it will not	Mt 12:32
Father and of the Son and of the **H**,	Mt 28:19
himself says by the **H**:	Mk 12:36

you speaking, but the **H**. | Mk 13:11
he will be filled with the **H** | Lk 1:15
The **H** will come upon you | Lk 1:35
Elizabeth was filled with the **H**. | Lk 1:41
Zechariah was filled with the **H** | Lk 1:67
and the **H** was on him. | Lk 2:25
and the **H** descended on | Lk 3:22
full of the **H**, and was | Lk 4:1
Father give the **H** to those who ask | Lk 11:13
For the **H** will teach you | Lk 12:12
the Counselor, the **H**, | Jn 14:26
said, "Receive the **H**. | Jn 20:22
you will be baptized with the **H** | Ac 1:5
power when the **H** has come | Ac 1:8
they were all filled with the **H** | Ac 2:4
from the Father the promised **H**, | Ac 2:33
you will receive the gift of the **H**. | Ac 2:38
Peter was filled with the **H** and said | Ac 4:8
You said through the **H**, | Ac 4:25
they were all filled with the **H** and | Ac 4:31
to lie to the **H** and keep back part | Ac 5:3
always resisting the **H**; | Ac 7:51
Stephen, filled by the **H**, gazed | Ac 7:55
Simon saw that the **H** was given | Ac 8:18
and be filled with the **H**. | Ac 9:17
encouragement of the **H**, | Ac 9:31
Jesus ... with the **H** and with power | Ac 10:38
H had been poured out on Gentiles | Ac 10:45
you will be baptized with the **H**. | Ac 11:16
the **H** said, "Set apart | Ac 13:2
with joy and the **H**. | Ac 13:52
by giving the **H**, just as He did | Ac 15:8
For it was the **H**'s decision | Ac 15:28
prevented by the **H** from | Ac 16:6
Did you receive the **H** when you | Ac 19:2
after town the **H** testifies to me | Ac 20:23
H has appointed you as overseers | Ac 20:28
This is what the **H** says: | Ac 21:11
H ... spoke through the prophet | Ac 28:25
in our hearts through the **H** | Rm 5:5
is testifying to me with the **H** | Rm 9:1
peace, and joy in the **H**. | Rm 14:17
by the power of the **H**. | Rm 15:13
your body is a sanctuary of the **H** | 1Co 6:19
"Jesus is Lord," except by the **H**. | 1Co 12:3
by kindness, by the **H**, by | 2Co 6:6
were sealed with the promised **H**. | Eph 1:13
don't grieve God's **H**, | Eph 4:30

but also in power, in the **H**, and | 1Th 1:5
with the joy from the **H**. | 1Th 1:6
and renewal by the **H**. | Ti 3:5
distributions (of gifts) from the **H** | Heb 2:4
became companions with the **H**, | Heb 6:4
H also testifies to us about this. | Heb 10:15
moved by the **H**, men spoke | 2Pt 1:21

HOMAGE

David bowed to the ground in **h**. | 1Sm 24:8
Bathsheba ... paid **h** to the king, | 1Kg 1:16
down and paid **h** to the LORD | 1Ch 29:20
came and paid **h** to the king. | 2Ch 24:17
Mordecai would not ... pay **h**. | Est 3:2
Pay **h** to the Son, or He will be | Ps 2:12
Nebuchadnezzar ... paid **h**
  to Daniel, | Dn 2:46
knees, they were paying Him **h**. | Mk 15:19

HOME

Return **h**, my daughters. | Ru 1:11
Uriah didn't go **h**, | 2Sm 11:10
and daughters, your wives and **h-s**. | Neh 4:14
Where is the road to the **h** of light? | Jb 38:19
Their graves are their eternal **h-s**, | Ps 49:11
evil is in their **h-s** and within them | Ps 55:15
God provides **h-s** for those who are | Ps 68:6
sparrow finds a **h**, and a swallow | Ps 84:3
stork makes its **h** in the pine | Ps 104:17
He has desired it for His **h**: | Ps 132:13
He blesses the **h** of the | Pr 3:33
her feet do not stay at **h**. | Pr 7:11
My husband isn't **h**; he went on a | Pr 7:19
will be at **h** among the wise. | Pr 15:31
man is headed to his eternal **h**, | Ec 12:5
And what place could be My **h**? | Is 66:1
He goes **h** and rests his hand | Am 5:19
was reported that He was at **h**. | Mk 2:1
Go back to your **h**, and tell all | Lk 8:39
Martha welcomed Him into her **h**. | Lk 10:38
to him and make Our **h** with him. | Jn 14:23
disciple took her into his **h**. | Jn 19:27
they took him **h** and explained | Ac 18:26
church that meets in their **h**. | Rm 16:5
is hungry, he should eat at **h**, | 1Co 11:34
ask their own husbands at **h**, | 1Co 14:35
church that meets in their **h**. | 1Co 16:19
while we are at **h** in the body we | 2Co 5:6
of the body and at **h** with the Lord. | 2Co 5:8
do not receive him into your **h**, | 2Jn 10

HOMELAND

exiled from their h until today.	2Kg 17:23
certainly go into exile from its h.	Am 7:11
that they are seeking a h.	Heb 11:14

HOMELESS

make them h wanderers and bring	Ps 59:11
the poor and h into your house,	Is 58:7
clothed, roughly treated, h;	1Co 4:11

HOMEMAKERS

pure, good h, and submissive	Ti 2:5

HOMEOWNER

If the h had known what time the	Mt 24:43
once the h gets up and shuts the	Lk 13:25

HOMETOWN

to Gibeah, Saul's {h},	1Sm 11:4
not without honor except in his h	Mt 13:57
No prophet is accepted in his h.	Lk 4:24

HOMOSEXUALS

male prostitutes, h,	1Co 6:9
for the sexually immoral and h,	1Tm 1:10

HONEST

We are h men and not spies.	Gn 42:31
You are to have h balances, h	Lv 19:36
You must have a full and h weight,	Dt 25:15
and I brought back an h report.	Jos 14:7
How painful h words can be!	Jb 6:25
An h witness does not deceive,	Pr 14:5
H balances and scales are the	Pr 16:11
who gives an h answer gives a kiss	Pr 24:26
Bloodthirsty men hate an h person,	Pr 29:10
You must have h balances, an h	Ezk 45:10
render h and peaceful judgments	Zch 8:16
word with an h and good heart,	Lk 8:15
he must do h work with his own	Eph 4:28

HONESTLY

The one who lives h,	Ps 15:2
and he loves one who speaks h.	Pr 16:13
no one pleads h.	Is 59:4

HONESTY

on my wages, my h will testify	Gn 30:33
or to beat a noble for his h.	Pr 17:26
square, and h cannot enter.	Is 59:14

HONEY

land flowing with milk and h	Ex 3:8
like wafers {made} with h.	Ex 16:31

it is flowing with milk and h,	Nm 13:27
a land flowing with milk and h.	Dt 6:3
him with h from the rock	Dt 32:13
a land flowing with milk and h.	Jos 5:6
of bees with h in the carcass.	Jdg 14:8
What is sweeter than h?	Jdg 14:18
ate the h, he had renewed energy.	1Sm 14:27
and a jar of h, and go to him.	1Kg 14:3
a land of olive trees and h	2Kg 18:32
flowing with h and cream.	Jb 20:17
sweeter than h—than h dripping	Ps 19:10
you with h from the rock.	Ps 81:16
{sweeter} than h to my mouth.	Ps 119:103
woman drip h and her words are	Pr 5:3
Eat h, my son, for it is good	Pr 24:13
If you find h, eat only what you	Pr 25:16
It is not good to eat too much h,	Pr 25:27
H and milk are under your tongue	Sg 4:11
I eat my honeycomb with my h.	Sg 5:1
he will be eating butter and h.	Is 7:15
a land flowing with milk and h,	Jr 11:5
was as sweet as h in my mouth.	Ezk 3:3
flowing with milk and h,	Ezk 20:6
his food was locusts and wild h.	Mt 3:4
was as sweet as h in my mouth,	Rv 10:10

HONEYCOMB

and dipped it into the h.	1Sm 14:27
Pleasant words are a h:	Pr 16:24
and the h is sweet to your	Pr 24:13
who is full tramples on a h,	Pr 27:7
drip {sweetness like} the h,	Sg 4:11
I eat my h with my honey.	Sg 5:1

HONEYMOON

and the bride her h chamber.	Jl 2:16

HONOR (n)

I will give you ... riches and h,	1Kg 3:13
Riches and h come from You,	1Ch 29:12
stripped me of my h and removed	Jb 19:9
yourself with h and glory.	Jb 40:10
will my h be insulted?	Ps 4:2
and leave my h in the dust.	Ps 7:5
crowned him with glory and h.	Ps 8:5
will rescue him and give him h.	Ps 91:15
in her left, riches and h.	Pr 3:16
and humility comes before h.	Pr 15:33
h is inappropriate for a fool.	Pr 26:1

Giving **h** to a fool is like   Pr 26:8
a humble spirit will gain **h**.   Pr 29:23
little folly outweighs wisdom and **h**.   Ec 10:1
if I am a father, where is My **h**?   Mal 1:6
is not without **h** except in his   Mt 13:57
but glory, **h**, and peace for   Rm 2:10
of pottery for **h** and another for   Rm 9:21
Outdo one another in showing **h**.   Rm 12:10
and **h** to those you owe **h**.   Rm 13:7
we clothe these with greater **h**,   1Co 12:23
and hold men like him in **h**,   Php 2:29
vessel in sanctification and **h**,   1Th 4:4
be **h** and glory forever and ever   1Tm 1:17
to whom be **h** and eternal might.   1Tm 6:16
crowned him with glory and **h**   Heb 2:7
No one takes this **h** on himself;   Heb 5:4
receive glory and **h** and power,   Rv 4:11
Blessing and **h** and glory and   Rv 5:13

HONOR (v)

H your father and your mother   Ex 20:12
the elderly and **h** the old.   Lv 19:32
My Sabbaths and **h** My sanctuary;   Lv 26:2
H your father and your mother,   Dt 5:16
You have **h-ed** your sons more   1Sm 2:29
I will **h** those who **h** Me,   1Sm 2:30
Please **h** me now before the   1Sm 15:30
king of Israel **h-ed** himself today!   2Sm 6:20
for the man the king wants to **h**?   Est 6:6
but **h-s** those who fear the LORD,   Ps 15:4
rescue you, and you will **h** Me.   Ps 50:15
a thank offering **h-s** Me,   Ps 50:23
and will **h** Your name.   Ps 86:9
H His holy name;   Ps 105:3
I will **h** Your name forever and   Ps 145:2
H the LORD with your possessions   Pr 3:9
who accepts rebuke will be **h-ed**.   Pr 13:18
who is kind to the needy **h-s** Him.   Pr 14:31
to **h** Me with lip-service   Is 29:13
I will **h** the holiness of My   Ezk 36:23
Your name be **h-ed** as holy.   Mt 6:9
H your father and your mother;   Mt 15:4
These people **h** Me with their   Mt 15:8
h your father and your mother;   Mt 19:19
Father, Your name be **h-ed** as holy.   Lk 11:2
will then be **h-ed** in the presence   Lk 14:10
people will **h** the Son just as they **h**   Jn 5:23
I **h** My Father and you dishonor   Jn 8:49
serves Me, the Father will **h** him.   Jn 12:26

if one member is **h-ed**, all the   1Co 12:26
H your father and mother   Eph 6:2
will be highly **h-ed** in my body,   Php 1:20
may spread rapidly and be **h-ed**,   2Th 3:1
Fear God. **H** the Emperor.   1Pt 2:17

HONORABLE

Jabez was more **h** than his   1Ch 4:9
It is **h** for a man to resolve a   Pr 20:3
the holy {day} of the LORD **h**;   Is 58:13
to do what is **h** in everyone's   Rm 12:17
greater honor to the less **h**,   1Co 12:24
making provision for what is **h**,   2Co 8:21
whatever is **h**, whatever is just   Php 4:8

HONORABLY

ourselves **h** in everything.   Heb 13:18
yourselves **h** among the Gentiles   1Pt 2:12

HONORARIUM

worthy of an ample **h**,   1Tm 5:17

HOOFBEATS

I hear the **h** of his horses?   Jdg 5:28

HOOK

I will put My **h** in your nose and   2Kg 19:28
captured Manasseh with **h-s**,   2Ch 33:11
Leviathan with a **h** or tie his   Jb 41:1
those who cast **h-s** into the Nile   Is 19:8
I will put **h-s** in your jaws and   Ezk 29:4
you will be taken away with **h-s**,   Am 4:2

HOOPOE

heron, the **h**, and
  the bat.   Lv 11:19; Dt 14:18

HOOVES

with divided **h** and that chews   Lv 11:3
chew the cud or have divided **h**,   Dt 14:7
than a bull with horns and **h**.   Ps 69:31
horns iron and your **h** bronze,   Mc 4:13

HOPE (n)

Even if I thought there was {still} **h**   Ru 1:12
were looking for a sign of **h**,   1Kg 20:33
are like a shadow, without **h**.   1Ch 29:15
but there is still **h** for Israel   Ezr 10:2
integrity of your life your **h**?   Jb 4:6
they come to an end without **h**.   Jb 7:6
the **h** of the godless will perish   Jb 8:13
so You destroy a man's **h**.   Jb 14:19
where then is my **h**? Who can see   Jb 17:15

He uproots my **h** like a tree. Jb 19:10
LORD, I turn my **h** to You. Ps 25:1
you who put your **h** in the LORD. Ps 31:24
I put my **h** in You, LORD; Ps 38:15
My **h** is in You. Ps 39:7
Put your **h** in God, for I will Ps 42:5
for my **h** comes from Him Ps 62:5
For You are my **h**, Lord GOD, Ps 71:5
for I put my **h** in Your word. Ps 119:74
Israel, put your **h** in the LORD. Ps 130:7
whose **h** is in the LORD his God, Ps 146:5
put their **h** in His faithful love. Ps 147:11
Delayed **h** makes the heart sick, Pr 13:12
your son while there is **h**; Pr 19:18
and your **h** will never fade. Pr 23:18
There is more **h** for a fool than Pr 29:20
But there is **h** for whoever is Ec 9:4
H of Israel, its Savior in time Jr 14:8
to give you a future and a **h**. Jr 29:11
and therefore I have **h**: Lm 3:21
and our **h** has perished; Ezk 37:11
of Achor into a gateway of **h**. Hs 2:15
and always put your **h** in God. Hs 12:6
you prisoners who have **h**; Zch 9:12
nations will put their **h** in His Mt 12:21
on whom you have set your **h**. Jn 5:45
And I have a **h** in God, Ac 24:15
Because of this **h** I am being Ac 26:7
Against **h**, with **h** he believed, Rm 4:18
we rejoice in the **h** of the glory Rm 5:2
This **h** does not disappoint, Rm 5:5
Him who subjected it—in the **h** Rm 8:20
yet **h** that is seen is not **h**, Rm 8:24
Rejoice in **h**; be patient in Rm 12:12
the Scriptures we may have **h**. Rm 15:4
may the God of **h** fill you with Rm 15:13
three remain: faith, **h**, and love. 1Co 13:13
have placed our **h** in Christ for 1Co 15:19
have placed our **h** in Him that He 2Co 1:10
wait for the **h** of righteousness Gl 5:5
already put our **h** in the Messiah Eph 1:12
what is the **h** of His calling, Eph 1:18
called to one **h** at your calling Eph 4:4
because of the **h** reserved for Col 1:5
Christ in you, the **h** of glory. Col 1:27
For who is our **h**, or joy, or 1Th 2:19
like the rest, who have no **h**. 1Th 4:13

a helmet of the **h** of salvation. 1Th 5:8
and of Christ Jesus, our **h**: 1Tm 1:1
has put her **h** in God and 1Tm 5:5
for the blessed **h** and the Ti 2:13
heirs with the **h** of eternal life Ti 3:7
to seize the **h** set before us. Heb 6:18
but a better **h** is introduced, Heb 7:19
birth into a living **h** through 1Pt 1:3
reason for the **h** that is in you 1Pt 3:15
who has this **h** in Him purifies 1Jn 3:3

HOPE (v)

He kills me, I will **h** in Him. Jb 13:15
But when I **h-d** for good, evil came Jb 30:26
We **h** for justice, but there is Is 59:11
We **h-d** for peace, but there was Jr 8:15
But we were **h-ing** that He was Lk 24:21
But if we **h** for what we do not Rm 8:25
in Him the Gentiles will **h**. Rm 15:12
all things, **h-s** all things 1Co 13:7
Now I **h** in the Lord Jesus to Php 2:19
the reality of what is **h-d** for, Heb 11:1
the holy women who **h-d** in God also 1Pt 3:5

HOPELESS

all this, it seemed **h** Ps 73:16
you say: It's **h**; I love strangers, Jr 2:25
will say: It's **h**. We will continue Jr 18:12

HOPHNI

One of Eli's wicked sons (1Sm 1:3; 2:34; 4:4,11,17).

HOR

Aaron at Mount **H** on the border Nm 20:23
old when he died on Mount **H**. Nm 33:39
died on Mount **H** and was gathered Dt 32:50

HOREB

Another name for Mt. Sinai (Ex 3:1; 17:16; Dt 5:2; 1Kg 19:8; Ps 106:19; Mal 4:4).

HORITES

Inhabitants of Mt. Seir (Gn 14:6; 36:20-30; Dt 2:12,22).

HORIZON

He laid out the **h** on the surface Jb 26:10
He laid out the **h** on the surface Pr 8:27
flashes from **h** to **h** and lights up Lk 17:24

HORMAH

City destroyed by Israel (Nm 21:3; Jdg 1:17).

HORN

caught by its h-s in the thicket.	Gn 22:13
When the ram's h sounds a long	Ex 19:13
rite on the h-s of the altar.	Ex 30:10
When there is a ... blast of the h	Jos 6:5
my h is lifted up by the LORD.	1Sm 2:1
blew the ram's h throughout the	1Sm 13:3
Then Joab blew the ram's h,	2Sm 2:28
blew the ram's h and shouted:	2Sm 20:1
My shield, the h of my salvation	2Sm 22:3
Then they blew the ram's h,	1Kg 1:39
hold of the h-s of the altar 1Kg 1:50; 2:28	
Chenaanah made iron h-s and	1Kg 22:11
blew the ram's h and proclaimed	2Kg 9:13
Do not lift up your h.	Ps 75:4
by Your favor our h is exalted.	Ps 89:17
His h will be exalted in honor.	Ps 112:9
I will make a h grow for David;	Ps 132:17
has raised up a h for His people	Ps 148:14
Moab's h is chopped off;	Jr 48:25
I will cause a h to sprout for	Ezk 29:21
you hear the sound of the h,	Dn 3:5
and it had 10 h-s.	Dn 7:7
words the h was speaking.	Dn 7:11
The two h-s were long, but one was	Dn 8:3
a conspicuous h between his eyes	Dn 8:5
Blow the h in Zion; sound the	Jl 2:1
If a ram's h is blown in a city	Am 3:6
I looked up and saw four h-s.	Zch 1:18
has raised up a h of salvation	Lk 1:69
He had seven h-s and seven eyes,	Rv 5:6
From the four h-s of the gold	Rv 9:13
having seven heads and	
10 h-s	Rv 12:3; 17:3

HORNET

will send the h in front of you	Ex 23:28
also send the h against them	Dt 7:20
I sent the h ahead of you,	Jos 24:12

HORRIBLE

Don't do this h thing Jdg 19:23; 2Sm 13:12	
A h, terrible thing has taken place	Jr 5:30
seen something h in the house	Hs 6:10

HORRIFIED

Be h at this, heavens;	Jr 2:12
to be deeply distressed and h.	Mk 14:33

HORROR

You will become an object of h,	Dt 28:37
h has overwhelmed me.	Ps 55:5
I suffer Your h-s; I am desperate	Ps 88:15
heart staggers; h terrifies me	Is 21:4
they will be a h to all mankind.	Is 66:24
What a h Babylon has become	Jr 50:23
an object of h and will never	Ezk 27:36

HORSE

all Pharaoh's h-s and chariots,	Ex 14:9
has thrown the h and its rider into	Ex 15:1
not acquire many h-s for himself	Dt 17:16
hamstrung their h-s and burned up	Jos 11:9
and he hamstrung all the h-s,	2Sm 8:4
Solomon's h-s were imported	1Kg 10:28
army you lost—h for h, chariot	1Kg 20:25
a chariot of fire with h-s of fire	2Kg 2:11
was covered with h-s and chariots	2Kg 6:17
give you 2,000 h-s if you're able	2Kg 18:23
laughs at the h and its rider.	Jb 39:18
a chariot, and others in h-s, but we	Ps 20:7
The h is a false hope for safety	Ps 33:17
impressed by the strength of a h;	Ps 147:10
A h is prepared for the day of	Pr 21:31
A whip for the h, a bridle for	Pr 26:3
seen slaves on h-s, but princes	Ec 10:7
for help and who depend on h-s!	Is 31:1
His h-s are swifter than eagles.	Jr 4:13
eat your fill of h-s and riders,	Ezk 39:20
appearance is like that of h-s,	Jl 2:4
the one riding a h will not save	Am 2:15
Do h-s run on rock, or does	Am 6:12
saw a man riding on a red h.	Zch 1:8
The first chariot had red h-s,	Zch 6:2
the mouths of h-s to make them	Jms 3:3
and there was a white h.	Rv 6:2
Then another h went out, a fiery	Rv 6:4
and there was a black h.	Rv 6:5
and there was a pale green h.	Rv 6:8
appearance of the locusts was like h-s	Rv 9:7
up to the h-s' bridles	Rv 14:20
and there was a white h!	Rv 19:11
flesh of h-s and of their riders,	Rv 19:18

HORSEFLY

but a **h** from the north is coming   Jr 46:20

HORSEMEN

chariots, his **h**, and his army   Ex 14:9
and 12,000 **h** and stationed them   1Kg 10:26
the chariots and **h**
    of Israel!   2Kg 2:12; 13:14
The **h** had breastplates that were   Rv 9:17

HOSANNA

H to the Son of David!   Mt 21:9
H in the highest heaven!   Mt 21:9
kept shouting: **H!** Blessed is He   Mk 11:9
kept shouting: "**H!** Blessed is He   Jn 12:13

HOSEA

Prophet in Israel near the end of the kingdom; his marriage modeled God's love and
Israel's unfaithfulness (Hs 1–3).

HOSHEA

1. Joshua (Nm 13:8,16).
2. Son of Elah; last king of Israel (2Kg
15:30; 17:1-6).
3. Ephraimite official (1Ch 27:20).
4. Signed Nehemiah's covenant (Neh
10:23).

HOSPITABLE

respectable, **h**, an able teacher   1Tm 3:2
but **h**, loving what is good   Ti 1:8
Be **h** to one another without   1Pt 4:9

HOSPITALITY

in their needs; pursue **h**.   Rm 12:13
up children, shown **h**, washed the   1Tm 5:10
neglect to show **h**, for by doing   Heb 13:2

HOST

whole heavenly **h** was standing   1Kg 22:19
whole heavenly **h** and served Baal   2Kg 17:16
whole heavenly **h** and served them   2Kg 21:3
and the whole heavenly **h**.   2Kg 23:4
the heavenly **h** worships You.   Neh 9:6
Restore us, God of **H-s**;   Ps 80:7
praise Him, all His **h-s**.   Ps 148:2
out the starry **h** by number;   Is 40:26
His name is Yahweh of **H-s**.   Is 48:2
whole heavenly **h**, which they   Jr 8:2
h-s of heaven cannot be counted;   Jr 33:22
LORD, the God of **H-s**, the God of   Jr 35:17
LORD, the God of **H-s**, the God of   Jr 38:17

LORD, the God of **H-s**, the God of   Jr 44:7
grew as high as the heavenly **h**,   Dn 8:10
Yahweh is the God of **H-s**;   Hs 12:5
the God of **H-s**, is His name.   Am 4:13
the rooftops to the heavenly **h**;   Zph 1:5
on the house of Yahweh of **H-s**,   Hg 1:14
of the heavenly **h** with the angel   Lk 2:13
up to worship the **h** of heaven,   Ac 7:42
If the Lord of **H-s** had not left us   Rm 9:29
the ears of the Lord of **H-s**.   Jms 5:4

HOSTAGES

the king's palace, and the **h**.   2Kg 14:14

HOSTILE

they had been **h** toward each   Lk 23:12
mindset of the flesh is **h** to God   Rm 8:7
alienated and **h** in mind because   Col 1:21
and are **h** to everyone,   1Th 2:15

HOSTILITY

I will put **h** between you and the   Gn 3:15
one also, so he named it **H**.   Gn 26:21
If you act with **h** toward Me   Lv 26:21
pushes a person without **h** or   Nm 35:22
Show no **h** toward Moab   Dt 2:9
H is in the house of his God!   Hs 9:8
tore down the dividing wall of **h**.   Eph 2:14
who endured such **h** from sinners   Heb 12:3
with the world is **h** toward God?   Jms 4:4

HOT

when the sun grew **h**, it melted.   Ex 16:21
My heart grew **h** within me;   Ps 39:3
and the furnace extremely **h**,   Dn 3:22
you are neither cold nor **h**.   Rv 3:15

HOT-TEMPERED

A **h** man stirs up conflict,   Pr 15:18
than with a nagging and **h** wife.   Pr 21:19
be a companion of a **h** man,   Pr 22:24
and a **h** man increases rebellion   Pr 29:22

HOUR

be given what to say at that **h**,   Mt 10:19
'These last men put in one **h**,   Mt 20:12
that day and **h** no one knows   Mt 24:36
is coming at an **h** you do not   Mt 24:44
know either the day or the **h**.   Mt 25:13
you stay awake with Me one **h**?   Mt 26:40
the **h** might pass from Him.   Mk 14:35
But this is your **h**—and the   Lk 22:53

My **h** has not yet come."	Jn 2:4	better to go to a **h** of mourning than	Ec 7:2
But an **h** is coming, and is now	Jn 4:23	of negligent hands the **h** leaks.	Ec 10:18
was the very **h** at which Jesus had	Jn 4:53	to the **h** of the God of Jacob.	Is 2:3
An **h** is coming, and is now here	Jn 5:25	those who add **h** to to **h** and join field	Is 5:8
Him because His **h** had not yet	Jn 7:30	for My **h** will be called a **h** of prayer	Is 56:7
because His **h** had not come.	Jn 8:20	**H** of Israel, can I not treat you	Jr 18:6
Aren't there 12 **h-s** in a day?	Jn 11:9	which the **h** of Israel profaned	Ezk 36:21
The **h** has come for the Son of	Jn 12:23	the winter **h** and the summer **h**;	Am 3:15
Father, save Me from this **h**?	Jn 12:27	They will build **h-s** but never live	Zph 1:13
that is why I came to this **h**.	Jn 12:27	while this **h** lies in ruins?	Hg 1:4
Father, the **h** has come.	Jn 17:1	glory of this **h** will be greater	Hg 2:9
Why are we in danger every **h**?	1Co 15:30	that there may be food in My **h**.	Mal 3:10
Children, it is the last **h**.	1Jn 2:18	who built his **h** on the rock.	Mt 7:24
no idea at what **h** I will come	Rv 3:3	When Jesus went into Peter's **h**,	Mt 8:14
keep you from the **h** of testing	Rv 3:10	Jesus came to the leader's **h**,	Mt 9:23
the **h** of His judgment has come.	Rv 14:7	lost sheep of the **h** of Israel.	Mt 10:6
in a single **h** she was destroyed	Rv 18:19	no city or **h** divided against itself	Mt 12:25
		someone enter a strong man's **h**	Mt 12:29
HOUSE		And everyone who has left **h-s**,	Mt 19:29
your father's **h** to the land	Gn 12:1	My **h** will be called a **h** of prayer.	Mt 21:13
born in my **h** will be my heir.	Gn 15:3	devour widows' **h-s** and make long	Mt 23:14
passed over the **h-s** of the	Ex 12:27	your **h** is left to you desolate.	Mt 23:38
Do not covet your neighbor's **h**.	Ex 20:17	in Bethany at the **h** of Simon,	Mt 26:6
mildew contamination in a **h**	Lv 14:34	there is no one who has left **h**,	Mk 10:29
when you sit in your **h** and	Dt 6:7	the master of the **h** is coming	Mk 13:35
Has any man built a new **h** and not	Dt 20:5	Joseph, of the **h** of David.	Lk 1:27
May your **h** become like the **h** of	Ru 4:12	reign over the **h** of Jacob	Lk 1:33
Your **h** and kingdom will endure	2Sm 7:16	he was of the **h** and family line	Lk 2:4
This is the **h** of the LORD God,	1Ch 22:1	Whatever **h** you enter, stay there	Lk 9:4
rebuild the LORD's **h** in Jerusalem.	Ezr 1:5	so that my **h** may be filled.	Lk 14:23
has the **h** of God been neglected?	Neh 13:11	salvation has come to this **h**,	Lk 19:9
He who filled their **h-s** with good	Jb 22:18	My Father's **h** into a marketplace	Jn 2:16
dwell in the **h** of the LORD as	Ps 23:6	Zeal for Your **h** will consume Me	Jn 2:17
I love the **h** where You dwell,	Ps 26:8	the **h** was filled with the fragrance	Jn 12:3
procession to the **h** of God,	Ps 42:4	In My Father's **h** are many	Jn 14:2
with the goodness of Your **h**,	Ps 65:4	the whole **h** where they were	Ac 2:2
zeal for Your **h** has consumed me	Ps 69:9	broke bread from **h** to to **h**.	Ac 2:46
the door of the **h** of my God than	Ps 84:10	who owned lands or **h-s** sold them,	Ac 4:34
to the **h** of Israel;	Ps 98:3	along with everyone in his **h**.	Ac 16:32
H of Aaron, trust in the LORD!	Ps 115:10	in public and from **h** to **h**.	Ac 20:20
Let us go to the **h** of the LORD.	Ps 122:1	years in his own rented **h**.	Ac 28:30
Unless the LORD builds a **h**,	Ps 127:1	Don't you have **h-s** to eat and	1Co 11:22
not enter my **h** or get into my	Ps 132:3	a **h** not made with hands,	2Co 5:1
H of Israel, praise the LORD!	Ps 135:19	Nympha and the church in her **h**.	Col 4:15
for her **h** sinks down to death	Pr 2:18	be idle, going from **h** to **h**;	1Tm 5:13
Her **h** is the road to Sheol,	Pr 7:27	Now in a large **h** there are not	2Tm 2:20
Wisdom has built her **h**;	Pr 9:1	church that meets in your **h**.	Phm 2
Every wise woman builds her **h**,	Pr 14:1	builder has more honor than the **h**.	Heb 3:3
A **h** is built by wisdom, and it	Pr 24:3		

Now every **h** is built by someone | Heb 3:4
covenant with the **h** of Israel | Heb 8:8
high priest over the **h** of God, | Heb 10:21
into a spiritual **h** for a holy | 1Pt 2:5

HOUSEHOLD

stole her father's **h** idols. | Gn 31:19
watches over the activities of her **h** | Pr 31:27
when your king is a **h** servant, | Ec 10:16
and if the **h** is worthy, let your | Mt 10:13
will be the members of his **h**. | Mt 10:36
in his hometown and in his **h**. | Mt 13:57
charge of his **h** servants to give | Lk 12:42
believed, along with his whole **h**. | Jn 4:53
God along with his whole **h**. | Ac 10:2
and all your **h** will be saved. | Ac 11:14
she and her **h** were baptized, | Ac 16:15
will be saved—you and your **h**. | Ac 16:31
believed God with his entire **h**. | Ac 16:34
Lord, along with his whole **h**; | Ac 18:8
baptize the **h** of Stephanas; | 1Co 1:16
who belong to the **h** of faith. | Gl 6:10
saints, and members of God's **h**, | Eph 2:19
those from Caesar's **h**. | Php 4:22
manages his own **h** competently, | 1Tm 3:4
people ought to act in God's **h**, | 1Tm 3:15
mercy to the **h** of Onesiphorus, | 2Tm 1:16
their way into **h-s** and capture | 2Tm 3:6
overthrow whole **h-s** by teaching for | Ti 1:11
as Moses was in all God's **h**. | Heb 3:2
as a Son over His **h**, whose **h** we are | Heb 3:6
judgment to begin with God's **h**; | 1Pt 4:17

HOUSETOP

A man on the **h** must not come | Mt 24:17
will be proclaimed on the **h-s**. | Lk 12:3

HOVER

Spirit of God was **h-ing** over the | Gn 1:2
an eagle and **h-s** over His young; | Dt 32:11
Like **h-ing** birds, so the LORD of | Is 31:5

HOW

H long will You hide Your face | Ps 13:1
H long, LORD? Will You be angry | Ps 79:5
H lovely is Your dwelling place | Ps 84:1
H good and pleasant it is when | Ps 133:1
You ask: "**H** do we rob You?" | Mal 3:8
H is it then that David, | Mt 22:43
H often I wanted to gather your | Mt 23:37
asked the angel, "**H** can this be, | Lk 1:34

H is it that You, a Jew, ask | Jn 4:9
was born blind? **H** then does he | Jn 9:19
H happy the man whom the Lord | Rm 4:8
H can we who died to sin still | Rm 6:2
But **h** can they call on Him in | Rm 10:14
this is **h** I write. | 2Th 3:17
h will he take care of God's | 1Tm 3:5
h will we escape if we neglect | Heb 2:3

HUGE

H crowds followed Him, and He | Mt 12:15
And a **h** crowd was following Him | Jn 6:2

HULDAH

Wife of Shallum; prophetess in Josiah's time (2Kg 22:14).

HUMAN

him with a **h** rod and with blows | 2Sm 7:14
don't let me fall into **h** hands. | 2Sm 24:14
You alone know every **h** heart, | 1Kg 8:39
H bones will be burned on you. | 1Kg 13:2
not gods but made by **h** hands | 2Kg 19:18
for You alone know the **h** heart, | 2Ch 6:30
He has only **h** strength, but we | 2Ch 32:8
or do You see as a **h** sees? | Jb 10:4
disappeared from the **h** race. | Ps 12:1
is exalted by the **h** race. | Ps 12:8
heaven on the **h** race to see if | Ps 14:2
offspring from the **h** race. | Ps 21:10
heaven on the **h** race to see if | Ps 53:2
the foe, for **h** help is worthless | Ps 60:11
Even **h** wrath will praise You; | Ps 76:10
wonderful works for the **h** race. | Ps 107:8
and gold, made by **h** hands. | Ps 115:4
He has given to the **h** race. | Ps 115:16
Redeem me from **h** oppression, | Ps 119:134
delighting in the **h** race. | Pr 8:31
LORD—how much more, **h** hearts. | Pr 15:11
H pride will be humbled, | Is 2:11
will fall, but not by **h** sword; | Is 31:8
appearance: They had **h** form, | Ezk 1:5
the **h** flock of My pasture, | Ezk 34:31
be shattered, not by **h** hands. | Dn 8:25
one with **h** likeness touched | Dn 10:16
I led them with **h** cords, with | Hs 11:4
You judge by **h** standards. | Jn 8:15
is He served by **h** hands, | Ac 17:25
image fashioned by **h** art and | Ac 17:29
I use a **h** argument: Is God | Rm 3:5

I am using a **h** analogy because | Rm 6:19
not depend on **h** will or effort, | Rm 9:16
is wiser than **h** wisdom, | 1Co 1:25
not in words taught by **h** wisdom, | 1Co 2:13
by you or by a **h** court. | 1Co 4:3
this from a **h** perspective? | 1Co 9:8
in Ephesus with only **h** hope, | 1Co 15:32
is one flesh for **h-s**, another for | 1Co 15:39
known Christ in a purely **h** way, | 2Co 5:16
boast from a **h** perspective, | 2Co 11:18
not based on a **h** point of view. | Gl 1:11
of the law no **h** being will be | Gl 2:16
I'm using a **h** illustration. | Gl 3:15
by **h** cunning with cleverness in | Eph 4:14
obey your **h** masters with fear | Eph 6:5
deceit based on **h** tradition, | Col 2:8
they are **h** commands and | Col 2:22
obey your **h** masters in | Col 3:22
welcomed it not as a **h** message, | 1Th 2:13
Submit to every **h** institution | 1Pt 2:13
no longer for **h** desires, but for | 1Pt 4:2
donkey spoke with a **h** voice and | 2Pt 2:16
according to **h** measurement, | Rv 21:17

HUMANITY

All **h** will come to You, | Ps 65:2
and it weighs heavily on **h**: | Ec 6:1
because this {is for} all **h**. | Ec 12:13
H is brought low, man is humbled | Is 5:15
and all **h** will see {it} together | Is 40:5
All **h** is grass, and all its | Is 40:6
pour out My Spirit on all **h**; | Jl 2:28
pour out My Spirit on all **h**; | Ac 2:17
you except what is common to **h**. | 1Co 10:13

HUMBLE (adj)

Moses was a very **h** man, | Nm 12:3
have heard the desire of the **h**; | Ps 10:17
The **h** will eat and be satisfied | Ps 22:26
He leads the **h** in what is right | Ps 25:9
the **h** will hear and be glad. | Ps 34:2
But the **h** will inherit the land | Ps 37:11
The **h** will see it and rejoice. | Ps 69:32
He takes note of the **h**; | Ps 138:6
He adorns the **h** with salvation. | Ps 149:4
but gives grace to the **h**. | Pr 3:34
to be lowly of spirit with the **h** | Pr 16:19
but a **h** spirit will gain honor. | Pr 29:23
one who is **h**, submissive in spirit, | Is 66:2
Seek the LORD, all you **h** of the earth | Zph 2:3

h and riding on a donkey, | Zch 9:9
I am gentle and **h** in heart, | Mt 11:29
instead, associate with the **h**. | Rm 12:16
who comforts the **h**, comforted us | 2Co 7:6
I who am **h** among you in person, | 2Co 10:1
the body of our **h** condition | Php 3:21
The brother of **h** circumstances | Jms 1:9
but gives grace to the **h**. | Jms 4:6
and be compassionate and **h**, | 1Pt 3:8
but gives grace to the **h**. | 1Pt 5:5

HUMBLE (v)

that He might **h** you and test you | Dt 8:2
He **h-s** and He exalts. | 1Sm 2:7
Ahab has **h-d** himself before Me | 1Kg 21:29
called by My name **h** themselves, | 2Ch 7:14
Then Hezekiah **h-d** himself for | 2Ch 32:26
every proud person and **h** him; | Jb 40:12
but You **h** those with haughty | Ps 18:27
I **h-d** myself with fasting, and my | Ps 35:13
despise a broken and **h-d** heart. | Ps 51:17
He **h-s** the spirit of leaders; | Ps 76:12
as many days as You have **h-d** us, | Ps 90:15
A person's pride will **h** him, | Pr 29:23
the loftiness of men will be **h-d**; | Is 2:17
whoever **h-s** himself like this child | Mt 18:4
who exalts himself will be **h-d**, | Lk 14:11
did I commit a sin by **h-ing** myself | 2Co 11:7
He **h-d** Himself by becoming | Php 2:8
H yourselves before the Lord, | Jms 4:10
H yourselves therefore under the | 1Pt 5:6

HUMBLY

and to walk **h** with your God. | Mc 6:8
h receive the implanted word, | Jms 1:21

HUMILIATE

because you have **h-d** her. | Dt 21:14
even more and **h** myself. | 2Sm 6:22
to kill me be disgraced and **h-d**; | Ps 35:4
But You have rejected and **h-d** us; | Ps 44:9
seek You be **h-d** because of me, | Ps 69:6
companion of gluttons **h** his father. | Pr 28:7
Be ashamed and **h-d** because of | Ezk 36:32
all His adversaries were **h-d**, | Lk 13:17
my God will again **h** me in your | 2Co 12:21

HUMILIATION

He remembered us in our **h** | Ps 136:23
They can no longer feel **h**. | Jr 6:15
and then in **h**, you will proceed | Lk 14:9

In His **h** justice was denied Him — Ac 8:33
rich {should boast} in his **h**, — Jms 1:10

HUMILITY
and Your **h** exalts me. — Ps 18:35
cause of truth, **h**, and justice. — Ps 45:4
but with **h** comes wisdom. — Pr 11:2
and **h** comes before honor. — Pr 15:33
but before honor comes **h**. — Pr 18:12
The result of **h** is fear of the — Pr 22:4
Seek righteousness, seek **h**; — Zph 2:3
serving the Lord with all **h**, — Ac 20:19
with all **h** and gentleness, — Eph 4:2
but in **h** consider others as more — Php 2:3
ascetic practices, **h**, and severe — Col 2:23
kindness, **h**, gentleness — Col 3:12
clothe yourselves with **h** toward one — 1Pt 5:5

HUNDRED
child be born to a **h**-year-old man? — Gn 17:17
reaped a **h** times {what was sown}. — Gn 26:12
least of them was a match for a **h**, — 1Ch 12:14
more than a **h** lashes into a fool. — Pr 17:10
man may father a **h** children and — Ec 6:3
commits crime a **h** times and — Ec 8:12
the youth will die at a **h** years, — Is 65:20
he was about a **h** years old — Rm 4:19

HUNGER (n)
for him because his **h** urges him — Pr 16:26
where he will die from **h**, — Jr 38:9
for there will be **h** within you. — Mc 6:14
by sleepless nights, by times of **h**, — 2Co 6:5
sleepless nights, **h** and thirst, — 2Co 11:27

HUNGER (v)
They will not **h** or thirst, — Is 49:10
Blessed are those who **h** and thirst — Mt 5:6
no longer will they **h**; — Rv 7:16

HUNGRY
He humbled you by letting you go **h**; — Dt 8:3
The people must be **h**, exhausted — 2Sm 17:29
They carry sheaves but go **h**. — Jb 24:10
Young lions lack food and go **h**, — Ps 34:10
If I were **h**, I would not tell — Ps 50:12
and filled the **h** with good — Ps 107:9
and giving food to the **h**. — Ps 146:7
not let the righteous go **h**, — Pr 10:3
your enemy is **h**, give him food — Pr 25:21
but to a **h** person, any bitter — Pr 27:7

like a **h** one who dreams he is eating, — Is 29:8
if you offer yourself to the **h**, — Is 58:10
bread to the **h** and covers the naked — Ezk 18:7
days and 40 nights, He was **h**. — Mt 4:2
disciples were **h** and began to — Mt 12:1
For I was **h** and you gave Me — Mt 25:35
out from Bethany, He was **h**. — Mk 11:12
satisfied the **h** with good things — Lk 1:53
Blessed are you who are **h** now, — Lk 6:21
who comes to Me will ever be **h**, — Jn 6:35
If your enemy is **h**, feed him. — Rm 12:20
one person is **h** while another is — 1Co 11:21
If anyone is **h**, he should eat at — 1Co 11:34
whether well-fed or **h**, whether — Php 4:12

HUNT
went to the field to **h** some game — Gn 27:5
though you are **h**-ing me down — 1Sm 24:11
You **h** me like a lion — Jb 10:16
relentlessly **h** down a violent — Ps 140:11

HUNTED
my enemies **h** me like a bird. — Lm 3:52

HUNTER
Nimrod, a powerful **h** — Gn 10:9
Esau became an expert **h**, — Gn 25:27
Escape like a gazelle from a **h**, — Pr 6:5

HUR
Descendant of Caleb who helped support Moses' hands (Ex 17:12) and assisted Moses (24:14).

HURAM *see* HIRAM

HURAM-ABI *see* HIRAM

HURL
He **h**-ed lightning bolts and routed — Ps 18:14
reproach they have **h**-ed at You, — Ps 79:12
but **h**-ed Pharaoh and his army
into — Ps 136:15
So I will **h** you from this land — Jr 16:13
intending to **h** Him over the cliff. — Lk 4:29
the altar, and **h**-ed it to the earth — Rv 8:5

HURRY (n)
You are to eat it in a **h**; — Ex 12:11
left the land of Egypt in a **h** — Dt 16:3
but one in a **h** to get rich will — Pr 28:20
A greedy man is in a **h** for wealth; — Pr 28:22
do not be in a **h**. Leave his — Ec 8:3

HURRY (v)

So Abraham h-ied into the tent and	Gn 18:6
However, the Levites did not h.	2Ch 24:5
God told me to h. Stop opposing	2Ch 35:21
H to help me, Lord, my Savior.	Ps 38:22
God, deliver me. H to help me,	Ps 70:1
and they h to commit murder	Pr 1:16
king got up and h-ied to the lions'	Dn 6:19
They h-ied off and found both Mary	Lk 2:16

HURT

They h his feet with shackles;	Ps 105:18
a wicked man will get h.	Pr 9:7
quarries stones may be h by them;	Ec 10:9
They haven't h me, for I was	Dn 6:22
out of him without h-ing him at all.	Lk 4:35
brother is h by what you eat	Rm 14:15
cheer me other than the one h?	2Co 2:2

HUSBAND

she also gave {some} to her h,	Gn 3:6
Your desire will be for your h,	Gn 3:16
Her h may confirm or cancel any	Nm 30:13
jealousy enrages a h, and he will	Pr 6:34
My h isn't home; he went on a	Pr 7:19
A capable wife is her h-'s crown,	Pr 12:4
heart of her h trusts in her,	Pr 31:11
Her h is known at the city gates	Pr 31:23
Her h also praises her:	Pr 31:28
For your h is your Maker	Is 54:5
you will call Me: My h,	Hs 2:16
for the h of her youth.	Jl 1:8
she divorces her h and marries	Mk 10:12
"Go call your h," He told her,	Jn 4:16
you've had five h-s, and the man	
you now have is not your h.	Jn 4:18
But if her h dies, she is free	Rm 7:3
woman should have her own h.	1Co 7:2
A h should fulfill his marital	1Co 7:3
a wife is not to leave her h.	1Co 7:10
and a h is not to leave his wife	1Co 7:11
the unbelieving h is sanctified	1Co 7:14
whether you will save your h?	1Co 7:16
how she may please her h.	1Co 7:34
But if her h dies, she is free	1Co 7:39
should ask their own h-s at home,	1Co 14:35
promised you in marriage to one h	2Co 11:2
for the h is head of the wife as	Eph 5:23
H-s, love your wives, just as also	Eph 5:25
the wife is to respect her h.	Eph 5:33

submissive to your h-s, as is fitting	Col 3:18
H-s, love your wives and don't	Col 3:19
the h of one wife,	1Tm 3:2
Deacons must be h-s of one wife,	1Tm 3:12
has been the wife of one h,	1Tm 5:9
is blameless, the h of one wife,	Ti 1:6
encourage ... women to love their h-s	Ti 2:4
submit yourselves to your own h-s	1Pt 3:1
H-s, in the same way, live with	1Pt 3:7
like a bride adorned for her h.	Rv 21:2

HUSHAI

David's friend and spy in Absalom's court (2Sm 15:32–17:15).

HUSKS

Let them be like h in the wind,	Ps 35:5
and even sell the wheat h!	Am 8:6

HYACINTH

were fiery red, h blue, and	Rv 9:17

HYENAS

H will howl in the fortresses,	Is 13:22

HYMENAEUS

Paul's former co-worker; backslider (1Tm 1:19-20; 2Tm 2:17-18).

HYMN

new song in my mouth, a h of praise	Ps 40:3
praying and singing h-s to God,	Ac 16:25
in psalms, h-s, and spiritual	Eph 5:19
singing psalms, h-s, and spiritual	Col 3:16
I will sing h-s to You in the	Heb 2:12

HYPNOTIZED

Who has h you, before whose eyes	Gl 3:1

HYPOCRISY

are full of h and lawlessness	Mt 23:28
knowing their h, He said to them	Mk 12:15
yeast of the Pharisees, which is h.	Lk 12:1
Love must be without h.	Rm 12:9
rest of the Jews joined his h,	Gl 2:13
through the h of liars whose	1Tm 4:2
without favoritism and h.	Jms 3:17
all deceit, h, envy, and all	1Pt 2:1

HYPOCRITE

or associate with h-s.	Ps 26:4
as the h-s do in the synagogues	Mt 6:2
you must not be like the h-s,	Mt 6:5
don't be sad-faced like the h-s.	Mt 6:16

H! First take the log out of Mt 7:5
H-s! Isaiah prophesied correctly Mt 15:7
Why are you testing Me, h-s? Mt 22:18
scribes and Pharisees, h-s! Mt 23:13
assign him a place with the h-s. Mt 24:51
H-s! You know how to interpret the Lk 12:56
H-s! Doesn't each one of you untie Lk 13:15

HYPOCRITICAL

not h, not drinking a lot of wine, 1Tm 3:8

HYRAX

the h, though it chews the cud Lv 11:5
the cliffs are a refuge for h-s. Ps 104:18
h-s are not a mighty people, Pr 30:26

HYSSOP

Take a cluster of h, dip it in Ex 12:22
yarn, and h, and dip them all Lv 14:6
and h to purify the house, Lv 14:49
take cedar wood, h, and crimson Nm 19:6
in Lebanon to the h growing out 1Kg 4:33
Purify me with h, and I will be Ps 51:7
of sour wine on h and held it up Jn 19:29
wool, and h, and sprinkled Heb 9:19

I

I AM

I WHO I. Ex 3:14
I Yahweh. Ex 6:2
live if he does them. I the LORD. Lv 18:5
I the LORD your God. Do not fear Jdg 6:10
Stop ... and know that I God, Ps 46:10
I Yahweh your God, who brought Ps 81:10
the first, and with the last—I He. Is 41:4
I Yahweh, that is My name; Is 42:8
I, I the LORD, and there is no other Is 43:11
I the first and I the last. There is no Is 44:6
nations will know that I Yahweh Ezk 36:23
in security, that thinks to herself: I, Zph 2:15
message to the people, "I with you" Hg 1:13
who do you say that I? Mt 16:15
I the God of Abraham and the God Mt 22:23
I with you always, to the end of Mt 28:20
"I," said Jesus, Mk 14:62
"I He," Jesus told her, Jn 4:26
"I the bread of life," Jesus told them. Jn 6:35

if you do not believe that I He, you Jn 8:24
then you will know that I He, Jn 8:28
Before Abraham was, I. Jn 8:58
I the light of the world. Jn 9:5
I the door of the sheep. Jn 10:7
I the good shepherd. Jn 10:11
I the resurrection and the life. Jn 11:25
you will believe that I He. Jn 13:19
I the way, the truth, and the life. Jn 14:6
I the vine; you are the branches. Jn 15:5
When He told them, "I He," they Jn 18:6
I Jesus, whom you are persecuting, Ac 9:5
For I with you, and no one will Ac 18:10
I the Alpha and the Omega, Rv 1:8
I the First and the Last, Rv 1:17
I coming quickly. Hold on to what Rv 3:11
I the Alpha and the Omega, the
  Beginning and the End. Rv 21:6
I the Root and the Offspring of
  David, the Bright Morning Star. Rv 22:16
Yes, I coming quickly. Rv 22:20

IBZAN

Judge from Bethlehem; practiced tribal intermarriage (Jdg 12:8-10).

ICE

become darkened because of i, Jb 6:16
I is formed by the breath of God Jb 37:10
Whose womb did the i come from? Jb 38:29

ICHABOD

Son of Phinehas, grandson of Eli (1Sm 4:19-22; 14:3).

ICONIUM

City in Asia Minor visited by Paul (Ac 13:51; 14:1,19,21; 2Tm 3:11).

IDDO

the Visions of I the Seer 2Ch 9:29
and of I the Seer 2Ch 12:15
the Writing of the Prophet I. 2Ch 13:22
I sent them to I, the leader at Ezr 8:17

IDEA

want to know what these i-s mean. Ac 17:20
is a judge of the i-s and thoughts Heb 4:12
and you have no i at what hour I Rv 3:3

IDENTITY

revealed his i to his brothers Gn 45:1

IDLE

Do not be deaf, God; do not be i.	Ps 83:1
I hands make one poor, but	Pr 10:4
her household and is never i.	Pr 31:27
they also learn to be i,	1Tm 5:13
and capture i women burdened	2Tm 3:6
rebellious people, i talkers and	Ti 1:10
pronounced long ago, is not i,	2Pt 2:3

IDOL

stole her father's household i-s.	Gn 31:19
Do not make an i for yourself,	Ex 20:4
Do not turn to i-s or make cast	Lv 19:4
makes a carved i or cast image,	Dt 27:15
made an ephod and household i-s,	Jdg 17:5
the household i was on the bed	1Sm 19:16
the detestable i of Moab,	1Kg 11:7
pursued worthless i-s and became	2Kg 17:15
the gods of the peoples are i-s,	Ps 96:5
Their i-s are silver and gold,	Ps 115:4
Their land is full of i-s;	Is 2:8
To an i?—{something that} a	
smelter casts	Is 40:19
makes a god or his i with the rest	Is 44:17
one offers incense, one praises an i	Is 66:3
who cling to worthless i-s forsake	Jnh 2:8
and I will destroy all her i-s.	Mc 1:7
What use is a carved i after its	Hab 2:18
and makes i-s that cannot speak.	Hab 2:18
For the i-s speak falsehood,	Zch 10:2
abstain from food offered to i-s,	Ac 15:29
that the city was full of i-s.	Ac 17:16
You who detest i-s, do you rob	Rm 2:22
About food offered to i-s:	1Co 8:1
we know that "an i is nothing	1Co 8:4
they eat food offered to an i,	1Co 8:7
or that an i is anything?	1Co 10:19
God's sanctuary have with i-s?	2Co 6:16
turned to God from i-s to serve	1Th 1:9
guard yourselves from i-s.	1Jn 5:21
to eat meat sacrificed to i-s.	Rv 2:20
demons and i-s of gold,	Rv 9:20

IDOLATER

babble like the i-s, since they	Mt 6:7
or greedy, an i or a reviler	1Co 5:11
immoral people, i-s, adulterers	1Co 6:9
greedy person, who is an i, has an	Eph 5:5
sorcerers, i-s, and all liars	Rv 21:8
murderers, the i-s, and everyone	Rv 22:15

IDOLATROUS

he did away with the i priests	2Kg 23:5

IDOLATRY

defiance is like wickedness and i.	1Sm 15:23
my dear friends, flee from i.	1Co 10:14
i, sorcery, hatreds, strife	Gl 5:20
desire, and greed, which is i.	Col 3:5
carousing, and lawless i.	1Pt 4:3

IGNITE

His anger may i at any moment.	Ps 2:12
I am about to i a fire in you,	Ezk 20:47
large a forest a small fire i-s.	Jms 3:5

IGNORANCE

who conceals {My} counsel	
with i?	Jb 42:3
foolish ones, will you love i?	Pr 1:22
unintentionally or through i.	Ezk 45:20
I know that you did it in i,	Ac 3:17
what you worship in i, this I	Ac 17:23
overlooked the times of i,	Ac 17:30
because of the i that is in them	Eph 4:18
it was out of i that I had acted	1Tm 1:13
of the people committed in i.	Heb 9:7
to the desires of your former i	1Pt 1:14
silence the i of foolish people	1Pt 2:15

IGNORANT

obscures {My} counsel with i words	Jb 38:2
for they are i and do wrong.	Ec 5:1
Everyone is stupid and i.	Jr 10:14
some people are i about God.	1Co 15:34
for we are not i of his	2Co 2:11
reject foolish and i disputes,	2Tm 2:23
those who are i and are going	Heb 5:2

IGNORE

sheep straying, you must not i it;	Dt 22:1
You i-d the Rock who gave you	Dt 32:18
and do not i my plea for help	Ps 55:1
and be wise; don't i it.	Pr 8:33
whoever i-s an insult is sensible.	Pr 12:16
Anyone who i-s instruction	Pr 15:32
Do not i my cry for relief.	Lm 3:56
the trumpet but i-s the warning,	Ezk 33:4
if anyone i-s this, he will be i-d.	1Co 14:38
They willfully i this:	2Pt 3:5

ILL

to David, and he became i.	2Sm 12:15

Hezekiah became terminally i.   2Kg 20:1
many are sick and i among you,   1Co 11:30

ILLEGAL

It's i for you to pick up your   Jn 5:10

ILLEGITIMATE

No one of i birth may enter the   Dt 23:2
they gave birth to i children.   Hs 5:7
then you are i children and not   Heb 12:8

ILL-GOTTEN

I gains do not profit anyone,   Pr 10:2

ILLNESSES

I will take away your i.   Ex 23:25
stomach and your frequent i.   1Tm 5:23

ILLUMINATE

pillar of fire by night, to i the way   Neh 9:12
my God i-s my darkness.   Ps 18:28
the earth was i-d by his splendor   Rv 18:1
God's glory i-s it, and its lamp   Rv 21:23

ILLUSION

exalted men, an i. On a balance   Ps 62:9
flattering things. Prophesy i-s.   Is 30:10
and the diviners see i-s;   Zch 10:2

ILLUSTRATE

How can we i the kingdom of God   Mk 4:30

ILLUSTRATION

Jesus gave them this i, but they   Jn 10:6
Brothers, I'm using a human i.   Gl 3:15
These things are i-s,   Gl 4:24
he also got him back as an i.   Heb 11:19

ILLYRICUM

all the way around to I.   Rm 15:19

IMAGE

Let Us make man in Our i,   Gn 1:26
God created man in His own i;   Gn 1:27
for God made man in His i.   Gn 9:6
made it into an i of a calf.   Ex 32:4
destroy all their stone i-s and cast   Nm 33:52
and burn up their carved i-s.   Dt 7:5
makes a carved idol or cast i,   Dt 27:15
made for themselves molded i-s   2Kg 17:16
Josiah removed the ... i-s, and all   2Kg 23:24
You will despise their i.   Ps 73:20
His jealousy with their carved i-s.   Ps 78:58
and worshiped the cast metal i.   Ps 106:19

exchanged their glory for the i of   Ps 106:20
for his cast i-s are a lie;   Jr 51:17
Whose i and inscription is this   Mt 22:20
an i fashioned by human art and   Ac 17:29
exchanged the glory ... for i-s   Rm 1:23
conformed to the i of His Son,   Rm 8:29
he is God's i and glory,   1Co 11:7
also bear the i of the heavenly   1Co 15:49
into the same i from glory to   2Co 3:18
of Christ, who is the i of God.   2Co 4:4
He is the i of the invisible God   Col 1:15
according to the i of his Creator.   Col 3:10
an i of the beast   Rv 13:14
worshiped the beast or his i,   Rv 20:4

IMAGINATION

the i-s of their hearts run wild.   Ps 73:7
in his i it is like a high wall   Pr 18:11
prophesy out of their own i: Ezk 13:2
fashioned by human art and i.   Ac 17:29

IMAGINE

since they i they'll be heard   Mt 6:7
who i that godliness is a way to   1Tm 6:5

IMITATE

Do not i their practices.   Ex 23:24
do not i the detestable customs   Dt 18:9
had commanded them not to i.   2Kg 17:15
i-ing the detestable practices of   2Ch 28:3
Join in i-ing me, brothers, and   Php 3:17
know how you must i us: 2Th 3:7
to you so that you would i us.   2Th 3:9
of their lives, i their faith.   Heb 13:7
do not i what is evil, but what is   3Jn 11

IMITATORS

I urge you, be i of me.   1Co 4:16
Be i of me, as I also am of   1Co 11:1
Therefore, be i of God, as   Eph 5:1
and you became i of us and of   1Th 1:6
became i of God's churches in   1Th 2:14
but i of those who inherit the   Heb 6:12

IMMANUEL

have a son, and name him I.   Is 7:14
will fill your entire land, I!   Is 8:8
they will name Him I, which is   Mt 1:23

IMMATURE

of the ignorant, a teacher of the i,   Rm 2:20

IMMEASURABLE

| and what is the i greatness of | Eph 1:19 |
| display the i riches of His | Eph 2:7 |

IMMEDIATELY

and did not drive them out i.	Jdg 2:23
I they left their nets and	Mt 4:20
I his disease was healed.	Mt 8:3
I they could see, and they	Mt 20:34
I after the tribulation of	Mt 24:29
I a rooster crowed,	Mt 26:74
I the Spirit drove Him into the	Mk 1:12
I the girl got up and began to	Mk 5:42
I his ears were opened, his	Mk 7:35
I his mouth was opened and his	Lk 1:64
piece of bread, he went out i.	Jn 13:30
I he began proclaiming Jesus in	Ac 9:20
I did not i consult with anyone	Gl 1:16
I I was in the Spirit, and there	Rv 4:2

IMMENSE

| through this i wilderness. | Dt 2:7 |
| Do you see this entire i horde? | 1Kg 20:13 |

IMMORAL

associate with sexually i people	1Co 5:9
who is sexually i or greedy,	1Co 5:11
no sexually i people, idolaters,	1Co 6:9
who is sexually i sins against	1Co 6:18
no sexually i or impure or	Eph 5:5
the sexually i and homosexuals	1Tm 1:10
there isn't any i or irreverent	Heb 12:16
God will judge i people and	Heb 13:4
unrestrained behavior of the i	2Pt 2:7
the error of the i and fall from	2Pt 3:17
murderers, sexually i, sorcerers	Rv 21:8
the sexually i, the murderers	Rv 22:15

IMMORALITY

to your indecency and sexual i,	Ezk 23:27
except in a case of sexual i,	Mt 5:32
sexual i-ies, thefts, false	Mt 15:19
except for sexual i, and marries	Mt 19:9
We weren't born of sexual i,	Jn 8:41
abstain ... from sexual i,	Ac 15:20
there is sexual i among you,	1Co 5:1
The body is not for sexual i but for	1Co 6:13
Flee from sexual i!	1Co 6:18
Let us not commit sexual i as some	1Co 10:8
sexual i, and promiscuity	2Co 12:21
sexual i, moral impurity	Gl 5:19

But sexual i and any impurity or	Eph 5:3
sexual i, impurity, lust, evil	Col 3:5
that you abstain from sexual i,	1Th 4:3
committed sexual i and practiced	Jd 7
want to repent of her sexual i.	Rv 2:21
drink the wine of her sexual i,	Rv 14:8

IMMORTAL

| glory of the i God for images | Rm 1:23 |
| the King eternal, i, invisible | 1Tm 1:17 |

IMMORTALITY

seek for glory, honor, and i;	Rm 2:7
mortal must be clothed with i.	1Co 15:53
the only One who has i, dwelling	1Tm 6:16
brought life and i to light	2Tm 1:10

IMMOVABLE

| the root of the righteous is i. | Pr 12:3 |
| be steadfast, i, always excelling | 1Co 15:58 |

IMPART

| that I may i to you some | Rm 1:11 |

IMPARTIAL

| You gave them i ordinances, | Neh 9:13 |
| A rod of correction i-s wisdom, | Pr 29:15 |

IMPARTIALLY

| They were divided i by lot, | 1Ch 24:5 |
| One who judges i based on each | 1Pt 1:17 |

IMPATIENT

but the people became i because	Nm 21:4
Then why shouldn't I be i?	Jb 21:4
Is the Spirit of the LORD i?	Mc 2:7
I became i with them, and they	Zch 11:8

IMPERFECTION

| darling, with no i in you. | Sg 4:7 |

IMPERIAL

| throughout the whole i guard, | Php 1:13 |

IMPERISHABLE

crown, but we an i one.	1Co 9:25
into an inheritance that is i,	1Pt 1:4
of perishable seed but of i	1Pt 1:23
the heart with the i quality of	1Pt 3:4

IMPLANTED

| humbly receive the i word, | Jms 1:21 |

IMPLORE

| petitioning and i-ing his God. | Dn 6:11 |

Now I i you, brothers, through | Rm 15:30
Now I i you, brothers, watch out | Rm 16:17
and i-ed each one of you to walk | 1Th 2:12

IMPORTANT

bring you every i case but judge | Ex 18:22
clan the least i of all the | 1Sm 9:21
than to act i but have no food. | Pr 12:9
greatest and most i commandment. | Mt 22:38
have neglected the more i matters | Mt 23:23
is far more {i} than all the burnt | Mk 12:33
a citizen of an i city. | Ac 21:39
on to you as most i what I also | 1Co 15:3
those recognized as i added nothing | Gl 2:6
others as more i than yourselves | Php 2:3

IMPORTED

horses were i from Egypt and Kue | 1Kg 10:28

IMPOSED

They ruthlessly i all this work | Ex 1:14
they i forced labor on the | Jos 17:13
that King Solomon had i to build | 1Kg 9:15
washings i until the time | Heb 9:10

IMPOSSIBLE

nothing they plan to do will be i | Gn 11:6
Is anything i for the LORD? | Gn 18:14
It is i for God {to do} wrong, | Jb 34:10
Nothing will be i for you. | Mt 17:20
With men this is i, but with God | Mt 19:26
For nothing will be i with God. | Lk 1:37
For it is i to renew to | Heb 6:4
in which it is i for God to lie | Heb 6:18
For it is i for the blood of | Heb 10:4
without faith it is i to please God, | Heb 11:6

IMPOSTERS

and i will become worse, | 2Tm 3:13

IMPRESS

I these words of Mine on your | Dt 11:18
He is not i-ed by the strength of a | Ps 147:10

IMPRESSION

and He gave the i that He was | Lk 24:28

IMPRESSIVE

Saul, an i young man. | 1Sm 9:2
massive stones! What i buildings! | Mk 13:1

IMPRISONED

So Joseph i them together for | Gn 42:17

Pharaoh Neco i him at Riblah in | 2Kg 23:33
the prophet was i in the guard's | Jr 32:2
I had those who believed in You i | Ac 22:19
For God has i all in disobedience, | Rm 11:32
Scripture has i everything under | Gl 3:22

IMPRISONMENT

confiscation of property, or i. | Ezr 7:26
by beatings, by i-s, by riots, by | 2Co 6:5
labors, many more i-s, far worse | 2Co 11:23
both in my i and in the defense | Php 1:7
that my i is for Christ. | Php 1:13
to cause {me} trouble in my i. | Php 1:17
Remember my i. | Col 4:18
so that in my i for the gospel | Phm 13
as well as bonds and i. | Heb 11:36

IMPROPER

He must not see anything i among | Dt 23:14
he finds something i about her, | Dt 24:1

IMPROPERLY

he is acting i toward his virgin | 1Co 7:36
does not act i; is not selfish | 1Co 13:5

IMPROVISE

They i songs to the sound of the | Am 6:5

IMPULSIVE

and do not be i to make a speech | Ec 5:2

IMPULSIVELY

He follows her i like an ox | Pr 7:22

IMPURE

immoral or i or greedy person, | Eph 5:5

IMPURITY

because of the Israelites' i-ies | Lv 16:16
during her menstrual i to have | Lv 18:19
the water {to remove} i; | Nm 19:9
by their i and detestable | Ezr 9:11
I will remove all your i-ies. | Is 1:25
a woman during her menstrual i. | Ezk 18:6
before Me was like menstrual i. | Ezk 36:17
cleanse you from all your i-ies | Ezk 36:25
{to wash away} sin and i. | Zch 13:1
dead men's bones and every i. | Mt 23:27
of their hearts to sexual i, | Rm 1:24
as slaves to moral i, | Rm 6:19
moral i, promiscuity, | Gl 5:19
of every kind of i with a desire | Eph 4:19
and any i or greed should | Eph 5:3
immorality, i, lust, evil desire | Col 3:5

For God has not called us to i, 1Th 4:7
escaped the world's i through 2Pt 2:20

INACCESSIBLE
Wisdom is i to a fool; Pr 24:7

INANIMATE
Even i things producing sounds 1Co 14:7

INAPPROPRIATE
honor is i for a fool. Pr 26:1

INAUGURATE
will serve to i a permanent Ex 40:15
covenant was i-d with blood. Heb 9:18
way that He has i-d for us, Heb 10:20

INCALCULABLE
to the Gentiles the i riches of Eph 3:8

INCAPABLE
will they be i of innocence? Hs 8:5
The people are i of doing right Am 3:10

INCENSE
spices ... for the fragrant i; Ex 25:6
an altar for the burning of i; Ex 30:1
the gold altar for i in front of Ex 40:5
put the i on the fire ... so that the
    cloud of i covers the mercy seat Lv 16:13
12 gold bowls full of i Nm 7:86
fire in it, put i on it, and Nm 16:18
they will set i before You and Dt 33:10
My altar, to burn i, and to wear 1Sm 2:28
and burned i on the high places 1Kg 3:3
burn i in the presence
    of the LORD 1Ch 23:13
prayer be set before You as i, Ps 141:2
Oil and i bring joy to the heart Pr 27:9
I despise {your} i. Is 1:13
You are burning i to other gods Jr 44:8
Each had an i burner in his hand Ezk 8:11
I and pure offerings will be Mal 1:11
to the right of the altar of i. Lk 1:11
the gold altar of i and the ark Heb 9:4
and gold bowls filled with i, Rv 5:8
The smoke of the i, with the Rv 8:4
cinnamon, spice, i, myrrh, and Rv 18:13

INCITED
and i the entire community Nm 14:36
because his wife Jezebel i him. 1Kg 21:25
against Israel and i David to count 1Ch 21:1

even though you i Me against him Jb 2:3
But the Jews i the religious Ac 13:50

INCLINATION
though man's i is evil from his Gn 8:21
carrying out the i-s of our flesh Eph 2:3

INCLINE
May He i our hearts toward Him 1Kg 8:58

INCLUDING
act to judgment, i every hidden Ec 12:14

INCOME
the i of the wicked. Pr 15:6
than great i with injustice. Pr 16:8
{is} never {satisfied} with i. Ec 5:10

INCOMPARABLE
an absolutely i eternal weight 2Co 4:17

INCORRUPTIBLE
and the dead will be raised i, 1Co 15:52

INCORRUPTION
Sown in corruption, raised in i; 1Co 15:42
corruption cannot inherit i. 1Co 15:50

INCREASE
the waters i-d and lifted up the Gn 7:17
so that you may live and i, Dt 8:1
If wealth i-s, pay no attention to it. Ps 62:10
You will i my honor and comfort Ps 71:21
You i-d strength within me. Ps 138:3
our flocks will i by thousands Ps 144:13
will listen and i his learning, Pr 1:5
and pleasant speech i-s learning. Pr 16:21
When the wicked i, rebellion Pr 29:16
a hot-tempered man i-s rebellion. Pr 29:22
as knowledge i-s, grief i-s. Ec 1:18
When good things i, the ones who Ec 5:11
many words, they i futility. Ec 6:11
the nation and i-d its joy. Is 9:3
and they will i and be fruitful Ezk 36:11
and knowledge will i. Dn 12:4
fruit i-d, the more he i-d the altars. Hs 10:1
reduce the measure while i-ing the Am 8:5
and produced a crop that i-d 30, Mk 4:8
And Jesus i-d in wisdom and Lk 2:52
said to the Lord, "I our faith." Lk 17:5
He must i, but I must decrease. Jn 3:30
added to the Lord in i-ing numbers Ac 5:14
Spirit, and it i-d in numbers. Ac 9:31

faith and were **i-d** in number daily   Ac 16:5
your seed and **i** the harvest of   2Co 9:10
fruit that is **i-ing** to your account   Php 4:17
cause you to **i** and overflow with   1Th 3:12
of you for one another is **i-ing**.   2Th 1:3
qualities are yours and are **i-ing**,   2Pt 1:8

INCREDIBLE
it may seem **i** to the remnant   Zch 8:6
We have seen **i** things today!   Lk 5:26
Why is it considered **i** by any of you   Ac 26:8

INCURABLE
intestines with an **i** disease.   2Ch 21:18
My wound is **i**, though I am   Jb 34:6
my wound **i**, refusing to be   Jr 15:18
Your injury is **i**; your wound   Jr 30:12
her wound is **i** and has reached   Mc 1:9

INDECENT
embarrassed by your **i** behavior.   Ezk 16:27
not to imitate your **i** behavior.   Ezk 23:48

INDECISIVE
An **i** man is unstable in all his   Jms 1:8

INDEED
I **i** it is flowing with milk and   Nm 13:27
But will God **i** live on earth?   1Kg 8:27
You will **i** drink My cup.   Mt 20:23
if **i** you remain grounded and   Col 1:23
and **i** our fellowship is with the   1Jn 1:3

INDEPENDENT
woman is not **i** of man, and man
     is not **i** of woman.   1Co 11:11

INDESCRIBABLE
Thanks be to God for His **i** gift.   2Co 9:15

INDESTRUCTIBLE
but based on the power of an **i** life.   Heb 7:16

INDIA
127 provinces from **I** to Cush.   Est 1:1; 8:9

INDICATING
Christ within them was **i** when He   1Pt 1:11

INDICT
Can anyone **i** me?   Jb 13:19

INDIGNANT
they became **i** with the two   Mt 20:24
the Son of David!" they were **i**   Mt 21:15

disciples saw it, they were **i**.   Mt 26:8
He was **i** and said to them,   Mk 10:14
i because Jesus had healed on   Lk 13:14

INDIGNATION
in my body because of Your **i**;   Ps 38:3
fury, **i**, and calamity   Ps 78:49
because of Your **i** and wrath;   Ps 102:10
for You filled me with **i**.   Jr 15:17
I will pour out My **i** on you;   Ezk 21:31
Who can withstand His **i**?   Nah 1:6
order to pour out My **i** on them,   Zph 3:8
but wrath and **i** to those who are   Rm 2:8
what **i**, what fear, what   2Co 7:11
and I do not burn with **i**?   2Co 11:29

INDISTINCTLY
For now we see **i**, as in a mirror   1Co 13:12

INDIVIDUAL
body of Christ, and **i** members   1Co 12:27
proper working of each **i** part.   Eph 4:16

INDIVIDUALLY
and **i** members of one another.   Rm 12:5

INDOORS
His disciples were **i** again,   Jn 20:26

INDUCES
Laziness **i** deep sleep, and a   Pr 19:15

INDULGE
Please **i** me, my lord.   Gn 33:15
the land and have **i-ed** yourselves.   Jms 5:5

INDULGENCE
of any value against fleshly **i**.   Col 2:23

INEDIBLE
bad figs, so bad they were **i**.   Jr 24:2
figs that are **i** because they are   Jr 29:17

INEFFECTIVE
why the law is **i** and justice   Hab 1:4
His grace toward me was not **i**.   1Co 15:10

INEXHAUSTIBLE
an **i** treasure in heaven, where   Lk 12:33

INEXPERIENCED
My son Solomon is young and **i**,   1Ch 22:5
trustworthy, making the **i** wise.   Ps 19:7
The LORD guards the **i**;   Ps 116:6
gives understanding to the **i**.   Ps 119:130

teaching shrewdness to the i, Pr 1:4
waywardness of the i will kill them, Pr 1:32
Whoever is i, enter here! Pr 9:4,16
The i believe anything, but the Pr 14:15
mocker, and the i learn a lesson; Pr 19:25
the i keep going and are punished. Pr 22:3
on milk is i with the message Heb 5:13

INEXPRESSIBLE
He heard i words, which a man is 2Co 12:4
rejoice with i and glorious joy 1Pt 1:8

INFANT
like i-s who never see daylight? Jb 3:16
mouths of children and nursing i-s, Ps 8:2
An i will play beside the Is 11:8
a nursing i will no longer live Is 65:20
The nursing i-'s tongue clings to Lm 4:4
learned and revealed them to i-s. Mt 11:25
mouths of children and nursing i-s Mt 21:16
even bringing i-s to Him so He Lk 18:15
but be i-s in evil and adult in 1Co 14:20
because he is an i. Heb 5:13
Like newborn i-s, desire the 1Pt 2:2

INFATUATED
He became i with Dinah, daughter Gn 34:3
son Amnon was i with her. 2Sm 13:1
would you be i with a forbidden Pr 5:20

INFECTION
will examine the i on the skin Lv 13:3
someone who has an i or leprosy 2Sm 3:29

INFECTIOUS
with an i skin disease is Lv 13:45
in a case of i skin disease, Dt 24:8

INFERIOR
jealousy with an i people; Dt 32:21
I am not i to you. Jb 12:3; 13:2
another kingdom, i to yours, and Dn 2:39
We are not i if we don't eat, 1Co 8:8
in no way i to the "super-apostles" 2Co 11:5
since I am in no way i to the 2Co 12:11
the i is blessed by the superior. Heb 7:7

INFERTILE
will be no i male or female Dt 7:14

INFINITE
His understanding is i. Ps 147:5

INFLAME
Mockers i a city, but the wise Pr 29:8
females and were i-d in their lust Rm 1:27

INFLATE
Look, his ego is i-d; Hab 2:4
none of you will be i-d with pride 1Co 4:6
Now some are i-d with pride, 1Co 4:18
And you are i-d with pride 1Co 5:2
Knowledge i-s with pride, but 1Co 8:1
realm and i-d without cause Col 2:18

INFLICT
on you I i-ed on the Egyptians Ex 15:26
and heals the wounds He i-ed. Is 30:26
After they had i-ed many blows Ac 16:23
Is God unrighteous to i wrath? Rm 3:5
and they i injury with them. Rv 9:19

INFORM
someone i-s him about the sin Lv 4:23
turn would go and i King David, 2Sm 17:17
how Mordecai had i-ed on Bigthana Est 6:2
If a man i-s on his friends for a price, Jb 17:5
when I question you, you will i Me. Jb 38:3
i-ing (all) people of Your mighty Ps 145:12
was accurately i-ed about the Way, Ac 24:22

INFORMATION
back to me with accurate i, 1Sm 23:23

INFORMER
Then an i came to David and 2Sm 15:13

INFURIATE
i-ing Him with what your hands Dt 31:29
They i-d the LORD, Jdg 2:12
David was i-d with the man and 2Sm 12:5

INGATHERING
the Festival of I at the end Ex 23:16
the Festival of I at the turn Ex 34:22

INHABIT
the upright will i the land, Pr 2:21
justice will i the wilderness, Is 32:16

INHABITANT
all the i-s of the cities Gn 19:25
the world and its i-s, belong to Ps 24:1
let all the i-s of the world stand Ps 33:8
the earth and all its i-s shake, Ps 75:3
cities lie in ruins without i-s, Is 6:11
is abandoned; no i is left. Jr 4:29

INHABITED

I was rejoicing in His i world,	Pr 8:31
says to Jerusalem: She will be i,	Is 44:26
but formed it to be i	Is 45:18
This city will be i forever.	Jr 17:25
never again be i or lived in	Jr 50:39
I will cause the cities to be i,	Ezk 36:33
But Judah will be i forever,	Jl 3:20
to the ends of the i world,	Rm 10:18

INHERIT

and they will i {it} forever.	Ex 32:13
You will i their land, since I	Lv 20:24
me and make me i the iniquities	Jb 13:26
the humble will i the land	Ps 37:11
righteous will i the land and	Ps 37:29
The wise will i honor, but He	Pr 3:35
his household will i the wind,	Pr 11:29
The gullible i foolishness,	Pr 14:18
and wealth are i-ed from fathers,	Pr 19:14
blameless will i what is good.	Pr 28:10
refuge in Me will i the land and	Is 57:13
Our fathers i-ed only lies	Jr 16:19
gentle, because they will i the earth.	Mt 5:5
more and will i eternal life.	Mt 19:29
i the kingdom prepared for you	Mt 25:34
must I do to i eternal life?	Lk 10:25; 18:18
that he would i the world	Rm 4:13
unjust will not i God's kingdom?	1Co 6:9
and blood cannot i the kingdom	1Co 15:50
slave will never i with the son	Gl 4:30
as the name He i-ed is superior to	Heb 1:4
who are going to i salvation?	Heb 1:14
of those who i the promises	Heb 6:12
he wanted to i the blessing,	Heb 12:17
so that you can i a blessing.	1Pt 3:9
The victor will i these things,	Rv 21:7

INHERITANCE

Aaron, "You will not have an i	Nm 18:20
to be a people for His i,	Dt 4:20
give you their land as an i,	Dt 4:38
Levi has no i among his brothers, the LORD is his i,	Dt 18:2
His people, Jacob, His own i.	Dt 32:9
are Your people and Your i;	1Kg 8:51
I will make the nations Your i	Ps 2:8
indeed, I have a beautiful i.	Ps 16:6
and their i will last forever.	Ps 37:18
chooses for us our i—the pride	Ps 47:4

You revived Your i when it	Ps 68:9
He gave their land as an i,	Ps 135:12
good man leaves an i to his	Pr 13:22
An i gained prematurely will not	Pr 20:21
Wisdom is as good as an i,	Ec 7:11
{Israel is} the tribe of His i;	Jr 51:19
do not make Your i a disgrace,	Jl 2:17
let's kill him and take his i!	Mt 21:38
He didn't give him an i in it,	Ac 7:5
For if the i is from the law,	Gl 3:18
In Him we were also made His i,	Eph 1:11
is the down payment of our i,	Eph 1:14
has an i in the kingdom of the	Eph 5:5
in the saints' i in the light.	Col 1:12
the promise of the eternal i,	Heb 9:15
was going to receive as an i;	Heb 11:8
and into an i that is imperishable,	1Pt 1:4

INIQUITY

for the i of the Amorites has	Gn 15:16
because our i-ies are higher than	Ezr 9:6
How many i-ies and sins have I	Jb 13:23
and You would cover over my i.	Jb 14:17
You and did not conceal my i.	Ps 32:5
The i of my foes surrounds me.	Ps 49:5
I-ies overwhelm me; only You can	Ps 65:3
and a wicked mouth swallows i.	Pr 19:28
terror to those who practice i.	Pr 21:15
people weighed down with i,	Is 1:4
crushed because of our i-ies;	Is 53:5
punished Him for the i of us all.	Is 53:6
and He will carry their i-ies.	Is 53:11
But your i-ies have built barriers	Is 59:2
conceive trouble and give birth to i.	Is 59:4
are with us, and we know our i-ies:	Is 59:12
or remember {our} i forever.	Is 64:9
not die for his father's i.	Ezk 18:17
I cleanse you from all your i-ies,	Ezk 36:33
removing i and passing over	Mc 7:18
He will vanquish our i-ies.	Mc 7:19
by bitterness and bound by i.	Ac 8:23

INJURE

When a man's ox i-s his neighbor's	Ex 21:35
and it is i-d or dies while its	Ex 22:14

INJURY

born prematurely, but there is no i,	Ex 21:22
Whatever i he inflicted on the	Lv 24:20
There is no remedy for your i;	Nah 3:19

INJUSTICE

for there is no i or partiality — 2Ch 19:7
and i shuts its mouth. — Jb 5:16
who drinks i like water? — Jb 15:16
If you banish i from your tent — Jb 22:23
if there is i on my hands, — Ps 7:3
and all i shuts its mouth. — Ps 107:42
than great income with i. — Pr 16:8
looked for justice but saw i, — Is 5:7
plowed wickedness and reaped i; — Hs 10:13
and founds a town with i! — Hab 2:12
Is there i with God? — Rm 9:14
Why not rather put up with i? — 1Co 6:7

INK

was writing on the scroll in i. — Jr 36:18
not written with i but with the — 2Co 3:3
to do so with paper and i. — 2Jn 12
to write to you with pen and i. — 3Jn 13

INLAID

Its interior is i with love by — Sg 3:10

INN

was no room for them at the i. — Lk 2:7
him to an i, and took care — Lk 10:34

INNER

sanctuary and the i sanctuary. — 1Kg 6:5
desire integrity in the i self, — Ps 51:6
The i man and the heart are — Ps 64:6
to someone in the i recesses of — Am 6:10
Look, he's in the i rooms! — Mt 24:26
For in my i self I joyfully — Rm 7:22
our i person is being renewed — 2Co 4:16
His Spirit in the i man, — Eph 3:16
that enters the i sanctuary — Heb 6:19

INNERMOST

and my i being was wounded — Ps 73:21
goes down to one's i being. — Pr 18:8
LORD, searching the i parts. — Pr 20:27
beatings cleanse the i parts. — Pr 20:30
My i being will cheer when your — Pr 23:16
goes down to one's i being. — Pr 26:22

INNKEEPER

two denarii, gave them to the i, — Lk 10:35

INNOCENCE

wash my hands in i and go around — Ps 26:6
wash my hands in i for nothing? — Ps 73:13
will they be incapable of i? — Hs 8:5

INNOCENT

Do not kill the i and the just, — Ex 23:7
the guilt of shedding i blood, — Dt 19:13
a bribe to kill an i person. — Dt 27:25
are forever i before the LORD — 2Sm 3:28
and the i will divide up his — Jb 27:17
or take a bribe against the i — Ps 15:5
and condemn the i to death. — Ps 94:21
They shed i blood—the blood of — Ps 106:38
hands that shed i blood, — Pr 6:17
not good to fine an i person, — Pr 17:26
the justice due the i. — Pr 18:5
and they rush to shed i blood. — Is 59:7
for I was found i before Him. — Dn 6:22
violate the Sabbath and are i? — Mt 12:5
would not have condemned the i. — Mt 12:7
sinned by betraying i blood, — Mt 27:4
I am i of this man's blood. — Mt 27:24
day that I am i of everyone's — Ac 20:26
is good, yet i about what is — Rm 16:19
holy, i, undefiled, separated — Heb 7:26

INNUMERABLE

enormous guilt and your i sins. — Jr 30:14
are many and your sins i. — Am 5:12
of heaven and as i as the grains — Heb 11:12

INQUIRE

So she went to i of the LORD. — Gn 25:22
Do not i about their gods, — Dt 12:30
the Israelites i-d of the LORD — Jdg 1:1; 20:27
Please i of God so we will know — Jdg 18:5
was going to i of God would say — 1Sm 9:9
So David i-d of the LORD: — 1Sm 23:2
Once again, David i-d of the LORD — 1Sm 23:4
He i-d of the LORD, but the LORD — 1Sm 28:6
later, David i-d of the LORD: — 2Sm 2:1
Then David i-d of the LORD: — 2Sm 5:19
years, so David i-d of the LORD. — 2Sm 21:1
Go i of Baal-zebub, — 2Kg 1:2
Go and i of the LORD for me, — 2Kg 22:13
but he did not i of the LORD. — 1Ch 10:14
who is sending you to i of Me: — Jr 37:7
not seek the LORD or i of Him. — Zph 1:6
They i-d into what time or what — 1Pt 1:11

INSANE

pretended to be i in their — 1Sm 21:13
and the inspired man is i, — Hs 9:7

INSCRIBE

tablets i-d by the finger of God.	Ex 31:18
They were i-d on both sides	Ex 32:15
stone tablets, i-d by God's finger	Dt 9:10
or were i-d in stone forever by an	Jb 19:24
presence and i it on a scroll;	Is 30:8
I have i-d you on the palms of My	Is 49:16
clearly i it on tablets so one	Hab 2:2
found an altar on which was i-d:	Ac 17:23
a new name is i-d that no one	Rv 2:17
names were i-d,	Rv 21:12

INSCRIPTION

wrote on it an i like the	Ex 39:30
but none could read the i	Dn 5:8
Whose image and i is this?	Mt 22:20
The i of the charge written	Mk 15:26
An i was above Him:	Lk 23:38
on the cross. The i was: JESUS	Jn 19:19
stands firm, having this i:	2Tm 2:19

INSECTS

All winged i that walk on all	Lv 11:20
All winged i are unclean for you	Dt 14:19

INSENSITIVE

Their hearts are hard and i,	Ps 119:70

INSIDE

it with pitch i and outside.	Gn 6:14
LORD his God from i the fish:	Jnh 2:1
but i they are full of greed and	Mt 23:25
First clean the i of the cup,	Mt 23:26
but i are full of dead men's	Mt 23:27
he will answer from i and say,	Lk 11:7
Those i the city must leave it,	Lk 21:21
you not judge those who are i?	1Co 5:12
struggles on the outside, fears i.	2Co 7:5
covered with eyes around and i.	Rv 4:8
writing on the i and on the back	Rv 5:1

INSIDES

And Eglon's i came out.	Jdg 3:22
and all his i spilled out.	Ac 1:18

INSIGHT

very great i, and understanding	1Kg 4:29
LORD give you i and	1Ch 22:12
a wise son with i and	2Ch 2:12
a man of i from the descendants	Ezr 8:18
his words are without i.	Jb 34:35
His instructions have good i.	Ps 111:10

I have more i than all my	Ps 119:99
you call out to i and lift your	Pr 2:3
A man is praised for his i,	Pr 12:8
I is a fountain of life for its	Pr 16:22
A person's i gives him patience	Pr 19:11
despise the i of your words.	Pr 23:9
i to say, "I burned half of it	Is 44:19
he was found to have i,	Dn 5:11
to understand my i about the	Eph 3:4

INSIGHTFUL

son Zechariah, an i counselor	1Ch 26:14

INSIGNIFICANT

I am so i. How can I answer You	Jb 40:4
I am i and despised, but I do	Ps 119:141
I will make you i among the	Ob 2
the world's i and despised	1Co 1:28

INSIST

I i on buying it from you for a	2Sm 24:24
I i on paying the full price,	1Ch 21:24
But he kept i-ing, "If I have to die	Mk 14:31
I want you to i on these things	Ti 3:8

INSPECT

Moses i-ed all the work they had	Ex 39:43
and I i-ed the walls of Jerusalem	Neh 2:13
You i him every morning, and put	Jb 7:18

INSPIRED

a fool, and the i man is insane	Hs 9:7
then that David, i by the Spirit	Mt 22:43
All Scripture is i by God and is	2Tm 3:16

INSTANT

a nation be delivered in an i?	Is 66:8
Sodom ... was overthrown in an i	Lm 4:6

INSTANTLY

I her flow of blood ceased,	Mk 5:29
and i she was restored and began	Lk 13:13
I he could see, and he began to	Lk 18:43
I the man got well, picked up	Jn 5:9
I she dropped dead at his feet.	Ac 5:10

INSTEAD

a crown of beauty i of ashes,	Is 61:3
release Barabbas to them i.	Mk 15:11
give him a snake i of a fish?	Lk 11:11

INSTINCT

creatures of i born to be caught	2Pt 2:12
they know by i, like unreasoning	Jd 10

INSTINCTIVELY

i do what the law demands,	Rm 2:14

INSTITUTED

those that exist are i by God.	Rm 13:1
By faith he i the Passover and	Heb 11:28

INSTITUTION

to every human i because of the	1Pt 2:13

INSTRUCT

I them about the statutes and	Ex 18:20
to do exactly as they i you.	Dt 17:10
Your good Spirit to i them.	Neh 9:20
You have i-ed many and have	Jb 4:3
the earth, and it will i you;	Jb 12:8
at night my conscience i-s me.	Ps 16:7
I will i you and show you the	Ps 32:8
The One who i-s nations, the One	Ps 94:10
for You Yourself have i-ed me.	Ps 119:102
I a wise man, and he will be	Pr 9:9
A wise heart i-s its mouth and	Pr 16:23
teaches him order; He i-s him.	Is 28:26
This man had been i-ed in the way	Ac 18:25
superior, being i-ed from the law,	Rm 2:18
and able to i one another.	Rm 15:14
Lord's mind, that he may i Him?	1Co 2:16
I those who are rich in the	1Tm 6:17
i-ing his opponents with	2Tm 2:25
are able to i you for salvation	2Tm 3:15
i-ing us to deny godlessness and	Ti 2:12

INSTRUCTION

commands, My statutes, and My i-s.	Gn 26:5
or not they will follow My i-s.	Ex 16:4
Moses gave us i, a possession	Dt 33:4
This book of i must not depart	Jos 1:8
I have carried out the LORD's i-s.	1Sm 15:13
carry out the i and the command	2Ch 14:4
book of the LORD's i with them.	2Ch 17:9
reliable i-s, and good decrees	Neh 9:13
his delight is in the LORD's i,	Ps 1:2
The i of the LORD is perfect,	Ps 19:7
The i of his God is in his heart	Ps 37:31
Your i resides within me.	Ps 40:8
You hate i and turn your back on	Ps 50:17
forsake My i and do not live	Ps 89:30
but I delight in Your i.	Ps 119:70
I from Your lips is better for	Ps 119:72
live, for Your i is my delight.	Ps 119:77
and Your i is true.	Ps 119:142

to those who love Your i;	Ps 119:165
and Your i is my delight.	Ps 119:174
fools despise wisdom and i.	Pr 1:7
Listen, my son, to your father's i,	Pr 1:8
Hold on to i; don't let go	Pr 4:13
Accept my i instead of silver,	Pr 8:10
Listen to i and be wise;	Pr 8:33
Whoever loves i loves knowledge	Pr 12:1
has contempt for i will pay the	Pr 13:13
fear of the LORD is wisdom's i,	Pr 15:33
and receive i so that you may be	Pr 19:20
If you stop listening to i,	Pr 19:27
yourself to i and listen to	Pr 23:12
I looked, and received i:	Pr 24:32
and loving i is on her tongue.	Pr 31:26
For i will go out of Zion and	Is 2:3
Seal up the i among my disciples	Is 8:16
for i will come from Me,	Is 51:4
people in whose heart is My i:	Is 51:7
but i will perish from the priests	Ezk 7:26
suitable for i in all wisdom,	Dn 1:4
by following His i-s that He set	Dn 9:10
For i will go out of Zion and	Mc 4:2
True i was in his mouth, and	Mal 2:6
Remember the i of Moses My	Mal 4:4
before was written for our i,	Rm 15:4
the training and i of the Lord.	Eph 6:4
not obey our i in this letter,	2Th 3:14
the goal of our i is love from a	1Tm 1:5
you this i in keeping with	1Tm 1:18

INSTRUCTOR

an i of the ignorant, a teacher	Rm 2:20
can have 10,000 i-s in Christ,	1Co 4:15

INSTRUMENT

joy accompanied by musical i-s	1Ch 15:16
LORD day after day with loud i-s.	2Ch 30:21
with the musical i-s of David,	Neh 12:36
play stringed i-s all the days	Is 38:20
their own musical i-s like David.	Am 6:5
is My chosen i to carry My name	Ac 9:15
will be a special i, set apart	2Tm 2:21

INSULT (n)

Make their i-s return on their own	Neh 4:4
I have endured i-s because of You	Ps 69:7
Take i and contempt away	
from me	Ps 119:22
whoever ignores an i is sensible.	Pr 12:16

endure the **i**-s of the nations. — Ezk 34:29
I will no longer allow the **i**-s of — Ezk 36:15
there began to yell **i**-s at Him: — Lk 23:39
weaknesses, in **i**-s, in — 2Co 12:10
i and slander must be removed — Eph 4:31
not paying back evil for evil or **i** for **i** — 1Pt 3:9

INSULT (v)
it is not an enemy who **i**-s me — Ps 55:12
of those who **i** You have fallen — Ps 69:9
Will the enemy **i** Your name — Ps 74:10
foolish people has **i**-ed Your name. — Ps 74:18
who mocks the poor **i**-s his Maker, — Pr 17:5
you when they **i** you and — Mt 5:11
exclude you, **i** you, and slander — Lk 6:22
say these things You **i** us too. — Lk 11:45
and He will be mocked, **i**-ed, spit — Lk 18:32
what Paul was saying by **i**-ing him. — Ac 13:45
of those who **i** You have fallen — Rm 15:3
and **i**-ed the Spirit of grace? — Heb 10:29

INTACT
The camp was **i**, and they had — 2Kg 7:7

INTEGRITY
if you walk before Me ... with **i** — 1Kg 9:4
since they worked with **i**. — 2Kg 12:15
hands since they work with **i**. — 2Kg 22:7
He was a man of perfect **i**, — Jb 1:1
He still retains his **i**, even though you — Jb 2:3
God does not reject a person of **i**, — Jb 8:20
will maintain my **i** until I die. — Jb 27:5
and He will recognize my **i**. — Jb 31:6
May **i** and uprightness keep me, — Ps 25:21
I have lived with **i** and have trusted — Ps 26:1
You supported me because of my **i** — Ps 41:12
You desire **i** in the inner self — Ps 51:6
pay attention to the way of **i**. — Ps 101:2
all who call out to Him with **i**. — Ps 145:18
who lives with **i** lives securely — Pr 10:9
The **i** of the upright guides them — Pr 11:3
lives with **i** fears the LORD, — Pr 14:2
who lives with **i** is righteous; — Pr 20:7
who lives with **i** than a rich man — Pr 28:6
despise the one who speaks with **i**. — Am 5:10
he is without **i**. But the righteous — Hab 2:4
with **i** and dignity in your teaching. — Ti 2:7

INTELLIGENCE
you have insight, **i**, and — Dn 5:14

INTELLIGENT
is no one as **i** and wise as you. — Gn 41:39
The woman was **i** and beautiful, — 1Sm 25:3
The **i** person restrains his words — Pr 17:27
I am the least **i** of men, and I — Pr 30:2
Sergius Paulus, an **i** man. — Ac 13:7

INTELLIGENTLY
Jesus saw that he answered **i**, — Mk 12:34

INTELLIGIBLE
use your tongue for **i** speech, — 1Co 14:9

INTEND
But if he didn't **i** any harm, — Ex 21:13
If the LORD had **i**-ed to kill us, — Jdg 13:23
since the LORD **i**-s to kill him. — 1Sm 2:25
My father Saul **i**-s to kill you. — 1Sm 19:2
Though they **i** to harm you and — Ps 21:11
the flock **i**-ed for slaughter. — Zch 11:4
Where does He **i** to go so we — Jn 7:35
kindness is **i**-ed to lead you to — Rm 2:4
other languages is **i**-ed as a sign, — 1Co 14:22

INTENSIFY
I will **i** your labor pains; — Gn 3:16
When the battle **i**-ed against Saul, — 1Sm 31:3

INTENT
at him without malicious **i** — Nm 35:22
Lord that the **i** of your heart — Ac 8:22
or impurity or an **i** to deceive. — 1Th 2:3

INTENTION
I ... find out my father has evil **i**-s — 1Sm 20:9
understands the **i** of every thought. — 1Ch 28:9
with no **i** of buying wisdom? — Pr 17:16
know the LORD's **i**-s or understand — Mc 4:12
and reveal the **i**-s of the hearts. — 1Co 4:5
we are not ignorant of his **i**-s. — 2Co 2:11

INTERCEDE
But Moses **i**-d with the LORD his — Ex 32:11
And Moses **i**-d for the people. — Nm 21:7
sins against the LORD, who can **i** — 1Sm 2:25
But Hezekiah had **i**-d for them, — 2Ch 30:18
sin of many and **i**-d for the rebels. — Is 53:12
amazed that there was no one **i**-ing; — Is 59:16
I will **i** for you in a time of — Jr 15:11
let them **i** with the LORD of — Jr 27:18
the Spirit Himself **i**-s for us with — Rm 8:26
because He **i**-s for the saints — Rm 8:27

right hand of God and **i**-s for us.   Rm 8:34
He always lives to **i** for them.   Heb 7:25

INTERCESSION
perseverance and **i** for all the   Eph 6:18
prayers, **i**-s, and thanksgivings   1Tm 2:1

INTERCOURSE
has sexual **i** with an animal   Ex 22:19
You are not to have sexual **i** with   Lv 18:9
who has sexual **i** with any animal.   Dt 27:21
left natural sexual **i** with females   Rm 1:27

INTEREST
you must not charge him **i**.   Ex 22:25
not profit or take **i** from him,   Lv 25:36
You may charge a foreigner **i**,   Dt 23:20
let us stop charging this **i**.   Neh 5:10
who does not lend his money at **i**   Ps 15:5
excessive **i** collects it for one who   Pr 28:8
doesn't lend at **i** or for profit   Ezk 18:8
received my money back with **i**.   Mt 25:27
not (only) for his own **i**-s, but also   Php 2:4
genuinely care about your **i**-s;   Php 2:20
all seek their own **i**-s, not those   Php 2:21
but having a sick **i** in disputes   1Tm 6:4

INTERIOR
overlaid the **i** of the temple   1Kg 6:21

INTERMARRY
i with us; give your daughters   Gn 34:9
Do not **i** with them.   Dt 7:3
and if you **i** or associate with   Jos 23:12
Do not **i** with them, and   1Kg 11:2
and **i** with the peoples who   Ezr 9:14

INTERPRET
but there is no one to **i** them.   Gn 40:8
a dream, and no one can **i** it.   Gn 41:15
tell fortunes, **i** omens, practice   Dt 18:10
and the ability to **i** dreams,   Dn 5:12
don't you know how to **i** this time?   Lk 12:56
He **i**-ed for them the things   Lk 24:27
speak in languages? Do all **i**?   1Co 12:30
unless he **i**-s so that the church   1Co 14:5
should pray that he can **i**.   1Co 14:13
and someone must **i**.   1Co 14:27

INTERPRETATION
Don't **i**-s belong to God?   Gn 40:8
"This is its **i**," Joseph said to   Gn 40:12

account of the dream and its **i**,   Jdg 7:15
who knows the **i** of a matter?   Ec 8:1
tell me the dream and its **i**,   Dn 2:5
I will give him the **i**.   Dn 2:24
is true, and its **i** certain.   Dn 2:45
they could not make its **i** known   Dn 4:7
This is the **i**, Your Majesty,   Dn 4:24
about you, that you can give **i**-s   Dn 5:16
inscription and give me its **i**,   Dn 5:16
he let me know the **i** of these things   Dn 7:16
to another, **i** of languages.   1Co 12:10
(another) language, or an **i**.   1Co 14:26
comes from one's own **i**,   2Pt 1:20

INTERPRETER
there was an **i** between them.   Gn 42:23
But if there is no **i**, that person   1Co 14:28

INTERVENED
But Phinehas stood up and **i**,   Ps 106:30
reported how God first **i** to take   Ac 15:14

INTESTINES
and spilled his **i** out on the   2Sm 20:10
including a disease of the **i**,   2Ch 21:15

INTIMATE
had never been **i** with a man.   Jdg 11:39
When he was **i** with her, the LORD   Ru 4:13
Then Elkanah was **i** with his wife   1Sm 1:19
but he was not **i** with them.   2Sm 20:3
but he was not **i** with her.   1Kg 1:4
I was then **i** with the prophetess   Is 8:3
I have not been **i** with a man?   Lk 1:34

INTIMATELY
Adam knew his wife Eve **i**,   Gn 4:1
Cain knew his wife **i**,   Gn 4:17
Adam knew his wife **i** again,   Gn 4:25
who had not known a man **i**.   Gn 24:16
he did not know her **i** again.   Gn 38:26
not know her **i** until she gave   Mt 1:25

INTIMIDATE
Do not be **i**-ed by anyone, for   Dt 1:17
they were all trying to **i** us,   Neh 6:9
Tobiah sent letters to **i** me.   Neh 6:19
Do not be **i**-ed by them or I will   Jr 1:17

INTOXICATE
fragrance of your perfume is **i**-ing;   Sg 1:3
Drink, be **i**-d with love!   Sg 5:1

INTRIGUE

king, skilled in **i**, will come to	Dn 8:23
seize the kingdom by **i**.	Dn 11:21

INTRODUCED

customs the kings of Israel had **i**.	2Kg 17:8
a better hope is **i**, through which	Heb 7:19

INVADE

Pul king of Assyria **i-d** the land,	2Kg 15:19
king of Assyria **i-d** the whole land	2Kg 17:5
nations have **i-d** Your inheritance	Ps 79:1
For a nation has **i-d** My land,	Jl 1:6
When Assyria **i-s** our land,	Mc 5:5

INVALIDATE

You completely **i** God's command	Mk 7:9

INVENT

i-ing them in your own mind.	Neh 6:8
and **i** their own musical instruments	Am 6:5
If a man of spirit comes and **i-s** lies:	Mc 2:11

INVENTORS

proud, boastful, **i** of evil,	Rm 1:30

INVESTIGATE

they came to **i** the entire land.	Jos 2:3
the report was **i-d** and verified,	Est 2:23
We have **i-d** this, and it is true!	Jb 5:27
glory of kings to **i** a matter.	Pr 25:2
hearts of kings cannot be **i-d**.	Pr 25:3
I have carefully **i-d** everything	Lk 1:3
I and you will see that no	Jn 7:52
were going to **i** his case more	Ac 23:15
to you searched and carefully **i-d**.	1Pt 1:10

INVESTIGATION

judges are to make a careful **i**,	Dt 19:18
After they made a thorough **i**,	Jdg 6:29
shatters the mighty without an **i**	Jb 34:24

INVISIBLE

His **i** attributes, that is, His	Rm 1:20
He is the image of the **i** God,	Col 1:15
visible and the **i**, whether	Col 1:16
immortal, **i**, the only God,	1Tm 1:17
as one who sees Him who is **i**.	Heb 11:27

INVITE

Did you **i** us here to rob us?	Jdg 14:15
Then **i** Jesse to the sacrifice,	1Sm 16:3
and Absalom **i-d** all the king's	2Sm 13:23
but he did not **i** Nathan	1Kg 1:10

Queen Esther **i-d** no one but me to	Est 5:12
opens his lips **i-s** his own ruin.	Pr 13:3
summon those **i-d** to the banquet	Mt 22:3
the city and **i** everyone you find	Mt 22:9
For many are **i-d**, but few are	Mt 22:14
the Pharisees **i-d** Him to eat with	Lk 7:36
a parable to those who were **i-d**,	Lk 14:7
a dinner, don't **i** your friends	Lk 14:12
a banquet, **i** those who are poor,	Lk 14:13
disciples were **i-d** to the wedding	Jn 2:2
Peter then **i-d** them in and gave	Ac 10:23
and were **i-d** to stay with them	Ac 28:14
of the unbelievers **i-s** you over	1Co 10:27
are those **i-d** to the marriage	Rv 19:9

INVOICE

'Take your **i**,' he told him	Lk 16:6

INVOKE

Israel will **i** blessings by you,	Gn 48:20
You must not **i** the names of	Ex 23:13
may the king **i** the LORD	2Sm 14:11
who **i** You deceitfully.	Ps 139:20
from the east who **i-s** My name.	Is 41:25
never again be **i-d** by anyone of	Jr 44:26
Yahweh's name must not be **i-d**.	Am 6:10

INVOLVE

I will not be **i-d** with evil.	Ps 101:4
I do not get **i-d** with things too	Ps 131:1
because fear **i-s** punishment.	1Jn 4:18

INWARD

was You who created my **i** parts;	Ps 139:13

INWARDLY

their mouths, but they curse **i**.	Ps 62:4
clothing but **i** are ravaging	Mt 7:15
a person is a Jew who is one **i**,	Rm 2:29

IRON

your sky like **i** and your land	Lv 26:19
His bed was made of **i**.	Dt 3:11
out of Egypt's **i** furnace to be	Dt 4:20
whose rocks are **i** and from whose	Dt 8:9
He will place an **i** yoke on your	Dt 28:48
even though they have **i** chariots	Jos 17:18
because those people had **i** chariots.	Jdg 1:19
Jabin had 900 **i** chariots,	Jdg 4:3
or any **i** tool was heard in the	1Kg 6:7
it there, and made the **i** float.	2Kg 6:6
He regards **i** as straw, and	Jb 41:27

break them with a rod of i; Ps 2:9
I sharpens i, and one man Pr 27:17
and cut the i bars in two. Is 45:2
land of Egypt, out of the i furnace. Jr 11:4
Take an i plate and set it up as Ezk 4:3
legs were i, and its feet were partly i Dn 2:33
strong, with large i teeth. Dn 7:7
threshed Gilead with i sledges. Am 1:3
them with an i scepter; Rv 2:27
all nations with an i scepter Rv 12:5
them with an i scepter. Rv 19:15

IRRATIONAL
judges of the earth to be i. Is 40:23
these people, like i animals 2Pt 2:12

IRRECONCILABLE
unloving, i, slanderers, without 2Tm 3:3

IRRESPONSIBLE
when I planned this, was I i? 2Co 1:17
we were not i among you; 2Th 3:7

IRRESPONSIBLY
who walks i and not according 2Th 3:6

IRREVERENCE
him dead on the spot for his i, 2Sm 6:7

IRREVERENT
the unholy and i, for those who 1Tm 1:9
to do with i and silly myths. 1Tm 4:7
to you, avoiding i, empty speech 1Tm 6:20
But avoid i, empty speech, for 2Tm 2:16
any immoral or i person like Heb 12:16

IRREVOCABLE
it is i and cannot be changed. Dn 6:8
gracious gifts and calling are i. Rm 11:29

IRRIGATED
sowed your seed and i by hand as Dt 11:10
life will be like an i garden, Jr 31:12

ISAAC
Son of Abraham and Sarah; fulfillment of a promise (Gn 17:17; 21:5). God tested Abraham by asking him to sacrifice Isaac (Gn 22; Heb 11:17-19). Married Rebekah (Gn 24). Heir to Abraham's promise (Gn 25:5,11; Ps 105:9; Rm 9:7). Father of Esau and Jacob (Gn 25:21-26); blessed Jacob (Gn 27). Lied to Abimelech in Gerar about Rebekah (26:7-11). Died in Hebron (35:27-29).

ISAIAH
Son of Amoz; prophet to four kings of Judah (Is 1:1). Called (Is 6). Sons' names were symbolic (7:3; 8:3).

ISCARIOT
Surname of Judas the betrayer (Mt 10:4; 26:14; Mk 3:19; 14:10; Lk 6:16; 22:3; Jn 12:4) and his father Simon (Jn 6:71; 13:2,26).

ISH-BOSHETH
Saul's son; tried to become king (2Sm 2:8-17; 3:6-16); was murdered (2Sm 4).

ISHMAEL
1. Son of Abraham and Hagar (Gn 16:11-15). Received a blessing but not the promise (17:18-21). Descendants are perpetual opponents of Israel (25:18).
2. Descendant of Jonathan (1Ch 8:38; 9:44).
3. Son of Nethaniah; assassinated Gedaliah (2Kg 25:25; Jr 40–41).
4. Jehoiadah's commander (2Ch 23:1).
5. Jew with foreign wife (Ezr 10:22).

ISHMAELITES
sell him to the I and not lay a Gn 37:27
him from the I who had brought Gn 39:1
earrings because they were I. Jdg 8:24
the tents of Edom and the I, Ps 83:6

ISLAND
the coasts and i-s bring tribute, Ps 72:10
the many coasts and i-s be glad. Ps 97:1
He lifts up the i-s like fine dust Is 40:15
Be silent before Me, i-s! Is 41:1
you i-s with your inhabitants. Is 42:10
and i-s were your regular markets. Ezk 27:15
the coasts and i-s are appalled at Ezk 27:35
must run aground on a certain i. Ac 27:26
to the leading man of the i, Ac 28:7
was on the i called Patmos Rv 1:9
mountain and i was moved from Rv 6:14
Every i fled, and the mountains Rv 16:20

ISN'T
I this the David they sing about 1Sm 29:5
I there a prophet of Yahweh 1Kg 22:7
i this what I said while I was Jnh 4:2

rebellion of Jacob? I it Samaria   Mc 1:5
I this Jesus the son of Joseph   Jn 6:42

ISOLATE
One who i-s himself pursues   Pr 18:1
they want to i you so you will   Gl 4:17

ISOLATION
of your kingdom, yet living in i.   Est 3:8

ISRAEL
Name God gave Jacob (Gn 32:28; 35:10). Also his descendants—God's chosen people—and their land (Ex 3:16; 1Sm 13:19; 15:35; 1Kg 4:1; Mt 2:6,20; Php 3:5). In the divided kingdom, the northern (1Kg 12:20).

ISRAELITE
Rehoboam reigned over the I-s   1Kg 12:17
The I-s persisted in all the sins   2Kg 17:22
evil the I-s and Judeans have done   Jr 32:32
I-s and Judeans will come together,   Jr 50:4
Judeans and the I-s will be gathered   Hs 1:11
LORD loves the I-s though they   Hs 3:1
about him, "Here is a true I;   Jn 1:47
They are I-s, and to them belong   Rm 9:4
For I too am an I, a descendant   Rm 11:1
Are they I-s? So am I.   2Co 11:22

ISSACHAR
1. Son of Jacob and Leah (Gn 30:18). Tribe with territory from Jezreel to Tabor (Jos 19:17-23); its troops who rallied to David understood the times (1Ch 12:32).
2. Korahite gatekeeper (1Ch 26:5).

ISSUE
King Cyrus to i a proclamation   Ezr 1:1
he i-d a decree concerning the   Ezr 6:3
the law was i-d in the fortress   Est 3:15
law was also i-d in the fortress   Est 8:14
his ruler will i from him.   Jr 30:21
The LORD has i-d a decree against   Lm 1:17
You as king have i a decree that   Dn 3:10
Therefore I i a decree that   Dn 3:29
I i a decree that in all my   Dn 6:26
From the i-ing of the decree to   Dn 9:25
Then he i-d a decree in Nineveh: Jnh 3:7

ITALIAN
what was called the I Regiment.   Ac 10:1

ITALY
come from I with his wife   Ac 18:2
that we were to sail to I,   Ac 27:1
Those who are from I greet you.   Heb 13:24

ITCH
they have an i to hear something   2Tm 4:3

ITEMS
the man to whom these i belong.   Gn 38:25

ITHAMAR
Fourth son of Aaron (Ex 6:23; 28:1; Nm 26:20; 1Ch 6:3; 24:1); took over priesthood when their brothers died (Lv 10:6,12,16; Nm 3:4; 1Ch 24:2); in charge of the Levites (Ex 38:21; Nm 4:28,33; 7:8).

ITHIEL
man's oration to I, to I and Ucal: Pr 30:1

ITINERANT
some of the i Jewish exorcists   Ac 19:13

ITSELF
You are not to reap what grows by i   Lv 25:5
will mourn, every family by i: Zch 12:12
tomorrow will worry about i.   Mt 6:34
divided against i will stand.   Mt 12:25
and dies, it remains by i.   Jn 12:24
in a separate place by i.   Jn 20:7
which opened to them by i.   Ac 12:10
that nothing is unclean in i.   Rm 14:14
have works, is dead by i.   Jms 2:17

ITTAI
But in response, I vowed to the   2Sm 15:21
one third under I the Gittite.   2Sm 18:2
I son of Ribai from Gibeah of   2Sm 23:29

ITUREA
the region of I and Trachonitis   Lk 3:1

IVORY
also made a large i throne and   1Kg 10:18
gold, silver, i, apes, and   1Kg 10:22
the i palace he built   1Kg 22:39
from i palaces harps bring you   Ps 45:8
His body is an i panel covered   Sg 5:14
Your neck is like a tower of i,   Sg 7:4
brought back i tusks and ebony   Ezk 27:15
{inlaid with} i will be destroyed,   Am 3:15
lie on beds {inlaid with} i,   Am 6:4
wood products; objects of i;   Rv 18:12

JABAL
Son of Lamech (Gn 4:20).

JABBOK
Jacob ... crossed the ford of J.	Gn 32:22
land from the Arnon to the J,	Nm 21:24
and up to the J River, the border	Dt 3:16

JABESH
City in Gilead, also called Jabesh-gilead. Wives taken for Benjaminites (Jdg 21:8-14); people rescued from Ammonites by Saul (1Sm 11:1-11); recovered Saul's bones (1Sm 31:11-13; 1Ch 10:11-12); rewarded by David (2Sm 2:4-5; 21:12).

JABEZ
Israelite who asked for and received a blessing (1Ch 4:9-10).

JABIN
A king of Canaan, whose commander Sisera was defeated by Israel (Jdg 4–5).

JACHIN
right pillar and named it J;	1Kg 7:21

JACINTH
the third row, a j, an agate	Ex 28:19
the eleventh j, the twelfth	Rv 21:20

JACKALS
a brother to j and a companion	Jb 30:29
in a haunt of j and have covered	Ps 44:19
they will become the j' prey.	Ps 63:10
will become a dwelling for j,	Is 34:13
a heap of rubble, a j' den.	Jr 9:11
Even j offer {their} breasts to	Lm 4:3
Israel, are like j among ruins.	Ezk 13:4
howl like the j and mourn like	Mc 1:8
his inheritance to the desert j.	Mal 1:3

JACOB
1. Son of Isaac and Rebekah; younger twin brother of Esau (Gn 25:21-26). Took birthright (25:33); fled Esau (27:41–28:5). Received the promise (28:10-22). Worked for his wives (29:1-30). Wrestled with God

(32:22-32); God changed his name to Israel (32:28; 49:2). Reconciled with Esau (33:4-16). Fathered the twelve tribes (29:21–30:24; 35:16-18). Went to Egypt (46:1-7). Died there, buried in Hebron (49:29–50:14). Ancestor of Jesus (Mt 1:2).

2. Father of Mary's husband, Joseph (Mt 1:15-16).

Even so, I loved J,	Mal 1:2
over the house of J forever,	Lk 1:33
J-'s well was there, and Jesus	Jn 4:6
and J went down to Egypt.	Ac 7:15
J I have loved, but Esau I have	Rm 9:13
By faith J, when he was dying	Heb 11:21

JAEL
Woman who killed Sisera (Jdg 4:17-22).

JAIL
and placed him in j in the house	Jr 37:15
doors of the j during the night	Ac 5:19
foundations of the j were shaken,	Ac 16:26
both men and women in j,	Ac 22:4

JAILER
When the J woke up and saw the	Ac 16:27

JAIR
Gileadite Judge (Jdg 10:3-5).

JAIRUS
Synagogue leader whose daughter Jesus restored (Mk 5:22-43; Lk 8:41-56).

JAMBRES
as Jannes and J resisted Moses,	2Tm 3:8

JAMES
1. Apostle; son of Zebedee; brother of John (Mt 4:21; 10:2). At transfiguration (17:1); in Gethsemane (26:36-37). Martyred (Ac 12:2).

2. Apostle; son of Alphaeus (Mt 10:3).

3. Brother of Jesus (Mt 13:55; Gl 1:19). Believed after the resurrection (Jn 7:3; Ac 1:14; 1Co 15:7). Leader of church in Jerusalem (Ac 15; 21:18; Gl 2:9). Author (Jms 1:1).

4. Father of the Apostle Judas who was called Thaddaeus (Lk 6:16; cp. Mt 10:3).

JANNES
as J and Jambres resisted Moses,	2Tm 3:8

JAPHETH

Son of Noah (Gn 5:32; 9:18-27).

JAR

drink from the j-s the young men	Ru 2:9
flour j will not become empty	1Kg 17:14
in the house except a j of oil.	2Kg 4:2
can tilt the water j-s of heaven	Jb 38:37
and the j is shattered at the	Ec 12:6
so he made it into another j,	Jr 18:4
with an alabaster j of pure and	Mk 14:3
"Fill the j-s with water," Jesus told	Jn 2:7
the woman left her water j,	Jn 4:28
A j full of sour wine was	Jn 19:29
have this treasure in clay j-s,	2Co 4:7
there was a gold j containing	Heb 9:4

JASHAR

this written in the Book of J?	Jos 10:13
It is written in the Book of J:	2Sm 1:18

JASON

Countryman of Paul (Rm 16:21) threatened for harboring Paul (Ac 17:5-9).

JASPER

row, a beryl, an onyx, and a j.	Ex 28:20
beryl, onyx, and j, sapphire	Ezk 28:13
looked like j and carnelian	Rv 4:3
stone, like a j stone, bright as	Rv 21:11

JAVAN

Son of Japheth (Gn 10:2,4; 1Ch 1:5,7) and progenitor of the Greek people (Is 66:19; Ezk 27:13,19).

JAVELIN

laughs at the whirring of a j.	Jb 41:29
Draw the spear and j against my	Ps 35:3
They grasp bow and j.	Jr 50:42

JAW

you from the j-s of distress to	Jb 36:16
or pierce his j with a hook?	Jb 41:2
Who can open his j-s, surrounded	Jb 41:14
a bridle on the j-s of the peoples	Is 30:28
hooks in your j-s and make the	Ezk 29:4
hooks in your j-s, and bring you	Ezk 38:4
eases the yoke from their j-s;	Hs 11:4

JAWBONE

He found a fresh j of a donkey,	Jdg 15:15

JEALOUS

His brothers were j of him,	Gn 37:11
LORD your God, am a j God,	Ex 20:5
LORD, being j by nature, is a j God.	Ex 34:14
and he becomes j of her though	Nm 5:14
Moses asked him, "Are you j	Nm 11:29
is a consuming fire, a j God.	Dt 4:24
He is a holy God. He is a j God;	Jos 24:19
Don't be j of sinners;	Pr 23:17
and I will be j for My holy name	Ezk 39:25
the LORD became j for His land	Jl 2:18
The LORD is a j and avenging God	Nah 1:2
I am extremely j for Jerusalem	Zch 1:14
I am extremely j for Zion;	Zch 8:2
Are you j because I'm generous?	Mt 20:15
the Jews became j, and when they	Ac 17:5
I will make you j of those who	Rm 10:19
the Gentiles to make Israel j.	Rm 11:11
For I am j over you with a godly	2Co 11:2

JEALOUSLY

watched David j from that day	1Sm 18:9
caused to live in us yearns j?	Jms 4:5

JEALOUSY

if a feeling of j comes over him	Nm 5:14
provoked His j with foreign gods	Dt 32:16
and j slays the gullible.	Jb 5:2
and provoked His j with their	Ps 78:58
Will Your j keep burning like	Ps 79:5
For j enrages a husband, and he	Pr 6:34
but j is rottenness to the bones	Pr 14:30
flood, but who can withstand j?	Pr 27:4
due to a man's j of his friend.	Ec 4:4
consumed by the fire of His j.	Zph 1:18
Sadducees, were filled with j.	Ac 5:17
were filled with j and began to	Ac 13:45
not in quarreling and j.	Rm 13:13
are we provoking the Lord to j?	1Co 10:22
jealous over you with a godly j,	2Co 11:2
may be quarreling, j, outbursts	2Co 12:20
hatreds, strife, j, outbursts of	Gl 5:20

JEBUS

Canaanite name for Jerusalem (Jos 18:28; Jdg 19:10-11; 1Ch 11:4-5).

JEBUSITES

Descendants of Canaan (Gn 10:16; 15:21; Ex 3:8; Dt 7:1; 20:17), inhabitants of Jebus (1Ch 11:4). Defeated by Judah and Benjamin, but not dispossessed (Jos 15:63; Jdg 1:8,21; 3:5); defeated by David (2Sm 5:6-9) and enslaved by Solomon (1Kg 9:20-21).

JECONIAH

Variant of Jehoiachin (1Ch 3:16-17).

JEDIDIAH

Name given to Solomon by Nathan (2Sm 12:25).

JEDUTHUN

Levite musician (1Ch 16:41-42; 25:1-6; 2Ch 5:12; Pss 62; 39; 77).

JEHOAHAZ

1. Son of Jehoram; king of Judah (2Ch 21:17). Also known as Ahaziah (22:1).

2. Son of Jehu; king of Israel (2Kg 13:1-9).

3. Son of Josiah; king of Judah (2Kg 23:30-34). Called Shallum (Jr 22:11).

JEHOASH

1. Alternate name of Joash son of Ahaziah, king of Judah (2Kg 12).

2. Son of Jehoahaz; king of Israel (2Kg 13:10–14:13).

JEHOIACHIN

Son of Jehoiakim; king of Judah (2Kg 24:6). Also called Jeconiah or Coniah (Jr 22:24; 24:1). Exiled (2Kg 24:10-17) but later favored (25:27-30).

JEHOIADA

Priest who protected Joash from Queen Athaliah, enthroned him, then advised him (2Kg 11–12; 2Ch 22–24).

JEHOIAKIM

Son of Josiah; king of Judah. Succeeded his brother Jehoahaz; name changed from Eliakim by Neco (2Kg 23:34). Burned Jeremiah's scroll (Jr 36). Became vassal of Babylon; later rebelled and was defeated (2Kg 24:1-6; Dn 1:2).

JEHORAM

1. Alternate form of Joram, son of Ahab; king of Israel (2Kg 3:1).

2. Reforming priest in Judah (2Ch 17:8).

3. Son of Jehoshaphat; king of Judah (2Kg 8:16-24; 2Ch 21). Ahab's son-in-law (2Kg 8:18). Edom gained independence during his reign (8:20).

JEHOSHABEATH

J, the king's daughter, rescued   2Ch 22:11

JEHOSHAPHAT

1. Son of Ahilud; court historian for David and Solomon (2Sm 8:16; 1Kg 4:3).

2. Son of Paruah; Issachar's official under Solomon (1Kg 4:17).

3. Son of Asa; king of Judah (1Kg 15:24). Initially faithful, strong, blessed (2Ch 17). Then married Ahab's daughter Athaliah and formed alliances with Ahab and Joram, kings of Israel (1Kg 22; 2Kg 3; 8:26; 2Ch 18; 20).

4. Jehu's father (2Kg 9:2).

5. Valley of judgment (Jl 3:2,12).

JEHOSHEBA

J, ... King Jehoram's daughter   2Kg 11:2

JEHOZABAD

Conspirator who killed Joash (2Kg 12:21).

JEHU

1. Son of Hanani; prophet against Baasha king of Israel (1Kg 16:1-12).

2. Son of Jehoshaphat; king of Israel. Anointed by Elisha's servant; executed Ahaziah king of Judah, Joram, Jezebel and the house of Ahab in Israel, and the worshipers of Baal (2Kg 9–10; cp. 1Kg 19:16-17).

3. Son of Obed of Judah (1Ch 2:38).

4. Son of Joshibiah of Simeon (1Ch 4:35).

5. Benjaminite archer who joined David (1Ch 12:3).

the driving is like that of J   2Kg 9:20

JEMIMAH

named his first {daughter} J,   Jb 42:14

JEOPARDIZED

If I had j my own life—and   2Sm 18:13

JEPHTHAH

Gileadite judge who made rash vow affecting his daughter (Jdg 11–12; 1Sm 12:11; Heb 11:32).

JEREMIAH

Prophet to Judah in the time leading up to the exile (Jr 1:1-3). Put in stocks (20:1-3), threatened (Jr 26), opposed (Jr 28), imprisoned (32:2; 37), censured (Jr 36), and thrown into a cistern (Jr 38). Taken to Egypt against his will (Jr 43).

JERICHO

City near the Jordan River north of the Dead Sea (Nm 22:1). Spied out (Jos 2) and conquered (Jos 6; Heb 11:30) by Joshua; rebuilt by Hiel (1Kg 16:34). Visited by Jesus (Mt 20:29-34; Mk 10:46-52; Lk 18:35; 19:1-10).

JEROBOAM

1. Son of Nebat; Solomon's servant; rebelled; first king of Israel (1Kg 11:26–12:20). Judged for notorious idolatry (12:25–14:20).

2. Son of Joash, king of Israel (2Kg 14:23-29).

JERUBBAAL

Name given to Gideon after he destroyed Baal's altar (Jdg 6:32).

JERUSALEM

Formerly called Salem (Gn 14:18; Ps 76:2) or Jebus (Jos 18:28; 1Ch 11:4). David conquered it and made it his capital (2Sm 5:5-9); Solomon built temple, palace, and fortifications (1Kg 3:1). Conquered by Babylon (2Kg 24:10-12). Rebuilt and resettled after the exile (Ezr 1; Neh 12:27). Jesus visited (Mt 21:1; Jn 2:13); mourned (Mt 23:37). Important city in early church (Ac 15:4). New Jerusalem promised (Rv 3:12; 21:2,10).

the Jebusites who lived in J.	Jos 15:63
Judah fought against J and captured	Jdg 1:8
in J he reigned 33 years over all	2Sm 5:5
names of those born to him in J:	2Sm 5:14
and because of J that I chose.	1Kg 11:13
J, the city I chose for Myself to put My name there.	1Kg 11:36
Going to J is too difficult for you.	1Kg 12:28
Jehoash went to J and broke down 200 yards of J-'s wall	2Kg 14:13
deceive you by promising that J	2Kg 19:10
Daughter J shakes her head	2Kg 19:21
For a remnant will go out from J,	2Kg 19:31
J is where I will put My name.	2Kg 21:4
about to bring such disaster on J	2Kg 21:12
I will reject this city J,	2Kg 23:27
king of Babylon marched up to J,	2Kg 24:10
land into exile from J to Babylon.	2Kg 24:15
the king of Babylon, entered J.	2Kg 25:8
exiles went up from Babylon to J.	Ezr 1:11
began to rebuild God's house in J.	Ezr 5:2
Judah and Benjamin gathered in J	Ezr 10:9
Come, let's rebuild J-'s wall,	Neh 2:17
men who volunteered to live in J.	Neh 11:2
to prosper; build the walls of J.	Ps 51:18
LORD in Zion and His praise in J,	Ps 102:21
Pray for the peace of J:	Ps 122:6
If I forget you, J, may my right	Ps 137:5
The LORD rebuilds J;	Ps 147:2
Young women of J, I charge you,	Sg 2:7; 3:5
Speak tenderly to J, and announce	Is 40:2
J, herald of good news, raise your	Is 40:9
His people; He has redeemed J.	Is 52:9
I will rejoice in J and be glad in	Is 65:19
J will be called, The LORD's Throne	Jr 3:17
I will make J a heap of rubble,	Jr 9:11
J has sinned grievously; therefore,	Lm 1:8
a brick, ... draw the city of J on it.	Ezk 4:1
See, I am against you, J,	Ezk 5:8
Samaria and Oholibah represents J.	Ezk 23:4
From ... rebuild J until Messiah	Dn 9:25
when I restore the fortunes of ... J,	Jl 3:1
J will be holy, and foreigners will	Jl 3:17
LORD ... raises His voice from J;	Am 1:2
and the word of the LORD from J.	Mc 4:2
I am extremely jealous for J	Zch 1:14
To measure J to determine its width	Zch 2:2
J will be inhabited without walls	Zch 2:4
He will once again choose J.	Zch 2:12
I will bring them back to live in J.	Zch 8:8
Shout in triumph, Daughter J!	Zch 9:9
living water will flow out from J,	Zch 14:8
that He must go to J and suffer	Mt 16:21
O J! J that kills the prophets and	Mt 23:37
brought Him up to J to present Him	Lk 2:22
Every year His parents traveled to J	Lk 2:41
for a prophet to perish outside of J!	Lk 13:33
J will be trampled by the Gentiles	Lk 21:24
Daughters of J, do not weep	Lk 23:28

to all the nations, beginning at J.   Lk 24:27
say that the place to worship is in J.   Jn 4:20
He commanded them not to leave J,   Ac 1:4
you will be My witnesses in J, in all   Ac 1:8
you have filled J with your teaching   Ac 5:28
apostles and elders in J concerning   Ac 15:2
And now I am on my way to J,   Ac 20:22
begged him not to go up to J.   Ac 21:12
to the poor among the saints in J.   Rm 15:26
to carry your gracious gift to J.   1Co 16:3
I did not go up to J to those who   Gl 1:17
corresponds to the present J,   Gl 4:25
the living God (the heavenly J),   Heb 12:22
the city of My God—the new J,   Rv 3:12
the Holy City, new J, coming down   Rv 21:2

JESHUA

1. Descendant of Aaron (1Ch 24:11).

2. Kore's assistant (2Ch 31:15).

3. Son of Jozadak; high priest; returned with Zerubbabel (Ezr 3:2; Neh 7:7).

4. Pahath-moab's descendant (Ezr 2:6; Neh 7:11).

5. Levite (Ezr 2:40; Neh 7:43).

6. Assisted Ezra in interpreting the law (Neh 8:7).

7. Village in Judah (Neh 11:26).

JESHURUN

Then J became fat and rebelled   Dt 32:15
is My servant; I have chosen J.   Is 44:2

JESSE

David's father (Ru 4:17-22; 1Sm 16; 1Ch 2:12-16; Mt 1:5-6; Lk 3:32).

JESUS

1. Messiah and Lord (Ac 2:36; Eph 3:11; 1Pt 3:15). Born in Bethlehem (Mt 1:18-25; Lk 2:1-7) to a virgin, Mary (Mt 1:20; Lk 1:26-38). Genealogy (Mt 1:1-17; Lk 3:23-38). Raised in Nazareth (Mt 2:19-23; Lk 2:39-40). Visited the temple at age 12 (Lk 2:41-50).

Baptized by John (Mt 3:13-17; Lk 3:21). Tempted in the wilderness (Mt 4:1-11; Lk 4:1-13). Chose apostles (Lk 5:1-11,27-28; 6:12-16; Jn 1:35-51).

Transformation (Mt 17:1-9; Mk 9:2-10). Triumphal entry into Jerusalem (Mt 21:1-11; Lk 19:28-40). Betrayal and arrest (Mt 26:17-25,47-56; Mk 14:17-21,43-50; Lk 22:1-

6,47-54), trial (Mt 26:57-66; 27:11-31; Mk 14:53-65; 15:1-20; Lk 22:66–23:25), crucifixion (Mt 27:32-56; Mk 15:21-39; Lk 23:32-49), and resurrection (Mt 28; Mk 16; Lk 24; Jn 20–21).

2. Jewish Christian, Paul's co-worker; called Justus (Col 4:11).

JETHER

Gideon's oldest son (Jdg 8:20).

JETHRO

Priest of Midian; Moses' father-in-law and advisor (Ex 3:1; 4:18; 18). Also called Reuel (2:18).

JEW

{they killed} the J-s and the   2Kg 25:25
Let ... the J-s rebuild this house   Ezr 6:7
What are these pathetic J-s doing?   Neh 4:2
He set out to destroy all ... the J-s,   Est 3:6
I see Mordecai the J sitting at   Est 5:13
Haman, the enemy of the J-s.   Est 8:1
that came to Jeremiah for all the J-s   Jr 44:1
There are some J-s you have   Dn 3:12
has been born King of the J-s?   Mt 2:2
Are You the King of the J-s?   Mt 27:11
Him: "Hail, King of the J-s!"   Mt 27:29
JESUS THE KING OF THE J-S   Mt 27:37
the J-s, will not eat unless they wash   Mk 7:3
How is it that You, a J, ask for a   Jn 4:9
For J-s do not associate with   Jn 4:9
salvation is from the J-s.   Jn 4:22
the J-s began persecuting Jesus   Jn 5:16
said to the J-s who had believed   Jn 8:31
Again the J-s picked up rocks to   Jn 10:31
"I'm not a J, am I?" Pilate   Jn 18:35
to the burial custom of the J-s.   Jn 19:40
There were J-s living in Jerusalem   Ac 2:5
Hellenistic J-s against the Hebraic J-s   Ac 6:1
the J-s conspired to kill him,   Ac 9:23
But the J-s incited the religious   Ac 13:50
Then some J-s came from Antioch   Ac 14:19
The J-s stirred up the crowd and   Ac 17:8
all the J-s to leave Rome.   Ac 18:2
refuted the J-s in public,   Ac 18:28
recognized that he was a J,   Ac 19:34
the J-s formed a conspiracy and   Ac 23:12
first to the J, and also to the   Rm 1:16
first to the J, and also to   Rm 2:9
a person is a J who is one inwardly,   Rm 2:29

JEWEL

what advantage does the J have?	Rm 3:1
Or is God for J-s only? Is He not	Rm 3:29
between J and Greek,	Rm 10:12
For the J-s ask for signs and the	1Co 1:22
block to the J-s and foolishness	1Co 1:23
To the J-s I became like a J,	1Co 9:20
one body—whether J-s or Greeks	1Co 12:13
I received from the J-s 40 lashes	2Co 11:24
If you, who are a J, live like a	Gl 2:14
There is no J or Greek, slave or	Gl 3:28
Here there is not Greek and J,	Col 3:11
who claim to be J-s and are not,	Rv 3:9

JEWEL

She is more precious than j-s;	Pr 3:15
is gold and a multitude of j-s,	Pr 20:15
is far more precious than j-s.	Pr 31:10
with one j of your necklace.	Sg 4:9
washed in milk and set like j-s.	Sg 5:12
Babylon, the j of the kingdoms	Is 13:19
adorns herself with her j-s.	Is 61:10
for they are like j-s in a crown,	Zch 9:16

JEWELRY

Egyptians for silver and gold j	Ex 12:35
mourned and didn't put on their j.	Ex 33:4
cheeks are beautiful with j,	Sg 1:10
wear all your children as j,	Is 49:18
Can a young woman forget her j	Jr 2:32
I adorned you with j,	Ezk 16:11
put on her rings and j,	Hs 2:13

JEWISH

annihilate all the J people	Est 3:13
and the J temple police arrested	Jn 18:12
the son of a believing J woman,	Ac 16:1
where there was a J synagogue.	Ac 17:1
of the itinerant J exorcists	Ac 19:13
I am a J man from Tarsus of	Ac 21:39
Neither against the J law,	Ac 25:8
an expert in all the J customs	Ac 26:3
may not pay attention to J myths	Ti 1:14

JEZEBEL

Wife of King Ahab of Israel, daughter of the king of Sidon; brought Baal worship to Israel (1Kg 16:31-33). Killed prophets and threatened Elijah (18:4,13; 19:1-2). Killed by Jehu (2Kg 9:30-37) in fulfillment of prophecy (1Kg 21). Name used as a label (Rv 2:20).

JEZREEL

1. A valley separating Galilee from Samaria, and a city of that valley (Jos 17:16; Jdg 6:33; Hs 1:5; 1Sm 29:11; 2Sm 4:4; 1Kg 18:45). Site of Naboth's vineyard (21:23). Scene of Jehu's massacre of Ahab (2Kg 9-10; Hs 1:4).

2. City near Ziph, where Ahinoam was from (1Sm 25:43).

JOAB

Son of Zeruiah; David's nephew and commander of his troops (1Ch 2:16; 11:6). Killed Abner (2Sm 3:22-39), Absalom (2Sm 18), Amasa, and Sheba (2Sm 20). Sided with Adonijah (1Kg 1:7,19); David told Solomon to execute him (2:5-6,28-35).

JOANNA

J the wife of Chuza, Herod's	Lk 8:3
Mary Magdalene, J, Mary the	Lk 24:10

JOASH

1. Father of Gideon (Jdg 6:11).
2. Son of Shelah (1Ch 4:21-22).
3. Son of Becher (1Ch 7:8).
4. One of David's warriors (1Ch 12:3).
5. One of David's officers (1Ch 27:28).
6. Son of Ahab (1Kg 22:26).
7. Son of Ahaziah; king of Judah (2Kg 12). Protected by Jehoiada (2Kg 11). Repaired temple (2Ch 24:4-14).
8. Alternate name of Jehoash son of Jehoahaz, king of Israel (2Kg 13:10).

JOB

Wealthy patriarch. His book tells of his testing (Jb 1–2), perseverance (Jb 3–37), rebuke (Jb 38-41), and vindication (Jb 42; Jms 5:11).

JOCHEBED

Levite, sister of Kohath, wife of Amram, mother of Miram, Aaron, and Moses (Ex 6:20; Nm 26:59).

JOEL

1. Dishonest son of Samuel (2Sm 8:2).
2. Levite (1Ch 6:36).
3. Reubenite (1Ch 5:4,8).
4. Levite leader who brought the ark to Jerusalem (1Ch 15:7,11,17).

5. Simeonite (1Ch 4:35).

6. Gadite chief (1Ch 5:12).

7. Issacharite chief (1Ch 7:3).

8. One of David's warriors (1Ch 11:38).

9. Manassite leader (1Ch 27:20).

10. Levite under Hezekiah (2Ch 29:12).

11. Son of Pethuel; prophet who urged priests to call Judah to repentance; depicted calamities (Jl 1:1–2:11); predicted the Messiah (2:21-32; Ac 2:16).

12. Israelite Ezra condemned for intermarriage (Ezr 10:43).

13. Benjaminite leader (Neh 9:11).

JOHANAN

1. High priest (1Ch 6:9-10).

2. Benjaminite who joined David (1Ch 12:4).

3. Gadite who joined David (1Ch 12:12).

4. Eldest son of Josiah (1Ch 3:15).

5. Commander; stayed in Judah and tried to protect Gedaliah (2Kg 25:23); forced Jeremiah to go to Egypt (Jr 40–43).

6. Leader under Ezra (Ezr 8:12).

7. Descendant of David (1Ch 3:24).

8. High priest (Neh 12:22-23).

JOHN

1. The baptizer; son of Zechariah; prophet. Annunciation and birth (Lk 1:5-25,57-66). Preached repentance, announced the coming Messiah (Mt 3:1-12; Mk 1:1-8; Lk 3:1-18; 7:27-28), and baptized Jesus (Mt 3:13-15; Mk 1:9; Lk 3:21-22). Fulfilled the role of Elijah (Mt 11:13-14; 17:12-13; Mk 9:12-13; Mt 3:4; cp. 2Kg 1:8). Asked Jesus to verify His identity (Mt 11:2-6; Lk 7:18-23). Beheaded by Herod Antipas (Mt 14:1-12; Mk 6:14-29; Lk 3:19-20; 9:7-9).

2. Apostle; son of Zebedee; brother of James. Call (Mt 4:21-22; Mk 1:19-20). Among the inner three at special occasions (Mk 9:2; 14:32-33). With James, called "Sons of Thunder" (Mk 3:17); asked for places of honor (Mk 10:35-41). Often with Peter (Ac 1:13; 3:1-11; 4:13-20; 8:14); a leader in Jerusalem (Gl 2:9). In his gospel, called the disciple Jesus loved (Jn 13:23; 19:26; 20:2; 21:7,20); also wrote three letters and Revelation.

3. Peter's father (Jn 1:42).

4. Member of Annas' family (Ac 4:6).

5. John Mark see MARK

JOIN

Do not j the wicked to be a	Ex 23:1
country have j-ed forces against us	Jos 10:6
or j a group of mockers!	Ps 1:1
as a city (should be), solidly j-ed	Ps 122:3
for whoever is j-ed with all the	Ec 9:4
to house and j field to field	Is 5:8
will come and j themselves to	Jr 50:5
Then j them together into a	Ezk 37:17
others will j them insincerely	Dn 11:34
mother and be j-ed to his wife,	Mt 19:5
what God has j-ed together,	Mt 19:6
of the rest dared to j them,	Ac 5:13
some men j-ed him and believed,	Ac 17:34
For if we have been j-ed with Him	Rm 6:5
the Spirit also j-s to help in our	Rm 8:26
that anyone j-ed to a prostitute	1Co 6:16
anyone j-ed to the Lord is one	1Co 6:17
of the Jews j-ed his hypocrisy,	Gl 2:13
mother and be j-ed to his wife,	Eph 5:31
encouraged and j-ed together in	Col 2:2

JOINTS

through the j of his armor.	1Kg 22:34
soul, spirit, j, and marrow;	Heb 4:12

JOKE

You make us a j among the	Ps 44:14
and I was a j to them.	Ps 69:11
he has become a j to his	Ps 89:41
and rulers are a j to them.	Hab 1:10

JOKING

sons-in-law thought he was j.	Gn 19:14
and says, "I was only j!	Pr 26:19
or crude j are not suitable	Eph 5:4

JONADAB

1. Friend and cousin of Amnon; encouraged him to have relations with his sister (2Sm 13:3-5,32-36).

2. First of the Rechabites (Jr 35:5-19); also called Jehonadab: accompanied Jehu against Baal (2Kg 10:15,23).

JONAH

1. Son of Amittai; prophet at the time of Jeroboam II (2Kg 14:23-27). Rejected God's call to preach in Nineveh; swallowed by a great fish (Jnh 1). Prayed (Jnh 2); preached repentance in Nineveh (Jnh 3); scolded by God for his anger (Jnh 4). Used as an example (Mt 12:39-41; 16:4; Lk 11:29-32).

2. Alternate spelling for Peter's father (Mt 16:17).

JONATHAN

1. Levite who served as priest (Jdg 17–18).

2. Son of Saul; friend of David (1Sm 18:1-4; 19:1-7; 20; 23:16-18). Killed in battle (31:1-13); mourned by David (2Sm 1:17-27).

3. Son of Abiathar the priest; served David (2Sm 15:24; 17:17,20; 1Kg 1:42-43).

4. David's uncle; his counselor and scribe (1Ch 27:32).

5. Son of David's brother Shimei; killed a Philistine giant (2Sm 21:21; 1Ch 20:7).

6. Son of Shamma; one of David's warriors (2Sm 23:32-33; 1Ch 11:34).

7. Son of Uzziah; in charge of David's storehouses (1Ch 27:25).

8. Owner of house where Jeremiah was jailed (Jr 37:15).

9. Priest (Neh 12:14).

10. Son of Joiada; priest (Neh 12:11).

11. Son of Asahel; supported foreign marriages (Ezr 10:15).

12. Jerahmeelite (1Ch 3:32-33).

JOPPA

Seaport (2Ch 2:16; Ezr 3:7; Jnh 1:3); scene of Tabitha's healing and Peter's vision (Ac 10).

JORAM

1. Son of King Toi of Hamath (2Sm 8:10).

2. Levite under David (1Ch 26:25).

3. Son of Ahab; king of Israel (2Kg 3). Succeeded his brother Ahaziah (1:17). Attacked Moab with the help of Judah, Edom, and Elisha (3:4-27). Wounded by Arameans (8:28); killed by Jehu (9:14-26).

4. Alternate form of Jehoram, son of Jehoshaphat; king of Judah (2Kg 8:16-24; 2Ch 21).

JORDAN

Lot chose the entire J Valley	Gn 13:11
the border will go down to the J	Nm 34:12
for you will not cross this J.	Dt 3:27
dry ground in the middle of the J,	Jos 3:17
the two of them stood by the J.	2Kg 2:7
and stood on the bank of the J.	2Kg 2:13
himself in the J seven times,	2Kg 5:14
the J turned back.	Ps 114:3
were baptized by him in the J River	Mt 3:6
Jesus came ... to John at the J,	Mt 3:13

JOSEPH

1. Son of Jacob and Rachel. Sold into slavery in Egypt (Gn 37); imprisoned on false accusations (Gn 39); became Pharaoh's second in command (41:39-45); sold grain to brothers (Gn 42–45); enabled his father and brothers to move to Egypt (Gn 46–47). Sons Ephraim and Manasseh each became tribes (Gn 48). Died in Egypt, buried in Canaan (50:22-26; Ex 13:19; Jos 24:32; Ac 7:16).

2. Descendant of Asaph (1Ch 25:9).

3. Descendant of Bani; married a foreigner (Ezr 10:42).

4. Descendant of Shebaniah; priest (Neh 12:14).

5. Ancestors of Jesus ((Lk 3:24,30).

6. Husband of Mary; foster father of Jesus (Mt 1:16,20; Lk 2:4; 3:23; 4:22; Jn 1:45; 6:42). Carpenter (Mt 13:55). Told in a dream not to divorce Mary (Mt 1:18-25); told in a dream to flee to Egypt (2:13-23).

7. Of Arimathea; a righteous member of the Sanhedrin who sought the kingdom of God; put Jesus' body in his tomb (Mt 27:57-60; Mk 15:43-46; Lk 23:50-53; Jn 19:38-42).

8. Brother of Jesus (Mt 13:55).

9. Brother of James (Mt 27:56).

10. Called Barsabbas or Justus; candidate to replace Judas (Ac 1:23).

JOSES

Brother of Jesus, also called Joseph (Mk 6:3; 15:40,47).

JOSHUA

1. Son of Nun; successor to Moses as leader of Israelites. Leader of Moses' army (Ex 17:8-13); Moses' servant on Mt. Sinai (32:17). Scouted Canaan and, along with Caleb, recommended invasion (Nm 13:30–14:38). Chosen, commissioned, and encouraged by God (Nm 27:15-23; Dt 31:14-15,23; Jos 1:1-9).

Conquered Canaan (Jos 2–11) and distributed the land (Jos 12–21). Renewed the covenant and charged the people (Jos 23–24).

2. Owner of the field where the ark returned (1Sm 6:14).

3. Governor (2Kg 23:8).

4. High priest who returned from Babylon (Hag 1:1; Zch 3:1).

JOSIAH

Son of Amon; king of Israel. Became king at age 8 (2Kg 21:19–22:2). Found the book of the law and instituted reforms (2Kg 22–23; 2Ch 34–35). Died resisting Pharaoh Neco (2Kg 23:29-30; 2Ch 35:20-25).

JOTHAM

1. Son of Gideon (Jdg 9).

2. Son of Uzziah/Azariah; co-regent (2Kg 15:5), then king of Judah (15:32-38).

JOURNEY

LORD had made his j a success.	Gn 24:21
about a day's j in every	Nm 11:31
ask Him for a safe j for us,	Ezr 8:21
How long will your j take,	Neh 2:6
he went on a long j.	Pr 7:19
like a man on a j, who left his	Mk 13:34
worn out from His j, sat down at	Jn 4:6
a Sabbath day's j away.	Ac 1:12
start by you on my j to Judea.	2Co 1:16
On frequent j-s, {I faced} dangers	2Co 11:26
them on their j in a manner	3Jn 6

JOURNEYED

Then Abram j by stages to the	Gn 12:9

JOY

and you will have abundant j.	Dt 16:15
so that he can bring j to the wife	Dt 24:5
you didn't serve your God with j	Dt 28:47
strength and j are in His place	1Ch 16:27
observed seven days with j,	2Ch 30:23
God had given them great j.	Neh 12:43
behold His face with a shout of j,	Jb 33:26
the sons of God shouted for j?	Jb 38:7
have put more j in my heart than	Ps 4:7
in Your presence is abundant j;	Ps 16:11
cheer him with j in Your presence.	Ps 21:6
but there is j in the morning.	Ps 30:5
altar of God, to God, my greatest j.	Ps 43:4
Let me hear j and gladness;	Ps 51:8
Restore the j of Your salvation	Ps 51:12
trees of the forest will shout for j	Ps 96:12
they are the j of my heart.	Ps 119:111
in tears will reap with shouts of j.	Ps 126:5
Your godly people shout for j.	Ps 132:9
A wise son brings j to his father,	Pr 10:1
The hope of the righteous is j,	Pr 10:28
those who promote peace have j.	Pr 12:20
may be sad, and j may end in grief.	Pr 14:13
the father of a fool has no j.	Pr 17:21
Justice executed is a j to	Pr 21:15
the nation and increased its j.	Is 9:3
crowned with unending j.	Is 35:10; 51:11
go out with j and be peacefully	Is 55:12
and eternal j will be theirs.	Is 61:7
will shout for j from a glad	Is 65:14
to me and the j of my heart,	Jr 15:16
turn their mourning into j,	Jr 31:13
the j of the whole earth?	Lm 2:15
Sing for j, Daughter Zion;	Zph 3:14
immediately receives it with j.	Mt 13:20
Share your master's j!'	Mt 25:21
the tomb with fear and great j,	Mt 28:8
baby leaped for j inside me!	Lk 1:44
news of great j that will be for	Lk 2:10
will be more j in heaven over	Lk 15:7
not believe because of {their} j	Lk 24:41
to Jerusalem with great j.	Lk 24:52
So this j of mine is complete.	Jn 3:29
and your j may be complete.	Jn 15:11
but your sorrow will turn to j.	Jn 16:20
no one will rob you of your j.	Jn 16:22
that your j may be complete.	Jn 16:24
they may have My j completed in	Jn 17:13
there was great j in that city.	Ac 8:8
filled with j and the Holy Spirit.	Ac 13:52
peace, and j in the Holy Spirit.	Rm 14:17
fill you with all j and peace in	Rm 15:13

all of you that my **j** is yours. 2Co 2:3
abundance of **j** and their deep 2Co 8:2
fruit of the Spirit is love, **j**, peace Gl 5:22
fulfill my **j** by thinking the same Php 2:2
brothers, my **j** and crown, stand Php 4:1
endurance and patience, with **j** Col 1:11
message with the **j** from the Holy 1Th 1:6
who is our hope, or **j**, or crown 1Th 2:19
so that I may be filled with **j**, 2Tm 1:4
For I have great **j** and Phm 7
who for the **j** that lay before Him Heb 12:2
Consider it a great **j**, my brothers Jms 1:2
mourning and your **j** to sorrow. Jms 4:9
inexpressible and glorious **j**, 1Pt 1:8
with great **j** at the revelation 1Pt 4:13
that our **j** may be complete 1Jn 1:4; 2Jn 12
I have no greater **j** than this: 3Jn 4
blameless and with great **j**, Jd 24

JOYFUL

with **j** and thankful shouts. Ps 42:4
will praise You with **j** lips. Ps 63:5
come before Him with **j** songs. Ps 100:2
great things for us; we were **j**. Ps 126:3
A **j** heart makes a face cheerful Pr 15:13
A **j** heart is good medicine, Pr 17:22
In the day of prosperity be **j**, Ec 7:14
Mountains break into **j** shouts! Is 49:13

JOYFULLY

giving **j** and willingly to You. 1Ch 29:17
will **j** proclaim Your faithful love Ps 59:16
Shout **j** to God, all the earth! Ps 66:1
let us shout **j** to the LORD, Ps 95:1
will **j** sing of Your righteousness. Ps 145:7
the one who **j** does what is right Is 64:5
came down and welcomed Him **j**. Lk 19:6
my inner self I **j** agree with Rm 7:22

JUBAL

Father of lyre and flute players (Gn 4:21).

JUBILANT

shout to God with a **j** cry. Ps 47:1
be **j**, shout for joy, and sing. Ps 98:4
Is this your **j** {city}, whose Is 23:7
The noise of the **j** has stopped. Is 24:8

JUBILANTLY

do not rejoice **j** as the nations Hs 9:1

JUBILATION

rest, commemoration and **j** Lv 23:24
will be a day of **j** for you. Nm 29:1

JUBILEE

It will be your **J**, when Lv 25:10
his field during the Year of **J**, Lv 27:17
When the **J** comes for the Nm 36:4

JUDAH

1. Son of Jacob and Leah (Gn 29:35); tribe with large territory west and south of Jerusalem (Jos 15:20-63). Tricked by daughter-in-law (Gn 38). Ancestor of David and Jesus (Gn 49:10; 1Sm 17:12; Mt 1:3,6,16; Rv 5:5). Name of the southern part of the divided kingdom (2Kg 12:20; 14:21; 23:27; Ezk 37:15-23) and the Persian province in the restoration (Neh 5:14; Hg 1:1).

2. Naphtalite border city (Jos 19:34).

3. Priest with Zerubbabel (Ezr 3:9; Neh 12:8).

4. Levite who married a foreigner (Ezr 10:23).

5. Benjaminite official who returned (Neh 11:9; 12:34).

6. Priest; musician (Neh 12:36).

JUDAHITES

J be taught The Song of the Bow. 2Sm 1:18
and expelled the **J** from Elath. 2Kg 16:6
J succeeded ... they depended on 2Ch 13:18

JUDAISM

my former way of life in **J**: Gl 1:13
and I advanced in **J** beyond many Gl 1:14
especially those from **J**. Ti 1:10

JUDAS

1. Iscariot; apostle (Mt 10:4); treasurer, miser, thief (Jn 12:4-6). Betrayed Jesus (Mt 26:21-25,44-50; Lk 22:3-6; Jn 13:21-30); committed suicide (Mt 27:3-10; Ac 1:16-20).

2. Son of James; apostle; called Thaddaeus (Mt 10:3; Mk 3:18; Lk 6:16; Jn 14:22).

3. Brother of Jesus (Mt 13:55; Mk 6:3); also called Jude.

4. Galilean revolutionary (Ac 5:37).

5. Owner of house in Damascus where Paul stayed (Ac 9:7-12).

6. Leader of Jerusalem church; messenger; prophet; called Barsabbas (Ac 15:22).

JUDE

Brother of Jesus; also called Judas; author (Mt 13:55; Jd 1:1).

JUDEA

Another name for the territory of Judah.

Jesus was born in Bethlehem of J	Mt 2:1
In the days of King Herod of J,	Lk 1:5
in Galilee, to J, to the city of	Lk 2:4
Pontius Pilate was governor of J,	Lk 3:1
He did not want to travel in J because	Jn 7:1
in Jerusalem, in all J and Samaria,	Ac 1:8
scattered throughout the land of J	Ac 8:1

JUDEAN

His J wife gave birth to Jered	1Ch 4:18
no one enslave his J brother.	Jr 34:9
Daniel, one of the J exiles, has	Dn 6:13

JUDEANS

become as numerous as the J.	1Ch 4:27
evil the Israelites and J have done	Jr 32:32
When all the J in Moab and among	Jr 40:11
Israelites and J will come together,	Jr 50:4
J and the Israelites will be gathered	Hs 1:11

JUDGE (n)

Won't the J of all the earth do	Gn 18:25
made you a leader and j over us?	Ex 2:14
and to the j who presides at	Dt 17:9
LORD raised up j-s, who saved them	Jdg 2:16
During the time of the j-s,	Ru 1:1
his sons as j-s over Israel.	1Sm 8:1
the time of the j-s who judged	2Kg 23:22
He appointed j-s in all the	2Ch 19:5
and j-s to judge all the people	Ezr 7:25
He blinds its j-s.	Jb 9:24
barefoot and makes j-s go mad.	Jb 12:17
Your throne as a righteous j.	Ps 9:4
for God is the j.	Ps 50:6
Rise up, J of the earth;	Ps 94:2
princes and all j-s of the earth,	Ps 148:11
and makes the j-s of the earth to	Is 40:23
will cut off the j from the land	Am 2:3
her j-s are wolves of the night,	Zph 3:3
will hand you over to the j,	Mt 5:25
this reason they will be your j-s.	Mt 12:27
appointed Me a j or arbitrator	Lk 12:14

a j in one town who didn't fear God	Lk 18:2
by God to be the J of the living	Ac 10:42
the righteous J, will give me	2Tm 4:8
to God who is the j of all,	Heb 12:23
There is one lawgiver and j	Jms 4:12
Look, the j stands at the door!	Jms 5:9

JUDGE (v)

May the LORD j between me and	Gn 16:5
Dan will j his people as one of	Gn 49:16
Moses sat down to j the people,	Ex 18:13
They j-d the people at all times;	Ex 18:26
assembly is to j between the	Nm 35:24
was on him, and he j-d Israel.	Jdg 3:10
The LORD will j the ends of the	1Sm 2:10
Samuel j-d Israel throughout his	1Sm 7:15
May the LORD j between you and	1Sm 24:12
who is able to j this great	1Kg 3:9
He is coming to j the earth.	1Ch 16:33
He j-s the world with righteousness;	Ps 9:8
to be condemned when he is j-d.	Ps 37:33
You are blameless when You j.	Ps 51:4
There is a God who j-s on earth!	Ps 58:11
for You j the peoples with	Ps 67:4
God rose up to j and to save all	Ps 76:9
He j-s among the gods:	Ps 82:1
How long will you j unjustly and	Ps 82:2
Rise up, God, j the earth, for	Ps 82:8
coming to j the earth. He will j the	Ps 96:13
coming to j the earth. He will j the	Ps 98:9
When he is j-d, let him be found	Ps 109:7
He will j the nations, heaping	Ps 110:6
For the LORD will j His people	Ps 135:14
on a throne to j sifts out all	Pr 20:8
Speak up, j righteously, and	Pr 31:9
He will not j by what He sees	Is 11:3
j between one sheep and another,	Ezk 34:17
to j all the surrounding nations.	Jl 3:12
Do not j, so that you won't be j-d.	Mt 7:1
j-ing the 12 tribes of Israel.	Mt 19:28
You have j-d correctly,	Lk 7:43
that He might j the world,	Jn 3:17
who believes in Him is not j-d,	Jn 3:18
The Father, in fact, j-s no one but	Jn 5:22
I j only as I hear, and My	Jn 5:30
Stop j-ing according to outward	Jn 7:24
rather j according to righteous	Jn 7:24
law doesn't j a man before it	Jn 7:51
You j by human standards. I j no	Jn 8:15

I did not come to j the world but | Jn 12:47
ruler of this world has been **j-d**. | Jn 16:11
Take Him yourselves and **j** Him | Jn 18:31
on which He is going to **j** the world | Ac 17:31
I am being **j-d** because of the hope | Ac 23:6
when you **j** another, you condemn | Rm 2:1
the law will be **j-d** by the law. | Rm 2:12
how will God **j** the world? | Rm 3:6
that the saints will **j** the world? | 1Co 6:2
know that we will **j** angels | 1Co 6:3
J for yourselves: Is it proper | 1Co 11:13
but when we are **j-d**, we are | 1Co 11:32
by all and is **j-d** by all. | 1Co 14:24
don't let anyone **j** you in regard to | Col 2:16
who is going to **j** the living and | 2Tm 4:1
God will **j** immoral people | Heb 13:4
those who will be **j-d** by the law | Jms 2:12
But if you **j** the law, you are | Jms 4:11
who are you to **j** your neighbor? | Jms 4:12
so that you will not be **j-d**. | Jms 5:9
the One who **j-s** impartially based | 1Pt 1:17
to the One who **j-s** justly. | 1Pt 2:23
who stands ready to **j** the living | 1Pt 4:5
He **j-s** and makes war. | Rv 19:11
who were given authority to **j**. | Rv 20:4
the dead were **j-d** according to | Rv 20:12

JUDGMENT

outstretched arm and great acts of **j**. | Ex 6:6
I will execute **j-s** against all the | Ex 12:12
act unjustly when rendering **j**. | Lv 19:15
not show partiality when
   rendering **j**; | Dt 1:17
for **j** belongs to God | Dt 1:17
that you may know there is a **j**. | Jb 19:29
the wicked will not survive the **j**, | Ps 1:5
You have ordained a **j**. | Ps 7:6
He executes **j** on the peoples | Ps 9:8
Your **j-s**, like the deepest sea. | Ps 36:6
rejoice because of Your **j-s**. | Ps 48:11
my mouth, for I hope in Your **j-s**. | Ps 119:43
Teach me good **j** and discernment | Ps 119:66
There, thrones for **j** are placed | Ps 122:5
he rebels against all sound **j**. | Pr 18:1
J-s are prepared for mockers, | Pr 19:29
It is not good to show partiality in **j**. | Pr 24:23
God will bring every act to **j**, | Ec 12:14
because of oppression and **j**; | Is 53:8
They ask Me for righteous **j-s**; | Is 58:2

will execute **j** on all flesh with | Is 66:16
He enters into **j** with all flesh | Jr 25:31
I will execute **j-s** against you and | Ezk 5:10
will you pass **j**, son of man? | Ezk 20:4
arrived and a **j** was given in | Dn 7:22
enter into **j** with them there | Jl 3:2
come to you in **j**, and I will be | Mal 3:5
murders will be subject to **j**. | Mt 5:21
more tolerable on the day of **j** for | Mt 10:15
Sodom on the day of **j** than for | Mt 11:24
j people will have to account for | Mt 12:36
is the **j**: the light has come into | Jn 3:19
but has given all **j** to the Son, | Jn 5:22
not come under **j** but has passed | Jn 5:24
to the resurrection of **j**. | Jn 5:29
as I hear, and My **j** is righteous | Jn 5:30
judge according to righteous **j**. | Jn 7:24
if I do judge, My **j** is true | Jn 8:16
I came into this world for **j**, | Jn 9:39
Now is the **j** of this world. | Jn 12:31
sin, righteousness, and **j**: | Jn 16:8
that you will escape God's **j**? | Rm 2:3
from one sin came the **j**, | Rm 5:16
His **j-s** and untraceable | Rm 11:33
stand before the **j** seat of God. | Rm 14:10
eats and drinks **j** on himself. | 1Co 11:29
before the **j** seat of Christ, | 2Co 5:10
of the dead, and eternal **j**. | Heb 6:2
die once—and after this, **j**— | Heb 9:27
a terrifying expectation of **j**, | Heb 10:27
Mercy triumphs over **j**. | Jms 2:13
we will receive a stricter **j**; | Jms 3:1
so that you won't fall under **j**. | Jms 5:12
has come for **j** to begin with | 1Pt 4:17
the day of **j** and destruction | 2Pt 3:7
confidence in the day of **j**; | 1Jn 4:17
for the **j** of the great day | Jd 6
a single hour your **j** has come. | Rv 18:10
because His **j-s** are true and | Rv 19:2

JUG

lower your water **j** so that I may | Gn 24:14
and the water **j** by Saul's head, | 1Sm 26:12
and the oil **j** will not run dry | 1Kg 17:14
shatter the **j** in the presence | Jr 19:10
man carrying a water **j** will meet | Mk 14:13

JUICE

He must not drink any grape **j** or | Nm 6:3

JULIUS

and J treated Paul kindly and — Ac 27:3

JUMPED

So he j up, stood, and started — Ac 3:8
And he j up and started to — Ac 14:10

JUNIPER

Be like a j bush in the — Jr 48:6

JURISDICTION

that He was under Herod's j, — Lk 23:7

JUST

Judge of all the earth do what is j? — Gn 18:25
all His ways are entirely j. — Dt 32:4
my j decisions were like a robe — Jb 29:14
LORD, hear a j cause; — Ps 17:1
his tongue speaks what is j. — Ps 37:30
The LORD is j; He is my rock — Ps 92:15
and Your judgments are j. — Ps 119:137
LORD upholds the j cause of the — Ps 140:12
of the righteous {are} j, — Pr 12:5
is righteous and j is more acceptable — Pr 21:3
for the LORD is a j God. — Is 30:18
and does what is j and right — Ezk 18:5; 33:14
are true and His ways are j. — Dn 4:37
you supposed to know what is j? — Mc 3:1
someone die for a j person — Rm 5:7
is holy and j and good. — Rm 7:12
and not j when I am with you. — Gl 4:18
whatever is j, whatever is pure — Php 4:8
received a j punishment, — Heb 2:2

JUSTICE

along with a crowd to pervert {j}. — Ex 23:2
must not deny j to the poor — Ex 23:6
He executes j for the fatherless — Dt 10:18
Pursue j and j alone, — Dt 16:20
Do not deny j to a foreign — Dt 24:17
took bribes, and perverted j. — 1Sm 8:3
for yourself to understand j, — 1Kg 3:11
Does God pervert j? — Jb 8:3
for help, but there is no j. — Jb 19:7
yet God has deprived me of j. — Jb 34:5
but He gives j to the afflicted — Jb 36:6
In His j and righteousness, — Jb 37:23
He has executed j, striking down — Ps 9:16
He loves righteousness and j; — Ps 33:5
your j like the noonday. — Ps 37:6
Your kingdom is a scepter of j. — Ps 45:6

Provide j for the needy and the — Ps 82:3
Righteousness and j are the — Ps 89:14
The mighty King loves j. — Ps 99:4
sing of faithful love and j; — Ps 101:1
of righteousness and j for all — Ps 103:6
happy are those who uphold j, — Ps 106:3
executing j for the exploited — Ps 146:7
guard the paths of j and protect — Pr 2:8
J executed is a joy to the — Pr 21:15
Evil men do not understand j, — Pr 28:5
By j a king brings stability to — Pr 29:4
a man receives j from the LORD. — Pr 29:26
Learn to do what is good. Seek j. — Is 1:17
And I will make j the measuring — Is 28:17
He will bring j to the nations. — Is 42:1
He has established j on earth. — Is 42:4
Preserve j and do what is right — Is 56:1
J is turned back, and — Is 59:14
For I the LORD love j; — Is 61:8
the LORD, showing faithful love, j, — Jr 9:24
I will shepherd them with j. — Ezk 34:16
Maintain love and j, and always — Hs 12:6
Those who turn j into wormwood — Am 5:7
establish j in the gate. — Am 5:15
But let j flow like water, — Am 5:24
Render true j. Show faithful — Zch 7:9
or "Where is the God of j?" — Mal 2:17
will proclaim j to the nations. — Mt 12:18
important matters of the law—j, — Mt 23:23
kind of herb, and you bypass j — Lk 11:42
'Give me j against my adversary. — Lk 18:3
His humiliation j was denied Him. — Ac 8:33
J does not allow him to live! — Ac 28:4
Your kingdom is a scepter of j. — Heb 1:8

JUSTIFICATION

and raised for our j. — Rm 4:25
came the gift, resulting in j. — Rm 5:16
there is life-giving j for everyone. — Rm 5:18

JUSTIFY

How can we j ourselves? — Gn 44:16
I will not j the guilty. — Ex 23:7
a person be j-ied before God? — Jb 9:2; 25:4
he had j-ied himself rather than God. — Jb 32:2
Israel will be j-ied and find glory — Is 45:25
The One who j-ies Me is near; — Is 50:8
righteous servant will j many, — Is 53:11
But wanting to j himself, he — Lk 10:29
You are the ones who j yourselves — Lk 16:15
down to his house j-ied rather than — Lk 18:14

who believes in Him is **j-ied**	Ac 13:39
You may be **j-ied** in Your words	Rm 3:4
no flesh will be **j-ied** in His sight	Rm 3:20
They are **j-ied** freely by His grace	Rm 3:24
that a man is **j-ied** by faith apart	Rm 3:28
God who will **j** the circumcised	Rm 3:30
and those He called, He also **j-ied;**	Rm 8:30
God is the One who **j-ies.**	Rm 8:33
you were **j-ied** in the name of the	1Co 6:11
no one is **j-ied** by the works of the	Gl 2:16
we might be **j-ied** by faith in Christ	Gl 2:16
while seeking to be **j-ied** by Christ,	Gl 2:17
that God would **j** the Gentiles by	Gl 3:8
that no one is **j-ied** before God	Gl 3:11
so that we could be **j-ied** by faith.	Gl 3:24
trying to be **j-ied** by the law are	Gl 5:4
in the flesh, **j-ied** in the Spirit,	1Tm 3:16
having been **j-ied** by His grace,	Ti 3:7
a man is **j-ied** by works and not	Jms 2:24

JUSTLY

because they refuse to act **j.**	Pr 21:7
No one makes claims **j;**	Is 59:4
anyone who acts **j,** who seeks to	Jr 5:1
Only to act **j,** to love	Mc 6:8
We are punished **j,** because we're	Lk 23:41
to the One who judges **j.**	1Pt 2:23

JUSTUS

1. Another name for Joseph Barsabbas (Ac 1:23).

2. Titius Justus, with whom Paul stayed in Corinth (Ac 18:7).

3. Another name for a man named Jesus who was a fellow minister of Paul (Col 4:11).

K

KADESH

Oasis, also called Kadesh-barnea. Where Abraham fought the Amalekites (Gn 14:7). Where the Israelites camped, they sent out spies, and Moses struck the rock (Nm 13:26; 20:1,11; 27:14; 32:8; Dt 1:46; 9:23; Jdg 11:16-17). Southern limit of Judah (Nm 34:4; Jos 10:41; 15:3).

KEDAR

lived among the tents of **K!**	Ps 120:5
I am dark like the tents of **K,**	Sg 1:5
the flocks of **K** will be gathered	Is 60:7

KEDESH

1. Another name for Kadesh-barnea (Jos 15:23).

2. City of Naphtali (Jos 12:22; 19:37); home of Barak (Jdg 4:6-11). Also called Kedesh in Galilee, a Levitical city (Jos 20:7; 21:32; 1Ch 6:76). Inhabitants exiled to Assyria (2Kg 15:29).

3. Levitical city in Issachar (1Ch 6:72), also called Kishion (Jos 21:28).

KEEP

I will **k** My covenant between Me	Gn 17:7
I have also **kept** you from sinning	Gn 20:6
who love Me and **k** My commands.	Ex 20:6
Fire must be **kept** burning on the	Lv 6:13
testimony to be **kept** as a sign for	Nm 17:10
you to **k** the Sabbath day	Dt 5:15
faithful God who **k-s** His gracious	Dt 7:9
and if you **k** My statutes and	1Kg 9:4
K the Passover of the LORD your	2Kg 23:21
be with me, and **k** me from harm	1Ch 4:10
who **k-s** His gracious covenant with	
those who ... **k** His commands,	Neh 1:5
who **k-s** his word whatever the cost	Ps 15:4
I have **kept** all His ordinances in	Ps 18:22
is great reward in **k-ing** them.	Ps 19:11
k Your servant from willful sins	Ps 19:13
to those who **k** His covenant	Ps 25:10
When I **kept** silent, my bones	Ps 32:3
K your tongue from evil and your	Ps 34:13
for the LORD and **k** His way,	Ps 37:34
The LORD will **k** him and preserve	Ps 41:2
these things, and I **kept** silent;	Ps 50:21
He **k-s** us alive and does not allow	Ps 66:9
committed to **k-ing** Your statutes!	Ps 119:5
How can a young man **k** his way	
pure? By **k-ing** Your word.	Ps 119:9
K me from the way of deceit,	Ps 119:29
I have **kept** my feet from every	Ps 119:101
K me safe from violent men	Ps 140:1
k watch at the door of my lips.	Ps 141:3
K my commands and live	Pr 4:4; 7:2
k your feet away from evil.	Pr 4:27
considered wise when he **k-s** silent,	Pr 17:28

one who **k-s** commands preserves   Pr 19:16
say, "I have **kept** my heart pure;   Pr 20:9
k going and are punished.   Pr 22:3; 27:12
A discerning son **k-s** the law,   Pr 28:7
K falsehood and deceitful words   Pr 30:8
a time to **k** and a time to throw   Ec 3:6
can one person alone **k** warm?   Ec 4:11
wealth **kept** by its owner to his   Ec 5:13
fear God and **k** His commands,   Ec 12:13
K listening, but do not understand;   Is 6:9
You will **k** in perfect peace the   Is 26:3
I will **k** you, and I make you a   Is 42:6
I will not **k** silent because of   Is 62:1
He will **k** his life like the   Jr 38:2
who **kept** watch of My sanctuary   Ezk 44:15
God who **k-s** His gracious covenant   Dn 9:4
K asking, and it will be given   Mt 7:7
into life, **k** the commandments   Mt 19:17
"I have **kept** all these," the young   Mt 19:20
But He **kept** silent and did not   Mk 14:61
the fields and **k-ing** watch at night   Lk 2:8
His mother **kept** all these things in   Lk 2:51
of God and **k** it are blessed!   Lk 11:28
if they were to **k** silent, the   Lk 19:40
Yet none of you **k-s** the law!   Jn 7:19
do know Him, and I **k** His word.   Jn 8:55
for He doesn't **k** the Sabbath!   Jn 9:16
hates his life in this world will **k** it   Jn 12:25
My words and doesn't **k** them,   Jn 12:47
loves Me, he will **k** My word.   Jn 14:23
just as I have **kept** My Father's   Jn 15:10
and they have **kept** Your word.   Jn 17:6
he **kept** back part of the proceeds   Ac 5:2
If you **k** yourselves from these   Ac 15:29
K it to yourself before God.   Rm 14:22
sacred secret **kept** silent for long   Rm 16:25
k-ing God's commandments does.   1Co 7:19
all things and **k** the traditions   1Co 11:2
is obligated to **k** the entire law   Gl 5:3
diligently **k-ing** the unity of the   Eph 4:3
K yourself pure.   1Tm 5:22
k a clear head about everything   2Tm 4:5
the race, I have **kept** the faith.   2Tm 4:7
k-ing our eyes on Jesus, the source   Heb 12:2
and to **k** oneself unstained   Jms 1:27
whoever **k-s** the entire law, yet   Jms 2:10
Go in peace, **k** warm, and eat   Jms 2:16
and unfading, **kept** in heaven for   1Pt 1:4

know Him: by **k-ing** His commands.   1Jn 2:3
Him because we **k** His commands   1Jn 3:22
for God is: to **k** His commands   1Jn 5:3
One who is born of God **k-s** him,   1Jn 5:18
loved by God ... and **kept** by Jesus   Jd 1
prophecy and **k** what is written   Rv 1:3
have **kept** My word, and not denied   Rv 3:8
I will also **k** you from the hour   Rv 3:10
and those who **k** the words of   Rv 22:9

KEEPER

they made me a **k** of the vineyards.   Sg 1:6
My Father is the vineyard **k**.   Jn 15:1

KEILAH

David rescued this city in the Judean foothills from the Philistines but fled when the
inhabitants would have turned him over to
Saul (1Sm 13:1-13).

KENITES

Canaanite tribe (Gn 15:19), perhaps metalworkers. Lived among Israelites (Jdg 1:16;
4:11,17); prophesied against by Balaam (Nm
24:21); spared by Saul (1Sm 15:6).

KENIZZITES

Canaanite tribe (Gn 15:19; Nm 32:12).

KETURAH

Abraham's second wife (Gn 25:1-4).

KEY

I will place the **k** of the House   Is 22:22
give you the **k-s** of the kingdom   Mt 16:19
taken away the **k** of knowledge!   Lk 11:52
and I hold the **k-s** of death and   Rv 1:18
the One who has the **k** of David,   Rv 3:7
The **k** to the shaft of the abyss   Rv 9:1
heaven with the **k** to the abyss   Rv 20:1

KICK

hard for you to **k** against the   Ac 26:14

KIDNAP

For I was **k-ped** from the land
  of the   Gn 40:15
Whoever **k-s** a person must be put   Ex 21:16
also had **k-ped** the women and   1Sm 30:2

KIDNAPPER

or sells him, the **k** must die.   Dt 24:7
homosexuals, for **k-s**, liars   1Tm 1:10

KIDNEYS

and the two k with the fat	Ex 29:13
and the two k with the fat	Lv 3:4
He pierces my k without mercy	Jb 16:13
with the fat of the k of rams.	Is 34:6
He pierced my k with His arrows	Lm 3:13

KIDRON

Valley between Jerusalem and the Mount of Olives (Jn 18:1). David fled across it from Absalom (2Sm 15:23); idols were burned there (1Kg 15:13; 2Kg 23:4,6,12; 2Ch 15:16; 29:16; 30:14).

KILL

his brother Abel and k-ed him.	Gn 4:8
whoever finds me will k me.	Gn 4:14
whoever k-s Cain will suffer	Gn 4:15
For I k-ed a man for wounding me,	Gn 4:23
let's k him and throw him into	Gn 37:20
Now I will k your firstborn son!	Ex 4:23
LORD k-ed every firstborn {male}	Ex 13:15
bring us out of Egypt to k us	Ex 17:3
k-s anyone, he must be put to death	Lv 24:17
Whoever k-s an animal is to make	Lv 24:18
to k us in the wilderness?	Nm 16:13
the one who k-s someone may flee	Nm 35:6
If the LORD had intended to k us,	Jdg 13:23
And the dead he k-ed at his death	Jdg 16:30
servant has k-ed lions and bears	1Sm 17:36
Saul has k-ed his thousands, but	1Sm 18:7
was determined to k David.	1Sm 20:33
altars, and k-ed Your prophets	1Kg 19:10
Am I God, k-ing and giving life	2Kg 5:7
k-ed Your prophets who warned	Neh 9:26
Even if He k-s me, I will hope in	Jb 13:15
he k-s the innocent in secret	Ps 10:8
a time to k and a time to heal;	Ec 3:3
Don't fear those who k the body but are not able to k the soul;	Mt 10:28
k-ed, and be raised the third day.	Mt 16:21
They will k Him, and on the	Mt 17:23
slaves, beat one, k-ed another, and	Mt 21:35
let's k him and take his	Mt 21:38
of them you will k and crucify,	Mt 23:34
The city who k-s the prophets and	Mt 23:37
do evil, to save life or to k?	Mk 3:4
and after He is k-ed, He will rise	Mk 9:31
way to arrest and k Him.	Mk 14:1

and your fathers k-ed them.	Lk 11:47
tower in Siloam fell on and k-ed	Lk 13:4
the Jews were trying to k Him.	Jn 7:1
Why do you want to k Me?	Jn 7:19
to steal and to k and to destroy	Jn 10:10
decided to also k Lazarus,	Jn 12:10
And you k-ed the source of life,	Ac 3:15
Get up, Peter; k and eat!	Ac 10:13
and was going to k himself,	Ac 16:27
and through it k-ed me.	Rm 7:11
they have k-ed Your prophets,	Rm 11:3
for the letter k-s, but the Spirit	2Co 3:6
as being chastened yet not k-ed;	2Co 6:9
They k-ed both the Lord Jesus and	1Th 2:15
to k by the sword, by famine,	Rv 6:8
were released to k a third of	Rv 9:15

KIND (adj)

you have been so k to me,	Ru 2:13
If you will be k to these people	2Ch 10:7
You, Lord, are k and ready to	Ps 86:5
A k man benefits himself, but a	Pr 11:17
but one who is k to the needy	Pr 14:31
for one who is k to the poor.	Pr 28:8
Love is patient; love is k.	1Co 13:4
And be k and compassionate to	Eph 4:32
and to be k, always showing	Ti 3:2

KIND (n)

in it, according to their k-s.	Gn 1:11
the birds according to their k-s,	Gn 6:20
your fields with two k-s of seed,	Lv 19:19
say every k of evil against	Mt 5:11
asked, "What k of man is this?	Mt 8:27
this k does not come out except	Mt 17:21
who and what k of woman this is	Lk 7:39
signify what k of death He was	Jn 12:33
signify by what k of death he	Jn 21:19
different k-s of languages,	1Co 12:10
What k of body will they have	1Co 15:35
of every k of impurity with	Eph 4:19
is a root of all k-s of evil,	1Tm 6:10
we have this k of high priest,	Heb 8:1
forgets what k of man he was.	Jms 1:24
of life bearing 12 k-s of fruit,	Rv 22:2

KINDLE

a quarrelsome man for k-ing strife.	Pr 26:21
Look, all you who k a fire,	Is 50:11
see that I, Yahweh, have k-d it.	Ezk 20:48

KINDNESS

For he did not think to show **k**,	Ps 109:16
whoever shows **k** to the poor will	Pr 14:21
K to the poor is a loan to the	Pr 19:17
human cords, with ropes of **k**.	Hs 11:4
that God's **k** is intended to lead	Rm 2:4
consider God's **k** and severity:	Rm 11:22
by patience, by **k**, by the Holy	2Co 6:6
patience, **k**, goodness, faith	Gl 5:22
grace in {His} **k** to us in Christ	Eph 2:7
compassion, **k**, humility	Col 3:12

KING

k-s of peoples will come from her.	Gn 17:16
A new **k**, who had not known	Ex 1:8
to appoint a **k** over us like all	Dt 17:14
days there was no **k** in Israel;	Jdg 17:6
said, "Give us a **k** to judge us	1Sm 8:6
have rejected Me as their **k**.	1Sm 8:7
shouted, "Long live the **k**!"	1Sm 10:24
the LORD your God is your **k**.	1Sm 12:12
here is the **k** you've chosen,	1Sm 12:13
anointed David **k** over the house	2Sm 2:4
Historical Record of Israel's **K-s**.	1Kg 14:19
in the Book of the **K-s** of Israel.	1Ch 9:1
Artaxerxes, **k** of **k-s**, to Ezra	Ezr 7:12
away to the **k** of terrors.	Jb 18:14
The **k-s** of the earth take their	Ps 2:2
have consecrated My **K** on Zion,	Ps 2:6
of my cry, my **K** and my God, for	Ps 5:2
The LORD is **K** forever and ever;	Ps 10:16
LORD, give victory to the **k**!	Ps 20:9
Who is this **K** of glory?	Ps 24:8
LORD sits enthroned, **K** forever.	Ps 29:10
A **k** is not saved by a large army	Ps 33:16
You are my **K**, my God, who	Ps 44:4
a great **K** over all the earth.	Ps 47:2
is the city of the great **K**.	Ps 48:2
k-s will bring tribute to You.	Ps 68:29
And let all **k-s** bow down to him,	Ps 72:11
feared by the **k-s** of the earth.	Ps 76:12
LORD of Hosts, my **K** and my God.	Ps 84:3
God, a great **K** above all gods.	Ps 95:3
All the **k-s** on earth will give You	Ps 138:4
of Zion rejoice in their **K**.	Ps 149:2
It is by me that **k-s** reign	
and rulers	Pr 8:15
Righteous lips are a **k-**'s delight,	Pr 16:13
A **k-**'s terrible wrath is like the	Pr 20:2

A **k-**'s heart is a water channel in	Pr 21:1
He will stand in the presence of **k-s**.	Pr 22:29
the glory of **k-s** to investigate	Pr 25:2
so the hearts of **k-s** cannot be	Pr 25:3
By justice a **k** brings stability	Pr 29:4
a servant when he becomes **k**,	Pr 30:22
locusts have no **k**, yet all of	Pr 30:27
yet it lives in **k-s**' palaces.	Pr 30:28
The words of **K** Lemuel, an oracle	Pr 31:1
efforts on those who destroy **k-s**.	Pr 31:3
it is not for **k-s** to drink wine or	Pr 31:4
he came from prison to be **k**,	Ec 4:14
Do not curse the **k** even in your	Ec 10:20
a **k** could be held captive in	Sg 7:5
In the year that **K** Uzziah died,	Is 6:1
my eyes have seen the **K**,	Is 6:5
a **k** will reign righteously,	Is 32:1
the LORD is our **K**.	Is 33:22
the Creator of Israel, your **K**.	Is 43:15
K-s will be your foster fathers,	Is 49:23
K-s will shut their mouths because	Is 52:15
in Zion, her **K** not in her midst	Jr 8:19
not fear You, **K** of the nations?	Jr 10:7
the living God and eternal **K**.	Jr 10:10
of Babylon, **k** of **k-s**, against Tyre	Ezk 26:7
Your Majesty, you are **k** of **k-s**.	Dn 2:37
10 horns are 10 **k-s** who will rise	Dn 7:24
installed **k-s**, but not through Me.	Hs 8:4
I give you a **k** in My anger and	Hs 13:11
See, your **K** is coming to you;	Zch 9:9
will become **K** over all the earth	Zch 14:9
I am a great **K**," says the LORD	Mal 1:14
who has been born **K** of the Jews?	Mt 2:2
it is the city of the great **K**.	Mt 5:35
governors and **k-s** because of Me,	Mt 10:18
See, your **K** is coming to you	Mt 21:5
be compared to a **k** who gave a	Mt 22:2
Are You the **K** of the Jews?	Mt 27:11
JESUS THE **K** OF THE JEWS	Mt 27:37
prophets and **k-s** wanted to see	Lk 10:24
Blessed is the **K** who comes in	Lk 19:38
The **k-s** of the Gentiles dominate	Lk 22:25
You are the **K** of Israel!	Jn 1:49
Him by force to make Him **k**,	Jn 6:15
"You are a **k** then?" Pilate asked	Jn 18:37
told the Jews, "Here is your **k**!"	Jn 19:14
We have no **k** but Caesar!	Jn 19:15
The **k-s** of the earth took their	Ac 4:26

that there is another **k**	Ac 17:7
to reign as **k-s** without us	1Co 4:8
Now to the **K** eternal, immortal	1Tm 1:17
for **k-s** and all those who are in	1Tm 2:2
K of **k-s**, and the Lord of lords,	1Tm 6:15
Melchizedek—**K** of Salem, priest	Heb 7:1
ruler of the **k-s** of the earth.	Rv 1:5
Lord of lords and **K** of **k-s**.	Rv 17:14
K OF **K-S** AND LORD OF	Rv 19:16
you may eat the flesh of **k-s**,	Rv 19:18

KINGDOM *see also*
   KINGDOM OF GOD;
   KINGDOM OF HEAVEN

His **k** started with Babylon,	Gn 10:10
you will be My **k** of priests and	Ex 19:6
and I will establish his **k**.	2Sm 7:12
to tear the **k** out of Solomon's	1Kg 11:31
Yours, LORD, is the **k**,	1Ch 29:11
scepter of Your **k** is a scepter	Ps 45:6
Nations rage, **k-s** topple;	Ps 46:6
to God, you **k-s** of the earth;	Ps 68:32
heaven, and His **k** rules over all	Ps 103:19
Your **k** is an everlasting **k**;	Ps 145:13
to tremble, who shook the **k-s**,	Is 14:16
longer be divided into two **k-s**.	Ezk 37:22
will set up a **k** that will never	Dn 2:44
His **k** is an eternal **k**,	Dn 4:3
and His **k** is one that will not	Dn 7:14
but the **k** will be the LORD's.	Ob 21
showed Him all the **k-s** of the world	Mt 4:8
Your **k** come. Your will be done	Mt 6:10
For Yours is the **k** and the power	Mt 6:13
Every **k** divided against itself	Mt 12:25
these are the sons of the **k**.	Mt 13:38
from His **k** everything that causes	Mt 13:41
I will give you the keys of the **k**	Mt 16:19
the Son of Man coming in His **k**.	Mt 16:28
other on Your left, in Your **k**.	Mt 20:21
nation, and **k** against **k**.	Mt 24:7
good news of the **k** will be	Mt 24:14
inherit the **k** prepared for you	Mt 25:34
will give you, up to half my **k**.	Mk 6:23
Blessed is the coming **k** of our	Mk 11:10
and His **k** will have no end.	Lk 1:33
But seek His **k**, and these	Lk 12:31
delights to give you the **k**.	Lk 12:32
I bestow on you a **k**, just as My	Lk 22:29
and drink at My table in My **k**.	Lk 22:30

me when You come into Your **k**!	Lk 23:42
My **k** is not of this world,	Jn 18:36
You restoring the **k** to Israel?	Ac 1:6
when He hands over the **k**	
to God	1Co 15:24
inheritance in the **k** of the Messiah	Eph 5:5
transferred us into the **k** of the Son	Col 1:13
calls you into His own **k** and glory.	1Th 2:12
me safely into His heavenly **k**.	2Tm 4:18
scepter of Your **k** is a scepter	Heb 1:8
faith conquered **k-s**, administered	Heb 11:33
are receiving a **k** that cannot be	Heb 12:28
and heirs of the **k** that He has	Jms 2:5
into the eternal **k** of our Lord	2Pt 1:11
and made us a **k**, priests to His	Rv 1:6
The **k** of the world has become	Rv 11:15

KINGDOM OF GOD (GOD'S KINGDOM)

But seek first the **k** and His	Mt 6:33
then the **k** has come to you.	Mt 12:28
for a rich person to enter the **k**.	Mt 19:24
prostitutes are entering	
the **k** before	Mt 21:31
the **k** will be taken away from you	Mt 21:43
fulfilled, and the **k** has come near.	Mk 1:15
secret of the **k** has been granted to	Mk 4:11
"The **k** is like this," He said.	Mk 4:26
How can we illustrate the **k**,	Mk 4:30
not taste death until they see the **k**	Mk 9:1
to enter the **k** with one eye than	Mk 9:47
for the **k** belongs to such as these.	Mk 10:14
welcome the **k** like a little child	Mk 10:15
those with wealth to enter the **k**!	Mk 10:23
how hard it is to enter the **k**!	Mk 10:24
You are not far from the **k**.	Mk 12:34
I drink it in a new way in the **k**.	Mk 14:25
himself looking forward to the **k**,	Mk 15:43
proclaim the good news about the **k**	Lk 4:43
are poor, because the **k** is yours.	Lk 6:20
the least in the **k** is greater than he.	Lk 7:28
telling the good news of the **k**.	Lk 8:1
to proclaim the **k** and to heal the sick.	Lk 9:2
you go and spread the news of the **k**.	Lk 9:60
plow and looks back is fit for the **k**.	Lk 9:62
What is the **k** like, and what can	Lk 13:18
prophets in the **k** but yourselves	Lk 13:28
recline at the table in the **k**.	Lk 13:29
will eat bread in the **k** is blessed!	Lk 14:15
news of the **k** has been proclaimed,	Lk 16:16

k is not coming with something   Lk 17:20
you see, the k is among you.   Lk 17:21
or children, because of the k,   Lk 18:29
thought the k was going to appear Lk 19:11
happening, know that the k is near. Lk 21:31
again until it is fulfilled in the k.   Lk 22:16
is born again, he cannot see the k.   Jn 3:3
and speaking about the k.   Ac 1:3
troubles on our way into the k.   Ac 14:22
proclaiming the k and teaching   Ac 28:31
the k is not eating and drinking,   Rm 14:17
the k is not in talk but in power.   1Co 4:20
will not inherit **God's kingdom**?   1Co 6:9
and blood cannot inherit the k,   1Co 15:50
such things will not inherit the k.   Gl 5:21
are my co-workers for the k,   Col 4:11
counted worthy of **God's kingdom**,   2Th 1:5

KINGDOM OF HEAVEN
Repent, because the k has come near! Mt 3:2
poor in spirit, because the k is theirs. Mt 5:3
will be called the least in the k.   Mt 5:19
unless ... you will never enter the k.   Mt 5:20
'Lord, Lord!' will enter the k,   Mt 7:21
at the table with ... Jacob in the k.   Mt 8:11
this: 'The k has come near.'   Mt 10:7
the least in the k is greater
     than he.   Mt 11:11
the k has been suffering violence,   Mt 11:12
secrets of the k have granted to   Mt 13:11
The k may be compared to a man Mt 13:24
The k is like a mustard seed   Mt 13:31
The k is like yeast   Mt 13:33
The k is like treasure, buried   Mt 13:44
the k is like a merchant in search Mt 13:45
the k is like a large net thrown   Mt 13:47
k is like a landowner who brings Mt 13:52
I will give you the keys of the k,   Mt 16:19
Who is greatest in the k?   Mt 18:1
unless you ... become like children,
     you will never enter the k.   Mt 18:3
this child ... is the greatest in the k.   Mt 18:4
the k can be compared to a king   Mt 18:23
k is made up of people like this.   Mt 19:14
for a rich person to enter the k!   Mt 19:23
For the k is like a landowner   Mt 20:1
The k may be compared to a king Mt 22:2
You lock up the k from people.   Mt 23:13
Then the k will be like 10 virgins   Mt 25:1

KINGSHIP
to the people the rights of k.   1Sm 10:25
so we can renew the k there.   1Sm 11:14
Saul assumed the k over Israel,   1Sm 14:47
has torn the k of Israel away   1Sm 15:28
as well ask the k for him,   1Kg 2:22
Israel gave the k over Israel to   2Ch 13:5
for k belongs to the LORD;   Ps 22:28

KIRIATH-ARBA
Former name of Hebron (Jos 14:15; Jdg
1:10); Sarah died there (Gn 23:2).

KIRIATH-JEARIM
City on the border of Dan in the south
(Jos 18:15); the ark was there temporarily
(1Sm 6:21–7:2).

KISHON
River in the Jezreel Valley; site of Deborah
and Barak's victory (Jdg 4:7,13; 5:21; Ps
83:9) and Elijah's slaughter of the priests of
Baal (1Kg 18:40).

KISS (n)
enticed and I threw them a k,   Jb 31:27
answer gives a k on the lips.   Pr 24:26
but the k-es of an enemy are   Pr 27:6
You gave Me no k, but she hasn't   Lk 7:45
betraying the Son of Man with a k? Lk 22:48
Greet . . . with a holy k.   Rm 16:16;
          1 Co 16:20; 2 Co 13:12; 1Th 5:26
one another with a k of love.   1Pt 5:14

KISS (v)
Please come closer and k me,   Gn 27:26
Then Jacob k-ed Rachel and wept Gn 29:11
father's face, wept and k-ed him.   Gn 50:1
he and Jonathan k-ed each other 1Sm 20:41
Amasa by the beard to k him.   2Sm 20:9
mouth that has not k-ed him.   1Kg 19:18
Please let me k my father and   1Kg 19:20
She grabs him and k-es him;   Pr 7:13
that he would k me with the   Sg 1:2
find you in public and k you,   Sg 8:1
men who sacrifice k the calves.   Hs 13:2
The One I k, He's the One;   Mt 26:48
embracing Paul, they k-ed him,   Ac 20:37

KITTIM
will come from the coast of K;   Nm 24:24
Ships of K will come against him, Dn 11:30

KNEAD

K three measures of fine flour	Gn 18:6
also took flour, k-ed it, and baked	1Sm 28:24
and the women k dough to make	Jr 7:18

KNEADING

with their k bowls wrapped up in	Ex 12:34

KNEE

every k that has not bowed to	1Kg 19:18
My k-s are weak from fasting,	Ps 109:24
hands, steady the shaking k-s!	Is 35:3
Every k will bow to Me, every	Is 45:23
shook and his k-s knocked together	Dn 5:6
the Lord, every k will bow to Me	Rm 14:11
reason I bow my k-s before the	Eph 3:14
of Jesus every k should bow	Php 2:10
tired hands and weakened k-s,	Heb 12:12

KNEEL

made the camels k beside a well	Gn 24:11
with everyone who k-s to drink.	Jdg 7:5
knelt down in front of the entire	2Ch 6:13
to the dust will k before Him	Ps 22:29
May desert tribes k before him	Ps 72:9
let us k before the LORD our	Ps 95:6
came up and knelt before Him,	Mt 8:2
came and knelt down before Him	Mt 9:18
But she came, knelt before Him,	Mt 15:25
approached and knelt down before	Mt 17:14
She knelt down to ask Him for	Mt 20:20
And they knelt down before Him	Mt 27:29
ran up, knelt down before Him	Mk 10:17
a stone's throw, knelt down,	Lk 22:41
He knelt down, prayed, and turning	Ac 9:40
he knelt down and prayed with all	Ac 20:36
After k-ing down on the beach to	Ac 21:5

KNIFE

and took the k to slaughter his	Gn 22:10
Make flint k-ves and circumcise the	Jos 5:2
he picked up a k, took hold of	Jdg 19:29
and stick a k in your throat if	Pr 23:2
whose fangs are k-ves, devouring	Pr 30:14
their spears into pruning k-ves.	Is 2:4
with a scribe's k and throw the	Jr 36:23
and your pruning k-ves into spears.	Jl 3:10
their spears into pruning k-ves.	Mc 4:3

KNIT

You k me together in my mother's	Ps 139:13
fitted and k together by every	Eph 4:16

KNOCK

k the teeth out of their mouths	Ps 58:6
My love is k-ing! Open to me, my	Sg 5:2
shook and his knees k-ed together.	Dn 5:6
Keep k-ing, and the door will be	Mt 7:7
demon k-ed him down and threw	Lk 9:42
Keep k-ing, and the door will be	Lk 11:9
so that when he comes and k-s,	Lk 12:36
outside and k on the door,	Lk 13:25
He k-ed at the door in the gateway	Ac 12:13
I stand at the door and k.	Rv 3:20

KNOW

God k-s that when you eat it your	Gn 3:5
be like God, k-ing good and evil.	Gn 3:5
and they knew they were naked;	Gn 3:7
like one of Us, k-ing good and evil	Gn 3:22
Adam knew his wife Eve intimately,	Gn 4:1
For now I k that you fear God,	Gn 22:12
this place, and I did not k it.	Gn 28:16
new king, who had not k-n Joseph,	Ex 1:8
You will k that I am Yahweh your	Ex 6:7
Egyptians will k that I am the	Ex 7:5
You said, 'I k you by name,	Ex 33:12
K that Yahweh your God is God,	Dt 7:9
to k what was in your heart,	Dt 8:2
you and your fathers had not k-n,	Dt 8:3
whom the LORD knew face to face.	Dt 34:10
and you k with all your heart	Jos 23:14
rose up who did not k the LORD	Jdg 2:10
will k that Israel has a God.	1Sm 17:46
because I thought, 'Who k-s?	2Sm 12:22
Angel of God, k-ing everything	2Sm 14:20
a people I had not k-n serve me.	2Sm 22:44
You alone k every human heart,	1Kg 8:39
earth may k that the LORD is God.	1Kg 8:60
he will k there is a prophet in Israel.	2Kg 5:8
But I k your sitting down,	2Kg 19:27
my son, k the God of your father,	1Ch 28:9
Who k-s, perhaps you have come	Est 4:14
{born only} yesterday and k nothing.	Jb 8:9
But I k my living Redeemer,	Jb 19:25
What does God k? Can He judge	Jb 22:13
If only I knew how to find Him,	Jb 23:3
Yet He k-s the way I have taken;	Jb 23:10
Certainly you k! Who stretched	Jb 38:5
too wonderful for me to k.	Jb 42:3
Those who k Your name trust in	Ps 9:10

Now I **k** that the LORD gives   Ps 20:6

since He **k-s** the secrets of the   Ps 44:21

and **k** that I am God,   Ps 46:10

This I **k**: God is for me   Ps 56:9

God is **k-n** in Judah; His name is   Ps 76:1

The LORD **k-s** man's thoughts;   Ps 94:11

For He **k-s** what we are made of,   Ps 103:14

and its place is no longer **k-n**.   Ps 103:16

You have searched me and **k-n** me.   Ps 139:1

You **k** when I sit down and when I   Ps 139:2

and I **k** {this} very well   Ps 139:14

Search me, God, and **k** my heart;   Ps 139:23

displeasure is **k-n** at once,   Pr 12:16

a young man is **k-n** by his actions   Pr 20:11

beat me, but I didn't **k** it!   Pr 23:35

But we didn't **k** about this,   Pr 24:12

He who protects your life **k**?   Pr 24:12

who **k-s** what disaster these two   Pr 24:22

for you don't **k** what a day might   Pr 27:1

the name of His Son—if you **k**?   Pr 30:4

Her husband is **k-n** at the city   Pr 31:23

I applied my mind to **k** wisdom   Ec 1:17

And who **k-s** whether he will be a   Ec 2:19

Who **k-s** if the spirit of people   Ec 3:21

For who **k-s** what is good for man   Ec 6:12

Yet no one **k-s** what will happen,   Ec 8:7

but the dead don't **k** anything.   Ec 9:5

No one **k-s** what will happen,   Ec 10:14

The ox **k-s** its owner, and the   Is 1:3

before the boy **k-s** to reject what   Is 7:16

and Egypt will **k** the LORD on   Is 19:21

say, "Who sees us? Who **k-s** us?"   Is 29:15

But I **k** your sitting down,   Is 37:28

Do you not **k**? Have you not heard?   Is 40:21

Then all flesh will **k** that I,   Is 49:26

My people will **k** My name;   Is 52:6

summon a nation you do not **k**,   Is 55:5

nation whose language you do not **k**   Jr 5:15

stork in the sky **k-s** her seasons.   Jr 8:7

that he understands and **k-s** Me   Jr 9:24

I will give them a heart to **k** Me,   Jr 24:7

I am He who **k-s**, and I am a   Jr 29:23

K the LORD, for they will all **k** Me,   Jr 31:34

will **k** that a prophet has been among   Ezk 2:5

Then they will **k** that I am Yahweh.   Ezk 6:14

I had made Myself **k-n** to Israel by   Ezk 20:9

nations will **k** that I am Yahweh   Ezk 36:23

Lord GOD, {only} You **k**.   Ezk 37:3

He **k-s** what is in the darkness,   Dn 2:22

I wanted to **k** the true meaning   Dn 7:19

K and understand this: From the   Dn 9:25

and you will **k** the LORD.   Hs 2:20

Let us strive to **k** the LORD.   Hs 6:3

but they never **knew** that I healed   Hs 11:3

you **k** no God but Me, and no   Hs 13:4

Who **k-s**? He may turn and relent   Jl 2:14

I have **k** only you out of all the   Am 3:2

Who **k-s**? God may turn and relent   Jnh 3:9

I **knew** that You are a merciful and   Jnh 4:2

but did not **k** her intimately   Mt 1:25

your left hand **k** what your right   Mt 6:3

your Father **k-s** the things you need   Mt 6:8

k how to give good gifts to your   Mt 7:11

I never **knew** you! Depart from Me,   Mt 7:23

hidden that won't be made **k-n**.   Mt 10:26

No one **k-s** the Son except the   Mt 11:27

K-ing their thoughts, He told them: Mt 12:25

for a tree is **k-n** by its fruit.   Mt 12:33

have been given for you to **k**,   Mt 13:11

You **k** how to read the   Mt 16:3

answered Jesus, "We don't **k**."   Mt 21:27

you don't **k** the Scriptures   Mt 22:29

that day and hour no one **k-s**   Mt 24:36

you don't **k** what day your Lord   Mt 24:42

I assure you: I do not **k** you!   Mt 25:12

you don't **k** either the day   Mt 25:13

an oath, "I don't **k** the man!"   Mt 26:72

But so you may **k** that the Son of   Mk 2:10

warn them not to make Him **k-n**.   Mk 3:12

so that you may **k** the certainty   Lk 1:4

which the Lord has made **k-n** to us.   Lk 2:15

Didn't you **k** that I had to be   Lk 2:49

But He **knew** their thoughts and told   Lk 6:8

but God **k-s** your hearts.   Lk 16:15

deny three times that you **k** Me!   Lk 22:34

He Himself **knew** what was in man   Jn 2:25

speak what We **k** and We testify   Jn 3:11

If you **knew** the gift of God,   Jn 4:10

We worship what we do **k**,   Jn 4:22

For Jesus **knew** from the beginning   Jn 6:64

believe and **k** that You are the Holy   Jn 6:69

I **k** Him because I am from Him,   Jn 7:29

you would also **k** My Father.   Jn 8:19

You will **k** the truth, and the   Jn 8:32

One thing I do **k**: I was blind   Jn 9:25

I **k** My own sheep, and they **k** Me,   Jn 10:14

He **knew** who would betray Him. Jn 13:11
people will **k** that you are My Jn 13:35
You **k** the way where I am going. Jn 14:4
k Me, you will also **k** My Father. Jn 14:7
slave doesn't **k** what his master Jn 15:15
Now we **k** that You **k** everything Jn 16:30
that they may **k** You, the only true Jn 17:3
The world has not **k-n** You. Jn 17:25
k-ing everything that was about to Jn 18:4
to Him, "You **k** that I love You. Jn 21:15
We **k** that his testimony is true Jn 21:24
not for you to **k** times or Ac 1:7
You, Lord, **k** the hearts of all; Ac 1:24
house of Israel **k** with certainty Ac 2:36
Jesus I **k**, and Paul I recognize Ac 19:15
not **k-ing** what I will encounter Ac 20:22
since what can be **k-n** about God is Rm 1:19
For though they **knew** God, they Rm 1:21
path of peace they have not **k-n**. Rm 3:17
would not have **k-n** sin if it were not Rm 7:7
searches the hearts **k-s** the Spirit's Rm 8:27
We **k** that all things work Rm 8:28
For who has **k-n** the mind of the Rm 11:34
the world did not **k** God through 1Co 1:21
I determined to **k** nothing among 1Co 2:2
no one **k-s** the concerns of God 1Co 2:11
is not able to **k** it since it is 1Co 2:14
who has **k-n** the Lord's mind, 1Co 2:16
Don't you **k** that you are God's 1Co 3:16
The Lord **k-s** the reasonings of 1Co 3:20
Do you not **k** that your body is a 1Co 6:19
how do you **k** whether you will 1Co 7:16
If anyone thinks he **k-s** anything, 1Co 8:2
Do you not **k** that the runners in 1Co 9:24
Now I **k** in part, but then I will **k**
    fully, as I am fully **k-n**. 1Co 13:12
k-ing that your labor in the Lord 1Co 15:58
every place the scent of **k-ing** Him. 2Co 2:14
k-ing that the One who raised the 2Co 4:14
k anyone in a purely human way. 2Co 5:16
One who did not **k** sin to be sin 2Co 5:21
out of the body, I don't **k**; God **k-s**. 2Co 12:2
when you didn't **k** God, you were Gl 4:8
or rather have become **k-n** by God, Gl 4:9
He made **k-n** to us the mystery of Eph 1:9
k the Messiah's love that surpasses Eph 3:19
and I don't **k** which one I should Php 1:22
the surpassing value of **k-ing** Christ Php 3:8

to **k** Him and the power of His Php 3:10
your requests be made **k-n** to God. Php 4:6
I **k** both how to have a little, Php 4:12
the Gentiles who don't **k** God, 1Th 4:5
because I **k** whom I have believed 2Tm 1:12
The Lord **k-s** those who are His, 2Tm 2:19
childhood you have **k-n** the sacred 2Tm 3:15
They profess to **k** God, but they Ti 1:16
'**K** the Lord,' ... they will all **k** Me Heb 8:11
k-ing that you yourselves have a Heb 10:34
went out, not **k-ing** where he was Heb 11:8
angels as guests without **k-ing** it. Heb 13:2
k-ing that the testing of your faith Jms 1:3
You don't even **k** what tomorrow Jms 4:14
for the person who **k-s** to do good Jms 4:17
k-ing that the same sufferings are 1Pt 5:9
for them not to have **k-n** the way 2Pt 2:21
who says, "I have come to **k** Him," 1Jn 2:4
does not **k** us is that it didn't **k** Him. 1Jn 3:1
We **k** that when He appears, 1Jn 3:2
sins has not seen Him or **k-n** Him. 1Jn 3:6
to **k** love: He laid down His life 1Jn 3:16
is how we will **k** we are of the 1Jn 3:19
our hearts and **k-s** all things. 1Jn 3:20
has been born of God and **k-s** God. 1Jn 4:7
This is how we **k** that we love 1Jn 5:2
so that you may **k** that you have 1Jn 5:13
We **k** that we are of God, 1Jn 5:19
I **k** your works Rv 2:2,19; 3:1,8,15
that no one **k-s** except the one who Rv 2:17
who haven't **k-n** the deep things of Rv 2:24
that no one **k-s** except Himself. Rv 19:12

KNOWLEDGE

the tree of the **k** of good and evil. Gn 2:9
for the LORD is a God of **k**, 1Sm 2:3
grant me wisdom and **k** so that I 2Ch 1:10
Can anyone teach God **k**, Jb 21:22
after night they communicate **k**. Ps 19:2
the One who teaches man **k** Ps 94:10
extraordinary **k** is beyond me. Ps 139:6
of the LORD is the beginning of **k**; Pr 1:7
and {you} fools hate **k**? Pr 1:22
and **k** rather than pure gold. Pr 8:10
The wise store up **k**, Pr 10:14
Whoever loves instruction loves **k**, Pr 12:1
A shrewd person conceals **k**, Pr 12:23
but **k** {comes} easily to the Pr 14:6
zeal is not good without **k**, Pr 19:2

by **k** the rooms are filled with | Pr 24:4
and I have no **k** of the Holy One | Pr 30:3
as **k** increases, grief increases | Ec 1:18
advantage of **k** is that wisdom | Ec 7:12
no work, planning, **k**, or wisdom | Ec 9:10
a Spirit of **k** and of the fear of | Is 11:2
as full of the **k** of the LORD as | Is 11:9
will be satisfied with His **k**. | Is 53:11
roam about, and **k** will increase. | Dn 12:4
are destroyed for lack of **k**. | Hs 4:6
the **k** of God rather than burnt | Hs 6:6
filled with the **k** of the LORD's | Hab 2:14
have taken away the key of **k**! | Lk 11:52
worthwhile to have God in their **k**, | Rm 1:28
in the law the full expression of **k** | Rm 2:20
for God, but not according to **k**. | Rm 10:2
of the wisdom and the **k** of God! | Rm 11:33
filled with all **k**, and able to | Rm 15:14
K inflates with pride, but love | 1Co 8:1
weak ... is ruined by your **k**. | 1Co 8:11
to another, a message of **k** | 1Co 12:8
all mysteries and all **k**, | 1Co 13:2
as for **k**, it will come to an end | 1Co 13:8
light of the **k** of God's glory | 2Co 4:6
by purity, by **k**, by patience, by | 2Co 6:6
raised up against the **k** of God, | 2Co 10:5
to know ... love that surpasses **k**, | Eph 3:19
filled with the **k** of His will in | Col 1:9
of wisdom and **k** are hidden. | Col 2:3
from the "**k**" that falsely bears | 1Tm 6:20
to come to a **k** of the truth. | 2Tm 3:7
with goodness, goodness with **k**, | 2Pt 1:5
in the grace and **k** of our Lord | 2Pt 3:18
Holy One, and you all have **k**. | 1Jn 2:20

KNOWLEDGEABLE

but **k** lips are a rare treasure. | Pr 20:15
with a discerning and **k** person, | Pr 28:2

KOHATH

Son of Levi (Gn 46:11). Transported the tabernacle's holy objects (Nm 4:15; 1Ch 15:5,12-15). Continued in service (2Ch 20:19; 29:12; 34:12; 1Ch 9:32).

KORAH

1. Son of Esau (Gn 36:5).
2. Led rebellion against Moses (Nm 16; Jd 11).

3. Kohathite Levite (Ex 6:21; 1Ch 6:22); ancestor of temple singers (2Ch 20:19; Pss 42; 44–49; 84–85; 87–88).

4. Son of Hebron (2Ch 2:43).

KOUM

and said to her, "Talitha **k**!" | Mk 5:41

KUE

were imported from Egypt and K. | 1Kg 10:28

L

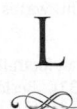

LABAN

1. Rebekah's brother (Gn 24:29); father of Leah and Rachel (Gn 29:15-30).

2. City in the Transjordanian wilderness (Dt 1:1).

LABOR (n)

I will intensify your **l** pains; | Gn 3:16
to oppress them with forced **l**. | Ex 1:11
imposed forced **l** on the | Jos 17:13
as forced **l** but never drove | Jdg 1:28
was in charge of forced **l**; | 2Sm 20:24
fruit of their **l** to the locust. | Ps 78:46
The **l** of the righteous leads to | Pr 10:16
laziness will lead to forced **l**. | Pr 12:24
it through **l** will multiply it | Pr 13:11
Give her the reward of her **l**, | Pr 31:31
and rejoice in his **l**. | Ec 5:19
in anguish like a woman in **l**. | Is 13:8
Yet as soon as Zion was in **l**, | Is 66:8
agony like a woman in **l**. | Jr 22:23
L pains come on him. | Hs 13:13
Zion, like a woman in **l**. | Mc 4:10
she who is in **l** has given birth | Mc 5:3
a woman is in **l** she has pain | Jn 16:21
together with **l** pains until now | Rm 8:22
reward according to his own **l**. | 1Co 3:8
that your **l** in the Lord is | 1Co 15:58
with far more **l**-s, many more | 2Co 11:23
l and hardship, many sleepless | 2Co 11:27
your work of faith, **l** of love | 1Th 1:3
and cried out in **l** and agony to | Rv 12:2
let them rest from their **l**-s, | Rv 14:13

LABOR (v)

You are to l six days and do all	Ex 20:9
You are to l six days and do all	Dt 5:13
why should I l in vain?	Jb 9:29
its builders l over it in vain;	Ps 127:1
you did not l over and did not	Jnh 4:10
they don't l or spin thread.	Mt 6:28
to reap what you didn't l for;	Jn 4:38

LABORER

The l is worthy of his wages.	1Tm 5:18

LACHISH

City in the Judean foothills, conquered by Joshua (Jos 10:3-33). Besieged by Assyria (2Kg 18; 2Ch 32; Is 36).

LACK

the whole city for l of five?	Gn 18:28
40 years, and you have l-ed nothing.	Dt 2:7
where you will l nothing;	Dt 8:9
Israel is a nation l-ing sense	Dt 32:28
40 years and they l-ed nothing.	Neh 9:21
anyone dying for l of clothing	Jb 31:19
shepherd; there is nothing I l.	Ps 23:1
LORD will not l any good thing.	Ps 34:10
who commits adultery l-s sense;	Pr 6:32
a young man l-ing sense.	Pr 7:7
To the one who l-s sense, she says	Pr 9:4,16
but fools die for l of sense.	Pr 10:21
chases fantasies l-s sense.	Pr 12:11
A leader who l-s understanding is	Pr 28:16
he will not l anything good.	Pr 31:11
what is l-ing cannot be counted.	Ec 1:15
it never l-s mixed wine.	Sg 7:2
exile because they l knowledge;	Is 5:13
scattered for l of a shepherd;	Ezk 34:5
destroyed for l of knowledge.	Hs 4:6
You l one thing: Go, sell all	Mk 10:21
or sandals, did you l anything?	Lk 22:35
a nation that l-s understanding.	Rm 10:19
Do not l diligence; be fervent	Rm 12:11
that you do not l any spiritual	1Co 1:7
of your l of self-control	1Co 7:5
they l understanding.	2Co 10:12
up what was l-ing in your ministry	Php 2:30
my flesh what is l-ing in Christ's	Col 1:24
for their l of understanding	2Tm 3:9
so that they will l nothing.	Ti 3:13
mature and complete, l-ing nothing.	Jms 1:4

Now if any of you l-s wisdom,	Jms 1:5
clothes and l-s daily food,	Jms 2:15
The person who l-s these things is	2Pt 1:9

LADY

girl when she ousts her l.	Pr 30:23
To the elect l and her children	2Jn 1

LAHMI

killed L the brother of Goliath	1Ch 20:5

LAISH

Peaceful northern Canaanite city seized and renamed by Dan (Jdg 18).

LAKE

was standing by L Gennesaret.	Lk 5:1
windstorm came down on the l;	Lk 8:23
were thrown alive into the l of fire	Rv 19:20
second death, the l of fire.	Rv 20:14
will be in the l that burns with	Rv 21:8

LAMB

but where is the l for the burnt	Gn 22:7
God Himself will provide the l	Gn 22:8
and slaughter the Passover l.	Ex 12:21
an unblemished year-old ewe l,	Lv 14:10
poor man had ... one small ewe l	2Sm 12:3
l-s will provide your clothing,	Pr 27:26
The wolf will live with the l,	Is 11:6
He gathers the l-s in His arms	Is 40:11
Like a l led to the slaughter	Is 53:7
The wolf and the l will feed	Is 65:25
like a docile l led to slaughter	Jr 11:19
like l-s to the slaughter,	Jr 51:40
dine on l-s from the flock and	Am 6:4
they sacrifice the Passover l,	Mk 14:12
you out like l-s among wolves.	Lk 10:3
L of God, who takes away the sin	Jn 1:29
"Feed My l-s," He told him.	Jn 21:15
as a l is silent before its shearer,	Ac 8:32
like that of a l without defect	1Pt 1:19
a slaughtered l standing between	Rv 5:6
L who was slaughtered is worthy	Rv 5:12
and from the wrath of the L,	Rv 6:16
by the blood of the L and by the	Rv 12:11
book of life of the L	Rv 13:8
who follow the L wherever He	Rv 14:4
and the song of the L:	Rv 15:3
to the marriage feast of the L!	Rv 19:9

and its lamp is the L.   Rv 21:23
written in the L-'s book of life.   Rv 21:27

LAME

no man who is blind, l,   Lv 21:18
if it is l or blind or has any   Dt 15:21
blind and the l will never enter   2Sm 5:8
son who is l in both feet.   2Sm 9:3
they did their l dance around   1Kg 18:26
to the blind and feet to the l.   Jb 29:15
a fool is like l legs that hang   Pr 26:7
the l will plunder it   Is 33:23
Then the l will leap like a deer   Is 35:6
blind and the l will be with them   Jr 31:8
I will make the l into a remnant   Mc 4:7
I will save the l and gather the   Zph 3:19
you present a l or sick {animal},   Mal 1:8
the blind see, the l walk,   Mt 11:5
you to enter life maimed or l,   Mt 18:8
the poor, maimed, blind, and l!   Lk 14:21
who was l from his mother's womb   Ac 3:2
what is l may not be dislocated,   Heb 12:13

LAMECH

1. Son of Methushael (Gn 4:18-24).
2. Son of Methuselah, father of Noah (Gn 5:25-31; 1Ch 1:3; Lk 3:36).

LAMENT (n)

the following l for Saul and his   2Sm 1:17
the king sang a l for Abner: 2Sm 3:33
You turned my l into dancing;   Ps 30:11
and no cry of l in our public   Ps 144:14
heard in Ramah, a l with bitter   Jr 31:15
Is a l and should be used as a l.   Ezk 19:14
This is a l that will be   Ezk 32:16
for you, a l, house of Israel: Am 5:1
we sang a l, but you didn't   Mt 11:17

LAMENT (v)

across the Jordan, they l-ed   Gn 50:10
but the widows could not l.   Ps 78:64
her gates will l and mourn;   Is 3:26
hooks into the Nile will l,   Is 19:8
you must not l or weep or let   Ezk 24:16
their wailing they l for you,   Ezk 27:32
Dress {in sackcloth} and l,   Jl 1:13
of this I will l and wail;   Mc 1:8
players and a crowd l-ing loudly.   Mt 9:23
who were mourning and l Him.   Lk 23:27

LAMENTATION

and l within Daughter Judah.   Lm 2:5
and all your songs into l;   Am 8:10

LAMP

Make seven l-s on it.   Ex 25:37
to keep the l burning continually.   Ex 27:20
Before the l of God had gone out   1Sm 3:3
not extinguish the l of Israel.   2Sm 21:17
will always have a l before Me   1Kg 11:36
God gave him a l in Jerusalem to   1Kg 15:4
to give a l to David and to   2Kg 8:19
and their l-s of pure gold   2Ch 4:20
and the l beside him is put out   Jb 18:6
How often is the l of the wicked   Jb 21:17
LORD, You light my l;   Ps 18:28
Your word is a l for my feet and   Ps 119:105
prepared a l for My anointed   Ps 132:17
For a commandment is a l,   Pr 6:23
the l of the wicked is extinguished.   Pr 13:9
his l will go out in deep   Pr 20:20
and her l never goes out at   Pr 31:18
I will search Jerusalem with l-s   Zph 1:12
It has seven l-s on it and seven   Zch 4:2
No one lights a l and puts it   Mt 5:15
The eye is the l of the body.   Mt 6:22
like 10 virgins who took their l-s   Mt 25:1
for service and have your l-s lit.   Lk 12:35
light a l, sweep the house   Lk 15:8
was a burning and shining l,   Jn 5:35
There were many l-s in the room   Ac 20:8
as to a l shining in a dismal   2Pt 1:19
the light of a l will never   Rv 18:23
and its l is the Lamb.   Rv 21:23

LAMPLIGHT

will not need l or sunlight,   Rv 22:5

LAMPSTAND

a l out of pure, hammered gold.   Ex 25:31
I see a solid gold l there with a bowl   Zch 4:2
but rather on a l, and it gives light   Mt 5:15
holy place," were the l, the table,   Heb 9:2
seven l-s are the seven churches.   Rv 1:20
and remove your l from its place   Rv 2:5
two l-s that stand before the Lord   Rv 11:4

LANCE

with a flashing spear and a l.   Jb 39:23
Polish the l-s; put on armor!   Jr 46:4

LAND

and let the dry l appear.	Gn 1:9
God called the dry l "earth,"	Gn 1:10
If you work the l, it will never	Gn 4:12
house to the l that I will show	Gn 12:1
I will give this l to your	Gn 12:7
Isn't the whole l before you?	Gn 13:9
to give you this l to possess.	Gn 15:7
I will give the l where you are	Gn 17:8
will go to my l and my family to	Gn 24:4
I will give this l to your	Gn 24:7
For I will give all these l-s to you	Gn 26:3
will bring you back to this l,	Gn 28:15
this l, and return to your native l.	Gn 31:13
The l that I gave to Abraham and	Gn 35:12
up from this l to the l He promised	Gn 50:24
a stranger in a foreign l.	Ex 2:22
a l flowing with milk and honey	Ex 3:8
the l they lived in as foreigners.	Ex 6:4
bring you to the l that I swore to give	Ex 6:8
brought you out of the l of Egypt,	Ex 20:2
the l will observe a Sabbath to	Lv 25:2
you are only ... residents on My l.	Lv 25:23
Send men to scout out the l of	Nm 13:2
distribute the l as an	Nm 34:17
can be no atonement for the l	Nm 35:33
bless you in the l the LORD your	Dt 28:8
the LORD showed him all the l:	Dt 34:1
and He will give you this l.	Jos 1:13
So Joshua took the entire l,	Jos 11:23
This is the l that remains:	Jos 13:2
divide this l as an inheritance	Jos 13:7
I gave you a l you did not labor	Jos 24:13
Canaanites refused to leave this l.	Jdg 1:27
day you buy the l from Naomi,	Ru 4:5
of Assyria invaded the whole l,	2Kg 17:5
the custom of the God of the l.	2Kg 17:26
Who among the gods of the l-s	2Kg 18:35
Judah went into exile from its l.	2Kg 25:21
forgive their sin, and heal their l.	2Ch 7:14
found in the l of the living.	Jb 28:13
nations will perish from His l.	Ps 10:16
in the l of the living.	Ps 27:13
the humble will inherit the l	Ps 37:11
He turned the sea into dry l,	Ps 66:6
He brought them to His holy l,	Ps 78:54
You showed favor to Your l;	Ps 85:1
His hands formed the dry l.	Ps 95:5
He gave them the l-s of	
the nations	Ps 105:44
scattering them throughout	
the l-s.	Ps 106:27
and has gathered them from the l-s	Ps 107:3
will be powerful in the l;	Ps 112:2
portion in the l of the living.	Ps 142:5
I am like parched l before You.	Ps 143:6
the upright will inhabit the l,	Pr 2:21
who works his l will have plenty	Pr 12:11
from a distant l is like cold	Pr 25:25
Woe to you, l, when your king is	Ec 10:16
pay attention, all you distant l-s;	Is 8:9
and your l will be married.	Is 62:4
Can a l be born in one day,	Is 66:8
My flock from all the l-s where I	Jr 23:3
the most beautiful of all l-s.	Ezk 20:6
will bring you into your own l.	Ezk 36:24
make them one nation in the l,	Ezk 37:22
also invade the beautiful l,	Dn 11:41
and strike the l with a curse.	Mal 4:6
was already over a mile from l,	Mt 14:24
travel over l and sea to make	Mt 23:15
darkness came over the whole l.	Mt 27:45
to put out a little from the l.	Lk 5:3
A rich man's l was very	Lk 12:16
since they were not far from l	Jn 21:8
those who owned l-s or houses sold	Ac 4:34
He gave their l to them as an	Ac 13:19
he himself was going by l.	Ac 20:13
this way, all got safely to l.	Ac 27:44
may have a long life in the l.	Eph 6:3
foreigner in the l of promise,	Heb 11:9
they now aspire to a better l	Heb 11:16
You have lived luxuriously on the l	Jms 5:5
gave rain and the l produced its	Jms 5:18
on the sea, his left on the l,	Rv 10:2

LANDOWNER

The l-'s slaves came to him and	Mt 13:27
is like a l who brings out	Mt 13:52
heaven is like a l who went out	Mt 20:1
was a man, a l, who planted	Mt 21:33

LANES

Go out into the highways and l	Lk 14:23

LANGUAGE

Each {group} had its own l.	Gn 10:5
the whole earth had the same l	Gn 11:1

LORD confused the l of the whole	Gn 11:9
a nation whose l you don't	Dt 28:49
children spoke the l of Ashdod	Neh 13:24
each ethnic group in its own l,	Est 1:22
I heard an unfamiliar l:	Ps 81:5
people who spoke a foreign l	Ps 114:1
powerful nation with a strange l,	Is 18:2
He will speak ... in a foreign l.	Is 28:11
to gather all nations and l-s;	Is 66:18
a nation whose l you do not know	Jr 5:15
difficult l but to the house of Israel.	Ezk 3:5
they will speak in new l-s;	Mk 16:17
and not using any figurative l.	Jn 16:29
began to speak in different l-s,	Ac 2:4
heard them speaking in his own l.	Ac 2:6
in our own l-s the magnificent	Ac 2:11
in {other} l-s and declaring	Ac 10:46
with {other} l-s and to prophesy.	Ac 19:6
different kinds of l-s, to another,	
interpretation of l-s.	1Co 12:10
managing, various kinds of l-s.	1Co 12:28
Do all speak in l-s?	1Co 12:30
If I speak the l-s of men and of	1Co 13:1
as for l-s, they will cease;	1Co 13:8
person who speaks in {another} l	1Co 14:2
I wish all of you spoke in other l-s,	1Co 14:5
For if I pray in {another} l,	1Co 14:14
speak in {other} l-s more than all	1Co 14:18
10,000 words in {another} l.	1Co 14:19
of other l-s and by the lips	1Co 14:21
not forbid speaking in {other} l-s.	1Co 14:39
and filthy l from your mouth.	Col 3:8
every tribe and l and people	Rv 5:9
people, and l, which no one	Rv 7:9
peoples, nations, l-s, and kings.	Rv 10:11
peoples, tribes, l-s, and nations	Rv 11:9
tribe, people, l, and nation.	Rv 13:7
nation, tribe, l, and people.	Rv 14:6
multitudes, nations, and l-s.	Rv 17:15

LAODICEA

City in southwest Asia Minor for which Paul was concerned (Col 2:1; 4:15-16); one of the seven churches (Rv 1:11; 3:14).

LAP

The lot is cast into the l,	Pr 16:33
will be poured into your l.	Lk 6:38

LAPPED

deliver you with the 300 men who l	Jdg 7:7

LARGE

The l house will be smashed to	Am 6:11
was an extremely l city,	Jnh 3:3
Such l crowds gathered around	Mt 13:2
Look at what l letters I have	Gl 6:11
also have such a l cloud of	Heb 12:1
though very l and driven by	Jms 3:4

LASHES

He may be flogged with 40 l,	Dt 25:3
than a hundred l into a fool.	Pr 17:10
L and wounds purge away evil,	Pr 20:30
from the Jews 40 l minus one.	2Co 11:24

LAST (adj)

He took his l breath and died at	Gn 25:8
These are the l words of David:	2Sm 23:1
In the l days the mountain of	Is 2:2
In the l days, I will restore	Jr 49:39
It will happen in the l days,	Ezk 38:16
what will happen in the l days.	Dn 2:28
to your people in the l days,	Dn 10:14
to His goodness in the l days.	Hs 3:5
In the l days the mountain of	Mc 4:1
are first will be l, and the l first.	Mt 19:30
to give this l man the same as	Mt 20:14
So the l will be first, and the first l.	Mt 20:16
he must be l of all and servant	Mk 9:35
that man's l condition is worse	Lk 11:26
until you have paid the l cent.	Lk 12:59
will raise him up on the l day.	Jn 6:40
On the l and most important day	Jn 7:37
the resurrection at the l day.	Jn 11:24
will judge him on the l day.	Jn 12:48
And it will be in the l days,	Ac 2:17
apostles, in l place, like men	1Co 4:9
The l enemy He abolishes is	1Co 15:26
the l Adam became a life-giving	1Co 15:45
of an eye, at the l trumpet.	1Co 15:52
times will come in the l days.	2Tm 3:1
In these l days, He has spoken	Heb 1:2
up treasure in the l days!	Jms 5:3
to be revealed in the l time.	1Pt 1:5
the l state is worse for them	2Pt 2:20
come in the l days to scoff,	2Pt 3:3
Children, it is the l hour.	1Jn 2:18
Your l works are greater than	Rv 2:19

LAST (adv)

Then l of all the woman died.	Mt 22:27
L of all, as to one abnormally	1Co 15:8

LAST (n)

This one, at l, is bone of my	Gn 2:23
breathes his l—where is he?	Jb 14:10
He will stand on the dust at l.	Jb 19:25
first, and with the l—I am He.	Is 41:4
I am the first and I am the l.	Is 44:6
am the first, I am also the l.	Is 48:12
a loud cry and breathed His l.	Mk 15:37
I am the First and the L,	Rv 1:17
First and the L, the Beginning	Rv 22:13

LAST (v)

For His anger l-s only a moment,	Ps 30:5
inheritance will l forever.	Ps 37:18
{his} assets, man will not l;	Ps 49:12
his throne as long as heaven l-s.	Ps 89:29
not even a crown l-s for all time.	Pr 27:24
all God does will l forever;	Ec 3:14
the food that l-s for eternal life	Jn 6:27

LASTING (adj)

establish a l dynasty for him	1Sm 2:35
to make a l dynasty for my	1Sm 25:28
build you a l dynasty just as	1Kg 11:38
l wealth and righteousness.	Pr 8:18
there is no l remembrance of the	Ec 2:16

LATE

the early and l rains,	Dt 11:14
vain you get up early and stay up l,	Ps 127:2
who gives the rain, both early and l,	Jr 5:24
certainly come and not be l.	Hab 2:3
and it is already l.	Mt 14:15
the early and the l rains.	Jms 5:7

LATER

LORD your God in l days and obey	Dt 4:30
Come back l. I'll give it tomorrow	Pr 3:28
rashly and l to reconsider his vows.	Pr 20:25
those who come l will not	Ec 4:16
Yet l he changed his mind and	Mt 21:29

LATIN

in Hebrew, L, and Greek.	Jn 19:20

LATRINE

of Baal and made it a l	2Kg 10:27

LATTER

LORD blessed the l part of Job's	Jb 42:12
that in the l times some will	1Tm 4:1

LATTICE

she {peered} through the l,	Jdg 5:28
through the l-d window of his	2Kg 1:2
my house I looked through my l.	Pr 7:6
windows, peering through the l.	Sg 2:9

LAUGH

Abraham fell to the ground, l-ed,	Gn 17:17
Why did Sarah l,	Gn 18:13
God has made me l, and everyone	Gn 21:6
You will l at destruction and	Jb 5:22
she l-s at the horse and its rider	Jb 39:18
He l-s at fear,	Jb 39:22
and he l-s at the whirring of a	Jb 41:29
The One enthroned in heaven l-s;	Ps 2:4
The Lord l-s at him because He	Ps 37:13
But You l at them, LORD;	Ps 59:8
in turn, will l at your calamity	Pr 1:26
and she can l at the time to	Pr 31:25
a time to weep and a time to l;	Ec 3:4
They l at every fortress and	Hab 1:10
And they started l-ing at Him.	Mt 9:24
weep now, because you will l.	Lk 6:21
Woe to you who are l-ing now,	Lk 6:25

LAUGHINGSTOCK

otherwise we will become a l.	Gn 38:23
I am a l to my friends,	Jb 12:4
a l among the peoples.	Ps 44:14
Wasn't Israel a l to you?	Jr 48:27
I am a l to all my people,	Lm 3:14

LAUGHTER

mouths were filled with l then,	Ps 126:2
Even in l a heart may be sad,	Pr 14:13
I said about l, "It is madness,"	Ec 2:2
Grief is better than l,	Ec 7:3
A feast is prepared for l,	Ec 10:19
Your l must change to mourning	Jms 4:9

LAUNDERER

white as no l on earth could	Mk 9:3

LAVISHED

You l your sexual favors on	Ezk 16:15
that He l on us with all wisdom	Eph 1:8

LAW

the stone tablets with the l	Ex 24:12

Moses began to explain this l,   Dt 1:5
Moses wrote down this l and gave it   Dt 31:9
read aloud all the words of the l   Jos 8:34
None of them ... observe ... the l   2Kg 17:34
I have found the book of the l   2Kg 22:8
if only your sons ... walk in My L   2Ch 6:16
abandoned the l of the LORD   2Ch 12:1
explained the l to the people   Neh 8:7
Do you know the l-s of heaven?   Jb 38:33
and refused to live by His l.   Ps 78:10
according to the l of the LORD!   Ps 119:1
see wonderful things in Your l.   Ps 119:18
I will always keep Your l,   Ps 119:44
I did not forget Your l.   Ps 119:61
reign and rulers enact just l;   Pr 8:15
who keep the l battle against them.   Pr 28:4
A discerning son keeps the l,   Pr 28:7
who keeps the l will be happy.   Pr 29:18
To the l and to the testimony!   Is 8:20
L after l, l after l, line after line,   Is 28:10
They have rejected My l.   Jr 6:19
for the l will never be lost   Jr 18:18
I will place My l within them   Jr 31:33
Her priests do violence to My l   Ezk 22:26
ten thousand points of My l,   Hs 8:12
This is why the l is ineffective   Hab 1:4
assume that I came to destroy the L   Mt 5:17
this is the L and the Prophets.   Mt 7:12
and the l prophesied until   Mt 11:13
All the L and the Prophets depend   Mt 22:40
more important matters of the l   Mt 23:23
everything according to the l   Lk 2:39
stroke of a letter in the l to drop   Lk 16:17
written about Me in the L   Lk 24:44
the l was given through Moses,   Jn 1:17
Our l doesn't judge a man   Jn 7:51
a teacher of the l who was   Ac 5:34
they are all zealous for the l.   Ac 21:20
disputed matters in their l,   Ac 23:29
who sinned without the l will also   Rm 2:12
the l is written on their hearts.   Rm 2:15
now, apart from the l, God's   Rm 3:21
what kind of l? By one of works?   Rm 3:27
by faith apart from works of l.   Rm 3:28
For the l produces wrath;   Rm 4:15
sin was in the world before the l,   Rm 5:13
are not under l but under grace   Rm 6:14
dies, she is free from that l.   Rm 7:3

Is the l sin? Absolutely not!   Rm 7:7
So then, the l is holy, and the   Rm 7:12
has set you free from the l of sin   Rm 8:2
What the l could not do since it   Rm 8:3
For Christ is the end of the l   Rm 10:4
Love ... is the fulfillment of the l.   Rm 13:10
like one under the l—though I
 myself am not under the l—
 to win those   1Co 9:20
and the power of sin is the l.   1Co 15:56
through the l I have died to the l,   Gl 2:19
by the works of the l or by hearing   Gl 3:2
The l, then, was our guardian until   Gl 3:24
to redeem those under the l,   Gl 4:5
you who want to be under the l,   Gl 4:21
obligated to keep the entire l.   Gl 5:3
justified by the l are alienated   Gl 5:4
For the entire l is fulfilled in   Gl 5:14
you are not under the l.   Gl 5:18
will fulfill the l of Christ.   Gl 6:2
as to the l, a Pharisee;   Php 3:5
Now we know that the l is good,   1Tm 1:8
quarrels, and disputes about the l,   Ti 3:9
for the l perfected nothing   Heb 7:19
I will put My l-s into their minds,   Heb 8:10
Since the l has (only) a shadow   Heb 10:1
I will put My l-s on their hearts   Heb 10:16
into the perfect l of freedom   Jms 1:25
For whoever keeps the entire l,   Jms 2:10
criticizes the l and judges the l.   Jms 4:11
sin is the breaking of l.   1Jn 3:4

LAWBREAKER

Depart from Me, you l-s!   Mt 7:23
but if you are a l, your   Rm 2:25
but you do murder, you are a l.   Jms 2:11

LAWFUL

doing what is not l to do on the   Mt 12:2
Is it l to heal on the Sabbath?   Mt 12:10
It's not l for you to have her!   Mt 14:4
Is it l for a man to divorce   Mt 19:3
Is it l to pay taxes to Caesar   Mt 22:17

LAWGIVER

the LORD is our l, the LORD is   Is 33:22
There is one l and judge who is   Jms 4:12

LAWLESS

Then some l men joined Jephthah   Jdg 11:3
you used l people to nail Him to   Ac 2:23

those whose l acts are forgiven	Rm 4:7
and then the l one will be	2Th 2:8
but for the l and rebellious,	1Tm 1:9
by day with the l deeds he saw	2Pt 2:8

LAWLESSNESS

Because l will multiply,	Mt 24:12
and to greater and greater l,	Rm 6:19
between righteousness and l?	2Co 6:14
and the man of l is revealed,	2Th 2:3
the mystery of l is already at	2Th 2:7
us from all l and to cleanse for	Ti 2:14
righteousness and hated l;	Heb 1:9

LAWSUIT

not testify in a l and go along	Ex 23:2
then l-s and dishonor will cease.	Pr 22:10
or suppressing a person's l	Lm 3:36
So l-s break out like poisonous	Hs 10:4
Listen to the LORD's l, you mountains	Mc 6:2
defeat for you that you have l-s	1Co 6:7

LAWYER

and a l named Tertullus.	Ac 24:1
help Zenas the l and Apollos on	Ti 3:13

LAY

Do not l a hand on the boy or	Gn 22:12
and his sons must l their hands on	Ex 29:10
He is to l his hand on the head	Lv 1:4
l his hand on the bull's head,	Lv 4:4
have the Israelites l their hands on	Nm 8:10
Joshua ... l your hands on him	Nm 27:18
came and laid the foundation	Ezr 5:16
you must not l a hand on Job	Jb 1:12
Or who laid its cornerstone	Jb 38:6
L a hand on him. You will	Jb 41:8
for He laid its foundation on the	Ps 24:2
l-ing the beams of His palace on	Ps 104:3
when He laid out the horizon on the	Pr 8:27
when He laid out the foundations of	Pr 8:29
Look, I have laid a stone in Zion	Is 28:16
the foundations laid long ago;	Is 58:12
that hatches eggs it didn't l.	Jr 17:11
of the LORD's temple was laid;	Hg 2:18
hands have laid the foundation of	Zch 4:9
laid the foundation of the earth,	Zch 12:1
Man has no place to l His head.	Mt 8:20
He laid His hands on them and	Mk 10:16
they will l hands on the sick,	Mk 16:18
in cloth and laid Him in a feeding	Lk 2:7

dug deep and laid the foundation	Lk 6:48
good shepherd l-s down his life	Jn 10:11
I l down My life for the sheep.	Jn 10:15
up from supper, laid aside His robe	Jn 13:4
Will you l down your life for	Jn 13:38
someone would l down his life	Jn 15:13
and laid them at the apostles' feet	Ac 4:35
who prayed and laid their hands on	Ac 6:6
Peter and John laid their hands on	Ac 8:17
so that anyone I l hands on may	Ac 8:19
prayed, and laid hands on them	Ac 13:3
when Paul had laid his hands on	Ac 19:6
and praying and l-ing his hands on	Ac 28:8
builder I have laid a foundation,	1Co 3:10
because no one can l any other	1Co 3:11
with the l-ing of hands by the	1Tm 4:14
too quick to l hands on anyone	1Tm 5:22
through the l-ing on of my hands	2Tm 1:6
not l-ing again the foundation of	Heb 6:1
ritual washings, l-ing on of hands	Heb 6:2
let us l aside every weight and	Heb 12:1
I l a stone in Zion, a chosen	1Pt 2:6
I will soon l aside my tent,	2Pt 1:14
He laid down His life for us.	1Jn 3:16
We should also l down our lives	1Jn 3:16
He laid His right hand on me,	Rv 1:17

LAZARUS

1. Poor man in Jesus' parable (Lk 16:19-31).

2. Brother of Mary and Martha; friend of Jesus (Jn 11:1-5). Died; revived by Jesus (11:3-44). Endangered because of fame (12:9-11,17).

LAZINESS

but l will lead to forced labor	Pr 12:24
L induces deep sleep, and a lazy	Pr 19:15
Because of l the roof caves in,	Ec 10:18

LAZY

A l man doesn't roast his game,	Pr 12:27
who is truly l in his work is	Pr 18:9
and a l person will go hungry.	Pr 19:15
You evil, l slave! If you knew	Mt 25:26
warn those who are l, comfort	1Th 5:14
liars, evil beasts, l gluttons.	Ti 1:12
so that you won't become l,	Heb 6:12

LEAD (n)

They sank like l in the mighty	Ex 15:10

bronze, iron, tin, and l	Nm 31:22
by an iron stylus and l!	Jb 19:24
blasting the l with fire.	Jr 6:29
tin, iron, and l inside the furnace;	Ezk 22:18
and l for your merchandise.	Ezk 27:12
Then a l cover was lifted,	Zch 5:7

LEAD (v)

so that you may l My people,	Ex 3:10
of cloud to l them on their way	Ex 13:21
You will l the people You have	Ex 15:13
l the people to the place I told	Ex 32:34
He led you through the great and	Dt 8:15
This led to sin; the people walked	1Kg 12:30
Jeroboam led Israel away from	2Kg 17:21
so that I may l these people,	2Ch 1:10
way of the wicked l-s to ruin.	Ps 1:6
l me in Your righteousness,	Ps 5:8
He l-s me beside quiet waters.	Ps 23:2
He l-s me along the right paths	Ps 23:3
He l-s the humble in what is right	Ps 25:9
way, LORD, and l me on a level	Ps 27:11
You l and guide me because of	Ps 31:3
l-ing the festive procession to the	Ps 42:4
and Your truth; let them l me.	Ps 43:3
He will l us eternally.	Ps 48:14
L me to a rock that is high above me	Ps 61:2
He l-s out the prisoners to	Ps 68:6
He led them with a cloud by day	Ps 78:14
He led them by the right path to	Ps 107:7
even there Your hand will l me;	Ps 139:10
l me in the everlasting way.	Ps 139:24
Spirit l me on level ground.	Ps 143:10
labor of the righteous l-s to life;	Pr 10:16
l-ing him in a way that is not good	Pr 16:29
own foolishness l-s him astray,	Pr 19:3
The fear of the LORD l-s to life;	Pr 19:23
The one who l-s the upright into	Pr 28:10
and a child will l them.	Is 11:6
He gently l-s those that are nursing.	Is 40:11
I will l the blind by a way they	Is 42:16
who l-s you in the way you should	Is 48:17
and l them to springs of water.	Is 49:10
Like a lamb led to the slaughter	Is 53:7
I will l him and comfort him and	Is 57:18
The LORD will always l you,	Is 58:11
You led Your people this way to	Is 63:14
a docile lamb led to slaughter.	Jr 11:19
them and l-ing My people astray	Jr 23:32

shepherds have led them astray,	Jr 50:6
those who l many to righteousness,	Dn 12:3
to persuade her, I her to the	Hs 2:14
I led them with human cords,	Hs 11:4
land of Egypt and led you 40 years	Am 2:10
Then Jesus was led up by the	Mt 4:1
is broad that l-s to destruction,	Mt 7:13
l astray, if possible, even the elect.	Mt 24:24
and led Him away to crucify Him.	Mt 27:31
sheep by name and l-s them out.	Jn 10:3
He was led like a sheep to the	Ac 8:32
someone to l him by the hand.	Ac 13:11
is intended to l you to repentance?	Rm 2:4
sin l-ing to death or of obedience	Rm 6:16
All those led by God's Spirit are	Rm 8:14
l-ing, with diligence;	Rm 12:8
to dumb idols—being led astray.	1Co 12:2
a scent of death l-ing to death,	2Co 2:16
your grief led to repentance.	2Co 7:9
and l-ing to salvation,	2Co 7:10
But if you are led by the Spirit,	Gl 5:18
to seek to l a quiet life,	1Th 4:11
so that we may l a tranquil and	1Tm 2:2
led along by a variety of passions	2Tm 3:6
the truth that l-s to godliness,	Tt 1:1
I took them by their hand to l them	Heb 8:9
Don't be led astray by various	Heb 13:9
that you are not led away by the	2Pt 3:17

LEADER

He will father 12 tribal l-s,	Gn 17:20
Who made you a l and judge over	Ex 2:14
When a l sins and	Lv 4:22
All the men were l-s in Israel.	Nm 13:3
Let's appoint a l and go back to	Nm 14:4
and you will become l of all the	Jdg 11:8
He chose Judah as l,	1Ch 28:4
l-s and officials have taken the lead	Ezr 9:2
the family l-s gave to the project.	Neh 7:70
and overthrows established l-s.	Jb 12:19
deprives the world's l-s of reason,	Jb 12:24
For the l-s of the earth belong to	Ps 47:9
He humbles the spirit of l-s;	Ps 76:12
He will crush l-s over the entire	Ps 110:6
Without l, administrator, or	Pr 6:7
A l who lacks understanding is	Pr 28:16
I will make youths their l-s,	Is 3:4
have a cloak—you be our l!	Is 3:6
My people, your l-s mislead you;	Is 3:12

will send them a savior and l,   Is 19:20
Jacob's l will be one of them;   Jr 30:21
the LORD as their l.   Mc 2:13
least among the l-s of Judah: Mt 2:6
out of you will come a l who will   Mt 2:6
of the synagogue l-s, named Jairus   Mk 5:22
priests and l-s handed Him over   Lk 24:20
Remember your l-s who
    have spoken   Heb 13:7
Obey your l-s and submit
    to them,   Heb 13:17

LEADING (adj)

I selected 12 of the l priests,   Ezr 8:24
took away the l men of the land   Ezk 17:13
of one of the l Pharisees,   Lk 14:1
both l men among the brothers.   Ac 15:22
as a number of the l women.   Ac 17:4
belonging to the l man of the   Ac 28:7

LEAF

they sewed fig l-ves together and   Gn 3:7
a plucked olive l in her beak.   Gn 8:11
the sound of a wind-driven l will   Lv 26:36
Will You frighten a wind-driven l?   Jb 13:25
and whose l does not wither   Ps 1:3
and Carmel shake off {their} l-ves.   Is 33:9
all of us wither like a l,   Is 64:6
food and their l-ves for medicine.   Ezk 47:12
found nothing on it except l-ves.   Mt 21:19
becomes tender and sprouts l-ves,   Mt 24:32
The l-ves of the tree are for   Rv 22:2

LEAFY

fronds, boughs of l trees, and   Lv 23:40
and under every l tree you lie   Jr 2:20
saw any high hill or l tree,   Ezk 20:28
and others spread l branches cut   Mk 11:8

LEAH

Wife of Jacob; mother of Reuben, Simeon, Levi, Judah, Issachar, Zebulun, and Dinah (Gn 29:16-35; 30:14-21).

LEAKS

of negligent hands the house l.   Ec 10:18

LEAN (adj)

the fat sheep and the l sheep.   Ezk 34:20

LEAN (v)

temple, so I can l against them.   Jdg 16:26
which if a man l-s on it will go   2Kg 18:21

I have l-ed on You from birth;   Ps 71:6
l-ing on the one she loves?   Sg 8:5
pierce the hand of anyone who l-s on   Is 36:6
and l on the God of Israel;   Is 48:2
the LORD; let him l on his God.   Is 50:10
they l-ed on you, you shattered   Ezk 29:7
Yet they l on the LORD, saying   Mc 3:11
So he l-ed back against Jesus and   Jn 13:25
the one who had l-ed back against   Jn 21:20
l-ing on the top of his staff.   Heb 11:21

LEANING (adj)

attack as if he were a l-ing wall or   Ps 62:3

LEAP

saw King David l-ing and dancing   2Sm 6:16
with my God I can l over a wall.   2Sm 22:30
at this and l-s from my chest.   Jb 37:1
with my God I can l over a wall.   Ps 18:29
Here he comes, l-ing over the   Sg 2:8
and wild goats will l about.   Is 13:21
the lame will l like a deer,   Is 35:6
greeting, the baby l-ed inside her   Lk 1:41
Rejoice in that day and l for joy!   Lk 6:23
walking, l-ing, and praising God.   Ac 3:8

LEARN

that they may l to fear Me all   Dt 4:10
will listen and l to fear the LORD   Dt 31:13
that I could l Your statutes.   Ps 119:71
so that I can l Your commands.   Ps 119:73
righteous man, and he will l more.   Pr 9:9
and the inexperienced l a lesson;   Pr 19:25
or you will l his ways and   Pr 22:25
L to do what is good.   Is 1:17
By the time he l-s to reject what   Is 7:15
L how the wildflowers of the   Mt 6:28
take up My yoke and l from Me,   Mt 11:29
l-ed from the Father comes to Me.   Jn 6:45
May we l about this new   Ac 17:19
to the doctrine you have l-ed.   Rm 16:17
so that you may l from us the   1Co 4:6
everyone may l and everyone
    may   1Co 14:31
if they want to l something,   1Co 14:35
I only want to l this from you: Gl 3:2
is not how you l-ed about the   Eph 4:20
for I have l-ed to be content in   Php 4:11
A woman should l in silence with   1Tm 2:11
they should l to practice their   1Tm 5:4

always l-ing and never able to | 2Tm 3:7
continue in what you have l-ed | 2Tm 3:14
people must also I to devote | Ti 3:14
He l-ed obedience through what He | Heb 5:8
no one could I the song except | Rv 14:3

LEARNED (n)

these things from the wise and I | Mt 11:25

LEARNING (n)

will listen and increase his I, | Pr 1:5
pleasant speech increases I. | Pr 16:21

LEASE

He l-d the vineyard to tenants. | Sg 8:11
He l-d it to tenant farmers and | Mt 21:33
and I his vineyard to other | Mt 21:41

LEASH

or put him on a I for your girls | Jb 41:5

LEAST

my clan the I important of all | 1Sm 9:21
the greatest of them to the I. | Jnh 3:5
are by no means I among the | Mic 2:6
will be called I in the kingdom | Mt 5:19
but the I in the kingdom of | Mt 11:11
you did for one of the I of these | Mt 25:40
For whoever is I among you | Lk 9:48
For I am the I of the apostles, | 1Co 15:9
to me—the I of all the saints | Eph 3:8

LEATHER

of linen or wool, or in I or | Lv 13:48
man with a I belt around his | 2Kg 1:8
garment with a I belt around his | Mt 3:4
garment with a I belt around his | Mk 1:6
Joppa with Simon, a I tanner. | Ac 9:43

LEAVE

This is why a man l-s his father | Gn 2:24
Get up, I this land, and return | Gn 31:13
he left his garment with me
    and ran | Gn 39:15
some people left part of it until | Ex 16:20
may not I any of it until morning. | Lv 7:15
Why did we ever I Egypt? | Nm 11:20
We left no survivors. | Dt 2:34
Let him I and return home. | Dt 20:5
He will not I you or forsake you | Dt 31:6
I will not I you or forsake you | Jos 1:5
Not a man was left in Ai or Bethel | Jos 8:17
to the sword, and left no survivors | Jos 10:30

The LORD left them to test Israel, | Jdg 3:4
persuade me to I you or go back | Ru 1:16
Spirit of the LORD had left Saul, | 1Sm 16:14
My faithful love will never I him | 2Sm 7:15
Is there anyone left of Saul's | 2Sm 9:3
sword will never I your house | 2Sm 12:10
he left behind 10 concubines to | 2Sm 15:16
May He not abandon us or I us. | 1Kg 8:57
I alone am left, and they are | 1Kg 19:10
Elisha left the oxen, ran to follow | 1Kg 19:20
of the people he left in the land | 2Kg 25:22
He won't I you or forsake you | 1Ch 28:20
God left him to test him and | 2Ch 32:31
should the work cease while I I it | Neh 6:3
or I me alone until I swallow my | Jb 7:19
and they I their surplus to | Ps 17:14
do not I me or abandon me, | Ps 27:9
my strength l-s me, and even | Ps 38:10
my head, and my courage l-s me. | Ps 40:12
Then they I their wealth to | Ps 49:10
When his breath l-s him, he returns | Ps 146:4
loyalty and faithfulness I you. | Pr 3:3
L inexperience behind, and you | Pr 9:6
A good man l-s an inheritance to | Pr 13:22
for the one who l-s the path; | Pr 15:10
because I must I it to the man | Ec 2:18
Hosts had not left us a few survivors, | Is 1:9
wouldn't they I some gleanings? | Jr 49:9
left to be vinedressers and farmers | Jr 52:16
the vision I had seen left me, | Ezk 11:24
What the devouring locust has left, | Jl 1:4
and relent and I a blessing | Jl 2:14
wouldn't they I some grapes? | Ob 5
LORD is l-ing His place and coming | Mic 1:3
Then the Devil left Him, and | Mt 4:11
Immediately they left their nets | Mt 4:20
I your gift there in front of | Mt 5:24
her hand, and the fever left her. | Mt 8:15
won't he I the 99 on the | Mt 18:12
we have left everything and | Mt 19:27
your house is left to you desolate | Mt 23:38
stone will be left here on another | Mt 24:2
one will be taken and one left. | Mt 24:40
and they left their father Zebedee | Mk 1:20
reason a man will I his father | Mk 10:7
and dying, left no offspring. | Mk 12:20
Then Jesus said, "L her alone. | Mk 14:6
She did not I the temple complex | Lk 2:37

the boats to land, **left** everything	Lk 5:11
and they will not **l** one stone on	Lk 19:44
He **left** them and was carried up	Lk 24:51
Then the woman **left** her water jar,	Jn 4:28
He has not **left** Me alone, because I	Jn 8:29
doesn't own the sheep, **l-s** them	Jn 10:12
I will not **l** you as orphans;	Jn 14:18
Peace **l** with you. My peace I	Jn 14:27
I am **l-ing** the world and going to	Jn 16:28
commanded them not to **l** Jerusalem,	Ac 1:4
He was not **left** in Hades, and His	Ac 2:31
of Hosts had not **left** us a seed,	Rm 9:29
am the only one **left**, and they are	Rm 11:3
you would have to **l** the world.	1Co 5:10
a wife is not to **l** her husband.	1Co 7:10
if the unbeliever **l-s**, let him **l**.	1Co 7:15
reason a man will **l** his father	Eph 5:31
The reason I **left** you in Crete was	Ti 1:5
By faith he **left** Egypt behind,	Heb 11:27
I will never **l** you or forsake	Heb 13:5

LEAVENED

Do not eat anything **l**;	Ex 12:20
must not eat **l** bread with it.	Dt 16:3
of the dough until it is **l**.	Hs 7:4
Offer **l** bread as a thank	Am 4:5

LEAVENS

A little yeast **l** the whole lump	Gl 5:9

LEBANON

Mountainous region of northern promised land (Dt 1:7; 11:24). Known for its cedars and lush growth (Jdg 9:15; 1Kg 5:6; 2Ch 2:8,16; Pss 72:16; 92:12; Sg 4:11,15; Is 2:13; Ezk 27:5; 31:3). God is greater (Pss 29:5-6; 104:16).

LEECH

The **l** has two daughters: Give,	Pr 30:15

LEEKS

cucumbers, melons, **l**, onions	Nm 11:5

LEFT (adj)

to the **l**, I will go to to the right;	Gn 13:9
put his **l** on Manasseh's head,	Gn 48:14
and pour it into his **l** palm.	Lv 14:15
not to turn aside to the right or the **l**.	Dt 5:32
from it to the right or the **l**,	Jos 1:7
their torches in their **l** hands,	Jdg 7:20
strayed to the right or to the **l**.	1Sm 6:12

l pillar and named it Boaz.	1Kg 7:21
he did not turn to the right or the **l**.	2Kg 22:2
using either their right or **l** hand,	1Ch 12:2
Don't turn to the right or to the **l**;	Pr 4:27
but a fool's heart to the **l**.	Ec 10:2
His **l** hand is under my head,	Sg 2:6; 8:3
the face of an ox on the **l**,	Ezk 1:10
down on your **l** side and place	Ezk 4:4
between their right and their **l**,	Jnh 4:11
on the right and **l** of the lampstand?	Zch 4:11
don't let your **l** hand know what	Mt 6:3
right and the other on Your **l**,	Mt 20:21
right, and the goats on the **l**.	Mt 25:33
also say to those on the **l**,	Mt 25:41
on the right and one on the **l**.	Mt 27:38
on the right hand and the **l**,	2Co 6:7
on the sea, his **l** on the land,	Rv 10:2

LEFT-HANDED

Ehud son of Gera, a **l** Benjaminite,	Jdg 3:15
700 choice men who were **l**	Jdg 20:16

LEFTOVER

up 12 baskets full of **l** pieces!	Mt 14:20
they collected the **l** pieces	Mt 15:37
Collect the **l-s** so that nothing	Jn 6:12

LEGAL

It's not **l** for us to put	Jn 18:31
that are not **l** for us as Romans	Ac 16:21
be decided in a **l** assembly.	Ac 19:39
Is it **l** for you to scourge a	Ac 22:25
based on a **l** command	Heb 7:16

LEGALLY

was {the method of} **l** binding a	Ru 4:7
married woman is **l** bound to her	Rm 7:2
through angels was **l** binding,	Heb 2:2
which has been **l** enacted on	Heb 8:6

LEGION

with more than 12 **l-s** of angels?	Mt 26:53
"My name is **L**," he answered Him	Mk 5:9
been demon-possessed by the **l**,	Mk 5:15

LEGITIMATELY

law is good, provided one uses it **l**.	1Tm 1:8

LEGS

is like lame **l** that hang limp.	Pr 26:7
His **l** are alabaster pillars set	Sg 5:15
Their **l** were straight, and the	Ezk 1:7
spread your **l** to everyone who	Ezk 16:25

its l were iron, and its feet | Dn 2:33
snatches two l or a piece of an | Am 3:12
they did not break His l since | Jn 19:33
his l were like fiery pillars, | Rv 10:1

LEMUEL
words of King **L**, an oracle that | Pr 31:1

LEND
If you l money to My people | Ex 22:25
to l him your silver with interest | Lv 25:37
cancel what he has **lent** his
  neighbor. | Dt 15:2
You will l to many nations, | Dt 28:12
He will l to you, but you won't | Dt 28:44
have been **l-ing** them money | Neh 5:10
who does not l his money at | Ps 15:5
generous, always **l-ing**, | Ps 37:26
come to a man who **l-s** generously | Ps 112:5
I did not l or borrow, yet | Jr 15:10
and **l-s** at interest or for profit | Ezk 18:13
And if you l to those from whom | Lk 6:34
and l, expecting nothing in return. | Lk 6:35
l me three loaves of bread, | Lk 11:5

LENDER
He will give a reward to the l. | Pr 19:17
borrower is a slave to the l. | Pr 22:7
buyer and seller, l and borrower, | Is 24:2

LENGTH
unfairly in measurements of l, | Lv 19:35
two cord **l-s** (of those) to be put to | 2Sm 8:2
measurements of volume and l. | 1Ch 23:29
l of days forever and ever. | Ps 21:4
go to great **l-s** to hide their plans | Is 29:15
the standard l plus three inches | Ezk 43:13
to determine its width and l. | Zch 2:2
Its l, width, and height are equal. | Rv 21:16

LENGTHEN
for the shadow to l 10 steps. | 2Kg 20:10
they will not l their days like | Ec 8:13
l your ropes, and drive your | Is 54:2
He will not l your exile. | Lm 4:22
and l their tassels. | Mt 23:5

LENGTHENING (adj)
My days are like a l shadow, | Ps 102:11
I fade away like a l shadow; | Ps 109:23

LENIENT
I come again, I will not be l, | 2Co 13:2

LENTIL
gave bread and l stew to Esau; | Gn 25:34
there was a field full of **l-s**. | 2Sm 23:11
barley, beans, l, millet, and | Ezk 4:9

LEOPARD
from the mountains of the **l-s**. | Sg 4:8
and the l will lie down with the | Is 11:6
A l keeps watch over their | Jr 5:6
his skin, or a l his spots? | Jr 13:23
It was like a l with four wings | Dn 7:6
will lurk like a l on the path. | Hs 13:7
Their horses are swifter than **l-s** | Hab 1:8
The beast I saw was like a l, | Rv 13:2

LEPROSY *see also* SKIN (disease)
an infection or l or a man who | 2Sm 3:29

LESS
and the poor may not give l, | Ex 30:15
and l from a smaller one | Nm 35:8
punished (us) l than our sins | Ezr 9:13
You made him little l than God | Ps 8:5
they (weigh) l than a vapor. | Ps 62:9
we think to be l honorable, | 1Co 12:23
you more, am I to be loved l? | 2Co 12:15

LESSER
the l light to have dominion over | Gn 1:16

LESSON
on up, and we'll teach you a l! | 1Sm 14:12
the inexperienced learn a l; | Pr 19:25

LET
L there be light, | Gn 1:3
He **l-s** me lie down in green | Ps 23:2
L the little children come to Me; | Mk 10:14

LETTER
In the l he wrote: Put Uriah at | 2Sm 11:15
So she wrote **l-s** in Ahab's name | 1Kg 21:8
When the king of Israel read the l, | 2Kg 5:7
wrote a l and sent (it) to Solomon | 2Ch 2:11
Then a l came to Jehoram from | 2Ch 21:12
The l was written in Aramaic and | Ezr 4:7
the text of the l that Tattenai | Ezr 5:6
who had an open l in his hand. | Neh 6:5
And Tobiah sent **l-s** to intimidate | Neh 6:19
He sent **l-s** with messages of peace | Est 9:30
the text of the l that Jeremiah | Jr 29:1
not the smallest l or one stroke | Mt 5:18
and requested **l-s** from him to the | Ac 9:2

wrote this l to be delivered	Ac 15:23
have written a l containing our	Ac 21:25
by the Spirit, not the l.	Rm 2:29
not in the old l of the law.	Rm 7:6
to you in a l not to associate	1Co 5:9
do we need l-s of recommendation	2Co 3:1
You yourselves are our l,	2Co 3:2
plain that you are Christ's l,	2Co 3:3
l kills, but the Spirit produces life.	2Co 3:6
chiseled in l-s on stones, came	2Co 3:7
I grieved you with my l,	2Co 7:8
His l-s are weighty and powerful	2Co 10:10
at what large l-s I have written	Gl 6:11
And when this l has been read	Col 4:16
Lord that this l be read to all	1Th 5:27
or by a l as if from us,	2Th 2:2
not obey our instruction in this l,	2Th 3:14
This is a sign in every l;	2Th 3:17
now the second l I've written	2Pt 3:1
these things in all his l-s,	2Pt 3:16

LEVEL (adj)

mason's l {used on} the house	2Kg 21:13
My foot stands on l ground;	Ps 26:12
LORD, and lead me on a l path.	Ps 27:11
Spirit lead me on l ground.	Ps 143:10
The path of the righteous is l;	Is 26:7
and righteousness the mason's l.	Is 28:17
and rough places into l ground.	Is 42:16
He stood on a l place with a	Lk 6:17

LEVEL (v)

its furrows and l-ing its ridges.	Ps 65:10
When he has l-ed its surface,	Is 28:25
mountain and hill will be l-ed;	Is 40:4
and will l all roads for him.	Is 45:13

LEVI

1. Son of Jacob and Leah (Gn 29:34). Ancestor of priestly tribe (Ex 32:25-29; Nm 3:11-13; Dt 10:6-9); received no allotment of land, only scattered towns and cities of refuge (Nm 18:20; 35:1-8; Jos 13:14,33); supported by tithes (Nm 18:21; Heb 7:5). Assisted descendants of Aaron in worship (Nm 3:5-9; 1Ch 6:16,31-32,49; 23:24-32; 2Ch 29:12-21); taught the word of God (2Ch 17:7-9; Neh 8:9-12).

2. Two ancestors of Jesus (Lk 3:24,29).

3. Apostle, called Matthew (Mk 2:14; Lk 5:27-29; cp. Mt 9:9).

LEVIATHAN

who are skilled in rousing L.	Jb 3:8
Can you pull in L with a hook or	Jb 41:1
ferocious {enough} to rouse L;	Jb 41:10
When L rises, the mighty are	Jb 41:25
You crushed the heads of L;	Ps 74:14
and L, which You formed	Ps 104:26
bring judgment on L, the fleeing	Is 27:1

LEVITICAL

Concerning the L cities, the	Lv 25:32
came through the L priesthood	Heb 7:11

LEWDNESS

actions, deceit, l, stinginess	Mk 7:22

LIAR

out to be a l who has falsely	Dt 19:18
can prove me a l and show that	Jb 24:25
from the womb; l-s err from birth	Ps 58:3
the mouths of l-s will be shut.	Ps 63:11
alarm I said, "Everyone is a l."	Ps 116:11
a l pays attention to a	Pr 17:4
children, you race of l-s,	Is 57:4
he is a l and the father of l-s.	Jn 8:44
I would be a l like you.	Jn 8:55
must be true, but everyone is a l,	Rm 3:4
for kidnappers, l-s, perjurers	1Tm 1:10
the hypocrisy of l-s whose	1Tm 4:2
are always l-s, evil beasts, lazy	Ti 1:12
we make Him a l, and His word is	1Jn 1:10
Who is the l, if not the one who	1Jn 2:22
hates his brother, he is a l.	1Jn 4:20
believe God has made Him a l,	1Jn 5:10
you have found them to be l-s.	Rv 2:2
and all l-s—their share will	Rv 21:8

LIBERALLY

Israelites gave l of the best	2Ch 31:5

LIBERATED

you have been l from sin and	Rm 6:22
Christ has l us into freedom.	Gl 5:1

LIBERATION

l and deliverance will come to	Est 4:14

LIBERATOR

The L will come from Zion;	Rm 11:26

LIBERTY

to proclaim l to the captives, Is 61:1

LIBNAH

1. Way station in the wilderness (Nm 33:20-21).

2. City conquered by Joshua (Jos 10:29-30); given to Aaron's descendants (21:13; 1Ch 6:57).

LIBRARY

searched in the l of Babylon Ezr 6:1

LIBYA

plus L and the men of the Ezk 30:5
Put and L were among her allies Nah 3:9
and the parts of L near Cyrene; Ac 2:10

LIBYANS

with him from Egypt—L, Sukkiim 2Ch 12:3
Cushites and L a vast army with 2Ch 16:8
The L and Cushites will also be Dn 11:43

LICE

shepherd picks l off his garment Jr 43:12

LICK

and it l-ed up the water that was 1Kg 18:38
where the dogs l-ed Naboth's 1Kg 21:19
the dogs will also l your blood! 1Kg 21:19
The dogs l-ed up his blood, 1Kg 22:38
and his enemies l the dust. Ps 72:9
and l the dust at your feet. Is 49:23
They will l the dust like a Mc 7:17
would come and l his sores. Lk 16:21

LIE (n)

you coat [the truth] with l-s; Jb 13:4
You destroy those who tell l-s; Ps 5:6
no one who tells l-s will remain Ps 101:7
people persecute me with l-s Ps 119:86
a dishonest witness utters l-s. Pr 14:5
one who utters l-s will not escape Pr 19:5
and one who utters l-s perishes. Pr 19:9
for his cast images are a l; Jr 10:14
Our fathers inherited only l-s, Jr 16:19
they prophesy a l to you so that Jr 27:10
to My people, who listen to l-s. Ezk 13:19
will speak l-s at the same table Dn 11:27
you have eaten the fruit of l-s. Hs 10:13
When he tells a l, he speaks Jn 8:44
exchanged the truth of God for a l, Rm 1:25
But if by my l God's truth is Rm 3:7

because no l comes from the truth. 1Jn 2:21
No l was found in their mouths; Rv 14:5

LIE (v) (prevaricate) see also LYING (n)

You must not ... l to one another. Lv 19:11
God is not a man who l-s, or a Nm 23:19
One of Israel does not l or change 1Sm 15:29
would I l to your face? Jb 6:28
Am I l-ing, or can I not recognize Jb 6:30
l-ing instead of speaking truthfully Ps 52:3
they l-d to Him with their tongues Ps 78:36
I will not l to David. Ps 89:35
your heart to l to the Holy Spirit Ac 5:3
You have not l-d to men but to God Ac 5:4
truth in Christ—I am not l-ing; Rm 9:1
Lord Jesus, knows I am not l-ing. 2Co 11:31
what I write to you, I'm not l-ing. Gl 1:20
Do not l to one another, since Col 3:9
telling the truth; I am not l-ing), 1Tm 2:7
God, who cannot l, promised Ti 1:2
it is impossible for God to l, Heb 6:18
don't brag and l in defiance of Jms 3:14
we are l-ing and are not practicing 1Jn 1:6
be Jews and are not, but are l-ing Rv 3:9

LIE (v) (recline)

when you l down and when Dt 6:7; 11:19
notice the place where he's l-ing, Ru 3:4
He told Samuel, "Go and l down. 1Sm 3:9
the troops were l-ing around him. 1Sm 26:7
The splendor of Israel l-s slain 2Sm 1:19
Jerusalem l-s in ruins and its Neh 2:17
but it will l down with him in Jb 20:11
He lets me l down in green Ps 23:2
The wicked l-s in wait for the Ps 37:32
you l down, you will not be afraid; Pr 3:24
Also, if two l down together Ec 4:11
tree falls, there it will l. Ec 11:3
the leopard will l down with the Is 11:6
L low, residents of Dedan, for I Jr 49:8
Then l down on your left side Ezk 4:4
they will l down in a good grazing Ezk 34:14
As I was l-ing in my bed, I also saw Dn 4:13
mind as he was l-ing in his bed. Dn 7:1
while this house l-s in ruins? Hg 1:4
and see the place where He lay? Mt 28:6
in cloth and l-ing in a manger. Lk 2:12
baby who was l-ing in the feeding Lk 2:16
saw the linen cloths l-ing there, Jn 20:5

the race that l-s before us, Heb 12:1
for the joy that lay before Him Heb 12:2

LIFE

the breath of l into his Gn 2:7
the tree of l in the midst Gn 2:9
I will require the l of every Gn 9:5
then you must give l for l, Ex 21:23
the l of a creature is in the blood, Lv 17:11
make restitution for it, l for l. Lv 24:18
blood is the l, and you must not eat Dt 12:23
set before you l and death, Dt 30:19
Choose l so that you and your Dt 30:19
I bring death and I give l; Dt 32:39
to you but they are your l, Dt 32:47
LORD brings death and gives l; 1Sm 2:6
who has redeemed my l from every 1Kg 1:29
not ask for long l or riches for 1Kg 3:11
You give l to all of them, Neh 9:6
your power; only spare his l. Jb 2:6
Remember that my l is {but} a breath. Jb 7:7
You gave me l and faithful love Jb 10:12
l of every living thing is in His Jb 12:10
dies, will he come back to l? Jb 14:14
they have no assurance of l. Jb 24:22
when God takes away his l? Jb 27:8
breath of the Almighty gives me l. Jb 33:4
may shine with the light of l. Jb 33:30
You reveal the path of l to me; Ps 16:11
He renews my l; He leads me Ps 23:3
will pursue me all the days of my l, Ps 23:6
LORD is the stronghold of my l Ps 27:1
Who is the man who delights in l, Ps 34:12
LORD, reveal to me the end of my l Ps 39:4
Your faithful love is better than l. Ps 63:3
for their **lives** are precious in his Ps 72:14
He protects the **lives** of His godly Ps 97:10
He redeems your l from the Pit; Ps 103:4
will sing to the LORD all my l; Ps 104:33
me l through Your righteousness. Ps 119:40
Your promise has given me l. Ps 119:50
the blessing—l forevermore. Ps 133:3
preserve my l from the anger Ps 138:7
none reach the paths of l. Pr 2:19
Long l is in her right hand; Pr 3:16
They will be l for you and Pr 3:22
Guard it, for it is your l. Pr 4:13
instructions are the way to l. Pr 6:23
doesn't know it will cost him his l. Pr 7:23

the one who finds me finds l Pr 8:35
righteous is a fountain of l, Pr 10:11
fear of the LORD prolongs l, Pr 10:27
instruction is a fountain of l, Pr 13:14
of the LORD is a fountain of l, Pr 14:27
the path of l leads upward, Pr 15:24
L and death are in the power of Pr 18:21
few days of his l God has given Ec 5:18
wisdom preserves the l of its owner. Ec 7:12
Enjoy l with the wife you love Ec 9:9
presenting to you the way of l and the Jr 21:8
and they came to l and stood on Ezk 37:10
risked their **lives** rather than serve Dn 3:28
awake, some to eternal l, and some Dn 12:2
covenant with him was one of l and Mal 2:5
Don't worry about your l, Mt 6:25
Isn't l more than food and Mt 6:25
the road that leads to l, Mt 7:14
Anyone finding his l will lose it, Mt 10:39
wants to save his l will lose it, Mt 16:25
gains whole world yet loses his l? Mt 16:26
must I do to have eternal l? Mt 19:16
to give His l—a ransom for many. Mt 20:28
the righteous into eternal l. Mt 25:46
and eternal l in the age to come Mk 10:30
one's l is not in the abundance of Lk 12:15
this very night your l is demanded Lk 12:20
even his own l—he cannot be My Lk 14:26
and worries of l, or that day Lk 21:34
L was in Him, and that l was the light Jn 1:4
in Him will have eternal l. Jn 3:15
not perish but have eternal l. Jn 3:16
believes in the Son has eternal l, Jn 3:36
springing up within him for eternal l. Jn 4:14
Son also gives l to anyone He Jn 5:21
but has passed from death to l. Jn 5:24
as the Father has l in Himself, Jn 5:26
"I am the bread of l," Jesus told Jn 6:35
to you are spirit and are l. Jn 6:63
that they may have l and have it Jn 10:10
lays down his l for the sheep. Jn 10:11
I give them eternal l, Jn 10:28
I am the resurrection and the l. Jn 11:25
I will lay down my l for You! Jn 13:37
the way, the truth, and the l. Jn 14:6
lay down his l for his friends. Jn 15:13
This is eternal l: that they may Jn 17:3
you may have l in His name. Jn 20:31

And you killed the source of l, Ac 3:15
appointed to eternal l believed. Ac 13:48
have risked their **lives** for the name Ac 15:26
gives everyone l and breath and Ac 17:25
who gives l to the dead and Rm 4:17
in eternal l through Jesus Rm 5:21
too may walk in a new way of l. Rm 6:4
gift of God is eternal l in Christ Rm 6:23
law of l in Christ Jesus Rm 8:2
that neither death nor l, Rm 8:38
mean but l from the dead? Rm 11:15
cases pertaining to this l, 1Co 6:4
hope in Christ for this l only, 1Co 15:19
a scent of l leading to l. 2Co 2:16
but the Spirit produces l. 2Co 3:6
that Jesus' l may also be revealed 2Co 4:11
death works in us, but l in you. 2Co 4:12
may be swallowed up by l. 2Co 5:4
The l I now live in the flesh, Gl 2:20
Hold firmly the message of l. Php 2:16
names are in the book of l. Php 4:3
and your l is hidden with the Col 3:3
Messiah, who is your l, is revealed, Col 3:4
present l and also for the l to come. 1Tm 4:8
God, who gives l to all, 1Tm 6:13
take hold of l that is real. 1Tm 6:19
in the concerns of everyday l. 2Tm 2:4
crown of l that He has promised Jms 1:12
who wants to love l and to see good 1Pt 3:10
required for l and godliness, 2Pt 1:3
that l was revealed, and we have 1Jn 1:2
we have passed from death to l 1Jn 3:14
lay down our **lives** for our brothers 1Jn 3:16
us eternal l, and this l is in His Son. 1Jn 5:11
The one who has the Son has l. 1Jn 5:12
is the true God and eternal l. 1Jn 5:20
to eat from the tree of l, Rv 2:7
I will give you the crown of l. Rv 2:10
his name from the book of l, Rv 3:5
in the book of l of the Lamb who Rv 13:8
They came to l and reigned with Rv 20:4
was opened, which is the book of l, Rv 20:12
in the Lamb's book of l. Rv 21:27
was the tree of l bearing 12 Rv 22:2
to the tree of l and may enter Rv 22:14

LIFEBLOOD

not eat meat with its l in it. Gn 9:4
since it is the l that makes Lv 17:11

LIFE-GIVING

listens to l rebukes will be Pr 15:31
act there is l justification for Rm 5:18
last Adam became a l Spirit. 1Co 15:45

LIFELESS

sacrifices offered to l gods. Ps 106:28

LIFESTYLE

and the pride in one's l 1Jn 2:16

LIFETIME

throughout Joshua's l and during Jdg 2:7
I will not do it during your l 1Kg 11:12
not bring the disaster during his l, 1Kg 21:29
peace and security during my l? 2Kg 20:19
only a moment, but His favor, a l. Ps 30:5
praises himself during his l Ps 49:18
will be like the l of a tree. Is 65:22
not be successful in his l. Jr 22:30

LIFT

waters increased and l-ed up the ark Gn 7:17
As for you, l up your staff Ex 14:16
moved out when the cloud l-ed. Nm 9:21
my horn is l-ed up by the LORD. 1Sm 2:1
poor from the dust and l-s the needy 1Sm 2:8
and the One who l-s up my head. Ps 3:3
L up your heads, you gates! Ps 24:7
You have l-ed me up and have Ps 30:1
has l-ed up his heel against me. Ps 41:9
Your name, I will l up my hands. Ps 63:4
of the righteous will be l-ed up. Ps 75:10
My hands were l-ed up all night Ps 77:2
But He l-s the needy out of their Ps 107:41
from the dust and l-s the needy Ps 113:7
I will l up my hands to Your Ps 119:48
L up your hands in the holy Ps 134:2
his companion can l him up; Ec 4:10
a day ... against all that is l-ed up Is 2:12
L up a banner on a barren Is 13:2
Now I will l Myself up. Is 33:10
Every valley will be l-ed up, Is 40:4
servant ... will be raised and l-ed up Is 52:13
He l-ed them up and carried them Is 63:9
Let us l up our hearts and Lm 3:41
The Spirit then l-ed me up, and I Ezk 3:12
Be l-ed up and thrown into the sea Mt 21:21
so the Son of Man must be l-ed up, Jn 3:14
When you l up the Son of Man, Jn 8:28
if I am l-ed up from the earth I Jn 12:32

The Son of Man must be l-**ed** up | Jn 12:34
same veil remains; it is not l-**ed**, | 2Co 3:14
l-**ing** up holy hands without anger | 1Tm 2:8

LIGAMENT

together by every supporting l, | Eph 4:16
held together by its l-**s** and tendons, | Col 2:19

LIGHT (adj)

but you, make it l-**er** on us! | 1Kg 12:10
yoke is easy and My burden is l. | Mt 11:30
our momentary l affliction is | 2Co 4:17

LIGHT (n)

"Let there be l," and there was l. | Gn 1:3
God called the l "day," | Gn 1:5
God made the two great l-**s** | Gn 1:16
Israelites had l where they lived. | Ex 10:23
pillar of fire to give them l at night, | Ex 13:21
is like the morning l when the sun | 2Sm 23:4
Why is l given to one burdened | Jb 3:20
the l of the wicked is extinguished; | Jb 18:5
Where is the road to the home of l? | Jb 38:19
The LORD is my l and my salvation | Ps 27:1
In Your l we will see l. | Ps 36:9
Send Your l and Your truth; | Ps 43:3
before God in the l of life. | Ps 56:13
L dawns for the righteous, | Ps 97:11
wraps Himself in l as if it were | Ps 104:2
L shines in the darkness for the | Ps 112:4
LORD is God and has given us l. | Ps 118:27
for my feet and a l on my path. | Ps 119:105
of Your words brings l and gives | Ps 119:130
darkness and l are alike to You | Ps 139:12
like the l of dawn, shining brighter | Pr 4:18
is a lamp, teaching is a l, | Pr 6:23
l of the righteous shines brightly, | Pr 13:9
the LORD gives l to the eyes of | Pr 29:13
over folly, like the advantage of l | Ec 2:13
L is sweet, and it is pleasing | Ec 11:7
let us walk in the LORD's l. | Is 2:5
who substitute darkness for l and l for | Is 5:20
in darkness have seen a great l; | Is 9:2
constellations will not give their l. | Is 13:10
people {and} a l to the nations | Is 42:6
darkness to l in front of them | Is 42:16
I form l and create darkness, | Is 45:7
make you a l for the nations | Is 49:6
your l will appear like the dawn, | Is 58:8
Arise, shine, for your l has come, | Is 60:1

Nations will come to your l, | Is 60:3
the LORD will be your everlasting l, | Is 60:19
who gives the sun for l by day, | Jr 31:35
the moon will not give its l. | Ezk 32:7
It will be darkness and not l. | Am 5:18
the LORD will be my l. | Mc 7:8
On that day there will be no l; | Zch 14:6
live in darkness have seen a great l, | Mt 4:16
You are the l of the world. | Mt 5:14
let your l shine before men, | Mt 5:16
whole body will be full of l. | Mt 6:22
the moon will not shed its l; | Mt 24:29
hidden except to come to l. | Mk 4:22
a l for revelation to the Gentiles | Lk 2:32
that the l in you is not darkness. | Lk 11:35
are more astute than the sons of l | Lk 16:8
and that life was the l of men. | Jn 1:4
The true l, who gives l to everyone, | Jn 1:9
loved darkness rather than the l | Jn 3:19
I am the l of the world. | Jn 8:12
While you have the l, believe in
the l so that you may become
sons of l. | Jn 12:36
a l from heaven suddenly flashed | Ac 9:3
and a l shone in the cell. | Ac 12:7
and put on the armor of l. | Rm 13:12
both bring to l what is hidden | 1Co 4:5
to give the l of the knowledge | 2Co 4:6
fellowship does l have with | 2Co 6:14
is disguised as an angel of l. | 2Co 11:14
Walk as children of l | Eph 5:8
are all sons of l and sons of | 1Th 5:5
dwelling in unapproachable l, | 1Tm 6:16
immortality to l through the | 2Tm 1:10
down from the Father of l-**s**; | Jms 1:17
darkness into His marvelous l. | 1Pt 2:9
God is l, and there is | 1Jn 1:5
walk in the l as He Himself is in the l | 1Jn 1:7
says he is in the l but hates his | 1Jn 2:9
The nations will walk in its l, | Rv 21:24
the Lord God will give them l. | Rv 22:5

LIGHT (v)

on the wood but not l the fire. | 1Kg 18:23
LORD, You l my lamp; | Ps 18:28
No one l-**s** a lamp and puts it | Mt 5:15
to horizon and l-**s** up the sky, | Lk 17:24

LIGHTEN

l your father's harsh service | 1Kg 12:4

into the sea to l the load. Jnh 1:5

they began to l the ship by Ac 27:38

LIGHTLY

Naaman off l by not accepting 2Kg 5:20

of blows will be beaten l. Lk 12:48

take the Lord's discipline l, Heb 12:5

LIGHTNING

L struck the earth, Ex 9:23

was thunder and l, a thick cloud Ex 19:16

He spreads His l around Him and Jb 36:30

He hurled l bolts and routed them. Ps 18:14

His l lights up the world; Ps 97:4

l and hail, snow and cloud Ps 148:8

He makes l for the rain and Jr 10:13

face like the brilliance of l, Dn 10:6

For as the l comes from the east Mt 24:27

His appearance was like l, Mt 28:3

From the throne came flashes of l, Rv 4:5

rumblings, l-s, and an earthquake Rv 8:5

There were l-s, rumblings Rv 11:19

There were l-s, rumblings, and Rv 16:18

LIKE

will make a helper who is l him. Gn 2:18

you will be l God, knowing good Gn 3:5

know there is no one l the LORD Ex 8:10

LORD, who is l You Ex 15:11

been no day l it before or since, Jos 10:14

There is no one holy l the LORD. 1Sm 2:2

There is no one l You, 2Sm 7:22

Get ready to answer Me l a man; Jb 38:3

LORD, who is l You, rescuing Ps 35:10

God, who is l You? Ps 71:19

What god is great l God? Ps 77:13

there is no one l You among the Ps 86:8

Who is l the LORD our God Ps 113:5

who make them are just l them, Ps 135:18

[I am] God, and no one is l Me. Is 46:9

LORD, there is no one l You. Jr 10:6

But it was not l that from the Mt 19:8

It must not be l that among you Mt 20:26

The second is l it: Love your Mt 22:39

The kingdom of God is l this, Mk 4:26

this generation, and what are they l? Lk 7:31

What is the kingdom of God l, Lk 13:18

It will be l that on the day the Lk 17:30

No man ever spoke l this! Jn 7:46

Some of you were l this; 1Co 6:11

that all people were just l me. 1Co 7:7

spoke l a child, I thought l a child, 1Co 13:11

L the man made of dust, so are 1Co 15:48

we no longer know Him l that. 2Co 5:16

become l me, for I also became l Gl 4:12

you will not grieve l the rest, 1Th 4:13

He had to be l His brothers in Heb 2:17

was a man with a nature l ours; Jms 5:17

we will be l Him, because we will 1Jn 3:2

was One l the Son of Man, Rv 1:13

His face was l the sun, Rv 10:1

and One l the Son of Man was Rv 14:14

Who is l the great city? Rv 18:18

LIKED

son Jonathan l David very much, 1Sm 19:1

LIKE-MINDED

have no one else l who will Php 2:20

you should be l and sympathetic 1Pt 3:8

LIKEN

What can I l you to, so that I Lm 2:13

LIKENESS

Our image, according to Our l. Gn 1:26

He made him in the l of God; Gn 5:1

he fathered {a child} in his l, Gn 5:3

one with human l touched my lips Dn 10:16

did not sin in the l of Adam's Rm 5:14

Joined with Him in the l of His death Rm 6:5

slave, taking on the l of men. Php 2:7

into the l of His glorious Php 3:21

men who are made in God's l. Jms 3:9

LILY

portico were shaped like l-ies, 1Kg 7:19

brim of a cup or of a l blossom. 1Kg 7:26

a rose of Sharon, a l of the valleys. Sg 2:1

Like a l among thorns, so is my Sg 2:2

he feeds among the l-ies. Sg 2:16; 6:3

His lips are l-ies, dripping with Sg 5:13

mound of wheat surrounded by l-ies. Sg 7:2

blossom like the l and take root Hs 14:5

LIMB

He tore them l from l with a great Jdg 15:8

into 12 pieces, l by l, and sent her Jdg 19:29

you will be torn l from l, Dn 2:5

will be torn l from l and his house Dn 3:29

LIME

because he burned to l the bones Am 2:1

LIMIT

or discover the l-s of the Almighty	Jb 11:7
You have set l-s he cannot pass,	Jb 14:5
He established a l for the rain	Jb 28:26
but Your command is without l.	Ps 119:96
{or} settle at the western l-s,	Ps 139:9
when He set a l for the sea so	Pr 8:29
there is no l to His understanding.	Is 40:28

LIMITED

Is the LORD's power l?	Nm 11:23
of the wind and l the water by	Jb 28:25
time, your strength is l.	Pr 24:10
Unless those days were l, no one	Mt 24:22
not do since it was l by the flesh,	Rm 8:3
of the body has a l benefit,	1Tm 4:8

LIMP

is like lame legs that hang l.	Pr 26:7

LINE

The boundary l-s have fallen for me	Ps 16:6
I will establish his l forever.	Ps 89:29
Don't move an ancient property l,	Pr 23:10
l after l, l after l, a little here	Is 28:10
measuring l and a plumb l over her	Is 34:11
A measuring l will once again	Jr 31:39
He stretched out a measuring l	Lm 2:8
with a measuring l in his hand,	Ezk 47:3
with a plumb l in His hand.	Am 7:7
and a measuring l will be	Zch 1:16
house and family l of David,	Lk 2:4

LINEN

him with fine l garments,	Gn 41:42
make them of finely spun l,	Ex 26:1
tunics of fine woven l for Aaron	Ex 39:27
on his l robe and l undergarments.	Lv 6:10
a holy l tunic, and l undergarments	Lv 16:4
He will put on the l garments,	Lv 16:32
made of both wool and l.	Dt 22:11
presence and wore a l ephod.	1Sm 2:18
David was ... wearing a l ephod.	2Sm 6:14
clothing is fine l and purple.	Pr 31:22
She makes and sells l garments;	Pr 31:24
buy yourself l underwear and	Jr 13:1
clothed in l, with writing equipment	Ezk 9:2
there was a man dressed in l,	Dn 10:5
body, wrapped it in clean, fine l,	Mt 27:59
but he left the l cloth behind	Mk 14:52
dress in purple and fine l,	Lk 16:19

he saw only the l cloths.	Lk 24:12
bound hand and foot with l strips	Jn 11:44
tomb and saw the l cloths lying	Jn 20:6
fine l represents the righteous acts	Rv 19:8

LINGER

Dan, why did you l at the ships?	Jdg 5:17
Those who l over wine, those who	Pr 23:30
who l into the evening, inflamed	Is 5:11

LINTEL

and the l of the houses	Ex 12:7
and brush the l and the two	Ex 12:22

LION

Judah is a young l	Gn 49:9
tore the l apart with his bare hands	Jdg 14:6
Whenever a l or a bear came	1Sm 17:34
on a snowy day and killed a l.	2Sm 23:20
Twelve l-s were standing there on	1Kg 10:20
When he left, a l met him	1Kg 13:24
donkey and the l standing beside	1Kg 13:28
When you leave me, a l will kill	1Kg 20:36
So the LORD sent l-s among them,	2Kg 17:25
If I am proud, You hunt me like a l	Jb 10:16
or they will tear me like a l,	Ps 7:2
mouths against me—l-s, mauling	Ps 22:13
Young l-s lack food and go hungry	Ps 34:10
tread on the l and the cobra;	Ps 91:13
A king's rage is like a l-'s roar,	Pr 19:12
says, "There's a l outside!'	Pr 22:13
righteous are as bold as a l.	Pr 28:1
a live dog is better than a dead l.	Ec 9:4
and the l will eat straw like an ox.	Is 11:7
the face of a l on the right,	Ezk 1:10
the third that of a l,	Ezk 10:14
cubs, and he became a young l.	Ezk 19:3
will be thrown into the l-s' den.	Dn 6:7
was like a l but had eagle's	Dn 7:4
For I am like a l to Ephraim and	Hs 5:14
Does a l roar in the forest when	Am 3:4
A l has roared; who will not	Am 3:8
who flees from a l only to have	Am 5:19
I was rescued from the l-'s mouth.	2Tm 4:17
shut the mouths of l-s,	Heb 11:33
prowling around like a roaring l,	1Pt 5:8
first living creature was like a l;	Rv 4:7
The L from the tribe of Judah,	Rv 5:5
their teeth were like l-s' teeth;	Rv 9:8
the horses were like l-s' heads,	Rv 9:17

LIPS

do whatever comes from your l,	Dt 23:23
and although her l were moving,	1Sm 1:13
May the LORD cut off all flattering l	Ps 12:3
Let lying l be quieted;	Ps 31:18
His praise will always be on my l.	Ps 34:1
With my l I proclaim all the	Ps 119:13
deliver me from lying l	Ps 120:2
keep watch at the door of my l.	Ps 141:3
and your l safeguard knowledge	Pr 5:2
but foolish l will be destroyed	Pr 10:8
one who controls his l is wise.	Pr 10:19
The l of the righteous feed many	Pr 10:21
Lying l are detestable to the	Pr 12:22
compresses his l brings about	Pr 16:30
discerning, when he seals his l.	Pr 17:28
answer gives a kiss on the l.	Pr 24:26
Smooth l with an evil heart are	Pr 26:23
a stranger, and not your own l.	Pr 27:2
but the l of a fool consume him	Ec 10:12
Your l are like a scarlet cord,	Sg 4:3
Your l drip {sweetness like} the	Sg 4:11
His l are lilies, dripping with	Sg 5:13
gliding past my l and teeth!	Sg 7:9
I am a man of unclean l	Is 6:5
their l, but far from their conscience.	Jr 12:2
human likeness touched my l.	Dn 10:16
You with praise from our l.	Hs 14:2
nothing wrong was found on his l.	Mal 2:6
people honors Me with their l,	Mt 15:8
Vipers' venom is under their l.	Rm 3:13
and by the l of foreigners,	1Co 14:21
fruit of our l that confess His	Heb 13:15
and his l from speaking deceit,	1Pt 3:10

LIP-SERVICE

honor Me with l—yet their hearts	Is 29:13

LIQUID

and an honest l measure;	Lv 19:36
and the l measure will be	Ezk 45:11

LIST (n)

support l unless she is at	1Tm 5:9

LIST (v)

old or more, and l their names.	Nm 3:40

LISTEN

Because you l-ed to your wife's	Gn 3:17
Sarah was l-ing at the entrance	Gn 18:10
Rebekah was l-ing to what Isaac	Gn 27:5
l-ed to Leah, and she conceived	Gn 30:17
They will l to what you say.	Ex 3:18
Pharaoh will not l to you,	Ex 7:4
Moses l-ed to his father-in-law and	Ex 18:24
The LORD l-ed to Israel's request,	Nm 21:3
L, Israel: The LORD our God	Dt 6:4
the LORD l-ed to me on that	Dt 9:19
your God would not l to Balaam,	Dt 23:5
Be silent, Israel, and l!	Dt 27:9
they did not l to their judges	Jdg 2:17
God l-ed to Manoah, and the Angel	Jdg 13:9
Speak, for Your servant is l-ing.	1Sm 3:10
L to Your servant's prayer	1Kg 8:28
So the LORD l-ed to Elijah's voice	1Kg 17:22
But they would not l.	2Kg 17:14
But don't l to Hezekiah when he	2Kg 18:32
All the people l-ed attentively to	Neh 8:3
L to this, Job.	Jb 37:14
L to my words, LORD;	Ps 5:1
LORD, l and be gracious to me;	Ps 30:10
You open my ears to l.	Ps 40:6
l to my prayer and do not ignore	Ps 55:1
the Lord would not have l-ed.	Ps 66:18
For the LORD l-s to the needy and	Ps 69:33
But My people did not l to Me;	Ps 81:11
I will l to what God will say;	Ps 85:8
L, LORD, to my cry for help.	Ps 140:6
L to my cry, for I am very weak	Ps 142:6
a wise man will l and increase	Pr 1:5
L, {my} sons, to a father's	Pr 4:1
Anyone who l-s to me is happy,	Pr 8:34
but whoever l-s to counsel is wise	Pr 12:15
A wicked person l-s to malicious	Pr 17:4
one gives an answer before he l-s	Pr 18:13
L to your father who gave you	Pr 23:22
Keep l-ing, but do not understand;	Is 6:9
L to Me, Jacob, and Israel, the	Is 48:12
L carefully to Me, and eat what	Is 55:2
no one has l-ed, no eye has seen	Is 64:4
hear! Lord, forgive! Lord, l and act!	Dn 9:19
because they have not l-ed to Him;	Hs 9:17
call for help and You do not l,	Hab 1:2
The LORD took notice and l-ed.	Mal 3:16
Anyone who has ears should l!	Mt 11:15
You will l and l, yet never	Mt 13:14
I take delight in Him. L to Him!	Mt 17:5
But if he won't l, take one or	Mt 18:16

L to another parable: Mt 21:33
Today as you l, this Scripture Lk 4:21
Therefore, take care how you l. Lk 8:18
Whoever l-s to you l-s to Me. Lk 10:16
If they don't l to Moses and Lk 16:31
you cannot l to My word. Jn 8:43
who is from God l-s to God's words Jn 8:47
that God doesn't l to sinners, Jn 9:31
and they will l to My voice. Jn 10:16
is of the truth l-s to My voice. Jn 18:37
You must l to Him in everything Ac 3:22
You will l and l, yet never Ac 28:26
to the Gentiles; they will l! Ac 28:28
even then, they will not l to Me, 1Co 14:21
not from God does not l to us. 1Jn 4:6
ear should l to what the Spirit says Rv 2:7
anyone has an ear, he should l: Rv 13:9

LITERATURE
the Chaldean language and l. Dn 1:4
in every kind of l and wisdom. Dn 1:17

LITTLE
who gathered a l had no shortage Ex 16:18
drive them out l by l ahead of you Ex 23:30
My l finger is thicker than my 1Kg 12:10
served Baal a l, but Jehu will 2Kg 10:18
grant them a l deliverance. 2Ch 12:7
You made him l less than God and Ps 8:5
Better the l that the righteous Ps 37:16
I am like a l child. Ps 131:2
A l sleep, a l slumber, Pr 6:10; 24:33
Better a l with the fear of the Pr 15:16
Better a l with righteousness Pr 16:8
so a l folly outweighs wisdom Ec 10:1
after line, a l here, , a l there. Is 28:10
another horn, a l one, came up Dn 7:8
planted much but harvested l. Hg 1:6
Once more, in a l while, I am Hg 2:6
more for you—you of l faith? Mt 6:30
are you fearful, you of l faith? Mt 8:26
one of these l ones because he Mt 10:42
You of l faith, why did you doubt? Mt 14:31
Jesus said, "You of l faith! Mt 16:8
"Because of your l faith," He told Mt 17:20
welcomes one l child such as Mk 9:37
Let the l children come to Me. Mk 10:14
the one who is forgiven l, loves l. Lk 7:47
Whoever is faithful in very l is also Lk 16:10
again a l while and you will see Me. Jn 16:16

who gathered l did not have too l. 2Co 8:15
A l yeast leavens the whole lump Gl 5:9
I know both how to have a l, Php 4:12
For in yet a very l while, Heb 10:37
and he had a l scroll opened in Rv 10:2

LIVE (adj)
since a l dog is better than a Ec 9:4

LIVE (v)
tree of life, and eat, and l forever. Gn 3:22
Methuselah l-d 782 years after the Gn 5:26
And Abraham l-d as a foreigner in Gn 21:34
for no one can see Me and l. Ex 33:20
a person will l if he does them Lv 18:5
man does not l on bread alone Dt 8:3
As the LORD l-s, if you had let Jdg 8:19
as the LORD l-s, I will. Ru 3:13
shouted, "Long l the king!" 1Sm 10:24
as the LORD l-s who saves Israel, 1Sm 14:39
No, as the LORD l-s, not a hair of 1Sm 14:45
as the LORD l-s, David will not be 1Sm 19:6
the LORD l-s and as you yourself l, 1Sm 20:3
day Jesse's son l-s on earth you 1Sm 20:31
LORD l-s and as you yourself l, 1Sm 25:26
as the LORD God of Israel l-s, 1Sm 25:34
As the LORD l-s, the LORD will 1Sm 26:10
as the LORD l-s, nothing bad will 1Sm 28:10
As the LORD l-s, you are an 1Sm 29:6
as the LORD l-s, {the One} who has 2Sm 4:9
surely as you l and by your life 2Sm 11:11
as the LORD l-s, the man who did 2Sm 12:5
"As the LORD l-s," he vowed 2Sm 14:11
As surely as you l, my lord the 2Sm 14:19
as the LORD l-s and as my lord
the king l-s, 2Sm 15:21
to Absalom, "Long l the king! 2Sm 16:16
saying, 'Long l King Adonijah!' 1Kg 1:25
and say, 'Long l King Solomon!' 1Kg 1:34
I will l among the Israelites 1Kg 6:13
But will God indeed l on earth? 1Kg 8:27
As the LORD God of Israel l-s, 1Kg 17:1
LORD your God l-s, I don't have 1Kg 17:12
the LORD your God l-s, there is no 1Kg 18:10
LORD of Hosts l-s, before whom I 1Kg 18:15
As the LORD l-s, I will say 1Kg 22:14
the LORD l-s and as you yourself l, 2Kg 2:2
LORD of Hosts l-s, I stand before 2Kg 3:14
the LORD l-s and as you yourself l, 2Kg 4:30
As the LORD l-s, I stand before 2Kg 5:16

and cried, "Long l the king!"	2Kg 11:12
so that you may l and not die.	2Kg 18:32
can I enter the temple and l?	Neh 6:11
a person will l if he does them	Neh 9:29
I give up! I will not l forever.	Jb 7:16
Who can l on Your holy mountain	Ps 15:1
The Lord l-s—may my rock be	Ps 18:46
of the Lord as long as I l.	Ps 23:6
will praise You as long as I l;	Ps 63:4
and I will l by Your truth.	Ps 86:11
The one who l-s under	
the protection	Ps 91:1
praise to my God while I l.	Ps 104:33
Jacob l-d as a foreigner in the	Ps 105:23
Let me l, and I will praise You	Ps 119:175
when brothers can l together!	Ps 133:1
upright will l in Your presence	Ps 140:13
to the Lord as long as I l.	Ps 146:2
Keep my commands and l	Pr 4:4; 7:2
who l-s with integrity l-s securely,	Pr 10:9
one who hates bribes will l.	Pr 15:27
yet it l-s in kings' palaces.	Pr 30:28
on those l-ing in the land of darkness,	Is 9:2
Your dead will l; their bodies	Is 26:19
these {promises} people l,	Is 38:16
As I l"—the Lord's declaration	Is 49:18
listen, so that you will l.	Is 55:3
and Exalted One who l-s forever,	Is 57:15
swear, As the Lord l-s, in truth	Jr 4:2
When they say, "As the Lord l-s,"	Jr 5:2
l because he listened to your	Ezk 3:21
L! Yes, I said to you as you lay	Ezk 16:6
just and right, he will certainly l;	Ezk 18:21
who does them will l by them.	Ezk 20:11
Son of man, can these bones l?	Ezk 37:3
swear an oath: As the Lord l-s!	Hs 4:15
house of Israel: Seek Me and l!	Am 5:4
"As your god l-s, Dan," or "As the	
way of Beer-sheba l-s"	Am 8:14
the righteous one will l by his faith.	Hab 2:4
Man must not l on bread alone	Mt 4:4
The people who l in darkness	Mt 4:16
If we had l-d in the days of our	Mt 23:30
Do this and you will l.	Lk 10:28
told him, "your son will l."	Jn 4:50
and those who hear will l.	Jn 5:25
this bread he will l forever.	Jn 6:51
in Me, even if he dies, will l.	Jn 11:25

Everyone who l-s and believes in	Jn 11:26
The Father who l-s in Me does His	Jn 14:10
Because I l, you will l too.	Jn 14:19
not l in shrines made by hands.	Ac 17:24
in Him we l and move and	Ac 17:28
religion I l-d as a Pharisee.	Ac 26:5
The righteous will l by faith.	Rm 1:17
that we will also l with Him,	Rm 6:8
but in that He l-s, He l-s to God.	Rm 6:10
man while her husband is l-ing,	Rm 7:3
know that nothing good l-s in me,	Rm 7:18
the Spirit of God l-s in you.	Rm 8:9
for if you l according to the flesh,	Rm 8:13
these things will l by them.	Rm 10:5
on your part, l at peace with	Rm 12:18
For none of us l-s to himself,	Rm 14:7
If we l, we l to the Lord;	Rm 14:8
As I l, says the Lord, every	Rm 14:11
the Spirit of God l-s in you?	1Co 3:16
a man is l-ing with his father's	1Co 5:1
as long as her husband is l-ing.	1Co 7:39
those who l should no longer l for	2Co 5:15
as dying and look—we l;	2Co 6:9
but He l-s by God's power.	2Co 13:4
l like a Gentile and not like a	Gl 2:14
I no longer l, but Christ l-s in me.	
The life I now l in the flesh,	
I l by faith	Gl 2:20
the righteous will l by faith.	Gl 3:11
these things will l by them.	Gl 3:12
If we l by the Spirit, we must	Gl 5:25
l your life in a manner worthy	Php 1:27
faith that first l-d in your	2Tm 1:5
the Holy Spirit who l-s in us,	2Tm 1:14
we will also l with Him;	2Tm 2:11
righteous one will l by faith;	Heb 10:38
we will l and do this or that.	Jms 4:15
You have l-d luxuriously on the	Jms 5:5
for as he l-d among them,	2Pt 2:8
so that we might l through Him.	1Jn 4:9
I know where you l	Rv 2:13
the One who l-s forever and ever,	Rv 4:9
who had the sword wound yet l-d.	Rv 13:14
of God who l-s forever and ever	Rv 15:7
and He will l with them.	Rv 21:3

LIVER

the fatty lobe of the l,	Ex 29:13
fatty lobe of the l from the sin	Lv 9:10

the flashing tip out of his l.   Jb 20:25
until an arrow pierces its l,   Pr 7:23
the idols, and observes the l.   Ezk 21:21

LIVESTOCK

Abram was very rich in l,   Gn 13:2
they brought their l to Joseph,   Gn 47:17
Egyptian l died, but none among   Ex 9:6
and every firstborn of the l.   Ex 12:29
along with a huge number of l,   Ex 12:38
We took only the l and the spoil   Dt 2:35
as well as its l with the sword   Dt 13:15
its spoil and l for yourselves.   Jos 8:2

LIVING (adj)

and the man became a l being.   Gn 2:7
into the ark two of every l thing   Gn 6:19
the voice of the l God speaking   Dt 5:26
defy the armies of the l God?   1Sm 17:26
Cut the l boy in two and give   1Kg 3:25
Assyria sent to mock the l God,   2Kg 19:4
But I know my l Redeemer, and He   Jb 19:25
I thirst for God, the l God.   Ps 42:2
flesh cry out for the l God.   Ps 84:2
the desire of every l thing.   Ps 145:16
let every l thing praise His   Ps 145:21
Me, the fountain of l water, and dug   Jr 2:13
should {any} l person complain   Lm 3:39
form of four l creatures came   Ezk 1:5
For He is the l God, and He   Dn 6:26
be called: Sons of the l God.   Hs 1:10
On that day l water will flow   Zch 14:8
Messiah, the Son of the l God!   Mt 16:16
By the l God I place You under   Mt 26:63
and He would give you l water.   Jn 4:10
I am the l bread that came down   Jn 6:51
have streams of l water flow   Jn 7:38
be called sons of the l God.   Rm 9:26
your bodies as a l sacrifice,   Rm 12:1
man Adam became a l being;   1Co 15:45
are the sanctuary of the l God,   2Co 6:16
have put our hope in the l God,   1Tm 4:10
word of God is l and effective   Heb 4:12
by the new and l way that He has   Heb 10:20
into the hands of the l God!   Heb 10:31
new birth into a l hope through   1Pt 1:3
yourselves, as l stones, are   1Pt 2:5
and the L One. I was dead,   Rv 1:18
throne were four l creatures   Rv 4:6
who had the seal of the l God.   Rv 7:2

them to springs of l waters,   Rv 7:17
showed me the river of l water,   Rv 22:1
take the l water as a gift   Rv 22:17

LIVING (n)

was the mother of all the l.   Gn 3:20
be found in the land of the l.   Jb 28:13
goodness in the land of the l.   Ps 27:13
you from the land of the l.   Ps 52:5
the LORD in the land of the l.   Ps 116:9
my portion in the land of the l.   Ps 142:5
more than the l, who are still   Ec 4:2
and the l should take it to heart.   Ec 7:2
For the l know that they will die,   Ec 9:5
consult the dead on behalf of the l?   Is 8:19
The l, only the l can thank You,   Is 38:19
cut off from the land of the l;   Is 53:8
splendor in the land of the l.   Ezk 26:20
terror in the land of the l.   Ezk 32:23
This is so the l will know that   Dn 4:17
God of the dead, but of the l.   Mt 22:32
looking for the l among the dead?   Lk 24:5
Judge of the l and the dead.   Ac 10:42
over both the dead and the l.   Rm 14:9
earn their l by the gospel.   1Co 9:14
l is Christ and dying is gain.   Php 1:21
to judge the l and the dead,   2Tm 4:1
to judge the l and the dead.   1Pt 4:5

LIZARD

a l can be caught in your hands   Pr 30:28

LOAD (n)

lying {helpless} under its l,   Ex 23:5
do not pick up a l and bring it   Jr 17:21
into the sea to lighten the l.   Jnh 1:5
tie up heavy l-s that are hard to   Mt 23:4
will have to carry his own l.   Gl 6:5

LOAD (v)

l-ed the grain on their donkeys   Gn 42:26
You l people with burdens that   Lk 11:46

LOAF

of Egypt into unleavened **loaves**,   Ex 12:39
flour and bake it into 12 **loaves**;   Lv 24:5
a l of barley bread came tumbling   Jdg 7:13
Give me five **loaves** of bread or   1Sm 21:3
taking 200 **loaves** of bread,   1Sm 25:18
Am I to set 20 **loaves** before 100   2Kg 4:43
fee is only a l of bread,   Pr 6:26

only have five **loaves** and two fish | Mt 14:17
took the seven **loaves** and the fish, | Mt 15:36
the five **loaves** for the 5,000 | Mt 16:9
and had only one l with them in | Mk 8:14
lend me three **loaves** of bread, | Lk 11:5
table, and the presentation **loaves**. | Heb 9:2

LOAN (n)
to the poor is a l to the LORD, | Pr 19:17
one ... who put up security for l-s. | Pr 22:26
him, and forgave him the l. | Mt 18:27

LOAN (v)
and freely l him enough for | Dt 15:8

LOATHE
and do not l His discipline; | Pr 3:11
They will l themselves because | Ezk 6:9
and you will l yourselves for | Ezk 20:43
and you will l yourselves for | Ezk 36:31
I l Jacob's pride and hate his | Am 6:8

LOBE
put {it} on the l of the right ear | Lv 14:14

LOCAL
When the l people saw the | Ac 28:4

LOCATION
see that the city's l is good, | 2Kg 2:19

LOCK (v)
upstairs room l-ed and thought he | Jdg 3:24
l-ed themselves in and went up | Jdg 9:51
my bride, {you are} a l-ed garden | Sg 4:12
You l up the kingdom of heaven | Mt 23:13
he l-ed John up in prison. | Lk 3:20
door is already l-ed, and my | Lk 11:7
with the doors l-ed because of | Jn 20:19
Even though the doors were l-ed, | Jn 20:26
We found the jail securely l-ed, | Ac 5:23
and l l-ed up many of the saints in | Ac 26:10

LOCUST
I will bring l-s into your territory. | Ex 10:4
eat these: the various kinds of l, | Lv 11:22
little, because l-s will devour it | Dt 28:38
the valley like a swarm of l-s, | Jdg 7:12
when there is blight, mildew, l, | 1Kg 8:37
Do you make him leap like a l? | Jb 39:20
fruit of their labor to the l. | Ps 78:46
He spoke and l-s came | Ps 105:34
I am shaken off like a l. | Ps 109:23

l-s have no king, yet all of them | Pr 30:27
be gathered as l-s are gathered; | Is 33:4
What the devouring l has left, the | Jl 1:4
I will repay you for the years that the
swarming l ate, | Jl 2:25
the l devoured your many gardens | Am 4:9
devour you like the young l. | Nah 3:15
his food was l-s and wild honey. | Mt 3:4
out of the smoke l-s came to the | Rv 9:3

LO-DEBAR
You'll find him in L at the house | 2Sm 9:4
you who rejoice over L and say, | Am 6:13

LODGE
evil cannot l with You. | Ps 5:4
He's gone to l with a sinful | Lk 19:7
He is l-ing with Simon, a tanner | Ac 10:6

LOFTY
Your l judgments are beyond his | Ps 10:5
It is l; I am unable to {reach} it. | Ps 139:6
against all that is proud and l, | Is 2:12
Lord seated on a high and l throne, | Is 6:1

LOG
Jordan where we can each get a l | 2Kg 6:2
along with cedar l-s, stonemasons | 1Ch 14:1
quantity of cedar l-s to David. | 1Ch 22:4
to prepare l-s for me in abundance | 2Ch 2:9
We will cut l-s from Lebanon, | 2Ch 2:16
Pile on the l-s and kindle the | Ezk 24:10
notice the l in your own eye | Mt 7:3
notice the l in your own eye | Lk 6:41

LOINCLOTHS
and made l for themselves. | Gn 3:7

LOINS
with the fat on them at the l; | Lv 3:4
Smash the l of his adversaries | Dt 33:11
is thicker than my father's l! | 1Kg 12:10
strength of his l and the power | Jb 40:16
For my l are full of burning pain, | Ps 38:7
and let their l continually shake. | Ps 69:23
to unloose the l of kings, | Is 45:1
knees tremble, l shake, every | Nah 2:10

LOIS
Timothy's grandmother (2Tm 1:5).

LONG (adj)
you may have a l life in the land | Ex 20:12

shouted, "L live the king!"	1Sm 10:24
How l are you going to mourn	1Sm 16:1
to Absalom, "L live the king!	2Sm 16:16
saying, 'L live King Adonijah!"	1Kg 1:25
and say, 'L live King Solomon!'	1Kg 1:34
did not ask for l life or riches	1Kg 3:11
How l will you hesitate between	1Kg 18:21
and cried, "L live the king!"	2Kg 11:12
you not heard? I designed it l ago;	2Kg 19:25
How l will your journey take,	Neh 2:6
already born; you have lived so l!	Jb 38:21
And You, LORD—how l?	Ps 6:3
How l will You hide Your face	Ps 13:1
while all day l people say to me	Ps 42:3
God, how l will the foe mock?	Ps 74:10
How l, LORD? Will You be angry	Ps 79:5
How l, LORD? Will You hide	Ps 89:46
LORD—how l? Turn and have	Ps 90:13
I will satisfy him with a l life	Ps 91:16
how l will the wicked gloat?	Ps 94:3
L ago You established the earth	Ps 102:25
sing to the LORD as l as I live.	Ps 146:2
L life is in her right hand;	Pr 3:16
How l will you stay in bed,	Pr 6:9
I declared to you l ago;	Is 48:5
How l, LORD, must I call for help	Hab 1:2
How l must I put up with you?	Mt 17:17
houses and make l prayers just	Mt 23:14
As l as they have the groom with	Mk 2:19
want to go around in l robes,	Mk 12:38
they would have repented l ago,	Lk 10:13
the son was still a l way off,	Lk 15:20
being put to death all day l;	Rm 8:36
All day l I have spread out My	Rm 10:21
if a man has l hair it is a disgrace	1Co 11:14
you may have a l life in the	Eph 6:3
L ago God spoke to the fathers	Heb 1:1
how l until You judge and avenge	Rv 6:10

LONG (v)

My heart l-s within me.	Jb 19:27
As a deer l-s for streams of water, so	Ps 42:1
I l and yearn for the courts of	Ps 84:2
them to the harbor they l-ed for.	Ps 107:30
How l I l for Your precepts!	Ps 119:40
I l for Your salvation;	Ps 119:81
I should go, because I l for You.	Ps 143:8
I l for You in the night;	Is 26:9
the god l-ed for by women,	Dn 11:37

Woe to you who l for the Day of	Am 5:18
people l-ed to see the things you	Mt 13:17
He l-ed to eat his fill from the	Lk 15:16
He l-ed to be filled with what fell	Lk 16:21
I l to see you so that I may be	2Tm 1:4
they will l to die, but death	Rv 9:6

LONGER

Your name will no l be Abram,	Gn 17:5
Your name will no l be Jacob,	Gn 32:28
when she could no l hide him,	Ex 2:3
I will no l drive out before	Jdg 2:21
the LORD now says, "No l!	1Sm 2:30
You will no l be called Deserted,	Is 62:4
you will no l use this proverb	Ezk 18:3
and no l call Me: My Baal.	Hs 2:16
and you will no l see Me;	Jn 16:10
and I no l live, but Christ	Gl 2:20

LONGING

overcome by l for Your judgments	Ps 119:20
l to put on our house from	2Co 5:2
He announced to us your deep l,	2Co 7:7
he has been l for all of you	Php 2:26

LONGINGLY

wife looked l at Joseph and said	Gn 39:7

LONG-SLEEVED

Tamar was wearing a l garment,	2Sm 13:18

LOOK

But his wife l-ed back and became	Gn 19:26
he was afraid to l at God.	Ex 3:6
anyone who is bitten l-s at it,	Nm 21:8
donkeys you went l-ing for have	1Sm 10:2
Do not l at his appearance or	1Sm 16:7
daughter Michal l-ed down from	2Sm 6:16
they are l-ing for me to take my	1Kg 19:10
Will You ever l away from me,	Jb 7:19
when I l-ed for light, darkness	Jb 30:26
then could I l at a young woman	Jb 31:1
the son of man that You l after him?	Ps 8:4
The LORD l-s down from heaven on	Ps 14:2
The LORD l-s down from heaven;	Ps 33:13
Those who l to Him are radiant	Ps 34:5
Lord, how long will You l on?	Ps 35:17
God l-s down from heaven on the	Ps 53:2
My eyes fail, l-ing for my God.	Ps 69:3
L down from heaven and see;	Ps 80:14
l-ed down from His holy heights	Ps 102:19

the end he will l in triumph on	Ps 112:8
The sea l-ed and fled; the Jordan	Ps 114:3
I will l in triumph on those who	Ps 118:7
Turn my eyes from l-ing at what	Ps 119:37
grow weary {l-ing} for what You	Ps 119:82
But my eyes {l} to You, Lord GOD	Ps 141:8
All eyes l to You, and You give	Ps 145:15
Let your eyes l forward;	Pr 4:25
but if someone l-s for trouble,	Pr 11:27
those who go l-ing for mixed wine.	Pr 23:30
I'll l for another {drink}.	Pr 23:35
anything, "L, this is new"?	Ec 1:10
and he l-ed on me with love.	Sg 2:4
He l-ed for justice but saw	Is 5:7
keep l-ing, but do not perceive.	Is 6:9
that day people will l to their Maker	Is 17:7
but you did not l to the One who	Is 22:11
They do not l to the Holy One of	Is 31:1
L at Zion, the city of our	Is 33:20
L to the rock from which you	Is 51:1
that He did not l like a man,	Is 52:14
that we should l at Him,	Is 53:2
LORD, l on my affliction,	Lm 1:9
end of 10 days they l-ed better and	Dn 1:15
yet I will l once more toward	Jnh 2:4
But as for me, I will l to the LORD;	Mc 7:7
L to the mountains—the feet of	Nah 1:15
eyes are too pure to l on evil,	Hab 1:13
will l at Me whom they pierced.	Zch 12:10
everyone who l-s at a woman to	Mt 5:28
L at the birds of the sky:	Mt 6:26
because they do not see,	Mt 13:13
you will l and l, yet never perceive.	Mt 13:14
two fish, and l-ing up to heaven,	Mt 14:19
Sanhedrin were l-ing for false	Mt 26:59
I know you are l-ing for Jesus who	Mt 28:5
they l to me like trees walking.	Mk 8:24
they were l-ing for a way to arrest	Mk 12:12
the plow and l-s back is fit for	Lk 9:62
'L there!' or 'L here!' Don't	Lk 17:23
L at the fig tree, and all the	Lk 21:29
L at My hands and My feet,	Lk 24:39
he said, "L! The Lamb of God!"	Jn 1:36
your eyes and l at the fields,	Jn 4:35
You are l-ing for Me, not because	Jn 6:26
You will l for Me, but you will	Jn 7:34
They will l at the One they	Jn 19:37
she stooped to l into the tomb.	Jn 20:11

do you stand l-ing up into heaven?	Ac 1:11
l-ed at him intently and said, "L at	Ac 3:4
you will l and l, yet never perceive.	Ac 28:26
eats must not l down on one who	Rm 14:3
were not able to l directly at	2Co 3:7
Everyone should l out not {only}	Php 2:4
he was l-ing forward to the city	Heb 11:10
is like a man l-ing at his own face	Jms 1:23
to l after orphans and widows in	Jms 1:27
Angels desire to l into these	1Pt 1:12
l-ing for anyone he can devour.	1Pt 5:8
L at how great a love the Father	1Jn 3:1
to open the scroll or even to l in it.	Rv 5:3

LOOKOUT

Balak took him to L Field on top	Nm 23:14
eyes are on the l for the helpless.	Ps 10:8
Lord has said to me, "Go, post a l;	Is 21:6
station myself on the l tower.	Hab 2:1

LOOM

my head with the web of a l	Jdg 16:13
He cuts me off from the l.	Is 38:12

LOOPS

Make l of blue yarn on the edge	Ex 26:4

LOOSE

whatever you l on earth is already	Mt 16:19
L him and let him go.	Jn 11:44
and everyone's chains came l.	Ac 16:26
a wife? Do not seek to be l-d.	1Co 7:27

LOOT

off a great supply of l.	2Ch 14:13
will take the l from those who	Ezk 39:10

LOOTED

houses will be l, and their	Is 13:16
is a people plundered and l,	Is 42:22
from those who l them and	Ezk 39:10
the houses l, and the women	Zch 14:2

LORD LD = LORD/Yahweh see also YAHWEH

at the time that the LD God made	Gn 2:4
began to call on the name of the LD.	Gn 4:26
Abram worshiped the LD there.	Gn 13:4
Abram believed the LD, and He	Gn 15:6
anything impossible for the LD?	Gn 18:14
and said, "My l-s, turn aside to	Gn 19:2
that place The LD Will Provide,	Gn 22:14
May the LD watch between you	Gn 31:49

The Lᴏʀᴅ, the God of the Hebrews	Ex 3:18	I am the Lᴏʀᴅ, the God of all flesh.	Jr 32:27
Moses replied to the Lᴏʀᴅ, "Please, L,	Ex 4:10	the glory of the Lᴏʀᴅ moved away	Ezk 10:18
I will sing to the Lᴏʀᴅ, for He is	Ex 15:1	you will know that I am the Lᴏʀᴅ.	Ezk 36:11
The Lᴏʀᴅ is my strength and my song	Ex 15:2	glory of the Lᴏʀᴅ filled His temple.	Ezk 44:4
The Lᴏʀᴅ is a warrior; Yahweh is	Ex 15:3	indeed God of gods, L of kings	Dn 2:47
I am the Lᴏʀᴅ your God, who brought	Ex 20:2	for the Day of the Lᴏʀᴅ is coming;	Jl 2:1
I, the Lᴏʀᴅ your God, am holy.	Lv 19:2	a city, hasn't the Lᴏʀᴅ done it?	Am 3:6
The Lᴏʀᴅ bless you and protect you	Nm 6:24	who long for the Day of the Lᴏʀᴅ!	Am 5:18
The Lᴏʀᴅ our God, the Lᴏʀᴅ is One.	Dt 6:4	For the Day of the Lᴏʀᴅ is near,	Ob 15
Love the Lᴏʀᴅ your God with all	Dt 6:5	what it is the Lᴏʀᴅ requires of you	Mc 6:8
For the Lᴏʀᴅ your God is the God of		But the Lᴏʀᴅ is in His holy temple	Hab 2:20
gods and L of l-s,	Dt 10:17	The great Day of the Lᴏʀᴅ is near,	Zph 1:14
family, we will worship the Lᴏʀᴅ.	Jos 24:15	A day of the Lᴏʀᴅ is coming when	Zch 14:1
all the l-s of Shechem,	Jdg 9:2	and awesome Day of the Lᴏʀᴅ comes.	Mal 4:5
There is no one holy like the Lᴏʀᴅ.	1Sm 2:2	Prepare the way for the L;	Mt 3:3
glory of the Lᴏʀᴅ filled the temple.	1Kg 8:11	Do not test the L your God.	Mt 4:7
Give thanks to the Lᴏʀᴅ; call on His	1Ch 16:8	who says to Me, 'L, L! will enter	Mt 7:21
I said, Lᴏʀᴅ God of heaven,	Neh 1:5	pray to the L of the harvest to	Mt 9:38
You alone are the Lᴏʀᴅ. You created	Neh 9:6	Son of Man is L of the Sabbath.	Mt 12:8
Lᴏʀᴅ gives, and the Lᴏʀᴅ takes away.	Jb 1:21	mercy on me, L, Son of David!	Mt 15:22
Then the Lᴏʀᴅ answered Job from the	Jb 38:1	who comes in the name of the L!	Mt 21:9
against the Lᴏʀᴅ and His Anointed	Ps 2:2	Love the L your God with all	Mt 22:37
The Lᴏʀᴅ is King forever and ever;	Ps 10:16	The L declared to my L,	Mt 22:44
I said to the Lᴏʀᴅ, "You are my L;	Ps 16:2	If, then, David calls Him 'L,' how	Mt 22:45
The Lᴏʀᴅ is my shepherd;	Ps 23:1	who comes in the name of the L!	Mt 23:39
the house of the Lᴏʀᴅ as long as I	Ps 23:6	The L our God, The L is One.	Mk 12:29
The Lᴏʀᴅ is my light and my salvation	Ps 27:1	the glory of the L shone around	Lk 2:9
the nation whose God is the Lᴏʀᴅ	Ps 33:12	a Savior, who is Messiah the L,	Lk 2:11
Sing a new song to the Lᴏʀᴅ;	Ps 96:1	the year of the L-'s favor.	Lk 4:19
ascribe to the Lᴏʀᴅ glory and strength.	Ps 96:7	you call Me 'L, L,' and don't do	Lk 6:46
The Lᴏʀᴅ declared to my L:	Ps 110:1	The L has certainly been raised	Lk 24:34
Not to us, Lᴏʀᴅ, not to us, but to	Ps 115:1	the arm of the L been revealed	Jn 12:38
thanks to the Lᴏʀᴅ, for He is good;	Ps 118:1	You call Me Teacher and L.	Jn 13:13
Unless the Lᴏʀᴅ builds a house,	Ps 127:1	to Him, "My L and my God!"	Jn 20:28
Give thanks to the L of l-s.	Ps 136:3	on the name of the L will be saved.	Ac 2:21
The fear of the Lᴏʀᴅ is the beginning of	Pr 1:7	The L said to my L, 'Sit at My	Ac 2:34
Trust in the Lᴏʀᴅ with all your	Pr 3:5	crucified, both L and Messiah!	Ac 2:36
but the Lᴏʀᴅ determines his steps.	Pr 16:9	"Who are You, L?" he said.	Ac 9:5
but the Lᴏʀᴅ evaluates the motives.	Pr 21:2	"No, L!" Peter said. "For I have	Ac 10:14
I saw the L seated on a high and	Is 6:1	Jesus Christ—He is L of all.	Ac 10:36
Holy, holy, holy is the Lᴏʀᴅ of Hosts;	Is 6:3	Father and the L Jesus Christ.	Rm 1:7
Yah, the Lᴏʀᴅ, is my strength	Is 12:2	with your mouth, "Jesus is L,"	Rm 10:9
other l-s than You have ruled over	Is 26:13	the name of the L will be saved.	Rm 10:13
who trust in the Lᴏʀᴅ will renew their	Is 40:31	If we live, we live to the L;	Rm 14:8
I, I am the Lᴏʀᴅ, and there is no other	Is 43:11	who boasts must boast in the L.	1Co 1:31
Lᴏʀᴅ has punished Him for the iniquity	Is 53:6	are many "gods" and many "l-s"	1Co 8:5
by Your name, Lᴏʀᴅ God of Hosts.	Jr 15:16	and one L, Jesus Christ,	1Co 8:6
brother, saying: Know the Lᴏʀᴅ, for	Jr 31:34	earth is the L-'s, and all that is	1Co 10:26

one can say, "Jesus is **L**," except	1Co 12:3
ministries, but the same **L**.	1Co 12:5
in the day of our **L** Jesus.	2Co 1:14
Now the **L** is the Spirit;	2Co 3:17
body and at home with the **L**.	2Co 5:8
who boasts must boast in the **L**.	2Co 10:17
one **L**, one faith, one baptism,	Eph 4:5
confess that Jesus Christ is **L**,	Php 2:11
Rejoice in the **L** always.	Php 4:4
The **L** is near.	Php 4:5
received Christ Jesus the **L**,	Col 2:6
you serve the **L** Christ.	Col 3:24
the Day of the **L** will come just	1Th 5:2
The **L** be with all of you.	2Th 3:16
King of kings, and the **L** of **l-s**,	1Tm 6:15
his brother, saying, 'Know the **L**,'	Heb 8:11
do not take the **L-**'s discipline	Heb 12:5
say, "If the **L** wills, we will	Jms 4:15
have tasted that the **L** is good.	1Pt 2:3
obeyed Abraham, calling him **l**.	1Pt 3:6
but set apart the Messiah as **L**	1Pt 3:15
the Day of the **L** will come like	2Pt 3:10
denying our only Master and **L**,	Jd 4
but said, "The **L** rebuke you!"	Jd 9
was in the Spirit on the **L-**'s day,	Rv 1:10
Holy, holy, holy, **L** God,	Rv 4:8
Our **L** and God, You are worthy to	Rv 4:11
because he is **L** of **l-s** and King of	Rv 17:14
KING OF KINGS AND **L** OF **L-S**	Rv 19:16
Amen! Come, **L** Jesus!	Rv 22:20

LORDING

not **l** it over those entrusted to	1Pt 5:3

LOSE

Why should I **l** you both in one	Gn 27:45
we heard this, we **lost** heart,	Jos 2:11
Foreigners **l** heart and come	2Sm 22:46
and **lost** their confidence,	Neh 6:16
Don't **l** sight of them; keep them	Pr 4:21
That wealth was **lost** in a bad	Ec 5:14
if the salt should **l** its taste,	Mt 5:13
better that you **l** one of the	Mt 5:29
finding his life will **l** it,	Mt 10:39
He will never **l** his reward!	Mt 10:42
but whoever **l-s** his life because	Mt 16:25
the whole world yet **l-s** his life?	Mt 16:26
100 sheep and **l-s** one of them,	Lk 15:4
not a hair of your head will be **lost**.	Lk 21:18
that I should **l** none of those He	Jn 6:39

who loves his life will **l** it,	Jn 12:25
I have not **lost** one of those You	Jn 18:9
not a hair will be **lost** from	Ac 27:34
it will be **lost**, but he will be saved;	1Co 3:15
won't grow weary and **l** heart.	Heb 12:3
so that you don't **l** what we have	2Jn 8

LOSS

l of children and widowhood.	Is 47:9
will be no **l** of any of your	Ac 27:22
experience any **l** from us.	2Co 7:9
everything to be a **l** in view of	Php 3:8

LOST (adj)

finds something **l** and lies about it;	Lv 6:3
perishing! We're **l**; we're all **l**!	Nm 17:12
I wander like a **l** sheep;	Ps 119:176
be **l** in her love forever.	Pr 5:19
and a time to count as **l**;	Ec 3:6
My people are **l** sheep;	Jr 50:6
go to the **l** sheep of the house	Mt 10:6
sent only to the **l** sheep of the	Mt 15:24
and go after the **l** one until he	Lk 15:4
he was **l** and is found!	Lk 15:24
them and not one of them is **l**,	Jn 17:12

LOST (n)

I will seek the **l**, bring back	Ezk 34:16
will not seek the **l** or heal the	Zch 11:16
of Man has come to save the **l**.	Mt 18:11
come to seek and to save the **l**.	Lk 19:10

LOT

   Abraham's nephew (Gn 11:27). Separated from Abraham; settled in Sodom (13:1-13). Rescued from kings (14:1-16); from Sodom (18:16–19:29; Lk 17:28-29; 2Pt 2:7-9). Fathered Moabites and Ammonites by his daughters (Gn 19:30-38).

LOT

who gathered a **l** had no surplus	Ex 16:18
goat chosen by **l** for Azazel is	Lv 16:10
The land must be divided by **l**;	Nm 26:55
inheritance by **l** according to	Nm 33:54
inheritance was by **l** as the LORD	Jos 14:2
Joshua cast **l-s** for them at Shiloh	Jos 18:10
Cast {the **l**} between me and my	1Sm 14:42
were divided impartially by **l**,	1Ch 24:5
Pur (that is, the **l**) was cast	Est 3:7
Pur (that is, the **l**) to crush	Est 9:24

you would cast {l-s} for a	Jb 6:27
and they cast l-s for my clothing	Ps 22:18
Throw in your l with us, and	Pr 1:14
The l is cast into the lap,	Pr 16:33
{Casting} the l ends quarrels	Pr 18:18
indeed, they are your l.	Is 57:6
This is your l, what I have	Jr 13:25
They cast l-s for My people;	Jl 3:3
and cast l-s for Jerusalem,	Ob 11
cast l-s, and the l singled out Jonah.	Jnh 1:7
divide the land by casting l-s.	Mc 2:5
They cast l-s for her dignitaries	Nah 3:10
His clothes by casting l-s.	Mt 27:35
that he was chosen by l,	Lk 1:9
and the l fell to Matthias.	Ac 1:26
and I know how to have a l.	Php 4:12
not drinking a l of wine, not	1Tm 3:8

LOTUS

He lies under the l plants,	Jb 40:21

LOUD

and I screamed as I as I could.	Gn 39:14
neighbor with a l voice early	Pr 27:14
Jesus cried out with a l voice,	Mt 27:46
I heard behind me a l voice like	Rv 1:10

LOUDLY

said, "Shout l, for he's a god!	1Kg 18:27
the people were shouting so l.	Ezr 3:13
Cry out l, don't hold back!	Is 58:1

LOVE (n)

redeemed with Your faithful l;	Ex 15:13
showing faithful l to a thousand	Ex 20:6
rich in faithful l and truth,	Ex 34:6
anger and rich in faithful l,	Nm 14:18
show faithful l to you as you	Ru 1:8
Your l for me was more wonderful	2Sm 1:26
My faithful l will never leave him	2Sm 7:15
than the l he had loved her	2Sm 13:15
His faithful l to Israel endures	Ezr 3:11
anger and rich in faithful l,	Neh 9:17
and faithful l will pursue me	Ps 23:6
save me by Your faithful l.	Ps 31:16
full of the LORD's unfailing l.	Ps 33:5
Your faithful l {reaches} to heaven,	Ps 36:5
according to Your faithful l;	Ps 51:1
Your faithful l in the morning.	Ps 59:16
Your faithful l is better than life.	Ps 63:3
not withdraw My faithful l from	Ps 89:33

Your faithful l in the morning	Ps 92:2
is good, and His l is eternal;	Ps 100:5
His faithful l endures forever.	Ps 106:1
His faithful l endures forever.	Ps 107:1
In return for my l they accuse me,	Ps 109:4
His faithful l endures forever.	Ps 118:1
His l is eternal.	Ps 136:1-26
Your faithful l in the morning,	Ps 143:8
be lost in her l forever.	Pr 5:19
Let's feast on each other's l!	Pr 7:18
but l covers all offenses.	Pr 10:12
where there is l than a fattened	Pr 15:17
conceals an offense promotes l,	Pr 17:9
and faithful l will find life,	Pr 21:21
reprimand than concealed l.	Pr 27:5
Their l, their hate, and their	Ec 9:6
your l is more delightful than wine.	Sg 1:2
and he looked on me with l.	Sg 2:4
stir up or awaken l until	Sg 2:7; 3:5; 8:4
Drink, be intoxicated with l!	Sg 5:1
I am my l-'s and my l is mine;	Sg 6:3
For l is as strong as death;	Sg 8:6
Mighty waters cannot extinguish l;	Sg 8:7
give all his wealth for l,	Sg 8:7
throne ... established by faithful l.	Is 16:5
My l will not be removed from you	Is 54:10
because of His l and compassion	Is 63:9
have loved you with an everlasting l;	Jr 31:3
LORD's faithful l we do not perish,	Lm 3:22
show l to a woman who is loved	Hs 3:1
slow to anger, rich in faithful l,	Jl 2:13
to become angry, rich in faithful l,	Jnh 4:2
bring {you} quietness with His l.	Zph 3:17
the l of many will grow cold.	Mt 24:12
bypass justice and l for God.	Lk 11:42
you have no l for God within	Jn 5:42
also loved you. Remain in My l.	Jn 15:9
No one has greater l than this,	Jn 15:13
because God's l has been poured	Rm 5:5
God proves His own l for us in that	Rm 5:8
separate us from the l of Christ?	Rm 8:35
L must be without hypocrisy.	Rm 12:9
L, therefore, is the fulfillment	Rm 13:10
inflates with pride, but l builds up.	1Co 8:1
L is patient; l is kind. L does not	1Co 13:4
But the greatest of these is l.	1Co 13:13
Pursue l and desire spiritual	1Co 14:1
For Christ's l compels us,	2Co 5:14

the proof of your l and of our	2Co 8:24
is faith working through l.	Gl 5:6
serve one another through l.	Gl 5:13
the fruit of the Spirit is l,	Gl 5:22
In l He predestined us to be adopted	Eph 1:4
and firmly established in l,	Eph 3:17
the Messiah's l that surpasses	Eph 3:19
But speaking the truth in l,	Eph 4:15
having the same l, sharing the	Php 2:2
and joined together in l,	Col 2:2
work of faith, labor of l,	1Th 1:3
armor of faith and l on our chests,	1Th 5:8
instruction is l from a pure	1Tm 1:5
in faith, l, and holiness, with	1Tm 2:15
in conduct, in l, in faith, in	1Tm 4:12
For the l of money is a root of	1Tm 6:10
godliness, faith, l, endurance	1Tm 6:11
faith, l, and peace, along	2Tm 2:22
patience, l, and endurance,	2Tm 3:10
sound in faith, l, and endurance	Ti 2:2
instead, on the basis of l.	Phm 9
to promote l and good works,	Heb 10:24
Let brotherly l continue.	Heb 13:1
be free from the l of money.	Heb 13:5
since l covers a multitude of sins.	1Pt 4:8
one another with a kiss of l.	1Pt 5:14
and brotherly affection with l.	2Pt 1:7
Look at how great a l the Father has	1Jn 3:1
to know l: He laid down His life	1Jn 3:16
not know God, because God is l.	1Jn 4:8
God's l was revealed among us in	1Jn 4:9
L consists in this: not that we	1Jn 4:10
in us and His l is perfected in us.	1Jn 4:12
God is l,	1Jn 4:16
who remains in l remains in God	1Jn 4:16
l is perfected with us so that	1Jn 4:17
no fear in l; instead perfect l drives	1Jn 4:18
this is what l for God is: to keep His	1Jn 5:3
this is l: that we walk according to	2Jn 6
and l be multiplied to you.	Jd 2
reefs at your l feasts.	Jd 12
yourselves in the l of God,	Jd 21
abandoned the l {you had} at first.	Rv 2:4

LOVE (v)

your only son Isaac, whom you l,	Gn 22:2
Rebekah ... Isaac l-d her,	Gn 24:67
Isaac l-d Esau ... but	
Rebekah l-d Jacob.	Gn 25:28

he l-d Rachel more than Leah.	Gn 29:30
Now Israel l-d Joseph more than	Gn 37:3
of those who l Me and keep My	Ex 20:6
but l your neighbor as yourself;	Lv 19:18
You are to l him as yourself,	Lv 19:34
Because He l-d your fathers,	Dt 4:37
L the LORD your God with all	Dt 6:5
because the LORD l-d you and kept	Dt 7:8
He will l you, bless you, and	Dt 7:13
the LORD your God l-s you.	Dt 23:5
to l the LORD your God, walk in	Jos 22:5
You hate me and don't l me!	Jdg 14:16
for he l-d her even though the	1Sm 1:5
he l-d him as he l-d himself.	1Sm 20:17
Solomon l-d the LORD by walking	1Kg 3:3
King Solomon l-d many foreign	1Kg 11:1
Because the LORD l-s His people,	2Ch 2:11
Your God l-d Israel enough to	2Ch 9:8
with those who l Him and keep	Neh 1:5
The king l-d Esther more than all	Est 2:17
I l You, LORD, my strength.	Ps 18:1
He l-s righteousness and justice;	Ps 33:5
l-ing a long life to enjoy what is	Ps 34:12
For the LORD l-s justice and will	Ps 37:28
let those who l Your salvation	Ps 40:16
You l righteousness and hate	Ps 45:7
Mount Zion, which He l-d.	Ps 78:68
The LORD l-s the gates of Zion	Ps 87:2
have distanced l-d one and	Ps 88:18
He l-d cursing—let it fall on	Ps 109:17
I l the LORD because He has	Ps 116:1
How I l Your teaching!	Ps 119:97
therefore, I l Your decrees.	Ps 119:119
He gives sleep to the one He l-s.	Ps 127:2
guards all those who l Him,	Ps 145:20
The LORD l-s the righteous.	Ps 146:8
LORD disciplines the one He l-s,	Pr 3:12
I her, and she will guard you.	Pr 4:6
I l those who l me, and those	Pr 8:17
all who hate me l death.	Pr 8:36
a wise man, and he will l you.	Pr 9:8
Whoever l-s instruction l-s	Pr 12:1
the one who l-s him disciplines	Pr 13:24
A friend l-s at all times,	Pr 17:17
One who l-s to offend l-s strife;	Pr 17:19
Don't l sleep, or you will	Pr 20:13
one who l-s pleasure will become	Pr 21:17
The one who l-s a pure heart and	Pr 22:11

a time to l and a time to hate;   Ec 3:8
one who l-s money is never satisfied Ec 5:10
with the wife you l all the days   Ec 9:9
I will sing about the one I l,   Is 5:1
I have l-d you with an everlasting   Jr 31:3
with those who l Him and keep   Dn 9:4
a woman who is l-d by another man   Hs 3:1
When Israel was a child, I l-d him,   Hs 11:1
I will freely l them, for My   Hs 14:4
Hate evil and l good;   Am 5:15
You hate good and l evil.   Mc 3:2
to act justly, to l faithfulness   Mc 6:8
Therefore, l truth and peace.   Zch 8:19
"I have l-d you," says the LORD.   Mal 1:2
Even so, I l-d Jacob,   Mal 1:2
l your enemies and pray for   Mt 5:44
because they l to pray standing   Mt 6:5
will hate one and l the other,   Mt 6:24
who l-s father or mother more   Mt 10:37
and l your neighbor as yourself   Mt 19:19
L the Lord your God with all   Mt 22:37
L your neighbor as yourself.   Mt 22:39
They l the place of honor at   Mt 23:6
Even sinners l those who l them.   Lk 6:32
which of them will l him more?   Lk 7:42
is forgiven little, l-s little.   Lk 7:47
For God l-d the world in this way   Jn 3:16
and people l-d darkness rather   Jn 3:19
The Father l-s the Son and has   Jn 3:35
you would l Me, because I   Jn 8:42
This is why the Father l-s Me,   Jn 10:17
Jesus l-d Martha, her sister, and   Jn 11:5
Jews said, "See how He l-d him!   Jn 11:36
The one who l-s his life will lose   Jn 12:25
He l-d them to the end.   Jn 13:1
the one Jesus l-d, was reclining   Jn 13:23
new commandment: l one another.   Jn 13:34
If you l Me, you will keep My   Jn 14:15
keeps them is the one who l-s Me.   Jn 14:21
If anyone l-s Me, he will keep My   Jn 14:23
Just as the Father has l-d me,   Jn 15:9
I have also l-d you.   Jn 15:9
l one another as I have l-d you.   Jn 15:12
For the Father Himself l-s you,   Jn 16:27
have l-d them as You have l-d Me.   Jn 17:23
Simon, son of John, do you l Me?   Jn 21:16
the good of those who l God: Rm 8:28
Jacob I have l-d, but Esau I have   Rm 9:13

not owe ... except to l one another,   Rm 13:8
for the one who l-s another has   Rm 13:8
for God l-s a cheerful giver.   2Co 9:7
l-d me and gave Himself for me.   Gl 2:20
the Messiah also l-d us and gave   Eph 5:2
Husbands, l your wives, just as   Eph 5:25
as also Christ l-d the church   Eph 5:25
He who l-s his wife l-s himself.   Eph 5:28
l your wives and don't become   Col 3:19
who has l-d us and given us   2Th 2:16
those who have l-d His appearing.   2Tm 4:8
because he l-d this present world   2Tm 4:10
young women to l their husbands   Ti 2:4
You have l-d righteousness and   Heb 1:9
Lord disciplines the one He l-s,   Heb 12:6
promised to those who l Him   Jms 1:12; 2:5
You shall l your neighbor as   Jms 2:8
You l Him, though you have not   1Pt 1:8
l one another earnestly from a   1Pt 1:22
who l-d the wages of   2Pt 2:15
Do not l the world or the things   1Jn 2:15
If anyone l-s the world, love for   1Jn 2:15
we should l one another,   1Jn 3:11
who does not l remains in death   1Jn 3:14
we must not l in word or speech   1Jn 3:18
l one another, because l is from God   1Jn 4:7
and everyone who l-s has been born 1Jn 4:7
we l-d God, but that He l-d us   1Jn 4:10
We l because He first l-d us.   1Jn 4:19
who l-s God must also l his brother. 1Jn 4:21
who l-s the parent also l-s his child. 1Jn 5:1
children, whom I l in truth   2Jn 1
l-d by God ... and kept by Jesus   Jd 1
Him who l-s us and has set us free   Rv 1:5
As many as I l, I rebuke and   Rv 3:19
for they did not l their lives   Rv 12:11

LOVELY

How l is Your dwelling place,   Ps 84:1
for praise is pleasant and l.   Ps 147:1
I am dark ... yet l like the curtains of Sg 1:5
is sweet, and your face is l.   Sg 2:14
How l and beautiful they will be   Zch 9:17
whatever is pure, whatever is l,   Php 4:8

LOVEMAKING

let's drink deeply of l until morning.   Pr 7:18

LOVER

He hates the l of violence.   Ps 11:5

now hear this, l of luxury, who Is 47:8
as a woman may betray her l, Jr 3:20
for all your l-s have been crushed Jr 22:20
All your l-s have forgotten you; Jr 30:14
never again pay fees for l-s. Ezk 16:41
I handed her over to her l-s, Ezk 23:9
went after her l-s, but forgot Me Hs 2:13
Pharisees, who were l-s of money, Lk 16:14
will be l-s of self, l-s of money 2Tm 3:2
l-s of pleasure rather than l-s
 of God 2Tm 3:4

LOVESICK
refresh me with apricots, for I am l. Sg 2:5
you find my love, tell him that I am l. Sg 5:8

LOVING (adj)
A l doe, a graceful fawn—let Pr 5:19
and l instruction is on her Pr 31:26

LOW
I am bent over and brought l; Ps 38:6
both l and high, rich and poor Ps 49:2
human pride will be brought l, Is 2:17
Lie l, residents of Dedan, for I Jr 49:8
and hill will be made l; Lk 3:5

LOWER
gave her the upper and l springs. Jos 15:19
descended to the l parts of the earth? Eph 4:9
You made him l than the angels Heb 2:7

LOWERED
they l the stretcher on which Mk 2:4
by night and l him in a large Ac 9:25

LOWEST
proceed to take the l place. Lk 14:9

LOWLIEST
and sets over it the l of men. Dn 4:17

LOWLY
He sets the l on high, Jb 5:11
to save all the l of the earth. Ps 76:9
Better to be l of spirit with Pr 16:19
with the oppressed and l of spirit, Is 57:15
exalt the l and bring down the Ezk 21:26
thrones and exalted the l. Lk 1:52

LOYAL
but I remained l to the LORD my Jos 14:8
LORD has found a man l to Him, 1Sm 13:14

the l have disappeared from the Ps 12:1
protects the l, but fully repays Ps 31:23
the way of His l followers. Pr 2:8
you shepherds who are l to Me, Jr 3:15

LOYALTY
faithful God who keeps covenant l Dt 7:9
Is this your l to your friend? 2Sm 16:17
He shows l to His anointed, 2Sm 22:51
Show l to the sons of Barzillai 1Kg 2:7
Never let l and faithfulness Pr 3:3
Many a man proclaims his own l, Pr 20:6
L and faithfulness deliver a Pr 20:28
I remember the l of your youth, Jr 2:2
Your l is like the morning mist Hs 6:4
For I desire l and not sacrifice Hs 6:6
but also pledge l to Milcom; Zph 1:5

LUD
Tarshish, Put, L (who are Is 66:19
{Men of} Persia, L, and Put were Ezk 27:10
Cush, Put, and L, and all the Ezk 30:5

LUKE
 Companion of Paul (2Tm 4:11; Phm 24);
physician (Col 4:14); author of Luke and
Acts (note "we" in Ac 16:10; 28:16).

LUKEWARM
because you are l, and neither Rv 3:16

LUMP
Let them take a l of figs and Is 38:21
make from the same l one piece Rm 9:21
leavens the whole l of dough. Gl 5:9

LURE
Then I will l Sisera commander Jdg 4:7
that no one l-s you with riches; Jb 36:18
You l-d us into a trap; You placed Ps 66:11
she l-s with her flattering talk. Pr 7:21
A violent man l-s his neighbor, Pr 16:29
doctrines to l the disciples Ac 20:30

LURK
wife or I have l-ed at his door, Jb 31:9
He l-s in secret like a lion in a Ps 10:9
like a young lion l-ing in ambush. Ps 17:12
They stir up strife, they l; Ps 56:6
she l-s at every corner Pr 7:12
I will l like a leopard on the Hs 13:7

LUSH

| Our bed is l with foliage; | Sg 1:16 |
| Israel is a l vine; it yields | Hs 10:1 |

LUST (n)

Because your l was poured out	Ezk 16:36
inflamed in their l for one another.	Rm 1:27
impurity, l, evil desire	Col 3:5
deny godlessness and worldly l-s	Ti 2:12
to scoff, following their own l-s,	2Pt 3:3
the l of the flesh, the l of the eyes	1Jn 2:16
world with its l is passing away	1Jn 2:17

LUST (v)

Don't l in your heart for her	Pr 6:25
She l-ed after her lovers,	Ezk 23:5
looks at a woman to l for her has	Mt 5:28

LUSTFUL

| and your {l} neighings, | Jr 13:27 |
| not with l desires, like the | 1Th 4:5 |

LUTE

| with a l I will praise You | Ps 71:22 |

LUXURIOUSLY

| You have lived l on the land and | Jms 5:5 |

LUXURY

L is not appropriate for a fool	Pr 19:10
now hear this, lover of l, who sits	Is 47:8
and live in l are in royal palaces.	Lk 7:25
grown wealthy from her excessive l.	Rv 18:3

LUZ

1. Original name of Bethel (Gn 28:19; 35:6; 48:3; Jos 16:2; 18:13; Jdg 1:23).

2. Town among the Hittites built by a former resident of Bethel (Jdg 1:26).

LYCAONIA

Region of Asia Minor where Paul preached (Ac 14:6,11).

LYDDA

City where Peter healed a paralytic (Ac 9:32-28).

LYDIA

First Philippian convert; seller of purple (Ac 16:12-15,40).

LYE

| and cleanse my hands with l, | Jb 9:30 |

| you wash with l and use a great | Jr 2:22 |
| fire and like cleansing l. | Mal 3:2 |

LYING (adj)

go and become a l spirit	1Kg 22:22
Let l lips be quieted;	Ps 31:18
against me with l tongues.	Ps 109:2
deliver me from l lips and a	Ps 120:2
arrogant eyes, a l tongue, hands	Pr 6:17
who conceals hatred has l lips,	Pr 10:18
forever, but a l tongue, only a	Pr 12:19
L lips are detestable to the	Pr 12:22
a fortune through a l tongue is	Pr 21:6
A l witness will perish, but the	Pr 21:28
A l tongue hates those it	Pr 26:28
is the prophet, the l teacher.	Is 9:15
the l pen of scribes has	Jr 8:8
and speak l divinations.	Ezk 13:6

LYING (n)

They take pleasure in l;	Ps 62:4
righteous hate l, but the wicked	Pr 13:5
Cursing, l, murder, stealing	Hs 4:2
Since you you put away l, Speak	Eph 4:25
who loves and practices l.	Rv 22:15

LYRE

who play the l and the flute.	Gn 4:21
prophesying. ... preceded by ... l-s.	1Sm 10:5
l-s, harps, tambourines, sistrums,	2Sm 6:5
to prophesy accompanied by l-s,	1Ch 25:1
tambourine and l and rejoicing	Jb 21:12
My l is {used} for mourning and	Jb 30:31
Praise the LORD with the l;	Ps 33:2
I will praise You with the l,	Ps 43:4
I explain my riddle with a l.	Ps 49:4
Wake up, harp and l!	Ps 57:8
Sing to the LORD with the l,	Ps 98:5
we hung up our l-s on the poplar	Ps 137:2
praise Him with harp and l.	Ps 150:3
At their feasts they have l,	Is 5:12
The joyful l has ceased.	Is 24:8
sound of your l-s will no longer	Ezk 26:13
flute, zither, l, harp, drum	Dn 3:5

LYSTRA

City where Paul preached and was persecuted (Ac 14:6-21; 2Tm 3:11); hometown of Timothy (Ac 16:1-2).

M

MAACAH

1. Son of Abraham's brother Nahor (Gn 22:24).

2. Caleb's concubine (1Ch 2:48).

3. Jeiel's wife (1Ch 8:29; 9:35).

4. David's wife; mother of Absalom (2Sm 3:3; 1Ch 3:2).

5. Mother of Judah's King Abijam (1Kg 15:2); promoted Asherah worship (15:13).

MACEDONIA

Region to which Paul went in response to a vision (Ac 16:9-10).

to pass through M and Achaia and	Ac 19:21
good-bye, departed to go to M.	Ac 20:1
for M and Achaia were pleased to	Rm 15:26
I will be traveling through M	1Co 16:5
and to go on to M with your help	2Co 1:16
granted to the churches of M:	2Co 8:1
who came from M supplied my	2Co 11:9
when I left M, no church shared	Php 4:15
the believers in M and Achaia.	1Th 1:7
I urged you when I went to M	1Tm 1:3

MACHIR

Son of Manasseh (Gn 50:23; Nm 26:29; 32:39-40; Dt 3:15; Jos 17:1).

MACHPELAH

Burial place of Sarah, Abraham, Jacob, Isaac, Rebekah, and Leah (Gn 23:9,17,19; 25:9; 49:29-31; 50:13).

MAD

will be driven m by what you see	Dt 28:34
therefore, the nations go m.	Jr 51:7
Too much study is driving you m!	Ac 26:24

MADMAN

He acted like a m around them,	1Sm 21:13
Jehu ... he drives like a m.	2Kg 9:20
Like a m who throws flaming	Pr 26:18
for every m who acts like	Jr 29:26
I'm talking like a m—I'm a better	2Co 11:23

MADNESS

and knowledge, m and folly;	Ec 1:17
m is in their hearts while	Ec 9:3
restrained the prophet's m	2Pt 2:16

MAGDALENE see MARY 2.

MAGGOT

didn't smell or have any m-s in it.	Ex 16:24
clothed with m-s and encrusted	Jb 7:5
how much less man, who is a m,	Jb 25:6
M-s are spread out under you,	Is 14:11
for their m-s will never die,	Is 66:24

MAGIC

There is no m curse against Jacob	Nm 23:23
seems like a m stone to its	Pr 17:8
women who sew {m} bands on	Ezk 13:18
practiced m collected their books	Ac 19:19

MAGICIAN

summoned all the m-s of Egypt	Gn 41:8
the m-s of Egypt, and they also did	Ex 7:11
the m-s of Egypt did the same	Ex 7:22
But the m-s did the same thing	Ex 8:7
The m-s tried to produce gnats	Ex 8:18
is the finger of God," the m-s said	Ex 8:19
the boils were on the m-s as well	Ex 9:11
cunning m, and necromancer.	Is 3:3

MAGISTRATES

appoint m and judges to judge	Ezr 7:25
judges, m, and all the rulers	Dn 3:2
them before the chief m	Ac 16:20

MAGNIFICENCE

her m come to the verge of ruin	Ac 19:27

MAGNIFICENT

from the hand of these m gods?	1Sm 4:8
LORD, our Lord, how m is Your name	Ps 8:1
For You are their m strength	Ps 89:17
How m are Your works, LORD,	Ps 92:5
own languages the m acts of God	Ac 2:11

MAGNIFY

Does a saw m itself above the	Is 10:15
will exalt and m himself above	Dn 11:36
name of the Lord Jesus was m-ied.	Ac 19:17
the Gentiles, I m my ministry,	Rm 11:13

MAGOG

1. Descendant of Japheth (Gn 10:2; 1Ch 1:5).

2. Land ruled by Gog, an apocalyptic foe from the north (Ezk 38:2; 39:6; Rv 20:8).

MAHANAIM

City of Gilead (Jos 13:26,30) named by Jacob (Gn 32:2). Levitical city (Jos 21:38) used as a refuge by Ish-bosheth (2Sm 2:8-9) and David (17:24-27).

MAHER-SHALAL-HASH-BAZ

Symbolic name of Isaiah's son (Is 8:1).

MAHLON

Son of Naomi, married Ruth (Ru 1:2).

MAIMED

animal ... that is blind, injured, m,	Lv 22:22
it is better for you to enter life m	Mt 18:8
invite those who are poor, m, lame,	Lk 14:13

MAINTAIN

m-ing faithful love to a thousand	Ex 34:7
loyalty he m-s his throne.	Pr 20:28
Because you m-ed an ancient	Ezk 35:5
M love and justice, and always	Hs 12:6
in order to m your tradition!	Mk 7:9

MAJESTIC

God thunders with His m voice.	Jb 37:4
You are resplendent and m	Ps 76:4
the LORD on high is m.	Ps 93:4
All that He does is splendid and m;	Ps 111:3
from His m splendor.	Is 2:10,19,21
For there the m One, the LORD	Is 33:21
in the m name of Yahweh His God	Mc 5:4
came to Him from the M Glory:	2Pt 1:17

MAJESTY

adversaries by Your great m.	Ex 15:7
aid on the clouds in His m.	Dt 33:26
Splendor and m are before Him;	1Ch 16:27
and the splendor and the m	1Ch 29:11
awesome m surrounds Him.	Jb 37:22
the heavens with Your m.	Ps 8:1
You confer m and splendor on him	Ps 21:5
In your m and splendor	Ps 45:3
He is robed in m;	Ps 93:1
Splendor and m are before Him;	Ps 96:6
clothed with m and splendor.	Ps 104:1
His m covers heaven and earth.	Ps 148:13
when You rise in Your m.	Is 33:3
right hand of the M on high.	Heb 1:3
throne of the M in the heavens,	Heb 8:1

we were eyewitnesses of His m. | 2Pt 1:16
our Lord, be glory, m, power | Jd 25

MAKE

Let Us m man in Our image,	Gn 1:26
God saw all that He had made	Gn 1:31
regretted that He had made man	Gn 6:6
I will m you into a great nation	Gn 12:2
never say, 'I made Abram rich.'	Gn 14:23
day the LORD made a covenant	Gn 15:18
Do not m an idol for yourself,	Ex 20:4
For the LORD made the heavens	Ex 20:11
m us a god who will go before us	Ex 32:1
and made it into an image of a calf	Ex 32:4
the LORD m His face shine on you	Nm 6:25
Moses made a bronze snake	Nm 21:9
Jonathan made a covenant with	1Sm 20:16
Jeroboam made a festival in the	1Kg 12:32
that the Samaritans had made.	2Kg 17:29
the bronze snake that Moses made	2Kg 18:4
made the heavens and the earth	2Kg 19:15
David had made to praise the LORD	2Ch 7:6
He m-s nations great, then	Jb 12:23
Almighty who has made me bitter,	Jb 27:2
have made a covenant with my eyes	Jb 31:1
The Spirit of God has made me,	Jb 33:4
You made him little less than God	Ps 8:5
m-ing the inexperienced wise.	Ps 19:7
The heavens were made by the word	Ps 33:6
m His praise glorious.	Ps 66:2
drunkards m up songs about me.	Ps 69:12
You made summer and winter.	Ps 74:17
M and keep your vows to the LORD	Ps 76:11
The sea is His; He made it.	Ps 95:5
but the LORD made the heavens.	Ps 96:5
He made us, and we are His	Ps 100:3
He knows what we are made of,	Ps 103:14
He made the moon to mark the	Ps 104:19
hand until I m Your enemies Your	Ps 110:1
and gold, made by human hands.	Ps 115:4
Those who m them are just like	Ps 115:8
is the day the LORD has made;	Ps 118:24
Your hands made me and formed	Ps 119:73
if I m my bed in Sheol, You are	Ps 139:8
I have been ... wonderfully made.	Ps 139:14
LORD made me at the beginning	Pr 8:22
the LORD made them both.	Pr 20:12; 22:2
She m-s her own bed coverings;	Pr 31:22

He has **made** everything appropriate Ec 3:11
God has **made** the one as well as the Ec 7:14
no end to the **m-ing** of many books Ec 12:12
to what their fingers have **made**. Is 2:8
I will **m** myself like the Most Is 14:14
they will **m** vows to the LORD and Is 19:21
do not look to the One who
  made it, Is 22:11
How can what is **made** say about its
  maker, "He didn't **m** me"? Is 29:16
m a straight highway for our God Is 40:3
I will **m** a way in the wilderness Is 43:19
All who **m** idols are nothing, Is 44:9
one forming it: What are you **m-ing**? Is 45:9
I **made** the earth, and created man Is 45:12
and he **m-s** it into a god. Is 46:6
My hand **made** all these things, Is 66:2
and the new earth, which I will **m**, Is 66:22
your gods you **made** for yourself? Jr 2:28
He **made** the earth by His power, Jr 10:12
Can one **m** gods for himself? Jr 16:20
when I will **m** a new covenant Jr 31:31
You Yourself **made** the heavens Jr 32:17
He **made** the earth by His power, Jr 51:15
I have **made** you a watchman Ezk 3:17; 33:7
it could not be **made** into a useful Ezk 15:5
and **m** yourselves a new heart Ezk 18:31
My Nile is my own; I **made** {it} Ezk 29:3
I will **m** a covenant of peace Ezk 34:25
I will **m** them one nation in the Ezk 37:22
Nebuchadnezzar **made** a gold statue, Dn 3:1
I **made** it all myself. Hs 12:8
The One who **made** the Pleiades Am 5:8
who **made** the sea and the dry land. Jnh 1:9
He **m-s** my feet like those of a deer Hab 3:19
with nothing to **m** {them} afraid. Zph 3:13
Didn't the one {God} **m** {us} with Mal 2:15
m His paths straight! Mt 3:3
and I will **m** you fish for people! Mt 4:19
you cannot **m** a single hair Mt 5:36
made them male and female, Mt 19:4
and **m** disciples of all nations, Mt 28:19
are willing, You can **m** me clean. Mk 1:40
Sabbath was **made** for man and not Mk 2:27
Let us **m** three tabernacles: Mk 9:5
But you have **made** it a den of Mk 11:17
build another not **made** by hands Mk 14:58
and hill will be **made** low; Lk 3:5

M every effort to enter through Lk 13:24
your mina has **made** five minas. Lk 19:18
until I **m** Your enemies Your Lk 20:43
m-ing Himself equal with God. Jn 5:18
being a man—**m** Yourself God. Jn 10:33
come to him and **m** Our home with Jn 14:23
until I **m** Your enemies Your Ac 2:35
God has **made** this Jesus ... Lord Ac 2:36
are the One who **made** the heaven, Ac 4:24
what their hands had **made**. Ac 7:41
in sanctuaries **made** with hands, Ac 7:48
Did not My hand **m** all these things? Ac 7:50
living God, who **made** the heaven Ac 14:15
The God who **made** the world and Ac 17:24
one man He has **made** every
  nation Ac 17:26
that gods **made** by hand are not Ac 19:26
through what He has **made**. Rm 1:20
the many will be **made** righteous. Rm 5:19
Why did you **m** me like this? Rm 9:20
to **m** from the same lump one Rm 9:21
and to **m** His power known Rm 9:22
m no plans to satisfy the fleshly Rm 13:14
Lord is able to **m** him stand. Rm 14:4
God **made** the world's wisdom 1Co 1:20
For who **m-s** you so superior? 1Co 4:7
in Christ all will be **made** alive. 1Co 15:22
a house not **made** with hands 2Co 5:1
made the One who did not know 2Co 5:21
made us alive with the Messiah Eph 2:5
m-ing the most of the time, Eph 5:16
and **m-ing** music to the Lord Eph 5:19
M your own attitude that of Php 2:5
He **made** you alive with Him and Col 2:13
m-ing the most of the time. Col 4:5
through whom He **made** the Heb 1:2
until I **m** Your enemies Your Heb 1:13
made him lower than the angels Heb 2:7
tabernacle not **made** with hands Heb 9:11
enemies are **made** His footstool. Heb 10:13
seen has been **made** from things Heb 11:3
who are **made** in God's likeness Jms 3:9
but **made** alive in the spiritual 1Pt 3:18
m every effort to confirm your 2Pt 1:10
m every effort to be found in 2Pt 3:14
not sinned," we **m** Him a liar 1Jn 1:10
and to **m** you stand in the presence Jd 24
and **made** us a kingdom, priests to Rv 1:6

and **made** them white in the blood Rv 7:14
to **m** an image of the beast, Rv 13:14
I am **m-ing** everything new. Rv 21:5
the holy go on being **made** holy. Rv 22:11

MAKER

or a man more pure than his **M**? Jb 4:17
my **M** would remove me in an Jb 32:22
Where is God my **M**, who provides Jb 35:10
ascribe righteousness to my **M**. Jb 36:3
kneel before the LORD our **M**. Ps 95:6
M of heaven and earth
      Ps 115:15; 121:2; 124:8; 134:3; 146:6
Let Israel celebrate its **M**; Ps 149:2
oppresses the poor insults their **M**, Pr 14:31
mocks the poor insults his **M** Pr 17:5
that day people will look to their **M** Is 17:7
can what is made say about its **m** Is 29:16
the LORD your **M** who shaped you Is 44:2
the one who argues with his **M** Is 45:9
m-s of idols go in humiliation Is 45:16
the LORD, your **M**, who stretched Is 51:13
For your husband is your **M** Is 54:5
forgotten his **M** and built Hs 8:14
Worship the **M** of heaven and Rv 14:7

MALACHI

Postexilic prophet (Mal 1:1).

MALCHISHUA

Saul's son, killed at Gilboa (1Sm 14:49; 31:2).

MALCHUS

High priest's slave, whose ear Peter cut off (Jn 8:10).

MALE

He created them **m** and female. Gn 1:27
each, **m** and female, entered the ark Gn 7:9
your **m-s** must be circumcised. Gn 17:10
unblemished animal, a year-old **m**; Ex 12:5
Consecrate every firstborn **m** to Me, Ex 13:2
Any **m** among the priests may eat Lv 6:29
names of every **m** 20 years old Nm 1:20
offering. Every **m** may eat it; Nm 18:10
waged war ... and killed every **m**. Nm 31:7
All your **m-s** are to appear three Dt 16:16
is not to wear **m** clothing, Dt 22:5
Completely destroy every **m** Jdg 21:11
I acquired **m** and female servants Ec 2:7

saying, "A **m** child is born to Jr 20:15
see whether a **m** can give birth. Jr 30:6
and you made **m** images so that Ezk 16:17
when she saw **m** figures carved Ezk 23:14
My Spirit on the **m** and female Jl 2:29
to massacre all the **m** children Mt 2:16
made them **m** and female, Mt 19:4
My Spirit on My **m** and female Ac 2:18
M-s committed shameless acts Rm 1:27
adulterers, **m** prostitutes 1Co 6:9
slave or free, **m** or female; Gl 3:28
she gave birth to a son—a **m** Rv 12:5

MALICE

trouble and **m** are under his Ps 10:7
while **m** is in their hearts. Ps 28:3
been aware of **m** in my heart, Ps 66:18
perceiving their **m**, Jesus said Mt 22:18
disputes, deceit, and **m**. Rm 1:29
with the yeast of **m** and evil, 1Co 5:8
anger, wrath, **m**, slander, Col 3:8
living in **m** and envy, hateful Ti 3:3

MALICIOUS

at him with **m** intent and he dies Nm 35:20
If a **m** witness testifies Dt 19:16
M witnesses come forward; Ps 35:11
on his bed he makes **m** plans. Ps 36:4
but destruction awaits the **m**. Pr 10:29
slandering us with **m** words. 3Jn 10

MALICIOUSLY

me without cause look at me **m**. Ps 35:19
My enemies speak **m** about me: Ps 41:5
They mock, and they speak **m**; Ps 73:8
men who had **m** accused Daniel Dn 6:24

MALIGNING

You sit, **m** your brother Ps 50:20

MALLOW

They plucked **m** among the shrubs Jb 30:4

MALTA

Island where Paul was shipwrecked (Ac 28:1).

MAMRE

Region where Abraham dwelt and was buried (Gn 13:18; 14:13; 18:1; 23:19; 25:9).

MAN *see also* MAN OF GOD

Let Us make **m** in Our image,	Gn 1:26
God formed the **m** out of the dust	Gn 2:7
not good for the **m** to be alone.	Gn 2:18
for she was taken from **m**.	Gn 2:23
This is why a **m** leaves his	Gn 2:24
Whoever sheds **m**-'s blood, his blood	Gn 9:6
saw three **men** standing near him.	Gn 18:2
and a **m** wrestled with him	Gn 32:24
Send **men** to scout out the land of	Nm 13:2
God is not a **m** who lies, or a	Nm 23:19
m does not live on bread alone	Dt 8:3
Bring out the **men** who came to you	Jos 2:3
favor with the LORD and with **men**	1Sm 2:26
has found a **m** loyal to Him,	1Sm 13:14
is not **m** who changes his mind.	1Sm 15:29
for **m** sees what is visible,	1Sm 16:7
replied to David, "You are the **m**!	2Sm 12:7
What is **m**, that You think so	Jb 7:17
For He is not a **m** like me,	Jb 9:32
M born of woman is short of days	Jb 14:1
What is **m**, that he should be	Jb 15:14
let God deal with him, not **m**.	Jb 32:13
Get ready to answer Me like a **m**;	Jb 38:3
How happy is the **m** who does not	Ps 1:1
what is **m** that You remember him,	Ps 8:4
nations know they are only **men**.	Ps 9:20
LORD, {save me} from **men**,	
from **men** of the world	Ps 17:14
But I am a worm and not a **m**,	
scorned by **men** and despised	Ps 22:6
every mortal **m** is only a vapor.	Ps 39:5
not fear. What can **m** do to me?	Ps 56:4
Men are only a vapor; exalted **men**,	
an illusion.	Ps 62:9
tent where He resided among **men**.	Ps 78:60
you will die like **men** and fall like	Ps 82:7
As for **m**, his days are like	Ps 103:15
M goes out to his work and to	Ps 104:23
How can a young **m** keep his way	Ps 119:9
what is **m**, that You care for him,	Ps 144:3
M is like a breath; his days are	Ps 144:4
Do not trust in nobles, in **m**, who	Ps 146:3
does not value the power of a **m**.	Ps 147:10
For a **m**-'s ways are before the	Pr 5:21
M cannot be made secure by	Pr 12:3
a way that seems right to a **m**	Pr 14:12
All a **m**-'s ways seem right in his	Pr 16:2

A **m**-'s heart plans his way,	Pr 16:9
Many plans are in a **m**-'s heart,	Pr 19:21
A **m**-'s steps are determined by the	Pr 20:24
and the way of a **m** with a young	Pr 30:19
concubines, the delights of **men**.	Ec 2:8
What is the advantage for **m**?	Ec 6:11
I have found one {true} **m**,	Ec 7:28
no more trust in **m**, who has only	Is 2:22
seven women will seize one **m**,	Is 4:1
you to try the patience of **men**?	Is 7:13
Egyptians are **men**, not God;	Is 31:3
that He did not look like a **m**,	Is 52:14
He was despised and rejected	
by **men**, a **m** of suffering	Is 53:3
a female will shelter a **m**.	Jr 31:22
never fail to have a **m** sitting	Jr 33:17
each their faces was that of a **m**,	Ezk 1:10
Son of **m**, I am sending you to	Ezk 2:3
You devour **men**	Ezk 36:13
I see four **men**, not tied, walking	Dn 3:25
mind be changed from that of a **m**,	Dn 4:16
One like a son of **m** coming with	Dn 7:13
someone who appeared with a **m**.	Dn 8:15
"Son of **m**," he said to me	Dn 8:17
I am God and not **m**, the Holy One	Hs 11:9
your old **men** will have dreams,	Jl 2:28
and reveals His thoughts to **m**,	Am 4:13
Will a **m** rob God? Yet you are	Mal 3:8
wise **men** from the east arrived	Mt 2:1
M must not live on bread alone	Mt 4:4
let your light shine before **men**	Mt 5:16
but the Son of **M** has no place to	Mt 8:20
What kind of **m** is this?	Mt 8:27
had given such authority to **men**.	Mt 9:8
will acknowledge Me before **men**	Mt 10:32
A **m** is worth far more than a	Mt 12:12
as doctrines the commands of **men**.	Mt 15:9
about God's concerns, but **m**-'s.	Mt 16:23
what will a **m** give in exchange	Mt 16:26
betrayed into the hands of **men**.	Mt 17:22
this reason a **m** will leave his	Mt 19:5
God has joined together, **m** must not	Mt 19:6
With **men** this is impossible,	Mt 19:26
will see the Son of **M** coming on	Mt 24:30
Then two **men** will be in the field	Mt 24:40
see the Son of **M** seated at the	Mt 26:64
an oath, "I don't know the **m**!"	Mt 26:72
for **m** and not **m** for the Sabbath	Mk 2:27

two **men** were talking with Him	Lk 9:30
A **m** had two sons. The younger	Lk 15:11
of John from heaven or from **men**?	Lk 20:4
"**M**, I am not!" Peter said.	Lk 22:58
suddenly two **men** stood by them in	Lk 24:4
that life was the light of **men**.	Jn 1:4
or of the will of **m**, but of God.	Jn 1:13
He Himself knew what was in **m**.	Jn 2:25
I don't receive **m**-'s testimony,	Jn 5:34
I do not accept glory from **men**	Jn 5:41
Some were saying, "He's a good **m**."	Jn 7:12
No **m** ever spoke like this!	Jn 7:46
the witness of two **men** is valid.	Jn 8:17
Do you believe in the Son of **M**?	Jn 9:35
You—being a **m**—make Yourself	Jn 10:33
that one **m** should die for	Jn 11:50
praise from **men** more than praise	Jn 12:43
Pilate said to them, "Here is the **m**!"	Jn 19:5
suddenly two **men** in white clothes	Ac 1:10
your young **men** will see visions,	Ac 2:17
have not lied to **men** but to God!	Ac 5:4
We must obey God rather than **men**.	Ac 5:29
and the Son of **M** standing at the	Ac 7:56
both **men** and women	
were baptized	Ac 8:12
Stand up! I myself am also a **m**.	Ac 10:26
voice of a god and not of a **m**!	Ac 12:22
son of Jesse, a **m** after My heart	Ac 13:22
that through this **m** forgiveness	Ac 13:38
down to us in the form of **men**!	Ac 14:11
We are **men** also, with the same	Ac 14:15
Greek women as well as **men**.	Ac 17:12
and said: "**Men** of Athens! I see	Ac 17:22
From one **m** He has made every	Ac 17:26
by the **M** He has appointed.	Ac 17:31
for images resembling mortal **m**,	Rm 1:23
is not from **men** but from God.	Rm 2:29
entered the world through one **m**,	Rm 5:12
What a wretched **m** I am!	Rm 7:24
to God and approved by **men**.	Rm 14:18
not be based on **men**-'s wisdom but	1Co 2:5
knows the concerns of a **m** except	1Co 2:11
But the natural **m** does not	1Co 2:14
So no one should boast in **men**	1Co 3:21
each **m** should have his own wife	1Co 7:2
Christ is the head of every **m**,	
and the **m** is the head	
of the woman,	1Co 11:3

languages of **men** and of angels,	1Co 13:1
When I became a **m**, I put aside	1Co 13:11
not speaking to **men** but to God,	1Co 14:2
since death came through a **m**	1Co 15:21
first **m** Adam became a living	1Co 15:45
the Lord but also before **men**.	2Co 8:21
not from **men** or by **m**, but by Jesus	Gl 1:1
create in Himself one new **m** from	Eph 2:15
put on the new **m**, the one	Eph 4:24
this reason a **m** will leave his	Eph 5:31
as to the Lord and not to **men**.	Eph 6:7
taking on the likeness of **men**.	Php 2:7
put off the old **m** with his	Col 3:9
done for the Lord and not for **men**,	Col 3:23
not to please **men**, but rather God	1Th 2:4
rejects this does not reject **m**	1Th 4:8
between God and **m**, a **m**, Christ	1Tm 2:5
or to have authority over a **m**;	1Tm 2:12
commit to faithful **men** who will	2Tm 2:2
commandments of **men** who reject	Ti 1:14
and love for **m** appeared from God	Ti 3:4
What is **m**, that You remember him	Heb 2:6
priest taken from **men** is appointed	Heb 5:1
the Lord set up, and not **m**.	Heb 8:2
But this **m**, after offering one	Heb 10:12
And therefore from one **m**	Heb 11:12
be afraid. What can **m** do to me?	Heb 13:6
m-'s anger does not accomplish	Jms 1:20
but no **m** can tame the tongue.	Jms 3:8
Elijah was a **m** with a nature	Jms 5:17
ever came by the will of **m**;	2Pt 1:21
Holy Spirit, **men** spoke from God.	2Pt 1:21
If we accept the testimony of **men**,	1Jn 5:9
was One like the Son of **M**	Rv 1:13
creature had a face like a **m**;	Rv 4:7
their faces were like **men**-'s faces;	Rv 9:7
it is the number of a **m**.	Rv 13:18
One like the Son of **M** was seated	Rv 14:14
God's dwelling is with **men**,	Rv 21:3

MAN OF GOD

blessing that Moses, the **m**, gave	Dt 33:1
told her husband, "A **m** came	Jdg 13:6
A **m** came to Eli and said	1Sm 2:27
there's a **m** in this city	1Sm 9:6
came to Shemaiah, the **m**:	1Kg 12:22
A **m** came from Judah to Bethel	1Kg 13:1
He is the **m** who disobeyed	1Kg 13:26
She said to Elijah, "**M**, what do	1Kg 17:18

the m ... said to the king of Israel, 1Kg 20:28
M, the king declares, 'Come down!' 2Kg 1:9
I know that the one ... is a holy m, 2Kg 4:9
death in the pot, m! 2Kg 4:40
came to the m with ... bread 2Kg 4:42
When Elisha the m heard 2Kg 5:8
The m repeatedly warned the king 2Kg 6:10
died, just as the m had predicted 2Kg 7:17
The m wept, 2Kg 8:11
The m was angry with him 2Kg 13:19
tomb of the m who came 2Kg 23:17
As for Moses the m, 1Ch 23:14
the command of David, the m. 2Ch 8:14
word ... came to Shemaiah, the m: 2Ch 11:2
a m came to him and said, 2Ch 25:7
the law of Moses the m. Ezr 3:2
as David the m had prescribed. Neh 12:24
Igdaliah, a m, who had a chamber Jr 35:4
you, m, run from these things; 1Tm 6:11
so that the m may be complete, 2Tm 3:17

MANAGE
and Abednego to m the province Dn 2:49
one who m-s his own household 1Tm 3:4
have children, m their
households, 1Tm 5:14

MANAGER
m his master will put in charge Lk 12:42
Then the m said to himself, Lk 16:3
and m-s of God's mysteries. 1Co 4:1
as God's m, must be blameless, Ti 1:7
as good m-s of the varied grace 1Pt 4:10

MANAGING (n)
gifts of healing, helping, m, 1Co 12:28

MANASSEH
1. Son of Joseph and Asenath (Gn 41:50-51). Adopted by Jacob as a tribe (Gn 48); allotted half of its territory east of the Jordan from Gerasa to Mt. Hermon in the far north and half west of the Jordan to the Mediterranean from the Yarkon River to Mt. Carmel (Nm 32:33-42; Jos 13:29-31; 17).
2. Son of Hezekiah; king of Judah (2Kg 21:1-18). Wickedness brought on God's judgment (21:10-15; Jr 15:4).
3. Names of two who had married foreigners (Ezr 10:30,33).

MANATEE
ram skins dyed red and m skins; Ex 25:5
and a covering of m skins on top Ex 26:14
this a covering made of m skin, Nm 4:6

MANDATE
listened to My voice and kept My m Gn 26:5
always keep His m and His statutes, Dt 11:1
They will keep My m. Ezk 44:16

MANDRAKES
give me some of your son's m. Gn 30:14
The m give off a fragrance, Sg 7:13

MANGER
in cloth and lying in a m. Lk 2:12

MANIFESTATION
A m of the Spirit is given to each 1Co 12:7

MANIFESTED
He was m in the flesh, justified 1Tm 3:16

MANKIND
Spirit will not remain with m forever, Gn 6:3
And this is a revelation for m 2Sm 7:19
But m is born for trouble as Jb 5:7
All m has seen it; people have Jb 36:25
His acts toward m are Ps 66:5
You return m to the dust, saying Ps 90:3
out to you; my cry is to m. Pr 8:4
since that is the end of all m Ec 7:2
All m will come to worship Me, Is 66:23
Cursed is the man who trusts in m, Jr 17:5
I will cut off m from the face Zph 1:3
who are left of m may seek the Ac 15:17
whom none of m has seen or can 1Tm 6:16

MAN-MADE
you will worship m gods of wood Dt 4:28
consists of] m rules learned Is 29:13

MANNA
Israel named the substance m. Ex 16:31
nothing to look at but this m! Nm 11:6
The m resembled coriander seed, Nm 11:7
then He gave you m to eat, Dt 8:3
the land, the m ceased. Jos 5:12
withhold Your m from their Neh 9:20
He rained m for them to eat; Ps 78:24
fathers ate the m in the desert, Jn 6:31,49
a gold jar containing the m Heb 9:4
victor some of the hidden m. Rv 2:17

MANNER

in the Lord in a **m** worthy of the	Rm 16:2
live your life in a **m** worthy of	Php 1:27
journey in a **m** worthy of God,	3Jn 6

MANOAH

Samson's father (Jdg 13).

MANSLAUGHTER

one could flee who committed **m**	Dt 4:42
who commits **m** can flee to these	Dt 19:3
who committed **m** may return home	Jos 20:6
for the one who commits **m**,	Jos 21:13-38

MANTLE

he tucked his **m** under his belt	1Kg 18:46
his face in his **m** and went out	1Kg 19:13
him and threw his **m** over him.	1Kg 19:19
picked up the **m** that had fallen	2Kg 2:13
Then he took the **m** Elijah had	2Kg 2:14
Tuck your **m** under your belt,	2Kg 4:29; 9:1

MANURE

will be like **m** on the surface	2Kg 9:37
they became **m** for the ground.	Ps 83:10
corpses will fall like **m** on the surface	Jr 9:22
fit for the soil or for the **m** pile;	Lk 14:35

MANY

become the father of **m** nations.	Gn 17:4
made a robe of **m** colors for him	Gn 37:3
must not acquire **m** wives for	Dt 17:17
There are still too **m** people.	Jdg 7:4
Solomon loved **m** foreign women	1Kg 11:1
How **m** iniquities and sins have I	Jb 13:23
M bulls surround me; strong ones	Ps 22:12
than the roar of **m** waters.	Ps 93:4
Him in the presence of **m**.	Ps 109:30
Your compassions are **m**, LORD;	Ps 119:156
When there are **m** words, sin is	Pr 10:19
but with **m** counselors there is	Pr 11:14
M plans are in a man's heart,	Pr 19:21
M women are capable, but you	Pr 31:29
For when there are **m** words,	Ec 6:11
end to the making of **m** books,	Ec 12:12
bore the sin of **m** and interceded	Is 53:12
Indeed, our rebellions are **m**;	Jr 14:7
You who reside by **m** waters,	Jr 51:13
because of her **m** transgressions	Lm 1:5
it refers to **m** days (in the future).	Dn 8:26
M of those who sleep in the dust	Dn 12:2

On that day **m** will say to Me,	Mt 7:22
give His life—a ransom for **m**.	Mt 20:28
For **m** are invited, but few are	Mt 22:14
and they will deceive **m**.	Mt 24:5
M false prophets will rise up	Mt 24:11
the love of **m** will grow cold.	Mt 24:12
it is shed for **m** for the	Mt 26:28
holy city, and appeared to **m**.	Mt 27:53
name is Legion ... because we are **m**.	Mk 5:9
her **m** sins have been forgiven;	Lk 7:47
M more believed because of what	Jn 4:41
house are **m** dwelling places;	Jn 14:2
Jesus performed **m** other signs in	Jn 20:30
overflowed to the **m** by the grace	Rm 5:15
way we who are **m** are one body	Rm 12:5
not **m** powerful, not **m** of noble	1Co 1:26
but you can't have **m** fathers.	1Co 4:15
as there are **m** "gods" and **m** "lords"	1Co 8:5
we who are **m** are one body,	1Co 10:17
body is one and has **m** parts,	1Co 12:12
once to bear the sins of **m**	Heb 9:28
even now **m** antichrists have	1Jn 2:18
and on His head were **m** crowns.	Rv 19:12

MARA

Call me **M**," she answered,	Ru 1:20

MARAH

that is why it was named **M**.	Ex 15:23

MARANATHA

a curse be on him. **M**!	1Co 16:22

MARAUDERS

He handed them over to **m**	Jdg 2:14
helped David against the **m**	1Ch 12:21

MARAUDING

suddenly they saw a **m**-ing band,	2Kg 13:21

MARCH

m around the city seven times,	Jos 6:4
the sound of **m**-ing in the tops	2Sm 5:24
when kings **m** out (to war),	2Sm 11:1
"**M** on," David replied to Ittai.	2Sm 15:22
You do not **m** out with our armies	Ps 44:9
when You **m**-ed through the desert	Ps 68:7
yet all of them **m** in ranks;	Pr 30:27
the South will **m** out to fight	Dn 11:11

MARDUK

Chief god of Babylon (Jr 50:2).

MARE

| a m among Pharaoh's chariots | Sg 1:9 |

MARITAL

| or m rights of the first wife. | Ex 21:10 |
| fulfill his m duty to his wife, | 1Co 7:3 |

MARK, JOHN

Missionary (Ac 12:12,25); Barnabas's cousin (Col 4:10); cause of split between Paul and Barnabas (Ac 15:36-40); later apparently reconciled to Paul (Col 4:10; 2Tm 4:11; Phm 24). Also close to Peter (1Pt 5:13). Wrote the Gospel of Mark.

MARK

He placed a m on Cain so that	Gn 4:15
or m-ed off the heavens	Is 40:12
and put a m on the foreheads of	Ezk 9:4
come near anyone who has the m.	Ezk 9:6
If I don't see the m of the nails	Jn 20:25
I carry the m-s of Jesus on my	Gl 6:17
to be given a m on his right	Rv 13:16
and receives a m on his forehead	Rv 14:9
who accepted the m of the beast	Rv 19:20

MARKER

stone that I have set up as a m	Gn 28:22
a stone and set it up as a m.	Gn 31:45
the m is a witness	Gn 31:52
Jacob set up a m at the place	Gn 35:14
Jacob set up a m on her grave;	Gn 35:20
your neighbor's boundary m	Dt 19:14
The wicked displace boundary m-s	Jb 24:2
Set up road m-s for yourself;	Jr 31:21
like those who move boundary m-s	Hs 5:10

MARKET

| islands were your regular m-s. | Ezk 27:15 |
| that is sold in the meat m | 1Co 10:25 |

MARKETPLACE

and deceit never leave its m.	Ps 55:11
sitting in the m-s who call out to	Mt 11:16
who love greetings in the m-s	Lk 20:46
My Father's house into a m!	Jn 2:16
and in the m every day with	Ac 17:17

MARRIAGE

must not violate his father's m bed.	Dt 22:30
He gave his 30 daughters in m	Jdg 12:9
daughter to a Benjaminite in m.	Jdg 21:1
an alliance with Ahab through m.	2Ch 18:1

to their sons in m or take their	Ezr 9:12
our daughters in m to the	Neh 10:30
daughters in m to their sons	Neh 13:25
though she was your m partner	Mal 2:14
nor are given in m but are like	Mt 22:30
and giving in m, until the day	Mt 24:38
promised you in m to one husband	2Co 11:2
They forbid m and demand	1Tm 4:3
M must be respected by all,	Heb 13:4
and the m bed kept undefiled,	Heb 13:4
the m of the Lamb has come,	Rv 19:7
invited to the m feast of the Lamb!	Rv 19:9

MARRIED (adj)

| a m woman is legally bound to | Rm 7:2 |
| a m man is concerned about | 1Co 7:33 |

MARROW

| and his bones are full of m. | Jb 21:24 |
| soul, spirit, joints, and m; | Heb 4:12 |

MARRY

die in battle and another man m her.	Dt 20:7
doesn't want to m his sister-in-law,	Dt 25:7
Egypt by m-ing Pharaoh's daughter.	1Kg 3:1
who have m-led foreign women	Ezr 10:14
an unloved woman when she m-ies	Pr 30:23
the children of the m-ied woman,	Is 54:1
Go and m a promiscuous wife	Hs 1:2
has m-ied the daughter of a foreign	Mal 2:11
whoever m-ies a divorced woman	Mt 5:32
divorces ... and m-ies another,	Mt 19:9
it's better not to m!	Mt 19:10
and drinking, m-ing and giving	Mt 24:38
I just got m-ied, and therefore	Lk 14:20
For all seven had m-ied her.	Lk 20:33
the dead neither m nor are given	Lk 20:35
it is better to m than to burn	1Co 7:9
if you do get m-ied, you have not	1Co 7:28
he who does not m will do better.	1Co 7:38
I want younger women to m,	1Tm 5:14

MARTHA

Sister of Mary and Lazarus (Lk 10:38-42; Jn 11:1–12:2).

MARVEL (n)

| Egypt and His m-s in the region | Ps 78:43 |

MARVEL (v)

| you scoffers, m and vanish away | Ac 13:41 |

MARVELOUS
of darkness into His **m** light   1Pt 2:9

MARVELOUSLY
for he was **m** helped until   2Ch 26:15

MARY
1. Mother of Jesus (Mt 1:16; Lk 1:26-56; 2:1-20,34-35). Present at the cross (Jn 19:25-27); among the believers (Ac 1:14).

2. Magdalene; delivered from demons (Lk 8:2); follower and supporter of Jesus (Mk 15:40-41). Witness to the crucifixion and resurrection (Mt 27:54–28:10; Mk 16:1-10; Lk 24:10; Jn 19:25–20:18).

3. Mother of James and Joseph/Joses; follower and supporter of Jesus (Mk 15:40-41). Witness to the crucifixion and resurrection (Mt 27:54–28:10; Mk 16:1-8; Lk 24:10).

4. Sister of Martha and Lazarus (Jn 11); anointed Jesus' feet (12:1-3).

5. Wife of Clopas (Jn 19:25).

6. Mother of John Mark (Ac 12:12).

7. Believer in Rome (Rm 16:6).

MASON
m-'s level (used on) the house of   2Kg 21:13
stonecutters, **m**-s, carpenters,   1Ch 22:15
and righteousness the **m**-'s level.   Is 28:17

MASSACRE
It is a sword for **m**, a sword for   Ezk 21:14
He gave orders to **m** all the male   Mt 2:16

MASSAH
Where Israel tested God (Ex 17:7; Dt 6:16; 9:22; 33:8; Ps 95:8).

MASSIVE
What **m** stones! What impressive   Mk 13:1

MAST
down on the top of a ship's **m**.   Pr 23:34
Lebanon to make a **m** for you.   Ezk 27:5

MASTER (n)
His **m** must pierce his ear with   Ex 21:6
are running away from their **m**-s.   1Sm 25:10
If only my **m** would go to the   2Kg 5:3
are our own—who can be our **m**?   Ps 12:4
a servant's eyes on His **m**-'s hand   Ps 123:2
Don't slander a servant to his **m**,   Pr 30:10
the donkey its **m**-'s feeding-trough,   Is 1:3

And if I am a **m**, where is   Mal 1:6
No one can be a slave of two **m**-s   Mt 6:24
or a slave above his **m**.   Mt 10:24
that fall from their **m**-s' table!   Mt 15:27
And do not be called **m**-s either,   Mt 23:10
you have one **M**, the Messiah.   Mt 23:10
That slave whose **m** finds him   Mt 24:46
His **m** said to him, 'Well done   Mt 25:21
know when the **m** of the house is   Mk 13:35
M, **M**, we're going to die!   Lk 8:24
M, it's good for us to be here!   Lk 9:33
slaves the **m** will find alert   Lk 12:37
Jesus, **M**, have mercy on us!   Lk 17:13
is not greater than his **m**,   Jn 13:16
doesn't know what his **m** is doing.   Jn 15:15
as a skilled **m** builder I have   1Co 3:10
obey your human **m**-s with fear   Eph 6:5
And **m**-s, treat them the same way   Eph 6:9
your human **m**-s in everything;   Col 3:22
you too have a **M** in heaven.   Col 4:1
have believing **m**-s should not be   1Tm 6:2
useful to the **M**, prepared for   2Tm 2:21
to their **m**-s in everything,   Ti 2:9
to your **m**-s with all respect,   1Pt 2:18
denying the **M** who bought them   2Pt 2:1
denying our only **M** and Lord,   Jd 4

MASTER (v)
is for you, but you must **m** it.   Gn 4:7

MATE
herself to an animal to **m** with it;   Lv 18:23
near any animal and **m**-s with it,   Lv 20:16

MATERIAL
garment made of two kinds of **m**.   Lv 19:19
Your decrees and not to **m** gain.   Ps 119:36
to minister to Jews in **m** needs.   Rm 15:27
if we reap **m** things from you   1Co 9:11
godliness is a way to **m** gain.   1Tm 6:5

MATTANIAH
King Zedekiah's original name (2Kg 24:17).

MATTER (n)
except in the **m** of Uriah   1Kg 15:5
the glory of kings to investigate a **m**. Pr 25:2
The end of a **m** is better than   Ec 7:8
the conclusion of the **m** is: Ec 12:13
more important **m**-s of the law   Mt 23:23

faithful in a very small **m** | Lk 19:17
About **m**-**s** of the spirit: | 1Co 12:1
there are some **m**-**s** that are hard | 2Pt 3:16

MATTER (v)

and uncircumcision does not **m** | 1Co 7:19
what **m**-**s** is faith working through | Gl 5:6
you can determine what really **m**-**s** | Php 1:10

MATTHEW

Apostle; former tax collector (Mt 9:9; 10:3). Also called Levi son of Alphaeus (Mk 2:14; cp. Lk 5:27-32). Wrote a gospel.

MATTHIAS

Chosen to replace Judas (Ac 1:23-26).

MATTOCKS

a shekel for plowshares and **m** | 1Sm 13:21

MATURE

among the **m** we do speak a wisdom | 1Co 2:6
{growing} into a **m** man | Eph 4:13
who are **m** should think this way. | Php 3:15
present everyone **m** in Christ. | Col 1:28
you can stand **m** and fully | Col 4:12
But solid food is for the **m** | Heb 5:14
that you may be **m** and complete, | Jms 1:4
he is a **m** man who is also able | Jms 3:2

MATURITY

age should speak and **m** should | Jb 32:7
also pray for this: your **m**. | 2Co 13:9
us go on to **m**, not laying | Heb 6:1

MAUL

the meat of a **m**-ed animal | Ex 22:31
or was **m**-ed by wild beasts, | Lv 22:8
lion had not ... **m**-ed the donkey. | 1Kg 13:28
bears ... **m**-ed 42 of the youths. | 2Kg 2:24
lions, **m**-ing and roaring. | Ps 22:13
The lion **m**-ed whatever its cubs | Nah 2:12

MAY

M the words of my mouth and the | Ps 19:14
so that I **m** not sin against | Ps 119:11
the LORD while He **m** be found; | Is 55:6
M it be done to me according to | Lk 1:38

MAYBE

m he has wandered away; | 1Kg 18:27
M this god will consider us, | Jnh 1:6

MEAL

Then Elisha said, "Get some **m**." | 2Kg 4:41
quarts of fine **m** {will sell} for | 2Kg 7:1
Better a **m** of vegetables where | Pr 15:17
in exchange for one **m**. | Heb 12:16

MEAN

What does this ritual **m** to you? | Ex 12:26
What do these stones **m** to you? | Jos 4:6
Go and learn what this **m**-s: | Mt 9:13
If you had known what this **m**-s: | Mt 12:7
and uncircumcision **m** nothing; | Gl 6:15
He ascended" **m** except that He | Eph 4:9

MEANING (n)

What is the **m** of the decrees, | Dt 6:20
and giving the **m** so that the | Neh 8:8
if I do not know the **m** of | 1Co 14:11
the secret **m** of the woman | Rv 17:7

MEANS (n)

are by no **m** least among the | Mt 2:6
for yourselves by **m** of the | Lk 16:9
that I may by all **m** save some. | 1Co 9:22
angels by **m** of a mediator. | Gl 3:19

MEANINGLESS

not **m** words to you but they are | Dt 32:47
man's thoughts; they are **m**. | Ps 94:11

MEASURE (n)

has not yet reached its full **m**. | Gn 15:16
honest dry **m**, and an honest liquid | Lv 19:36
a full and honest dry **m**, | Dt 25:15
of these articles was beyond **m**. | 2Kg 25:16
Differing weights and varying **m**-s | Pr 20:10
The dry **m** and the liquid **m** will
be uniform | Ezk 45:11
can reduce the **m** while increasing | Am 8:5
accursed short **m** in the house | Mc 6:10
and with the **m** you use, it will be | Mt 7:2
a good **m**—pressed down, shaken | Lk 6:38
He gives the Spirit without **m**. | Jn 3:34
might become sinful beyond **m**. | Rm 7:13
distributed a **m** of faith to each | Rm 12:3
will not boast beyond **m**, but | 2Co 10:13
to the **m** of the Messiah's | Eph 4:7

MEASURE (v)

that he stopped **m**-ing it because | Gn 41:49
Who has **m**-d the waters in the | Is 40:12
If the heavens above can be **m**-d | Jr 31:37

the sand of the sea cannot be **m-d**. Jr 33:22
He **m-d** the thickness of the Ezk 40:5
which cannot be **m-d** or counted. Hs 1:10
To **m** Jerusalem to determine its Zch 2:2
you use, it will be **m-d** to you. Mt 7:2
But in **m-ing** themselves by 2Co 10:12
with a stature **m-d** by Christ's Eph 4:13
Go and **m** God's sanctuary and Rv 11:1
He **m-d** the city with the rod at Rv 21:16

MEASUREMENTS

You must not act unfairly in **m** Lv 19:35
side also had the same **m**. Ezk 40:10
are the **m** of the altar Ezk 43:13
These are the city's **m**: Ezk 48:16

MEASURING (adj)

stretch over Jerusalem the **m** line 2Kg 21:13
will make justice the **m** line Is 28:17
m line will once again stretch Jr 31:39
and a **m** rod in his hand. Ezk 40:3
went out east with a **m** line Ezk 47:3
land be divided up with a **m** line. Am 7:17
saw a man with a **m** line in his hand Zch 2:1
It's a **m** basket that is Zch 5:6
was given a **m** reed like a rod Rv 11:1
had a gold **m** rod to measure Rv 21:15

MEAT

LORD will give you **m** to eat Ex 16:8
said, "Who will feed us **m**? Nm 11:4
While the **m** was still between Nm 11:33
whatever the **m** fork brought up. 1Sm 2:14
He rained **m** on them like dust, Ps 78:27
city is the pot, and we are the **m**. Ezk 11:3
no **m** or wine entered my mouth, Dn 10:3
It is a noble thing not to eat **m**, Rm 14:21
I will never again eat **m**, so that I 1Co 8:13
that is sold in the **m** market, 1Co 10:25

MEDDLER

thief, an evildoer, or as a **m**. 1Pt 4:15

MEDDLES

A passerby who **m** in a quarrel Pr 26:17

MEDES

People of Media, conquerors of Babylon (Is 13:17; 21:2; Jr 51:11,28); Darius (Dn 5:31; 9:1; 11:1); present at Pentecost (Ac 2:9).

MEDIA

Country of the Medes, north of Elam and west of Assyria (Ezr 6:2); ally of Persia (Est 1:3; Dn 5:28; 8:20); cursed by Jeremiah (Jr 25:25).

MEDIATOR

your **m-s** have rebelled against Me. Is 43:27
through angels by means of a **m**. Gl 3:19
one God and one **m** between God 1Tm 2:5
He is the **m** of a better Heb 8:6
He is the **m** of a new covenant Heb 9:15
to Jesus (**m** of a new covenant), Heb 12:24

MEDICINE

A joyful heart is good **m**, Pr 17:22
{no} **m** has been applied and no Ezk 30:21
for food and their leaves for **m**. Ezk 47:12

MEDITATE

he **m-s** on it day and night. Ps 1:2
I am on You during the night Ps 63:6
I think of God; I groan; I **m**; Ps 77:3
and **m** on Your actions. Ps 77:12
I will **m** on Your precepts Ps 119:15
I **m** on all You have done; Ps 143:5
mind will **m** on the {past} terror: Is 33:18
in her heart and **m-ing** on them Lk 2:19

MEDITATION

and hinder **m** before Him. Jb 15:4
mouth and the **m** of my heart Ps 19:14
heart's **m** {brings} understanding. Ps 49:3
my **m** be pleasing to Him Ps 104:34
It is my **m** all day long. Ps 119:97

MEDITERRANEAN SEA

Western border of Israel (Ex 23:31; Nm 34:6; Dt 11:24; 34:2; Jos 1:4; 23:4; Ezk 47:15-20), including several of the tribal territories (Jos 15:4,11,12,47; 16:3,8; 17:9).

MEDIUM

Do not turn to **m-s** or consult Lv 19:31
A man or woman who is a **m** Lv 20:27
consult a **m** or a familiar spirit Dt 18:11
removed the **m-s** and spiritists 1Sm 28:3
a woman at Endor who is a **m**. 1Sm 28:7
and consulted **m-s** and spiritists 2Kg 21:6
removed the **m-s**, the spiritists 2Kg 23:24
diviner-priests, **m-s**, sorcerers Dn 2:2
called out to bring in the **m-s** Dn 5:7

MEEK

I will leave a **m** and humble — Zph 3:12

MEET

and God's angels **met** him. — Gn 32:1
The LORD ... has **met** with us. — Ex 3:18
I will **m** with you there above — Ex 25:22
Let us **m** at the house of God — Neh 6:10
For You **m** him with rich blessings; — Ps 21:3
faithful God will come to **m** me; — Ps 59:10
place where You **met** with us. — Ps 74:4
for a man to **m** a bear robbed — Pr 17:12
Messenger races to **m** messenger, — Jr 51:31
together without agreeing to **m**? — Am 3:3
Israel, prepare to **m** your God! — Am 4:12
and went out to **m** the groom. — Mt 25:1
Jesus often **met** there with His — Jn 18:2
year they **met** with the church — Ac 11:26
from them and **met** separately with — Ac 19:9
church that **m-s** in their home. — Rm 16:5
church that **m-s** in their home. — 1Co 16:19
in the clouds to **m** the Lord in — 1Th 4:17
church that **m-s** in your house. — Phm 2
who **met** Abraham and blessed him — Heb 7:1

MEETING (n)

In the tent of **m** outside the — Ex 27:21
roared in the **m** place where — Ps 74:4
not staying away from our **m-s** — Heb 10:25

MEGIDDO

City near Jezreel, defeated and allotted but not dispossessed at first (Jos 12:21; 17:11; Jdg 1:27); possessed by the time of Solomon (1Kg 4:12). Scene of many key events (2Kg 9:27; 23:29; Zch 12:11). *see also* ARMEGEDDON

MELCHIZEDEK

King of Salem and priest (Gn 14:18); represents undying priesthood (Ps 110:4; Heb 5:6,10; 6:20; 7).

MELONS

the cucumbers, **m**, leeks, onions — Nm 11:5

MELT

mountains **m-ed** before the LORD — Jdg 5:5
heart is like wax, **m-ing** within — Ps 22:14
the earth **m-s** when He lifts His — Ps 46:6
The mountains **m** like wax at the — Ps 97:5

and every man's heart will **m**. — Is 13:7
elements will **m** with the heat. — 2Pt 3:12

MEMBER

will be the **m-s** of his household — Mt 10:36
individually **m-s** of one another. — Rm 12:5
your bodies are the **m-s** of Christ? — 1Co 6:15
if one **m** suffers, all the **m-s** suffer — 1Co 12:26
the saints, and **m-s** of God's — Eph 2:19
co-heirs, **m-s** of the same body — Eph 3:6
we are **m-s** of one another — Eph 4:25
since we are **m-s** of His body. — Eph 5:30

MEMORIAL

This day is to be a **m** for you, — Ex 12:14
of the ephod as **m** stones for — Ex 28:12
will burn this **m** portion of it — Lv 2:2
these stones will always be a **m** for — Jos 4:7
a **m** and a name better than sons — Is 56:5
come up as a **m** offering before — Ac 10:4

MEMORY

blot out the **m** of Amalek — Ex 17:14; Dt 25:19
{All} **m** of him perishes from the — Jb 18:17
the very **m** of them has perished. — Ps 9:6
let Him cut off {all} **m** of them — Ps 109:15
is no **m** of those who came before; — Ec 1:11
will also be told in **m** of her. — Mt 26:13
you always have good **m** of us, — 1Th 3:6

MEMPHIS

City in Egypt (Is 19:13; Jr 2:16; 44:1; 46:14,19; Ezk 30:13,16; Hs 9:6).

MENAHEM

King of Israel; obtained throne by force (2Kg 15:10-16). Paid tribute to the king of Assyria (15:19-20).

MENE

inscribed: M, M, TEKEL, PARSIN — Dn 5:25

MENSTRUAL

during her **m** impurity — Lv 18:19
before Me was like **m** impurity. — Ezk 36:17

MENSTRUATION

unclean because of her **m** for seven — Lv 15:19

MENTION

I will **m** those who know Me: — Ps 87:4
I have never commanded or **m-ed**; — Jr 19:5
that I constantly **m** you, — Rm 1:9
shameful even to **m** what is done — Eph 5:12

my God when I **m** you in my   Phm 4
m-ed the exodus of the sons of   Heb 11:22

MENTORS
or listen closely to my **m**.   Pr 5:13

MEPHIBOSHETH
1. Son of Jonathan; granted privilege in David's court (2Sm 4:4; 9; 16; 19).

2. Son of Saul whom David delivered to the Gibeonites (2Sm 21:1-9). His mother guarded his body until he was buried (21:10-14).

MERAB
Saul's eldest daughter (1Sm 14:49); promised to David but not given (18:17-19).

MERARI
Third son of Levi (Gn 46:11; Nm 3:35-37; 1Ch 26:10-19; Ezr 8:19).

MERCHANDISE
for money or treat her as **m**   Dt 21:14
peoples bring **m** or any kind of   Neh 10:31
When your **m** was unloaded from   Ezk 27:33
no one buys their **m** any longer   Rv 18:11

MERCHANT
She was the **m** among the nations   Is 23:3
m of the peoples to many coasts   Ezk 27:3
like a **m** in search of fine pearls.   Mt 13:45
and the **m**-s of the earth have   Rv 18:3

MERCIFULLY
He has dealt **m** with our fathers   Lk 1:72

MERCIFUL
your God is gracious and **m**;   2Ch 30:9
but {even} the **m** acts of the   Pr 12:10
that You are a **m** and   Jnh 4:2
Blessed are the **m**, because they   Mt 5:7
Be **m**, just as your Father also is **m**.   Lk 6:36
a **m** and faithful high priest   Heb 2:17
I will be **m** to their wrongdoing,   Heb 8:12
is very compassionate and **m**.   Jms 5:11

MERCY
Make a **m** seat of pure gold,   Ex 25:17
Put the **m** seat on the ark of the   Ex 26:34
He set the **m** seat on top of the ark.   Ex 40:20
in the cloud above the **m** seat.   Lv 16:2
sprinkle it against the **m** seat   Lv 16:15

from above the **m** seat that was   Nm 7:89
with them and show them no **m**.   Dt 7:2
hands because His **m-ies**
    are great,   2Sm 24:14
with You for **m** in this temple,   1Kg 8:33
Have **m** on me, my friends, have **m**,   Jb 19:21
listen to my plea for **m**.   Ps 86:6
He has heard my appeal for **m**.   Ps 116:1
plead aloud to the LORD for **m**.   Ps 142:1
and renounces them will find **m**.   Pr 28:13
LORD is waiting to show you **m**   Is 30:18
yet I will show **m** to you with My   Is 60:10
They are cruel and show no **m**.   Jr 6:23
for His **m-ies** never end.   Lm 3:22
by showing **m** to the needy.   Dn 4:27
In {Your} wrath remember **m**!   Hab 3:2
You withhold **m** from Jerusalem   Zch 1:12
because they will be shown **m**.   Mt 5:7
I desire **m** and not sacrifice.   Mt 9:13
shouting, "Have **m** on us, Son of   Mt 9:27
I desire **m** and not sacrifice,   Mt 12:7
of the law—justice, **m**, and faith.   Mt 23:23
His **m** is from generation to   Lk 1:50
Lord had shown her His great **m**   Lk 1:58
The one who showed **m** to him,   Lk 10:37
I will show **m** to whom I show **m**,   Rm 9:15
effort, but on God who shows **m**.   Rm 9:16
on objects of **m** that He prepared   Rm 9:23
so that He may have **m** on all.   Rm 11:32
by the **m-ies** of God, I urge   Rm 12:1
by the Lord's **m** is trustworthy.   1Co 7:25
the Father of **m-ies** and the God of   2Co 1:3
as we have received **m**, we do not   2Co 4:1
But God, who is abundant in **m**,   Eph 2:4
if any affection and **m**   Php 2:1
God had **m** on him, and not   Php 2:27
in unbelief, I received **m**   1Tm 1:13
that he obtain **m** from the Lord   2Tm 1:18
according to His **m**, through the   Ti 3:5
we may receive **m** and find grace   Heb 4:16
it overshadowing the **m** seat.   Heb 9:5
law, he dies without **m**, based on   Heb 10:28
M triumphs over judgment.   Jms 2:13
to His great **m**, He has given us   1Pt 1:3
had not received **m**, but now you   1Pt 2:10
expecting the **m** of our Lord   Jd 21

MERIBAH

Where Israel tested God and He gave them water (Ex 17:7; Nm 20:13,24; Dt 33:8; Pss 81:7; 95:8; 106:32).

MERIB-BAAL

Another name for Mephibosheth (1Ch 8:34).

MERODACH-BALADAN

King of Babylon who sent ambassadors to Hezekiah (2Kg 20:12; Is 39:1).

MESH

Construct a grate for it of bronze **m**   Ex 27:4
net, and he strays into its **m**.   Jb 18:8

MESHA

1. King of Moab (2Kg 3:4).
2. Descendant of Judah (1Ch 2:42).
3. Descendant of Benjamin (1Ch 8:9).

MESHACH

Daniel's companion; originally called Mishael (Dn 1:7; 3:12 30).

MESOPOTAMIA

The region of the Tigris and Euphrates Rivers (Ac 2:9); Abraham's home (7:2).

MESSAGE

speak only the **m** God puts in my   Nm **22:38**
the LORD put a **m** in Balaam's   Nm 23:5
we recognize a **m** the LORD has   Dt 18:21
But the **m** is very near you,   Dt 30:14
I have a secret **m** for you.   Jdg 3:19
What was the **m** He gave you?   1Sm 3:17
Their **m** has gone out to all the   Ps 19:4
one who sends a **m** by a fool's   Pr 26:6
I have heard a **m** from the LORD;   Jr 49:14
speak whatever **m** I will speak,   Ezk 12:25
a **m** was revealed to Daniel,   Dn 10:1
Listen to this **m** that the LORD   Am 3:1
Listen to this **m**, you cows of   Am 4:1
Listen to this **m** that I am   Am 5:1
and preach the **m** that I tell you   Jnh 3:2
because His **m** had authority.   Lk 4:32
So the sisters sent a **m** to Him: Jn 11:3
Lord, who has believed our **m**?   Jn 12:38
believe in Me through their **m**.   Jn 17:20
to speak God's **m** with boldness.   Ac 4:31
house and to hear a **m** from you.   Ac 10:22
Then God's **m** flourished and   Ac 12:24

if you have any **m** of   Ac 13:15
welcomed the **m** with eagerness   Ac 17:11
this way the Lord's **m** flourished   Ac 19:20
Lord, who has believed our **m**?   Rm 10:16
comes through the **m** about
   Christ.   Rm 10:17
perishing the **m** of the cross is   1Co 1:18
one is given a **m** of wisdom   1Co 12:8
committed the **m** of reconciliation   2Co 5:19
Hold firmly the **m** of life.   Php 2:16
to make God's **m** fully known,   Col 1:25
you welcomed the **m** with the joy   1Th 1:6
but as it truly is, the **m** of God,   1Th 2:13
but God's **m** is not bound.   2Tm 2:9
so that God's **m** will not be slandered.   Ti 2:5
Now this is the **m** we have heard   1Jn 1:5

MESSENGER

m was still speaking when another   Jb 1:18
—a band of deadly **m-s**   Ps 78:49
and making the winds His **m-s**   Ps 104:4
A king's fury is a **m** of death   Pr 16:14
a trustworthy **m** is like the   Pr 25:13
or deaf like My **m** I am sending?   Is 42:19
M races to meet **m**,   Jr 51:31
he is the **m** of the LORD of Hosts.   Mal 2:7
See, I am going to send My **m**,   Mal 3:1
am sending My **m** ahead of You   Mt 11:10
After John's **m-s** left, He began   Lk 7:24
a **m** is not greater than the one who   Jn 13:16
are the **m-s** of the churches   2Co 8:23
a **m** of Satan to torment me so   2Co 12:7

MESSIAH

until **M** the Prince will be seven   Dn 9:25
62 weeks the **M** will be cut off   Dn 9:26
to Jesus who is called the **M**.   Mt 1:16
You are the **M**, the Son of the   Mt 16:16
What do you think about the **M**?   Mt 22:42
'I am the **M**' and they will deceive   Mt 24:5
False **m-s** and false prophets   Mt 24:24
if You are the **M**, the Son of God   Mt 26:63
or Jesus who is called **M**?   Mt 27:17
Are You the **M**, the Son of   Mk 14:61
today a Savior, who is **M** the Lord,   Lk 2:11
before he saw the Lord's **M**.   Lk 2:26
whether John might be the **M**.   Lk 3:15
If You are the **M**, tell us.   Lk 22:67
Didn't the **M** have to suffer   Lk 24:26
the **M** would suffer and rise from   Lk 24:46

he declared: "I am not the M."   Jn 1:20
told him, "We have found the M!"   Jn 1:41
I know that M is coming   Jn 4:25
Could this be the M?   Jn 4:29
When the M comes, He won't   Jn 7:31
that you may believe Jesus is the M   Jn 20:31
you crucified, both Lord and M!   Ac 2:36
good news that the M is Jesus.   Ac 5:42
proving that this One is the M.   Ac 9:22
showing that the M had to suffer   Ac 17:3
Scriptures that Jesus is the M.   Ac 18:28
that the M must suffer, and that   Ac 26:23
the {crucified} body of the M   Rm 7:4
came the M, who is God over all,   Rm 9:5
For even the M did not please   Rm 15:3
just as the M also accepted you   Rm 15:7
everything together in the M   Eph 1:10
{power} in the M by raising Him   Eph 1:20
alive with the M even though we   Eph 2:5
time you were without the M   Eph 2:12
incalculable riches of the M   Eph 3:8
and that the M may dwell in your   Eph 3:17
how you learned about the M   Eph 4:20
as the M also loved us and gave   Eph 5:2
kingdom of the M and of God.   Eph 5:5
and the M will shine on you.   Eph 5:14
in the circumcision of the M.   Col 2:11
the substance is the M.   Col 2:17
have been raised with the M   Col 3:1
is hidden with the M in God.   Col 3:3
When the M, who is your life, is   Col 3:4
And let the peace of the M   Col 3:15
message about the M dwell richly   Col 3:16
to speak the mystery of the M   Col 4:3
of the M if we hold firmly   Heb 3:14
the M did not exalt Himself to   Heb 5:5
elementary message about the M   Heb 6:1
Now the M has appeared, high   Heb 9:11
more will the blood of the M   Heb 9:14
For the M did not enter a   Heb 9:24
so also the M, having been   Heb 9:28
set apart the M as Lord in your   1Pt 3:15
sufferings of the M rejoice,   1Pt 4:13
who denies that Jesus is the M?   1Jn 2:22
Jesus is the M has been born of God,   1Jn 5:1
kingdom of our Lord and of His M   Rv 11:15
with the M for 1,000 years   Rv 20:4
be priests of God and the M   Rv 20:6

MESSIANIC
In the M Age, when the Son of   Mt 19:28

METALWORKER
and a m plates with gold   Is 40:19
The craftsman encourages the m;   Is 41:7

METHUSELAH
Son of Enoch; grandfather of Noah (Gn 5:21-29; Lk 3:36-37).

MICAH
1. Ephraimite idolater (Jdg 17–18).

2. Descendant of Reuben (1Ch 5:5).

3. Grandson of Jonathan (1Ch 8:34; 9:40).

4. Levite leader (1Ch 23:20; 24:24-25).

5. Prophet to Israel and Judah in the days of kings Jotham, Ahaz, and Hezekiah of Judah (Jr 26:18; Mc 1:1).

MICAIAH
1. Son of Imlah; prophet against Ahab (1Kg 22: 5-28; 2Ch 18:4-27).

2. Wife of Rehoboam; mother of Abijah (2Ch 13:2).

3. Grandson of Shaphan; told officials about Jeremiah's scroll (Jr 36:11-13).

4. Reforming teacher in Judah (2Ch 17:7).

5. Priest; trumpeter (Neh 12:41).

MICE
and five gold m   1Sm 6:4

MICHAEL
1. Archangel; guardian of Israel (Dn 10:13,21; 12:1). Disputed with the Devil (Jd 9); will fight the dragon (Rv 12:7).

2. Benjaminite chief (1Ch 8:16).

3. Manassite who joined David (1Ch 12:20).

4. Son of Jehoshaphat (2Ch 21:2).

MICHAL
Daughter of Saul (1Sm 14:49); offered to David to endanger him (18:20-29); warned David of a plot (19:11-17). Given to Palti (25:44); taken back (2Sm 3:12-16). Despised David dancing before the Lord (6:14-23; 1Ch 15:29).

MICHMASH

Site of Jonathan's battle with the Philistines (1Sm 13:16–14:15).

MIDDAY

brighter and brighter until **m**.	Pr 4:18
was shining like the sun at **m**.	Rv 1:16

MIDDLE

tree in the **m** of the garden,	Gn 3:3
12 stones in the **m** of the Jordan	Jos 4:9
sun stopped in the **m** of the sky	Jos 10:13
sanctuary will be in the **m** of it.	Ezk 48:8
a tree in the **m** of the earth,	Dn 4:10
will lie down in the **m** of it,	Zph 2:14
boat was in the **m** of the sea,	Mk 6:47
sanctuary was split down the **m**.	Lk 23:45
side, with Jesus in the **m**.	Jn 19:18
down the **m** of the broad street	Rv 22:2

MID-HEAVEN

eagle, flying in **m**, saying in a	Rv 8:13
saw another angel flying in **m**	Rv 14:6
to all the birds flying in **m**	Rv 19:17

MIDIAN

Son of Abraham and Keturah (Gn 25:2); father of the Midianites.

went to live in the land of M	Ex 2:15
Jethro, the priest of M.	Ex 3:1
They waged war against M,	Nm 31:7
handed them over to M seven years,	Jdg 6:1
an exile in the land of M	Ac 7:29

MIDIANITE

When M traders passed by, they	Gn 37:28
came bringing a M woman to his	Nm 25:6
the Israelites against the M-s.	Nm 31:2

MIDNIGHT

About **m** I will go throughout	Ex 11:4
At **m**, Boaz was startled, turned	Ru 3:8
I rise at **m** to thank You for	Ps 119:62
whether in the evening or at **m**	Mk 13:35
goes to him at **m** and says to him	Lk 11:5
About **m** Paul and Silas were	Ac 16:25
extended his message until **m**.	Ac 20:7

MIDWIFE

the **m** said to her, "Don't be afraid,	Gn 35:17
the **m** took it and tied a scarlet	Gn 38:28
of Egypt said to the Hebrew **m-ves**	Ex 1:15
Since the **m-ves** feared God, He	Ex 1:21

MIGDOL

1. Encampment on the exodus (Ex 14:2; Nm 33:7).

2. City in Egypt where Jews fled (Jr 44:1).

MIGHT

with all his **m** before the LORD	2Sm 6:14
In Your hand are power and **m**	1Ch 29:12
Power and **m** are in Your hand,	2Ch 20:6
we will sing and praise Your **m**.	Ps 21:13
and vindicate me by Your **m**!	Ps 54:1
He rules forever by His **m**;	Ps 66:7
of the LORD, His **m**, and the	Ps 78:4
and will declare Your **m**	Ps 145:11
Where is Your zeal and Your **m**?	Is 63:15
mighty must not boast in his **m**;	Jr 9:23
Not by strength or by **m**, but by My	Zch 4:6
according to His glorious **m**	Col 1:11
to whom be honor and eternal **m**.	1Tm 6:16
who are greater in **m** and power,	2Pt 2:11

MIGHTIER

a greater and **m** nation than they	Nm 14:12

MIGHTY

hands of the M One of Jacob,	Gn 49:24
deeds and **m** acts like Yours?	Dt 3:24
the great, **m**, and awesome God	Dt 10:17
The LORD is with you, **m** warrior.	Jdg 6:12
How the **m** have fallen!	2Sm 1:19
He shatters the **m** without an	Jb 34:24
strong and **m**, the LORD, **m** in battle.	Ps 24:8
M warrior, strap your sword at	Ps 45:3
because of the **m** acts of the	Ps 71:16
The **m** King loves justice.	Ps 99:4
the LORD's **m** acts or proclaim	Ps 106:2
a vow to the M One of Jacob:	Ps 132:5
and will proclaim Your **m** acts.	Ps 145:4
Praise Him in His **m** heavens.	Ps 150:1
hyraxes are not a **m** people,	Pr 30:26
M waters cannot extinguish love	Sg 8:7
Counselor, M God, Eternal Father	Is 9:6
Redeemer, the M One of Jacob.	Is 60:16
the **m** must not boast in his	Jr 9:23
great in counsel and **m** in deed,	Jr 32:19
because the M One has done great	Lk 1:49
has toppled the **m** from their	Lk 1:52
under the **m** hand of God,	1Pt 5:6
Lord God who judges her is **m**.	Rv 18:8
city, Babylon, the **m** city!	Rv 18:10

MILCOM

God of the Ammonites (1Kg 11:5,7,33; 2Kg 23:13; Jr 49:1,3; Zph 1:5).

MILDEW

fabric is contaminated with m	Lv 13:47
in the house, it is harmful m;	Lv 14:44
heat, drought, blight, and m;	Dt 28:22
when there is blight, m, locust	1Kg 8:37
I struck you with blight and m;	Am 4:9
with blight, m, and hail, but	Hg 2:17

MILE

if anyone forces you to go one m,	Mt 5:41
was already over a m from land,	Mt 14:24
about seven m-s from Jerusalem	Lk 24:13
rowed about three or four m-s	Jn 6:19
Jerusalem (about two m-s away).	Jn 11:18
bridles for about 180 m-s.	Rv 14:20

MILETUS

Where Paul met Ephesian elders (Ac 20:15,17) and left Trophimus (2Tm 4:20).

MILK

a land flowing with m and honey	Ex 3:8
a young goat in its mother's m.	Ex 23:19
asked for water; she gave him m.	Jdg 5:25
They took two m cows, hitched	1Sm 6:10
pour me out like m and curdle me	Jb 10:10
churning of m produces butter	Pr 30:33
Honey and m are under your tongue.	Sg 4:11
buy wine and m without money and	Is 55:1
will nurse on the m of nations,	Is 60:16
than snow, whiter than m;	Lm 4:7
and the hills will flow with m.	Jl 3:18
I fed you m, not solid food	1Co 3:2
not drink the m from the flock?	1Co 9:7
You need m, not solid food.	Heb 5:12
the unadulterated spiritual m	1Pt 2:2

MILL

while the sound of the m fades;	Ec 12:4
will be grinding at the m:	Mt 24:41
the sound of a m will never be	Rv 18:22

MILLSTONE

or an upper m as security for a	Dt 24:6
portion of a m on Abimelech's	Jdg 9:53
drop an upper m on him	
from the	2Sm 11:21

better for him if a heavy m were	Mt 18:6
like a large m and threw it	Rv 18:21

MINA

Your m will equal 60 shekels.	Ezk 45:12
gave them 10 m-s, and told them	Lk 19:13

MIND

change their m-s and return to	Ex 13:17
LORD changed His m about the	Ex 32:14
a son of man who changes His m.	Nm 23:19
not given you a m to understand,	Dt 29:4
is not man who changes his m.	1Sm 15:29
You with their whole m and heart	1Kg 8:48
everything that was on her m.	1Kg 10:2
with all his m and with all his	2Kg 23:3
a whole heart and a willing m,	1Ch 28:9
with all their m and all their	2Ch 15:12
His m rejoiced in the LORD's	2Ch 17:6
put it into the m of King Cyrus	Ezr 1:1
But I also have a m; I am not	Jb 12:3
or gave the m understanding?	Jb 38:36
I keep the LORD in m always.	Ps 16:8
examine my heart and m.	Ps 26:2
me an undivided m to fear Your	Ps 86:11
but a twisted m is despised.	Pr 12:8
The m of the righteous person	Pr 15:28
and apply your m to my knowledge	Pr 22:17
I applied my m to seek and	Ec 1:13
my m still guiding me with	Ec 2:3
I applied my m to know wisdom	Ec 8:16
Dull the m-s of these people;	Is 6:10
understand with their m-s, turn back,	Is 6:10
You will keep in perfect peace the m	Is 26:3
I, the LORD, examine the m,	Jr 17:10
I call this to m, and therefore	Lm 3:21
be given the m of an animal	Dn 4:16
all your soul, and with all your m.	Mt 22:37
dressed and in his right m;	Mk 5:15
opened their m-s to understand	Lk 24:45
them over to a worthless m	Rm 1:28
with my m I myself am a slave to	Rm 7:25
has known the m of the Lord?	Rm 11:34
by the renewing of your m,	Rm 12:2
fully convinced in his own m.	Rm 14:5
who has known the Lord's m	1Co 2:16
But we have the m of Christ.	1Co 2:16
say that you are out of your m-s	1Co 14:23
But their m-s were closed.	2Co 3:14
has blinded the m-s of the	2Co 4:4

For if we are out of our **m**   2Co 5:13
be of the same **m**, be at peace   2Co 13:11
renewed in the spirit of your **m**-s;   Eph 4:23
spirit, with one **m**, working side   Php 1:27
and your **m**-s in Christ Jesus   Php 4:7
Set your **m**-s on what is above,   Col 3:2
quiet life, to **m** your own business,   1Th 4:11
among men whose **m**-s
  are depraved   1Tm 6:5
who are corrupt in **m**, worthless   2Tm 3:8
their **m** and conscience are defiled.   Ti 1:15
and He will not change His **m**,   Heb 7:21
will put My laws into their **m**-s,   Heb 8:10
I will write them on their **m**-s   Heb 10:16
get your **m**-s ready for action,   1Pt 1:13
One who examines **m**-s and hearts,   Rv 2:23
Here is the **m** with wisdom: Rv 17:9

MIND-SET
For the **m** of the flesh is death   Rm 8:6
hearts knows the Spirit's **m**   Rm 8:27

MINE
both man and animal; it is M.   Ex 13:2
although all the earth is M   Ex 19:5
creatures of the field are M.   Ps 50:11
Gilead is M, Manasseh is M,   Ps 60:7
am my love's and my love is m;   Sg 6:3
"They will be M," says the LORD   Mal 3:17
Everything the Father has is M.   Jn 16:15

MINISTER (n)
Levites to be **m**-s before the ark   1Ch 16:4
speak of you as **m**-s of our God   Is 61:6
wail, you **m**-s of the altar.   Jl 1:13
be a **m** of Christ Jesus to the   Rm 15:16
competent to be **m**-s of a new   2Co 3:6
as God's **m**-s, we commend   2Co 6:4
a faithful **m** of the Messiah   Col 1:7
Paul, have become a **m** of it   Col 1:23
a **m** of the sanctuary and the   Heb 8:2

MINISTER (v)
{worn by} Aaron whenever he **m**-s   Ex 28:35
not able to continue **m**-ing   1Kg 8:11
They **m**-ed with song in front   1Ch 6:32
the LORD and to **m** before Him   1Ch 15:2
of the LORD, to **m** to Him,   1Ch 23:13
convert to the LORD, **m** to Him, love Is 56:6
women who had ... **m**-ed to Him   Mt 27:55
they were **m**-ing to the Lord   Ac 13:2

how much he **m**-ed at Ephesus   2Tm 1:18
stands day after day **m**-ing and   Heb 10:11

MINISTERING (adj)
Are they not all **m** spirits sent   Heb 1:14

MINISTRY
garments for **m** in the sanctuary   Ex 39:1
in the **m** of God's temple   1Ch 9:13
As He began {His **m**}, Jesus was   Lk 3:23
prayer and to the preaching **m**.   Ac 6:4
have a fruitful **m** among you,   Rm 1:13
are different **m**-ies, but the same   1Co 12:5
Now if the **m** of death, chiseled   2Co 3:7
since we have this **m**, as we have   2Co 4:1
gave us the **m** of reconciliation,   2Co 5:18
sharing in the **m** to the saints,   2Co 8:4
of the area {of **m**} that God has   2Co 10:13
of the saints in the work of **m**   Eph 4:12
was lacking in your **m** to me.   Php 2:30
attention to the **m** you have   Col 4:17
appointing me to the **m**   1Tm 1:12
an evangelist, fulfill your **m**.   2Tm 4:5
he is useful to me in the **m**.   2Tm 4:11
has now obtained a superior **m**   Heb 8:6

MINT
pay a tenth of **m**, dill, and cumin,   Mt 23:23

MIRACLE
Perform a **m**, tell Aaron: Ex 7:9
How great are His **m**-s,   Dn 4:3
and do many **m**-s in Your name?   Mt 7:22
For if the **m**-s that were done in   Mt 11:21
did not do many **m**-s there because Mt 13:58
was not able to do any **m**-s there,   Mk 6:5
will perform a **m** in My name who   Mk 9:39
to see some **m** performed by Him.   Lk 23:8
pointed out to you by God with **m**-s, Ac 2:22
extraordinary **m**-s by Paul's hands   Ac 19:11
to another, the performing of **m**-s,   1Co 12:10
Are all teachers? Do all do **m**-s?   1Co 12:29
signs but also wonders and **m**-s.   2Co 12:12
the Spirit and work **m**-s among you   Gl 3:5
with all kinds of false **m**-s, signs,   2Th 2:9
testified by signs ... various **m**-s,   Heb 2:4

MIRACULOUS
so that I may do these **m** signs   Ex 10:1
and gave him a **m** sign.   2Ch 32:24
performed His **m** signs in Egypt   Ps 78:43

performed His **m** signs among Ps 105:27
by the power of **m** signs and Rm 15:19

MIRIAM

1. Sister of Moses and Aaron; daughter of Jochabed and Amram (Nm 26:59; 1Ch 6:3). Watched over baby Moses (Ex 2:4-8). Prophetess; led dancing at Red Sea (15:20-21). Struck with skin disease for criticizing Moses (Nm 12; Dt 24:9); died in Kadesh (Nm 20:1).

MIRROR

{bronze} **m**-s of the women who Ex 38:8
as hard as a cast metal **m**? Jb 37:18
as in a **m**, but then face to face. 1Co 13:12
looking at his own face in a **m**; Jms 1:23

MIRY

Rescue me from the **m** mud; Ps 69:14

MISCARRY

and female goats have not **m**-ied Gn 31:38
No woman will **m** or be barren in Ex 23:26
I not hidden like a **m**-ied child, Jb 3:16
like a woman's **m**-ied {child}, they Ps 58:8
a womb that **m**-ies and breasts that Hs 9:14

MISERABLE

You are all **m** comforters. Jb 16:2
days of the oppressed are **m** Pr 15:15
this **m** task to keep them occupied. Ec 1:13
Be **m** and mourn and weep. Jms 4:9

MISERY

I have observed the **m** of My people Ex 3:7
He became weary of Israel's **m**. Jdg 10:16
What **m** that I have stayed in Ps 120:5
but the wicked are full of **m**. Pr 12:21
LORD has added **m** to my pain! Jr 45:3
gloat over their **m** in the day of Ob 13
wail over the **m**-ies that are coming Jms 5:1

MISFORTUNE

to the wicked and **m** to evildoers? Jb 31:3
who rejoice at my **m** be disgraced Ps 35:26
You caused ... troubles and **m**-s, Ps 71:20
my enemies have heard of my **m**; Lm 1:21

MISHAEL

1. Cousin of Moses who helped bury Nadab and Abihu (Ex 6:22; Lv 10:4).

2. One who stood with Ezra (Neh 8:4).
3. Meshach's original name (Dn 1:7).

MISLEAD

Isn't Hezekiah **m**-ing you to give 2Ch 32:11
My people, your leaders **m** you; Is 3:12
and **m**-led a considerable number Ac 19:26

MISMATCHED

Do not be **m** with unbelievers. 2Co 6:14

MISS

a stone at a hair and not **m**. Jdg 20:16
you'll be **m**-ed because your seat 1Sm 20:18
a twin, and not one **m**-ing. Sg 4:2; 6:6
nor will any be **m**-ing. Jr 23:4
how I deeply **m** all of you with Php 1:8
that none of you should **m** it. Heb 4:1

MISSION

If you don't report our **m** Jos 2:14
I went on the **m** the LORD gave 1Sm 15:20
king gave me a **m**, but he told me 1Sm 21:2
and he will succeed in his **m**. Is 48:15
had completed their relief **m** Ac 12:25

MIST

lying tongue is a vanishing **m** Pr 21:6
cloud, and your sins like a **m**. Is 44:22
Your loyalty is like the morning **m** Hs 6:4
will be like the morning **m** Hs 13:3
Suddenly a **m** and darkness fell Ac 13:11
m-s driven by a whirlwind. 2Pt 2:17

MISTAKE

thought it was a **m** and took his Gn 48:17
sinned, my **m** concerns only me. Jb 19:4
do not say ... that it was a **m**. Ec 5:6

MISTREAT

Then Sarai **m**-ed her so much that Gn 16:6
If you **m** my daughters or take Gn 31:50
You must not **m** any widow or Ex 22:22
But the Egyptians **m**-ed Dt 26:6
Whom have I wronged or **m**-ed? 1Sm 12:3
and you **m** me without shame. Jb 19:3
pray for those who **m** you. Lk 6:28
he saw one of them being **m**-ed Ac 7:24
Remember ... the **m**-ed, as though Heb 13:3

MISTRESS

she looked down on her **m**. Gn 16:4
girl's eyes on her **m**-'s hand, Ps 123:2

servant and **m**, buyer and seller	Is 24:2
no longer be called **m** of kingdoms.	Is 47:5
the attractive **m** of sorcery,	Nah 3:4

MISUSE

Do not **m** the name of the LORD	Ex 20:7
Do not **m** the name of the LORD	Dt 5:11

MIX

holy people has become **m-ed** with	Ezr 9:2
separated all those of **m-ed** descent	Neh 13:3
she has **m-ed** her wine;	Pr 9:2
it never lacks **m-ed** wine.	Sg 7:2
who are fearless at **m-ing** beer,	Is 5:22
The LORD has **m-ed** within her a	Is 19:14
You saw the iron **m-ed** with clay,	Dn 2:41
to get **m-ed** up with the nations.	Hs 7:8
and **m-ed** into 50 pounds of flour	Mt 13:33
gave Him wine **m-ed** with gall	Mt 27:34
m-ed full strength in the cup	Rv 14:10
cup in which she **m-ed**, **m** a double	Rv 18:6

MIXTURE

it spread through the entire **m**.	Lk 13:21

MIZPAH or MIZPEH

1. City in Gilead (Gn 31:22-55).
2. City in Moab (Jdg 20:1; 1Sm 7:5; 22:3-5; 2Kg 25:23; Neh 3:15; Jr 40:6).
3. City in Benjamin (Jos 18:26).

MOAB

1. Son of Lot (Gn 19:37).
2. Country east of the Dead Sea (Nm 21:11,13; Dt 1:5; Ru 1:1; 2Kg 3:5; Ps 60:8; Is 15:1; Jr 48:1; Ezk 25:11; Am 2:1; Zph 2:8).

MOABITE

the father of the M-s of today.	Gn 19:37
So the M-s said to the elders of	Nm 22:4
No Ammonite or M may enter the	Dt 23:3
Her sons took M women as their	Ru 1:4
no Ammonite or M should ever	Neh 13:1

MOABITESS

her daughter-in-law Ruth the M.	Ru 1:22
will also acquire Ruth the M	Ru 4:5

MOAN

a crane; I **m** like a dove.	Is 38:14
I have heard Ephraim **m-ing**:	Jr 31:18
m like the sound of doves,	Nah 2:7

MOB

from the **m** of evildoers,	Ps 64:2
A large **m**, with swords and clubs	Mt 26:47

MOCK

have **m-ed** me and told me lies!	Jdg 16:10
At noon Elijah **m-ed** them.	1Kg 18:27
Assyria sent to **m** the living God	2Kg 19:4
When I stand up, they **m** me.	Jb 19:18
Everyone who sees me **m-s** me;	Ps 22:7
God, how long will the foe **m**?	Ps 74:10
He **m-s** those who **m**, but gives grace	Pr 3:34
if you **m**, you alone will bear	Pr 9:12
Fools **m** at making restitution,	Pr 14:9
The one who **m-s** the poor insults	Pr 17:5
A worthless witness **m-s** justice,	Pr 19:28
look, I am **m-ed** by their songs.	Lm 3:63
over to the Gentiles to be **m-ed**	Mt 20:19
down before Him and **m-ed** Him:	Mt 27:29
and elders, **m-ed** Him and said,	Mt 27:41
The soldiers also **m-ed** Him.	Lk 23:36
God is not **m-ed**. For whatever a man	Gl 6:7
others experienced **m-ings** and	Heb 11:36

MOCKER

Surely **m-s** surround me and my	Jb 17:2
or join a group of **m-s**!	Ps 1:1
How long will {you} **m-s** enjoy	Pr 1:22
one who corrects a **m** will bring	Pr 9:7
Don't rebuke a **m**, or he will	Pr 9:8
but a **m** doesn't listen to rebuke	Pr 13:1
A **m** doesn't love one who	Pr 15:12
Judgments are prepared for **m-s**,	Pr 19:29
Wine is a **m**, beer is a brawler	Pr 20:1
When a **m** is punished, the	Pr 21:11
person, named "M," acts with	Pr 21:24
Drive out a **m**, and conflict goes	Pr 22:10
and a **m** is detestable to people	Pr 24:9
M-s inflame a city, but the wise	Pr 29:8
you **m-s** who rule this people in	Is 28:14

MOCKERY

a source of **m** and ridicule to	Ps 44:13
plunder and a **m** to the rest	Ezk 36:4
with **m** and riddles about him?	Hab 2:6

MODEL

according to the **m** ... you have been shown on the mountain.	Ex 25:40
King Ahaz sent a **m** of the altar	2Kg 16:10
hands (only a **m** of the true one)	Heb 9:24

MODEST

dress themselves in **m** clothing, 1Tm 2:9

MOLECH

God of the Ammonites (Lv 18:21; 20:2-5; 2Kg 23:10; Jr 32:35).

MOLES

to the **m** and the bats. Is 2:20

MOMENT

for a brief **m**, grace has come Ezr 9:8
godless has lasted only a **m**? Jb 20:5
His anger may ignite at any **m**. Ps 2:12
For His anger lasts only a **m**, Ps 30:5
but a lying tongue, only a **m**. Pr 12:19
I deserted you for a brief **m** Is 54:7
At one **m** I might announce Jr 18:7
servant was cured that very **m**. Mt 8:13
was made well from that **m**. Mt 9:22
And from that **m** her daughter Mt 15:28
and from that **m** the boy was Mt 17:18
At that very **m**, three men who Ac 11:11
at the appointed **m**, Christ died for Rm 5:6
in a **m**, in the twinkling of an eye, 1Co 15:52

MOMENTARY

For our **m** light affliction is 2Co 4:17

MONEY

return each man's **m** to his sack, Gn 42:25
you must not sell her for **m** or Dt 21:14
All the dedicated **m** brought to 2Kg 12:4
loves **m** is never satisfied with **m** Ec 5:10
and **m** is the answer for everything. Ec 10:19
you without **m**, come, buy, and eat! Is 55:1
Why do you spend **m** on what is not Is 55:2
cannot be slaves of God and of **m**. Mt 6:24
overturned the **m** changers' Mt 21:12
ground, and hid his master's **m**. Mt 25:18
treasury, since it is blood **m**. Mt 27:6
the soldiers a large sum of **m** Mt 28:12
no traveling bag, no bread, no **m**; Lk 9:3
make friends ... by ... unrighteous **m** Lk 16:9
were lovers of **m**, were listening Lk 16:14
poured out the **m** changers' coins Jn 2:15
brought the **m**, and laid it at Ac 4:37
God could be obtained with **m**! Ac 8:20
for a large amount of **m**. Ac 22:28
a lot of wine, not greedy for **m**. 1Tm 3:8
For the love of **m** is a root of 1Tm 6:10

will be lovers of self, lovers of **m**, 2Tm 3:2
not a bully, not greedy for **m**, Ti 1:7
be free from the love of **m**. Heb 13:5
not for the **m** but eagerly; 1Pt 5:2

MONEY-BAG

Don't carry a **m**, traveling bag Lk 10:4
Make **m-s** for yourselves that won't Lk 12:33
When I sent you out without **m** Lk 22:35
charge of the **m** and would steal Jn 12:6
Since Judas kept the **m**, some Jn 13:29

MONSTER

or a sea **m**, that You keep me under Jb 7:12
of the sea **m-s** in the waters; Ps 74:13
all sea **m-s** and ocean depths, Ps 148:7
He will slay the **m** that is in Is 27:1
pieces, who pierced the sea **m**? Is 51:9
has swallowed me like a sea **m**; Jr 51:34
you are like a **m** in the seas. Ezk 32:2

MONTH

she hid him for three **m-s**. Ex 2:2
it is the first **m** of your year. Ex 12:2
Each **m** they will bear fresh fruit Ezk 47:12
In the sixth **m**, the angel Lk 1:26
is the sixth **m** for her who was Lk 1:36
There are still four more **m-s** Jn 4:35
You observe {special} days, **m-s**, Gl 4:10
by his parents for three **m-s** Heb 11:23
to torment {them} for five **m-s**; Rv 9:5
authority to act for 42 **m-s**. Rv 13:5
producing its fruit every **m**. Rv 22:2

MONTHLY

I am having my **m** period. Gn 31:35
This is the **m** burnt offering for Nm 28:14

MONUMENT

he set up a **m** for himself. 1Sm 15:12
called Absalom's **M** today 2Sm 18:18
You build **m-s** to the prophets Lk 11:47

MOOD

was in a good **m** and very drunk, 1Sm 25:36
is in a good **m** from the wine. 2Sm 13:28

MOON

this time the sun, **m**, and 11 stars Gn 37:9
bow down to the sun, **m**, or all the Dt 17:3
sun stood still and the **m** stopped, Jos 10:13
is the New **M**, and I'm supposed 1Sm 20:5
It's neither New **M** or Sabbath. 2Kg 4:23

to the sun, **m**, constellations 2Kg 23:5
Sabbaths, New **M-s**, and the three 2Ch 8:13
the **m** and the stars, which You set Ps 8:3
abound until the **m** is no more. Ps 72:7
established the **m** and the sun. Ps 74:16
like the **m**, established forever Ps 89:37
He made the **m** to mark the Ps 104:19
you by day, or the **m** by night. Ps 121:6
the **m** and stars to rule by night Ps 136:9
Praise Him, sun and **m**; Ps 148:3
beautiful as the **m**, bright as Sg 6:10
hate your New **M-s** and prescribed Is 1:14
The **m** will be put to shame and Is 24:23
fixed order of **m** and stars for Jr 31:35
and the **m** will not give its Ezk 32:7
The sun and **m** grow dark, and the Jl 2:10
the **m** to blood before the great Jl 2:31
The sun and **m** will grow dark, Jl 3:15
will the New **M** be over so we may Am 8:5
Sun and **m** stand still in Hab 3:11
and the **m** will not shed its light; Mt 24:29
signs in the sun, **m**, and stars; Lk 21:25
the **m** to blood, before the great Ac 2:20
another of the **m**, and another 1Co 15:41
or a new **m** or a sabbath day Col 2:16
the entire **m** became like blood; Rv 6:12
a third of the **m**, and a third Rv 8:12
with the **m** under her feet, Rv 12:1
the sun or the **m** to shine on it Rv 21:23

MOONLIGHT

sunlight and **m** will diminish. Zch 14:6

MORAL

as slaves to **m** impurity, Rm 6:19
sexual immorality, **m** impurity Gl 5:19
if there is any **m** excellence and Php 4:8
of all **m** filth and evil Jms 1:21

MORALS

Bad company corrupts good **m**. 1Co 15:33

MORDECAI

1. Cousin and legal guardian of Esther (Est 2:7). Uncovered assassination plot (2:21-23). Offended Haman (3:1-7); Haman sought genocide (3:7-15); Mordecai led Esther to thwart the attempt (Est 4–5). Honored by the king (Est 6); wrote revenge edict (Est 8).

2. Man who returned with Zerubbabel (Ezr 2:2; Neh 7:7).

MORE

of Job's life **m** than the earlier Jb 42:12
They are **m** desirable than gold Ps 19:10
and the wicked will be no **m**; Ps 37:10
and will praise You **m** and **m**. Ps 71:14
abound until the moon is no **m**. Ps 72:7
I have **m** insight than all my Ps 119:99
commandments **m** than gold, Ps 119:127
m than watchmen for the morning Ps 130:6
because they were no **m**. Mt 2:18
be 'no' Anything **m** than this is Mt 5:37
Isn't life **m** than food and the Mt 6:25
you are worth **m** than many Mt 10:31
whoever has, {**m**} will be given Mt 13:12
they assumed they would get **m** Mt 20:10
who has, **m** will be given Mt 25:29
Do not sin any **m**, so that Jn 5:14
from now on do not sin any **m**. Jn 8:11
that it will produce **m** fruit. Jn 15:2
do you love Me **m** than these? Jn 21:15
grace multiplied even **m** Rm 5:20
things we are **m** than victorious Rm 8:37
how much **m** will their full Rm 11:12
all, in order to win **m** people. 1Co 9:19
languages **m** than all of you 1Co 14:18
m labors, many **m** imprisonments 2Co 11:23
If I love you, am I to be 2Co 12:15
with a desire for **m** and **m**. Eph 4:19
in the flesh, I have **m**: Php 3:4
you are doing—do so even **m**. 1Th 4:1
as a slave, but **m** than a slave Phm 16
you will do even **m** than I say. Phm 21
and all the **m** as you see the day Heb 10:25
"Yet once **m**," indicates Heb 12:27
are still two **m** woes to come Rv 9:12

MORIAH

Where Abraham offered Isaac (Gn 22:2); where the temple was built (2Ch 3:1; see 2Sm 24:18).

MORNING

came, and then **m**: the first day. Gn 1:5
Do not let any of it remain until **m**; Ex 12:10
In the **m** there was a layer of Ex 16:13
m you will say, 'If only it were Dt 28:67
the **m** stars sang together Jb 38:7

but there is joy in the **m**.	Ps 30:5
Your faithful love in the **m**.	Ps 59:16
in the **m** my prayer meets You	Ps 88:13
Satisfy us in the **m** with	Ps 90:14
faithful love in the **m**	Ps 92:2
more than watchmen for the **m**	Ps 130:6
a loud voice early in the **m**	Pr 27:14
Shining **m** star, how you have fallen	Is 14:12
They are new every **m**;	Lm 3:23
He applies His justice **m** by **m**;	Zph 3:5
in the **m**, 'Today will be stormy	Mt 16:3
in the **m** to hire workers	Mt 20:1
rooster or early in the **m**	Mk 13:35
very early in the **m**, on the first day	Mk 16:2
it's only nine in the **m**	Ac 2:15
and the **m** star arises in your hearts.	2Pt 1:19
also give him the **m** star	Rv 2:28
of David, the Bright **M** Star.	Rv 22:16

MORON

'You **m**' will be subject to hellfire.	Mt 5:22

MORTAL

Do not let a mere **m** hinder You.	2Ch 14:11
every **m** man is only a vapor.	Ps 39:5
whose dwelling is not with **m**-s.	Dn 2:11
for images resembling **m** man,	Rm 1:23
let sin reign in your **m** body,	Rm 6:12
also bring your **m** bodies to life	Rm 8:11
and this **m** must be clothed with	1Co 15:53
be revealed in our **m** flesh.	2Co 4:11

MORTALITY

that **m** may be swallowed up	2Co 5:4

MORTALLY

for I'm **m** wounded, but my life	2Sm 1:9

MORTAR

for stone and asphalt for **m**.	Gn 11:3
a fool in a **m** with a pestle	Pr 27:22

MOSES

Leader of Israel; Levite; brother of Aaron and Miriam (1Ch 6:3). Born under Egyptian oppression (Ex 1); set adrift on Nile; rescued and raised by Pharaoh's daughter (2:1-10). Killed Egyptian; fled to Midian and married Zipporah (2:11-22). Called by God from burning bush (Ex 3–4). Announced ten plagues (Ex 7–11).

Divided the Red Sea (Ex 14). Brought water from a rock (17:1-7); held up God's staff and defeated Amalek (17:8-13). Delegated judging (18:13-26).

God spoke to him at Sinai: law (Ex 19–23); tabernacle, equipment, and garments (Ex 25–28; 30); consecration of priests (Ex 29). Discovered golden calf and broke tablets (Ex 32). Saw God's glory (33:12–34:28). Ordained Aaron and his sons (Lv 8–9).

Opposed by Aaron and Miram (Nm 12); opposed by Korah (Nm 16). Excluded from promised land for striking rock (Nm 20:1-13; 27:12-14; Dt 32:51). Made a bronze snake for healing (Nm 21:4-9; Jn 3:14). Wrote the book of the law (Jos 23:6; 2Ch 34:14). Saw promised land from a distance (Dt 3:23-27; 34:1-4); commissioned Joshua as successor (Nm 27:12-23); buried by God (34:5-8).

MOST

serpent was the **m** cunning of all	Gn 3:1
he was a priest to God **M** High.	Gn 14:18
holy place and the **m** holy place.	Ex 26:33
sin offering is **m** holy and must	Lv 6:25
concerns the **m** holy objects.	Nm 4:4
consecrate the **m** holy things,	1Ch 23:13
Then he made the **m** holy place;	2Ch 3:8
man who feared God more than **m**.	Neh 7:2
name of the LORD, the **M** High.	Ps 7:17
I call to God **M** High, to God who	Ps 57:2
you are all sons of the **M** High.	Ps 82:6
protection of the **M** High dwells	Ps 91:1
m beautiful of women	Sg 1:8; 5:9; 6:1
make myself like the **M** High.	Is 14:14
servants of the **M** High God	Dn 3:26
that the **M** High is ruler over	Dn 4:25
of the holy ones of the **M** High,	Dn 7:22
Jesus, Son of the **M** High God?	Mk 5:7
is the **m** important of all?	Mk 12:28
called the Son of the **M** High,	Lk 1:32
the power of the **M** High will	Lk 1:35
You are the **m** blessed of women,	Lk 1:42
you will be sons of the **M** High.	Lk 6:35
the slaves of the **M** High God,	Ac 16:17
on to you as **m** important what I	1Co 15:3
making the **m** of the time	Eph 5:16; Col 4:5

priest of the **M** High God, who   Heb 7:1
up in your **m** holy faith   Jd 20

MOST HIGH

he was a priest to God **M.**   Gn 14:18
has knowledge from the **M,**   Nm 24:16
When the **M** gave the nations   Dt 32:8
name of the LORD, the **M.**   Ps 7:17
the **M** projected His voice.   Ps 18:13
dwelling place of the **M.**   Ps 46:4
pay your vows to the **M.**   Ps 50:14
I call to God **M,** to God who   Ps 57:2
rock, the **M** God, their   Ps 78:35
you are all sons of the **M.**   Ps 82:6
under the protection of the **M**   Ps 91:1
despised the counsel of the **M.**   Ps 107:11
I will make myself like the **M.**   Is 14:14
come from the mouth of the **M?**   Lm 3:38
know that the **M** is ruler over   Dn 4:17
holy ones of the **M** will receive   Dn 7:18
Jesus, Son of the **M** God?   Mk 5:7
called the Son of the **M,**   Lk 1:32
the **M** does not dwell in sanctuaries   Ac 7:48
the slaves of the **M** God,   Ac 16:17
of Salem, priest of the **M** God,   Heb 7:1

MOTH

dust, who are crushed like a **m!**   Jb 4:19
like a **m** what is precious   Ps 39:11
a garment; a **m** will devour them   Is 50:9
where **m** and rust destroy and   Mt 6:19

MOTH-EATEN

rotten, like a **m** garment.   Jb 13:28
your clothes are **m;**   Jms 5:2

MOTHER

a man leaves his father and **m**   Gn 2:24
she was the **m** of all the living   Gn 3:20
Honor your father and your **m** so   Ex 20:12
If anyone curses his father or **m**   Lv 20:9
Deborah, I arose, a **m** in Israel.   Jdg 5:7
Each year his **m** made him a   1Sm 2:19
a city that is like a **m** in Israel.   2Sm 20:19
Naked I came from my **m-'s** womb,   Jb 1:21
the joyful **m** of children.   Ps 113:9
little weaned child with its **m;**   Ps 131:2
knit me together in my
   m-'s womb.   Ps 139:13
don't reject your **m-'s** teaching,   Pr 1:8

son, heartache to his **m.**   Pr 10:1
Let your father and **m** have joy,   Pr 23:25
oracle that his **m** taught him: Pr 31:1
she is the favorite of her **m**   Sg 6:9
house of my **m** who taught me.   Sg 8:2
As a **m** comforts her son, so I   Is 66:13
my **m** might have been my grave,   Jr 20:17
Amorite and your **m** a Hittite.   Ezk 16:3
Like **m,** like daughter.   Ezk 16:44
saw the child with Mary His **m**   Mt 2:11
a daughter against her **m,**   Mt 10:35
father or **m** more than Me is   Mt 10:37
suddenly His **m** and brothers were   Mt 12:46
Who is My **m** and who are My   Mt 12:48
Isn't His **m** called Mary, and His   Mt 13:55
Honor your father and your **m;**   Mt 15:4
leave his father and **m** and be joined   Mt 19:5
sisters, father or **m,** children,   Mt 19:29
Then the **m** of Zebedee's sons   Mt 20:20
while still in his **m-'s** womb.   Lk 1:15
that the **m** of my Lord should   Lk 1:43
His father and **m** were amazed at   Lk 2:33
His **m** kept all these things in   Lk 2:51
He was his **m-'s** only son, and she   Lk 7:12
against father, **m** against daughter,   Lk 12:53
not hate his own father and **m**   Lk 14:26
Jesus' **m** told Him, "They don't have   Jn 2:3
he enter his **m-'s** womb a second   Jn 3:4
whose father and **m** we know?   Jn 6:42
the cross of Jesus were His **m**   Jn 19:25
to the disciple, "Here is your **m.**"   Jn 19:27
also his **m**—and mine.   Rm 16:13
is free, and she is our **m.**   Gl 4:26
leave his father and **m** and be   Eph 5:31
your father and **m**—which is the   Eph 6:2
as a nursing **m** nurtures her own   1Th 2:7
older women as **m-s,** and with all   1Tm 5:2
then in your **m** Eunice, and that   2Tm 1:5
without father, **m,** or genealogy   Heb 7:3
THE **M** OF PROSTITUTES   Rv 17:5

MOTHER-IN-LAW

a daughter-in-law is against her **m;**   Mc 7:6
a daughter-in-law against her **m;**   Mt 10:35
Simon's **m** was suffering from   Lk 4:38

MOTIVES

but the LORD weighs the **m.**   Pr 16:2
whether out of false **m** or   Php 1:18

MOUND

This **m** is a witness between me   Gn 31:48
must remain a **m** of ruins forever   Dt 13:16
stood on their **m**-s except Hazor,   Jos 11:13
piled a huge **m** of stones over   2Sm 18:17
Your waist is a **m** of wheat   Sg 7:2
city will be rebuilt on its **m**;   Jr 30:18

MOUNT (n) *see also* CARMEL, EBAL,
         GERAZIM, GILBOA, GILEAD,
         HERMON, HOR, HOREB,
         MORIAH, NEBO,
         MOUNT OF OLIVES, SEIR, SINAI,
         SION, ZION

The LORD came down on M Sinai,   Ex 19:20
the blessing at M Gerizim and   Dt 11:29
south of the M of Destruction,   2Kg 23:13
Abijah stood on M Zemaraim,   2Ch 13:4
peaks of Hermon, from M Mizar.   Ps 42:6
M Zion on the slopes of the north is   Ps 48:2
M Bashan is God's towering   Ps 68:15
{Remember} M Zion where You   Ps 74:2
M Zion, which He loved.   Ps 78:68
trust in the LORD are like M Zion.   Ps 125:1
head crowns you like M Carmel,   Sg 7:5
on the **m** of the {gods'} assembly,   Is 14:13
and the temple **m** a forested hill.   Jr 26:18
the temple **m** will be a thicket.   Mc 3:12
LORD will rule over them in M Zion   Mc 4:7
the Holy One from M Paran.   Hab 3:3
The M of Olives will be split in   Zch 14:4
was sitting on the M of Olives,   Mt 24:3
they went out to the M of Olives.   Mt 26:30
from the **m** called Olive Grove   Ac 1:12
Now Hagar is M Sinai in Arabia   Gl 4:25
you have come to M Zion, to the   Heb 12:22
and there on M Zion stood the   Rv 14:1

MOUNT (v)

Rebekah ... **m**-ed the camels,   Gn 24:61
snake and **m**-ed it on a pole.   Nm 21:9
Harness the horses; **m** the steeds;   Jr 46:4
gentle, and **m**-ed on a donkey,   Mt 21:5

MOUNT OF OLIVES

David was climbing ... the M,   2Sm 15:30
day His feet will stand on the M,   Zch 14:4
The M will be split in half   Zch 14:4
came to Bethphage at the M,   Mt 21:1
While He was sitting on the M,   Mt 24:3
psalms, they went out to the M.   Mt 26:30

came near the path down the M,   Lk 19:37
made His way as usual to the M,   Lk 22:39
But Jesus went to the M.   Jn 8:1

MOUNTAIN

m-s were covered as the waters   Gn 7:20
will be provided on the LORD's **m**.   Gn 22:14
came to Horeb, the **m** of God.   Ex 3:1
who touches the **m** will be put to   Ex 19:12
I stayed on the **m** 40 days and 40   Dt 10:10
nights to Horeb, the **m** of God.   1Kg 19:8
a god of the **m**-s and not a god   1Kg 20:28
He removes **m**-s without their   Jb 9:5
But as a **m** collapses and   Jb 14:18
My King on Zion, My holy **m**.   Ps 2:6
He answers me from His holy **m**.   Ps 3:4
Who can live on Your holy **m**?   Ps 15:1
my God, my **m** where I seek refuge   Ps 18:2
may ascend the **m** of the LORD?   Ps 24:3
and the **m**-s topple into the depths   Ps 46:2
May the **m**-s bring prosperity to   Ps 72:3
Before the **m**-s were born, before   Ps 90:2
The **m**-s melt like wax at the   Ps 97:5
The **m**-s skipped like rams, the   Ps 114:4
I raise my eyes toward the **m**-s.   Ps 121:1
Jerusalem—the **m**-s surround her   Ps 125:2
make my way to the **m** of myrrh   Sg 4:6
young stag on the **m**-s of spices   Sg 8:14
last days the **m** of the LORD's house   Is 2:2
let us go up to the **m** of the LORD,   Is 2:3
every **m** and hill will be leveled;   Is 40:4
beautiful on the **m**-s are the feet   Is 52:7
Though the **m**-s move and the   Is 54:10
m-s and the hills will break into   Is 55:12
m-s would quake at Your presence   Is 64:1
or destroy on My entire holy **m**   Is 65:25
prophesy to the **m**-s of Israel   Ezk 36:1
The **m**-s will be thrown down,   Ezk 38:20
became a great **m** and filled the   Dn 2:35
will say to the **m**-s, "Cover us!"   Hs 10:8
sound the alarm on My holy **m**!   Jl 2:1
who forms the **m**-s, creates the   Am 4:13
as you have drunk on My holy **m**   Ob 16
The **m**-s will melt beneath Him,   Mc 1:4
last days the **m** of the LORD's house   Mc 4:1
let us go up to the **m** of the LORD,   Mc 4:2
m-s quake before Him,   Nah 1:5
Look to the **m**-s—the feet of   Nah 1:15
again be haughty on My holy **m**.   Zph 3:11

the **m** of the LORD of Hosts,	Zch 8:3
so that half the **m** will move to	Zch 14:4
to a very high **m** and showed Him	Mt 4:8
went up on the **m**, and after He	Mt 5:1
When He came down from the **m**	Mt 8:1
up on a high **m** by themselves.	Mt 17:1
will tell this **m**, 'Move from	Mt 17:20
in Judea must flee to the **m-s**!	Mt 24:16
and every **m** and hill will be	Lk 3:5
went out to the **m** to pray and	Lk 6:12
and went up on the **m** to pray.	Lk 9:28
fathers worshiped on this **m**	Jn 4:20
Jesus went up a **m** and sat down	Jn 6:3
again to the **m** by Himself.	Jn 6:15
all faith, so that I can move **m-s**,	1Co 13:2
that was shown to you on the **m**.	Heb 8:5
we were with Him on the holy **m**.	2Pt 1:18
and every **m** and island was moved	Rv 6:14
fled, and the **m-s** disappeared.	Rv 16:20
a great and high **m** and showed me	Rv 21:10

MOUNTAINTOP

and stand before Me on the **m**.	Ex 34:2
let them cry out from the **m-s**.	Is 42:11

MOURN

Israel **m-ed** for him 30 days	Nm 20:29
And David **m-ed** for his son	2Sm 13:37
He's **m-ing** over Absalom.	2Sm 19:1
Do not **m** or weep." For all	Neh 8:9
grief, like one **m-ing** a mother.	Ps 35:14
a time to **m** and a time to dance;	Ec 3:4
to a house of **m-ing** than to go	Ec 7:2
The earth **m-s** and withers;	Is 24:4
to comfort all who **m**,	Is 61:2
will **m** for Him as one **m-s** for	Zch 12:10
and great **m-ing**, Rachel weeping	Mt 2:18
Blessed are those who **m**, because	Mt 5:4
sang a lament, but you didn't **m**!	Mt 11:17
peoples of the earth will **m**;	Mt 24:30
laughing now, because you will **m**	Lk 6:25
Be miserable and **m** and weep.	Jms 4:9
of the earth will **m** over Him.	Rv 1:7

MOURNER

eat the bread of **m-s**	Ezk 24:17,22
will be like the bread of **m-s**;	Hs 9:4
and professional **m-s** to wail.	Am 5:16

MOURNING (n)

and their **m** into a holiday.	Est 9:22

day long I go around in **m**.	Ps 38:6
festive oil instead of **m**,	Is 61:3
I will turn their **m** into joy,	Jr 31:13
our dancing has turned to **m**.	Lm 5:15
I will turn your feasts into **m**	Am 8:10
must change to **m** and your joy	Jms 4:9

MOUTH

Who made the human **m**?	Ex 4:11
earth opened its **m** and swallowed	Nm 16:32
the LORD opened the donkey's **m**	Nm 22:28
comes from the **m** of the LORD.	Dt 8:3
I will put My words in his **m**	Dt 18:18
is very near you, in your **m** and in	Dt 30:14
must not depart from your **m**;	Jos 1:8
Your own **m** condemns you, not I;	Jb 15:6
from the **m-s** of children	Ps 8:2
May the words of my **m** and	Ps 19:14
They open their **m-s** against me	Ps 22:13
person who does not open his **m**.	Ps 38:13
He put a new song in my **m**	Ps 40:3
My **m** speaks wisdom;	Ps 49:3
and my **m** will declare Your	Ps 51:15
listen to the words of my **m**.	Ps 54:2
bless with their **m-s**, but they curse	Ps 62:4
my **m** will praise You with joyful	Ps 63:5
Open your **m** wide, and I will	Ps 81:10
with my **m** I will proclaim Your	Ps 89:1
and all injustice shuts its **m**.	Ps 107:42
They have **m-s**, but cannot speak	Ps 115:5
{sweeter} than honey to my **m**.	Ps 119:103
LORD, set up a guard for my **m**;	Ps 141:3
My **m** will declare the LORD's	Ps 145:21
from His **m** come knowledge and	Pr 2:6
by the words of your **m**.	Pr 6:2
but the **m** of the wicked conceals	Pr 10:6
who guards his **m** protects his	Pr 13:3
but the **m** of fools blurts out	Pr 15:2
A wise heart instructs its **m**	Pr 16:23
of a man's **m** are deep waters	Pr 18:4
A fool's **m** is his devastation,	Pr 18:7
avoid someone with a big **m**.	Pr 20:19
The **m** of the forbidden woman is	Pr 22:14
A proverb in the **m** of a fool is	Pr 26:7,9
too weary to bring it to his **m**.	Pr 26:15
and a flattering **m** causes ruin.	Pr 26:28
praise you, and not your own **m**	Pr 27:2
eats and wipes her **m** and says,	Pr 30:20
She opens her **m** with wisdom,	Pr 31:26

Do not let your **m** bring guilt on Ec 5:6
His **m** is sweetness. Sg 5:16
He touched my **m** {with it} and Is 6:7
approach Me with their **m-s** Is 29:13
for the **m** of the LORD has spoken Is 40:5
I have put My words in your **m** Is 51:16
yet He did not open His **m**. Is 53:7
comes from My **m** will not return Is 55:11
For the **m** of the LORD has spoken. Is 58:14
will not depart from your **m** Is 59:21
I have filled your **m** with My words. Jr 1:9
come from the **m** of the Most High Lm 3:38
was as sweet as honey in my **m**. Ezk 3:3
and shut the lions' **m-s**. Dn 6:22
it had a **m** that spoke arrogantly. Dn 7:8
killed them with the words of My **m**. Hs 6:5
that comes from the **m** of God. Mt 4:4
the **m** speaks from the overflow Mt 12:34
It's not what goes into the **m** that Mt 15:11
praise from the **m-s** of children Mt 21:16
so He does not open His **m**. Ac 8:32
that by my **m** the Gentiles would Ac 15:7
so that every **m** may be shut and Rm 3:19
in your **m** and in your heart. Rm 10:8
if you confess with your **m** Rm 10:9
talk should come from your **m** Eph 4:29
filthy language from your **m**. Col 3:8
Out of the same **m** come blessing Jms 3:10
their **m-s** utter arrogant words, Jd 16
going to vomit you out of My **m**. Rv 3:16
was as sweet as honey in my **m** Rv 10:10
A **m** was given to him to speak Rv 13:5
From His **m** came a sharp sword, Rv 19:15

MOVE

pillar of cloud **m-d** from in Ex 14:19
I will never be **m-d** Ps 10:6
these things will never be **m-d**. Ps 15:5
My heart is **m-d** by a noble theme Ps 45:1
and everything that **m-s** in them, Ps 69:34
Don't **m** an ancient property line Pr 22:28
and those who **m** with the flocks Jr 31:24
did not turn as they **m-d**; Ezk 1:9
glory of the LORD **m-d** away Ezk 10:18
like those who **m** boundary Hs 5:10
the mountain will **m** to the north Zch 14:4
'M from here to there' and it will Mt 17:20
M-ed with compassion, Jesus Mt 20:34
to lift a finger to **m** them. Mt 23:4

in His spirit and deeply **m-d**. Jn 11:33
in Him we live and **m** and exist, Ac 17:28
so that I can **m** mountains, 1Co 13:2
instead, I am **m-d** by the Holy Spirit 2Pt 1:21

MUCH

how **m** better it is than gold! Pr 16:16
might have too **m** and deny You, Pr 30:9
For with **m** wisdom is **m** sorrow; Ec 1:18
and **m** study wearies the body. Ec 12:12
You have planted **m** but harvested Hg 1:6
that's why she loved **m**. Lk 7:47
M will be required of everyone
  who has been given **m**. Lk 12:48
little is also faithful in **m** Lk 16:10
and I in him produces **m** fruit, Jn 15:5
gathered **m** did not have too **m**, 2Co 8:15

MUCK

its waters churn up mire and **m**. Is 57:20

MUD

Rescue me from the miry **m**; Ps 69:14
and Jeremiah sank in the **m**. Jr 38:6
made some **m** from the saliva, Jn 9:6
and a sow ... wallows in the **m**. 2Pt 2:22

MUDDY (adj)

out of the **m** clay, and set my feet Ps 40:2

MUDDY (v)

Must you also **m** the rest with Ezk 34:18

MULBERRY

you can say to this **m** tree, Lk 17:6

MULE

and each fled on his **m**. 2Sm 13:29
m went under the tangled
  branches 2Sm 18:9
Solomon ride on King David's **m** 1Kg 1:38
Do not be like a horse or **m** Ps 32:9

MULTI-FACETED

so that God's **m** wisdom may now Eph 3:10

MULTIPLY

Be fruitful, **m**, fill the earth, Gn 1:28
But you, be fruitful and **m**; Gn 9:7
I will greatly **m** your offspring Gn 16:10
and I will **m** you greatly. Gn 17:2
fruitful, increased rapidly, **m-ied**, Ex 1:7
you may prosper and **m** greatly, Dt 6:3
and your silver and gold **m**, Dt 8:13

The sorrows ... m;   Ps 16:4
it through labor will m it.   Pr 13:11
the ones who consume them m;   Ec 5:11
Yet the fool m-ies words.   Ec 10:14
our transgressions have m-ied   Is 59:12
I will m them in number like a   Ezk 36:37
The more they m-ied, the more they   Hs 4:7
Because lawlessness will m   Mt 24:12
in Jerusalem m-ied greatly,   Ac 6:7
message flourished and m-ied.   Ac 12:24
where sin m-ied, grace m-ied   Rm 5:20
sin in order that grace may m?   Rm 6:1
will provide and m your seed   2Co 9:10
grace and peace be m-ied to you.   1Pt 1:2
and peace be m-ied to you through   2Pt 1:2
peace, and love be m-ied to you.   Jd 2

MULTITUDE

A vast m from beyond the Dead   2Ch 20:2
The m of your foes will be like   Is 29:5
great m, but the m will be handed   Dn 11:11
M-s, m-s in the valley of decision!   Jl 3:14
there was a m of the heavenly   Lk 2:13
A great m of the people followed   Lk 23:27
Now the m of those who believed   Ac 4:32
and cover a m of sins.   Jms 5:20
since love covers a m of sins.   1Pt 4:8
there was a vast m from every   Rv 7:9
are peoples, m-s, nations, and   Rv 17:15
voice of a vast m in heaven,   Rv 19:1

MURDER

Do not m.   Ex 20:13; Dt 5:17
m-ed them (in a time) of peace   1Kg 2:5
foreigner and m the fatherless.   Ps 94:6
and they hurry to commit m.   Pr 1:16
Do you steal, m, commit   Jr 7:9
Cursing, lying, m, stealing, and   Hs 4:2
Do not m, and whoever m-s will   Mt 5:21
evil thoughts, m-s, adulteries,   Mt 15:19
Jesus answered, Do not m;   Mt 19:18
of those who m-ed the prophets.   Mt 23:31
who had committed m during the   Mk 15:7
whom you had m-ed by hanging   Ac 5:30
breathing threats and m against   Ac 9:1
full of envy, m, disputes   Rm 1:29
you shall not m, you shall not   Rm 13:9
adultery, also said, Do not m.   Jms 2:11
You m and covet and cannot   Jms 4:2

evil one and m-ed his brother   1Jn 3:12
they did not repent of their m-s   Rv 9:21

MURDERER

the m must be put to death.   Nm 35:16
dwelt in her—but now, m-s   Is 1:21
He was a m from the beginning   Jn 8:44
asked to have a m given to   Ac 3:14
This man is probably a m   Ac 28:4
fathers and mothers, for m-s   1Tm 1:9
should suffer as a m, a thief   1Pt 4:15
who hates his brother is a m   1Jn 3:15
no m has eternal life   1Jn 3:15
vile, m-s, sexually immoral   Rv 21:8

MURMUR

He stilled the storm to a m   Ps 107:29

MUSED

as I m, a fire burned.   Ps 39:3

MUSIC

In charge of the m in the LORD's   1Ch 6:31
were to lead the m with lyres   1Ch 15:21
and skillful in m for the LORD,   1Ch 25:7
sing and make m to the LORD.   Ps 27:6
make m to Him with a   Ps 33:2
At night I remember my m;   Ps 77:6
harp and the m of a lyre.   Ps 92:3
and make m to Him with   Ps 149:3
walks (to the m) of a flute,   Is 30:29
every kind of m, you are to fall   Dn 3:5
not listen to the m of your harps.   Am 5:23
house, he heard m and dancing.   Lk 15:25
singing and making m to the Lord   Eph 5:19

MUSICAL

accompanied by m instruments   1Ch 15:16
play and m instruments of God   1Ch 16:42
the m instruments of the LORD,   2Ch 7:6
singers with m instruments   2Ch 23:13
the m instruments of David   Neh 12:36
their own m instruments like David.   Am 6:5

MUSICIAN

While the m played, the LORD's   2Kg 3:15
lead the way, with m-s following   Ps 68:25
sound of harpists, m-s, flutists   Rv 18:22

MUST

say that Elijah m come first?   Mt 17:10
For offenses m come, but woe to   Mt 18:7
And the good news m first be   Mk 13:10

you that you **m** be born again. Jn 3:7
people by which we **m** be saved. Ac 4:12
We **m** obey God rather than men. Ac 5:29
near to Him **m** believe that He Heb 11:6
show you what **m** take place after Rv 4:1
he **m** be released for a short Rv 20:3

MUSTACHE
do not cover {your} **m** or eat Ezk 24:17

MUSTARD
is like a **m** seed that a man Mt 13:31
faith the size of a **m** seed, Mt 17:20
It's like a **m** seed that, when Mk 4:31
It's like a **m** seed that a man Lk 13:19
have faith the size of a **m** seed, Lk 17:6

MUTE
Who makes him **m** or deaf, seeing Ex 4:11
tongue of the **m** will sing for Is 35:6
all of them are **m** dogs, Is 56:10
and you will be **m** and unable to Ezk 3:26
will speak and no longer be **m**. Ezk 24:27
opened and I was no longer **m**. Ezk 33:22
You **m** and deaf spirit, I command Mk 9:25
the man who had been **m**, spoke Lk 11:14

MUTILATE
watch out for those who **m** the flesh. Php 3:2

MUTTER
the spiritists who chirp and **m** Is 8:19
Pharisees heard the crowd **m-ing** Jn 7:32

MUTUALLY
to be **m** encouraged by each Rm 1:12

MUZZLE
Do not **m** an ox while it treads Dt 25:4
my mouth with a **m** as long as the Ps 39:1
Do not **m** an ox while it treads 1Co 9:9
You must not **m** an ox that is 1Tm 5:18

MYRIADS
to **m** of angels in festive Heb 12:22

MYRRH
and a half pounds of liquid **m** Ex 30:23
with oil of **m** for six months Est 2:12
M, and cassia {perfume Ps 45:8
I've perfumed my bed with **m** Pr 7:17
the mountain of **m** and the hill Sg 4:6
frankincense, **m** and aloes, with Sg 4:14
My hands dripped with **m**, my fingers Sg 5:5

gold, frankincense, and **m**. Mt 2:11
to give Him wine mixed with **m** Mk 15:23
about 75 pounds of **m** and aloes. Jn 19:39
spice, incense, **m**, and Rv 18:13

MYRTLE
olive, wild olive, **m**, palm, and Neh 8:15
acacias, **m-s**, and olive trees Is 41:19
of the brier, a **m** will come up; Is 55:13
standing among the **m** trees in Zch 1:8

MYSELF
and said, "By M I have sworn Gn 22:16
Israel might brag: 'I did it **m**' Jdg 7:2
By M I have sworn; Is 45:23
For by M I have sworn"—the Jr 49:13
If I testify about M, My testimony Jn 5:31
Even if I testify about M Jn 8:14
"If I glorify M," Jesus answered Jn 8:54
I will draw all {people} to M. Jn 12:32
come back and receive you to M Jn 14:3
him and will reveal M to him. Jn 14:21

MYSTERIOUS
inner man and the heart are **m**. Ps 64:6

MYSTERY
He reveals **m-ies** from the darkness Jb 12:22
I will speak **m-ies** from the past Ps 78:2
The **m** was then revealed to Daniel Dn 2:19
a God in heaven who reveals **m-ies** Dn 2:28
and that no **m** puzzles you, Dn 4:9
to be unaware of this **m**: Rm 11:25
God's hidden wisdom in a **m** 1Co 2:7
Christ and managers of God's **m-ies**. 1Co 4:1
understand all **m-ies** and all 1Co 13:2
he speaks **m-ies** in the Spirit. 1Co 14:2
I am telling you a **m**: 1Co 15:51
known to us the **m** of His will, Eph 1:9
about the **m** of the Messiah. Eph 3:4
This **m** is profound, but I am Eph 5:32
boldness the **m** of the gospel. Eph 6:19
the **m** hidden for ages and Col 1:26
have the knowledge of God's **m** Col 2:2
to speak the **m** of the Messiah Col 4:3
For the **m** of lawlessness is 2Th 2:7
holding the **m** of the faith with 1Tm 3:9
the **m** of godliness is great: 1Tm 3:16

MYTHS
pay attention to **m** and endless 1Tm 1:4

do with irreverent and silly **m**.　　1Tm 4:7
truth and will turn aside to **m**.　　2Tm 4:4
attention to Jewish **m** and the　　Ti 1:14
contrived **m** when we made known　2Pt 1:16

N

NAAMAN

Aramean commander; cured of skin disease by Elisha (2Kg 5; Lk 4:27).

NABAL

Husband of Abigail; struck dead for refusing to support David (1Sm 25:4-38).

NABOTH

Jezreelite killed by Jezebel for his vineyard (1Kg 21:1-16). Avenged by Jehu (21:17-29; 2Kg 9:21–10:11).

NADAB

1. Priest (Ex 28:1), son of Aaron (Ex 6:23), died for offering unauthorized fire (Lv 10:1-2; Nm 26:60-61).

2. Son of Jeroboam; king of Israel (1Kg 15:25-32).

3. Son of Shammai; Judahite (1Ch 2:28).

4. Son of Jeiel; Benjaminite (1Ch 8:30).

NAGGED

because she had **n** him so　　　Jdg 14:17
Because she **n** him day after　　Jdg 16:16

NAGGING (adj)

share a house with a **n** wife　　　Pr 21:9
with a **n** and hot-tempered　　　Pr 21:19
house shared with a **n** wife　　　Pr 25:24
rainy day and a **n** wife are　　　Pr 27:15

NAGGING (n)

a wife's **n** is an endless　　　Pr 19:13

NAHASH

Ammonite ruler who besieged Jabesh-gilead and was defeated by Saul(1Sm 11:1-11); friendly with David (2Sm 10:2).

NAHOR

1. Abraham's grandfather (Gn 11:22-25; Lk 3:34).

2. Abraham's brother (Gn 11:26-29; 22:20).

3. Mesopotamian hometown of Rebekah (Gn 24:10).

NAHUM

Prophet against Nineveh (Nah 1:1).

NAIL (n)

weight of the **n**-s was 20 ounces　2Ch 3:9
are like firmly embedded **n**-s.　　Ec 12:11
with **n**-s so that it will not fall　Is 41:7
hammer and **n**-s, so it won't totter.　Jr 10:4
finger into the mark of the **n**-s　Jn 20:25

NAIL (v)

people to **n** Him to a cross　　　Ac 2:23
the way by **n**-ing it to the cross　Col 2:14

NAIN

Town where Jesus raised the widow's son (Lk 7:11).

NAIOTH

City in Ramah where David and Samuel stayed (1Sm 19:18–20:1).

NAKED

the man and his wife were **n**　　Gn 2:25
Who told you that you were **n**?　Gn 3:11
saw his father **n** and told his　　Gn 9:22
{and lay} **n** all that day　　　1Sm 19:24
N I came from my mother's womb,　Jb 1:21
Sheol is **n** before God, and　　Jb 26:6
Isaiah has gone **n** and barefoot　Is 20:3
to clothe the **n** when you see him　Is 58:7
you were stark **n** and lying in　Ezk 16:22
and covers the **n** with clothing.　Ezk 18:7
will strip her **n** and expose her　Hs 2:3
will flee **n** on that day　　　Am 2:16
I was **n** and you clothed Me;　Mt 25:36
cloth behind and ran away **n**.　Mk 14:52
we will not be found **n**.　　　2Co 5:3
all things are **n** and exposed to　Heb 4:13
pitiful, poor, blind, and **n**　　Rv 3:17

NAKEDNESS

they covered their father's **n**.　　Gn 9:23
so that your **n** is not exposed on　Ex 20:26
in famine, thirst, **n**, and a lack　Dt 28:48

Your **n** will be uncovered, and	Is 47:3
in order to look at their **n**!	Hab 2:15
or famine or **n** or danger or	Rm 8:35
your shameful **n** not be exposed,	Rv 3:18

NAME (n)

The man gave **n-s** to all the	Gn 2:20
to call on the **n** of the LORD.	Gn 4:26
will make your **n** great,	Gn 12:2
Your **n** will no longer be Abram,	Gn 17:5
Sarai, for Sarah will be her **n**.	Gn 17:15
This is My **n** forever;	Ex 3:15
and to make My **n** known in all	Ex 9:16
Yahweh is His **n**.	Ex 15:3
not misuse the **n** of the LORD	Ex 20:7
not invoke the **n-s** of other gods	Ex 23:13
and proclaimed {His} **n** Yahweh.	Ex 34:5
blasphemes the **N**, he is to be	Lv 24:16
each man's **n** on his staff.	Nm 17:2
not misuse the **n** of the LORD	Dt 5:11
and take {your} oaths in His **n**.	Dt 6:13
the place to have His **n** dwell.	Dt 12:11
so his **n** will not be blotted out	Dt 25:6
you are called by the LORD's **n**	Dt 28:10
this glorious and awesome **n**	Dt 28:58
blot out his **n** under heaven,	Dt 29:20
build a temple for the **n** of the LORD	1Kg 5:3
My people who are called by My **n**	2Ch 7:14
who love Your **n** boast about You	Ps 5:11
magnificent is Your **n** throughout	Ps 8:1
who know Your **n** trust in You	Ps 9:10
I will sing about Your **n**.	Ps 18:49
we take pride in the **n** of the LORD	Ps 20:7
the right paths for His **n-'s** sake	Ps 23:3
the LORD the glory due His **n**;	Ps 29:2
let us exalt His **n** together.	Ps 34:3
Your **n**, God, like Your praise	Ps 48:10
They will sing praise to Your **n**.	Ps 66:4
on the clouds—His **n** is Yahweh	Ps 68:4
the dwelling place of Your **n**.	Ps 74:7
people has insulted Your **n**.	Ps 74:18
poor and needy praise Your **n**.	Ps 74:21
and we will call on Your **n**.	Ps 80:18
alone—whose **n** is Yahweh—are	Ps 83:18
him because he knows My **n**.	Ps 91:14
Sing to the LORD, praise His **n**;	Ps 96:2
Your great and awe-inspiring **n**.	Ps 99:3
thanks to Him and praise His **n**.	Ps 100:4
within me, praise His holy **n**.	Ps 103:1

to the LORD, call on His **n**;	Ps 105:1
Let the **n** of the LORD be praised	Ps 113:2
but to Your **n** give glory because	Ps 115:1
in the **n** of the LORD I destroyed	Ps 118:10
who comes in the **n** of the LORD.	Ps 118:26
I remember Your **n** in the night,	Ps 119:55
help is in the **n** of the LORD,	Ps 124:8
of Your **n**, Yahweh, let me	Ps 143:11
He gives **n-s** to all of them.	Ps 147:4
for His **n** alone is exalted.	Ps 148:13
The **n** of the LORD is a strong	Pr 18:10
A good **n** is to be chosen over	Pr 22:1
What is His **n**, and what is the	Pr 30:4
A good **n** is better than fine	Ec 7:1
Declare that His **n** is exalted.	Is 12:4
He calls all of them by **n**.	Is 40:26
I am Yahweh, that is My **n**;	Is 42:8
His **n** is Yahweh of Hosts.	Is 48:2
waves roar—His **n** is Yahweh of	Is 51:15
His **n** is Yahweh of Hosts	Is 54:5
it will make a **n** for the LORD as	Is 55:13
whose **n** is Holy says this:	Is 57:15
by a new **n** that the LORD's	Is 62:2
make a glorious **n** for Yourself.	Is 63:14
where I made My **n** dwell at first	Jr 7:12
to swear by My **n**, 'As the LORD	Jr 12:16
prophesy a lie in My **n** have said:	Jr 23:25
I have sworn by My great **n**	Jr 44:26
I acted for the sake of My **n**	Ezk 20:9
I had concern for My holy **n**	Ezk 36:21
and made Your **n** {renowned} as it	Dn 9:15
calls on the **n** of Yahweh will	Jl 2:32
of the earth—Yahweh is His **n**.	Am 5:8
because Yahweh's **n** must not be	Am 6:10
of the earth. Yahweh is His **n**.	Am 9:6
will walk in the **n** of Yahweh our	Mc 4:5
in the majestic **n** of Yahweh His	Mc 5:4
may call on the **n** of Yahweh and	Zph 3:9
will trust in the **n** of Yahweh.	Zph 3:12
one who swears falsely by My **n**.	Zch 5:4
Yahweh alone, and His **n** alone.	Zch 14:9
How have we despised Your **n**?	Mal 1:6
and My **n** will be feared among	Mal 1:14
and had high regard for His **n**.	Mal 3:16
Your **n** be honored as holy.	Mt 6:9
didn't we prophesy in Your **n**	Mt 7:22
These are the **n-s** of the 12	Mt 10:2
by everyone because of My **n**.	Mt 10:22

will put their hope in His **n**.	Mt 12:21
like this in My **n** welcomes Me.	Mt 18:5
are gathered together in My **n**	Mt 18:20
who comes in the **n** of the Lord!	Mt 21:9
who comes in the **n** of the Lord!	Mt 23:39
For many will come in My **n**	Mt 24:5
them in the **n** of the Father	Mt 28:19
To Simon, He gave the **n** Peter;	Mk 3:16
He gave the **n** "Boanerges"	Mk 3:17
"My **n** is Legion," he answered	Mk 5:9
as this in My **n** welcomes Me.	Mk 9:37
In My **n** they will drive out	Mk 16:17
and you will call His **n** JESUS.	Lk 1:31
wrote: HIS **N** IS JOHN	Lk 1:63
and slander your **n** as evil,	Lk 6:22
that your **n-s** are written in heaven.	Lk 10:20
to those who believe in His **n**	Jn 1:12
I have come in My Father's **n**	Jn 5:43
He calls His own sheep by **n**	Jn 10:3
you ask in My **n**, I will do it so	Jn 14:13
you ask the Father in My **n**	Jn 15:16
have asked for nothing in My **n**.	Jn 16:24
you may have life in His **n**.	Jn 20:31
calls on the **n** of the Lord will	Ac 2:21
in the **n** of Jesus the Messiah	Ac 2:38
By faith in His **n**, His name has	Ac 3:16
there is no other **n** under heaven	Ac 4:12
not to speak in the **n** of Jesus	Ac 5:40
much he must suffer for My **n**!	Ac 9:16
baptized in the **n** of Jesus Christ.	Ac 10:48
The **n** of God is blasphemed among	Rm 2:24
calls on the **n** of the Lord will	Rm 10:13
were you baptized in Paul's **n**?	1Co 1:13
the **n** that is above every **n**,	Php 2:9
so that at the **n** of Jesus every	Php 2:10
whose **n-s** are in the book	Php 4:3
do everything in the **n** of the Lord	Col 3:17
so that the **n** of our Lord Jesus	2Th 1:12
that falsely bears that **n**.	1Tm 6:20
Everyone who names the **n** of	2Tm 2:19
just as the **n** He inherited is	Heb 1:4
of our lips that confess His **n**.	Heb 13:15
Don't they blaspheme the noble **n**	Jms 2:7
ridiculed for the **n** of Christ,	1Pt 4:14
forgiven on account of His **n**.	1Jn 2:12
believe in the **n** of His Son	1Jn 3:23
believe in the **n** of the Son of	1Jn 5:13
set out for the sake of the **n**	3Jn 7
never erase his **n** from the book	Rv 3:5
not denied My **n**, look, I have	Rv 3:8
beast's **n** or the number of his **n**.	Rv 13:17
His Father's **n** written on their	Rv 14:1
a cryptic **n** was written:	Rv 17:5
the earth whose **n-s** were not	Rv 17:8
He had a **n** written that no one	Rv 19:12
His **n** is called the Word of God.	Rv 19:13
the **n-s** of the 12 tribes of the	Rv 21:12
His **n** will be on their foreheads.	Rv 22:4

NAME (v)

Adam **n-ed** his wife Eve because	Gn 3:20
you will no longer be **n-ed** Jacob	Gn 35:10
n-ed him Moses, "Because	Ex 2:10
will be **n-ed** Wonderful Counselor	Is 9:6
and you are to **n** Him Jesus,	Mt 1:21
where Christ has not been **n-ed**	Rm 15:20
in heaven and on earth is **n-ed**.	Eph 3:15
Everyone who **n-s** the name of	2Tm 2:19

NAOMI

Ruth's mother-in-law (Ru 1:2-4).

NAPHTALI

Son of Jacob and Bilhah (Gn 30:1-8). Tribe with territory north and west of the Sea of Galilee (Jos 19:32-39); praised by Deborah (Jdg 5:18); produced Hiram the craftsman (1Kg 7:13-14).

NARD

choicest fruits, henna with **n**	Sg 4:13
expensive fragrant oil of **n**.	Mk 14:3
expensive **n**—anointed Jesus' feet,	Jn 12:3

NARRATIVE

to compile a **n** about the events	Lk 1:1
I wrote the first **n**, Theophilus	Ac 1:1

NARROW

Enter through the **n** gate.	Mt 7:13
How **n** is the gate and difficult	Mt 7:14
to enter through the **n** door,	Lk 13:24

NATHAN

1. Prophet to David; told David he would never fail to have a descendant on the throne (2Sm 7:4-17); confronted David about Bathsheba (2Sm 12:1-15). Anointed Solomon (1Kg 1).
2. Son of David (2Sm 5:14).

3. Returning exile whom Ezra sent to bring ministers (Ezr 8:15-17); perhaps the same one who married a foreigner (10:39).

NATHANAEL

Apostle "in whom is no deceit"; invited by Philip; asked if anything good comes out of Nazareth (Jn 1:45-49; 21:2); possibly also called Bartholomew (Mt 10:3).

NATION

I will make you into a great n	Gn 12:2
become the father of many n-s.	Gn 17:4
all the n-s of the earth will	Gn 18:18
you destroy a n even though it	Gn 20:4
Two n-s are in your womb;	Gn 25:23
kingdom of priests and My holy n.	Ex 19:6
I will scatter you among the n-s	Lv 26:33
For what great n is there that	Dt 4:7
just like those n-s that the LORD	2Kg 17:11
makes n-s great, then destroys	Jb 12:23
Why do the n-s rebel and the	Ps 2:1
I will make the n-s Your	Ps 2:8
Happy is the n whose God is the	Ps 33:12
and scatter us among the n-s.	Ps 44:11
N-s rage, kingdoms topple;	Ps 46:6
exalted among the n-s,	Ps 46:10
God reigns over the n-s;	Ps 47:8
Your salvation among all n-s.	Ps 67:2
down to him, all n-s serve him.	Ps 72:11
all n-s be blessed by him and	Ps 72:17
He drove out n-s before them.	Ps 78:55
for all the n-s belong to You.	Ps 82:8
Declare His glory among the n-s	Ps 96:3
Say among the n-s: "The LORD	Ps 96:10
Then the n-s will fear the name	Ps 102:15
wandering from n to n and from	Ps 105:13
will judge the n-s, heaping up	Ps 110:6
is exalted above all the n-s	Ps 113:4
Why should the n-s say, "Where	Ps 115:2
Righteousness exalts a n, but sin	Pr 14:34
All n-s will stream to it,	Is 2:2
N-s will not take up the sword	Is 2:4
the n-s are like a drop in a	Is 40:15
He will bring justice to the n-s	Is 42:1
make you a light for the n-s	Is 49:6
will bring justice to the n-s.	Is 51:5
a house of prayer for all n-s.	Is 56:7
N-s will come to your light,	Is 60:3
to a n that was not called by My	Is 65:1

or a n be delivered in an instant?	Is 66:8
proclaim My glory among the n-s.	Is 66:19
you a prophet to the n-s.	Jr 1:5
Has a n {ever} exchanged its	Jr 2:11
not fear You, King of the n-s?	Jr 10:7
to be a n before Me forever.	Jr 31:36
n-s will know that I am Yahweh	Ezk 36:23
make them one n in the land,	Ezk 37:22
occurred since n-s came into being	Dn 12:1
n-s that are called by My name	Am 9:12
N will not take up the sword against	Mc 4:3
treasures of all the n-s will come,	Hg 2:7
Many n-s will join themselves to	Zch 2:11
will proclaim peace to the n-s.	Zch 9:10
gather all the n-s against	Zch 14:2
name will be great among the n-s	Mal 1:11
will proclaim justice to the n-s	Mt 12:18
n-s will put their hope in His	Mt 12:21
and given to a n producing its	Mt 21:43
For n will rise up against n	Mt 24:7
world as a testimony to all n-s.	Mt 24:14
All the n-s will be gathered	Mt 25:32
and make disciples of all n-s	Mt 28:19
a house of prayer for all n-s?	Mk 11:17
first be proclaimed to all n-s	Mk 13:10
he loves our n and has built us	Lk 7:5
in His name to all the n-s	Lk 24:47
rather than the whole n perish.	Jn 11:50
was going to die for the n	Jn 11:51
men from every n under heaven.	Ac 2:5
has made every n of men to live	Ac 17:26
he became the father of many n-s	Rm 4:18
of those who are not a n;	Rm 10:19
the n-s will be blessed in you	Gl 3:8
a royal priesthood, a holy n,	1Pt 2:9
and language and people and n,	Rv 5:9
a vast multitude from every n	Rv 7:9
because it is given to the n-s	Rv 11:2
tribe, people, language, and n.	Rv 13:7
are Your ways, King of the N-s.	Rv 15:3
The n-s will walk in its light,	Rv 21:24
the tree are for healing the n-s	Rv 22:2

NATIVE

house and from my n land,	Gn 24:7
to both the n and the foreigner	Ex 12:49
both the n and the foreigner who	Lv 16:29
of us, in our own n language?	Ac 2:8
cut off from your n wild olive,	Rm 11:24

NATURAL

exchanged n sexual intercourse	Rm 1:26
did not spare the n branches,	Rm 11:21
the n man does not welcome	1Co 2:14
sown a n body, raised a	1Co 15:44
had n fathers discipline us	Heb 12:9

NATURALLY

animal that dies n or is mauled	Lv 7:24
animal that died n or was mauled	Lv 22:8
If these men die {n} as all people	Nm 16:29
animal that died n or was mauled	Ezk 44:31

NATURE

being jealous by n, is a jealous	Ex 34:14
he speaks from his own n, because	Jn 8:44
men also, with the same n as you,	Ac 14:15
that the divine n is like gold	Ac 17:29
His eternal power and divine n	Rm 1:20
and against n were grafted into	Rm 11:24
Does not even n itself teach you	1Co 11:14
and by n we were children under	Eph 2:3
of God's n dwells bodily,	Col 2:9
the exact expression of His n	Heb 1:3
was a man with a n like ours;	Jms 5:17
you may share in the divine n	2Pt 1:4

NAVEL

Your n is a rounded bowl;	Sg 7:2

NAZARENE

that He will be called a N.	Mt 2:23
"Jesus the N," they answered.	Jn 18:5
the name of Jesus Christ the N	Ac 3:6
of the sect of the N-s!	Ac 24:5

NAZARETH

Hometown of Jesus (Mt 2:23; Lk 2:51; 4:16; Jn 1:45-46).

NAZIRITE

a special vow, a N vow,	Nm 6:2
boy will be a N to God from	Jdg 13:5
because I am a N to God from	Jdg 16:17
some of your young men as N-s.	Am 2:11

NEAR

that has a god n to it as the LORD	Dt 4:7
But the message is very n you,	Dt 30:14
The LORD is n the brokenhearted	Ps 34:18
salvation is very n those who fear	Ps 85:9
You are n, LORD,	Ps 119:151
The LORD is n all who call out	Ps 145:18

For the day of the LORD is n.	Is 13:6
call to Him while He is n.	Is 55:6
the Day of the LORD is n	Jl 1:15
For the Day of the LORD is n	Ob 15
The great Day of the LORD is n	Zph 1:14
kingdom of heaven has come n!	Mt 3:2
know that He is n—at the door!	Mt 24:33
The message is n you, in your	Rm 10:8
have been brought n by the blood	Eph 2:13
and peace to those who were n.	Eph 2:17
The Lord is n.	Php 4:5
let us draw n with a true heart	Heb 10:22
Draw n to God, and He will draw n	Jms 4:8
because the Lord's coming is n.	Jms 5:8
Now the end of all things is n;	1Pt 4:7
because the time is n!	Rv 1:3
because the time is n.	Rv 22:10

NEARBY

Then she went and sat down n	Gn 21:16
a neighbor n than a brother	Pr 27:10

NEARER

our salvation is n than when we	Rm 13:11

NEAREST

his n relative may come and	Lv 25:25
to the n relative of his	Nm 27:11

NEARLY

my steps n went astray.	Ps 73:2
he was so sick that he n died.	Php 2:27

NEBO

Mountain from which Moses viewed the promised land (Dt 32:49; 34:1).

NEBUCHADNEZZAR

King of Babylon; defeated and exiled Judah (2Kg 24–25; 1Ch 6:15; 2Ch 36; Jr 39). Dreams interpreted by Daniel (Dn 2; 4); threw Shadrach, Meshach, and Abednego into the furnace (Dn 3); temporarily insane (Dn 4); praised God (2:47; 3:28; 4:34-37).

NEBUZARADAN

Commander of Nebuchadnezzar's army (2Kg 25:8).

NECESSARY

but one thing is n.	Lk 10:42
It was n that God's message be	Ac 13:46
burden on you than these n things:	Ac 15:28

that seem to be weaker are **n**.   1Co 12:22
in the flesh is more **n** for you.   Php 1:24
It is **n** to silence them;   Ti 1:11

NECESSITY
not out of regret or out of **n**   2Co 9:7

NECK
do not redeem it, break its **n**.   Ex 13:13
break the cow's **n** there by the   Dt 21:4
and heavy, his **n** broke and he   1Sm 4:18
Strength resides in his **n**   Jb 41:22
the water has risen to my **n**.   Ps 69:1
Tie them around your **n**;   Pr 3:3
you and adornment for your **n**.   Pr 3:22
Your **n** is like the tower of   Sg 4:4
Your **n** is like a tower of ivory   Sg 7:4
place a yoke on her fine **n**.   Hs 10:11
waters engulfed me up to the **n**;   Jnh 2:5
millstone were hung around his **n**   Mt 18:6
threw his arms around his **n**   Lk 15:20
risked their own **n-s** for my life   Rm 16:4

NECKLACE
rings, **n-s**, and all kinds   Ex 35:22
pride is their **n**,   Ps 73:6
your neck with its **n**.   Sg 1:10
with one jewel of your **n**.   Sg 4:9

NECO
Pharaoh who killed Josiah (2Kg 23:29)
and installed Jehoiakim (23:33-35).

NECROMANCER
cunning magician, and **n**.   Is 3:3

NEED (n)
enough for whatever **n** he has.   Dt 15:8
paid attention to Hannah's {**n**},   1Sm 2:21
a robber, your **n**, like a bandit.   Pr 24:34
to the poor will not be in **n**   Pr 28:27
when he was in **n** and hungry   Mk 2:25
to all, as anyone had a **n**.   Ac 2:45
each person as anyone had a **n**   Ac 4:35
hands have provided for my **n-s**   Ac 20:34
with the saints in their **n-s**;   Rm 12:13
supplying the **n-s** of the   2Co 9:12
from Macedonia supplied my **n-s**   2Co 11:9
to share with anyone in **n**.   Eph 4:28
and minister to my **n**   Php 2:25
whether in abundance or in **n**.   Php 4:12

supply all your **n-s** according   Php 4:19
brother in **n** but shuts off   1Jn 3:17

NEED (v)
and I have everything I **n**.   Gn 33:11
as much as he **n-ed** to eat.   Ex 16:18
honey, eat only what you **n**;   Pr 25:16
feed me with the food I **n**.   Pr 30:8
Father knows the things you **n**   Mt 6:8
who are well don't **n** a doctor   Mt 9:12
say that the Lord **n-s** them,   Mt 21:3
as though He **n-ed** anything, since   Ac 17:25
say to the hand, "I don't **n** you!"   1Co 12:21
having everything you **n**   2Co 9:8
who doesn't **n** to be ashamed,   2Tm 2:15
the kind of high priest we **n**:   Heb 7:26
you don't **n** anyone to teach   1Jn 2:27
become wealthy, and **n** nothing,'   Rv 3:17
The city does not **n** the sun   Rv 21:23

NEEDLE
eye of a **n**   Mt 19:24; Mk 10:25; Lk 18:25

NEEDY
and lifts the **n** from the garbage   1Sm 2:8
They push the **n** off the road;   Jb 24:4
I was a father to the **n**,   Jb 29:16
the LORD listens to the **n**   Ps 69:33
Rescue the poor and **n**;   Ps 82:4
But He lifts the **n** out of their   Ps 107:41
and lifts the **n** from the garbage   Ps 113:7
will satisfy its **n** with bread.   Ps 132:15
of the poor, justice for the **n**.   Ps 140:12
is kind to the **n** honors Him.   Pr 14:31
cause of the oppressed and **n**.   Pr 31:9
she extends her hands to the **n**.   Pr 31:20
defended the rights of the **n**.   Jr 5:28
he oppresses the poor and **n**   Ezk 18:12
and a **n** person for a pair of sandals. Am 2:6
there was not a **n** person among   Ac 4:34

NEGATIVE
So they gave a **n** report to the   Nm 13:32

NEGEV
Arid land south of Judah (Gn 13:1; 20:1;
Nm 13:22; Jos 10:40; 1Sm 30:1; 2Sm 24:7;
Ps 126:4; Ob 19-20).

NEGLECT
has the house of God been **n-ed**?   Neh 13:11
you have **n-ed** the more important   Mt 23:23

Do not **n** the gift that is in you | 1Tm 4:14
we escape if we **n** such a great | Heb 2:3
Don't **n** to show hospitality, | Heb 13:2
Don't **n** to do good and to share | Heb 13:16

NEGLIGENT
because of **n** hands the house | Ec 10:18

NEHEMIAH
1. Exile who returned with Zerubbabel (Ezr 2:2; Neh 7:7).

2. Son of Azbuk; helped Nehemiah son of Hacaliah rebuild the walls (Neh 3:16).

3. Cupbearer to King Artaxerxes of Babylon (Neh 1:11); obtained permission for, planned, and supervised rebuilding Jerusalem's walls despite opposition (Neh 2–6). Was appointed governor of Judah (5:14). Dedicated wall (12:27-43). Promoted reforms (Neh 8–10; 13). Prayed frequently (1:4-11; 2:4; 4:4-5,9; 5:19; 6:9,14; 13:14,22,29,31).

NEIGH
each **n-ing** after someone else's wife. | Jr 5:8
and your {lustful} **n-ings** | Jr 13:27
grain and **n** like stallions, | Jr 50:11

NEIGHBOR
false testimony against your **n**. | Ex 20:16
Do not covet your **n-'s** wife, | Ex 20:17
but love your **n** as yourself; | Lv 19:18
testimony against your **n**. | Dt 5:20
desire your **n-'s** wife or covet | Dt 5:21
move your **n-'s** boundary marker | Dt 19:14
given it to your **n** who is better | 1Sm 15:28
and gave it to your **n** David. | 1Sm 28:17
everyone—from all your **n-s**. | 2Kg 4:3
his friend or discredit his **n**, | Ps 15:3
adversaries and even by my **n-s**. | Ps 31:11
an object of reproach to our **n-s** | Ps 44:13
who secretly slanders his **n**; | Ps 101:5
Don't say to your **n**, "Go away! | Pr 3:28
security for your **n** or entered | Pr 6:1
one who despises his **n** sins, | Pr 14:21
against your **n** without cause. | Pr 24:28
set foot in your **n-'s** house; | Pr 25:17
better a **n** nearby than a brother | Pr 27:10
one blesses his **n** with a loud | Pr 27:14
man against man, **n** against **n**; | Is 3:5
one teach his **n** or his brother, | Jr 31:34

He does not defile his **n-'s** wife | Ezk 18:6
to him who gives his **n-s** drink, | Hab 2:15
Love your **n** and hate your enemy | Mt 5:43
and love your **n** as yourself. | Mt 19:19
Love your **n** as yourself. | Mt 22:39
asked Jesus, "And who is my **n**?" | Lk 10:29
proved to be a **n** to the man who | Lk 10:36
or your rich **n-s**, because they | Lk 14:12
calls his friends and **n-s** together, | Lk 15:6
shall love your **n** as yourself. | Rm 13:9
Love does no wrong to a **n**. | Rm 13:10
must please his **n** for his good, | Rm 15:2
shall love your **n** as yourself. | Gl 5:14
shall love your **n** as yourself, | Jms 2:8

NEITHER
Give me **n** poverty nor wealth; | Pr 30:8
where **n** moth nor rust destroys, | Mt 6:20
N will I tell you by what | Mt 21:27
N this man nor his parents | Jn 9:3
persuaded that **n** death nor life | Rm 8:38
in Christ Jesus **n** circumcision | Gl 5:6
that you are **n** cold nor hot. | Rv 3:15

NEPHEW
his wife Sarai, his **n** Lot, all | Gn 12:5

NEPHILIM
Ancient race of powerful men (Gn 6:4; Nm 13:33).

NEST (n)
your **n** is set in the cliffs. | Nm 24:21
a bird's **n** with chicks or eggs, | Dt 22:6
watches over His **n** like an eagle | Dt 32:11
command and make its **n** on high? | Jb 39:27
home, and a swallow, a **n** for herself | Ps 84:3
you elevate your **n** like the eagle, | Jr 49:16
and make your **n** among the stars | Ob 4
house to place his **n** on high, | Hab 2:9
and birds of the sky have **n-s** | Mt 8:20

NEST (v)
of the sky **n-ed** in its branches | Ezk 31:6
sky come and **n** in its branches. | Mt 13:32

NET
me and caught me in His **n**. | Jb 19:6
will pull my feet out of the **n**. | Ps 25:15
They hid their **n** for me without | Ps 35:7
They prepared a **n** for my steps; | Ps 57:6
a bird from the hunter's **n**; | Ps 124:7

they spread a n along the path	Ps 140:5
to spread a n where any bird can	Pr 1:17
spreads a n for his feet.	Pr 29:5
like fish caught in a cruel n	Ec 9:12
street like an antelope in a n.	Is 51:20
will be a place to spread n-s.	Ezk 26:14
gather them in their fishing n;	Hab 1:15
they left their n-s and followed	Mt 4:20
is like a large n thrown into	Mt 13:47
let down your n-s for a catch	Lk 5:4
Cast the n on the right side of	Jn 21:6
so many, the n was not torn.	Jn 21:11

NEVER

My faithful love will n leave him	2Sm 7:15
will n fail to have a man	1Kg 2:4; 8:25; 9:5
does these things will n be moved.	Ps 15:5
their fire will n go out,	Is 66:24
for His mercies n end.	Lm 3:22
kingdom that will n be destroyed,	Dn 2:44
You eat but n have enough	Hg 1:6
with fire that n goes out.	Mt 3:12
to them, 'I n knew you!	Mt 7:23
but My words will n pass away.	Mt 24:35
Holy Spirit n has forgiveness	Mk 3:29
heard this they said, "No—n!"	Lk 20:16
will n get thirsty again—ever!	Jn 4:14
he will n see death—ever!"	Jn 8:51
and they will n perish—ever!	Jn 10:28
Love n ends.	1Co 13:8
it can n perfect the worshipers	Heb 10:1
I will n leave you or forsake	Heb 13:5
because it will n be night there.	Rv 21:25

NEW

A n king, who had not known	Ex 1:8
Israel chose n gods, then war	Jdg 5:8
If they tie me up with n ropes	Jdg 16:11
They set the ark of God on a n cart	2Sm 6:3
Today is a day of good n-s.	2Kg 7:9
giving us n life, so that we	Ezr 9:9
their grain and n wine abound.	Ps 4:7
Sing a n song to Him;	Ps 33:3
He put a n song in my mouth,	Ps 40:3
Sing a n song to the LORD;	Ps 96:1
Sing a n song to the LORD,	Ps 98:1
I will sing a n song to You;	Ps 144:9
Sing to the LORD a n song,	Ps 149:1
there is nothing n under the sun.	Ec 1:9
Sing a n song to the LORD;	Is 42:10

I am about to do something n;	Is 43:19
will be called by a n name that	Is 62:2
will create a n heaven and a n earth;	Is 65:17
I will make a n covenant with	Jr 31:31
They are n every morning;	Lm 3:23
heart and put a n spirit within	Ezk 11:19
a n heart and a n spirit.	Ezk 18:31
you a n heart and put a n spirit	Ezk 36:26
overflow with n wine and olive	Jl 2:24
And no one puts n wine into old	Mt 9:17
what is n and what is old.	Mt 13:52
good n-s of the kingdom will	Mt 24:14
I drink it in a n way in My	Mt 26:29
A n teaching with authority!	Mk 1:27
they will speak in n languages;	Mk 16:17
This cup is the n covenant	Lk 22:20
I give you a n commandment:	Jn 13:34
A n tomb was in the garden;	Jn 19:41
telling or hearing something n.	Ac 17:21
may walk in a n way of life.	Rm 6:4
This cup is the n covenant in My	1Co 11:25
be ministers of a n covenant,	2Co 3:6
Christ, there is a n creation;	2Co 5:17
instead is a n creation.	Gl 6:15
you put on the n man,	Eph 4:24
and have put on the n man,	Col 3:10
He must not be a n convert,	1Tm 3:6
an itch to hear something n.	2Tm 4:3
I will make a n covenant with	Heb 8:8
the mediator of a n covenant,	Heb 9:15
by the n and living way that He	Heb 10:20
He gave us a n birth by the	Jms 1:18
He has given us a n birth into a	1Pt 1:3
we wait for n heavens and	
a n earth,	2Pt 3:13
writing you a n command,	1Jn 2:7,8
on the stone a n name is	Rv 2:17
of My God—the n Jerusalem	Rv 3:12
And they sang a n song:	Rv 5:9
I saw a n heaven and a n earth,	Rv 21:1
I am making everything n.	Rv 21:5

NEWBORN

Like n infants, desire the	1Pt 2:2

NEWLY

a n created people will praise	Ps 102:18

NEWS

the people heard this bad n	Ex 33:4

He will not fear bad n;   Ps 112:7
good n strengthens the bones.   Pr 15:30
Good n from a distant land is   Pr 25:25
Zion, herald of good n, go up on a   Is 40:9
who brings n of good things,   Is 52:7
Then the n about Him spread   Mt 4:24
the poor are told the good n.   Mt 11:5
Repent and believe in the good n!   Mk 1:15
And the good n must first be   Mk 13:10
good n of great joy that   Lk 2:10
the good n that the Messiah is Jesus.   Ac 5:42
was telling the good n about Jesus   Ac 17:18

NEXT

bear to you at this time n year.   Gn 17:21
At this time n year you will have   2Kg 4:16
the n generation will be told   Ps 22:30
their children the n generation.   Jl 1:3

NICODEMUS

Pharisee and member of the Sanhedrin.
Visited Jesus at night (Jn 3:1-21); defended
Jesus to the Sanhedrin (7:45-52); helped
prepare Jesus' body for burial (19:39).

NICOLAITANS

Heretical sect (Rv 2:6,15).

NIGHT

and He called the darkness "n."   Gn 1:5
on the earth 40 days and 40 n-s   Gn 7:4
and day and n will not cease.   Gn 8:22
It was a n of vigil in honor of   Ex 12:42
pillar of fire to give them light at n   Ex 13:21
the mountain 40 days and 40 n-s.   Ex 24:18
with the LORD 40 days and 40 n-s   Ex 34:28
you are to recite it day and n   Jos 1:8
marching all n from Gilgal.   Jos 10:9
in the daytime, he did it at n.   Jdg 6:27
don't spend the n in the square.   Jdg 19:20
he walked 40 days and 40 n-s   1Kg 19:8
They went by n and surrounded   2Kg 6:14
Then at n he set out to attack   2Kg 8:21
I went out at n through the   Neh 2:13
provides {us} with songs in the n   Jb 35:10
he meditates on it day and n.   Ps 1:2
even at n my conscience   Ps 16:7
n after n they communicate   Ps 19:2
may spend the n, but there is joy   Ps 30:5
song will be with me in the n   Ps 42:8
The day is Yours, also the n;   Ps 74:16

not fear the terror of the n   Ps 91:5
and Your faithfulness at n   Ps 92:2
I remember Your name in the n   Ps 119:55
stand in the LORD's house at n!   Ps 134:1
The n shines like the day;   Ps 139:12
will sleep at n without danger.   Pr 19:23
She rises while it is still n   Pr 31:15
even at n, his mind does not   Ec 2:23
against the terror of the n.   Sg 3:8
I long for You in the n;   Is 26:9
and your n will be like noonday   Is 58:10
and My covenant with the n so   Jr 33:20
watching in the n visions,   Dn 7:7,13
fish three days and three n-s.   Jnh 1:17
appeared in a n and perished in a n.   Jnh 4:10
it will be n for you—without   Mc 3:6
and His mother during the n   Mt 2:14
He had fasted 40 days and 40 n-s   Mt 4:2
belly of the great fish ... three n-s,   Mt 12:40
came during the n and stole Him   Mt 28:13
watch at n over their flock.   Lk 2:8
all n long and caught nothing!   Lk 5:5
and spent all n in prayer to God   Lk 6:12
who cry out to Him day and n?   Lk 18:7
man came to Him at n and said,   Jn 3:2
N is coming when no one can work   Jn 9:4
If anyone walks during the n   Jn 11:10
out immediately. And it was n.   Jn 13:30
previously come to Him at n   Jn 19:39
but that n they caught nothing.   Jn 21:3
said to Paul in a n vision,   Ac 18:9
The n is nearly over,   Rm 13:12
on the n when He was betrayed,   1Co 11:23
come just like a thief in the n.   1Th 5:2
We're not of the n or of darkness.   1Th 5:5
Day and n they never stop,   Rv 4:8
them before our God day and n.   Rv 12:10
day and n forever and ever   Rv 20:10
it will never be n there.   Rv 21:25
N will no longer exist, and   Rv 22:5

NILE

River of Egypt (Gn 41:1; Ex 1:22; 2:3; Is
7:18; 19:7-8; Ezk 29:3-10; Nah 3:8; Zch
10:11); floods periodically (Jr 46:7-8; Am
8:8; 9:5); struck by the plagues (Ex 7:20-21;
8:3).

NIMROD

Grandson of Ham (Gn 10:8-9).

NINE

n cities from these two tribes.	Jos 21:16
He was n feet, n inches tall	1Sm 17:4
went out about n in the morning	Mt 20:3
Now it was n in the morning when	
10 cleansed? Where are the n?	Mk 15:25
since it's only n in the morning	Lk 17:17
to go to Caesarea at n tonight.	Ac 2:15
	Ac 23:23

NINETY-YEAR-OLD

Can Sarah, a n woman, give birth	Gn 17:17

NINEVEH

Capital of Assyria (Gn 10:11-12; 2Kg 19:36; Is 37:37); Jonah preached against (Jnh 3:2-4) and the people repented (3:5-7; Mt 12:41; Lk 11:30-32); prophets condemned (Nah 1:1; Zph 2:13).

NIPPLES

and their virgin n caressed.	Ezk 23:3

NISAN

In the first month, the month of N,	Est 3:7

NOAH

1. Son of Lamech; descendant of Seth; a righteous man (Gn 5:28-29; 6:9; Ezk 14:14; 2Pt 2:5; Heb 11:7). Built an ark, entered it with animals and his family, and survived the flood (Gn 6:14–8:19; 1Pt 3:20). Received God's promise (Gn 8:20–9:17). Got drunk and cursed Canaan (9:20-27). Flood a symbol of sudden judgment (Mt 24:37-38; Lk 17:26-27).

2. Daughter of Zelophehad (Nm 26:33; 27:1; 36:11; Jos 17:3).

NOB

City in Benjamin (Neh 11:32; Is 10:32) where priests aided David (1Sm 21:1-9) and were executed by Saul (22:9-23).

NOBLE (adj)

a prominent man of n character	Ru 2:1
you are a woman of n character.	Ru 3:11
one of the king's most n officials.	Est 6:9
they are the n ones in whom is	Ps 16:3
My heart is moved by a n theme as I	Ps 45:1
for I speak of n things, and	Pr 8:6
But a n person plans n things;	Is 32:8
She has done a n thing for Me.	Mt 26:10

It is a n thing not to eat meat	Rm 14:21
powerful, not many of n birth.	1Co 1:26
overseer, he desires a n work.	1Tm 3:1
blaspheme the n name that you	Jms 2:7

NOBLE (n)

The n-s of the people hollowed it	Nm 21:18
but their n-s did not lift a finger	Neh 3:5
I accused the n-s and officials,	Neh 5:7
I rebuked the n-s of Judah and	Neh 13:17
The n-s of the peoples have	Ps 47:9
contempt on n-s and makes them	Ps 107:40
in order to seat them with n-s	Ps 113:8
in the LORD than to trust in n-s.	Ps 118:9
Do not trust in n-s, in man, who	Ps 146:3
as do n-s {and} all righteous	Pr 8:16
or to beat a n for his honesty.	Pr 17:26
you in plain view of a n.	Pr 25:7
when your king is a son of n-s	Ec 10:17
to Babylon along with all the n-s	Jr 27:20
slaughtered all Judah's n-s.	Jr 39:6
and my n-s sought me out,	Dn 4:36
1,000 of his n-s and drank wine	Dn 5:1
all her n-s were bound in chains.	Nah 3:10
Herod gave a banquet for his n-s	Mk 6:21
the earth, the n-s, the military	Rv 6:15

NOBLEMAN

He seats them with n-men and	1Sm 2:8
Where now is the n-'s house?	Jb 21:28
The n-men's voices were hushed,	Jb 29:10
A n traveled to a far country	Lk 19:12

NOD

Land where Cain was banished (Gn 4:16).

NOISE

that's the n you heard.	1Kg 1:45
Athaliah heard the n from	2Kg 11:13
Pharaoh king of Egypt was all n;	Jr 46:17
like the n of an army.	Ezk 1:24
an end to the n of your songs,	Ezk 26:13
there was a n, a rattling sound	Ezk 37:7
from Me the n of your songs!	Am 5:23
will pass away with a loud n	2Pt 3:10

NOISY

The n city, the jubilant town	Is 22:2
It will be n with people.	Mc 2:12

NOMADIC

| he was the father of the **n** | |
| herdsmen. | Gn 4:20 |

NONE

"There's **n** like it!" David said.	1Sm 21:9
N of you cares about me or tells	1Sm 22:8
should be as though they had **n**	1Co 7:29

NONSENSE

| words seemed like **n** to them, | Lk 24:11 |
| thinking became **n**, and their | Rm 1:21 |

NOON

At **n** Elijah mocked them.	1Kg 18:27
pestilence that ravages at **n**.	Ps 91:6
will make the sun go down at **n**;	Am 8:9
When it was **n**, darkness came	Mk 15:33
on the housetop at about **n**.	Ac 10:9
about **n** an intense light from	Ac 22:6

NOONDAY

life will be brighter than **n**;	Jb 11:17
dawn, your justice like the **n**.	Ps 37:6
and your night will be like **n**.	Is 58:10

NORTH

Mount Zion on the slopes of the **n**	Ps 48:2
N and south—You created them.	Ps 89:12
The **n** wind produces rain, and a	Pr 25:23
turning to the **n**, turning	Ec 1:6
falls to the south or the **n**	Ec 11:3
Awaken, **n** wind—come, south	Sg 4:16
have raised up one from the **n**	Is 41:25
bringing disaster from the **n**	Jr 4:6
a whirlwind coming from the **n**	Ezk 1:4
from the remotest parts of the **n**.	Ezk 39:2
king of the **N** to seal the agreement.	Dn 11:6
the king of the **N** will come,	Dn 11:15
Leave the land of the **n'**	Zch 2:6
east and west, from **n** and south	Lk 13:29

NORTHEASTER

| wind called the "**n**" rushed down | Ac 27:14 |

NORTHERN

army is coming from a **n** land;	Jr 6:22
to bring them from the **n** land.	Jr 31:8
My Spirit in the **n** land.	Zch 6:8

NOSE

| I put the ring on her **n** and the | Gn 24:47 |
| My hook in your **n** and My bit in | 2Kg 19:28 |

or pierce his **n** with snares?	Jb 40:24
cord through his **n** or pierce his	Jb 41:2
n-s, but cannot smell.	Ps 115:6
and twisting a **n** draws blood,	Pr 30:33
Your **n** is like the tower of	Sg 7:4
signet rings, **n** rings,	Is 3:21
putting the branch to their **n**?	Ezk 8:17
a ring in your **n**, earrings on	Ezk 16:12
will cut off your **n** and ears,	Ezk 23:25

NOSTRILS

the breath of life into his **n**	Gn 2:7
up at the blast of Your **n**;	Ex 15:8
until it comes out of your **n**	Nm 11:20
an end by the breath of His **n**.	Jb 4:9
from God remains in my **n**	Jb 27:3
billows from his **n** as from a	Jb 41:20
rose from His **n**, and consuming	Ps 18:8
blast of the breath of Your **n**.	Ps 18:15
has only the breath in his **n**.	Is 2:22
practices are smoke in My **n**	Is 65:5
of your camp to fill your **n**	Am 4:10

NOTE

He takes **n** of the humble;	Ps 138:6
Take **n**: I have told you in	Mt 24:25
N this: some are last who will	Lk 13:30
Take **n**! I, Paul, tell you that	Gl 5:2
letter, take **n** of that person;	2Th 3:14
Take **n**! I will make those from	Rv 3:9

NOTHING

N can keep the LORD from saving	1Sm 14:6
offerings that cost [me] **n**.	2Sm 24:24
40 years and they lacked **n**.	Neh 9:21
Does Job fear God for **n**?	Jb 1:9
He hangs the earth on **n**.	Jb 26:7
my shepherd; there is **n** I lack.	Ps 23:1
for those who fear Him lack **n**.	Ps 34:9
life span as **n** in Your sight.	Ps 39:5
You sell Your people for **n**;	Ps 44:12
he dies, he will take **n** at all;	Ps 49:17
And I desire **n** on earth but You	Ps 73:25
You created everyone for **n**?	Ps 89:47
of the wicked will come to **n**.	Ps 112:10
n you desire compares with her.	Pr 3:15
and **n** desirable can compare with	Pr 8:11
she is gullible and knows **n**.	Pr 9:13
and struggle adds **n** to it.	Pr 10:22
his expectation comes to **n**	Pr 11:7

pretends to be rich but has **n**;	Pr 13:7
If you do **n** in a difficult time	Pr 24:10
there is **n** new under the sun.	Ec 1:9
he will take **n** for his efforts	Ec 5:15
nations are as **n** before Him;	Is 40:17
you will become absolutely **n**.	Is 41:12
N is too difficult for You!	Jr 32:17
of the earth are counted as **n**	Dn 4:35
GOD does **n** without revealing	Am 3:7
with **n** to make {them} afraid.	Zph 3:13
N will be impossible for you.	Mt 17:20
lend, expecting **n** in return.	Lk 6:35
I can do **n** on My own.	Jn 5:30
you can do **n** without Me.	Jn 15:5
have asked for **n** in My name.	Jn 16:24
were dispersed and came to **n**.	Ac 5:36
might bring to **n** the things that	1Co 1:28
N beyond what is written.	1Co 4:6
that "an idol is **n** in the world,	1Co 8:4
but do not have love, I am **n**.	1Co 13:2
even though I am **n**.	2Co 12:11
law, then Christ died for **n**.	Gl 2:21
and uncircumcision mean **n**;	Gl 6:15
that our labor might be for **n**.	1Th 3:5
For we brought **n** into the world,	1Tm 6:7
He left **n** not subject to him.	Heb 2:8
mature and complete, lacking **n**.	Jms 1:4
need **n**,' and you don't know that	Rv 3:17

NOTHINGNESS
by Him as **n** and emptiness.	Is 40:17

NOTICE
Why are you so kind to **n** me,	Ru 2:10
May He take **n** and plead my	1Sm 24:15
eye but don't **n** the log in your	Mt 7:3

NOTORIOUS
she became **n** among women.	Ezk 23:10
they had a **n** prisoner called	Mt 27:16
judgment of the **n** prostitute who	Rv 17:1

NOURISH
He **n**-ed him with honey from the	Dt 32:13
n-ed and held together by its	Col 2:19
n-ed by the words of the faith	1Tm 4:6

NOW
but **n** my eyes have seen You.	Jb 42:5
I have been young and **n** I am old,	Ps 37:25
of John the Baptist until **n**	Mt 11:12

the world until **n** and never will	Mt 24:21
Blessed are you who are hungry **n**,	Lk 6:21
is coming, and is **n** here,	Jn 4:23; 5:25
doing you don't understand **n**	Jn 13:7
going you cannot follow Me **n**	Jn 13:36
I have told you **n** before it	Jn 14:29
but you can't bear them **n**.	Jn 16:12
N You're speaking plainly and	Jn 16:29
N, Father, glorify Me in Your	Jn 17:5
no condemnation **n** exists for	Rm 8:1
but **n** have received mercy	Rm 11:30
N I know in part, but then I	1Co 13:12
N we have this treasure in clay	2Co 4:7
n is the day of salvation.	2Co 6:2
The life I **n** live in the flesh,	Gl 2:20
But **n** in Christ Jesus, you who	Eph 2:13
N to Him who is able to do above	Eph 3:20
but **n** even more in my absence,	Php 2:12
but **n** you have received mercy.	1Pt 2:10
God's children **n**, and what we	1Jn 3:2
N to Him who is able to protect	Jd 24

NUMBER (n)
give {you} the full **n** of your days.	Ex 23:26
troops so I can know their **n**.	2Sm 24:2
wonders without **n**.	Jb 5:9; 9:10
end of my life and the **n** of my days.	Ps 39:4
were few in **n**, very few indeed	Ps 105:12

O

❦

OAK
beside the **o**-**s** of Mamre	Gn 13:18
So Jacob named it **O** of Weeping.	Gn 35:8
He sat under the **o** that was in	Jdg 6:11
direction of the Diviners' **O**.	Jdg 9:37
Absalom hanging in an **o** tree!	2Sm 18:10
him sitting under an **o** tree.	1Kg 13:14
and he was as sturdy as the **o**-**s**;	Am 2:9
Wail, **o**-**s** of Bashan, for the	Zch 11:2

OATH
the two of them swore an **o**.	Gn 21:31
Its owner must accept {the **o**},	Ex 22:11
a person may speak rashly in an **o**	Lv 5:4
a vow to the LORD or swears an **o**	Nm 30:2

and take {your} o-s in His name.	Dt 6:13
and kept the o He swore to your	Dt 7:8
to Him and take o-s in His name.	Dt 10:20
free from the o you made us	Jos 2:20
community swore an o to them.	Jos 9:15
placed the troops under an o:	1Sm 14:24
to take an o before Your altar	1Kg 8:31
All Judah rejoiced over the o,	2Ch 15:15
a sworn o to follow the law	Neh 10:29
I forced them to take an o	Neh 13:25
I have sworn an o to David My	Ps 89:3
I have sworn an o by My holiness	Ps 89:35
The LORD has sworn an o and will	Ps 110:4
The LORD swore an o to David,	Ps 132:11
an o, so for the one who fears an o.	Ec 9:2
to establish the o I swore to your	Jr 11:5
not swear an o: as the LORD lives!	Hs 4:15
I tell you, don't take an o at all:	Mt 5:34
because of his o-s and his guests.	Mt 14:9
whoever takes an o by the gold of	Mt 23:16
living God I place You under o:	Mt 26:63
again he denied it with an o	Mt 26:72
the o that He swore to our father	Lk 1:73
a confirming o ends every dispute.	Heb 6:16
others became priests without an o,	Heb 7:20
by earth or with any other o.	Jms 5:12
He swore an o by the One who	Rv 10:6

OBADIAH

1. Man in charge of Ahab's palace; sheltered 100 prophets from Jezebel (1Kg 18:3-16).

2. Gadite who joined David (1Ch 12:8-9).

3. Sent by Jehoshaphat to teach the law (2Ch 17:7-9).

4. Merarite Levite appointed by Josiah to repair the temple (2Ch 34:12).

5. Prophet against Edom (Ob 1).

6. Descendant of David (1Ch 3:21).

7. Issacharite (1Ch 7:3).

8. Benjaminite (1Ch 8:38; 9:44).

9. Levite who returned from exile (1Ch 9:16).

10. Priest who returned with Ezra (Ezr 8:9) and put his seal on an agreement (Neh 10:5).

11. Gatekeeper under Ezra (Neh 12:25).

OBED

1. Son of Boaz and Ruth; grandfather of David; ancestor of Christ (Ru 4:17-22; Mt 1:5).

2. Father of Jehu (1Ch 2:37-38).

3. One of David's warriors (1Ch 11:47).

4. Temple gatekeeper (1Ch 26:7).

OBED-EDOM

1. Gittite at whose house David stored the ark (2Sm 6:10-12).

2. Gatekeeper and musician (1Ch 15:18-24; 16:5).

OBEDIENCE

o of the peoples belongs to Him.	Gn 49:10
and despises o to a mother,	Pr 30:17
to draw near in o than to offer	Ec 5:1
to bring about the o of faith	Rm 1:5
through the one man's o the many	Rm 5:19
or of o leading to righteousness?	Rm 6:16
The report of your o has reached	Rm 16:19
to advance the o of faith among	Rm 16:26
they will glorify God for your o to	2Co 9:13
thought captive to the o of Christ.	2Co 10:5
Since I am confident of your o	Phm 21
He learned o through what He	Heb 5:8
for o and {for the} sprinkling	1Pt 1:2

OBEDIENT

give Your servant an o heart	1Kg 3:9
If you are willing and o, you will eat	Is 1:19
to Nazareth and was o to them.	Lk 2:51
priests became o to the faith.	Ac 6:7
to someone as o slaves,	Rm 6:16
becoming o to the point of death	Php 2:8
As o children, do not be	1Pt 1:14

OBEY

you have o-ed My command	Gn 22:18
that I should o Him by letting	Ex 5:2
If you will carefully o the LORD	Ex 15:26
We will do and o everything that	Ex 24:7
God in later days and o Him.	Dt 4:30
Be careful to o all these things	Dt 12:28
son who does not o his father or	Dt 21:18
Now if you faithfully o the LORD	Dt 28:1
But if you do not o the LORD	Dt 28:15
and o Him with all your heart	Dt 30:2
We will worship ... and o Him.	Jos 24:24
But you have not o-ed Me.	Jdg 2:2

to **o** is better than sacrifice,	1Sm 15:22
soon as they hear, they **o** me.	Ps 18:44
and I will **o** it and follow it	Ps 119:34
and have not **o-ed** My voice.	Jr 3:13
O Me, and then I will be your God,	Jr 7:23
and time again: **O** My voice.	Jr 11:7
we will **o** the voice of the LORD	Jr 42:6
have not **o-ed** the voice of the	Dn 9:10
when you fully **o** the LORD your	Zch 6:15
the winds and the sea **o** Him!	Mt 8:27
unclean spirits, and they **o** Him.	Mk 1:27
in the sea,' and it will **o** you.	Lk 17:6
We must **o** God rather than men.	Ac 5:29
are slaves of that one you **o**	Rm 6:16
you **o-ed** from the heart that	Rm 6:17
But all did not **o** the gospel.	Rm 10:16
Children, **o** your parents in the Lord,	Eph 6:1
Slaves, **o** your human masters with	Eph 6:5
just as you have always **o-ed**	Php 2:12
o your parents in everything,	Col 3:20
o your human masters in	Col 3:22
those who don't **o** the gospel of	2Th 1:8
salvation to all who **o** Him,	Heb 5:9
o-ed and went out to a place he	Heb 11:8
O your leaders and submit to	Heb 13:17
of horses to make them **o** us,	Jms 3:3
as Sarah **o-ed** Abraham, calling	1Pt 3:6
we love God and **o** His commands.	1Jn 5:2

OBJECT

touch the holy **o-s** or they will	Nm 4:15
He has made me an **o** of scorn to	Jb 17:6
I have become an **o** of ridicule	Ps 109:25
will become an **o** of contempt,	Is 16:14
will become an **o** of execration,	Jr 42:18
and become an **o** of cursing	Jr 44:8
You will be an **o** of ridicule and	Ezk 23:32
and an **o** of people's gossip	Ezk 36:3
have become an **o** of ridicule to	Dn 9:16
an **o** of scorn among the nations	Jl 2:17
residents an **o** of contempt;	Mc 6:16
much patience **o-s** of wrath ready	Rm 9:22
so-called god or **o** of worship,	2Th 2:4
o-s of ivory; **o-s** of expensive wood	Rv 18:12

OBLIGATED

I am **o** by vows to You, God;	Ps 56:12
I am **o** both to Greeks and	Rm 1:14
are not **o** to the flesh to	Rm 8:12

are not **o** to save up for	2Co 12:14
he is **o** to keep the entire	Gl 5:3

OBLIGATION

hears about her vow or the **o** she	Nm 30:4
confirms all her vows and **o-s**,	Nm 30:14
be free from **o** to the LORD	Nm 32:22
keep your **o** to the LORD	1Kg 2:3
Pay your **o-s** to everyone:	Rm 13:7
strong have an **o** to bear the	Rm 15:1
because an **o** is placed on	1Co 9:16
the certificate of debt, with its **o-s**,	Col 2:14
deed might not be out of **o**,	Phm 14

OBLIVION

righteousness in the land of **o**?	Ps 88:12

OBSCENE

she had made an **o** image of	1Kg 15:13
and Oholibah, those **o** women.	Ezk 23:44

OBSCURES

He **o** the view of {His} throne	Jb 26:9
Who is this who **o** {My} counsel	Jb 38:2

OBSERVE

O the Festival of	Ex 23:15
You must **o** My Sabbaths,	Ex 31:13
Israelites are to **o** the Passover at	Nm 9:2
O the month of Abib and	Dt 16:1
carefully **o** everything written in it.	Jos 1:8
Josiah **o-d** the LORD's Passover	2Ch 35:1
exiles **o-d** the Passover on the	Ezr 6:19
When I **o** Your heavens, the work	Ps 8:3
from heaven; He **o-s** everyone.	Ps 33:13
You **o** my travels and my rest;	Ps 139:3
Go to the ant ... **O** its ways	Pr 6:6
and let your eyes **o** my ways.	Pr 23:26
and carefully **o** My ordinances.	Ezk 36:27
teaching them to **o** everything I	Mt 28:20
We **o-d** His glory, the glory as the	Jn 1:14
were to **o** the Son of Man ascending	Jn 6:62
finger here and **o** My hands.	Jn 20:27
benefits you if you **o** the law,	Rm 2:25
Whoever **o-s** the day, **o-s** it to the	Rm 14:6
let us **o** the feast, not	1Co 5:8
You **o** {special} days, months,	Gl 4:10
and **o** those who live according	Php 3:17
may, by **o-ing** your good works,	1Pt 2:12
when they **o** your pure, reverent	1Pt 3:2
we have **o-d**, and have touched	1Jn 1:1

OBSERVER

The king saw an o, a holy one,   Dn 4:23

OBSTACLE

remove {every} o from My   Is 57:14

OBSTINATE

his heart o in order to hand
  him over   Dt 2:30
practices or their o ways.   Jdg 2:19
they became o like their   2Kg 17:14
Don't become o now like your   2Ch 30:8
He became o and hardened his   2Ch 36:13
or pay attention but became o;   Jr 7:26; 17:23
children are o and hardhearted   Ezk 2:4
For Israel is as o as a stubborn   Hs 4:16

OBTAIN

was desirable for o-ing wisdom   Gn 3:6
me finds life and o-s favor from   Pr 8:35
Wealth o-ed by fraud will dwindle   Pr 13:11
who finds a wife ... o-s favor from   Pr 18:22
of God could be o-ed with money!   Ac 8:20
have o-ed access by faith into   Rm 5:2
have o-ed righteousness   Rm 9:30
but to o salvation through our   1Th 5:9
that they also may o salvation,   2Tm 2:10
Abraham o-ed the promise.   Heb 6:15
Jesus has now o-ed a superior   Heb 8:6
having o-ed eternal redemption.   Heb 9:12
justice, o-ed promises, shut   Heb 11:33
murder and covet and cannot o.   Jms 4:2
those who have o-ed a faith of   2Pt 1:1

OBVIOUS

their fasting is o to people.   Mt 6:16
For an o sign, evident to all   Ac 4:16
each one's work will become o   1Co 3:13
it is o that He who puts   1Co 15:27
the works of the flesh are o: Gl 5:19
good works are o, and those that   1Tm 5:25

OCCASION

seeking an o against the Philistines. Jdg 14:4
There is an o for everything,   Ec 3:1

OCCULT

same thing by their o practices.   Ex 7:11

OCCUPATION

Pharaoh ... asks, 'What is your o?'   Gn 46:33
and his o is sorrowful;   Ec 2:23
the same o, stayed with them   Ac 18:3

OCCUPY

miserable task to keep them o-ied.   Ec 1:13
given people to keep them o-ied.   Ec 3:10
God keeps him o-ied with the joy   Ec 5:20
will rebuild and o ruined cities,   Am 9:14
Paul was o-ied with preaching the   Ac 18:5

OCEAN

The o depths say, "It's not in   Jb 28:14
all sea monsters and o depths,   Ps 148:7

ODED

  Prophet (2Ch 28:9).

ODIOUS

making me o to the inhabitants   Gn 34:30

OFFEND

and his baker o-ed their master,   Gn 40:1
who loves to o loves strife;   Pr 17:19
o-ed brother is {harder to reach}   Pr 18:19
anyone is not o-ed because of Me   Mt 11:6
And they were o-ed by Him.   Mt 13:57
But, so we won't o them, go to   Mt 17:27
asked them, "Does this o you?   Jn 6:61

OFFENSE

or repaid us according to our o-s.   Ps 103:10
but love covers all o-s.   Pr 10:12
conceals an o promotes love,   Pr 17:9
his virtue is to overlook an o.   Pr 19:11
calmness puts great o-s to rest   Ec 10:4
Pharisees took o when they heard   Mt 15:12
You are an o to Me because   Mt 16:23
o-s must come, but woe to that   Mt 18:7
many will take o, betray one   Mt 24:10
Give no o to the Jews or the   1Co 10:32
that case the o of the cross has   Gl 5:11

OFFENSIVE

My breath is o to my wife,   Jb 19:17
if there is any o way in me;   Ps 139:24
the o statue that provokes   Ezk 8:3

OFFER

and o him there as a burnt   Gn 22:2
Then Jacob o-ed a sacrifice on   Gn 31:54
This is what you are to o regularly   Ex 29:38
You must not o unauthorized   Ex 30:9
forced myself to o the burnt   1Sm 13:12
He o-ed 1,000 burnt offerings   1Kg 3:4
O sacrifices in righteousness   Ps 4:5
I will o sacrifices in His tent   Ps 27:6

o You a sacrifice of thanksgiving Ps 116:17
Let him o {his} cheek to the one Lm 3:30
and they o-ed a sacrifice to the Jnh 1:16
if you are o-ing your gift on Mt 5:23
on the cheek, o the other also. Lk 6:29
hands, he o-ed them money, Ac 8:18
abstain from food o-ed to idols, Ac 15:29
o yourselves to God, Rm 6:13
His own Son, but o-ed Him up for Rm 8:32
About food o-ed to idols: 1Co 8:1
the gospel and o it free of 1Co 9:18
This is food o-ed to an idol, 1Co 10:28
to o both gifts and sacrifices Heb 5:1
once for all when He o-ed Himself. Heb 7:27
o-ed Himself without blemish Heb 9:14
not do this to o Himself many Heb 9:25
having been o-ed once to bear Heb 9:28
continually o year after year Heb 10:1
after o-ing one sacrifice for Heb 10:12
faith Abel o-ed to God a better Heb 11:4
he was tested, o-ed up Isaac Heb 11:17
let us continually o up to God a Heb 13:15
to o spiritual sacrifices acceptable 1Pt 2:5

OFFERING (n) *see also* BURNT,
    CONTRIBUTION, DRINK,
    FELLOWSHIP, FREEWILL, GRAIN,
    PRESENTATION, REMEM-
    BRANCE,
    RESTITUTION, SIN,
    THANK, VOW

LORD had regard for Abel and his o. Gn 4:4
offered burnt o-s on the altar. Gn 8:20
provide the lamb for the burnt o, Gn 22:8
a freewill o to the LORD, Ex 35:29
When any of you brings an o Lv 1:2
This is the law of the sin o Lv 6:25
Don't respect their o. Nm 16:15
and My food as My fire o, Nm 28:2
o-s only in the place the LORD Dt 12:14
they offered burnt o-s to the LORD Jos 8:31
not send it without {an o}. 1Sm 6:3
Saul ... offered the burnt o. 1Sm 13:9
take pleasure in burnt o-s ... as
    much as in obeying the LORD? 1Sm 15:22
burnt o-s and fellowship o-s. 2Sm 24:25
and consumed the burnt o 1Kg 18:38
and consumed the burnt o 2Ch 7:1
willing hearts brought burnt o-s. 2Ch 29:31

a freewill o for the house of God Ezr 1:4
daily grain o, the regular burnt o, Neh 10:33
offer burnt o-s for all of them. Jb 1:5
May He remember all your o-s Ps 20:3
You do not delight in sacrifice and o Ps 40:6
Sacrifice a thank o to God, Ps 50:14
You are not pleased with a burnt o. Ps 51:16
bring an o and enter His courts. Ps 96:8
accept my willing o-s of praise, Ps 119:108
Stop bringing useless o-s. Is 1:13
You make Him a restitution o Is 53:10
burnt o-s are not acceptable Jr 6:20
he will put a stop to sacrifice and o. Dn 9:27
of God rather than burnt o-s. Hs 6:6
o-s have been cut off from the house Jl 1:9
I will accept no o from your hands. Mal 1:10
the o-s ... will please the LORD Mal 3:4
important than all the burnt o-s Mk 12:33
dropping their o-s into the Lk 21:1
bring Me o-s and sacrifices Ac 7:42
that the o of the Gentiles Rm 15:16
share in the o-s of the altar 1Co 9:13
and fragrant o to God. Eph 5:2
if I am poured out as a drink o Php 2:17
a fragrant o, a welcome Php 4:18
being poured out as a drink o 2Tm 4:6
You did not want sacrifice and o, Heb 10:5
by one o He has perfected Heb 10:14
is no longer an o for sin. Heb 10:18

OFFICE
I will remove you from your o; Is 22:19
Matthew sitting at the tax o Mt 9:9
Levi sitting at the tax o Lk 5:27
the priestly o have a Heb 7:5
by death from remaining in o. Heb 7:23

OFFICIAL
and David's sons were chief o-s. 2Sm 8:18
the o-s contributed 1,000 bulls 2Ch 30:24
His o-s also donated willingly for 2Ch 35:8
o-s have taken the lead in
    unfaithfulness Ezr 9:2
Therefore, I rebuked the o-s, Neh 13:11
one o protects another o, and higher Ec 5:8
be placed on the o support list 1Tm 5:9

OFFSPRING
I will give this land to your o. Gn 12:7
You have given me no o, so a slave Gn 15:3

God has even let me see your o.   Gn 48:11
your son, your own o, will build it   1Kg 8:19
know that your o will be many   Jb 5:25
His o will continue forever,   Ps 89:36
and their o will be established   Ps 102:28
The o of evildoers will never be   Is 14:20
and My blessing on your o.   Is 44:3
does the One seek? A godly o.   Mal 2:15
The seven also left no o.   Mk 12:22
from David's o and from the town   Jn 7:42
said, 'For we are also His o.'   Ac 17:28
Being God's o, then, we   Ac 17:29
but to help Abraham's o.   Heb 2:16
war against the rest of her o   Rv 12:17
I am the Root and the O of David,   Rv 22:16

OFTEN

How o I wanted to gather your   Mt 23:37
because Jesus o met there with   Jn 18:2
For as o as you eat this bread   1Co 11:26

OG

Amorite king of Bashan defeated by Israel before they crossed the Jordan (Nm 21:33-35; Dt 3:1-13).

OH

O, that he would kiss me   Sg 1:2
O, the depth of the riches both   Rm 11:33

OHOLAH

A name used to represent Samaria (Ezk 23).

OHOLIAB

Tabernacle craftsman (Ex 31:6; 38:23).

OHOLIBAH

A name used to represent Jerusalem (Ezk 23).

OIL

He poured o on top of it   Gn 28:18
o for the light; spices for the
  anointing o   Ex 25:6
it will be holy anointing o.   Ex 30:25
Take the anointing o, and anoint   Ex 40:9
the anointing o on Aaron's head   Lv 8:12
a land of olive o and honey;   Dt 8:8
your grain, new wine, and o.   Dt 11:14
Samuel took the flask of o   1Sm 10:1
So Samuel took the horn of o   1Sm 16:13
and the o jug did not run dry,   1Kg 17:16

and pour o into all these   2Kg 4:4
prophet poured the o on his head   2Kg 9:6
treatments with o of myrrh for   Est 2:12
You anoint my head with o;   Ps 23:5
companions, with the o of joy.   Ps 45:7
I have been anointed with o.   Ps 92:10
and go into his bones like o.   Ps 109:18
It is like fine o on the head,   Ps 133:2
it is o for my head;   Ps 141:5
her words are smoother than o   Pr 5:3
wind and grasps o with his right   Pr 27:16
flies make a perfumer's o ferment   Ec 10:1
festive o instead of mourning,   Is 61:3
grain, the new wine, and the o.   Hs 2:8
grain, new wine, and olive o.   Jl 2:19
with ten thousand streams of o?   Mc 6:7
you fast, put o on your head   Mt 6:17
sensible ones took o in their flasks   Mt 25:4
of very expensive fragrant o.   Mt 26:7
many sick people with o   Mk 6:13
didn't anoint My head with o   Lk 7:46
wounds, pouring on o and wine.   Lk 10:34
Why wasn't this fragrant o sold   Jn 12:5
anointed you ... with the o of joy.   Heb 1:9
him with olive o in the name of   Jms 5:14
harm the olive o and the wine.   Rv 6:6

OINTMENT

and o to spread on your eyes so   Rv 3:18

OLD

borne him a son in his o age.   Gn 21:7
the child of his o age.   Gn 44:20
Remember the days of o;   Dt 32:7
The God of o is {your} dwelling   Dt 33:27
is not {only} the o who are wise   Jb 32:9
I have been young and now I am o,   Ps 37:25
Don't discard me in my o age: Ps 71:9
Even when I am o and gray,   Ps 71:18
days of o, years long past   Ps 77:5
will still bear fruit in o age,   Ps 92:14
I remember the days of o;   Ps 143:5
the splendor of o men is gray   Pr 20:29
even when he is o he will not   Pr 22:6
your mother when she is o.   Pr 23:22
delicacy—new as well as o.   Sg 7:13
young and o men {rejoice} together   Jr 31:13
your o men will have dreams,   Jl 2:28
O men and women will again sit   Zch 8:4
as in days of o and years gone   Mal 3:4

puts new wine into o wineskins.   Mt 9:17
what is new and what is o.   Mt 13:52
(She was 12 years o.)   Mk 5:42
conceived a son in her o age,   Lk 1:36
When He was 12 years o, they went   Lk 2:42
ministry, Jesus was about 30 years o   Lk 3:23
after drinking o wine, wants new,   Lk 5:39
can anyone be born when he is o?   Jn 3:4
when you grow o, you will   Jn 21:18
and your o men will dream dreams   Ac 2:17
he was about a hundred years o   Rm 4:19
we know that our o self was   Rm 6:6
the reading of the o covenant,   2Co 3:14
o things have passed away,   2Co 5:17
the o man that is corrupted   Eph 4:22
have put off the o man with his   Col 3:9
And what is o and aging is about   Heb 8:13
The o command is the message you   1Jn 2:7

OLDER

and the o will serve the younger   Gn 25:23
the o was named Leah,   Gn 29:16
Now his o son was in the field   Lk 15:25
The o will serve the younger.   Rm 9:12
not rebuke an o man, but exhort   1Tm 5:1
o women as mothers, and with all   1Tm 5:2
O men are to be self-controlled   Ti 2:2
o women are to be reverent in   Ti 2:3

OLIVE   *see also* MOUNT OF OLIVES

was a plucked o leaf in her beak   Gn 8:11
vineyards and o groves that you   Dt 6:11
a land of o oil and honey;   Dt 8:8
vineyards and o groves you did   Jos 24:13
They said to the tree, "Reign   Jdg 9:8
two cherubim ... out of o wood.   1Kg 6:23
a land of o trees and honey   2Kg 18:32
a flourishing o tree in the   Ps 52:8
like young o trees around your   Ps 128:3
you will press o-s but not anoint   Mc 6:15
though the o crop fails and the   Hab 3:17
are also two o trees beside it,   Zch 4:3
you, though a wild o branch,   Rm 11:17
Can fig tree produce o-s,   Jms 3:12
do not harm the o oil and the   Rv 6:6
are the two o trees and the two   Rv 11:4

OMEGA

the Alpha and the O   Rv 1:8; 21:6; 22:13

OMEN

not go to seek o-s as on previous   Nm 24:1
interpret o-s, practice sorcery,   Dt 18:10
divination and interpreted o-s.   2Kg 17:17
as a sign and o against Egypt   Is 20:3
destroys the o-s of the false prophets   Is 44:25

OMRI

1. Grandson of Benjamin (1Ch 7:8).

2. Issacharite officer under David (1Ch 27:18).

3. Army commander; king of Israel; founded the city of Samaria (1Kg 16:15-28).

ONAN

Judah's second son (Gn 38:4-9; 46:12).

ONCE

O a year Aaron is to perform   Ex 30:10
they marched around the city o   Jos 6:14
I have spoken o, and I will not   Jb 40:5
God has spoken o; I have heard   Ps 62:11
O more, in a little while, I am   Hg 2:6
He died to sin o for all;   Rm 6:10
O I was alive apart from the law   Rm 7:9
For you were o darkness, but now   Eph 5:8
although I o had confidence in   Php 3:4
And you were o alienated and   Col 1:21
and you o walked in these things   Col 3:7
those who were o enlightened,   Heb 6:4
He did this o for all when He   Heb 7:27
the holy of holies o for all,   Heb 9:12
appointed for people to die o   Heb 9:27
been offered o to bear the sins   Heb 9:28
of Jesus Christ o and for all.   Heb 10:10
Yet o more I will shake not only   Heb 12:26
O you were not a people, but now   1Pt 2:10
suffered for sins o for all,   1Pt 3:18

ONE   *see* ONE AND ONLY SON

and they become o flesh.   Gn 2:24
The LORD our God, the LORD is o.   Dt 6:4
Not o of all the good promises   1Kg 8:56
no o who does good, not even o.   Ps 14:3
have asked o thing from the LORD;   Ps 27:4
his bones; not o of them is broken.   Ps 34:20
provoked the Holy O of Israel.   Ps 78:41
in the assembly of the holy o-s   Ps 89:5
before a single o of them began.   Ps 139:16
knew that o fate comes
  to them both.   Ec 2:14

Better o handful with rest,	Ec 4:6
Two are better than o because they	Ec 4:9
how can o person alone keep warm?	Ec 4:11
has made the o as well as the other,	Ec 7:14
by adding o thing to another	Ec 7:27
I have found o true man,	Ec 7:28
there is o fate for the righteous and	Ec 9:2
but o sinner can destroy much good.	Ec 9:18
sayings are given by o Shepherd.	Ec 12:11
captured my heart with o glance of	Sg 4:9
day seven women will seize o man,	Is 4:1
make them o nation in the land,	Ezk 37:22
Don't all of us have o Father?	
Didn't o God create us?	Mal 2:10
For he is the o spoken of	Mt 3:3
forces you to go o mile, go ... two.	Mt 5:41
but deliver us from the evil o.	Mt 6:13
cold water to o of these little o-s	Mt 10:42
Are You the Coming O,	Mt 11:3
to enter life with o eye, rather than	Mt 18:9
the two will become o flesh?	Mt 19:5
they each received o denarius.	Mt 20:9
because you have o Teacher,	Mt 23:8
o will be taken and o left.	Mt 24:40
O of you will betray Me.	Mt 26:21
stay awake with Me o hour?	Mt 26:40
You certainly are o of them,	Mt 26:73
O of whom I said, 'The O coming	Jn 1:15
This is the O I told you about:	Jn 1:30
We have found the O Moses wrote	Jn 1:45
You are the Holy O of God!	Jn 6:69
I did o work, and you are all amazed	Jn 7:21
said. "We have o Father—God."	Jn 8:41
O thing I do know: I was blind,	Jn 9:25
there will be o flock, o shepherd.	Jn 10:16
The Father and I are o.	Jn 10:30
advantage that o man should die	Jn 11:50
No o comes to the Father except	Jn 14:6
they may be o as We are o.	Jn 17:11
and not o of them is lost,	Jn 17:12
May they be made completely o,	Jn 17:23
I have not lost o of those You	Jn 18:9
that o man should die for the	Jn 18:14
Not o of His bones will be broken.	Jn 19:36
were of o heart and soul,	Ac 4:32
From o man He has made every	Ac 17:26
There is no o righteous, not even o;	Rm 3:10
by the o man's trespass, death	Rm 5:17

who are many are o body in Christ	Rm 12:5
that o for whom Christ died.	Rm 14:15
joined to a prostitute is o body	1Co 6:16
yet for us there is o God,	1Co 8:6
but only o receives the prize?	1Co 9:24
we who are many are o body,	1Co 10:17
baptized by o Spirit into o body	1Co 12:13
if O died for all, then all died.	2Co 5:14
you are all o in Christ Jesus.	Gl 3:28
made both groups o and tore down	Eph 2:14
o Lord, o faith, o baptism,	Eph 4:5
the two will become o flesh.	Eph 5:31
firm in o spirit, with o mind,	Php 1:27
same feelings, focusing on o goal.	Php 2:2
But o thing I do: forgetting	Php 3:13
you were also called in o body,	Col 3:15
For there is o God and o mediator	1Tm 2:5
the husband of o wife,	1Tm 3:2; Ti 1:6
after offering o sacrifice for sins	Heb 10:12
from o man ... came offspring	Heb 11:12
entire law, yet fails in o point,	Jms 2:10
You believe that God is o;	Jms 2:19
from o-'s own interpretation,	2Pt 1:20
the Lord o day is like 1,000 years,	2Pt 3:8
the O who is in you is greater than	1Jn 4:4
The Holy O, the True O, the O who	Rv 3:7

ONE AND ONLY SON

glory as the O from the Father,	Jn 1:14
No one has ever seen God. The O	Jn 1:18
He gave His O, so that everyone	Jn 3:16
not believed in the name of the O	Jn 3:18
God sent His O into the world so	1Jn 1:8

ONE-FIFTH

he must add o to its value.	Lv 27:31

ONESIMUS

    Slave of Philemon converted by Paul (Phm 10); became a messenger (Col 4:9).

ONESIPHORUS

    Ephesian Christian praised by Paul (2Tm 1:16; 4:19).

ONE-TENTH

to collect the o offering in all	Neh 10:37

ONIONS

melons, leeks, o, and garlic.	Nm 11:5

ONLY   *see* ONE AND ONLY SON

If o Ishmael could live in Your	Gn 17:18

"Take your son," He said, "your o   Gn 22:2
I am the o remaining prophet of   1Kg 18:22
o spare his life.   Jb 2:6
Should we accept o good from God   Jb 2:10
And who is a rock? O our God.   Ps 18:31
O goodness and faithful love   Ps 23:6
For His anger lasts o a moment,   Ps 30:5
darkness is my {o} friend.   Ps 88:18
Lord your God, and serve o Him.   Mt 4:10
I was sent o to the lost sheep   Mt 15:24
Don't be afraid. O believe.   Mk 5:36
but o what He sees the Father   Jn 5:19
invisible, the o God, be honor   1Tm 1:17
to the o God our Savior,   Jd 25

ONYX

bdellium and o are also there.   Gn 2:12
Take two o stones and engrave   Ex 28:9
diamond, beryl, o, and jasper   Ezk 28:13

OPEN (adj)

their throat is an o grave;   Ps 5:9
His ears are o to their cry for   Ps 34:15
Better an o reprimand than   Pr 27:5
like a lamb in an o meadow?   Hs 4:16
Their throat is an o grave;   Rm 3:13
before you an o door that no one   Rv 3:8
there in heaven was an o door.   Rv 4:1

OPEN (v)

eyes will be o-ed and you will be   Gn 3:5
The earth o-ed its mouth and   Nm 16:32
Then the LORD o-ed the donkey's   Nm 22:28
the LORD o-ed the servant's eyes.   2Kg 6:17
Ezra o-ed the book in full view   Neh 8:5
They o their mouths against me   Ps 22:13
who does not o his mouth.   Ps 38:13
Lord, o my lips, and my mouth   Ps 51:15
when You o Your hand,   Ps 104:28
O my eyes so that I may see   Ps 119:18
The LORD o-s the eyes of the blind.   Ps 146:8
A gift o-s doors for a man and   Pr 18:16
o your eyes, and you'll have enough   Pr 20:13
O to me, my sister, my darling   Sg 5:2
what he o-s, no one can close;   Is 22:22
eyes of the blind will be o-ed   Is 35:5
in order to o blind eyes, to   Is 42:7
yet He did not o His mouth.   Is 53:7
heavens o-ed and I saw visions   Ezk 1:1
and the books were o-ed   Dn 7:10

fountain will be o-ed for the   Zch 13:1
if I will not o the floodgates   Mal 3:10
and the door will be o-ed to you   Mt 7:7
I will o My mouth in parables;   Mt 13:35
they said to Him, "o our eyes!"   Mt 20:33
Immediately his ears were o-ed   Mk 7:35
Then their eyes were o-ed, and   Lk 24:31
Then He o-ed their minds to   Lk 24:45
we don't know who o-ed his eyes.   Jn 9:21
angel of the Lord o-ed the doors   Ac 5:19
see the heavens o-ed and the Son   Ac 7:56
so He does not o His mouth.   Ac 8:32
door for effective ministry has o-ed   1Co 16:9
door was o-ed to me by the Lord   2Co 2:12
our heart has been o-ed wide.   2Co 6:11
us that God may o a door to us   Col 4:3
His ears are o to their request   1Pt 3:12
who o-s and no one will close,   Rv 3:7
hears My voice and o-s the door,   Rv 3:20
Who is worthy to o the scroll   Rv 5:2
I saw the Lamb o one of the   Rv 6:1
I saw heaven o-ed, and there was   Rv 19:11
and books were o-ed.   Rv 20:12

OPENLY

could no longer enter a town o.   Mk 1:45
He was o talking about this.   Mk 8:32
went up, not o but secretly.   Jn 7:10
I have spoken o to the world,   Jn 18:20
We have spoken o to you   2Co 6:11

OPEN-MINDED

here were more o than those   Ac 17:11

OPERATE

passions o-d through the law   Rm 7:5
plan, which o-s by faith   1Tm 1:4

OPHEL

Hill south of the temple, fortified by Israel
(2Ch 27:3; 33:14; Neh 3:19-27; 11:21).

OPHIR

Place famous for trade, especially in gold
(1Kg 9:28; 10:11; 22:48; 1Ch 29:4; Jb
22:24; 28:16; Ps 45:9; Is 13:12).

OPINION

call the girl and ask her o.   Gn 24:57
you hesitate between two o-s?   1Kg 18:21
only wants to show off his o-s.   Pr 18:2
wise in their own o and clever   Is 5:21

OPPONENT

his o-s with gentleness	2Tm 2:25
that the o will be ashamed	Ti 2:8

OPPORTUNITY

looking for a good o to betray Him.	Mt 26:16
lead to an o for you to witness.	Lk 21:13
sin, seizing an o	Rm 7:8,11
freedom as an o for the flesh,	Gl 5:13
as we have o, we must work for	Gl 6:10
and don't give the Devil an o.	Eph 4:27
but lacked the o {to show it}.	Php 4:10
adversary no o to accuse us.	1Tm 5:14
patience ... as {an o for} salvation,	2Pt 3:15

OPPOSE

I came out to o you, because	Nm 22:32
Who has o-d Him and come out	Jb 9:4
who can o Him? He does what He	Jb 23:13
of Persia o-d me for 21 days.	Dn 10:13
to be a sign that will be o-d	Lk 2:34
authority is o-ing God's command,	Rm 13:2
o-d him to his face because he	Gl 2:11
was against us and o-d to us,	Col 2:14
He o-s and exalts himself above	2Th 2:4

OPPOSITION

God to you in spite of great o.	1Th 2:2

OPPRESS

be enslaved and o-ed 400 years.	Gn 15:13
more they o-ed them, the more	Ex 1:12
way the Egyptians are o-ing them	Ex 3:9
You must not o a foreign resident;	Ex 23:9
You must not o your neighbor	Lv 19:13
LORD severely o-ed the people	1Sm 5:6
it good for You to o, to reject	Jb 10:3
LORD is a refuge for the o-ed	Ps 9:9
for the fatherless and the o-ed	Ps 10:18
and justice for all the o-ed.	Ps 103:6
raises up those who are o-ed	Ps 146:8
one who o-es the poor insults	Pr 14:31
leader who o-es the poor is like	Pr 28:3
the cause of the o-ed and needy.	Pr 31:9
the tears of those who are o-ed;	Ec 4:1
He was o-ed and afflicted,	Is 53:7
to set the o-ed free,	Is 58:6
if you no longer o the alien,	Jr 7:6
will no longer o My people but	Ezk 45:8
Do not o the widow or the	Zch 7:10
against those who o the widow	Mal 3:5

to the blind, to set free the o-ed,	Lk 4:18
would enslave and o them for 400	Ac 7:6
avenged the o-ed man by striking	Ac 7:24
Don't the rich o you and drag	Jms 2:6

OPPRESSION

Because of the o of the afflicted	Ps 12:5
Place no trust in o, or false hope in	Ps 62:10
them from o and violence,	Ps 72:14
humbled by cruel o and	Ps 107:39
I observed all the acts of o	Ec 4:1
If you see o of the poor and	Ec 5:8
have trusted in o and deceit	Is 30:12
because of o and judgment	Is 53:8
Put away violence and o and	Ezk 45:9
seen the o of My people	Ac 7:34

OPPRESSIVE

crooked statutes and writing o laws	Is 10:1

OPPRESSOR

crying out because of their o-s	Ex 3:7
hear the voice of {their} o.	Jb 3:18
help the poor, and crush the o,	Ps 72:4
do not leave me to my o-s.	Ps 119:121
The poor and the o have this in	Pr 29:13
Correct the o. Defend the rights	Is 1:17
because of the fury of the o	Is 51:13
I will punish all his o-s.	Jr 30:20
and no o will march against them	Zch 9:8

ORACLE

The o of Balaam son of Beor,	Nm 24:3
uttered this o against him:	2Kg 9:25
An o within my heart concerning	Ps 36:1
of Agur son of Jakeh. The o.	Pr 30:1
an o that his mother taught him	Pr 31:1
An o against Babylon that Isaiah	Is 13:1
An o against Moab:	Is 15:1
An o against Damascus:	Is 17:1
An o against Egypt:	Is 19:1
An o against the desert by the	Is 21:1
An o against Dumah:	Is 21:11
An o against Arabia:	Is 21:13
An o against the Valley of Vision:	Is 22:1
An o against Tyre:	Is 23:1
An o about the animals of the	Is 30:6
the wise, or an o from the prophet.	Jr 18:18
their own tongues to deliver an o.	Jr 23:31
saw o-s for you that were empty	Lm 2:14
This o is about the prince in	Ezk 12:10

The o concerning Nineveh. Nah 1:1
The o that Habakkuk the prophet Hab 1:1
An O The word of the LORD Zch 9:1; 12:1
An o: The word of the LORD to Mal 1:1
received living o-s to give to us. Ac 7:38
{should be} like the o-s of God; 1Pt 4:11

ORATION
The man's o to Ithiel, to Ithiel Pr 30:1

ORCHARD
while Lebanon will become an o Is 29:17
the desert will become an o Is 32:15

ORDAIN
then anoint, o, and consecrate Ex 28:41
the way you will o Aaron and his Ex 29:9
who o-s victories for Jacob. Ps 44:4
He has o-ed His covenant forever Ps 111:9
He has o-ed a lot for them; Is 34:17
unless the Lord has o-ed {it}? Lm 3:37

ORDEAL
when the fiery o arises among 1Pt 4:12

ORDER (n)
seated before him in o by age, Gn 43:33
Put your affairs in o, 2Kg 20:1
give His angels o-s concerning Ps 91:11
an o that will never pass away. Ps 148:6
will also give o-s to the clouds Is 5:6
His God teaches him o; Is 28:26
If this fixed o departs from My Jr 31:36
He gave o-s to heat the furnace Dn 3:19
give His angels o-s concerning Mt 4:6
vacant, swept, and put in o. Mt 12:44
So he sent o-s and had John Mt 14:10
gave the disciples o-s to tell no one Mt 16:20
given o-s through the Holy Spirit Ac 1:2
sin in o that grace may multiply? Rm 6:1
must be done decently and in o. 1Co 14:40
But each in his own o: 1Co 15:23
see your good o and the strength Col 2:5
forever in the o of Melchizedek. Heb 5:6

ORDER (v)
and whoever o-s his conduct, Ps 50:23
because He has o-ed it by my Is 34:16
Then He o-ed them to tell no one Mk 7:36
He o-ed them to tell no one what Mk 9:9
and o-ed them not to preach Ac 4:18
o-ed them not to speak in the name Ac 5:40

ORDERLY
to write to you in o sequence, Lk 1:3
to them in an o sequence, Ac 11:4

ORDINANCE
These are the o-s that you Ex 21:1
Keep My statutes and o-s; Lv 18:5
because the rejected My o-s Lv 26:43
careful to keep these o-s Dt 7:12
and o-s, so that you may live Dt 30:16
David established this policy as
a law and an o for Israel 1Sm 30:25
You gave them impartial o-s Neh 9:13
the o-s of the LORD are reliable Ps 19:9
I have set Your o-s {before me}. Ps 119:30
her people have rejected My o-s Ezk 5:6
and carefully observe My o-s. Ezk 36:27
that no edict or o the king Dn 6:15

ORDINARY
There is no o bread on hand. 1Sm 21:4
some for special use, some for o. 2Tm 2:20

ORDINATION
the ram of Aaron's o Ex 29:26
offering, the o offering Lv 7:37
second ram, the ram of o, and Aaron Lv 8:22
your days of o are completed, Lv 8:33

ORGIES
drunkenness, o, carousing, 1Pt 4:3

ORIGIN
whose o was in ancient times, Is 23:7
Your o and your birth were in Ezk 16:3
His o is from antiquity, Mc 5:2
that they did not know its o. Lk 20:7
kingdom does not have its o here. Jn 18:36

ORIGINAL
be rebuilt on its {o} site Ezr 5:15
just as the o eyewitnesses Lk 1:2
have renounced their o pledge 1Tm 5:12

ORIGINATE
Did the word of God o from you, 1Co 14:36

ORIGINATOR
the O of God's creation says Rv 3:14

ORION
the Bear, O, the Pleiades, and Jb 9:9
or loosen the belt of O? Jb 38:31
who made the Pleiades and O Am 5:8

ORNAMENT

the crescent o-s that were   Jdg 8:21
a gold ring or an o of gold.   Pr 25:12
wearing of gold o-s or fine clothes.   1Pt 3:3

ORNAN *see* ARAUNAH

ORPAH

Naomi's daughter-in-law (Ru 1:4,14).

ORPHANS

Abandon your o; I will preserve   Jr 49:11
We have become o, fatherless;   Lm 5:3
I will not leave you as o;   Jn 14:18
to look after o and widows in   Jms 1:27

OSTRICH

the o, the short-eared owl,   Lv 11:16
wings of the o flap joyfully,   Jb 39:13
for jackals, an abode for o-es.   Is 34:13
like o-es in the wilderness   Lm 4:3
the jackals and mourn like o-es.   Mc 1:8

OTHER

Do not have o gods besides Me.   Ex 20:3
on earth below; there is no o.   Dt 4:39
They went after o gods from the   Jdg 2:12
they had worshiped o gods.   2Kg 17:7
there is no o Savior but Me.   Is 43:11
I am the LORD, and there is no o;   Is 45:5
LORD your God, and there is no o.   Jl 2:27
cheek, turn the o to him also.   Mt 5:39
he will hate one and love the o,   Mt 6:24
as you want o-s to do for you,   Lk 6:31
gospel o than what we have preached   Gl 1:8
consider o-s as more important   Php 2:3
people not to teach o doctrine   1Tm 1:3
If anyone teaches o doctrine   1Tm 6:3
will be able to teach o-s also.   2Tm 2:2
should use it to serve o-s,   1Pt 4:10

OTHNIEL

Judge; defeated Arameans (Jdg 3:7-11);
Caleb's nephew (Jos 15:17; Jdg 1:13).

OUGHT

you also o to wash one another's   Jn 13:14
I o to have been
  recommended by   2Co 12:11
how people o to act in God's   1Tm 3:15
farmer who o to be the first to   2Tm 2:6
by this time you o to be teachers,   Heb 5:12

OUR

Let Us make man in O image,   Gn 1:26
O Father in heaven,   Mt 6:9

OUSTS

serving girl when she o her lady.   Pr 30:23

OUTBREAK

It is a scaly o, a skin disease   Lv 13:30

OUTBURST

that place an O Against Uzzah,   2Sm 6:8
jealousy, o-s of anger, selfish   2Co 12:20
jealousy, o-s of anger, selfish   Gl 5:20

OUTCAST

they will call you The O,   Jr 30:17

OUTCOME

will be the o of these things?   Dn 12:8
the temple police to see the o.   Mt 26:58
observe the o of their lives,   Heb 13:7
what will the o be for those who   1Pt 4:17

OUTCRY

the o against its people is great   Gn 19:13
He heard the o of the afflicted   Jb 34:28
and the o of the harvesters has   Jms 5:4

OUTDO

O one another in showing honor.   Rm 12:10

OUTDOOR

Complete your o work, and   Pr 24:27

OUTDOORSMAN

Esau ... an expert hunter, an o,   Gn 25:27

OUTER

be thrown into the o darkness.   Mt 8:12
throw him into the o darkness,   Mt 22:13
slave into the o darkness.   Mt 25:30
though our o person is being   2Co 4:16

OUTLAWS

And He was counted among o.   Mk 15:28
And He was counted among the o.   Lk 22:37

OUTLIVED

of the elders who o Joshua.   Jdg 2:7

OUTNUMBER

Israelites who o the Levites,   Nm 3:46
who are with us o those who are   2Kg 6:16
they would o the grains of sand   Ps 139:18

OUTRAGE

committed an o against Israel	Gn 34:7
has committed an o in Israel by	Dt 22:21
and committed an o in Israel	Jos 7:15
Tell us, how did this o occur?	Jdg 20:3
have committed an o in Israel	Jr 29:23

OUTRAGEOUS

will say o things against the God	Dn 11:36

OUTRAGEOUSLY

treated them o and killed them.	Mt 22:6
suffered and been o treated	1Th 2:2

OUTRAN

of the plain and o the Cushite.	2Sm 18:23
other disciple o Peter and got	Jn 20:4

OUTSIDE

o the camp; it is a sin offering.	Ex 29:14
bring the bull o the camp	Lv 4:21
flesh and the hide o the camp.	Lv 9:11
must be brought o the camp	Lv 16:27
slacker says, "There's a lion o!	Pr 22:13
You clean the o of the cup and	Mt 23:25
prophet to perish o of Jerusalem!	Lk 13:33
But Mary stood o facing the tomb	Jn 20:11
person can commit is o the body,	1Co 6:18
To those who are o the law,	1Co 9:21
Jesus also suffered o the gate,	Heb 13:12
us then go to Him o the camp,	Heb 13:13
O are the dogs, the sorcerers	Rv 22:15

OUTSIDER

But no o may share it.	Lv 22:13
what is it to me to judge o-s?	1Co 5:12
Walk in wisdom toward o-s,	Col 4:5
properly in the presence of o-s	1Th 4:12
a good reputation among o-s	1Tm 3:7

OUTSKIRTS

and consumed the o of the camp.	Nm 11:1
will only see the o of their camp;	Nm 23:13

OUTSTANDING

They are o among the apostles,	Rm 16:7

OUTSTRETCHED

you with an o arm and great acts	Ex 6:6
by a strong hand and an o arm,	Dt 4:34
by Your great power and o arm.	Dt 9:29
a strong hand and an o arm,	Dt 26:8
with great power and an o arm.	2Kg 17:36

with a strong hand and o arm.	Ps 136:12
By My great strength and o arm,	Jr 27:5
a strong hand, an o arm,	Ezk 20:33

OUTWARD

Stop judging according to o	Jn 7:24
pride in the o appearance rather	2Co 5:12
should not consist of o things	1Pt 3:3

OUTWARDLY

person is not a Jew who is one o,	Rm 2:28

OUTWEIGH

For then it would o the sand of	Jb 6:3
but aggravation from a fool o-s them	Pr 27:3
a little folly o-s wisdom	Ec 10:1

OVEN

like an o heated by a baker	Hs 7:4

OVEN-FIRED

Come, let us make o bricks.	Gn 11:3

OVERCAST

a day of clouds and dense o,	Jl 2:2

OVERCOME

is Jewish, you won't o him,	Est 6:13
the torments of Sheol o-came me;	Ps 116:3
am continually o by longing for	Ps 119:20
my heart is o with dismay.	Ps 143:4
No disaster {o-s} the righteous,	Pr 12:21
{Woe} to those o with wine.	Is 28:1
will not o you, for I am with you	Jr 15:20
like a man o by wine,	Jr 23:9
and the current o-came me.	Jnh 2:3
yet the darkness did not o it.	Jn 1:5
When he was o by sleep he fell	Ac 20:9
I am o with joy in all our	2Co 7:4

OVERCONFIDENT

and you have become o.	2Kg 14:10

OVEREXTENDING

For we are not o ourselves,	2Co 10:14

OVERFLOW

Now the Jordan o-s its banks	Jos 3:15
my cup o-s.	Ps 23:5
Your ways o with plenty.	Ps 65:11
The wilderness pastures o	Ps 65:12
and drink in their o-ing waters.	Ps 73:10
your vats will o with new wine.	Pr 3:10
My eyes will o with tears,	Jr 13:17

My eyes o unceasingly,	Lm 3:49
the vats will o with new wine	Jl 2:24
will again o with prosperity;	Zch 1:17
speaks from the o of the heart.	Mt 12:34
so that you may o with hope by	Rm 15:13
our comfort o-s through Christ	2Co 1:5
thanksgiving to o to God's glory	2Co 4:15
poverty o-ed into the wealth	2Co 8:2
to make every grace o to you,	2Co 9:8
to increase and o with love	1Th 3:12
and the grace of our Lord o-ed,	1Tm 1:14

OVERJOYED

the ark, they were o to see it.	1Sm 6:13
The king was o and gave orders	Dn 6:23
saw the star, they were o	Mt 2:10
Abraham was o that he would see	Jn 8:56

OVERLAID

He o them with gold and made	Ex 36:34
he o it with pure gold.	1Kg 6:20

OVERLOOK

his virtue is to o an offense.	Pr 19:11
widows were being o-ed in the	Ac 6:1
having o-ed the times of ignorance	Ac 17:30

OVERLY

Why then have I been o wise?	Ec 2:15
and don't be o wise.	Ec 7:16

OVERNIGHT

not to leave his corpse on the tree o	Dt 21:23
Please agree to stay o and enjoy	Jdg 19:6

OVERPOWER

Jews' enemies had hoped to o them,	Est 9:1
if somebody o-s one person, two	Ec 4:12
forces of Hades will not o it.	Mt 16:18
leaped on them, o-ed them all,	Ac 19:16

OVERRUN

Their land was o with frogs,	Ps 105:30
foreigners will never o it again.	Jl 3:17

OVERSEE

who o-saw the LORD's temple.	2Kg 12:11
those who o the LORD's temple.	2Kg 22:5
not o-ing out of compulsion but	1Pt 5:2

OVERSEER

o-s insisted, "Finish your	Ex 5:13
has appointed you as o-s	Ac 20:28

including the o-s and deacons	Php 1:1
If anyone aspires to be an o	1Tm 3:1
an o, as God's manager, must	Ti 1:7

OVERSHADOW

the Lord has o-ed Daughter Zion	Lm 2:1
of the Most High will o you.	Lk 1:35
a cloud appeared and o-ed them.	Lk 9:34
above it o-ing the mercy seat.	Heb 9:5

OVERSTEPPED

transgressed teachings, o decrees,	Is 24:5

OVERTAKE

disaster will o me, and I will die.	Gn 19:19
o him because the distance is	Dt 19:6
blessings will come and o you,	Dt 28:2
sword of your enemy o-ing you	1Ch 21:12
the thing I feared has o-n me,	Jb 3:25
Terrors o him like a flood;	Jb 27:20
may an enemy pursue and o me;	Ps 7:5
I pursue my enemies and o them;	Ps 18:37
my sins have o-n me;	Ps 40:12
let Your burning anger o them.	Ps 69:24
Trouble and distress have o-n me,	Ps 119:143
Joy and gladness will o (them),	Is 35:10
sword you fear will o you there	Jr 42:16
the plowman will o the reaper	Am 9:13
No calamity will o us.	Mc 3:11
so that darkness doesn't o you.	Jn 12:35
temptation has o-n you except	1Co 10:13
and wrath has o-n them completely	1Th 2:16
this day would o you like a thief.	1Th 5:4

OVERTHROW

He o-threw these cities, the entire	Gn 19:25
and o-s established leaders.	Jb 12:19
The wicked are o-n and perish,	Pr 12:7
Gomorrah when God o-threw them.	Is 13:19
Gomorrah were o-n along with their	Jr 49:18
which was o-n in an instant	Lm 4:6
I o-threw some of you as I o-threw	Am 4:11
In 40 days Nineveh will be o-n!	Jnh 3:4
work is of men, it will be o-n;	Ac 5:38
they o whole households by	Ti 1:11

OVERTURN

I will o royal thrones and	Hg 2:22
o-ed the money changers' tables	Mt 21:12

o-ed the money changers' tables Mk 11:15
coins and o-ed the tables. Jn 2:15
and are o-ing the faith of some. 2Tm 2:18

OVERWHELM

grief that would o my father. Gn 44:34
I was o-ed with fear Neh 2:2
he falls, he will not be o-ed, Ps 37:24
Iniquities o me; only You can Ps 65:3
anger o-s me because my foes Ps 119:139
when the o-ing scourge passes Is 28:15
on you an o-ing urge to sleep; Is 29:10
rivers, they will not o you. Is 43:2
Nineveh with an o-ing flood, Nah 1:8
and astonishment o-ed them. Mk 16:8
were completely o-ed—beyond 2Co 1:8
may be o-ed by excessive grief. 2Co 2:7

OWE

forgive whatever your brother o-s Dt 15:3
one who o-d 10,000 talents Mt 18:24
and said, 'Pay what you o' Mt 18:28
o-d 500 denarii, and the other Lk 7:41
How much do you o my master? Lk 16:5
not ... a gift, but as something o-d. Rm 4:4
taxes to those you o taxes, Rm 13:7
Do not o anyone anything, except Rm 13:8
you o me even your own self. Phm 19

OWL

the little o, ... the long-eared o Lv 11:17
little o, ... long-eared o, ... white o Dt 14:16
desert o, like an o among the ruins. Ps 102:6
and o-s will fill the houses. Is 13:21
the screech o will stay there Is 34:14
desert o and ... screech o will roost Zph 2:14

OWN (adj)

God created man in His o image; Gn 1:27
seems right in his o eyes. Dt 12:8
be put to death for his o sin. Dt 24:16
each to his o inheritance. Jos 24:28
to make you His o people. 1Sm 12:22
Israel Your o people forever, 2Sm 7:24
eat from his o vine and his o fig 2Kg 18:31
my o mouth would condemn me; Jb 9:20
and take my life in my o hands? Jb 13:14
comes back on his o head, Ps 7:16
chosen to be His o possession! Ps 33:12
rely on your o understanding; Pr 3:5

water from your o cistern, Pr 5:15
way is right in his o eyes, Pr 12:15
ways seem right in his o eyes, Pr 16:2
man who is wise in his o eyes? Pr 26:12
stranger, and not your o lips. Pr 27:2
way will fall into his o pit, Pr 28:10
all have turned to our o way; Is 53:6
will die for his o wrongdoing. Jr 31:30
die for his o iniquity Ezk 18:18
his blood is on his o hands. Ezk 33:5
will return on your o head. Ob 15
are the people in his o home. Mc 7:6
notice the log in your o eye? Mt 7:3
let the dead bury their o dead. Mt 8:22
has no honor in his o country. Jn 4:44
He calls his o sheep by name and Jn 10:3
speaking in his o language. Ac 2:6
did not even spare His o Son, Rm 8:32
be wise in your o estimation. Rm 12:16
fully convinced in his o mind. Rm 14:5
over his o body, but his wife does. 1Co 7:4
no one ever hates his o flesh, Eph 5:29
not {only} for his o interests, Php 2:4
work out your o salvation with Php 2:12
all seek their o interests, Php 2:21
one who manages his o household 1Tm 3:4
provide for his o relatives, 1Tm 5:8
but by His o blood, Heb 9:12
from one's o interpretation, 2Pt 1:20

OWN (n)

will eat what grows on its o, 2Kg 19:29
is not the case; I am on my o. Jb 9:35
not despise His o who are Ps 69:33
has enough trouble of its o. Mt 6:34
He came to His o, Jn 1:11
I can do nothing on My o. Jn 5:30
For I didn't come on My o Jn 8:42
but I lay it down on My o. Jn 10:18
Having loved His o who were in Jn 13:1
would love {you as} its o. Jn 15:19
You are not your o, 1Co 6:19

OWN (v)

all that he o-ed under Joseph's Gn 39:6
and strike everything he o-s, Jb 1:11
everything he o-s in exchange Jb 2:4
Solomon o-ed a vineyard in Sg 8:11
those who o-ed lands or houses Ac 4:34

OWNER

its **o** must also be put to death.	Ex 21:29
must make restitution to its **o**.	Ex 22:12
like a magic stone to its **o**;	Pr 17:8
preserves the life of its **o**.	Ec 7:12
ox knows its **o**, and the donkey	Is 1:3
what will the **o** of the vineyard	Lk 20:15
profit for her **o-s** by	Ac 16:16
though he is the **o** of everything.	Gl 4:1

OX

or female slave, his **o** or donkey,	Ex 20:17
When an **o** gores a man	Ex 21:28
your enemy's stray **o** or donkey,	Ex 23:4
an **o** and a ram for a fellowship	Lv 9:4
Do not muzzle an **o** while it treads	Dt 25:4
in from the field behind his **oxen**.	1Sm 11:5
because the **oxen** had stumbled.	2Sm 6:6
Here are the **oxen** for a burnt	2Sm 24:22
He has lavishly sacrificed **oxen**	1Kg 1:19
It stood on 12 **oxen**, three facing	1Kg 7:25
Elisha left the **oxen**, ran to follow	1Kg 19:20
500 yoke of **oxen**,	Jb 1:3
Would the wild **o** be willing to	Jb 39:9
1,000 yoke of **oxen**,	Jb 42:12
from the horns of the wild **oxen**.	Ps 22:21
Sirion, like a young wild **o**.	Ps 29:6
please the LORD more than an **o**,	Ps 69:31
for the image of a grass-eating **o**.	Ps 106:20
impulsively like an **o** going to	Pr 7:22
Where there are no **oxen**,	Pr 14:4
The **o** knows its owner, and the	Is 1:3
lion will eat straw like the **o**	Is 11:7; 65:5
the face of an **o** on the left,	Ezk 1:10
one of you untie his **o** or donkey	Lk 13:15
son or **o** falls into a well,	Lk 14:5
I have bought five yoke of **oxen**	Lk 14:19
not muzzle an **o** while it treads	1Co 9:9
Is God really concerned with **oxen**?	1Co 9:9
not muzzle an **o** that is	1Tm 5:18

OXGOAD

down 600 Philistines with an **o**.	Jdg 3:31
for putting a point on an **o**.	1Sm 13:21

P

PACK

P your bags for exile	Jr 46:19
p your bags for exile and go	Ezk 12:3

PADDAN-ARAM

Land where Abraham came from, and where Isaac and Jacob got their wives (Gn 25:20; 28:2-7; 31:18; 33:18; 35:9,26; 46:15; 48:7).

PAGAN (adj)

He removed the **p** altars and	2Ch 14:3
yourself will die on **p** soil,	Am 7:17
the names of the **p** priests	Zph 1:4

PAGANS

when you were **p**, you were led	1Co 12:2
spent in doing the will of the **p**:	1Pt 4:3
accepting nothing from **p**.	3Jn 7

PAIN

I will intensify your labor **p-s**;	Gn 3:16
her labor **p-s** came on her.	1Sm 4:19
I gave birth to him in **p**.	1Ch 4:9
so that I will not cause any **p**.	1Ch 4:10
I would leap for joy in unrelenting **p**	Jb 6:10
on his bed with **p** and constant	Jb 33:19
Many **p-s** come to the wicked,	Ps 32:10
and my **p** is constantly with me.	Ps 38:17
struck me, but I feel no **p**!	Pr 23:35
LORD gives you rest from your **p**,	Is 14:3
P grips me, like the **p** of a woman in	Is 21:3
and He carried our **p-s**;	Is 53:4
Your **p** has no cure!	Jr 30:15
Labor **p-s** come on him.	Hs 13:13
are the beginning of birth **p-s**.	Mt 24:8
a woman is in labor she has **p**	Jn 16:21
ending the **p-s** of death,	Ac 2:24
with labor **p-s** until now.	Rm 8:22
if I cause you **p**, then who will	2Co 2:2
am in the **p-s** of childbirth for	Gl 4:19
like labor **p-s** on a pregnant woman,	1Th 5:3
pierced themselves with many **p-s**.	1Tm 6:10
and **p** will exist no longer,	Rv 21:4

PAINFUL

by means of p labor all the	Gn 3:17
How p honest words can be!	Jb 6:25
to you on another p visit.	2Co 2:1
enjoyable at the time, but p.	Heb 12:11

PAINT (n)

you enlarge your eyes with p?	Jr 4:30

PAINTED

so she p-ed her eyes,	2Kg 9:30
You bathed, p-ed your eyes,	Ezk 23:40

PAIR

and seven p-s, male and female,	Gn 7:3
began to send them out in p-s	Mk 6:7
a p of turtledoves or two young	Lk 2:24
sent them ahead of Him in p-s	Lk 10:1

PALACE

and they built a p for David.	2Sm 5:11
his entire p complex after 13 years	1Kg 7:1
and a royal p for himself.	2Ch 2:12
Esther was also taken to the p	Est 2:8
from ivory p-s harps bring you joy	Ps 45:8
yet it lives in kings' p-s.	Pr 30:28
For the p will be forsaken,	Is 32:14
capable of serving in the king's p	Dn 1:4
forgotten his Maker and built p-s;	Hs 8:14
wear soft clothes are in kings' p-s.	Mt 11:8
in the p of the high priest,	Mt 26:3
live in luxury are in royal p-s.	Lk 7:25

PALATE

words as the p tastes food?	Jb 12:11; 34:3
honeycomb is sweet to your p;	Pr 24:13

PALE

his face will no longer be p.	Is 29:22
labor and every face turned p?	Jr 30:6
his face turned p,	Dn 5:6
before them; all faces turn p.	Jl 2:6
and there was a p green horse.	Rv 6:8

PALM

springs of water and 70 date p-s,	Ex 15:27
and pour it into his left p.	Lv 14:15
p fronds, boughs of leafy trees,	Lv 23:40
Jericho, the City of P-s,	Dt 34:3
p trees and flower blossoms	1Kg 6:29
thrive like a p tree and grow	Ps 92:12
I will climb the p tree and take	Sg 7:8
you on the p-s of My hands;	Is 49:16

was decorated with p trees.	Ezk 40:16
they took p branches and went	Jn 12:13
robed in white with p branches in	Rv 7:9

PALTI or PALTIEL

Man to whom Saul gives Michal (1Sm 25:44; 2Sm 3:15).

PAMPERED

A slave p from his youth will	Pr 29:21
no longer be called p and spoiled.	Is 47:1

PAMPHYLIA

Region on the coast of Asia Minor represented at Pentecost (Ac 2:10) and visited by Paul (13:13; 14:24; 15:38).

PANELED (adj)

to live in your p houses,	Hg 1:4

PANELED (v)

p the interior temple walls	1Kg 6:15
It was p with cedar from the	1Kg 7:7

PANIC

the land is p-king because of you.	Jos 2:9
the p in the Philistine camp	1Sm 14:19
P, pit, and trap await you,	Jr 48:43
have experienced p and pitfall,	Lm 3:47
There will be p on the mountains	Ezk 7:7
that day a great p from the LORD	Zch 14:13

PANT

I p with open mouth because I	Ps 119:131
sun sets; p-ing, {it returns} to	Ec 1:5
donkeys stand ... p-ing for air like	Jr 14:6

PAPER

give divorce p-s and to send her	Mt 19:7
I don't want to do so with p and ink.	2Jn 12

PAPHOS

Paul visited (Ac 13:6-13).

PAPYRUS

she got a p basket for him and	Ex 2:3
Does p grow where there is no	Jb 8:11
will be grass, reeds, and p.	Is 35:7

PARABLE

understanding a proverb or a p,	Pr 1:6
and speak a p to the house	Ezk 17:2
Now speak a p to the rebellious	Ezk 24:3
I gave p-s through the prophets.	Hs 12:10
He told them many things in p-s	Mt 13:3

Why do You speak to them in p-s? Mt 13:10
listen to the p of the sower: Mt 13:18
speak anything to them without
a p Mt 13:34
I will open My mouth in p-s; Mt 13:35
Explain this p to us. Mt 15:15
Now learn this p from the fig Mt 24:32
had said this p against them, Mk 12:12
but to the rest it is in p-s, so that Lk 8:10
are You telling this p to us or to Lk 12:41

PARADE

p him on the horse through the city Est 6:9

PARADISE

branches are a p of pomegranates Sg 4:13
you will be with Me in p Lk 23:43
was caught up into p. 2Co 12:4
tree of life, which is in the p of God. Rv 2:7

PARALYTIC

the epileptics, and the p-s. Mt 4:24
brought to Him a p lying on a Mt 9:2
He told the p, "Get up, pick up your Mt 9:6
told the p, "Son, your sins are Mk 2:5

PARALYZED

he had a seizure and became p. 1Sm 25:37
my servant is lying at home p, Mt 8:6
He saw a man who had a p hand. Mt 12:10
the sick—blind, lame, and p Jn 5:3
many who were p and lame were Ac 8:7
who was p and had been bedridden Ac 9:33

PARAN

1. Wilderness south of Judah. Ishmael settled (Gn 21:21); Israel camped (Nm 10:12; 12:16; 13:3-26); David hid (1Sm 25:1); Hadad went through (1Kg 11:18).

2. Mountain, perhaps another name for Sinai (Dt 33:2; Hab 3:3).

PARCHED

my throat is p. My eyes fail Ps 69:3
I am like p land before You. Ps 143:6
like cold water to a p throat. Pr 25:25
and Egypt's canals will be p. Is 19:6
the p ground will become a pool Is 35:7
lead you, satisfy you in a p land, Is 58:11

PARCHMENTS

the scrolls, especially the p. 2Tm 4:13

PARDON

Please p the wrongdoing of this Nm 14:19
may the LORD p your servant: 2Kg 5:18
p-ed King Jehoiachin of Judah 2Kg 25:27
my sin and p my transgression? Jb 7:21
her iniquity has been p-ed, Is 40:2
I will p their bloodguilt, Jl 3:21

PARENT

even rise up against their p-s Mt 10:21
Every year His p-s traveled to Lk 2:41
Her p-s were astounded, but He Lk 8:56
one who has left ... p-s or children Lk 18:29
who sinned, this man or his p-s, Jn 9:2
evil, disobedient to p-s, Rm 1:30
save up for their p-s, but p-s for 2Co 12:14
Children, obey your p-s in the Lord, Eph 6:1
obey your p-s in everything, Col 3:20
family first and to repay their p-s, 1Tm 5:4
disobedient to p-s, ungrateful, 2Tm 3:2
hidden by his p-s for three Heb 11:23
who loves the p also loves his child. 1Jn 5:1

PARSIN

MENE, MENE, TEKEL, P. Dn 5:25

PART (n)

the latter p of Job's life more Jb 42:12
You who created my inward p-s; Ps 139:13
searching the innermost p-s. Pr 20:27
cleanse the innermost p-s. Pr 20:30
wash you, you have no p with Me. Jn 13:8
he kept back p of the proceeds Ac 5:2
do not offer any p-s of it to sin Rm 6:13
see a different law in the p-s of my Rm 7:23
as we have many p-s in one body, Rm 12:4
the body is one and has many p-s 1Co 12:12
know in p, and we prophesy in p. 1Co 13:9
Now I know in p, but then I will 1Co 13:12
to the lower p-s of the earth? Eph 4:9
working of each individual p. Eph 4:16
sending him—a p of myself Phm 12
though the tongue is a small p Jms 3:5

PART (v)

which p-ed to the right and left. 2Kg 2:8
p-ed the heavens and came down Ps 18:9
p Your heavens and come down. Ps 144:5
that they p-ed company, Ac 15:39

PARTIAL

Do not be **p** to the poor or	Lv 19:15
I will be **p** to no one, and I	Jb 32:21
God is not **p** to princes and does	Jb 34:19
a **p** hardening has come to Israel	Rm 11:25
the **p** will come to an end.	1Co 13:10

PARTIALITY

Do not show **p** when rendering	Dt 1:17
showing no **p** and taking no bribe.	Dt 10:17
Do not deny justice or show **p**	Dt 16:19
p or taking bribes with the LORD	2Ch 19:7
you show **p** to Him or argue	Jb 13:8
and show **p** to the wicked?	Ps 82:2
not good to show **p**	Pr 18:5; 24:23; 28:21
but are showing **p** in	Mal 2:9
to no one, for You don't show **p**	Mt 22:16
You don't show **p** but teach	Mk 12:14
You don't show **p**, but teach	Lk 20:21

PARTIALLY

as you have **p** understood us	2Co 1:14

PARTICIPANT

also a **p** in the glory about to be	1Pt 5:1

PARTICIPATE

circumcised, and then he may **p**;	Ex 12:48
don't **p** in the fruitless works of	Eph 5:11

PARTICIPATION

I pray that your **p** in the faith	Phm 6

PARTICULAR

On this **p** day you are not to do	Lv 23:28
in a **p** matter may the LORD	2Kg 5:18

PARTLY

feet were **p** iron and **p** fired clay.	Dn 2:33

PARTNER

To be a thief's **p** is to hate	Pr 29:24
your marriage **p** and your wife	Mal 2:14
who were Simon's **p**-s.	Lk 5:10
I may become a **p** in its benefits.	1Co 9:23
you to be **p**-s with demons!	1Co 10:20
Titus, he is my **p** and co-worker	2Co 8:23
and **p**-s of the promise in Christ	Eph 3:6
do not become their **p**-s.	Eph 5:7
and you are all **p**-s with me in	Php 1:7
So if you consider me a **p**	Phm 17

PARTNERSHIP

For what **p** is there between	2Co 6:14

because of your **p** in the gospel	Php 1:5

PARTRIDGE

who pursues a **p** in the mountains	1Sm 26:20
a **p** that hatches eggs it didn't lay.	Jr 17:11

PARTY

Assuming He was in the traveling **p**,	Lk 2:44
the strictest **p** of our religion	Ac 26:5
those from the circumcision **p**.	Gl 2:12

PASHHUR

1. Priest and chief officer in the temple; persecuted Jeremiah (Jr 20:1-2).

2. Zedekiah's messenger (Jr 21:1).

3. Head of priestly family that returned from exile (1Ch 9:12; Ezr 2:38; 10:22; Neh 7:41; 10:3; 11:12).

PASS

torch appeared and **p**-ed between	Gn 15:17
see the blood, I will **p** over you.	Ex 12:13
My goodness to **p** in front of you	Ex 33:19
your children **p** through the fire	Lv 18:21
son or daughter **p** through the fire,	Dt 18:10
At that moment, the LORD **p**-ed by	1Kg 19:11
made his son **p** through the fire	2Kg 16:3
and daughters **p** through the fire	2Kg 17:17
or his daughter **p** through the fire	2Kg 23:10
fish of the sea **p**-ing through	Ps 8:8
are right when You **p** sentence;	Ps 51:4
when the wind **p**-es over it, it	Ps 103:16
his days are like a **p**-ing shadow	Ps 144:4
calling to those who **p** by,	Pr 9:15
when you **p** through the waters,	Is 43:2
nothing to you, all you who **p**	Lm 1:12
p-ed by you and saw you lying in	Ezk 16:6
your children **p** through the fire	Ezk 20:31
I will make you **p** under the rod	Ezk 20:37
for I will **p** among you.	Am 5:17
stroke of a letter will **p** from the law	Mt 5:18
generation will certainly not **p**	Mt 24:34
Heaven and earth will **p** away, but My words will never **p** away.	Mt 24:35
let this cup **p** from Me.	Mt 26:39
sea and wanted to **p** by them.	Mk 6:48
who was **p**-ing by, to carry	Mk 15:21
He **p**-ed right through the crowd	Lk 4:30
he **p**-ed by on the other side.	Lk 10:31

Jesus the Nazarene is **p-ing** by,	Lk 18:37
but has **p-ed** from death to life.	Jn 5:24
God **p-ed** over the sins previously	Rm 3:25
in its current form is **p-ing** away	1Co 7:31
all **p-ed** through the sea,	1Co 10:1
Lord what I also **p-ed** on to you:	1Co 11:23
For I **p-ed** on to you as most	1Co 15:3
old things have **p-ed** away,	2Co 5:17
we may appear to **p** the test,	2Co 13:7
priest who has **p-ed** through the	Heb 4:14
because when he **p-es** the test he	Jms 1:12
heavens will **p** away with a loud	2Pt 3:10
darkness is **p-ing** away and the	1Jn 2:8
we have **p-ed** from death to life	1Jn 3:14
first woe has **p-ed**. There are still	Rv 9:12
previous things have **p-ed** away.	Rv 21:4

PASSAGE

grant me (safe) **p** until I reach	Neh 2:7
the Scripture **p** he was reading	Ac 8:32
He also says in another **p**	Ac 13:35
said in another **p**, You are a	Heb 5:6

PASSERBY

A **p** who meddles in a quarrel	Pr 26:17

PASSIONATE

if you are **p** for what is good?	1Pt 3:13

PASSIONS

them over to degrading **p**.	Rm 1:26
flesh, the sinful **p** operated	Rm 7:5
flesh with its **p** and desires.	Gl 5:24
Flee from youthful **p**, and pursue	2Tm 2:22
led along by a variety of **p**	2Tm 3:6
captives of various **p** and pleasures,	Ti 3:3

PASSOVER

it is the LORD's **P**.	Ex 12:11
of the **P** Festival must not remain	Ex 34:25
The **P** to the LORD comes in the	Lv 23:5
observe the **P** at its appointed time.	Nm 9:2
celebrate the **P** to the LORD	Dt 16:1
they kept the **P** on the evening	Jos 5:10
Josiah observed the LORD's **P**	2Ch 35:1
observed the **P** on the fourteenth	Ezr 6:19
you are to celebrate the **P**	Ezk 45:21
I am celebrating the **P** at your place	Mt 26:18
parents ... to Jerusalem for the **P**	Lk 2:41
the **P** lamb had to be sacrificed.	Lk 22:7
eat this **P** with you before I suffer.	Lk 22:15

The Jewish **P** was near, so Jesus	Jn 2:13
Now the **P**, a Jewish festival	Jn 6:4
The Jewish **P** was near, and many	Jn 11:55
Six days before the **P**, Jesus came to	Jn 12:1
It was the preparation day for the **P**,	Jn 19:14
out to the people after the **P**.	Ac 12:4
Christ our **P** has been sacrificed.	1Co 5:7
By faith he instituted the **P**	Heb 11:28

PAST

either in the **p** or recently or	Ex 4:10
days of old, years long **p**.	Ps 77:5
speak mysteries from the **p**	Ps 78:2
Do not hold **p** sins against us;	Ps 79:8
For now the winter is **p**;	Sg 2:11
Do not remember the **p** events,	Is 43:18
the **p** events will not be	Is 65:17
never existed in ages **p** and never will	Jl 2:2
In **p** generations He allowed all	Ac 14:16
if she is **p** marriageable age,	1Co 7:36
in the **p**, when you didn't know God,	Gl 4:8
even though she was **p** the age,	Heb 11:11
For in the **p**, the holy women who	1Pt 3:5
who in the **p** were disobedient,	1Pt 3:20
the cleansing from his **p** sins.	2Pt 1:9

PASTORS

some **p** and teachers,	Eph 4:11

PASTURE (n)

I took you from the **p** and from	2Sm 7:8
lets me lie down in green **p-s**	Ps 23:2
glory of the **p-s**, will fade	Ps 37:20
The **p-s** are clothed with flocks	Ps 65:13
against the sheep of Your **p**?	Ps 74:1
sheep of Your **p**, will thank You	Ps 79:13
and we are the people of His **p**	Ps 95:7
His people, the sheep of His **p**.	Ps 100:3
Sharon will be a **p** for flocks,	Is 65:10
and scatter the sheep of My **p**!	Jr 23:1
I will tend them with good **p**	Ezk 34:14
flock of My **p**, and I am your	Ezk 34:31
When they had **p**, they became	Hs 13:6
confusion since they have no **p**.	Jl 1:18
the wilderness **p-s** have turned	Jl 2:22
they will find **p** there.	Zph 2:7
But they will **p** and lie down,	Zph 3:13
come in and go out and find **p**.	Jn 10:9

PASTURE (v)

while he was **p-ing** the donkeys	Gn 36:24

p-ing {the flocks} at Shechem	Gn 37:13
Where do you p your sheep?	Sg 1:7

PASTURELAND

The open p ... may not be sold,	Lv 25:34
Levites to live in and p	Nm 35:2
Levites these cities with their p-s	Jos 21:3
were given ... Libnah and its p-s,	1Ch 6:57
Levites left their p-s and their	2Ch 11:14
The seacoast will become p-s	Zph 2:6

PATCH

scarecrows in a cucumber p	Jr 10:5
because the p pulls away from	Mt 9:16
No one sews a p of unshrunk	Mk 2:21
No one tears a p from a new	Lk 5:36

PATH

a viper beside the p, that bites	Gn 49:17
turn from the p I have commanded	Dt 31:29
No bird of prey knows that p;	Jb 28:7
He stands watch over all my p-s.	Jb 33:11
or take the p of sinners,	Ps 1:1
You reveal the p of life to me;	Ps 16:11
My steps are on Your p-s;	Ps 17:5
the right p-s for His name's	Ps 23:3
teach me Your p-s.	Ps 25:4
LORD, and lead me on a level p.	Ps 27:11
have not strayed from Your p.	Ps 44:18
for my feet and a light on my p.	Ps 119:105
and integrity—every good p.	Pr 2:9
none reach the p-s of life.	Pr 2:19
will guide you on the right p-s.	Pr 3:6
and all her p-s, peaceful.	Pr 3:17
is on the p to life,	Pr 10:17
but another p leads to death.	Pr 12:28
the p of the upright is a highway.	Pr 15:19
the p of life leads upward,	Pr 15:24
don't know the p of the wind,	Ec 11:5
You clear a straight p for the	Is 26:7
taught Him the p-s of justice?	Is 40:14
and a p through surging waters,	Is 43:16
Ask about the ancient p-s:	Jr 6:16
make His p-s straight!	Mt 3:3
some seeds fell along the p,	Mt 13:4
You have revealed the p-s of life	Ac 2:28
perverting the straight p-s of	Ac 13:10
and the p of peace they have not	Rm 3:17
make straight p-s for your feet,	Heb 12:13

abandoning the straight p, they have ... followed the p of Balaam,	2Pt 2:15

PATHETIC

What are these p Jews doing?	Neh 4:2

PATHROS

Upper Egypt; dwelling place of Jewish exiles (Is 11:11; Jr 44:1,15; Ezk 29:14; 30:14).

PATHWAYS

His p are ancient.	Hab 3:6

PATIENCE

P is better than power,	Pr 16:32
A person's insight gives him p,	Pr 19:11
ruler can be persuaded through p,	Pr 25:15
you also try the p of my God?	Is 7:13
In Your p, don't take me away.	Jr 15:15
restraint, and p, not	Rm 2:4
we eagerly wait for it with p.	Rm 8:25
endured with much p objects of	Rm 9:22
by knowledge, by p, by kindness,	2Co 6:6
love, joy, peace, p, kindness,	Gl 5:22
with p, accepting one another	Eph 4:2
all endurance and p, with joy	Col 1:11
humility, gentleness, and p,	Col 3:12
Jesus ... demonstrate the utmost p	1Tm 1:16
faith, p, love, and endurance.	2Tm 3:10
and encourage with great p	2Tm 4:2
an example of suffering and p.	Jms 5:10
regard the p of our Lord as	2Pt 3:15

PATIENT

A p person {shows} great	Pr 14:29
Be p with me, and I pay you	Mt 18:26
Rejoice in hope; be p in affliction;	Rm 12:12
Love is p; love is kind.	1Co 13:4
the weak, be p with everyone.	1Th 5:14
able to teach, and p,	2Tm 2:24
be p until the Lord's coming.	Jms 5:7
but is p with you, not wanting any	2Pt 3:9

PATIENTLY

I waited p for the LORD,	Ps 40:1
Happy are all who wait p for Him.	Is 30:18
when God p waited in the days of	1Pt 3:20

PATMOS

Island where John was banished (Rv 1:9).

PATRIARCH

speak to you about the **p** David:	Ac 2:29
Jacob, and Jacob with the 12 **p-s**	Ac 7:8
even Abraham the **p** gave a tenth	Heb 7:4

PATRIARCHAL

the strict view of our **p** law.	Ac 22:3

PATROL

LORD has sent to **p** the earth.	Zch 1:10
they wanted to go **p** the earth,	Zch 6:7

PATTERN

according to the **p** the LORD had	Nm 8:4
according to the **p** he had seen.	Ac 7:44
that **p** of teaching you were	Rm 6:17
Hold on to the **p** of sound	2Tm 1:13
into the same **p** of disobedience	Heb 4:11
according to the **p** that was shown	Heb 8:5

PAUL

Early church missionary, theologian, and writer. Also called Saul (Ac 13:9). Citizen of Tarsus, a Benjaminite, raised in Jerusalem as a rabbinical student and Pharisee (21:39; 22:3,28; 26:5; Gl 1:14; Php 3:5). Persecuted Christians, including Stephen (Ac 8:1; 26:9-11); converted on the way to Damascus (9:1-19); began preaching Christ in Arabia and Damascus and was threatened (9:20-22; Gl 1:17; 2Co 11:32-33).

Introduced to the church at Jerusalem by Barnabas (Ac 9:26-30); carried money with Barnabas from Antioch to Judea (11:27-30). Set apart with Barnabas to go through Cyprus and Galatia as missionaries (Ac 13–14); stoned (14:19-20). Focused on Gentile evangelism (9:15; Gl 2:7; Eph 3:8). Attended Jerusalem council (Ac 15). Split with Barnabas over John Mark (15:36-39).

Traveled with Silas and Timothy through Asia Minor and Greece (15:39–16:3). Hindered by the Spirit from entering Bithynia; called to Macedonia in a vision (16:7-10). Beaten, imprisoned, and released in Philippi (16:16-40). Spoke at Areopagus in Athens (17:19-34). Preached at Corinth and Ephesus (Ac 18–19). Said farewell in Ephesus (20:17-38).

Arrested at riot in Jerusalem (21:26-36); testified before the Sanhedrin (23:1-10), Governors Felix and Festus (24:10-21; 25:1-12), and King Agrippa (Ac 26); appealed to Caesar (25:11). Shipwrecked on the way to Rome (Ac 27); ministered in Malta, then Rome (Ac 28).

PAVEMENT

like a **p** made of sapphire	Ex 24:10
on a mosaic **p** of red feldspar,	Est 1:6
Thirty chambers faced the **p**	Ezk 40:17
in a place called the Stone P	Jn 19:13

PAVILION

how ... thunder roars from God's **p**?	Jb 36:29
he will pitch his **p** over them.	Jr 43:10

PAW

who rescued me from the **p** of the lion and the **p** of the bear will	1Sm 17:37
He **p-s** in the valley and rejoices	Jb 39:21

PAY

they **p** the penalty for their sin,	Lv 26:43
He is to **p** full compensation,	Nm 5:7
You will **p** the redemption price	Nm 18:16
You are to **p** him his wages each	Dt 24:15
to **p** attention (is better) than	1Sm 15:22
he must **p** four lambs for that	2Sm 12:6
sell the oil and **p** your debt;	2Kg 4:7
I insist on **p-ing** the full price	1Ch 21:24
P homage to the Son, or He will	Ps 2:12
p your vows to the Most High.	Ps 50:14
p attention to my prayer.	Ps 61:1
I will **p** You my vows.	Ps 66:13
P back sevenfold to our	Ps 79:12
I will **p** attention to the way of	Ps 101:2
happy is the one who **p-s** you back	Ps 137:8
My son, **p** attention to my words	Pr 4:20
he must **p** seven times as much;	Pr 6:31
and **p** attention to your herds,	Pr 27:23
never again **p** fees for lovers	Ezk 16:41
He **paid** the fare and went down into	Jnh 1:3
until you have **paid** the last penny!	Mt 5:26
If he **p-s** no attention to them,	Mt 18:17
and said, 'P what you owe!'	Mt 18:28
Is it lawful to **p** taxes to Caesar	Mt 22:17
You **p** a tenth of mint, dill, and	Mt 23:23
I'll **p** back four times as much!	Lk 19:8
p is not considered as a gift,	Rm 4:4

for this reason you p taxes,	Rm 13:6
P your obligations to everyone:	Rm 13:7
is troubling you will p the penalty.	Gl 5:10
wrongdoer will be **paid** back for	Col 3:25
These will p the penalty of	2Th 1:9
or to p attention to myths and	1Tm 1:4
and may not p attention to	Ti 1:14
has **paid** tithes through Abraham,	Heb 7:9
The p that you withheld from the	Jms 5:4
not p-ing back evil for evil or	1Pt 3:9
P her back the way she also **paid**	Rv 18:6

PAYMENT

her priests teach for p,	Mc 3:11
opposing p of taxes to Caesar,	Lk 23:2
Spirit as a down p in our hearts.	2Co 1:22
gave us the Spirit as a down p.	2Co 5:5
He is the down p of our	Eph 1:14
harm as the p for unrighteousness.	2Pt 2:13

PEACE

I will give p to the land,	Lv 26:6
favor on you and give you p.	Nm 6:26
I grant him My covenant of p.	Nm 25:12
you must make an offer of p.	Dt 20:10
Never seek p or friendship with	Dt 23:6
Gibeon had made p with Israel	Jos 10:1
No city made p with the Israelites	Jos 11:19
Abner, and he went in p.	2Sm 3:21
murdered them {in a time} of p	1Kg 2:5
What do you have to do with p?	2Kg 9:18
Make p with me and surrender	2Kg 18:31
will be p ... during my lifetime?	2Kg 20:19
I will give p and quiet to Israel	1Ch 22:9
and go down to Sheol in p.	Jb 21:13
to terms with God and be at p;	Jb 22:21
both lie down and sleep in p	Ps 4:8
seek p and pursue it.	Ps 34:14
will declare p to His people,	Ps 85:8
Abundant p belongs to those	Ps 119:165
Pray for the p of Jerusalem:	Ps 122:6
P be with Israel.	Ps 125:5; 128:6
those who promote p have joy.	Pr 12:20
a dry crust with p than a house	Pr 17:1
time for war and a time for p.	Ec 3:8
Eternal Father, Prince of P.	Is 9:6
You will keep in perfect p the mind	Is 26:3
There is no p ... for the wicked.	Is 48:22
who proclaims p, who brings news	Is 52:7
for our p was on Him,	Is 53:5

P, p to the one who is far or near	Is 57:19
have not known the path of p	Is 59:8
make p flow to her like a river,	Is 66:12
P, p, when there is no p.	Jr 6:14; 8:11
We hoped for p, but	Jr 8:15; 14:19
They will seek p, but	Ezk 7:25
saying: P, when there is no p,	Ezk 13:10
I will make a covenant of p	Ezk 34:25; 37:26
During a time of p, he will come	Dn 11:24
proclaim p when they have food	Mc 3:5
There will be p.	Mc 5:5
good news and proclaiming p!	Nah 1:15
I will provide p in this place	Hg 2:9
He will proclaim p to the nations.	Zch 9:10
is worthy, let your p be on it.	Mt 10:13
I did not come to bring p,	Mt 10:34
and p on earth to people He favors!	Lk 2:14
can dismiss Your slave in p	Lk 2:29
P I leave with you. My p I give	Jn 14:27
so that in Me you may have p.	Jn 16:33
the good news of p through Jesus	Ac 10:36
Grace to you and p from God our	Rm 1:7
we have p with God through our	Rm 5:1
of the Spirit is life and p.	Rm 8:6
part, live at p with everyone.	Rm 12:18
God of p will soon crush Satan	Rm 16:20
God has called you to p.	1Co 7:15
not a God of disorder but of p.	1Co 14:33
God of love and p will be with	2Co 13:11
fruit of the Spirit is love, joy, p,	Gl 5:22
For He is our p, who made both	Eph 2:14
with the p that binds {us}.	Eph 4:3
readiness for the gospel of p.	Eph 6:15
And the p of God, which surpasses	Php 4:7
by making p through the blood	Col 1:20
And let the p of the Messiah,	Col 3:15
When they say, "P and security,"	1Th 5:3
Be at p among yourselves.	1Th 5:13
the Lord of p Himself give you p	2Th 3:16
pursue ... faith, love, and p,	2Tm 2:22
of Salem," meaning "king of p";	Heb 7:2
Pursue p with everyone,	Heb 12:14
is sown in p by those who make p.	Jms 3:18
He must seek p and pursue it,	1Pt 3:11
May grace and p be multiplied to	2Pt 1:2
to take p from the earth,	Rv 6:4

PEACEABLY

bring themselves to speak p to him.	Gn 37:4

PEACEFUL
My people will dwell in a **p** place, Is 32:18

PEACE-LOVING
first pure, then **p**, gentle Jms 3:17

PEACEMAKERS
Blessed are the **p**, because they Mt 5:9

PEACOCKS
silver, ivory, apes, and **p**. 1Kg 10:22

PEAKS
and the mountain **p** are His. Ps 95:4

PEARL
price of wisdom is beyond **p-s.** Jb 28:18
or toss your **p-s** before pigs, Mt 7:6
When he found one priceless **p** Mt 13:46
gold, **p-s**, or expensive 1Tm 2:9
silver, precious stones, and **p-s** Rv 18:12
gate was made of a single **p**. Rv 21:21

PEELED
and **p** (the bark), exposing white Gn 30:37

PEG
hammered the **p** into his temple Jdg 4:21
drive him, like a **p**, into a firm Is 22:23
its tent **p-s** will not be pulled up Is 33:20
and drive your **p-s** deep. Is 54:2

PEKAH
King of Israel; assassin (2Kg 15:25-31).

PEKAHIAH
Son of Menahem; king of Israel; assassinated by his captain, Pekah (2Kg 15:22-26).

PELEG
Son of Eber (Gn 10:25; 11:16-19; 1Ch 1:19,25); ancestor of Christ (Lk 3:35).

PEN (n)
confined their calves in the **p**. 1Sm 6:10
my tongue is the **p** of a skillful Ps 45:1
write on it with an ordinary **p**: Is 8:1
enter the sheep **p** by the door Jn 10:1
to write to you with **p** and ink. 3Jn 13

PEN (v)
p-ned this epistle in the Lord Rm 16:22

PENALTY
will pay the **p** for their sin, Lv 26:41
and bear the **p** for your acts Nm 14:33

for instruction will pay the **p**, Pr 13:13
the appropriate **p** for their Rm 1:27
troubling you will pay the **p**. Gl 5:10
will pay the **p** of everlasting 2Th 1:9

PENETRATING
p as far as to divide soul Heb 4:12

PENIEL
Where Jacob wrestled with God (Gn 32:30).

PENINNAH
Hannah's rival (1Sm 1:2,4).

PENIS
or whose **p** has been cut off Dt 23:1

PENNY
until you have paid the last **p**! Mt 5:26
two sparrows sold for a **p**? Mt 10:29
five sparrows sold for two **p-ies**? Lk 12:6

PENTECOST
When the day of **P** had arrived, Ac 2:1
If possible, for the day of **P**. Ac 20:16
I will stay in Ephesus until **P** 1Co 16:8

PENUEL
Place where Jacob wrestled with God (Gn 32:31); city destroyed by Gideon (Jdg 8:8-17) and rebuilt by Jeroboam (1Kg 12:25).

PEOPLE
as one **p** all having the same Gn 11:6
kings of **p-s** will come from her. Gn 17:16
Let My **p** go, Ex 5:1
take you as My **p**, and I will be Ex 6:7
Sacrifice the **p-'s** offering Lv 9:7
who set you apart from the **p-s**. Lv 20:24
to be a **p** for His inheritance, Dt 4:20
you were the fewest of all **p-s**. Dt 7:7
You will be blessed above all **p-s**; Dt 7:14
the LORD's portion is His **p**, Dt 32:9
your **p** will be my **p**, Ru 1:16
Because I was afraid of the **p**, I 1Sm 15:24
You will shepherd My **p** Israel 2Sm 5:2
proclaim His deeds among the **p-s**. 1Ch 16:8
and My **p** who are called by My 2Ch 7:14
you are the **p**, and wisdom will Jb 12:2
and the **p-s** plot in vain? Ps 2:1
The LORD judges the **p-s**; Ps 7:8
a **p** I had not known serve me. Ps 18:43

by men and despised by **p**. Ps 22:6
LORD blesses His **p** with peace. Ps 29:11
Clap your hands, all you **p-s**; Ps 47:1
let all the **p-s** praise You. Ps 67:3
and we are the **p** of His pasture Ps 95:7
He judges the **p-s** fairly. Ps 96:10
His **p**, the sheep of His pasture. Ps 100:3
proclaim His deeds among the **p-s**. Ps 105:1
Let all the **p** say, "Amen! Ps 106:48
And the LORD surrounds His **p**, Ps 125:2
Happy are the **p** whose God is the Ps 144:15
kings of the earth and all **p-s**, Ps 148:11
LORD takes pleasure in His **p**; Ps 149:4
but sin is a disgrace to any **p**. Pr 14:34
the ants are not a strong **p** Pr 30:25
For the fate of **p** and the fate Ec 3:19
The **p** walking in darkness have Is 9:2
Comfort, comfort My **p**, Is 40:1
indeed, the **p** are grass. Is 40:7
The **p** I formed for Myself will Is 43:21
Raise a banner for the **p-s**. Is 62:10
customs of the **p-s** are worthless. Jr 10:3
They will be My **p**, and I will be Jr 24:7
the city {once} crowded with **p**! Lm 1:1
God, and they will be My **p**. Ezk 37:27
Name him Not My **P**, for you are not Hs 1:9
just the preacher for this **p**! Mc 2:11
P-s will stream to it, Mc 4:1
on that day and become My **p**. Zch 2:11
a heavy stone for all the **p-s**; Zch 12:3
will save His **p** from their sins. Mt 1:21
For this **p-'s** heart has grown Mt 13:15
Who do **p** say that the Son of Mt 16:13
then all the **p-s** of the earth Mt 24:30
joy that will be for all the **p**: Lk 2:10
in favor with God and with **p**. Lk 2:52
but they feared the **p**. Lk 20:19
they were afraid of the **p**. Lk 22:2
and His own **p** did not receive Jn 1:11
should die for the **p** rather than Jn 11:50
one man should die for the **p**. Jn 18:14
having favor with all the **p**. Ac 2:47
the Gentiles a **p** for His name. Ac 15:14
commands all **p** everywhere to Ac 17:30
I have many **p** in this city. Ac 18:10
to make his defense to the **p**. Ac 19:33
you are not My **p**, there they Rm 9:26
has God rejected His **p**? Rm 11:1

all the **p-s** should praise Him! Rm 15:11
spiritual **p** but as **p** of the flesh, 1Co 3:1
God, and they will be My **p**. 2Co 6:16
Or am I striving to please **p**? Gl 1:10
He gave gifts to **p**. Eph 4:8
we didn't seek glory from **p** 1Th 2:6
cleanse for Himself a special **p**, Ti 2:14
God, and they will be My **p**. Heb 8:10
The Lord will judge His **p**. Heb 10:30
a holy nation, a **p** for His possession, 1Pt 2:9
you were not a **p**, but now you
  are God's **p**; 1Pt 2:10
and language and **p** and nation. Rv 5:9
nation, tribe, **p**, and language Rv 7:9
prophesy again about many **p-s** Rv 10:11
over every tribe, **p**, language Rv 13:7
nation, tribe, language, and **p**. Rv 14:6
will be His **p**, and God Himself Rv 21:3

PEOR

1. Mountain from which Balaam viewed
Israel (Nm 23:28).

2. Abbreviation for **BAAL OF PEOR** (Nm
25:18; 31:16; Jos 22:17).

PERCEIVE

I **p** him, but not near. Nm 24:17
if I go west, I cannot **p** Him. Jb 23:8
keep looking, but do not **p**. Is 6:9
p-ing their thoughts, Jesus said Mt 9:4
look and look, yet never **p**. Mt 13:14
p-ing their malice, Jesus said Mt 22:18
look and look, yet never **p**. Ac 28:26

PERCENT

Bring the full 10 **p** into the Mal 3:10

PERCEPTION

no one has the **p** or insight to say, Is 44:19

PERCEPTIVE

of them are clear to the **p**, Pr 8:9
knowledge {comes} easily to the **p**. Pr 14:6
knowledgeable, **p**, and Dn 1:4

PERES

P {means that} your kingdom has Dn 5:28

PEREZ

Son of Judah and Tamar; twin to Zerah
(Gn 38:29-30; Lk 3:33).

PERFECT (adj)

The Rock—His work is p;	Dt 32:4
God—His way is p;	2Sm 22:31
He makes my way p.	2Sm 22:33
He was a man of p integrity,	Jb 1:1
one who has p knowledge is with	Jb 36:4
God—His way is p;	Ps 18:30
strength and makes my way p.	Ps 18:32
The instruction of the LORD is p,	Ps 19:7
my darling, my dove, my p one.	Sg 5:2
will keep in p peace the mind	Is 26:3
full of wisdom and p in beauty.	Ezk 28:12
Be p, therefore, as your heavenly	Mt 5:48
"If you want to be p," Jesus said	Mt 19:21
pleasing, and p will of God.	Rm 12:2
But when the p comes,	1Co 13:10
love—the p bond of unity.	Col 3:14
and more p tabernacle not	Heb 9:11
and every p gift is from above,	Jms 1:17
into the p law of freedom	Jms 1:25
instead, p love drives out fear,	1Jn 4:18

PERFECT (v)

for power is p-ed in weakness,	2Co 12:9
After He was p-ed, He became the	Heb 5:9
(for the law p-ed nothing)	Heb 7:19
a Son, who has been p-ed forever.	Heb 7:28
by one offering He has p-ed	Heb 10:14
and by works, faith was p-ed.	Jms 2:22
in him the love of God is p-ed.	1Jn 2:5
and His love is p-ed in us.	1Jn 4:12

PERFECTER

the source and p of our faith	Heb 12:2

PERFECTION

From Zion, the p of beauty,	Ps 50:2
I have seen a limit to all p,	Ps 119:96
was called the p of beauty,	Lm 2:15
You were the seal of p,	Ezk 28:12
If ... p came through the Levitical	Heb 7:11
has not reached p in love.	1Jn 4:18

PERFORM

I will p wonders in the presence	Ex 34:10
He p-ed His miraculous signs	Ps 78:43
They p-ed His miraculous signs	Ps 105:27
With God we will p valiantly;	Ps 108:13
hoping to see some miracle p-ed	Lk 23:8
Jesus p-ed this first sign in	Jn 2:11
What are You going to p?	Jn 6:30

Jesus p-ed many other signs in	Jn 20:30
signs were being p-ed through	Ac 2:43
another, the p-ing of miracles,	1Co 12:10
repeatedly, p-ing their ministry,	Heb 9:6
He also p-s great signs, even	Rv 13:13

PERFUME

and then with p-s and cosmetics	Est 2:12
p-d my bed with myrrh, aloes	Pr 7:17
fragrance of your p is intoxicating;	Sg 1:3
and prepared spices and p-s.	Lk 23:56

PERFUMER

blend, the work of a p;	Ex 30:25
your daughters to become p-s,	1Sm 8:13
flies make a p-'s oil ferment	Ec 10:1

PERGA

City visited by Paul (Ac 13:13-14; 14:25).

PERGAMUM

One of the seven churches (Rv 1:11; 2:12).

PERHAPS

P the LORD will be with me	Jos 14:12
P the LORD will help us.	1Sm 14:6
P the LORD will see my	2Sm 16:12
P the LORD your God will hear	2Kg 19:4
P my children have sinned,	Jb 1:5
P this is the Son of David!	Mt 12:23
a good person p someone might	Rm 5:7
P God will grant them repentance	2Tm 2:25

PERIOD

I am having my monthly p.	Gn 31:35
has a discharge beyond her p,	Lv 15:25
an animal for seven p-s of time.	Dn 4:16
them for a certain p of time.	Dn 7:12
times or p-s that the Father	Ac 1:7

PERISH

You will p among the nations;	Lv 26:38
to Moses, "Look, we're p-ing!	Nm 17:12
the weapons of war have p-ed!	2Sm 1:27
If I p, I p.	Est 4:16
the hope of the godless will p.	Jb 8:13
But the wicked will p;	Ps 37:20
he is like the animals that p.	Ps 49:12
far from You will certainly p;	Ps 73:27
They will p, but You will endure;	Ps 102:26
and one who utters lies p-es.	Pr 19:9
who abandon the LORD will p.	Is 1:28

both will **p** together. Is 31:3
righteous one **p-es**, and no one Is 57:1
Truth has **p-ed** Jr 7:28
LORD's faithful love we do not **p**, Lm 3:22
will **p** from the priests Ezk 7:26
and our hope has **p-ed**; Ezk 37:11
don't let us **p** because of this Jnh 1:14
in a night and **p-ed** in a night. Jnh 4:10
one of these little ones **p**. Mt 18:14
up a sword will **p** by a sword. Mt 26:52
repent, you will all **p** as well! Lk 13:3
in Him will not **p** but have Jn 3:16
Don't work for food that **p-es** but for Jn 6:27
and they will never **p**—ever! Jn 10:28
rather than the whole nation **p**. Jn 11:50
will also **p** without the law, Rm 2:12
to those who are **p-ing** the message 1Co 1:18
asleep in Christ have also **p-ed**. 1Co 15:18
and among those who are **p-ing**. 2Co 2:15
is veiled to those who are **p-ing**. 2Co 4:3
{They **p**} because they did not 2Th 2:10
they will **p**, but You remain. Heb 1:11
which **p-es** though refined by 1Pt 1:7
world of that time **p-ed** when it 2Pt 3:6
not wanting any to **p**, but all to 2Pt 3:9

PERISHABLE

do it to receive a **p** crown, 1Co 9:25
fathers, not with **p** things, 1Pt 1:18
not of **p** seed but of 1Pt 1:23

PERIZZITES

Ancient people of the promised land (Gn 13:7; 34:30; Dt 20:17); dispossessed by Israel (Ex 23:23; Dt 7:1; Jos 3:10), especially Joseph's descendants (Jos 17:15), though some remained (Jdg 3:5; 1Kg 9:20).

PERJURER

better to be a poor man than a **p**. Pr 19:22
for kidnappers, liars, **p-s**, 1Tm 1:10

PERJURY

do not love **p**, for I hate all Zch 8:17

PERMANENT

your generations as a **p** statute. Ex 12:14
inaugurate a **p** priesthood Ex 40:15
This is a **p** statute throughout Lv 3:17
for it is their **p** possession Lv 25:34

burned Ai and left it a **p** ruin, Jos 8:28
{This is} a **p** statute Ezk 46:14

PERMANENTLY

land is not to be **p** sold because Lv 25:23
in the walled city is **p** transferred Lv 25:30
is **p** dedicated ... belongs to you. Nm 18:14
LORD would have **p** established 1Sm 13:13
the land and dwell in it **p**. Ps 37:29
is **p** dedicated ... will belong to Ezk 44:29
you might get him back **p**, Phm 15
He holds His priesthood **p**, Heb 7:24

PERMEATES

a little yeast **p** the whole batch 1Co 5:6

PERMISSION

And He gave them **p**. Mk 5:13
Pilate gave him **p**, so he Jn 19:38

PERMISSIBLE

Everything is **p** for me, 1Co 6:12
"Everything is **p**," but not 1Co 10:23

PERMIT

Moses **p-ted** you to divorce Mt 19:8
But He would not **p** the demons to Mk 1:34
begged Him to **p** them to enter Lk 8:32
for they are not **p-ted** to speak, 1Co 14:34
And we will do this if God **p-s**. Heb 6:3
They were not **p-ted** to kill them Rv 9:5
he was **p-ted** to wage war against Rv 13:7

PERPETUAL

generations as a **p** covenant. Ex 31:16
Sabbath day as a **p** covenant Lv 24:8
This is a **p** statute for them. Nm 19:21
covenant of **p** priesthood for Nm 25:13

PERPETUATE

to **p** the deceased man's name Ru 4:10

PERPLEXED

Peter was deeply **p** about what Ac 10:17
we are **p** but not in despair; 2Co 4:8

PERSECUTE

Why do you **p** me as God {does}? Jb 19:22
people **p** me with lies Ps 119:86
Princes **p-d** me without Ps 119:161
insult you and **p** you and falsely Mt 5:11
how they **p-d** the prophets who Mt 5:12
and pray for those who **p** you, Mt 5:44
When they **p** you in one town, Mt 10:23

lay their hands on you and p you. Lk 21:12
they p-d Me, they will also p you. Jn 15:20
did your fathers not p? Ac 7:52
Saul, Saul, why are you p-ing Me? Ac 9:4
I p-d this Way to the death, Ac 22:4
Bless those who p you; Rm 12:14
when we are p-d, we endure it; 1Co 4:12
because I p-d the church of God 1Co 15:9
we are p-d but not abandoned; 2Co 4:9
formerly p-d us now preaches Gl 1:23
circumcision, why am I still p-d? Gl 5:11
as to zeal, p-ing the church; Php 3:6
in Christ Jesus will be p-d. 2Tm 3:12

PERSECUTION
When pressure or p comes Mt 13:21
they will hand you over for p, Mt 24:9
fields, with p-s—and eternal life Mk 10:30
a severe p broke out against Ac 8:1
scattered as a result of the p Ac 11:19
stirred up p against Paul Ac 13:50
or anguish or p or famine or Rm 8:35
in catastrophes, in p-s, 2Co 12:10
we were going to suffer p, 1Th 3:4
endurance and faith in all the p-s 2Th 1:4

PERSECUTOR
my enemies and from my p-s. Ps 31:15
My p-s and foes are many. Ps 119:157
formerly a blasphemer, a p, and 1Tm 1:13

PERSEVERANCE
with all p and intercession Eph 6:18
through faith and p Heb 6:12
and p in Jesus, Rv 1:9

PERSEVERE
forever if he p-s in keeping My 1Ch 28:7
p in these things, for by doing 1Tm 4:16
for he p-ed, as one who sees Heb 11:27
law of freedom and p-s in it, Jms 1:25

PERSIA
Nation that conquered Babylon and permitted the return of the Jewish exiles (2Ch 36:20-23; Ezr 1:1-4; Est 1:1-3; Dn 5:28-31; 6:28; 10:1).

PERSIST
Israelites p-ed in all the sins 2Kg 17:22
and don't p in a bad cause, Ec 8:3
p in it whether convenient or not; 2Tm 4:2

PERSISTENCE
because of his p, he will get up Lk 11:8

PERSISTENT
seduces him with her p pleading; Pr 7:21
wear me out by her p coming. Lk 18:5
be p in prayer. Rm 12:12

PERSON
received in their own p-s the Rm 1:27
consist of the hidden p of the heart 1Pt 3:4

PERSONAL
I, Paul, make a p appeal to you 2Co 1:10

PERSONALLY
You can hold me p accountable! Gn 43:9

PERSPECTIVE
not many are wise from a human p 1Co 1:26
I saying this from a human p? 1Co 9:8
many boast from a human p 2Co 11:18

PERSUADE
Do not p me to leave you or go Ru 1:16
sinners entice you, don't be p-d. Pr 1:10
A ruler can be p-d through Pr 25:15
I am going to p her, Hs 2:14
p-d the crowds to ask for Mt 27:20
not be p-d if someone rises Lk 16:31
and tried to p both Jews and Ac 18:4
this man Paul has p-d and misled Ac 19:26
Are you going to p me to become Ac 26:28
Some were p-d by what he said, Ac 28:24
For I am p-d that neither death Rm 8:38
I know and am p-d by the Lord Rm 14:14
fear of the Lord, we p people. 2Co 5:11
Since I am p-d of this, I know Php 1:25
and am p-d that He is able 2Tm 1:12

PERSUASION
This p did not come from Him who Gl 5:8

PERSUASIVE
were not with p words of wisdom 1Co 2:4
deceive you with p arguments. Col 2:4

PERTAIN
speak of things p-ing to this life? 1Co 6:3

PERVERSE
for they are a p generation Dt 32:20
You son of a p and rebellious 1Sm 20:30
of them are deceptive or p. Pr 8:8

evil conduct, and p speech. Pr 8:13

but a p tongue will be cut out. Pr 10:31

the wicked, {only} what is p. Pr 10:32

PERVERSION

to mate with it; it is a p. Lv 18:23

of the poor and p of justice Ec 5:8

penalty for their p. Rm 1:27

immorality and practiced p-s, Jd 7

PERVERSITY

enjoy doing evil and celebrate p, Pr 2:14

plots evil with p in his heart Pr 6:14

the p of the treacherous destroys Pr 11:3

and the city full of p. Ezk 9:9

PERVERT

with a crowd to p {justice}. Ex 23:2

took bribes, and p-ed justice. 1Sm 8:3

Does God p justice? Jb 8:3

Almighty does not p justice. Jb 34:12

whoever p-s his ways will be found Pr 10:9

partiality to the guilty by p-ing the Pr 18:5

for they have p-ed their way; Jr 3:21

you p the words of the living God, Jr 23:36

and p everything that is right, Mc 3:9

Won't you ever stop p-ing the Ac 13:10

PERVERTED (adj)

p men of the city surrounded Jdg 19:22

justice comes out p. Hab 1:4

in a crooked and p generation, Php 2:15

such a person is p and sins, Ti 3:11

PESTERING

because this widow keeps p me, Lk 18:5

PESTILENCE

ravaged by p and bitter plague; Dt 32:24

when there is p, when there is 1Kg 8:37

or if I send p on My people, 2Ch 7:13

or judgment, p or famine—we 2Ch 20:9

or the p that ravages at noon. Ps 91:6

and p follows in His steps. Hab 3:5

PESTLE

grind a fool in a mortar with a p Pr 27:22

PETALS

and its calyxes and p. Ex 25:31

from its base to its flower p. Nm 8:4

PETER

Apostle; originally named Simon; also called Simeon (Ac 15:14) and Cephas. A fisherman in business with James and John (Lk 5:2-3,10); married, lived in Capernaum (Mk 1:21,29-30).

Walked on water (Mt 14:28-31). Confessed Jesus as Messiah (Mt 16:13-20; Mk 8:27-30; Lk 9:18-21). At transfiguration (Mt 17:1-9; Mk 9:2-8; Lk 9:28-36; 2Pt 1:16-18). Jesus predicted he would deny Him (Mt 26:31-35; Mk 14:27-31; Lk 22:31-34; Jn 13:36-38); denial (Mt 26:69-75; Mk 14:66-72; Lk 22:54-62; Jn 18:15-18,25-27); restoration to "feed My sheep" (Jn 21:15-19).

Spoke at Pentecost (Ac 2:14-40). Healed people (3:1-10; 5:15; 9:34); raised Tabitha from the dead (9:36-43). Arrested and forbidden to preach (4:1-31; 5:17-41). Saw vision: sent to Cornelius (Ac 10); reported Gentile conversions (Ac 11; 15); confronted by Paul for inconsistency (Gl 2:11-14). Imprisoned by Herod; freed by angel (Ac 12:1-19).

Focused on Jewish evangelism (Gl 2:7). Wrote two letters (1Pt 1:1; 2Pt 1:1).

PETITION

may the God of Israel grant the p 1Sm 1:17

Hear the p of Your servant and 1Kg 8:30

I have heard your prayer and p 1Kg 9:3

He heard his p and granted his 2Ch 33:13

{This is} my p and my request: Est 5:7

the king my p that he not return Jr 38:26

anyone who p-s any god or man Dn 6:7

to seek Him by prayer and p-s Dn 9:3

prayer and p with thanksgiving, Php 4:6

I urge that p-s, prayers, 1Tm 2:1

and day in her p-s and prayers; 1Tm 5:5

PHARAOH

the LORD struck P and his house Gn 12:17

Then P sent for Joseph, Gn 41:14

P-'s daughter went down to bathe Ex 2:5

I am sending you to P Ex 3:10

to see what I will do to P: Ex 6:1

But I will harden P-'s heart and Ex 7:3

firstborn of P who sits on his Ex 11:5

when I receive glory through P, Ex 14:18

Solomon made an alliance with P 1Kg 3:1

by marrying P-'s daughter.	1Kg 3:1
P Neco king of Egypt marched	2Kg 23:29
signs and wonders against P	Neh 9:10
against P and all his officials	Ps 135:9
but hurled P and his army into	Ps 136:15
to a mare among P-'s chariots.	Sg 1:9
shelter under P-'s protection	Is 30:2
am about to hand over P Hophra,	Jr 44:30
P king of Egypt was all noise;	Jr 46:17
P and those trusting in him.	Jr 46:25
am against you, P king of Egypt	Ezk 29:3
P-'s daughter adopted and raised	Ac 7:21
For the Scripture tells P:	Rm 9:17
refused to be called ... son of P-'s	Heb 11:24

PHARISEE

When he saw many of the P-s	Mt 3:7
surpasses that of the scribes and P-s	Mt 5:20
we and the P-s fast often	Mt 9:14
the P-s said, "He drives out	Mt 9:34
the P-s went out and plotted	Mt 12:14
know that the P-s took offense	Mt 15:12
yeast of the P-s and Sadducees.	Mt 16:6
Some P-s approached Him to test	Mt 19:3
the P-s heard His parables,	Mt 21:45
Then the P-s went and plotted	Mt 22:15
When the P-s heard that He had	Mt 22:34
woe to you, scribes and P-s,	Mt 23:13
Blind P! First clean the inside	Mt 23:26
and the P-s gathered before	Mt 27:62
He entered the P-'s house and	Lk 7:36
a P asked Him to dine with him.	Lk 11:37
Now you P-s clean the outside	Lk 11:39
But woe to you P-s!	Lk 11:42
and the P-s began to oppose	Lk 11:53
P-s, who were lovers of money	Lk 16:14
by the P-s when the kingdom	Lk 17:20
one a P and the other a tax	Lk 18:10
they had been sent from the P-s	Jn 1:24
man from the P-s named Nicodemus	Jn 3:1
P-s heard the crowd muttering	Jn 7:32
Or any of the P-s?	Jn 7:48
and the P-s brought a woman	Jn 8:3
went to the P-s and told them	Jn 11:46
because of the P-s they did not	Jn 12:42
A P named Gamaliel, a teacher of	Ac 5:34
party of the P-s stood up and	Ac 15:5
and the other part were P-s	Ac 23:6
I am a P, a son of P-s!	Ac 23:6

but the P-s affirm them all.	Ac 23:8
as to the law, a P;	Php 3:5

PHILADELPHIA

One of the seven churches (Rv 1:11; 3:7).

PHILEMON

Convert of Paul and recipient of his letter (Phm 1,28).

PHILETUS

Heretical teacher (2Tm 2:17).

PHILIP

1. Name of two Herods (Mk 6:17; Lk 3:1).

2. Apostle (Mt 10:3; Jn 12:21-22). Invited Nathanael to "come and see" (Jn 1:43-51); questioned how to feed the 5,000 (6:5-7); asked Jesus to show them the Father (14:8-9).

3. One of the first seven deacons (Ac 6:1-6); evangelized Simon the sorcerer in Samaria (8:5-13) and an Ethiopian eunuch (8:26-39).

PHILIPPI

City in Macedonia where Paul preached (Ac 16:12; 20:6; 1Th 2:2) and to whom he wrote (Php 1:1; 4:15).

PHILISTIA

Coastal plain of southwestern Palestine; land of the Philistines (Ex 15:14; Ps 60:8; 83:7; Is 9:12; Jl 3:4).

PHILISTINES

People of Philistia (Gn 10:14; 26:1). Originated in Caphtor (Jr 47:4; Am 9:7) as the Casluhim (Gn 10:14).

Enemies of Israel: Moses and Joshua did not defeat them (Ex 13:17; Jos 13:2; Jdg 3:1-3). In conflict with Shamgar (3:31); with Samson (Jdg 13–16); with Samuel (1Sm 4–7); with Saul (1Sm 13–14; 17; 23:27-28; 28:5,15; 31:1-6); with David (17:20-57; 18:20-27; 19:8; 23:1-5; 30:16; 2Sm 5:17-25; 8:1; 21:15-22; 23:9-13); with Jehoram (2Ch 21:16); with Uzziah (26:6-7); with Ahaz (28:18); and with Hezekiah (2Kg 18:8). David hid among them (1Sm 27:1,7,11; 29:11) but did not fight for them (27:8-12; 29:9).

Prophesied against (Is 11:14; 14:29-32; Jr 47; Ezk 25:15-17; Am 1:6-8; Ob 19; Zph 2:4-7; Zch 9:5-7).

PHILOSOPHER

and Stoic p-s argued with him.	Ac 17:18
Where is the p? Where is the	1Co 1:20

PHILOSOPHY

captive through p and empty	Col 2:8

PHINEHAS

1. Grandson of Aaron; high priest (Ex 6:25; Nm 25:7-13; Ps 106:30).

2. One of Eli's wicked sons (1Sm 2:12-17,34; 4:4-19).

PHOEBE

Significant woman in the church in Cenchrea, commended by Paul (Rm 16:1).

PHOENICIA

Northern coastal region, visited by evangelists (Ac 11:19) including Paul (15:3; 21:2).

PHRYGIA

Region near Galatia represented at Pentecost (Ac 2:10) and visited by Paul (16:6; 18:23).

PHYSICAL

who has a p defect is to come	Lv 21:17
men without any p defect	Dn 1:4
in a p appearance like a dove.	Lk 3:22
my countrymen by p descent.	Rm 9:3
but his p presence is weak,	2Co 10:10
though my p condition was a trial	Gl 4:14
you by His p body through His	Col 1:22
concerning p descent but	Heb 7:16
are p regulations and only	Heb 9:10

PHYSICALLY

A man who is p uncircumcised,	Rm 2:27

PHYSICIAN

who were p-s to embalm his	Gn 50:2
didn't seek the LORD but the p-s	2Ch 16:12
Is there no p there?	Jr 8:22
Luke, the loved p, and Demas	Col 4:14

PICK

Get up, p up your stretcher,	Mt 9:6
and began to p and eat some	Mt 12:1

PIECE

laid the p-s opposite each other,	Gn 15:10
sold him for 20 p-s of silver to	Gn 37:28
cherubim of one p with the mercy	Ex 25:19
branches are to be of one p.	Ex 25:36
the horns are to be of one p.	Ex 27:2
on the ephod must be of one p	Ex 28:8
cut her into 12 p-s, limb by limb	Jdg 19:29
Take 10 p-s for yourself,	1Kg 11:31
in order to pass between its p-s.	Jr 34:18
two legs or a p of an ear	Am 3:12
my wages, 30 p-s of silver.	Zch 11:12
weighed out 30 p-s of silver for	Mt 26:15
They took the 30 p-s of silver,	Mt 27:9
baskets full of p-s of bread and	Mk 6:43
large baskets of leftover p-s.	Mk 8:8
one I give the p of bread to	Jn 13:26
woven in one p from the top.	Jn 19:23

PIERCE

His master must p his ear with	Ex 21:6
will go into his palm and p it.	2Kg 18:21
they p-d my hands and my feet.	Ps 22:16
until an arrow p-s its liver,	Pr 7:23
But He was p-d because of our	Is 53:5
will look at Me whom they p-d.	Zch 12:10
a sword will p your own soul	Lk 2:35
the soldiers p-d His side with	Jn 19:34
will look at the One they p-d.	Jn 19:37
they were p-d to the heart and	Ac 2:37
p-d themselves with many pains.	1Tm 6:10
including those who p-d Him.	Rv 1:7

PIETY

Isn't your p your confidence,	Jb 4:6

PIG

the p, though it has divided	Lv 11:7
like a gold ring in a p-'s snout.	Pr 11:22
or toss your pearls before p-s,	Mt 7:6
a large herd of p-s was feeding.	Mt 8:30
him into his fields to feed p-s.	Lk 15:15

PIGEON

a turtledove, and a young p.	Gn 15:9
two turtledoves or two young p-s	Lv 5:7
of turtledoves or two young p-s	Lk 2:24

PI-HAHIROTH

Israelite camp before crossing the Red Sea (Ex 14:2,9).

PILATE, PONTIUS

Governor of Judea; presided over Jesus' trial and sentencing (Mt 27:11-26; Mk 15:1-15; Lk 23:1-25; Jn 18:28–19:16); warned by his wife (Mt 27:19); gave Jesus' body to Joseph of Arimathea (Mt 27:58; Mk 15:45; Lk 23:52; Jn 19:38); assigned guards to the tomb (Mt 27:65).

PILGRIMAGE

My p has lasted 130 years.	Gn 47:9
whose hearts are set on p.	Ps 84:5
or make a p to Beth-aven,	Hs 4:15

PILLAGE

breaks in; a gang p-s outside.	Hs 7:1

PILLAR

back and became a p of salt.	Gn 19:26
p of cloud by day and the p of fire	Ex 13:22
smash their sacred p-s,	Ex 34:13
and do not set up a sacred p;	Dt 16:22
at the tent in a p of cloud,	Dt 31:15
had him stand between the p-s.	Jdg 16:25
Absalom had erected ... a p	2Sm 18:18
He cast two (hollow) bronze p-s:	1Kg 7:15
standing by the p according to	2Kg 11:14
As for the two p-s, the one	2Kg 25:16
I am the One who steadies its p-s.	Ps 75:3
she has carved out her seven p-s	Pr 9:1
alabaster p-s set on pedestals	Sg 5:15
of Egypt and a p to the Lord	Is 19:19
recognized as p-s, acknowledged	Gl 2:9
the p and foundation of the truth.	1Tm 3:15
will make him a p in the	Rv 3:12
his legs were like fiery p-s	Rv 10:1

PILLOW

I dampen my p and drench my bed	Ps 6:6

PILOT

wherever the will of the p directs.	Jms 3:4

PIN

thinking, "I'll p David to the	1Sm 18:11
Saul tried to p David to the	1Sm 19:10

PINE

I am like a flourishing p tree;	Hs 14:8

PINNACLE

stand on the p of the temple,	Mt 4:5; Lk 4:9

PISGAH

Mountain where Balaam viewed Israel's camp (Nm 21:20; 23:14), and from which Moses viewed the promised land (Dt 3:17,27; 34:1). Marked the edge of Sihon's and Reuben's land (Jos 12:3; 13:20).

PISHON

One of the four rivers of Eden (Gn 2:11).

PISIDIA

Area visited by Paul (Ac 13:14; 14:24).

PISTACHIOS

gum and resin, p and almonds.	Gn 43:11

PIT

contained many asphalt p-s,	Gn 14:10
and threw him into the p.	Gn 37:24
When a man ... digs a p,	Ex 21:33
down into a p on a snowy day	2Sm 23:20
God spares his soul from the P	Jb 33:18
fallen into the p they made;	Ps 9:15
Your Faithful One to see the P.	Ps 16:10
like those going down to the P.	Ps 28:1
me up from a desolate p	Ps 40:2
redeems your life from the P;	Ps 103:4
The arrogant have dug p-s for me	Ps 119:85
For a prostitute is a deep p	Pr 23:27
one who digs a p will fall into	Pr 26:27
one who digs a p may fall into	Ec 10:8
Panic, p, and trap await you	Jr 48:43
They dropped me alive into a p	Lm 3:53
people who descend to the P.	Ezk 31:14
You raised my life from the P	Jnh 2:6
fell into a p on the Sabbath,	Mt 12:11
blind, both will fall into a p.	Mt 15:14
dug out a p for a winepress,	Mk 12:1

PITCH (n)

and cover it with p inside and	Gn 6:14
coated it with asphalt and p.	Ex 2:3

PITCH (v)

Jacob had p-ed his tent in the	Gn 31:25
He will p his royal tents	Dn 11:45

PITCHER

and an empty p with a torch	Jdg 7:16

PITFALL

a p and a retribution to them.	Rm 11:9

block or **p** in your brother's	Rm 14:13
dissensions and **p-s** contrary to	Rm 16:17

PITHOM

Storage city in Egypt built by Hebrew slaves (Ex 1:11).

PITY (n)

and not look on them with **p**.	Dt 7:16
must not show **p**: life for life	Dt 19:21
was moved to **p** whenever they	Jdg 2:18
done this thing and shown no **p**	2Sm 12:6
He will have **p** on the poor and	Ps 72:13
allow no mercy, **p**, or compassion	Jr 13:14
Have **p** on Your people, LORD	Jl 2:17

PITY (v)

but **p** the one who falls without	Ec 4:10

PITIED (adj)

we should be **p** more than anyone.	1Co 15:19
you are wretched, **p**, poor, blind	Rv 3:17

PIVOTING

without **p** as they moved.	Ezk 10:11

PLACE (n) *see also* HIGH PLACE, HOLY PLACE

Surely the LORD is in this **p**,	Gn 28:16
for the **p** where you are standing	Ex 3:5
between the holy **p** and the most	Ex 26:33
I will destroy your high **p-s**,	Lv 26:30
the stars, which You set in **p**,	Ps 8:3
fallen for me in pleasant **p-s**;	Ps 16:6
He made darkness His hiding **p**	Ps 18:11
me out to a wide-open **p**;	Ps 18:19
Who may stand in His holy **p**?	Ps 24:3
You are my hiding **p**;	Ps 32:7
You put them in slippery **p-s**;	Ps 73:18
How lovely is Your dwelling **p**,	Ps 84:1
and its **p** is no longer known.	Ps 103:16
All are going to the same **p**;	Ec 3:20
do not both go to the same **p**?	Ec 6:6
and the rough **p-s** a plain.	Is 40:4
My dwelling **p** will be with them	Ezk 37:27
I will depart and return to My **p**	Hs 5:15
of Man has no **p** to lay His head.	Mt 8:20
They love the **p** of honor at	Mt 23:6
in the holy **p**" (let the reader	Mt 24:15
until all these things take **p**.	Mt 24:34
and see the **p** where He lay.	Mt 28:6

house are many dwelling **p-s**;	Jn 14:2
going away to prepare a **p** for you.	Jn 14:2
Judas left to go to his own **p**.	Ac 1:25
to have first **p** in everything.	Col 1:18

PLACE (v)

I will **p** My law within them and	Jr 31:33
I will **p** My Spirit within you	Ezk 36:27

PLAGUE

to send all My **p-s** against you,	Ex 9:14
will bring one more **p** on Pharaoh	Ex 11:1
No **p** will be among you to	Ex 12:13
LORD inflicted a **p** on the people	Ex 32:35
them with a very severe **p**.	Nm 11:33
saw that the **p** had begun among	Nm 16:47
Then the **p** on the Israelites was	Nm 25:8
or to have a **p** in your land	2Sm 24:13
{when there is} any **p** or illness,	1Kg 8:37
the **p** that stalks in darkness,	Ps 91:6
sword, famine, and **p**.	Jr 14:12; Ezk 6:11
P goes before Him, and	Hab 3:5
This will be the **p** the LORD	Zch 14:12
diseases, **p-s**, and evil spirits	Lk 7:21
and famines and **p-s** in various	Lk 21:11
have found this man to be a **p**	Ac 24:5
was killed by these three **p-s**	Rv 9:18
angels with the seven last **p-s**	Rv 15:1
blasphemed God for the **p** of hail	Rv 16:21
add to him the **p-s** that are	Rv 22:18

PLAIN

God destroyed the cities of the **p**,	Gn 19:29
camped in the **p-s** of Moab near	Nm 22:1
crossed to the **p-s** of Jericho	Jos 4:13
let's fight with them on the **p**;	1Kg 20:25
and the rough places a **p**.	Is 40:4
I got up and went out to the **p**.	Ezk 3:23
will be changed into a **p**.	Zch 14:10

PLAINLY

If You are the Messiah, tell us **p**.	Jn 10:24
Jesus then told them **p**, "Lazarus	Jn 11:14
You're speaking **p** and not using	Jn 16:29

PLAN

nothing they **p** to do will be	Gn 11:6
You **p-ned** evil against me;	Gn 50:20
tabernacle according to the **p**	Ex 26:30
of the altar and complete **p-s**	2Kg 16:10
David gave ... Solomon the **p-s**	1Ch 28:11

But they were **p-ning** to harm me. Neh 6:2
no **p** of Yours can be thwarted. Jb 42:2
He thwarts the **p-s** of the peoples. Ps 33:10
and Your **p-s** for us; Ps 40:5
and **p-ned** before a single one Ps 139:16
who **p** evil in their hearts. Ps 140:2
on that day his **p-s** die. Ps 146:4
those who **p** good find loyalty Pr 14:22
P-s fail when there is no Pr 15:22
A man's heart **p-s** his way, but Pr 16:9
Many **p-s** are in a man's heart, Pr 19:21
Finalize **p-s** through counsel, Pr 20:18
p-s of the diligent certainly Pr 21:5
for their hearts **p** violence, Pr 24:2
is no work, **p-ning**, knowledge Ec 9:10
Devise a **p**; it will fail. Is 8:10
p-s {formed} long ago, Is 25:1
a noble person **p-s** noble things; Is 32:8
I have **p-ned** it; I will also do it. Is 46:11
not bring the disaster ... I had **p-ned**. Jr 18:8
am now **p-ning** a disaster against Mc 2:3
God's ... **p** and foreknowledge, Ac 2:23
Your **p** had predestined to take place Ac 4:28
to you the whole **p** of God. Ac 20:27
and make no **p-s** to satisfy the Rm 13:14
what I **p**, do I **p** in a purely human 2Co 1:17
good pleasure that He **p-ned** in Him Eph 1:9
rather than God's **p**, 1Tm 1:4
God's hidden **p** will be completed Rv 10:7
to carry out His **p** by having one Rv 17:17

PLANT (n)

given you every seed-bearing **p** Gn 1:29
will eat the **p-s** of the field. Gn 3:18
The hail beat down every **p** Ex 9:25
Then our sons will be like **p-s** Ps 144:12
grew up before Him like a young **p** Is 53:2
the LORD God appointed a **p** Jnh 4:6
Every **p** that My heavenly Father Mt 15:13

PLANT (v)

LORD God **p-ed** a garden in Eden, Gn 2:8
was the first to **p** a vineyard. Gn 9:20
Abraham **p-ed** a tamarisk tree in Gn 21:33
and **p** any kind of tree for food, Lv 19:23
groves that you did not **p** Dt 6:11
You will **p** a vineyard but not Dt 28:30
and olive groves you did not **p**. Jos 24:13
like a tree **p-ed** beside streams Ps 1:3
root Your right hand has **p-ed**, Ps 80:15

P-ed in the house of the LORD, Ps 92:13
cedars of Lebanon that He **p-ed**. Ps 104:16
a time to **p** and a time to uproot; Ec 3:2
p-ed it with the finest vines Is 5:2
are barely **p-ed**, barely sown Is 40:24
they will **p** vineyards and eat Is 65:21
be like a tree **p-ed** by water Jr 17:8
I will **p** them and not uproot Jr 24:6
P gardens and eat their produce. Jr 29:28
to build and to **p** them, Jr 31:28
I will **p** them on their land, Am 9:15
p vineyards but never drink Zph 1:13
You have **p-ed** much but harvested Hg 1:6
A man **p-ed** a vineyard, leased it Lk 20:9
I **p-ed**, Apollos watered, but God 1Co 3:6
Who **p-s** a vineyard and does not 1Co 9:7

PLASTER

and the **p** that is scraped off Lv 14:41
you are to cover them with **p**. Dt 27:4
a wall they **p** it with whitewash Ezk 13:10
Her prophets **p** with whitewash Ezk 22:28
writing on the **p** of the king's Dn 5:5

PLATFORM

Ezra ... stood on a high wooden **p** Neh 8:4

PLATTER

the Baptist's head here on a **p**! Mt 14:8
the Baptist's head on a **p** Mk 6:25

PLAY

the father of all who **p** the lyre Gn 4:21
who knows how to **p** the harp. 1Sm 16:16
was **p-ing** {the harp} as usual 1Sm 18:10
David was **p-ing** {the harp}, 1Sm 19:9
While the musician **p-ed**, 2Kg 3:15
p skillfully on the strings, Ps 33:3
which You formed to **p** there. Ps 104:26
I will **p** on a ten-stringed harp Ps 144:9
An infant will **p** beside the Is 11:8
they have **p-ed** the fool. Jr 5:4
voice and **p-s** skillfully Ezk 33:32
p-ed the flute for you, but you Mt 11:17
p-ed the flute for you, but you Lk 7:32
eat and drink, and got up to **p**. 1Co 10:7
will what is **p-ed** on the flute 1Co 14:7

PLEA

LORD has heard my **p** for help; Ps 6:9
do not ignore my **p** for help. Ps 55:1

Let my p reach You;	Ps 119:170
You hear my p:	Lm 3:56

PLEAD

Let Baal p his case with him,	Jdg 6:32
after day and pled with him until	Jdg 16:16
David p-ed with God for the boy.	2Sm 12:16
I would p my case before Him and	Jb 23:4
at daybreak I p my case to You	Ps 5:3
the sound of my p-ing when I cry	Ps 28:2
him with her persistent p-ing;	Pr 7:21
P the widow's cause.	Is 1:17
came to Him, p-ing with Him,	Mt 8:5
Jesus' feet and p-ed with Him to	Lk 8:41
he p-s with God against Israel	Rm 11:2
we p on Christ's behalf,	2Co 5:20
p-ed with the Lord three times	2Co 12:8

PLEASANT

have fallen for me in p places;	Ps 16:6
despised the p land and did not	Ps 106:24
How good and p it is when	Ps 133:1
for praise is p and lovely.	Ps 147:1
and your sleep will be p.	Pr 3:24
but p words are pure.	Pr 15:26
P words are a honeycomb:	Pr 16:24
beautiful you are and how p	Sg 7:6
My sleep had been most p to me.	Jr 31:26
They turned a p land into a	Zch 7:14

PLEASE

if it doesn't p you to worship	Jos 24:15
P allow me to make one more test	Jdg 6:39
everything the king did p-d them.	2Sm 3:36
do with me whatever p-s Him.	2Sm 15:26
p them by speaking kind words	2Ch 10:7
young woman who p-s the king	Est 2:4
Call out if you p. Will anyone	Jb 5:1
LORD, be p-d to deliver me;	Ps 40:13
You are not p-d with a burnt	Ps 51:16
will p the LORD more than an ox,	Ps 69:31
heaven and does whatever He p-s.	Ps 115:3
does whatever He p-s in heaven	Ps 135:6
When a man's ways p the LORD,	Pr 16:7
The one who p-s God will escape	Ec 7:26
LORD was p-d, because of His	Is 42:21
the LORD was p-d to crush Him,	Is 53:10
it will accomplish what I p,	Is 55:11
you do as you p on the day of	Is 58:3
your sacrifices do not p Me.	Jr 6:20

I give it to anyone I p.	Jr 27:5
sacrifices will not p Him.	Hs 9:4
was greatly p-d with the plant.	Jnh 4:6
Would the LORD be p-d with	Mc 6:7
Would he be p-d with you or	Mal 1:8
offerings ... will p the LORD as	Mal 3:4
danced before them and p-d	Mt 14:6
The wind blows where it p-s,	Jn 3:8
because I always do what p-s Him.	Jn 8:29
he saw that it p-d the Jews	Ac 12:3
the flesh are unable to p God.	Rm 8:8
one of us must p his neighbor	Rm 15:2
the Messiah did not p Himself.	Rm 15:3
God was p-d to save those who	1Co 1:21
how he may p the Lord.	1Co 7:32
how he may p his wife	1Co 7:33
But God was not p-d with most	1Co 10:5
as I also try to p all people in all	1Co 10:33
am p-d in weaknesses, in insults,	2Co 12:10
am I striving to p people?	Gl 1:10
in order to p men, but	Eph 6:6; Col 3:22
God was p-d {to have} all His	Col 1:19
how you must walk and p God	1Th 4:1
good, and it p-s God our Savior,	1Tm 2:3
their parents, for this p-s God.	1Tm 5:4
To p the recruiter, no one	2Tm 2:4
he was approved, having p-d God.	Heb 11:5
it is impossible to p God,	Heb 11:6
for God is p-d with such	Heb 13:16

PLEASING (adj)

every tree p in appearance	Gn 2:9
the LORD smelled the p aroma	Gn 8:21
is a p aroma, a fire offering	Ex 29:18
a fire offering of a p aroma to the	Lv 1:9
something was found p to the	1Kg 14:13
sacrifices of p aroma to the	Ezr 6:10
The sacrifice p to God is a	Ps 51:17
May my meditation be p to Him;	Ps 104:34
For it is p if you keep them	Pr 22:18
one who is p in God's sight.	Ec 2:26
it is p for the eyes to see the sun.	Ec 11:7
living sacrifice, holy and p to God;	Rm 12:1
the good, p, and perfect will	Rm 12:2
make it our aim to be p to	2Co 5:9
what is p to the Lord.	Eph 5:10
welcome sacrifice, p to God.	Php 4:18
the Lord, fully p {to Him},	Col 1:10
for this is p in the Lord.	Col 3:20

in us what is **p** in His sight,   Heb 13:21
do what is **p** in His sight.   1Jn 3:22

PLEASURE

Does the LORD take **p** in burnt   1Sm 15:22
in Your right hand are eternal **p-s.**   Ps 16:11
since He takes **p** in him.   Ps 22:8
In Your good **p,** cause Zion to   Ps 51:18
the LORD takes **p** in His people;   Ps 149:4
and take **p** in the wife of your   Pr 5:18
The one who loves **p** will become   Pr 21:17
I will test you with **p** and enjoy   Ec 2:1
of fools is in a house of **p.**   Ec 7:4
shepherd, he will fulfill all My **p**   Is 44:28
seeking your own **p,**   Is 58:13
I take no **p** in anyone's death.   Ezk 18:32
choked with worries, riches, and **p-s** Lk 8:14
because this was Your good **p.**   Lk 10:21
according to His good **p**   Eph 1:9
lovers of **p** rather than lovers   2Tm 3:4
captives of various passions and **p-s,** Ti 3:3
My soul has no **p** in him.   Heb 10:38
enjoy the short-lived **p** of sin.   Heb 11:25
spend it on your desires for **p.**   Jms 4:3

PLEDGE (n)

loads himself with goods taken in **p.** Hab 2:6
renounced their original **p.**   1Tm 5:12
but the **p** of a good conscience   1Pt 3:21

PLEDGE (v)

They **p-d** to send their wives away Ezr 10:19
I **p-d** Myself to you,   Ezk 16:8
LORD but also **p** loyalty to Milcom. Zph 1:5

PLEIADES

the Bear, Orion, the **P,** and the   Jb 9:9
Can you fasten the chains of the **P** Jb 38:31
One who made the **P** and Orion,   Am 5:8

PLENTY

and there is **p** left over because 2Ch 31:10
Your ways overflow with **p.**   Ps 65:11
land will have **p** of food,   Pr 12:11; 28:19
You will have **p** to eat and be   Jl 2:26
there was **p** of water there.   Jn 3:23

PLOT (n)

p of land at Jezreel 1Kg 21:23; 2Kg 9:10,36
middle of the **p** and defended it 1Ch 11:14
but their **p** became known to Saul Ac 9:24
than 40 who had formed this **p.** Ac 23:13

PLOT (v)

had **p-ted** against the Jews   Est 9:24
and the peoples **p** in vain?   Ps 2:1
The one who **p-s** evil will be   Pr 24:8
Whatever you **p** against the LORD Nah 1:9
and do not **p** evil in your hearts Zch 7:10
went out and **p-ted** against Him, Mt 12:14
went and **p-ted** how to trap Him Mt 22:15
the people **p-ted** against Jesus Mt 27:1
the peoples **p** futile things?   Ac 4:25

PLOW (n)

swords into **p-s** and their spears Is 2:4
will beat their swords into **p-s,** Mc 4:3
his hand to the **p** and looks back Lk 9:62

PLOW (v)

Do not **p** with an ox and a donkey Dt 22:10
If you hadn't **p-ed** with my young Jdg 14:18
Elisha ... as he was **p-ing.**   1Kg 19:19
Will it **p** the valleys behind you Jb 39:10
slacker does not **p** during planting Pr 20:4
Zion will be **p-ed** like a field, Jr 26:18
have **p-ed** wickedness and reaped Hs 10:13
or does someone **p** {it} with oxen? Am 6:12
Zion will be **p-ed** like a field, Mc 3:12
he who **p-s** ought to **p** in hope, 1Co 9:10

PLOWMAN

when the **p** will overtake the   Am 9:13

PLOWSHARES

Philistines to sharpen their **p** 1Sm 13:20
Hammer your **p** into swords and Jl 3:10

PLUCK

you may **p** heads of grain with Dt 23:25
He **p-ed** off its topmost shoot, Ezk 17:4

PLUMAGE

feathers and **p** like the stork's? Jb 39:13
and full of **p** of many colors came Ezk 17:3

PLUMB LINE

a measuring line and a **p** over her Is 34:11
I am setting a **p** among My people Am 7:8
will rejoice when they see the **p** Zch 4:10

PLUNDER (n)

little children will become **p.**   Nm 14:3
who you said would be **p**   Dt 1:39
they rushed to the **p,** took sheep 1Sm 14:32
they did not seize any **p.**   Est 9:10

and fill our houses with **p**.	Pr 1:13
than to divide **p** with the proud	Pr 16:19
The **p** from the poor is in your	Is 3:14
have become **p**, with no one to	Is 42:22
Their wealth will become **p**	Zph 1:13
and divides up his **p**.	Lk 11:22
gave a tenth of the **p**!	Heb 7:4

PLUNDER (v)

So you will **p** the Egyptians.	Ex 3:22
this way they **p-ed** the Egyptians.	Ex 12:36
you may **p** its spoil and	Jos 8:2
out and **p-ed** the Aramean camp	2Kg 7:16
The brave-hearted have been **p-ed**;	Ps 76:5
All who pass by **p** him;	Ps 89:41
and will **p** those who **p** them.	Pr 22:23
and all who **p** you will be **p-ed**.	Jr 30:16
and **p** those who **p** them.	Ezk 39:10
P the silver! **P** the gold!	Nah 2:9
Since you have **p-ed** many nations	Hab 2:8

PLUNGE

which **p** people into ruin and	1Tm 6:9
that you don't **p** with them into	1Pt 4:4
kingdom was **p-d** into darkness.	Rv 16:10

PLUS

standard length **p** three inches.	Ezk 40:5

PODS

from the carob **p** the pigs were	Lk 15:16

POEM

Balaam proclaimed his **p**:	Nm 23:7
A **p** by Hezekiah king of Judah	Is 38:9

POETS

Therefore the **p** say: Come to	Nm 21:27
some of your own **p** have said,	Ac 17:28

POINT (n)

LORD has helped us to this **p**.	1Sm 7:12
him ten thousand **p-s** of My law,	Hs 8:12
in sorrow—to the **p** of death.	Mt 26:38
obedient to the **p** of death	Php 2:8
to the **p** of being bound like a	2Tm 2:9
Now the main **p** of what is being	Heb 8:1
resisted to the **p** of shedding	Heb 12:4
yet fails in one **p**, is guilty	Jms 2:10

POINT (v)

was a man **p-ed** out to you by God	Ac 2:22
If you **p** these things out to the	1Tm 4:6

POISON

venom, the deadly **p** of cobras.	Dt 32:33
He will suck the **p** of cobras;	Jb 20:16
Lethal **p** has been poured into	Ps 41:8
you have turned justice into **p**	Am 6:12
evil, full of deadly **p**.	Jms 3:8

POISONED (v)

I see you are **p** by bitterness	Ac 8:23
stirred up and **p** the minds	Ac 14:2

POISONED (adj)

He has given us **p** water to drink,	Jr 8:14

POISONOUS

the LORD sent **p** snakes among	Nm 21:6
wilderness with its **p** snakes	Dt 8:15
no root among you bearing **p**	Dt 29:18
and give them **p** waters to drink.	Jr 9:15

POLE

Insert the **p-s** into the rings on	Ex 25:14
and chop down their Asherah **p-s**.	Ex 34:13
snake and mounted it on a **p**.	Nm 21:9
cut down their Asherah **p-s**,	Dt 7:5
The **p-s** were so long that their	1Kg 8:8
Asherah **p-s** on every high hill	2Kg 17:10
a {solitary} **p** on a mountaintop	Is 30:17

POLICE

was sitting with the temple **p**,	Mk 14:54
and temple **p** how he could hand	Lk 22:4
sent temple **p** to arrest Him.	Jn 7:32
The **p** answered, "No man ever	Jn 7:46
Jewish temple **p** arrested Jesus	Jn 18:12
But when the temple **p** got there,	Ac 5:22
Then the **p** reported these words	Ac 16:38

POLISHED

like the gleam of **p** bronze	Ezk 1:7; Dn 10:6

POLLUTE

because they have **p-d** My land.	Jr 16:18
it **p-s** the whole body,	Jms 3:6

POLLUTED (adj)

the land became **p** with blood.	Ps 106:38
a muddied spring or a **p** well.	Pr 25:26
earth is **p** by its inhabitants.	Is 24:5
acts are like a **p** garment;	Is 64:6
abstain from things **p** by idols,	Ac 15:20

POLLUTING (adj)

follow the **p-ing** desires of the	2Pt 2:10

POMEGRANATE

gold bells and **p**-s alternate	Ex 28:34
made **p**-s of finely spun blue	Ex 39:24
also {took} some **p**-s and figs	Nm 13:23
under the **p** tree in Migron	1Sm 14:2
of **p**-s on the one grating	1Kg 7:18
brow is like a slice of **p**	Sg 4:3; 6:7
budding and the **p**-s blooming.	Sg 6:11
to drink from my **p** juice.	Sg 8:2
p, the date palm, and the	Jl 1:12
fig, the **p**, and the olive	Hg 2:19

POMP

came with great **p** and entered	Ac 25:23

PONDERS

in my heart, and my spirit **p**.	Ps 77:6

PONTUS

Province south of the Black Sea, represented at Pentecost (Ac 2:9); home of Aquila (18:2); addressees of Peter (1Pt 1:1).

POOL

he made the **p** and the tunnel	2Kg 20:20
a desert into a **p** of water,	Ps 107:35
the rock into a **p** of water,	Ps 114:8
your eyes like **p**-s in Heshbon	Sg 7:4
parched ground will become a **p**	Is 35:7
desert into a **p** of water	Is 41:18
there is a **p**, called Bethesda	Jn 5:2
wash in the **p** of Siloam	Jn 9:7

POOR

since I am such a **p** speaker?	Ex 6:12
must not deny justice to the **p**	Ex 23:6
and the **p** may not give less,	Ex 30:15
Leave them for the **p** and	Lv 19:10
Do not be partial to the **p** or give	Lv 19:15
There will be no **p** among you,	Dt 15:4
there will never cease to be **p**	Dt 15:11
younger men, whether rich or **p**.	Ru 3:10
He raises the **p** from the dust	1Sm 2:8
but the **p** man had nothing except	2Sm 12:3
So the **p** have hope,	Jb 5:16
I rescued the **p** man who cried	Jb 29:12
This **p** man cried, and the LORD	Ps 34:6
rescuing the **p** from one too	Ps 35:10
is one who cares for the **p**;	Ps 41:1
You provided for the **p**	Ps 68:10
lives of Your **p** people forever.	Ps 74:19

let the **p** and needy praise Your	Ps 74:21
me, for I am **p** and needy.	Ps 86:1
He distributes freely to the **p**;	Ps 112:9
He raises the **p** from the dust	Ps 113:7
Idle hands make one **p**,	Pr 10:4
pretends to be **p** but has great	Pr 13:7
but a **p** man hears no threat.	Pr 13:8
A **p** man is hated even by his	Pr 14:20
oppresses the **p** insults their	Pr 14:31
who mocks the **p** insults his	Pr 17:5
Better a **p** man who walks in	Pr 19:1
Kindness to the **p** is a loan to	Pr 19:17
better to be a **p** man than a perjurer.	Pr 19:22
who is reckless only becomes **p**.	Pr 21:5
rich and the **p** have this in common:	Pr 22:2
and the glutton will become **p**,	Pr 23:21
a **p** man who lives with integrity	Pr 28:6
who gives to the **p** will not be	Pr 28:27
Her hands reach out to the **p**	Pr 31:20
Better is a **p** but wise youth	Ec 4:13
wisdom of the **p** man is despised	Ec 9:16
He will judge the **p** righteously	Is 11:4
been a stronghold for the **p**	Is 25:4
Me to bring good news to the **p**.	Is 61:1
some of the **p** people of the land	Jr 52:16
have oppressed the **p** and needy	Ezk 22:29
and deprive the **p** of justice at	Am 5:12
We can buy the **p** with silver and	Am 8:6
stranger or the **p**, and do not	Zch 7:10
Blessed are the **p** in spirit,	Mt 5:3
So whenever you give to the **p**	Mt 6:2
and the **p** are told the good news	Mt 11:5
belongings and give to the **p**	Mt 19:21
You always have the **p** with you,	Mt 26:11
And a **p** widow came and dropped	Mk 12:42
invite those who are **p**,	Lk 14:13
give half of my possessions to the **p**,	Lk 19:8
contribution to the **p** among	Rm 15:26
all my goods to feed the **p**	1Co 13:3
as **p** yet enriching many;	2Co 6:10
for your sake He became **p**,	2Co 8:9
has given to the **p**;	2Co 9:9
only that we would remember the **p**,	Gl 2:10
and a **p** man dressed in dirty	Jms 2:2
God choose the **p** in this world	Jms 2:5
pitiful, **p**, blind, and naked,	Rv 3:17
rich and **p**, free and slave	Rv 13:16

POOREST

Except for the **p** people of the   2Kg 24:14
some of the **p** of the land to   2Kg 25:12

POORLY

we are **p** clothed, roughly   1Co 4:11

POPLAR

then took branches of fresh **p**   Gn 30:37
up our lyres on the **p** trees,   Ps 137:2

POPULAR

Mordecai ... highly **p** with many   Est 10:3

POPULATED

them the whole earth was **p**.   Gn 9:19

POPULATION

A large **p** is a king's splendor,   Pr 14:28
in spite of a very large **p**   Is 16:14

POPULOUS

will become a **p** nation.   Gn 48:19
became ... powerful, and **p** nation.   Dt 26:5

PORCIUS see FESTUS

PORE

You **p** over the Scriptures   Jn 5:39

PORTICO

The **p** in front of the temple   1Kg 6:3
between the **p** and the altar,   Ezk 8:16
he measured the **p** of the gate;   Ezk 40:8
weep between the **p** and the altar.   Jl 2:17

PORTION

it is to be your **p**.   Ex 29:26
it as their **p** from My fire   Lv 6:17
It is a holy **p** for the priest,   Nm 6:20
Levi does not have a **p**   Dt 10:9
But the LORD's **p** is His people,   Dt 32:9
Levites among you do not get a **p**,   Jos 18:7
he gave a double **p** to Hannah,   1Sm 1:5
We have no **p** in David, no   2Sm 20:1
What **p** do we have in David?   1Kg 12:16
be a double **p** of your spirit   2Kg 2:9
required **p**-s for the priests   Neh 12:44
LORD, You are my **p** and my cup   Ps 16:5
strength of my heart, my **p** forever.   Ps 73:26
The LORD is my **p**;   Ps 119:57
my **p** in the land of the living.   Ps 142:5
and **p**-s for her servants.   Pr 31:15
must give his **p** to a man who has   Ec 2:21

For that is your **p** in life and   Ec 9:9
I will give Him the many as a **p**,   Is 53:12
Jacob's **P** is not like these   Jr 10:16
The LORD is my **p**, therefore I   Lm 3:24
will be Dan—one **p**.   Ezk 48:1
Judah as His **p** in the Holy Land,   Zch 2:12
and brought a **p** of it and laid   Ac 5:2
mix a double **p** for her.   Rv 18:6

PORTRAYED

Christ was vividly **p** as crucified?   Gl 3:1

POSITION

and restore you to your **p**.   Gn 40:13
P yourselves, stand still, and see   2Ch 20:17
strengthened his **p** by killing   2Ch 21:4
strengthened his **p** and led his   2Ch 25:11
strengthened his **p** by rebuilding   2Ch 32:5
let another take over his **p**.   Ps 109:8
third highest **p** in the kingdom.   Dn 5:7
men of high **p** exercise power   Mt 20:25
Let someone else take his **p**.   Ac 1:20
angels who did not keep their own **p**   Jd 6

POSSESS

to give you this land to **p**.   Gn 15:7
I will give it to you to **p**   Lv 20:24
I have given you the land to **p**.   Nm 33:53
the land you are entering to **p**.   Dt 28:21
the land remains to be **p**-ed.   Jos 13:1
you may **p** whatever your god   Jdg 11:24
so that you may **p** this good land   1Ch 28:8
are entering to **p** is an impure   Ezr 9:11
to go in and **p** the land You had   Neh 9:15
They will live there and **p** it.   Ps 69:35
I **p** good advice and competence;   Pr 8:14
they will **p** the land forever;   Is 60:21
the kingdom and **p** it forever,   Dn 7:18
so that they may **p** the remnant   Am 9:12
while Benjamin will **p** Gilead.   Ob 19
those **p**-ed fell down before Him   Mk 3:11
has put in everything she **p**-ed   Mk 12:44
came out of many who were **p**-ed   Ac 8:7
buy as though they did not **p**   1Co 7:30
nothing yet **p**-ing everything.   2Co 6:10
knows how to **p** his own vessel   1Th 4:4

POSSESSION

Canaan—as an eternal **p**,   Gn 17:8
you will be My own **p**   Ex 19:5
We must go up and take **p**   Nm 13:30

Enter and take **p** of the land | Dt 1:8
God has chosen you to be His own **p** | Dt 7:6
go in and take **p** of the land | Jos 1:11
failed to take **p** of | Jdg 1:27
the ends of the earth Your **p**. | Ps 2:8
Save Your people, bless Your **p**, | Ps 28:9
He has chosen to be His own **p**! | Ps 33:12
rush around in vain, gathering **p-s** | Ps 39:6
as the tribe for Your own **p**. | Ps 74:2
Israel as His treasured **p**. | Ps 135:4
Honor the LORD with your **p-s** | Pr 3:9
I am their **p**. | Ezk 44:28
the flock that is Your **p**. | Mc 7:14
The LORD will take **p** of Judah | Zch 2:12
a special **p** on the day I am | Mal 3:17
because he had many **p-s**. | Mt 19:22
him in charge of all his **p-s**. | Mt 24:47
in the abundance of his **p-s**. | Lk 12:15
say good-bye to all his **p-s** cannot | Lk 14:33
was squandering his **p-s** | Lk 16:1
half of my **p-s** to the poor, | Lk 19:8
sold their **p-s** and property | Ac 2:45
that any of his **p-s** was his own, | Ac 4:32
for the redemption of the **p**, | Eph 1:14
the confiscation of your **p-s**, | Heb 10:34
you have a better and enduring **p**. | Heb 10:34
a holy nation, a people for His **p**, | 1Pt 2:9

POSSESSOR

a fountain of life for its **p**, | Pr 16:22

POSSIBLE

but with God all things are **p**. | Mt 19:26
astray, if **p**, even the elect | Mt 24:24
If it is **p**, let this cup pass | Mt 26:39
Everything is **p** to the one who | Mk 9:23
All things are **p** for You. | Mk 14:36
it is not **p** for a prophet to | Lk 13:33
with men is **p** with God. | Lk 18:27
If **p**, on your part, live at | Rm 12:18
you that, if **p**, you would have | Gl 4:15
It is not **p** to speak about these | Heb 9:5

POT

a smoking fire **p** and a flaming | Gn 15:17
when we sat by **p-s** of meat and | Ex 16:3
kettle or caldron or cooking **p**. | 1Sm 2:14
There's death in the **p**, | 2Kg 4:40
as from a boiling **p**. | Jb 41:20
I see a boiling **p**, its mouth | Jr 1:13

shattered **p**, a jar no one wants | Jr 22:28
The city is the **p**, and we are | Ezk 11:3
like flesh for the cooking **p** | Mc 3:3

POTIPHAR

Egyptian officer of Pharaoh who bought Joseph (Gn 37:36; 39:1); threw him in prison (39:7-20).

POTTER

as if the **p** were the same as the | Is 29:16
like a **p** who treads the clay. | Is 41:25
we are the clay, and You are our **p**; | Is 64:8
Just like clay in the **p-'s** hand, | Jr 18:6
Go, buy a **p-'s** clay jug. | Jr 19:1
one shatters a **p-'s** jar that can | Jr 19:11
jars, the work of a **p-'s** hands! | Lm 4:2
Throw it to the **p**, | Zch 11:13
and bought the **p-'s** field with it | Mt 27:7
Or has the **p** no right over His | Rm 9:21

POTTERY

Job took a piece of broken **p** to scrape | Jb 2:8
You will shatter them like **p**. | Ps 2:9
a dead person—like broken **p**. | Ps 31:12
the nations like discarded **p**. | Hs 8:8
lump one piece of **p** for honor | Rm 9:21
He will shatter them like **p** | Rv 2:27

POUCH

stones ... and put them in the **p** | 1Sm 17:40

POUND (n)

Mary took a **p** of fragrant oil | Jn 12:3
about 75 **p-s** of myrrh and aloes | Jn 19:39

POUND (v)

winds blew and **p-ed** that house. | Mt 7:25

POUR

blood; **p** it on the ground like water | Dt 12:16
been **p-ing** out my heart before | 1Sm 1:15
be like water **p-ed** out on the | 2Sm 14:14
Instead, he **p-ed** it out to the | 2Sm 23:16
who used to **p** water on Elijah's | 2Kg 3:11
Did You not **p** me out like milk | Jb 10:10
Now my life is **p-ed** out before | Jb 30:16
after day they **p** out speech; | Ps 19:2
I am **p-ed** out like water, | Ps 22:14
this as I **p** out my heart: | Ps 42:4
p out your hearts before Him. | Ps 62:8
P out Your wrath on the nations | Ps 79:6
I **p** out my complaint before Him | Ps 142:2

then I will **p** out my spirit on   Pr 1:23
your name is perfume **p-ed** out.   Sg 1:3
I will **p** out My Spirit on your   Is 44:3
P out Your wrath on the nations   Jr 10:25
P out your heart like water   Lm 2:19
for I will **p** out My Spirit on   Ezk 39:29
I will **p** out My Spirit on all   Jl 2:28
His wrath is **p-ed** out like fire,   Nah 1:6
Then I will **p** out a spirit of   Zch 12:10
of heaven and **p** out a blessing   Mal 3:10
the jar and **p-ed** it on His head.   Mk 14:3
over—will be **p-ed** into your   Lk 6:38
wounds, **p-ing** on oil and wine   Lk 10:34
that I will **p** out My Spirit on   Ac 2:17
has **p-ed** out what you both see   Ac 2:33
Spirit had been **p-ed** out on the   Ac 10:45
love has been **p-ed** out in our   Rm 5:5
even if I am **p-ed** out as a drink   Php 2:17
already being **p-ed** out as a   2Tm 4:6
This {Spirit} He **p-ed** out on us   Ti 3:6
Go and **p** out the seven bowls of   Rv 16:1

POVERTY

The LORD brings **p** and gives   1Sm 2:7
your **p** will come like a   Pr 6:11; 24:34
the **p** of the poor is their   Pr 10:15
P and disgrace {come to} those   Pr 13:18
endless talk leads only to **p**.   Pr 14:23
will have his fill of **p**.   Pr 28:19
Give me neither **p** nor wealth;   Pr 30:8
but she out of her **p** has put in   Mk 12:44
she out of her **p** has put in all   Lk 21:4
joy and their deep **p** overflowed   2Co 8:2
so that by His **p** you might   2Co 8:9
I know your tribulation and **p**   Rv 2:9

POWDER

of it into a fine **p** and put some   Ex 30:36
falls, it will grind him to **p**!   Mt 21:44

POWER

this purpose: to show you My **p**   Ex 9:16
right hand is glorious in **p**.   Ex 15:6
My **p** and my own ability have   Dt 8:17
LORD, is the greatness and the **p**   1Ch 29:11
for God has the **p** to help or to   2Ch 25:8
reach Him—He is exalted in **p**!   Jb 37:23
no escape by its great **p**.   Ps 33:17
my life from the **p** of Sheol,   Ps 49:15
Ascribe **p** to God. His majesty is   Ps 68:34

Our Lord is great, vast in **p**;   Ps 147:5
Patience is better than **p**,   Pr 16:32
death are in the **p** of the tongue,   Pr 18:21
wicked come to **p**, people hide   Pr 28:12,28
and His **p** establishes His rule.   Is 40:10
He made the earth by His **p**,   Jr 10:12; 51:15
for wisdom and **p** belong to Him.   Dn 2:20
that nation, but without its **p**.   Dn 8:22
I am filled with **p** by the Spirit   Mc 3:8
slow to anger but great in **p**;   Nah 1:3
This is where His **p** is hidden.   Hab 3:4
kingdom and the **p** and the glory   Mt 6:13
why supernatural **p-s** are at work   Mt 14:2
position exercise **p** over them.   Mt 20:25
the Scriptures or the **p** of God.   Mt 22:29
the celestial **p-s** will be shaken   Mt 24:29
of heaven with **p** and great glory   Mt 24:30
right hand of the **P** and coming   Mt 26:64
in Himself that **p** had gone out   Mk 5:30
the kingdom of God come in **p**.   Mk 9:1
in the spirit and **p** of Elijah,   Lk 1:17
and the **p** of the Most High will   Lk 1:35
Galilee in the **p** of the Spirit,   Lk 4:14
And the Lord's **p** to heal was in   Lk 5:17
because **p** was coming out from   Lk 6:19
He gave them **p** and authority   Lk 9:1
over all the **p** of the enemy;   Lk 10:19
He has no **p** over Me.   Jn 14:30
you will receive **p** when the Holy   Ac 1:8
by our own **p** or godliness we   Ac 3:12
And with great **p** the apostles   Ac 4:33
is called the Great **P** of God!   Ac 8:10
Give me this **p** too, so that   Ac 8:19
the Holy Spirit and with **p**,   Ac 10:38
and from the **p** of Satan to God,   Ac 26:18
it is God's **p** for salvation to   Rm 1:16
His eternal **p** and divine nature   Rm 1:20
nor things to come, nor **p-s**,   Rm 8:38
that I may display My **p** in you,   Rm 9:17
wrath and to make His **p** known,   Rm 9:22
and by the **p** of God's Spirit.   Rm 15:19
to Him who has **p** to strengthen   Rm 16:25
are being saved it is God's **p**.   1Co 1:18
and Greeks, Christ is God's **p**   1Co 1:24
demonstration of the Spirit and **p**,   1Co 2:4
on men's wisdom but on God's **p**.   1Co 2:5
of God is not in talk but in **p**.   1Co 4:20
and with the **p** of our Lord Jesus   1Co 5:4

rule and all authority and **p**.	1Co 15:24
sown in weakness, raised in **p**;	1Co 15:43
and the **p** of sin is the law.	1Co 15:56
extraordinary **p** may be from God	2Co 4:7
of truth, by the **p** of God;	2Co 6:7
for **p** is perfected in weakness.	2Co 12:9
but He lives by God's **p**.	2Co 13:4
greatness of His **p** to us who	Eph 1:19
to me by the working of His **p**.	Eph 3:7
according to the **p** that works in	Eph 3:20
the world **p-s** of this darkness	Eph 6:12
know Him and the **p** of His	Php 3:10
you be strengthened with all **p**	Col 1:11
only, but also in **p**, in the Holy	1Th 1:5
fearfulness, but one of **p**, love,	2Tm 1:7
relying on the **p** of God,	2Tm 1:8
of religion but denying its **p**.	2Tm 3:5
one holding the **p** of death	Heb 2:14
word and the **p-s** of the coming age,	Heb 6:5
but based on the **p** of an	Heb 7:16
by God's **p** through faith for	1Pt 1:5
and **p-s** subjected to Him	1Pt 3:22
For His divine **p** has given us	2Pt 1:3
known to you the **p** and coming of	2Pt 1:16
glory, majesty, **p**, and authority	Jd 25
receive glory and honor and **p**	Rv 4:11
and honor and **p** and strength,	Rv 7:12
glory, and **p** belong to our God,	Rv 19:1
death has no **p** over these,	Rv 20:6

POWERFUL

They were the **p** men of old,	Gn 6:4
was the first **p** man on earth	Gn 10:8
after me is more **p** than I.	Mt 3:11
was a Prophet **p** in action	Lk 24:19
who was **p** in the Scriptures	Ac 18:24
established as the **p** Son of	Rm 1:4
many **p**, not many of noble	1Co 1:26
are **p** through God for the	2Co 10:4
letters are weighty and **p**	2Co 10:10
toward you, but **p** among you.	2Co 13:3
all things by His **p** word.	Heb 1:3
of the righteous is very **p**.	Jms 5:16

POWERFULLY

strength that works **p** in me.	Col 1:29

PRACTICE (n)

Do not imitate their **p-s**.	Ex 23:24
not follow the **p-s** of the land	Lv 18:3
This was Job's regular **p**.	Jb 1:5
This is my {**p**}: I obey Your	Ps 119:56
the **p** of every kind of impurity	Eph 4:19
insisting on ascetic **p-s**	Col 2:18
off the old man with his **p-s**	Col 3:9
you hate the **p-s** of the	Rv 2:6

PRACTICE (v)

You are not to **p** divination or	Lv 19:26
assembly and **p** self-denial;	Lv 23:27
the fire and **p-d** divination	2Kg 17:17
you **p** injustice in your hearts;	Ps 58:2
whoever **p-s** and teaches	Mt 5:19
Be careful not to **p** your	Mt 6:1
they don't **p** what they teach.	Mt 23:3
everyone who **p-s** wicked things	Jn 3:20
previously **p-d** sorcery in that	Ac 8:9
for us as Romans to adopt or **p**.	Ac 16:21
who had **p-d** magic collected	Ac 19:19
those who **p** such things	Rm 1:32; 5:21
and promiscuity they **p-d**.	2Co 12:21
P these things;	1Tm 4:15
should learn to **p** their religion	1Tm 5:4
and are not **p-ing** the truth	1Jn 1:6
everyone who loves and **p-s** lying.	Rv 22:15

PRAISE (n)

in holiness, revered with **p-s**,	Ex 15:11
consecrated as a **p** offering to	Lv 19:24
He is your **p** and He is your God,	Dt 10:21
the nations He has made in **p**	Dt 26:19
I will sing **p** to the LORD God of	Jdg 5:3
Sing to Him; sing **p** to Him;	1Ch 16:9
and rejoice in Your **p**.	1Ch 16:35
instruments were leading the **p**.	2Ch 23:13
Levites to sing **p** to the LORD	2Ch 29:30
and for **p** in the gates of the	2Ch 31:2
above all blessing and **p**.	Neh 9:5
were in charge of the **p** songs.	Neh 12:8
to the LORD, who is worthy of **p**,	Ps 18:3
enthroned on the **p-s** of Israel.	Ps 22:3
p from the upright is beautiful.	Ps 33:1
His **p** will always be on my lips.	Ps 34:1
a hymn of **p** to our God.	Ps 40:3
Sing **p** to God, sing **p**;	Ps 47:6
my mouth will declare Your **p**.	Ps 51:15
P is rightfully Yours, God,	Ps 65:1
make His **p** glorious.	Ps 66:2
and His courts with **p**.	Ps 100:4
Sing to Him, sing **p** to Him;	Ps 105:2

God of my p, do not be silent.	Ps 109:1
His p endures forever.	Ps 111:10
a man, by the p he receives.	Pr 27:21
proclaim the p-s of the LORD.	Is 60:6
Jerusalem the p of the earth.	Is 62:7
be saved, for You are my p.	Jr 17:14
and the earth is full of His p.	Hab 3:3
have prepared p from the mouths	Mt 21:16
they saw it, gave p to God.	Lk 18:43
For they loved p from men more	Jn 12:43
His p is not from men but from	Rm 2:29
And then p will come to each one	1Co 4:5
to the p of His glorious grace	Eph 1:6
might bring p to His glory.	Eph 1:12
to the p of His glory.	Eph 1:14
to the glory and p of God.	Php 1:11
and if there is any p—dwell on	Php 4:8
up to God a sacrifice of p,	Heb 13:15
cheerful? He should sing p-s.	Jms 5:13
proclaim the p-s of the One who	1Pt 2:9

PRAISE (v)

P the LORD, the God of Shem;	Gn 9:26
This time I will p the LORD.	Gn 29:35
This is my God, and I will p Him,	Ex 15:2
LORD is great and is highly p-d;	1Ch 16:25
4,000 are to p the LORD with	1Ch 23:5
They worshiped and p-d the LORD	2Ch 7:3
priests p-d the LORD day after	2Ch 30:21
their positions to p the LORD,	Ezr 3:10
LORD lives—may my rock be p-d!	Ps 18:46
I will p You in the congregation.	Ps 22:22
highly p-d in the city of our God.	Ps 48:1
whose word I p, in God I trust;	Ps 56:4
let all the peoples p You.	Ps 67:3
Let heaven and earth p Him,	Ps 69:34
Even human wrath will p You;	Ps 76:10
the heavens p Your wonders	Ps 89:5
It is good to p the LORD, to	Ps 92:1
LORD is great and is highly p-d;	Ps 96:4
My soul, p the LORD, and all	Ps 103:1
be p-d from everlasting to	Ps 106:48
LORD be p-d both now and forever.	Ps 113:2
Let me live, and I will p You;	Ps 119:175
House of Israel, p the LORD!	Ps 135:19
May the LORD be p-d from Zion;	Ps 135:21
I will p You, because I have	Ps 139:14
May the LORD my rock be p-d,	Ps 144:1
All You have made will p You,	Ps 145:10

My soul, p the LORD.	Ps 146:1
P the LORD from the heavens;	Ps 148:1
P God in His sanctuary.	Ps 150:1
that breathes p the LORD.	Ps 150:6
Let another p you, and not your	Pr 27:2
Her husband also p-s her:	Pr 31:28
who fears the LORD will be p-d.	Pr 31:30
let her works p her at the city	Pr 31:31
Death cannot p You,	Is 38:18
temple, where our fathers p-d You,	Is 64:11
Daniel p-d the God of heaven	Dn 2:19
Then I p-d the Most High and	Dn 4:34
p-d their gods made of gold and	Dn 5:4
You will p the name of Yahweh	Jl 2:26
Jesus said, "I p You, Father,	Mt 11:25
host with the angel, p-ing God	Lk 2:13
glorifying and p-ing God for all	Lk 2:20
began to p God joyfully with	Lk 19:37
p-ing God and having favor with	Ac 2:47
walking, leaping, and p-ing God.	Ac 3:8
all the peoples should p Him!	Rm 15:11
I p you because you remember	1Co 11:2
p you? I do not p you for this!	1Co 11:22
do evil and to p those who do	1Pt 2:14
P our God, all you His servants	Rv 19:5

PRANCING

along with p steps, jingling	Is 3:16

PRAY

Then Abraham p-ed to God, and	Gn 20:17
Moses, and he p-ed to the LORD,	Nm 11:2
Manoah p-ed to the LORD	Jdg 13:8
Hannah p-ed to the LORD	1Sm 1:10
against the LORD by ceasing to p	1Sm 12:23
the courage to p this prayer to	2Sm 7:27
servant p-s toward this place	1Kg 8:29
Solomon finished p-ing this	1Kg 8:54
your God and p for me so that my	1Kg 13:6
Hezekiah p-ed before the LORD	2Kg 19:15
by My name humble themselves, p	2Ch 7:14
While Ezra p-ed and confessed,	Ezr 10:1
So I p-ed to the God of heaven	Neh 2:4
we p-ed to our God and stationed	Neh 4:9
My servant Job will p for you.	Jb 42:8
and my God, for I p to You.	Ps 5:2
who is faithful p to You at a	Ps 32:6
P for the peace of Jerusalem:	Ps 122:6
do not p for these people.	Jr 7:16; 11:14
for he p-s three times a day.	Dn 6:13

Jonah **p-ed** ... from inside the fish: Jnh 2:1
and **p** for those who persecute you, Mt 5:44
Whenever you **p**, you must not be Mt 6:5
you should **p** like this: Mt 6:9
p to the Lord of the harvest to Mt 9:38
the mountain by Himself to **p**. Mt 14:23
put His hands on them and **p**. Mt 19:13
while I go over there and **p**. Mt 26:36
facedown and **p-ed**, "My Father! Mt 26:39
things you **p** and ask for—believe Mk 11:24
you stand **p-ing**, if you have Mk 11:25
teach us to **p**, just as John Lk 11:1
p always ... not become discouraged Lk 18:1
to **p**, one a Pharisee Lk 18:10
be alert at all times, **p-ing** Lk 21:36
I have **p-ed** for you that your faith Lk 22:32
P that you may not enter into Lk 22:40
I **p** for them. I am not praying for Jn 17:9
I **p** not only for these, but also Jn 17:20
When they had **p-ed**, the place Ac 4:31
Please **p** to the Lord for me, Ac 8:24
afternoon, I was **p-ing** in my Ac 10:30
and **p-ed** with fasting, Ac 14:23
and Silas were **p-ing** and singing Ac 16:25
knelt down and **p-ed** with all of Ac 20:36
know what to **p** for as we should Rm 8:26
Every man who **p-s** or prophesies 1Co 11:4
for a woman to **p** to God with her 1Co 11:13
For if I **p** in {another} language 1Co 14:14
{I **p**} that the God of our Lord Eph 1:17
p at all times in the Spirit, Eph 6:18
P that I might be bold enough in Eph 6:20
always **p-ing** with joy for all of Php 1:4
And I **p** this: that your love Php 1:9
we haven't stopped **p-ing** for you Col 1:9
p also for us that God may open Col 4:3
P constantly. 1Th 5:17
Brothers, **p** for us also. 1Th 5:25
we always **p** for you that our God 2Th 1:11
Finally, **p** for us, brothers 2Th 3:1
the men in every place to **p** 1Tm 2:8
P for us; for we are convinced Heb 13:18
suffering? He should **p**. Jms 5:13
and **p** for one another Jms 5:16
p-ed earnestly that it would not Jms 5:17
not saying he should **p** about that. 1Jn 5:16
faith and **p-ing** in the Holy Spirit, Jd 20

PRAYER

courage to pray this **p** to You. 2Sm 7:27
God answered **p** for the land. 2Sm 21:14
LORD answered **p** on behalf of 2Sm 24:25
may You hear their **p** 1Kg 8:45
I have heard your **p** and petition 1Kg 9:3
attentive to **p** from this place. 2Ch 7:15
and their **p** came into His holy 2Ch 30:27
and my **p** is pure. Jb 16:17
the LORD accepted Job's {**p**}. Jb 42:9
gracious to me and hear my **p**. Ps 4:1
the LORD accepts my **p**. Ps 6:9
and my **p** was genuine. Ps 35:13
p-s of David son of Jesse are Ps 72:20
May my **p** reach Your presence; Ps 88:2
LORD, hear my **p**; let my cry for Ps 102:1
the **p** of the upright is His delight. Pr 15:8
He hears the **p** of the righteous. Pr 15:29
even his **p** is detestable. Pr 28:9
even if you offer countless **p-s** Is 1:15
a house of **p** for all nations. Is 56:7
so that no **p** can pass through Lm 3:44
I have come because of your **p-s**. Dn 10:12
out except by **p** and fasting. Mt 17:21
will be called a house of **p**. Mt 21:13
whatever you ask for in **p**. Mt 21:22
and make long **p-s** just for show. Mt 23:14
because your **p** has been heard. Lk 1:13
and day with fastings and **p-s**. Lk 2:37
disciples fast often and say **p-s** Lk 5:33
spent all night in **p** to God. Lk 6:12
were continually united in **p** Ac 1:14
breaking of bread, and to **p-s**. Ac 2:42
devote ourselves to **p** and to Ac 6:4
but **p** was being made earnestly Ac 12:5
thought there was a place of **p**. Ac 16:13
be persistent in **p**. Rm 12:12
to devote yourselves to **p**. 1Co 7:5
you as I remember you in my **p-s**. Eph 1:16
for all of you in my every **p** Php 1:4
everything, through **p** and petition Php 4:6
Devote yourselves to **p**; Col 4:2
petitions, **p-s**, intercessions, 1Tm 2:1
by the word of God and by **p**. 1Tm 4:5
you in my **p-s** night and day. 2Tm 1:3
God when I mention you in my **p-s** Phm 4
He offered **p-s** and appeals Heb 5:7
The **p** of faith will save the Jms 5:15

PREACH

The intense **p** of the righteous	Jms 5:16
so that your **p-s** will not be	1Pt 3:7
which are the **p-s** of the saints.	Rv 5:8

PREACH

the south and **p** against it.	Ezk 20:46
Nineveh and **p**	Jnh 1:2; 3:2
"Stop your **p-ing**," they **p**.	Mc 2:6
John ... came, **p-ing** in the Wilderness	Mt 3:1
From then on Jesus began to **p**	Mt 4:17
p-ing the good news of	Mt 4:23; 9:35
to teach and **p** in their towns.	Mt 11:1
p-ing a baptism of repentance	Mk 1:4
Galilee, **p-ing** in their synagogues	Mk 1:39
to send them out to **p**	Mk 3:14
p-ed that people should repent.	Mk 6:12
the world and **p** the gospel to	Mk 16:15
anointed Me to **p** good news to	Lk 4:18
have the good news **p-ed** to them.	Lk 7:22
them not to **p** or teach at all	Ac 4:18
the **p-ing** about God flourished	Ac 6:7
Samaria and **p-ed** the Messiah to	Ac 8:5
after the baptism that John **p-ed**	Ac 10:37
you by the Jesus whom Paul **p-es**!	Ac 19:13
I went about **p-ing** the kingdom,	Ac 20:25
I am eager to **p** the good news to	Rm 1:15
You who **p**, "You must not steal	Rm 2:21
how can they **p** unless they are	Rm 10:15
foolishness of the message **p-ed**.	1Co 1:21
but we **p** Christ crucified,	1Co 1:23
who **p** the gospel should earn	1Co 9:14
woe to me if I do not **p** the gospel!	1Co 9:16
so that after **p-ing** to others,	1Co 9:27
our **p-ing** is without foundation	1Co 15:14
comes and **p-es** another Jesus,	2Co 11:4
if anyone **p-es** to you a gospel	Gl 1:9
so that I could **p** Him among the	Gl 1:16
p Christ out of envy and strife	Php 1:15
seen by angels, **p-ed** among the	1Tm 3:16
work hard at **p-ing** and teaching.	1Tm 5:17
gospel was also **p-ed** to	1Pt 4:6

PREACHER

be just the **p** for this people!	Mc 2:11
He seems to be a **p** of foreign	Ac 17:18
how can they hear without a **p**?	Rm 10:14
Noah, a **p** of righteousness,	2Pt 2:5

PRECEPTS

The **p** of the LORD are right,	Ps 19:8
How I long for Your **p**!	Ps 119:40

PRECIOUS

He also gave **p** gifts to her	Gn 24:53
today you considered my life **p**.	1Sm 26:21
and it had a **p** stone {in it}.	2Sm 12:30
Whatever is **p** to you, they will	1Kg 20:6
their lives are **p** in his sight.	Ps 72:14
She is more **p** than jewels;	Pr 3:15
wisdom is better than **p** stones,	Pr 8:11
She is far more **p** than jewels.	Pr 31:10
a tested stone, a **p** cornerstone	Is 28:16
Because you are **p** in My sight	Is 43:4
but with the **p** blood of Christ,	1Pt 1:19
us very great and **p** promises,	2Pt 1:4

PREDESTINED

Your plan had **p** to take place.	Ac 4:28
He also **p** to be conformed	Rm 8:29
which God **p** before the ages for	1Co 2:7
He **p** us to be adopted through	Eph 1:5
p according to the purpose of	Eph 1:11

PREDICT

sanctuary, just as God had **p-ed**.	2Kg 24:13
Who **p-ed** this long ago?	Is 45:21
And just as Isaiah **p-ed**:	Rm 9:29

PREDICTION

Make a **p-ion**; it will not happen.	Is 8:10
had a spirit of **p-ion** and made a	Ac 16:16

PREFECTS

So the satraps, **p**, governors	Dn 3:3

PREFERABLE

it is **p** to silver.	Pr 16:16

PREFERENCE

poor or give **p** to the rich	Lv 19:15

PREGNANT

with Hagar, and she became **p**.	Gn 16:4
became **p** by their father	Gn 19:36
Sarah became **p** and bore a son to	Gn 21:2
I am **p** by the man to whom these	Gn 38:25
and hit a **p** woman so that her	Ex 21:22
to inform David: "I am **p**."	2Sm 11:5
ripped open all the **p** women.	2Kg 15:16
See, he is **p** with evil	Ps 7:14
in the womb of a **p** woman,	Ec 11:5
my grave, her womb eternally **p**.	Jr 20:17
ripped open the **p** women of Gilead	Am 1:13
that she was **p** by the Holy	Mt 1:18
will become **p** and give birth to	Mt 1:23

Woe to **p** women and nursing	Mt 24:19
was engaged to him and was **p.**	Lk 2:5
Rebekah became **p** by Isaac our	Rm 9:10
like labor pains on a **p** woman,	1Th 5:3
She was **p** and cried out in labor	Rv 12:2

PREJUDICE

faithful God, without **p,**	Dt 32:4
observe these things without **p,**	1Tm 5:21

PREMATURELY

that her children are born {**p**},	Ex 21:22
inheritance gained **p** will not be	Pr 20:21
don't judge anything **p,**	1Co 4:5

PREPARATION

David made lavish **p-s** for it	1Ch 22:5
make **p-s** for your brothers	2Ch 35:6
Make the **p-s** for us there.	Mk 14:15
was **p** day (that is, the day before	Mk 15:42
Since it was the **p** day,	Jn 19:31
the Jewish **p** and since the	Jn 19:42

PREPARE

you to the place I have **p-d.**	Ex 23:20
Let her **p** food in my presence so	2Sm 13:5
to the banquet Esther had **p-d.**	Est 5:5
You **p** a table before me in the	Ps 23:5
They **p-d** a net for my steps;	Ps 57:6
will go before Him to **p** the way	Ps 85:13
it **p-s** its provisions in summer;	Pr 6:8
LORD has **p-d** everything for His	Pr 16:4
Judgments are **p-d** for mockers,	Pr 19:29
A horse is **p-d** for the day of	Pr 21:31
outdoor work, and **p** your field;	Pr 24:27
P the way of the LORD in the	Is 40:3
build it up, **p** the way, remove	Is 57:14
p a way for the people!	Is 62:10
the nations: **P** for holy war;	Jl 3:9
Israel, **p** to meet your God!	Am 4:12
the LORD has **p-d** a sacrifice;	Zph 1:7
P the way for the Lord;	Mt 3:3
he will **p** Your way before You.	Mt 11:10
it has been **p-d** by My Father	Mt 20:23
You have **p-d** praise from the	Mt 21:16
inherit the kingdom **p-d** for you	Mt 25:34
eternal fire **p-d** for the Devil	Mt 25:41
she has **p-d** Me for burial.	Mt 26:12
You want us to **p** the Passover so	Mt 26:17
for those it has been **p-d** for.	Mk 10:40
ready for the Lord a **p-d** people	Lk 1:17

before the Lord to **p** His ways,	Lk 1:76
have **p-d** {it} in the presence	Lk 2:31
your minds not to **p** your defense	Lk 21:14
they returned and **p-d** spices	Lk 23:56
going away to **p** a place for you	Jn 14:2
mercy that He **p-d** beforehand	Rm 9:23
what God has **p-d** for those who	1Co 2:9
sound, who will **p** for battle?	1Co 14:8
And the One who **p-d** us for this	2Co 5:5
which God **p-d** ahead of time so	Eph 2:10
and having **p-d** everything,	Eph 6:13
the Master, **p-d** for every good	2Tm 2:21
also **p** a guest room for me,	Phm 22
but You **p-d** a body for Me.	Heb 10:5
for He has **p-d** a city for them.	Heb 11:16
p-d like a bride adorned for	Rv 21:2

PRESCRIBED

hadn't observed it often, as **p.**	2Ch 30:5
offer what Moses **p** for your	Mk 1:44
to the custom **p** by Moses,	Ac 15:1
the gifts **p** by the law.	Heb 8:4
the royal law **p** in Scripture,	Jms 2:8

PRESENCE

out from the LORD's **p** and lived	Gn 4:16
Ishmael could live in Your **p**!	Gn 17:18
the bread of the **P** on the table	Ex 25:30
My **p** will go {with you},	Ex 33:14
to rise in the **p** of the elderly	Lv 19:32
to treat Me as holy in their **p.**	Dt 32:51
Samuel served in the LORD's **p**	1Sm 2:18
the bread of the **P** that had been	1Sm 21:6
I am terrified in His **p**;	Jb 23:15
boastful cannot stand in Your **p**;	Ps 5:5
in Your **p** is abundant joy;	Ps 16:11
will be satisfied with Your **p.**	Ps 17:15
In the **p** of my enemies;	Ps 23:5
in the protection of Your **p**;	Ps 31:20
Do not banish me from Your **p** or	Ps 51:11
May my prayer reach Your **p**;	Ps 88:2
walk in the light of Your **p.**	Ps 89:15
enter His **p** with thanksgiving;	Ps 95:2
in the very **p** of all His people	Ps 116:18
Where can I flee from Your **p**?	Ps 139:7
upright will live in Your **p.**	Ps 140:13
will stand in the **p** of kings.	Pr 22:29
Leave his **p,** and don't persist	Ec 8:3
nations will tremble at Your **p**!	Is 64:2
you will stand in My **p.**	Jr 15:19

was fleeing from the LORD's **p**,   Jnh 1:10
silent in the **p** of the Lord GOD,   Zph 1:7
who stands in the **p** of God,   Lk 1:19
in the **p** of all peoples   Lk 2:31
and slaughter them in my **p**.   Lk 19:27
He took it and ate in their **p**.   Lk 24:43
I have seen in the **p** of the Father,   Jn 8:38
performed so many signs in their **p**   Jn 12:37
glorify Me in Your **p** with that glory   Jn 17:5
me with gladness in Your **p**.   Ac 2:28
come from the **p** of the Lord,   Ac 3:19
that no one can boast in His **p**.   1Co 1:29
over the **p** of Stephanas,   1Co 16:17
is for you in the **p** of Christ,   2Co 2:10
but his physical **p** is weak,   2Co 10:10
not only in my **p**, but now even   Php 2:12
in the **p** of our God and Father,   1Th 1:3
boasting in the **p** of our Lord   1Th 2:19
away from the Lord's **p**   2Th 1:9
In the **p** of God, who gives life   1Tm 6:13
from me in the **p** of many   2Tm 2:2
appear in the **p** of God for us.   Heb 9:24
convince our hearts in His **p**   1Jn 3:19
stand in the **p** of His glory,   Jd 24
who stand in the **p** of God;   Rv 8:2
was remembered in God's **p**;   Rv 16:19

PRESENT (adj)

of this **p** time are not worth   Rm 8:18
nor things **p**, nor things to   Rm 8:38
death or things **p** or things to   1Co 3:22
Up to the **p** hour we are both   1Co 4:11
absent in body but **p** in spirit,   1Co 5:3
good because of the **p** distress: 1Co 7:26
that when I am **p** I will not need   2Co 10:2
rescue us from this **p** evil age,   Gl 1:4
corresponds to the **p** Jerusalem,   Gl 4:25
promise for the **p** life and also   1Tm 4:8
because he loved this **p** world,   2Tm 4:10
and godly way in the **p** age,   Ti 2:12

PRESENT (v)

they **p**-ed themselves before God.   Jos 24:1
of God came to **p** themselves   Jb 1:6
When you **p** a blind {animal} for   Mal 1:8
and **p**-ed Him with gifts: gold,   Mt 2:11
Jerusalem to **p** Him to the Lord   Lk 2:22
also **p**-ed Himself alive to them   Ac 1:3
and widows and **p**-ed her alive.   Ac 9:41

God **p**-ed Him as a propitiation   Rm 3:25
I urge you to **p** your bodies as a   Rm 12:1
to **p** a pure virgin to Christ.   2Co 11:2
He did this to **p** the church to   Eph 5:27
His death, to **p** you holy   Col 1:22
so that we may **p** everyone mature   Col 1:28
Be diligent to **p** yourself   2Tm 2:15

PRESENTABLE

our **p** parts have no need   1Co 12:24

PRESENTATION

them as a **p** offering before   Ex 29:24
waved as a **p** offering before   Lv 7:30
sheaf of the **p** offering   Lv 23:15
them as a **p** offering before   Nm 6:20
the LORD as a **p** offering   Nm 8:11
Israelites' **p** offerings   Nm 18:11

PRESERVE

sent me ahead of you to **p** life.   Gn 45:5
refuses to **p** his brother's name   Dt 25:7
have no son to **p** the memory of   2Sm 18:18
the one who cannot **p** his life.   Ps 22:29
LORD, You **p** man and beast.   Ps 36:6
I will always **p** My faithful love   Ps 89:28
You will **p** my life from the   Ps 138:7
who keeps commands **p**-s himself;   Pr 19:16
that wisdom **p**-s the life of its   Ec 7:12
P justice and do what is right,   Is 56:1
orphans; I will **p** them;   Jr 49:11
just and right, he will **p** his life.   Ezk 18:27
loses his life will **p** it.   Lk 17:33

PRESS

and Your hand has **p**-ed down on   Ps 38:2
diseases were **p**-ing toward Him   Mk 3:10
following and **p**-ing against Him.   Mk 5:24
good measure—**p**-ed down, shaken   Lk 6:38

PRESSURE (n)

When **p** or persecution comes   Mt 13:21
by hardship, by **p**-s,   2Co 6:4
there is the daily **p** on me: 2Co 11:28
in persecutions, and in **p**-s.   2Co 12:10

PRESSURED (v)

We are **p** in every way but not   2Co 4:8
I am **p** by both.   Php 1:23

PRESUME

And don't **p** to say to yourselves,   Mt 3:9

PRESUMPTUOUS

your p heart has deceived you.	Jr 49:16
Your p heart has deceived you,	Ob 3

PRESUMPTUOUSLY

The prophet has spoken it p	Dt 18:22

PRETEND

so he p-ed to be insane in their	1Sm 21:13
on your bed and p you're sick.	2Sm 13:5
He told her, "P to be in	2Sm 14:2
when he p-ed to be insane in the	Ps 34:1
the LORD would p submission to	Ps 81:15
One man p-s to be rich but has	Pr 13:7
spies who p-ed to be righteous	Lk 20:20
Who do You p to be?	Jn 8:53
p-ing that they were going to	Ac 27:30

PRETENSE

with all her heart—only in p.	Jr 3:10

PREVAIL

God and with men and have p-ed.	Gn 32:28
hand, Israel p-ed, but whenever	Ex 17:11
Our own hand has p-ed;	Dt 32:27
for a man does not p by	1Sm 2:9
certainly entice him and p.	1Kg 22:22
Do not let man p;	Ps 9:19
a wicked plan, they will not p.	Ps 21:11
but the LORD's decree will p.	Pr 19:21
no counsel {will p} against the	Pr 21:30
He p-s over His enemies.	Is 42:13
but never p over you,	Jr 1:19
not faithfulness p in the land,	Jr 9:3
holding it in, and I cannot p.	Jr 20:9
struggled with the Angel and p-ed;	Hs 12:4
one will not p by his strength,	Am 2:14
message flourished and p-ed.	Ac 19:20
but he could not p,	Rv 12:8

PREVENT

who p-ed me from harming you,	1Sm 25:34
they were p-ed from recognizing	Lk 24:16
and p these from being baptized,	Ac 10:47
were p-ed by the Holy Spirit from	Ac 16:6
to you (but was p-ed until now)	Rm 1:13
who p-ed you from obeying	Gl 5:7
since they are p-ed by death	Heb 7:23

PREVIOUS

So the p commandment	
is annulled	Heb 7:18
because the p things have passed	Rv 21:4

PREVIOUSLY

without p hating him.	Dt 4:42
John had p proclaimed a baptism	Ac 13:24
over the sins p committed.	Rm 3:25
in which you p walked according	Eph 2:2
We too all p lived among them in	Eph 2:3
we told you p that we were going	1Th 3:4
the words p spoken by the holy	2Pt 3:2

PREY

Birds of p came down on the	Gn 15:11
the morning he devours the p	Gn 49:27
No bird of p knows that path;	Jb 28:7
from the mountains of p.	Ps 76:4
the birds of p will gather there	Is 34:15
Can the p be taken from the	Is 49:24
After he learned to tear p	Ezk 19:3
a roaring lion tearing {its} p:	Ezk 22:25
no longer be p for the nations,	Ezk 34:28
in the forest when it has no p?	Am 3:4

PRICE

for the full p, as a burial	Gn 23:9
pay a redemption p for his life	Ex 21:30
the redemption p for a month-old	Nm 18:16
I insist on paying the full p,	1Ch 21:24
The p of wisdom is beyond pearls	Jb 28:18
the p of redeeming him is too	Ps 49:8
this magnificent p I was valued	Zch 11:13
the p of Him whose p was set by	Mt 27:9
you sell the field for this p?	Ac 5:8
for you were bought at a p;	1Co 6:20
You were bought at a p;	1Co 7:23

PRICELESS

When he found one p pearl,	Mt 13:46

PRIDE

will break down your strong p.	Lv 26:19
and lifted your eyes in p?	2Kg 19:22
Some take p in a chariot, and	Ps 20:7
the p of Jacob, whom He	Ps 47:4
Therefore, p is their necklace	Ps 73:6
I hate arrogant p, evil conduct	Pr 8:13
When p comes, disgrace follows	Pr 11:2
P comes before destruction,	Pr 16:18
the p of sons is their fathers.	Pr 17:6
A person's p will humble him,	Pr 29:23
So human p will be brought low,	Is 2:17
the land will be the p and glory	Is 4:2

make you an object of eternal **p**,	Is 60:15
sanctuary, the **p** of your power	Ezk 24:21
to humble those who walk in **p**.	Dn 4:37
has sworn by the **P** of Jacob:	Am 8:7
blasphemy, **p**, and foolishness.	Mk 7:22
inflated with **p** in favor of one	1Co 4:6
Knowledge inflates with **p**,	1Co 8:1
that we are your reason for **p**	2Co 1:14
those who take **p** in the outward	2Co 5:12
I have great **p** in you.	2Co 7:4
and the **p** in one's lifestyle	1Jn 2:16

PRIEST

he was a **p** to God Most High.	Gn 14:18
Now the **p** of Midian had seven	Ex 2:16
be My kingdom of **p-s** and My holy	Ex 19:6
serve Me as **p**—Aaron, his sons	Ex 28:1
Aaron's sons the **p-s** are to present	Lv 1:5
this way the **p** will make atonement	Lv 4:31
The **p** will make atonement on his	Lv 19:22
for the **p** is holy to his God.	Lv 21:7
and Eleazar his son became **p**	Dt 10:6
this law and gave it to the **p-s**,	Dt 31:9
said to the **p-s**, "Take the ark	Jos 3:6
while the **p-s** blow the trumpets.	Jos 6:4
Phinehas ... the **p** said to ... Gad,	Jos 22:31
one of his sons to be his **p**.	Jdg 17:5
and be my father and **p**,	Jdg 17:10
Eli the **p** was sitting on a chair	1Sm 1:9
up a faithful **p** for Myself.	1Sm 2:35
p gave him the consecrated bread,	1Sm 21:6
had killed the **p-s** of the LORD.	1Sm 22:21
p-s and the Levites brought the ark	1Kg 8:4
the time of Jehoiada the **p**, Joash	2Ch 24:2
Hilkiah the **p** found the book of	2Ch 34:14
along with the **p-s** and Levites	Ezr 1:5
Ezra the **p** and scribe	Neh 8:9
p-s fell by the sword, but the	Ps 78:64
You are a **p** like Melchizedek.	Ps 110:4
clothe its **p-s** with salvation	Ps 132:16
p and prophet stagger because of	Is 28:7
will be called the LORD's **p-s**;	Is 61:6
and the guilt of her **p-s**	Lm 4:13
p-s do violence to My law and	Ezk 22:26
for My case is against you **p-s**.	Hs 4:4
her **p-s** teach for payment,	Mc 3:11
will also be a **p** on His throne,	Zch 6:13
show yourself to the **p**, and offer	Mt 8:4
Iscariot—went to the chief **p-s**	Mt 26:14

Then the high **p** tore his robes	Mt 26:65
led Jesus away to the high **p**	Mk 14:53
But the chief **p-s** stirred up the	Mk 15:11
A **p** happened to be going	Lk 10:31
struck the high **p-'s** slave and	Lk 22:50
p-s decided to also kill Lazarus,	Jn 12:10
Annas the high **p**, Caiaphas, John	Ac 4:6
serving as a **p** of God's good	Rm 15:16
faithful high **p** in service to	Heb 2:17
apostle and high **p** of our	Heb 3:1
a great high **p** who has passed	Heb 4:14
not have a high **p** who is unable	Heb 4:15
You are a **p** forever in the order	Heb 5:6
King of Salem, **p** of the Most	Heb 7:1
of God—remains a **p** forever.	Heb 7:3
is the kind of high **p** we need:	Heb 7:26
every day, as high **p-s** do	Heb 7:27
on earth, He wouldn't be a **p**, since	Heb 8:4
But the high **p** alone enters the	Heb 9:7
a great high **p** over the house	Heb 10:21
made us a kingdom, **p-s** to His	Rv 1:6
a kingdom and **p-s** to our God,	Rv 5:10
but they will be **p-s** of God and	Rv 20:6

PRIESTHOOD

The **p** is to be theirs by a	Ex 29:9
a permanent **p** for them	Ex 40:15
you are seeking the **p** as well.	Nm 16:10
the work of the **p** as a gift,	Nm 18:7
of perpetual **p** for him and his	Nm 25:13
inheritance is the **p** of the LORD.	Jos 18:7
for defiling the **p** as well as	Neh 13:29
during the high **p** of Annas and	Lk 3:2
there is a change of the **p**	Heb 7:12
He holds His **p** permanently.	Heb 7:24
house for a holy **p** to offer	1Pt 2:5
race, a royal **p**, a holy nation	1Pt 2:9

PRIME

youth and the **p** of life are	Ec 11:10

PRINCE

The **p-s** dug the well;	Nm 21:18
God is not partial to **p-s** and	Jb 34:19
P-s have persecuted me without	Ps 119:161
by me, **p-s** lead, as do nobles	Pr 8:16
for a slave to rule over **p-s**!	Pr 19:10
slaves on horses, but **p-s** walking	Ec 10:7
and your **p-s** feast	Ec 10:16,17
Eternal Father, **P** of Peace.	Is 9:6

He reduces p-s to nothing and | Is 40:23
David will be their p forever. | Ezk 37:25
even stand against the P of p-s. | Dn 8:25
until Messiah the P will be seven | Dn 9:25
them except Michael, your p. | Dn 10:21
many days without king or p, | Hs 3:4
king and his p-s will go into exile | Am 1:15

PRINCESS

wives who were p-es and 300 | 1Kg 11:3
beautiful are your sandaled feet, p! | Sg 7:1
The p among the provinces has | Lm 1:1

PRINCIPLE

So I discover this p: | Rm 7:21
again the basic p-s of God's | Heb 5:12

PRISCILLA

Wife of Aquila (Ac 18:2,18,26; 1Co 16:19);
also called Prisca (Rm 16:3; 2Tm 4:19).

PRISON

So Joseph was there in p. | Gn 39:20
Put this guy in p and feed him | 1Kg 22:27
changed his p clothes, | 2Kg 25:29
Free me from p so that I can | Ps 142:7
in darkness from the p house. | Is 42:7
and you will be thrown into p. | Mt 5:25
John heard in p what the Messiah | Mt 11:2
and had John beheaded in the p. | Mt 14:10
threw him into p until he could | Mt 18:30
I was in p and you visited Me. | Mt 25:36
he locked John up in p. | Lk 3:20
the bailiff throw you into p. | Lk 12:58
and women, and put them in p. | Ac 8:3
Peter was kept in p, but prayer | Ac 12:5
saw the doors of the p open, | Ac 16:27
Felix left Paul in p. | Ac 24:27
Messiah—for which I am in p— | Col 4:3
to the spirits in p | 1Pt 3:19
Satan will be released from his p | Rv 20:7

PRISONER

groans of the p-s reach You; | Ps 79:11
The LORD frees p-s. | Ps 146:7
and freedom to the p-s; | Is 61:1
a notorious p called Barabbas. | Mt 27:16
release for the people a p | Mk 15:6
the p-s were listening to them | Ac 16:25
and taking me p to the law of | Rm 7:23
p of Christ Jesus on behalf | Eph 3:1

therefore, the p in the Lord | Eph 4:1
fellow p, greets you, as does | Col 4:10
Paul, a p of Christ Jesus, | Phm 1
Remember the p-s, as though | Heb 13:3

PRIVATE

go into your p room, shut your | Mt 6:6
go and rebuke him in p. | Mt 18:15
in p rooms will be proclaimed | Lk 12:3

PRIVATELY

approached Him p and said, | Mt 24:3
P, however, He would explain | Mk 4:34
John, and Andrew asked Him p | Mk 13:3
but p to those recognized | Gl 2:2

PRIVILEGE

for the p of sharing in the ministry | 2Co 8:4

PRIZE

but only one receives the p? | 1Co 9:24
as my goal the p promised by | Php 3:14

PROBABLY

This man is p a murderer, | Ac 28:4

PROBLEMS

explain riddles, and solve p-s. | Dn 5:12

PROCEDURE

about the proper p-s. | 1Ch 15:13
there is a right time and p, | Ec 8:6

PROCEED

for they p from one evil to | Jr 9:3
each man p-s on his own path. | Jl 2:8
Spirit of truth who p-s from the | Jn 15:26
Jews, he p-ed to arrest Peter | Ac 12:3

PROCEEDS (n)

and distributed the p to all, | Ac 2:45
brought the p of the things | Ac 4:34
part of the p from the field | Ac 5:3

PROCESSION

What do you mean by this whole p | Gn 33:8
walked behind the funeral p. | 2Sm 3:31
leading the festive p to the house | Ps 42:4
People have seen Your p, God, | Ps 68:24

PROCLAIM

and I will p the name Yahweh | Ex 33:19
passed in front of him and p-ed: | Ex 34:6
Balaam p-ed his poem: | Nm 23:7
For I will p the LORD's name. | Dt 32:3

P His salvation from day to day.   1Ch 16:23
p His deeds among the peoples.   Ps 9:11
and the sky p-s the work of His   Ps 19:1
I will p Your name to my   Ps 22:22
The heavens p His righteousness   Ps 50:6
I will p Your righteousness,   Ps 71:16
p His salvation from day to day.   Ps 96:2
The heavens p His righteousness;   Ps 97:6
p His deeds among the peoples.   Ps 105:1
I will live and p what the LORD   Ps 118:17
Many a man p-s his own loyalty,   Pr 20:6
news of things, who p-s salvation,   Is 52:7
to p liberty to the captives,   Is 61:1
to p the year of the LORD's favor,   Is 61:2
He will p peace to the nations.   Zch 9:10
in a whisper, p on the housetops.   Mt 10:27
and He will p justice to the   Mt 12:18
kingdom will be p-ed in all the   Mt 24:14
Wherever this gospel is p-ed   Mt 26:13
them, the more they would p it.   Mk 7:36
must first be p-ed to all nations.   Mk 13:10
He has sent Me to p freedom to   Lk 4:18
to p the year of the Lord's favor.   Lk 4:19
will be p-ed on the housetops.   Lk 12:3
of sins would be p-ed in His name   Lk 24:47
teaching and p-ing the good news   Ac 5:42
on their way p-ing the message   Ac 8:4
Immediately he began p-ing Jesus   Ac 9:20
p-ing the good news   Ac 10:36; 11:20
in ignorance, this I p to you.   Ac 17:23
p-ing the kingdom of God   Ac 28:31
My name may be p-ed in all the   Rm 9:17
the message of faith that we p: Rm 10:8
I have fully p-ed the good news   Rm 15:19
you p the Lord's death until He   1Co 11:26
we are not p-ing ourselves but   2Co 4:5
motives or true, Christ is p-ed.   Php 1:18
has been p-ed in all creation   Col 1:23
We p Him, warning and teaching   Col 1:28
p the message; persist in it   2Tm 4:2
so that you may p the praises of   1Pt 2:9

PROCLAMATION

they sent a p throughout the   Ex 36:6
gospel and the p of Jesus Christ   Rm 16:25
My speech and my p were not with   1Co 2:4
went and made a p to the spirits   1Pt 3:19

PROCONSUL

was with the p, Sergius Paulus   Ac 13:7
While Gallio was p of Achaia,   Ac 18:12

PRODUCE (n)

and the land will yield its p,   Lv 26:4
tenth of all the p grown in your   Dt 14:22
ate from the p of the land,   Jos 5:12
supplying all kinds of p;   Ps 144:13
Honor the LORD ... with the first p   Pr 3:9
Plant gardens and eat their p.   Jr 29:5,28

PRODUCE (v)

Let the earth p vegetation: Gn 1:11
stirring up anger p-s strife.   Pr 30:33
Therefore p fruit consistent   Mt 3:8
that doesn't p good fruit will   Mt 3:10
A good tree can't p bad fruit;   Mt 7:18
A good man p-s good things from   Mt 12:35
on good ground, and p-d a crop: Mt 13:8
to a nation p-ing its fruit.   Mt 21:43
if it dies, it p-s a large crop.   Jn 12:24
that does not p fruit He removes   Jn 15:2
that affliction p-s endurance,   Rm 5:3
p-d in me coveting of every   Rm 7:8
kills, but the Spirit p-s life.   2Co 3:6
godly grief p-s a repentance   2Co 7:10
for this will p an even greater   2Tm 2:16
of your faith p-s endurance.   Jms 1:3
Can a fig tree p olives, my   Jms 3:12

PROFANE

Whoever p-s it must be put to   Ex 31:14
Do not p the name of your God;   Lv 18:21
Israel by p-ing the Sabbath   Neh 13:18
name, so that it would not be p-d   Ezk 20:9
holy things and p My Sabbaths.   Ezk 22:8
You p-d your sanctuaries   Ezk 28:18
they p-d My holy name   Ezk 36:20
no longer allow it to be p-d.   Ezk 39:7
Her priests p the sanctuary;   Zph 3:4
Judah has p-d the LORD's sanctuary   Mal 2:11
temple and has p-d this holy   Ac 21:28
regarded as p the blood of the   Heb 10:29
Nothing p will ever enter it: Rv 21:27

PROFESS

By p-ing it, some people have   1Tm 6:21
They p to know God, but they   Ti 1:16

PROFESSIONAL

to mourn, and p mourners to wail.   Am 5:16

PROFIT (n)

There is **p** in all hard work,	Pr 14:23
She sees that her **p-s** are good,	Pr 31:18
everyone is gaining **p** unjustly.	Jr 6:13; 8:10
that their hope of **p** was gone,	Ac 16:19
not seeking my own **p**, but the **p**	1Co 10:33
trade in God's message {for **p**},	2Co 2:17
and do business and make a **p**.	Jms 4:13

PROFIT (v)

Do not **p** or take interest from	Lv 25:36
things that can't **p** or deliver you;	1Sm 12:21
What does it **p** You, and what	Jb 35:3
what they treasure does not **p**.	Is 44:9
your works—they will not **p** you.	Is 57:12

PROFITABLE

she is more **p** than silver	Pr 3:14
Wealth is not **p** on a day of	Pr 11:4
to you anything that was **p**	Ac 20:20
this because it is **p** for	2Co 8:10
is in no way **p** and leads	2Tm 2:14
God and is **p** for teaching	2Tm 3:16
are good and **p** for everyone	Ti 3:8

PROFOUND

LORD, how **p** Your thoughts!	Ps 92:5
This mystery is **p**, but I am	Eph 5:32

PROGRESS

so that your **p** may be evident to	1Tm 4:15

PROHIBIT

if her father **p-s** her on the day	Nm 30:5

PROJECT

the Most High **p-ed** His voice.	Ps 18:13

PROLONG

and He will **p** your life in the	Dt 30:20
The fear of the LORD **p-s** life,	Pr 10:27
hates unjust gain **p-s** his life.	Pr 28:16
a hundred times and **p-s** his life	Ec 8:12
He will **p** His days,	Is 53:10

PROMINENT

He was a **p** man of noble	Ru 2:1
p member of the Sanhedrin who	Mk 15:43
number of the **p** Greek women	Ac 17:12
and **p** men of the city.	Ac 25:23

PROMISCUITY

priest's daughter defiles herself by **p**	Lv 21:9
they are the children of **p**.	Hs 2:4

P, wine, and new wine take	Hs 4:11
a spirit of **p**	Hs 4:12; 5:4
not in sexual impurity and **p**;	Rm 13:13
immorality, and **p** they	2Co 12:21
moral impurity, **p**,	Gl 5:19
over to **p** for the practice	Eph 4:19
turning the grace of our God into **p**	Jd 4

PROMISCUOUS

You engaged in **p** acts with	Ezk 16:26
Go and marry a **p** wife	Hs 1:2
Don't be **p** or belong to any man,	Hs 3:3
will be **p** but not multiply,	Hs 4:10

PROMISCUOUSLY

in Egypt behaving **p** in their youth.	Ezk 23:3

PROMISE (n)

None of the good **p-s** the LORD	Jos 21:45
not one **p** has failed.	Jos 23:14
the good **p-s** He made through	1Kg 8:56
kept Your **p**, for You are righteous.	Neh 9:8
Is {His} **p** at an end	Ps 77:8
For He remembered His holy **p**	Ps 105:42
they believed His **p-s** and sang	Ps 106:12
Your **p** has given me life.	Ps 119:50
oath to David, a **p** He will not	Ps 132:11
name and Your **p** above everything	Ps 138:2
will confirm My **p** concerning you	Jr 29:10
{This is} the **p** I made to you	Hg 2:5
but to wait for the Father's **p**.	Ac 1:4
For the **p** is for you and for	Ac 2:39
to fulfill the **p** that God had	Ac 7:17
the hope of the **p** made by God to	Ac 26:6
and the **p** is canceled.	Rm 4:14
This is why the **p** is by faith,	Rm 4:16
waver in unbelief at God's **p**	Rm 4:20
to them belong ... the **p-s**.	Rm 9:4
children of the **p** are considered seed	Rm 9:8
this is the statement of the **p**:	Rm 9:9
of God's **p-s** is "Yes" in Him.	2Co 1:20
receive the **p** of the Spirit through	Gl 3:14
the **p-s** were spoken to Abraham	Gl 3:16
it is no longer from the **p**;	Gl 3:18
law therefore contrary to God's **p-s**?	Gl 3:21
heirs according to the **p**.	Gl 3:29
like Isaac, are children of **p**.	Gl 4:28
to the covenants of the **p**,	Eph 2:12
partners of the **p** in Christ Jesus	Eph 3:6
first commandment with a **p**	Eph 6:2
since it holds **p** for the present	1Tm 4:8

while the **p** remains of entering Heb 4:1
inherit the **p**-s through faith Heb 6:12
Abraham obtained the **p**. Heb 6:15
obtained **p**-s, shut the mouths Heb 11:33
us very great and precious **p**-s, 2Pt 1:4
Where is the **p** of His coming? 2Pt 3:4
The Lord does not delay His **p** 2Pt 3:9
this is the **p** that He Himself made 1Jn 2:25

PROMISE (v)

I have **p**-d you that I will bring you Ex 3:17
to the land I **p**-d to Abraham, Ex 33:1
not act, or **p** and not fulfill? Nm 23:19
and bless you as He **p**-d you. Dt 1:11
This is the land I **p**-d Abraham, Dt 34:4
Do as You have **p**-d, 2Sm 7:25
and made me a dynasty as He **p**-d 1Kg 2:24
the LORD **p**-d my father David 1Kg 5:5
LORD has fulfilled what He **p**-d. 1Kg 8:20
I have **p**-d to keep Your words. Ps 119:57
sending you what My Father **p**-d. Lk 24:49
which He **p**-d long ago through Rm 1:2
He had **p**-d He was also able Rm 4:21
for He who **p**-d is faithful. Heb 10:23
One who had **p**-d was faithful. Heb 11:11
did not receive what was **p**-d, Heb 11:39
They **p** them freedom, but they 2Pt 2:19

PROMISED (adj)

from the Father the **p** Holy Spirit, Ac 2:33
sealed with the **p** Holy Spirit. Eph 1:13

PROMOTE

He **p**-d him in rank and gave him Est 3:1
but those who **p** peace have joy. Pr 12:20
conceals an offense **p**-s love, Pr 17:9
the king **p**-d Daniel and gave Dn 2:48
pursue what **p**-s peace and what Rm 14:19
the teaching that **p**-s godliness 1Tm 6:3
in order to **p** love and good Heb 10:24

PROMPTED

whose hearts **p** them to bring Ex 35:29
And **p** by her mother, she Mt 14:8

PRONOUNCE

he must **p** him unclean. Lv 13:3
Levi ... to serve Him and **p** blessings Dt 21:5
he could not **p** it correctly, Jdg 12:6
and to **p** blessings in His name 1Ch 23:13
From heaven You **p**-d judgment. Ps 76:8

I will **p** My judgments against Jr 1:16
condemnation, {**p-d**} long ago, is 2Pt 2:3

PROOF

to them by many convincing **p**-s Ac 1:3
He has provided **p** of this to Ac 17:31
show them the **p** of your love and 2Co 8:24
since you seek **p** of Christ 2Co 13:3
the **p** of what is not seen. Heb 11:1

PROPER

give them food at the **p** time? Mt 24:45
of what is **p**, and so that you 1Co 7:35
Is it **p** for a woman to pray to 1Co 11:13
in love by the **p** working of each Eph 4:16
among you, as is **p** for saints. Eph 5:3
a testimony at the **p** time. 1Tm 2:6
as is **p** for women who affirm 1Tm 2:10
grace to help us at the **p** time. Heb 4:16

PROPERLY

If we were **p** evaluating 1Co 11:31
you may walk **p** in the presence 1Th 4:12

PROPERTY

move about, and acquire **p** in it. Gn 34:10
because he is his {owner's} **p**. Ex 21:21
Don't move an ancient **p** line, Pr 23:10
sold their possessions and **p** Ac 2:45
his wife, sold a piece of **p**. Ac 5:1

PROPHECY

to seal up vision and **p**, Dn 9:24
living and give {your} **p**-ies there, Am 7:12
Isaiah's **p** is fulfilled in them, Mt 13:14
If **p**, use it according to the Rm 12:6
miracles, to another, **p**, 1Co 12:10
If I have {the gift of} **p**, 1Co 13:2
But as for **p**-ies, they will come to 1Co 13:8
or knowledge or **p** or teaching? 1Co 14:6
But **p** is not for unbelievers but 1Co 14:22
Don't despise **p**-ies, 1Th 5:20
in keeping with the **p**-ies 1Tm 1:18
it was given to you through **p**, 1Tm 4:14
no **p** of Scripture comes from 2Pt 1:20
no **p** ever came by the will 2Pt 1:21
those who hear the words of this **p** Rv 1:3
about Jesus is the spirit of **p**. Rv 19:10

PROPHESY

Spirit rested on them, they **p-ied**, Nm 11:25

and he **p-ied** along with them. 1Sm 10:10

and they also started **p-ing**. 1Sm 19:20

he never **p-ies** good about me, 1Kg 22:8

the prophets were **p-ing** the same 1Kg 22:12

to **p** accompanied by lyres, 1Ch 25:1

Do not **p** the truth to us. Is 30:10

prophets who **p** a lie in My name Jr 23:25

Ammonites and **p** against them. Ezk 25:2

toward Sidon and **p** against it. Ezk 28:21

king of Egypt and **p** against him Ezk 29:2

p against the shepherds of Ezk 34:2

Mount Seir and **p** against it. Ezk 35:2

P concerning these bones and Ezk 37:4

P to the breath, **p**, son of man. Ezk 37:9

sons and your daughters will **p**, Jl 2:28

GOD has spoken; who will not **p**? Am 3:8

Lord, didn't we **p** in Your name, Mt 7:22

and the law **p-ied** until John; Mt 11:13

Isaiah **p-ied** correctly about you Mt 15:7

P to us, Messiah! Who hit You? Mt 26:68

with the Holy Spirit and **p-ied**: Lk 1:67

that year he **p-ied** that Jesus was Jn 11:51

sons and your daughters will **p** Ac 2:17

languages and to **p**. Ac 19:6

four virgin daughters who **p-ied**. Ac 21:9

who prays or **p-ies** with her head 1Co 11:4

know in part, and we **p** in part. 1Co 13:9

and above all that you may **p**. 1Co 14:1

who **p-ies** builds up the church. 1Co 14:4

The person who **p-ies** is greater 1Co 14:5

But if all are **p-ing**, and some 1Co 14:24

For you can all **p** one by one, 1Co 14:31

be eager to **p**, and do not forbid 1Co 14:39

prophets who **p-ied** about the grace 1Pt 1:10

from Adam, **p-ied** about them: Jd 14

You must **p** again about many Rv 10:11

and they will **p** for 1,260 days, Rv 11:3

PROPHET

for he is a **p**, and he will pray Gn 20:7

your brother will be your **p**. Ex 7:1

all the LORD's people were **p-s**, Nm 11:29

If a **p** or someone who has Dt 13:1

God will raise up for you a **p** like Dt 18:15

When a **p** speaks in the LORD's Dt 18:22

No **p** has arisen again in Israel Dt 34:10

a woman who was a **p** and the wife Jdg 4:4

the LORD sent a **p** to them. Jdg 6:8

Saul also among the **p-s**? 1Sm 10:12; 19:24

The old **p** deceived him, 1Kg 13:18

and took 100 **p-s** and hid them, 1Kg 18:4

450 **p-s** of Baal and the 400 **p-s** 1Kg 18:19

Isn't there a **p** of Yahweh here 1Kg 22:7

the sons of the **p-s** said to Elisha, 2Kg 2:16

summon to me all the **p-s** of Baal 2Kg 10:19

through Your servants the **p-s** Ezr 9:11

There is no longer a **p**. Ps 74:9

anointed ones, or harm My **p-s**. Ps 105:15

appointed you a **p** to the nations. Jr 1:5

Where are your **p-s** who Jr 37:19

know that a **p** has been among Ezk 2:5

prophesy against the **p-s** of Israel Ezk 13:2

us through His servants the **p-s**. Dn 9:10

The **p** is a fool, Hs 9:7

I was not a **p** or the son of a **p**; Am 7:14

I am not a **p**; I am a tiller of the Zch 13:5

send you Elijah the **p** before the Mal 4:5

is what was written by the **p**: Mt 2:5

persecuted the **p-s** who were Mt 5:12

to destroy the Law or the **P-s**. Mt 5:17

this is the Law and the **P-s**. Mt 7:12

welcomes a **p** ... will receive a **p's** Mt 10:41

A **p**? Yes ... and far more than a **p**. Mt 11:9

A **p** is not without honor except Mt 13:57

Jeremiah or one of the **p-s**. Mt 16:14

This is the **p** Jesus from Nazareth Mt 21:11

everyone thought John was a **p**. Mt 21:26

Law and the **P-s** depend on these Mt 22:40

tombs of the **p-s** and decorate Mt 23:29

kills the **p-s** and stones those Mt 23:37

messiahs and false **p-s** will Mt 24:24

be called a **p** of the Most High, Lk 1:76

No **p** is accepted in his hometown. Lk 4:24

A great **p** has risen among us, Lk 7:16

if He were a **p**, would know who Lk 7:39

possible for a **p** to perish outside Lk 13:33

They have Moses and the **p-s**; Lk 16:29

who was a **P** powerful in action Lk 24:19

"Are you the **P**?" "No," Jn 1:21

This really is the **P** Jn 6:14

will see that no **p** arises from Jn 7:52

up for you a **P** like me from Ac 3:22

Which of the **p-s** did your fathers Ac 7:52

All the **p-s** testify about Him Ac 10:43

a Jewish false **p** named Bar-Jesus Ac 13:6

who were also **p-s** themselves, Ac 15:32

a p named Agabus came down
  from Ac 21:10
Agrippa, do you believe the **p-s**? Ac 26:27
attested by the Law and the **P-s**, Rm 3:21
killed Your **p-s**, torn down Your Rm 11:3
first apostles, second **p-s**, 1Co 12:28
are under the control of the **p-s**, 1Co 14:32
thinks he is a **p** or spiritual, 1Co 14:37
foundation of the apostles and **p-s**, Eph 2:20
apostles, some **p-s**, some Eph 4:11
One of their very own **p-s** said, Ti 1:12
fathers by the **p-s** at different Heb 1:1
take the **p-s** who spoke in the Jms 5:10
the **p-s** who prophesied about the 1Pt 1:10
were also false **p-s** among the 2Pt 2:1
many false **p-s** have gone out 1Jn 4:1
these two **p-s** tormented those Rv 11:10
blood of the saints and the **p-s** Rv 16:6
from the mouth of the false **p.** Rv 16:13
apostles, and **p-s**, because God Rv 18:20
and along with him the false **p** Rv 19:20
the beast and the false **p** are, Rv 20:10

PROPHETESS

Miriam the **p**, Aaron's sister, Ex 15:20
Asaiah went to the **p** Huldah, 2Kg 22:14
also Noadiah the **p** and the other Neh 6:14
I was then intimate with the **p**, Is 8:3
There was also a **p**, Anna, Lk 2:36
calls herself a **p**, and teaches Rv 2:20

PROPHETIC

p visions were not widespread. 1Sm 3:1
that the **p** Scriptures would Mt 26:56
known through the **p** Scriptures, Rm 16:26
we have the **p** word strongly 2Pt 1:19
who keeps the **p** words of this book. Rv 22:7

PROPHETICALLY

called, **p**, Sodom and Egypt, Rv 11:8

PROPITIATION

Him as a **p** through faith Rm 3:25
to make **p** for the sins of the Heb 2:17
Himself is the **p** for our sins, 1Jn 2:2
Son to be the **p** for our sins. 1Jn 4:10

PROPORTION

p to the years left until ... Jubilee, Lv 27:18
p to how the LORD ... has blessed Dt 16:10

PROPOSAL

p pleased the whole company Ac 6:5

PROPOSED

So they **p** two: Joseph, called Ac 1:23

PROPRIETY

with all **p**, the younger women 1Tm 5:2

PROSECUTE

Let me know why You **p** me. Jb 10:2
Would He **p** me forcefully? Jb 23:6

PROSELYTE

land and sea to make one **p** Mt 23:15
from Rome, both Jews and **p-s**, Ac 2:10
and Nicolaus, a **p** from Antioch. Ac 6:5
Jews and devout **p-s** followed Paul Ac 13:43

PROSPER

and I will cause you to **p**, Gn 32:9
so that you may **p** in the land Dt 5:16
you may live, **p**, and have a long Dt 5:33
For then you will **p** and succeed Jos 1:8
and wherever he went, he **p-ed**. 2Kg 18:7
He **p-ed**, and all Israel obeyed 1Ch 29:23
to seek his God, and he **p-ed**. 2Ch 31:21
Whatever he does **p-s**. Ps 1:3
good pleasure, cause Zion to **p**; Ps 51:18
May those who love you **p**; Ps 122:6
conceals his sins will not **p** Pr 28:13
trusts in the LORD will **p**. Pr 28:25
will **p** in what I send it {to do}. Is 55:11
does the way of the wicked **p**? Jr 12:1
Daniel **p-ed** during the reign of Dn 6:28
cause deceit to **p** through his Dn 8:25
save to the extent that he **p-s**, 1Co 16:2
I pray that you may **p** in every way 3Jn 2

PROSPERITY

set before you life and **p**, Dt 30:15
Your wisdom and **p** far exceed 1Kg 10:7
Never seek their peace or **p**, Ezr 9:12
and my **p** has passed by like Jb 30:15
they will end their days in **p** Jb 36:11
restored his **p** and doubled Jb 42:10
and will enjoy abundant **p** Ps 37:11
I saw the **p** of the wicked. Ps 73:3
You restored Jacob's **p**. Ps 85:1
In the day of **p** be joyful, Ec 7:14
vast, and its **p** will never Is 9:7
when it has **p**, you will prosper. Jr 29:7

will again overflow with **p**; Zch 1:17
know that our **p** is derived Ac 19:25

PROSTITUTE (n)

treated our sister like a **p**? Gn 34:31
he thought she was a **p**, Gn 38:15
daughter by making her a **p**, Lv 19:29
no Israelite man is to be a cult **p**. Dt 23:17
Do not bring a female **p-'s** wages Dt 23:18
a **p** named Rahab, and stayed there. Jos 2:1
two women who were **p-s** came 1Kg 3:16
There were even male shrine **p-s** 1Kg 14:24
For a **p-'s** fee is only a loaf Pr 6:26
For a **p** is a deep pit, Pr 23:27
consorts with **p-s** destroys his Pr 29:3
your beauty and acted like a **p** Ezk 16:15
who acted like **p-s** in Egypt, Ezk 23:3
loved the wages of a **p** on every Hs 9:1
p-s are entering kingdom Mt 21:31
devoured your assets with **p-s**, Lk 15:30
male **p-s**, homosexuals, 1Co 6:9
and make them members of a **p**? 1Co 6:15
joined to a **p** is one body with her? 1Co 6:16
faith Rahab the **p** received the Heb 11:31
Rahab the **p** also justified Jms 2:25
the notorious **p** who sits on many Rv 17:1
THE MOTHER OF **P-S** Rv 17:5

PROSTITUTE (v)

they **p** themselves with their gods Ex 34:15
they **p-d** themselves with other Jdg 2:17
p-d themselves with the gods 1Ch 5:25
the house of Ahab **p-d** itself, 2Ch 21:13
p-d themselves by their deeds. Ps 106:39
Judah ... also went and **p-d** herself. Jr 3:8

PROTECT

Angel before you to **p** you Ex 23:20
The LORD bless you and **p** you; Nm 6:24
He is the shield that **p-s** you, Dt 33:29
also **p-ed** us all along the way Jos 24:17
the LORD your God **p-s** the living 1Sm 25:29
P me, God, for I take refuge in You. Ps 16:1
You **p** me from trouble. Ps 32:7
He **p-s** all his bones; Ps 34:20
P my life from the terror of the Ps 64:1
to **p** you in all your ways. Ps 91:11
He **p-s** the lives of His godly ones; Ps 97:10
The LORD **p-s** you; Ps 121:5
They will **p** you from an evil woman Pr 6:24

the lips of the wise **p** them. Pr 14:3
righteous run to it and are **p-ed**. Pr 18:10
Won't He who **p-s** your life know? Pr 24:12
official **p-s** another official Ec 5:8
the LORD of Hosts will **p** Jerusalem Is 31:5
He **p-s** His flock like a shepherd Is 40:11
in awe of John and was **p-ing** him Mk 6:20
concerning you, to **p** you, Lk 4:10
p them by Your name that You Jn 17:11
but that You **p** them from the Jn 17:15
are being **p-ed** by God's power 1Pt 1:5
who is able to **p** you from Jd 24

PROTECTION

come under the **p** of my roof. Gn 19:8
Their **p** has been removed Nm 14:9
hide them in the **p** of Your presence Ps 31:20
lives under the **p** of the Most High Ps 91:1
my God is the rock of my **p**. Ps 94:22
I come to You for **p**. Ps 143:9
For wisdom is **p** as money is **p**, Ec 7:12
no trouble for me and is a **p** for you. Php 3:1

PROTECTIVE

His faithfulness will be a **p** shield. Ps 91:4

PROTECTOR

the **P** of Israel does not slumber Ps 121:4

PROTOTYPE

He is a **p** of the Coming One. Rm 5:14

PROUD

become **p** and you forget the LORD Dt 8:14
If I am **p**, You hunt me like a Jb 10:16
Look on every **p** person and Jb 40:12
turned to the **p** or to those who Ps 40:4
repay the **p** what they deserve. Ps 94:2
LORD, my heart is not **p**; Ps 131:1
destroys the house of the **p** Pr 15:25
Everyone with a **p** heart is Pr 16:5
to divide plunder with the **p**. Pr 16:19
downfall a man's heart is **p**, Pr 18:12
is better than a **p** spirit. Ec 7:8
Do not be **p**, for the LORD has Jr 13:15
and their hearts became **p**. Hs 13:6
He has scattered the **p** because Lk 1:51
arrogant, **p**, boastful, inventors Rm 1:30
Do not be **p**; instead, associate Rm 12:16
money, boastful, **p**, blasphemers 2Tm 3:2

God resists the **p**, but gives   Jms 4:6
because God resists the **p**, but   1Pt 5:5

PROUDLY
Do not boast so **p**, or let   1Sm 2:3
not walk so **p** because it will   Mc 2:3

PROVE
the pure You **p** Yourself pure,   2Sm 22:27
but were unable to **p** that their   Ezr 2:59
But what does your rebuke **p**?   Jb 6:25
Yet no one **p**-ed Job wrong;   Jb 32:12
the pure You **p** Yourself pure,   Ps 18:26
you think **p**-ed to be a neighbor   Lk 10:36
much fruit and **p** to be My   Jn 15:8
in Damascus by **p**-ing that this One   Ac 9:22
But God **p**-s His own love for us   Rm 5:8
if they **p** blameless, then they   1Tm 3:10

PROVEN
endurance produces **p** character,   Rm 5:4
so I may know your **p** character,   2Co 2:9
But you know his **p** character,   Php 2:22

PROVERB
As the old **p** says, 'Wickedness   1Sm 24:13
Solomon composed 3,000 **p-s**,   1Kg 4:32
memorable sayings are **p-s** of ash;   Jb 13:12
I turn my ear to a **p**;   Ps 49:4
The **p-s** of Solomon son of David,   Pr 1:1
understanding a **p** or a parable,   Pr 1:6
Solomon's **p-s**: A wise son brings   Pr 10:1
These too are **p-s** of Solomon,   Pr 25:1
A **p** in the mouth of a fool is   Pr 26:7,9
and arranged many **p-s**.   Ec 12:9
what is this **p** you {people} have   Ezk 12:22
uses **p-s** will say this **p** about you: Ezk 16:44
no longer use this **p** in Israel.   Ezk 18:3
you will quote this **p** to Me: Lk 4:23
them according to the true **p**:   2Pt 2:22

PROVIDE
God Himself will **p** the lamb   Gn 22:8
that place The LORD Will **P**,   Gn 22:14
It will be **p-d** on the LORD's   Gn 22:14
p-d for them in the wilderness   Neh 9:21
God's power **p-s** this.   Jb 12:6
Who **p-s** the raven's food   Jb 38:41
goodness You **p-d** for the poor,   Ps 68:10
Is God able to **p** food in the   Ps 78:19
the LORD will **p** what is good,   Ps 85:12

has **p-d** food for those who fear   Ps 111:5
p-s the animals with their food   Ps 147:9
lambs will **p** your clothing,   Pr 27:26
and **p-s** food for her household   Pr 31:15
because I **p** water in the wilderness,   Is 43:20
and it grew up to **p** shade over   Jnh 4:6
all these things will be **p-d** for you.   Mt 6:33
these hands have **p-d** for my needs   Ac 20:34
He will also **p** a way of escape,   1Co 10:13
the One who **p-s** seed for
    the sower   2Co 9:10
flesh, but **p-s** and cares for it,   Eph 5:29
if anyone does not **p** for his own   1Tm 5:8
richly **p-s** us with all things   1Tm 6:17
God had **p-d** something better   Heb 11:40
from the strength God **p-s**,   1Pt 4:11

PROVINCE
the message in the **p** of Asia.   Ac 16:6
inhabitants of the **p** of Asia,   Ac 19:10
have any work to do in these **p-s**,   Rm 15:23
took place in the **p** of Asia: 2Co 1:8
churches in the **p** of Asia.   Rv 1:4

PROVISION
Their entire **p** of bread was dry   Jos 9:5
Solomon's **p-s** for one day were   1Kg 4:22
I've made **p** for the house   1Ch 29:2
it prepares its **p-s** in summer;   Pr 6:8
daily **p-s** from the royal food   Dn 1:5
who eat his **p-s** will destroy him   Dn 11:26
making **p** for what is honorable,   2Co 8:21

PROVOKE
and do not **p** them to battle,   Dt 2:9
You **p-d** the LORD at Horeb, and   Dt 9:8
You continued to **p** the LORD at   Dt 9:22
They have **p-d** My jealousy with   Dt 32:21
So I will **p** their jealousy with   Dt 32:21
taunt her severely just to **p** her,   1Sm 1:6
In order to **p** Me, you have   1Kg 14:9
Ahab did more to **p** the LORD God   1Kg 16:33
did evil things, **p**-ing the LORD.   2Kg 17:11
and those who **p** God are secure;   Jb 12:6
tested God and **p-d** the Holy One   Ps 78:41
p-d the LORD with their deeds   Ps 106:29
and his mouth **p-s** a beating.   Pr 18:6
continually **p** Me to My face,   Is 65:3
But are they really **p**-ing Me?   Jr 7:19
do not **p** Me to anger by the work of   Jr 25:6

to other gods to **p** Me to anger.   Jr 32:29
statue that **p-s** jealousy was   Ezk 8:3
your fathers **p-d** Me to anger,   Zch 8:14
are we **p-ing** the Lord to jealousy   1Co 10:22
is not selfish; is not **p-d**;   1Co 13:5
conceited, **p-ing** one another,   Gl 5:26
Therefore I was **p-d** with this   Heb 3:10

PROWLING
the Devil is **p** around like a   1Pt 5:8

PRUDENT
who gathers during summer is **p**;   Pr 10:5
counsel perished from the **p**?   Jr 49:7

PRUNES
and He **p** every branch that   Jn 15:2

PRUNING (adj)
and their spears into **p-ing** knives.   Is 2:4
swords and your **p-ing** knives into   Jl 3:10
and their spears into **p-ing** knives.   Mc 4:3

PSALM
After singing **p-s**, they went out   Mt 26:30
After singing **p-s**, they went out   Mk 14:26
himself says in the Book of **P-s**:   Lk 20:42
and the **P-s** must be fulfilled.   Lk 24:44
it is written in the Book of **P-s**   Ac 1:20
it is written in the second **P**:   Ac 13:33
and I will sing **p-s** to Your name.   Rm 15:9
each one has a **p**, a teaching   1Co 14:26
speaking to one another in **p-s**,   Eph 5:19
wisdom, and singing **p-s**, hymns   Col 3:16

PSEUDO-INTELLECTUAL
What is this **p** trying to say?   Ac 17:18

PUBLIC
find you in **p** and kiss you,   Sg 8:1
the day of his **p** appearance to   Lk 1:80
it to you in **p** and from house to   Ac 20:20
are God's **p** servants,   Rm 13:6
your attention to **p** reading,   1Tm 4:13

PUBLICLY
and he will sleep with them **p**.   2Sm 12:11
Moses was read **p** to the people.   Neh 13:1
not wanting to disgrace her **p**   Mt 1:19
nobody was talking **p** about Him   Jn 7:13
and disgraced them **p**;   Col 2:15
P rebuke those who sin, so that   1Tm 5:20

PUBLIUS
Roman official who welcomed Paul (Ac 28:7-8).

PUL
King of Assyria (2Kg 15:19; 1Ch 5:26).

PULL
He **p-ed** me out of deep waters.   Ps 18:16
for He will **p** my feet out of the   Ps 25:15
they **p-ed** him up with the ropes   Jr 38:13
will not immediately **p** him out   Lk 14:5

PULVERIZE
p them like dust before the   Ps 18:42
a sledgehammer that **p-s** rock?   Jr 23:29

PUNISH
p-ing the children for the father's   Ex 20:5
will take the man and **p** him.   Dt 22:18
May God **p** me severely if you   1Sm 14:44
may God **p** Jonathan and do   1Sm 20:13
May God **p** me, and even more if   1Sm 25:22
May God **p** Abner and do so   2Sm 3:9
May God **p** me and do so   2Sm 3:35; 19:13
May God **p** me and do so severely   1Kg 2:23
May the gods **p** me and do   1Kg 19:2; 20:10
May God **p** me and do so severely   2Kg 6:31
p-ed {us} less than our sins   Ezr 9:13
because God's anger does not **p**   Jb 35:15
P them, God; let them fall by   Ps 5:10
refuge in Him will not be **p-ed**.   Ps 34:22
do not **p** me in Your anger or   Ps 38:1
keep going and are **p-ed**.   Pr 22:3; 27:12
the LORD has **p-ed** Him for the   Is 53:6
Should I not **p** them for these   Jr 5:9
I will **p** you according to what   Jr 21:14
But He will **p** your iniquity,   Lm 4:22
I will **p** them for their ways and   Hs 4:9
I will not relent from **p-ing**   Am 1:3
so I will **p** the leaders.   Zch 10:3
ready to **p** any disobedience,   2Co 10:6
p-es every son whom He receives.   Heb 12:6
to **p** those who do evil   1Pt 2:14

PUNISHMENT
My **p** is too great to bear!   Gn 4:13
What will you do on the day of **p**   Is 10:3
p for our peace was on Him,   Is 53:5
So I will choose their **p**,   Is 66:4
the year of their **p**.   Jr 11:23

Zion, your p is complete;	Lm 4:22
son won't suffer p for the father's	Ezk 18:20
The days of p have come;	Hs 9:7
they will go away into eternal p,	Mt 25:46
These will receive harsher p.	Mk 12:40
The p by the majority is sufficient	2Co 2:6
unrighteous under p until the day	2Pt 2:9
because fear involves p	1Jn 4:18
undergoing the p of eternal	Jd 7

PUPIL

guarded him as the p of His eye.	Dt 32:10
as you would the p of your eye.	Pr 7:2
you touches the p of His eye.	Zch 2:8

PUR

He cast the P (that is, the lot)	Est 9:24

PURCHASED

p a section of the field from	Gn 33:19
until the people whom You p	Ex 15:16
You p long ago and redeemed	Ps 74:2
which He p with His own blood.	Ac 20:28

PURE

Make a mercy seat of p gold,	Ex 25:17
he overlaid it with p gold.	1Kg 6:20
or a man more p than his Maker?	Jb 4:17
if you are p and upright, then	Jb 8:6
and I am p in Your sight.	Jb 11:4
What is man, that he should be p,	Jb 15:14
heavens are not p in His sight,	Jb 15:15
I am p, without transgression;	Jb 33:9
words of the LORD are p words,	Ps 12:6
with the p You prove Yourself p,	Ps 18:26
the word of the LORD is p.	Ps 18:30
The fear of the LORD is p,	Ps 19:9
who has clean hands and a p heart,	Ps 24:4
to Israel, to the p in heart.	Ps 73:1
can a young man keep his way p?	Ps 119:9
but pleasant words are p.	Pr 15:26
say, "I have kept my heart p;	Pr 20:9
eyes are too p to look on evil,	Hab 1:13
I will then restore p speech to	Zph 3:9
Blessed are the p in heart,	Mt 5:8
commended yourselves to be p	2Co 7:11
to present a p virgin to Christ	2Co 11:2
whatever is just, whatever is p,	Php 4:8
is love from a p heart,	1Tm 1:5
Keep yourself p.	1Tm 5:22
call on the Lord from a p heart.	2Tm 2:22

To the p, everything is p, but to	Ti 1:15
to be sensible, p, good	Ti 2:5
our bodies washed in p water.	Heb 10:22
P and undefiled religion before	Jms 1:27
wisdom from above is first p	Jms 3:17
earnestly from a p heart,	1Pt 1:22
himself just as He is p.	1Jn 3:3
wear fine linen, bright and p.	Rv 19:8
the city was p gold like clear	Rv 21:18

PURELY

do I plan in a p human way	2Co 1:17
know anyone in a p human way.	2Co 5:16
known Christ in a p human way,	2Co 5:16

PUREST

than gold, even the p gold,	Ps 119:127
His head is p gold.	Sg 5:11

PURGE

You must p the evil from you.	Dt 13:5
Lashes and wounds p away evil,	Pr 20:30
I will p your uncleanness.	Ezk 22:15

PURIFICATION

Aaron is to perform the p rite	Ex 30:10
until completing her days of p.	Lv 12:4
be purified with the p water.	Nm 31:23
the days of their p according to	Lk 2:22
been set there for Jewish p.	Jn 2:6
completion of the p days when	Ac 21:26
After making p for sins, He sat	Heb 1:3
for the p of the flesh,	Heb 9:13

PURIFY

and hyssop to p the house,	Lv 14:49
He will p the {most} holy place	Lv 16:16
The Levites p-ied themselves and	Nm 8:21
He is to p himself with the	Nm 19:12
Levites had p-ied themselves,	
they p-ied the people,	Neh 12:30
earthen furnace, p-ied seven times.	Ps 12:6
P me with hyssop, and I will be	Ps 51:7
go out from her, p yourselves,	Is 52:11
They will p the altar just as	Ezk 43:22
and p the sanctuary.	Ezk 45:18
Many will be p-ied, cleansed, and	Dn 12:10
He will p the sons of Levi and	Mal 3:3
p yourself along with them,	Ac 21:24
everything is p-ied with blood,	Heb 9:22
sinners, and p your hearts,	Jms 4:8

having **p-ied** yourselves for sincere | 1Pt 1:22
hope in Him **p-ies** himself just as | 1Jn 3:3

PURIM

reason these days are called **P**, | Est 9:26

PURITY

rescued by the **p** of your hands. | Jb 22:30
with God-given sincerity and **p** | 2Co 1:12
by **p**, by knowledge, by patience, | 2Co 6:6
and **p** of the truth. | Eph 4:24
in love, in faith, in **p**. | 1Tm 4:12

PURPLE

blue, **p**, and scarlet yarn; | Ex 28:5
clothing is fine linen and **p**. | Pr 31:22
and they clothed Daniel in **p**, | Dn 5:29
They dressed Him in a **p** robe, | Mk 15:17
rich man who would dress in **p** | Lk 16:19
crown of thorns and the **p** robe. | Jn 19:5
a dealer in **p** cloth from the | Ac 16:14
was dressed in **p** and scarlet, | Rv 17:4
fabrics of linen, **p**, silk, and | Rv 18:12

PURPOSE

I have let you live for this **p**: | Ex 9:16
and fulfill your whole **p**. | Ps 20:4
who fulfills {His **p**} for me. | Ps 57:2
will fulfill {His **p**} for me. | Ps 138:8
has prepared everything for His **p** | Pr 16:4
a man for My **p** from a far | Is 46:11
because I was sent for this **p**. | Lk 4:43
I have appeared to you for this **p**, | Ac 26:16
are called according to His **p**. | Rm 8:28
so that God's **p** according to | Rm 9:11
unless you believed to no **p**. | 1Co 15:2
according to the **p** of the ages, | Eph 3:11
will and to act for His good **p**. | Php 2:13
to His own **p** and grace, | 2Tm 1:9
of God was revealed for this **p**: | 1Jn 3:8

PURSUE

They **p-d** worthless idols and | 2Kg 17:15
what is worthless and **p** a lie? | Ps 4:2
love will **p** me all the days | Ps 23:6
seek peace and **p** it. | Ps 34:14
Disaster **p-s** sinners, but good | Pr 13:21
one who **p-s** righteousness and | Pr 21:21
flee when no one is **p-ing** {them}, | Pr 28:1
I will **p** them with sword, famine | Jr 29:18
their hearts **p** unjust gain. | Ezk 33:31

who did not **p** righteousness, | Rm 9:30
they did not **p** it by faith, | Rm 9:32
we must **p** what promotes peace | Rm 14:19
P love and desire spiritual | 1Co 14:1
but always **p** what is good for | 1Th 5:15
but **p** righteousness, godliness | 1Tm 6:11
and **p** righteousness, faith, | 2Tm 2:22
P peace with everyone, and | Heb 12:14
He must seek peace and **p** it, | 1Pt 3:11

PURSUERS

save me from all my **p** and rescue me, | Ps 7:1

PURSUIT

The Egyptians set out in **p** | Ex 14:23
a vanishing mist, a **p** of death. | Pr 21:6
futile, a **p** of the wind. | Ec 1:14
in the morning in **p** of beer, | Is 5:11

PUSH

They do not **p** each other; | Jl 2:8

PUT

I will **p** hostility between you | Gn 3:15
P your hand inside your cloak. | Ex 4:6
The LORD **p** it into the mind of | Ezr 1:1
You **p** everything under his feet | Ps 8:6
do not let me be **p** to shame, | Ps 25:20
I **p** my hope in You, LORD; | Ps 38:15
He **p** a new song in my mouth, | Ps 40:3
P your hope in God, for I will | Ps 42:5
of the wicked will be **p** out. | Pr 24:20
p your hand over your mouth. | Pr 30:32
He has also **p** eternity in their | Ec 3:11
P no more trust in man, | Is 2:22
I have **p** My Spirit on Him; | Is 42:1
a new heart and **p** a new spirit | Ezk 36:26
I will **p** My Spirit on Him, | Mt 12:18
and He will not **p** out a | Mt 12:20
They **p** them at His feet, | Mt 15:30
How long must I **p** up with you? | Mt 17:17
Him so He might **p** His hands on | Mt 19:13
hand until I **p** Your enemies | Mt 22:44
so they could **p** Him to death. | Mt 26:59
had already **p** it into the heart | Jn 13:2
for us to **p** anyone to death | Jn 18:31
I don't know where they've **p** Him. | Jn 20:13
p my finger into the mark of the | Jn 20:25
But **p** on the Lord Jesus Christ, | Rm 13:14
P away the evil person from | 1Co 5:13
Why not rather **p** up with | 1Co 6:7

you **p** up with it splendidly!	2Co 11:4
For you gladly **p** up with fools	2Co 11:19
into Christ have **p** on Christ.	Gl 3:27
you **p** on the new man, the one	Eph 4:24
P on the full armor of God so	Eph 6:11
p to death whatever in you is	Col 3:5
since you have **p** off the old man	Col 3:9
p on heartfelt compassion,	Col 3:12
be sober and **p** the armor of faith	1Th 5:8
has **p** her hope in God and	1Tm 5:5
I will **p** My laws into their	Heb 8:10
For God has **p** it into their	Rv 17:17

PUZZLES

and that no mystery **p** you,	Dn 4:9

Q

QUAIL

So at evening **q** came	Ex 16:13
and blew **q** in from the sea	Nm 11:31
and He brought **q** and satisfied	Ps 105:40

QUAKE

Then the earth shook and **q-d**;	Ps 18:7
the mountains **q** with its turmoil.	Ps 46:3
Let the earth **q**.	Ps 99:1
mountains would **q** at Your	Is 64:1
The earth **q-s** before them;	Jl 2:10
won't the land **q** and all who	Am 8:8
earth **q-d** and the rocks were split.	Mt 27:51

QUALITY

will test the **q** of each one's	1Co 3:13
the imperishable **q** of a gentle	1Pt 3:4
For if these **q-ies** are yours and are	2Pt 1:8

QUANTITY

produce the same **q** of bricks.	Ex 5:18
an immeasurable **q** of bronze,	1Ch 22:3

QUARANTINE

the priest must **q** the infected	Lv 13:4
its doorway and **q** the house for	Lv 14:38
He lived in **q** with a serious skin	2Ch 26:21

QUARREL (n)

the lot ends **q-s** and separates	Pr 18:18
fool can get himself into a **q**.	Pr 20:3
meddles in a **q** that's not his	Pr 26:17
that there are **q-s** among you.	1Co 1:11
genealogies, **q-s**, and disputes	Ti 3:9

QUARREL (v)

of Gerar **q-ed** with Isaac's	Gn 26:20
When men **q** and one strikes the	Ex 21:18
The people **q-ed** with Moses	Nm 20:3
The Lord's slave must not **q**,	2Tm 2:24

QUARRELING (n)

Lot, "Please, let's not have **q**	Gn 13:8
not in **q** and jealousy.	Rm 13:13
there may be **q**, jealousy	2Co 12:20
come envy, **q**, slanders,	1Tm 6:4

QUARRELSOME

schemes of men, from **q** tongues.	Ps 31:20
so is a **q** man for kindling strife.	Pr 26:21
but gentle, not **q**, not greedy	1Tm 3:3

QUARRY

cut at the **q** so that no hammer	1Kg 6:7
the **q** from which you were cut.	Is 51:1

QUART

A **q** of wheat for a denarius,	Rv 6:6

QUARTERMASTER

in the care of the **q** and ran to	1Sm 17:22

QUARTZ

Coral and **q** are not worth	Jb 28:18

QUEEN

The **q** of Sheba heard about	1Kg 10:1
But **Q** Vashti refused to come	Est 1:12
head and made her **q** in place of	Est 2:17
the **q** ... stands at your right hand.	Ps 45:9
are 60 **q-s** and 80 concubines	Sg 6:8
burn incense to the **q** of heaven	Jr 44:17
The **q** of the south will rise up	Mt 12:42
of Candace, **q** of the Ethiopians	Ac 8:27
says in her heart, 'I sit as **q**;	Rv 18:7

QUENCHED

and it will not be **q**.	2Kg 22:17
wrath will burn and not be **q**.	Jr 7:20
not die, and the fire is not **q**.	Mk 9:44
q the raging of fire,	Heb 11:34

QUESTION (n)

David. "It was just a **q**."	1Sm 17:29
to test him with difficult **q-s**.	1Kg 10:1
I will also ask you one **q**,	Mt 21:24
asked a **q** to test Him:	Mt 22:35
to them and asking them **q-s**.	Lk 2:46
kept asking Him **q-s**, but Jesus	Lk 23:9
asking no **q-s** for conscience' sake	1Co 10:25

QUESTION (v)

when I **q** you, you will inform Me.	Jb 38:3
no one dared to **q** Him any more.	Mt 22:46
Why ... **q** Me? **Q** those who heard	Jn 18:21

QUICK

A **q**-tempered man acts foolishly,	Pr 14:17
but a **q**-tempered one promotes	Pr 14:29
Don't be too **q** to lay hands on	1Tm 5:22
not arrogant, not **q** tempered,	Ti 1:7
everyone must be **q** to hear,	Jms 1:19

QUICKLY

They have **q** turned from the way	Ex 32:8
you will perish **q** from the good	Dt 11:17
My strength, come **q** to help me.	Ps 22:19
I am in distress. Answer me **q**!	Ps 69:17
answer me **q** when I call.	Ps 102:2
the sentence ... is not carried out **q**,	Ec 8:11
Reach a settlement **q** with your	Mt 5:25
they sprang up **q** since the soil	Mt 13:5
did the fig tree wither so **q**?	Mt 21:20
Then go **q** and tell His disciples	Mt 28:7
What you're doing, do **q**.	Jn 13:27
that you are so **q** turning away	Gl 1:6
I am coming **q**. Hold on to what	Rv 3:11
Yes, I am coming **q**.	Rv 22:20

QUIET

but Jacob was a **q** man	Gn 25:27
fight for you; you must be **q**.	Ex 14:14
to a **q** and unsuspecting people.	Jdg 18:27
Be a **q** for now, my sister.	2Sm 13:20
He said, "Yes, I know. Be **q**."	2Kg 2:3
He leads me beside **q** waters.	Ps 23:2
Calm down and be **q**.	Is 7:4
will lie in **q** confidence.	Is 30:15
will be **q** confidence forever.	Is 32:17
have calm and **q** with no one to	Jr 30:10
Be **q**, and come out of him!	Mk 1:25
Many people told him to keep **q**	Mk 10:48
seek to lead a **q** life,	1Th 4:11

a tranquil and **q** life in all	1Tm 2:2
of a gentle and **q** spirit,	1Pt 3:4

QUIETED (v)

Let lying lips be **q**;	Ps 31:18
have calmed and **q** myself like	Ps 131:2

QUIETLY

Groan **q**;	Ezk 24:17
q working, they may eat their own	2Th 3:12

QUIETNESS

bring {you} **q-ness** with His love	Zph 3:17

QUIRINIUS

Governor of Syria (Lk 2:2).

QUIVER

your **q** and bow, and go out	Gn 27:3
A **q** rattles at his side, along	Jb 39:23
who has filled his **q** with them.	Ps 127:5
He hid me in His **q**.	Is 49:2
Their **q** is like an open grave;	Jr 5:16
Sharpen the arrows! Fill the **q-s**!	Jr 51:11

QUOTA

require the same **q** of bricks	Ex 5:8
reduce your daily **q** of bricks,	Ex 5:19

QUOTE

No doubt you will **q** this proverb	Lk 4:23

R

⟨∞⟩

RABBAH

Capitol of Ammon (Dt 3:11; Jos 13:25); captured by David (2Sm 11:1; 12:26-31); prophesied against (Jr 49:2-3; Ezk 21:20; 25:5; Am 1:14).

RABBI

and to be called '**R**' by people.	Mt 23:7
do not be called '**R**' because you	Mt 23:8
Surely not I, **R**?	Mt 26:25
right up to Him and said, "**R**!"	Mk 14:45
said to Him, "**R**" (which means	Jn 1:38

RABBOUNI

"**R**," the blind man told Him,	Mk 10:51
she said to Him in Hebrew, "**R**!"	Jn 20:16

RAB-MAG

Title of a Babylonian official (Jr 39:3,13).

RAB-SARIS

Title of Assyrian and Babylonian officials (2Kg 18:17; Jr 39:3,13).

RABSHAKEH

Title of an Assyrian official (2Kg 18:17–19:8; Is 36:2–37:8).

RACE (n)

the r is not to the swift,	Ec 9:11
I have finished the r, I have kept	2Tm 4:7
endurance the r that lies before	Heb 12:1
you are a chosen r, a royal	1Pt 2:9

RACE (v)

Messenger r-s to meet messenger,	Jr 51:31
the runners in a stadium all r,	1Co 9:24

RACHEL

Daughter of Laban; wife and cousin of Jacob (Gn 29:10,18-30); mother of Joseph and Benjamin (30:24; 35:16-20); stole her father's household idols (31:19).

R weeping for her children,	Jr 31:15
R weeping for her children;	Mt 2:18

RADIANCE

From the r of His presence,	Ps 18:12
God appears in r.	Ps 50:2
to the brightness of your r.	Is 60:3
He is the r of His glory,	Heb 1:3

RADIANT

Moses' face was r.	Ex 34:35
who look to Him are r with joy;	Ps 34:5
Then you will see and be r,	Is 60:5
they will be r with joy because	Jr 31:12

RAFTS

make them into r to go by sea to	1Kg 5:9

RAGE (n)

homage, he was filled with r.	Est 3:5
A king's r is like a lion's roar	Pr 19:12
and a covert bribe, fierce r.	Pr 21:14
a people destined for My r,	Is 10:6
I will not come in r.	Hs 11:9

RAGE (v)

Nations r, kingdoms topple;	Ps 46:6
his heart r-s against the LORD	Pr 19:3

Then he will r against the holy	Dn 11:30
the Gentiles r, and the peoples	Ac 4:25

RAGING (adj)

Unleash your r anger;	Jb 40:11
hurry to my shelter from the r wind	Ps 55:8
the r waters would have swept	Ps 124:5

RAGING (n)

nations rage like the r of ... waters.	Is 17:13
and the sea stopped its r.	Jnh 1:15

RAGS

grogginess will clothe {them} in r.	Pr 23:21

RAHAB

Prostitute in Jericho who hid the Israelite spies (Jos 2; Heb 11:31); spared by Joshua (6:17,22-25). Mother of Boaz (Mt 1:5).

RAID

R-ing parties went out from the	1Sm 13:17
Where did you r today?	1Sm 27:10

RAILING

make a r around your roof,	Dt 22:8

RAIN (n)

and the r fell on the earth 40	Gn 7:12
I will give you r at the right	Lv 26:4
I will provide r for your land	Dt 11:14
Let my teaching fall like r	Dt 32:2
May You send r on Your land that	1Kg 8:36
will be no dew or r during these	1Kg 17:1
He gives r to the earth and	Jb 5:10
Does the r have a father?	Jb 38:28
You, God, showered abundant r;	Ps 68:9
is like a cloud with spring r.	Pr 16:15
like clouds and wind without r.	Pr 25:14
the r has ended and gone away.	Sg 2:11
a refuge from the r, a shade	Is 25:4
For just as r and snow fall from	Is 55:10
God, who gives the r, both early	Jr 5:24
Torrential r will come, and I	Ezk 13:11
righteousness on you like the r.	Hs 10:12
autumn and spring r as before.	Jl 2:23
I sent r on one city but no r on	Am 4:7
and sends r on the righteous and	Mt 5:45
The r fell, the rivers rose, and	Mt 7:25
giving you r from heaven and	Ac 14:17
For the ground has drunk the r	Heb 6:7

RAIN (v)

God had not made it r on the land,	Gn 2:5
the LORD r-ed burning sulfur	Gn 19:24
r-ed hail on the land of Egypt.	Ex 9:23
I am going to r bread from	Ex 16:4
He r-ed manna for them to eat;	Ps 78:24
fire and sulfur r-ed from heaven	Lk 17:29
prayed earnestly that it would not r	Jms 5:17
it does not r during the days	Rv 11:6

RAINBOW

was like that of a r in a cloud	Ezk 1:28
A r that looked like an emerald	Rv 4:3
with a r over his head.	Rv 10:1

RAINSTORM

for there is the sound of a r.	1Kg 18:41

RAINY

dripping on a r day and a nagging	Pr 27:15

RAISE

I will r up for them a prophet	Dt 18:18
LORD r-d up judges, who saved	Jdg 2:16
the LORD r-d up Othniel son of	Jdg 3:9
and He r-d up Ehud son of Gera,	Jdg 3:15
r-s the poor from the dust and	1Sm 2:8
Then I will r up a faithful priest	1Sm 2:35
I will r up after you your	2Sm 7:12
I would not r my hand against	2Sm 18:12
be gracious to me and r me up;	Ps 41:10
I r my eyes toward the mountains	Ps 121:1
The LORD r-s up those who are	Ps 146:8
hand is still r-d (to strike).	Is 9:12
herald of good news, r your voice	Is 40:9
and My highways will be r-d up.	Is 49:11
I will r up a righteous Branch	Jr 23:5
LORD has r-d up prophets for	Jr 29:15
and I will r up David their king	Jr 30:9
It was r-d up on one side, with	Dn 7:5
on the third day He will r us up	Hs 6:2
I am r-ing up the Chaldeans,	Hab 1:6
I am about to r up a shepherd in	Zch 11:16
God is able to r up children for	Mt 3:9
Heal the sick, r the dead,	Mt 10:8
dead are r-d, and the poor are	Mt 11:5
killed, and be r-d the third day.	Mt 16:21
the third day He will be r-d up	Mt 17:23
He has been r-d from the dead.	Mt 27:64
Nation will be r-d up against	Lk 21:10
and I will r it up in three days.	Jn 2:19

as the Father r-s the dead and	Jn 5:21
and I will r him up on the last	Jn 6:40
after He was r-d from the dead.	Jn 21:14
r-d Him up, ending the pains	Ac 2:24
God of our fathers r-d up Jesus	Ac 5:30
God will r up for you a Prophet	Ac 7:37
But God r-d Him from the dead,	Ac 13:30
and r-d for our justification.	Rm 4:25
as Christ was r-d from the dead	Rm 6:4
then He who r-d Christ from the	Rm 8:11
believe in your heart that God r-d	Rm 10:9
r-d up the Lord and will also r us	1Co 6:14
that He was r-d on the third	1Co 15:4
and if Christ has not been r-d	1Co 15:14
whom He did not r up if in fact	1Co 15:15
If the dead are not r-d at all,	1Co 15:29
dead will be r-d incorruptible,	1Co 15:52
but in God who r-s the dead.	2Co 1:9
who r-d the Lord Jesus will r us	2Co 4:14
the Father who r-d Him from the	Gl 1:1
He also r-d us up with Him and	Eph 2:6
were also r-d with Him through	Col 2:12
have been r-d with the Messiah	Col 3:1
heaven, whom He r-d from the	1Th 1:10
to be able even to r someone	Heb 11:19
and the Lord will r him up;	Jms 5:15
r-d Him from the dead and gave	1Pt 1:21

RAISIN

or eat fresh grapes or r-s.	Nm 6:3
and a r cake to each	2Sm 6:19
Sustain me with r-s;	Sg 2:5
for the r cakes of Kir-hareseth.	Is 16:7
to other gods and love r cakes.	Hs 3:1

RAISING (n)

r of my hands as the evening	Ps 141:2

RAM

up and saw a r caught by its	Gn 22:13
lay their hands on the r-'s head.	Ex 29:15
an unblemished r from the flock	Lv 5:15
second ram, the r of ordination,	Lv 8:22
with the atonement r by which	Nm 5:8
(is better) than the fat of r-s.	1Sm 15:22
with the fragrant smoke of r-s;	Ps 66:15
The mountains skipped like r-s	Ps 114:4
r-s of Nebaioth will serve you	Is 60:7
there was a r standing beside	Dn 8:3

If a r-'s horn is blown in a city	Am 3:6
be pleased with thousands of r-s	Mc 6:7

RAMAH

1. Town(s) in Asher and Naphtali (Jos 19:29,36).

2. City in Benjamin between Israel and Judah (Jos 18:25; Jdg 19:13; 1Kg 15:16-22; 2Ch 16:1,5-6; Is 10:29); site of Rachel's tomb (1Sm 10:2; Jr 31:15; Mt 2:18); home of Deborah (Jdg 4:5); staging area for exile and return (Jr 40:1; Ezr 2:26; Neh 7:30).

3. City in Simeon, also called Ramoth of the Negev (Jos 19:8; 1Sm 30:27).

4. Home of Samuel (1Sm 1:19; 2:11; 7:17; 8:4; 15:34; 25:1); David fled to him there 19:18-23).

RAMESES

Egyptian supply city built by Hebrew slaves (Ex 1:11).

RAMOTH-GILEAD

City of refuge and Levitical city (Dt 4:43; Jos 20:8; 21:38); made a district capital by Solomon (1Kg 4:13); contested by Syria—Ahab killed (22:3,29-40; 2Kg 9:14); where Elisha anointed Jehu (2Kg 9:1-6).

RAMPART

note its r-s; tour its citadels	Ps 48:13
is established as walls and r-s.	Is 26:1
whose r was the sea,	Nah 3:8

RANGE

eyes of the LORD r throughout	2Ch 16:9

RANK

brought your r-s out of the land	Ex 12:17
I defy the r-s of Israel today.	1Sm 17:10
Take her out between the r-s	2Kg 11:15
promoted him in r and gave him	Est 3:1
yet all of them march in r-s;	Pr 30:27
his front r-s into the Dead Sea,	Jl 2:20
higher in r than the angels	Heb 1:4

RANSOM (n)

the men must pay a r for himself	Ex 30:12
not to accept a r for the life	Nm 35:31
to the Pit; I have found a r,	Jb 33:24
do not let a large r lead you astray.	Jb 36:18
Yet these cannot ... pay his r to God	Ps 49:7
Riches are a r for a man's life	Pr 13:8

The wicked are a r for the	Pr 21:18
to give His life—a r for many.	Mt 20:28
to give His life—a r for many.	Mk 10:45
gave Himself—a r for all, a	1Tm 2:6

RANSOM (v)

r me because of my enemies.	Ps 69:18
r-ed of the LORD will return 51:11	Is 35:10;
for the LORD has r-ed Jacob and	Jr 31:11
I will r them from the power of	Hs 13:14

RANTING

You know the sort and their r.	2Kg 9:11

RAPED

he took her and r her.	Gn 34:2
the man who r her must die.	Dt 22:25
They r her and abused her all	Jdg 19:25
than she was, he r her.	2Sm 13:14
be looted, and their wives r.	Is 13:16
Women are r in Zion,	Lm 5:11
looted, and the women r.	Zch 14:2

RAPIDLY

near, near and r approaching.	Zph 1:14
may spread r and be honored,	2Th 3:1

RARE

the word of the LORD was r	1Sm 3:1
and mankind more r than the gold	Is 13:12

RARELY

For r will someone die for a	Rm 5:7

RASH

her vows or the r commitment	Nm 30:6
That is why my words are r.	Jb 6:3
calm and not do anything r.	Ac 19:36

RASHLY

a person may speak r in an oath	Lv 5:4
and he spoke r with his lips.	Ps 106:33
There is one who speaks r,	Pr 12:18
something r and later to reconsider	Pr 20:25

RATHER

I would r be at the door of the	Ps 84:10
LORD be darkness r than light,	Am 5:20

RATIFIED

human covenant that has been r	Gl 3:15

RATTLING

a noise, a r sound, and the bones	Ezk 37:7

RAVAGE

the pestilence that r-s at noon.   Ps 91:6
by night—how r-d you will be!   Ob 5
Saul, however, was r-ing the church, Ac 8:3

RAVAGES (n)

Rescue my life from their r-s   Ps 35:17

RAVAGING (adj)

your prophets like a r lion.   Jr 2:30
but inwardly are r wolves.   Mt 7:15

RAVE

he began to r inside the palace.   1Sm 18:10
they kept on r-ing until the   1Kg 18:29
ranting and r-ing but no resolution. Pr 29:9

RAVEN

he sent out a r.   Gn 8:7
The r-s kept bringing him bread   1Kg 17:6
provides the r-'s food when its   Jb 38:41
and the young r-s, what they cry   Ps 147:9
hair is wavy and black as a r.   Sg 5:11
Consider the r-s: they don't sow   Lk 12:24

RAVINE

hill with a r between them.   1Sm 17:3
come and settle in the steep r-s   Is 7:19

RAW

Do not eat any of it r   Ex 12:9
boiled meat from you—only r.   1Sm 2:15

RAYS

eyes are like the r of dawn.   Jb 41:18
r are flashing from His hand.   Hab 3:4

RAZOR

Like a sharpened r, your tongue   Ps 52:2
Lord will use a r hired from   Is 7:20

REACH

with its top r-ing heaven,   Gn 28:12
and my cry to Him r-ed His ears.   Ps 18:6
r-ed down from on high and took   Ps 18:16
r-es to the ends of the earth;   Ps 48:10
faithfulness r-es to the clouds.   Ps 57:10
May my prayer r Your presence;   Ps 88:2
Let my cry r You, LORD;   Ps 119:169
I am unable to {r} it.   Ps 139:6
R down from on high; rescue me   Ps 144:7
offended brother is {harder to r}   Pr 18:19
whose top r-ed to the sky and   Dn 4:20
to us, {which} r-es even to you.   2Co 10:13

until we all r unity in the faith   Eph 4:13
not that I have already r-ed   Php 3:12
behind and r-ing forward to what   Php 3:13

READ

scroll and r {it} aloud to   Ex 24:7
you are to r this law aloud   Dt 31:11
Joshua r aloud all the words of   Jos 8:34
he r all the words of the book   2Kg 23:2
They r the book of the law   Neh 8:8
I can't r it, because it is sealed. Is 29:11
as Jehudi would r three or four   Jr 36:23
but none could r the inscription   Dn 5:8
tablets so one may easily r it.   Hab 2:2
haven't you r in the Law that   Mt 12:5
Sabbath day and stood up to r.   Lk 4:16
you understand what you're r-ing?   Ac 8:30
recognized and r by everyone,   2Co 3:2
Moses is r, a veil lies over   2Co 3:15
letter has been r among you,   Col 4:16
your attention to public r-ing,   1Tm 4:13
Blessed is the one who r-s   Rv 1:3

READER

(let the r understand),   Mt 24:15; Mk 13:14

READINESS

feet sandaled with r for the gospel Eph 6:15

READY

are kind and r to forgive,   Ps 86:5
May Your hand be r to help me,   Ps 119:173
The banquet is r, but those who   Mt 22:8
This is why you also must be r   Mt 24:44
those who were r went in with   Mt 25:10
r for the Lord a prepared people.   Lk 1:17
You also be r, because the Son   Lk 12:40
I'm r to go with You both to   Lk 22:33
for they are r for harvest.   Jn 4:35
And we are r to punish any   2Co 10:6
to be r for every good work,   Ti 3:1
and always be r to give a   1Pt 3:15

REAL

My flesh is r food and My blood   Jn 6:55
The r widow, left all alone, has   1Tm 5:5
take hold of life that is r.   1Tm 6:19

REALITY

faith is the r of what is hoped   Heb 11:1

REALIZE

Then Manoah r-d that it was the   Jdg 13:21

REALLY

Did God r say, 'You can't eat from	Gn 3:1
did you r fast for Me?	Zch 7:5
This man r was God's Son!	Mt 27:54
This man r was righteous!	Lk 23:47
sets you free, you r will be free.	Jn 8:36
God is r among you.	1Co 14:25
what they r were makes no	Gl 2:6
determine what r matters and can	Php 1:10

REALM

in the fleshly r but made alive	1Pt 3:18
judged by men in the fleshly r	1Pt 4:6

REAP

you are not to r to the very edge	Lv 19:9
who sow trouble r the same.	Jb 4:8
sow in tears will r with shouts	Ps 126:5
sows injustice will r disaster,	Pr 22:8
looks at the clouds will not r.	Ec 11:4
the wind and r the whirlwind.	Hs 8:7
yourselves and r faithful love;	Hs 10:12
You will sow but not r;	Mc 6:15
they don't sow or r or gather	Mt 6:26
r-ing where you haven't sown	Mt 25:24
One sows and another r-s.	Jn 4:37
too much if we r material things	1Co 9:11
will also r sparingly,	2Co 9:6
a man sows he will also r,	Gl 6:7
the Spirit will r eternal life	Gl 6:8
r, for the time to r has come,	Rv 14:15

REAPER

will be as if a r had gathered	Is 17:5
the plowman will overtake the r	Am 9:13
harvest time I'll tell the r-s:	Mt 13:30
so the sower and r can rejoice	Jn 4:36

REAR

God of Israel is your r guard.	Is 52:12

REASON (n)

many hate me for no r.	Ps 38:19
Who has wounds for no r?	Pr 23:29
They hated Me for no r.	Jn 15:25
For this r I raised you up:	Rm 9:17
asks you for a r for the hope	1Pt 3:15

REASON (v)

upright man could r with Him,	Jb 23:7
and the Pharisees began to r:	Lk 5:21
So he r-ed in the synagogue with	Ac 17:17

He r-ed in the synagogue every	Ac 18:4
a child, I r-ed like a child.	1Co 13:11

REBEKAH

Sister of Laban; wife of Isaac (Gn 24); mother of Jacob and Esau (25:21-26). Passed off as Isaac's sister (26:6-11). Encouraged Jacob to secure Isaac's blessing (27:1-17).

REBEL (n)

and don't associate with r-s.	Pr 24:21
were known as a r from birth.	Is 48:8
and was counted among the r-s;	Is 53:12
many and interceded for the r-s.	Is 53:12

REBEL (v)

Only don't r against the LORD,	Nm 14:9
because you both r-led against	Nm 20:24
r against the LORD's command,	1Sm 12:14
Are you r-ling against the king?	Neh 2:19
disobedient and r-led against	Neh 9:26
those who r against the light.	Jb 24:13
Why do the nations r and the peoples	Ps 2:1
for they r against You.	Ps 5:10
because they r-led against God's	Ps 107:11
he r-s against all sound judgment.	Pr 18:1
but they have r-led against Me.	Is 1:2
All of you have r-led against Me.	Jr 2:29
But they r-led against Me	Ezk 20:8
acted wickedly, r-led, and turned	Dn 9:5
them, for they r-led against Me.	Hs 7:13
Bethel and r; r even more at Gilgal!	Am 4:4
And if Satan r-s against himself	Mk 3:26
For who heard and r-led?	Heb 3:16

REBELLION

he has urged r against the LORD	Dt 13:5
For r is like the sin of divination,	1Sm 15:23
For he adds r to his sin;	Jb 34:37
of my youth or my acts of r;	Ps 25:7
compassion, blot out my r.	Ps 51:1
only You can atone for our r-s.	Ps 65:3
An evil man seeks only r;	Pr 17:11
the wicked increase, r increases	Pr 29:16
Indeed, our r-s are many;	Jr 14:7
he has preached r against the	Jr 29:32
the r that makes desolate,	Dn 8:13
What is the r of Jacob?	Mc 1:5
When you hear of wars and r-s	Lk 21:9
into prison for r and murder.	Lk 23:25

harden your hearts as in the r | Heb 3:8
and have perished in Korah's r. | Jd 11

REBELLIOUS

has a stubborn and r son who | Dt 21:18
I will teach the r Your ways, | Ps 51:13
a stubborn and r generation, | Ps 78:8
day long to a r people who walk | Is 65:2
because their r acts are many, | Jr 5:6
for they are a r house. | Ezk 2:6
all their leaders are r. | Hs 9:15
unbelieving and r generation! | Mt 17:17
there are also many r people, | Ti 1:10

REBUILD

to go up and r the LORD's house | Ezr 1:5
Come, let's r Jerusalem's wall | Neh 2:17
for the LORD will r Zion; | Ps 102:16
The LORD r-s Jerusalem; | Ps 147:2
He will r My city, and set My | Is 45:13
They will r the ancient ruins; | Is 61:4
and the ruins will be rebuilt. | Ezk 36:33
to restore and r Jerusalem until | Dn 9:25
and r it as in the days of old, | Am 9:11
sanctuary and r it in three days. | Mt 26:61
and will r David's tent, | Ac 15:16

REBUKE (n)

tremble, astounded at His r. | Jb 26:11
exposed, at Your r, LORD, at the | Ps 18:15
they perish at the r of Your | Ps 80:16
At Your r the waters fled; | Ps 104:7
a mocker doesn't listen to r. | Pr 13:1
ear that listens to life-giving r-s | Pr 15:31
A r cuts into a perceptive | Pr 17:10
to listen to r from a wise | Ec 7:5

REBUKE (v)

r-d them, cursed them, beat some | Neh 13:25
do not r me in Your anger; | Ps 6:1
You have r-d the nations: | Ps 9:5
one who r-s a wicked man will | Pr 9:7
r a wise man, and he will love you. | Pr 9:8
r the discerning, and he gains | Pr 19:25
One who r-s a person will later | Pr 28:23
The LORD r you, Satan! | Zch 3:2
He got up and r-d the winds | Mt 8:26
Peter ... began to r Him, | Mt 16:22
Then Jesus r-d the demon, | Mt 17:18
go and r him in private. | Mt 18:15
But the disciples r-d them. | Mt 19:13

r-d their unbelief and hardness | Mk 16:14
stood over her and r-d the fever, | Lk 4:39
brother sins, r him, | Lk 17:3
Teacher, r Your disciples. | Lk 19:39
Do not r an older man, | 1Tm 5:1
Publicly r those who sin, | 1Tm 5:20
profitable for teaching, for r-ing, | 2Tm 3:16
r, correct, and encourage with | 2Tm 4:2
So, r them sharply, that they | Ti 1:13
him, but said, "The Lord r you!" | Jd 9
many as I love, I r and discipline. | Rv 3:19

REBURIED

that a man found and r. | Mt 13:44

RECEDED

The water steadily r from the earth, | Gn 8:3

RECEIVE

I will r glory by means of Pharaoh | Ex 14:4
He will r blessing from the LORD | Ps 24:5
You r-d gifts from people, | Ps 68:18
who asks r-s, and the one who | Mt 7:8
You have r-d free of charge; | Mt 10:8
and immediately r-s it with joy | Mt 13:20
you will r whatever you ask for | Mt 21:22
believe that you have r-d them, | Mk 11:24
you have r-d your comfort. | Lk 6:24
from whom you expect to r | Lk 6:34
The blind r their sight, the | Lk 7:22
His own people did not r Him. | Jn 1:11
But to all who did r Him, He gave | Jn 1:12
have all r-d grace after grace | Jn 1:16
who r-s whomever I send r-s Me, | Jn 13:20
come back and r you to Myself, | Jn 14:3
Ask and you will r, | Jn 16:24
and said, "R the Holy Spirit. | Jn 20:22
But you will r power when the | Ac 1:8
and they r-d the Holy Spirit. | Ac 8:17
Did you r the Holy Spirit when | Ac 19:2
is more blessed to give than to r. | Ac 20:35
What do you have that you didn't r? | 1Co 4:7
but only one r-s the prize? | 1Co 9:24
For I r-d from the Lord what I | 1Co 11:23
most important what I also r-d: | 1Co 15:3
Don't r God's grace in vain. | 2Co 6:1
Did you r the Spirit by the | Gl 3:2
you r-d me as an angel of God, | Gl 4:14
as you have r-d Christ Jesus | Col 2:6
himself, who r-s tithes, | Heb 7:9

but they did not r what was	Heb 11:39
punishes every son whom He r-s.	Heb 12:6
should not expect to r anything	Jms 1:7
ask and don't r because you ask	Jms 4:3
had not r-d mercy, but now you	1Pt 2:10
Based on the gift they have r-d,	1Pt 4:10
and can r whatever we ask from	1Jn 3:22
do not r him into your home,	2Jn 10
what you have r-d and heard;	Rv 3:3
are worthy to r glory and honor	Rv 4:11
anyone who r-s the mark of his	Rv 14:11

RECITE

Moses r-d aloud every single	Dt 31:30
you are to r it day and night,	Jos 1:8
noble theme as I r my verses to	Ps 45:1
What right do you have to r My	Ps 50:16

RECKLESS

worthless and r men with this	Jdg 9:4
who is r only becomes poor.	Pr 21:5
which (leads to) r actions,	Eph 5:18
traitors, r, conceited, lovers of	2Tm 3:4

RECLINE

and r at the table with Abraham,	Mt 8:11
as He was r-ing at the table,	Mk 14:3
loved, was r-ing close beside	Jn 13:23

RECOGNITION

while he's seeking public r.	Jn 7:4
to give r to those who labor	1Th 5:12

RECOGNIZE

did not r him, because his hands	Gn 27:23
r-d his brothers, they did not r him	Gn 42:8
She does not r that it is I who gave	Hs 2:8
You'll r them by their fruit.	Mt 7:16
come, and they didn't r him.	Mt 17:12
these things, r that He is near	Mt 24:33
opened, and they r-d Him, but	Lk 24:31
yet the world did not r Him.	Jn 1:10
him because they r his voice	Jn 10:4
Jesus I know, and Paul I r—but	Ac 19:15
sin, in order to be r-d as sin,	Rm 7:13
on the flute or harp be r-d?	1Co 14:7
Therefore r such people.	1Co 16:18
But from those r-d as important	Gl 2:6

RECOMMENDATION

do we need letters of r-ation to you	2Co 3:1

RECOMPENSE

Him, and His r is before Him.	Is 62:11

RECONCILE

First go and be r-d with your	Mt 5:24
and tried to r them peacefully,	Ac 7:26
we were r-d to God through the	Rm 5:10
unmarried or be r-d to her	1Co 7:11
who r-d us to Himself through	2Co 5:18
was r-ing the world to Himself	2Co 5:19
Christ's behalf, "Be r-d to God."	2Co 5:20
that He might r both to God	Eph 2:16
through Him to r everything to	Col 1:20

RECONCILIATION

whom we have now received r.	Rm 5:11
if their being rejected is world r,	Rm 11:15
and gave us the ministry of r:	2Co 5:18
committed the message of r to us.	2Co 5:19

RECONSIDER

R; don't be unjust. R;	Jb 6:29
rashly and later to r his vows.	Pr 20:25

RECORD (n)

These are the r-s of the heavens	Gn 2:4
r-s of the descendants of Adam.	Gn 5:1
These are the family r-s of Noah.	Gn 6:9
the family r-s of Noah's sons,	Gn 10:1
These are the family r-s of Shem.	Gn 11:10
These are the family r-s of Terah.	Gn 11:27
are the family r-s of ... Ishmael,	Gn 25:12
These are the family r-s of Isaac	Gn 25:19
These are the family r-s of Esau	Gn 36:1
These are the family r-s of Jacob.	Gn 37:2
the family r-s of Aaron and Moses	Nm 3:1
written about in the Historical R	1Kg 14:19
r-s, but they could not be found,	Ezr 2:62
I found the genealogical r of those	Neh 7:5
The historical r of Jesus Christ	Mt 1:1
does not keep a r of wrongs;	1Co 13:5

RECORD (v)

I r-ed it on a scroll, sealed it	Jr 32:10
you what is r-ed in the book	Dn 10:21

RECOVER

bitten looks at it, he will r.	Nm 21:8
Will I r from this sickness?	2Kg 8:8

RECOVERY

shattered instantly—beyond r.	Pr 6:15
the captives and r of sight to	Lk 4:18

RECRUCIFYING

they are r the Son of God   Heb 6:6

RECRUITER

To please the r-er, no one serving   2Tm 2:4

RED

Let me eat some of that r stuff,   Gn 25:30
an unblemished r cow that has no   Nm 19:2
water ... was r like blood.   2Kg 3:22
for no reason? Who has r eyes?   Pr 23:29
Don't gaze at wine when it is r,   Pr 23:31
they are as r as crimson,   Is 1:18
Why is Your clothing r,   Is 63:2
shields of his warriors are dyed r;   Nah 2:3
saw a man riding on a r horse.   Zch 1:8
good weather because the sky is r.   Mt 16:2
another horse went out, a fiery r one,   Rv 6:4
There was a great fiery r dragon   Rv 12:3

RED SEA

Crossed by Israel (Ex 13:18; 14:15-31; Nm 21:4; Dt 11:4; Jos 2:10; 4:23; 24:6; Neh 9:9; Pss 106:7,9-11,22; 136:13-15; Ac 7:36; Heb 11:29); southern extent of the promised land (Ex 23:31); location of Solomon's fleet (1Kg 9:26).

REDDISH

one came out r, covered with   Gn 25:25

REDEEM

I will r you with an outstretched arm   Ex 6:6
You must r every firstborn   Ex 13:13
people You have r-ed with Your   Ex 15:13
One of his brothers may r him.   Lv 25:48
must certainly r the firstborn   Nm 18:15
and the LORD your God r-ed you;   Dt 15:15
who has r-ed my life from every   2Sm 4:9
to r a people for Himself,   2Sm 7:23
who has r-ed my life from every   1Kg 1:29
In famine He will r you from death,   Jb 5:20
r-ed my soul from going down to   Jb 33:28
r me and be gracious to me.   Ps 26:11
The LORD r-s the life of His   Ps 34:22
the price of r-ing him is too costly,   Ps 49:8
But God will r my life from   Ps 49:15
because You have r-ed me   Ps 71:23
With power You r-ed Your people,   Ps 77:15
He r-s your life from the Pit;   Ps 103:4
And He will r Israel from all   Ps 130:8

Is My hand too short to r?   Is 50:2
and you will be r-ed without silver.   Is 52:3
Though I want to r {them},   Hs 7:13
I will r them from death.   Hs 13:14
One who was about to r Israel.   Lk 24:21
Christ has r-ed us from the curse   Gl 3:13
to r those under the law,   Gl 4:5
Himself for us to r us from all   Ti 2:14
you were r-ed from your empty   1Pt 1:18
and You r-ed {people} for God by   Rv 5:9
144,000 who had been r-ed   Rv 14:3

REDEEMED (n)

Let the r of the LORD   Ps 107:2
But the r will walk {on it},   Is 35:9
a road for the r to pass over?   Is 51:10

REDEEMER

for you are a family r.   Ru 3:9
has not left you without a family r   Ru 4:14
I know my living R, and He will   Jb 19:25
LORD, my rock and my R.   Ps 19:14
the Most High God, their R.   Ps 78:35
for their R is strong,   Pr 23:11
Your R is the Holy One of Israel.   Is 41:14
LORD, your R, the Holy One   Is 48:17
The R will come to Zion,   Is 59:20
Your name is our R.   Is 63:16
Their R is strong; the LORD   Jr 50:34
God sent as a ruler and a r   Ac 7:35

REDEMPTION

You are to allow the r of any land   Lv 25:24
Take my right of r, because I can't   Ru 4:6
and with Him is r in abundance.   Ps 130:7
you own the right of r to buy it.   Jr 32:7
forward to the r of Jerusalem.   Lk 2:38
because your r is near!   Lk 21:28
through the r that is in Christ   Rm 3:24
adoption, the r of our bodies.   Rm 8:23
sanctification, and r,   1Co 1:30
In Him we have r through His   Eph 1:7
sealed you for the day of r.   Eph 4:30
in whom we have r,   Col 1:14
having obtained eternal r.   Heb 9:12

REDUCE

You cannot r your daily quota   Ex 5:19
the LORD began to r the size of   2Kg 10:32
He r-s princes to nothing and   Is 40:23
can r the measure while increasing   Am 8:5

REED

the basket among the r-s	Ex 2:5
Do r-s flourish without water?	Jb 8:11
He will not break a bruised r,	Is 42:3
A r swaying in the wind?	Mt 11:7
He will not break a bruised r	Mt 12:20
placed a r in His right hand	Mt 27:29
fixed it on a r, and offered	Mt 27:48
hitting Him on the head with a r	Mk 15:19

REEFS

like dangerous r at your love feasts.	Jd 12

REELED

they r and staggered like drunken	Ps 107:27

REFER

vision r-s to the time of the end.	Dn 8:17
He was r-ring to Judas,	Jn 6:71
your seed, r-ring to one,	Gl 3:16

REFINE

and a place where gold is r-d.	Jb 28:1
like silver r-d in an earthen furnace,	Ps 12:6
You r-d us as silver is r-d.	Ps 66:10
Look, I have r-d you, but not	Is 48:10
I am about to r them and test	Jr 9:7
fall so that they may be r-d,	Dn 11:35
I will r them as silver is r-d	Zch 13:9
and r them like gold and silver.	Mal 3:3
perishes though r-d by fire	1Pt 1:7
from Me gold r-d in the fire so	Rv 3:18

REFINER

a r—so you may know and assay	Jr 6:27
For He will be like a r-'s fire	Mal 3:2

REFLECT

on your bed, r in your heart	Ps 4:4
I r on the work of Your hands.	Ps 143:5
water r-s the face, so the heart r-s	Pr 27:19
No one r-s,	Is 44:19
are r-ing the glory of the Lord	2Co 3:18

REFLECTIONS

The r of the heart belong to man,	Pr 16:1

REFRAIN

But if you r from making a vow,	Dt 23:22
R from anger	Ps 37:8
no right to r from working?	1Co 9:6

REFRESH

day He rested and was r-ed.	Ex 31:17

he r-es the life of his masters.	Pr 25:13
r me with apricots,	Sg 2:5
r my heart in Christ.	Phm 20

REFRESHING (adj)

drink from Your r stream,	Ps 36:8

REFRESHING (n)

that seasons of r may come	Ac 3:19

REFUGE

will include six cities of r,	Nm 35:6
your cities of r, as I	Jos 20:2
come and find r in my shade.	Jdg 9:15
whose wings you have come for r.	Ru 2:12
my mountain where I seek r.	2Sm 22:3
to all who take r in Him.	2Sm 22:31
those who take r in Him are happy.	Ps 2:12
a r for the oppressed, a r in times of	Ps 9:9
I have taken r in the LORD.	Ps 11:1
God, for I take r in You.	Ps 16:1
God is our r and strength,	Ps 46:1
I will seek r in the shadow of	Ps 57:1
you will take r under His wings.	Ps 91:4
But the LORD is my r;	Ps 94:22
better to take r in the LORD	Ps 118:8
my shield, and I take r in Him;	Ps 144:2
and his children have a r.	Pr 14:26
righteous have a r when they die.	Pr 14:32
shield to those who take r in Him.	Pr 30:5
a r from the rain, a shade	Is 25:4
we have made falsehood our r	Is 28:15
and take r in Egypt's shadow.	Is 30:2
LORD will be a r for His people,	Jl 3:16
cares for those who take r in Him.	Nah 1:7
we who have fled for r might	Heb 6:18

REFUSE

But if you r to let My people go,	Ex 10:4
But Queen Vashti r-d to come	Est 1:12
oil for my head; let me not r it.	Ps 141:5
because they r to act justly.	Pr 21:7
because his hands r to work.	Pr 21:25
I did not r myself any pleasure	Ec 2:10
But if you r and rebel,	Is 1:20
but they r-d to accept discipline.	Jr 5:3
they r to know Me.	Jr 9:6
people, who r to listen to Me,	Jr 13:10
r-ing to be comforted for her	Jr 31:15
listen, and let the one who r-s, r	Ezk 3:27
and she r-d to be consoled	Mt 2:18

but the one who **r-s** to believe — Jn 3:36
But the Jews who **r-d** to believe — Ac 14:2
But **r** to enroll younger widows; — 1Tm 5:11
r-d to be called the son of — Heb 11:24

REFUTE

not one of you **r-d** his arguments. — Jb 32:12
and you will **r** any accusation — Is 54:17
For he vigorously **r-d** the Jews in — Ac 18:28
and to **r** those who contradict it. — Ti 1:9

REGAIN

so he may **r** his sight. — Ac 9:12

REGARD (n)

The LORD had **r** for Abel and his — Gn 4:4
They have no **r** for God. — Ps 54:3
I will have no **r** for your — Am 5:22
and had high **r** for His name. — Mal 3:16
judge you in **r** to food and drink — Col 2:16
worthless in **r** to the faith. — 2Tm 3:8

REGARD (v)

You are to **r** only the LORD of — Is 8:13
but we in turn **r-ed** Him stricken, — Is 53:4
He **r-s** them no more. — Lm 4:16
since they **r-ed** him as a prophet. — Mt 14:5
they **r-ed** Him as a prophet. — Mt 21:46
R-ing the gospel, they are enemies — Rm 11:28
r-ed as profane the blood of the — Heb 10:29
r the patience of our Lord as — 2Pt 3:15

REGENERATION

through the washing of **r** and — Ti 3:5

REGION

Joshua conquered the whole **r** — Jos 10:40
from remote **r-s** of the earth — Jr 31:8
withdrew to the **r** of Galilee. — Mt 2:22
went to the **r** of Judea across — Mt 19:1
to the **r** of the Gerasenes. — Mk 5:1
to beg Him to leave their **r**. — Mk 5:17
In the same **r**, shepherds were — Lk 2:8
the gospel to the **r-s** beyond you — 2Co 10:16

REGISTER

r-ed them in the Wilderness — Nm 1:19
Beer-sheba and **r** the troops so — 2Sm 24:2
All Israel was **r-ed** in the — 1Ch 9:1
people to be **r-ed** by genealogy — Neh 7:5
that the whole empire should be **r-ed**. — Lk 2:1

REGRET

LORD **r-ted** that He had made man — Gn 6:6
I **r** that I made Saul king, — 1Sm 15:11
He died to no one's **r** — 2Ch 21:20
I do not **r** it—even though I did **r** it — 2Co 7:8
a repentance not to be **r-ted** — 2Co 7:10
not out of **r** or out of necessity, — 2Co 9:7

REGULATIONS

law of the commandments in **r**, — Eph 2:15
Why do you submit to **r**: — Col 2:20
They are physical **r** and only — Heb 9:10

REGULAR

This will be a **r** burnt offering — Ex 29:42
fine flour as a **r** grain offering — Lv 6:20
The **r** bread {offering} is to be — Nm 4:7
This was Job's **r** practice. — Jb 1:5

REGULARLY

so that the lamp will burn **r**. — Lv 24:2

REHOBOAM

Son of Solomon; king of Judah (1Kg 11:43). Answered people harshly; the kingdom was divided (12:1-19; 2Ch 10:1-19).

REIGN

The LORD will **r** forever and ever! — Ex 15:18
that Saul should not **r** over us? — 1Sm 11:12
but now your **r** will not endure. — 1Sm 13:14
God **r-s** over the nations; — Ps 47:8
The LORD **r-s**! He is robed in — Ps 93:1
The LORD **r-s**. The world is — Ps 96:10
The LORD **r-s**! Let the earth — Ps 97:1
The LORD **r-s**! Let the peoples — Ps 99:1
The LORD **r-s** forever; — Ps 146:10
It is by me that kings **r** — Pr 8:15
He will **r** on the throne of David — Is 9:7
a king will **r** righteously, — Is 32:1
who says to Zion, "Your God **r-s**!" — Is 52:7
not have a son **r-ing** on his throne, — Jr 33:21
and bring in a **r** of violence. — Am 6:3
He will **r** over the house of — Lk 1:33
death **r-ed** from Adam to Moses, — Rm 5:14
sin **r-ed** in death ... grace will **r** — Rm 5:21
do not let sin **r** in your mortal — Rm 6:12
I wish you did **r**, so that we also — 1Co 4:8
For He must **r** until He puts all — 1Co 15:25
we will also **r** with Him; — 2Tm 2:12
and they will **r** on the earth. — Rv 5:10

and He will **r** forever and ever!	Rv 11:15
the Almighty, has begun to **r**!	Rv 19:6
will **r** with Him for 1,000 years.	Rv 20:6
And they will **r** forever and ever.	Rv 22:5

REIMBURSE

when I come back I'll **r** you	Lk 10:35

REJECT

you have **r**-ed the LORD who is	Nm 11:20
they have **r**-ed Me as their king.	1Sm 8:7
LORD, He has **r**-ed you as king.	1Sm 15:23
They **r**-ed His statutes and His	2Kg 17:15
So the LORD **r**-ed all the	2Kg 17:20
forsake Him, He will **r** you forever	1Ch 28:9
Why have You **r**-ed me?	Ps 43:2
God, You have **r**-ed us;	Ps 60:1
Will the Lord **r** forever and	Ps 77:7
The stone the builders **r**-ed has	Ps 118:22
You **r** all who stray from Your	Ps 119:118
do not **r** Your anointed one.	Ps 132:10
and don't **r** your mother's	Pr 1:8
the one who **r**-s correction goes	Pr 10:17
time he learns to **r** what is bad	Is 7:15
Because you have **r**-ed this message	Is 30:12
He was despised and **r**-ed by men,	Is 53:3
The Lord has **r**-ed His altar	Lm 2:7
Lord will not **r** {us} forever.	Lm 3:31
because they **r**-ed My ordinances,	Ezk 20:16
Because you have **r**-ed knowledge,	Hs 4:6
Israel has **r**-ed what is good;	Hs 8:3
because they have **r**-ed the law	Am 2:4
as though I had never **r**-ed them.	Zch 10:6
the builders **r**-ed has become	Mt 21:42
suffer many things, and be **r**-ed	Mk 8:31
they **r**-ed the plan of God for	Lk 7:30
Whoever **r**-s you **r**-s Me.	Lk 10:16
The one who **r**-s Me and doesn't	Jn 12:48
This Moses, whom they **r**-ed	Ac 7:35
has God **r**-ed His people?	Rm 11:1
who **r**-s this does not **r** man,	1Th 4:8
Some have **r**-ed these and have	1Tm 1:19
should be **r**-ed if it is received	1Tm 4:4
R a divisive person after a	Ti 3:10
not escape when they **r**-ed Him	Heb 12:25
r-ed by men but chosen and	1Pt 2:4
The stone that the builders **r**-ed	1Pt 2:7

REJOICE

and **r** before the LORD your God	Lv 23:40
R during your festival	Dt 16:14
My heart **r**-s in the LORD;	1Sm 2:1
to the city of David with **r**-ing.	2Sm 6:12
heavens be glad and the earth **r**,	1Ch 16:31
The righteous see {this} and **r**;	Jb 22:19
and **r** with trembling.	Ps 2:11
all who take refuge in You **r**;	Ps 5:11
my heart is glad, and my spirit **r**-s;	Ps 16:9
R in the LORD, you righteous	Ps 33:1
Then I will **r** in the LORD;	Ps 35:9
the bones You have crushed **r**.	Ps 51:8
righteous will **r** when he sees	Ps 58:10
But the king will **r** in God;	Ps 63:11
The humble will see it and **r**.	Ps 69:32
They **r** in Your name all day long	Ps 89:16
be glad and the earth **r**;	Ps 96:11
Let the earth **r**;	Ps 97:1
The upright see it and **r**,	Ps 107:42
let us **r** and be glad in it.	Ps 118:24
I **r** over Your promise like one	Ps 119:162
I **r**-d with those who said to me,	Ps 122:1
I was **r**-ing in His inhabited world,	Pr 8:31
the righteous thrive, a city **r**-s,	Pr 11:10
one who **r**-s over disaster will	Pr 17:5
the people **r**, but when the	Pr 29:2
R, young man, while you are	Ec 11:9
people will **r** in the Holy One	Is 29:19
But you will **r** in the LORD;	Is 41:16
R, barren one, who did not give	Is 54:1
I greatly **r** in the LORD, I exult	Is 61:10
as a bridegroom **r**-s over {his} bride,	
so your God will **r** over you.	Is 62:5
young and old men {**r**} together.	Jr 31:13
I will **r** over them to do what is	Jr 32:41
r and be glad, for the LORD has done	Jl 2:21
Do not **r** over me, my enemy!	Mc 7:8
He will **r** over you with gladness.	Zph 3:17
R greatly, Daughter Zion!	Zch 9:9
Be glad and **r**, because your	Mt 5:12
and many will **r** at his birth.	Lk 1:14
spirit has **r**-d in God my Savior,	Lk 1:47
but **r** that your names are written	Lk 10:20
same hour He **r**-d in the Holy	Lk 10:21
whole crowd was **r**-ing over all	Lk 13:17
R with me, because I have found	Lk 15:6,9
and reaper can **r** together.	Jn 4:36
see My day; he saw it and **r**-d.	Jn 8:56
would have **r**-d that I am going	Jn 14:28

and wail, but the world will **r**. | Jn 16:20
r-ing that they were counted | Ac 5:41
But he went on his way **r-ing**. | Ac 8:39
but we also **r** in our afflictions | Rm 5:3
R in hope; be patient in | Rm 12:12
R with those who **r**; | Rm 12:15
who **r** as though they did not **r**, | 1Co 7:30
but **r-s** in the truth; | 1Co 13:6
as grieving yet always **r-ing**; | 2Co 6:10
Finally, brothers, **r**. | 2Co 13:11
R, O barren woman who does not | Gl 4:27
And in this I **r**. Yes, and I will **r** | Php 1:18
R in the Lord always. I will say it
again: **R**! | Php 4:4
r-d in the Lord greatly that now | Php 4:10
Now I **r** in my sufferings for you | Col 1:24
R always! | 1Th 5:16
in Him and **r** with inexpressible | 1Pt 1:8
Therefore **r**, O heavens, | Rv 12:12

RELATION
you were put to death in **r** to the law | Rm 7:4

RELATIONS
not had sexual **r** with a man. | Gn 19:8
sexual **r** with the same girl, | Am 2:7
not to have **r** with a woman. | 1Co 7:1

RELATIONSHIP
What **r** do you have with the | Jos 22:24
had revealed her **r** to Mordecai. | Est 8:1
If the **r** of a man with his wife | Mt 19:10

RELATIVE
not to come near any close **r** for | Lv 18:6
The man is a close **r**. | Ru 2:20
r-s stop coming by, | Jb 19:14
my **r-s** stand at a distance. | Ps 38:11
call understanding {your} **r**. | Pr 7:4
in his hometown, among his **r-s**, | Mk 6:4
consider your **r** Elizabeth | Lk 1:36
None of your **r-s** has that name. | Lk 1:61
called together his **r-s** and close | Ac 10:24
does not provide for his own **r-s**, | 1Tm 5:8

RELEASE (n)
the LORD's **r** of debts has been | Dt 15:2

RELEASE (v)
goat ... and he will **r** it there. | Lv 16:22
It is to be **r-d** at the Jubilee, | Lv 25:28
a conflict is to **r** a flood; | Pr 17:14

r-d him, and forgave the loan. | Mt 18:27
do you want me to **r** for you? | Mt 27:21
Then he **r-d** Barabbas to them. | Mt 27:26
Do you want me to **r** the King | Mk 15:9
Pilate made every effort to **r** Him. | Jn 19:12
shouted, "If you **r** this man, | Jn 19:12
when he had decided to **r** Him. | Ac 3:13
After they were **r-d**, they went | Ac 4:23
the name of Jesus and **r-d** them. | Ac 5:40
sent orders for you to be **r-d**. | Ac 16:36
could have been **r-d** if he had | Ac 26:32
we have been **r-d** from the law, | Rm 7:6
R the four angels | Rv 9:14
Satan will be **r-d** from his prison | Rv 20:7

RELENT
but the LORD **r-ed** concerning | 2Sm 24:16
r-ed according to the abundance | Ps 106:45
I will not **r** or turn back from it. | Jr 4:28
so that I might **r** concerning the | Jr 26:3
not show pity, and I will not **r**. | Ezk 24:14
and He **r-s** from sending disaster. | Jl 2:13
may turn and **r** and leave a blessing | Jl 2:14
I will not **r** | Am 1:3,6,9,11,13; 2:1,4,6
The LORD **r-ed** concerning this. | Am 7:3,6
God may turn and **r**; | Jnh 3:9
so God **r-ed** from the disaster | Jnh 3:10
and One who **r-s** from {sending | Jnh 4:2
and would not **r**," says the LORD | Zch 8:14

RELIABLE
leaders don't think you are **r**. | 1Sm 29:6
the ordinances of the LORD are **r** | Ps 19:9
testimonies are completely **r**; | Ps 93:5
to teach you true and **r** words, | Pr 22:21
mirage to me—water that is not **r**. | Jr 15:18

RELIANCE
spoke boldly, in **r** on the Lord, | Ac 14:3

RELIEF
saying, "This one will bring us **r** | Gn 5:29
But when Pharaoh saw there was **r**, | Ex 8:15
soon as they had **r**, they again | Neh 9:28
Do not ignore my cry for **r**. | Lm 3:56
determined to send **r** to | Ac 11:29
had completed their **r** mission, | Ac 12:25

RELIEVE
when you **r** yourself, dig a hole | Dt 23:13
thought he was **r-ing** himself in | Jdg 3:24

and he went in to r himself.   1Sm 24:3
if I speak, my suffering is not **r-d**,   Jb 16:6

RELIGION
disagreements ... about their own r   Ac 25:19
the strictest party of our r I lived   Ac 26:5
practice their r toward their own   1Tm 5:4
holding to the form of r but denying   2Tm 3:5
his r is useless.   Jms 1:26
and undefiled r before our God   Jms 1:27

RELIGIOUS
are extremely r in every respect.   Ac 17:22
If anyone thinks he is r,   Jms 1:26

RELY
says: 'What are you **r-ing** on?'   2Kg 18:19
people **r-ied** on the words of King   2Ch 32:8
For the king **r-ies** on the LORD;   Ps 21:7
He **r-ies** on the LORD; let Him   Ps 22:8
not did believe God or r on His   Ps 78:22
for I r on Your commands.   Ps 119:66
do not r on your own understanding;   Pr 3:5
You have **r-ied** on your swords,   Ezk 33:26
Do not r on a friend; don't trust   Mc 7:5
all who {r on} the works of the law   Gl 3:10
gospel, **r-ing** on the power of God.   2Tm 1:8

REMAIN
My Spirit will not r with mankind   Gn 6:3
let any of it r until morning;   Ex 12:10
those you allow to r will become   Nm 33:55
of the land **r-s** to be possessed.   Jos 13:1
LORD, for no faithful one **r-s**;   Ps 12:1
with their **r-ing** wrath.   Ps 76:10
tells lies will r in my presence.   Ps 101:7
cannot be shaken; it **r-s** forever.   Ps 125:1
He **r-s** faithful forever,   Ps 146:6
wicked will not r on the earth.   Pr 10:30
comes, but the earth **r-s** forever.   Ec 1:4
my wisdom also **r-ed** with me.   Ec 2:9
the word of our God **r-s** forever.   Is 40:8
to Babylon and will r there until I   Jr 27:22
the wrath of God **r-s** on him.   Jn 3:36
you say, 'We see'—your sin **r-s**.   Jn 9:41
in Me would not r in darkness.   Jn 12:46
R in Me, and I in you.   Jn 15:4
R in My love.   Jn 15:9
and that your fruit should r,   Jn 15:16
If I want him to r until I come,   Jn 21:22
if you r in His kindness.   Rm 11:22

Each person should r in the life   1Co 7:20
three r: faith, hope, and love.   1Co 13:13
most of whom r to the present,   1Co 15:6
old covenant, the same veil **r-s**;   2Co 3:14
but to r in the flesh is more   Php 1:24
faithless, He **r-s** faithful, for   2Tm 2:13
they will perish, but You r.   Heb 1:11
Since it **r-s** for some to enter   Heb 4:6
of God—**r-s** a priest forever   Heb 7:3
no longer **r-s** a sacrifice for sins,   Heb 10:26
who says he **r-s** in Him should   1Jn 2:6
God's word **r-s** in you,   1Jn 2:14
they would have **r-ed** with us.   1Jn 2:19
Everyone who **r-s** in Him does not   1Jn 3:6
way we know that He **r-s** in us is   1Jn 3:24
the one who **r-s** in love **r-s** in God,
    and God **r-s** in him.   1Jn 4:16
Be alert and strengthen what **r-s**,   Rv 3:2
he must r for a little while.   Rv 17:10

REMARKABLE
and look at this r sight.   Ex 3:3
great and r day of the Lord comes.   Ac 2:20

REMARKABLY
been r and wonderfully made.   Ps 139:14

REMEDY
His people that there was no r.   2Ch 36:16
suddenly—and without a r.   Pr 29:1
You have multiplied **r-ies** in vain;   Jr 46:11
There is no r for your injury;   Nah 3:19

REMEMBER
God **r-ed** Noah,   Gn 8:1
will r My covenant between Me   Gn 9:15
Then God **r-ed** Rachel.   Gn 30:22
cupbearer did not r Joseph;   Gn 40:23
r-ed His covenant with Abraham,   Ex 2:24
R to dedicate the Sabbath day   Ex 20:8
I cause My name to be **r-ed**   Ex 20:24
R that you were a slave in   Dt 5:15
R the days of old; consider   Dt 32:7
Israelites did not r the LORD   Jdg 8:34
Hannah, and the LORD **r-ed** her.   1Sm 1:19
R the wonderful works He has   1Ch 16:12
R that my life is {but} a breath.   Jb 7:7
what is man that You r him,   Ps 8:4
Do not r the sins of my youth   Ps 25:7
I r this as I pour out my heart: Ps 42:4
{R} Mount Zion where You dwell.   Ps 74:2

At night I **r** my music; Ps 77:6
They **r-ed** that God was their rock, Ps 78:35
R how short my life is. Ps 89:47
made of, **r-ing** that we are dust. Ps 103:14
R the wonderful works He has Ps 105:5
R me, LORD, when You show Ps 106:4
He **r-s** His covenant forever. Ps 111:5
LORD **r-s** us and will bless us. Ps 115:12
r David and all the hardships Ps 132:1
and wept when we **r-ed** Zion. Ps 137:1
Yet no one **r-ed** that poor man. Ec 9:15
So **r** your Creator in the days Ec 12:1
own sake and **r** your sins no more. Is 43:25
do not ... **r** {our} iniquity forever. Is 64:9
R Your covenant with us; Jr 14:21
and never again **r** their sin. Jr 31:34
Yahweh, **r** what has happened to us. Lm 5:1
your survivors will **r** Me among Ezk 6:9
In {Your} wrath **r** mercy! Hab 3:2
Don't you **r** the five loaves Mt 16:9
Peter **r-ed** the words Jesus Mt 26:75
And **r**, I am with you always, Mt 28:20
and **r-ed** His holy covenant Lk 1:72
R Lot's wife! Lk 17:32
r me when You come into Your Lk 23:42
R how He spoke to you when He Lk 24:6
disciples **r-ed** that He had said this. Jn 2:22
asked only that we would **r** the poor, Gl 2:10
r that at one time you were Eph 2:11
R my imprisonment. Col 4:18
r-ing you constantly in our 1Th 1:3
constantly **r** you in my prayers 2Tm 1:3
R-ing your tears, I long to see you 2Tm 1:4
man, that You **r** him, or the Heb 2:6
will never again **r** their sins Heb 8:12; 10:17
R the earlier days when, Heb 10:32
R the prisoners, as though Heb 13:3
R your leaders who have Heb 13:7
so that you can **r** the words 2Pt 3:2
R then how far you have fallen; Rv 2:5

REMEMBRANCE

a grain offering for **r** Nm 5:15
there is no **r** of You in death; Ps 6:5
The **r** of the righteous is a blessing, Pr 10:7
is no lasting **r** of the wise man Ec 2:16
So a book of **r** was written Mal 3:16
Do this in **r** of Me. Lk 22:19; 1Co 11:24
to my God for every **r** of you, Php 1:3

REMIND

r you of everything I have told you. Jn 14:26
R them of these things, 2Tm 2:14
I will always **r** you about these 2Pt 1:12
Now I want to **r** you, though you Jd 5

REMINDER

and as a **r** on your forehead, Ex 13:9
scroll as a **r** and recite it Ex 17:14
there is a **r** of sins every year. Heb 10:3
to wake you up with a **r**, 2Pt 1:13

REMNANT

establish you as a **r** within the land Gn 45:7
For a **r** will go out from 2Kg 19:31
our God to preserve a **r** for us Ezr 9:8
The **r** will return, the **r** of Jacob, Is 10:21
sand of the sea, only a **r** of them Is 10:22
as a vine the **r** of Israel. Jr 6:9
I will gather the **r** of My flock Jr 23:3
forgive those I leave as a **r**. Jr 50:20
I will leave a **r** when you are Ezk 6:8
I will collect the **r** of Israel. Mc 2:12
will become a **r** for our God; Zch 9:7
only the **r** will be saved; Rm 9:27
present time a **r** chosen by grace Rm 11:5

REMORSE

was full of **r** and returned the Mt 27:3

REMOTE

gather them from **r** regions of Jr 31:8
by boat to a **r** place to be alone. Mt 14:13
to a **r** place and rest a little. Mk 6:31

REMOTEST

in the **r** parts of the North. Is 14:13
from the **r** parts of the north Ezk 38:6

REMOVAL

result of the **r** of his sin will be Is 27:9
for the **r** of sin by the sacrifice Heb 9:26
the **r** of what can be shaken Heb 12:27
not the **r** of the filth of the flesh, 1Pt 3:21

REMOVE

r his sandal from his foot, and spit Dt 25:9
R the sandals from your feet, Jos 5:15
the redeemer **r-d** his sandal and Ru 4:8
and **r-d** all of the idols 1Kg 15:12
He **r-d** the high places and 2Kg 18:4
Josiah also **r-d** all the shrines 2Kg 23:19
I will also **r** Judah from My 2Kg 23:27

He r-s mountains without their   Jb 9:5
You r-d my sackcloth and clothed   Ps 30:11
R Your torment from me;   Ps 39:10
so far has He r-d our   Ps 103:12
R sorrow from your heart,   Ec 11:10
His anger is not r-d,   Is 5:25; 9:12; 10:4
My love will not be r-d from you   Is 54:10
you will be r-d from your land.   Jr 27:10
I will r your heart of stone and   Ezk 36:26
r-s kings and establishes kings   Dn 2:21
LORD has r-d your punishment;   Zph 3:15
I have r-d your guilt from you,   Zch 3:4
"R the stone," Jesus said.   Jn 11:39
saw that the stone had been r-d   Jn 20:1
to the Lord, the veil is r-d.   2Co 3:16
slander must be r-d from you,   Eph 4:31
come to you and r your lampstand   Rv 2:5

RENDER

partiality when r-ing judgment;   Dt 1:17
Hosts says this: R true justice.   Zch 7:9
R service with a good attitude,   Eph 6:7

RENEW

so we can r the kingship there.   1Sm 11:14
He r-s my life; He leads me along   Ps 23:3
and r a steadfast spirit within me. Ps 51:10
youth is r-ed like the eagle.   Ps 103:5
and You r the face of the earth.   Ps 104:30
the LORD will r their strength;   Is 40:31
r our days as in former times,   Lm 5:21
by the r-ing of your mind,   Rm 12:2
person is being r-ed day by day.   2Co 4:16
you are being r-ed in the spirit   Eph 4:23
last you have r-ed your care for   Php 4:10
who is being r-ed in knowledge   Col 3:10
is impossible to r to repentance   Heb 6:4

RENEWAL

regeneration and r by the Holy Spirit.   Ti 3:5

RENOUNCE

care about myself; I r my life.   Jb 9:21
and r-s them will find mercy.   Pr 28:13
have r-d shameful secret things,   2Co 4:2
have r-d their original pledge.   1Tm 5:12

RENOVATE

r-d the altar of the LORD that   2Ch 15:8
it to heart to r the LORD's   2Ch 24:4

RENTED

If it was r, the loss is covered by   Ex 22:15
whole years in his own r house.   Ac 28:30

REPAIR

he r-ed the LORD's altar that   1Kg 18:30
priests had not r-ed the damage   2Kg 12:6
LORD's temple to r the damage.   2Kg 22:5
walls, and r-ing its foundations.   Ezr 4:12
I will r its gaps, restore its   Am 9:11

REPAY

have you repaid evil for good?   Gn 44:4
he must r double.   Ex 22:4
Is this how you r the LORD,   Dt 32:6
Vengeance belongs to Me; I will r.   Dt 32:35
God has repaid me for what I have   Jdg 1:7
May the LORD r you with good   1Sm 24:19
Should God r {you} on your terms   Jb 34:33
LORD repaid me according to my   Ps 18:24
R them according to the work   Ps 28:4
but fully r-s the arrogant.   Ps 31:23
They r me evil for good, making   Ps 35:12
For You r each according to his   Ps 62:12
deserve or repaid us according to   Ps 103:10
How can I r the LORD all the good   Ps 116:12
righteous will be repaid on earth,   Pr 11:31
Won't He r a person according to   Pr 24:12
I will not keep silent, but I will r;   Is 65:6
I will first r them double for   Jr 16:18
Should good be repaid with evil?   Jr 18:20
He will certainly r.   Jr 51:56
will be repaid at the resurrection   Lk 14:14
He will r each one according to   Rm 2:6
Do not r anyone evil for evil.   Rm 12:17
I will r, says the Lord.   Rm 12:19
each may be repaid for what he   2Co 5:10
that no one r-s evil for evil   1Th 5:15
first and to r their parents,   1Tm 5:4
The Lord will r him according to   2Tm 4:14
I will r it—not to mention   Phm 19
Vengeance belongs to Me, I will r   Heb 10:30
is with Me to r each person   Rv 22:12

REPEAT

R them to your children.   Dt 6:7
remember the battle and never r it!   Jb 41:8
so a fool r-s his foolishness.   Pr 26:11
God r-s what has passed.   Ec 3:15

REPEATEDLY
priests enter the first room r   Heb 9:6

REPEL
the blind and lame can r you,   2Sm 5:6

REPENT
and r and petition You   1Kg 8:47
and r in dust and ashes.   Jb 42:6
they r-ed and searched for God.   Ps 78:34
After I returned, I r-ed;   Jr 31:19
R, r of your evil ways!   Ezk 33:11
because they refused to r.   Hs 11:5
R, because the kingdom of heaven   Mt 3:2
would have r-ed in sackcloth   Mt 11:21
R and believe in the good news!   Mk 1:15
but unless you r, you will all   Lk 13:3
one sinner who r-s than over 99   Lk 15:7
and if he r-s, forgive him.   Lk 17:3
R ... and be baptized,   Ac 2:38
Therefore r and turn back,   Ac 3:19
all people everywhere to r.   Ac 17:30
they should r and turn to God,   Ac 26:20
r, and do the works you did at first.   Rv 2:5
they did not r and give Him glory.   Rv 16:9

REPENTANCE
Take words {of r} with you   Hs 14:2
fruit consistent with r.   Mt 3:8
baptize you with water for r.   Mt 3:11
a baptism of r for the forgiveness   Mk 1:4
righteous, but sinners to r.   Lk 5:32
people who don't need r.   Lk 15:7
r for forgiveness of sins will be   Lk 24:47
God has granted r resulting   Ac 11:18
baptism of r to all the people   Ac 13:24
with a baptism of r,   Ac 19:4
and do works worthy of r.   Ac 26:20
kindness is intended to lead you to r   Rm 2:4
godly grief produces a r   2Co 7:10
will grant them r to know   2Tm 2:25
foundation of r from dead works,   Heb 6:1
renew to r those who were   Heb 6:4
find any opportunity for r   Heb 12:17
to perish, but all to come to r.   2Pt 3:9

REPHAIM
Pre-Israelite inhabitants of Palestine (Gn 14:5; Dt 2:11,20,21; 3:11,13; Jos 12:4; 13:12; 17:15); valley near Jerusalem named for them (Jos 15:8; 18:16; 2Sm 5:18,22; 23:13).

REPLANTED
and have r what was desolate   Ezk 36:36

REPLASTER
plaster to r the house.   Lv 14:42

REPLICA
Look at the r of the LORD's altar   Jos 22:28

REPORT (n)
You must not spread a false r.   Ex 23:1
gave a negative r to the   Nm 13:32

REPORT (v)
a messenger came to Job and r-ed: Jb 1:14
r back to me so that I too can   Mt 2:8
Go and r to John what you hear   Mt 11:4
It has been r-ed to me about you   1Co 1:11
It is widely r-ed that there is   1Co 5:1

REPRESENT
one to r the people before God   Ex 18:19
and Oholibah r-s Jerusalem.   Ezk 23:4
that you saw r-s the kings   Dn 8:20
the women r the two covenants.   Gl 4:24
fine linen r-s the righteous   Rv 19:8

REPRIMAND (n)
Better an open r than concealed   Pr 27:5

REPRIMAND (v)
never once r-ed him by saying   1Kg 1:6

REPROACH
You make us an object of r to   Ps 44:13
you will no longer experience r   Ezk 36:30
must be above r, the husband of   1Tm 3:2
message is to be sound beyond r,   Ti 2:8
For he considered r for the sake   Heb 11:26

REPTILE
animals, birds, r-s, and fish.   1Kg 4:33
hiding places like r-s slithering   Mc 7:17
animals and r-s of the earth,   Ac 10:12
four-footed animals, and r-s.   Rm 1:23
animal or bird, r or fish—is tamed   Jms 3:7

REPUDIATED
You have **r** the covenant with	Ps 89:39
His altar, **r** His sanctuary;	Lm 2:7

REPULSIVE
eaten on the third day, it is a **r** thing;	Lv 19:7
and Israel is now **r** to the	1Sm 13:4
you have become **r** to your father	2Sm 16:21
and my own children find me **r**.	Jb 19:17
You have made me **r** to them.	Ps 88:8

REPUTATION
His **r** extended to all the	1Kg 4:31
Your **r**, LORD, through all	Ps 135:13
seven men of good **r**,	Ac 6:3
who has a good **r** with the whole	Ac 10:22
having a good **r** with all the	Ac 22:12
these have a **r** of wisdom	Col 2:23
have a good **r** among outsiders,	1Tm 3:7
you have a **r** for being alive,	Rv 3:1

REQUEST (n)
And God granted his **r**.	1Ch 4:10
spare my life—[this is] my **r**;	Est 7:3
May the LORD fulfill all your **r-s**.	Ps 20:5
have not denied the **r** of his lips.	Ps 21:2
every prayer and **r**, pray at all	Eph 6:18
your **r-s** be made known to God.	Php 4:6
His ears are open to their **r**.	1Pt 3:12

REQUEST (v)
the evil of **r-ing** a king	1Sm 12:19
and you have not **r-ed** riches,	2Ch 1:11
the people a prisoner they **r-ed**.	Mk 15:6
and **r-ed** letters from him to the	Ac 9:2

REQUIRE
I will **r** the life of every	Gn 9:5
what it is the LORD **r-s** of you:	Mc 6:8
Much will be **r-d** of everyone	Lk 12:48
reveal it as I am **r-d** to speak.	Col 4:4
given us everything **r-d** for life	2Pt 1:3

REQUIREMENT
do not know the **r-s** of the LORD	Jr 8:7
commandments and **r-s** of the	Lk 1:6
man keeps the law's **r-s**,	Rm 2:26
in order that the law's **r** would	Rm 8:4

RESCUE
So the people **r-d** Jonathan,	1Sm 14:45
LORD who **r-d** me from the paw	1Sm 17:37
Turn, LORD! **R** me;	Ps 6:4

r-d me because He delighted in me.	Ps 18:19
You **r** me from violent men.	Ps 18:48
relies on the LORD; let Him **r** him;	Ps 22:8
those who fear Him, and **r-s** them.	Ps 34:7
R my life from their ravages,	Ps 35:17
I will **r** you, and you will honor	Ps 50:15
R me from the miry mud;	Ps 69:14
R the poor and needy;	Ps 82:4
r-d them many times, but they	Ps 106:43
He **r-d** them from the Pit.	Ps 107:20
R me from my enemies, LORD;	Ps 143:9
It will **r** you from a forbidden	Pr 2:16
righteousness **r-s** from death.	Pr 10:2; 11:4
speech of the upright **r-s** them.	Pr 12:6
if you **r** him, you'll have to do	Pr 19:19
and you will **r** his life from	Pr 23:14
R those being taken off to death,	Pr 24:11
But even if He does not **r** us,	Dn 3:18
been able to **r** you from the lions?	Dn 6:20
not be able to **r** them on the day	Zph 1:18
His trust in God; let God **r** Him	Mt 27:43
Who will **r** me from this body of	Rm 7:24
to **r** us from this present evil age,	Gl 1:4
has **r-d** us from the domain of	Col 1:13
r-s us from the coming wrath.	1Th 1:10
the Lord **r-d** me from them all.	2Tm 3:11
I was **r-d** from the lion's mouth.	2Tm 4:17
The Lord will **r** me from every	2Tm 4:18
Lord knows how to **r** the godly	2Pt 2:9

RESCUER
and there will be no **r**.	Ps 50:22

RESEMBLE
we would **r** Gomorrah.	Is 1:9
God for images **r-ing** mortal man,	Rm 1:23
but **r-ing** the Son of God	Heb 7:3

RESERVE
which I hold in **r** for times of	Jb 38:23
the hope **r-d** for you in heaven	Col 1:5
there is **r-d** for me the crown	2Tm 4:8
darkness has been **r-d** for them.	2Pt 2:17
for whom is **r-d** the blackness	Jd 13

RESERVOIR
He made the cast {metal} **r**,	1Kg 7:23

RESIDE
the foreigner who **r-s** among you.	Ex 12:49
for I, the LORD, **r** among	Nm 35:34

the place where Your glory r-s.   Ps 26:8
Your instruction r-s within me.   Ps 40:8
the tent where He r-d among men.   Ps 78:60
are those who r in Your house,   Ps 84:4
Wisdom r-s in the heart of the   Pr 14:33
Christ's power may r in me.   2Co 12:9
has eternal life r-ing in him.   1Jn 3:15
how can God's love r in him?   1Jn 3:17

RESIDENCE

I will place My r among you,   Lv 26:11
David took up r in the   2Sm 5:9
servants' r, his attendants'   1Kg 10:5
a place for Your r forever.   2Ch 6:2
be a royal r and to display   Dn 4:30
flesh and took up r among us.   Jn 1:14
this time of temporary r.   1Pt 1:17

RESIDENT

whether a foreign r or native   Ex 12:19
the poor and the foreign r   Lv 19:10
and temporary r-s in Canaan,   Ps 105:12
temporary r-s on the earth.   Heb 11:13
To the temporary r-s of the   1Pt 1:1
as aliens and temporary r-s to   1Pt 2:11

RESIST

one person, two can r him.   Ec 4:12
tell you, don't r an evildoer.   Mt 5:39
are always r-ing the Holy Spirit; Ac 7:51
For who can r His will?   Rm 9:19
the one who r-s the authority is Rm 13:2
may be able to r in the evil day Eph 6:13
as Jannes and Jambres r-ed Moses,
  so these also r the truth,   2Tm 3:8
have not yet r-ed to the point   Heb 12:4
r-s the proud, but gives grace to Jms 4:6
But r the Devil, and he will flee Jms 4:7
because God r-s the proud, but   1Pt 5:5
R him, firm in the faith,   1Pt 5:9

RESOLUTION

be ranting and raving but no r.   Pr 29:9

RESOLVE

am r-d to obey Your statutes to Ps 119:112
for a man to r a dispute,   Pr 20:3
All who r to go to Egypt to live Jr 42:17
As I r-d to treat you badly when Zch 8:14
Paul r-d in the Spirit to pass   Ac 19:21
arm yourselves also with the same r 1Pt 4:1

RESOUND

sea and all that fills it r.   Ps 96:11
and those who live in it, r.   Ps 98:7
Praise Him with r-ing cymbals; Ps 150:5
and destruction r in her.   Jr 6:7
the tumult of their voice r-s   Jr 51:55

RESPECT (n)

showing no r for the old and   Dt 28:50
elders are shown no r.   Lm 5:12
extremely religious in every r.   Ac 17:22
r to those you owe r,   Rm 13:7
be worthy of r, not hypocritical 1Tm 3:8
masters to be worthy of all r,   1Tm 6:1
worthy of r, sensible, and sound Ti 2:2
to your masters with all r,   1Pt 2:18
do this with gentleness and r,   1Pt 3:16

RESPECT (v)

Each of you is to r his mother   Lv 19:3
The priests are not r-ed;   Lm 4:16
'They will r my son,' he said.   Mt 21:37
who didn't fear God or r man.   Lk 18:2
the wife is to r her husband.   Eph 5:33
discipline us, and we r-ed them. Heb 12:9
Marriage must be r-ed by all,   Heb 13:4

RESPECTABLE

sensible, r, hospitable, an able   1Tm 3:2

RESPECTFULLY

to deal r with the holy offerings Lv 22:2

RESPLENDENT

You are r and majestic   Ps 76:4

RESPOND

advise me to r to these people?   1Kg 12:6

RESPONSIBLE

I myself am r for the lives   1Sm 22:22
hold you r for his blood.   Ezk 3:18; 33:8
may be held r for the blood   Lk 11:50

RESPONSIBILITY

the boy's r-ies and mission be?   Jdg 13:12
their r-ies to offer praise   2Ch 8:14
is your r, and we support you.   Ezr 10:4

REST (n)

ark came to r in the seventh month, Gn 8:4
be a Sabbath of complete r,   Ex 31:15
and I will give you r.   Ex 33:14
LORD your God will give you r,   Jos 1:13

give you r from all your enemies. 2Sm 7:11
and there the weary find r. Jb 3:17
by night, yet I have no r. Ps 22:2
I would fly away and find r. Ps 55:6
I am at r in God alone; Ps 62:1
They will not enter My r. Ps 95:11
Return to your r, my soul, Ps 116:7
observe my travels and my r; Ps 139:3
folding of the arms to r, Pr 6:10; 24:33
Better one handful with r, Ec 4:6
LORD gives you r from your pain Is 14:3
This is the place of r, let the weary r Is 28:12
and find r for yourselves. Jr 6:16
and I will give you r. Mt 11:28
you will find r for yourselves. Mt 11:29
but to the r it is in parables, Lk 8:10
waterless places looking for r, Lk 11:24
I had no r in my spirit because 2Co 2:13
into Macedonia, we had no r. 2Co 7:5
you will not grieve like the r, 1Th 4:13
{to reward} with r you who are 2Th 1:7
They will not enter My r. Heb 3:11
A Sabbath r remains, therefore Heb 4:9
every effort to enter that r, Heb 4:11
There is no r day or night for Rv 14:11

REST (v)
He r-ed on the seventh day Gn 2:2
people r-ed on the seventh day. Ex 16:30
six days but r on the seventh Ex 23:12
As the Spirit r-ed on them, they Nm 11:25
God's friendship r-ed on my tent, Jb 29:4
my body also r-s securely. Ps 16:9
at night, his mind does not r. Ec 2:23
Spirit of the LORD will r on Him Is 11:2
Are you still sleeping and r-ing? Mt 26:45
to a remote place and r a while. Mk 6:31
like a dove, and He r-ed on Him. Jn 1:32
to them and r-ed on each one of Ac 2:3
yourself a Jew, and r in the law, Rm 2:17
seventh day God r-ed from all Heb 4:4
of glory and of God r-s on you. 1Pt 4:14
let them r from their labors, Rv 14:13

RESTING PLACE
but the dove found no r for her foot. Gn 8:9
you have not yet come into the r Dt 12:9
there will be no r for ... your foot. Dt 28:65
to build a house as a r for the ark 1Ch 28:2
God, {come} to Your r, 2Ch 6:41

may my cry for help find no r. Jb 16:18
LORD, come to Your r, Ps 132:8
This is My r forever; Ps 132:14
His r will be glorious. Is 11:10
they have forgotten their r. Jr 50:6
What sort of house ... what is My r? Ac 7:49

RESTITUTION
A thief must make full r. Ex 22:3
make full r for it and add a fifth Lv 6:5
this is the law of the r offering; Lv 7:1
Fools mock at making r, Pr 14:9
When You make Him a r offering, Is 53:10

RESTLESS
You will be a r wanderer Gn 4:12
I am r and in turmoil with my Ps 55:2
It is a r evil, full of deadly Jms 3:8

RESTORATION
until the times of the r of all things, Ac 3:21
until the time of r. Heb 9:10

RESTORE
r-d the chief cupbearer to his Gn 40:21
then He will r your fortunes, Dt 30:3
May You r them to the land You 1Kg 8:34
whose son he had r-d to life, 2Kg 8:1
God will r his righteousness to him. Jb 33:26
the LORD r-d his prosperity and Jb 42:10
When the LORD r-s His captive Ps 14:7
R the joy of Your salvation to me, Ps 51:12
When God r-s His captive people Ps 53:6
You have been angry. R us! Ps 60:1
R us, God; look {on us} with Ps 80:3
R our fortunes, LORD, like Ps 126:4
I will r your judges to what Is 1:26
bring them up and r them to this Jr 27:22
R me, and I will return, for you Jr 31:18
LORD, r us to Yourself, so we Lm 5:21
kingdom will be r-d to you as Dn 4:26
of the decree to r and rebuild Dn 9:25
when I r the fortunes of Judah Jl 3:1
that I will r double to you. Zch 9:12
is coming and will r everything, Mt 17:11
it out, and his hand was r-d. Mk 3:5
are You r-ing the kingdom to Israel? Ac 1:6
Be r-d, be encouraged, 2Co 13:11
spiritual should r such a person Gl 6:1
prayers I will be r-d to you. Phm 22
Jesus, will personally r, establish, 1Pt 5:10

RESTRAIN

I will not r my mouth.	Jb 7:11
intelligent person r-s his words,	Pr 17:27
all this, will You r Yourself?	Is 64:12
they set out to r Him, because	Mk 3:21
no one was able to r him any more	Mk 5:3
know what currently r-s {him},	2Th 2:6
r-ing the four winds of the earth	Rv 7:1

RESTRAINT

have cast off r in my presence.	Jb 30:11
free ourselves from their r-s.	Ps 2:3
of His kindness, r, and patience,	Rm 2:4
because in His r God passed over	Rm 3:25
not to put a r on you, but	1Co 7:35

RESTRICT

who was r-ed {to his house}.	Neh 6:10
commanded Baruch, "I am r-ed;	Jr 36:5
For the wicked r the righteous;	Hab 1:4

RESULT

to bring about the present r	Gn 50:20
The r of humility is fear of the	Pr 22:4
judgment, r-ing in condemnation,	Rm 5:16
with you was not without r.	1Th 2:1

RESURRECTED

and He will be r on the third	Mt 20:19
have been r, I will go ahead	Mt 26:32
For He has been r, just as He said.	Mt 28:6
He has been r! He is not here!	Mk 16:6
saw Him after He had been r.	Mk 16:14
God has r this Jesus.	Ac 2:32

RESURRECTION

Sadducees, who say there is no r,	Mt 22:23
in the r, whose wife will she be	Mt 22:28
out of the tombs after His r,	Mt 27:53
repaid at the r of the righteous.	Lk 14:14
since they are sons of the r.	Lk 20:36
the r of life ... the r of judgment.	Jn 5:29
rise again in the r at the last day.	Jn 11:24
I am the r and the life.	Jn 11:25
a witness with us of His r.	Ac 1:22
news about Jesus and the r.	Ac 17:18
hope of the r of the dead	Ac 23:6
there is going to be a r	Ac 24:15
Son of God by the r from the dead	Rm 1:4
be in the likeness of His r,	Rm 6:5
if there is no r of the dead,	1Co 15:13

So it is with the r of the dead:	1Co 15:42
know Him and the power of His r	Php 3:10
saying that the r has already	2Tm 2:18
of hands, the r of the dead,	Heb 6:2
they might gain a better r,	Heb 11:35
through the r of Jesus	1Pt 1:3; 3:21
This is the first r.	Rv 20:5

RETAIN

tribes is to r its inheritance.	Nm 36:9
Do you still r your integrity?	Jb 2:9
r {the sins of} any, they are r-ed.	Jn 20:23

RETRIBUTION

will rejoice when he sees the r;	Ps 58:10
God's r is coming;	Is 35:4
for the LORD is a God of r;	Jr 51:56
the days of r have come.	Hs 9:7
I will bring r on your heads.	Jl 3:7
a pitfall and a r to them.	Rm 11:9

RETRIEVED

r the body of Saul	1Sm 31:12

RETURN (n)

lend, expecting nothing in r.	Lk 6:35

RETURN (v)

you are dust, and you will r to dust.	Gn 3:19
and r to Him with all your heart	Dt 30:10
and when they r to You with	1Kg 8:48
away from you if you r to Him.	2Ch 30:9
But if you r to Me and carefully	Neh 1:9
and sinners will r to You.	Ps 51:13
R, God of Hosts.	Ps 80:14
You r mankind to the dust,	Ps 90:3
leaves him, he r-s to the ground	Ps 146:4
None r who go to her;	Pr 2:19
As a dog r-s to its vomit, so a	Pr 26:11
{it r-s} to its place where it	Ec 1:5
from dust, and all r to dust.	Ec 3:20
the spirit r-s to God who gave	Ec 12:7
a remnant of them will r.	Is 10:22
the Lord will r and come to Zion	Is 51:11
mouth will not r to Me empty,	Is 55:11
For I will r them to their land	Jr 16:15
they will r to Me with all	Jr 24:7
Restore me, and I will r,	Jr 31:18
After I r-ed, I repented;	Jr 31:19
restore us to Yourself, so we may r;	Lm 5:21
Come, let us r to the LORD.	Hs 6:1

But you must r to your God.	Hs 12:6
and r to the LORD your God.	Jl 2:13
yet you did not r to Me	Am 4:6
R to Me ... and I will r to you,	Zch 1:3
R to Me, and I will r to you,	Mal 3:7
let your peace r to you.	Mt 10:13
shepherds r-ed, glorifying and	Lk 2:20
Her spirit r-ed, and she got up	Lk 8:55
the apostles r-ed, they reported	Lk 9:10
but if not, it will r to you.	Lk 10:6
And r-ing, it finds {the house}	Lk 11:25
He did not revile in r;	1Pt 2:23
A dog r-s to its own vomit, and	2Pt 2:22

REUBEN

Son of Jacob and Leah; eldest (Gn 29:32). Lost birthright for sleeping with father's concubine (35:22; 49:4; 1Ch 5:1). Tried to rescue Joseph (Gn 37:21-29); offered to protect Benjamin (42:37). Tribe with territory east of the Dead Sea, north of the Arnon River (Nm 32; Jos 13:15-23).

REVEAL

that God had r-ed Himself to him	Gn 35:7
but the r-ed things belong to us	Dt 29:29
LORD had not yet been r-ed to	1Sm 3:7
r-s mysteries from the darkness	Jb 12:22
The LORD has r-ed Himself;	Ps 9:16
You r the path of life to me;	Ps 16:11
r to me the end of my life and	Ps 39:4
R to me the way I should go,	Ps 143:8
The one who r-s secrets is a	Pr 20:19
will be r-ed in the assembly	Pr 26:26
the arm of the LORD been r-ed to	Is 53:1
God in heaven who r-s mysteries,	Dn 2:28
nothing without r-ing His counsel	Am 3:7
and r-s His thoughts to man,	Am 4:13
learned and r-ed them to infants	Mt 11:25
whom the Son desires to r Him.	Mt 11:27
blood did not r this to you,	Mt 16:17
is concealed except to be r-ed,	Mk 4:22
of many hearts may be r-ed.	Lk 2:35
the day the Son of Man is r-ed.	Lk 17:30
Father's side—He has r-ed Him.	Jn 1:18
him and will r Myself to him.	Jn 14:21
Jesus r-ed Himself again to His	Jn 21:1
righteousness is r-ed from faith	Rm 1:17
God's wrath is r-ed from heaven	Rm 1:18
that is going to be r-ed to us.	Rm 8:18

for God's sons to be r-ed.	Rm 8:19
God has r-ed them to us by the	1Co 2:10
because it will be r-ed by fire;	1Co 3:13
of his heart will be r-ed,	1Co 14:25
to r His Son in me, so that I	Gl 1:16
until the coming faith was r-ed.	Gl 3:23
as it is now r-ed to His holy	Eph 3:5
God will r this to you also.	Php 3:15
but now r-ed to His saints.	Col 1:26
is r-ed, then you also will be r-ed	Col 3:4
the man of lawlessness is r-ed	2Th 2:3
is ready to be r-ed in the last	1Pt 1:5
that life was r-ed, and we have	1Jn 1:2
we will be has not yet been r-ed.	1Jn 3:2
God's love was r-ed among us in	1Jn 4:9

REVEL

and drink, then got up to r.	Ex 32:6

REVELATION

this is a r for mankind,	2Sm 7:19
But a r from God came to	1Kg 12:22
r of Your words brings	Ps 119:130
Without r people run wild,	Pr 29:18
light for r to the Gentiles	Lk 2:32
according to the r of the	Rm 16:25
eagerly wait for the r of our Lord	1Co 1:7
has a psalm, a teaching, a r,	1Co 14:26
visions and r-s of the Lord.	2Co 12:1
it came by a r from Jesus	Gl 1:12
was made known to me by r,	Eph 3:3
you by a r from the Lord:	1Th 4:15
at the r of the Lord Jesus	2Th 1:7
basic principles of God's r.	Heb 5:12
at the r of Jesus Christ	1Pt 1:7
joy at the r of His glory.	1Pt 4:13
The r of Jesus Christ that God gave	Rv 1:1

REVENGE

Do not take r or bear a grudge	Lv 19:18
show no mercy when he takes r.	Pr 6:34

REVENUE

and her r is better than gold.	Pr 3:14

REVERE

and r My sanctuary;	Lv 19:30
who delight to r Your name.	Neh 1:11
descendants of Israel, r Him!	Ps 22:23
so that You may be r-d.	Ps 130:4

You who r the LORD, praise Ps 135:20
and he r-d Me and stood in awe Mal 2:5

REVERED (adj)
glorious in holiness, r with praises, Ex 15:11

REVERENCE
for it produces r for You. Ps 119:38
he was heard because of His r. Heb 5:7
in r built an ark to deliver Heb 11:7
serve God acceptably, with r Heb 12:28
conduct yourselves in r during this 1Pt 1:17

REVERENT
Happy is the one who is always r, Pr 28:14
it will go well ... for they are r Ec 8:12
older women are to be r in behavior, Ti 2:3
observe your pure, r lives. 1Pt 3:2

REVERENTIAL
Serve the LORD with r awe, Ps 2:11
holy temple in r awe of You. Ps 5:7

REVILE
all who r-d you will fall down Is 60:14
Do you dare r God's high priest? Ac 23:4
When we are r-d, we bless; 1Co 4:12
when r-d, He did not r in return; 1Pt 2:23

REVILER
a r, a drunkard or a swindler. 1Co 5:11
drunkards, r-s, or swindlers 1Co 6:10

REVIVE
bones, the man r-d and stood up! 2Kg 13:21
LORD is perfect, r-ing the soul; Ps 19:7
but You will r me again. Ps 71:20
Will You not r us again so that Ps 85:6
to r the spirit of the lowly and r the Is 57:15
He will r us after two days, Hs 6:2
R {Your work} in these years; Hab 3:2

REVOKE
Media, so that it cannot be r-d: Est 1:19
a word that will not be r-d: Is 45:23
You r God's word by your tradition Mk 7:13
later, does not r a covenant that Gl 3:17

REVOLT
There have been r-s in it since Ezr 4:15

REVOLTING (adj)
one who is r and corrupt Jb 15:16

corrupt; their actions are r. Ps 14:1
people is r in God's sight Lk 16:15

REWARD (n)
your r will be very great. Gn 15:1
there is great r in keeping them. Ps 19:11
there is a r for the righteous! Ps 58:11
from the LORD, children, a r. Ps 127:3
sows righteousness, a true r. Pr 11:18
This was my r for all my struggles. Ec 2:10
they have a good r for their Ec 4:9
His r is with Him, and His gifts Is 40:10
is coming, His r is with Him, Is 62:11
the r for your work will come Jr 31:16
your r is great in heaven. Mt 5:12
love you, what r will you have? Mt 5:46
They've got their r! Mt 6:2,5,16
will receive a prophet's r. Mt 10:41
He will never lose his r! Mt 10:42
receive his own r according to 1Co 3:8
survives, he will receive a r. 1Co 3:14
What then is my r? To preach the 1Co 9:18
his attention was on the r. Heb 11:26
quickly, and My r is with Me Rv 22:12

REWARD (v)
May the LORD r you for what you Ru 2:12
LORD r-ed me according to my Ps 18:20
respects a command will be r-ed. Pr 13:13
head, and the LORD will r you. Pr 25:22
who sees in secret will r you. Mt 6:4,6,18
then He will r each according Mt 16:27
when he comes will be r-ed. Mt 24:46
He exists and r-s those who seek Heb 11:6

REZIN
King of Aram (2Kg 15:37; 16:5-9; Is 7:1-8; 9:11).

RHODA
Servant, answered the door (Ac 12:13).

RIB
God made the r ... into a woman Gn 2:22
with three r-s in its mouth Dn 7:5

RICH (adj)
Abram was very r in livestock, Gn 13:2
can never say, 'I made Abram r.' Gn 14:23
younger men, whether r or poor. Ru 3:10
The r man had a large number of 2Sm 12:2
Do not be afraid when a man gets r, Ps 49:16

You satisfy me as with r food; Ps 63:5
A r man's wealth is his Pr 10:15
pretends to be r but has nothing Pr 13:7
wine and oil will not get r. Pr 21:17
Don't wear yourself out to get r; Pr 23:4
in a hurry to get r will not Pr 28:20
and do not curse a r person even Ec 10:20
LORD because I have become r! Zch 11:5
hard for a r person to enter Mt 19:23
a r man from Arimathea named Mt 27:57
Many r people were putting in Mk 12:41
woe to you who are r, Lk 6:24
A r man's land was very Lk 12:16
The r man also died and was Lk 16:22
tax collector, and he was r. Lk 19:2
Lord of all is r to all who call Rm 10:12
you were made r in everything 1Co 1:5
Already you are r! 1Co 4:8
His poverty you might become r. 2Co 8:9
who want to be r fall into 1Tm 6:9
do good, to be r in good works, 1Tm 6:18
r {should boast} in his humiliation, Jms 1:10
Come now, you r people! Jms 5:1
and poverty, yet you are r. Rv 2:9
Because you say, 'I'm r; Rv 3:17

RICH (n)

or give preference to the r; Lv 19:15
not favor the r over the poor, Jb 34:19
The r and the poor have this in Pr 22:2
the r must not boast in his riches. Jr 9:23
and sent the r away empty. Lk 1:53
Don't the r oppress you and drag Jms 2:6

RICHES

and you have not requested r 2Ch 1:11
and boast of their abundant r. Ps 49:6
trusted in the abundance of his r, Ps 52:7
Wealth and r are in his house, Ps 112:3
in her left, r and honor. Pr 3:16
but diligent hands bring r. Pr 10:4
trusting in his r will fall, Pr 11:28
R are a ransom for a man's Pr 13:8
are still not content with r. Ec 4:8
gives a man r, wealth, and Ec 6:2
to the wise, or r to the discerning, Ec 9:11
of darkness and r from secret Is 45:3
and you will boast in their r. Is 61:6
the rich must not boast in his r. Jr 9:23
choked with worries, r, Lk 8:14

do you despise the r of His kindness, Rm 2:4
make known the r of His glory Rm 9:23
Oh, the depth of the r Rm 11:33
according to the r of His Eph 1:7
immeasurable r of His grace Eph 2:7
incalculable r of the Messiah Eph 3:8
to the r of His glory, Eph 3:16
according to His r in glory Php 4:19
receive power and r and wisdom Rv 5:12

RICHLY

the Messiah dwell r among you, Col 3:16
who r provides us with all 1Tm 6:17
Christ will be r supplied to you 2Pt 1:11

RID

Get r of the gods your ancestors Jos 24:14

RIDDLE

directly, openly, and not in r-s; Nm 12:8
"Let me tell you a r," Samson said Jdg 14:12
I explain my r with a lyre. Ps 49:4
words of the wise, and their r-s. Pr 1:6
pose a r and speak a parable to Ezk 17:2
dreams, explain r-s, and solve Dn 5:12

RIDE

who r-s the heavens to your aid Dt 33:26
He had 30 sons who rode on 30 Jdg 10:4
on the wind and make me r {it}; Jb 30:22
He rode on a cherub and flew, Ps 18:10
in your splendor r triumphantly Ps 45:4
Exalt Him who r-s on the clouds Ps 68:4
LORD r-s on a swift cloud and Is 19:1
humble and r-ing on a donkey, Zch 9:9

RIDER

horse and its r into the sea. Ex 15:1,21
able to supply r-s for them! 2Kg 18:23
laughs at the horse and its r. Jb 39:18
When he sees r-s—pairs of Is 21:7
will smash the horse and its r; Jr 51:21
Its r is called Faithful and True, Rv 19:11

RIDICULE (n)

r among all the peoples Dt 28:37; 1Kg 9:7
mockery and r to those around Ps 44:13
an object of r to my accusers; Ps 109:25
object of scorn, r, and cursing Jr 24:9
an object of r to all those Dn 9:16

RIDICULE (v)

he r-d the LORD's anointed 2Sm 19:21

laughs; the Lord r-s them.   Ps 2:4
You r all the nations.   Ps 59:8
The arrogant constantly r me,   Ps 119:51
They r-d him: "You're that man's   Jn 9:28
the dead, some began to r him.   Ac 17:32
If you are r-d for the name of   1Pt 4:14

RIGHT (adj)
Your r hand is glorious in power.   Ex 15:6
Do what is r and good   Dt 6:18
doing what is r in the LORD's sight.   Dt 12:25
I will never affirm that you are r.   Jb 27:5
in Your r hand are eternal   Ps 16:11
The precepts of the LORD are r,   Ps 19:8
So You are r when You pass   Ps 51:4
Your r hand holds on to me.   Ps 63:8
them their food at the r time.   Ps 104:27
He stands at the r hand of the   Ps 109:31
Sit at My r hand until I make   Ps 110:1
may my r hand forget {its skill}.   Ps 137:5
Your r hand will save me.   Ps 138:7
will guide you on the r paths.   Pr 3:6
Long life is in her r hand;   Pr 3:16
fool's way is r in his own eyes,   Pr 12:15
way that seems r to a man, Pr 14:12; 16:25
ways of a man seem r to him,   Pr 21:2
and his r hand embraces me.   Sg 2:6; 8:3
and does what is just and r Ezk 18:5; 33:14
For the ways of the LORD are r,   Hs 14:9
Is it r for you to be angry?   Jnh 4:4
If your r eye causes you to sin   Mt 5:29
know what your r hand is doing,   Mt 6:3
Sit at My r hand until I put   Mt 22:44
seated at the r hand of the   Mt 26:64
dressed and in his r mind;   Mk 5:15
sat down at the r hand of God.   Mk 16:19
Mary has made the r choice,   Lk 10:42
to my Lord, 'Sit at My r hand   Ac 2:34
standing at the r hand of God,   Ac 7:55
your heart is not r before God.   Ac 8:21
He also is at the r hand of God   Rm 8:34
they gave the r hand of fellowship   Gl 2:9
seating Him at His r hand in the   Eph 1:20
in the Lord, because this is r.   Eph 6:1
seated at the r hand of God.   Col 3:1
Sit at My r hand until I make   Heb 1:13
sat down at the r hand of God.   Heb 10:12
In His r hand He had seven stars   Rv 1:16
a mark on his r hand or on his   Rv 13:16

RIGHT (n)
If you do r, won't you be   Gn 4:7
the left, I will go to the r;   Gn 13:9
or marital r-s of the first wife.   Ex 21:10
his r of redemption will last   Lv 25:29
not to turn aside to the r or the left. Dt 5:32
he has the r-s of the firstborn.   Dt 21:17
Take my r of redemption,   Ru 4:6
Even if I were in the r,   Jb 9:15,20
What r do you have to recite My   Ps 50:16
Don't turn to the r or to the left;   Pr 4:27
rich man who distorts r and wrong. Pr 28:6
person knows the r-s of the poor,   Pr 29:7
man's heart {goes} to the r   Ec 10:2
Defend the r-s of the fatherless.   Is 1:17
between their r and their left,   Jnh 4:11
Don't I have the r to do what I   Mt 20:15
one on Your r and the other on   Mt 20:21
He will put the sheep on His r   Mt 25:33
one on the r and one on the left   Mt 27:38
gave them the r to be children   Jn 1:12
granted Him the r to pass judgment Jn 5:27
and I have the r to take it up again. Jn 10:18
the potter no r over His clay,   Rm 9:21
that this r of yours in no   1Co 8:9
I have used none of these r-s   1Co 9:15
do not have a r to eat.   Heb 13:10
they may have the r to the tree   Rv 22:14

RIGHTEOUS (adj)
Noah was a r man,   Gn 6:9
The LORD is the R One,   Ex 9:27
what great nation has r statutes   Dt 4:8
You are more r than I,   1Sm 24:17
Can a person be more r than God,   Jb 4:17
The r see {this} and rejoice;   Jb 22:19
because he was r in his own eyes.   Jb 32:1
you say, "I am r before God"?   Jb 35:2
For You, LORD, bless the r one;   Ps 5:12
God is a r judge, and a God who   Ps 7:11
For the LORD is r; He loves r deeds. Ps 11:7
are reliable and altogether r.   Ps 19:9
will delight in r sacrifices,   Ps 51:19
Your decrees are r forever.   Ps 119:144
no one alive is r in Your sight.   Ps 143:2
The LORD is r in all His ways   Ps 145:17
The R One considers the house of Pr 21:12
there is a r man who perishes in   Ec 7:15
Don't be excessively r,   Ec 7:16

you will be called the **R** City,	Is 1:26
on to you with My **r** right hand.	Is 41:10
My **r** servant will justify many,	Is 53:11
The **r** one perishes, and no one	Is 57:1
our **r** acts are like a polluted garment.	Is 64:6
raise up a **r** Branch of David.	Jr 23:5
Now if a **r** person turns from his	Ezk 3:20
LORD our God is **r** in all He has	Dn 9:14
they sell a **r** person for silver	Am 2:6
But the **r** one will live by his faith.	Hab 2:4
The **r** LORD is in her;	Zph 3:5
Joseph, being a **r** man, and not	Mt 1:19
r will receive a **r** person's reward.	Mt 10:41
prophets and **r** people longed to	Mt 13:17
separate the evil people from the **r**	Mt 13:49
from the blood of **r** Abel to	Mt 23:35
Both were **r** in God's sight,	Lk 1:6
than over 99 **r** people who don't	Lk 15:7
that they were **r** and looked down	Lk 18:9
saying, "This man really was **r**!"	Lk 23:47
was a good and **r** man named	Lk 23:50
My judgment is **r**, because I do	Jn 5:30
the coming of the **R** One,	Ac 7:52
the law are not **r** before God,	Rm 2:13
is no one **r**, not even one;	Rm 3:10
have been declared **r** by faith,	Rm 5:1
the many will be made **r**.	Rm 5:19
the law is not meant for a **r** person,	1Tm 1:9
the Lord, the **r** Judge,	2Tm 4:8
is good, sensible, **r**, holy,	Ti 1:8
But My **r** one will live by faith;	Heb 10:38
he was approved as a **r** man,	Heb 11:4
if He rescued **r** Lot, distressed	2Pt 2:7
is faithful and **r** to forgive us	1Jn 1:9
Jesus Christ the **r** One.	1Jn 2:1
does what is right is **r**, just as He is **r**.	1Jn 3:7
r and true are Your ways, King	Rv 15:3
represents the **r** acts of the	Rv 19:8

RIGHTEOUS (n)

sweep away the **r** with the wicked	Gn 18:23
watches over the way of the **r**	Ps 1:6
examines the **r** and the wicked.	Ps 11:5
eyes of the LORD are on the **r**,	Ps 34:15
I have not seen the **r** abandoned	Ps 37:25
the **r** will enter through it.	Ps 118:20
He blesses the home of the **r**;	Pr 3:33
will not let the **r** go hungry,	Pr 10:3
labor of the **r** leads to life;	Pr 10:16

but what the **r** desires will be	Pr 10:24
The **r** will never be shaken,	Pr 10:30
The **r** is rescued from trouble;	Pr 11:8
When the **r** thrive, a city	Pr 11:10
but the **r** will flourish like	Pr 11:28
but good rewards the **r**.	Pr 13:21
wealth is stored up for the **r**.	Pr 13:22
He hears the prayer of the **r**.	Pr 15:29
the **r** run to it and are protected.	Pr 18:10
but the **r** give and don't hold	Pr 21:26
When the **r** triumph, there is	Pr 28:12
When the **r** flourish, the people	Pr 29:2
but the **r** will see their	Pr 29:16
will judge the **r** and the wicked	Ec 3:17
fate for the **r** and the wicked,	Ec 9:2
sends rain on the **r** and the	Mt 5:45
I didn't come to call the **r**	Mt 9:13
Then the **r** will shine like the	Mt 13:43
but the **r** into eternal life.	Mt 25:46
at the resurrection of the **r**.	Lk 14:14
The **r** will live by faith.	Rm 1:17
because the **r** will live by faith.	Gl 3:11
prayer of the **r** is very powerful	Jms 5:16
the **r** for the unrighteous,	1Pt 3:18

RIGHTEOUSLY

He will judge the world **r**	Ps 98:9
Speak up, judge **r**, and defend	Pr 31:9
a king will reign **r**,	Is 32:1
The one who lives **r** and speaks	Is 33:15
how devoutly, **r**, and blamelessly	1Th 2:10

RIGHTEOUSNESS

He credited it to him as **r**.	Gn 15:6
possess this land because of my **r**.	Dt 9:4
LORD repay every man for his **r**	1Sm 26:23
repaid me according to my **r**	2Sm 22:25
my **r** is still the issue.	Jb 6:29
I will cling to my **r**	Jb 27:6
and ascribe **r** to my Maker.	Jb 36:3
He judges the world with **r**;	Ps 9:8
Save me by Your **r**.	Ps 31:1
tongue will proclaim Your **r**,	Ps 35:28
You love **r** and hate wickedness;	Ps 45:7
The heavens proclaim His **r**	Ps 50:6
r and peace will embrace.	Ps 85:10
R and justice are the foundation	Ps 89:14
His **r** endures forever.	Ps 111:3; 112:3
Give me life through Your **r**.	Ps 119:40
Your **r** is an everlasting **r**,	Ps 119:142

Then you will understand r   Pr 2:9
but r rescues from death.   Pr 10:2; 11:4
There is life in the path of r,   Pr 12:28
R exalts a nation, but sin is   Pr 14:34
is established through r.   Pr 16:12
who pursues r and faithful love   Pr 21:21
perishes in spite of his r,   Ec 7:15
R and faithfulness will be a belt   Is 11:5
and their r is from Me.   Is 54:17
He put on r like a breastplate,   Is 59:17
until her r shines like   Is 62:1
will be named: The LORD Is Our R.   Jr 23:6
Branch of r to sprout up for David,   Jr 33:15
The r of the righteous person   Ezk 18:20
to bring in everlasting r,   Dn 9:24
those who lead many to r,   Dn 12:3
Sow r for yourselves and reap   Hs 10:12
Seek r, seek humility;   Zph 2:3
the sun of r will rise with   Mal 4:2
way for us to fulfill all r.   Mt 3:15
who hunger and thirst for r,   Mt 5:6
unless your r surpasses that   Mt 5:20
kingdom of God and His r,   Mt 6:33
about sin, r, and judgment: Jn 16:8
judge the world in r by the Man   Ac 17:31
in it God's r is revealed   Rm 1:17
apart from the law, God's r has   Rm 3:21
It was credited to him for r.   Rm 4:3
grace will reign through r   Rm 5:21
to God as weapons for r.   Rm 6:13
offer them as slaves to r   Rm 6:19
not pursue r, have obtained r—namely
    the r that comes from faith.   Rm 9:30
end the law for r to everyone   Rm 10:4
become the r of God in Him.   2Co 5:21
weapons of r on the right   2Co 6:7
if r comes through the law   Gl 2:21
was credited to him for r   Gl 3:6
r like armor on your chest,   Eph 6:14
not having a r of my own from   Php 3:9
pursue r, godliness, faith, love,   1Tm 6:11
for correcting, for training in r,   2Tm 3:16
reserved for me the crown of r,   2Tm 4:8
not by works of r that we had done,   Ti 3:5
means "king of r," then   Heb 7:2
peace and r to those who   Heb 12:11
anger does not accomplish God's r.   Jms 1:20
was credited to him for r   Jms 2:23

fruit of r is sown in peace   Jms 3:18
died to sins, we might live for r;   1Pt 2:24
if you should suffer for r,   1Pt 3:14
a preacher of r, and seven   2Pt 2:5
in r He judges and makes   Rv 19:11

RIGHTFULLY
Praise is r Yours, God,   Ps 65:1

RING (n)
Whose signet r, cord, and staff   Gn 38:25
Cast four gold r-s for it and   Ex 25:12
sealed with the royal signet r.   Est 3:12
is like a gold r in a pig's snout.   Pr 11:22
signet r-s, nose r-s,   Is 3:21
I put a r in your nose, earrings   Ezk 16:12
his own signet r and with the   Dn 6:17
and make you like My signet r,   Hg 2:23
put a r on his finger and   Lk 15:22
your meeting wearing a gold r   Jms 2:2

RING (v)
Lord's message rang out from you,   1Th 1:8

RINGLEADER
and a r of the sect of the   Ac 24:5

RIOT
so there won't be r-ing   Mt 26:5
but that a r was starting   Mt 27:24
risk of being charged with r-ing   Ac 19:40

RIP
You will r open their pregnant   2Kg 8:12
they r-ped open the pregnant   Am 1:13

RIPE
because the harvest is r.   Jl 3:13
and then the r grain on the head   Mk 4:28
the harvest of the earth is r.   Rv 14:15

RISE
generation rose up who did not   Jdg 2:10
man lies down never to r again.   Jb 14:12
R up, LORD!   Ps 3:7; 7:6; 9:19; 10:12; 17:13
Smoke rose from His nostrils,   Ps 18:8
R up, ancient doors!   Ps 24:7
for the water has r-n to my neck.   Ps 69:1
when God rose up to judge and to   Ps 76:9
R up, Judge of the earth;   Ps 94:2
mountains rose and valleys sank   Ps 104:8
From the r-ing of the sun to its   Ps 113:3
I r at midnight to thank You for   Ps 119:62

She **r-s** while it is still night | Pr 31:15
Her sons **r** up and call her blessed. | Pr 31:28
The sun **r-s** and the sun sets; | Ec 1:5
their bodies will **r**. | Is 26:19
know from the **r-ing** of the sun to | Is 45:6
glory of the LORD **rose** from above | Ezk 10:4
will rest, then **r** to your destiny | Dn 12:13
Israel will never **r** again. | Am 5:2
from the **r-ing** of the sun to its | Mal 1:11
will **r** with healing in its wings, | Mal 4:2
causes His sun to **r** on the evil | Mt 5:45
the rivers **rose**, the winds blew | Mt 7:27
For nation will **r** up against | Mt 24:7
After three days I will **r** again. | Mt 27:63
Son of Man had **r-n** from the dead. | Mk 9:9
what "**r-ing** from the dead" meant. | Mk 9:10
Children will **r** up against | Mk 13:12
after He had **r-n**, He appeared | Mk 16:9
the fall and **r** of many in Israel | Lk 2:34
A great prophet has **r-n** among us, | Lk 7:16
of the ancient prophets had **r-n**. | Lk 9:8
if someone **r-s** from the dead. | Lk 16:31
would suffer and **r** from the dead | Lk 24:46
Your brother will **r** again, | Jn 11:23
to suffer and **r** from the dead, | Ac 17:3
the first to **r** from the dead, | Ac 26:23
sleeper, and **r** up from the dead, | Eph 5:14
that Jesus died and **rose** again, | 1Th 4:14
dead in Christ will **r** first. | 1Th 4:16

RISEN (adj)
Jesus Christ, **r** from the dead, | 2Tm 2:8

RISK
blood of men who **r-ed** their lives | 2Sm 23:17
have **r-ed** their lives for the name | Ac 15:26
r-ing his life to make up what | Php 2:30

RITUAL
What does this **r** mean to you? | Ex 12:26
perform the **r** washing before | Lk 11:38
teaching about **r** washings, | Heb 6:2

RITUALLY
unless they wash their hands **r**, | Mk 7:3
of Asia found me **r** purified in | Ac 24:18

RIVAL
a woman as a **r** to her sister | Lv 18:18
Her **r** would taunt her severely | 1Sm 1:6

RIVALRY
proclaim Christ out of **r** | Php 1:17
Do nothing out of **r** or conceit, | Php 2:3

RIVER
A **r** went out from Eden to water | Gn 2:10
in the Nile will die, the **r** will stink, | Ex 7:18
from the Euphrates **R** to the land | 1Kg 4:21
and Pharpar, the **r-s** of Damascus | 2Kg 5:12
from crossing the **r** {of death}. | Jb 33:18
{There is} a **r**—its streams | Ps 46:4
You dried up ever-flowing **r-s**. | Ps 74:15
Let the **r-s** clap their hands; | Ps 98:8
turns **r-s** into desert, springs | Ps 107:33
By the **r-s** of Babylon—there we | Ps 137:1
are deep waters, a flowing **r**, | Pr 18:4
r-s cannot sweep it away. | Sg 8:7
through the **r-s**, they will not | Is 43:2
way in wilderness, **r-s** in the desert. | Is 43:19
make peace flow to her like a **r**, | Is 66:12
be life everywhere the **r** goes. | Ezk 47:9
were baptized by him in the Jordan **R** | Mt 3:6
The rain fell, the **r-s** rose, | Mt 7:25
dangers from **r-s**, | 2Co 11:26
a third of the **r-s** and springs | Rv 8:10
showed me the **r** of living water | Rv 22:1

RIVERBANK
Pharaoh's daughter ... along the **r**. | Ex 2:5

RIZPAH
Saul's concubine. Abner was accused of an affair with her (2Sm 3:7). She defended her sons' bodies (21:8-11).

ROAD
and when you walk along the **r**, | Dt 6:7
or maybe he's on the **r**. | 1Kg 18:27
don't travel that **r** with them | Pr 1:15
Her house is the **r** to Sheol, | Pr 7:27
There's a lion in the **r** | Pr 26:13
sea-bed into a **r** for the | Is 51:10
Mark out a **r** that the sword can | Ezk 21:20
r is broad that leads to destruction, | Mt 7:13
and spreading them on the **r**. | Mt 21:8
happened to be going down that **r**. | Lk 10:31
He was talking with us on the **r** | Lk 24:32
on the **r**, Saul had seen the Lord, | Ac 9:27

ROAM
From **r-ing** through the earth, | Jb 1:7; 2:2

but a fool's eyes r to the ends | Pr 17:24
it r-s through waterless places | Mt 12:43

ROAR (n)

to deep in the r of Your waterfalls; | Ps 42:7
than the r of many waters | Ps 93:4
like the r of mighty waters | Ezk 43:2
Listen to the r of young lions, | Zch 11:3

ROAR (v)

though its waters r and foam | Ps 46:3
The young lions r for their prey | Ps 104:21
The LORD r-s from on high; | Jr 25:30
LORD; He will r like a lion | Hs 11:10
The LORD will r from Zion and | Jl 3:16
LORD r-s from Zion and raises | Am 1:2
Does a lion r in the forest when | Am 3:4
A lion has r-ed; who will not fear? | Am 3:8

ROARING (adj)

Then there comes a r sound; | Jb 37:4
prowling around like a r lion, | 1Pt 5:8
a loud voice like a r lion. | Rv 10:3

ROARING (n)

wrath is like the r of a lion; | Pr 20:2

ROAST

they should eat it, r-ed over the fire | Ex 12:8
Give the priest {some} meat to r, | 1Sm 2:15
r-ed the Passover {lambs} with | 2Ch 35:13
A lazy man doesn't r his game, | Pr 12:27

ROB

a wild bear r-bed of her cubs. | 2Sm 17:8
to meet a bear r-bed of her cubs | Pr 17:12
Don't r a poor man because he is | Pr 22:22
Will a man r God? Yet you are | Mal 3:8
Then he can r his house. | Mt 12:29
no one will r you of your joy. | Jn 16:22
do you r their temples? | Rm 2:22
I r-bed other churches by taking | 2Co 11:8

ROBBER

The tents of r-s are safe, | Jb 12:6
poverty will come like a r, | Pr 6:11; 24:34
she sets an ambush like a r | Pr 23:28
Who gave Jacob to the r, and Israel | Is 42:24
this house ... become a den of r-s | Jr 7:11
and fell into the hands of r-s. | Lk 10:30
other way, is a thief and a r. | Jn 10:1
not temple r-s or blasphemers | Ac 19:37
dangers from r-s, dangers from | 2Co 11:26

ROBBERY

or false hope in r. | Ps 62:10
I hate r and injustice; | Is 61:8

ROBE

and he made a r of many colors | Gn 37:3
and dipped the r in its blood. | Gn 37:31
and his r-s in the blood of grapes. | Gn 49:11
The r must be {worn by} Aaron | Ex 28:35
cut off the corner of Saul's r. | 1Sm 24:4
my just decisions were like a r | Jb 29:14
in light as if it were a r, | Ps 104:2
down Aaron's beard, on his r-s. | Ps 133:2
and His r filled the temple. | Is 6:1
wrapped me in a r of righteousness, | Is 61:10
their r-s were unaffected | Dn 3:27
clothe you with splendid r-s | Zch 3:4
If I can just touch His r, | Mt 9:21
only touch the tassel on His r. | Mt 14:36
spread their r-s on the road; | Mt 21:8
and dressed Him in a scarlet r. | Mt 27:28
and his r was as white as snow. | Mt 28:3
want to go around in long r-s | Mk 12:38
A man dressed in soft r-s? | Lk 7:25
Bring out the best r and put it on | Lk 15:22
crown of thorns and the purple r. | Jn 19:5
laid their r-s at the feet | Ac 7:58
showing him the r-s and clothes | Ac 9:39
in a dazzling r stood before me | Ac 10:30
they will be changed like a r. | Heb 1:12
So a white r was given to each | Rv 6:11
He wore a r stained with blood, | Rv 19:13
are those who wash their r-s | Rv 22:14

ROBED (v)

Your power, r with strength; | Ps 65:6
He is r in majesty; | Ps 93:1
are these people r in white, | Rv 7:13

ROCK

when you hit the r, water will | Ex 17:6
will put you in the crevice of the r | Ex 33:22
and struck the r twice with his | Nm 20:11
The R—His work is perfect; | Dt 32:4
with honey from the r and oil | Dt 32:13
But their "r" is not like our R; | Dt 32:31
And there is no r like our God. | 1Sm 2:2
stopped there near a large r. | 1Sm 6:14
He cuts out channels in the r-s | Jb 28:10
The LORD is my r, | Ps 18:2

And who is a r? Only our God.   Ps 18:31
LORD lives—may my r be praised!   Ps 18:46
LORD, my r and my Redeemer.   Ps 19:14
He will set me high on a r.   Ps 27:5
and set my feet on a r,   Ps 40:2
say to God, my r, "Why have You   Ps 42:9
Lead me to a r that is high   Ps 61:2
you with honey from the r.   Ps 81:16
my God is the r of my protection.   Ps 94:22
and dashes them against the r-s.   Ps 137:9
May the LORD my r be praised,   Ps 144:1
the way of a snake on a r,   Pr 30:19
Go into the r-s and hide in the   Is 2:10
and a r to trip over,   Is 8:14
the LORD, is an everlasting r!   Is 26:4
shade of a massive r in an arid land. Is 32:2
no (other) R; I do not know any.   Is 44:8
Look to the r from which you   Is 51:1
sledgehammer that pulverizes r?   Jr 23:29
Do horses run on r,   Am 6:12
in clefts of the r in your home   Ob 3
who built his house on the r.   Mt 7:24
on this r I will build My church,   Mt 16:18
quaked and the r-s were split.   Mt 27:51
Him in a tomb cut out of the r   Mk 15:46
Other seed fell on the r;   Lk 8:6
called Cephas" (which means "R").   Jn 1:42
and a r to trip over,   Rm 9:33
drank from a spiritual r that followed
    them, and that r was Christ.   1Co 10:4
and a r that trips them up.   1Pt 2:8
to the r-s, "Fall on us   Rv 6:16

ROCKY

Others fell on r ground, where   Mt 13:5

ROD

discipline him with a human r   2Sm 7:14
no r from God (strikes) them.   Jb 21:9
his limbs are like iron r-s.   Jb 40:18
break them with a r of iron;   Ps 2:9
Your r and Your staff—they   Ps 23:4
but a r is for the back of the one   Pr 10:13
not use the r hates his son,   Pr 13:24
r of discipline will drive it away   Pr 22:15
beat him with a r, he will not die.   Pr 23:13
and a r for the backs of fools.   Pr 26:3
A r of correction imparts wisdom,   Pr 29:15
His arms are r-s of gold   Sg 5:14
Assyria, the r of My anger   Is 10:5

pass under the r and will bring   Ezk 20:37
and a measuring r in his hand.   Ezk 40:3
the r and the One who ordained it.   Mc 6:9
Should I come to you with a r,   1Co 4:21
Three times I was beaten
    with r-s.   2Co 11:25
the manna, Aaron's r that budded,   Heb 9:4
a measuring reed like a r,   Rv 11:1
a gold measuring r to measure   Rv 21:15

ROLE

and each has the r the Lord has   1Co 3:5

ROLL

Today I have r-ed away the disgrace   Jos 5:9
Call the r and determine who   1Sm 14:17
whoever r-s a stone—it will come   Pr 26:27
The skies will r up like a scroll,   Is 34:4
R (in the dust), you leaders of   Jr 25:34
after r-ing a great stone against the Mt 27:60
Who will r away the stone from   Mk 16:3
very large—had been r-ed away.   Mk 16:4
found the stone r-ed away from   Lk 24:2
You will r them up like a cloak,   Heb 1:12
like a scroll being r-ed up;   Rv 6:14

ROMAN

not legal for us as R-s to adopt   Ac 16:21
Paul and Silas were R citizens.   Ac 16:38
Tell me—are you a R citizen?   Ac 22:27
learned that he is a R citizen.   Ac 23:27
into the hands of the R-s   Ac 28:17

ROME

    Italian city, capital of the Roman Empire;
represented at Pentecost (Ac 2:10); Jews
expelled (18:2); Paul addressed a letter to
the church there (Rm 1:7,15) and went
there (Ac 19:21; 23:11; 28:14-16; 2Tm
1:17).

ROOF

make a railing around your r,   Dt 22:8
up to the r and hidden them   Jos 2:6
From the r he saw a woman   2Sm 11:2
stuck to the r of their mouths.   Jb 29:10
sticks to the r of my mouth.   Ps 22:15
stick to the r of my mouth if I   Ps 137:6
live on the corner of a r than   Pr 21:9; 25:24
clings to the r of his mouth   Lm 4:4
stick to the r of your mouth,   Ezk 3:26

walking on the **r** of the royal — Dn 4:29
to have You come under my **r**. — Mt 8:8
went up on the **r** and lowered him — Lk 5:19

ROOFTOPS

them be like grass on the **r** — Ps 129:6
grass on the **r**, blasted — Is 37:27
worship on the **r** to the heavenly — Zph 1:5

ROOM

Make **r-s** in the ark, — Gn 6:14
himself in the cool **r**. — Jdg 3:24
by knowledge the **r-s** are filled — Pr 24:4
you pray, go into your private **r**, — Mt 6:6
show you a large **r** upstairs, — Mk 14:15
there was no **r** for them at the — Lk 2:7
has been done, and there's still **r**. — Lk 14:22
went to the **r** upstairs where — Ac 1:13
instead, leave **r** for His wrath. — Rm 12:19
also prepare a guest **r** for me, — Phm 22
enter the first **r** repeatedly, — Heb 9:6

ROOSTER

a strutting **r**, a goat, and a king — Pr 30:31
before the **r** crows, you will — Mt 26:34
Immediately a **r** crowed, — Mt 26:74
at the crowing of the **r** or early — Mk 13:35

ROOT

no **r** among you bearing poisonous — Dt 29:18
will again take **r** downward and — 2Kg 19:30
I have seen a fool taking **r** — Jb 5:3
the **r** of the righteous is immovable. — Pr 12:3
the **r** of the righteous produces
  fruit. — Pr 12:12
On that day the **r** of Jesse will — Is 11:10
and like a **r** out of dry ground. — Is 53:2
vine bent its **r-s** toward him! — Ezk 17:7
for its **r-s** extended to abundant — Ezk 31:7
fruit above and his **r-s** beneath. — Am 2:9
to strike the **r** of the trees! — Mt 3:10
they had no **r**, they withered. — Mt 13:6
tree withered from the **r-s** up. — Mk 11:20
And if the **r** is holy, so are the — Rm 11:16
the **r**, but the **r** sustains you. — Rm 11:18
The **r** of Jesse will appear, — Rm 15:12
r-ed and firmly established — Eph 3:17
r-ed and built up in Him and — Col 2:7
of money is a **r** of all kinds — 1Tm 6:10
and that no **r** of bitterness — Heb 12:15
dead, pulled out by the **r-s**; — Jd 12

of Judah, the **R** of David, — Rv 5:5
I am the **R** and the Offspring of — Rv 22:16

ROPE

them down by a **r** through the — Jos 2:15
up with two new **r-s** and led him — Jdg 15:13
Delilah took new **r-s**, tied him — Jdg 16:12
tie his tongue down with a **r**? — Jb 41:1
The **r-s** of death were wrapped — Ps 18:4
The **r-s** of Sheol entangled me; — Ps 18:5
He has cut the **r-s** of the wicked — Ps 129:4
in the **r-s** of his own sin. — Pr 5:22
instead of a belt, a **r**; — Is 3:24
lengthen your **r-s**, and drive your — Is 54:2
lowering Jeremiah with **r-s**. — Jr 38:6
cords, with **r-s** of kindness. — Hs 11:4

ROSE (n)

I am a **r** of Sharon, a lily of — Sg 2:1
rejoice and blossom like a **r**. — Is 35:1

ROT

the name of the wicked will **r**. — Pr 10:7
So I am like **r** to Ephraim — Hs 5:12
tongues will **r** in their mouths. — Zch 14:12

ROTE

man-made rules learned {by **r**} — Is 29:13

ROTTEN

and bronze as **r** wood. — Jb 41:27
Trusting ... is like a **r** tooth — Pr 25:19
make them like **r** figs — Jr 29:17
No **r** talk should come from your — Eph 4:29

ROTTENNESS

causes shame is like **r** in his bones. — Pr 12:4
jealousy is **r** to the bones. — Pr 14:30
R entered my bones; — Hab 3:16

ROUGH

and the **r** places a plain. — Is 40:4
straight, the **r** ways smooth, — Lk 3:5

ROUGHLY

but the rich one answers **r**. — Pr 18:23

ROUND

from brim to brim, perfectly **r**. — 1Kg 7:23
they make the **r-s** on its walls. — Ps 55:10

ROUT

One of you **r-ed** a thousand, — Jos 23:10
lightning bolts and **r-ed** them. — Ps 18:14

ROUTE
to their own country by another r.   Mt 2:12

ROW
After they had r-ed about three   Jn 6:19

ROWDY
The woman Folly is r;   Pr 9:13

ROYAL
live in the r city with you?   1Sm 27:5
and captured the r fortress.   2Sm 12:26
to annihilate all the r heirs.   2Kg 11:1
the LORD and a r palace for himself.   2Ch 2:1
but you wear your r attire.   2Ch 18:29
may use the r treasury to pay   Ezr 7:20
He placed the r crown on her   Est 2:17
the r daughter is all glorious,   Ps 45:13
It is Solomon's r litter   Sg 3:7
and a r diadem in the palm of   Is 62:3
provisions from the r food and   Dn 1:5
took off his r robe, put on sackcloth,   Jnh 3:6
in luxury are in r palaces.   Lk 7:25
was a certain r official whose   Jn 4:46
dressed in r robes and seated on   Ac 12:21
carry out the r law prescribed   Jms 2:8
a chosen race, a r priesthood, a   1Pt 2:9

RUBIES
I will make your battlements of r,   Is 54:12

RUDDER
by a very small r wherever the   Jms 3:4

RUG
and she covered him with a r.   Jdg 4:18

RUIN (n)
remain a mound of r-s forever;   Dt 13:16
house of our God and repair its r-s,   Ezr 9:9
Jerusalem lies in r-s   Neh 2:17
way of the wicked leads to r.   Ps 1:6
to the everlasting r-s,   Ps 74:3
and turned Jerusalem into r-s.   Ps 79:1
like an owl among the r-s.   Ps 102:6
his lips invites his own r.   Pr 13:3
speech will fall into r.   Pr 17:20
He brings the wicked to r.   Pr 21:12
a fortified city, into a r;   Is 25:2
you will rebuild the ancient r-s;   Is 58:12
land will become a desolate r   Jr 25:11
A r, a r, I will make it a r!   Ezk 21:27
grieve over the r of Joseph.   Am 6:6

My house still lies in r-s   Hg 1:9
I will rebuild its r-s and will set it   Ac 15:16
desires, which plunge people into r   1Tm 6:9
leads to the r of the hearers.   2Tm 2:14

RUIN (v)
and the stone wall was r-ed.   Pr 24:31
foxes that r the vineyards   Sg 2:15
Woe is me, for I am r-ed,   Is 6:5
I will r the great pride of both Judah   Jr 13:9
The cities that were once r-ed   Ezk 36:35
and the skins are r-ed.   Mt 9:17
r-s God's sanctuary, God will r   1Co 3:17
Your wealth is r-ed: Jms 5:2

RUINED (adj)
rebuild and occupy r cities,   Am 9:14

RULE (n)
His power establishes His r.   Is 40:10
when He abolishes all r and all   1Co 15:24
he competes according to the r-s.   2Tm 2:5

RULE (v)
They will r the fish of the sea   Gn 1:26
Are you really going to r us?   Gn 37:8
who comes from Jacob will r;   Nm 24:19
said to Gideon, "R over us,   Jdg 8:22
king who will r over them.   1Sm 8:9
we must have a king r over us   1Sm 12:12
who r-s in the fear of God,   2Sm 23:3
so that godless men should not r   Jb 34:30
do not let them r over me.   Ps 19:13
He r-s forever by His might;   Ps 66:7
You r the raging sea;   Ps 89:9
and His kingdom r-s over all.   Ps 103:19
R over Your surrounding enemies.   Ps 110:2
the sun to r by day,   Ps 136:8
wise servant will r over a   Pr 17:2
for a slave to r over princes!   Pr 19:10
the wicked r, people groan.   Pr 29:2
you acknowledge that Heaven r-s.   Dn 4:26
will sit on His throne and r.   Zch 6:13
don't want this man to r over us!   Lk 19:14
Death no longer r-s over Him.   Rm 6:9
For sin will not r over you,   Rm 6:14
who rises to r the Gentiles;   Rm 15:12

RULER
Joseph ... is r over all the land   Gn 45:26
from following the sheep to be r   2Sm 7:8

and the r-s conspire together against	Ps 2:2
Without leader, administrator, or r,	Pr 6:7
by me ... r-s enact just law;	Pr 8:15
much worse are lies for a r.	Pr 17:7
When you sit down to dine with a r,	Pr 23:1
A r can be persuaded through	Pr 25:15
If a r listens to lies, all his	Pr 29:12
wine or for r-s {to desire} beer.	Pr 31:4
All your r-s have fled together,	Is 22:3
Most High is r over the kingdom	Dn 4:32
One will come from you to be r	Mc 5:2
demons by the r of the demons!	Mt 9:34
know that the r-s of the Gentiles	Mt 20:25
Nicodemus, a r of the Jews.	Jn 3:1
Have any of the r-s believed in Him?	Jn 7:48
Now the r of this world will be	Jn 12:31
believe in Him even among the r-s,	Jn 12:42
the r of the world is coming.	Jn 14:30
the r of this world has been judged.	Jn 16:11
appointed you a r and a judge?	Ac 7:35
nor angels nor r-s, nor things	Rm 8:38
For r-s are not a terror to good	Rm 13:3
None of the r-s of this age knew	1Co 2:8
above every r and authority,	Eph 1:21
according to the r of the	Eph 2:2
but against the r-s, against	Eph 6:12
dominions or r-s or authorities	Col 1:16
disarmed the r-s and authorities	Col 2:15
Remind them to be submissive to r-s	Ti 3:1
the r of the kings of the earth.	Rv 1:5

RUMOR

he will hear a r and return to	2Kg 19:7
I had heard r-s about You, but now	Jb 42:5
there will be r after r.	Ezk 7:26
to hear of wars and r-s of wars.	Mt 24:6
you hear of wars and r-s of wars	Mk 13:7

RUN

But Esau ran to meet him,	Gn 33:4
r-ning in front of his chariots.	1Sm 8:11
David ran quickly to the battle	1Sm 17:48
Ahimaaz ran by way of the plain	2Sm 18:23
and ran ahead of Ahab	1Kg 18:46
r-ning down Aaron's beard,	Ps 133:2
His word r-s swiftly.	Ps 147:15

their feet r toward trouble	Pr 1:16
when you r, you will not stumble.	Pr 4:12
feet eager to r to evil,	Pr 6:18
righteous r to it and are protected.	Pr 18:10
revelation people r wild,	Pr 29:18
they will r and not grow weary;	Is 40:31
Do horses r on rock, or does	Am 6:12
I will never r away!	Mt 26:33
shaken together, and r-ning over	Lk 6:38
He ran, threw his arms around his	Lk 15:20
we must r aground on a certain	Ac 27:26
R in such a way that you may win	1Co 9:24
not r like one who r-s aimlessly,	1Co 9:26
not be r-ning, or have r, in vain.	Gl 2:2
You were r-ning well.	Gl 5:7
that I didn't r in vain or labor	Php 2:16
you, man of God, r from these	1Tm 6:11
and r with endurance the race	Heb 12:1

RUNNER

My days fly by faster than a r;	Jb 9:25
the r-s in a stadium all race, but	1Co 9:24

RURAL

explains why the r Jews who live	Est 9:19

RUSH

Why did you r on the plunder	1Sm 15:19
They r-ed him out of there.	2Ch 26:20
frantically r around in vain,	Ps 39:6
they r to shed innocent blood.	Is 59:7
sound ... of a violent r-ing wind	Ac 2:2

RUST

the pot that has r inside it,	Ezk 24:6
where moth and r destroy and	Mt 6:19

RUTH

Moabitess; widowed daughter-in-law of Naomi (Ru 1:1-5); married Boaz; ancestor of David and Christ (Ru 4:1; Mt 1:5-6,16).

RUTHLESS

a gang of r men seeks my life.	Ps 86:14
For the r one will vanish,	Is 29:20
r men from the nations,	Ezk 28:7

RUTHLESSLY

They worked the Israelites r	Ex 1:13

S

SABACHTHÁNI

voice, "Elí, Elí, lemá s?"	Mt 27:46
voice, "Eloi, Eloi, lemá s?"	Mk 15:34

SABBATH

rest, a holy S to the LORD.	Ex 16:23
Remember to dedicate the S day:	Ex 20:8
the LORD blessed the S day	Ex 20:11
You must observe My S-s,	Ex 31:13
You must keep My S-s and honor	Lv 26:2
rest and make up for its S-s.	Lv 26:34
man gathering wood on the S day.	Nm 15:32
and the land enjoyed its S rest	2Ch 36:21
New Moons and S-s,	Is 1:13
if you call the S a delight,	Is 58:13
you must consecrate the S day,	Jr 17:22
I also gave them My S-s	Ezk 20:12
through the grainfields on the S.	Mt 12:1
may not be in winter or on a S.	Mt 24:20
The S was made for man and not	Mk 2:27
Son of Man is Lord even of the S.	Mk 2:28
whether He would heal him on the S.	Mk 3:2
lawful on the S to do good or to	Mk 3:4
pull him out on the S day?	Lk 14:5
Now that day was the S,	Jn 5:9
you circumcise a man on the S.	Jn 7:22
mud and opened his eyes was a S.	Jn 9:14
for that S was a special day	Jn 19:31
Jerusalem—a S day's journey	Ac 1:12
On the S day they went into the	Ac 13:14
on three S days reasoned with	Ac 17:2
synagogue every S and tried to	Ac 18:4
or a new moon or a s day.	Col 2:16
A S rest remains, therefore, for	Heb 4:9

SABBATIC

You are to count seven s years,	Lv 25:8

SACHET

My love is a s of myrrh to me,	Sg 1:13

SACK

each man's money to his s,	Gn 42:25
cup was found in Benjamin's s.	Gn 44:12

SACKCLOTH

s around his waist, and mourned	Gn 37:34
put on s, and mourn over Abner.	2Sm 3:31
took s and spread it out for	2Sm 21:10
there was s under his clothes	2Kg 6:30
I have sewn s over my skin;	Jb 16:15
You removed my s and clothed me	Ps 30:11
were sick, my clothing was s;	Ps 35:13
instead of fine clothes, s;	Is 3:24
with fasting, s, and ashes.	Dn 9:3
proclaimed a fast and dressed in s	Jnh 3:5
would have repented in s and ashes	Mt 11:21
black like s made of goat hair;	Rv 6:12
for 1,260 days, dressed in s."	Rv 11:3

SACRED

You are to hold a s assembly	Ex 12:16
and smash their s pillars to	Ex 23:24
and do not set up a s pillar;	Dt 16:22
set up for themselves s pillars	2Kg 17:10
He broke the s pillars	2Kg 23:14
Announce a s fast;	Jl 1:14
they ate the s bread,	Mt 12:4
revelation of the s secret kept	Rm 16:25
you have known the s Scriptures,	2Tm 3:15

SACRIFICE (n)

Jacob offered a s on the mountain	Gn 31:54
is the Passover s to the LORD,	Ex 12:27
If his offering is a fellowship s,	Lv 3:1
If the s he offers is a vow or a	Lv 7:16
to obey is better than s,	1Sm 15:22
Offer s-s in righteousness and	Ps 4:5
You do not delight in s and offering;	Ps 40:6
You do not want a s, or I would	Ps 51:16
The s pleasing to God is a broken	Ps 51:17
Let them offer s-s of thanksgiving	Ps 107:22
offer You a s of thanksgiving	Ps 116:17
The s of the wicked is detestable	Pr 15:8
more acceptable to the LORD than s.	Pr 21:3
than to offer the s as fools do,	Ec 5:1
What are all your s-s to Me?	Is 1:11
your s-s do not please Me.	Jr 6:20
put a stop to s and offering.	Dn 9:27
abolish the daily s and set up	Dn 11:31
time the daily s is abolished	Dn 12:11
For I desire loyalty and not s,	Hs 6:6
Bring your s-s every morning,	Am 4:4
the LORD has prepared a s;	Zph 1:7

present a blind {animal} for s, Mal 1:8
I desire mercy and not s. Mt 9:13
mercy and not s, you would not Mt 12:7
than all the burnt offerings and s-s. Mk 12:33
and to offer a s (according to Lk 2:24
offerings and s-s for 40 years Ac 7:42
your bodies as a living s, Rm 12:1
a welcome s, pleasing to God. Php 4:18
need to offer s-s every day, Heb 7:27
with better s-s than these. Heb 9:23
of sin by the s of Himself. Heb 9:26
offering one s for sins forever Heb 10:12
no longer remains a s for sins, Heb 10:26
offer up to God a s of praise, Heb 13:15
for God is pleased with such s-s. Heb 13:16
offer spiritual s-s acceptable to 1Pt 2:5

SACRIFICE (v)
so that we may s to the LORD our Ex 5:3
Whoever s-s to any gods, except Ex 22:20
When you s a thank offering to Lv 22:29
S a thank offering to God, Ps 50:14
They s-d their sons ... to demons. Ps 106:37
They kept s-ing to the Baals and Hs 11:2
I will s to You with a voice of Jnh 2:9
the Passover lamb had to be s-d. Lk 22:7
our Passover has been s-d. 1Co 5:7
they s to demons and not to God. 1Co 10:20

SACRIFICED (adj)
from food s to idols, Ac 21:25
to eat meat s-d to idols Rv 2:14,20

SACRIFICIAL
took the fire and the s knife, Gn 22:6
s and fragrant offering to God. Eph 5:2

SAD
had never been s in his presence, Neh 2:1
in laughter a heart may be s, Pr 14:13
when a face is s, a heart may be Ec 7:3
guests be s while the groom Mt 9:15
s, because he was very rich. Lk 18:23

SADDLEBAG
put them in the s of the camel, Gn 31:34

SADDUCEES
S coming to the place of his baptism, Mt 3:7
and S approached, and as a test, Mt 16:1
of the yeast of the Pharisees and S. Mt 16:6

S, who say there is
no resurrection, Mt 22:23
He had silenced the S, Mt 22:34
and the S confronted them, Ac 4:1
the S, were filled with jealousy. Ac 5:17
between the Pharisees and the S, Ac 23:7

SAD-FACED
don't be s like the hypocrites. Mt 6:16

SAFE
The tents of robbers are s, Jb 12:6
They are kept s forever, Ps 37:28
that I can be s and be concerned Ps 119:117
Keep me s from violent men Ps 140:1,4
who walks in wisdom will be s. Pr 28:26
he has him back s and sound. Lk 15:27

SAFEGUARD
and your lips s knowledge. Pr 5:2
one who s-s understanding finds Pr 19:8

SAFELY
you ever return s, the LORD has 1Kg 22:28
He led them s, and they were not Ps 78:53
Then you will go s on your way; Pr 3:23
In this way, all got s to land. Ac 27:44
will bring me s into His 2Tm 4:18

SAFETY
and Israel lived in s from Dan 1Kg 4:25
His children are far from s. Jb 5:4
about and lie down in s. Jb 11:18
LORD, make me live in s. Ps 4:8
The horse is a false hope for s; Ps 33:17
impoverished will lie down in s, Is 14:30

SAIL (n)
Your s was {made of} fine Ezk 27:7

SAIL (v)
from there they s-ed to Cyprus. Ac 13:4
had decided to s past Ephesus so Ac 20:16
that we were to s to Italy, Ac 27:1
advice not to s from Crete and Ac 27:21

SAILOR
your s-s and helmsmen, Ezk 27:27
s-s were afraid, and each cried Jnh 1:5
Some s-s tried to escape from Ac 27:30
the s-s, and all who do business Rv 18:17

SAINT
bodies of the s-s who had gone Mt 27:52

loved by God, called as s-s. Rm 1:7
intercedes for the s-s according Rm 8:27
Christ Jesus and called as s-s, 1Co 1:2
not know that the s-s will judge 1Co 6:2
in all the churches of the s-s, 1Co 14:33
the ministry to the s-s, 2Co 9:1
His inheritance among the s-s, Eph 1:18
me—the least of all the s-s! Eph 3:8
training of the s-s in the work Eph 4:12
among you, as is proper for s-s. Eph 5:3
intercession for all the s-s. Eph 6:18
Greet every s in Christ Jesus. Php 4:21
but now revealed to His s-s. Col 1:26
our Lord Jesus with all His s-s. 1Th 3:13
glorified by His s-s and to be 2Th 1:10
to the s-s once for all. Jd 3
are the prayers of the s-s. Rv 5:8
drunk with the blood of the s-s Rv 17:6
the righteous acts of the s-s. Rv 19:8
the encampment of the s-s, Rv 20:9

SAKE

for the s of the 50 righteous Gn 18:24
man Absalom gently for my s. 2Sm 18:5
My s and for the s of My servant 2Kg 19:34
right paths for His name's s. Ps 23:3
for My own s, indeed, My own, Is 48:11
us, LORD, act for Your name's s. Jr 14:7
not for your s that I will act, Ezk 36:22,32
for Your own s, do not delay, Dn 9:19
no questions for conscience's, 1Co 10:25
for your s He became poor, 2Co 8:9
reproach for the s of the Heb 11:26
set out for the s of the name, 3Jn 7

SALAMIS

City in Cyprus where Paul preached (Ac 13:5).

SALEM

Jerusalem (Gn 14:18; Ps 76:2; Heb 7:1-2).

SALIVA

and letting s run down his beard. 1Sm 21:13
me alone until I swallow my s? Jb 7:19
some mud from the s, and spread Jn 9:6

SALOME

1. Wife of Zebedee, mother of James and John (Mk 15:40; 16:1; cp. Mt 27:56); possibly Mary's sister (Jn 19:25).

2. Daughter of Herodias (Mt 14:6-11; Mk 6:17-28).

SALT

back and became a pillar of s. Gn 19:26
it is to be seasoned with s, Ex 30:35
s of the covenant ... present s with
   each of your offerings. Lv 2:13
It is a perpetual covenant of s Nm 18:19
the City of S, and En-gedi—six Jos 15:62
the city and sowed it with s. Jdg 9:45
Edomites in the Valley of S. 2Sm 8:13
forever by a covenant of s? 2Ch 13:5
Is bland food eaten without s? Jb 6:6
not rubbed with s or wrapped in Ezk 16:4
You are the s of the earth. Mt 5:13
S is good, but if the s should lose Mk 9:50
seasoned with s, so that you may Col 4:6

SALTED

everyone will be s with fire. Mk 9:49

SALTWATER

Neither can a s spring yield Jms 3:12

SALTY

lose its taste, how can it be made s? Mt 5:13

SALUTE

they began to s Him, "Hail, King Mk 15:18

SALVATION

I wait for Your s, LORD. Gn 49:18
Stand firm and see the LORD's s Ex 14:13
He has become my s. Ex 15:2
and scorned the Rock of his s. Dt 32:15
because I rejoice in Your s. 1Sm 2:1
He not bring about my whole s 2Sm 23:5
Proclaim His s from day to day. 1Ch 16:23
S belongs to the LORD; Ps 3:8
rejoice in Your s within the Ps 9:14
my shield and the horn of my s, Ps 18:2
The God of my s is exalted. Ps 18:46
for You are the God of my s; Ps 25:5
The LORD is my light and my s Ps 27:1
Restore the joy of Your s to me, Ps 51:12
my s comes from Him. Ps 62:1
God is a God of s, Ps 68:20
who love Your s continually say, Ps 70:4
His s is very near those who fear Ps 85:9
proclaim His s from day to day. Ps 96:2
take the cup of s and worship Ps 116:13

He has become my s. Ps 118:14
S is far from the wicked because Ps 119:155
my song, He has become my s. Is 12:2
and our s in time of trouble. Is 33:2
who proclaims s, who says to Is 52:7
earth will see the s of our God. Is 52:10
and a helmet of s on His head; Is 59:17
Look, your s is coming, Is 62:11
but the s of Israel is only in the LORD Jr 3:23
S is from the LORD! Jnh 2:9
will rejoice in the God of my s! Hab 3:18
up a horn of s for us in the Lk 1:69
For my eyes have seen Your s. Lk 2:30
everyone will see the s of God. Lk 3:6
Today s has come to this house, Lk 19:9
because s is from the Jews. Jn 4:22
There is s in no one else, Ac 4:12
to bring s to the ends of the earth. Ac 13:47
s has come to the Gentiles to Rm 11:11
now our s is nearer than when Rm 13:11
now is the day of s. 2Co 6:2
be regretted and leading to s, 2Co 7:10
the helmet of s, and the sword Eph 6:17
work out your own s with fear Php 2:12
on a helmet of the hope of s. 1Th 5:8
has chosen you for s through 2Th 2:13
instruct you for s through faith 2Tm 3:15
appeared, with s for all people, Ti 2:11
if we neglect such a great s? Heb 2:3
better things connected with s. Heb 6:9
Concerning this s, the prophets 1Pt 1:10
S belongs to our God, who is Rv 7:10
S, glory, and power belong to Rv 19:1

SAMARIA

Capital and namesake of the northern kingdom (1Kg 13:32; 16:24; 2Kg 17:24; Is 7:9; Ezk 16:46; 23:4; Hos 8:5; Ob 19; Mc 1:1); captured by Assyria (2Kg 17:6).

In NT times, region of central hill country between Judah and Galilee (Lk 17:11; Ac 1:8; 8:1,5,14, often shunned by Jews (Jn 4:4-9); home of Samaritans.

SAMARITAN

places that the S-s had made. 2Kg 17:29
and don't enter any S town. Mt 10:5
a village of the S-s to make Lk 9:52
But a S on his journey came up Lk 10:33
thanking Him. And he was a S. Lk 17:16

Jews do not associate with S-s. Jn 4:9
You're a S and have a demon? Jn 8:48
evangelizing ... the S-s. Ac 8:25

SAME

even the Gentiles do the s? Mt 5:47
to do for you, do also the s for them Mt 7:12
told him, "Go and do the s." Lk 10:37
you, the judge, do the s things. Rm 2:1
since the s Lord of all is rich Rm 10:12
different gifts, but the s Spirit. 1Co 12:4
my joy by thinking the s way, Php 2:2
Jesus Christ is the s yesterday, Heb 13:8
Out of the s mouth come blessing Jms 3:10

SAMSON

Son of Manoah; Danite judge. Birth announced; to be a Nazirite (Jdg 13). Rashly married a Philistine; posed a riddle (Jdg 14). Took revenge on Philistines: set fire to fields; killed 1,000 with donkey's jawbone (Jdg 15). Married Delilah; was betrayed (16:4-21). Slaughter in Dagon's temple (16:23-30; Heb 11:32-34).

SAMUEL

Son of Elkanah and Hannah; Ephraimite judge, kingmaker, priest, and prophet. Born in answer to prayer (1Sm 1:1-20); raised at Shiloh by Eli (1:25-28; 2:11); called (3:1-18). Served as military and judicial judge (1Sm 7). Warned people about the nature of a king (8:10-18; 10:25); anointed Saul (10:1); rejected Saul (13:11-14; 15:10-29). Anointed David (16:1-13); protected David from Saul (19:18-24). Death (25:1); appearance to Saul after death (28:3-19).

SANBALLAT

Governor of Samaria, opponent of Nehemiah (Neh 2:10; 4:7-8; 6:1-14).

SANCTIFICATION

which results in s Rm 6:19,22
righteousness, s, and redemption 1Co 1:30
making our s complete in the 2Co 7:1
For this is God's will, your s: 1Th 4:3
salvation through s by the 2Th 2:13

SANCTIFY

temple I have s-ied for My name. 1Kg 9:7
that I, the LORD, s Israel. Ezk 37:28

or the altar that **s-ies** the gift?   Mt 23:19
S them by the truth;   Jn 17:17
they also may be **s-ied** by the truth.   Jn 17:19
among all who are **s-ied.**   Ac 20:32
who are **s-ied** by faith in Me.   Ac 26:18
be acceptable, **s-ied** by the Holy   Rm 15:16
who are **s-ied** in Christ Jesus   1Co 1:2
washed, you were **s-ied,** you were   1Co 6:11
husband is **s-ied** by the wife,   1Co 7:14
the God of peace Himself s you   1Th 5:23
since it is **s-ied** by the word of   1Tm 4:5
the One who **s-ies** and those who   Heb 2:11
we have been **s-ied** through the   Heb 10:10

SANCTUARY

They are to make a s for Me   Ex 25:8
Whenever he enters the s,   Ex 28:29
and revere My s;   Lv 19:30
standard s shekel.   Lv 27:3; Nm 3:50; 7:13
for sin against the s.   Nm 18:1
his sons are defiling the s,   1Sm 3:13
the s and the inner s.   1Kg 6:5
and all the utensils of the s,   1Ch 9:29
up my hands toward Your holy s.   Ps 28:2
gaze on You in the s to see Your   Ps 63:2
until I entered God's s.   Ps 73:17
They set Your s on fire;   Ps 74:7
and beauty are in His s.   Ps 96:6
Judah became His s,   Ps 114:2
Praise God in His s.   Ps 150:1
He will be a s;   Is 8:14
to beautify the place of My s,   Is 60:13
so that I must depart from My s?   Ezk 8:6
while I have been a s for them   Ezk 11:16
I am about to desecrate My s,   Ezk 24:21
and will set My s among them   Ezk 37:26
then the s will be restored.   Dn 8:14
will destroy the city and the s.   Dn 9:26
Whoever takes an oath by the s,   Mt 23:16
between the s and the altar.   Mt 23:35
Destroy this s, and I will raise   Jn 2:19
dwell in **s-ies** made with hands,   Ac 7:48
that you are God's s   1Co 3:16
your body is a s of the Holy   1Co 6:19
does God's s have with idols?   2Co 6:16
For we are the s of the living   2Co 6:16
into a holy s in the Lord,   Eph 2:21
so that he sits in God's s,   2Th 2:4
for ministry and an earthly s.   Heb 9:1

not enter a s made with hands   Heb 9:24
to enter the s through the blood   Heb 10:19
him a pillar in the s of My God,   Rv 3:12
Him day and night in His s.   Rv 7:15
measure God's s and the altar,   Rv 11:1
the heavenly s—the tabernacle   Rv 15:5
Almighty and the Lamb are its s.   Rv 21:22

SAND

and the s on the seashore   Gn 22:17
offspring like the s of the sea,   Gn 32:12
and hid him in the s.   Ex 2:12
as the s on the seashore   Jos 11:4; 1Sm 13:5
as numerous as the s by the sea;   1Kg 4:20
outweigh the s of the seas!   Jb 6:3
would outnumber the grains of s;   Ps 139:18
as numerous as the s of the sea,   Is 10:22
will be like the s of the sea,   Hs 1:10
who built his house on the s.   Mt 7:26
the grains of s by the seashore   Heb 11:12
He stood on the s of the sea.   Rv 12:18

SANDAL

Take your **s-s** off your feet,   Ex 3:5
remove his s from his foot,   Dt 25:9
s-s on your feet did not wear out;   Dt 29:5
Remove the **s-s** from your feet,   Jos 5:15
removed his s and said to Boaz,   Ru 4:8
on Edom I throw My s.   Ps 60:8; 108:9
needy person for a pair of **s-s.**   Am 2:6
not worthy to take off His **s-s.**   Mt 3:11
extra shirt, **s-s,** or a walking   Mt 10:10
the **s-s** off your feet, because   Ac 7:33
told him, "and put on your **s-s.**"   Ac 12:8
to untie the **s-s** on His feet.'   Ac 13:25

SANDALED

beautiful are your s feet,   Sg 7:1
your feet s with readiness   Eph 6:15

SANHEDRIN

will be subject to the **S.**   Mt 5:22
hand you over to **s-s** and flog   Mt 10:17
and the whole **S** were looking for   Mk 14:55
and brought Him before their **S.**   Lk 22:66
named Joseph, a member of the **S,**   Lk 23:50
had ordered them to leave the **S,**   Ac 4:15
had them stand before the **S,**   Ac 5:27
sitting in the **S** looked intently   Ac 6:15
out in the **S,** "Brothers, I am   Ac 23:6

SANITY

heaven, and my s returned to me.   Dn 4:34

SAPPHIRA

Wife of Ananias, lied about a gift and died (Ac 5:1).

SAPPHIRE

a turquoise, a s, and a diamond;	Ex 28:18
Its rocks are a source of s,	Jb 28:6
an ivory panel covered with s-s.	Sg 5:14
and lay your foundations in s-s.	Is 54:11
appearance of s stone was above	Ezk 1:26
jasper, the second s, the third	Rv 21:19

SARAH

Wife and half sister of Abraham; originally named Sarai (Gn 11:29-31; 20:12); barren (11:30). Twice passed off as Abraham's sister (12:10-20; 20). Gave Hagar to Abraham, then sent her away (Gn 16; 21:9-21). Laughed when she heard the promise of a son (18:9-15). Bore Isaac (21:1-7; Heb 11:11). Died; buried at Machpelah (Gn 23; 25:10; 49:31).

SARDIS

One of the seven churches (Rv 1:11; 3:1).

SASH

woven tunic, a turban, and a s.	Ex 28:4
Aaron, wrapped the s around him,	Lv 8:7
gold s-es wrapped around their	Rv 15:6

SATAN

S stood up against Israel and	1Ch 21:1
LORD asked S, "Where have you	Jb 1:7
LORD said to S: "The LORD rebuke	Zch 3:2
Jesus told him, "Go away, S!	Mt 4:10
If S drives out S, he is divided	Mt 12:26
told Peter, "Get behind Me, S!	Mt 16:23
40 days, being tempted by S.	Mk 1:13
S comes and takes away the word	Mk 4:15
I watched S fall from heaven	Lk 10:18
S has bound this woman, a	Lk 13:16
Then S entered Judas, called	Lk 22:3
S has asked to sift you like	Lk 22:31
piece of bread, S entered him.	Jn 13:27
why has S filled your heart to	Ac 5:3
and from the power of S to God,	Ac 26:18
soon crush S under your feet	Rm 16:20
that one over to S for the	1Co 5:5

S may tempt you because of your	1Co 7:5
not be taken advantage of by S;	2Co 2:11
For S himself is disguised as an	2Co 11:14
messenger of S to torment me so	2Co 12:7
and again—but S hindered us.	1Th 2:18
and I have delivered them to S,	1Tm 1:20
already turned away to follow S.	1Tm 5:15
synagogue of S.	Rv 2:9; 3:9
you live—where S-'s throne is!	Rv 2:13
who is called the Devil and S,	Rv 12:9
serpent who is the Devil and S,	Rv 20:2
S will be released from his	Rv 20:7

SATISFACTION

I will gain s against My foes;	Is 1:24

SATISFY

you will eat but not be s-ied.	Lv 26:26
and when you eat and are s-ied,	Dt 6:11
if you are not s-ied with her,	Dt 21:14
I will be s-ied with Your presence.	Ps 17:15
humble will eat and be s-ied;	Ps 22:26
You s me as with rich food;	Ps 63:5
ate and were completely s-ied,	Ps 78:29
S us in the morning with Your	Ps 90:14
He s-ies you with goodness;	Ps 103:5
For He has s-ied the thirsty and	Ps 107:9
I will s its needy with bread.	Ps 132:15
let her breasts always s you;	Pr 5:19
A man will be s-ied with good	Pr 12:14
but the diligent is fully s-ied.	Pr 13:4
and Abaddon are never s-ied,	Pr 27:20
Three things are never s-ied;	Pr 30:15
The eye is not s-ied by seeing or	Ec 1:8
is never s-ied with money,	Ec 5:10
but they are [still] not s-ied.	Is 9:20
and He will be s-ied with His	Is 53:11
your wages on what does not s?	Is 55:2
My people will be s-ied with My	Jr 31:14
them, you were still not s-ied.	Ezk 16:28
They will eat but not be s-ied;	Hs 4:10
have plenty to eat and be s-ied.	Jl 2:26
drink water but were not s-ied,	Am 4:8
like Death he is never s-ied.	Hab 2:5
never have enough to be s-ied.	Hg 1:6
the children to be s-ied first,	Mk 7:27
has s-ied the hungry with good	Lk 1:53
make no plans to s the fleshly	Rm 13:14
Be s-ied with what you have, for	Heb 13:5

SATRAPS

to the royal s and governors	Ezr 8:36
Jews, to the s, the governors,	Est 8:9
sent word to assemble the s,	Dn 3:2
to appoint 120 s over the	Dn 6:1

SATURATING

there without s-ing the earth,	Is 55:10

SAUL

1. First King of united Israel. Son of Kish; tall, handsome Benjaminite (1Sm 9:1-2). Met Samuel while looking for donkeys (9:3-27). Anointed privately (10:1); chosen by lot and announced publicly (10:17-24); delivered Jabesh-gilead (11:1-11); confirmed king at Gilgal (11:12-15). Rebuked and rejected (13:8-15; 15:11-30). Attempted to kill David (18:11,17,25; 19:10-17; 23:8,25; 24:2; 26:2); spared by David (1Sm 24; 26). Among the prophets (10:9-13; 19:18-24). Consulted a medium to inquire of Samuel (1Sm 28). Killed by Philistines (1Sm 31).

2. Paul's Hebrew name. see PAUL

SAVAGE

my departure s wolves will come	Ac 20:29

SAVE

you s-d a blessing for me?	Gn 27:36
That day the LORD s-d Israel	Ex 14:30
you, a people s-d by the LORD?	Dt 33:29
a deliverer to s the Israelites.	Jdg 3:9
said, "How can this guy s us?"	1Sm 10:27
can keep the LORD from s-ing,	1Sm 14:6
or by spear that the LORD s-s,	1Sm 17:47
S us, God of our salvation;	1Ch 16:35
So the LORD s-d Hezekiah	2Ch 32:22
s-s the needy from their sharp	Jb 5:15
God will s the humble.	Jb 22:29
s me because of Your faithful	Ps 6:4
and I was s-d from my enemies.	Ps 18:3
S Your people,	Ps 28:9
S me by Your righteousness.	Ps 31:1
king is not s-d by a large army;	Ps 33:16
heard {him} and s-d him from all	Ps 34:6
S me from the guilt of bloodshed,	Ps 51:14
down from heaven and s-s me,	Ps 57:3
S with Your right hand, and	Ps 60:5
s Your servant who trusts in You.	Ps 86:2
Yet He s-d them because of His	Ps 106:8
s me according to Your faithful	Ps 109:26
I was helpless, and He s-d me.	Ps 116:6
Your right hand will s me.	Ps 138:7
in nobles, in man, who cannot s.	Ps 146:3
and s those stumbling toward	Pr 24:11
Turn to Me and be s-d, all the ends	Is 45:22
hand is not too short to s,	Is 59:1
powerful to s.	Is 63:1
I am with you to s you	Jr 15:20
s me, and I will be s-d,	Jr 17:14
LORD, s Your people, the remnant	Jr 31:7
In those days Judah will be s-d,	Jr 33:16
I will s you from all your	Ezk 36:29
on the name of Yahweh will be s-d,	Jl 2:32
the brave will not s his life.	Am 2:14
is among you, a warrior who s-s.	Zph 3:17
Jesus, because He will s His people	Mt 1:21
saying, "Lord, s {us}!	Mt 8:25
whoever wants to s his life will	Mt 16:25
asked, "Then who can be s-d?"	Mt 19:25
it in three days, s Yourself!	Mt 27:40
He s-d others, but He cannot s	Mt 27:42
to s life or to kill?	Mk 3:4
and is baptized will be s-d,	Mk 16:16
Your faith has s-d you. Go in peace.	Lk 7:50
they may not believe and be s-d.	Lk 8:12
are there few being s-d?	Lk 13:23
come to seek and to s the lost.	Lk 19:10
the Messiah? S Yourself and us!	Lk 23:39
world might be s-d through Him.	Jn 3:17
enters by Me, he will be s-d	Jn 10:9
Father, s Me from this hour	Jn 12:27
the world but to s the world.	Jn 12:47
name of the Lord will be s-d.	Ac 2:21
Be s-d from this corrupt generation!	Ac 2:40
people by which we must be s-d.	Ac 4:12
Sirs, what must I do to be s-d?	Ac 16:30
will we be s-d by His life!	Rm 5:10
Now in this hope we were s-d,	Rm 8:24
from the dead, you will be s-d.	Rm 10:9
on the name of the Lord will be s-d.	Rm 10:13
this way all Israel will be s-d,	Rm 11:26
us who are being s-d it is God's	1Co 1:18
be lost, but he will be s-d,	1Co 3:15
his spirit may be s-d in the Day	1Co 5:5
whether you will s your husband?	1Co 7:16
that I may by all means s some.	1Co 9:22

of many, that they may be **s-d**. 1Co 10:33
You are also **s-d** by it, if you hold 1Co 15:2
are being **s-d** and among those 2Co 2:15
By grace you are **s-d**! Eph 2:5
grace you are **s-d** through faith, Eph 2:8
came into the world to **s** sinners 1Tm 1:15
wants everyone to be **s-d** 1Tm 2:4
But she will be **s-d** through 1Tm 2:15
this you will **s** both yourself 1Tm 4:16
who has **s-d** us and called us with 2Tm 1:9
He **s-d** us—not by works of Ti 3:5
was able to **s** Him from death, Heb 5:7
word, which is able to **s** you. Jms 1:21
have works? Can his faith **s** him? Jms 2:14
who is able to **s** and to destroy. Jms 4:12
of faith will **s** the sick person, Jms 5:15
s his life from death and cover Jms 5:20
people—were **s-d** through water. 1Pt 3:20
to this, now **s-s** you (not the 1Pt 3:21
righteous is **s-d** with difficulty 1Pt 4:18

SAVIOR

my refuge, and my **S**, 2Sm 22:3
Hurry to help me, Lord, my **S**. Ps 38:22
still praise Him, my **S** and my God. Ps 42:5
They forgot God their **S**, Ps 106:21
GOD, my strong **S**, You shield my Ps 140:7
will send them a **s** and leader, Is 19:20
and there is no other **S** but Me. Is 43:11
but Me, a righteous God and **S**; Is 45:21
I the LORD, am your **S**, Is 49:26; 60:16
and He became their **S**. Is 63:8
its **S** in time of distress, Jr 14:8
and no **S** exists besides Me. Hs 13:4
S-s will ascend Mount Zion to Ob 21
spirit has rejoiced in God my **S**, Lk 1:47
a **S**, who is Messiah the Lord. Lk 2:11
really is the **S** of the world. Jn 4:42
His right hand as ruler and **S**, Ac 5:31
God brought the **S**, Jesus, Ac 13:23
He is the **S** of the body. Eph 5:23
we also eagerly wait for a **S**, Php 3:20
God, who is the **S** of everyone, 1Tm 4:10
appearing of our **S** Christ Jesus, 2Tm 1:10
Father and Christ Jesus our **S**. Ti 1:4
glory of our great God and **S**, Ti 2:13
for man appeared from God our **S**, Ti 3:4
of our Lord and **S** Jesus Christ. 2Pt 3:18

sent the Son as **S** of the world. 1Jn 4:14
only God our **S**, through Jesus Jd 25

SAW

and put {them to work} with **s-s**, 2Sm 12:31
cut to size and **s-ed** with **s-s** 1Kg 7:9
and put them to work with **s-s**, 1Ch 20:3
above the one who **s-s** with it? Is 10:15
they were **s-ed** in two, Heb 11:37

SAY

Did God really **s**, 'You can't eat Gn 3:1
who do you **s** that I am? Mt 16:15

SAYING (n)

listen closely to my **s-ings**. Pr 4:20
s-ings of the wise are like goads, Ec 12:11
s-ings are given by one Shepherd. Ec 12:11
This **s** Is trustworthy 1Tm 1:15; 4:9
This **s** is trustworthy 2Tm 2:11; Ti 3:8

SCALE

that has fins and **s-s**, Lv 11:9
One **s** is so close to another that Jb 41:16
On a balance **s**, they go up; Ps 62:9
Dishonest **s-s** are detestable Pr 11:1
balances and **s-s** are the LORD's; Pr 16:11
and dishonest **s-s** are unfair. Pr 20:23
as a speck of dust on the **s-s**; Is 40:15
with dishonest **s-s** in his hands. Hs 12:7
and cheat with dishonest **s-s**. Am 8:5
Can I excuse wicked **s-s** Mc 6:11
something like **s-s** fell from his Ac 9:18
had a balance **s** in his hand. Rv 6:5

SCALY

It is a **s** outbreak, a skin disease Lv 13:30

SCARE

and no one will **s** them away. Dt 28:26

SCARECROWS

Like **s** in a cucumber patch, Jr 10:5

SCARLET

and tied a **s** {thread} around Gn 38:28
blue, purple, and **s** yarn, with a Ex 26:1
cedar wood, **s** yarn, and hyssop Lv 14:4
tie this **s** cord to the window Jos 2:18
clothed you in **s**, with luxurious 2Sm 1:24
Your lips are like a **s** cord, Sg 4:3
Though your sins are like **s**, Is 1:18
that you dress yourself in **s**, Jr 4:30

valiant men are dressed in **s**. Nah 2:3
Him and dressed Him in a **s** robe. Mt 27:28
with water, **s** wool, and hyssop Heb 9:19
sitting on a **s** beast that was Rv 17:3

SCATTER

otherwise, we will be **s-ed** over the Gn 11:4
But I will **s** you among the Lv 26:33
The LORD will **s** you among the Dt 4:27
like sheep and **s** us among the Ps 44:11
God arises. His enemies **s**, Ps 68:1
He **s-s** frost like ashes; Ps 147:16
I will **s** them among nations that Jr 9:16
and **s** the sheep of My pasture! Jr 23:1
One who **s-ed** Israel will gather Jr 31:10
and the sheep will be **s-ed**; Zch 13:7
who does not gather with Me **s-s**. Mt 12:30
and gather where I haven't **s-ed**, Mt 25:26
sheep of the flock will be **s-ed**. Mt 26:31
A man **s-s** seed on the ground; Mk 4:26
and the sheep will be **s-ed**. Mk 14:27
wolf then snatches and **s-s** them. Jn 10:12
unite the **s-ed** children of God. Jn 11:52
will be **s-ed** to his own home, Jn 16:32
apostles were **s-ed** throughout Ac 8:1
who had been **s-ed** as a result Ac 11:19
written: He has **s-ed**; He has given 2Co 9:9

SCENT

the **s** of knowing Him. 2Co 2:14
To some we are a **s** of death 2Co 2:16

SCEPTER

s will not depart from Judah, Gn 49:10
and a **s** will arise from Israel. Nm 24:17
if the king extends the golden **s** Est 4:11
of Your kingdom is a **s** of justice. Ps 45:6
Judah is My **s**. Ps 60:7; 108:8
extend Your mighty **s** from Zion. Ps 110:2
The **s** of the wicked will not Ps 125:3
The **s** of My son, the sword Ezk 21:10
of Your kingdom is a **s** of justice. Heb 1:8
shepherd them with an
   iron **s**; Rv 2:27; 19:15

SCEVA

Seven sons of **S**, a Jewish chief Ac 19:14

SCHEME

every **s** his mind thought of was Gn 6:5
a shelter from the **s-s** of men, Ps 31:20

but He condemns a man who **s-s**. Pr 12:2
and a man who **s-s** is hated. Pr 14:17
plots evil will be called a **s-r**. Pr 24:8
but they pursued many **s-s**. Ec 7:29

SCHOLAR

Where is the **s**? Where is the 1Co 1:20

SCOFF

he **s-s** at all his adversaries. Ps 10:5
all these things and **s-ing** at Him. Lk 16:14
and even the leaders kept **s-ing**: Lk 23:35

SCOFFERS

Look, you **s**, marvel and vanish Ac 13:41
s will come in the last days to 2Pt 3:3
s walking according to their own Jd 18

SCORCH

rebellious live in a **s-ed** land. Ps 68:6
on coals without **s-ing** his feet? Pr 6:28
his speech is like a **s-ing** fire. Pr 16:27
will not be **s-ed** when you walk Is 43:2
s-ing heat or sun will not strike Is 49:10
God appointed a **s-ing** east wind. Jnh 4:8
the sun came up they were **s-ed**, Mt 13:6

SCORCHER

you say, 'It's going to be a **s**!' Lk 12:55

SCORN

and **s-ed** the Rock of his salvation. Dt 32:15
s-ed by men and despised by people. Ps 22:6
despises you and **s-s** you: Is 37:22
My face from **s** and spitting. Is 50:6

SCORNER

the voice of the **s** and reviler, Ps 44:16
the **s** will disappear, Is 29:20

SCORPION

its poisonous snakes and **s-s**, Dt 8:15
you and you live among **s-s**, Ezk 2:6
to trample on snakes and **s-s** Lk 10:19
asks for an egg, will give him a **s**? Lk 11:12
like the power that **s-s** have Rv 9:3

SCOUNDREL

they had brought together some **s-s** Ac 17:5

SCOURGE

s a man who is a Roman citizen Ac 22:25

SCOUT

Send men to **s** out the land Nm 13:2

Valley of Eshcol, s-ing the land.	Dt 1:24
s the land, especially Jericho.	Jos 2:1
So the men went up and s-ed Ai.	Jos 7:2
emissaries ... to s out the city,	2Sm 10:3

SCREAM

when I s-ed for help, he left	Gn 39:18

SCREEN

make a s embroidered with	Ex 26:36
and s off the ark with the veil.	Ex 40:3

SCRIBE

asked Ezra the s to bring the	Neh 8:1
lying pen of s-s has produced	Jr 8:8
seize Baruch the s and Jeremiah	Jr 36:26
surpasses that of the s-s and	Mt 5:20
authority, and not like their s-s.	Mt 7:29
A s approached Him and said,	Mt 8:19
woe to you, s-s and Pharisees,	Mt 23:13
Beware of the s-s, who want to	Mk 12:38
priests and the s-s were looking	Mk 14:1

SCRIPTURE

don't know the S-s or the power	Mt 22:29
But the S-s must be fulfilled.	Mk 14:49
the S was fulfilled that says:	Mk 15:28
Today ... this S has been fulfilled.	Lk 4:21
concerning Himself in all the S-s.	Lk 24:27
You pore over the S-s because you	Jn 5:39
and the S cannot be broken	Jn 10:35
to fulfill the S that says:	Jn 19:24
the S had to be fulfilled that	Ac 1:16
Now the S passage he was reading	Ac 8:32
reasoned with them from the S-s,	Ac 17:2
examined the S-s daily to see if	Ac 17:11
man who was powerful in the S-s,	Ac 18:24
For what does the S say?	Rm 4:3
For the S tells Pharaoh:	Rm 9:17
died ... according to the S-s	1Co 15:3
But the S has imprisoned	Gl 3:22
you have known the sacred S-s,	2Tm 3:15
All S is inspired by God and is	2Tm 3:16
For it stands in S:	1Pt 2:6
no prophecy of S comes from one's	2Pt 1:20

SCROLL

curses on a s and wash {them}	Nm 5:23
which are written in this s,	Dt 28:58
about me in the volume of the s.	Ps 40:7
presence and inscribe it on a s;	Is 30:8

Baruch wrote on a s all the	Jr 36:4
had burned the s with the words	Jr 36:27
Eat this s, then go and speak to	Ezk 3:1
and saw a flying s.	Zch 5:1
The s of the prophet Isaiah was	Lk 4:17
as well as the s-s, especially	2Tm 4:13
open the s and break its seals?	Rv 5:2
like a s being rolled up	Rv 6:14
he had a little s opened in his	Rv 10:2

SCYTHIAN

barbarian, S, slave and free;	Col 3:11

SEA

gathering of the water "s-s."	Gn 1:10
and blew them into the Red S.	Ex 10:19
through the s on dry ground,	Ex 14:22
horse and its rider into the s.	Ex 15:1
And it is not across the s,	Dt 30:13
Am I the s or a s monster,	Jb 7:12
Who enclosed the s behind doors	Jb 38:8
through the currents of the s-s.	Ps 8:8
depths of the s became visible,	Ps 18:15
He laid its foundation on the s-s	Ps 24:2
topple into the depths of the s-s,	Ps 46:2
The s is His; He made it.	Ps 95:5
Let the s and all that fills it,	Ps 98:7
Others went to s in ships,	Ps 107:23
a limit for the s so that the	Pr 8:29
flow to the s, yet the s is never full.	Ec 1:7
I dry up the s by My rebuke;	Is 50:2
are like the storm-tossed s,	Is 57:20
sand as the boundary of the s,	Jr 5:22
huge beasts came up from the s,	Dn 7:3
stagger from s to s and roam from	Am 8:12
sins into the depths of the s.	Mc 7:19
rebukes the s so that it dries	Nah 1:4
as the waters cover the s.	Hab 2:14
the winds and the s obey Him!	Mt 8:27
toward them walking on the s.	Mt 14:25
up and thrown into the s,	Mt 21:21
they saw Jesus walking on the s.	Jn 6:19
earth, and the s, and everything	Ac 4:24
all passed through the s,	1Co 10:1
doubter is like the surging s,	Jms 1:6
was something like a s of glass,	Rv 4:6
a beast coming up out of the s.	Rv 13:1
standing on the s of glass with	Rv 15:2
Then the s gave up its dead,	Rv 20:13
and the s existed no longer.	Rv 21:1

SEACOAST

Woe, inhabitants of the **s**,	Zph 2:5
The **s** will become pasturelands	Zph 2:6

SEAL (n)

stone must be engraved like a **s**,	Ex 28:21
Set me as a **s** on your heart,	Sg 8:6
You were the **s** of perfection,	Ezk 28:12
set His **s** of approval on Him.	Jn 6:27
circumcision as a **s** of the	Rm 4:11
for you are the **s** of my	1Co 9:2
the scroll and break its **s-s**?"	Rv 5:2
When He opened the second **s**,	Rv 6:3
When He opened the seventh **s**,	Rv 8:1
not have God's **s** on their foreheads.	Rv 9:4

SEAL (v)

Ahab's name and **s-ed** them with	1Kg 21:8
s-ed with the royal signet ring	Est 8:8
My rebellion would be **s-ed** up	Jb 14:17
locked garden and a **s-ed** spring.	Sg 4:12
S up the instruction among my	Is 8:16
I can't read it, because it is **s-ed**.	Is 29:11
s up the vision because it refers	Dn 8:26
to **s** up vision and prophecy,	Dn 9:24
s the book until the time of the end.	Dn 12:4
tomb secure by **s-ing** the stone	Mt 27:66
He has also **s-ed** us and given us	2Co 1:22
were **s-ed** with the promised Holy	Eph 1:13
who **s-ed** you for the day of	Eph 4:30
s-ed with seven seals.	Rv 5:1
s the slaves ... on their foreheads.	Rv 7:3
S up what the seven thunders	Rv 10:4
Don't **s** the prophetic words of	Rv 22:10

SEAMLESS

tunic, which was **s**, woven in one	Jn 19:23

SEARED

liars whose consciences are **s-ed**.	1Tm 4:2

SEARCH

the LORD **s-es** every heart and	1Ch 28:9
they repented and **s-ed** for God.	Ps 78:34
S for the LORD and for His	Ps 105:4
You have **s-ed** me and known me.	Ps 139:1
S me, God, and know my heart;	Ps 139:23
and those who **s** for me find me.	Pr 8:17
a time to **s** and a time to count	Ec 3:6
Me when you **s** for Me with all	Jr 29:13
I Myself will **s** for My flock and	Ezk 34:11

Go and **s** carefully for the child.	Mt 2:8
Keep **s-ing**, and you will find.	Mt 7:7
and go and **s** for the stray?	Mt 18:12
returned to Jerusalem to **s** for Him.	Lk 2:45
and **s** carefully until she finds	Lk 15:8
And He who **s-es** the hearts knows	Rm 8:27
for the Spirit **s-es** everything,	1Co 2:10
prophets ... **s-ed** and carefully	1Pt 1:10

SEASHORE

and the sand on the **s**.	Gn 22:17
saw the Egyptians dead on the **s**.	Ex 14:30
numerous as the sand on the **s**	Jos 11:4
numerous as the sand on the **s**.	1Sm 13:5
as {vast} as the sand on the **s**.	1Kg 4:29
as the grains of sand by the **s**.	Heb 11:12

SEASON

of sheaves is gathered in its **s**.	Jb 5:26
that bears its fruit in **s**	Ps 1:3
made the moon to mark the **s-s**;	Ps 104:19
does not plow during planting **s**;	Pr 20:4
stork in the sky knows her **s-s**.	Jr 8:7
He changes the times and **s-s**;	Dn 2:21
it was not the **s** for figs.	Mk 11:13
so that **s-s** of refreshing may	Ac 3:19
days, months, **s-s**, and years.	Gl 4:10
About the times and the **s-s**:	1Th 5:1

SEASONED

it is to be **s** with salt,	Ex 30:35
be gracious, **s** with salt, so	Col 4:6

SEAT (n)

Make a mercy **s** of pure gold,	Ex 25:17
I sit in the **s** of gods	Ezk 28:2
the Ancient of Days took His **s**.	Dn 7:9
the front **s-s** in the synagogues,	Mt 23:6
love the front **s** in the	Lk 11:43
before the judgment **s** of God.	Rm 14:10
before the judgment **s** of Christ,	2Co 5:10
overshadowing the mercy **s**.	Heb 9:5

SEAT (v)

God is **s-ed** on His holy throne.	Ps 47:8
in order to **s** them with nobles	Ps 113:8
I saw the Lord **s-ed** on a high and	Is 6:1
are **s-ed** in the chair of Moses.	Mt 23:2
s-ed at the right hand of the	Mt 26:64
robes and **s-ed** on the throne,	Ac 12:21
and **s-ing** Him at His right hand	Eph 1:20

up with Him and **s-ed** us with Him | Eph 2:6
s-ed at the right hand of God. | Col 3:1
God, who is **s-ed** on the throne, | Rv 19:4

SEAWEED
s was wrapped around my head. | Jnh 2:5

SECOND
and then morning: the s day. | Gn 1:8
The s is like it: Love your | Mt 22:39
womb a s time and be born? | Jn 3:4
the s man is from heaven. | 1Co 15:47
Behind the s curtain, | Heb 9:3
appear a s time, not to bear | Heb 9:28
never be harmed by the s death. | Rv 2:11
the s living creature was like a | Rv 4:7
The s death has no power over | Rv 20:6
This is the s death, the lake of | Rv 20:14
sulfur, which is the s death." | Rv 21:8

SECRET
You acted in s, but I will do | 2Sm 12:12
show you the **s-s** of wisdom, | Jb 11:6
The s counsel of the LORD is for | Ps 25:14
He knows the **s-s** of the heart? | Ps 44:21
our s sins in the light of Your | Ps 90:8
from You when I was made in s, | Ps 139:15
goes around revealing a s, | Pr 11:13
who reveals **s-s** is a constant | Pr 20:19
A s gift soothes anger, and a | Pr 21:14
without revealing another's s; | Pr 25:9
I have not spoken in s | Is 45:19; 48:16
keep these words s and seal the | Dn 12:4
so that your giving may be in s. | Mt 6:4
Father who sees in s will reward you. | Mt 6:4
Because the **s-s** of the kingdom | Mt 13:11
things kept from the | Mt 13:35
I haven't spoken anything in s. | Jn 18:20
judges what people have kept s, | Rm 2:16
of the sacred s kept silent for | Rm 16:25
The **s-s** of his heart will be | 1Co 14:25
renounced shameful s things, | 2Co 4:2
what is done by them in s. | Eph 5:12
I have learned the s {of being | Php 4:12

SECRETARY
Seraiah was court s; | 2Sm 8:17
Sheva was court s; | 2Sm 20:25
king sent the court s Shaphan | 2Kg 22:3
Some of the Levites were **s-ies**, | 2Ch 34:13

SECRETLY
Israelites s did what was not | 2Kg 17:9
and bread {eaten} s is tasty! | Pr 9:17
A wicked man s takes a bribe to | Pr 17:23
decided to divorce her s. | Mt 1:19
Then Herod s summoned the wise | Mt 2:7
also went up, not openly but s. | Jn 7:10
but s because of his fear of the | Jn 19:38
who came in s to spy on our | Gl 2:4

SECT
of the s of the Nazarenes | Ac 24:5
the Way, which they call a s, | Ac 24:14
concerning this s, we are aware | Ac 28:22

SECTION
made repairs to another s, | Neh 3:11
Scripture says in the Elijah s | Rm 11:2

SECURE
Their homes are s and free of | Jb 21:9
His ways are always s; | Ps 10:5
making me s while at my mother's | Ps 22:9
When I was s, I said, "I will | Ps 30:6
on a rock, making my steps s. | Ps 40:2
but the righteous are s forever. | Pr 10:25
flock will be s in their land. | Ezk 34:27
to those who feel s on the hill | Am 6:1
and made the tomb s by sealing | Mt 27:66
to make his life s will lose it, | Lk 17:33

SECURELY
that you may live s in the land. | Lv 25:18
who were there were living s, | Jdg 18:7
my body also rests s. | Ps 16:9
and sets me s on the heights. | Ps 18:33
dwell in the land and live s. | Ps 37:3
lives with integrity lives s, | Pr 10:9
lover of luxury, who sits s, | Is 47:8
enable the people to rest s. | Hs 2:18
They will live s, for then His | Mc 5:4

SECURITY
around you and you live in s, | Dt 12:10
upper millstone as s for a debt, | Dt 24:6
not take a widow's garment as s. | Dt 24:17
shouldn't I find s for you, | Ru 3:1
He gives them a sense of s, | Jb 24:23
you have put up s for your | Pr 6:1
puts up s for a stranger, | Pr 11:15
and puts up s for his friend. | Pr 17:18

he has put up **s** for a stranger; Pr 20:16
who put up **s** for loans. Pr 22:26
he has put up **s** for a stranger; Pr 27:13
nation at ease, one living in **s.** Jr 49:31
So Jerusalem will dwell in **s.** Zch 14:11
say, "Peace and **s,**" then sudden 1Th 5:3

SEDAN
Solomon made a a **s** chair for Sg 3:9

SEDUCE
When a man **s-s** a virgin who was Ex 22:16
wives **s-d** him {to follow} other 1Kg 11:4
She **s-s** him with her persistent Pr 7:21
looking for sin, **s-ing** unstable 2Pt 2:14

SEDUCTION
and the **s** of wealth choke
    the word, Mt 13:22

SEE
And God **saw** that it was good. Gn 1:10
I have **s-n** God face to face, Gn 32:30
when I **s** the blood, I will pass Ex 12:13
no one can **s** Me and live. Ex 33:20
but the LORD **s-s** the heart. 1Sm 16:7
yet I will **s** God in my flesh. Jb 19:26
The upright will **s** His face. Ps 11:7
Taste and **s** that the LORD is Ps 34:8
Come and **s** the works of God; Ps 66:5
They say, "The LORD doesn't **s** it. Ps 94:7
One who formed the eye not **s?** Ps 94:9
eyes, but cannot **s.** Ps 115:5
so that I may **s** wonderful things Ps 119:18
S if there is any offensive way Ps 139:24
hearing ear and the **s-ing** eye Pr 20:12
Have you **s-n** the one I love? Sg 3:3
I **saw** the Lord seated on a high Is 6:1
because my eyes have **s-n** the King, Is 6:5
they might **s** with their eyes Is 6:10
darkness have **s-n** a great light; Is 9:2
ends of the earth will **s** the salvation Is 52:10
He will **s** {His} seed, Is 53:10
your young men will **s** visions. Jl 2:28
darkness have **s-n** a great light, Mt 4:16
in heart, because they will **s** God. Mt 5:8
that they may **s** your good works Mt 5:16
of people, to be **s-n** by them. Mt 6:1
Father who **s-s** in secret will Mt 6:4
this has ever been **s-n** in Israel! Mt 9:33
because looking they do not **s,** Mt 13:13

people longed to **s** the things you
    s yet didn't **s** them; Mt 13:17
We have **s-n** incredible things today! Lk 5:26
No one has ever **s-n** God. Jn 1:18
"Come and **s,**" Philip answered. Jn 1:46
We testify to what We have **s-n,** Jn 3:11
from God. He has **s-n** the Father. Jn 6:46
overjoyed that he would **s** My day; Jn 8:56
I was blind, and now I can **s!** Jn 9:25
do not **s** will **s** and those who do **s**
    will become blind. Jn 9:39
Sir, we want to **s** Jesus. Jn 12:21
who has **s-n** Me has **s-n** the Father. Jn 14:9
the world will **s** Me no longer, Jn 14:19
I have **s-n** the Lord! Jn 20:18
Because you have **s-n** Me, you have Jn 20:29
about what we have **s-n** and heard. Ac 4:20
been clearly **s-n,** being understood Rm 1:20
What no eye has **s-n** and no ear has 1Co 2:9
Have I not **s-n** Jesus our Lord? 1Co 9:1
For now we **s** indistinctly, 1Co 13:12
So we do not focus on what is **s-n,** 2Co 4:18
received and heard and **s-n** in me, Php 4:9
in the Spirit, **s-n** by angels, 1Tm 3:16
none of mankind has **s-n** or can **s,** 1Tm 6:16
though you have not **s-n** Him. 1Pt 1:8
what we have **s-n** with our eyes, 1Jn 1:1
because we will **s** Him as He is. 1Jn 3:2
No one has ever **s-n** God. 1Jn 4:12
whom he has **s-n** cannot love God 1Jn 4:20
clouds, and every eye will **s** Him, Rv 1:7
They will **s** His face, and His Rv 22:4

SEED
bearing fruit with **s** in it, Gn 1:11
and between your **s** and her **s.** Gn 3:15
will sow your **s** in vain because Lv 26:16
In the morning sow your **s,** Ec 11:6
the holy is the stump. Is 6:13
He will see {His} **s,** Is 53:10
and providing **s** to sow and food Is 55:10
who sowed good **s** in his field. Mt 13:24
like a mustard **s** that a man took Mt 13:31
faith the size of a mustard **s,** Mt 17:20
and the **s** sprouts and grows Mk 4:27
Other **s** fell on the rock; Lk 8:6
The **s** is the word of God. Lk 8:11
And in your **s** all the families Ac 3:25
in Isaac your **s** will be called. Rm 9:7

of Hosts had not left us a s, Rm 9:29
to each of the s-s its own body. 1Co 15:38
One who provides s for the sower 2Co 9:10
He does not say "and to s-s," Gl 3:16
are Abraham's s, heirs according Gl 3:29
In Isaac your s will be called. Heb 11:18
not of perishable s but of 1Pt 1:23
because His s remains in him; 1Jn 3:9

SEEDTIME

earth endures, s and harvest, Gn 8:22

SEEK

when you s Him with all your Dt 4:29
If you s Him, He will be found 1Ch 28:9
pray and s My face, and turn 2Ch 7:14
and have decided to s God. 2Ch 19:3
so he resolved to s the LORD. 2Ch 20:3
sought the LORD with all his heart. 2Ch 22:9
Josiah began to s the God of his 2Ch 34:3
is gracious to all who s Him, Ezr 8:22
who s the LORD will not lack any Ps 34:10
s peace and pursue it. Ps 34:14
one who is wise and who s-s God. Ps 53:2
You are my God; I eagerly s You. Ps 63:1
sought You with all my heart; Ps 119:10
but those who s the LORD Pr 28:5
sought him, but did not find him. Sg 3:1
Learn to do what is good. S justice. Is 1:17
The nations will s Him, Is 11:10
S the LORD while He may be found; Is 55:6
found by those who did not s Me. Is 65:1
stupid: they don't s the LORD. Jr 10:21
You will s Me and find Me when Jr 29:13
I will s the lost, bring back Ezk 34:16
is time to s the LORD until He Hs 10:12
house of Israel: S Me and live! Am 5:4
from north to east, s-ing the word Am 8:12
the Lord you s will suddenly Mal 3:1
But s first the kingdom of God Mt 6:33
come to s and to save the lost. Lk 19:10
because I do not s My own will, Jn 5:30
I do not s My glory; Jn 8:50
that they might s God, and Ac 17:27
there is no one who s-s God. Rm 3:11
from a wife? Do not s a wife. 1Co 7:27
No one should s his own {good}, 1Co 10:24
I am not s-ing what is yours, 2Co 12:14
all s their own interests, Php 2:21
s what is above, where the Messiah Col 3:1

and rewards those who s Him. Heb 11:6
He must s peace and pursue it, 1Pt 3:11

SEEM

they s-ed like only a few days Gn 29:20
a way that s-s right to
  a man, Pr 14:12; 16:25
a man's ways s right in his own Pr 16:2
state his case s-s right until Pr 18:17
ways of a man s right to him, Pr 21:2
No discipline s-s enjoyable at the Heb 12:11

SEER

today was formerly called the s. 1Sm 9:9
every prophet and every s, 2Kg 17:13
in the Events of Samuel the S, 1Ch 29:29
and the Events of Gad the S, 1Ch 29:29
of Iddo the S concerning 2Ch 9:29
Hanani the s came to King Asa of 2Ch 16:7
words of the s-s who spoke to 2Ch 33:18
say to the s-s, "Do not see," Is 30:10
said to Amos, "Go away, you s! Am 7:12
Then the s-s will be ashamed and Mc 3:7

SEIR

A mountain range in Edom (Gn 14:6; Dt
1:2); another name for Edom (Gn 32:3; Dt
2:4,12; 2Ch 20:22-23); prophesied against
(Ezk 35:2).

SEIZE

s the city, for the LORD Jos 8:7
S the prophets of Baal! 1Kg 18:40
Trembling s-d them there, agony Ps 48:6
Distress has s-d us—pain like Jr 6:24
They covet fields and s them; Mc 2:2
have been s-ing it by force. Mt 11:12
Often a spirit s-s him; Lk 9:39
They s-d Him, led Him away, Lk 22:54
Then they tried to s Him. Jn 7:30
But no one s-d Him, because His Jn 8:20
they were trying again to s Him, Jn 10:39
s-d Paul and Silas and dragged Ac 16:19
Then they all s-d Sosthenes, Ac 18:17
s-ing an opportunity through the Rm 7:8

SEIZURES

because he has s and suffers Mt 17:15

SELA

Major fortified city in Edom (Jdg 1:36;
2Kg 14:7; Is 16:1; 42:11).

SELAH

is no help for him in God." S   Ps 3:2

Holy One from Mount Paran. S   Hab 3:3

SELDOM

S set foot in your neighbor's   Pr 25:17

SELF

desire integrity in the inner s,   Ps 51:6

that our old s was crucified   Rm 6:6

For people will be lovers of s,   2Tm 3:2

that you owe me even your own s.   Phm 19

SELF-CONDEMNED

is perverted and sins, being s.   Ti 3:11

SELF-CONTROL

righteousness, s, and the   Ac 24:25

you because of your lack of s.   1Co 7:5

But if they do not have s,   1Co 7:9

exercises s in everything.   1Co 9:25

gentleness, s. Against such   Gl 5:23

without s, brutal, without   2Tm 3:3

knowledge with s, s with endurance,   2Pt 1:6

SELF-CONTROLLED

of one wife, s, sensible,   1Tm 3:2

not slanderers, s, faithful in   1Tm 3:11

sensible, righteous, holy, s,   Ti 1:8

men are to be s, worthy of   Ti 2:2

SELF-COUNSEL

of a friend is better than s.   Pr 27:9

SELF-DENIAL

to practice s and do no work,   Lv 16:29

sacred assembly and practice s;   Lv 23:27

seventh month and practice s;   Nm 29:7

SELF-DISCIPLINED

minds ready for action, being s,   1Pt 1:13

SELF-INDULGENCE

they are full of greed and s!   Mt 23:25

SELF-INDULGENT

she who is s is dead even while   1Tm 5:6

SELFISH

himself pursues {s} desires;   Pr 18:1

is not s; is not provoked;   1Co 13:5

of anger, s ambitions, slander   2Co 12:20

outbursts of anger, s ambitions,   Gl 5:20

envy and s ambition   Jms 3:14,16

SELF-SEEKING

to those who are s and disobey   Rm 2:8

SELL

First s me your birthright.   Gn 25:31

let's s him to the Ishmaelites   Gn 37:27

redeem what his brother has **sold**.   Lv 25:25

unless their Rock had **sold** them,   Dt 32:30

He **sold** them to the enemies

around   Jdg 2:14

Go s the oil and pay your debt;   2Kg 4:7

You s Your people for nothing;   Ps 44:12

Joseph, who was **sold** as a slave.   Ps 105:17

and do not s—truth, wisdom   Pr 23:23

makes and s-s linen garments;   Pr 31:24

You were **sold** for nothing, and you   Is 52:3

You **sold** the people of Judah and   Jl 3:6

because they s a righteous   Am 2:6

two sparrows **sold** for a penny?   Mt 10:29

joy he goes and s-s everything   Mt 13:44

buying and s-ing in the temple.   Mt 21:12

s all you have and give to the poor,   Mk 10:21

sold for more than 300 denarii and   Mk 14:5

buying, s-ing, planting,   Lk 17:28

sword should s his robe and buy   Lk 22:36

So they **sold** their possessions and   Ac 2:45

sold a field he owned, brought the   Ac 4:37

sold into sin's power.   Rm 7:14

that is **sold** in the meat market   1Co 10:25

sold his birthright in exchange   Heb 12:16

one can buy or s unless he has   Rv 13:17

SEMEN

he released his s on the ground   Gn 38:9

When a man has an emission of s,   Lv 15:16

a man who has an emission of s,   Lv 22:4

SEND

and he **sent** out a raven.   Gn 8:7

I AM has **sent** me to you.   Ex 3:14

I will s an angel ahead of you   Ex 33:2

Moses **sent** them to scout out   Nm 13:17

The LORD **sent** me to anoint you   1Sm 15:1

Samuel told Jesse, "S for him.   1Sm 16:11

LORD will s His faithful love   Ps 42:8

slacker is to the one who s-s him   Pr 10:26

The one who s-s a message by a   Pr 26:6

S your bread on the surface of   Ec 11:1

Who should I s? ... Here I am. S me.   Is 6:8

I will s him against a godless   Is 10:6

He will s them a savior and | Is 19:20
the Lord GOD has sent me | Is 48:16
He has sent Me to heal the | Is 61:1
to everyone I s you to and speak | Jr 1:7
It was not I who sent
or commanded | Jr 23:32
I will s fire against | Am 1:4,7,10,12; 2:2,5
s you into exile beyond Damascus. | Am 5:27
I am going to s My messenger, | Mal 3:1
I am going to s you Elijah the | Mal 4:5
s-s rain on the righteous and | Mt 5:45
of the harvest to s out workers | Mt 9:38
sent out these 12 after giving | Mt 10:5
s-ing you out like sheep among | Mt 10:16
Me welcomes Him who sent Me. | Mt 10:40
s-ing My messenger ahead of You; | Mt 11:10
of Man will s out His angels, | Mt 13:41
S the crowds away so they can go | Mt 14:15
I was sent only to the lost sheep of | Mt 15:24
Finally, he sent his son to them. | Mt 21:37
He will s out His angels with a | Mt 24:31
At harvest time he sent a slave to | Mk 12:2
has sent Me to proclaim freedom | Lk 4:18
was not sent to any of them | Lk 4:26
I was sent for this purpose. | Lk 4:43
the Baptist sent us to ask You, | Lk 7:20
named John who was sent from God. | Jn 1:6
For God did not s His Son into | Jn 3:17
the will of Him who sent Me. | Jn 5:30; 6:38
who sent Me testifies about Me. | Jn 8:18
but the One who sent Me is true, | Jn 8:26
The One who sent Me is with Me. | Jn 8:29
come on My own, but He sent Me. | Jn 8:42
of Siloam" (which means "Sent"). | Jn 9:7
so they may believe You sent Me. | Jn 11:42
the Father will s Him in My name | Jn 14:26
If I go, I will s Him to you. | Jn 16:7
One You have sent—Jesus Christ. | Jn 17:3
As You sent Me into the world, | Jn 17:18
Father has sent Me, I also s you. | Jn 20:21
sin in the flesh by s-ing His own | Rm 8:3
they preach unless they are sent? | Rm 10:15
but you should s him on his way | 1Co 16:11
time came, God sent His Son, born | Gl 4:4
the Holy Spirit sent from heaven. | 1Pt 1:12
God sent His One and Only Son into | 1Jn 4:9
He loved us and sent His Son to be | 1Jn 4:10

the Father has sent the Son as | 1Jn 4:14
have sent My angel to attest these | Rv 22:16

SENNACHERIB

King of Assyria; laid siege to Jerusalem (2Kg 18:13–19:37; 2Ch 32:1-21; Is 36–37).

SENSE

Israel is a nation lacking s | Dt 32:28
and when they come to their s-s | 1Kg 8:47
who commits adultery lacks s; | Pr 6:32
To the one who lacks s, she says, | Pr 9:4,16
but fools die for lack of s. | Pr 10:21
chases fantasies lacks s. | Pr 12:11
acquires good s loves himself; | Pr 19:8
when he came to his s-s, he said, | Lk 15:17
with decency and good s; | 1Tm 2:9
may come to their s-s and escape | 2Tm 2:26

SENSIBLE

whoever ignores an insult is s. | Pr 12:16
but the s watch their steps. | Pr 14:15
who heeds correction is s. | Pr 15:5
but a s wife is from the LORD. | Pr 19:14
A s person sees danger and takes | Pr 22:3
like a s man who built his house on | Mt 7:24
were foolish and five were s. | Mt 25:2
self-controlled, s, respectable, | 1Tm 3:2
is good, s, righteous, holy, | Ti 1:8
to be s, pure, good homemakers, | Ti 2:5

SENSUAL

but is earthly, s, demonic. | Jms 3:15

SENTENCE

You are right when You pass s; | Ps 51:4
and this is the s of the Most | Dn 4:24
know full well God's just s | Rm 1:32
will execute His s completely | Rm 9:28
had a death s within ourselves | 2Co 1:9

SENTENCED

Him over to be s to death, | Lk 24:20

SEPARATE (adj)

out from among them and be s, | 2Co 6:17

SEPARATE (v)

God s-d the light from the darkness. | Gn 1:4
s the Levites from the rest | Nm 8:14
but death s-s you and me. | Ru 1:17
Levites have not s-d themselves | Ezr 9:1
and a gossip s-s friends. | Pr 16:28

gossips about it s-s friends. Pr 17:9
ends quarrels and s-s powerful Pr 18:18
you will not s his foolishness Pr 27:22
joined together, man must not s. Mt 19:6
just as a shepherd s-s the sheep Mt 25:32
Who can s us from the love of Rm 8:35
undefiled, s-d from sinners, Heb 7:26

SEPARATION
veil will make a s for you between Ex 26:33

SEQUENCE
to write to you in orderly s, Lk 1:3
explain to them in an orderly s, Ac 11:4

SERAPHIM
S were standing above Him; Is 6:2
Then one of the s flew to me, Is 6:6

SERGIUS PAULUS
Proconsul of Cyprus, converted by Paul (Ac 13:7).

SERPENT
Now the s was the most cunning Gn 3:1
the woman said, "It was the s. Gn 3:13
his staff, and it became a s. Ex 7:12
wine is s-s' venom, the deadly Dt 32:33
His hand pierced the fleeing s. Jb 26:13
trample the young lion and the s. Ps 91:13
from its egg comes a flying s. Is 14:29
as shrewd as s-s and as harmless Mt 10:16
as the s deceived Eve by his 2Co 11:3
the ancient s, who is called Rv 12:9
that ancient s who is the Devil Rv 20:2

SERVANT
Not so with My s Moses; Nm 12:7
Moses My s is dead. Jos 1:2
Speak, for Your s is listening. 1Sm 3:10
Gehazi, the s of the man of God, 2Kg 8:4
through My s-s the prophets. 2Kg 17:13
Have you considered My s Job? Jb 1:8
Your s is warned by them; Ps 19:11
redeems the life of His s-s, Ps 34:22
save Your s who trusts in You. Ps 86:2
I have found David My s; Ps 89:20
LORD, I am indeed Your s; Ps 116:16
Like a s-'s eyes on His master's Ps 123:2
Because of Your s David, do not Ps 132:10
Give praise, you s-s of the LORD Ps 135:1
Better to be dishonored, yet have a s, Pr 12:9

A wise s will rule over a Pr 17:2
Don't slander a s to his master, Pr 30:10
a s when he becomes king, a fool Pr 30:22
when your king is a household s, Ec 10:16
s and master, female s and mistress, Is 24:2
This is My S; I strengthen Him, Is 42:1
or blind like the s of the LORD? Is 42:19
and My s whom I have chosen, Is 43:10
listen, Jacob My s, Israel whom Is 44:1
See, My s will act wisely; Is 52:13
righteous s will justify many, Is 53:11
sent all My s-s the prophets to Jr 7:25
send for My s Nebuchadnezzar Jr 43:10
shepherd, My s David, and he Ezk 34:23
us through His s-s the prophets. Dn 9:10
about to bring My s, the Branch. Zch 3:8
word, and my s will be cured. Mt 8:8
Here is My S whom I have chosen, Mt 12:18
great among you must be your s, Mt 20:26
among you will be your s. Mt 23:11
he must be last of all and s of all. Mk 9:35
us in the house of His s David, Lk 1:69
Where I am, there My s also will be Jn 12:26
this world, My s-s would fight, Jn 18:36
has glorified His S Jesus, Ac 3:13
against Your holy S Jesus, Ac 4:27
For government is God's s, Rm 13:4
as s-s of Christ and managers of 1Co 4:1
Are they s-s of Christ? 2Co 11:23
I was made a s of this {gospel} Eph 3:7
be a good s of Christ Jesus, 1Tm 4:6
was faithful as a s in all God's Heb 3:5
to His s-s the prophets. Rv 10:7
blood of His s-s that was on her Rv 19:2

SERVE
s Him with all your heart and all Jos 22:5
the wild ox be willing to s you? Jb 39:9
S the LORD with reverential awe, Ps 2:11
a people I had not known s me. Ps 18:43
S the LORD with gladness; Ps 100:2
so will you s strangers in a land Jr 5:19
God, whom you s continually, Dn 6:16
and s Him with a single purpose. Zph 3:9
It is useless to s God. Mal 3:14
Lord your God, and s only Him. Mt 4:10
did not come to be s-d, but to s, Mt 20:28
and she began to s them. Mk 1:31
clutches, to s Him without fear Lk 1:74

sister has left me to s alone?   Lk 10:40
am among you as the One who s-s.   Lk 22:27
If anyone s-s Me, he must follow   Jn 12:26
Neither is He s-d by human hands,   Ac 17:25
s-ing the Lord with all humility,   Ac 20:19
The older will s the younger.   Rm 9:12
fervent in spirit; s the Lord.   Rm 12:11
Whoever s-s the Messiah in this   Rm 14:18
but s one another through love.   Gl 5:13
you s the Lord Christ.   Col 3:24
God from idols to s the living   1Th 1:9
no one s-ing as a soldier gets   2Tm 2:4
dead works to s the living God?   Heb 9:14
they were not s-ing themselves   1Pt 1:12
should use it to s others,   1Pt 4:10
and they s Him day and night in   Rv 7:15

SERVICE

will think he is offering s to God.   Jn 16:2
if s, in s; if teaching, in teaching;   Rm 12:7
Render s with a good attitude,   Eph 6:7
faithfulness, s, and endurance.   Rv 2:19

SET

Everything s apart is especially   Lv 27:28
today I have s before you life   Dt 30:15
city and everything in it are s apart Jos 6:17
what was s apart for destruction   1Sm 15:21
of a deer and s-s me securely   Ps 18:33
You have s my feet in a spacious   Ps 31:8
muddy clay, and s my feet on a   Ps 40:2
since I s my hope on You,   Ps 86:4
Seldom s foot in your neighbor's   Pr 25:17
The sun rises and the sun s-s;   Ec 1:5
to s free the oppressed,   Lk 4:18
if the Son s-s you free,   Jn 8:36
One the Father s apart and sent   Jn 10:36
S apart for Me Barnabas and Saul   Ac 13:2
because He has s a day on which   Ac 17:31
in Christ Jesus has s you free   Rm 8:2
everything that is s before you,   1Co 10:27
of you is to s something aside   1Co 16:2
my mother's womb s me apart and   Gl 1:15
I do not s aside the grace of   Gl 2:21
S your minds on what is above,   Col 3:2
instrument, s apart, useful to   2Tm 2:21
S an example of good works   Ti 2:7
the Father and s apart by the   1Pt 1:2
but s apart the Messiah as Lord   1Pt 3:15

SETH

Third son of Adam and Eve (Gn 4:25; 5:3); ancestor of Jesus (Lk 3:38).

SETTLE

You can s in the land of Goshen   Gn 45:10
take possession of the land and s   Nm 33:53
speech s-d on them {like dew}.   Jb 29:22
horizon {or} s at the western   Ps 139:9
who wanted to s accounts with   Mt 18:23
slaves came and s-d accounts   Mt 25:19
make an effort to s with him on   Lk 12:58

SETTLEMENT

Reach a s quickly with your   Mt 5:25

SEVEN

and s pairs, male and female, of   Gn 7:3
So Jacob worked s years for   Gn 29:20
The s good cows are s years,   Gn 41:26
Make s lamps on it.   Ex 25:37
Have s priests carry s ram's-horn   Jos 6:4
march around the city s times,   Jos 6:4
The boy sneezed s times and   2Kg 4:35
Go wash s times in the Jordan   2Kg 5:10
Joash was s years old when he   2Ch 24:1
He had s sons and three   Jb 1:2
furnace, purified s times.   Ps 12:6
I praise You s times a day for   Ps 119:164
s are detestable to Him: Pr 6:16
a righteous man falls s times,   Pr 24:16
for there are s abominations in   Pr 26:25
On that day s women will seize   Is 4:1
an animal for s periods of time   Dn 4:16
will be s weeks and 62 weeks.   Dn 9:25
These s eyes of the LORD, which   Zch 4:10
brings with it s other spirits   Mt 12:45
forgive him? As many as s times?   Mt 18:21
Jesus said to him, "but 70 times s.   Mt 18:22
Now there were s brothers among   Mt 22:25
of whom He had driven s demons.   Mk 16:9
her husband s years after her   Lk 2:36
goes and brings s other spirits   Lk 11:26
against you s times in a day,   Lk 17:4
from among you s men of good   Ac 6:3
S sons of Sceva, a Jewish chief   Ac 19:14
one of the S, and stayed with   Ac 21:8
To the s churches in the province   Rv 1:4
turned I saw s gold lampstands,   Rv 1:12
secret of the s stars you saw   Rv 1:20

the back, sealed with s seals. Rv 5:1
I saw the s angels who stand Rv 8:2
the s thunders spoke with their Rv 10:3
red dragon having s heads and 10 Rv 12:3
s angels with the s last plagues, Rv 15:1
having s heads and 10 horns. Rv 17:3
They are also s kings: Rv 17:10
Then one of the s angels, Rv 21:9

SEVENFOLD
Pay back s to our neighbors the Ps 79:12

SEVENTH
By the s day, God completed His Gn 2:2
ark came to rest in the s month, Gn 8:4
the s day is a Sabbath to Ex 20:10
the s year you are to let it rest Ex 23:11
but rest on the s day so that Ex 23:12
rest for the land in the s year, Lv 25:4
must set him free in the s year. Dt 15:12
And on the s day God rested from Heb 4:4
in the s {generation} from Adam, Jd 14
When He opened the s seal, Rv 8:1
The s angel blew his trumpet, Rv 11:15
Then the s poured out his bowl Rv 16:17

SEVENTY *see also* 70
Our lives last s years or, Ps 90:10
S weeks are decreed about your Dn 9:24
The S returned with joy, saying, Lk 10:17

SEVENTY-SEVEN *see also* 77
for Lamech it will be s times! Gn 4:24

SEVERE
the famine in the land was s. Gn 12:10
will bring a s plague against Ex 9:3
The famine was s in Samaria. 1Kg 18:2
famine was so s in the city that 2Kg 25:3
is incurable; your wound most s. Jr 30:12
that day a s persecution broke Ac 8:1
there would be a s famine Ac 11:28
and s treatment of the body, Col 2:23
in spite of s persecution, 1Th 1:6
that plague was extremely s. Rv 16:21

SEVERELY
my brokenness—I am s wounded! Jr 10:19

SEVERITY
consider God's kindness and s: Rm 11:22

SEW
so they s-ed fig leaves together Gn 3:7
I have s-n sackcloth over my skin; Jb 16:15
a time to tear and a time to s; Ec 3:7
to the women who s {magic}
  bands Ezk 13:18
No one s-s a patch of unshrunk Mk 2:21

SEX
so we can have s with them! Gn 19:5
are not to have s with your Lv 18:8
so we can have s with him! Jdg 19:22

SEXUAL
s intercourse with an animal must Ex 22:19
must not have s intercourse with Lv 18:7
You lavished your s favors on Ezk 16:15
offered her s favors to them; Ezk 23:7
except in a case of s immorality, Mt 5:32
adulteries, s immoralities, Mt 15:19
except for s immorality, Mt 19:9
We weren't born of s immorality, Jn 8:41
strangled, and from s immorality. Ac 15:29
not in s impurity and Rm 13:13
that there is s immorality among 1Co 5:1
body is not for s immorality but 1Co 6:13
Flee from s immorality! 1Co 6:18
Let us not commit s immorality 1Co 10:8
s immorality and any impurity Eph 5:3
you abstain from s immorality, 1Th 4:3
and to commit s immorality. Rv 2:14
the wine of her s immorality, Rv 18:3

SEXUALLY
not to associate with s immoral 1Co 5:9
no s immoral people, idolaters, 1Co 6:9
the person who is s immoral sins 1Co 6:18
no s immoral or impure or greedy Eph 5:5
for the s immoral and 1Tm 1:10
vile, murderers, s immoral, Rv 21:8

SHACK
like a s in a cucumber field, Is 1:8

SHACKLES
I will now ... tear off your s. Nah 1:13
by chains and s, he would snap Lk 8:29

SHADE
plants cover him with their s; Jb 40:22
I delight to sit in his s, Sg 2:3
be a booth for s from heat by Is 4:6

SHADOW

the rain, a s from the heat.	Is 25:4
in the s of its branches.	Ezk 17:23
great nations lived in its s.	Ezk 31:6
return and live beneath his s.	Hs 14:7
to provide s over Jonah's	Jnh 4:6
birds of the sky can nest in its s.	Mk 4:32

SHADOW

let the s go back 10 steps.	2Kg 20:10
Our days on earth are like a s,	1Ch 29:15
Our days on earth are but a s.	Jb 8:9
and the s of death covers my	Jb 16:16
is like death's s to them.	Jb 24:17
you seen the gates of death's s?	Jb 38:17
hide me in the s of Your wings	Ps 17:8
refuge in the s of Your wings.	Ps 36:7
man walks about like a mere s.	Ps 39:6
refuge in the s of Your wings	Ps 57:1
rejoice in the s of Your wings.	Ps 63:7
dwells in the s of the Almighty.	Ps 91:1
days are like a lengthening s,	Ps 102:11
fade away like a lengthening s;	Ps 109:23
his days are like a passing s.	Ps 144:4
life that he spends like a s?	Ec 6:12
day breaks and the s-s flee,	Sg 2:17; 4:6
and take refuge in Egypt's s.	Is 30:2
He hid me in the s of His hand.	Is 49:2
covered you in the s of My hand,	Is 51:16
in darkness and the s of death,	Lk 1:79
least his s might fall on some	Ac 5:15
These are a s of what was to	Col 2:17
as a copy and s of the heavenly	Heb 8:5
law has {only} a s of the good	Heb 10:1
variation or s cast by turning	Jms 1:17

SHADOWLAND

those living in the s of death,	Mt 4:16

SHADRACH

Daniel's companion; originally called Hananiah (Dn 1:7; 3:12-30).

SHAFT

His spear s was like a weaver's	1Sm 17:7
He opened the s of the abyss,	Rv 9:2

SHAGGY

The s goat represents the king	Dn 8:21

SHAKE

whole mountain shook violently.	Ex 19:18
loud shout that the ground shook.	1Sm 4:5
Then the earth shook and quaked;	2Sm 22:8
as a reed s-s in water.	1Kg 14:15
established; it cannot be s-n.	1Ch 16:30
over me and made all my bones s.	Jb 4:14
s-s the earth from its place so	Jb 9:6
they sneer and s their heads:	Ps 22:7
of the LORD s-s the wilderness;	Ps 29:8
I said, "I will never be s-n."	Ps 30:6
never allow the righteous to be s-n.	Ps 55:22
stronghold; I will never be s-n.	Ps 62:2
let their loins continually s.	Ps 69:23
trembled. Even the depths shook.	Ps 77:16
foundations of the earth are s-n.	Ps 82:5
He will never be s-n.	Ps 112:6
The righteous will never be s-n,	Pr 10:30
Stand up, s the dust off	Is 52:2
covenant of peace will not be s-n,	Is 54:10
speak of him you s {your head}.	Jr 48:27
he s-s the arrows, consults the	Ezk 21:21
his hip joints shook and his knees	Dn 5:6
and I will s the house of Israel	Am 9:9
knees tremble, loins s,	Nah 2:10
He stands and s-s the earth;	Hab 3:6
I am going to s the heavens and	Hg 2:6
s the dust off your feet when you	Mt 10:14
the celestial powers will be s-n.	Mt 24:29
insults at Him, s-ing their heads	Mt 27:39
pressed down, s-n together,	Lk 6:38
against that house and couldn't s it,	Lk 6:48
my right hand, I will not be s-n.	Ac 2:25
where they were assembled was s-n,	Ac 4:31
s-ing the dust off their feet	Ac 13:51
foundations of the jail were s-n,	Ac 16:26
he shook out his clothes and told	Ac 18:6
he shook the creature off into the	Ac 28:5
once more I will s not only the	Heb 12:26
that what is not s-n might remain.	Heb 12:27

SHALLUM

1. King of Israel; assassinated Zechariah; was assassinated by Menahem (2Kg 15:10-15).

2. Alternate name for Jehoahaz (2Kg 23:30-34; Jr 22:11). see JEHOAHAZ

3. Gatekeeper (1Ch 9:17,19,31; cp. Ezr 2:42; Neh 7:45).

4. Chief priest (1Ch 6:13; Ezr 7:2).

5. Judahite (1Ch 2:40).

6. Doorkeeper (Jr 35:4).

7. Simeonite (1Ch 4:25).

8. Naphtalite (1Ch 7:13).

9. Gatekeeper who married a foreigner (Ezr 10:24).

10. Israelite who married a foreigner (Ezr 10:42).

11. Supervisor who helped rebuild the wall (Neh 3:12).

SHALMANESER

King of Assyria; captured Samaria and deported Israel (2Kg 17:3-6; 18:9-11).

SHALOM

| and called it Yahweh S. | Jdg 6:24 |

SHAME

were naked, yet felt no s.	Gn 2:25
do not let me be put to s,	Ps 25:20
I endure—my s and disgrace.	Ps 69:19
see and be put to s because You,	Ps 86:17
in idols, will be put to s.	Ps 97:7
will wear their s like a cloak.	Ps 109:29
a wife who causes s is like	Pr 12:4
a wicked man comes, s does also,	Pr 18:3
moon will be put to s and the	Is 24:23
protection will become your s,	Is 30:3
hope in Me will not be put to s.	Is 49:23
will forget the s of your youth,	Is 54:4
The wise will be put to s;	Jr 8:9
some to s and eternal contempt.	Dn 12:2
I will expose her s in the sight	Hs 2:10
consecrated themselves to S,	Hs 9:10
will never again be put to s.	Jl 2:26
one who does wrong knows no s.	Zph 3:5
on Him will not be put to s.	Rm 9:33
foolish things to s the wise,	1Co 1:27
I'm not writing this to s you,	1Co 4:14
I say this to your s	1Co 6:5; 15:34
I say this to {our} s:	2Co 11:21
their glory is in their s.	Php 3:19
a cross and despised the s,	Heb 12:2
in Him will never be put to s!	1Pt 2:6
Christian life will be put to s.	1Pt 3:16

SHAMEFUL

As s conduct is pleasure for a	Pr 10:23
is a disgraceful and s son.	Pr 19:26
have renounced s secret things,	2Co 4:2
For it is s even to mention what	Eph 5:12

SHAMEFULLY

| on the head and treated him s. | Mk 12:4 |
| too, treated him s, and sent him | Lk 20:11 |

SHAMELESS

| Males committed s acts with males | Rm 1:27 |

SHAMGAR

Judge; killed 600 Philistines with an oxgoad (Jdg 3:31; 5:6).

SHAPE (n)

in the s of any figure:	Dt 4:16
yourself in the s of anything	Dt 5:8
one who crafts its s trusts in	Hab 2:18

SHAPE (v)

Your hands s-d me and formed me.	Jb 10:8
Can the One who s-d the ear not	Ps 94:9
Maker who s-d you from birth;	Is 44:2

SHAPELY

| but Rachel was s and beautiful. | Gn 29:17 |

SHAPHAN

Josiah's court secretary or scribe (2Kg 22:3-14); his sons were friends of Jeremiah (Jr 26:24; 36:10; 39:14).

SHARE (n)

and Mamre—they can take their s.	Gn 14:24
You have no s in the LORD!	Jos 22:25
as the s of the one who remains	1Sm 30:24
Father, give me the s of the estate	Lk 15:12
allotted a s in this ministry.	Ac 1:17
will take away his s of the tree	Rv 22:19

SHARE (v)

It s-d his meager food and drank	2Sm 12:3
and no outsider s-s in its joy.	Pr 14:10
of a roof than to s a house with	Pr 21:9
Is it not to s your bread with	Is 58:7
S your master's joy!	Mt 25:21
two shirts must s with someone	Lk 3:11
Take this and s it among	Lk 22:17
S with the saints in their needs;	Rm 12:13
the Gentiles have s-d in their	Rm 15:27
You cannot s in the Lord's table	1Co 10:21
message must s his goods with	Gl 6:6
has something to s with anyone	Eph 4:28
rejoice and s your joy with me.	Php 2:18
church s-d with me in the matter	Php 4:15
enabled you to s in the saints'	Col 1:12

to be generous, willing to s,   1Tm 6:18
S in suffering as a good soldier   2Tm 2:3
so that we can s His holiness.   Heb 12:10
neglect to do good and to s,   Heb 13:16
as you s in the sufferings of the   1Pt 4:13
that you will not s in her sins,   Rv 18:4

SHARON

Fertile plain on the coast south of Mt. Carmel (1Ch 27:29; Is 33:9; 35:2; 65:10; Ac 9:35).

I am a rose of S, a lily of the   Sg 2:1

SHARP

their tongues are s swords.   Ps 57:4
their tongues as s as a snake's   Ps 140:3
as s as a double-edged sword.   Pr 5:4
you into a s threshing board   Is 41:15
He made my words like a s sword;   Is 49:2
man, take a s sword, use it as   Ezk 5:1
There was such a s disagreement   Ac 15:39
mouth came a s two-edged sword   Rv 1:16
and a s sickle in His hand.   Rv 14:14
From His mouth came a s sword,   Rv 19:15

SHARPEN

went to the Philistines to s their   1Sm 13:20
repent, God will s His sword;   Ps 7:12
who s their tongues like swords   Ps 64:3
s-s iron, and one man s-s another.   Pr 27:17
and one does not s its edge,   Ec 10:10
sword is s-ed and also polished.   Ezk 21:9

SHARPER

and s than any two-edged sword,   Heb 4:12

SHARPLY

So, rebuke them s, that they may   Ti 1:13

SHATTER

and s-ed every tree in the field.   Ex 9:25
I was at ease, but He s-ed me;   Jb 16:12
You will s them like pottery.   Ps 2:9
He s-s bows and cuts spears to   Ps 46:9
the jar is s-ed at the spring,   Ec 12:6
The city of chaos is s-ed;   Is 24:10
iron crushes and s-s everything,   Dn 2:40
even rocks are s-ed before Him.   Nah 1:6
He will s them like pottery   Rv 2:27

SHAVE

He is to s off all his hair   Lv 14:9
s the edge of their beards,   Lv 21:5

Nazirite is to s his consecrated   Nm 6:18
She must s her head, trim her   Dt 21:12
If I am s-d, my strength will leave   Jdg 16:17
emissaries, s-d off half their   2Sm 10:4
use a razor hired ... to s the head,   Is 7:20
all those who s their temples;   Jr 25:23
and s your head and beard.   Ezk 5:1
S yourselves bald and cut off   Mc 1:16
He s-d his head at Cenchreae,   Ac 18:18
for them to get their heads s-d.   Ac 21:24
the same as having her head s-d.   1Co 11:5

SHEAF

your s-ves ... bowed down to my s.   Gn 37:7
the first s of your harvest   Lv 23:10
shouts of joy, carrying his s-ves.   Ps 126:6
arms of the one who binds s-ves.   Ps 129:7
wagon full of s-ves crushes {grain}   Am 2:13
them like s-ves to the threshing   Mc 4:12
like a flaming torch among s-ves;   Zch 12:6

SHEALTIEL

Father of Zerubbabel and ancestor of Christ (Ezr 3:8; Neh 12:1; Hg 1:1; Lk 3:27).

SHEAR

Laban had gone to s his sheep,   Gn 31:19
heard that Nabal was s-ing sheep,   1Sm 25:4

SHEARER

a sheep silent before her s-s,   Is 53:7
a lamb is silent before its s,   Ac 8:32

SHEATHE

said to Peter, "S your sword!   Jn 18:11

SHEBA

1. Son of Raamah (Gn 10:7).

2. Son of Joktan (Gn 10:28).

3. Son of Jokshan; grandson of Abraham (Gn 25:3).

4. Benjaminite; revolted against David (2Sm 20).

5. Gadite (1Ch 5:13).

6. Nation whose queen came to see Solomon (1Kg 10; 2Ch 9); also called Sabeans (Jb 1:15; Jl 3:8).

SHEBNA or SHEBNAH

Court secretary or scribe to Hezekiah (2Kg 18:18-37); deposed as steward (Is 22:15-21).

SHECHEM

1. City in the hill country of Ephraim. Simeon and Levi destroyed the city in revenge for the rape of Dinah (Gn 34); Joshua renewed the covenant there (Jos 24:1-28); served as first capital of the Northern Kingdom (1Kg 12:25).

2. Son of Hamor; raped Dinah (Gn 34).

3. Name of two descendants of Manasseh (Nm 26:31; 1Ch 7:19).

SHED

Whoever s-s man's blood, his blood	Gn 9:6
because you have s so much blood	1Ch 22:8
s innocent blood—the blood	Ps 106:38
hands that s innocent blood,	Pr 6:17
they rush to s innocent blood.	Is 59:7
bribes in order to s blood.	Ezk 22:12
blood they had s on the land,	Ezk 36:18
righteous blood s on the earth	Mt 23:35
the moon will not s its light;	Mt 24:29
covenant; it is s for many for the	Mt 26:28
the covenant; it is s for many.	Mk 14:24
My blood; it is s for you.	Lk 22:20
witness Stephen was being s,	Ac 22:20
Their feet are swift to s blood;	Rm 3:15
and to s light for all about the	Eph 3:9
without the s-ding of blood there	Heb 9:22
the point of s-ding your blood.	Heb 12:4

SHEEP

Rachel came with her father's s,	Gn 29:9
be like s without a shepherd.	Nm 27:17
sound of s and cattle I hear?	1Sm 15:14
hills like s without a shepherd.	1Kg 22:17
are counted as s to be slaughtered.	Ps 44:22
against the s of Your pasture	Ps 74:1
people, the s of Your pasture	Ps 79:13
pasture, the s under His care.	Ps 95:7
people, the s of His pasture.	Ps 100:3
I wander like a lost s;	Ps 119:176
We all went astray like s;	Is 53:6
and like a s silent before her	Is 53:7
away like s to slaughter,	Jr 12:3
scatter the s of My pasture!	Jr 23:1
My people are lost s;	Jr 50:6
As a shepherd looks for his s	Ezk 34:12
judge between one s and another,	Ezk 34:17
a young lion among flocks of s,	Mc 5:8
and the s will be scattered;	Zch 13:7

like s without a shepherd.	Mt 9:36
go to the lost s of the house of	Mt 10:6
you out like s among wolves.	Mt 10:16
if he had a s that fell into a	Mt 12:11
lost s of the house of Israel.	Mt 15:24
If a man has 100 s, and one	Mt 18:12
separates the s from the goats.	Mt 25:32
the s of the flock will be scattered.	Mt 26:31
because I have found my lost s!	Lk 15:6
He calls his own s by name	Jn 10:3
I am the door of the s.	Jn 10:7
I lay down My life for the s.	Jn 10:15
But I have other s that are not	Jn 10:16
because you are not My s.	Jn 10:26
My s hear My voice, I know them,	Jn 10:27
"Shepherd My s," He told him.	Jn 21:16
"Feed My s," Jesus said.	Jn 21:17
was led like a s to the slaughter,	Ac 8:32
are counted as s to be slaughtered.	Rm 8:36
the great Shepherd of the s	Heb 13:20
you were like s going astray,	1Pt 2:25

SHEEPFOLDS

While you lie among the s,	Ps 68:13
and took him from the s;	Ps 78:70

SHEEPSHEARERS

went up to Timnah to the s.	Gn 38:12
Absalom's s were at Baal-hazor	2Sm 13:23

SHEEPSKINS

about in s, in goatskins,	Heb 11:37

SHEET

hammered out thin s-s of gold,	Ex 39:3
a large s being lowered to	Ac 10:11

SHEKEL

who is registered must pay half a s	Ex 30:13
for a male is 20 s-s and for a female	Lv 27:5
12 quarts of barley {sold} for a s,	2Kg 7:16
I bought her for 15 s-s of silver	Hs 3:2

SHELTER

conceal me in His s in the day	Ps 27:5
under the s of Your wings.	Ps 61:4
You are my s and my shield;	Ps 119:114
the LORD is a s right by your	Ps 121:5
I say, "You are my s, my portion	Ps 142:5
Each will be like a s from the wind,	Is 32:2
land—a female will s a man.	Jr 31:22

made himself a s there and sat   Jnh 4:5
on the throne will s them: Rv 7:15

SHEM
Son of Noah (Gn 6:10); blessed (9:20-27);
ancestor of Abraham and Jesus (11:10-26;
Lk 3:36).

SHEMAIAH
Prophet to Rehoboam in Judah (2Ch 11:2-
4; 12:5-8).

SHEMER
Previous owner of hill on which Samaria
was built (1Kg 16:24).

SHEOL
I will go down to S to my son,   Gn 37:35
gray hairs down to S   Gn 42:38; 44:29,31
that they go down alive into S,   Nm 16:30
sends {some} to S, and He raises   1Sm 2:6
The ropes of S entangled me;   2Sm 22:6
gray head descend to S in peace.   1Kg 2:6
goes down to S will never rise   Jb 7:9
would hide me in S and conceal   Jb 14:13
it go down to the gates of S,   Jb 17:16
S is naked before God,   Jb 26:6
who can thank You in S?   Ps 6:5
The wicked will return to S   Ps 9:17
You will not abandon me to S;   Ps 16:10
my life from the power of S,   Ps 49:15
troubles, and my life is near S.   Ps 88:3
himself from the power of S?   Ps 89:48
the torments of S overcame me;   Ps 116:3
make my bed in S, You are there.   Ps 139:8
alive, like S, still healthy   Pr 1:12
her steps head straight for S.   Pr 5:5
Her house is the road to S,   Pr 7:27
S and Abaddon lie open before   Pr 15:11
you will rescue his life from S.   Pr 23:14
S and Abaddon are never   Pr 27:20
S; a barren womb; earth, which   Pr 30:16
or wisdom in S where you are   Ec 9:10
love is as unrelenting as S.   Sg 8:6
have made an agreement with S;   Is 28:15
For S cannot thank You;   Is 38:18
who went down to S with their   Ezk 32:27
S, where is your sting?   Hs 13:14
they dig down to S, from there   Am 9:2
out for help in the belly of S;   Jnh 2:2
He enlarges his appetite like S,   Hab 2:5

SHEPHERD (n)
Now Abel became a s of a flock,   Gn 4:2
s-s are abhorrent to Egyptians.   Gn 46:34
s-s in the wilderness for 40 years   Nm 14:33
hills like sheep without a s.   1Kg 22:17
The LORD is my s; there is   Ps 23:1
from tending ewes to be s over His   Ps 78:71
The sayings are given by one S.   Ec 12:11
and like sheep without a s,   Is 13:14
He protects His flock like a s;   Is 40:11
Cyrus: My s, he will fulfill all My   Is 44:28
And they are s-s who have no   Is 56:11
give you s-s who are loyal to Me,   Jr 3:15
For the s-s are stupid: Jr 10:21
Woe to the s-s who destroy   Jr 23:1
He will watch over him as a s   Jr 31:10
their s-s have led them astray,   Jr 50:6
prophesy against the s-s of Israel.   Ezk 34:2
were scattered for lack of a s;   Ezk 34:5
the s-s feed themselves   Ezk 34:8
I will appoint over them a single s   Ezk 34:23
will be one s for all of them.   Ezk 37:24
As the s snatches two legs or a   Am 3:12
My anger burns against the s-s,   Zch 10:3
Woe to the worthless s who   Zch 11:17
Strike the s, and the sheep will   Zch 13:7
like sheep without a s.   Mt 9:36
just as a s separates the sheep   Mt 25:32
I will strike the s, and the sheep   Mt 26:31
s-s were staying out in the fields   Lk 2:8
I am the good s. The good s lays   Jn 10:11
I am the good s. I know My own   Jn 10:14
there will be one flock, one s.   Jn 10:16
the great S of the sheep   Heb 13:20
the s and guardian of your souls.   1Pt 2:25
And when the chief S appears,   1Pt 5:4

SHEPHERD (v)
You will s My people Israel   2Sm 5:2
Death will s them.   Ps 49:14
leader who will s My people   Mt 2:6
"S My sheep," He told him.   Jn 21:16
overseers, to s the church of God,   Ac 20:28
Or who s-s a flock and does not   1Co 9:7
s God's flock among you, not   1Pt 5:2
and He will s them with an iron   Rv 2:27
of the throne will s them;   Rv 7:17

SHESHBAZZAR

Prince or governor of Judah, began rebuilding the temple (Ezr 1:8,11; 5:14,16).

SHIBBOLETH

they told him, "Please say S."   Jdg 12:6

SHIELD

I am your s; your reward will be   Gn 15:1
He is the s that protects you,   Dt 33:29
the s of the mighty was defiled   2Sm 1:21
He is a s to all who take refuge   2Sm 22:31
You, LORD, are a s around me, my   Ps 3:3
My s is with God, who saves the   Ps 7:10
my s and the horn of my salvation,   Ps 18:2
LORD is my strength and my s;   Ps 28:7
He is our help and s.   Ps 33:20
For the LORD God is a sun and s.   Ps 84:11
will be a protective s.   Ps 91:4
He is their help and s.   Ps 115:9
You are my shelter and my s;   Ps 119:114
He is my s, and I take refuge in   Ps 144:2
He is a s for those who live with   Pr 2:7
He is a s to those who take refuge   Pr 30:5
The s-s of his warriors are dyed   Nah 2:3
situation take the s of faith,   Eph 6:16

SHILOH

Site of the tabernacle (Jos 18:1,8-10; Jdg 18:31; 1Sm 1:24; 3:21; 1Kg 14:2); abandoned (Ps 78:60; Jr 7:12-14; 26:6).

SHIMEI

Benjaminite who cursed David (2Sm 16:5-13); David spared him (16:10-12; 19:16-23); Solomon executed him (1Kg 2:8-9,36-46).

SHINAR

Land of the Tower of Babel (Gn 11:2).

SHINE

Moses, the skin of his face shone!   Ex 34:30
the LORD make His face s on you,   Nm 6:25
moon does not s and the stars   Jb 25:5
righteousness s like the dawn,   Ps 37:6
Light s-s in the darkness for   Ps 112:4
The night s-s like the day;   Ps 139:12
s-ing brighter and brighter   Pr 4:18
of the righteous s-s brightly,   Pr 13:9
Who is this who s-s like the dawn   Sg 6:10
and the moon will not s.   Is 13:10

S-ing morning star, how you have   Is 14:12
Arise, s, for your light has   Is 60:1
and the earth shone with His glory.   Ezk 43:2
Those who are wise will s like   Dn 12:3
the stars will cease their s-ing.   Jl 3:15
let your light s before men,   Mt 5:16
righteous will s like the sun   Mt 13:43
and His face shone like the sun.   Mt 17:2
glory of the Lord shone around them,   Lk 2:9
That light s-s in the darkness,   Jn 1:5
was a burning and s-ing lamp,   Jn 5:35
and a light shone in the cell.   Ac 12:7
Light shall s out of darkness   2Co 4:6
and the Messiah will s on you.   Eph 5:14
among whom you s like stars in   Php 2:15
to a lamp s-ing in a dismal place,   2Pt 1:19
the true light is already s-ing.   1Jn 2:8
His face was s-ing like the sun   Rv 1:16
the sun or the moon to s on it,   Rv 21:23

SHIP

and will be a harbor for s-s,   Gn 49:13
a fleet of s-s at Ezion-geber,   1Kg 9:26
for the king had s-s of Tarshish   1Kg 10:22
because the s-s were wrecked at   1Kg 22:48
went to sea in s-s, conducting   Ps 107:23
the way of a s at sea,   Pr 30:19
She is like the merchant s-s,   Pr 31:14
and found a s going to Tarshish   Jnh 1:3
a sandbar and ran the s aground.   Ac 27:41
consider s-s: though very large   Jms 3:4
third of the s-s were destroyed.   Rv 8:9

SHIPHRAH

A Hebrew midwife (Ex 1:15).

SHIPWRECK

Three times I was s-ed.   2Co 11:25
suffered the s of their faith.   1Tm 1:19

SHIRT

to sue you and take away your s,   Mt 5:40
road, or an extra s, sandals,   Mt 10:10
who has two s-s must share with   Lk 3:11

SHISHAK

King of Egypt (1Kg 11:40; 14:25; 2Ch 12:2-9).

SHOOT (n)

a s will grow from the stump   Is 11:1

SHOOT (v)

He **shot** His arrows and scattered	Ps 18:14
They **s** at him suddenly and are	Ps 64:4
s Your arrows and rout them.	Ps 144:6

SHORE

the whole crowd stood on the **s**.	Mt 13:2
daybreak came, Jesus stood on the **s**.	Jn 21:4

SHORT

Remember how **s** my life is.	Ps 89:47
Is My hand too **s** to redeem?	Is 50:2
hand is not too **s** to save,	Is 59:1
the crowd, since he was a man.	Lk 19:3
sinned and fall **s** of the glory	Rm 3:23
than the angels for a **s** time;	Heb 2:7
that no one falls **s** of the grace	Heb 12:15
though now for a **s** time you have	1Pt 1:6
he knows he has a **s** time.	Rv 12:12
must be released for a **s** time.	Rv 20:3

SHORTAGE

I have such a **s** of crazy people	1Sm 21:15
but a **s** of people is a ruler's	Pr 14:28

SHORT-LIVED

to enjoy the **s** pleasure of sin.	Heb 11:25

SHORTSIGHTED

these things is blind and **s**,	2Pt 1:9

SHOULDERS

government will be on His **s**.	Is 9:6
and put them on people's **s**,	Mt 23:4
he joyfully puts it on his **s**,	Lk 15:5

SHOUT (n)

the people gave a great **s** of praise	Ezr 3:11
His works with **s-s** of joy.	Ps 107:22
will reap with **s-s** of joy.	Ps 126:5
descend from heaven with a **s**,	1Th 4:16

SHOUT (v)

until the time I say, '**S**!' Then you	Jos 6:10
s for joy, all you upright in	Ps 32:11
s for joy and be glad;	Ps 35:27
s to God with a jubilant cry.	Ps 47:1
S joyfully to God, all the earth!	Ps 66:1
s in triumph to the God of Jacob.	Ps 81:1
s triumphantly to the rock of our	Ps 95:1
S to the LORD, all the earth;	Ps 98:4
S triumphantly to the LORD,	Ps 100:1
S in triumph, Daughter Jerusalem!	Zch 9:9

they kept **s-ing**, "Crucify Him!"	Mt 27:23
They kept **s-ing**: "Hosanna!	Jn 12:13
Break forth and **s**, you who are	Gl 4:27

SHOVEL

ashes, and its **s-s**, basins, meat	Ex 27:3
pots, **s-s**, basins, meat forks,	Ex 38:3
meatforks, **s-s**, and basins—all	Nm 4:14
the basins, the **s-s**, and the	1Kg 7:40
the pots, the **s-s**, and sprinkling	1Kg 7:45
the pots, the **s-s**, the wick	2Kg 25:14
pots, the **s-s**, and the bowls.	2Ch 4:11
pots, the **s-s**, the forks, and	2Ch 4:16
with winnowing **s** and fork.	Is 30:24
the pots, the **s-s**, the wick	Jr 52:18
His winnowing **s** is in His hand,	Mt 3:12
His winnowing **s** is in His hand	Lk 3:17

SHOVELED

he **s** six {measures} of barley	Ru 3:15

SHOW

to the land that I will **s** you.	Gn 12:1
the LORD **s-ed** him all the land:	Dt 34:1
have **s-n** more kindness now than	Ru 3:10
He **s-s** loyalty to His anointed,	Ps 18:50
He **s-s** sinners the way.	Ps 25:8
will **s** him the salvation of God.	Ps 50:23
S us Your faithful love, LORD,	Ps 85:7
S us favor, LORD, **s** us favor, for	Ps 123:3
he **s-s** everyone he is a fool.	Ec 10:3
LORD is waiting to **s** you mercy,	Is 30:18
elders are **s-n** no respect.	Lm 5:12
s love to a woman who is loved	Hs 3:1
The Lord GOD **s-ed** me this:	Am 7:1
S faithful love and compassion	Zch 7:9
high mountain and **s-ed** Him all	Mt 4:8
because they will be **s-n** mercy.	Mt 5:7
asked Him to **s** them a sign from	Mt 16:1
S Me the coin used for the tax.	Mt 22:19
make long prayers just for **s**.	Mt 23:14
but go and **s** yourself to the	Mk 1:44
The one who **s-ed** mercy to him,	Lk 10:37
I will **s** you the One to fear:	Lk 12:5
and **s** yourselves to the priests.	Lk 17:14
He **s-ed** them His hands and feet.	Lk 24:40
loves the Son and **s-s** Him everything	Jn 5:20
s Yourself to the world.	Jn 7:4
I have **s-n** you many good works	Jn 10:32
s us the Father, and that's enough	Jn 14:8

s-ed them His hands and His side.   Jn 20:20
that God doesn't s favoritism,   Ac 10:34
explaining and s-ing that the   Ac 17:3
I will s mercy to whom I s mercy,   Rm 9:15
but on God who s-s mercy.   Rm 9:16
He s-s mercy to whom He wills,   Rm 9:18
And I will s you an even better   1Co 12:31
God does not s favoritism   Gl 2:6
the opportunity {to s it}.   Php 4:10
But if you s favoritism, you   Jms 2:9
to the one who hasn't s-n mercy.   Jms 2:13
S me your faith without works,   Jms 2:18
He should s his works by good   Jms 3:13
s you what must take place after   Rv 4:1
Come, I will s you the bride,   Rv 21:9

SHOWERS

grass and s on tender plants   Dt 32:2
soften it with s and bless its   Ps 65:10
like spring s that water the   Ps 72:6
is why the s haven't come   Jr 3:3
Or can the skies alone give s?   Jr 14:22
s in ... season—s of blessing.   Ezk 34:26
like the spring s that water   Hs 6:3
He sends s for you, both autumn   Jl 2:23
He will give them s of rain   Zch 10:1

SHREWD

crooked You prove Yourself s.   Ps 18:26
Learn to be s, you who are   Pr 8:5
A s person conceals knowledge,   Pr 12:23
Therefore be as s as serpents   Mt 10:16

SHREWDNESS

for teaching s to the   Pr 1:4

SHRINE

This man Micah had a s,   Jdg 17:5
built s-s on the high places   1Kg 12:31
were even male s prostitutes   1Kg 14:24
in the s-s of the high places   2Kg 17:29
removed all the s-s of the high   2Kg 23:19
not live in s-s made by hands.   Ac 17:24
who made silver s-s of Artemis,   Ac 19:24

SHRINK

and that I did not s back from   Ac 20:20
did not s back from declaring   Ac 20:27

SHRIVEL

After I have become s-ed up and   Gn 18:12

your thigh s and your belly   Nm 5:21
have s-ed me up   Jb 16:8

SHROUD

will destroy the {burial} s,   Is 25:7

SHUDDER

everyone who hears about it will s.   1Sm 3:11
everyone who hears about it will s   Jr 19:3
The mountains see You and s;   Hab 3:10
also believe—and they s.   Jms 2:19

SHULAMMITE

Come back, come back, S!   Sg 6:13

SHUNAMMITE

they found Abishag the S   1Kg 1:3
give me Abishag the S as a wife.   1Kg 2:17
Gehazi, "Call this S woman."   2Kg 4:12

SHUR

   Region of northeastern Egypt (Gn 16:7;
20:1; Ex 15:22; 1Sm 15:7; 27:8).

SHUT

Then the LORD s him in.   Gn 7:16
the skies are s and there is no   1Kg 8:35
Then go in and s the door behind   2Kg 4:4
the mouths of liars will be s.   Ps 63:11
I am s in and cannot go out.   Ps 88:8
s-s his ears to the cry of the poor   Pr 21:13
for He has s their eyes so they   Is 44:18
fire ... s up in my bones.   Jr 20:9
and s the lions' mouths.   Dn 6:22
room, s your door, and pray to   Mt 6:6
and they have s their eyes;   Mt 13:15
banquet, and the door was s.   Mt 25:10
when the sky was s up for three   Lk 4:25
gets up and s-s the door.   Lk 13:25
and they have s their eyes;   Ac 28:27
that every mouth may be s   Rm 3:19
need but s-s off his compassion   1Jn 3:17

SICK

lay down and pretended to be s.   2Sm 13:6
Hezekiah had been s.   2Kg 20:12
Delayed hope makes the heart s,   Pr 13:12
you'll get s from it and vomit.   Pr 25:16
he'll get s of you and hate you.   Pr 25:17
to crush Him, and He made Him s.   Is 53:10
the weak, healed the s, bandaged   Ezk 34:4
the princes are s with the heat   Hs 7:5
stolen, lame, or s animals.   Mal 1:13

and healed all who were s,	Mt 8:16
need a doctor, but the s do.	Mt 9:12
I was s and you took care of Me;	Mt 25:36
her brother Lazarus who was s.	Jn 11:2
is why many are s and ill among	1Co 11:30
because you heard that he was s.	Php 2:26
but having a s interest in	1Tm 6:4
Trophimus I left s at Miletus.	2Tm 4:20
Is anyone among you s?	Jms 5:14

SICKBED

You will not get up from your s;	2Kg 1:16
LORD will sustain him on his s;	Ps 41:3

SICKENING

There is a s tragedy I have seen	Ec 5:13
This is futile and a s tragedy.	Ec 6:2

SICKLE

mattocks, axes, and s-s.	1Sm 13:20
wields the s at harvest time.	Jr 50:16
Swing the s because the harvest	Jl 3:13
sends for the s, because harvest	Mk 4:29
and a sharp s in His hand.	Rv 14:14

SICKLY

other cows, s and thin, came up	Gn 41:3

SICKNESS

LORD will remove all s from you;	Dt 7:15
Will I recover from this s?	2Kg 8:8
man's spirit can endure s,	Pr 18:14
of suffering who knew what s was.	Is 53:3
He Himself bore our s-es,	Is 53:4
healing every disease and every s.	Mt 9:35
to heal every disease and s.	Mt 10:1
healed of evil spirits and s-es:	Lk 8:2
This s will not end in death	Jn 11:4

SIDE

had given him rest on every s	2Sm 7:1
He gave them rest on every s.	2Ch 32:22
for true wisdom has two s-s.	Jb 11:6
Terrors frighten him on every s	Jb 18:11
terror is on every s.	Ps 31:13
Though a thousand fall at your s	Ps 91:7
If the LORD had not been on our s	Ps 124:1
Terror is on every s!	Jr 20:10
lie down on your left s	Ezk 4:4
It was raised up on one s,	Dn 7:5
he passed by on the other s.	Lk 10:31
by the angels to Abraham's s.	Lk 16:22

One who is at the Father's s	Jn 1:18
Him, one on either s, with Jesus	Jn 19:18
pierced His s with a spear,	Jn 19:34
showed them His hands and His s.	Jn 20:20
net on the right s of the boat,	Jn 21:6

SIDON

1. Firstborn son of Canaan (Gn 10:15).

2. Phoenician port city, sister city to Tyre (Gn 10:19; 49:13; Jos 19:28; Jdg 1:31); prophesied against (Is 23:12; Ezk 28:21; Jl 3:4; Zch 9:2); Jesus visited (Mt 15:21; Mk 3:8; 7:24); Paul visited (Ac 27:3).

SIEGE

When you lay s to a city	Dt 20:19
Jerusalem ... came under s.	2Kg 24:10
Then lay s against it:	Ezk 4:2

SIEVE

sift the nations in a s of destruction	Is 30:28
as one shakes a s, but not a	Am 9:9

SIFT

s-s out all evil with his eyes.	Pr 20:8
comes to s the nations in a sieve	Is 30:28
has asked to s you like wheat.	Lk 22:31

SIGH (n)

we end our years like a s.	Ps 90:9

SIGH (v)

LORD; consider my s-ing.	Ps 5:1
my s-ing is not hidden from You.	Ps 38:9
sorrow and s-ing will flee.	Is 35:10; 51:11
He s-ed deeply and said to him,	Mk 7:34
But s-ing deeply in His spirit,	Mk 8:12

SIGHT

earth was corrupt in God's s,	Gn 6:11
and look at this remarkable s.	Ex 3:3
what was evil in the LORD's s.	Jdg 2:11
I am cut off from Your s.	Ps 31:22
and done this evil in Your s.	Ps 51:4
lives are precious in his s.	Ps 72:14
For in Your s a thousand years	Ps 90:4
is valuable in the LORD's s.	Ps 116:15
you are precious in My s	Is 43:4
have been banished from Your s,	Jnh 2:4
The blind receive their s,	Lk 7:22
against heaven and in your s.	Lk 15:18,21
is revolting in God's s.	Lk 16:15

justified in His **s** by the works | Rm 3:20
for we walk by faith, not by **s** | 2Co 5:7

SIGN

will serve as **s**-**s** for festivals | Gn 1:14
This is the **s** of the covenant I | Gn 9:12
to serve as a **s** of the covenant | Gn 17:11
and multiply My **s**-**s** and wonders | Ex 7:3
by trials, **s**-**s**, wonders, and war | Dt 4:34
What is the **s** that the LORD will | 2Kg 20:8
miraculous **s**-**s** in Egypt and His | Ps 78:43
Show me a **s** of Your goodness. | Ps 86:17
Ask for a **s** from the LORD your | Is 7:11
will give you a **s**: The virgin | Is 7:14
an everlasting **s** that will not | Is 55:13
performs **s**-**s** and wonders in the | Dn 6:27
we want to see a **s** from You. | Mt 12:38
demands a **s**, but no **s** will be given
   to it except the **s** of ... Jonah. | Mt 12:39
can't read the **s**-**s** of the times. | Mt 16:3
s of Your coming and of the end | Mt 24:3
perform great **s**-**s** and wonders to | Mt 24:24
Then the **s** of the Son of Man | Mt 24:30
these **s**-**s** will accompany those | Mk 16:17
This will be the **s** for you: | Lk 2:12
Israel and to be a **s** that will | Lk 2:34
there will be **s**-**s** in the sun, | Lk 21:25
this first **s** in Cana of Galilee | Jn 2:11
What **s** {of authority} will You | Jn 2:18
s-**s** You do unless God were with him. | Jn 3:2
{people} see **s**-**s** and wonders, | Jn 4:48
was the second **s** Jesus performed | Jn 4:54
perform more **s**-**s** than this man | Jn 7:31
Jesus performed many other **s**-**s** | Jn 20:30
heaven above and **s**-**s** on the | Ac 2:19
Many **s**-**s** and wonders were being | Ac 5:12
by granting that **s**-**s** and wonders | Ac 14:3
received the **s** of circumcision | Rm 4:11
of miraculous **s**-**s** and wonders, | Rm 15:19
Jews ask for **s**-**s** and the Greeks | 1Co 1:22
languages is intended as a **s**, | 1Co 14:22
only **s**-**s** but also wonders and | 2Co 12:12
false miracles, **s**-**s**, and wonders, | 2Th 2:9
testified by **s**-**s** and wonders, | Heb 2:4
A great **s** appeared in heaven: | Rv 12:1
of demons performing **s**-**s**, | Rv 16:14

SIGNAL

His betrayer had given them a **s**. | Mk 14:44

SIGNATURE

Here is my **s**; let the Almighty | Jb 31:35
rains, serve as His **s** to all mankind, | Jb 37:7

SIGNET

Whose **s** ring, cord, and staff | Gn 38:25
removed his **s** ring from his hand | Gn 41:42
with the royal **s** ring. | Est 3:12; 8:8
were a **s** ring on My right hand, | Jr 22:24
and make you like My **s** ring, | Hg 2:23

SIGNIFY

He said this to **s** what kind of | Jn 12:33
be fulfilled **s**-**ing** what sort of | Jn 18:32
said this to **s** by what kind of | Jn 21:19

SIGNPOSTS

Set up road markers ... establish **s**! | Jr 31:21

SIHON

Amorite king (Nm 21:21-32; 32:33; Jdg 11:19-21).

SILAS

Early church leader and prophet; also called Silvanus. Brought news from Jerusalem to Antioch (Ac 15:22,32); worked with Paul and Peter in missions and writing letters (15:40-41; 16:19-40; 17:10-15; 18:5; 2Co 1:19; 1Th 1:1; 2Th 1:1; 1Pt 5:12).

SILENCE (n)

soon rest in the **s** {of death}. | Ps 94:17
sit in **s** and go into darkness. | Is 47:5
should learn in **s** with full | 1Tm 2:11
there was **s** in heaven for about | Rv 8:1

SILENCE (v)

the wicked are **s**-**d** in darkness, | 1Sm 2:9
to **s** the enemy and the avenger. | Ps 8:2
You **s** the roar of the seas, | Ps 65:7
warriors will be **s**-**d** in that day. | Jr 50:30
that He had **s**-**d** the Sadducees, | Mt 22:34
said to the sea, "**S**! Be still!" | Mk 4:39
It is necessary to **s** them; | Ti 1:11
s the ignorance of foolish | 1Pt 2:15

SILENT

If you keep **s** at this time, | Est 4:14
Teach me, and I will be **s**. | Jb 6:24
If You remain **s** to me, I will be | Ps 28:1
When I kept **s**, my bones became | Ps 32:3
LORD; do not be **s**. | Ps 35:22

Be s before the LORD and wait   Ps 37:7
He will not be s!   Ps 50:3
God of my praise, do not be s.   Ps 109:1
man with understanding keeps s.   Pr 11:12
considered wise when he keeps s,   Pr 17:28
a time to be s and a time to speak;   Ec 3:7
and like a sheep s before her   Is 53:7
will not keep s because of Zion   Is 62:1
on earth be s in His presence.   Hab 2:20
Be s in the presence of the Lord   Zph 1:7
But Jesus kept s.   Mt 26:63
or to kill?" But they were s.   Mk 3:4
were to keep s, the stones would   Lk 19:40
at His answer, they became s.   Lk 20:26
and as a lamb is s before its   Ac 8:32
women should be s in the   1Co 14:34
instead, she is to be s.   1Tm 2:12

SILK

and covered you with s.   Ezk 16:10
linen, purple, s, and scarlet;   Rv 18:12

SILLY

to do with irreverent and s myths.   1Tm 4:7

SILOAM

1. Tower in Jerusalem (Lk 13:4).
2. Pool in Jerusalem (Jn 9:7,11).

SILVANUS

Paul's co-worker (2Co 1:19; 1Th 1:1; 2Th 1:1; 1Pt 5:12).

SILVER

rich in livestock, s, and gold.   Gn 13:2
He must not acquire ... s and gold   Dt 17:17
but they took no spoil of s.   Jdg 5:19
The king made s as common in   1Kg 10:27
Though he piles up s like dust   Jb 27:16
like s refined in an earthen   Ps 12:6
You refined us as s is refined.   Ps 66:10
thousands of gold and s pieces.   Ps 119:72
she is more profitable than s,   Pr 3:14
my instruction instead of s,   Pr 8:10
of the righteous is pure s;   Pr 10:20
crucible is for s and a smelter   Pr 17:3
favor is better than s and gold.   Pr 22:1
like golden apples on a s tray.   Pr 25:11
before its s cord is snapped,   Ec 12:6
Your s has become dross,   Is 1:22
I have refined you, but not as s;   Is 48:10

you will be redeemed without s.   Is 52:3
They are called rejected s,   Jr 6:30
We can buy the poor with s and   Am 8:6
The s and gold belong to Me   Hg 2:8
my wages, 30 pieces of s.   Zch 11:12
refine them as s is refined and   Zch 13:9
a refiner and purifier of s;   Mal 3:3
30 pieces of s for him.   Mt 26:15
I have neither s nor gold, but   Ac 3:6
May your s be destroyed with   Ac 8:20
with gold, s, costly stones,   1Co 3:12

SILVERSMITH

of silver and gave it to a s.   Jdg 17:4
vessel will be produced for a s.   Pr 25:4
a s who made silver shrines of   Ac 19:24

SIMEON

1. Son of Jacob and Leah (Gn 29:33); with Levi, avenged Dinah's rape by Shechem (34:25-31; 49:5); held as hostage by Joseph (42:24). Tribe with territory within Judah (Jos 19:1-9; Jdg 1:3,17).

2. Devout Jew who blessed the baby Jesus (Lk 2:25-35).

3. Ancestor of Jesus (Lk 3:30).

4. Early church prophet (Ac 13:1).

5. Jewish variation of Simon (Ac 15:14; 2Pt 1:1). see PETER

SIMON

1. Apostle Peter's original name (Mt 4:18). see PETER

2. Apostle; called the Zealot (Mt 10:4; Mk 3:18; Lk 6:15; Ac 1:13).

3. Father of Judas (Jn 6:71).

4. Jesus' brother (Mt 13:55).

5. Pharisee who hosted Jesus (Lk 7:36-50).

6. Leper who hosted Jesus (Mt 26:6-13).

7. Cyrenian forced to carry Jesus' cross (Mk 15:21).

8. Sorcerer who wanted to buy the power of the Spirit (Ac 8:9-24).

9. Tanner of Joppa who hosted Peter, where Peter saw the vision (Ac 9:43).

SIN

Wilderness region in Sinai (Ex 16:1; 17:1; Nm 33:11-12).

SIN (n)

s is crouching at the door.	Gn 4:7
their s is extremely serious.	Gn 18:20
Please forgive my s once more	Ex 10:17
if You would only forgive their s.	Ex 32:32
bull as a s offering for the s he has	Lv 4:3
This is the law of the s offering.	Lv 6:25
bear the consequences of his s.	Lv 24:15
The person is to confess the s	Nm 5:7
he died because of his own s,	Nm 27:3
be sure your s will catch up with	Nm 32:23
be put to death for his own s.	Dt 24:16
is like the s of divination,	1Sm 15:23
LORD has taken away your s;	2Sm 12:13
This led to s; the people walked	1Kg 12:30
because of Jeroboam's s-s	1Kg 14:16
be put to death for his own s.	2Kg 14:6
forgive their s, and heal their land.	2Ch 7:14
keep Your servant from willful s-s;	Ps 19:13
not remember the s-s of my youth	Ps 25:7
and take away all my s-s.	Ps 25:18
is forgiven, whose s is covered!	Ps 32:1
Then I acknowledged my s to You	Ps 32:5
You took away the guilt of my s.	Ps 32:5
guilt, and cleanse me from my s.	Ps 51:2
and my s is always before me.	Ps 51:3
and atone for our s-s,	Ps 79:9
You covered all their s.	Ps 85:2
He forgives all your s;	Ps 103:3
not dealt with us as our s-s deserve	Ps 103:10
don't let s dominate me.	Ps 119:133
if You considered s-s, Lord, who	Ps 130:3
many words, s is unavoidable,	Pr 10:19
but s is a disgrace to any people.	Pr 14:34
conceals his s-s will not prosper,	Pr 28:13
Though your s-s are like scarlet,	Is 1:18
and your s is atoned for.	Is 6:7
and remember your s-s no more.	Is 43:25
yet He bore the s of many	Is 53:12
and your s-s have made Him hide	Is 59:2
never again remember their s.	Jr 31:34
confessing my s and the s of my	Dn 9:20
They feed on the s of My people;	Hs 4:8
preserved; his s is stored up.	Hs 13:12
Forgive all {our} s	Hs 14:2
cast all our s-s into the depths	Mc 7:19
{to wash away} s and impurity.	Zch 13:1

save His people from their s-s.	Mt 1:21
as they confessed their s-s.	Mt 3:6
authority on earth to forgive s-s	Mt 9:6
forgiven every s and blasphemy,	Mt 12:31
many for the forgiveness of s-s.	Mt 26:28
baptism ... for the forgiveness of s-s.	Mk 1:4
Who can forgive s-s but God alone?	Mk 2:7
but is guilty of an eternal s	Mk 3:29
forgive us our s-s, for we	Lk 11:4
takes away the s of the world!	Jn 1:29
The one without s among you	Jn 8:7
that you will die in your s-s.	Jn 8:24
who commits s is a slave of s.	Jn 8:34
among you can convict Me of s?	Jn 8:46
You were born entirely in s,	Jn 9:34
you say, 'We see'—your s remains.	Jn 9:41
will convict the world about s,	Jn 16:8
over to you has the greater s.	Jn 19:11
If you forgive the s-s of any,	Jn 20:23
that your s-s may be wiped out	Ac 3:19
wash away your s-s by calling on	Ac 22:16
law {comes} the knowledge of s.	Rm 3:20
and whose s-s are covered!	Rm 4:7
just as s entered the world	Rm 5:12
but s is not charged to one's	Rm 5:13
But where s multiplied, grace	Rm 5:20
we continue in s in order that	Rm 6:1
He died to s once for all;	Rm 6:10
For s will not rule over you,	Rm 6:14
you used to be slaves of s,	Rm 6:17
For the wages of s is death,	Rm 6:23
Is the law s? Absolutely not!	Rm 7:7
And s, seizing an opportunity	Rm 7:8
it is the s that lives in me.	Rm 7:20
free from the law of s and of death.	Rm 8:2
when I take away their s-s.	Rm 11:27
that is not from faith is s.	Rm 14:23
s a person can commit is outside	1Co 6:18
Christ died for our s-s according to	1Co 15:3
you are still in your s-s.	1Co 15:17
Now the sting of death is s,	1Co 15:56
who did not know s to be s for us,	2Co 5:21
is Christ then a promoter of s?	Gl 2:17
dead in your trespasses and s-s	Eph 2:1
the forgiveness of s-s.	Col 1:14
Some people's s-s are evident,	1Tm 5:24
making purification for s-s,	Heb 1:3
way as we are, yet without s.	Heb 4:15

their own **s-s**, then for those	Heb 7:27
never again remember their **s-s**.	Heb 8:12
removal of **s** by the sacrifice	Heb 9:26
once to bear the **s-s** of many,	Heb 9:28
one sacrifice for **s-s** forever,	Heb 10:12
is no longer an offering for **s**.	Heb 10:18
the short-lived pleasure of **s**.	Heb 11:25
weight and the **s** that so easily	Heb 12:1
high priest as a **s** offering are	Heb 13:11
gives birth to **s**, and when **s** is fully	Jms 1:15
and doesn't do it, it is a **s**.	Jms 4:17
confess your **s-s** to one another	Jms 5:16
and cover a multitude of **s-s**.	Jms 5:20
did not commit **s**, and no deceit	1Pt 2:22
Himself bore our **s-s** in His body	1Pt 2:24
having died to **s-s**, we might	1Pt 2:24
suffered for **s-s** once for all,	1Pt 3:18
love covers a multitude of **s-s**.	1Pt 4:8
His Son cleanses us from all **s**.	1Jn 1:7
confess our **s-s**, He is faithful	1Jn 1:9
us our **s-s** and to cleanse	1Jn 1:9
is the propitiation for our **s-s**,	1Jn 2:2
your **s-s** have been forgiven	1Jn 2:12
s is the breaking of law.	1Jn 3:4
and there is no **s** in Him.	1Jn 3:5
be the propitiation for our **s-s**.	1Jn 4:10
There is **s** that brings death.	1Jn 5:16
free from our **s-s** by His blood,	Rv 1:5
you will not share in her **s-s**,	Rv 18:4

SIN (v)

When you **s** unintentionally and	Nm 15:22
when one man **s-s**, will You vent	Nm 16:22
Israelites said, "We have **s-ned**.	Jdg 10:15
but if a man **s** against the LORD,	1Sm 2:25
s against the LORD by eating	1Sm 14:34
Saul said, "I have **s-ned**.	1Sm 15:30
Saul responded, "I have **s-ned**.	1Sm 26:21
I have **s-ned** against the LORD.	2Sm 12:13
When they **s** against You—for	1Kg 8:46
who had caused Israel to **s**.	1Kg 22:52
has also caused Judah to **s**,	2Kg 21:11
Job did not **s** or blame God for	Jb 1:22
Job did not **s** in what he said	Jb 2:10
Be angry and do not **s**;	Ps 4:4
for I have **s-ned** against You."	Ps 41:4
You—You alone—I have **s-ned**	Ps 51:4
so that I may not **s** against You.	Ps 119:11
who despises his neighbor **s-s**,	Pr 14:21

a man may **s** for a piece of bread.	Pr 28:21
who does good and never **s-s**.	Ec 7:20
you have said: I have not **s-ned**.	Jr 2:35
Jerusalem has **s-ned** grievously;	Lm 1:8
fathers **s-ned**; they no longer	Lm 5:7
who **s-s** is the one who will die.	Ezk 18:4
we have **s-ned**, done wrong, acted	Dn 9:5
your right eye causes you to **s**,	Mt 5:29
If your brother **s-s** against you,	Mt 18:15
I have **s-ned** by betraying	Mt 27:4
I have **s-ned** against heaven and	Lk 15:18
If your brother **s-s**, rebuke him,	Lk 17:3
And if he **s-s** against you seven	Lk 17:4
Do not **s** any more, so that	Jn 5:14
from now on do not **s** any more.	Jn 8:11
Rabbi, who **s-ned**, this man or	Jn 9:2
those who **s-ned** without the law	Rm 2:12
For all have **s-ned** and fall short	Rm 3:23
you are **s-ning** against Christ.	1Co 8:12
right-minded and stop **s-ning**,	1Co 15:34
Be angry and do not **s**.	Eph 4:26
deliberately **s** after receiving	Heb 10:26
spare the angels who **s-ned**,	2Pt 2:4
say, "We have not **s-ned**," we make	1Jn 1:10
so that you may not **s**.	1Jn 2:1
But if anyone does **s**, we have an	1Jn 2:1
who remains in Him does not **s**;	1Jn 3:6
for the Devil has **s-ned** from the	1Jn 3:8
is not able to **s**, because he has	1Jn 3:9
has been born of God does not **s**,	1Jn 5:18

SINAI

Mountain where God revealed the Law (Ex 19:20; 31:18; 34:32; Lv 25:1; Ac 7:38; Gl 4:25). The wilderness region (Ex 19:1; Lv 7:38).

SINCERE

by the Holy Spirit, by **s** love,	2Co 6:6
good conscience, and a **s** faith.	1Tm 1:5
recalling your **s** faith that	2Tm 1:5
for **s** love of the brothers,	1Pt 1:22

SINCERELY

of rivalry, not **s**, seeking to	Php 1:17

SINCERITY

and worship Him in **s** and truth.	Jos 24:14
speak what they know with **s**.	Jb 33:3
unleavened bread of **s** and truth.	1Co 5:8
with God-given **s** and purity,	2Co 1:12

but as those with **s**, we speak in   2Co 2:17
in the **s** of your heart, as   Eph 6:5

SINFUL

considered their demand **s**,   1Sm 8:6
I was **s** when my mother conceived   Ps 51:5
how much more the wicked and **s**.   Pr 11:31
Oh—**s** nation, people weighed   Is 1:4
and have put **s** stumbling blocks   Ezk 14:3
adulterous and **s** generation,   Mk 8:38
from me, because I'm a **s** man, Lord!   Lk 5:8
were more **s** than all Galileans   Lk 13:2
gone to lodge with a **s** man!   Lk 19:7
into the hands of **s** men,   Lk 24:7
can a **s** man perform such signs?   Jn 9:16

SING

I will **s** to the LORD, for He is   Ex 15:1
I hear the sound of **s-ing**!   Ex 32:18
Spring up, well—**s** to it!   Nm 21:17
Awake! Awake, **s** a song!   Jdg 5:12
women **sang**: Saul has killed his   1Sm 18:7
Don't they **s** about him during   1Sm 21:11
the David they **s** about during   1Sm 29:5
David **sang** the following lament   2Sm 1:17
I will **s** about Your name.   2Sm 22:50
S to Him; **s** praise to Him;   1Ch 16:9
S to the LORD, all the earth.   1Ch 16:23
appointed some to **s** for the LORD   2Ch 20:21
joyous dedication with ... **s-ing**   Neh 12:27
the morning stars **sang** together   Jb 38:7
S to the LORD, who dwells in   Ps 9:11
I will **s** to the LORD because He   Ps 13:6
S to the LORD, you His faithful   Ps 30:4
S a new song to Him;   Ps 33:3
S praise to God, **s** praise;   Ps 47:6
and my tongue will **s** of Your   Ps 51:14
I will **s**; I will **s** praises.   Ps 57:7
S the glory of His name;   Ps 66:2
S to God! **S** praises to His name.   Ps 68:4
S for joy to God our strength;   Ps 81:1
I will **s** about the LORD's   Ps 89:1
S a new song to the LORD   Ps 96:1; 98:1
I will **s** of faithful love and   Ps 101:1
will **s** to the LORD all my life;   Ps 104:33
S to Him, **s** praise to Him;   Ps 105:2
will **s** praises to You among the   Ps 108:3
s praise to His name, for it is   Ps 135:3
S us one of the songs of Zion.   Ps 137:3
They will **s** of the LORD's ways,   Ps 138:5

I will **s** a new song to You;   Ps 144:9
will **s** to the LORD as long as I   Ps 146:2
S to the LORD a new song,   Ps 149:1
S-ing songs to a troubled heart   Pr 25:20
The time of **s-ing** has come,   Sg 2:12
and they **s** her praises: Sg 6:9
I will **s** about the one I love,   Is 5:1
S to the LORD, for He has done   Is 12:5
S a new song to the LORD;   Is 42:10
and come to Zion with **s-ing**,   Is 51:11
the LORD says: **S** with joy for   Jr 31:7
S for joy, Daughter Zion;   Zph 3:14
sang a lament, but you didn't   Mt 11:17
After **s-ing** psalms, they went out   Mt 26:30
praying and **s-ing** hymns to God,   Ac 16:25
I will **s** psalms to Your name.   Rm 15:9
s with the spirit, and I will also **s**   1Co 14:15
s-ing and making music to the   Eph 5:19
s-ing psalms, hymns, and spiritual   Col 3:16
I will **s** hymns to You in the   Heb 2:12
cheerful? He should **s** praises.   Jms 5:13
they **sang** a new song: You are   Rv 5:9
They **sang** a new song before the   Rv 14:3
sang the song of God's servant   Rv 15:3

SINGED

not a hair of their heads was **s**,   Dn 3:27

SINGER

David ... the favorite **s** of Israel: 2Sm 23:1
harps and lyres for the **s-s**.   1Kg 10:12
to appoint their relatives as **s-s**   1Ch 15:16
harps and lyres for the **s-s**.   2Ch 9:11
the **s-s** with musical instruments   2Ch 23:13
Levites, **s-s**, gatekeepers,   Ezr 2:70; 7:7
gatekeepers, **s-s**, and Levites   Neh 7:1
the Levites and **s-s** together and   Neh 13:11
S-s lead the way, with musicians   Ps 68:25
male and female **s-s** for myself,   Ec 2:8

SINGLE

on the testimony of a **s** witness.   Dt 17:6
every **s** word of this law,   Dt 31:24
planned before a **s** one of them   Ps 139:16
you cannot make a **s** hair white   Mt 5:36
any of you add a **s** cubit to his   Mt 6:27
in a **s** hour your judgment has   Rv 18:10
gate was made of a **s** pearl.   Rv 21:21

SINK

they **sank** to the depths like a   Ex 15:5

while you s lower and lower.   Dt 28:43
Your arrows have **sunk** into me,   Ps 38:2
we have **sunk** down to the dust;   Ps 44:25
I have **sunk** in deep mud,   Ps 69:2
from the miry mud; don't let me s.   Ps 69:14
mountains rose and valleys **sank**   Ps 104:8
up to the sky, s-ing down to   Ps 107:26
her house s-s down to death   Pr 2:18
and Jeremiah **sank** in the mud.   Jr 38:6
Babylon will s and never rise   Jr 51:64
the ancient hills s down.   Hab 3:6
And beginning to s he cried out,   Mt 14:30
so full that they began to s.   Lk 5:7

SINNER

or take the path of s-s,   Ps 1:1
and s-s will not be in the community   Ps 1:5
therefore He shows s-s the way.   Ps 25:8
not destroy me along with s-s,   Ps 26:9
Your ways, and s-s will return   Ps 51:13
s-s vanish from the earth and   Ps 104:35
My son, if s-s entice you, don't   Pr 1:10
but wickedness undermines the s.   Pr 13:6
Disaster pursues s-s, but good   Pr 13:21
Don't be jealous of s-s;   Pr 23:17
but to the s He gives the task   Ec 2:26
Although a s commits crime   Ec 8:12
but one s can destroy much good.   Ec 9:18
The s-s in Zion are afraid;   Is 33:14
All the s-s among My people,   Am 9:10
s-s came as guests with Jesus   Mt 9:10
to call the righteous, but s-s.   Mt 9:13
friend of tax collectors and s-s!   Mt 11:19
betrayed into the hands of s-s.   Mt 26:45
Even s-s do that.   Lk 6:33
is touching Him—she's a s!   Lk 7:39
in heaven over one s who repents   Lk 15:7
turn Your wrath from me—a s!   Lk 18:13
or not He's a s, I don't know.   Jn 9:25
that God doesn't listen to s-s,   Jn 9:31
while we were still s-s Christ died   Rm 5:8
the many were made s-s,   Rm 5:19
Jews by birth and not "Gentile s-s";   Gl 2:15
came into the world to save s-s   1Tm 1:15
separated from s-s, and exalted   Heb 7:26
endured such hostility from s-s   Heb 12:3
your hands, s-s, and purify your   Jms 4:8
s from the error of his way will   Jms 5:20
become of the ungodly and the s?   1Pt 4:18

SION

Another name for Mt. Hermon (Dt 4:48).

SIRION

Another name for Mt. Hermon (Dt 3:9; Ps 29:6).

SISERA

Commander of the Canaanite forces (Jdg 4–5; 1Sm 12:9; Ps 83:9).

SISTER

say you're my s   Gn 12:13
his wife Sarah, "She is my s."   Gn 20:2
she really is my s, the daughter   Gn 20:12
said, "She is my s," for he was   Gn 26:7
he had defiled their s Dinah.   Gn 34:13
Then his s stood at a distance   Ex 2:4
sexual intercourse with your s,   Lv 18:9
the one who sleeps with his s,   Dt 27:22
had a beautiful s named Tamar,   2Sm 13:1
to the worm: My mother or my s,   Jb 17:14
Say to wisdom, "You are my s,"   Pr 7:4
my heart, my s, my bride.   Sg 4:9
Our s is young;   Sg 8:8
her treacherous s Judah saw it.   Jr 3:7
Your older s was Samaria, who   Ezk 16:46
Oholah, and her s was Oholibah.   Ezk 23:4
is My brother and s and mother.   Mt 12:50
His s-s, aren't they all with   Mt 13:56
brothers or s-s, father or   Mt 19:29
She had a s named Mary, who also   Lk 10:39
Jesus loved Martha, her s, and   Jn 11:5
His mother, His mother's s,   Jn 19:25
son of Paul's s, hearing about   Ac 23:16
the younger women as s-s.   1Tm 5:2
If a brother or s is without   Jms 2:15
your elect s send you greetings.   2Jn 13

SISTER-IN-LAW

man doesn't want to marry his s,   Dt 25:7
your s has gone back to her   Ru 1:15

SIT

Moses sat down to judge   Ex 18:13
The people sat down to eat and   Ex 32:6
her custom to s under the palm   Jdg 4:5
there was Eli s-ting on his chair   1Sm 4:13
the one who is to s on my throne?   1Kg 1:13
the LORD s-ting on His throne,   1Kg 22:19
the LORD s-s enthroned forever;   Ps 9:7

and I do not s with the wicked.   Ps 26:5
The LORD sat enthroned at the   Ps 29:10
Those who s at the city gate   Ps 69:12
You who s enthroned {on} the   Ps 80:1
S at My right hand until I make   Ps 110:1
sons will also s on your throne,   Ps 132:12
there we sat down and wept when   Ps 137:1
You know when I s down
    and when   Ps 139:2
I delight to s in his shade,   Sg 2:3
justice will s on the throne   Is 16:5
I call her: Rahab Who Just S-s.   Is 30:7
I know your s-ting down, your   Is 37:28
Why are we just s-ting here?   Jr 8:14
will never fail to have a man s-ting   Jr 33:17
she s-s alone, the city {once}   Lm 1:1
Son of Man s-s on His glorious   Mt 19:28
But to s at My right and left is   Mt 20:23
S at My right hand until I put   Mt 22:44
Every day I used to s, teaching   Mt 26:55
he was s-ting on the judge's   Mt 27:19
into heaven and sat down at the   Mk 16:19
to the attendant, and sat down.   Lk 4:20
He sat down and was teaching   Lk 5:3
you will s on thrones judging   Lk 22:30
said, "Have the people s down."   Jn 6:10
a young donkey and sat on it,   Jn 12:14
to my Lord, 'S at My right hand   Ac 2:34
Eutychus was s-ting on a window   Ac 20:9
The people sat down to eat and   1Co 10:7
that he s-s in God's sanctuary,   2Th 2:4
sat down at the right hand of   Heb 1:3
S at My right hand until I make   Heb 1:13
say, "S here in a good place,"   Jms 2:3
give him the right to s with Me   Rv 3:21
prostitute who s-s on many waters.   Rv 17:1
saw a woman s-ting on a scarlet   Rv 17:3
she says in her heart, 'I s as queen;   Rv 18:7

SITE

at the s David had prepared   2Ch 3:1
on its {original} s.   Ezr 2:68; 5:15; 6:7

SITUATED

A city s on a hill cannot be   Mt 5:14

SITUATION

in whatever s he was called.   1Co 7:24
In every s take the shield of   Eph 6:16

SIX

For s days you may gather it,   Ex 16:26
are to labor s days and do all   Ex 20:9
S things the LORD hates;   Pr 6:16
each one had s wings: with two   Is 6:2
There are s days when work   Lk 13:14
it was about s in the morning.   Jn 19:14
living creatures had s wings;   Rv 4:8

SIXTH

and then morning: the s day.   Gn 1:31
s day He will give you two days'   Ex 16:29
blessing for you in the s year,   Lv 25:21
the s month, the angel Gabriel   Lk 1:26
Then I saw Him open the s seal.   Rv 6:12
The s poured out his bowl on the   Rv 16:12

SIZE

have faith the s of a mustard   Mt 17:20

SKILL

filled them with s to do all the   Ex 35:35
Hiram had great s, understanding,   1Kg 7:14
may my right hand forget {its s}.   Ps 137:5

SKILLED

to instruct all the s craftsmen,   Ex 28:3
Let all the s craftsmen among   Ex 35:10
and people s in every kind of   1Ch 22:15
Levites were all s on musical   2Ch 34:12
He was a scribe s in the law of   Ezr 7:6
I was a s craftsman beside Him.   Pr 8:30
Do you see a man s in his work?   Pr 22:29
looks for a s craftsman to set   Is 40:20
insolent king, s in intrigue,   Dn 8:23
a s master builder I have laid   1Co 3:10

SKILLFUL

the music because he was s.   1Ch 15:22
tongue is the pen of a s writer.   Ps 45:1
guided them with his s hands.   Ps 78:72
labor and all s work is due to   Ec 4:4
send for the s women.   Jr 9:17

SKILLFULLY

He made s designed devices in   2Ch 26:15
who performed s before
    the LORD.   2Ch 30:22
play s on the strings, with a   Ps 33:3
He made the heavens s.   Ps 136:5
I labored at s under the sun.   Ec 2:19

Play s, sing many a song, and   Is 23:16
How s you pursue love;   Jr 2:33

SKIN

clothing out of s-s for Adam and   Gn 3:21
but I am a man with smooth s.   Gn 27:11
Moses, the s of his face shone!   Ex 34:30
a disease on the s of his body,   Lv 13:2
unclean; he has a s disease.   Lv 13:8
This is the law regarding s disease   Lv 14:57
who is afflicted with a s disease,   Nm 5:2
Miriam's {s} suddenly became   Nm 12:10
a case of infectious s disease,   Dt 24:8
Naaman ... had a s disease.   2Kg 5:1
Naaman's s disease will cling to   2Kg 5:27
Four men with s diseases were   2Kg 7:3
a s disease broke out on his   2Ch 26:19
in quarantine with s disease   2Ch 26:21
"S for s!" Satan answered   Jb 2:4
I have sewn sackcloth over my s;   Jb 16:15
escaped by the s of my teeth.   Jb 19:20
Even after my s has been destroyed,   Jb 19:26
My s blackens and flakes off,   Jb 30:30
Can the Cushite change his s,   Jr 13:23
Our s is as hot as an oven from   Lm 5:10
flesh grew, and s covered them,   Ezk 37:8
You tear off the s of people and   Mc 3:2
a man with a serious s disease came   Mt 8:2
Otherwise, the s-s burst,   Mt 9:17
cleanse those with s diseases,   Mt 10:8
Simon who had a serious s disease,   Mk 14:3
10 men with serious s diseases   Lk 17:12

SKIP

their children s about,   Jb 21:11
He makes Lebanon s like a calf,   Ps 29:6
The mountains s-ped like rams,   Ps 114:4

SKIRTS

s are stained with the blood   Jr 2:34
will pull your s up over your   Jr 13:26
uncleanness {stains} her s.   Lm 1:9
will lift your s over your face   Nah 3:5

SKULL

head and fractured his s.   Jdg 9:53
did not find anything but her s,   2Kg 9:35
Golgotha (which means S Place),   Mt 27:33
at the place called The S,   Lk 23:33
out to what is called S Place,   Jn 19:17

SKY

God called the expanse "s."   Gn 1:8
The s above you will be bronze,   Dt 28:23
sun stopped in the middle of the s   Jos 10:13
When the s-ies are shut   1Kg 8:35
the s grew dark with clouds and   1Kg 18:45
and the s proclaims the work of   Ps 19:1
Your faithfulness to the s-ies.   Ps 36:5
a faithful witness in the s.   Ps 89:37
spreading out the s like a canopy,   Ps 104:2
who covers the s with clouds,   Ps 147:8
when He placed the s-ies above,   Pr 8:28
s-ies will roll up like a scroll,   Is 34:4
good weather because the s is red.   Mt 16:2
Son of Man will appear in the s,   Mt 24:30
the earth to the end of the s.   Mk 13:27
when the s was shut up for three   Lk 4:25
and the s gave rain and the land   Jms 5:18
the s separated like a scroll   Rv 6:14
to close the s so that it does not   Rv 11:6

SLACKER

You are s-s. S-s! That is why you   Ex 5:17
Go to the ant, you s!   Pr 6:6
will you stay in bed, you s?   Pr 6:9
so the s is to the one who
   sends him   Pr 10:26
The s craves, yet has nothing,   Pr 13:4
s-'s way is like a thorny hedge,   Pr 15:19
The s buries his hand in the Pr 19:24; 26:15
The s does not plow during   Pr 20:4
s-'s craving will kill him because   Pr 21:25
The s says, "There's a lion Pr 22:13; 26:13
by the field of a s and by the   Pr 24:30
on its hinge, and a s, on his bed.   Pr 26:14
a s is wiser than seven men who   Pr 26:16

SLANDER (n)

You must not go about spreading s   Lv 19:16
and whoever spreads s is a fool.   Pr 10:18
ambitions, s, gossip, arrogance   2Co 12:20
insult and s must be removed   Eph 4:31
wrath, malice, s, and filthy   Col 3:8
quarreling, s-s, evil suspicions   1Tm 6:4
hypocrisy, envy, and all s.   1Pt 2:1
{I know} the s of those who say   Rv 2:9

SLANDER (v)

s-ed your servant to my lord   2Sm 19:27
who does not s with his tongue,   Ps 15:3

destroy anyone who secretly **s-s** — Ps 101:5
Don't **s** a servant to his master, — Pr 30:10
when people ... **s** your name — Lk 6:22
s-ing the Way in front of the crowd, — Ac 19:9
when we are **s-ed**, we entreat. — 1Co 4:13
am I **s-ed** because of something — 1Co 10:30
God's message will not be **s-ed**. — Ti 2:5
to **s** no one, to avoid fighting, — Ti 3:2
of dissipation—and they **s** you. — 1Pt 4:4
s-ing us with malicious words. — 3Jn 10

SLANDERER

not let a **s** stay in the land. — Ps 140:11
s-s, God-haters, arrogant, proud, — Rm 1:30
worthy of respect, not **s-s**, — 1Tm 3:11
irreconcilable, **s-s**, without — 2Tm 3:3
behavior, not **s-s**, not addicted — Ti 2:3

SLANDEROUS

do not bring a **s** charge against — 2Pt 2:11

SLANDEROUSLY

as some people **s** claim we say, — Rm 3:8

SLAP

if anyone **s-s** you on your right — Mt 5:39
and beat Him; others **s-ped** Him — Mt 26:67

SLASH

S to the right; turn to the left — Ezk 21:16

SLAUGHTER

and took the knife to **s** his son. — Gn 22:10
S the bull before the LORD at — Ex 29:11
He is to **s** the male lamb at the — Lv 14:13
them in a great **s** at Gibeon, — Jos 10:10
Jezebel **s-ed** the LORD's prophets. — 1Kg 18:4
Kishon and **s-ed** them there. — 1Kg 18:40
the king's sons and **s-ed** all 70, — 2Kg 10:7
They **s-ed** Zedekiah's sons before — 2Kg 25:7
They **s-ed** the Passover lamb on — 2Ch 30:15
Passover and **s-ed** the Passover — 2Ch 35:1
for the **s** of the Jews. — Est 4:7
are counted as sheep to be **s-ed**. — Ps 44:22
like an ox going to the **s**, — Pr 7:22
save those stumbling toward **s**. — Pr 24:11
Like a lamb led to the **s** — Is 53:7
of Hinnom, but the Valley of **S**. — Jr 7:32
was like a docile lamb led to **s**. — Jr 11:19
You **s-ed** My children — Ezk 16:21
the flock intended for **s**. — Zch 11:4
s-ed the fattened calf for him. — Lk 15:30

and **s** them in my presence. — Lk 19:27
was led like a sheep to the **s**, — Ac 8:32
are counted as sheep to be **s-ed**. — Rm 8:36
your hearts for the day of **s**. — Jms 5:5
The Lamb who was **s-ed** is worthy — Rv 5:12
those **s-ed** because of God's word — Rv 6:9
life of the Lamb who was **s-ed**. — Rv 13:8

SLAVE

Canaan will be his **s**. — Gn 9:26
s born in my house will be my heir. — Gn 15:3
an Egyptian **s** named Hagar. — Gn 16:1
Drive out this **s** with her son, — Gn 21:10
The Hebrew **s** you brought to us — Gn 39:17
and said, "We are your **s-s**!" — Gn 50:18
do any work ... male or female **s**, — Ex 20:10
not covet ... male or female **s**, — Ex 20:17
When you buy a Hebrew **s**, — Ex 21:2
They are not to be sold as **s-s**, — Lv 25:42
Remember that you were a **s** in — Dt 5:15
not consign the Israelites to be **s-s** — 2Ch 8:9
fool will be a **s** to someone — Pr 11:29
much less for a **s** to rule over — Pr 19:10
borrower is a **s** to the lender. — Pr 22:7
A **s** pampered from his youth will — Pr 29:21
had **s-s** who were born in my house. — Ec 2:7
I have seen **s-s** on horses, — Ec 10:7
Is Israel a **s**? — Jr 2:14
free their male and female **s-s** — Jr 34:10
S-s rule over us; — Lm 5:8
No one can be a **s** of two masters — Mt 6:24
to my **s**, 'Do this!' and he does it. — Mt 8:9
teacher, or a **s** above his master. — Mt 10:24
first among you must be your **s**; — Mt 20:27
sent his **s-s** to the farmers to collect — Mt 21:34
And the others seized his **s-s**, — Mt 22:6
is a faithful and sensible **s**, — Mt 24:45
starts to beat his fellow **s-s**, — Mt 24:49
Well done, good and faithful **s**! — Mt 25:21
high priest's **s** and cut off his — Mt 26:51
"I am the Lord's **s**," said Mary. — Lk 1:38
You can dismiss Your **s** in peace, — Lk 2:29
A centurion's **s**, who was highly — Lk 7:2
that's who knew his master's will, — Lk 12:47
s-s; we've only done our duty. — Lk 17:10
who commits sin is a **s** of sin. — Jn 8:34
I do not call you **s-s** anymore, — Jn 15:15
because a **s** doesn't know what — Jn 15:15
The **s-**'s name was Malchus. — Jn 18:10

Then the **s** girl who was the | Jn 18:17
men are the **s-s** of the Most High | Ac 16:17
Paul, a **s** of Christ Jesus, | Rm 1:1
you are **s-s** of that one you obey | Rm 6:16
you used to be **s-s** of sin, | Rm 6:17
offer them as **s-s** to righteousness, | Rm 6:19
I myself am a **s** to the law of God, | Rm 7:25
Were you called while a **s**? | 1Co 7:21
as a free man is Christ's **s**. | 1Co 7:22
do not become **s-s** of men. | 1Co 7:23
I have made myself a **s** to all, | 1Co 9:19
or Greeks, whether **s-s** or free | 1Co 12:13
no Jew or Greek, **s** or free, male | Gl 3:28
are no longer a **s**, but a son; | Gl 4:7
Throw out the **s** and her son, | Gl 4:30
S-s, obey your human masters | Eph 6:5
by assuming the form of a **s**, | Php 2:7
barbarian, Scythian, **s** and free; | Col 3:11
S-s, obey your human masters in | Col 3:22
The Lord's **s** must not quarrel, | 2Tm 2:24
S-s are to be submissive to their | Ti 2:9
no longer as a **s**, but more than a **s** | Phm 16
As God's **s-s**, {live} as free | 1Pt 2:16
are **s-s** of corruption, | 2Pt 2:19
until we seal the **s-s** of our God | Rv 7:3
I am a fellow **s** with you, | Rv 22:9

SLAVERY

out of Egypt, out of the place of **s**, | Ex 13:3
not consign the Israelites to **s**; | 1Kg 9:22
has not abandoned us in our **s**. | Ezr 9:9
redeemed you from that place of **s**. | Mc 6:4
you did not receive a spirit of **s** | Rm 8:15
we ... were in **s** under the elemental | Gl 4:3
don't submit again to a yoke of **s**. | Gl 5:1

SLAIN (n)

will no longer conceal her **s**. | Is 26:21
night over the **s** of my dear | Jr 9:1
and fill the land with the **s**. | Ezk 30:11

SLAY

The splendor of Israel lies **s-n** | 2Sm 1:19
and jealousy **s-s** the gullible. | Jb 5:2
Because of You we are **s-n** all day | Ps 44:22
He will **s** the monster that is in | Is 27:1
and many will be **s-n** by the LORD. | Is 66:16

SLEDGES

threshed Gilead with iron **s**. | Am 1:3

SLEEP (n)

God caused a deep **s** to come over | Gn 2:21
a deep **s** fell on Abram, | Gn 15:12
When Jacob awoke from his **s**, | Gn 28:16
slipped into their {final} **s**. | Ps 76:5
the Lord awoke as if from **s**, | Ps 78:65
He gives **s** to the one He loves. | Ps 127:2
and your **s** will be pleasant. | Pr 3:24
A little **s**, a little slumber, | Pr 6:10; 24:33
Don't love **s**, or you will become | Pr 20:13
The **s** of the worker is sweet, | Ec 5:12
My **s** had been most pleasant to | Jr 31:26
fell into a deep **s**, with my face | Dn 8:18
overcome by **s** he fell down | Ac 20:9
hour for you to wake up from **s**, | Rm 13:11

SLEEP (v)

came and **slept** with her father; | Gn 19:33
But Uriah **slept** at the door of the | 2Sm 11:9
slept in his arms, and it was like | 2Sm 12:3
S with your father's concubines | 2Sm 16:21
Perhaps he's **s-ing** | 1Kg 18:27
both lie down and **s** in peace, | Ps 4:8
otherwise, I will **s** in death, | Ps 13:3
Why are You **s-ing**? Get up! | Ps 44:23
of Israel does not slumber or **s**. | Ps 121:4
I will not allow my eyes to **s** | Ps 132:4
they can't **s** unless they | Pr 4:16
the son who **s-s** during harvest | Pr 10:5
I **s**, but my heart is awake. | Sg 5:2
on you an overwhelming urge to **s**; | Is 29:10
Many of those who **s** in the dust | Dn 12:2
the girl isn't dead, but **s-ing**. | Mt 9:24
disciples and found them **s-ing**. | Mt 26:40
But He was in the stern, **s-ing** | Mk 4:38
come suddenly and find you **s-ing**. | Mk 13:36
was **s-ing** between two soldiers, | Ac 12:6
we must not **s**, like the rest, | 1Th 5:6
their destruction does not **s**. | 2Pt 2:3

SLEEPER

Get up, **s**, and rise up from the | Eph 5:14

SLEEPLESS

by labors, by **s** nights, by times | 2Co 6:5
hardship, many **s** nights, hunger | 2Co 11:27

SLIME

a slug that moves along in **s**, | Ps 58:8

SLING

could **s** a stone at a hair and	Jdg 20:16
Philistine with a **s** and a stone.	1Sm 17:50
is like binding a stone in a **s**.	Pr 26:8
and **s** you into a wide land.	Is 22:18
am **s-ing** out the land's residents	Jr 10:18

SLIP

In time their foot will **s**,	Dt 32:35
my feet have not **s-ped**.	Ps 17:5
does not allow our feet to **s**.	Ps 66:9
as for me, my feet almost **s-ped**;	Ps 73:2
will not allow your foot to **s**;	Ps 121:3

SLIPPERY

Let their way be dark and **s**,	Ps 35:6
Indeed You put them in **s** places;	Ps 73:18
be to them like **s** paths in the	Jr 23:12

SLOPE

Zion on the **s-s** of the north is	Ps 48:2

SLOW

I am **s** and hesitant in speech.	Ex 4:10
s to anger and rich in faithful	Ex 34:6
The LORD is **s** to anger and rich	Nm 14:18
a vow ... do not be **s** to keep it,	Dt 23:21
s to anger and rich in faithful	Neh 9:17
s to anger	Ps 86:15; 103:8; 145:8
a man **s** to anger calms strife.	Pr 15:18
compassionate, **s** to anger, rich	Jl 2:13
s to become angry,	Jnh 4:2
The LORD is **s** to anger but great	Nah 1:3
and **s** you are to believe	Lk 24:25
you have become **s** to understand.	Heb 5:11
to hear, **s** to speak, and **s** to anger,	Jms 1:19

SLUG

Like a **s** that moves along in	Ps 58:8

SLUMBER

people as they **s** on {their} beds	Jb 33:15
your Protector will not **s**.	Ps 121:3
eyes to sleep or my eyelids to **s**	Ps 132:4
your eyes or **s** to your eyelids	Pr 6:4
A little sleep, a little **s**,	Pr 6:10; 24:33
no one **s-s** or sleeps.	Is 5:27

SLY

s wink of the eye causes grief,	Pr 10:10
yet **s** as I am, I took you in by	2Co 12:16

SMALL

it's only a **s** place, isn't it?	Gn 19:20
Four things on earth are **s**,	Pr 30:24
There was a **s** city with few men	Ec 9:14
This place is too **s** for me;	Is 49:20
rise to power with a **s** nation.	Dn 11:23
Jacob survive since he is so **s**?	Am 7:2,5
you are **s** among the clans of	Mc 5:2
and a few **s** fish.	Mt 15:34
faithful in a very **s** matter,	Lk 19:17
the tongue is a **s** part	Jms 3:5
saw the dead, the great and the **s**,	Rv 20:12

SMALLEST

from the **s** of Israel's tribes	1Sm 9:21
not the **s** letter or one stroke	Mt 5:18
It's the **s** of all the seeds,	Mt 13:32
unworthy to judge the **s** cases?	1Co 6:2

SMASH

and **s** their sacred pillars	Ex 23:24
he **s-ed** the Asherah poles and	2Ch 34:7
With you I will **s** nations;	Jr 51:20
like iron that **s-es**, it will crush	Dn 2:40
chains and **s-ed** the shackles.	Mk 5:4

SMELL (n)

s of my son is like the **s** of a field	Gn 27:27
there was no **s** of fire on them	Dn 3:27
where would be the sense of **s**?	1Co 12:17

SMELL (v)

When the LORD **s-ed** the pleasing	Gn 8:21
and the river **s-ed** so bad the	Ex 7:21
cannot see, hear, eat, or **s**.	Dt 4:28
s-s the battle from a distance;	Jb 39:25
noses, but cannot **s**.	Ps 115:6

SMELTER

and a **s** for gold,	Pr 17:3

SMILE

change my expression, and **s**,	Jb 9:27
If I **s-d** at them, they couldn't	Jb 29:24

SMOKE

s-ing fire pot and a flaming	Gn 15:17
and he saw that **s** was going up	Gn 19:28
Sinai was ... enveloped in **s**	Ex 19:18
and **s** from the city was rising	Jos 8:20
whole city was going up in **s**.	Jdg 20:40
S billows from his nostrils as	Jb 41:20
S rose from His nostrils, and	Ps 18:8

they will fade away like s.	Ps 37:20
As s is blown away, so You blow	Ps 68:2
For my days vanish like s,	Ps 102:3
to the teeth and s to the eyes,	Pr 10:26
wilderness like columns of s,	Sg 3:6
the temple was filled with s.	Is 6:4
Its s will go up forever.	Is 34:10
the heavens will vanish like s,	Is 51:6
blood, fire, and columns of s.	Jl 2:30
blood and fire and a cloud of s.	Ac 2:19
and s came up out of the shaft	Rv 9:2
was filled with s from God's	Rv 15:8
Her s ascends forever and ever!	Rv 19:3

SMOLDERING (adj)

of these two s stubs of	Is 7:4
will not put out a s wick	Is 42:3; Mt 12:20

SMOLDERS

Their anger s all night;	Hs 7:6

SMOOTH

but I am a man with s skin.	Gn 27:11
and chose five s stones from	1Sm 17:40
buttery words are s, but war is	Ps 55:21
S lips with an evil heart are	Pr 26:23
the uneven ground will become s,	Is 40:4
with water by a s way where they	Jr 31:9
straight, the rough ways s,	Lk 3:5
and by s talk and flattering	Rm 16:18

SMOOTHER

and her words are s than oil,	Pr 5:3

SMOOTHLY

In the cup and goes down s.	Pr 23:31
flowing s for my love	Sg 7:9

SMUGGLED

because of false brothers s in,	Gl 2:4

SMYRNA

One of the seven churches (Rv 1:11; 2:8).	

SNAKE

He will be a s by the road,	Gn 49:17
the ground, and it became a s.	Ex 4:3
the staff that turned into a s.	Ex 7:15
made a bronze s and mounted it	Nm 21:9
the bronze s that Moses made,	2Kg 18:4
venom like the venom of a s,	Ps 58:4
In the end it bites like a s	Pr 23:32
the way of a s on a rock,	Pr 30:19

If the s bites before it is	Ec 10:11
only to have a s bite him.	Am 5:19
for a fish, will give him a s?	Mt 7:10
S-s! Brood of vipers! How can	Mt 23:33
they will pick up s-s;	Mk 16:18
you authority to trample on s-s	Lk 10:19
as Moses lifted up the s in the	Jn 3:14
and were destroyed by s-s.	1Co 10:9
their tails, like s-s, have heads,	Rv 9:19

SNAP

before the silver cord is s-ped,	Ec 12:6

SNARE

their gods, it will be a s for you.	Ex 23:33
they will become a s among you.	Ex 34:12
for that will be a s to you.	Dt 7:16
will become a s and a trap for	Jos 23:13
and it became a s to Gideon and	Jdg 8:27
the s-s of death confronted me.	2Sm 22:6
the s-s of death confronted me.	Ps 18:5
table set before them be a s,	Ps 69:22
idols, which became a s to them.	Ps 106:36
and from the s-s of evildoers.	Ps 141:9
will keep your foot from a s.	Pr 3:26
like a bird darting into a s	Pr 7:23
from the s-s of death.	Pr 13:14; 14:27
are thorns and s-s on the path	Pr 22:5
The fear of man is a s,	Pr 29:25
and s {await} you who dwell on	Is 24:17
he will be caught in	
My s.	Ezk 12:13; 17:20
a fowler's s on all his ways.	Hs 9:8
feasting become a s and a trap,	Rm 11:9

SNARED

they will be s and captured.	Is 8:15

SNARL

s-ing like dogs and prowling	Ps 59:6

SNATCH

s-ed the spear out of	2Sm 23:21
infant is s-ed from the breast;	Jb 24:9
As the shepherd s-es two legs or	Am 3:12
burning stick s-ed from a fire,	Am 4:11
burning stick s-ed from the fire?"	Zch 3:2
one comes and s-es away what	
was	Mt 13:19
The wolf then s-es and scatters	Jn 10:12

SNEER

No one will s them out of My   Jn 10:28
save others by s-ing {them} from   Jd 23

SNEER

they s and shake their heads: Ps 22:7
But some s-ed and said, "They're   Ac 2:13

SNEEZED

The boy s seven times and opened   2Kg 4:35

SNORTING

His proud s {fills one with} terror.   Jb 39:20
From Dan is heard the s of horses.   Jr 8:16

SNOUT

like a gold ring in a pig's s.   Pr 11:22

SNOW

his hand was diseased, like s.   Ex 4:6
diseased, as {white} as s.   Nm 12:10
diseased—{white} as s.   2Kg 5:27
where the s is stored?   Jb 38:22
and I will be whiter than s.   Ps 51:7
He spreads s like wool;   Ps 147:16
the coolness of s on a harvest   Pr 25:13
Like s in summer and rain at   Pr 26:1
for her household when it s-s,   Pr 31:21
they will be as white as s;   Is 1:18
as rain and s fall from heaven   Is 55:10
His clothing was white like s,   Dn 7:9
and his robe was as white as s.   Mt 28:3
head and hair were ... white as s,   Rv 1:14

SNOWY

into a pit on a s day and killed   2Sm 23:20

SNUFFERS

Its s and firepans must be of   Ex 25:38

SNUGLY

she wrapped Him s in cloth and   Lk 2:7
s in cloth and lying in a manger.   Lk 2:12

SOAK

s-ing its furrows and leveling   Ps 65:10
land will be s-ed with blood,   Is 34:7

SOAP

if you ... use a great amount of s,   Jr 2:22

SOAR

Does the eagle s at your command   Jb 39:27
s-ing on the wings of the wind.   Ps 18:10
will s on wings like eagles;   Is 40:31

be like an eagle s-ing upward,   Jr 49:22
you seem to s like an eagle   Ob 4

SOBER

but we must stay awake and be s.   1Th 5:6
Be s! Be on the alert!   1Pt 5:8

SOBERED

the morning when Nabal
  s-ed up,   1Sm 25:37

SO-CALLED

My jealousy with {their} s gods;   Dt 32:21
For even if there are s gods,   1Co 8:5
above every s god or object   2Th 2:4

SOCKET

and dislocated his hip s.   Gn 32:25
and my arm be pulled from its s.   Jb 31:22

SODA

or like {pouring} vinegar on s.   Pr 25:20

SODOM

  City on the plain, where Lot settled (Gn
10:19; 13:10; 14:11-12); destroyed along
with Gomorrah by God (Gn 18:20; 19:24).
  Came to symbolize debauchery (Dt
32:32; Is 3:9; Jr 23:14; Ezk 16:46-56; Mt
10:15; 11:23-24; 2Pt 2:6; Jd 7; Rv 11:8) and
the resulting devastation (Dt 29:23; Is 1:9;
13:19; Jr 49:18; 50:40; Lm 4:6; Am 4:11;
Zph 2:9; Lk 17:29; Rm 9:29).

SOFT

there was a voice, a s whisper.   1Kg 19:12
A man dressed in s clothes?   Mt 11:8

SOFTEN

You s it with showers and bless   Ps 65:10

SOFTER

His words are s than oil, but   Ps 55:21

SOIL

a man of the s, was the first to   Gn 9:20
from this good s that He gave to   1Kg 14:15
the LORD's song on foreign s?   Ps 137:4
one plows and breaks up the s,   Ps 141:7
not a prophet; I am a tiller of the s,   Zch 13:5
quickly since the s wasn't deep.   Mt 13:5
s produces a crop by itself   Mk 4:28
fit for the s or for the manure   Lk 14:35

SOJOURNER

foreigners and s-s in Your	1Ch 29:15
with You, a s like all my	Ps 39:12

SOLDERING

saying of the s, "It is good."	Is 41:7

SOLDIER

put him in command of the s-s,	1Sm 18:5
having s-s under my command.	Mt 8:9
the governor's s-s took Jesus	Mt 27:27
gave the s-s a large sum of money	Mt 28:12
Some s-s ... "What should we do?"	Lk 3:14
The s-s also mocked Him.	Lk 23:36
s-s also twisted together a crown	Jn 19:2
four parts, a part for each s.	Jn 19:23
one of the s-s pierced His side	Jn 19:34
and a devout s,	Ac 10:7
with the s who guarded him	Ac 28:16
and fellow s, as well as your	Php 2:25
as a good s of Christ Jesus.	2Tm 2:3
no one serving as a s gets entangled	2Tm 2:4
to Archippus our fellow s,	Phm 2

SOLE

place the s of your foot treads	Dt 11:24
no ... place for the s of your foot.	Dt 28:65
place where the s of your foot treads,	Jos 1:3
From the s of his foot to the	2Sm 14:25
boils from the s of his foot to	Jb 2:7
From the s of the foot even to	Is 1:6

SOLEMN

It is a s gathering; you are not to	Lv 23:36
a s assembly for Baal.	2Kg 10:20
s assemblies—I cannot stand	Is 1:13
the stench of your s assemblies.	Am 5:21
ourselves under a s curse that	Ac 23:14

SOLEMNLY

s warn them and tell them about	1Sm 8:9
made the troops s swear,	1Sm 14:28
I have s sworn to keep Your	Ps 119:106
to s testify that He is the One	Ac 10:42
s testified to the Jews that	Ac 18:5
I s charge you, before God and	1Tm 5:21
and His kingdom, I s charge you:	2Tm 4:1

SOLID

I fed you milk, not s food,	1Co 3:2
God's s foundation stands firm,	2Tm 2:19

You need milk, not s food.	Heb 5:12
But s food is for the mature	Heb 5:14

SOLITARY

I am like a s bird on a roof.	Ps 102:7

SOLOMON

Son of David and Bathsheba; third king of Israel (2Sm 12:24; 1Kg 1:30-40). Asked for wisdom (3:5-15); knew many proverbs and songs (4:32; Pss 72; 127; Pr 1:1; 10:1; 25:1; Sg 1:1); wisdom demonstrated in child dispute (1Kg 3:16-28) and the visit of the Queen of Sheba (10:1-13). Built and dedicated the temple (1Kg 5–8). Accumulated vast wealth (9:26-28; 10:26-29); had many wives and concubines, who influenced him toward idolatry (11:1-8).

SOME

s 100, s 60, and s 30 times	Mt 13:8,23
And they said, "S say John the	Mt 16:14
they worshiped, but s doubted.	Mt 28:17
gave s to be apostles, s prophets, s	Eph 4:11

SOMEBODY

Theudas rose up, claiming to be s,	Ac 5:36
while claiming to be s great.	Ac 8:9

SOMEHOW

that if it is s in God's will,	Rm 1:10
if I can s make my own people	Rm 11:14
assuming that I will s reach the	Php 3:11

SOMEONE

or should we expect s else?	Mt 11:3
S stands among you, but you don't	Jn 1:26
S is coming after me, and I am	Ac 13:25

SOMETHING

your brother has s against you,	Mt 5:23
Simon, I have s to say to you.	Lk 7:40
considers himself to be s when he is	Gl 6:3

SOMEWHERE

But one has s testified:	Heb 2:6
for s He has spoken about the	Heb 4:4

SON see also SON OF DAVID,
SON OF GOD, SON OF MAN,
SONS OF GOD

wife Sarah will bear you a s,	Gn 17:19
and bore a s to Abraham in his	Gn 21:2
"Take your s," He said, "your only	Gn 22:2

Jacob had 12 s-s:	Gn 35:22	No one knows the S except the	Mt 11:27
My s Joseph is still alive.	Gn 45:28	Isn't this the carpenter's s?	Mt 13:55
I will kill your firstborn s!	Ex 4:23	Messiah, the S of the living God!	Mt 16:16
not give your daughters to their s-s	Dt 7:3	Then the s-s are free,	Mt 17:26
If a man has a ... rebellious s	Dt 21:18	that these two s-s of mine may	Mt 20:21
A s has been born to Naomi,	Ru 4:17	A man had two s-s.	Mt 21:28
Eli's s-s were wicked men;	1Sm 2:12	'They will respect my s,' he said.	Mt 21:37
Are these all the s-s you have?	1Sm 16:11	how then can the Messiah be	
and he will be a s to Me.	2Sm 7:14	his S?	Mt 22:45
My s Absalom! My s, my s	2Sm 18:33	that you are s-s of those who	Mt 23:31
Then the s-s of the prophets	2Kg 2:3	For He said, 'I am God's S.'	Mt 27:43
wives of the s-s of the prophets	2Kg 4:1	This man really was God's S!	Mt 27:54
Did I ask my lord for a s?	2Kg 4:28	and of the S and of the Holy Spirit,	Mt 28:19
The s-s of the prophets were	2Kg 4:38	called the S of the Most High,	Lk 1:32
The s-s of the prophets said to	2Kg 6:1	gave birth to her firstborn S,	Lk 2:7
These were David's s-s	1Ch 3:1	thought to be the s of Joseph,	Lk 3:23
I have chosen him to be My s,	1Ch 28:6	of Seth, {s} of Adam, {s} of God.	Lk 3:38
If his s-s receive honor,	Jb 14:21	you will be s-s of the Most High.	Lk 6:35
He said to Me, "You are My S;	Ps 2:7	He was his mother's only s,	Lk 7:12
Pay homage to the S, or He will be	Ps 2:12	You S of the Most High God?	Lk 8:28
are all s-s of the Most High.	Ps 82:6	If a s of peace is there, your	Lk 10:6
S-s are indeed a heritage from	Ps 127:3	father against s, s against father,	Lk 12:53
If your s-s keep My covenant and	Ps 132:12	longer worthy to be called your s.	Lk 15:19
When I was a s with my father,	Pr 4:3	Now his older s was in the	Lk 15:25
A wise s brings joy to his father,	Pr 10:1	s-s of this age are more astute	Lk 16:8
Discipline your s, and he will	Pr 29:17	he too is a s of Abraham.	Lk 19:9
and what is the name of His S	Pr 30:4	s-s of this age marry and are	Lk 20:34
s of my womb? What, s of my vows?	Pr 31:2	One and Only S from the Father	Jn 1:14
Her s-s rise up and call her	Pr 31:28	seen God. The One and Only S	Jn 1:18
The virgin will conceive, have a s,	Is 7:14	He gave His One and Only S,	Jn 3:16
born for us, a s will be given to us,	Is 9:6	not send His S into the world	Jn 3:17
s-s will come from far away,	Is 60:4	believes in the S has eternal life,	Jn 3:36
Does Israel have no s-s?	Jr 49:1	Him to come down and heal his s,	Jn 4:47
fathers will eat {their} s-s	Ezk 5:10	The S is not able to do anything	Jn 5:19
fourth looks like a s of the gods.	Dn 3:25	has given all judgment to the S,	Jn 5:22
be called: S-s of the living God.	Hs 1:10	who sees the S and believes in	Jn 6:40
and out of Egypt I called My s.	Hs 11:1	but a s does remain forever.	Jn 8:35
He is not a wise s;	Hs 13:13	you may become s-s of light.	Jn 12:36
then your s-s and your daughters	Jl 2:28	Glorify Your S so that the S may	Jn 17:1
a prophet or the s of a prophet;	Am 7:14	except the s of destruction,	Jn 17:12
A s honors {his} father,	Mal 1:6	mother, "Woman, here is your s."	Jn 19:26
He will purify the s-s of Levi	Mal 3:3	then your s-s and your daughters	Ac 2:17
until she gave birth to a s.	Mt 1:25	are the s-s of the prophets and	Ac 3:25
Out of Egypt I called My S.	Mt 2:15	translated Encouragement,	Ac 4:36
beloved S. I take delight in Him!	Mt 3:17	and said, "You s of the Devil,	Ac 13:10
you may be s-s of your Father	Mt 5:45	Psalm: You are My S; today I	Ac 13:33
if his s asks him for bread,	Mt 7:9	s-s of Sceva, a Jewish chief	Ac 19:14
But the s-s of the kingdom will	Mt 8:12	sending His own S in flesh like	Rm 8:3

by God's Spirit are God's s-s. Rm 8:14
for God's s-s to be revealed. Rm 8:19
conformed to the image of His S, Rm 8:29
He did not even spare His own S, Rm 8:32
will be called s-s of the living Rm 9:26
into fellowship with His S, 1Co 1:9
then the S Himself will also be 1Co 15:28
you will be s-s and daughters 2Co 6:18
God sent His S, born of a woman Gl 4:4
might receive adoption as s-s. Gl 4:5
slave, but a s; and if a s, then an heir Gl 4:7
Throw out the slave and her s, Gl 4:30
to wait for His S from heaven, 1Th 1:10
are all s-s of light and s-s of the day. 1Th 5:5
the s of destruction. 2Th 2:3
He has spoken to us by {His} S, Heb 1:2
did He ever say, You are My S; Heb 1:5
but about the S: Your throne, O Heb 1:8
was faithful as a S over His Heb 3:6
Though a S, He learned obedience Heb 5:8
to be called the s of Pharaoh's Heb 11:24
that addresses you as s-s: Heb 12:5
punishes every s whom He Heb 12:6
illegitimate children and not s-s. Heb 12:8
is My beloved S. I take delight 2Pt 1:17
blood of Jesus His S cleanses us 1Jn 1:7
No one who denies the S can 1Jn 2:23
remain in the S and in the 1Jn 2:24
One and Only S into the world 1Jn 4:9
loved us and sent His S to be 1Jn 4:10
The one who has the S has life. 1Jn 5:12
But she gave birth to a S Rv 12:5
be his God, and he will be My s. Rv 21:7

SON OF DAVID

proverbs of Solomon s, Pr 1:1
words of the Teacher, s, Ec 1:1
the S, the Son of Abraham: Mt 1:1
Have mercy on us, S! Mt 9:27
Perhaps this is the S! Mt 12:23
Hosanna to the S! Mt 21:9

SON OF GOD

If You are the S, Mt 4:3,6
Truly You are the S! Mt 14:33
If You are the S, come Mt 27:40
of Jesus Christ, the S. Mk 1:1
will be called the S. Lk 1:35
saying, "You are the S!" Lk 4:41
Are You, then, the S? Lk 22:70

that He is the S! Jn 1:34
replied, "You are the S! Jn 1:49
of the One and Only S. Jn 3:18
hear the voice of the S, Jn 5:25
because I said: I am the S? Jn 10:36
He made Himself the S. Jn 19:7
Jesus Christ is the S. Ac 8:37
He is the S. Ac 9:20
established as the powerful S by Rm 1:4
I live by faith in the S, Gl 2:20
they are recrucifying the S Heb 6:6
resembling the S—remains a priest Heb 7:3
has trampled on the S, Heb 10:29
confesses that Jesus is the S 1Jn 4:15
one who believes that Jesus is the S? 1Jn 5:5

SON OF MAN

or a s who changes His mind. Nm 23:19
and the s, who is a worm! Jb 25:6
s that You look after Him? Ps 8:4
with the s You have made Ps 80:17
s, that You think of him? Ps 144:3
or a s who is given up like grass. Is 51:12
He said to me, "S, Ezk 2:1
I saw One like a s coming Dn 7:13
"S," he said to me, Dn 8:17
S has no place to lay His Mt 8:20
The S came eating and drinking, Mt 11:19
S is Lord of the Sabbath. Mt 12:8
a word against the S, Mt 12:32
three nights, so the S will be in Mt 12:40
the good seed is the S; Mt 13:37
Who do people say that the S is? Mt 16:13
S coming in His kingdom. Mt 16:28
until the S is raised from the dead. Mt 17:9
The S is about to be betrayed Mt 17:22
The S will be handed over Mt 20:18
the coming of the S. Mt 24:27
When the S comes in His glory, Mt 25:31
S will be handed over to Mt 26:2
The S will go just as it Mt 26:24
S seated at the right hand Mt 26:64
the S must suffer many things, Mk 8:31
S ... not come to be served Mk 10:45
S seated at the right hand Mk 14:62
long to see one of the days of the S Lk 17:22
S has come to seek and to save Lk 19:10
so the S must be lifted up, Jn 3:14
Do you believe in the S? Jn 9:35

Who is this S?   Jn 12:34
S standing at the right hand of God!   Ac 7:56
or the s, that You care for him?   Heb 2:6
lampstands was One like the S,   Rv 1:13
One like the S was seated on   Rv 14:14

SONG

The LORD is my strength and my s;   Ex 15:2
Then Israel sang this s: Nm 21:17
write down this s for yourselves   Dt 31:19
David spoke the words of this s   2Sm 22:1
and his s-s numbered 1,005.   1Kg 4:32
They ministered with s in front   1Ch 6:32
God with s-s and with lyres,   1Ch 13:8
rejoicing and s ordained by   2Ch 23:18
singing the s, and blowing   2Ch 29:28
in charge of the praise s-s.   Neh 12:8
with s-s in the night,   Jb 35:10
and I praise Him with my s.   Ps 28:7
Sing a new s to Him;   Ps 33:3
He put a new s in my mouth,   Ps 40:3
His s will be with me in the night   Ps 42:8
drunkards make up s-s about me.   Ps 69:12
Sing a new s to the LORD   Ps 96:1; 98:1
come before Him with joyful s-s.   Ps 100:2
LORD is my strength and my s;   Ps 118:14
my s during my earthly life.   Ps 119:54
Sing us one of the s-s of Zion.   Ps 137:3
I will sing a new s to You;   Ps 144:9
Sing to the LORD a new s,   Ps 149:1
Singing s-s to a troubled heart   Pr 25:20
the daughters of s grow faint   Ec 12:4
Solomon's Finest S   Sg 1:1
a s about my loved one's vineyard: Is 5:1
strength and my s, He has become   Is 12:2
On that day this s will be sung   Is 26:1
Sing a new s to the LORD;   Is 42:10
burst into s and shout, you who   Is 54:1
mocked by their s-s all day long.   Lm 3:14
I am mocked by their s-s.   Lm 3:63
an end to the noise of your s-s,   Ezk 26:13
from Me the noise of your s-s!   Am 5:23
They improvise s-s to the sound   Am 6:5
psalms, hymns, and spiritual s-s,   Eph 5:19
psalms, hymns, and spiritual s-s,   Col 3:16
sang a new s: You are worthy   Rv 5:9
could learn the s except the   Rv 14:3
the s of the Lamb: Rv 15:3

SON-IN-LAW

I should become the king's s?   1Sm 18:18
for he was a s to Ahab's family.   2Kg 8:27
had become a s to Sanballat   Neh 13:28

SONS-IN-LAW

Lot went out and spoke to his s,   Gn 19:14

SONS OF GOD

the s saw that the daughters of man Gn 6:2
One day the s came   Jb 1:6; 2:1
and all the s shouted for joy?   Jb 38:7
peacemakers ... will be called s.   Mt 5:9
they are like angels and are s,   Lk 20:36
you are all s through faith in Christ Gl 3:26

SOON

for My salvation is coming s,   Is 56:1

SOOTH

A secret gift s-es anger, and a   Pr 21:14
bandaged, or s-ed with oil.   Is 1:6

SORCERER

Pharaoh called the wise men and s-s Ex 7:11
or your s-s who say to you: Jr 27:9
mediums, s-s, and Chaldeans to   Dn 2:2
against s-s and adulterers;   Mal 3:5
But Elymas, the s, which is how   Ac 13:8
immoral, s-s, idolaters,   Rv 21:8
the dogs, the s-s, the sexually   Rv 22:15

SORCERESS

You must not allow a s to live.   Ex 22:18
you sons of a s,   Is 57:3

SORCERY

not to practice divination or s.   Lv 19:26
interpret omens, practice s,   Dt 18:10
witchcraft, divination, and s,   2Ch 33:6
the attractive mistress of s,   Nah 3:4
practiced s in that city   Ac 8:9
idolatry, s, hatreds, strife,   Gl 5:20
nations were deceived by your s,   Rv 18:23

SORES

and festering s not cleansed,   Is 1:6
Lazarus, covered with s,   Lk 16:20
severely painful s broke out   Rv 16:2

SORREL

him were red, s, and white   Zch 1:8

SORROW

gray hairs down to Sheol in s.	Gn 42:38
their s was turned into rejoicing	Est 9:22
s-s of those who take another god	Ps 16:4
my eyes are worn out from angry s	Ps 31:9
the best of them are struggle and s;	Ps 90:10
man fathers a fool to his own s;	Pr 17:21
Who has woe? Who has s?	Pr 23:29
For with much wisdom is much s;	Ec 1:18
his days, with much s, sickness,	Ec 5:17
Remove s from your heart, and	Ec 11:10
and s and sighing will flee. Is 35:10; 51:11	
My soul is swallowed up in s	Mt 26:38
s has filled your heart.	Jn 16:6
but your s will turn to joy.	Jn 16:20
I have intense s and continual	Rm 9:2
to mourning and your joy to s.	Jms 4:9

SORROWFUL

grief, and his occupation is s;	Ec 2:23

SORT

signifying what s of death He	Jn 18:32

SOSTHENES

A ruler of the synagogue in Corinth (Ac 18:17). Possibly the same man as Paul's co-worker (1Co 1:1).

SOUL

all your s, and with all your strength.	Dt 6:5
all your heart and all your s.	Jos 22:5
with all his s in order to carry out	2Ch 34:31
God spares his s from the Pit,	Jb 33:18
LORD is perfect, reviving the s;	Ps 19:7
My s, praise the LORD, and all	Ps 103:1
because of the bitterness of my s,	Is 38:15
to destroy both s and body in hell.	Mt 10:28
beloved in whom My s delights;	Mt 12:18
with all your s, and with all	Mt 22:37
My s is swallowed up in sorrow	Mt 26:38
a sword will pierce your own s	Lk 2:35
Now My s is troubled.	Jn 12:27
will not leave my s in Hades,	Ac 2:27
were of one heart and s,	Ac 4:32
may your spirit, s, and body be	1Th 5:23
as far as to divide s, spirit, joints,	Heb 4:12
sure and firm anchor of the s	Heb 6:19
watch over your s-s as those who	Heb 13:17
the salvation of your s-s.	1Pt 1:9
shepherd and guardian of your s-s.	1Pt 2:25

health, just as your s prospers.	3Jn 2
under the altar the s-s of those	Rv 6:9
also {saw} the s-s of those who	Rv 20:4

SOUND (adj)

rebels against all s judgment.	Pr 18:1
wage war with s guidance Pr 20:18; 24:6	
is contrary to the s teaching	1Tm 1:10
the pattern of s teaching that	2Tm 1:13
will not tolerate s doctrine,	2Tm 4:3
to encourage with s teaching and	Ti 1:9

SOUND (n)

There is a s of war in the camp.	Ex 32:17
When you hear the s of marching	2Sm 5:24
camp to hear the s of chariots,	2Kg 7:6
Dreadful s-s fill their ears;	Jb 15:21
cannot make a s with their throats.	Ps 115:7
one rises at the s of a bird,	Ec 12:4
eliminate ... the s of the millstones	Jr 25:10
you hear its s, but you don't	Jn 3:8
if the trumpet makes an unclear s,	1Co 14:8
voice like the s of cascading waters.	Rv 1:15
s of their wings was like	Rv 9:9
the s of a mill will never be	Rv 18:22
like the s of cascading waters,	Rv 19:6

SOUND (v)

voice s-ed like ... mighty waters,	Ezk 43:2
s the alarm on My holy mountain!	Jl 2:1
don't s a trumpet before you,	Mt 6:2
the trumpet will s, and the dead	1Co 15:52

SOUNDNESS

There is no s in my body because	Ps 38:3

SOUR

The fathers have eaten s grapes,	Jr 31:29
The fathers eat s grapes, and	Ezk 18:2
sponge full of s wine on hyssop	Jn 19:29

SOURCE

Guard your heart ... it is the s of life.	Pr 4:23
And you killed the s of life,	Ac 3:15
I did not receive it from a human s	Gl 1:12
make the s of their salvation	Heb 2:10
He became the s of eternal	Heb 5:9
s and perfecter of our faith,	Heb 12:2
What is the s of the wars and	Jms 4:1

SOUTH

Gusting to the s, turning to the	Ec 1:6
falls to the s or the north,	Ec 11:3

north wind—come, s wind. Sg 4:16
The king of the S will grow Dn 11:5
queen of the s will rise up at Mt 12:42
And when the s wind is blowing, Lk 12:55
When a gentle s wind sprang up, Ac 27:13

SOUTHERN
the constellations of the s sky. Jb 9:9

SOVEREIGN
{He is} the blessed and only S, 1Tm 6:15

SOVEREIGNTY
Rehoboam had established his s 2Ch 12:1
High God gave s, greatness, Dn 5:18
s will come to Daughter Mc 4:8
views of justice and s stem from Hab 1:7

SOW (n)
a s, after washing itself, wallows 2Pt 2:22

SOW (v)
a hundred times {what was sown}. Gn 26:12
S your land for six years and Ex 23:10
not ... s your fields with two kinds Lv 19:19
You may s your field for six years, Lv 25:3
the city and s-ed it with salt. Jdg 9:45
those who s trouble reap the same. Jb 4:8
Those who s in tears will reap Ps 126:5
the one who s-s righteousness, Pr 11:18
who s-s injustice will reap disaster, Pr 22:8
who watches the wind will not s, Ec 11:4
In the morning s your seed, Ec 11:6
Happy are you who s seed beside Is 32:20
are barely planted, barely sown, Is 40:24
the wilderness, in a land not sown. Jr 2:2
do not s among the thorns. Jr 4:3
when I will s the house of Israel Jr 31:27
s the wind and reap the whirlwind. Hs 8:7
S righteousness for yourselves Hs 10:12
You will s but not reap; Mc 6:15
they don't s or reap or gather Mt 6:26
As he was s-ing, some seeds fell Mt 13:4
the one sown along the path. Mt 13:19
a man who s-ed good seed Mt 13:24
The One who s-s the good seed is Mt 13:37
and reap what you didn't s. Lk 19:21
One s-s and another reaps. Jn 4:37
we have sown spiritual things 1Co 9:11
What you s does not come to life 1Co 15:36
Sown in corruption, raised in 1Co 15:42

person who s-s sparingly will 2Co 9:6
whatever a man s-s he will also Gl 6:7
righteousness is sown in peace by Jms 3:18

SOWER
Consider the s who went out to Mt 13:3
listen to the parable of the s: Mt 13:18
The s sows the word. Mk 4:14
so the s and reaper can rejoice Jn 4:36
One who provides seed for the s 2Co 9:10

SPACE
He named it Open S-s Gn 26:22
empty s; He hangs the earth on Jb 26:7
residential and open s. Ezk 48:15

SPACIOUS
to a good and s land, Ex 3:8
in the s and fertile land You Neh 9:35
distress to a s and unconfined Jb 36:16
have set my feet in a s place. Ps 31:8
me {and put me} in a s place. Ps 118:5

SPAIN
I will go by way of you to S. Rm 15:28

SPAN
marked off the heavens with the s Is 40:12

SPARE
s-ing ... for the sake of the 50 Gn 18:24
Saul and the troops s-d Agag, 1Sm 15:9
in your power; only s his life. Jb 2:6
God s-s his soul from the Pit, Jb 33:18
He did not s them from death, Ps 78:50
He did not even s His own Son, Rm 8:32
For if God did not s the natural Rm 11:21
and I am trying to s you. 1Co 7:28
it was to s you that I did not 2Co 1:23
if God didn't s the angels who 2Pt 2:4

SPARINGLY
person who sows s will also reap s, 2Co 9:6

SPARK
as surely as s-s fly upward. Jb 5:7
become tinder, and his work a s; Is 1:31

SPARKLING
living water, s like crystal, Rv 22:1

SPARROW
Even a s finds a home, Ps 84:3

Aren't two **s-s** sold for a penny? Mt 10:29
are worth more than many **s-s**. Mt 10:31

SPATTER
their blood **s-ed** My garments, Is 63:3

SPEAK
Then God **spoke** to Noah, Gn 8:15
I have ventured to **s** to the Lord Gn 18:27
all that the LORD has **spoken**. Ex 19:8
face to face, just as a man **s-s** with Ex 33:11
I **s** with him directly, openly, Nm 12:8
s only the message God puts in Nm 22:38
seen that God **s-s** with a person, Dt 5:24
who dares to **s** in My name a Dt 18:20
let me **s** one more time. Jdg 6:39
by **s-ing** kind words to them, 1Kg 12:7
He was still **s-ing** when another Jb 1:16
You **s** as a foolish woman **s-s**, Jb 2:10
if only God would **s** Jb 11:5
my spirit compels me {to **s**}. Jb 32:18
Surely I **spoke** about things I did not Jb 42:3
He **spoke**, and it came into being; Ps 33:9
God has **spoken** in His sanctuary: Ps 60:6
I am troubled and cannot **s**. Ps 77:4
but cannot **s**, eyes, but cannot see. Ps 115:5
I will **s** of Your glorious Ps 145:5
A word **spoken** at the right time is Pr 25:11
you see a man who **s-s** too soon? Pr 29:20
S up for those who have no voice, Pr 31:8
to be silent and a time to **s**; Ec 3:7
not be hasty to **s**, and do not be Ec 5:2
So He will **s** to this people with Is 28:11
S tenderly to Jerusalem, Is 40:2
the mouth of the LORD has **spoken**. Is 40:5
I have **spoken**; so I will also bring Is 46:11
and had not **spoken** deceitfully. Is 53:9
I **spoke** and they didn't hear; Is 66:4
I won't mention Him or **s** any longer Jr 20:9
and **s** tenderly to her. Hs 2:14
GOD has **spoken**; who will not Am 3:8
the one who **s-s** with integrity. Am 5:10
S truth to one another; Zch 8:16
worry about ... what you should **s**. Mt 10:19
you are not **s-ing**, but the Spirit Mt 10:20
But whoever **s-s** against the Holy Mt 12:32
Why do You **s** to them in parables? Mt 13:10
they will **s** in new languages; Mk 16:17
and would not allow them to **s**, Lk 4:41
when all people **s** well of you, Lk 6:26

his mouth **s-s** from the overflow Lk 6:45
all that the prophets have **spoken**! Lk 24:25
We **s** what We know Jn 3:11
the One **s-ing** to you. Jn 4:26
No man ever **spoke** like this! Jn 7:46
He is the One **s-ing** with you. Jn 9:37
Isaiah ... **spoke** about Him. Jn 12:41
I do not **s** on My own. Jn 14:10
but He will **s** whatever He hears. Jn 16:13
Now You're **s-ing** plainly and not Jn 16:29
began to **s** in different languages, Ac 2:4
Do all **s** in languages? 1Co 12:30
If I **s** the languages of men and 1Co 13:1
was a child, I **spoke** like a child, 1Co 13:11
the person who **s-s** in languages, 1Co 14:5
do not forbid **s-ing** in {other} 1Co 14:39
But **s-ing** the truth in love, let Eph 4:15
He has **spoken** to us by {His} Son, Heb 1:2
dead, he still **s-s** through this. Heb 11:4
quick to hear, slow to **s**, Jms 1:19
S and act as those who will be Jms 2:12
Holy Spirit, men **spoke** from God. 2Pt 1:21
was given to him to **s** boasts and Rv 13:5

SPEAKER
since I am such a poor **s**? Ex 6:12

SPEAR
His **s** shaft was like a weaver's 1Sm 17:7
it is not by sword or by **s** that 1Sm 17:47
As the **s** struck the wall, David 1Sm 19:10
Saul threw his **s** at Jonathan to 1Sm 20:33
Their teeth are **s-s** and arrows; Ps 57:4
their **s-s** into pruning knives. Is 2:4; Mc 4:3
your pruning knives into **s-s**. Jl 3:10
pierced His side with a **s**, Jn 19:34

SPECIAL
a **s** vow, a Nazirite vow, Nm 6:2
has chosen you to be His **s** people Dt 14:2
his bow without taking **s** aim 1Kg 22:34
They will be Mine ... a **s** possession Mal 3:17
for that Sabbath was a **s** day Jn 19:31
some for **s** use, some for 2Tm 2:20
cleanse for Himself a **s** people, Ti 2:14

SPECIFICATION
and according to every **s**. 1Kg 6:38
restored God's temple to its **s-s** 2Ch 24:13
statutes, design **s-s**, and laws. Ezk 43:11

SPECIFIES

He s a certain day—today   Heb 4:7

SPECK

are considered as a s of dust on   Is 40:15
the s in your brother's eye,   Mt 7:3

SPECKLED

sheep that is s or spotted,   Gn 30:32

SPECTACLE

I made a s of you before kings.   Ezk 28:17
I will make a s of you.   Nah 3:6
that had gathered for this s,   Lk 23:48
we have become a s to the world   1Co 4:9

SPECULATIONS

promote empty s rather than   1Tm 1:4

SPEECH

not understand one another's s.   Gn 11:7
I am slow and hesitant in s.   Ex 4:10
my s settled on them {like dew}.   Jb 29:22
Day after day they pour out s;   Ps 19:2
There is no s; there are no words;   Ps 19:3
confuse and confound their s,   Ps 55:9
Excessive s is not appropriate   Pr 17:7
with stammering s and in a   Is 28:11
a people whose s is difficult to   Is 33:19
of unintelligible s or difficult   Ezk 3:5
man who also had a s difficulty,   Mk 7:32
Spirit gave them ability for s.   Ac 2:4
with brilliance of s or wisdom.   1Co 2:1
s should always be gracious,   Col 4:6
example to the believers in s,   1Tm 4:12
irreverent, empty s   1Tm 6:20; 2Tm 2:16

SPEECHLESS

I was s and quiet;   Ps 39:2
face toward the ground and was s.   Dn 10:15
wedding clothes?' The man was s.   Mt 22:12

SPELLS

cast s, consult a medium or   Dt 18:11
who skillfully weave s.   Ps 58:5
and the potency of your s.   Is 47:9

SPEND

I have spent my strength for nothing   Is 49:4
Why do you s money on what is not   Is 55:2
had spent all she had on doctors   Lk 8:43
for whatever extra you s.   Lk 10:35
After he had spent everything,   Lk 15:14

gladly s and be spent for you.   2Co 12:15
so that you may s it on your desires   Jms 4:3
s a year there and do business   Jms 4:13

SPICES

s for the anointing oil   Ex 25:6
great quantity of s, and precious   1Kg 10:10
I gather my myrrh with my s.   Sg 5:1
stag on the mountains of s.   Sg 8:14
meat well and mix in the s!   Ezk 24:10
Salome bought s, so they could   Mk 16:1
and prepared s and perfumes.   Lk 23:56
cloths with the aromatic s,   Jn 19:40

SPILL

the skins burst, the wine s-s out,   Mt 9:17
and all his insides s-ed out.   Ac 1:18

SPIN

they don't labor or s   Mt 6:28; Lk 12:27

SPINDLE

a man who can only work a s   2Sm 3:29
and her hands hold the s.   Pr 31:19

SPIRIT see also HOLY SPIRIT,
             SPIRIT OF GOD,
             SPIRIT OF THE LORD

My S will not remain with mankind   Gn 6:3
breath of the s of life in its   Gn 7:22
have filled with a s of wisdom,   Ex 28:3
I have filled him with God's S,   Ex 31:3
Everyone ... whose s prompted
   him   Ex 35:21
I will take some of the S ... on you   Nm 11:17
My servant Caleb has a different s   Nm 14:24
God of the s-s of all flesh,   Nm 16:22; 27:16
a man who has the S in him,   Nm 27:18
consult a medium or a familiar s,   Dt 18:11
God sent an evil s between   Jdg 9:23
an evil s from the LORD began   1Sm 16:14
next day an evil s from God took   1Sm 18:10
Now an evil s from the LORD came   1Sm 19:9
Saul said, "Consult a s for me.   1Sm 28:8
has put a lying s into the mouth   1Kg 22:23
double portion of your s on me.   2Kg 2:9
Wasn't my s there when the man   2Kg 5:26
I am about to put a s in him,   2Kg 19:7
sent Your good S to instruct   Neh 9:20
and withdrew the s and breath He   Jb 34:14
Into Your hand I entrust my s;   Ps 31:5

renew a steadfast s within me.	Ps 51:10
or take Your Holy S from me.	Ps 51:11
pleasing to God is a broken s.	Ps 51:17
I meditate; my s becomes weak.	Ps 77:3
in my heart, and my s ponders.	Ps 77:6
and whose s was not faithful to God.	Ps 78:8
Do departed s-s rise up to praise	Ps 88:10
broke their s-s with hard labor;	Ps 107:12
Where can I go to escape Your S?	Ps 139:7
My s is weak within me;	Ps 143:4
then I will pour out my s on you	Pr 1:23
to the land of the departed s-s.	Pr 2:18
that the departed s-s are there,	Pr 9:18
a devious tongue breaks the s.	Pr 15:4
and an arrogant s before a fall.	Pr 16:18
but who can survive a broken s?	Pr 18:14
assembly of the departed s-s.	Pr 21:16
Who knows if the s of people rises	Ec 3:21
the s returns to God who gave	Ec 12:7
a S of wisdom and understanding,	Is 11:2
my s within me diligently seeks	Is 26:9
departed s-s do not rise up.	Is 26:14
their horses are flesh, not s.	Is 31:3
He will gather them by His S,	Is 34:16
I have put My S on Him;	Is 42:1
I will pour out My S on your	Is 44:3
Lord GOD has sent me and His S.	Is 48:16
to revive the s of the lowly and	Is 57:15
The S of the Lord GOD is on Me,	Is 61:1
and grieved His Holy S.	Is 63:10
the S entered me and set me on	Ezk 2:2
and put a new s within them;	Ezk 11:19
follow their own s and have seen	Ezk 13:3
a new heart and a new s.	Ezk 18:31
and put a new s within you;	Ezk 36:26
I will place My S within you and	Ezk 36:27
I will put My S in you, and you	Ezk 37:14
out My S on the house of Israel.	Ezk 39:29
the s of the holy gods is in him	Dn 4:8
to have an extraordinary s,	Dn 5:12
a s of promiscuity leads them	Hs 4:12
pour out My S on all humanity	Jl 2:28
If a man of s comes and invents	Mc 2:11
stirred up the s of Zerubbabel	Hg 1:14
but by My S,' says the LORD	Zch 4:6
and formed the s of man within	Zch 12:1
was led up by the S into the	Mt 4:1
Blessed are the poor in s,	Mt 5:3
them authority over unclean s-s,	Mt 10:1
I will put My S on Him, and He	Mt 12:18
against the S will not be	Mt 12:31
seven other s-s more evil than	Mt 12:45
The s is willing, but the flesh	Mt 26:41
and gave up His s.	Mt 27:50
open and the S descending to Him	Mk 1:10
But sighing deeply in His s,	Mk 8:12
in the s and power of Elijah,	Lk 1:17
Guided by the S, he entered the	Lk 2:27
Galilee in the power of the S,	Lk 4:14
Her s returned, and she got up	Lk 8:55
into Your hands I entrust My s.	Lk 23:46
I watched the S descending from	Jn 1:32
is born of water and the S,	Jn 3:5
He gives the S without measure.	Jn 3:34
God is s, and those who worship	
Him must worship in s and truth.	Jn 4:24
The S is the One who gives life.	Jn 6:63
for the S had not yet been	Jn 7:39
angry in His s and deeply moved	Jn 11:33
troubled in His s and testified,	Jn 13:21
He is the S of truth.	Jn 14:17
the S of truth who proceeds from	Jn 15:26
When the S of truth comes,	Jn 16:13
His head, He gave up His s.	Jn 19:30
as the S gave them ability for	Ac 2:4
pour out My S on all humanity	Ac 2:17
full of the S and wisdom,	Ac 6:3
Lord Jesus, receive my s!	Ac 7:59
The S told Philip, "Go and join	Ac 8:29
but the S of Jesus did not allow	Ac 16:7
met us who had a s of prediction	Ac 16:16
his s was troubled within him	Ac 17:16
being fervent in s, he spoke and	Ac 18:25
had the evil s leaped on them,	Ac 19:16
resolved in the S to pass	Ac 19:21
bound in my s, not knowing what	Ac 20:22
no resurrection, and no angel or s,	Ac 23:8
according to the S of holiness.	Rm 1:4
I serve with my s in {telling}	Rm 1:9
the heart—by the S, not the letter.	Rm 2:29
new way of the S and not in the	Rm 7:6
are not in the flesh, but in the S,	Rm 8:9
led by God's S are God's sons.	Rm 8:14
testifies together with our s that we	Rm 8:16
have the S as the firstfruits	Rm 8:23
S ... joins to help in our weakness,	Rm 8:26

hearts knows the S-'s mind-set,	Rm 8:27
God gave them a s of stupor,	Rm 11:8
and by the power of God's S.	Rm 15:19
revealed them to us by the S,	1Co 2:10
man except the s of the man that	1Co 2:11
in love and a s of gentleness?	1Co 4:21
absent in body but present in s,	1Co 5:3
that his s may be saved in the	1Co 5:5
be holy both in body and in s.	1Co 7:34
About matters of the s:	1Co 12:1
different gifts, but the same S.	1Co 12:4
distinguishing between s-s,	1Co 12:10
baptized by one S into one body	1Co 12:13
language, my s prays, but my	1Co 14:14
the prophets' s-s are under the	1Co 14:32
Adam became a life-giving S.	1Co 15:45
the S as a down payment	2Co 1:22; 5:5
no rest in my s because I did	2Co 2:13
letter kills, but the S produces life.	2Co 3:6
Now the Lord is the S;	2Co 3:17
we have the same s of faith in	2Co 4:13
After beginning with the S,	Gl 3:3
the one born according to the S,	Gl 4:29
walk by the S and you will not	Gl 5:16
But the fruit of the S is love,	Gl 5:22
we must also follow the S.	Gl 5:25
who sows to the S will reap eternal	Gl 6:8
would give you a s of wisdom and	Eph 1:17
There is one body and one S,	Eph 4:4
but be filled with the S:	Eph 5:18
sword of the S, which is God's	Eph 6:17
pray at all times in the S,	Eph 6:18
help from the S of Jesus Christ	Php 1:19
you are standing firm in one s,	Php 1:27
if any fellowship with the S,	Php 2:1
Jesus Christ be with your s.	Php 4:23
I am with you in s, rejoicing to	Col 2:5
Don't stifle the S.	1Th 5:19
And may your s, soul, and body	1Th 5:23
either by a s or by a message or	2Th 2:2
through sanctification by the S	2Th 2:13
justified in the S, seen by angels,	1Tm 3:16
deceitful s-s and the teachings	1Tm 4:1
not given us a s of fearfulness,	2Tm 1:7
all ministering s-s sent out to	Heb 1:14
to divide soul, s, joints, and	Heb 4:12
the eternal S offered Himself	Heb 9:14
and insulted the S of grace?	Heb 10:29

submit ... to the Father of s-s	Heb 12:9
the s-s of righteous people made	Heb 12:23
the body without the s is dead,	Jms 2:26
the S He has caused to live in us	Jms 4:5
the S of Christ within	1Pt 1:11
quality of a gentle and quiet s,	1Pt 3:4
proclamation to the s-s in prison	1Pt 3:19
is from the S He has given us	1Jn 3:24
not believe every s, but test the s-s	1Jn 4:1
Every s who confesses that Jesus	1Jn 4:2
This is the s of the antichrist;	1Jn 4:3
He has given to us from His S.	1Jn 4:13
the S is the One who testifies,	1Jn 5:6
the S, the water, and the blood	1Jn 5:8
natural, not having the S.	Jd 19
from the seven s-s before His throne;	Rv 1:4
was in the S on the Lord's day,	Rv 1:10
listen to what the S says to the	Rv 2:7
the seven s-s of God	Rv 3:1; 4:5; 5:6
to give a s to the image	Rv 13:15
saw three unclean s-s like frogs	Rv 16:13

SPIRIT OF GOD

S was hovering over the surface	Gn 1:2
a man who has the s in him?	Gn 41:38
the S descended on him,	Nm 24:2
Then the S took control of him,	1Sm 10:10
S suddenly took control of him,	1Sm 11:6
the S came on Saul's agents,	1Sm 19:20
The S also came on him,	1Sm 19:23
The S came on Azariah	2Ch 15:1
The S took control of Zechariah	2Ch 24:20
S has made me, and the breath	Jb 33:4
in a vision from the S.	Ezk 11:24
He saw the S descending like a dove	Mt 3:16
If I drive out demons by the S,	Mt 12:28
since the S lives in you.	Rm 8:9
the concerns of God except the S.	1Co 2:11
and that the S lives in you?	1Co 3:16
And I think that I also have the S.	1Co 7:40
no one speaking by the S says,	1Co 12:3
the ones who serve by the S,	Php 3:3
This is how you know the S:	1Jn 4:2

SPIRIT OF THE LORD

The S was on him, and he judged	Jdg 3:10
The S enveloped Gideon,	Jdg 6:34
The S came on Jephthah,	Jdg 11:29
Then the S began to direct him	Jdg 13:25
S took control of him,	Jdg 14:6,19; 15:14

The S will control you,								1Sm 10:6
S took control of David from that				1Sm 16:13
the S had left Saul, and an evil				1Sm 16:14
The S spoke through me,							2Sm 23:2
the S may carry you off							1Kg 18:12
the S leave me to speak to You?					1Kg 22:24
Maybe the S has carried him away				2Kg 2:16
the S came on Jahaziel							2Ch 20:14
The S will rest on Him							Is 11:2
Who has directed the S,							Is 40:13
The S of the Lord GOD is on Me,					Is 61:1
the S gave them rest.							Is 63:14
Then the S came on me,							Ezk 11:5
Is the S impatient?								Mc 2:7
I am filled with power by the S,				Mc 3:8
S is on Me ... He has appointed Me				Lk 4:18
Why did you agree to test the S?				Ac 5:9
the S carried Philip away,						Ac 8:39
where the S is, there is freedom.				2Co 3:17

SPIRITIST

not turn to mediums or consult s-s,				Lv 19:31
a s must be put to death.						Lv 20:27
Saul had removed ... s-s						1Sm 28:3
and consulted mediums and s-s.					2Kg 21:6
Josiah removed mediums, the s-s,				2Kg 23:24
the s-s who chirp and mutter,					Is 8:19

SPIRITUAL

For we know that the law is s;					Rm 7:14
this is your s worship.							Rm 12:1
explaining s things to s people.				1Co 2:13
The s person, however, can						1Co 2:15
speak to you as s people but as					1Co 3:1
They all ate the same s food,					1Co 10:3
Pursue love and desire s gifts,					1Co 14:1
thinks he is a prophet or s,					1Co 14:37
a natural body, raised a s body.				1Co 15:44
who are s should restore such					Gl 6:1
blessed us with every s blessing				Eph 1:3
hymns, and s songs,				Eph 5:19; Col 3:16
against the s forces of evil in					Eph 6:12
all wisdom and s understanding,					Col 1:9
desire the unadulterated s milk,				1Pt 2:2
priesthood to offer s sacrifices				1Pt 2:5
but made alive in the s realm.					1Pt 3:18
live by God in the s realm.						1Pt 4:6

SPIRITUALLY

grew up and became s strong,					Lk 1:80
know it since it is evaluated s.				1Co 2:14

SPIT

If the man with the discharge s-s on			Lv 15:8
father had merely s in her face,				Nm 12:14
from his foot, and s in his face.				Dt 25:9
did not hide My face from ... s-ting.			Is 50:6
Then they s in His face and beat				Mt 26:67
in the man's ears and s-ting,					Mk 7:33
S-ting on his eyes and laying					Mk 8:23
He will be mocked, insulted, s					Lk 18:32
He s on the ground, made some mud				Jn 9:6

SPITE

in s of this you did not trust
	the LORD									Dt 1:32
Will they escape in s of such sin?				Ps 56:7
who lives long in s of his evil.				Ec 7:15
in s of this it still belongs					1Co 12:15

SPLENDID

All that He does is s and majestic;				Ps 111:3
s clothes instead of despair.					Is 61:3
One who is s in His apparel,					Is 63:1
I will clothe you with s robes.					Zch 3:4
All your s and glamorous things					Rv 18:14

SPLENDIDLY

rising s, is the joy of the whole				Ps 48:2
you put up with it s!							2Co 11:4

SPLENDOR

The s of Israel lies slain on					2Sm 1:19
S and majesty are before Him;					1Ch 16:27
Worship the LORD in the s of					1Ch 16:29
glory and the s and the majesty				1Ch 29:11
some to praise the s of							2Ch 20:21
or at the moon moving in s,						Jb 31:26
Adorn yourself with majesty and s,				Jb 40:10
Worship the LORD in the s of					Ps 29:2
In your majesty and s							Ps 45:3
S and majesty are before Him;					Ps 96:6
are clothed with majesty and s.					Ps 104:1
I will speak of Your glorious s					Ps 145:5
large population is a king's s,					Pr 14:28
and the s of old men is gray hair.				Pr 20:29
and from His majestic s					Is 2:10,19,21
had no form or s that we should					Is 53:2
All her s has vanished from						Lm 1:6

wisdom and will defile your **s**.	Ezk 28:7
His **s** covers the heavens,	Hab 3:3
of the world and their **s**.	Mt 4:8
not even Solomon in all his **s** was	Mt 6:29
but the **s** of the heavenly bodies	1Co 15:40
the church to Himself in **s**,	Eph 5:27

SPLINTERED

in Egypt, that **s** reed of a staff	Is 36:6

SPLIT

the ground beneath them **s** open.	Nm 16:31
He **s** the sea and brought them	Ps 78:13
He **s** rocks in the wilderness and	Ps 78:15
He **s** the rock, and water gushed	Is 48:21
and the valleys will **s** apart,	Mc 1:4
Mount of Olives will be **s** in half	Zch 14:4
curtain of the sanctuary was **s**	Mt 27:51
quaked and the rocks were **s**.	Mt 27:51

SPOIL

burn up the city and all its **s**	Dt 13:16
You may enjoy the **s**	Dt 20:14
I saw among the **s-s** a beautiful	Jos 7:21
you may plunder its **s**	Jos 8:2
to take **s-s**, to plunder,	Is 10:6
He will receive the mighty as **s**,	Is 53:12
his life like the **s-s** {of war}.	Jr 21:9
Your despoilers will become **s**,	Jr 30:16

SPOKESMAN

He will be your **s**,	Ex 4:16
you will be My **s**.	Jr 15:19

SPONGE

a **s** full of sour wine on hyssop	Jn 19:29

SPOT

or **s** on the skin of his body,	Lv 13:2
his skin, or a leopard his **s-s**?	Jr 13:23
without **s** or wrinkle or any such	Eph 5:27
without **s** or blame until	1Tm 6:14
in peace without **s** or blemish	2Pt 3:14

SPOTTED

sheep that is speckled or **s**,	Gn 30:32

SPRAWL

with} ivory, **s-ed** out on their	Am 6:4
of those who **s** out will come to	Am 6:7

SPREAD

s out over the earth and multiply	Gn 9:7
and has not **s** on the skin,	Lv 13:5

S your cloak over me,	Ru 3:9
s out his hands toward heaven.	1Kg 8:22
letter ... **s** it out before the LORD.	2Kg 19:14
fell on my knees and **s** out my hands	Ezr 9:5
S Your faithful love over those	Ps 36:10
I **s** out my hands to You.	Ps 88:9
s-ing out the sky like a canopy,	Ps 104:2
they **s** a net along the path	Ps 140:5
He **s-s** snow like wool;	Ps 147:16
is foolish to **s** a net where any	Pr 1:17
whoever **s-s** slander is a fool.	Pr 10:18
and **s** the fragrance of its spices.	Sg 4:16
and **s-s** them out like a tent	Is 40:22
I **s** out My hands all day long to	Is 65:2
trees and **s-ing** them on the road	Mt 21:8
the news about Him **s** even more,	Lk 5:15
so this does not **s** any further	Ac 4:17
of the Lord **s** through the whole	Ac 13:49
day long I have **s** out My hands	Rm 10:21
message may **s** rapidly and be	2Th 3:1
their word will **s** like gangrene,	2Tm 2:17

SPRING (adj)

is like a cloud with **s** rain.	Pr 16:15
why there has been no **s** rain.	Jr 3:3
like the **s** showers that water	Hs 6:3
at the time the **s** crop first	Am 7:1

SPRING (n)

She down to the **s**, filled her jug	Gn 24:16
In the **s** when kings march out	2Sm 11:1
and stop up every **s** of water.	2Kg 3:19
You opened up **s-s** and streams;	Ps 74:15
s-s of water into thirsty ground,	Ps 107:33
Should your **s-s** flow in the streets,	Pr 5:16
like a muddied **s** or a polluted	Pr 25:26
a locked garden and a sealed **s**.	Sg 4:12
water from the **s-s** of salvation,	Is 12:3
and the thirsty land **s-s** of water.	Is 35:7
and dry land into **s-s** of water.	Is 41:18
and his **s** will run dry.	Hs 13:15
can a saltwater **s** yield fresh	Jms 3:12
These people are **s-s** without water,	2Pt 2:17
guide them to **s-s** of living waters	Rv 7:17
from the **s** of living water as a gift.	Rv 21:6

SPRING (v)

S up, well—sing to it!	Nm 21:17
Truth will **s** up from the earth,	Ps 85:11
and righteousness **s** up with it.	Is 45:8

SPRINKLE

Does a trap s from the ground	Am 3:5
they **sprang** up quickly since	Mt 13:5
well of water s-ing up within him	Jn 4:14
sin **sprang** to life	Rm 7:9
no root of bitterness s-s up,	Heb 12:15

SPRINKLE

took the blood, s-d it on the people,	Ex 24:8
s {it} on all sides of the altar.	Ex 29:16
blood and s some of it seven times	Lv 4:6
s-d some of the oil on the altar	Lv 8:11
and s-d {them} on Aaron	Lv 8:30
S them with the purification water.	Nm 8:7
s-d the blood ... on the altar.	2Kg 16:13
so He will s many nations.	Is 52:15
will also s clean water on you,	Ezk 36:25
ashes of a heifer s-ing those who	Heb 9:13
hearts s-d {clean} from an evil	Heb 10:22
and the s-ing of the blood,	Heb 11:28
and to the s-d blood, which says	Heb 12:24
s-ing with the blood of Jesus Christ.	1Pt 1:2

SPROUT

no plant of the field had yet s-ed,	Gn 2:5
staff of the man I choose will s,	Nm 17:5
If it is cut down, it will s again,	Jb 14:7
in the morning it s-s and grows;	Ps 90:6
though the wicked s like grass	Ps 92:7
cause a Branch ... to s up for David,	Jr 33:15
cause a horn to s for ... Israel,	Ezk 29:21
becomes tender and s-s leaves,	Mt 24:32
seed s-s and grows—he doesn't	Mk 4:27

SPUN

make them of finely s linen,	Ex 26:1

SPY (n)

said to them, "You are s-ies.	Gn 42:9
After Moses sent s-ies to Jazer,	Nm 21:32
Joshua ... sent two men as s-ies	Jos 2:1
They sent s-ies to Bethel	Jdg 1:23
and sent s-ies who pretended to	Lk 20:20
received the s-ies in peace and	Heb 11:31

SPY (v)

Danites sent out five ... to s out	Jdg 18:2
hasn't David sent ... to ... s on it,	2Sm 10:3
in secretly to s on our freedom	Gl 2:4

SQUADS

assigned four s of four soldiers	Ac 12:4

SQUANDERED

he s his estate in foolish living.	Lk 15:13

SQUARE

rather spend the night in the s.	Gn 19:2
don't spend the night in the s.	Jdg 19:20
and took my seat in the town s,	Jb 29:7
raises her voice in the public s-s.	Pr 1:20
a lion in the public s!	Pr 26:13
The city is laid out in a s;	Rv 21:16

STABILITY

By justice a king brings s to a land,	Pr 29:4
and fall from your own s.	2Pt 3:17

STAFF

crossed over this Jordan with my s,	Gn 32:10
ring, cord, and s are these?	Gn 38:25
or the s from between his feet,	Gn 49:10
Moses took God's s in his hand.	Ex 4:20
threw down his s before Pharaoh	Ex 7:10
lift up your s, stretch out your	Ex 14:16
s of the man I choose will sprout,	Nm 17:5
struck the rock twice with his s,	Nm 20:11
the end of the s he was carrying	1Sm 14:27
place my s on the boy's face.	2Kg 4:29
rod and Your s—they comfort me.	Ps 23:4
has broken the s of the wicked,	Is 14:5
that splintered reed of a s,	Is 36:6
is shattered, the glorious s!	Jr 48:17
took two s-s, calling one Favor	Zch 11:7
leaning on the top of his s.	Heb 11:21

STAG

like a gazelle or a young s	Sg 2:9,17; 8:14

STAGES

Abram journeyed by s to the Negev.	Gn 12:9
He went by s from the Negev to	Gn 13:3
these are the s {listed} by their	Nm 33:2

STAGGER

He makes them s like drunken men.	Jb 12:25
a wine to drink that made us s.	Ps 60:3
cup that {causes people} to s.	Is 51:17
drink, s, and go out of their minds	Jr 25:16
three cities s-ed to another city	Am 4:8
Jerusalem a cup that causes s-ing	Zch 12:2

STAIN (n)

the s of your guilt is still in	Jr 2:22

STAIN (v)
and all My clothes were **s-ed**.   Is 63:3
He wore a robe **s-ed** with blood,   Rv 19:13

STAIRWAY
A s was set on the ground with   Gn 28:12
the shadow ... on Ahaz's **s**.   2Kg 20:11

STALKS
the plague that s in darkness,   Ps 91:6

STALL
Solomon had 40,000 **s-s** of horses   1Kg 4:26
pen and no cattle in the **s-s**,   Hab 3:17

STALLIONS
well-fed, eager s, each neighing   Jr 5:8
was like that of **s**.   Ezk 23:20

STAMMER
to this people with **s-ing** speech   Is 28:11
and the **s-ing** tongue will speak   Is 32:4

STAMP
Clap your hands, s your feet,   Ezk 6:11

STAND
where you are **s-ing** is holy ground.   Ex 3:5
S firm and see the LORD's   Ex 14:13
will be able to s against you;   Dt 7:24
to s before the LORD to serve   Dt 10:8
place where you are **s-ing** is holy.   Jos 5:15
And the sun **stood** still and   Jos 10:13
Who is able to s in the presence   1Sm 6:20
s still, and see the salvation   2Ch 20:17
and He will s on the dust at last.   Jb 19:25
take their s and the rulers   Ps 2:2
LORD, why do You s so far away?   Ps 10:1
Who may s in His holy place?   Ps 24:3
counsel of the LORD **s-s** forever,   Ps 33:11
Who takes a s for me against   Ps 94:16
stood before Him in the breach   Ps 106:23
let an accuser s at his right   Ps 109:6
considered sins, Lord, who could s?   Ps 130:3
who s in the house of the LORD,   Ps 135:2
when I sit down and when I s up;   Ps 139:2
He will s in the presence of kings.   Pr 22:29
If you do not s firm ... will not s at all. Is 7:9
S by the roadways and look.   Jr 6:16
have a man to always s before Me.   Jr 35:19
and s in the gap before Me   Ezk 22:30
but she will not s with him or   Dn 11:17
saw the LORD **s-ing** beside the altar, Am 9:1

His feet will s on the Mount   Zch 14:4
will be able to s when He appears?   Mal 3:2
love to pray **s-ing** in the synagogues Mt 6:5
and found others **s-ing** around,   Mt 20:6
against itself, that house cannot s.   Mk 3:25
a child, had him s among them,   Mk 9:36
And whenever you s praying,   Mk 11:25
But the tax collector, **s-ing** far off, Lk 18:13
You are the ones who **stood** by Me   Lk 22:28
He Himself **stood** among them.   Lk 24:36
Someone **s-s** among you,   Jn 1:26
S-ing by the cross of Jesus were   Jn 19:25
why do you s looking up into   Ac 1:11
kings of the earth took their s,   Ac 4:26
you are **s-ing** is holy ground.   Ac 7:33
Son of Man **s-ing** at the right   Ac 7:56
into this grace in which we s,   Rm 5:2
according to election might s,   Rm 9:11
by unbelief, but you s by faith.   Rm 11:20
he **s-s** or falls. And s he will!   Rm 14:4
   For the Lord is able to make
       him s.   Rm 14:4
For we will all s before the   Rm 14:10
thinks he **s-s** must be careful   1Co 10:12
alert, s firm in the faith, be brave   1Co 16:13
joy, because you s by faith.   2Co 1:24
Therefore s firm and don't   Gl 5:1
so that you can s against the   Eph 6:11
everything, to take your s.   Eph 6:13
S, therefore, with truth like a   Eph 6:14
joy and crown, s firm in the Lord,   Php 4:1
if you s firm in the Lord.   1Th 3:8
God's solid foundation **s-s** firm,   2Tm 2:19
every priest **s-s** day after day   Heb 10:11
grace of God. Take your s in it!   1Pt 5:12
to make you s in the presence   Jd 24
I s at the door and knock.   Rv 3:20
And who is able to s?"   Rv 6:17
and the small, **s-ing** before the   Rv 20:12

STANDARD
will judge you by their own **s-s**.   Ezk 23:24
You judge by human **s-s**.   Jn 8:15
it according to the s of faith;   Rm 12:6
on all those who follow this s,   Gl 6:16

STAR
God made ... as well as the **s-s**.   Gn 1:16
numerous as the **s-s** in the sky   Gn 22:17
A s will come from Jacob, and a   Nm 24:17

the s-s are not pure in His sight,	Jb 25:5
the morning s-s sang together	Jb 38:7
moon and the s-s, which You set	Ps 8:3
moon and s-s to rule by night.	Ps 136:9
praise Him, all you shining s-s.	Ps 148:3
Shining morning s, how you have	Is 14:12
order of moon and s-s for light	Jr 31:35
like the s-s forever and ever.	Dn 12:3
and the s-s will cease their	Jl 3:15
we saw His s in the east	Mt 2:2
the s-s will fall from the sky,	Mt 24:29
signs in the sun, moon, and s-s;	Lk 21:25
for s differs from s in splendor.	1Co 15:41
you shine like s-s in the world.	Php 2:15
numerous as the s-s of heaven	Heb 11:12
and the morning s arises in your	2Pt 1:19
wandering s-s for whom is	Jd 13
In His right hand He had seven s-s;	Rv 1:16
also give him the morning s.	Rv 2:28
s-s of heaven fell to the earth	Rv 6:13
The name of the s is Wormwood,	Rv 8:11
a crown of 12 s-s on her head.	Rv 12:1
of David, the Bright Morning S.	Rv 22:16

STARE

people look and s at me.	Ps 22:17
not s at me because I am dark,	Sg 1:6

STARRY

brings out the s host by number;	Is 40:26

STARTED

He who s a good work in you	Php 1:6

STATE

The first to s his case seems	Pr 18:17
last s is worse for them than	2Pt 2:20

STATELY

even four are s in their walk:	Pr 30:29

STATIONED (v)

garden of Eden He s cherubim	Gn 3:24
prayed to our God and s a guard	Neh 4:9

STATUE

offensive s that provokes jealousy	Ezk 8:3
a colossal s appeared.	Dn 2:31
Nebuchadnezzar made a gold s,	Dn 3:1

STATURE

boy Samuel grew in s and in favor	1Sm 2:26
look at his appearance or his s,	1Sm 16:7

extraordinary s with six fingers	1Ch 20:6
Your s is like a palm tree;	Sg 7:7
Jesus increased in wisdom and s,	Lk 2:52
a s measured by Christ's fullness.	Eph 4:13

STATUTE

Abraham kept ... My s-s,	Gn 26:5
to be theirs by a permanent s.	Ex 29:9
Keep My s-s and ordinances;	Lv 18:5
the Passover s and its ordinances.	Nm 9:14
listen to the s-s and ordinances I	Dt 4:1
keep My s-s and commandments	1Kg 3:14
rejected His s-s and His covenant	2Kg 17:15
and have not disregarded His s-s.	Ps 18:22
For this is a s for Israel,	Ps 81:4
committed to keeping Your s-s!	Ps 119:5
teach me Your s-s.	Ps 119:12,26,64,68,135
s-s are {the theme of} my song	Ps 119:54
for You teach me Your s-s.	Ps 119:171
and have not walked in My s-s.	Ezk 5:6
cause you to follow My s-s	Ezk 36:27

STATUTORY

be a s ordinance for	Nm 27:11; 35:29

STAY

persuaded him, so he s-ed	Jdg 19:7
Help me s on the path of Your	Ps 119:35
you get up early and s up late,	Ps 127:2
S away from a foolish man;	Pr 14:7
is a friend who s-s closer than	Pr 18:24
and s awake with Me.	Mt 26:38
s there until you leave that	Mk 6:10
today I must s at your house.	Lk 19:5
S with us, because it's almost	Lk 24:29
where are You s-ing?	Jn 1:38
was sick, He s-ed two more days	Jn 11:6
fine for a man to s as he is.	1Co 7:26
S away from every form of evil.	1Th 5:22

STEADFAST

me and renew a s spirit within	Ps 51:10
dear brothers, be s, immovable,	1Co 15:58
grounded and s in the faith,	Col 1:23

STEADY

hands remained s until the sun	Ex 17:12
Make my steps s through Your	Ps 119:133

STEAL

Do not s.	Ex 20:15
or I might have nothing and s,	Pr 30:9

Do you **s**, murder, commit — Jr 7:9
who **s** My words from each other. — Jr 23:30
wouldn't they **s** only what they — Ob 5
where thieves break in and **s**. — Mt 6:19
house and **s** his possessions — Mt 12:29
adultery; do not **s**; do not bear — Mt 19:18
may come, **s** Him, and tell — Mt 27:64
comes only to **s** and to kill and — Jn 10:10
preach, "You must not **s**"—do you — Rm 2:21
The thief must no longer **s**. — Eph 4:28
Slaves ... not talking back or **s-ing**, — Ti 2:10

STEALTH
long ago, have come in by **s**; — Jd 4

STEEP
rushed down the **s** bank into the — Mt 8:32

STENCH
Instead of perfume there will be a **s**; — Is 3:24
and the **s** of their corpses will — Is 34:3
His **s** will rise; — Jl 2:20
I can't stand the **s** of your solemn — Am 5:21

STEP
must not go up to My altar on **s-s**, — Ex 20:26
guards the **s-s** of His faithful — 1Sm 2:9
is but a **s** between me and death. — 1Sm 20:3
let the shadow go back 10 **s-s**. — 2Kg 20:10
would count my **s-s** but would not — Jb 14:16
and He observes all his **s-s**. — Jb 34:21
My **s-s** are on Your paths; — Ps 17:5
man's **s-s** are established by the — Ps 37:23
his **s-s** do not falter. — Ps 37:31
on a rock, making my **s-s** secure. — Ps 40:2
my **s-s** nearly went astray. — Ps 73:2
Make my **s-s** steady through Your — Ps 119:133
your **s-s** will not be hindered; — Pr 4:12
but the LORD determines his **s-s**. — Pr 16:9
man's **s-s** are determined by the — Pr 20:24
walks determines his own **s-s**. — Jr 10:23
you should follow in His **s-s**. — 1Pt 2:21

STEPHEN
Foremost of the first seven deacons (Ac 6:1-7). First Christian martyr (6:8–7:60); Saul approved of his death (8:1; 22:20); start of persecution and dispersion (11:19).

STEW
Once when Jacob was cooking a **s**, — Gn 25:29
they ate the **s** they cried out, — 2Kg 4:40

STEWARDSHIP
I am entrusted with a **s**. — 1Co 9:17

STICK (n)
take a single **s** and write on it: — Ezk 37:16
were like a burning **s** snatched — Am 4:11
this man **s** snatched from the fire? — Zch 3:2

STICK (v)
and his unseen bones **s** out. — Jb 33:21
my tongue **s-s** to the roof of my — Ps 22:15
my flesh **s-s** to my bones. — Ps 102:5
May my tongue **s** to the roof of — Ps 137:6
and **s** a knife in your throat if — Pr 23:2
mouth and **s-ing** out your tongue — Is 57:4

STIFFEN
resisted, **s-ed** their necks, — Neh 9:29

STIFF-NECKED
Even though this is a **s** people, — Ex 34:9
for you are a **s** people. — Dt 9:6
how rebellious and **s** you are. — Dt 31:27
One who becomes **s**, after many — Pr 29:1
You **s** people with uncircumcised — Ac 7:51

STIFLE
He **s-d** his compassion, — Am 1:11
Don't **s** the Spirit. — 1Th 5:19

STILL (adj)
reflect in your heart and be **s**. — Ps 4:4
Silence! Be **s**!" The wind ceased — Mk 4:39

STILL (adv)
And the sun stood **s** and the moon — Jos 10:13
Hope in God, for I will **s** praise Him, — Ps 42:5
when I wake up, I am **s** with You. — Ps 139:18
while we were **s** sinners — Rm 5:8
We who are **s** alive at the Lord's — 1Th 4:15
while it is **s** called today, — Heb 3:13
he is dead, he **s** speaks through — Heb 11:4

STILL (v)
its waves surge, You **s** them. — Ps 89:9
He **s-ed** the storm to a murmur, — Ps 107:29

STILLBORN
Why was I not **s**; — Jb 3:11
I say that a **s** child is better — Ec 6:3

STING
Sheol, where is your **s**? — Hs 13:14

O Death, where is your s?	1Co 15:55
Now the s of death is sin,	1Co 15:56

STINGERS

and they had tails with s,	Rv 9:10

STINGS

In the end it ... s like a viper.	Pr 23:32

STINGY

don't have a s heart when you	Dt 15:10
Don't eat a s person's bread,	Pr 23:6

STINK

the river will s,	Ex 7:18
make a perfumer's oil ferment and s;	Ec 10:1
Lord, he already s-s.	Jn 11:39

STIR

and one who s-s up trouble among	Pr 6:19
Hatred s-s up conflicts,	Pr 10:12
but a harsh word s-s up wrath.	Pr 15:1
hot-tempered man s-s up conflict,	Pr 15:18
and their words s up trouble.	Pr 24:2
An angry man s-s up conflict,	Pr 29:22
s-ring up anger produces strife.	Pr 30:33
do not s up or awaken love	Sg 2:7; 3:5; 8:4
my feelings were s-red for him.	Sg 5:4
He s-s up the spirits of the departed	Is 14:9
My compassion is s-red!	Hs 11:8
The LORD s-red up the spirit of	Hg 1:14
from time to time and s up the water.	Jn 5:4
The whole city was s-red up,	Ac 21:30
fathers, don't s up anger in your	Eph 6:4

STOCKS

You put my feet in the s	Jb 13:27
He puts my feet in the s;	Jb 33:11
prophet beaten and put him in the s	Jr 20:2
secured their feet in the s.	Ac 16:24

STOIC

the Epicurean and S philosophers	Ac 17:18

STOLE

Rachel s her father's household	Gn 31:19
So Absalom s the hearts of the	2Sm 15:6
s Him while we were sleeping.	Mt 28:13

STOLEN

S water is sweet,	Pr 9:17
You bring s, lame, or sick	Mal 1:13

STOMACH

the s of the wicked is empty.	Pr 13:25
a man's s is satisfied;	Pr 18:20
All man's labor is for his s,	Ec 6:7
passes into the s and is eliminated?	Mt 15:17
Foods the s and the s for foods,	1Co 6:13
their god is their s;	Php 3:19
a little wine because of your s	1Tm 5:23
I ate it, my s became bitter.	Rv 10:10

STONE (n)

had brick for s and asphalt for	Gn 11:3
had spoken to him—a s marker.	Gn 35:14
sank to the depths like a s.	Ex 15:5
Take two onyx s-s and engrave on	Ex 28:9
12 s-s are to correspond to the	Ex 28:21
s tablets inscribed by ... God.	Ex 31:18
Cut two s tablets like the first	Ex 34:1
Take 12 s-s from ... the Jordan	Jos 4:3
see this s—it will be a witness	Jos 24:27
five smooth s-s from the wadi	1Sm 17:40
Philistine with a sling and a s.	1Sm 17:50
as water wears away s-s	Jb 14:19
strike your foot against a s.	Ps 91:12
The s that the builders rejected	Ps 118:22
wisdom is better than precious s-s,	Pr 8:11
like a magic s to its owner;	Pr 17:8
whoever rolls a s—It will come	Pr 26:27
A s is heavy and sand, a burden,	Pr 27:3
a time to throw s-s and a time to	Ec 3:5
one who quarries s-s may be hurt	Ec 10:9
He will be a s to stumble over	Is 8:14
have laid a s in Zion, a tested s,	Is 28:16
and to a s: You gave birth to me.	Jr 2:27
I will remove their heart of s	Ezk 11:19
worshiping wood and s,	Ezk 20:32
remove your heart of s and give	Ezk 36:26
a s broke off without a hand	Dn 2:34
the s-s will cry out from the wall	Hab 2:11
to mute s: Come alive!	Hab 2:19
children for Abraham from these s-s!	Mt 3:9
tell these s-s to become bread."	Mt 4:3
strike your foot against a s.	Mt 4:6
for bread, will give him a s?	Mt 7:9
The s that the builders rejected	Mt 21:42
Not one s will be left ... on another	Mt 24:2
massive s-s! What impressive	Mk 13:1
Who will roll away the s from	Mk 16:3
silent, the s-s would cry out!	Lk 19:40

from them about a s-'s throw,   Lk 22:41
be the first to throw a s at her.   Jn 8:7
picked up s-s to throw at Him.   Jn 8:59
"Remove the s," Jesus said.   Jn 11:39
{Jesus} is The s despised by you   Ac 4:11
stumbled over the stumbling s.   Rm 9:32
I am putting a s s in Zion to   Rm 9:33
silver, costly s-s, wood, hay,   1Co 3:12
not on s tablets but on tablets   2Co 3:3
to Him, a living s—rejected by   1Pt 2:4
as living s-s, are being built   1Pt 2:5
I lay a s in Zion, a chosen and   1Pt 2:6
The s that the builders rejected   1Pt 2:7
A s that causes men to stumble,   1Pt 2:8
I will also give him a white s,   Rv 2:17
angel picked up a s like a large   Rv 18:21
with every kind of precious s: Rv 21:19

STONE (v)
s-d him at the king's command   2Ch 24:21
s-s those who are sent to her!   Mt 23:37
works are you s-ing Me for?   Jn 10:32
were s-ing Stephen as he called   Ac 7:59
s-d Paul, they dragged him   Ac 14:19
Once I was s-d. Three times   2Co 11:25
They were s-d, they were sawed   Heb 11:37

STONECUTTERS
and 80,000 s in the mountains,   1Kg 5:15

STONEMASONS
carpenters, and s, and they   2Sm 5:11

STOOP
s-s down to look on the heavens   Ps 113:6
s-ed down and started writing   Jn 8:6

STOP
and the rain from the sky s-ped.   Gn 8:2
stood still and the moon s-ped,   Jos 10:13
let us s charging this interest.   Neh 5:10
S {your fighting} and know that I   Ps 46:10
s the dispute before it breaks out.   Pr 17:14
Instantly her bleeding s-ped.   Lk 8:44
he ordered the chariot to s,   Ac 8:38
I never s giving thanks for you   Eph 1:16
haven't s-ped praying for you.   Col 1:9
Day and night they never s,   Rv 4:8

STORAGE
with all the s cities that he   2Ch 8:4
fortresses and s cities in Judah   2Ch 17:12

in an earthen s jar so they will   Jr 32:14

STORE
So Joseph s-d up grain in such   Gn 41:49
{place} where the snow is s-d?   Jb 38:22
goodness that You have s-d up for   Ps 31:19
s-s up success for the upright;   Pr 2:7
The wise s up knowledge,   Pr 10:14
sinner's wealth is s-d up for   Pr 13:22
yet they s up their food in the   Pr 30:25
Ephraim's ... sin is s-d up.   Hs 13:12
those who s up violence and   Am 3:10
have anywhere to s my crops?   Lk 12:17
you are s-ing up wrath for yourself   Rm 2:5
s-ing up for themselves a good   1Tm 6:19
You s-d up treasure in the last   Jms 5:3

STOREHOUSE
Joseph opened up {all the s-s}   Gn 41:56
will open for you His abundant s,   Dt 28:12
Or have you seen the s-s of hail,   Jb 38:22
brings the wind from His s-s.   Ps 135:7
Our s-s will be full, supplying all   Ps 144:13
for you—a s of salvation,   Is 33:6
brings the wind from His s-s.   Jr 10:13; 51:16
full 10 percent into the s   Mal 3:10

STOREROOM
good things from his s of good,   Mt 12:35
brings out of his s what is new and   Mt 13:52
they don't have a s or a barn;   Lk 12:24

STORK
the s, the various kinds of heron,   Lv 11:19
and plumage like the s-'s?   Jb 39:13
the s makes its home in the pine   Ps 104:17
Even the s in the sky knows her   Jr 8:7
wings were like those of a s,   Zch 5:9

STORM
and a s rages around Him.   Ps 50:3
from the raging wind and the s.   Ps 55:8
He stilled the s to a murmur,   Ps 107:29
and shelter from s and rain.   Is 4:6
like a devastating hail s,   Is 28:2
Look, a s from the LORD!   Jr 23:19
such a violent s arose on the sea   Jnh 1:4
path is in the whirlwind and s,   Nah 1:3
a violent s arose on the sea,   Mt 8:24
you say, 'A s is coming,'   Lk 12:54

STORM-TOSSED

Poor [Jerusalem], **s**, and not   Is 54:11
the wicked are like the **s** sea,   Is 57:20

STORMY

will be **s** because the sky is red   Mt 16:3

STORY

And this **s** has been spread among   Mt 28:15

STRAIGHT

will advance, each man **s** ahead.   Jos 6:5
The cows went **s** up the road to   1Sm 6:12
make Your way **s** before me.   Ps 5:8
fix your gaze **s** ahead.   Pr 4:25
understanding walks a **s** path.   Pr 15:21
make a highway for our God in   Is 40:3
Each creature went **s** ahead.   Ezk 1:12; 10:22
for the Lord; make His paths **s**!   Mt 3:3
Let's go **s** to Bethlehem and see   Lk 2:15
the crooked will become **s**,   Lk 3:5
Make **s** the way of the Lord   Jn 1:23
and go to the street called **S**,   Ac 9:11
and make **s** paths for your feet,   Heb 12:13
abandoning the **s** path, they have   2Pt 2:15

STRAIGHTEN

What is crooked cannot be **s-ed**;   Ec 1:15
for who can **s** out what He has   Ec 7:13

STRAIN

You **s** out a gnat, yet gulp down   Mt 23:24

STRANDS

cord of three **s-s** is not easily   Ec 4:12

STRANGE

must not be a **s** god among you;   Ps 81:9
Your eyes will see **s** things,   Pr 23:33
nation with a **s** language,   Is 18:2,7
do His work, His **s** work,   Is 28:21
For what you say sounds **s** to us,   Ac 17:20
by various kinds of **s** teachings;   Heb 13:9

STRANGER

Your offspring will be **s-s** in a land   Gn 15:13
he treated them like **s-s**   Gn 42:7
a **s** in a foreign land.   Ex 2:22; 18:3
I have become a **s** to my brothers   Ps 69:8
I am a **s** on earth; do not hide   Ps 119:19
from a **s** with her flattering   Pr 2:16
or embrace the breast of a **s**?   Pr 5:20
puts up security for a **s**,   Pr 11:15

Instead, a **s** will enjoy them.   Ec 6:2
S-s will stand and feed your   Is 61:5
I was a **s** and you took Me in;   Mt 25:35
They will never follow a **s**;   Jn 10:5
would be **s-s** in a foreign country   Ac 7:6
no longer foreigners and **s-s**,   Eph 2:19
this [you are doing] for **s-s**;   3Jn 5

STRANGLE

I prefer **s-ing**, death rather than life   Jb 7:15
eating anything that has been **s-d**,   Ac 15:20

STRAP

and no sandal **s** broken.   Is 5:27
whose sandal **s** I'm not worthy to   Jn 1:27

STRAW

go and gather **s** for themselves.   Ex 5:7
Are they like **s** before the wind,   Jb 21:18
lion will eat **s** like the ox   Is 11:17; 65:25
costly stones, wood, hay, or **s**,   1Co 3:12

STRAY (adj)

your enemy's **s** ox or donkey,   Ex 23:4
Israel is a **s** lamb, chased by   Jr 50:17

STRAY (n)

seek the lost, bring back the **s-s**,   Ezk 34:16
and go and search for the **s**?   Mt 18:12

STRAY (v)

your brother's ox or sheep **s-ing**,   Dt 22:1
have not **s-ed** from Your path.   Ps 44:18
reject all who **s** from Your   Ps 119:118
don't **s** onto her paths.   Pr 7:25
Why, LORD, do You make us **s**   Is 63:17
may no longer **s** from following   Ezk 14:11
among you **s-s** from the truth,   Jms 5:19

STREAKED

The **s** sheep will be your wages,   Gn 31:8

STREAM (n)

land with **s-s** of water,   Dt 8:7
dams up the **s-s** from flowing so   Jb 28:11
planted beside **s-s** of water   Ps 1:3
drink from Your refreshing **s**,   Ps 36:8
a deer longs for **s-s** of water,   Ps 42:1
its **s-s** delight the city of God,   Ps 46:4
God's **s** is filled with water,   Ps 65:9
brought **s-s** out of the stone and   Ps 78:16
flowed like a **s** in the desert.   Ps 105:41
pour out **s-s** of tears because   Ps 119:136

s-s of water in the public squares? Pr 5:16
All the s-s flow to the sea, Ec 1:7
like doves beside s-s of water, Sg 5:12
like s-s of water in a dry land Is 32:2
and s-s in the desert; Is 35:6
like a rushing s driven by the Is 59:19
like an unfailing s. Am 5:24
s-s of living water flow from Jn 7:38

STREAM (v)
flock of goats s-ing down Sg 4:1; 6:5
All nations will s to it, Is 2:2
nations will no longer s to him; Jr 51:44
Peoples will s to it, Mc 4:1

STREET
Wisdom calls out in the s; Pr 1:20
your springs flow in the s-s, Pr 5:16
make His voice heard in the s-s. Is 42:2
dash madly through the s-s; Nah 2:4
on the s corners to be seen by people. Mt 6:5
and You taught in our s-s! Lk 13:26
quickly into the s-s and alleys Lk 14:21
and go to the s called Straight, Ac 9:11
s of the city was pure gold, Rv 21:21

STRENGTH
out of Egypt by the s of His hand. Ex 13:16
The LORD is my s and my song; Ex 15:2
all your soul, and with all your s. Dt 6:5
My s ... is now as it was then. Jos 14:11
March on, my soul, in s! Jdg 5:21
where his great s comes from, Jdg 16:5
the feeble are clothed with s. 1Sm 2:4
does not prevail by {his own} s. 1Sm 2:9
I will cut off your s and the s of 1Sm 2:31
David found s in the LORD his 1Sm 30:6
clothed me with s for battle; 2Sm 22:40
Then on the s from that food, 1Kg 19:8
for the LORD and for His s; 1Ch 16:11
ascribe to the LORD glory and s. 1Ch 16:28
your s {comes from} rejoicing in Neh 8:10
Wisdom and s belong to God; Jb 12:13
Do you give s to the horse? Jb 39:19
I love You, LORD, my s. Ps 18:1
He clothes me with s Ps 18:32
s is dried up like baked clay; Ps 22:15
The LORD is my s and my shield; Ps 28:7
give the LORD glory and s. Ps 29:1
not be delivered by great s. Ps 33:16

God is our refuge and s, a helper Ps 46:1
gives power and s to His people. Ps 68:35
but God is the s of my heart, Ps 73:26
They go from s to s; Ps 84:7
ascribe to the LORD glory and s. Ps 96:7
The LORD is my s and my song; Ps 118:14
impressed by the s of a horse; Ps 147:10
glory of young men is their s, Pr 20:29
man of knowledge than one of s; Pr 24:5
S and honor are her clothing, Pr 31:25
Wisdom is better than s, Ec 9:16
the LORD, is my s and my song, Is 12:2
He gives s to the weary and Is 40:29
in the LORD will renew their s; Is 40:31
LORD is righteousness and s. Is 45:24
LORD, my s and my stronghold, Jr 16:19
their s is their god. Hab 1:11
Not by s or by might, but by My Zch 4:6
your mind, and with all your s. Mk 12:30
is stronger than human s. 1Co 1:25
to the working of His vast s. Eph 1:19
by the Lord and by His vast s. Eph 6:10
striving with His s that works Col 1:29
from the s God provides, 1Pt 4:11
Because you have limited s, Rv 3:8
and honor and power and s, Rv 7:12

STRENGTHEN
S me, God, just once more. Jdg 16:28
But now, {my God,} s me. Neh 6:9
many and have s-ed weak hands. Jb 4:3
s me through Your word. Ps 119:28
S the weak hands, steady the Is 35:3
the weary and s-s the powerless. Is 40:29
I will s you; I will help you; Is 41:10
You have not s-ed the weak, Ezk 34:4
I will s them in the LORD, Zch 10:12
have turned back, s your brothers. Lk 22:32
s-ing the hearts of the disciples Ac 14:22
was s-ed in his faith Rm 4:20
be s-ed with power through His Eph 3:16
be s-ed by the Lord and by His Eph 6:10
things through Him who s-s me. Php 4:13
May you be s-ed with all power, Col 1:11
your hearts and s you in every 2Th 2:17
Lord, who has s-ed me, 1Tm 1:12
Lord stood with me and s-ed me, 2Tm 4:17
Therefore s your tired hands Heb 12:12
Be alert and s what remains, Rv 3:2

STRESS

when trouble and s overcome you. Pr 1:27

STRETCH

I will s out My hand and strike Ex 3:20
s-ed out his hand over the waters Ex 8:6
S out your hand over the sea so Ex 14:26
the hand he s-ed out ... withered 1Kg 13:4
Then he s-ed himself out over 1Kg 17:21
will s out its hands to God. Ps 68:31
s-ed out His hand over the sea; Is 23:11
Maker, who s-ed out the heavens Is 51:13
let your tent curtains be s-ed out; Is 54:2
for I will s out My hand against Jr 6:12
I will s out My hand against Ezk 6:14
I will s out My hand against Zph 1:4
told the man, "S out your hand." Mt 12:13
old, you will s out your hands Jn 21:18

STRETCHER

lowered the s on which the paralytic Mk 2:4
pick up your s, and go home. Mk 2:11
the sick on s-s to wherever they Mk 6:55

STRICKEN

but we in turn regarded Him s, Is 53:4

STRICT

He gave them s orders that no Mk 5:43
educated according to the s view of Ac 22:3
and bring it under s control, 1Co 9:27

STRICTER

we will receive a s judgment; Jms 3:1

STRICTEST

according to the s party of our Ac 26:5

STRICTLY

And He s warned them to tell no Mk 8:30
But He s warned and instructed Lk 9:21
Didn't we s order you not to Ac 5:28

STRIDE

Three things are stately in their s, Pr 30:29

STRIFE

They stir up s, they lurk; Ps 56:6
leads to nothing but s, Pr 13:10
but a man slow to anger calms s. Pr 15:18
a house full of feasting with s. Pr 17:1
One who loves to offend loves s; Pr 17:19
A fool's lips lead to s, Pr 18:6
quarrelsome man for kindling s. Pr 26:21

stirring up anger produces s. Pr 30:33
S is ongoing, and conflict Hab 1:3
there is envy and s among you, 1Co 3:3
sorcery, hatreds, s, jealousy, Gl 5:20
preach Christ out of envy and s, Php 1:15

STRIKE

s your head, and you will s his heel. Gn 3:15
wounding me, a boy for s-ing me. Gn 4:23
Whoever s-s his father or Ex 21:15
and struck the rock twice Nm 20:11
"S me!" But the man refused to s 1Kg 20:35
s this nation with blindness. 2Kg 6:18
king of Israel, "S the ground!" 2Kg 13:18
for God's hand has struck me. Jb 19:21
You s all my enemies on the cheek; Ps 3:7
He struck the rock and water Ps 78:20
He struck all the firstborn Ps 78:51
you will not s your foot against Ps 91:12
The sun will not s you by day, Ps 121:6
Let the righteous one s me Ps 141:5
calamity will s him suddenly; Pr 6:15
S a mocker, and the inexperienced Pr 19:25
S him with a rod, and you will Pr 23:14
struck me, but I feel no pain! Pr 23:35
His hand is still raised (to s). Is 5:25; 9:12
not turn to Him who struck them; Is 9:13
will s Egypt, s-ing and healing. Is 19:22
Him stricken, struck down by God, Is 53:4
I struck you in My wrath, Is 60:10
Let the sword s two times, Ezk 21:14
S the capitals of the pillars so Am 9:1
S the shepherd, and the sheep will Zch 13:7
and s the land with a curse. Mal 4:6
the ax is ready to s the root of Mt 3:10
you will not s your foot against Mt 4:6
I will s the shepherd, and the Mt 26:31
struck the high priest's slave, Jn 18:10
S-ing Peter on the side, he woke Ac 12:7
God is going to s you, you Ac 23:3
were struck down in the desert. 1Co 10:5
struck down but not destroyed. 2Co 4:9
no longer will the sun s them, Rv 7:16
and to s the earth with any Rv 11:6
with it He might s the nations. Rv 19:15

STRING

He has strung His bow and Ps 7:12
For look, the wicked s the bow; Ps 11:2
able to handle and s the bow. Jr 46:9

STRINGS

play skillfully on the s,	Ps 33:3
praise Him with flute and s.	Ps 150:4

STRIP

Philistines came to s the slain,	1Sm 31:8
S yourselves bare and put	Is 32:11
will s off your clothes	Ezk 16:39; 23:26
will s her naked and expose	Hs 2:3
They s-ped him, beat him up,	Lk 10:30

STRIVE

s-ing to take hold of You.	Is 64:7
Let us s to know the LORD.	Hs 6:3
Don't keep s-ing for	Lk 12:29
Or am I s-ing to please people?	Gl 1:10
s-ing with His strength that works	Col 1:29
In fact, we labor and s for this,	1Tm 4:10

STROKE

And every s of the appointed staff	Is 30:32
or one s of a letter will pass from	Mt 5:18
than for one s of a letter ... to drop	Lk 16:17

STROLLED

s around on the roof of the palace.	2Sm 11:2
s down the road to her house	Pr 7:8

STRONG

you out of Egypt with a s hand.	Ex 13:9
Be s and courageous;	Dt 31:6
be s and very courageous	Jos 1:7
God is my s refuge;	2Sm 22:33
for they were too s for me.	Ps 18:17
s ones of Bashan encircle me.	Ps 22:12
LORD, s and mighty, the LORD,	Ps 24:8
Be s and courageous, all you who	Ps 31:24
a s tower in the face of the	Ps 61:3
or, if we are s, eighty years.	Ps 90:10
with a s hand and outstretched	Ps 136:12
GOD, my s Savior, You shield	Ps 140:7
of the LORD one has s confidence	Pr 14:26
The name of the LORD is a s tower;	Pr 18:10
Redeemer is s, and He will take	Pr 23:11
wise warrior is better than a s one,	Pr 24:5
the ants are not a s people,	Pr 30:25
to the swift, or the battle to the s,	Ec 9:11
For love is as s as death;	Sg 8:6
The s one will become tinder,	Is 1:31
Their Redeemer is s; the LORD	Jr 50:34
It had s branches, {fit} for	Ezk 19:11

part of the kingdom will be s,	Dn 2:42
can someone enter a s man's house	Mt 12:29
grew up and became spiritually s,	Lk 1:80
The boy grew up and became s,	Lk 2:40
I'm not s enough to dig;	Lk 16:3
his feet and ankles became s.	Ac 3:7
Now we who are s have an	Rm 15:1
weak things to shame the s.	1Co 1:27
We are weak, but you are s!	1Co 4:10
be brave and s.	1Co 16:13
For when I am weak, then I am s.	2Co 12:10
when we are weak and you are s.	2Co 13:9
sends them a s delusion so that	2Th 2:11
be s in the grace that is in	2Tm 2:1
because you are s, God's word	1Jn 2:14

STRONGER

greater and s than you	Dt 4:38; 9:1; 11:23
When Israel became s, they made	Jdg 1:28
David growing s and the house	2Sm 3:1
But when one s than he attacks	Lk 11:22
God's weakness is s than human	1Co 1:25

STRONGHOLD

the mountains, caves, and s-s.	Jdg 6:2
whole time David was in the s.	1Sm 22:4
and his men went up to the s.	1Sm 24:22
David did capture the s of Zion,	2Sm 5:7
my salvation, my s, my refuge,	2Sm 22:3
to David at his s in the desert.	1Ch 12:8
its s is on a rocky crag.	Jb 39:28
He is a s of salvation for His	Ps 28:8
the God of Jacob is our s.	Ps 46:7,11
strength, because God is my s.	Ps 59:9
For You have been a s for me,	Ps 59:16
my rock and my salvation, my s;	Ps 62:2,6
way of the LORD is a s for the	Pr 10:29
You have been a s for the poor,	Is 25:4
The LORD is good, a s in a day	Nah 1:7
for the demolition of s-s.	2Co 10:4

STRUGGLE (n)

the days of my s until my relief	Jb 14:14
best of them are s and sorrow;	Ps 90:10
and s adds nothing to it.	Pr 10:22
there is no end to all his s-es,	Ec 4:8
and in your s under the sun.	Ec 9:9
womb to see {only} s and sorrow,	Jr 20:18

s-es on the outside, fears inside. 2Co 7:5
how great a s I have for you, Col 2:1

STRUGGLE (v)

children inside her s-d with each Gn 25:22
s-d with God ... and have prevailed Gn 32:28
s-ing against sin, you have not Heb 12:4

STRUTTING

a s rooster, a goat, and a king Pr 30:31

STUBBLE

Egypt to gather s for straw. Ex 5:12
it consumed them like s. Ex 15:7
you will give birth to s. Is 33:11
carries them away like s. Is 40:24
Look, they are like s; Is 47:14
but the house of Esau will be s; Ob 18
commits wickedness will become s. Mal 4:1

STUBBORN

son of ours is s and rebellious; Dt 21:20
a s and rebellious generation, Ps 78:8
I gave them over to their s hearts Ps 81:12
is as obstinate as a s cow. Hs 4:16

STUBBORNLY

When Pharaoh s refused to let us Ex 13:15

STUBBORNNESS

Disregard this people's s-ness, Dt 9:27
follow the s-ness of their evil Jr 3:17

STUDENT

every s of Scripture Mt 13:52

STUDY

Ezra had determined ... to s the law Ezr 7:10
and much s wearies the body. Ec 12:12
Too much s is driving you mad! Ac 26:24

STUFF

Let me eat some of that red s, Gn 25:30

STUMBLE

ark, because the oxen had s-d. 1Ch 13:9
power to help or to make one s. 2Ch 25:8
steadied the one who was s-ing, Jb 4:4
they s and perish before You. Ps 9:3
death, even my feet from s-ing, Ps 56:13
they s-d, and there was no one Ps 107:12
from tears, my feet from s-ing. Ps 116:8
nothing makes them s. Ps 119:165
men who plan to make me s. Ps 140:4

your foot will not s. Pr 3:23
when you run, you will not s. Pr 4:12
don't know what makes them s. Pr 4:19
save those s-ing toward slaughter. Pr 24:11
your heart rejoice when he s-s, Pr 24:17
None of them grows weary or s-s; Is 5:27
be a stone to s over and a rock Is 8:14
Many will s over these; Is 8:15
and young men s and fall, Is 40:30
We s at noon as though it were Is 59:10
For truth has s-d in the public Is 59:14
so that they did not s. Is 63:13
smooth way where they will not s, Jr 31:9
arrogant will s and fall with no Jr 50:32
longer cause your nation to s. Ezk 36:15
but he will s, fall, and be no more. Dn 11:19
for you have s-d in your sin. Hs 14:1
of the word, immediately he s-s. Mt 13:21
cause one of these little ones to s. Lk 17:2
walk during the day, he doesn't s, Jn 11:9
told you ... to keep you from s-ing. Jn 16:1
They s-d over the s-ing stone. Rm 9:32
putting a stone in Zion to s over, Rm 9:33
have they s-d so as to fall? Rm 11:11
by their s-ing, salvation has Rm 11:11
to cause s-ing by what he eats. Rm 14:20
We give no opportunity for s-ing 2Co 6:3
Who is made to s, and I do not 2Co 11:29
for we all s in many ways. Jms 3:2
anyone does not s in what he says Jms 3:2
A stone that causes men to s, 1Pt 2:8
They s by disobeying the message; 1Pt 2:8
these things you will never s. 2Pt 1:10
is no cause for s-ing in him. 1Jn 2:10
who is able to protect you from s-ing Jd 24

STUMBLING BLOCK

or put a s in front of the blind, Lv 19:14
I am going to place s-s before Jr 6:21
and I put a s in front of him, Ezk 3:20
s-s that brought about their iniquity Ezk 7:19
idols ... sinful s-s before their faces. Ezk 14:3
turn ... so they will not be a s Ezk 18:30
idols and became a sinful s Ezk 44:12
but instead decide not to put a s Rm 14:13
Christ crucified, a s to the Jews 1Co 1:23
this right ... in no way becomes a s 1Co 8:9
who taught Balak to place a s in Rv 2:14

STUMP

the holy seed is the s.	Is 6:13
shoot will grow from the s of Jesse,	Is 11:1
leave the s with its roots	Dn 4:15,23

STUNNED

I sat there s for seven days.	Ezk 3:15
was s for a moment,	Dn 4:19
But he was s at this demand,	Mk 10:22

STUPID

as cattle, as s in your sight?	Jb 18:3
Pay attention, you s people!	Ps 94:8
one who hates correction is s.	Pr 12:1
wisest advisers give s advice!	Is 19:11
For the shepherds are s:	Jr 10:21

STUPIDITY

wickedness is s and folly is madness	Ec 7:25

STUPOR

God gave them a spirit of s,	Rm 11:8

STYLUS

forever by an iron s and lead!	Jb 19:24
line, he outlines it with a s;	Is 44:13
Judah is written with an iron s.	Jr 17:1

SUBDUE

fill the earth, and s it.	Gn 1:28
the land had been s-d by them.	Jos 18:1
That day God s-d Jabin	Jdg 4:23
Philistines were s-d and did not	1Sm 7:13
I will also s all your enemies.	1Ch 17:10
You s my adversaries beneath me.	Ps 18:39
He s-s peoples under us	Ps 47:3
He s-s my people under me.	Ps 144:2
hand I have grasped to s nations	Is 45:1
no one was strong enough to s him.	Mk 5:4

SUBJECT

became David's s-s	2Sm 8:2,6
will be s to judgment.	Mt 5:21
the creation was s-ed to futility	Rm 8:20
And when everything is s to Him,	1Co 15:28
Son Himself will also be s to Him	1Co 15:28
who s-ed everything to Him,	1Co 15:28
that enables Him to s everything	Php 3:21
s-ed everything under his feet.	Heb 2:8
authorities, and powers s-ed to Him	1Pt 3:22
younger men, be s to the elders.	1Pt 5:5

SUBMISSION

who hate the LORD would pretend s	Ps 81:15
not yield in s to these people	Gl 2:5
learn in silence with full s.	1Tm 2:11

SUBMISSIVE

who is humble, s in spirit,	Is 66:2
not ... to speak, but should be s,	1Co 14:34
Wives, be s to your husbands, as	Col 3:18
homemakers, and s to their	Ti 2:5
are to be s to their masters	Ti 2:9
Remind them to be s to rulers	Ti 3:1

SUBMIT

your mistress and s to her	Gn 16:9
Foreigners s to me grudgingly;	Ps 18:44
He s-ted Himself to death,	Is 53:12
the demons s to us in Your name.	Lk 10:17
it does not s itself to God's law,	Rm 8:7
s to the governing authorities,	Rm 13:1
also to s to such people,	1Co 16:16
don't s again to a yoke of slavery.	Gl 5:1
s-ting to one another	Eph 5:21
Wives, s to your own husbands	Eph 5:22
Now as the church s-s to Christ,	Eph 5:24
Why do you s to regulations:	Col 2:20
Shouldn't we s even more to the	Heb 12:9
Obey your leaders and s to them,	Heb 13:17
Therefore, s to God. But resist	Jms 4:7
S to every human institution	1Pt 2:13
s yourselves to your masters	1Pt 2:18
s yourselves to your own husbands	1Pt 3:1

SUBSIDE

and the water began to s.	Gn 8:1
until your brother's anger s-s	Gn 27:44
Then the king's anger s-d.	Est 7:10
surge and then s like the Nile	Am 8:8

SUBSTANCE

the s is the Messiah.	Col 2:17

SUBVERT

takes a bribe to s the course of	Pr 17:23
found this man s-ing our nation,	Lk 23:2

SUCCEED

the LORD's command? It won't s.	Nm 14:41
but with many advisers they s.	Pr 15:22
wherever he turns, he s-s.	Pr 17:8
you don't know which will s,	Ec 11:6

of the LORD will s by His hand.	Is 53:10
weapon formed against you will s,	Is 54:17

SUCCESS

he prayed, "grant me s today,	Gn 24:12
you will have s wherever you go.	Jos 1:7
you will have s in everything	1Kg 2:3
sought the LORD, God gave him s.	2Ch 26:5
Give Your servant s today,	Neh 1:11
LORD, please grant us s!	Ps 118:25
He stores up s for the upright;	Pr 2:7
understands a matter finds s,	Pr 16:20
understanding finds s.	Pr 19:8
of wisdom is that it brings s.	Ec 10:10
I make s and create disaster;	Is 45:7

SUCCESSFUL

Joseph, and he became a s man,	Gn 39:2
David ... was s in everything Saul	1Sm 18:5

SUCCOTH

1. City in Gad (1Kg 7:46); visited by Jacob (Gn 33:17); didn't help Gideon (Jdg 8:5-7,13-16).

2. Encampment on the exodus (Ex 12:37; Nm 33:5).

SUCH

of God belongs to s as these.	Mk 10:14
if we neglect s a great	Heb 2:3
we also have s a large cloud	Heb 12:1
is pleased with s sacrifices.	Heb 13:16
s and s a city and spend a year	Jms 4:13
we ought to support s men,	3Jn 8

SUDDEN

then s destruction comes on	1Th 5:3

SUDDENLY

their destruction will come s;	Pr 24:22
you seek will s come to His temple,	Mal 3:1
he might come s and find you	Mk 13:36
S there was a multitude of the	Lk 2:13

SUE

one who wants to s you and take	Mt 5:40

SUEZ

LORD will divide the Gulf of S.	Is 11:15

SUFFER

If these men ... s the fate of all,	Nm 16:29
Fools s-ed affliction because of	Ps 107:17
security for a stranger, he will s	Pr 11:15

companion of fools will s harm.	Pr 13:20
I've s-ed terribly in a dream	Mt 27:19
Son of Man must s many things,	Mk 8:31
Passover with you before I s.	Lk 22:15
s these things and enter into His	Lk 24:26
Messiah would s and rise from	Lk 24:46
After He had s-ed, He also presented	Ac 1:3
that His Messiah would s	Ac 3:18
how much he must s for My name!	Ac 9:16
the Messiah had to s and rise	Ac 17:3
that the Messiah must s,	Ac 26:23
we s with Him so that we also may	Rm 8:17
one member s-s, all ... s with it;	1Co 12:26
Did you s so much for nothing	Gl 3:4
but also to s for Him,	Php 1:29
I have s-ed the loss of all things	Php 3:8
share in s-ing for the gospel,	2Tm 1:8
For this I s, to the point of	2Tm 2:9
Himself was tested and has s-ed,	Heb 2:18
obedience through what He s-ed.	Heb 5:8
would have had to s many times	Heb 9:26
chose to s with the people of God	Heb 11:25
Jesus also s-ed outside the gate,	Heb 13:12
Is anyone among you s-ing?	Jms 5:13
But when you do good and s,	1Pt 2:20
Christ also s-ed for you,	1Pt 2:21
when s-ing, He did not threaten,	1Pt 2:23
it is better to s for doing good,	1Pt 3:17
Christ also s-ed for sins once	1Pt 3:18
since Christ s-ed in the flesh,	1Pt 4:1
if {anyone s-s} as a Christian,	1Pt 4:16
those who s according to God's	1Pt 4:19
after you have s-ed a little.	1Pt 5:10
s-ing harm as the payment for	2Pt 2:13
afraid of what you are about to s.	Rv 2:10

SUFFERING (n)

and I know about their s-s.	Ex 3:7
his s was very intense	Jb 2:13
man of s who knew what sickness	Is 53:3
In all their s, He suffered,	Is 63:9
she no longer remembers the s	Jn 16:21
will have s in this world.	Jn 16:33
the s-s of this present time are not	Rm 8:18
as the s of Christ overflow	2Co 1:5
that as you share in the s-s,	2Co 1:7
the fellowship of His s-s,	Php 3:10
I rejoice in my s-s for you,	Col 1:24
because of the s of death.	Heb 2:9

salvation perfect through s-s.   Heb 2:10
as an example of s and patience.   Jms 5:10
testified ... to the messianic s-s   1Pt 1:11
share in the s-s of the Messiah   1Pt 4:13
witness to the s-s of the Messiah,   1Pt 5:1
the same s-s are being experienced   1Pt 5:9

SUFFICIENT
the majority is s for such a   2Co 2:6
My grace is s for you,   2Co 12:9

SUITABLE
or crude joking are not s,   Eph 5:4

SULFUR
LORD rained burning s on Sodom   Gn 19:24
He will rain ... s on the wicked;   Ps 11:6
fire and s rained from heaven   Lk 17:29
lake that burns with fire and s,   Rv 21:8

SUM
how vast their s is!   Ps 139:17

SUMMED
all are s up by this: Rm 13:9

SUMMER
cold and heat, s and winter,   Gn 8:22
was drained as in the s-'s heat.   Ps 32:4
You made s and winter.   Ps 74:17
it prepares its provisions in s;   Pr 6:8
who gathers during s is prudent;   Pr 10:5
Like snow in s and rain at   Pr 26:1
store up their food in the s;   Pr 30:25
winter house and the s house;   Am 3:15
showed me this: A basket of s fruit.   Am 8:1
leaves, you know that s is near.   Mt 24:32

SUMMON
I will s the grain and make it   Ezk 36:29
his slaves to s those invited to   Mt 22:3

SUN
s, moon, and 11 stars were bowing   Gn 37:9
And the s stood still   Jos 10:13
who love Him be like rising of the s   Jdg 5:31
burned up the chariots of the s.   2Kg 23:11
have gazed at the s when it was   Jb 31:26
He has pitched a tent for the s.   Ps 19:4
he continue while the s endures,   Ps 72:5
the LORD God is a s and shield.   Ps 84:11
rising of the s to its setting,   Ps 113:3
s will not strike you by day,   Ps 121:6

Praise Him, s and moon;   Ps 148:3
The s rises and the s sets;   Ec 1:5
there is nothing new under the s.   Ec 1:9
pleasing for the eyes to see the s.   Ec 11:7
for the s has gazed on me.   Sg 1:6
bright as the s, awe-inspiring   Sg 6:10
be called the City of the S.   Is 19:18
So the s-'s shadow went back the   Is 38:8
rising of the s to its setting   Is 45:6
The s will no longer be your   Is 60:19
s set while it was still day;   Jr 15:9
who gives the s for light by day   Jr 31:35
The s will be turned to darkness   Jl 2:31
s will set on these prophets,   Mc 3:6
s and moon stand still   Hab 3:11
the s of righteousness will rise   Mal 4:2
For He causes His s to rise on   Mt 5:45
the righteous will shine like the s   Mt 13:43
and His face shone like the s.   Mt 17:2
The s will be darkened,   Mt 24:29
there will be signs in the s,   Lk 21:25
s will be turned to darkness,   Ac 2:20
There is a splendor of the s,   1Co 15:41
Don't let the s go down on your   Eph 4:26
His face was shining like the s   Rv 1:16
s turned black like sackcloth   Rv 6:12
longer will the s strike them,   Rv 7:16
and a third of the s was struck,   Rv 8:12
a woman clothed with the s,   Rv 12:1
poured out his bowl on the s.   Rv 16:8
saw an angel standing in the s,   Rv 19:17
not need the s or the moon to   Rv 21:23

SUNLIGHT
and the s will be seven times   Is 30:26
s and moonlight will diminish.   Zch 14:6
will not need lamplight or s,   Rv 22:5

SUNRISE
Jericho, eastward toward the s.   Nm 34:15
they went to the tomb at s.   Mk 16:2

SUNSET
return it to him before s.   Ex 22:26

SUPER-APOSTLES
no way inferior to the "s."   2Co 11:5; 12:11

SUPERFICIALLY
treated My people's brokenness s,   Jr 6:14
have treated s the brokenness   Jr 8:11

SUPERIOR

approve the things that are s,	Rm 2:18
For who makes you so s?	1Co 4:7
He inherited is s to theirs.	Heb 1:4
inferior is blessed by the s.	Heb 7:7
has now obtained a s ministry,	Heb 8:6

SUPERNATURAL

why s powers are at work in him.	Mt 14:2

SUPPER

took the cup after s and said,	Lk 22:20
He got up from s, laid aside His	Jn 13:4
leaned back against Jesus at the s	Jn 21:20
not really to eat the Lord's S.	1Co 11:20
cup, after s, and said, "This	1Co 11:25
together for the great s of God,	Rv 19:17

SUPPLEMENT

to s your faith with goodness,	2Pt 1:5

SUPPLIES

he is, hidden among the s-ies.	1Sm 10:22
while 200 stayed with the s-ies.	1Sm 25:13
one who remains with the s-ies.	1Sm 30:24

SUPPLY (adj)

and Rameses as s cities for Pharaoh.	Ex 1:11

SUPPLY (v)

Don't continue to s the people with	Ex 5:7
from Macedonia s-ied my needs.	2Co 11:9
does God s you with the Spirit	Gl 3:5
am fully s-ied, having received	Php 4:18
And my God will s all your needs	Php 4:19
entry ... will be richly s-ied to you.	2Pt 1:11

SUPPORT

Aaron and Hur s-ed his hands,	Ex 17:12
the pillars s-ing the temple,	Jdg 16:26
but the LORD was my s.	2Sm 22:19
strongly s-ed him in his reign	1Ch 11:10
and He will not s evildoers.	Jb 8:20
but the LORD s-s the righteous.	Ps 37:17
on the LORD, and He will s you;	Ps 55:22
Your faithful love will s me,	Ps 94:18
His angels ... will s you	Mt 4:6
by every s-ing ligament,	Eph 4:16
we don't have the right (to s),	2Th 3:9
S widows who are genuinely	1Tm 5:3
we ought to s such men,	3Jn 8

SUPPOSE

again, "S 40 are found there?	Gn 18:29
Now s he has a son who sees all	Ezk 18:14
these people are not drunk, as you s,	Ac 2:15

SUPPRESS

unrighteousness s the truth,	Rm 1:18

SUPREME

Wisdom is s—so get wisdom.	Pr 4:7
the Emperor as the s authority,	1Pt 2:13

SURE

be s your sin will catch up with	Nm 32:23
answer me with Your s salvation.	Ps 69:13
cornerstone, a s foundation;	Is 28:16
appearance is as s as the dawn.	Hs 6:3
I am s of this, that He who	Php 1:6
a s and firm anchor of the soul	Heb 6:19

SURELY

S the LORD is in this place,	Gn 28:16
S You desire integrity in the	Ps 51:6
S the darkness will hide me,	Ps 139:11
to say to Him, "S not I, Lord?"	Mt 26:22
S the Messiah doesn't come from	Jn 7:41

SURFACE

over the s of the waters.	Gn 1:2
ark floated on the s of the water.	Gn 7:18
water covered the s of the whole	Gn 8:9

SURGE

its waves s, You still them.	Ps 89:9
doubter is like the s-ing sea,	Jms 1:6

SURPASS

King Solomon s-ed all the kings	1Kg 10:23
capable, but you s them all!	Pr 31:29
Whom do you s in loveliness?	Ezk 32:19
unless your righteousness s-es	Mt 5:20
One coming after me has s-ed me,	Jn 1:15
because of the glory that s-es it.	2Co 3:10
you because of the s-ing grace of	2Co 9:14
love that s-es knowledge,	Eph 3:19
view of the s-ing value of knowing	Php 3:8
peace of God, which s-es every	Php 4:7

SURPLUS

they all gave out of their s,	Mk 12:44
your s is (available) for their need,	2Co 8:14

SURPRISE

Let death take them by s;	Ps 55:15

Pilate was **s-d** that He was already Mk 15:44
they are **s-d** that you don't plunge 1Pt 4:4
test you, don't be **s-d** by it, 1Pt 4:12
not be **s-d** ... if the world hates you. 1Jn 3:13

SURRENDER
He **s-ed** His people to the sword Ps 78:62
but whoever **s-s** to the Chaldeans Jr 38:2
How can I **s** you, Israel? Hs 11:8

SURROUND
population, **s-ed** the house. Gn 19:4
must completely **s** the king with 2Kg 11:8
You **s** him with favor like a Ps 5:12
Many bulls **s** me; Ps 22:12
You **s** me with joyful shouts of Ps 32:7
have faithful love **s-ing** him. Ps 32:10
without number have **s-ed** me; Ps 40:12
Your faithfulness **s-s** You. Ps 89:8
All the nations **s-ed** me; Ps 118:10
And the LORD **s-s** His people, Ps 125:2
when you see Jerusalem **s-ed** by Lk 21:20
large cloud of witnesses **s-ing** us, Heb 12:1
the earth and **s-ed** the encampment Rv 20:9

SURVEY
They are to go and **s** the land, Jos 18:4

SURVIVAL
result—the **s** of many people. Gn 50:20

SURVIVE
The **s-ing** remnant of the house 2Kg 19:30
for we **s** as a remnant today. Ezr 9:15
wicked will not **s** the judgment, Ps 1:5
but who can **s** a broken spirit? Pr 18:14
How then can we **s**? Ezk 33:10
How will Jacob **s** since he is Am 7:2,5
were limited, no one would **s**. Mt 24:22
built **s-s**, he will receive a reward. 1Co 3:14

SURVIVOR
everyone in it, leaving no **s-s**. Jos 10:28
heirs for the **s-s** of Benjamin, Jdg 21:17
s-s from Mount Zion. The zeal 2Kg 19:31
Let every **s**, wherever he lives, Ezr 1:4
of Hosts had not left us a few **s-s**, Is 1:9
Even so, there will be **s-s** left in it, Ezk 14:22
hand over their **s-s** in the day Ob 14

SUSA
Winter capital of the Persian Empire (Ezr 4:9; Neh 1:1; Est 1:2; Dn 8:2).

SUSANNA
Follower and supporter of Jesus (Lk 8:3).

SUSPENDED
kept going, so he was **s** in midair. 2Sm 18:9

SUSPENSE
are You going to keep us in **s**? Jn 10:24

SUSPICIONS
quarreling, slanders, evil **s**, 1Tm 6:4

SUSTAIN
Didn't He make you and **s** you? Dt 32:6
and **s** you in your old age. Ru 4:15
wake again because the LORD **s-s** me. Ps 3:5
The LORD will **s** him on his Ps 41:3
and bread that **s-s** man's heart. Ps 104:15
S me with raisins; Sg 2:5
establish and **s** it with justice Is 9:7
have been **s-ed** from the womb, Is 46:3
to know how to **s** the weary with Is 50:4
not **s** the root, but the root **s** you. Rm 11:18
and He **s-s** all things by His Heb 1:3

SUSTAINER
the Lord is the **s** of my life. Ps 54:4

SWALLOW (n)
and a **s**, a nest for herself Ps 84:3
sparrow or a fluttering **s**, Pr 26:2
The turtledove, **s**, and crane are Jr 8:7

SWALLOW (v)
heads of grain **s-ed** up the seven Gn 41:7
Aaron's staff **s-ed** their staffs. Ex 7:12
earth opened its mouth and **s-ed** Nm 16:32
me alone until I **s** my saliva? Jb 7:19
Let's **s** them alive, like Sheol, Pr 1:12
and a wicked mouth **s-s** iniquity. Pr 19:28
has **s-ed** me like a sea monster; Jr 51:34
He has **s-ed** up Israel. Lm 2:5
a great fish to **s** Jonah, Jnh 1:17
My soul is **s-ed** up in sorrow Mt 26:38
has been **s-ed** up in victory. 1Co 15:54
mortality may be **s-ed** up by life. 2Co 5:4

SWAMPED
the boat was already being **s**. Mk 4:37

SWARM (n)
and chased you like a **s** of bees. Dt 1:44
and there was a **s** of bees with Jdg 14:8

SWARM (v)

Let the water s with living	Gn 1:20
The Nile will s with frogs;	Ex 8:3
houses will s with flies,	Ex 8:21
creatures that s on the ground	Lv 11:29

SWARMING (adj)

left, the s locust has eaten;	Jl 1:4
years that the s locust ate,	Jl 2:25

SWAY (n)

is under the s of the evil one.	1Jn 5:19

SWAYING (v)

A reed s in the wind?	Mt 11:7; Lk 7:24

SWEAR

Now s to me here by God that you	Gn 21:23
By Myself I have sworn, says	Gn 22:16
I will have you s by the LORD,	Gn 24:3
Jacob said, "S to me first."	Gn 25:33
I will confirm the oath that I swore	Gn 26:3
And Jacob said, "S to me."	Gn 47:31
the land that I swore to give to	Ex 6:8
that You swore to Your servants	Ex 32:13
Or [if] someone s-s rashly to do	Lv 5:4
You must not s falsely by My	Lv 19:12
I s that none of you will enter	Nm 14:30
had sworn an oath at Mizpah:	Jdg 21:1
made the troops solemnly s,	1Sm 14:28
So David swore to Saul.	1Sm 24:22
many times must I make you s	1Kg 22:16
with Abraham, swore to Isaac,	1Ch 16:16
and who has not sworn deceitfully.	Ps 24:4
all who s by Him will boast,	Ps 63:11
I have sworn an oath to David	Ps 89:3
love that You swore to David	Ps 89:49
swore in My anger, 'They will not	Ps 95:11
LORD has sworn an oath and will	Ps 110:4
LORD swore an oath to David,	Ps 132:11
Your enemies s {by You} falsely.	Ps 139:20
By Myself I have sworn;	Is 45:23
in the land will s by the God of	Is 65:16
ways of My people—to s by My	Jr 12:16
I swore to them that I would bring	Ezk 20:6
do not s an oath: As the LORD lives!	Hs 4:15
Those who s by the guilt of	Am 8:14
Neither should you s by your head,	Mt 5:36
to curse and to s with an oath,	Mt 26:74
oath that He swore to our father	Lk 1:73
swore in My anger, "They will not	Heb 3:11

s that they would not enter His	Heb 3:18
to s by, He swore by Himself:	Heb 6:13
For men s by something greater	Heb 6:16
Lord has sworn, and He will not	Heb 7:21
brothers, do not s, either by	Jms 5:12

SWEAT

eat bread by the s of your brow	Gn 3:19
His s became like drops of blood	Lk 22:44

SWEEP

Will You really s away the	Gn 18:23
or you will be swept away!	Gn 19:17
like chaff a storm s-s away?	Jb 21:18
Your billows have swept over me.	Ps 42:7
terrors of death s over me.	Ps 55:4
and a flood s-s over me.	Ps 69:2
torrent would have swept over us;	Ps 124:4
I will s her away with a broom of	Is 14:23
is I who s away your transgressions	Is 43:25
bloodshed will s through you,	Ezk 5:17
and Your billows swept over me.	Jnh 2:3
I will completely s away everything	Zph 1:2
vacant, swept, and put in order.	Mt 12:44
flood came and swept them all	Mt 24:39
not light a lamp, s the house,	Lk 15:8
His tail swept away a third of the	Rv 12:4
to s her away in a torrent.	Rv 12:15

SWEET

of the strong came something s.	Jdg 14:14
Though evil tastes s in his	Jb 20:12
How s Your word is to my taste	Ps 119:103
Stolen water is s,	Pr 9:17
Desire fulfilled is s to the taste,	Pr 13:19
Pleasant words are ... s to the taste	Pr 16:24
The sleep of the worker is s,	Ec 5:12
and his fruit is s to my taste.	Sg 2:3
your voice is s, and your face	Sg 2:14
bitter for s and s for bitter.	Is 5:20
it was as s as honey in my mouth.	Ezk 3:3
will drip with s wine,	Jl 3:18; Am 9:13
Does a spring pour out s and bitter	Jms 3:11
was as s as honey in my mouth,	Rv 10:10

SWEETER

What is s than honey?	Jdg 14:18
and s than honey—than honey	Ps 19:10

SWEETNESS

Should I stop giving my s	Jdg 9:11

and the s of a friend is better | Pr 27:9
His mouth is s. He is absolutely | Sg 5:16

SWELL
thigh shrivel and your belly s. | Nm 5:21
feet did not s these 40 years. | Dt 8:4
that he would s up or suddenly | Ac 28:6

SWIFT
that the race is not to the s, | Ec 9:11
Escape will fail the s, | Am 2:14
Their feet are s to shed blood; | Rm 3:15
bring s destruction on themselves. | 2Pt 2:1

SWIFTLY
and He will s destroy you. | Dt 7:4
My days pass more s than a weaver's | Jb 7:6
His word runs s. | Ps 147:15
He will s grant them justice. | Lk 18:8

SWINDLER
or a reviler, a drunkard or a s. | 1Co 5:11
or s-s will inherit God's kingdom. | 1Co 6:10

SWINE
in secret places, eating s's flesh, | Is 65:4

SWOLLEN
My eyes are s from grief; | Ps 6:7
man whose body was s with fluid. | Lk 14:2

SWOOP
Sabeans s-ed down and took them | Jb 1:15
He will s down like an eagle and | Jr 48:40
like an eagle, s-ing to devour. | Hab 1:8

SWORD
flaming, whirling s to guard the | Gn 3:24
It was not by your s or bow. | Jos 24:12
The s of the LORD and of Gideon! | Jdg 7:18
not by s ... that the LORD saves, | 1Sm 17:47
Saul took his s and fell on it. | 1Sm 31:4
terrified of the s of the LORD's | 1Ch 21:30
Deliver my life from the s, | Ps 22:20
and my s does not bring me | Ps 44:6
their tongues are sharp s-s. | Ps 57:4
speaks rashly, like a piercing s; | Pr 12:18
will turn their s-s into plows | Is 2:4
Nations will not take up the s against | Is 2:4
will fall, but not by human s; | Is 31:8
The LORD's s is covered with | Is 34:6
those {destined} for the s, to the s. | Jr 15:2
plague, the s, and the famine | Jr 21:7

A s is against the diviners, | Jr 50:36
Outside, the s takes the | Lm 1:20
take a sharp s, use it as you | Ezk 5:1
proclaim: A s! A s is sharpened | Ezk 21:9
I will shatter bow, s, and weapons | Hs 2:18
Hammer your plowshares into s-s | Jl 3:10
confront us, will die by the s. | Am 9:10
will beat their s-s into plows, | Mc 4:3
take up the s against nation, | Mc 4:3
S, awake against My shepherd, | Zch 13:7
come to bring peace, but a s. | Mt 10:34
who take up a s will perish by a s. | Mt 26:52
you come out with s-s and clubs, | Mt 26:55
a s will pierce your own soul | Lk 2:35
doesn't have a s should sell his | Lk 22:36
said, "look, here are two s-s." | Lk 22:38
said to Peter, "Sheathe your s! | Jn 18:11
or nakedness or danger or s? | Rm 8:35
does not carry the s for no reason. | Rm 13:4
and the s of the Spirit, | Eph 6:17
sharper than any two-edged s, | Heb 4:12
mouth came a sharp two-edged s; | Rv 1:16
them with the s of My mouth. | Rv 2:16
From His mouth came a sharp s, | Rv 19:15

SYCAMORE
he made cedar as abundant as s | 1Kg 10:27
the s-s have been cut down, but we | Is 9:10
and I took care of s figs. | Am 7:14
he climbed up a s tree to see | Lk 19:4

SYCHAR
Town in Samaria where Jesus spoke to the woman at the well (Jn 4:5).

SYMBOL
a s on your forehead | Ex 13:16; Dt 6:8
let them be a s on your foreheads. | Dt 11:18
should have {a s of} authority | 1Co 11:10
is a s for the present time, | Heb 9:9

SYMPATHETIC
you should be like-minded and s, | 1Pt 3:8

SYMPATHIZE
a high priest who is unable to s | Heb 4:15
you s-d with the prisoners and | Heb 10:34

SYMPATHY
to go and offer s and comfort to | Jb 2:11
They offered him s and comfort | Jb 42:11
I waited for s, but there was none; | Ps 69:20

SYNAGOGUE

teaching in their **s-s**, preaching	Mt 4:23
love to pray standing in the **s-s**	Mt 6:5
the front seats in the **s-s**,	Mt 23:6
will flog in your **s-s** and hound	Mt 23:34
One of the **s** leaders, named Jairus,	Mk 5:22
He entered the **s** on the Sabbath	Lk 4:16
he would be banned from the **s**.	Jn 9:22
would not be banned from the **s**.	Jn 12:42
They will ban you from the **s**.	Jn 16:2
taught in the **s** and in the temple	Jn 18:20
proclaiming Jesus in the **s-s**:	Ac 9:20
in the **s-s** every Sabbath day.	Ac 15:21
reasoned in the **s** every Sabbath	Ac 18:4
began to speak boldly in the **s**.	Ac 18:26
s after **s** I had those who believed	Ac 22:19
but are a **s** of Satan.	Rv 2:9
make those from the **s** of Satan,	Rv 3:9

SYRIA

The region north of Galilee (Mt 4:24; Lk 2:2; Ac 15:23,41; Gl 1:21). Called Aram in the OT (2Kg 5:1; Lk 4:27).

SYROPHOENICIAN

A person from the areas of Syria or Phoenicia, which were combined under Roman rule (Mk 7:26).

TABERAH

Camp where some were consumed by fire (Nm 11:1-3; Dt 9:22).

TABERNACLE

the design of the **t**	Ex 25:9
glory of the LORD filled the **t**.	Ex 40:34
anointed the **t** and everything	Lv 8:10
On the day the **t** was set up,	Nm 9:15
near the LORD's **t** will die.	Nm 17:13
all the service of the **t**,	1Ch 6:48
He abandoned the **t** at Shiloh,	Ps 78:60
I will make three **t-s** here:	Mt 17:4
Jewish Festival of **T-s** was near,	Jn 7:2

the true **t**, which the Lord set up,	Heb 8:2
more perfect **t** not made with	Heb 9:11

TABITHA

Aramaic counterpart to the Greek name Dorcas (Ac 9:36-42).

TABLE

construct a **t** of acacia wood,	Ex 25:23
pure {gold} **t** before the LORD.	Lv 24:6
will always eat meals at my **t**.	2Sm 9:7
the gold **t** that the bread of the	1Kg 7:48
the food at his **t**, his servants'	1Kg 10:5
He made 10 **t-s** and placed them in	2Ch 4:8
and the **t** for the rows {of the	2Ch 29:18
You prepare a **t** before me in the	Ps 23:5
Let their **t** ... be a snare,	Ps 69:22
she has also set her **t**.	Pr 9:2
all their **t-s** are covered with vomit;	Is 28:8
say: "The LORD's **t** is contemptible."	Mal 1:7
recline at the **t** with Abraham,	Mt 8:11
crumbs ... fall from their masters' **t**	Mt 15:27
overturned the money changers' **t-s**	Mt 21:12
as He was reclining at the **t**.	Mt 26:7
dogs under the **t** eat the	Mk 7:28
recline at the **t** in the kingdom	Lk 13:29
betraying Me is at the **t** with Me!	Lk 22:21
and drink at My **t** in My kingdom.	Lk 22:30
coins and overturned the **t-s**.	Jn 2:15
about God to wait on **t-s**.	Ac 6:2
the Lord's **t** and the **t** of demons.	1Co 10:21
the lampstand, the **t**, and the	Heb 9:2

TABLET

that I may give you the stone **t-s**	Ex 24:12
t-s inscribed by the finger	Ex 31:18
Moses ... threw the **t-s** ... smashing	Ex 32:19
Cut two stone **t-s** like the first	Ex 34:1
wrote down on the **t-s** the words	Ex 34:28
which He wrote on two stone **t-s**.	Dt 4:13
to receive the stone **t-s**,	Dt 9:9
Cut two stone **t-s** like the	Dt 10:1
placed the **t-s** in the ark I had	Dt 10:5
the two stone **t-s** that Moses had	1Kg 8:9
except the two **t-s** that Moses	2Ch 5:10
them on the **t** of your heart.	Pr 3:3; 7:3
engraved on the **t** of their hearts	Jr 17:1
not on stone **t-s** but on **t-s**	2Co 3:3
and the **t-s** of the covenant.	Heb 9:4

TABOR

1. Mountain near Jezreel (Jos 19:22; Jdg 4:6-14; 8:18; Ps 89:12; Jr 46:18; Hs 5:1).

2. Levitical city (1Ch 6:77).

3. Plain near Gibea (1Sm 10:3).

TACTICS

against the t of the Devil.   Eph 6:11

TADMOR

Solomon's trade city (2Ch 8:4).

TAHPANHES

City in Egypt where Jews fled with Jeremiah (Jr 2:16; 43:7; 44:1) against his advice (42:19; 46:14,19).

TAIL

your hand and grab it by the t.	Ex 4:4
make you the head and not the t;	Dt 28:13
the head, and you will be the t.	Dt 28:44
torch between each pair of t-s.	Jdg 15:4
He stiffens his t like a cedar	Jb 40:17
cut Israel's head and t,	Is 9:14
and they had t-s with stingers,	Rv 9:10
because their t-s, like snakes,	Rv 9:19
His t swept away a third of the	Rv 12:4

TAKE

for she was **taken** from man.	Gn 2:23
not there, because God **took** him.	Gn 5:24
"T your son," He said, "your	Gn 22:2
I will t you as My people,	Ex 6:7
not t revenge or bear a grudge	Lv 19:18
Enter and t possession of the	Dt 1:8
and t {your} oaths in His name.	Dt 6:13
anything to it or t anything away	Dt 12:32
T this book of the law and place	Dt 31:26
and **took** the wife Uriah	2Sm 12:10
LORD has **taken** away your sin;	2Sm 12:13
But God would not t away a life;	2Sm 14:14
boast like the one who t-s it off.	1Kg 20:11
gives, and the LORD t-s away.	Jb 1:21
He knows the way I have **taken**;	Jb 23:10
of the wicked, or t the path of sinners,	Ps 1:1
since He t-s pleasure in him.	Ps 22:8
dies, he will t nothing at all;	Ps 49:17
or t Your Holy Spirit from me.	Ps 51:11
Let death t them by surprise;	Ps 55:15
took me from my mother's womb.	Ps 71:6
let another t over his position.	Ps 109:8

an oath and will not t it back:	Ps 110:4
is gained by those who t advice.	Pr 13:10
T his garment, for he has put up	Pr 20:16
those being **taken** off to death,	Pr 24:11
no adding to it or t-ing from it.	Ec 3:14
will t nothing for his efforts	Ec 5:15
Nations will not t up the sword	Is 2:4
can t {anything} from My hand.	Is 43:13
He was **taken** away because of	Is 53:8
and no one t-s it to heart;	Is 57:1
the armies **took** the whole remnant	Jr 43:5
I will t you from the nations	Ezk 36:24
T words {of repentance} with you	Hs 14:2
the LORD **took** me from following	Am 7:15
LORD, please t my life from me,	Jnh 4:3
Nation will not t up the sword	Mc 4:3
Devil **took** Him to a very high	Mt 4:8
sue you and t away your shirt,	Mt 5:40
Himself **took** our weaknesses and	Mt 8:17
will be **taken** away from them,	Mt 9:15
whoever doesn't t up his cross	Mt 10:38
t up My yoke and learn from Me,	Mt 11:29
has will be **taken** away from him.	Mt 13:12
deny himself, t up his cross,	Mt 16:24
one will be **taken** and one left.	Mt 24:40
has will be **taken** away from him.	Mt 25:29
a stranger and you **took** Me in;	Mt 25:35
T and eat it; this is My body.	Mt 26:26
because all who t up a sword	Mt 26:52
T this cup away from Me.	Mk 14:36
Jesus was **taken** up into heaven	Mk 16:19
T care of him. When I come back	Lk 10:35
T it easy; eat, drink, and enjoy	Lk 12:19
who t-s away the sin of the world!	Jn 1:29
My life so I may t it up again.	Jn 10:17
because He will t from what is	Jn 16:14
they've **taken** away my Lord,	Jn 20:13
He was **taken** up as they were	Ac 1:9
the Lord Jesus **took** bread,	1Co 11:23
t up the full armor of God,	Eph 6:13
t-ing on the likeness of men.	Php 2:7
also have been **taken** hold of by	Php 3:12
in the world, **taken** up in glory.	1Tm 3:16
world, and we can t nothing out.	1Tm 6:7
which can never t away sins.	Heb 10:11
Enoch was **taken** away so that he	Heb 11:5
do not t the Lord's discipline	Heb 12:5
And if anyone t-s away from the	Rv 22:19

TALENTS

who owed 10,000 t was brought	Mt 18:24
To one he gave five t;	Mt 25:15

TALITHA

hand and said to her, "T koum!"	Mk 5:41

TALK (n)

Should he argue with useless t or	Jb 15:3
stranger with her flattering t,	Pr 2:16; 7:5
but endless t leads only to poverty.	Pr 14:23
of God is not in t but in power.	1Co 4:20
No rotten t should come from your	Eph 4:29

TALK (v)

T about them when you sit in	Dt 6:7
fool nobody can t to him!	1Sm 25:17
saw those unable to speak t-ing,	Mt 15:31
hearts ablaze ... while He was t-ing	Lk 24:32
that He was t-ing with a woman.	Jn 4:27
I will not t with you much longer,	Jn 14:30
anyone who t-s back to God?	Rm 9:20
I'm t-ing like a madman—I'm a	2Co 11:23
I am t-ing about Christ and the	Eph 5:32
and we will t face to face.	3Jn 14

TALKERS

idle t and deceivers, especially those	Ti 1:10

TALL

people as t as the Anakim,	Dt 2:10
He was nine feet, nine inches t	1Sm 17:4
who was seven and a half feet t.	1Ch 11:23
gallows 75 feet t at Haman's	Est 7:9
a nation t and smooth-skinned,	Is 18:2

TALLER

are larger and t than we are;	Dt 1:28
He stood a head t than anyone	1Sm 9:2
it comes up and grows t than all	Mk 4:32

TAMAR

1. Judah's daughter-in-law; widow of Er and Onan; mother of Judah's sons (Gn 38).

2. Daughter of David; raped by Amnon; avenged by Absalom (2Sm 13).

3. Daughter of Absalom (2Sm 14:27).

4. City near the Dead Sea (1Kg 9:18; 2Ch 8:4; Ezk 47:19; 48:28).

TAMARISK

Abraham planted a t tree in	Gn 21:33

under the t tree at the high	1Sm 22:6
them under the t tree in Jabesh	1Sm 31:13

TAMBOURINE

Aaron's sister, took a t	Ex 15:20
singing to the t and lyre and	Jb 21:12
young women playing t-s.	Ps 68:25
Praise Him with t and dance;	Ps 150:4
lyre, harp, t, flute,	Is 5:12
The joyful t-s have ceased.	Is 24:8

TAME

but no man can t the tongue.	Jms 3:8

TANGLED

Foolishness is t up in the heart	Pr 22:15

TANNER

in Joppa with Simon, a leather t.	Ac 9:43

TAPESTRIES

were weaving t for Asherah.	2Kg 23:7

TARGET

Why have You made me Your t,	Jb 7:20
set me as the t for His arrow.	Lm 3:12

TARSHISH

1. Son of Javan (Gn 10:4; 1Ch 1:7).

2. Benjaminite warrior (1Ch 7:10).

3. Persian official (Est 1:14).

4. Distant Mediterranean port city known for sea trade (1Kg 10:22; 22:48; Ps 48:7; 72:10; Is 2:16; 23:1,6,10,14; 66:19; Jr 10:9; Ezk 27:12,25; 38:13); Jonah fled toward it (Jnh 1:3).

TARSUS

Cilician city, hometown of Saul (Ac 9:11,30; 22:3); visited by Barnabas (11:25).

TARTAN

the king of Assyria sent the T,	2Kg 18:17

TASK

this miserable t to keep them	Ec 1:13
He gives the t of gathering	Ec 2:26
was distracted by her many t-s,	Lk 10:40

TASKMASTERS

Egyptians assigned t over the	Ex 1:11

TASSEL

are to make t-s for the corners	Nm 15:38
Make t-s on the four corners of	Dt 22:12

and touched the **t** on His robe,   Mt 9:20
and lengthen their **t-s**.   Mt 23:5

TASTE (n)

How sweet Your word is to my **t**   Ps 119:103
sweet to the **t** and health to the   Pr 16:24
and his fruit is sweet to my **t**.   Sg 2:3
if the salt should lose its **t**,   Mt 5:13

TASTE (v)

and **t-d** like wafers {made} with   Ex 16:31
It **t-d** like a pastry cooked with   Nm 11:8
Can your servant **t** what he eats   2Sm 19:35
words as the palate **t-s** food?   Jb 12:11; 34:3
T and see that the LORD is good.   Ps 34:8
who will not **t** death until they   Mt 16:28
the chief servant **t-d** the water   Jn 2:9
he will never **t** death—ever!'   Jn 8:52
handle, don't **t**, don't touch"?   Col 2:21
grace He might **t** death for   Heb 2:9
who **t-d** the heavenly gift,   Heb 6:4
since you have **t-d** that the Lord   1Pt 2:3

TASTY

bread {eaten} secretly is **t**!   Pr 9:17

TATTENAI

Persian governor who opposed Ezra (Ezr 5:3,6; 6:6,13).

TATTOO

not ... put **t** marks on yourselves;   Lv 19:28

TAUNT (n)

do not make me the **t** of fools.   Ps 39:8
not be shattered by their **t-s**.   Is 51:7
exposed to **t-s** and afflictions,   Heb 10:33

TAUNT (v)

Her rival would **t** her severely   1Sm 1:6
My adversaries **t** me, as if   Ps 42:10
My enemies **t** me all day long;   Ps 102:8
I can answer anyone who **t-s** me.   Pr 27:11
crucified with Him kept **t-ing** Him.   Mt 27:44

TAX (n) *see also* TAX COLLECTOR

exempt from paying **t-es**   1Sm 17:25
t must not be ... on any priests,   Ezr 7:24
Matthew sitting at the **t** office,   Mt 9:9
Teacher pay the double-drachma **t**?   Mt 17:24
lawful to pay **t-es** to Caesar or not?   Mt 22:17
Levi sitting at the **t** office,   Lk 5:27

opposing payment of **t-es** to Caesar,   Lk 23:2
t-es to those you owe **t-es**,   Rm 13:7

TAX (v)

Pharaoh's command he **t-ed** the   2Kg 23:35

TAX COLLECTOR

will arise who will send out a **t**   Dn 11:20
Don't even the **t-s** do the same?   Mt 5:46
Why does your Teacher eat with **t-s**   Mt 9:11
and Matthew the **t**;   Mt 10:3
a friend of **t-s** and sinners!   Mt 11:19
like an unbeliever and a **t** to you.   Mt 18:17
T-s and prostitutes are entering   Mt 21:31
T-s also came to be baptized,   Lk 3:12
saw a **t** named Levi   Lk 5:27
one a Pharisee and the other a **t**.   Lk 18:10
Zacchaeus who was a chief **t**,   Lk 19:2

TEACH

and I will **t** you what to say.   Ex 4:12
please **t** me Your ways,   Ex 33:13
T them to your children   Dt 4:9; 11:19
I will **t** you the good and right   1Sm 12:23
the Levites who **taught** all Israel   2Ch 35:3
Can anyone **t** God knowledge,   Jb 21:22
t me Your paths.   Ps 25:4
I will **t** you the fear of the   Ps 34:11
I will **t** the rebellious Your ways,   Ps 51:13
have **taught** me from my youth,   Ps 71:17
T us to number our days   Ps 90:12
the One who **t-es** man knowledge   Ps 94:10
t me Your statutes   Ps 119:12,64,124,
    135,171
T me to do Your will,   Ps 143:10
t a righteous man, and he will   Pr 9:9
T a youth about the way he   Pr 22:6
he constantly **taught** the people   Ec 12:9
house of my mother who **taught** me.   Sg 8:2
He will **t** us about His ways so   Is 2:3
Who is he trying to **t**?   Is 28:9
Who **taught** Him knowledge   Is 40:14
children will be **taught** by the LORD   Is 54:13
No longer will one **t** his neighbor   Jr 31:34
was I who **taught** Ephraim to walk,   Hs 11:3
her priests **t** for payment,   Mc 3:11
mute stone: Come alive! Can it **t**?   Hab 2:19
Galilee, **t-ing** in their synagogues,   Mt 4:23
breaks ... and **t-es** people to do so   Mt 5:19
t-ing as doctrines the commands   Mt 15:9

they don't practice what they t.	Mt 23:3
t-ing them to observe everything	Mt 28:20
t-ing them as one having authority.	Mk 1:22
He **taught** them many things in	Mk 4:2
as He **taught** in the temple	Mk 12:35
t us to pray, just as John also **taught**	Lk 11:1
Spirit will t you at that very	Lk 12:12
And they will all be **taught** by God.	Jn 6:45
But just as the Father **taught** Me,	Jn 8:28
and are you trying to t us?	Jn 9:34
Holy Spirit ... will t you all things	Jn 14:26
always **taught** in the synagogue	Jn 18:20
all that Jesus began to do and t	Ac 1:1
not to preach or t at all in the name	Ac 4:18
continued t-ing and proclaiming	Ac 5:42
taught ... about Jesus accurately,	Ac 18:25
t another, do you not t yourself?	Rm 2:21
but in those **taught** by the Spirit,	1Co 2:13
nature itself t you that if a	1Co 11:14
in order to t others also,	1Co 14:19
human source and I was not **taught**	Gl 1:12
you heard Him and were **taught**	Eph 4:21
warning and t-ing everyone with	Col 1:28
in the faith, just as you were **taught**,	Col 2:7
t-ing and admonishing one another	Col 3:16
are **taught** by God to love	1Th 4:9
to the traditions you were **taught**,	2Th 2:15
people not to t other doctrine	1Tm 1:3
may be **taught** not to blaspheme	1Tm 1:20
allow a woman to t or to have	1Tm 2:12
If anyone t-es other doctrine and	1Tm 6:3
will be able to t others also.	2Tm 2:2
correctly t-ing the word of truth.	2Tm 2:15
able to t, and patient,	2Tm 2:24
by t-ing for dishonest gain	Ti 1:11
need someone to t you again the	Heb 5:12
each person will not t his fellow	Heb 8:11
you don't need anyone to t you.	1Jn 2:27

TEACHER

the t along with the pupil.	1Ch 25:8
Who is a t like Him?	Jb 36:22
have more insight than all my t-s	Ps 119:99
The words of the T, son of David,	Ec 1:1
but your T will not hide Himself	Is 30:20
A disciple is not above his t,	Mt 10:24
you have one T, and you are all	Mt 23:8
Good T, what must I do	Mk 10:17
complex sitting among the t-s,	Lk 2:46

"Rabbi" (which means "T"),	Jn 1:38
You have come from God as a t,	Jn 3:2
Are you a t of Israel and don't	Jn 3:10
if I, your Lord and T, have washed	Jn 13:14
Gamaliel, a t of the law	Ac 5:34
Antioch there were prophets and t-s:	Ac 13:1
of the ignorant, a t of the immature,	Rm 2:20
prophets, third t-s, next, miracles	1Co 12:28
must share his goods with the t.	Gl 6:6
some pastors and t-s,	Eph 4:11
They want to be t-s of the law,	1Tm 1:7
and a t of the Gentiles in faith	1Tm 2:7
hospitable, an able t,	1Tm 3:2
accumulate t-s for themselves	2Tm 4:3
this time you ought to be t-s,	Heb 5:12
Not many should become t-s,	Jms 3:1
will be false t-s among you.	2Pt 2:1

TEACHING (n)

Let my t fall like rain and	Dt 32:2
How I love Your t! It is my	Ps 119:97
don't reject your mother's t	Pr 1:8; 6:20
is a lamp, t is a light,	Pr 6:23
were astonished at His t,	Mt 7:28; 22:33
A new t with authority!	Mk 1:27
This t is hard! Who can accept it?	Jn 6:60
My t isn't Mine but is from the One	Jn 7:16
devoted ... to the apostles' t,	Ac 2:42
May we learn about this new t	Ac 17:19
if service, in service; if t, in t;	Rm 12:7
knowledge or prophecy or t?	1Co 14:6
around by every wind of t,	Eph 4:14
is contrary to the sound t	1Tm 1:10
reading, exhortation, and t.	1Tm 4:13
work hard at preaching and t.	1Tm 5:17
pattern of sound t that you	2Tm 1:13
and is profitable for t,	2Tm 3:16
is consistent with sound t.	Ti 2:1
integrity and dignity in your t.	Ti 2:7
various kinds of strange t-s;	Heb 13:9
Anyone who does not remain in the t	2Jn 9

TEAMS

Twelve t of oxen were in front	1Kg 19:19

TEAR (n)

prayer; I have seen your t-s.	2Kg 20:5
with my t-s I dampen my pillow	Ps 6:6
do not be silent at my t-s.	Ps 39:12
My t-s have been my food day and	Ps 42:3

Put my t-s in Your bottle.   Ps 56:8
You fed them the bread of t-s   Ps 80:5
and mingle my drinks with t-s   Ps 102:9
Those who sow in t-s will reap   Ps 126:5
drench Heshbon ... with my t-s.   Is 16:9
wipe away the t-s from every face   Is 25:8
a fountain of t-s, I would weep   Jr 9:1
overflow with t-s   Jr 9:18; 13:17; 14:17
cover the LORD's altar with t-s,   Mal 2:13
to wash His feet with her t-s.   Lk 7:38
warning each one of you with t-s.   Ac 20:31
I wrote to you with many t-s   2Co 2:4
now say again with t-s,   Php 3:18
Remembering your t-s, I long to   2Tm 1:4
though he sought it with t-s.   Heb 12:17
away every t from their eyes   Rv 7:17; 21:4

TEAR (v)

not there, he tore his clothes.   Gn 37:29
Joseph has been **torn** to pieces!   Gn 37:33
T down their altars, smash their   Dt 12:3
Then Joshua tore his clothes   Jos 7:6
hem of his robe, and it tore.   1Sm 15:27
has torn the kingship out of your   1Sm 28:17
king stood up, tore his clothes,   2Sm 13:31
cloak ... tore it into 12 pieces,   1Kg 11:30
words, he tore his clothes,   1Kg 21:27
king of Israel tore his clothes,   2Kg 5:8
tore down the pillar of Baal.   2Kg 10:27
of the law, he tore his clothes.   2Kg 22:11
king tore down the altars   2Kg 23:12
because ... you tore your clothes   2Ch 34:27
each man tore his robe and threw   Jb 2:12
or they will t me like a lion,   Ps 7:2
foolish one t-s it down with her   Pr 14:1
a time to t down and a time to   Ec 3:3
the yoke and torn off the fetters.   Jr 5:5
I will t {them} to pieces and   Hs 5:14
For He has torn {us}, and He will   Hs 6:1
T your hearts, not just your   Jl 2:13
feet, turn, and t you to pieces.   Mt 7:6
high priest tore his robes and   Mt 26:65
and their nets began to t.   Lk 5:6
No one t-s a patch from a new   Lk 5:36
I'll t down my barns and build   Lk 12:18
Let's not t it, but toss for it   Jn 19:24
so many, the net was not torn.   Jn 21:11
Barnabas and Paul tore their robes   Ac 14:14
up and not for t-ing you down,   2Co 10:8

you would have **torn** out your eyes   Gl 4:15
and tore down the dividing wall   Eph 2:14

TEKEL

T {means that} you have been   Dn 5:27

TEKOA

  City in Judah, home of "a clever woman"
(2Sm 14:2-9) and Amos (Am 1:1).

TEL-ABIB

  City in Babylon where Ezekiel spoke to
exiles (Ezk 3:15).

TELL

Who **told** you that you were naked?   Gn 3:11
Do not t it in Gath,   2Sm 1:20
I alone have escaped to t you!   Jb 1:15
T {Me}, if you know all this.   Jb 38:18
that you can t a future generation: Ps 48:13
If I were hungry, I would not t you,   Ps 50:12
I will t what He has done for me.   Ps 66:16
t about all His wonderful works!   Ps 105:2
He has told you men what is good   Mc 6:8
But I t you,   Mt 5:22;
See that you don't t anyone;   Mt 8:4
I have told you in advance.   Mt 24:25
be told in memory of her.   Mt 26:13
t us if You are the Messiah,   Mt 26:63
quickly and t His disciples,   Mt 28:7
This is the One I told you about: Jn 1:30
found ... and told him,   Jn 1:41,43,45
see a man who told me everything   Jn 4:29
if not, I would have told you.   Jn 14:2
I have told you now before it   Jn 14:29

TEMPER

one's t, than capturing a city.   Pr 16:32
not control his t is like a city whose Pr 25:28
not quick t-ed, not addicted to wine,   Ti 1:7

TEMPEST

pursue them with Your t   Ps 83:15
noise, storm, t, and a flame   Is 29:6

TEMPLE

with a tent peg through his t!   Jdg 4:22
son ... will build the t for My name.   1Kg 5:5
Solomon finished building the t,   1Kg 6:14
glory of the LORD filled the t.   1Kg 8:11
come and pray toward this t   1Kg 8:42
The LORD is in His holy t;   Ps 11:4
From His t He heard my voice,   Ps 18:6

and seeking {Him} in His t.   Ps 27:4
and His robe filled the t.   Is 6:1
the t of the LORD, the t of the LORD,   Jr 7:4
to the threshold of the t.   Ezk 9:3; 10:4
But the LORD is in His holy t;   Hab 2:20
will suddenly come to His t,   Mal 3:1
stand on the pinnacle of the t,   Mt 4:5
something greater than the t is here!   Mt 12:6
buying and selling in the t.   Mk 11:15
they found Him in the t complex   Lk 2:46

TEMPORARY
A t resident or hired hand may   Ex 12:45
few indeed, and t residents in   1Ch 16:19
and t residents in Canaan,   Ps 105:12
what is seen is t, but what is   2Co 4:18
were foreigners and t residents   Heb 11:13
you as aliens and t residents to   1Pt 2:11

TEMPT
wilderness to be t-ed by the Devil.   Mt 4:1
otherwise, Satan may t you   1Co 7:5
Let us not t Christ as some of   1Co 10:9
allow you to be t-ed beyond what   1Co 10:13
so you won't be t-ed also.   Gl 6:1
and He Himself doesn't t anyone.   Jms 1:13

TEMPTATION
And do not bring us into t,   Mt 6:13
pray, so that you won't enter into t.   Mt 26:41
No t has overtaken you except   1Co 10:13
who want to be rich fall into t,   1Tm 6:9

TEMPTER
Then the t approached Him and   Mt 4:3
fearing that the t had tempted you   1Th 3:5

TEN see also 10
covenant—the T Commandments.   Ex 34:28
David his t-s of thousands.   1Sm 18:7; 29:5
and t thousand at your right hand,   Ps 91:7
notable among t thousand.   Sg 5:10

TENANT
He leased the vineyard to t-s.   Sg 8:11
He leased it to t farmers and   Mt 21:33

TEND
right now he's t-ing the sheep.   1Sm 16:11
brought him from t-ing ewes to   Ps 78:71
but you do not t the flock.   Ezk 34:3
I will t My flock and let them   Ezk 34:15

of Hosts has t-ed His flock,   Zch 10:3
Then the men who t-ed them fled.   Mt 8:33

TENDER
your heart was t and you humbled   2Kg 22:19
branch becomes t and sprouts   Mt 24:32

TENDERLY
Speak t to Jerusalem, and   Is 40:2
wilderness, and speak t to her.   Hs 2:14

TENDONS
me together with bones and t.   Jb 10:11
I will put t on you, make flesh   Ezk 37:6
together by its ligaments and t,   Col 2:19

TEN-STRINGED
make music to Him with a t harp.   Ps 33:2
will play on a t harp for You   Ps 144:9

TENT
east of Bethel and pitched his t,   Gn 12:8
In the t of meeting outside the   Ex 27:21
beautiful are your t-s, Jacob,   Nm 24:5
in the ground inside my t,   Jos 7:21
ark of God sits inside t curtains.   2Sm 7:2
LORD, who can dwell in Your t?   Ps 15:1
live in Your t forever and   Ps 61:4
grumbled in their t-s and did   Ps 106:25
victory in the t-s of the righteous: Ps 118:15
from me like a shepherd's t.   Is 38:12
Enlarge the site of your t,   Is 54:2
and will rebuild David's t,   Ac 15:16
our earthly house, a t, is destroyed,   2Co 5:1
we who are in this t groan,   2Co 5:4
as long as I am in this t,   2Pt 1:13
that I will soon lay aside my t,   2Pt 1:14

TENTH
Abram gave him a t of everything.   Gn 14:20
give to You a t of all that You give   Gn 28:22
Every t ... is holy to the LORD.   Lv 27:30
I have given the Levites every t   Nm 18:21
to the LORD—a t of the t.   Nm 18:26
the best part of the t,   Nm 18:30
set aside a t of all the   Dt 14:22
The offering, the t, and the   2Ch 31:12
Levites when they collect the t,   Neh 10:38
your t-s every three days.   Am 4:4
You pay a t of mint, dill, and   Mt 23:23
I give a t of everything I get.   Lk 18:12
Abraham gave him a t of   Heb 7:2

TENTMAKERS

for they were t by trade. Ac 18:3

TERAH

Father of Abraham (Gn 11:24-32; Jos 24:2; 1Ch 1:26; Lk 3:34).

TERRACE

he then built the t-s. 1Kg 9:24

TERRIBLE

the great and t wilderness Dt 1:19; 8:15
of our evil deeds and t guilt Ezr 9:13
Israel has done a most t thing. Jr 18:13
Day of the LORD is t and dreadful Jl 2:11
us from such a t death, 2Co 1:10

TERRIBLY

I've suffered t in a dream Mt 27:19

TERRIFY

Don't be t-ied or afraid of them! Dt 1:29
and t me with visions, Jb 7:14
I am t-ied in His presence; Jb 23:15
You hid Your face, I was t-ied. Ps 30:7
when He rises to t the earth. Is 2:19
thoughts so t-ied him that his Dn 5:6
on the sea, they were t-ied. Mt 14:26
fell facedown and were t-ied. Mt 17:6
they were t-ied and asked one Mk 4:41
around them, and they were t-ied. Lk 2:9
I am trying to t you with my 2Co 10:9
a t-ing expectation of judgment, Heb 10:27
It is a t-ing thing to fall into Heb 10:31
was so t-ing that Moses said, Heb 12:21

TERRITORY

plague all your t with frogs. Ex 8:2
enlarges your t as He swore to Dt 19:8
this as their t: From Aroer on Jos 13:16
sent her throughout Israel's t, Jdg 20:6
possess the t-ies of Ephraim Ob 19

TERROR

I will cause the people ... to feel t Ex 23:27
the t of the LORD fell on the 1Sm 11:7
shook, and t from God spread 1Sm 14:15
t of them fell on every Est 9:2
God's t-s are arrayed against me. Jb 6:4
T-s frighten him on every side Jb 18:11
with the t-s of death's shadow Jb 24:17
Put t in them, LORD; Ps 9:20
will be filled with t—t like no other Ps 53:5

t-s of death sweep over me. Ps 55:4
not fear the t of the night, Ps 91:5
Justice ... a t to those who Pr 21:15
against the t of the night. Sg 3:8
away from the t of the LORD and Is 2:19
T is on every side! Jr 20:10; 49:29
who {once} spread t in the land Ezk 32:23
but a great t fell on them, Dn 10:7
are not a t to good conduct Rm 13:3

TERTULLUS

Paul's accuser (Ac 24:1).

TEST

God t-ed Abraham Gn 22:1
Why are you t-ing the LORD? Ex 17:2
for God has come to t you, Ex 20:20
Do not t the LORD your God Dt 6:16
your God is t-ing you to know Dt 13:3
The LORD left them to t Israel, Jdg 3:4
so she came to t Solomon with 2Ch 9:1
when He has t-ed me, I will emerge Jb 23:10
You have t-ed my heart; You have Ps 17:3
T me, LORD, and try me; Ps 26:2
They deliberately t-ed God, Ps 78:18
t-ed you at the waters of Meribah. Ps 81:7
where your fathers t-ed Me; Ps 95:9
t me and know my concerns. Ps 139:23
Silver is {t-ed} in a crucible, Pr 27:21
I will t you with pleasure and Ec 2:1
I will not ask. I will not t the LORD. Is 7:12
stone in Zion, a t-ed stone, Is 28:16
You t whether my heart is with Jr 12:3
Please t your servants for 10 days. Dn 1:12
refined and t them as gold is t-ed. Zch 13:9
T Me in this way," says the LORD Mal 3:10
Do not t the Lord your God. Mt 4:7
approached Him to t Him. Mt 19:3
are you t-ing Me, hypocrites? Mt 22:18
a sign from heaven to t Him. Mk 8:11
and depart in a time of t-ing. Lk 8:13
expert in the law stood up to t Him Lk 10:25
He asked this to t him, for He knew Jn 6:6
did you agree to t the Spirit Ac 5:9
are you now t-ing God by putting Ac 15:10
the fire will t the quality of 1Co 3:13
t-ing the genuineness of your love. 2Co 8:8
T yourselves {to see} if you are 2Co 13:5
t all things. Hold on to what 1Th 5:21
they must also be t-ed first; 1Tm 3:10

He Himself was t-ed and has   Heb 2:18
who has been t-ed in every way   Heb 4:15
knowing that the t-ing of your   Jms 1:3
but t the spirits to determine   1Jn 4:1
have t-ed those who call themselves   Rv 2:2

TESTATOR

death of the t must be established.   Heb 9:16

TESTER

but the LORD is a t of hearts.   Pr 17:3

TESTICLE

rash, scabs, or a crushed t.   Lv 21:20
No man whose {t} have been   Dt 23:1

TESTIFY

Do not t in a lawsuit and go along   Ex 23:2
wicked men t-ied against Naboth   1Kg 21:13
your own lips t against you.   Jb 15:6
Don't t against your neighbor   Pr 24:28
hears the curse but will not t.   Pr 29:24
and our sins t against us.   Is 59:12
T against Me!   Mc 6:3
You therefore t against yourselves   Mt 23:31
John t-ied concerning Him   Jn 1:15
is Another who t-ies about Me,   Jn 5:32
the Scriptures ... t about Me.   Jn 5:39
who sent Me t-ies about Me.   Jn 8:18
the Spirit ... He will t about Me.   Jn 15:26
He who saw this has t-ied so that   Jn 19:35
the prophets t about Him that   Ac 10:43
the Holy Spirit t-ies to me that   Ac 20:23
so you must also t in Rome.   Ac 23:11
Spirit Himself t-ies together   Rm 8:16
because we have t-ied about God   1Co 15:15
when He t-ied in advance to   1Pt 1:11
t-ing that this is the true grace of   1Pt 5:12
the Spirit is the One who t-ies,   1Jn 5:6
For there are three that t: 1Jn 5:7

TESTIMONY

Do not give false t against your   Ex 20:16
t that I will give you into the ark.   Ex 25:16
gave him the two tablets of the t,   Ex 31:18
based on the t of one witness.   Nm 35:30
gave him the t, and made
    him king.   2Kg 11:12
the t of the LORD is trustworthy,   Ps 19:7
He established a t in Jacob   Ps 78:5
Your t-ies are completely reliable;   Ps 93:5

Bind up the t. Seal up the   Is 8:16
To the law and to the t!   Is 8:20
so that by the t of two or three   Mt 18:16
looking for false t against Jesus   Mt 26:59
Yet their t did not agree   Mk 14:59
Why do we need any more t,   Lk 22:71
This is John's t when the Jews   Jn 1:19
heard, yet no one accepts His t.   Jn 3:32
We know that his t is true.   Jn 21:24
as the t about Christ was confirmed   1Co 1:6
On the t of two or three   2Co 13:1
ashamed of the t about our Lord,   2Tm 1:8
the t of men, God's t is greater,   1Jn 5:9
And this is the t: 1Jn 5:11
and you know that our t is true.   3Jn 12
t about Jesus   Rv 1:2,9; 12:17; 19:10; 20:4
Lamb and by the word of their t,   Rv 12:11

TETRARCH

Herod was t of Galilee,   Lk 3:1
Herod the t heard about everything   Lk 9:7
a close friend of Herod the t,   Ac 13:1

THADDAEUS see also JUDAS

Apostle; also called Judas son of James
(not Iscariot) (Mt 10:3; Mk 3:18; Jn 14:22).

THANK (adj)

When you sacrifice a t offering   Lv 22:29
t offerings to the LORD's temple.   2Ch 29:31
Sacrifice a t offering to God,   Ps 50:14

THANK (v)

who can t You in Sheol?   Ps 6:5
only the living can t You,   Is 38:19
Does he t that slave because he   Lk 17:9
I t You that I'm not like other   Lk 18:11
I t my God through Jesus Christ   Rm 1:8
always t my God for you because   1Co 1:4
I t God that I speak in {other}   1Co 14:18
must always t God for you,   2Th 1:3; 2:13
I always t my God when I mention   Phm 4

THANKS

Give t to the LORD;   1Ch 16:8,34
I appointed two ... that gave t.   Neh 12:31
We give t to You, God;   Ps 75:1
Give t to Him and praise His name.   Ps 100:4
Give t to the LORD, for He is good;   Ps 118:1
Give t to the LORD, for He is good.   Ps 136:1
I offer t and praise to You,   Dn 2:23

and He gave t, broke them,	Mt 15:36
and after giving t, He gave it	Mt 26:27
since he gives t to God;	Rm 14:6
gave t, broke it, and said,	1Co 11:24
But t be to God, who gives us	1Co 15:57
T be to God for His indescribable	2Co 9:15
I never stop giving t for you	Eph 1:16
giving t always for everything	Eph 5:20
Give t in everything, for this	1Th 5:18
honor, and t to the One seated	Rv 4:9

THANKFUL
Be t.	Col 3:15

THANKFULNESS
and overflowing with t.	Col 2:7

THANKSGIVING
If he presents it for t,	Lv 7:12
raising my voice in t	Ps 26:7
Let us enter His presence with t;	Ps 95:2
Enter His gates with t and	Ps 100:4
I will offer You a sacrifice of t	Ps 116:17
to You with a voice of t.	Jnh 2:9
may cause t to overflow to God's	2Co 4:15
through prayer and petition with t,	Php 4:6
stay alert in it with t.	Col 4:2
if it is received with t,	1Tm 4:4
and wisdom and t and honor and	Rv 7:12

THEFTS
immoralities, t, false testimonies,	Mt 15:19
sexual immorality, or their t.	Rv 9:21

THEME
moved by a noble t as I recite	Ps 45:1
statutes are {the t of} my song	Ps 119:54

THEMSELVES
But in measuring t by t	2Co 10:12

THEOPHILUS
Addressee of Luke and Acts (Lk1:3; Ac 1:1).

THESSALONICA
City in Macedonia where Paul visited and was persecuted (Ac 17:1); he wrote them two letters (1Th 1:1; 2Th 1:1).

THICK
T swarms of flies went into	Ex 8:24
a t cloud on the mountain,	Ex 19:16
and t darkness on the mountain;	Dt 5:22
He would dwell in t darkness,	1Kg 8:12

Can He judge through t darkness?	Jb 22:13
Clouds and t darkness surround	Ps 97:2

THICKER
finger is t than my father's	1Kg 12:10

THICKET
caught by its horns in the t.	Gn 22:13
up from the t-s of the Jordan to	Jr 50:44
of the temple mount will be a t.	Mc 3:12
for the t-s of the Jordan are	Zch 11:3

THIEF
A t must make full restitution.	Ex 22:3
When you see a t, you make	Ps 50:18
People don't despise the t if he	Pr 6:30
To be a t-'s partner is to hate	Pr 29:24
are rebels, friends of t-ves.	Is 1:23
the shame of a t when he is	Jr 2:26
through the windows like t-ves.	Jl 2:9
If t-ves came to you, if marauders	Ob 5
for every t will be removed	Zch 5:3
and where t-ves break in and steal.	Mt 6:19
you are making it a den of t-ves!	Mt 21:13
what time the t was coming,	Mt 24:43
other way, is a t and a robber.	Jn 10:1
A t comes only to steal and to	Jn 10:10
the poor but because he was a t.	Jn 12:6
t-ves, greedy people, drunkards,	1Co 6:10
The t must no longer steal.	Eph 4:28
come just like a t in the night.	1Th 5:2
as a murderer, a t, an evildoer,	1Pt 4:15
of the Lord will come like a t;	2Pt 3:10
come like a t, and you have no	Rv 3:3
Look, I am coming like a t.	Rv 16:15

THIGH
Place your hand under my t,	Gn 24:2
give the right t to the priest	Lv 7:32
He makes your t shrivel and your	Nm 5:21
curves of your t-s are like	Sg 7:1
good piece—t and shoulder.	Ezk 24:4
its stomach and t-s were bronze,	Dn 2:32
and on His t He has a name	Rv 19:16

THIN
The sickly, t cows ate the	Gn 41:4

THING
I have asked one t from the LORD;	Ps 27:4
Glorious t-s are said about you,	Ps 87:3
are satisfied with good t-s.	Ps 104:28

see wonderful t-s in Your law. Ps 119:18
involved with t-s too great or Ps 131:1
Three t-s are never satisfied; Pr 30:15
all these t-s will be provided Mt 6:33
give good t-s to those who ask Mt 7:11
with God all t-s are possible. Mt 19:26
to God the t-s that are God's. Mt 22:21
were faithful over a few t-s; Mt 25:21
You lack one t: Go, sell you all Mk 10:21
kept all these t-s in her heart. Lk 2:51
apart from Him not one t was created Jn 1:3
even the deep t-s of God. 1Co 2:10
Just one t: live your life in a Php 1:27
But one t I do: forgetting Php 3:13
any praise—dwell on these t-s. Php 4:8
able to do all t-s through Him Php 4:13
and by Him all t-s hold together. Col 1:17
t-s should not be this way. Jms 3:10

THINK *see also* THOUGHT (n)
on my bed, I t of You, I meditate Ps 63:6
son of man, that You t of him? Ps 144:3
person t-s before answering Pr 15:28
as he t-s within himself, so he is. Pr 23:7
But what do you t? A man had two Mt 21:28
What do you t about the Messiah? Mt 22:42
and was **thought** to be the son Lk 3:23
because you t you have eternal Jn 5:39
you **thought** the gift of God Ac 8:20
their t-ing became nonsense, Rm 1:21
not to t of himself more highly than Rm 12:3
anyone among you t-s he is wise 1Co 3:18
If anyone t-s he knows anything, 1Co 8:2
whoever t-s he stands must be 1Co 10:12
a child, I **thought** like a child, 1Co 13:11
don't be childish in your t-ing, 1Co 14:20
beyond all that we ask or t Eph 3:20
my joy by t-ing the same way, Php 2:2
If anyone t-s he is religious, Jms 1:26

THIRD
and then morning: the t day. Gn 1:13
and on the t day He will raise Hs 6:2
killed, and be raised the t day. Mt 16:21
and on the t day He will be Mt 17:23
be resurrected on the t day. Mt 20:19
away again and prayed a t time, Mt 26:44
He asked him the t time, "Simon, Jn 21:17
raised on the t day according to 1Co 15:4
caught up into the t heaven 2Co 12:2

So a t of the earth was burned Rv 8:7
A t of the human race was killed Rv 9:18

THIRST (n)
You gave them water for their t. Neh 9:20
for my t they gave me vinegar Ps 69:21
the wild donkeys quench their t. Ps 104:11
tongues are parched with t. Is 41:17

THIRST (v)
the people t-ed there for water, Ex 17:3
I t for God, the living God. Ps 42:2
They will not hunger or t, Is 49:10
who hunger and t for righteousness, Mt 5:6
no longer will they t; Rv 7:16

THIRSTY
a t land where there was no Dt 8:15
He became very t and called out Jdg 15:18
David was extremely t and said, 2Sm 23:15
and if he is t, give him water Pr 25:21
and like a t one who dreams he Is 29:8
and deprives the t of drink. Is 32:6
and the t land springs of water. Is 35:7
everyone who is t, come to the Is 55:1
I satisfy the t person and feed Jr 31:25
wilderness, in a dry and t land. Ezk 19:13
was t and you gave Me something Mt 25:35
this water will get t again. Jn 4:13
in Me will ever be t again. Jn 6:35
If anyone is t, he should come Jn 7:37
be fulfilled, He said, "I'm t!" Jn 19:28
If he is t, give him something to Rm 12:20
the one who is t should come Rv 22:17

THIRTY
Among the T were: 2Sm 23:24
written for you t sayings about Pr 22:20

THISTLE
produce thorns and t-s for you, Gn 3:18
The t that was in Lebanon once 2Kg 14:9
T-s had come up everywhere, weeds Pr 24:31
from thornbushes or figs from t-s? Mt 7:16

THOMAS
Apostle; sought evidence of resurrection; made confession of faith (Jn 20:24-29).

THORN
It will produce t-s and thistles Gn 3:18
remain will become t-s in your Nm 33:55
They will be t-s in your sides, Jdg 2:3

There are t-s and snares on the	Pr 22:5
a fool is like a stick with t-s,	Pr 26:9
of {burning} t-s under the pot,	Ec 7:6
lily among t-s, so is my darling	Sg 2:2
sown wheat but harvested t-s.	Jr 12:13
I will block her way with t-s;	Hs 2:6
fell among t-s, and the t-s came up	Mt 13:7
twisted together a crown of t-s,	Mt 27:29
t in the flesh was given to me,	2Co 12:7

THORNBUSHES

Are grapes gathered from t or	Mt 7:16

THORNY

slacker's way is like a t hedge,	Pr 15:19

THOUGHT (n)

t of was nothing but evil all the time,	Gn 6:5
understands ... intention of every t	1Ch 28:9
The One who examines the t-s	Ps 7:9
LORD, how profound Your t-s!	Ps 92:5
The LORD knows man's t-s;	Ps 94:11
You understand my t-s from far	Ps 139:2
curse the king even in your t-s,	Ec 10:20
My t-s are not your t-s,	Is 55:8
harbor malicious t-s within you?	Jr 4:14
never entertained the t	Jr 7:31; 19:5; 32:35
reveals His t-s to man, the One	Am 4:13
dismiss any t of the evil day	Am 6:3
But perceiving their t-s, Jesus said,	Mt 9:4
from the heart come evil t-s,	Mt 15:19
knowing the t-s of their hearts,	Lk 9:47
taking every t captive to the	2Co 10:5
surpasses every t, will guard	Php 4:7
the ideas and t-s of the heart.	Heb 4:12

THOUSAND

may you become t-s upon ten t-s.	Gn 24:60
love to a t {generations}	Ex 20:6; 34:7
to the countless t-s of Israel.	Nm 10:36
increase you a t times more,	Dt 1:11
How could one man pursue a t,	Dt 32:30
his t-s, but David his tens of t-s.	1Sm 18:7
David his tens of t-s?"	1Sm 21:11; 29:5
He ordained for a t generations,	1Ch 16:15
answer God once in a t {times}.	Jb 9:3
the cattle on a t hills.	Ps 50:10
God's chariots are tens of t-s,	Ps 68:17
courts than a t {anywhere else}.	Ps 84:10
in Your sight a t years are like	Ps 90:4
Though a t fall at your side and	Ps 91:7

me than t-s of gold and silver	Ps 119:72
And if he lives a t years twice,	Ec 6:6
among a t {people} I have found	Ec 7:28
ten t times ten t stood before Him.	Dn 7:10
out for him ten t points of My	Hs 8:12
be pleased with t-s of rams,	Mc 6:7
Lord comes with t-s of His holy	Jd 14
was countless t-s, plus t-s of t-s.	Rv 5:11

THREAD

tied a scarlet {t} around it,	Gn 38:28
has come, your life t is cut.	Jr 51:13

THREADBARE

their feet and t clothing on	Jos 9:5

THREAT

but a poor man hears no t.	Pr 13:8
will flee} at the t of one,	Is 30:17
Lord, consider their t-s, and grant	Ac 4:29
Saul, still breathing t-s and murder	Ac 9:1

THREATEN

After t-ing them further, they	Ac 4:21
the same way, without t-ing them,	Eph 6:9
when suffering, He did not t,	1Pt 2:23

THREE

and he saw t men standing	Gn 18:2
The t branches are t days.	Gn 40:12
T times a year all your males	Ex 23:17
testimony of two or t witnesses.	Dt 17:6
I am offering you t {choices}.	2Sm 24:12
he struck the ground t times	2Kg 13:18
Now when Job's t friends	Jb 2:11
T things are never satisfied;	Pr 30:15
T things are beyond me;	Pr 30:18
earth trembles under t things;	Pr 30:21
T things are stately in their	Pr 30:29
cord of t strands is not easily	Ec 4:12
Didn't we throw t men, bound,	Dn 3:24
punishing ... for t crimes, even four	Am 1:3
was in the fish t days and t nights,	Jnh 1:17
the great fish t days and t nights,	Mt 12:40
I will make t tabernacles here:	Mt 17:4
testimony of two or t witnesses	Mt 18:16
For where two or t are gathered	Mt 18:20
you will deny Me t times!	Mt 26:34
and rebuild it in t days.	Mt 26:61
killed, and rise after t days.	Mk 8:31
And at t Jesus cried out with a	Mk 15:34

He was unable to see for t days, | Ac 9:9
This happened t times, and then | Ac 10:16
Now these t remain: faith, hope, | 1Co 13:13
or at the most t, each in turn, | 1Co 14:27
pleaded with the Lord t times to | 2Co 12:8
two or t witnesses | 2Co 13:1; Heb 10:28
For there are t that testify: | 1Jn 5:7
was killed by these t plagues | Rv 9:18
There were t gates on the east, | Rv 21:13

THREE-DAY

please let us go on a t trip | Ex 3:18
extremely large city, a t walk. | Jnh 3:3

THRESH

t-ing will continue until grape | Lv 26:5
making them like dust at t-ing. | 2Kg 13:7
drives the t-ing wheel over them. | Pr 20:26
My downtrodden and t-ed people, | Is 21:10
but is not t-ed endlessly. | Is 28:28
will t mountains and pulverize | Is 41:15
young cow that loves to t, | Hs 10:11
because they t-ed Gilead with | Am 1:3
Rise and t, Daughter Zion, for I | Mc 4:13
he who t-es should do so in hope | 1Co 9:10
muzzle an ox that is t-ing grain, | 1Tm 5:18

THRESHING FLOOR

put a fleece of wool here on the t. | Jdg 6:37
She went down {to} the t and | Ru 3:6
Nacon's t, Uzzah reached out | 2Sm 6:6
David bought the t | 2Sm 24:24
site David had prepared on the t | 2Ch 3:1
He will clear His t | Mt 3:12

THRESHOLD

house with her hands on the t. | Jdg 19:27
broken off and lying on the t. | 1Sm 5:4
was crossing the t of the house, | 1Kg 14:17
builds a high t invites injury. | Pr 17:19
to the t of the temple. | Ezk 9:3; 10:4
pillars so that the t-s shake; | Am 9:1

THRIVE

The righteous t like a palm tree | Ps 92:12
the righteous t, a city rejoices | Pr 11:10

THROAT

their t is an open grave; | Ps 5:9
a knife in your t if you have a | Pr 23:2
like cold water to a parched t. | Pr 25:25
Sheol enlarges its t and opens wide | Is 5:14

Keep ... your t from thirst. | Jr 2:25
Their t is an open grave; | Rm 3:13

THRONE

establish the t of David over | 2Sm 3:10
will establish the t of his kingdom | 2Sm 7:13
never fail to have a man on the t | 1Kg 2:4
seated me on the t of my father | 1Kg 2:24
David's t will remain established | 1Kg 2:45
I saw the LORD sitting on His t, | 1Kg 22:19
established His t for judgment. | Ps 9:7
the LORD's t is in heaven. | Ps 11:4
Your t, God, is forever and ever; | Ps 45:6
God is seated on His holy t. | Ps 47:8
justice are the foundation of Your t; | Ps 89:14
Your t has been established from | Ps 93:2
has established His t in heaven, | Ps 103:19
sons will also sit on your t, | Ps 132:12
since a t is established through | Pr 16:12
loyalty he maintains his t. | Pr 20:28
seated on a high and lofty t, | Is 6:1
He will reign on the t of David | Is 9:7
Heaven is My t, and earth is My | Is 66:1
called, The LORD's T, and all | Jr 3:17
They will sit on the t of David, | Jr 17:25
have no one to sit on David's t, | Jr 36:30
t-s were set in place, | Dn 7:9
and will sit on His t and rule. | Zch 6:13
heaven, because it is God's t; | Mt 5:34
Son of Man sits on His glorious t, | Mt 19:28
will also sit on 12 t-s, judging | Mt 19:28
give Him the t of His father | Lk 1:32
whether t-s or dominions or | Col 1:16
Your t, O God, is forever and | Heb 1:8
let us approach the t of grace with | Heb 4:16
at the right hand of God's t. | Heb 12:2
you live—where Satan's t is! | Rv 2:13
and on the t-s sat 24 elders | Rv 4:4
cast their crowns before the t, | Rv 4:10
great white t and One seated on it. | Rv 20:11
flowing from the t of God | Rv 22:1

THROW

t every son ... into the Nile, | Ex 1:22
He has t-n the horse and its rider | Ex 15:1
He threw stones at David | 2Sm 16:6
and he said, "T her down!" | 2Kg 9:33
they threw the man into Elisha's | 2Kg 13:21
a time to t stones and a time to | Ec 3:5
So I threw you down to the earth; | Ezk 28:17

The mountains will be t-n down, Ezk 38:20
worship will be t-n into a furnace Dn 3:11
will be t-n into the lions' den. Dn 6:7
Pick me up and t me into the sea Jnh 1:12
silver and **threw** it into the house Zch 11:13
be cut down and t-n into the fire. Mt 3:10
but to be t-n out and trampled Mt 5:13
gouge it out and t it away. Mt 5:29
here today and t-n into the Mt 6:30
So he **threw** the silver into the Mt 27:5
children's bread and t it to the dogs. Mk 7:27
neck and he were t-n into the sea. Mk 9:42
should be the first to t a stone at her. Jn 8:7
was t-n into the lake of fire Rv 20:10

THRUST

My love t his hand through the Sg 5:4
for the LORD has t him down. Jr 46:15

THUMB

on the t-s of their right hands, Ex 29:20
on the t of his right hand, Lv 14:14
cut off his t-s and big toes. Jdg 1:6

THUMMIM

the Urim and T in the breastpiece Ex 28:30
Your T and Urim belong to Your Dt 33:8
could consult the Urim and T. Ezr 2:63
could consult the Urim and T. Neh 7:65

THUNDER (n)

and the LORD sent t and hail. Ex 9:23
and God answered him in the t. Ex 19:19
Who can understand His mighty t? Jb 26:14
by the LORD of Hosts with t, Is 29:6
"Boanerges" (that is, "Sons of T"); Mk 3:17
heard it and said it was t. Jn 12:29
of lightning, rumblings, and t. Rv 4:5
the seven t-s spoke Rv 10:3
and like the rumbling of loud t. Rv 14:2
and like the rumbling of loud t, Rv 19:6

THUNDER (v)

The LORD t-ed loudly against the 1Sm 7:10
Can you t with a voice like His? Jb 40:9
The LORD t-ed from heaven; Ps 18:13
The storm clouds t-ed; Ps 77:17

THUNDERCLOUD

I answered you from the t. Ps 81:7

THWART

no plan of Yours can be t-ed. Jb 42:2
He t-s the plans of the peoples. Ps 33:10

THYATIRA

Home of Lydia (Ac 16:14); one of the
seven churches (Rv 1:11; 2:18).

TIBERIAS

A city on the Sea of Galilee (Jn 6:23), and
another name for the sea (6:1; 21:1).

TIBNI

Attempted to become king of Israel; killed
by Omri (1Kg 16:21-22).

TIE

t this scarlet cord to the window Jos 2:18
t them around your neck. Pr 6:21
he first t-s up the strong man? Mt 12:29
They t up heavy loads that are Mt 23:4
hands and someone else will t you Jn 21:18

TIGLATH-PILESER

King of Assyria (2Kg 15:29; 16:7,10).

TIGRIS

River of Babylon (Dn 10:4); one of the
four rivers in Eden (Gn 2:14).

TILLER

not a prophet; I am a t of the soil, Zch 13:5

TIMBER

the cedar and cypress t. 1Kg 5:8
to buy t and quarried stone 2Kg 12:12
I have also provided t and stone, 1Ch 22:14
he will give me t to rebuild the Neh 2:8

TIME

Three t-s a year all your males Ex 23:17
march around the city seven t-s, Jos 6:4
Go wash seven t-s in the Jordan 2Kg 5:10
for such a t as this. Est 4:14
a refuge in t-s of trouble. Ps 9:9
will praise the LORD at all t-s; Ps 34:1
their refuge in a t of distress. Ps 37:39
Trust in Him at all t-s, you people; Ps 62:8
give them their food in due t. Ps 145:15
friend loves at all t-s, and a brother Pr 17:17
a righteous man falls seven t-s, Pr 24:16
spoken at the right t is like golden Pr 25:11
a t for every activity under heaven: Ec 3:1
t and chance happen to all of them. Ec 9:11

accomplish it quickly in its **t**.   Is 60:22
animal for seven periods of **t**.   Dn 4:16
for a **t**, **t-s**, and half a **t**.   Dn 7:25; 12:7
In those **t-s** many will rise up   Dn 11:14
sealed until the **t** of the end.   Dn 12:9
is **t** to seek the LORD until He   Hs 10:12
will keep silent at such a **t**,   Am 5:13
is yet for the appointed **t**;   Hab 2:3
The **t** has not come for the house   Hg 1:2
them the exact **t** the star   Mt 2:7
to torment us before the **t**?   Mt 8:29
can't read the signs of the **t-s**.   Mt 16:3
said to him, "but 70 **t-s** seven.   Mt 18:22
Teacher says: My **t** is near;   Mt 26:18
you will deny Me three **t-s**!   Mt 26:34
receive 100 **t-s** more, now at this **t**   Mk 10:30
t came for her to give birth.   Lk 2:6
100 **t-s** {what was sown}.   Lk 8:8
I'll pay back four **t-s** as much!   Lk 19:8
until the **t-s** of the Gentiles   Lk 21:24
womb a second **t** and be born?"   Jn 3:4
at what **t** he got better.   Jn 4:52
My **t** has not yet arrived,   Jn 7:6
a **t** is coming when anyone who   Jn 16:2
He asked him the third **t**,   Jn 21:17
It is not for you to know **t-s**   Ac 1:7
determined their appointed **t-s**   Ac 17:26
At this **t** I will come, and Sarah   Rm 9:9
you agree, for a **t**, to devote   1Co 7:5
Look, now is the acceptable **t**;   2Co 6:2
when the completion of the **t** came,   Gl 4:4
pray at all **t-s** in the Spirit,   Eph 6:18
making the most of the **t**.   Col 4:5
About the **t-s** and the seasons: 1Th 5:1
a testimony at the proper **t**.   1Tm 2:6
the latter **t-s** some will depart   1Tm 4:1
will bring about in His own **t**.   1Tm 6:15
in Christ Jesus before **t** began.   2Tm 1:9
difficult **t-s** will come in the   2Tm 3:1
different **t-s** and in different   Heb 1:1
appear a second **t**, not to bear   Heb 9:28
seems enjoyable at the **t**,   Heb 12:11
to be revealed in the last **t**.   1Pt 1:5
inquired into what **t** or what   1Pt 1:11
that He may exalt you in due **t**,   1Pt 5:6
In the end **t** there will be   Jd 18
because the **t** is near!   Rv 1:3

she was fed for a **t**, **t-s**, and half a **t**.   Rv 12:14
book, because the **t** is near.   Rv 22:10

TIMELY
and a **t** word—how good that is!   Pr 15:23

TIMON
One of the first seven deacons (Ac 6:5).

TIMOTHY
Companion of Paul (Ac 16–20; Rm 16:21; 2Co 1:1; 1Th 1:1; 2Th 1:1; Php 1:1; Phm 1). Sent by Paul to Corinth (1Co 4:17); to Philippi (Php 2:19); to Thessalonica (1Th 3:2). Pastored Ephesian church (1Tm 1:3). Received two letters from Paul (1Tm 1:2; 2Tm 1:2) and a plea to come (4:9).

TIP
to dip the **t** of his finger   Lk 16:24

TIRED
am **t** of putting up with {them}.   Is 1:14
I am **t** of holding it back.   Jr 6:11
I am **t** of showing compassion.   Jr 15:6
I become **t** of holding it in,   Jr 20:9
must not get **t** of doing good,   Gl 6:9
strengthen your **t** hands and   Heb 12:12

TIRZAH
1. One of the daughters of Zelophehad (Nm 26:33; 36:11; Jos 17:3).

2. City in Israel (Jos 12:24; 2Kg 15:14,16; Sg 6:4); capital from Jeroboam until Omri (1Kg 14:17; 15:21,33; 16:8,23-24).

TITLE
not give anyone an {undeserved} **t**.   Jb 32:21
far above ... every **t** given,   Eph 1:21

TITUS
Gentile co-worker with Paul (Gl 2:1-3; 2Co 8:23). Sent to Corinth (2:1-4; 7:13-15; 8:16-17); in charge of church in Crete (Ti 1:5); went to Dalmatia (2Tm 4:10).

TOBIAH
1. Adversary against Nehemiah's efforts to rebuild Jerusalem's walls (Neh 2:10,19; 4:1-9; 6; 13:4-9).

2. Head of a clan who returned (Ezr 2:59-60; Neh 7:61-62).

TODAY

t I have set before you life and	Dt 30:15
t I have become Your Father.	Ps 2:7
T, if you hear His voice:	Ps 95:7
write down t's date, this very day.	Ezk 24:2
Give us t our daily bread.	Mt 6:11
which is here t and thrown into	Mt 6:30
t a Savior, who is Messiah the	Lk 2:11
T as you listen, this Scripture has	Lk 4:21
T salvation has come to this	Lk 19:9
T you will be with Me in paradise.	Lk 23:43
t I have become Your Father.	Ac 13:33
t I have become Your Father,	Heb 1:5; 5:5
T, if you hear His voice,	Heb 3:7
while it is still called t,	Heb 3:13
T, if you hear His voice, do not	Heb 3:15
T if you hear His voice, do not	Heb 4:7
same yesterday, t, and forever.	Heb 13:8

TODDLER

and a t will put his hand into a	Is 11:8

TOE

on the big t-s of their right	Ex 29:20
and on the big t of his right	Lv 14:14
cut off his thumbs and big t-s.	Jdg 1:6
hand and six t-s on each foot	2Sm 21:20
You saw the feet and t-s, partly	Dn 2:41

TOGETHER

Therefore what God has joined t,	Mt 19:6
all things work t for the good	Rm 8:28
and by Him all things hold t.	Col 1:17

TOLA

Issacharite judge (Jdg 10:1-2).

TOLERABLE

It will be more t on the day of	Mt 10:15
it will be more t for Tyre and	Mt 11:22

TOLERATE

not in the king's best interest to t	Est 3:8
I cannot t anyone with haughty	Ps 101:5
and You cannot t wrongdoing.	Hab 1:13
they will not t sound doctrine,	2Tm 4:3
and that you cannot t evil.	Rv 2:2
you t the woman Jezebel, who	Rv 2:20

TOMB

bury me there in the t that I hewed	Gn 50:5
threw the man into Elisha's t.	2Kg 13:21
but not in the t-s of the kings.	2Ch 21:20

carving your t on the height	Is 22:16
You are like whitewashed t-s,	Mt 23:27
t-s also were opened and many	Mt 27:52
and made the t secure by sealing	Mt 27:66
He lived in the t-s.	Mk 5:3
he placed Him in a t cut out of	Mk 15:46
they went to the t at sunrise.	Mk 16:2
stone rolled away from the t.	Lk 24:2
already been in the t four days.	Jn 11:17
out of the t and raised him	Jn 12:17
his t is with us to this day.	Ac 2:29

TOMORROW

Purify yourselves ... for t,	Nm 11:18
to consecrate themselves t,	Jos 7:13
I'll give it t"—when it is there	Pr 3:28
Don't boast about t, for you don't	Pr 27:1
Let us eat and drink, for t we die!	Is 22:13
and t will be like today, only	Is 56:12
and thrown into the furnace t,	Mt 6:30
Therefore don't worry about t,	Mt 6:34
travel today, t, and the next	Lk 13:33
us eat and drink, for t we die.	1Co 15:32
don't even know what t will bring	Jms 4:14

TONS

3,775 t of gold, 37,750 t of silver,	1Ch 22:14

TONGUE

His word was on my t.	2Sm 23:2
and he conceals it under his t,	Jb 20:12
and my t will not utter deceit.	Jb 27:4
they flatter with their t-s.	Ps 5:9
my t sticks to the roof of my	Ps 22:15
Keep your t from evil and your	Ps 34:13
And my t will proclaim Your	Ps 35:28
so that I may not sin with my t;	Ps 39:1
and my t will sing of Your	Ps 51:14
their t-s are sharp swords.	Ps 57:4
lying lips and a deceitful t.	Ps 120:2
Before a word is on my t, You	Ps 139:4
They make their t-s as sharp as a	Ps 140:3
arrogant eyes, a lying t, hands that	Pr 6:17
The t of the righteous is pure	Pr 10:20
a perverse t will be cut out.	Pr 10:31
but a lying t, only a moment.	Pr 12:19
The t that heals is a tree of	Pr 15:4
death are in the power of the t,	Pr 18:21
and a gentle t can break a bone.	Pr 25:15
lying t hates those it crushes,	Pr 26:28

Honey and milk are under your t.   Sg 4:11
and the t of the mute will sing   Is 35:6
every t will swear allegiance.   Is 45:23
and sticking out your t at?   Is 57:4
Their t-s are deadly arrows   Jr 9:8
and spitting, He touched his t.   Mk 7:33
finger in water and cool my t,   Lk 16:24
And t-s, like flames of fire that   Ac 2:3
they deceive with their t-s.   Rm 3:13
and every t will give praise to   Rm 14:11
you use your t for intelligible   1Co 14:9
and every t should confess that   Php 2:11
controlling his t but deceiving   Jms 1:26
but no man can tame the t.   Jms 3:8
must keep his t from evil and   1Pt 3:10

TOOL

Tubal-cain, who made ... iron t-s. Gn 4:22
You must have a digging t in your   Dt 23:13
must not use any iron t on them.   Dt 27:5
which no iron t has been used.   Jos 8:31
or any iron t was heard in the   1Kg 6:7

TOOTH

his teeth are whiter than milk.   Gn 49:12
for eye, t for t, Ex 21:24; Lv 24:20; Dt 19:21
meat was still between
   their teeth,   Nm 11:33
escaped by the skin of my teeth.   Jb 19:20
You break the teeth of the wicked. Ps 3:7
they gnashed their teeth at me.   Ps 35:16
knock the teeth out of their mouths; Ps 58:6
vinegar to the teeth and smoke to   Pr 10:26
like a rotten t or a faltering   Pr 25:19
Your teeth are like a flock of   Sg 4:2; 6:6
love gliding past my lips and teeth! Sg 7:9
children's teeth are set on edge   Jr 31:29
children's teeth are set on edge?   Ezk 18:2
strong, with large iron teeth.   Dn 7:7
for an eye and a t for a t.   Mt 5:38
weeping and gnashing of teeth.   Mt 8:12
and gnashed their teeth at him.   Ac 7:54

TOP

a tower with its t in the sky.   Gn 11:4
split in two from t to bottom;   Mt 27:51
woven in one piece from the t.   Jn 19:23

TOPAZ

of carnelian, t, and emerald;   Ex 28:17
T from Cush cannot compare with   Jb 28:19

are rods of gold set with t.   Sg 5:14
body was like t, his face like   Dn 10:6
eighth beryl, the ninth t,   Rv 21:20

TOPHETH

   Valley outside Jerusalem (2Kg 23:10; Is 30:33; Jr 7:31-32; 19:6-14).

TOPPLE

the mountains t into the depths   Ps 46:2
Nations rage, kingdoms t;   Ps 46:6
He has t-d the mighty from their   Lk 1:52

TORCH

fire pot and a flaming t appeared   Gn 15:17
empty pitcher with a t inside it   Jdg 7:16
He took t-es, turned the foxes   Jdg 15:4
her salvation like a flaming t.   Is 62:1
eyes like flaming t-es,   Dn 10:6
look like t-es; they dart back   Nah 2:4
like a flaming t among sheaves;   Zch 12:6
lanterns, t-es, and weapons.   Jn 18:3
throne were seven fiery t-es,   Rv 4:5
blazing like a t, fell from   Rv 8:10

TORMENT (n)

the t-s of Sheol overcame me;   Ps 116:3
will lie down in a place of t.   Is 50:11
And being in t in Hades, he   Lk 16:23
smoke of their t will go up   Rv 14:11

TORMENT (v)

evil spirit from God is t-ing you. 1Sm 16:15
How long will you t me   Jb 19:2
come here to t us before the time? Mt 8:29
beg You before God, don't t me!   Mk 5:7
those t-ed by unclean spirits   Lk 6:18
of Satan to t me so I would not   2Co 12:7
they will be t-ed day and night   Rv 20:10

TORMENTORS

songs, and our t, for rejoicing: Ps 137:3

TORRENT

the t-s of destruction terrified me. 2Sm 22:5
the t would have swept over us;   Ps 124:4
His breath is like an overflowing t Is 30:28
to sweep her away in a t.   Rv 12:15

TORRENTIAL

it will fall. T rain will come,   Ezk 13:11

TORTURED

Some men were t, not accepting   Heb 11:35

TOSS

and I t and turn until dawn.	Jb 7:4
or t your pearls before pigs,	Mt 7:6
tear it, but t for it, to see	Jn 19:24
t-ed by the waves and blown	Eph 4:14
driven and t-ed by the wind.	Jms 1:6

TOTAL

T darkness is reserved for his	Jb 20:26
gave Jacob over to t destruction	Is 43:28
and t darkness the peoples;	Is 60:2
shatter them with t destruction.	Jr 17:18
it is already a t defeat for you	1Co 6:7

TOTTER

hammer and nails, so it won't t.	Jr 10:4

TOUCH

You must not eat it or t it,	Gn 3:3
Anyone who t-es the mountain	Ex 19:12
they are not to t the holy objects	Nm 4:15
who t-es a body of a person	Nm 19:13
men whose hearts God had t-ed	1Sm 10:26
Suddenly, an angel t-ed him.	1Kg 19:5
When he t-ed Elisha's bones,	2Kg 13:21
Do not t My anointed ones or	1Ch 16:22
no harm will t you in seven.	Jb 5:19
t-es the mountains, and they pour	Ps 104:32
no one who t-es her will go	Pr 6:29
t-ed my mouth {with it} and said:	Is 6:7
Do not t anything unclean;	Is 52:11
out His hand, t-ed my mouth,	Jr 1:9
off without a hand t-ing it,	Dn 2:34
he t-ed me, made me stand up,	Dn 8:18
and with his fold t-es bread,	Hg 2:12
who t-es you t-es the pupil His eye.	Zch 2:8
t-ed him, saying, "I am willing;	Mt 8:3
If I can just t His robe,	Mt 9:21
And as many as t-ed it were made	Mt 14:36
to Him and begged Him to t him.	Mk 8:22
to Him so He might t them,	Mk 10:13
woman this is who is t-ing Him	Lk 7:39
"Who t-ed Me?" Jesus asked.	Lk 8:45
T Me and see, because a ghost	Lk 24:39
aprons that had t-ed his skin	Ac 19:12
do not t any unclean thing,	2Co 6:17
"Don't handle, don't taste, don't t"?	Col 2:21
even an animal t-es	
the mountain,	Heb 12:20

and have t-ed with our hands,	1Jn 1:1
and the evil one does not t him.	1Jn 5:18

TOUGH

{If} you knew I was a t man,	Lk 19:22

TOWEL

took a t, and tied it around Himself.	Jn 13:4

TOWER

a t with its top in the sky.	Gn 11:4
He is a t of salvation for His	2Sm 22:51
Zion, encircle it; count its t-s,	Ps 48:12
a refuge for me, a strong t	Ps 61:3
name of the LORD is a strong t;	Pr 18:10
neck is like the t of David,	Sg 4:4
He built a t in the middle of it	Is 5:2
to build a t, doesn't first sit down	Lk 14:28

TOWN

with its t-s and villages;	Jos 15:45,47
had Beth-shean with its t-s,	Jos 17:11
described it by t-s in a	Jos 18:9
gave these t-s ... to the Levites.	1Ch 6:64
When you enter any t or village,	Mt 10:11
and hound from t to t.	Mt 23:34
went up from the t of Nazareth	Lk 2:4
had gone into t to buy food.	Jn 4:8
and from the t of Bethlehem,	Jn 7:42
in t after t the Holy Spirit	Ac 20:23
to appoint elders in every t:	Ti 1:5

TRACED

offspring will be t through Isaac.	Gn 21:12
Israel's ... rebellion can be t to you.	Mc 1:13

TRACK

from there I will t them down	Am 9:3

TRACKLESS

wander in a t wasteland.	Jb 12:24; Ps 107:40

TRADE

who make a t in God's message	2Co 2:17

TRADERS

When Midianite t passed by,	Gn 37:28
king's t bought them from Kue	1Kg 10:28
crowns, whose t are princes,	Is 23:8
and set it in a city of t.	Ezk 17:4

TRADING

Tarshish was your t partner	Ezk 27:12

TRADITION

disciples break the t of the elders?	Mt 15:2
you keep the t of men.	Mk 7:8
You revoke God's word by your t	Mk 7:13
and keep the t-s just as I	1Co 11:2
I was ... zealous for the t-s	Gl 1:14
empty deceit based on human t,	Col 2:8
hold to the t-s you were taught	2Th 2:15
not according to the t received	2Th 3:6

TRAGEDY

a sickening t	Ec 5:13,16; 6:1

TRAIN

He t-s my hands for war;	2Sm 22:35
who t-s my hands for battle and	Ps 144:1
will never again t for war.	Is 2:4; Mc 4:3
is fully t-ed will be like his teacher.	Lk 6:40
Rather, t yourself in godliness,	1Tm 4:7
have been t-ed to distinguish	Heb 5:14
those who have been t-ed by it.	Heb 12:11
and with hearts t-ed in greed.	2Pt 2:14

TRAINING

them up in the t and instruction	Eph 6:4
t of the body has a limited benefit,	1Tm 4:8
correcting, for t in righteousness,	2Tm 3:16

TRAITOR

you t never betrayed!	Is 33:1
He allots our fields to t-s.	Mc 2:4
Judas Iscariot, who became a t.	Lk 6:16
t-s, reckless, conceited,	2Tm 3:4

TRAMPLE

people t-d him in the gateway,	2Kg 7:20
may he t me to the ground and	Ps 7:5
t them like mud in the streets.	Ps 18:42
Your name we t our enemies.	Ps 44:5
He will t our foes.	Ps 108:13
its wall, and it will be t-d.	Is 5:5
t-d them in My anger	Is 63:3
The Lord has t-d Virgin Daughter	Lm 1:15
it t-d with its feet whatever	Dn 7:7
that time she will be t-d like	Mc 7:10
You t down the nations in wrath.	Hab 3:12
You will t the wicked, for they	Mal 4:3
be thrown out and t-d on by men.	Mt 5:13
pearls before pigs, or they will t them	Mt 7:6
you the authority to t on snakes	Lk 10:19
Jerusalem will be t-d by the	Lk 21:24

who has t-d on the Son of God,	Heb 10:29
they will t the holy city for	Rv 11:2
He will also t the winepress of	Rv 19:15

TRAMPLING (n)

you—{this} t of My courts?	Is 1:12

TRANQUIL

A t heart is life to the body,	Pr 14:30
we may lead a t and quiet life	1Tm 2:2

TRANSFER

darkness and t-red us into the	Col 1:13

TRANSFORM

be t-ed into a different person.	1Sm 10:6
He was t-ed in front of them,	Mt 17:2
be t-ed by the renewing of your	Rm 12:2
are being t-ed into the same image	2Co 3:18
He will t the body of our humble	Php 3:21

TRANSFORMATION

prior to his t he was approved	Heb 11:5

TRANSGRESS

I have t-ed the LORD's command	1Sm 15:24
for they have t-ed teachings,	Is 24:5
ancestors have t-ed against Me	Ezk 2:3
who rebel and t against Me.	Ezk 20:38
because they t My covenant and	Hs 8:1
means one must not t against and	1Th 4:6
woman was deceived and t-ed.	1Tm 2:14

TRANSGRESSION

not remove your t-s and sins.	Jos 24:19
Reveal to me my t and sin.	Jb 13:23
Have I covered my t-s as others	Jb 31:33
I am pure, without t;	Jb 33:9
though I am without t.	Jb 34:6
is the one whose t is forgiven,	Ps 32:1
will confess my t-s to the LORD,	Ps 32:5
Deliver me from all my t-s;	Ps 39:8
has He removed our t-s from us.	Ps 103:12
It is I who sweep away your t-s	Is 43:25
was pierced because of our t-s,	Is 53:5
Tell My people their t,	Is 58:1
For our t-s are with us,	Is 59:12
t-s have been formed into a yoke,	Lm 1:14
and turn from all your t-s,	Ezk 18:30
I give my firstborn for my t,	Mc 6:7
where there is no law, there is no t.	Rm 4:15
sin in the likeness of Adam's t.	Rm 5:14

added because of t-s until the | Gl 3:19
from the t-s {committed} under | Heb 9:15

TRANSGRESSORS

But t will all be eliminated; | Ps 37:38
are convicted by the law as t. | Jms 2:9

TRANSITORY

Let me know how t I am. | Ps 39:4

TRANSLATE

The letter you sent us has been t-d | Ezr 4:18
law ... t-ing and giving the meaning | Neh 8:8
Immanuel ... t-d "God is with us." | Mt 1:23
which is t-d, "Little girl, I | Mk 5:41
which is t-d, "My God, My God, | Mk 15:34
is t-d Son of Encouragement, | Ac 4:36
Tabitha, which is t-d Dorcas. | Ac 9:36
Elymas ... is how his name is t-d, | Ac 13:8

TRANSMIT

so that they do not t holiness | Ezk 44:19

TRANSPARENT

was pure gold, like t glass. | Rv 21:21

TRANSPORT

They are to t the tabernacle | Nm 4:25
on a new cart and t-ed it from | 2Sm 6:3

TRAP

become a snare and a t for you, | Jos 23:13
their gods will be a t to you. | Jdg 2:3
She'll be a t for him, and the | 1Sm 18:21
t-s the wise in their craftiness | Jb 5:13
Let their table ... be a t | Ps 69:22
Protect me from the t they have set | Ps 141:9
like a bird from a fowler's t. | Pr 6:5
like a bird bounding toward a t | Pr 7:22
his lips are a t for his life. | Pr 18:7
a rock to trip over, and a t | Is 8:14
Panic, pit, and t await you, | Jr 48:43
Does a t spring from the ground | Am 3:5
Those who eat your bread will set a t | Ob 7
to t Him by what He said. | Mt 22:15
day will come ... like a t. | Lk 21:35
feasting become a snare and a t, | Rm 11:9
into disgrace and the Devil's t. | 1Tm 3:7
senses and escape the Devil's t, | 2Tm 2:26

TRAVEL

so that they could t day or night. | Ex 13:21
who t on the road, give praise! | Jdg 5:10

You observe my t-s and my rest; | Ps 139:3
don't t that road with them | Pr 1:15
are deserted; t has ceased. | Is 33:8
You t over land and sea to make | Mt 23:15
I must t today, tomorrow, and | Lk 13:33
A nobleman t-ed to a far country | Lk 19:12
we will t to such and such | Jms 4:13

TRAVELING (adj)

no bread, no t bag, no money | Mk 6:8
were Paul's t companions. | Ac 19:29

TRAVELER

t-s kept to the side roads. | Jdg 5:6
for I opened my door to the t. | Jb 31:32
like a t stopping only for the | Jr 14:8

TRAY

golden apples on a silver t. | Pr 25:11

TREACHEROUS

but the t are trapped by their | Pr 11:6
overthrows the words of the t. | Pr 22:12
The t act treacherously; | Is 24:16
and her t sister Judah saw it. | Jr 3:7
a solemn assembly of t people. | Jr 9:2
Her prophets are reckless—t men. | Zph 3:4
looking for a t way to arrest and kill | Mk 14:1

TREACHEROUSLY

those who act t without cause | Ps 25:3
the treacherous deal very t. | Is 24:16
Why then do we act t against one | Mal 2:10

TREACHERY

It's t, Ahaziah! | 2Kg 9:23
abhors a man of bloodshed and t. | Ps 5:6
because of the t he has engaged | Ezk 18:24
Me by committing t against Me: | Ezk 20:27

TREAD

your foot t-s will be yours. | Dt 11:24
an ox while it t-s out grain. | Dt 25:4
the heavens and t-s on the waves | Jb 9:8
they t the winepresses, | Jb 24:11
You will t on the lion and the | Ps 91:13
like a potter who t-s the clay. | Is 41:25
like one who t-s a winepress? | Is 63:2
a shout, like those who t {grapes}, | Jr 25:30
and {you will t} grapes but not | Mc 6:15
ox while it t-s out the grain. | 1Co 9:9

TREASON

Athaliah ... screamed "T! T!" 2Kg 11:14

TREASURE (n)

and the hidden t-s of the sand.	Dt 33:19
showed them his whole t house	2Kg 20:13
search for it more than for hidden t,	Jb 3:21
like one who finds vast t.	Ps 119:162
and search for it like hidden t,	Pr 2:4
there is no limit to their t-s;	Is 2:7
fear of the LORD is Zion's t.	Is 33:6
you trust in your works and t-s,	Jr 48:7
for yourselves t-s on earth,	Mt 6:19
For where your t is, there your	Mt 6:21
The kingdom of heaven is like t,	Mt 13:44
and you will have t in heaven.	Mt 19:21
one who stores up t for himself	Lk 12:21
Now we have this t in clay jars,	2Co 4:7
Him all the t-s of wisdom and	Col 2:3
wealth than the t-s of Egypt,	Heb 11:26
stored up t in the last days!	Jms 5:3

TREASURE (v)

have t-d the words of His mouth	Jb 23:12
I have t-d Your word in my heart	Ps 119:11
Israel as His t-d possession.	Ps 135:4
my words, and t my commands.	Pr 7:1
and what they t does not profit.	Is 44:9
you are a man t-d {by God}.	Dn 10:11
But Mary was t-ing up all these	Lk 2:19

TREASURY

and must go into the LORD's t.	Jos 6:19
is to be paid from the royal t.	Ezr 6:4
and filling their t-ies.	Pr 8:21
not lawful to put it into the temple t,	Mt 27:6
crowd dropped money into the t.	Mk 12:41
who was in charge of her entire t.	Ac 8:27

TREAT

Should he have t-ed our sister	Gn 34:31
he t-ed them like strangers and	Gn 42:7
I must be t-ed as holy among the	Lv 22:32
they t-ed the LORD's offering with	1Sm 2:17
t-ed the LORD with ... contempt	2Sm 12:14
t-ed them outrageously and	Mt 22:6
and be t-ed with contempt?	Mk 9:12
used to t the prophets.	Lk 6:23
outrageously t-ed in Philippi,	1Th 2:2
Yet don't t him as an enemy,	2Th 3:15

TREATMENT

them the required beauty t-s.	Est 2:3
and severe t of the body,	Col 2:23

TREATY

Make no t with them	Dt 7:2
Please make a t with us.	Jos 9:6
Go and break your t with Baasha	1Kg 15:19
So he made a t with him and	1Kg 20:34
and broke a t of brotherhood.	Am 1:9

TREE see also TREE OF LIFE

fruit t-s on the earth bearing fruit	Gn 1:11
the t of the knowledge of good and	Gn 2:9
to eat from any t of the garden.	Gn 2:16
Did you eat from the t that I had	Gn 3:11
hung {on a t} is under God's curse.	Dt 21:23
The t-s set out to anoint a king	Jdg 9:8
in the tops of the balsam t-s,	2Sm 5:24
head was caught fast in the t.	2Sm 18:9
He described t-s, from the cedar	1Kg 4:33
under a broom t and prayed	1Kg 19:4
There is hope for a t: If it is cut	Jb 14:7
He is like a t planted beside	Ps 1:3
like a flourishing native t.	Ps 37:35
all the t-s of the forest will	Ps 96:12
up our lyres on the poplar t-s,	Ps 137:2
whether a t falls to the south	Ec 11:3
Like an apricot t among the t-s	Sg 2:3
climb the palm t and take hold	Sg 7:8
all the t-s of the field will clap	Is 55:12
will be called righteous t-s,	Is 61:3
named you a flourishing olive t,	Jr 11:16
will be like a t planted by water:	Jr 17:8
under every green t	Ezk 6:13
the tall t, and make the low t tall.	Ezk 17:24
There was a t in the middle of	Dn 4:10
and the fig t is withered;	Jl 1:12
every t that doesn't produce good	Mt 3:10
good t produces good fruit,	Mt 7:17
for a t is known by its fruit.	Mt 12:33
At once the fig t withered.	Mt 21:19
this parable from the fig t:	Mt 24:32
look to me like t-s walking.	Mk 8:24
A man had a fig t that was	Lk 13:6
up a sycamore t to see Jesus,	Lk 19:4
you I saw you under the fig t?	Jn 1:50
murdered by hanging Him on a t.	Ac 5:30
Him by hanging Him on a t.	Ac 10:39
grafted into their own olive t?	Rm 11:24

Cursed is everyone ... hung on a t.   Gl 3:13
Can a fig t produce olives,   Jms 3:12
our sins in His body on the t,   1Pt 2:24
t-s in late autumn—fruitless,   Jd 12
as a fig t drops its unripe   Rv 6:13
third of the t-s were burned up,   Rv 8:7
two olive t-s and the two lampstands   Rv 11:4
leaves of the t are for healing   Rv 22:2

TREE OF LIFE

the t in the midst of the garden,   Gn 2:9
also take from the t, and eat,   Gn 3:22
sword to guard the way to the t.   Gn 3:24
She is a t to those who embrace her,   Pr 3:18
The fruit of the righteous is a t,   Pr 11:30
but fulfilled desire is a t.   Pr 13:12
The tongue that heals is a t,   Pr 15:4
victor the right to eat from the t,   Rv 2:7
the t bearing 12 kinds of fruit,   Rv 22:2
that they may have a right to the t   Rv 22:14
will take away his share of the t   Rv 22:19

TREMBLE

saw {it} they t-d and stood at   Ex 20:18
t before Him, all the earth.   1Ch 16:30
Everyone who t-d at the words of   Ezr 9:4
foundations of the mountains t-d;   Ps 18:7
though the earth t-s and the   Ps 46:2
t before Him, all the earth.   Ps 96:9
T, earth, at the presence of the   Ps 114:7
I t in awe of You;   Ps 119:120
earth t-s under three things;   Pr 30:21
I will make the heavens t,   Is 13:13
nations will t at Your presence   Is 64:2
You who t at His word, hear the   Is 66:5
Do you not t before Me, the One   Jr 5:22
people must t in fear before the   Dn 6:26
all the residents of the land t,   Jl 2:1
I heard, and I t-d within;   Hab 3:16
They do not t when they blaspheme   2Pt 2:10

TREMBLING (adj)

LORD will give you a t heart,   Dt 28:65

TREMBLING (n)

t will seize the leaders of Moab;   Ex 15:15
reverential awe, and rejoice with t.   Ps 2:11
Son of man, eat your bread with t   Ezk 12:18
because t and astonishment   Mk 16:8
in fear, and in much t.   1Co 2:3
received him with fear and t.   2Co 7:15

obey your ... masters with fear and t,   Eph 6:5
your own salvation with fear and t.   Php 2:12

TRENCH

he made a t around the altar   1Kg 18:32

TRESPASS

delivered up for our t-es and raised   Rm 4:25
by the one man's t the many died,   Rm 5:15
law came along to multiply the t.   Rm 5:20
not counting their t-es against   2Co 5:19
forgiveness of our t-es, according to   Eph 1:7
you were dead in your t-es and sins   Eph 2:1
when you were dead in t-es   Col 2:13

TRESSES

could be held captive in your t.   Sg 7:5

TRIAL

will not die until he stands t   Nm 35:12
out of another nation, by t-s, signs,   Dt 4:34
keep the poor from getting a fair t   Is 10:2
ones who stood by Me in My t-s.   Lk 22:28
they beat us in public without a t,   Ac 16:37
now I stand on t for the hope   Ac 26:6
physical condition was a t for you,   Gl 4:14
you experience various t-s,   Jms 1:2
Blessed is a man who endures t-s,   Jms 1:12
No one undergoing a t should say,   Jms 1:13
to be distressed by various t-s   1Pt 1:6
how to rescue the godly from t-s   2Pt 2:9

TRIBE

These are the t-s of Israel, 12   Gn 49:28
12 pillars for the 12 t-s of Israel   Ex 24:4
man from each t is to be with you,   Nm 1:4
Do not register ... the t of Levi   Nm 1:49
one t is {missing} in Israel today?   Jdg 21:3
redeemed as the t for Your own   Ps 74:2
He chose instead the t of Judah,   Ps 78:68
where ... the t-s of the LORD, go up   Ps 122:4
raising up the t-s of Jacob and   Is 49:6
these are the names of the t-s: Ezk 48:1
judging the 12 t-s of Israel.   Mt 19:28
{promise} our 12 t-s hope to attain   Ac 26:7
a different t, from which no one   Heb 7:13
To the 12 t-s in the Dispersion.   Jms 1:1
The Lion from the t of Judah,   Rv 5:5
from every t and language and people   Rv 5:9
sealed from every t of the sons   Rv 7:4
inscribed, the names of the 12 t-s   Rv 21:12

TRIBULATION

that time there will be great t,	Mt 24:21
brother and partner in the t,	Rv 1:9
and you will have t for 10 days.	Rv 2:10
I will throw ... into great t,	Rv 2:22
ones coming out of the great t.	Rv 7:14

TRIBUTE

Set aside a t for the LORD from	Nm 31:28
Israelites sent ... king of Moab ... t	Jdg 3:15
the Moabites ... brought t.	2Sm 8:2
all the kingdoms ... offered t	1Kg 4:21
Hoshea ... paid him t money.	2Kg 17:3
Then all Judah brought him t,	2Ch 17:5
t, ... not be imposed on ... priests	Ezr 7:24
kings will bring t to You.	Ps 68:29
around Him bring t to the	Ps 76:11

TRIMMED

got up and t their lamps.	Mt 25:7

TRIP

and his own schemes t him up.	Jb 18:7
over and a rock to t over,	Is 8:14
a rock to t over, yet the one who	Rm 9:33
and a rock that t-s them up.	1Pt 2:8

TRIUMPH

not allowed my enemies to t over	Ps 30:1
I will t! I will divide up	Ps 108:7
he will look in t on his foes.	Ps 112:8
When the righteous t, there is great	Pr 28:12
yet I will t in the LORD;	Hab 3:18
and t when You judge.	Rm 3:4
He t-ed over them by Him.	Col 2:15
Mercy t-s over Judgment.	Jms 2:13

TRIUMPHAL

the godly celebrate in t glory;	Ps 149:5

TRIUMPHANT

enemies, but Israel will be t.	Nm 24:18

TRIUMPHANTLY

shout t to the rock of our	Ps 95:1
Shout t to the LORD, all the	Ps 100:1

TRIVIAL

Is it t in your sight to become	1Sm 18:23
sin of Jeroboam ... were a t matter	1Kg 16:31

TROAS

City in Asia Minor visited by Paul (Ac 16:8-11; 20:6; 2Co 2:12; 2Tm 4:13).

TROPHIMUS

and Tychicus and T from Asia.	Ac 20:4
previously seen T the Ephesian	Ac 21:29
T I left sick at Miletus.	2Tm 4:20

TROUBLE (n)

t-s and afflictions will come	Dt 31:17
mankind is born for t as surely as	Jb 5:7
Man ... is short of days and full of t.	Jb 14:1
a refuge in times of t.	Ps 9:9
Consider my affliction and t,	Ps 25:18
You protect me from t.	Ps 32:7
For t-s without number have	Ps 40:12
is always found in times of t.	Ps 46:1
for me, a refuge in my day of t.	Ps 59:16
have had enough t-s, and my life	Ps 88:3
to the LORD in their t;	Ps 107:6,13,19,28
T and distress have overtaken me,	Ps 119:143
I reveal my t to Him.	Ps 142:2
feet run toward t and they hurry	Pr 1:16
who stirs up t among brothers.	Pr 6:19
The righteous is rescued from t;	Pr 11:8
but if someone looks for t,	Pr 11:27
but t accompanies the income of	Pr 15:6
and their words stir up t.	Pr 24:2
and remember his t no more.	Pr 31:7
and our salvation in time of t.	Is 33:2
they conceive t and give birth	Is 59:4
intercede for you in a time of t,	Jr 15:11
a day of t and distress,	Zph 1:15
Each day has enough t of its own.	Mt 6:34
rescued him out of all his t-s.	Ac 7:10
pass through many t-s on our way	Ac 14:22
such people will have t in this life,	1Co 7:28
write to you again about this is no t	Php 3:1

TROUBLE (v)

evil spirit from God {t-s} you,	1Sm 16:16
dishonestly t-s his household,	Pr 15:27
had dreams that t-d him,	Dn 2:1
Lord, don't t Yourself, since I	Lk 7:6
is t-ing you will pay the penalty,	Gl 5:10

TROUBLED (adj)

Singing songs to a t heart is like	Pr 25:20
she was deeply t by this	Lk 1:29
Why are you t?	Lk 24:38
Now My soul is t. What should	Jn 12:27
Your heart must not be t.	Jn 14:1

heart must not be t or fearful. Jn 14:27
spirit was t within him when Ac 17:16
be easily upset in mind or t, 2Th 2:2

TROUGH

peeled branches in the t-s in front Gn 30:38
and laid Him in a feeding t Lk 2:7
who was lying in the feeding t. Lk 2:16
the feeding t on the Sabbath, Lk 13:15

TRUE

and the message does not come t Dt 18:22
He is righteous and t. Dt 32:4
he says is sure to come t. 1Sm 9:6
You are God; Your words are t, 2Sm 7:28
Israel has been without the t God, 2Ch 15:3
All Your commands are t Ps 119:86,151
sows righteousness, a t reward. Pr 11:18
to teach you t and reliable Pr 22:21
I have found one {t} man, but Ec 7:28
But the LORD is the t God; Jr 10:10
may the LORD be a t and faithful Jr 42:5
carries out t justice between Ezk 18:8
The dream is t, and its Dn 2:45
says this: Render t justice. Zch 7:9
T instruction was in his mouth, Mal 2:6
The t light, who gives light to Jn 1:9
when the t worshipers will Jn 4:23
of the One who sent Him is t, Jn 7:18
My judgment is t, because I am Jn 8:16
I am the t vine, and My Father Jn 15:1
You, the only t God, and the One Jn 17:3
His testimony is t Jn 19:35; 21:24
and {t} circumcision is not Rm 2:28
God must be t, but everyone is a Rm 3:4
good report; as deceivers yet t; 2Co 6:8
whatever is t, whatever is Php 4:8
This testimony is t. So, rebuke them Ti 1:13
(only a model of the t one) Heb 9:24
that this is the t grace of God. 1Pt 5:12
which is t in Him and in you, 1Jn 2:8
and is t and is not a lie; 1Jn 2:27
so that we may know the t One. 1Jn 5:20
Holy One, the T One, the One who Rv 3:7
the faithful and t Witness, Rv 3:14
rider is called Faithful and T, Rv 19:11
these words are faithful and t. Rv 21:5; 22:6

TRULY

T You are the Son of God! Mt 14:33
t in him the love of God is perfected. 1Jn 2:5

TRUMPET

the sound of the t grew louder Ex 19:19
Make two t-s of hammered silver Nm 10:2
priests carry seven ram's-horn t-s Jos 6:4
Gideon's men blew their 300 t-s, Jdg 7:22
were to blow t-s before the ark 1Ch 15:24
were 120 priests blowing t-s. 2Ch 5:12
Wherever you hear the t sound, Neh 4:20
With t-s and the blast of the ram's Ps 98:6
Praise Him with t blast; Ps 150:3
When a t sounds, listen! Is 18:3
hears the sound of the t but ignores Ezk 33:4
horn in Gibeah, the t in Ramah; Hs 5:8
give ... don't sound a t before you, Mt 6:2
send out His angels with a loud t, Mt 24:31
if the t makes an unclear sound, 1Co 14:8
at the last t. For the t will sound, 1Co 15:52
with the t of God, and the dead in 1Th 4:16
behind me a loud voice like a t Rv 1:10
seven t-s were given to them. Rv 8:2

TRUST (n)

Put no more t in man, who has Is 2:22
put His t in God; let God rescue Mt 27:43

TRUST (v)

Hezekiah t-ed in the LORD God 2Kg 18:5
you now t in Egypt, the stalk 2Kg 18:21
he t-s in is in a spider's web. Jb 8:14
and t in the LORD. Ps 4:5
who know Your name t in You Ps 9:10
they t-ed, and You rescued them. Ps 22:4
t in You. Do not let me be disgraced. Ps 25:2
t-ed in the LORD without wavering. Ps 26:1
idols, but I t in the LORD. Ps 31:6
T in the LORD and do what is good; Ps 37:3
t in Him, and He will act, Ps 37:5
For I do not t in my bow, and my Ps 44:6
When I am afraid, I will t in You. Ps 56:3
in God I t; ... What can man do Ps 56:4,11
T in Him at all times, you Ps 62:8
happy is the person who t-s in You! Ps 84:12
fortress, my God, in whom I t. Ps 91:2
Israel, t in the LORD! Ps 115:9
in the LORD than to t in man. Ps 118:8
taunts me, for I t in Your word. Ps 119:42

T in the LORD with all your | Pr 3:5
t-ing in his riches will fall, | Pr 11:28
who t-s in the LORD will be happy. | Pr 16:20
T-ing an unreliable person in a | Pr 25:19
t-s in the LORD will prosper. | Pr 28:25
one who t-s in himself is a fool, | Pr 28:26
heart of her husband t-s in her, | Pr 31:11
I will t {Him} and not be afraid. | Is 12:2
those who t in the LORD will renew | Is 40:31
forgotten Me and t-ed in Falsehood. | Jr 13:25
Blessed is the man who t-s in the | Jr 17:7
Because you have t-ed in Me, | Jr 39:18
but he t-s in his righteousness | Ezk 33:13
rescued His servants who t-ed | Dn 3:28
uninjured, for he t-ed in his God. | Dn 6:23
don't t in a close companion. | Mc 7:5
to some who t-ed in themselves | Lk 18:9
so that we would not t in ourselves, | 2Co 1:9
Again, I will t in Him. | Heb 2:13

TRUSTWORTHY

the testimony of the LORD is t, | Ps 19:7
are righteous and altogether t. | Ps 119:138
but the t keeps a confidence. | Pr 11:13
a t courier {brings} healing. | Pr 13:17
but who can find a t man? | Pr 20:6
The wounds of a friend are t, | Pr 27:6
I have appointed t witnesses | Is 8:2
This saying is t | 1Tm 1:15; 3:1; 4:9
This saying is t | 2Tm 2:11; Ti 3:8

TRUTH

worship Him in sincerity and t. | Jos 24:14
swear ... to tell me ... the t | 1Kg 22:16
have not spoken the t about Me, | Jb 42:7
acknowledges the t in his heart | Ps 15:2
Guide me in Your t and teach me, | Ps 25:5
love and t will always guard | Ps 40:11
T will spring up from the earth, | Ps 85:11
The entirety of Your word is t, | Ps 119:160
Buy—and do not sell—t, | Pr 23:23
to accurately write words of t. | Ec 12:10
T has gone from My mouth, | Is 45:23
For t has stumbled in the public | Is 59:14
will be blessed by the God of t, | Is 65:16
T has perished—it has disappeared | Jr 7:28
no one tells the t. | Jr 9:5
horn will throw t to the ground | Dn 8:12
There is no t, no faithful love, | Hs 4:1
Speak t to one another; | Zch 8:16

from the Father, full of grace and t. | Jn 1:14
grace and t came through Jesus | Jn 1:17
worship the Father in spirit and t. | Jn 4:23
the t, and the t will set you free. | Jn 8:32
because there is no t in him. | Jn 8:44
am the way, the t, and the life. | Jn 14:6
He is the Spirit of t. | Jn 14:17
Spirit of t who proceeds from | Jn 15:26
When the Spirit of t comes, He will
    guide you into all the t. | Jn 16:13
Sanctify them by the t; Your word | Jn 17:17
"What is t?" said Pilate. | Jn 18:38
I'm speaking words of t | Ac 26:25
exchanged the t of God for a lie | Rm 1:25
I speak the t in Christ—I am not | Rm 9:1
but rejoices in the t; | 1Co 13:6
not ... to do anything against the t, | 2Co 13:8
But speaking the t in love, | Eph 4:15
Speak the t, each one to his | Eph 4:25
with t like a belt around your | Eph 6:14
did not accept the love of the t | 2Th 2:10
pillar and foundation of the t. | 1Tm 3:15
teaching the word of t, | 2Tm 2:15
to come to a knowledge of the t. | 2Tm 3:7
any among you strays from the t, | Jms 5:19
the way of t will be blasphemed. | 2Pt 2:2
and are not practicing the t. | 1Jn 1:6
and the t is not in us. | 1Jn 1:8
or speech, but in deed and t; | 1Jn 3:18
From this we know the Spirit of t | 1Jn 4:6
whom I love in t | 2Jn 1; 3Jn 1
you are walking in the t. | 3Jn 3

TRUTHFUL

T lips endure forever, but a lying | Pr 12:19
A t witness rescues lives, | Pr 14:25
we know that You are t and teach | Mt 22:16

TRUTHFULLY

lying instead of speaking t. | Ps 52:3
should speak My word t, | Jr 23:28
and teach t the way of God. | Mt 22:16

TRY

have t-ied me and found nothing | Ps 17:3
Test me, LORD, and t me; | Ps 26:2
fathers tested Me; they t-ied Me, | Ps 95:9
also t the patience of my God? | Is 7:13
fathers tested Me, t-ied {Me}, | Heb 3:9

TUBAL

Son of Japheth (Gn 10:2; 1Ch 1:5); descendants were prophesied about (Is 66:19; Ezk 27:13; 32:26; 38:3; 39:1).

TUBAL-CAIN

Son of Lamech; ancestor of metalworkers (Gn 4:22).

TUCK

he t-ed his mantle under his belt	1Kg 18:46
T your mantle under your belt	2Kg 4:29; 9:1

TUMOR

boils of Egypt, t-s, a festering	Dt 28:27
and its territory with t-s.	1Sm 5:6
Five gold t-s and five gold mice	1Sm 6:4

TUMULT

and the t of the nations.	Ps 65:7
Listen, a t on the mountains,	Is 13:4
the t of their voice resounds,	Jr 51:55

TUNIC

Make t-s, ...for Aaron's sons	Ex 28:40
He is to wear a holy linen t,	Lv 16:4
took the t, which was seamless,	Jn 19:23

TUNNEL

Hezekiah's ... pool and the t	2Kg 20:20

TURBAN

make a t of fine linen,	Ex 28:39
place the holy diadem on the t.	Ex 29:6
holy diadem, on the front of the t,	Lv 8:9
were like a robe and a t.	Jb 29:14
Remove the t, and take off the	Ezk 21:26
So a clean t was placed on his head,	Zch 3:5

TURMOIL

Why this t within me?	Ps 42:5,11; 43:5
Lord than great treasure with t.	Pr 15:16
rest to the earth but t to ... Babylon.	Jr 50:34
you infamous one full of t.	Ezk 22:5

TURN

in the Nile was t-ed to blood.	Ex 7:20
T from Your great anger and	Ex 32:12
Do not t to idols or make cast	Lv 19:4
Do not t to mediums or consult	Lv 19:31
you are not to t aside to the	Dt 5:32
they will t your sons away	Dt 7:4
He t-ed the curse into a blessing	Dt 23:5
Do not t aside to the right or	Dt 28:14
Do not t from it to the right or	Jos 1:7
and they t from their sins	1Kg 8:35
T from your evil ways and keep	2Kg 17:13
he did not t to the right or the	2Kg 22:2
He will not t {His} face away	2Ch 30:9
and t-s away from evil.	Jb 1:8; 2:3
to t from evil is understanding.	Jb 28:28
T, Lord! Rescue me;	Ps 6:4
All have t-ed away; all alike have	Ps 14:3
and have not t-ed from my God to	Ps 18:21
T to me and be gracious to me,	Ps 25:16
You t-ed my lament into dancing;	Ps 30:11
He t-ed to me and heard my cry	Ps 40:1
T Your face away from my sins	Ps 51:9
we will not t away from You;	Ps 80:18
t-ed from Your burning anger.	Ps 85:3
T to me and be gracious to me.	Ps 86:16
T my heart to Your decrees and	Ps 119:36
T to me and be gracious to me,	Ps 119:132
If you t to my discipline,	Pr 1:23
but fools hate to t from evil.	Pr 13:19
A gentle answer t-s away anger,	Pr 15:1
wherever he t-s, he succeeds.	Pr 17:8
A door t-s on its hinge, and a	Pr 26:14
t back, and be healed.	Is 6:10
T to Me and be saved, all the	Is 45:22
He was like one people t-ed away	Is 53:3
we all have t-ed to our own way;	Is 53:6
T, each one from his evil way of	Jr 35:15
He spread a net ... and t-ed me	Lm 1:13
creatures did not t as they moved;	Ezk 1:9
if you warn ... and he does not t	Ezk 3:19
Repent and t away from your	Ezk 14:6
if a wicked person t-s from the	Ezk 18:27
should t from his way and live.	Ezk 33:11
t to Me with all your heart,	Jl 2:12
He may t and relent and leave a	Jl 2:14
The sun will be t-ed to darkness	Jl 2:31
Each must t from his evil ways	Jnh 3:8
Who knows? God may t and relent;	Jnh 3:9
{they cry,} but no one t-s back.	Nah 2:8
And he will t the hearts of fathers	Mal 4:6
right cheek, t the other to him	Mt 5:39
t, and tear you to pieces.	Mt 7:6
I came to t a man against his	Mt 10:35
understand with their hearts and t	Mt 13:15
to t the hearts of fathers to	Lk 1:17
you, when you have t-ed back,	Lk 22:32

Stop t-ing My Father's house into	Jn 2:16
where He had t-ed the water into	Jn 4:46
but your sorrow will t to joy.	Jn 16:20
sun will be t-ed to darkness,	Ac 2:20
Therefore repent and t back,	Ac 3:19
saw him and t-ed to the Lord.	Ac 9:35
who believed t-ed to the Lord.	Ac 11:21
we now t to the Gentiles!	Ac 13:46
those who t to God from among	Ac 15:19
that they may t from darkness to	Ac 26:18
they should repent and t to God,	Ac 26:20
have t-ed away, together they	Rm 3:12
t that one over to Satan for the	1Co 5:5
{and are t-ing} to a different gospel	Gl 1:6
how you t-ed to God from idols	1Th 1:9
truth and will t aside to myths.	2Tm 4:4
variation or shadow cast by t-ing.	Jms 1:17
that whoever t-s a sinner from	Jms 5:20
must t away from evil and do good.	1Pt 3:11
the waters to t them into blood,	Rv 11:6

TURTLEDOVE

may take two t-s or two young	Lv 12:8
is to bring two t-s or two young	Nm 6:10
the t-'s cooing is heard in our	Sg 2:12
pair of t-s or two young pigeons	Lk 2:24

TWELVE see also 12

T teams of oxen were in front of	1Kg 19:19
at the table with the T.	Mt 26:20
one of the T, suddenly arrived	Mt 26:47
He appointed the T:	Mk 3:16
When He was alone with the T,	Mk 4:10
"T," they told Him.	Mk 8:19
went out to Bethany with the T.	Mk 11:11
one of the T—the one who	Mk 14:20
who was numbered among the T.	Lk 22:3
and one of the T named Judas was	Lk 22:47
Didn't I choose you, the T?	Jn 6:70
Then the T summoned the whole	Ac 6:2
to Cephas, then to the T.	1Co 15:5

TWICE

For he has cheated me t now.	Gn 27:36
they gathered t as much food,	Ex 16:22
struck the rock t with his staff,	Nm 20:11
worth t the wages of a hired	Dt 15:18
who had appeared to him t.	1Kg 11:9
if he lives a thousand years t,	Ec 6:6
you make him t as fit for hell	Mt 23:15

before the rooster crows t,	Mk 14:30
I fast t a week; I give a tenth	Lk 18:12
fruitless, t dead, pulled out	Jd 12

TWILIGHT

will slaughter the animals at t.	Ex 12:6
and at t offer the other lamb.	Ex 29:39
t on the fourteenth day of the	Lv 23:5
day of this month at t;	Nm 9:3
adulterer's eye watches for t,	Jb 24:15
at noon as though it were t;	Is 59:10

TWIN

were indeed t-s in her womb.	Gn 25:24
there were t-s in her womb.	Gn 38:27
each one having a t,	Sg 4:2; 6:6
two fawns, t-s of a gazelle,	Sg 4:5; 7:3
Thomas (called "T"), was not	Jn 20:24
with the T Brothers as its	Ac 28:11

TWINKLING

in a moment, in the t of an eye,	1Co 15:52

TWIST

and must t off its head and burn	Lv 1:15
of the wise and t-s the words	Dt 16:19
They t my words all day long;	Ps 56:5
with t-ed minds are detestable	Pr 11:20
insight, but a t-ed mind is	Pr 12:8
and t-ing a nose draws blood,	Pr 30:33
young camel t-ing and turning	Jr 2:23
soldiers also t-ed together a crown	Jn 19:2
and unstable t them to their own	2Pt 3:16

TWO

God made the t great lights	Gn 1:16
into the ark t of every living	Gn 6:19
T nations are in your womb;	Gn 25:23
He gave him the t tablets of the	Ex 31:18
may take t turtledoves or t young	Lv 12:8
He wrote them on t stone tablets,	Dt 5:22
gave me the t stone tablets,	Dt 9:10
the testimony of t or three	Dt 17:6; 19:15
for true wisdom has t sides.	Jb 11:6
T things I ask of You; don't	Pr 30:7
The leech has t daughters:	Pr 30:15
than t handfuls with effort and	Ec 4:6
T are better than one because	Ec 4:9
with t he covered his face,	Is 6:2
They will no longer be t nations	Ezk 37:22
had t horns. The t horns were long,	Dn 8:3

Can t walk together without	Am 3:3
to go one mile, go with him t.	Mt 5:41
No one can be a slave of t masters,	Mt 6:24
Aren't t sparrows sold for a	Mt 10:29
five loaves and t fish here,	Mt 14:17
than to have t eyes and be	Mt 18:9
the testimony of t or three	Mt 18:16
If t of you on earth agree about	Mt 18:19
where t or three are gathered	Mt 18:20
are no longer t, but one flesh.	Mt 19:6
A man had t sons. He went to	Mt 21:28
depend on these t commandments.	Mt 22:40
Then t men will be in the field:	Mt 24:40
Then t criminals were crucified	Mt 27:38
was split in t from top to	Mt 27:51
dropped in t tiny coins worth	Mk 12:42
turtledoves or t young pigeons	Lk 2:24
The one who has t shirts must	Lk 3:11
said, "look, here are t swords."	Lk 22:38
t of them were on their way to	Lk 24:13
the witness of t men is valid.	Jn 8:17
The t will become one flesh.	1Co 6:16
the testimony of t or three	2Co 13:1
women represent the t covenants.	Gl 4:24
one new man from the t,	Eph 2:15
and the t will become one flesh.	Eph 5:31
supported by t or three witnesses.	1Tm 5:19
I will empower my t witnesses,	Rv 11:3
he had t horns like a lamb,	Rv 13:11

TWO-EDGED

and a t sword in their hands,	Ps 149:6
and sharper than any t sword,	Heb 4:12
His mouth came a sharp t sword;	Rv 1:16
who has the sharp, t sword says:	Rv 2:12

TYCHICUS

Paul's fellow worker (Ac 20:4; Eph 6:21; Col 4:7; 2Tm 4:12; Ti 3:12).

TYPE

vineyard with two t-s of seed;	Dt 22:9

TYRANNY

were under the t of the Devil,	Ac 10:38

TYRE

Phoenician port city (Jos 19:29; Ps 87:4; Neh 13:16); associated with Sidon (Ezr 3:7; Jl 3:4; 1Ch 22:4; Mt 11:21; Ac 12:20). Home of Hiram (2Sm 5:11; 2Kg 5:1). Proph-

esied against (Is 23:1; Jr 25:22; 47:4; Ezk 26:2–28:18; Am 1:9; Zch 9:2). Jesus visited (Mt 15:21; Mk 3:8; 7:24); used it as an example (Mt 11:21). Paul visited (Ac 21:3,7).

U

UGLY

u cows ate the first seven	Gn 41:20

ULAI

Canal north of Susa; scene of Daniel's visions (Dn 8:2,16).

ULTERIOR

he brings it with u motives!	Pr 21:27

ULTIMATELY

will not be blessed u.	Pr 20:21

UMBILICAL

your u cord wasn't cut on the	Ezk 16:4

UNADULTERATED

desire the u spiritual milk,	1Pt 2:2

UNAFRAID

be firmly established and u.	Jb 11:15
you want to be u of the authority?	Rm 13:3

UNANIMOUSLY

the prophets are u favorable for	1Kg 22:13
we have u decided to select men	Ac 15:25

UNAPPROACHABLE

dwelling in u light, whom none	1Tm 6:16

UNAUTHORIZED

must not offer u incense on it,	Ex 30:9
and presented u fire before the	Lv 10:1
Any u person who comes near {it}	Nm 1:51

UNAVOIDABLE

there are many words, sin is u,	Pr 10:19

UNBELIEF

miracles there because of their u.	Mt 13:58
And He was amazed at their u.	Mk 6:6
I do believe! Help my u.	Mk 9:24
He rebuked their u and hardness	Mk 16:14

will their **u** cancel God's · Rm 3:3
not waver in **u** at God's promise · Rm 4:20
they were broken off by **u**, · Rm 11:20
ignorance that I had acted in **u**, · 1Tm 1:13
unable to enter because of **u**. · Heb 3:19

UNBELIEVER

let him be like an **u** and a tax · Mt 18:17
assign him a place with the **u**-s. · Lk 12:46
Don't be an **u**, but a believer. · Jn 20:27
against brother, and that before **u**-s! · 1Co 6:6
But if the **u** leaves, let him leave. · 1Co 7:15
If one of the **u**-s invites you over · 1Co 10:27
not to believers but to **u**-s. · 1Co 14:22
has blinded the minds of the **u**-s · 2Co 4:4
Do not be mismatched with **u**-s. · 2Co 6:14
have in common with an **u**? · 2Co 6:15
faith and is worse than an **u**. · 1Tm 5:8
cowards, **u**-s, vile, murderers · Rv 21:8

UNBELIEVING (adj)

You **u** and rebellious generation! · Mt 17:17
If any brother has an **u** wife, · 1Co 7:12
defiled and **u** nothing is pure; · Ti 1:15
for the **u**, The stone that the · 1Pt 2:7

UNBLEMISHED

You must have an **u** animal, · Ex 12:5
of one **u** year-old male · Nm 6:14
are to present an **u** male goat as · Ezk 43:22

UNCERTAINTY

set their hope on the **u** of wealth, · 1Tm 6:17

UNCHANGEABLE

so that through two **u** things, · Heb 6:18

UNCIRCUMCISED

But no **u** person may eat it. · Ex 12:48
and if their **u** hearts will be · Lv 26:41
who is this **u** Philistine that · 1Sm 17:26
their ear is **u**, so they cannot · Jr 6:10
all the circumcised yet **u**: · Jr 9:25
house of Israel is **u** in heart. · Jr 9:26
and be laid to rest with the **u**! · Ezk 32:19
u in both heart and flesh, · Ezk 44:7
people with **u** hearts and ears! · Ac 7:51
A man who is physically **u**, · Rm 2:27
by faith and the **u** through faith. · Rm 3:30
faith ... Abraham had while still **u**. · Rm 4:12
Was anyone called while **u**? · 1Co 7:18

with the gospel for the **u**, · Gl 2:7
called "the **u**" by those called · Eph 2:11

UNCIRCUMCISION

your circumcision has become **u**. · Rm 2:25
matter and **u** does not matter, · 1Co 7:19
circumcision nor **u** accomplishes · Gl 5:6
circumcision and **u**, barbarian, · Col 3:11

UNCLE

Jacob saw his **u** Laban's daughter · Gn 29:10
His **u** or cousin may redeem him, · Lv 25:49
daughter of ... the **u** of Mordecai · Est 2:15

UNCLEAN

clean animals, **u** animals, birds, · Gn 7:8
{if} someone touches anything **u** · Lv 5:2
between ... the clean and the **u**, · Lv 10:10
These will make you **u**. · Lv 11:24
who are clean or **u** may eat it, · Dt 12:15
I am a man of **u** lips and live among · Is 6:5
and the **u** will no longer enter · Is 52:1
between the clean and the **u**. · Ezk 44:23
and the **u** spirit from the land. · Zch 13:2
gave them authority over **u** spirits, · Mt 10:1
He commands even the **u** spirits, · Mk 1:27
Whenever the **u** spirits saw Him, · Mk 3:11
u spirits ... entered the pigs · Mk 5:13
eating their bread with **u** ... hands. · Mk 7:2
I have never eaten anything ... **u**! · Ac 10:14
that I must not call any person ... **u**. · Ac 10:28
am persuaded ... that nothing is **u** · Rm 14:14
your children would be **u**, · 1Co 7:14
do not touch any **u** thing, · 2Co 6:17
I saw three **u** spirits like frogs · Rv 16:13

UNCLEANNESS

Her **u** {stains} her skirts. · Lm 1:9
I will save you from all your **u**. · Ezk 36:29
and have not repented of the **u**, · 2Co 12:21

UNCLEAR

if the trumpet makes an **u** sound, · 1Co 14:8

UNCLOTHED

do not want to be **u** but clothed, · 2Co 5:4

UNCORRUPTED

imperishable, **u**, and unfading, · 1Pt 1:4

UNCOVER (v)

go in and **u** his feet, and lie down. · Ru 3:4
He **u**-s their ears at that time · Jb 33:16

UNCOVERED (adj)

with {his} eyes u:	Nm 24:4,16
covered that won't be u,	Mt 10:26
with her head u dishonors her	1Co 11:5
pray to God with her head u?	1Co 11:13

UNCULTIVATED

| to let it rest and leave it u, | Ex 23:11 |
| {the land} u in the seventh | Neh 10:31 |

UNCUT

| Use u stones to build the altar | Dt 27:6 |
| an altar of u stones on which no | Jos 8:31 |

UNDEFILED

priest we need: holy, innocent, u,	Heb 7:26
and the marriage bed kept u,	Heb 13:4
Pure and u religion before our	Jms 1:27

UNDENIABLE

| these things are u, you must | Ac 19:36 |

UNDER

LORD put his enemies u his feet.	1Kg 5:3
You put everything u his feet:	Ps 8:6
there is nothing new u the sun.	Ec 1:9
each man will sit u his grapevine	Mc 4:4
to be put u a basket or u a bed?	Mk 4:21
you I saw you u the fig tree?	Jn 1:50
no other name u heaven given to	Ac 4:12
who sinned u the law will be	Rm 2:12
you are not u law but u grace.	Rm 6:14
to those u the law, like one u the	1Co 9:20
has put everything u His feet.	1Co 15:27
born of a woman, born u the law,	Gl 4:4
And He put everything u His feet	Eph 1:22
and on earth and u the earth	Php 2:10
subjected everything u his feet.	Heb 2:8
or on earth or u the earth was	Rv 5:3

UNDERGARMENTS

| Make them linen u to cover | Ex 28:42 |

UNDERGOING

| No one u a trial should say, | Jms 1:13 |

UNDERMINE

| but wickedness u-s the sinner. | Pr 13:6 |

UNDERNEATH

| and u are the everlasting arms. | Dt 33:27 |
| in his tent, with the money u. | Jos 7:22 |

UNDERSTAND

they will not u one another's	Gn 11:7
u-stood the times and knew what	1Ch 12:32
LORD ... u-s the intention of every	1Ch 28:9
I spoke about things I did not u,	Jb 42:3
Then I u-stood their destiny.	Ps 73:17
I u more than the elders because	Ps 119:100
You u my thoughts from far away.	Ps 139:2
for u-ing a proverb or a parable,	Pr 1:6
then you will u the fear of the LORD	Pr 2:5
Then you will u righteousness,	Pr 2:9
Evil men do not u justice,	Pr 28:5
Keep listening, but do not u;	Is 6:9
shut ... their minds so they cannot u.	Is 44:18
and whose speech you do not u.	Jr 5:15
whose words you cannot u.	Ezk 3:6
Daniel also u-stood visions and	Dn 1:17
u that the vision refers to ... the end.	Dn 8:17
u-stood from ... Jeremiah	Dn 9:2
none of the wicked will u, but	Dn 12:10
Let whoever is wise u these things,	Hs 14:9
listen and listen, yet never u;	Mt 13:14
u with their hearts and turn back	Mt 13:15
Have you u-stood all these things?	Mt 13:51
Then they u-stood that He did not	Mt 16:12
the disciples u-stood that He spoke	Mt 17:13
holy place" (let the reader u),	Mt 24:15
they did not u this statement,	Mk 9:32
Then He opened their minds to u	Lk 24:45
Why don't you u what I say?	Jn 8:43
did not u these things at first.	Jn 12:16
What I'm doing you don't u now,	Jn 13:7
Do you u what you're reading?	Ac 8:30
u with their heart, and be converted	Ac 28:27
u-stood through what He has made.	Rm 1:20
no one who u-s, there is no one	Rm 3:11
For I do not u what I am doing,	Rm 7:15
But I ask, "Did Israel not u?"	Rm 10:19
those who have not heard will u.	Rm 15:21
and u all mysteries and all	1Co 13:2
but u what the Lord's will is.	Eph 5:17
he is conceited, u-ing nothing,	1Tm 6:4
By faith we u that the universe	Heb 11:3
about things they don't u,	2Pt 2:12

promise, as some u delay, but is 2Pt 3:9
some matters that are hard to u. 2Pt 3:16

UNDERSTANDING (adj)
nation is indeed a wise and u people. Dt 4:6
I will give you a wise and u heart, 1Kg 3:12
Who is wise and u among you? Jms 3:13

UNDERSTANDING (n)
LORD has given them wisdom and u Ex 36:1
Solomon ... u as {vast} as the sand 1Kg 4:29
counsel and u are His. Jb 12:13
and where is u located? Jb 28:12,20
and to turn from evil is u. Jb 28:28
Who ... gave the mind u? Jb 38:36
I gain u from Your precepts; Ps 119:104
and gives u to the inexperienced. Ps 119:130
Give me u, and I will live. Ps 119:144
His u is infinite. Ps 147:5
and do not rely on your own u; Pr 3:5
established the heavens by u. Pr 3:19
whatever else you get, get u. Pr 4:7
knowledge of the Holy One is u. Pr 9:10
acquire u—it is preferable to silver. Pr 16:16
A fool does not delight in u, Pr 18:2
Buy ... wisdom, instruction, and u. Pr 23:23
A house ... is established by u; Pr 24:3
a Spirit of wisdom and u, Is 11:2
Who gave Him u and taught Him Is 40:14
there is no limit to His u. Is 40:28
the heavens by His u. Jr 10:12; 51:15
By your wisdom and u you have Ezk 28:4
and new wine take away {one's} u. Hs 4:11
Are even you still lacking in u? Mt 15:16
to love Him ... with all your u, Mk 12:33
astounded at His u and His answers. Lk 2:47
I will also pray with my u. 1Co 14:15
speak five words with my u, 1Co 14:19
to themselves, they lack u. 2Co 10:12
are darkened in their u, Eph 4:18
all wisdom and spiritual u, Col 1:9
Lord will give you u in everything. 2Tm 2:7
and has given us u so that we 1Jn 5:20
one who has u must calculate Rv 13:18

UNDERWEAR
buy yourself linen u and put it Jr 13:1

UNDERWORLD
to death, to the u, among the Ezk 31:14

UNDESERVED
an u curse goes nowhere. Pr 26:2

UNDESIRABLE
gather together, u nation, Zph 2:1

UNDISCERNING
u, untrustworthy, unloving, and Rm 1:31

UNDIVIDED
Give me an u mind to fear Your Ps 86:11

UNDONE
Joshua did, leaving nothing u Jos 11:15
was to set right what was left u Ti 1:5

UNDYING
all who have u love for our Lord Eph 6:24

UNEDUCATED
that they were u and untrained Ac 4:13

UNENDING
singing, crowned with u joy. Is 35:10; 51:11

UNEVEN
the u ground will become smooth, Is 40:4
you and level the u places; Is 45:2

UNEXPECTEDLY
or that day will come on you u Lk 21:34

UNFADING
and u, kept in heaven 1Pt 1:4
receive the u crown of glory. 1Pt 5:4

UNFAILING
earth is full of the LORD's u love. Ps 33:5
anger, for I am u in My love. Jr 3:12
righteousness, like an u stream. Am 5:24

UNFAIR
and dishonest scales are u. Pr 20:23
Is it My way that is u? Ezk 18:25

UNFAIRLY
must not act u in measurements Lv 19:35

UNFAITHFUL
wife goes astray, is u to him, Nm 5:12
But they were u to the God of 1Ch 5:25
We have been u to our God by Ezr 10:2
destroy all who are u to You. Ps 73:27
you seen what u Israel has done? Jr 3:6

UNFAITHFULLY

| because they have acted **u**." | Ezk 15:8 |
| because they dealt **u** with Me. | Ezk 39:23 |

UNFAITHFULNESS

their **u** that they practiced	Lv 26:40
to Babylon because of their **u**.	1Ch 9:1
Saul died for his **u** to the LORD	1Ch 10:13
because of the **u** of the exiles,	Ezr 9:4
I will heal your **u**.	Jr 3:22

UNFRUITFUL

the water is bad and the land **u**.	2Kg 2:19
choke the word, and it becomes **u**.	Mt 13:22
but my understanding is **u**.	1Co 14:14
so that they will not be **u**.	Ti 3:14
or **u** in the knowledge of our Lord	2Pt 1:8

UNGODLY

defend my cause against an **u** nation;	Ps 43:1
both prophet and priest are **u**,	Jr 23:11
who declares righteous the **u**,	Rm 4:5
moment, Christ died for the **u**.	Rm 5:6
law is ... meant ... for the **u** and	1Tm 1:9
kept until the ... destruction of **u**	2Pt 3:7
convict them of all their **u** deeds	Jd 15

UNGRATEFUL

| disobedient to parents, **u**, unholy, | 2Tm 3:2 |

UNHARMED

| walking around in the fire **u**; | Dn 3:25 |

UNHOLY

| for the **u** and irreverent, | 1Tm 1:9 |
| to parents, ungrateful, **u**, | 2Tm 3:2 |

UNINFORMED

how will the **u** person	
say "Amen"	1Co 14:16
We do not want you to be **u**,	1Th 4:13

UNINHABITED

| will be reduced to **u** ruins. | Jr 4:7 |
| It will be **u** for 40 years. | Ezk 29:11 |

UNINTELLIGIBLE

| to a people of **u** speech or | Ezk 3:5 |

UNINTENTIONAL

| be forgiven, for the sin was **u**. | Nm 15:25 |
| Who perceives his **u** sins? | Ps 19:12 |

UNINTENTIONALLY

| When someone sins **u** against any | Lv 4:2 |

| who kills someone **u** | Nm 35:11; Jos 20:3 |
| everyone who sins **u** or through | Ezk 45:20 |

UNION

| calling one Favor and the other **U**, | Zch 11:7 |

UNIQUE

| my dove, my virtuous one, is **u**; | Sg 6:9 |
| was offering up his **u** son, | Heb 11:17 |

UNITED

Israel gathered **u** against the city.	Jdg 20:11
were continually **u** in prayer,	Ac 1:14
Christ with a **u** mind and voice.	Rm 15:6
and that you be **u** with the same	1Co 1:10
they were not **u** with those who	Heb 4:2

UNITY

keeping the **u** of the Spirit with	Eph 4:3
until we all reach **u** in the faith	Eph 4:13
love—the perfect bond of **u**.	Col 3:14

UNIVERSE

| and through whom He made the **u**. | Heb 1:2 |
| understand that the **u** was | Heb 11:3 |

UNJUST

one who hates **u** gain prolongs	Pr 28:16
An **u** man is detestable to the	Pr 29:27
Listen to what the **u** judge says.	Lk 18:6
know that the **u** will not inherit	1Co 6:9
For God is not **u**; He will not	Heb 6:10

UNJUSTLY

How long will you judge **u**	Ps 82:2
everyone is gaining profit **u**.	Jr 6:13; 8:10
Instead, you act **u** and cheat	1Co 6:8
endures grief from suffering **u**.	1Pt 2:19

UNKNOWN

not stand in the presence of **u** men.	Pr 22:29
TO AN **U** GOD	Ac 17:23
as **u** yet recognized;	2Co 6:9
personally **u** to the Judean	Gl 1:22

UNLEASH

| You **u** your mouth for evil and | Ps 50:19 |
| **u**-es His winds, and the waters | Ps 147:18 |

UNLEAVENED

and baked **u** bread for them,	Gn 19:3
observe the {Festival of} **U** Bread	Ex 12:17
they ate **u** bread and roasted grain	Jos 5:11
Take the meat with the **u** bread,	Jdg 6:20

observed the Festival of **U** Bread   Ezr 6:22
On the first day of **U** Bread   Mt 26:17
a new batch, since you are **u**.   1Co 5:7

UNLESS

not let You go **u** You bless me.   Gn 32:26
U the LORD builds a house,   Ps 127:1
u the Lord has ordained {it}?   Lm 3:37
can come to Me **u** the Father who   Jn 6:44
U a grain of wheat falls into   Jn 12:24

UNLOVED

the LORD saw that Leah was **u**,   Gn 29:31
one loved and the other **u**,   Dt 21:15
an **u** woman when she marries,   Pr 30:23
and she who is "**U**," "Beloved."   Rm 9:25

UNLOVING

untrustworthy, **u**, and unmerciful.   Rm 1:31
u, irreconcilable, slanderers,   2Tm 3:3

UNMARKED

You are like **u** graves;   Lk 11:44

UNMARRIED

I say to the **u** and to widows: 1Co 7:8
she must remain **u** or be   1Co 7:11
An **u** man is concerned about the   1Co 7:32

UNMERCIFUL

untrustworthy, unloving, and **u**.   Rm 1:31

UNNATURAL

intercourse for what is **u**.   Rm 1:26

UNNECESSARY

it is **u** for me to write to you.   2Co 9:1

UNPLOWED

Break up the **u** ground;   Jr 4:3

UNPREPARED

come with me and find you **u**,   2Co 9:4

UNPRESENTABLE

and our **u** parts have a better   1Co 12:23

UNPROFITABLE

for they are **u** and worthless.   Ti 3:9
because it was weak and **u**   Heb 7:18
for that would be **u** for you.   Heb 13:17

UNPUNISHED

will not leave {the guilty} **u**,   Ex 34:7
So don't let him go **u**,   1Kg 2:9
no one who touches her will go **u**.   Pr 6:29

that the wicked will not go **u**,   Pr 11:21
A false witness will not go **u**,   Pr 19:5,9
hurry to get rich will not go **u**.   Pr 28:20
can you possibly remain **u**?   Jr 49:12

UNQUENCHABLE

and go to hell—the **u** fire,   Mk 9:43

UNREASONING

know by instinct, like **u** animals   Jd 10

UNRELENTING

ardent love is as **u** as Sheol.   Sg 8:6

UNREPENTANT

because of your hardness and **u** heart   Rm 2:5

UNRESTRAINED

carrying on in **u** behavior,   1Pt 4:3
Many will follow their **u** ways,   2Pt 2:2
distressed by the **u** behavior of   2Pt 2:7

UNRIGHTEOUS

rain on the righteous and the **u**.   Mt 5:45
whoever is **u** in very little is also   Lk 16:10
not like other people—greedy, **u**,   Lk 18:11
Is God **u** to inflict wrath?   Rm 3:5
dare go to law before the **u**,   1Co 6:1
the righteous for the **u**,   1Pt 3:18
to keep the **u** under punishment
   until   2Pt 2:9

UNRIGHTEOUSNESS

and there is no **u** in Him.   Ps 92:15
who builds his palace through **u**,   Jr 22:13
true, and there is no **u** in Him.   Jn 7:18
against all godlessness and **u**   Rm 1:18
disobey the truth, but are obeying **u**;   Rm 2:8
But if our **u** highlights God's   Rm 3:5
of it to sin as weapons for **u**.   Rm 6:13
finds no joy in **u**, but rejoices   1Co 13:6
must turn away from **u**.   2Tm 2:19
harm as the payment for **u**.   2Pt 2:13
and to cleanse us from all **u**.   1Jn 1:9
All **u** is sin, and there is sin   1Jn 5:17

UNRIPE

that drops its **u** grapes   Jb 15:33
drops its **u** figs when shaken   Rv 6:13

UNSEARCHABLE

He does great and **u** things,   Jb 5:9; 9:10
His greatness is **u**.   Ps 145:3
How **u** His judgments and   Rm 11:33

UNSEEN
but Your footprints were **u**. Ps 77:19
temporary, but what is **u** is eternal. 2Co 4:18

UNSHRUNK
an old garment with **u** cloth, Mt 9:16

UNSPOKEN
for us with **u** groanings. Rm 8:26

UNSTABLE
know that her ways are **u**. Pr 5:6
indecisive man is **u** in all his ways. Jms 1:8
looking for sin, seducing **u** people, 2Pt 2:14
The untaught and **u** twist them to 2Pt 3:16

UNSTAINED
to keep oneself **u** by the world. Jms 1:27

UNSTOPPED
and the ears of the deaf **u**. Is 35:5

UNSUSPECTING
went into the **u** city, and killed Gn 34:25
living securely ... quiet and **u**. Jdg 18:7
deceive the hearts of the **u**. Rm 16:18

UNTAUGHT
The **u** and unstable twist them to 2Pt 3:16

UNTIE
to **u** the ropes of the yoke, Is 58:6
U them and bring them to Me. Mt 21:2
Doesn't each one of you **u** his ox Lk 13:15
sandal strap I'm not worthy to **u**. Jn 1:27
not worthy to **u** the sandals Ac 13:25

UNTRACEABLE
His judgments and **u** His ways! Rm 11:33

UNTRAINED
they were uneducated and **u** men, Ac 4:13
Though **u** in public speaking, 2Co 11:6

UNTRUSTWORTHY
undiscerning, **u**, unloving, and Rm 1:31

UNTURNED
Ephraim is **u** bread, baked on a Hs 7:8

UNUSUAL
as if something **u** were happening 1Pt 4:12

UNVEILED
We all, with **u** faces, are reflecting 2Co 3:18

UNWASHED
but eating with **u** hands does not Mt 15:20

UNWILLING
Suppose the woman is **u** to follow Gn 24:5
For a while he was **u**, but later he Lk 18:4

UNWISE
not as **u** people but as wise Eph 5:15

UNWORTHY
consider yourselves **u** of eternal Ac 13:46
cup of the Lord in an **u** way 1Co 11:27
u to be called an apostle, 1Co 15:9

UPHAZ
gold from **U** Jr 10:9; Dn 10:5

UPHOLD
hear their prayer ... **u** their cause. 1Kg 8:45
For You have **upheld** my just cause; Ps 9:4
happy are those who **u** justice, Ps 106:3
that the LORD **u-s** the just cause Ps 140:12
On the contrary, we **u** the law. Rm 3:31

UPON
The Holy Spirit will come **u** you, Lk 1:35
the Holy Spirit has come **u** you, Ac 1:8
casting all your care **u** Him, 1Pt 5:7

UPRIGHT
Let me die the death of the **u**; Nm 23:10
God, who saves the **u** in heart. Ps 7:10
The **u** will see His face. Ps 11:7
The LORD is good and **u**; Ps 25:8
praise from the **u** is beautiful. Ps 33:1
all the **u** in heart offer praise. Ps 64:10
The **u** see it and rejoice, Ps 107:42
of the **u** will be blessed. Ps 112:2
the **u** will live in Your presence. Ps 140:13
He stores up success for the **u**; Pr 2:7
For the **u** will inhabit the land, Pr 2:21
integrity of the **u** guides them, Pr 11:3
prayer of the **u** is His delight. Pr 15:8
the path of the **u** is a highway. Pr 15:19
but the **u** care about him. Pr 29:10
God made people **u**, but they Ec 7:29
there is no one **u** among the Mc 7:2
centurion, an **u** and God-fearing Ac 10:22

UPRIGHTNESS
and that You are pleased with **u**. 1Ch 29:17
May integrity and **u** keep me, Ps 25:21

UPRISINGS

city has had u against kings	Ezr 4:19

UPROAR

Why is the town in such an u?	1Kg 1:41
After the u was over, Paul sent	Ac 20:1

UPROOT

LORD u-ed them from their land	Dt 29:28
He will u Israel from this good	1Kg 14:15
He u-s my hope like a tree.	Jb 19:10
He will u you from the land of	Ps 52:5
the treacherous u-ed from it.	Pr 2:22
a time to plant and a time to u;	Ec 3:2
and kingdoms to u and tear down,	Jr 1:10
and I will u the house of Judah	Jr 12:14
over them to u and to tear them	Jr 31:28
I have planted I am about to u	Jr 45:4
kingdom will be u-ed and will go	Dn 11:4
never again be u-ed from the land	Am 9:15
you might also u the wheat with	Mt 13:29
Be u-ed and planted in the sea,	Lk 17:6

UPSIDE

wiping it and turning it u down.	2Kg 21:13
who have turned the world u down	Ac 17:6

UPSTAIRS

He will show you a large room u,	Mk 14:15
to the room u where they were	Ac 1:13

UPWARD

will only move u and never	Dt 28:13
as surely as sparks fly u.	Jb 5:7
the path of life leads u,	Pr 15:24
of people rises u and the spirit	Ec 3:21
root downward and bear fruit u.	Is 37:31
My eyes grow weak looking u.	Is 38:14

UR

City in lower Mesopotamia; birthplace of
Abraham (Gn 11:28,31; 15:7; Neh 9:7).

URGE (n)

you an overwhelming u to sleep;	Is 29:10

URGE (v)

the angels u-d Lot on: "Get up!	Gn 19:15
is strongly u-d to enter it.	Lk 16:16
the disciples kept u-ing Him,	Jn 4:31
testified and strongly u-d them,	Ac 2:40
I u you to present your bodies as	Rm 12:1
strongly u-d him to come to you	1Co 16:12

u you to walk worthy of the	Eph 4:1
I u Euodia and I u Syntyche to agree	Php 4:2
first of all, then, I u that petitions,	1Tm 2:1

URGENT

since the king's mission was u.	1Sm 21:8
command was so u and the furnace	Dn 3:22

URIAH

1. Hittite; husband of Bathsheba. One of
David's warriors (2Sm 23:39); David
arranged his death (2Sm 11).

2. High priest under Ahaz (2Kg 16:10-16;
Is 8:2).

3. Prophet against Jehoiakim (Jr 26:20-23).

4. Priest who returned from exile (Ezr
8:33; Neh 3:4,21).

5. Priest under Ezra (Neh 8:4).

URIM

Place the U and Thummim in the	Ex 28:30
him with the decision of the U.	Nm 27:21
Thummim and U belong to Your	Dt 33:8
answer him in dreams or by the U	1Sm 28:6
could consult the U and Thummim.	Ezr 2:63
could consult the U	
and Thummim.	Neh 7:65

URINE

and drink their own u?	2Kg 18:27

US

it will not happen. For God is with u.	Is 8:10
Immanuel ... "God is with u."	Mt 1:23
Whoever is not against u is for u.	Mk 9:40
If God is for u, who is against u?	Rm 8:31

USE

Can a man be of {any} u to God?	Jb 22:2
We u-d to have close fellowship;	Ps 55:14
Every day I u-d to sit, teaching	Mt 26:55
only don't u this freedom as an	Gl 5:13
is destroyed by being u-d up;	Col 2:22
but u a little wine because of	1Tm 5:23
don't u your freedom as a way	1Pt 2:16
everyone should u it to serve	1Pt 4:10

USEFUL

Can it be u for anything?	Ezk 15:4
set apart, u to the Master,	2Tm 2:21
for he is u to me in the	2Tm 4:11
but now he is u to both you and	Phm 11

USELESS

Stop bringing **u** offerings.	Is 1:13
by Baal and followed **u** idols.	Jr 2:8
You have said: It is **u** to serve God.	Mal 3:14
together they have become **u**;	Rm 3:12
Once he was **u** to you, but now he	Phm 11
his religion is **u**.	Jms 1:26
that faith without works is **u**?	Jms 2:20

USUAL

As **u**, He entered the synagogue	Lk 4:16
made His way as **u** to the Mount	Lk 22:39

USUALLY

as He **u** did, He began teaching	Mk 10:1

UTENSIL

also made the **u-s** that would be	Ex 37:16
He made all the altar's **u-s**:	Ex 38:3
All the **u-s** that Hiram made for	1Kg 7:45
silver and all the **u-s** found in	2Kg 14:14
Ahaz gathered up the **u-s**	2Ch 28:24

UTTER

and my tongue will not **u** deceit.	Jb 27:4
of the righteous **u-s** wisdom;	Ps 37:30
a dishonest witness **u-s** lies.	Pr 14:5

UTTERLY

for love, it would be **u** scorned.	Sg 8:7
were **u** astonished and asked,	Mt 19:25

UZZAH

Man struck down for touching the ark (2Sm 6:3-8).

UZZIAH

1. Descendant of Levi (1Ch 6:24).

2. Son of Amaziah; king of Judah; also known as Azariah (2Kg 15:1-7). Made king by popular acclaim (2Ch 26:1); expanded and fortified Judah (26:6-15); struck with skin disease when he attempted to serve as priest (26:16-21).

V

❦

VACANT

it finds {the house} **v**, swept,	Mt 12:44

VAIN

You will sow your seed in **v**	Lv 26:16
and the peoples plot in **v**?	Ps 2:1
its builders labor over it in **v**;	Ps 127:1
They worship Me in **v**,	Mt 15:9
labor in the Lord is not in **v**.	1Co 15:58
Don't receive God's grace in **v**.	2Co 6:1
be running, or have run, in **v**.	Gl 2:2
I didn't run in **v** or labor for	Php 2:16

VALIANT

He is also a **v** man, a warrior,	1Sm 16:18

VALIANTLY

With God we will perform **v**;	Ps 60:12

VALID

Myself, My testimony is not **v**.	Jn 5:31
My testimony is **v**, because I know	Jn 8:14
For a will is **v** only when people	Heb 9:17

VALLEY

the entire Jordan **V** for himself.	Gn 13:11
moon, over the **v** of Aijalon.	Jos 10:12
and not a god of the **v-s**,	1Kg 20:28
when I go through the darkest **v**,	Ps 23:4
rose of Sharon, a lily of the **v-s**.	Sg 2:1
Every **v** will be lifted up,	Is 40:4
the **v**; it was full of bones.	Ezk 37:1
multitudes in the **v** of decision!	Jl 3:14
and the **v-s** will split apart,	Mc 1:4
Every **v** will be filled, and every	Lk 3:5
His disciples across the Kidron **V**,	Jn 18:1

VALUABLE

Your faithful love is so **v** that people	Ps 36:7
The death of His faithful ones is **v**	Ps 116:15
your faith—more **v** than gold,	1Pt 1:7
a chosen and **v** cornerstone,	1Pt 2:6
which is very **v** in God's eyes.	1Pt 3:4

VALUATION

a vow ... that involves the **v**	Lv 27:2

VALUE

the priest will set a **v** for him.	Lv 27:8
Wisdom cannot be **v-d** in the gold	Jb 28:16
The LORD **v-s** those who fear Him,	Ps 147:11
despised, and we didn't **v** Him.	Is 53:3
So they calculated their **v**,	Ac 19:19
count my life of no **v** to myself,	Ac 20:24
the surpassing **v** of knowing	Php 3:8
are not of any **v** against fleshly	Col 2:23

VANDAL

lazy in his work is brother to a v.   Pr 18:9

VANISH

As a cloud fades away and v-es,   Jb 7:9
For my days v like smoke,   Ps 102:3
wind passes over it, it v-es,   Ps 103:16
a lying tongue is a v-ing mist,   Pr 21:6
the heavens will v like smoke,   Is 51:6
like the early dew that v-es.   Hs 6:4; 13:3
for a little while, then v-es.   Jms 4:14

VAPOR

every mortal man is only a v.   Ps 39:5
Men are only a v; exalted men,   Ps 62:9

VARIATION

with Him there is no v or shadow   Jms 1:17

VARIETY

led along by a v of passions,   2Tm 3:6

VARIOUS

the v kinds of locust, the   Lv 11:22
stones of v colors, all kinds   1Ch 29:2
suffering from v diseases and   Mt 4:24
and earthquakes in v places,   Mt 24:7
you experience v trials,   Jms 1:2

VASHTI

Queen of Persia; wife of Ahasuerus;
deposed for insubordination (Est 1:9–2:17).

VAST

how v their sum is!   Ps 139:17
the working of His v strength.   Eph 1:19
the Lord and by His v strength.   Eph 6:10
loud voice of a v multitude in   Rv 19:1

VAT

v-s will overflow with new   Pr 3:10; Jl 2:24

VEGETABLE

by hand as in a v garden.   Dt 11:10
Better a meal of v-s where there   Pr 15:17
Let us be given v-s to eat and   Dn 1:12
one who is weak eats only v-s.   Rm 14:2

VEGETATION

said, "Let the earth produce v: Gn 1:11
devoured all the v in their land   Ps 105:35
hills, and dry up all their v.   Is 42:15

VEIL

So she took her v and covered   Gn 24:65

so the v will make a separation   Ex 26:33
he put a v over his face.   Ex 34:33
Behind your v, your   Sg 4:1,3; 6:7
remove your v, strip off {your}   Is 47:2
old covenant, the same v remains;   2Co 3:14
it is v-ed to those who are perishing.   2Co 4:3

VENGEANCE

V belongs to Me; I will repay.   Dt 32:35
gives me v and subdues peoples   Ps 18:47
LORD, God of v—God of v, appear.   Ps 94:1
For the LORD has a day of v,   Is 34:8
and the day of our God's v;   Is 61:2
let me see Your v on them,   Jr 11:20
is the LORD's v, v for His temple.   Jr 51:11
The LORD takes v against His foes;   Nah 1:2
it is written: V belongs to Me;   Rm 12:19
who has said, V belongs to Me,   Heb 10:30

VENOM

turns into cobras' v inside him.   Jb 20:14
They have v like the v of a snake,   Ps 58:4
viper's v is under their lips.   Ps 140:3
Vipers' v is under their lips.   Rm 3:13

VENT

fool gives full v to his anger,   Pr 29:11

VENTURED

Since I have v to speak to the   Gn 18:27

VERDICT

God's v is on the lips of a king;   Pr 16:10

VERSES

as I recite my v to the king;   Ps 45:1

VESSEL

and a v will be produced for a   Pr 25:4
gold v-s ... from the temple,   Dn 5:3
possess his own v in   1Th 4:4
and all the v-s of worship with   Heb 9:21

VICTOR

I will give the v the right to   Rv 2:7
The v: I will make him a pillar   Rv 3:12
The v: I will give him the right   Rv 3:21
he went out as a v to conquer.   Rv 6:2
The v will inherit these things,   Rv 21:7

VICTORIOUS

LORD made David v wherever   2Sm 8:6,14
are more than v through Him who   Rm 8:37
has been v so that He may open   Rv 5:5

VICTORY

LORD brought about a great **v**.	2Sm 23:12
LORD's ... arrow of **v** over Aram.	2Kg 13:17
gives great **v-ies** to His king;	Ps 18:50
LORD gives **v** to His anointed;	Ps 20:6
and holy arm have won Him **v**.	Ps 98:1
the One who gives **v** to kings,	Ps 144:10
but **v** comes from the LORD.	Pr 21:31
v comes with many counselors.	Pr 24:6
until He has led justice to **v**.	Mt 12:20
has been swallowed up in **v**.	1Co 15:54
O Death, where is your **v**?	1Co 15:55
gives us the **v** through our Lord	1Co 15:57
you have had **v** over the evil one.	1Jn 2:13
This is the **v** that has conquered	1Jn 5:4
had won the **v** from the beast,	Rv 15:2

VIEW (n)

you will not accept any other **v**.	Gl 5:10

VIEW (v)

Although you will **v** the land	Dt 32:52
continually **v** the face of My	Mt 18:10
to be a loss in **v** of the	Php 3:8
nations will **v** their bodies for	Rv 11:9

VIGOR

approach the grave in full **v**,	Jb 5:26

VIGOROUS

for they are **v** and give birth	Ex 1:19

VILE

AND OF THE **V** THINGS OF	Rv 17:5

VILLAGE

with the cities and their **v-s**.	Jos 13:23
Jews who live in **v-s** observe the	Est 9:19
go up against a land of open **v-s**;	Ezk 38:11
can go into the **v-s** and buy food	Mt 14:15
Go into the **v** ahead of you.	Mt 21:2
going around the **v-s** in a circuit,	Mk 6:6
many **v-s** of the Samaritans	Ac 8:25

VINDICATE

LORD will indeed **v** His people	Dt 32:36
me when I call, God, who **v-s** me.	Ps 4:1
v me, LORD, according to my	Ps 7:8
V me, LORD, because I have lived	Ps 26:1
V me, LORD, my God, in keeping	Ps 35:24
V me, God, and defend my cause	Ps 43:1
Your name, and **v** me by Your	Ps 54:1
May he **v** the afflicted among the	Ps 72:4

Yet wisdom is **v-d** by her deeds.	Mt 11:19
wisdom is **v-d** by all her children.	Lk 7:35

VINE

dream there was a **v** in front of me.	Gn 40:9
He ties his donkey to a **v**,	Gn 49:11
For their **v** is from the **v** of Sodom	Dt 32:32
under his own **v** and his own fig	1Kg 4:25
You uprooted a **v** from Egypt;	Ps 80:8
like a fruitful **v** within your	Ps 128:3
see if the **v-s** were budding and	Sg 6:11
I planted you, a choice **v**	Jr 2:21
was like a **v** in your vineyard	Ezk 19:10
Israel is a lush **v**; it yields fruit	Hs 10:1
there is no fruit on the **v-s**,	Hab 3:17
the **v** will yield its fruit,	Zch 8:12
fruit of the **v** until that day	Mt 26:29
I am the true **v**, and My Father	Jn 15:1
unless it remains on the **v**,	Jn 15:4
I am the **v**; you are the	Jn 15:5

VINEDRESSERS

of the land to be **v** and farmers.	2Kg 25:12

VINEGAR

must not drink **v** made from wine	Nm 6:3
and dip it in the **v** sauce.	Ru 2:14
thirst they gave me **v** to drink.	Ps 69:21
Like **v** to the teeth and smoke to	Pr 10:26
or like {pouring} **v** on soda.	Pr 25:20

VINEYARD

Noah ... was the first to plant a **v**.	Gn 9:20
the best of his own field or **v**.	Ex 22:5
not strip your **v** bare or gather	Lv 19:10
Naboth the Jezreelite had a **v**;	1Kg 21:1
by the **v** of a man lacking sense.	Pr 24:30
little foxes that ruin the **v-s**	Sg 2:15
He leased the **v** to tenants.	Sg 8:11
abandoned like a shelter in a **v**,	Is 1:8
a song about my loved one's **v**:	Is 5:1
or shouting for joy in the **v-s**.	Is 16:10
wine, a land of bread and **v-s**.	Is 36:17
You will plant **v-s** again on the	Jr 31:5
build houses, and plant **v-s**.	Ezk 28:26
plant **v-s** and drink their wine,	Am 9:14
to hire workers for his **v**.	Mt 20:1
who planted a **v**, put a fence	Mt 21:33
and My Father is the **v** keeper.	Jn 15:1
Who plants a **v** and does not eat	1Co 9:7
grapes from earth's **v**,	Rv 14:18

VINTAGE

for the **v** will fail and the	Is 32:10

VIOLATE

he has **v-d** his neighbor's fianceé.	Dt 22:24
They have **v-d** My covenant that I	Jos 7:11
I will not **v** My covenant or	Ps 89:34
in the temple **v** the Sabbath and	Mt 12:5

VIOLENCE

and the earth was filled with **v**.	Gn 6:11
I cry out: **V!** but get no	Jb 19:7
He hates the lover of **v**.	Ps 11:5
rise up against me, breathing **v**.	Ps 27:12
v covers them like a garment.	Ps 73:6
of the land are full of **v**.	Ps 74:20
and drink the wine of **v**.	Pr 4:17
mouth of the wicked conceals **v**.	Pr 10:6
The **v** of the wicked sweeps them	Pr 21:7
although He had done no **v**	Is 53:9
V will never again be heard of	Is 60:18
There will be **v** in the land with	Jr 51:46
and the city is filled with **v**.	Ezk 7:23
Her priests do **v** to My law and	Ezk 22:26
Put away **v** and oppression and do	Ezk 45:9
who store up **v** and destruction	Am 3:10
day and bring in a reign of **v**.	Am 6:3
Oppression and **v** are right in	Hab 1:3
of heaven has been suffering **v**,	Mt 11:12

VIOLENT

You rescue me from **v** men.	2Sm 22:49
Keep me safe from **v** men	Ps 140:1
Don't envy a **v** man or	Pr 3:31
but **v** men gain {only} riches.	Pr 11:16
A **v** man lures his neighbor,	Pr 16:29
city of **v** people will fear You.	Is 25:3
is with me like a **v** warrior.	Jr 20:11
V men will enter it and profane	Ezk 7:22
and the **v** have been seizing it	Mt 11:12
like that of a **v** rushing wind	Ac 2:2

VIOLENTLY

the earth is **v** shaken.	Is 24:19

VIPER

a **v-'s** fangs will kill him.	Jb 20:16
v-'s venom is under their lips.	Ps 140:3
a snake and stings like a **v**.	Pr 23:32
a **v** will come out of the root	Is 14:29
and lion, of **v** and flying serpent,	Is 30:6

he said to them, "Brood of **v-s!**	Mt 3:7
Brood of **v-s!** How can you speak	Mt 12:34
Snakes! Brood of **v-s!** How can	Mt 23:33
a **v** came out because of the heat	Ac 28:3
V-s' venom is under their lips.	Rm 3:13

VIRGIN

When a man seduces a **v**	Ex 22:16
The **v** will conceive, have a son,	Is 7:14
for the **v** daughter of my people	Jr 14:17
Return, **V** Israel! Return to	Jr 31:21
console you, **V** Daughter Zion?	Lm 2:13
and their **v** nipples caressed.	Ezk 23:3
V Israel will never rise again.	Am 5:2
the **v** will become pregnant and	Mt 1:23
be like 10 **v-s** who took their	Mt 25:1
The **v-'s** name was Mary.	Lk 1:27
This man had four **v** daughters	Ac 21:9
and if a **v** marries,	1Co 7:28
to present a pure **v** to Christ.	2Co 11:2

VIRGINITY

didn't find {any} evidence of her **v**,	Dt 22:14
with my friends and mourn my **v**.	Jdg 11:37
for they have kept their **v**.	Rv 14:4

VIRILITY

and the firstfruits of my **v**,	Gn 49:3
he is the firstfruits of his **v**;	Dt 21:17

VIRTUE

his **v** is to overlook an offense.	Pr 19:11

VISIBLE

man sees what is **v**, but the LORD	1Sm 16:7
circumcision is not something **v**	Rm 2:28
on earth, the **v** and the invisible,	Col 1:16
made from things that are not **v**.	Heb 11:3

VISION

the LORD came to Abram in a **v**:	Gn 15:1
make Myself known to him in a **v**;	Nm 12:6
thoughts from **v-s** in the night,	Jb 4:13
chased away like a **v** in the night.	Jb 20:8
You once spoke in a **v** to Your	Ps 89:19
The **v** concerning Judah and	Is 1:1
oracle against the Valley of **V**:	Is 22:1
like a dream, a **v** in the night.	Is 29:7
receive no **v** from the LORD.	Lm 2:9
heavens opened and I saw **v-s**	Ezk 1:1
For the **v** concerning all its	Ezk 7:13
and carried me in **v-s** of God to	Ezk 8:3

see false **v**-s and speak lying	Ezk 13:6
In **v**-s of God He took me to the	Ezk 40:2
also understood **v**-s and dreams	Dn 1:17
to Daniel in a **v** at night,	Dn 2:19
must seal up the **v** because it	Dn 8:26
and your young men will see **v**-s.	Jl 2:28
The **v** of Obadiah.	Ob 1
be night for you—without **v**-s;	Mc 3:6
The book of the **v** of Nahum the	Nah 1:1
Don't tell anyone about the **v** until	Mt 17:9
they had seen a **v** of angels who	Lk 24:23
your young men will see **v**-s,	Ac 2:17
In a **v** he has seen a man named	Ac 9:12
but thought he was seeing a **v**.	Ac 12:9
the night a **v** appeared to Paul:	Ac 16:9
Lord said to Paul in a night **v**,	Ac 18:9
disobedient to the heavenly **v**.	Ac 26:19
move on to **v**-s and revelations	2Co 12:1

VISIONARY

he went into a **v** state.	Ac 10:10
I went into a **v** state	Ac 22:17
claiming access to a **v** realm	Col 2:18

VISIT

You **v** the earth and water it	Ps 65:9
you will be **v**-ed by the LORD of	Is 29:6
was in prison and you **v**-ed Me.	Mt 25:36
has **v**-ed and provided redemption	Lk 1:68
God has **v**-ed His people.	Lk 7:16
to you on another painful **v**.	2Co 2:1

VISITATION

recognize the time of your **v**.	Lk 19:44
glorify God in a day of **v**.	1Pt 2:12

VISITOR

You the only **v** in Jerusalem who	Lk 24:18

VITALITY

will give up your **v** to others	Pr 5:9

VIVIDLY

Jesus Christ was **v** portrayed as	Gl 3:1

VOCABULARY

had the same language and **v**.	Gn 11:1

VOICE

God heard the **v** of the boy,	Gn 21:17
The **v** is the **v** of Jacob,	Gn 27:22
didn't see a form; there was only a **v**	Dt 4:12
LORD listened to the **v** of a man,	Jos 10:14

Is that your **v**, David my son?	1Sm 24:16
Is that your **v**, my son David?	1Sm 26:17
after the fire there was a **v**, a soft	1Kg 19:12
before my eyes. I heard a quiet **v**:	Jb 4:16
thunders with His majestic **v**.	Jb 37:4
you thunder with a **v** like His?	Jb 40:9
daybreak, LORD, You hear my **v**;	Ps 5:3
From His temple He heard my **v**,	Ps 18:6
no words; their **v** is not heard.	Ps 19:3
The **v** of the LORD is above the	Ps 29:3
earth melts when He lifts His **v**.	Ps 46:6
He thunders with His powerful **v**!	Ps 68:33
Today, if you hear His **v**:	Ps 95:7
Listen to my **v** when I call on	Ps 141:1
with a loud **v** early in the	Pr 27:14
up for those who have no **v**,	Pr 31:8
me hear your **v**; for your **v** is sweet,	Sg 2:14
A **v** of one crying out:	Is 40:3
He will not ... make His **v** heard	Is 42:2
watchmen—they lift up their **v**-s,	Is 52:8
v from the temple—the **v** of the	Is 66:6
A **v** was heard in Ramah, a lament	Jr 31:15
the **v** of the bridegroom and the	Jr 33:11
will certainly obey the **v** of the LORD	Jr 42:6
facedown and heard a **v** speaking.	Ezk 1:28
who has a beautiful **v** and plays	Ezk 33:32
a **v** came from heaven:	Dn 4:31
and raise His **v** from Jerusalem;	Jl 3:16
and raises His **v** from Jerusalem;	Am 1:2
belly of Sheol; You heard my **v**.	Jnh 2:2
A **v** was heard in Ramah, weeping,	Mt 2:18
A **v** of one crying out in the	Mt 3:3
And there came a **v** from heaven:	Mt 3:17
no one will hear His **v** in the	Mt 12:19
Jesus cried out with a loud **v**,	Mt 27:46
with a loud **v** and gave up His	Mt 27:50
with loud **v**-s that He be crucified	Lk 23:23
greatly at the groom's **v**.	Jn 3:29
dead will hear the **v** of the Son	Jn 5:25
and the sheep hear his **v**.	Jn 10:3
Then a **v** came from heaven:	Jn 12:28
This **v** came, not for Me	Jn 12:30
who is of the truth listens to My **v**.	Jn 18:37
screamed at the top of their **v**-s,	Ac 7:57
Their **v** has gone out to all the	Rm 10:18
Christ with a united mind and **v**.	Rm 15:6
with the archangel's **v**, and with	1Th 4:16
Today, if you hear His **v**,	Heb 3:7,15; 4:7

His **v** shook the earth at that	Heb 12:26
v came to Him from the Majestic	2Pt 1:17
donkey spoke with a human **v**	2Pt 2:16
If anyone hears My **v** and opens	Rv 3:20
there were loud **v**-s in heaven	Rv 11:15

VOLUME

about me in the **v** of the scroll.	Ps 40:7
Me in the **v** of the scroll	Heb 10:7

VOLUNTEER (n)

of Zichri, the **v** of the LORD,	2Ch 17:16

VOLUNTEER (v)

when the people **v**, praise the	Jdg 5:2
all the men who **v**-ed to live in	Neh 11:2
Your people will **v** on Your day	Ps 110:3

VOMIT (n)

As a dog returns to its **v**,	Pr 26:11
as a drunkard staggers in his **v**.	Is 19:14
A dog returns to its own **v**,	2Pt 2:22

VOMIT (v)

land will **v** out its inhabitants.	Lv 18:25
Drink, get drunk, and **v**.	Jr 25:27
and it **v**-ed Jonah onto dry land.	Jnh 2:10
I am going to **v** you out of My	Rv 3:16

VOW (n)

Jacob made a **v**: "If God will	Gn 28:20
to fulfill a **v** or as a freewill	Lv 22:21
makes a special **v** to the LORD	Lv 27:2
makes a special **v**, a Nazirite **v**,	Nm 6:2
Israel made a **v** to the LORD,	Nm 21:2
When a woman ... makes a **v**	Nm 30:3
If you make a **v** to the LORD your	Dt 23:21
Jephthah made this **v** to the LORD:	Jdg 11:30
Making a **v**, she pleaded, "LORD	1Sm 1:11
and you will fulfill your **v**-s.	Jb 22:27
I will fulfill my **v**-s before those	Ps 22:25
pay your **v**-s to the Most High.	Ps 50:14
I am obligated by **v**-s to You,	Ps 56:12
v-s to You will be fulfilled.	Ps 65:1
keep your **v**-s to the LORD your	Ps 76:11
making a **v** to the Mighty One of	Ps 132:2
today I've fulfilled my **v**-s.	Pr 7:14
and later to reconsider his **v**-s.	Pr 20:25
What, son of my **v**-s?	Pr 31:2
they will make **v**-s to the LORD	Is 19:21
to the LORD and made **v**-s.	Jnh 1:16
because he had taken a **v**.	Ac 18:18
obligated themselves with a **v**.	Ac 21:23

VOW (v)

Fulfill what you **v**.	Ec 5:4
Better that you do not **v** than that you	Ec 5:5
I will fulfill what I have **v**-ed.	Jnh 2:9

VULGAR

like a **v** person would expose	2Sm 6:20

VULNERABLE

of the wall, at the **v** areas.	Neh 4:13

VULTURE

not eat ... bearded **v**, the black **v**,	Dt 14:12
carcass is, there the **v**-s will gather.	Mt 24:28

W

WADI

five smooth stones from the **w**	1Sm 17:40
exhausted to cross the W Besor.	1Sm 30:10
hide yourself at the W Cherith	1Kg 17:3
the **w** will be filled with water	2Kg 3:17
are as treacherous as a **w**,	Jb 6:15
The **w**-s evaporate in warm weather;	Jb 6:17
and a **w** becomes parched and dry,	Jb 14:11
I will lead them to **w**-s {filled} with	Jr 31:9

WAFER

tasted like **w**-s {made} with honey.	Ex 16:31
unleavened **w**-s coated with oil.	Ex 29:2

WAGE (n)

goats. {Such} will be my **w**-s.	Gn 30:32
me and changed my **w**-s 10 times.	Gn 31:7
me, and I will pay your **w**-s."	Ex 2:9
pay him his **w**-s each day	Dt 24:15
The wicked man earns an empty **w**,	Pr 11:18
your **w**-s on what does not satisfy?	Is 55:2
w-s into a bag with a hole in it.	Hg 1:6
they weighed my **w**-s, 30 pieces	Zch 11:12
and cheat the **w** earner;	Mal 3:5
be satisfied with your **w**-s.	Lk 3:14
the worker is worthy of his **w**-s.	Lk 10:7
For the **w**-s of sin is death,	Rm 6:23

laborer is worthy of his w-s. 1Tm 5:18
loved the w-s of unrighteousness, 2Pt 2:15

WAGE (v)

w war with sound guidance Pr 20:18; 24:6
I see a different law ... w-ing war Rm 7:23
we do not w war in a fleshly way, 2Co 10:3
is able to w war against him? Rv 13:4
together to w war against Rv 19:19

WAIL

W! For the day of the LORD is Is 13:6
W, you shepherds, and cry out. Jr 25:34
GOD says: W: Alas for the day! Ezk 30:2
rather, they w on their beds. Hs 7:14
people weeping and w-ing loudly. Mk 5:38
You will weep and w, but the world Jn 16:20
Weep and w over the miseries that Jms 5:1

WAILING (n)

a loud w throughout Egypt Ex 12:30

WAIST

a leather belt around his w. 2Kg 1:8
Your w is a mound of wheat Sg 7:2
will be a belt around His w. Is 11:5
From what seemed to be His w up, Ezk 1:27
of gold from Uphaz around his w. Dn 10:5
a leather belt around his w, Mt 3:4
truth like a belt around your w, Eph 6:14

WAISTBAND

artistically woven w ... on the ephod Ex 28:8

WAIT

I w for Your salvation, LORD. Gn 49:18
willing to w for them to grow up? Ru 1:13
"W, my daughter," she said, Ru 3:18
W for the LORD; be courageous Ps 27:14
W for the LORD and keep His way, Ps 37:34
I w-ed patiently for the LORD, Ps 40:1
I {w} ... more than watchmen Ps 130:6
I will w for the LORD, who is hiding Is 8:17
w-ed for Him, and He has saved us. Is 25:9
Happy are all who w patiently for Is 30:18
behalf of the one who w-s for Him. Is 64:4
is good to w quietly for deliverance Lm 3:26
I will w for the God of my Mc 7:7
Though it delays, w for it, Hab 2:3
like people w-ing for their master Lk 12:36
but to w for the Father's promise. Ac 1:4
give up preaching ... to w on tables. Ac 6:2

creation eagerly w-s with Rm 8:19
eagerly w-ing for adoption, Rm 8:23
we eagerly w for it with patience. Rm 8:25
as you eagerly w for the revelation 1Co 1:7
to eat, w for one another 1Co 11:33
Spirit we eagerly w for the hope Gl 5:5
we also eagerly w for a Savior, Php 3:20
to w for His Son from heaven, 1Th 1:10
while we w for the blessed hope Ti 2:13
to those who are w-ing for Him. Heb 9:28
now w-ing until His enemies Heb 10:13
the farmer w-s for the precious Jms 5:7
God patiently w-ed in the days 1Pt 3:20
you w for ... the day of God, 2Pt 3:12

WAKE

and no one woke up; 1Sm 26:12
I w again because the LORD Ps 3:5
I will w up the dawn. Ps 57:8; 108:2
I w up, I am still with You. Ps 139:18
W up, w up! Is 51:9; 52:1
they woke Him up and said to Him, Mk 4:38
Peter on the side, he woke him up Ac 12:7

WALK (n)

four are stately in their w: Pr 30:29

WALK (v)

the LORD God w-ing in the garden Gn 3:8
Enoch w-ed with God, and he was Gn 5:24
Noah w-ed with God. Gn 6:9
God by w-ing in all His ways, Dt 10:12
and when you w along the road, Dt 11:19
God w-s throughout your camps Dt 23:14
I w-ed through darkness by His Jb 29:3
we w-ed with the crowd into the Ps 55:14
they w in the light of Your Ps 89:15
w-ing on the wings of the wind, Ps 104:3
I will w before the LORD in the Ps 116:9
If I w in the thick of danger, Ps 138:7
Can a man w on coals without Pr 6:28
one who w-s with the wise will Pr 13:20
but one who w-s in wisdom will Pr 28:26
but the fool w-s in darkness. Ec 2:14
come and let us w in the LORD's light. Is 2:5
people w-ing in darkness have Is 9:2
This is the way. W in it. Is 30:21
But the redeemed will w {on it}, Is 35:9
they will w and not faint. Is 40:31
when you w through the fire Is 43:2

w-ing around in the fire unharmed; Dn 3:25
It was I who taught Ephraim to w, Hs 11:3
and the righteous w in them, Hs 14:9
Can two w together without Am 3:3
and to w humbly with your God. Mc 6:8
He w-ed with Me in peace and Mal 2:6
or to say, 'Get up and w'? Mt 9:5
the blind see, the lame w, Mt 11:5
saw Him w-ing on the sea, Mt 14:26
and began to w along with them. Lk 24:15
pick up your bedroll and w! Jn 5:8
will never w in the darkness, Jn 8:12
If anyone w-s during the day, Jn 11:9
W while you have the light so Jn 12:35
In the name of Jesus ... get up and w! Ac 3:6
and who had never w-ed, Ac 14:8
we too may w in a new way of life. Rm 6:4
who do not w according to the flesh Rm 8:4
Let us w with decency, as in the Rm 13:13
no longer w-ing according to love. Rm 14:15
we w by faith, not by sight 2Co 5:7
w by the Spirit and you will not Gl 5:16
you previously w-ed according to Eph 2:2
so that we should w in them. Eph 2:10
And w in love, as the Messiah Eph 5:2
W as children of light Eph 5:8
so that you may w worthy of the Col 1:10
Christ Jesus the Lord, w in Him, Col 2:6
us how you must w and please God 1Th 4:1
But if we w in the light as He 1Jn 1:7
in Him should w just as He w-ed. 1Jn 2:6
darkness, w-s in the darkness 1Jn 2:11
to find ... your children w-ing in truth, 2Jn 4
w-ing according to their desires; Jd 16
who w-s among the seven gold Rv 2:1
are not able to see, hear, or w. Rv 9:20
The nations will w in its light, Rv 21:24

WALL
shout, and the w collapsed. Jos 6:20
turned his face to the w and prayed 2Kg 20:2
let's rebuild Jerusalem's w, Neh 2:17
with my God I can leap over a w. Ps 18:29
the water stood firm like a w. Ps 78:13
imagination it is like a high w. Pr 18:11
a city whose w is broken down. Pr 25:28
If she is a w, we will build a Sg 8:9
grope along a w like the blind; Is 59:10
will name your w-s salvation, Is 60:18

tore down the w-s of Jerusalem. Jr 39:8
I will be a w of fire around it, Zch 2:5
strike you, you whitewashed w! Ac 23:3
down the dividing w of hostility. Eph 2:14
By faith the w-s of Jericho fell Heb 11:30
{The city} had a massive high w, Rv 21:12

WALLOWS
after washing itself, w in the mud. 2Pt 2:22

WANDER
He made them w
  in the wilderness Nm 32:13
My father was a w-ing Aramean. Dt 26:5
and makes them w in a trackless Jb 12:24
they w in darkness. Ps 82:5
don't let me w from Your Ps 119:10
I w like a lost sheep; Ps 119:176
is like a bird w-ing from its nest. Pr 27:8
Truly they love to w; Jr 14:10
So they w-ed aimlessly. Lm 4:15
{the people} w like sheep; Zch 10:2
have w-ed away from the faith 1Tm 6:10
w-ing stars for whom is reserved Jd 13

WANDERER
will be a restless w on the earth. Gn 4:12
make them homeless w-s Ps 59:11
they will become w-s among the Hs 9:17

WANT
You do not w a sacrifice, or I Ps 51:16
He gives it to anyone He w-s. Dn 4:25
For whoever w-s to save his life Mk 8:35
We don't w this man to rule over Lk 19:14
I do not practice what I w to do, Rm 7:15
who w-s everyone to be saved and 1Tm 2:4
not w-ing any to perish, 2Pt 3:9

WAR
return to Egypt if they face w. Ex 13:17
There is a sound of w in the camp. Ex 32:17
the land had rest from w. Jos 11:23; 14:15
He trains my hands for w; 2Sm 22:35
though w break out against me, Ps 27:3
makes w-s cease throughout the Ps 46:9
the sword, and the weapons of w. Ps 76:3
when I speak, they are for w. Ps 120:7
wage w with sound guidance Pr 20:18; 24:6
a time for w and a time for Ec 3:8
will never again train for w. Is 2:4

we will not see w or hear the Jr 42:14
until the end there will be w; Dn 9:26
hear of w-s and rumors of w-s. Mt 24:6
Or what king, going to w against Lk 14:31
waging w against the law of my Rm 7:23
Who ever goes to w at his own 1Co 9:7
we do not wage w in a fleshly 2Co 10:3
What is the source of the w-s and Jms 4:1
desires that w against you. 1Pt 2:11
Then w broke out in heaven: Rv 12:7
He judges and makes w. Rv 19:11

WARFARE

weapons of our w are not fleshly, 2Co 10:4

WARM

bedclothes, he could not get w. 1Kg 1:1
the boy's flesh became w. 2Kg 4:34
lie down together, they can keep w; Ec 4:11
takes some of it and w-s himself, Is 44:15
but never have enough to get w. Hg 1:6
she saw Peter w-ing himself, Mk 14:67
Go in peace, keep w, and eat well, Jms 2:16

WARN

The man specifically w-ed us: Gn 43:3
Go down and w the people not to Ex 19:21
Your servant is w-ed by them; Ps 19:11
if you w a wicked person Ezk 3:19; 33:9
his trumpet to w the people. Ezk 33:3
And being w-ed in a dream Mt 2:12,22
Who w-ed you to flee from the Mt 3:7
w-ed them not to make Him
known, Mt 12:16
I did not stop w-ing each one of Ac 20:31
to w you as my dear children. 1Co 4:14
were written as a w-ing to us, 1Co 10:11
I gave w-ing, and I give w-ing 2Co 13:2
w-ing and teaching everyone with Col 1:28
w those who are lazy, 1Th 5:14
an enemy, but w him as a brother 2Th 3:15
after a first and second w-ing, Ti 3:10
Moses was w-ed when he Heb 8:5
Noah, after being w-ed about Heb 11:7
rejected Him who w-ed them Heb 12:25

WARRIOR

LORD is a w; Yahweh is His name. Ex 15:3
The LORD is with you, mighty w. Jdg 6:12
been a w since he was young. 1Sm 17:33

He charges at me like a w. Jb 16:14
in the hand of a w are the sons Ps 127:4
A wise w is better than a strong Pr 24:5
The LORD advances like a w; Is 42:13
the w-s will flee naked that day Am 2:16
God is among you, a w who saves. Zph 3:17

WASH

you may w your feet and rest Gn 18:4
Go w seven times in the Jordan 2Kg 5:10
If I w myself with snow, and Jb 9:30
I w my hands in innocence and go Ps 26:6
W away my guilt, and cleanse me Ps 51:2
w me, and I will be whiter than Ps 51:7
he will w his feet in the blood Ps 58:10
purify my heart and w my hands Ps 73:13
ewes coming up from w-ing, Sg 6:6
W yourselves. Is 1:16
the Lord has w-ed away the filth Is 4:4
W the evil from your heart, Jr 4:14
and you weren't w-ed clean with Ezk 16:4
a fountain ... (to w away) sin Zch 13:1
when you fast ... w your face, Mt 6:17
they don't w their hands when Mt 15:2
w-ed his hands ... "I am innocent Mt 27:24
will not eat unless they w
their hands Mk 7:3
began to w His feet with her tears. Lk 7:38
w in the pool of Siloam Jn 9:7
began to w His disciples' feet Jn 13:5
the night and w-ed their wounds. Ac 16:33
and w away your sins by calling Ac 22:16
but you were w-ed, you were 1Co 6:11
in the w-ing of water by the word. Eph 5:26
w-ed the saints' feet, helped 1Tm 5:10
through the w-ing of regeneration Ti 3:5
sow, after w-ing itself, wallows 2Pt 2:22
w-ed their robes and made them Rv 7:14
Blessed ... who w their robes, Rv 22:14

WASHINGS

teaching about ritual w, laying Heb 6:2
and various w imposed until Heb 9:10

WASHBASIN

Moab is My w; Ps 60:8; 108:9

WASTE (n)

I will lay w mountains and hills, Is 42:15
I will make the land a desolate w, Ezk 6:14

WASTE (v)

will w away because of their sin;	Lv 26:39
His flesh w-s away to nothing,	Jb 33:21
and my bones w away.	Ps 31:10
their form will w away in Sheol,	Ps 49:14
the world w-s away and withers;	Is 24:4
I w away! I w away! Woe is me.	Is 24:16
Why has this fragrant oil been w-d?	Mk 14:4
leftovers so that nothing is w-d.	Jn 6:12
my labor for you has been w-d.	Gl 4:11

WASTELAND

makes them wander in a ... w.	Jb 12:24
and fruitful land into salty w,	Ps 107:34
I did not say ... Seek Me in a w.	Is 45:19
the earth will become a w	Mc 7:13

WATCH (n)

on You during the night w-es	Ps 63:6
keep w at the door of my lips.	Ps 141:3
keeping w at night over their flock.	Lk 2:8
for they keep w over your souls	Heb 13:17

WATCH (v)

May the LORD w between you and	Gn 31:49
the days when God w-ed over me,	Jb 29:2
the LORD w-es over the way of	Ps 1:6
The LORD w-es over the blameless	Ps 37:18
unless the LORD w-es over a city,	Ps 127:1
Discretion will w over you,	Pr 2:11
wisdom, and she will w over you;	Pr 4:6
She w-es over the activities of her	Pr 31:27
who w-es the wind will not sow,	Ec 11:4
I, the LORD, w over it;	Is 27:3
He will w over him as a shepherd	Jr 31:10
As you were w-ing, a stone broke	Dn 2:34
W the road!	Nah 2:1
W! Be alert! For you don't know	Mk 13:33
Pharisees were w-ing Him closely,	Lk 6:7
{work only} while being w-ed,	Eph 6:6
don't work only while being w-ed,	Col 3:22

WATCHER

have I done to You, W of mankind?	Jb 7:20

WATCHMAN

The w looked out and saw a man	2Sm 18:24
The w reported, "The messenger	2Kg 9:18
the w stays alert in vain.	Ps 127:1
more than w-men for the morning	Ps 130:6
W, what is {left} of the night?	Is 21:11

w-men—they lift up their voices,	Is 52:8
Israel's w-men are blind, all of	Is 56:10
appointed w-men on your walls;	Is 62:6
I appointed w-men over you	Jr 6:17
be a day when w-men will call out	Jr 31:6
I have made you a w	Ezk 3:17; 33:7
I will hold the w accountable for	Ezk 33:6
Ephraim's w is with my God.	Hs 9:8

WATCHTOWER

And you, w for the flock,	Mc 4:8
winepress in it, and built a w.	Mt 21:33

WATER (n)

w covered the earth.	Gn 7:6
I'll also draw w for your camels	Gn 24:19
Turbulent as w, you will no longer	Gn 49:4
I drew him out of the w.	Ex 2:10
I will strike the w in the Nile	Ex 7:17
So the w-s were divided,	Ex 14:21
there was no w for the people	Ex 17:1
and He will bless ... your w.	Ex 23:25
the bitter w that brings a curse.	Nm 5:18
Must we bring w out of this rock	Nm 20:10
feed him only bread and w until	1Kg 22:27
When He withholds the w-s,	Jb 12:15
as w wears away stones and	Jb 14:19
who drinks injustice like w?	Jb 15:16
You gave no w to the thirsty and	Jb 22:7
a tree planted beside streams of w	Ps 1:3
I am poured out like w,	Ps 22:14
He leads me beside quiet w-s.	Ps 23:2
voice of the LORD is above the w-s.	Ps 29:3
though its w-s roar and foam and	Ps 46:3
in a land that is ... without w.	Ps 63:1
we went through fire and w,	Ps 66:12
for the w has risen to my neck.	Ps 69:1
Your path through the great w-s,	Ps 77:19
the w stood firm like a wall.	Ps 78:13
At Your rebuke the w-s fled;	Ps 104:7
He turns a desert into a pool of w,	Ps 107:35
the w-s would have engulfed us;	Ps 124:4
Drink w from your own cistern,	Pr 5:15
Stolen w is sweet,	Pr 9:17
who gives a drink of w will receive	Pr 11:25
Counsel in a man's heart is deep w;	Pr 20:5
A king's heart is a w channel in	Pr 21:1
is thirsty, give him w to drink;	Pr 25:21
land is like cold w to a parched	Pr 25:25
bread on the surface of the w-s,	Ec 11:1

a well of flowing w streaming | Sg 4:15
w-s cannot extinguish love; | Sg 8:7
as the sea is filled with w. | Is 11:9
measured the w-s in the hollow | Is 40:12
turn the desert into a pool of w | Is 41:18
when you pass through the w-s, | Is 43:2
who is thirsty, come to the w-s; | Is 55:1
abandoned ... fountain of living w, | Jr 2:13
{their} knees will turn to w. | Ezk 7:17
will also sprinkle clean w on you, | Ezk 36:25
like the roar of mighty w-s, | Ezk 43:2
w-s engulfed me up to the neck; | Jnh 2:5
glory, as the w-s cover the sea. | Hab 2:14
that day living w will flow out | Zch 14:8
I baptize you with w for repentance, | Mt 3:11
a cup of cold w to one of these | Mt 10:42
Peter started walking on the w | Mt 14:29
the chief servant tasted the w | Jn 2:9
is born of w and the Spirit, | Jn 3:5
there was plenty of w there. | Jn 3:23
and He would give you living w. | Jn 4:10
time to time and stir up the w. | Jn 5:4
of living w flow from deep | Jn 7:38
at once blood and w came out. | Jn 19:34
John baptized with w, but you will be | Ac 1:5
eunuch said, "Look, there's w! | Ac 8:36
Can anyone withhold w | Ac 10:47
in the washing of w by the word. | Eph 5:26
Don't continue drinking only w, | 1Tm 5:23
sweet and bitter w from the same | Jms 3:11
eight ... were saved through w. | 1Pt 3:20
people are springs without w, | 2Pt 2:17
and through w by the word of God. | 2Pt 3:5
the One who came by w and blood; | 1Jn 5:6
the Spirit, the w, and the blood | 1Jn 5:8
like the sound of cascading w-s. | Rv 1:15
them to springs of living w-s, | Rv 7:17
third of the w-s became wormwood. | Rv 8:11
spring of living w as a gift. | Rv 21:6
showed me the river of living w, | Rv 22:1

WATER (v)

and w the entire surface of the land. | Gn 2:6
to w their father's flock | Ex 2:16
visit the earth and w it abundantly, | Ps 65:9
spring showers that w the earth. | Ps 72:6
I planted, Apollos w-ed, but God | 1Co 3:6

WATERFALLS

calls to deep in the roar of Your w; | Ps 42:7

WATERLESS

roams through w places looking | Mt 12:43
They are w clouds carried along | Jd 12

WATERY

sources of the w depths burst open, | Gn 7:11
The w depths congealed in the | Ex 15:8
the w depths overcame me; | Jnh 2:5

WAVE

sons and w them as a presentation | Ex 29:24
breast is to be w-d as a | Lv 7:30
He will w the sheaf before the | Lv 23:11
will w his hand over the spot | 2Kg 5:11
may it w on the tops of the | Ps 72:16
As if a staff could w those who lift | Is 10:15
He will w His hand over the | Is 11:15

WAVER

he did not w in obeying the LORD | 2Ch 27:6
trusted in the LORD without w-ing. | Ps 26:1
idols from My presence and do not w, | Jr 4:1
He did not w in unbelief at God's | Rm 4:20
of our hope without w-ing, | Heb 10:23

WAVES

treads on the w of the sea. | Jb 9:8
your proud w stop here"? | Jb 38:11
roar of their w, and the tumult | Ps 65:7
the w of the sea were hushed. | Ps 107:29
righteousness like the w of the sea | Is 48:18
was being swamped by the w. | Mt 8:24
battered by the w, because the | Mt 14:24
even the winds and the w, | Lk 8:25
little children, tossed by the w | Eph 4:14
wild w of the sea, foaming up | Jd 13

WAX

my heart is like w, melting within | Ps 22:14
As w melts before the fire, | Ps 68:2
mountains melt like w at the | Ps 97:5

WAY

teach them the w to live | Ex 18:20
please teach me Your w-s, | Ex 33:13
fear ... by walking in all His w-s, | Dt 10:12
all His w-s are entirely just. | Dt 32:4
now going the w of all the earth, | Jos 23:14
teach you the good and right w. | 1Sm 12:23
God—His w is perfect; | 2Sm 22:31
Turn from your evil w-s | 2Kg 17:13
did not walk in the w of the LORD | 2Kg 21:22

before I go the **w** of no return.   Jb 16:22
He has blocked my **w** so that I   Jb 19:8
Yet He knows the **w** I have taken;   Jb 23:10
watches over the **w** of the righteous   Ps 1:6
He will show him the **w**   Ps 25:12
show me Your **w**, LORD, and lead   Ps 27:11
Commit your **w** to the LORD;   Ps 37:5
I will teach the rebellious Your **w-s**,   Ps 51:13
Your **w** went through the sea,   Ps 77:19
Teach me Your **w**, LORD, and I   Ps 86:11
He revealed His **w-s** to Moses,   Ps 103:7
nations and adopted their **w-s.**   Ps 106:35
happy ... whose **w** is blameless,   Ps 119:1
can a young man keep his **w** pure?   Ps 119:9
thought about my **w-s** and turned   Ps 119:59
therefore I hate every false **w.**   Ps 119:104
will sing of the LORD's **w-s,**   Ps 138:5
See if there is any offensive **w**
  in me; lead me in
  the everlasting **w.**   Ps 139:24
Reveal to me the **w** I should go,   Ps 143:8
The LORD is righteous all His **w-s**   Ps 145:17
think about Him in all your **w-s,**   Pr 3:6
I am teaching you the **w** of wisdom;   Pr 4:11
For a man's **w-s** are before the   Pr 5:21
instructions are the **w** to life.   Pr 6:23
w of the LORD is a stronghold   Pr 10:29
A fool's **w** is right in his own eyes,   Pr 12:15
There is a **w** that seems right   Pr 14:12
but its end is the **w** to death.   Pr 14:12
When a man's **w-s** please the LORD,   Pr 16:7
All the **w-s** of a man seem right   Pr 21:2
strays from the **w** of wisdom will   Pr 21:16
youth about the **w** he should go;   Pr 22:6
and the **w** of a man with a young   Pr 30:19
He will teach us about His **w-s**   Is 2:3
This is the **w.** Walk in it.   Is 30:21
it will be called the Holy **W.**   Is 35:8
Prepare the **w** of the LORD in the   Is 40:3
My **w** is hidden from the LORD,   Is 40:27
I will make a **w** in the wilderness,   Is 43:19
we all have turned to our own **w;**   Is 53:6
the wicked one abandon his **w,**   Is 55:7
and your **w-s** are not My **w-s.**   Is 55:8
so My **w-s** are higher than your **w-s,** Is 55:9
by a smooth **w** where they will   Jr 31:9
will give them one heart and one **w**   Jr 32:39
you say: The Lord's **w** isn't fair.   Ezk 18:25

the **w-s** of the LORD are right,   Hs 14:9
he will clear the **w** before Me.   Mal 3:1
Test Me in this **w**," says the LORD   Mal 3:10
Prepare the **w** for the Lord;   Mt 3:3
he will prepare Your **w**   Mt 11:10
teach truthfully the **w** of God.   Mt 22:16
guide our feet into the **w** of peace.   Lk 1:79
God loved the world in this **w:**   Jn 3:16
You know the **w** where I am going.   Jn 14:4
I am the **w**, the truth, and the life.   Jn 14:6
found any who belonged to the **W,**   Ac 9:2
proclaiming ... the **w** of salvation.   Ac 16:17
explained the **w** of God to him   Ac 18:26
slandering the **W** in front of the   Ac 19:9
a major disturbance about the **W.**   Ac 19:23
to the **W,** which they call   Ac 24:14
too may walk in a new **w** of life.   Rm 6:4
and untraceable His **w-s!**   Rm 11:33
will also provide a **w** of escape,   1Co 10:13
will show you an even better **w.**   1Co 12:31
be like His brothers in every **w,**   Heb 2:17
tested in every **w** as we are,   Heb 4:15
the new and living **w** that He has   Heb 10:20
man is unstable in all his **w-s.**   Jms 1:8
for we all stumble in many **w-s.**   Jms 3:2
the error of his **w** will save his   Jms 5:20
the **w** of truth will be blasphemed.   2Pt 2:2
righteous and true are Your **w-s,**   Rv 15:3

WEAK

I will become **w**   Jdg 16:7,11,17
my spirit is **w** within me,   Ps 142:3
spirit is willing, but the flesh is **w.**   Mt 26:41
it is necessary to help the **w**   Ac 20:35
Accept anyone who is **w** in faith,   Rm 14:1
but one who is **w** eats only   Rm 14:2
God has chosen the ... **w** things   1Co 1:27
We are **w,** but you are strong!   1Co 4:10
conscience, being **w,** is defiled.   1Co 8:7
I became **w,** in order to win the **w.**   1Co 9:22
but his physical presence is **w,**   2Co 10:10
Who is **w,** and I am not **w?**   2Co 11:29
For when I am **w,** then I am   2Co 12:10
help the **w,** be patient with   1Th 5:14

WEAKEN

because he is **w-ing** the morale of   Jr 38:4
without **w-ing** in the faith.   Rm 4:19
your tired hands and **w-ed** knees,   Heb 12:12

WEAKER

the house of Saul becoming w.   2Sm 3:1
that seem to be w are necessary.   1Co 12:22
understanding of their w nature   1Pt 3:7

WEAKEST

my family is the w in Manasseh,   Jdg 6:15

WEAKLING

Let even the w say: I am a warrior.   Jl 3:10

WEAKNESS

took our w-es and carried our   Mt 8:17
also joins to help in our w,   Rm 8:26
and God's w is stronger than   1Co 1:25
was with you in w, in fear, and   1Co 2:3
sown in w, raised in power;   1Co 15:43
I will boast about my w-es.   2Co 11:30
for power is perfected in w.   2Co 12:9
was crucified in w, but He lives   2Co 13:4
unable to sympathize with
  our w-es   Heb 4:15
he himself is also subject to w.   Heb 5:2

WEALTH

God gives you the power to gain w, Dt 8:18
have not requested ... w, or glory, 2Ch 1:11
They trust in their w   Ps 49:6
If w increases, pay no attention   Ps 62:10
W and riches are in his house,   Ps 112:3
A rich man's w is his fortified   Pr 10:15
W is not profitable on a day of   Pr 11:4
and hope placed in w vanishes.   Pr 11:7
to be poor but has great w.   Pr 13:7
W obtained by fraud will dwindle, Pr 13:11
W attracts many friends,   Pr 19:4
name is to be chosen over great w; Pr 22:1
for w is not forever;   Pr 27:24
Give me neither poverty nor w;   Pr 30:8
and whoever loves w {is} never   Ec 5:10
were to give all his w for love,   Sg 8:7
w of the nations will come to you.   Is 60:5
seduction of w choke the word,   Mt 13:22
hard it is for those who have w to Mk 10:23
into the w of their generosity   2Co 8:2
the glorious w of this mystery,   Col 1:27
hope on the uncertainty of w,   1Tm 6:17
to be greater w than the   Heb 11:26
the sea became rich from her w;   Rv 18:19

WEALTHY

have become w, and need nothing, Rv 3:17

WEANED

When she had w him, she took   1Sm 1:24
like a little w child with its mother; Ps 131:2

WEAPON

Saul and ... Jonathan had {w-s}.   1Sm 13:22
Wisdom is better than w-s of war,   Ec 9:18
No w formed against you will   Is 54:17
I will repel the w-s of war in your   Jr 21:4
with lanterns, torches, and w-s.   Jn 18:3
to God as w-s for righteousness.   Rm 6:13
through w-s of righteousness on   2Co 6:7
the w-s of our warfare are not   2Co 10:4

WEAR

Your clothing did not w out,   Dt 8:4
woman is not to w male clothing,   Dt 22:5
sandals of ours are worn out from   Jos 9:13
him until she wore him out,   Jdg 16:16
that the king himself has worn   Est 6:8
but the righteous will w {it},   Jb 27:17
My eyes are worn out from crying.   Ps 88:9
He wore cursing like his coat   Ps 109:18
Don't w yourself out to get rich;   Pr 23:4
will w all your children as jewelry,   Is 49:18
the earth will w out like a garment,   Is 51:6
eyes are worn out from weeping;   Lm 2:11
He has worn away my flesh   Lm 3:4
about your body, what you will w.   Mt 6:25
they were weary and worn out,   Mt 9:36
those who w soft clothes are in   Mt 11:8
wore a camel-hair garment with   Mk 1:6
so she doesn't w me out by her   Lk 18:5
there, and Jesus, worn out from His   Jn 4:6
They will all w out like clothing;   Heb 1:11
and the w-ing of gold ornaments   1Pt 3:3

WEARISOME

All things are w; man is unable   Ec 1:8

WEARY (adj)

and there the w find rest.   Jb 3:17
I am w from my groaning;   Ps 6:6
I am w from my crying;   Ps 69:3
I am w from grief;   Ps 119:28
eyes grow w {looking for} Your   Ps 119:123
they will run and not grow w;   Is 40:31
to sustain the w with a word.   Is 50:4

were **w** and worn out, like sheep　Mt 9:36
Come to Me, all of you who are **w**　Mt 11:28
do not grow **w** in doing good.　2Th 3:13
you won't grow **w** and lose heart.　Heb 12:3
and have not grown **w**.　Rv 2:3

WEARY (v)

and much study **w-ies** the body.　Ec 12:12
have **w-ied** Me with your iniquities.　Is 43:24
You have **w-ied** the LORD with　Mal 2:17

WEATHER

will be good **w** because the sky　Mt 16:2

WEAVE　see also WOVEN (adj)

You are to **w** the tunic from fine　Ex 28:39
wove me together with bones and　Jb 10:11
who skillfully **w** spells.　Ps 58:5
eggs and **w** spider's webs.　Is 59:5

WEAVER

spear shaft was like a **w-'s** beam,　1Sm 17:7
his spear was like a **w-'s** beam.　2Sm 21:19
pass more swiftly than a **w-'s** shuttle;　Jb 7:6
have rolled up my life like a **w**;　Is 38:12

WEB

on my head with the **w** of a loom　Jdg 16:13
he trusts in is a spider's **w**.　Jb 8:14

WEDDING

His young women had no **w** songs.　Ps 78:63
placed on him the day of his **w**　Sg 3:11
Can the **w** guests be sad while　Mt 9:15
king who gave a **w** banquet for　Mt 22:2
get in here without **w** clothes?'　Mt 22:12
in with him to the **w** banquet,　Mt 25:10
their master to return from the **w**　Lk 12:36
by someone to a **w** banquet,　Lk 14:8
a **w** took place in Cana of Galilee.　Jn 2:1

WEEDS

w among the wheat,　Mt 13:25

WEEK

He finished the **w** {of celebration}　Gn 29:28
Observe the Festival of **W-s**　Ex 34:22
count seven complete **w-s**　Lv 23:15
Seventy **w-s** are decreed　Dn 9:24
will be seven **w-s** and 62 **w-s**.　Dn 9:25
first day of the **w** was dawning,　Mt 28:1
I fast twice a **w**; I give a tenth　Lk 18:12

On the first day of the **w**,　Ac 20:7
On the first day of the **w**,　1Co 16:2

WEEP

turned away from them and **wept**.　Gn 42:24
Hannah **wept** and would not eat.　1Sm 1:7
and **wept**, but when he died,　2Sm 12:21
of Olives, **w-ing** as he ascended.　2Sm 15:30
The man of God **wept**,　2Kg 8:11
And Hezekiah **wept** bitterly.　2Kg 20:3
who had seen the first temple,
　　wept　Ezr 3:12
shouting from that of the **w-ing**,　Ezr 3:13
these words, I sat down and **wept**.　Neh 1:4
Do not mourn or **w**.　Neh 8:9
face has grown red with **w-ing**,　Jb 16:16
for the LORD has heard ... my **w-ing**.　Ps 6:8
W-ing may spend the night, but　Ps 30:5
Though one goes along **w-ing**,　Ps 126:6
wept when we remembered Zion.　Ps 137:1
a time to **w** and a time to laugh;　Ec 3:4
GOD of Hosts called for **w-ing**,　Is 22:12
w-ing and crying will no longer be　Is 65:19
I would **w** day and night over the　Jr 9:1
They will come **w-ing**, but I will　Jr 31:9
Rachel **w-ing** for her children,　Jr 31:15
My eyes are worn out from **w-ing**,　Lm 2:11
not lament or **w** or let your　Ezk 24:16
turn to Me ... with fasting, **w-ing**,　Jl 2:12
for Him as one **w-s** for a firstborn.　Zch 12:10
Rachel **w-ing** for her children;　Mt 2:18
there will be **w-ing** and gnashing　Mt 8:12
he went outside and **wept** bitterly.　Mt 26:75
w-ing? The child is not dead　Mk 5:39
Blessed are you who **w** now,　Lk 6:21
His feet, **w-ing**, and began to wash　Lk 7:38
and saw the city, He **wept** over it,　Lk 19:41
not **w** for Me, but **w** for yourselves　Lk 23:28
Jesus **wept**.　Jn 11:35
You will **w** and wail, but the world　Jn 16:20
who rejoice; **w** with those who **w**.　Rm 12:15
who **w** as though they did not **w**,　1Co 7:30
with her will **w** and mourn over　Rv 18:9

WEIGH

and actions are **w-ed** by Him.　1Sm 2:3
would **w** the hair from his head　2Sm 14:26
If only my grief could be **w-ed**　Jb 6:2
together they {**w**} less than a　Ps 62:9
in a man's heart **w-s** it down,　Pr 12:25

but the LORD w-s the motives.   Pr 16:2
won't He who w-s hearts consider   Pr 24:12
and it w-s heavily on humanity: Ec 6:1
Who has ... w-ed the mountains   Is 40:12
you have been w-ed in the balance   Dn 5:27
they w-ed out 30 pieces of silver   Mt 26:15

WEIGHT

honest balances, honest w-s,   Lv 19:36
When God fixed the w of the wind   Jb 28:25
an accurate w is His delight.   Pr 11:1
all the w-s in the bag are His   Pr 16:11
Differing w-s ... detestable to   Pr 20:10,23
Can I excuse ... deceptive w-s?   Mc 6:11
incomparable eternal w of glory.   2Co 4:17
lay aside every w and the sin that   Heb 12:1

WEIGHTY

His letters are w and powerful,   2Co 10:10

WELCOME

one who w-s you w-s Me,   Mt 10:40
whoever w-s one child like this   Mt 18:5
hear the word, w it, and produce   Mk 4:20
How w are the feet of those who   Rm 10:15
natural man does not w what   1Co 2:14
a w sacrifice, pleasing to God.   Php 4:18
some have w-d angels as guests   Heb 13:2
says, "W," to him shares in his evil   2Jn 11

WELFARE

Seek the w of the city I have   Jr 29:7
plans for {your} w, not for disaster,   Jr 29:11

WE'LL

then w come back to you.   Gn 22:5

WELL (adj)

Those who are w don't need a   Mt 9:12
Your faith has made you w.   Mt 9:22

WELL (adv)

and I know {this} very w.   Ps 139:14
will go w with God-fearing people,   Ec 8:12
master said to him, 'W done,   Mt 25:21
that it may go w with you and   Eph 6:3
that God is one; you do w.   Jms 2:19

WELL (n)

W of the Living One Who Sees   Gn 16:14
of Midian, and sat down by a w.   Ex 2:15
w-s dug that you did not dig,   Dt 6:11
from the w at ... Bethlehem!   2Sm 23:15

water flowing from your own w.   Pr 5:15
a forbidden woman is a narrow w;   Pr 23:27
a w of flowing water streaming   Sg 4:15
Jacob's w was there, and Jesus,   Jn 4:6

WELL-BEING

many days, a full life, and w.   Pr 3:2
Do not pray for the w of these   Jr 14:11

WELL-FED

cows ate the healthy, w cows.   Gn 41:4
content—whether w or hungry,   Php 4:12

WELL-WATERED

entire Jordan Valley ... was w   Gn 13:10

WENT see GO

WE'RE

Don't you care that w going to die?   Mk 4:38

WEST

strong w wind, and it carried off   Ex 10:19
and if I go w, I cannot perceive Him.   Jb 23:8
far as the east is from the w,   Ps 103:12
and gather you from the w.   Is 43:5
They will fear ... the LORD in the w,   Is 59:19
male goat ... coming from the w   Dn 8:5
many will come from east and w,   Mt 8:11
and flashes as far as the w,   Mt 24:27
you see a cloud rising in the w,   Lk 12:54

WHATEVER

W he does prospers.   Ps 1:3
The LORD does w He pleases in   Ps 135:6
And w else you get, get   Pr 4:7
W your hands find to do, do with   Ec 9:10
W you ask in My name, I will do   Jn 14:13
you eat or drink, or w you do,   1Co 10:31
brothers, w is true, w is honorable,   Php 4:8
w you do, in word or in deed,   Col 3:17
W you do, do it enthusiastically,   Col 3:23

WHEAT

firstfruits of the w harvest,   Ex 34:22
Isn't the w harvest today?   1Sm 12:17
He satisfies you with the finest w.   Ps 147:14
Your waist is a mound of w   Sg 7:2
have sown w but harvested thorns.   Jr 12:13
and gather His w into the barn.   Mt 3:12
sowed weeds among the w,   Mt 13:25
has asked to sift you like w.   Lk 22:31

Unless a grain of w falls into — Jn 12:24
A quart of w for a denarius, — Rv 6:6

WHEEL

caused their chariot w-s to swerve — Ex 14:25
and the w is broken into the well; — Ec 12:6
{chariot} w-s are like a whirlwind. — Is 5:28
was like a w within a w. — Ezk 1:16
of the whip and rumble of the w, — Nah 3:2

WHEREVER

w he turns, he succeeds. — Pr 17:8
He directs it w He chooses. — Pr 21:1
W this gospel is proclaimed in — Mt 26:13

WHETHER

W it's right in the sight of God — Ac 4:19
Therefore, w we live or die, we — Rm 14:8
W he was in the body or out of — 2Co 12:2

WHIP (n)

A w for the horse, a bridle for — Pr 26:3
The crack of the w and rumble of — Nah 3:2
After making a w out of cords, — Jn 2:15

WHIPPED

I will have Him w and — Lk 23:16

WHIRL

w-ing sword to guard the way to — Gn 3:24
A sword will w through his — Hs 11:6

WHIRLWIND

Elijah up to heaven in a w. — 2Kg 2:1
LORD answered Job from the w. — Jb 38:1
your calamity comes like a w, — Pr 1:27
When the w passes, the wicked — Pr 10:25
a w carries them away like stubble. — Is 40:24
His chariots are like the w — Is 66:15
there was a w coming from the — Ezk 1:4
sow the wind and reap the w. — Hs 8:7
His path is in the w and storm, — Nah 1:3
mists driven by a w. — 2Pt 2:17

WHISPER

there was a voice, a soft w. — 1Kg 19:12
my ears caught a w of it. — Jb 4:12
All who hate me w together about — Ps 41:7
What you hear in a w, proclaim — Mt 10:27
and what you have w-ed in an ear — Lk 12:3

WHISTLE

distant nations and w-s for them — Is 5:26

the LORD will w to the fly that — Is 7:18
I will w and gather them because — Zch 10:8

WHITE

hair in the infection has turned w — Lv 13:3
became diseased, as {w} as snow. — Nm 12:10
diseased—{w} as snow. — 2Kg 5:27
scarlet, they will be as w as snow; — Is 1:18
His clothing was w like snow, — Dn 7:9
were red, sorrel, and w horses. — Zch 1:8
make a single hair w or black. — Mt 5:36
and his robe was as w as snow. — Mt 28:3
extremely w as no launderer — Mk 9:3
two angels in w sitting there, — Jn 20:12
head and hair were w like wool — Rv 1:14
in w, because they are worthy. — Rv 3:4
looked, and there was a w horse. — Rv 6:2
and made them w in the blood — Rv 7:14
I saw a great w throne and One — Rv 20:11

WHITEN

as no launderer ... could w them. — Mk 9:3

WHITER

and his teeth are w than milk. — Gn 49:12
and I will be w than snow. — Ps 51:7

WHITEWASH

the wall you plastered with w — Ezk 13:14
plaster with w for them by — Ezk 22:28
You are like w-ed tombs, — Mt 23:27
strike you, you w-ed wall! — Ac 23:3

WHO

w do you say that I am? — Mt 16:15

WHOEVER

w calls on the name of the Lord — Ac 2:21

WHOLE

over the face of the w earth. — Gn 11:4
Isn't the w land before you? — Gn 13:9
Let the w earth tremble before — Ps 33:8
is the joy of the w earth. — Ps 48:2
Your glory be over the w earth. — Ps 57:11
the w earth is filled with His glory. — Ps 72:19
His glory fills the w earth. — Is 6:3
than for your w body to be — Mt 5:29
your w body will be full of light. — Mt 6:22
if he gains the w world yet loses — Mt 16:26
declaring ... the w plan of God. — Ac 20:27
we know that the w creation has — Rm 8:22

If the w body were an eye, 1Co 12:17
also for those of the w world. 1Jn 2:2

WHOLEHEARTED
Asa was w his entire life. 2Ch 15:17

WHOLEHEARTEDLY
but {work} w, fearing the Lord. Col 3:22

WHOM
my salvation—w should I fear? Ps 27:1
W do I have in heaven but You? Ps 73:25
because I know w I have believed 2Tm 1:12

WHOSE
the people w God is the LORD. Ps 144:15
W image and inscription is this? Mt 22:20
the Messiah? W Son is He? Mt 22:42

WHY
My God, my God, w have You Ps 22:1
My God, My God, w have You Mt 27:46
W did you make me like this? Rm 9:20

WICK
will not put out a smoldering w; Is 42:3
extinguished, quenched like a w Is 43:17
will not put out a smoldering w, Mt 12:20

WICKED
the righteous with the w? Gn 18:23
but the w are silenced in darkness, 1Sm 2:9
Do you help the w and love those 2Ch 19:2
Why do the w continue to live, Jb 21:7
does not follow the advice of the w, Ps 1:1
Therefore the w will not survive Ps 1:5
Let the evil of the w come to an end, Ps 7:9
You have destroyed the w; Ps 9:5
The w will return to Sheol Ps 9:17
Why has the w despised God? Ps 10:13
For look, the w string the bow; Ps 11:2
and I do not sit with the w. Ps 26:5
and the w will be no more; Ps 37:10
The w go astray from the womb; Ps 58:3
I saw the prosperity of the w. Ps 73:3
cut off all the horns of the w, Ps 75:10
and show partiality to the w? Ps 82:2
save them from the hand of the w, Ps 82:4
than to live in the tents of the w. Ps 84:10
how long will the w gloat? Ps 94:3
flames consumed the w. Ps 106:18
Set a w person over him; Ps 109:6
The w man will see {it} and be Ps 112:10

Salvation is far from the w Ps 119:155
He frustrates the ways of the w. Ps 146:9
the w will be cut off from the land, Pr 2:22
Don't set foot on the path of the w; Pr 4:14
a heart that plots w schemes, Pr 6:18
who rebukes a w man will get Pr 9:7
mouth of the w conceals
   violence. Pr 10:6,11
What the w dreads will come Pr 10:24
years of the w are cut short. Pr 10:27
When the w dies, his expectation Pr 11:7
the w will not go unpunished, Pr 11:21
the hope of the w {leads to} Pr 11:23
lamp of the w is extinguished Pr 13:9
sacrifice of the w is detestable to Pr 15:8
The LORD is far from the w, Pr 15:29
even the w for the day of disaster. Pr 16:4
A w person desires evil; Pr 21:10
He brings the w to ruin. Pr 21:12
and don't envy the w. Pr 24:19
Remove the w from the king's Pr 25:5
when the w come to power, Pr 28:12,28
all his servants will be w. Pr 29:12
When the w increase, rebellion Pr 29:16
the upright is detestable to the w. Pr 29:27
judge the righteous and the w, Ec 3:17
Don't be excessively w, Ec 7:17
it will not go well with the w, Ec 8:13
one fate for the righteous and the w, Ec 9:2
is no peace ... for the w. Is 48:22; 57:21
They made His grave with the w, Is 53:9
Let the w one abandon his way, Is 55:7
the w are like the storm-tossed sea, Is 57:20
does the way of the w prosper? Jr 12:1
But if you warn a w person and Ezk 3:19
Now if the w person turns from Ezk 18:21
pleasure in the death of the w? Ezk 18:23
if you warn a w person to turn Ezk 33:9
no pleasure in the death of the w, Ezk 33:11
But when a w person turns from Ezk 33:19
but the w will act wickedly; Dn 12:10
between the righteous and the w, Mal 3:18
You w slave! I forgave you all that Mt 18:32
But if that w slave says in his heart, Mt 24:48
who practices w things hates the Jn 3:20
those who have done w things, Jn 5:29

WICKEDLY
faithfully, while we have acted w. Neh 9:33

WICKEDNESS (continued)

God does not act w	Jb 34:12
gone astray and have acted w.	Ps 106:6
have sinned, done wrong, acted w,	Dn 9:5
but the wicked will act w;	Dn 12:10

WICKEDNESS

saw that man's w was widespread	Gn 6:5
W comes from wicked people.	1Sm 24:13
Isn't your w abundant and aren't	Jb 22:5
are not a God who delights in w;	Ps 5:4
You love righteousness and hate w;	Ps 45:7
They eat the bread of w	Pr 4:17
and w is detestable to my lips.	Pr 8:7
but w undermines the sinner.	Pr 13:6
W is atoned for by loyalty and	Pr 16:6
and to know that w is stupidity	Ec 7:25
For w burns like a fire that	Is 9:18
You were secure in your w;	Is 47:10
and he does not turn from his w	Ezk 3:19
wicked person turns from the w	Ezk 18:27
your ways until w was found in	Ezk 28:15
turns from his w and does what	Ezk 33:19
You have plowed w and reaped	Hs 10:13
their w has confronted Me.	Jnh 1:2
do those who commit w prosper,	Mal 3:15
repent of this w of yours,	Ac 8:22
evil, greed, and w.	Rm 1:29
from you, along with all w.	Eph 4:31
So rid yourselves of all w,	1Pt 2:1

WIDE

open their mouths w against me	Ps 35:21
Open your mouth w, and I will	Ps 81:10
Sheol ... opens w its enormous	Is 5:14
the gate is w and the road is broad	Mt 7:13
because a w door for effective	1Co 16:9
our heart has been opened w.	2Co 6:11

WIDELY

It is w reported that there is	1Co 5:1

WIDEN

You w {a place} beneath me for	2Sm 22:37

WIDE-OPEN

unsuspecting people and a w land,	Jdg 18:10
He brought me out to a w place;	2Sm 22:20

WIDESPREAD

wickedness was w on the earth	Gn 6:5
prophetic visions were not w.	1Sm 3:1

WIDOW

Remain a w in your father's	Gn 38:11
not mistreat any w or fatherless	Ex 22:22
not to marry a w, a divorced	Lv 21:14
Any vow a w ... puts herself under	Nm 30:9
justice for the fatherless and the w,	Dt 10:18
You sent w-s away empty-handed,	Jb 22:9
I made the w-'s heart rejoice.	Jb 29:13
and a champion of w-s is God	Ps 68:5
They kill the w and the foreigner	Ps 94:6
be fatherless and his wife a w.	Ps 109:9
helps the fatherless and the w,	Ps 146:9
but He protects the w-'s territory.	Pr 15:25
Plead the w-'s cause.	Is 1:17
let your w-s trust in Me.	Jr 49:11
the nations has become like a w.	Lm 1:1
devour w-s' houses and make long	Mt 23:14
a poor w came and dropped in	Mk 12:42
and was a w for 84 years.	Lk 2:37
because this w keeps pestering	Lk 18:5
their w-s were being overlooked	Ac 6:1
I say to the unmarried and to w-s:	1Co 7:8
Support w-s who are genuinely w-s.	1Tm 5:3
look after ... w-s in their distress	Jms 1:27
I am not a w, and I will never	Rv 18:7

WIDOWHOOD

in one day: loss of children and w.	Is 47:9
no longer remember ... your w.	Is 54:4

WIDTH

what is the breadth and w, height	Eph 3:18

WIELDS

well as him who w the sickle	Jr 50:16
and the one who w the scepter	Am 1:5,8

WIFE

and mother and bonds with his w,	Gn 2:24
But his w looked back	Gn 19:26
Do not covet your neighbor's w,	Ex 20:17
If any man's w goes astray,	Nm 5:12
If a man has two w-ves, one loved	Dt 21:15
Manoah and his w were watching.	Jdg 13:19
do about w-ves for the survivors?	Jdg 21:7
w of Uriah the Hittite.	2Sm 11:3
700 w-ves who ... turned his heart	1Kg 11:3
send away all the {foreign} w-ves	Ezr 10:3
His w said to him, "Do you still	Jb 2:9
been seduced by {my neighbor's} w	Jb 31:9
Your w will be like a fruitful	Ps 128:3

pleasure in the **w** of your youth.	Pr 5:18
who sleeps with another man's **w**;	Pr 6:29
A capable **w** is her husband's	Pr 12:4
A man who finds a **w** finds a good	Pr 18:22
and a **w**-'s nagging is an endless	Pr 19:13
but a sensible **w** is from the LORD.	Pr 19:14
Who can find a capable **w**?	Pr 31:10
Enjoy life with the **w** you love	Ec 9:9
has called you, like a **w** deserted	Is 54:6
and my **w** died in the evening.	Ezk 24:18
Go and marry a promiscuous **w**	Hs 1:2
against the **w** of your youth.	Mal 2:15
afraid to take Mary as your **w**,	Mt 1:20
everyone who divorces his **w**,	Mt 5:32
mother and is joined to his **w**,	Mt 19:5
whose **w** will she be of the seven?	Mt 22:28
his **w** sent word to him,	Mt 27:19
you to have your brother's **w**!	Mk 6:18
does not hate his ... **w**	
and children,	Lk 14:26
Remember Lot's **w**!	Lk 17:32
has left a house, **w** or brothers,	Lk 18:29
with his **w**-'s knowledge,	Ac 5:2
each man should have his own **w**,	1Co 7:2
his marital duty to his **w**,	1Co 7:3
brother has an unbelieving **w**,	1Co 7:12
how he may please his **w**	1Co 7:33
A **w** is bound as long as her	1Co 7:39
be accompanied by a Christian **w**,	1Co 9:5
W-ves, submit to your	Eph 5:22
the husband is head of the **w**	Eph 5:23
Husbands, love your **w**-ves,	Eph 5:25
mother and be joined to his **w**,	Eph 5:31
W-ves, be submissive to your	Col 3:18
Husbands, love your **w**-ves	Col 3:19
husband of one **w**,	1Tm 3:2
W-ves, too, must be worthy of	1Tm 3:11
must be husbands of one **w**,	1Tm 3:12
has been the **w** of one husband,	1Tm 5:9
of one **w**, having faithful	Ti 1:6
W-ves, in the same way, submit	1Pt 3:1
message by the way their **w**-ves live,	1Pt 3:1
with your **w**-ves with understanding	1Pt 3:7
the bride, the **w** of the Lamb.	Rv 21:9

WILD

each **w** animal and each bird	Gn 2:19
This man will be {like} a **w** ass.	Gn 16:12
as well as animals in the **w**,	Ps 8:7

of their hearts run **w**.	Ps 73:7
supply water for every **w** beast;	Ps 104:11
w animals and all cattle,	Ps 148:10
Without revelation people run **w**,	Pr 29:18
w animals will lie down there,	Is 13:21
to live with the **w** animals.	Dn 4:25
food was locusts and **w** honey.	Mt 3:4
He was with the **w** animals,	Mk 1:13
you, though a **w** olive branch,	Rm 11:17
If I fought **w** animals in Ephesus	1Co 15:32

WILDERNESS

by a spring of water in the **w**,	Gn 16:7
Your corpses will fall in this **w**	Nm 14:29
I led you 40 years in the **w**;	Dt 29:5
in a barren, howling **w**;	Dt 32:10
able to provide food in the **w**?	Ps 78:19
Some wandered in the desolate **w**,	Ps 107:4
He led His people in the **w**.	Ps 136:16
to live in a **w** than with a	Pr 21:19
coming up from the **w**,	Sg 3:6; 8:5
who turned the world into a **w**,	Is 14:17
Prepare the way of the LORD in the **w**	Is 40:3
I will make a way in the **w**,	Is 43:19
Have I been a **w** to Israel	Jr 2:31
lead her to the **w**, and speak tenderly	Hs 2:14
voice of one crying out in the **w**:	Mt 3:3
into the **w** to be tempted	Mt 4:1
This place is a **w**, and it is	Mt 14:15
tell you, 'Look, he's in the **w**!'	Mt 24:26
lifted up the snake in the **w**,	Jn 3:14
fathers ate the manna in the **w**,	Jn 6:31,49

WILDFLOWERS

Consider how the **w** grow:	Lk 12:27

WILDLIFE

So God made the **w** of the earth	Gn 1:25
They {entered it} with all the **w**	Gn 7:14

WILDNESS

not accused of **w** or rebellion.	Ti 1:6

WILL (n)

I delight to do Your **w**, my God;	Ps 40:8
Teach me to do Your **w**,	Ps 143:10
Your **w** be done on earth as it is	Mt 6:10
one who does the **w** of My Father	Mt 7:21
Yet not as I **w**, but as You **w**.	Mt 26:39
flesh, or of the **w** of man, but of God.	Jn 1:13
My food is to do the **w** of Him	Jn 4:34

own w, but the w of Him who sent | Jn 5:30
If anyone wants to do His w, | Jn 7:17
has appointed you to know His w, | Ac 22:14
it does not depend on human w | Rm 9:16
For who can resist His w? | Rm 9:19
the good, pleasing, and perfect w | Rm 12:2
according to His favor and w, | Eph 1:5
understand what the Lord's w is. | Eph 5:17
do God's w from your heart. | Eph 6:6
filled with the knowledge of His w | Col 1:9
this is God's w, your sanctification: | 1Th 4:3
Give thanks ... is God's w for you | 1Th 5:18
the Holy Spirit according to His w. | Heb 2:4
Where a w exists, the death of the | Heb 9:16
See, I have come to do Your w. | Heb 10:9
with all that is good to do His w, | Heb 13:21
ask anything according to His w, | 1Jn 5:14
because of Your will they exist | Rv 4:11

WILL (v)

and He hardens whom He w-s. | Rm 9:18
w and to act for His good purpose. | Php 2:13
say, "If the Lord w-s, we will | Jms 4:15

WILLFUL

keep Your servant from w sins; | Ps 19:13

WILLFULLY

If a person w acts against his | Ex 21:14
They w ignore this: | 2Pt 3:5

WILLING (adj)

Let everyone whose heart is w bring | Ex 35:5
and give me a w spirit. | Ps 51:12
and works with w hands. | Pr 31:13
If you are w and obedient, | Is 1:19
Lord, if You are w, You can make | Mt 8:2
her wings, yet you were not w! | Mt 23:37
The spirit is w, but the flesh | Mt 26:41
if You are w, take this cup away | Lk 22:42
If ... she is w to live with him, | 1Co 7:12
isn't w to work, he should not eat. | 2Th 3:10

WILLINGLY

w open your hand to your ... poor | Dt 15:11
giving joyfully and w to You. | 1Ch 29:17
counselors have w given to the | Ezr 7:15
was subjected to futility—not w, | Rm 8:20
if I do this w, I have a reward | 1Co 9:17

WILLINGNESS

because of their leaders' w to give, | 1Ch 29:9

WIN

you have won your brother. | Mt 18:15
in order to w more people. | 1Co 9:19
Run in such a way that you may w. | 1Co 9:24
I now trying to w the favor of | Gl 1:10
they may be won over without a | 1Pt 3:1

WIND

God caused a w to pass over the | Gn 8:1
east w had brought in the locusts. | Ex 10:13
a powerful east w all that night | Ex 14:21
but the LORD was not in the w. | 1Kg 19:11
A w passed by me, and I shuddered | Jb 4:15
a storm w sweeps him away | Jb 27:20
God fixed the weight of the w | Jb 28:25
chaff the w blows away. | Ps 1:4
soaring on the wings of the w. | Ps 18:10
when the w passes over it, | Ps 103:16
making the w-s His messengers, | Ps 104:4
brings the w from His storehouses. | Ps 135:7
w that executes His command, | Ps 148:8
will inherit the w, | Pr 11:29
like clouds and w without rain. | Pr 25:14
controls the w and grasps oil | Pr 27:16
turning, turning, goes the w, | Ec 1:6
to be futile, a pursuit of the w. | Ec 1:14
who watches the w will not sow, | Ec 11:4
don't know the path of the w, | Ec 11:5
Awaken, north w—come, south w. | Sg 4:16
The prophets become {only} w, | Jr 5:13
from the four w-s and breathe | Ezk 37:9
they sow the w and reap the | Hs 8:7
Ephraim chases the w and pursues | Hs 12:1
the One who ... creates the w, | Am 4:13
appointed a scorching east w. | Jnh 4:8
w-s blew and pounded that house | Mt 7:25
the w-s and the sea obey Him! | Mt 8:27
A reed swaying in the w? | Mt 11:7
got into the boat, the w ceased. | Mt 14:32
The w blows where it pleases, | Jn 3:8
sound ... of a violent rushing w | Ac 2:2
around by every w of teaching, | Eph 4:14
He makes His angels w-s, | Heb 1:7
driven and tossed by the w. | Jms 1:6
clouds carried along by w-s; | Jd 12
restraining the four w-s of the earth | Rv 7:1

WINDOW

Noah opened the w of the ark | Gn 8:6
down by a rope through the w, | Jos 2:15

she lowered David from the w, 1Sm 19:12
LORD were to make w-s in heaven, 2Kg 7:2
gazing through the w-s, Sg 2:9
Death has climbed through our w-s; Jr 9:21
The w-s in its upper room opened Dn 6:10
enter through the w-s like thieves. Jl 2:9
Eutychus was sitting on a w sill Ac 20:9
let down in a basket through a w 2Co 11:33

WINDSTORM

A fierce w arose, and the waves Mk 4:37

WINE

drank some of the w,
  became drunk, Gn 9:21
not to drink w ... when you enter Lv 10:9
offering will be one quart of w. Lv 23:13
he is to abstain from w and beer. Nm 6:3
He will bless ... your grain, new w, Dt 7:13
She must not ... drink w Jdg 13:14
Royal w flowed freely, Est 1:7
drinking w in their oldest brother's Jb 1:13
when their grain and new w abound. Ps 4:7
a w to drink that made us stagger. Ps 60:3
w that makes man's heart glad Ps 104:15
vats will overflow with new w. Pr 3:10
and drink the w of violence. Pr 4:17
W is a mocker, beer is a brawler, Pr 20:1
whoever loves w and oil will not Pr 21:17
with those who drink too much w, Pr 23:20
Don't gaze at w when it is red, Pr 23:31
it is not for kings to drink w Pr 31:4
and w to one whose life is bitter. Pr 31:6
drink your w with a cheerful heart, Ec 9:7
your love is more delightful than w. Sg 1:2
Your mouth is like fine w Sg 7:9
buy w and milk without money Is 55:1
Take this cup of the w of wrath Jr 25:15
I will preach to you about w Mc 2:11
Moreover, w betrays; Hab 2:5
no one puts new w into old Mt 9:17
they gave Him w mixed with gall Mt 27:34
and will never drink w or beer. Lk 1:15
wounds, pouring on oil and w. Lk 10:34
water (after it had become w), Jn 2:9
said, "They're full of new w!" Ac 2:13
not to eat meat, or drink w, Rm 14:21
And don't get drunk with w, Eph 5:18
not addicted to w, 1Tm 3:3; Ti 1:7
not drinking a lot of w, 1Tm 3:8

a little w because of your stomach 1Tm 5:23
do not harm the olive oil and the w. Rv 6:6
also drink the w of God's wrath, Rv 14:10

WINEPRESS

threshing floor, and your w. Dt 15:14
I trampled the w alone, Is 63:3
because the w is full; Jl 3:13
a fence around it, dug a w in it, Mt 21:33
trample the w of the fierce anger of Rv 19:15

WINESKIN

w-s were new when we filled Jos 9:13
is about to burst like new w-s. Jb 32:19
like a w {dried} by smoke Ps 119:83
no one puts new wine into old w-s. Mt 9:17

WING

I carried you on eagles' w-s Ex 19:4
He spreads His w-s, catches him, Dt 32:11
under whose w-s you have come Ru 2:12
soaring on the w-s of the wind. 2Sm 22:11
One w of the {first} cherub was 1Kg 6:24
beneath the w-s of the cherubim. 1Kg 8:6
hide me in the shadow of Your w-s Ps 17:8
soaring on the w-s of the wind. Ps 18:10
refuge in the shadow of Your w-s Ps 36:7
shadow of Your w-s until danger Ps 57:1
under the shelter of Your w-s. Ps 61:4
in the shadow of Your w-s. Ps 63:7
you will take refuge under His w-s. Ps 91:4
walking on the w-s of the wind, Ps 104:3
each had six w-s: with two Is 6:2
will soar on w-s like eagles; Is 40:31
was like a lion but had eagle's w-s. Dn 7:4
rise with healing in its w-s, Mal 4:2
gathers her chicks under her w-s, Mt 23:37
living creatures had six w-s; Rv 4:8
given two w-s of a great eagle, Rv 12:14

WINK

w-s his eyes, signals with his Pr 6:13
A sly w of the eye causes grief, Pr 10:10

WINNOW

You will w them and a wind will Is 41:16
His w-ing shovel is in His hand, Mt 3:12

WINTER

summer and w, and day and night Gn 8:22
You made summer and w. Ps 74:17
For now the w is past; Sg 2:11

I will demolish the **w** house and   Am 3:15
Pray it won't happen in **w**.   Mk 13:18
even spend the **w**, that you may   1Co 16:6
every effort to come before **w**.   2Tm 4:21

WIPE

I will **w** off the face of the earth: Gn 6:7
tribe of Israel will not be **w-d** out.   Jdg 21:17
will **w** Jerusalem clean as one
   w-s a bowl—**w-ing** it and
   turning it   2Kg 21:13
she eats and **w-s** her mouth and   Pr 30:20
Lord GOD will **w** away the tears   Is 25:8
She **w-d** His feet with the hair   Lk 7:38
your sins may be **w-d** out so that   Ac 3:19
W this person off the earth   Ac 22:22
will **w** away every tear   Rv 7:17; 21:4

WISDOM

was desirable for obtaining **w**.   Gn 3:6
with **w** ... and ability in every craft   Ex 31:3
will [show] your **w** and   Dt 4:6
God gave Solomon **w**,   1Kg 4:29
secrets of **w**, for true **w** has two sides   Jb 11:6
the people, and **w** will die with you!   Jb 12:2
W is found with the elderly,   Jb 12:12
W and strength belong to God;   Jb 12:13
The fear of the Lord—that is **w**,   Jb 28:28
In **w** You have made them all;   Ps 104:24
of the LORD is the beginning of **w**;   Ps 111:10
fools despise **w** and instruction.   Pr 1:7
W calls out in the street;   Pr 1:20
W is supreme—so get **w**.   Pr 4:7
W has built her house;   Pr 9:1
of the LORD is the beginning of **w**,   Pr 9:10
but with humility comes **w**.   Pr 11:2
No **w** ... will prevail against the   Pr 21:30
A house is built by **w**,   Pr 24:3
She opens her mouth with **w**,   Pr 31:26
explore through **w** all that is done   Ec 1:13
For with much **w** is much sorrow;   Ec 1:18
Then I turned to consider **w**,   Ec 2:12
W is better than strength,   Ec 9:16
a Spirit of **w** and understanding,   Is 11:2
w of their wise men will vanish,   Is 29:14
the wise must not boast in his **w**;   Jr 9:23
established the world by His **w**,   Jr 10:12
He gives **w** to the wise and   Dn 2:21
How did this **w** and these   Mt 13:54
increased in **w** and stature,   Lk 2:52

Yet **w** is vindicated by all her   Lk 7:35
full of the Spirit and **w**,   Ac 6:3
both of the **w** and the knowledge   Rm 11:33
I will destroy the **w** of the wise,   1Co 1:19
Christ is God's power and God's **w**,   1Co 1:24
not be based on men's **w** but on   1Co 2:5
the **w** of this world is foolishness   1Co 3:19
not by fleshly **w** but by God's grace   2Co 1:12
God's multi-faceted **w** may now be   Eph 3:10
the treasures of **w** and knowledge   Col 2:3
Walk in **w** toward outsiders,   Col 4:5
Now if any of you lacks **w**,   Jms 1:5
But the **w** from above is first   Jms 3:17
and riches and **w** and strength   Rv 5:12

WISE

indeed a **w** and understanding people.   Dt 4:6
I will give you a **w** ... heart.   1Kg 3:12
He traps the **w** in their craftiness   Jb 5:13
will not find a **w** man among you.   Jb 17:10
to see if there is one who is **w**,   Ps 14:2
making the inexperienced **w**.   Ps 19:7
to see if there is one who is **w**   Ps 53:2
Don't consider yourself to be **w**;   Pr 3:7
rebuke a **w** man, and he will love   Pr 9:8
w son brings joy to his father,   Pr 10:1; 15:20
one who controls his lips is **w**.   Pr 10:19
walks with the **w** will become **w**,   Pr 13:20
Every **w** woman builds her house,   Pr 14:1
will be at home among the **w**.   Pr 15:31
is considered **w** when he keeps   Pr 17:28
pay attention to the words of the **w**,   Pr 22:17
a man who is **w** in his own eyes   Pr 26:12
but a **w** man holds it in check.   Pr 29:11
small, yet they are extremely **w**:   Pr 30:24
a poor but **w** youth than an old   Ec 4:13
and don't be overly **w**.   Ec 7:16
a poor **w** man was found in the   Ec 9:15
sayings of the **w** are like goads,   Ec 12:11
Where then are your **w** men?   Is 19:12
The **w** must not boast in his wisdom;   Jr 9:23
Those who are **w** will shine like   Dn 12:3
the **w** person will keep silent at   Am 5:13
w men from the east arrived   Mt 2:1
hidden these things from the **w**   Mt 11:25
both to the **w** and the foolish.   Rm 1:14
Claiming to be **w**, they became   Rm 1:22
Do not be **w** in your own   Rm 12:16
to the only **w** God, through Jesus   Rm 16:27

not many are **w** from a human 1Co 1:26
foolish things to shame the **w**, 1Co 1:27
He catches the **w** in their craftiness 1Co 3:19
but you are **w** in Christ! 1Co 4:10
not as unwise people but as **w** Eph 5:15

WISELY
See, My servant will act **w**; Is 52:13
He will reign **w** as king and Jr 23:5

WISER
He was **w** than anyone 1Kg 4:31
and makes us **w** than the birds Jb 35:11
makes me **w** than my enemies Ps 119:98
wise man, and he will be **w** still; Pr 9:9
the inexperienced become **w**; Pr 21:11
In his own eyes, a slacker is **w** Pr 26:16
God's foolishness is **w** than human 1Co 1:25

WISH
I **w** I had never existed Jb 10:19
how I **w** it were already set ablaze! Lk 12:49
For I could **w** that I myself were Rm 9:3
I **w** that all people were just like me. 1Co 7:7
I **w** all of you spoke in other 1Co 14:5
I **w** that you were cold or hot. Rv 3:15

WITCHCRAFT
and **w** from your mother Jezebel? 2Kg 9:22
practiced **w** and divination, 2Kg 21:6

WITHDRAW
don't ever **w** your faithful love 1Sm 20:15
then **w** from him so that he is 2Sm 11:15
I will not **w** My faithful love Ps 89:33
became aware of this, He **w-drew** Mt 12:15
He **w-drew** to the area of Tyre and Mt 15:21
He often **w-drew** to deserted places Lk 5:16
He took them along and **w-drew** Lk 9:10
He **w-drew** again to the mountain Jn 6:15
he **w-drew** and separated himself, Gl 2:12

WITHER
seven heads of grain—**w-ed**, thin, Gn 41:23
the hand he stretched out ... **w-ed**, 1Kg 13:4
and whose leaf does not **w**. Ps 1:3
they **w** quickly like grass and Ps 37:2
is afflicted, **w-ed** like grass; Ps 102:4
The earth mourns and **w-s**; Is 24:4
The grass **w-s**, the flowers fade Is 40:7
and even the leaf will **w**. Jr 8:13
Their leaves will not **w**, Ezk 47:12

attacked the plant, and it **w-ed**. Jnh 4:7
they had no root, they **w-ed**. Mt 13:6
At once the fig tree **w-ed**. Mt 21:19
aside like a branch and he **w-s**. Jn 15:6
the rich man will **w** away while Jms 1:11
grass **w-s**, and the flower drops 1Pt 1:24

WITHHOLD
have not **w-held** your only son Gn 22:12,16
not **w** Your compassion from me; Ps 40:11
He does not **w** the good from those Ps 84:11
don't **w** good from the one to Pr 3:27
another **w-s** what is right, only Pr 11:24
Don't **w** correction from a youth; Pr 23:13
Your sins have **w-held** {My} bounty Jr 5:25
But I **w-held** My hand Ezk 20:22
the skies have **w-held** the dew Hg 1:10
Can anyone **w** water and prevent Ac 10:47
that you **w-held** from the workers Jms 5:4

WITHIN
foreigner who is **w** your gates. Ex 20:10
destruction is **w** them; Ps 5:9
and all that is **w** me, praise His Ps 103:1
place My law **w** them and write it Jr 31:33
place My Spirit **w** you and cause Ezk 36:27
For from **w**, out of people's hearts, Mk 7:21

WITHOUT
like sheep **w** a shepherd. 2Ch 18:16
W guidance, people fall, but Pr 11:14
W revelation people run wild, Pr 29:18
like sheep **w** a shepherd. Mt 9:36
A prophet is not **w** honor except Mt 13:57
He gives the Spirit **w** measure. Jn 3:34
sinned **w** the law will also perish **w** Rm 2:12
no hope and **w** God in the world Eph 2:12
every way as we are, yet **w** sin. Heb 4:15
Now **w** faith it is impossible to Heb 11:6
that faith **w** works is useless Jms 2:20

WITNESS
mound is a **w** between me and Gn 31:48
I call heaven and earth as **w-es** Dt 4:26
the testimony of two or three **w-es**. Dt 19:15
it is to be a **w** between us and you, Jos 22:27
You are **w-es** against yourselves Jos 24:22
The LORD is our **w** if we don't do Jdg 11:10
are **w-es** today that I am buying Ru 4:9
Even now my **w** is in heaven, Jb 16:19
Malicious **w-es** come forward; Ps 35:11

a faithful **w** in the sky.   Ps 89:37
A truthful **w** rescues lives,   Pr 14:25
false **w** will not go unpunished,   Pr 19:5,9
A worthless **w** mocks justice,   Pr 19:28
have appointed trustworthy **w-es**   Is 8:2
true and faithful **w** against us.   Jr 42:5
LORD has been a **w** between you   Mal 2:14
two or three **w-es** every fact may   Mt 18:16
do not bear false **w**;   Mt 19:18
many false **w-es** came forward.   Mt 26:60
He came as a **w** to testify about   Jn 1:7
will be My **w-es** in Jerusalem,   Ac 1:8
We are all **w-es** of this.   Ac 2:32
the dead; we are **w-es** of this.   Ac 3:15
We are **w-es** of these things, and   Ac 5:32
w-es appointed beforehand   Ac 10:41
are now His **w-es** to the people.   Ac 13:31
you will be a **w** for Him to all   Ac 22:15
to be false **w-es** about God,   1Co 15:15
I call on God as a **w** against me: 2Co 1:23
two or three **w-es** every word will   2Co 13:1
you, I'm not lying. God is my **w**.   Gl 1:20
For God is my **w**, how I deeply   Php 1:8
You are **w-es**, and so is God, of   1Th 2:10
supported by two or three **w-es**.   1Tm 5:19
confession before many **w-es**.   1Tm 6:12
testimony of two or three **w-es**.   Heb 10:28
large cloud of **w-es** surrounding   Heb 12:1
from Jesus Christ, the faithful **w**,   Rv 1:5
empower my two **w-es**, and they   Rv 11:3
the blood of the **w-es** to Jesus.   Rv 17:6

WOE

If I am wicked, **w** to me!   Jb 10:15
Who has **w**? Who has sorrow?   Pr 23:29
W to you, land, when your king   Ec 10:16
W to those who   Is 5:8,11,18,20,21,22
W is me, for I am ruined,   Is 6:5
W to you, Jerusalem!   Jr 13:27
after all your evil—**W, w** to you!   Ezk 16:23
W to the shepherds of Israel,   Ezk 34:2
W to the worthless shepherd who   Zch 11:17
W to you, Chorazin! **W** to you,   Mt 11:21
but **w** to that man by whom the   Mt 18:7
w to you, scribes and Pharisees,   Mt 23:13
w to that man by whom the Son   Mt 26:24
W to you who are full now,   Lk 6:25
And **w** to me if I do not preach   1Co 9:16
W! W! W to those who live on   Rv 8:13

The first **w** has passed. There are   Rv 9:12
W to the earth and the sea,   Rv 12:12
W, w, the great city,   Rv 18:10,16,19

WOLF

The **w** will live with the lamb,   Is 11:6
The **w** and the lamb will feed   Is 65:25
but inwardly are ravaging **w-ves**.   Mt 7:15
you out like sheep among **w-ves**.   Mt 10:16
The **w** then snatches and scatters   Jn 10:12
savage **w-ves** will come in   Ac 20:29

WOMAN

this one will be called **w**,   Gn 2:23
hostility between you and the **w**,   Gn 3:15
to sleep with a man as with a **w**;   Lv 18:22
require the **w** to take an oath   Nm 5:19
A **w** is not to wear male clothing,   Dt 22:5
Jael is most blessed of **w-en**,   Jdg 5:24
you are a **w** of noble character.   Ru 3:11
Solomon loved many foreign **w-en**   1Kg 11:1
who had married foreign **w-en**.   Ezr 10:17
How can one born of **w** be pure?   Jb 25:4
then could I look at a young **w**?   Jb 31:1
agony like that of a **w** in labor,   Ps 48:6
gives the childless **w** a household,   Ps 113:9
keep you from a forbidden **w**,   Pr 7:5
The **w** Folly is rowdy; she is   Pr 9:13
A gracious **w** gains honor, but   Pr 11:16
Every wise **w** builds her house,   Pr 14:1
the way of a man with a young **w**,   Pr 30:19
Don't spend your energy on **w-en**   Pr 31:3
w who fears the LORD ... be praised.   Pr 31:30
all these I have not found a true **w**.   Ec 7:28
most beautiful of **w-en**   Sg 1:8; 5:9; 6:1
My people, and **w-en** rule over them.   Is 3:12
Can a **w** forget her nursing   Is 49:15
the god longed for by **w-en**,   Dn 11:37
w-en who oppress the poor and   Am 4:1
who looks at a **w** to lust for her   Mt 5:28
a **w** who had suffered ... 12 years   Mt 9:20
born of **w-en** no one greater   Mt 11:11
5,000 men, besides **w-en** and   Mt 14:21
4,000 men, besides **w-en** and   Mt 15:38
Two **w-en** will be grinding   Mt 24:41
a **w** ... with an alabaster jar   Mt 26:7
There were also **w-en** looking on   Mk 15:40
are the most blessed of **w-en**,   Lk 1:42
kind of **w** this is who is touching   Lk 7:39
w-en ... were telling the apostles   Lk 24:10

concern of yours to do with Me, w? Jn 2:4
a drink from me, a Samaritan w? Jn 4:9
brought a w caught in adultery Jn 8:3
His mother, "W, here is your son." Jn 19:26
in prayer, along with the w-en, Ac 1:14
religious w-en of high standing Ac 13:50
prominent Greek w-en as well as Ac 17:12
a w named Damaris, Ac 17:34
not to have relations with a w. 1Co 7:1
the man is the head of the w, 1Co 11:3
if a w-'s head is not covered, 1Co 11:6
man was not created for w, but w 1Co 11:9
w-en should be silent in 1Co 14:34
God sent His Son, born of a w, Gl 4:4
w-en represent the two covenants. Gl 4:24
the w-en are to dress ... in modest 1Tm 2:9
A w should learn in silence with 1Tm 2:11
I do not allow a w to teach 1Tm 2:12
but the w was deceived 1Tm 2:14
older w-en as mothers, and with 1Tm 5:2
capture idle w-en burdened down 2Tm 3:6
older w-en are to be reverent Ti 2:3
holy w-en who hoped in God also 1Pt 3:5
you tolerate the w Jezebel, Rv 2:20
a w clothed with the sun, Rv 12:1
the ones not defiled with w-en, Rv 14:4
I saw a w sitting on a scarlet Rv 17:3

WOMB

Two nations are in your w; Gn 25:23
Naked I came from my mother's w, Jb 1:21
carried from the w to the grave. Jb 10:19
You took me from the w, Ps 22:9
The wicked go astray from the w; Ps 58:3
from the w of the dawn, Ps 110:3
me together in my mother's w. Ps 139:13
Sheol; a barren w; earth, Pr 30:16
who formed you from the w, Is 44:24
me from the w to be His servant Is 49:5
before I formed you in the w; Jr 1:5
Spirit while still in his mother's w. Lk 1:15
The w that bore You ... blessed! Lk 11:27
his mother's w a second time Jn 3:4
from my mother's w set me apart Gl 1:15

WONDER

so that My w-s may be multiplied Ex 11:9
by trials, signs, w-s, and war, Dt 4:34
proclaims a sign or w to you, Dt 13:1
the LORD will do w-s among you Jos 3:5

where are all His w-s Jdg 6:13
w-s without number. Jb 5:9; 9:10
Stop and consider God's w-s. Jb 37:14
be praised, who alone does w-s. Ps 72:18
Do You work w-s for the dead? Ps 88:10
that I can meditate on Your w-s. Ps 119:27
confound ... people with w after w. Is 29:14
out of Egypt with signs and w-s, Jr 32:21
and how mighty His w-s! Dn 4:3
signs and w-s in the heavens Dn 6:27
will display w-s in the heavens Jl 2:30
signs and w-s to lead astray, Mt 24:24
Unless you ... see signs and w-s, Jn 4:48
I will display w-s in the heaven Ac 2:19
many w-s and signs were being Ac 2:43
signs and w-s were being done Ac 5:12
false miracles, signs, and w-s, 2Th 2:9
God also testified by signs and w-s, Heb 2:4

WONDERFUL

My name ... since it is w. Jdg 13:18
more w than the love of a woman 2Sm 1:26
things too w for me to know. Jb 42:3
I will declare all Your w works. Ps 9:1
and did not believe His w works. Ps 78:32
tell about all His w works! Ps 105:2
it is w in our eyes. Ps 118:23
that I may see w things in Your Ps 119:18
Your works are w, and I know Ps 139:14
He will be named W Counselor, Is 9:6
He gives w advice; Is 28:29
like all His {past} w works Jr 21:2
and is w in our eyes? Mt 21:42

WONDERFULLY

for He has w shown His faithful Ps 31:21
been remarkably and w made. Ps 139:14

WONDROUSLY

God, who has dealt w with you. Jl 2:26

WOOD

other gods, of w and stone. Dt 28:36
Without w, fire goes out; Pr 26:20
by human hands—w and stone. Is 37:19
I will bow down to a block of w. Is 44:19
by worthless idols {made of} w! Jr 10:8
worshiping w and stone, Ezk 20:32
gods made of ... iron, w, and stone. Dn 5:4
who says to w: Wake up! Hab 2:19
costly stones, w, hay, or straw, 1Co 3:12

also those of w and earthenware 2Tm 2:20
idols of ... bronze, stone, and w, Rv 9:20

WOODCUTTER

Gibeonites became w-s and water Jos 9:21

WOODEN

You broke a w yoke bar, but Jr 28:13
people consult their w {idols}, Hs 4:12

WOOL

made of both w and linen. Dt 22:11
will put a fleece of w here on Jdg 6:37
She selects w and flax and works Pr 31:13
as crimson, they will be like w. Is 1:18
You eat the fat, wear the w, Ezk 34:3
hair of His head like whitest w. Dn 7:9
head and hair were white like w Rv 1:14

WORD

Then God spoke all these w-s: Ex 20:1
These are the w-s Moses spoke to Dt 1:1
to report the w of the LORD to you, Dt 5:5
bread alone but on every w that Dt 8:3
these w-s of Mine on your hearts Dt 11:18
I'll reveal the w of God to you. 1Sm 9:27
the w of the LORD is pure. 2Sm 22:31
These are the last w-s of David: 2Sm 23:1
spoke through me, His w was on 2Sm 23:2
How painful honest w-s can be! Jb 6:25
this stream of w-s go unanswered Jb 11:2
the ear test w-s as the palate Jb 12:11
{no} end to your empty w-s? Jb 16:3
me and crush me with w-s? Jb 19:2
I am full of w-s, and my spirit Jb 32:18
take back {my w-s} and repent in Jb 42:6
Listen to my w-s, LORD; Ps 5:1
the w of the LORD is pure. Ps 18:30
there are no w-s; their voice is Ps 19:3
May the w-s of my mouth and the Ps 19:14
For the w of the LORD is right, Ps 33:4
In God, whose w I praise, in God Ps 56:4
his way pure? By keeping Your w. Ps 119:9
treasured Your w in my heart so Ps 119:11
give me life through Your w. Ps 119:25,107
Never take the w of truth from Ps 119:43
I put my hope in Your w. Ps 119:74,81
LORD, Your w is forever; Ps 119:89
sweet Your w is to my taste Ps 119:103
Your w is a lamp for my feet Ps 119:105
revelation of Your w-s brings Ps 119:130

Your w is completely pure, Ps 119:140
The entirety of Your w is truth, Ps 119:160
Before a w is on my tongue, Ps 139:4
His w runs swiftly. Ps 147:15
heart must hold on to my w-s. Pr 4:4
Where there are many w-s, sin is Pr 10:19
but a good w cheers it up. Pr 12:25
but a harsh w stirs up wrath. Pr 15:1
and a timely w—how good that Pr 15:23
teach you true and reliable w-s, Pr 22:21
A w spoken at the right time is Pr 25:11
Every w of God is pure; Pr 30:5
Don't add to His w-s, or He will Pr 30:6
so let your w-s be few. Ec 5:2
For when there are many w-s, Ec 6:11
accurately write w-s of truth. Ec 12:10
despised the w of the Holy One Is 5:24
will be like the w-s of a sealed Is 29:11
w of our God remains forever. Is 40:8
a w that will not be revoked: Is 45:23
I have put My w-s in your mouth, Is 51:16
My w ... not return to Me empty, Is 55:11
and who trembles at My w. Is 66:2
filled your mouth with My w-s. Jr 1:9
Your w-s were found, and I ate Jr 15:16
who has My w should speak My w Jr 23:28
None of My w-s will be delayed Ezk 12:28
killed them with the w-s of My Hs 6:5
but of hearing the w-s of the LORD. Am 8:11
Don't My w-s bring good to the Mc 2:7
wearied the LORD with your w-s. Mal 2:17
bread alone but on every w that Mt 4:4
be heard for their many w-s. Mt 6:7
hears these w-s of Mine and acts Mt 7:24
only say the w, and my servant Mt 8:8
for every careless w they speak. Mt 12:36
but My w-s will never pass away. Mt 24:35
The sower sows the w. Mk 4:14
You revoke God's w by your Mk 7:13
amazed by the gracious w-s that Lk 4:22
pressing in on Jesus to hear God's w, Lk 5:1
And they remembered His w-s. Lk 24:8
beginning was the W, and
    the W was with God,
    and the W was God. Jn 1:1
The W became flesh and took up Jn 1:14
You have the w-s of eternal life. Jn 6:68
continue in My w, you really are Jn 8:31

anyone keeps My w, he will never   Jn 8:51
The w that you hear is not Mine   Jn 14:24
in Me and My w-s remain in you,   Jn 15:7
by the truth; Your w is truth.   Jn 17:17
as though the w of God has failed.   Rm 9:6
not with clever w-s, so that the   1Co 1:17
in w-s taught by human wisdom,   1Co 2:13
rather speak five w-s with my   1Co 14:19
Did the w of God originate from   1Co 14:36
the washing of water by the w.   Eph 5:26
of the Spirit, which is God's w.   Eph 6:17
whatever you do, in w or in deed,   Col 3:17
did not come to you in w only,   1Th 1:5
sanctified by the w of God and   1Tm 4:5
disputes and arguments over w-s;   1Tm 6:4
not to fight about w-s;   2Tm 2:14
correctly teaching the w of truth.   2Tm 2:15
all things by His powerful w.   Heb 1:3
For the w of God is living and   Heb 4:12
was created by the w of God,   Heb 11:3
humbly receive the implanted w,   Jms 1:21
doers of the w and not hearers   Jms 1:22
living and enduring w of God.   1Pt 1:23
through water by the w of God.   2Pt 3:5
concerning the W of life   1Jn 1:1
whoever keeps His w, truly in   1Jn 2:5
God's w remains in you,   1Jn 2:14
we must not love in w or speech,   1Jn 3:18
testified to God's w and to the   Rv 1:2
hear the w-s of this prophecy   Rv 1:3
His name is called the W of God.   Rv 19:13
These w-s are faithful and true.   Rv 22:6
who keeps the ... w-s of this book.   Rv 22:7
takes away from the w-s of this   Rv 22:19

WORK (n)

seventh day, God completed His w   Gn 2:2
six days and do all your w,   Ex 20:9
So Moses finished the w.   Ex 40:33
not to do any daily w.   Lv 23:7,21,28,35
Levites ... perform the LORD's w.   Nm 8:11
God has blessed you in all the w   Dt 2:7
The Rock—His w is perfect;   Dt 32:4
heavens, the w of Your fingers,   Ps 8:3
lord over the w-s of Your hands;   Ps 8:6
declare all Your wonderful w-s.   Ps 9:1
proclaims the w of His hands.   Ps 19:1
wonderful w-s and Your plans   Ps 40:5
repay each according to his w-s.   Ps 62:12

Come and see the w-s of God;   Ps 66:5
How magnificent are Your w-s,   Ps 92:5
His wonderful w-s among all   Ps 96:3
heavens are the w of Your hands.   Ps 102:25
w-s for the human race.   Ps 107:8,15,21,31
w-s of His hands are truth and   Ps 111:7
eating food earned by hard w;   Ps 127:2
w-s are wonderful, and I know   Ps 139:14
will declare Your w-s to the next   Ps 145:4
There is profit in all hard w,   Pr 14:23
repay a person according to his w?   Pr 24:12
your outdoor w, and prepare your   Pr 24:27
her w-s praise her at the city gates.   Pr 31:31
I hated all my w at which I   Ec 2:18
God has already accepted your w-s.   Ec 9:7
because there is no w, planning,   Ec 9:10
bow down to the w of their hands,   Is 2:8
to do His w, His strange w,   Is 28:21
we all are the w of Your hands.   Is 64:8
provoke ... by the w of their hands   Jr 32:30
because all His w-s are true   Dn 4:37
see your good w-s and give glory   Mt 5:16
powers are at w in him.   Mk 6:14
six days when w should be done;   Lk 13:14
third day I will complete My w.   Lk 13:32
show Him greater w-s than these   Jn 5:20
is the w of God: that you believe   Jn 6:29
The w-s that I do in My Father's   Jn 10:25
which of these w-s are you stoning   Jn 10:32
don't believe Me, believe the w-s.   Jn 10:38
do even greater w-s than these,   Jn 14:12
completing the w You gave Me to   Jn 17:4
I am doing a w in your days,   Ac 13:41
and do w-s worthy of repentance.   Ac 26:20
show that the w of the law is   Rm 2:15
by faith apart from w-s of law.   Rm 3:28
If Abraham was justified by w-s,   Rm 4:2
to the one who w-s, pay is not   Rm 4:4
righteousness apart from w-s: Rm 4:6
if by grace, then it is not by w-s;   Rm 11:6
test the quality of each one's w.   1Co 3:13
Are you not my w in the Lord?   1Co 9:1
excelling in the Lord's w,   1Co 15:58
he is doing the Lord's w,   1Co 16:10
you may excel in every good w.   2Co 9:8
will be according to their w-s.   2Co 11:15
because by the w-s of the law no   Gl 2:16
by the w-s of the law or by hearing   Gl 3:5

Now the **w-s** of the flesh are | Gl 5:19
person should examine his own **w**, | Gl 6:4
not from **w-s**, so that no one can | Eph 2:9
in Christ Jesus for good **w-s**, | Eph 2:10
the saints in the **w** of ministry, | Eph 4:12
he must do honest **w** with his own | Eph 4:28
started a good **w** in you will | Php 1:6
in every good **w** and growing | Col 1:10
your **w** of faith, labor of love, | 1Th 1:3
of lawlessness is already at **w**; | 2Th 2:7
you in every good **w** and word. | 2Th 2:17
with good **w-s**, as is proper for | 1Tm 2:10
Likewise, good **w-s** are obvious, | 1Tm 5:25
not according to our **w-s**, | 2Tm 1:9
prepared for every good **w**. | 2Tm 2:21
equipped for every good **w**. | 2Tm 3:17
do the **w** of an evangelist, | 2Tm 4:5
repay him according to his **w-s**. | 2Tm 4:14
but they deny Him by their **w-s**. | Ti 1:16
special people, eager to do good **w-s**. | Ti 2:14
not by **w-s** of righteousness that | Ti 3:5
devote themselves to good **w-s**. | Ti 3:8,14
heavens are the **w-s** of Your hands; | Heb 1:10
has rested from his own **w-s**, | Heb 4:10
of repentance from dead **w-s**, | Heb 6:1
cleanse ... from dead **w-s** to serve | Heb 9:14
to promote love and good **w-s**, | Heb 10:24
has faith, but does not have **w-s**? | Jms 2:14
faith, if it doesn't have **w-s**, is dead | Jms 2:17
Abraham ... justified by **w-s** | Jms 2:21
impartially, based on each one's **w**, | 1Pt 1:17
by observing your good **w-s**, glorify | 1Pt 2:12
to destroy the Devil's **w-s**. | 1Jn 3:8
Because his **w-s** were evil, and | 1Jn 3:12
I know your **w-s** | Rv 2:2,19; 3:1,8,15
and do the **w-s** you did at first. | Rv 2:5
of you according to your **w-s**. | Rv 2:23
for their **w-s** follow them! | Rv 14:13
judged according to their **w-s**. | Rv 20:13

WORK (v)

they **w-ed** with integrity. | 2Kg 12:15; 22:7
people had the will to keep **w-ing**. | Neh 4:6
w-ed with one hand and held a | Neh 4:17
You are the God who **w-s** wonders; | Ps 77:14
My son, go, **w** in the vineyard | Mt 21:28
master finds him **w-ing** when he | Mt 24:46
the Lord **w-ing** with them | Mk 16:20
My Father is still **w-ing**, and I | Jn 5:17

Don't **w** for the food that | Jn 6:27
that all things **w** together for | Rm 8:28
matters is faith **w-ing** through love. | Gl 5:6
to the power that **w-s** in you | Eph 3:20
w out your own salvation with | Php 2:12
For it is God who is **w-ing** in you, | Php 2:13
strength that **w-s** powerfully in | Col 1:29
don't **w** only while being watched, | Col 3:22
isn't willing to **w**, he should not eat | 2Th 3:10
w-ing in us what is pleasing in | Heb 13:21

WORKER

A **w-'s** appetite works for him | Pr 16:26
The sleep of the **w** is sweet, | Ec 5:12
abundant, but the **w-s** are few. | Mt 9:37
to hire **w-s** for his vineyard. | Mt 20:1
the **w** is worthy of his wages. | Lk 10:7
watch out for evil **w-s**, | Php 3:2
a **w** who doesn't need to be | 2Tm 2:15

WORKING (n)

by the proper **w** of each | Eph 4:16
faith in the **w** of God, | Col 2:12

WORLD

He judges the **w** with righteousness; | Ps 9:8
foundations of the **w** were exposed, | Ps 18:15
the **w** and everything in it is Mine. | Ps 50:12
The **w** is firmly established; | Ps 96:10
rejoicing in His inhabited **w**, | Pr 8:31
I will bring disaster on the **w**, | Is 13:11
You are the light of the **w**. | Mt 5:14
from the foundation of the **w**. | Mt 13:35
the field is the **w**; | Mt 13:38
gains the whole **w** yet loses his | Mt 16:26
is proclaimed in the whole **w**, | Mt 26:13
Go into all the **w** and preach the | Mk 16:15
yet the **w** did not recognize Him. | Jn 1:10
who takes away the sin of the **w**! | Jn 1:29
For God loved the **w** in this way: | Jn 3:16
His Son into the **w** that He might | Jn 3:17
this really is the Savior of the **w**. | Jn 4:42
The **w** cannot hate you, but it | Jn 7:7
I am the light of the **w**. | Jn 8:12; 9:5
You are of this **w**; I am not | Jn 8:23
the **w** has gone after Him! | Jn 12:19
life in this **w** will keep it for | Jn 12:25
The **w** is unable to receive Him | Jn 14:17
not give to you as the **w** gives. | Jn 14:27
the ruler of the **w** is coming. | Jn 14:30

were of the w, the w would love   Jn 15:19
wail, but the w will rejoice.   Jn 16:20
I have conquered the w.   Jn 16:33
I am not praying for the w but for   Jn 17:9
The w has not known You.   Jn 17:25
My kingdom is not of this w,   Jn 18:36
not even the w itself could contain   Jn 21:25
as sin entered the w through one   Rm 5:12
chosen the w-'s foolish things   1Co 1:27
wisdom of this w is foolishness   1Co 3:19
you would have to leave the w.   1Co 5:10
the saints will judge the w?   1Co 6:2
reconciling the w to Himself,   2Co 5:19
the w has been crucified to me,   Gl 6:14
before the foundation of the w,   Eph 1:4
and without God in the w.   Eph 2:12
the elemental forces of the w,   Col 2:8,20
we brought nothing into the w,   1Tm 6:7
because he loved this present w,   2Tm 4:10
since the foundation of the w,   Heb 4:3; 9:26
The w was not worthy of them.   Heb 11:38
keep oneself unstained by the w.   Jms 1:27
friendship with the w is hostility   Jms 4:4
before the foundation of the w,   1Pt 1:20
He didn't spare the ancient w,   2Pt 2:5
also for those of the whole w.   1Jn 2:2
Do not love the w or the things   1Jn 2:15
the w with its lust is passing away,   1Jn 2:17
The reason the w does not know   1Jn 3:1
greater than the one who is in the w.   1Jn 4:4
Son into the w so that we might   1Jn 4:9
been born of God conquers the w.   1Jn 5:4
The kingdom of the w has become   Rv 11:15
written from the foundation of the w   Rv 13:8

WORLDLY

but w grief produces death.   2Co 7:10
walked according to this w age,   Eph 2:2
to death whatever in you is w: Col 3:5
godlessness and w lusts and to   Ti 2:12

WORM

and to the w: My mother   Jb 17:14
and the son of man, who is a w!   Jb 25:6
But I am a w and not a man,   Ps 22:6
Do not fear, you w Jacob,   Is 41:14
God appointed a w that attacked   Jnh 4:7
where Their w does not die,   Mk 9:44

became infected with w-s
and died.   Ac 12:23
who w their way into households   2Tm 3:6

WORMWOOD

in the end she's as bitter as w   Pr 5:4
I am about to feed this people w   Jr 9:15
Those who turn justice into w   Am 5:7
The name of the star is W,   Rv 8:11

WORRY

Don't w because of evildoers,   Pr 24:19
Don't w about your life,   Mt 6:25
don't w about tomorrow,   Mt 6:34
the w-ies of this age and the   Mt 13:22
don't w beforehand what you will   Mk 13:11
Martha, you are w-ied and upset   Lk 10:41
and w-ies of life, or that day will   Lk 21:34
Don't w about anything, but in   Php 4:6

WORSE

acts w than ... her sister.   Ezk 23:11
condition is w than the first.   Mt 12:45
that something w doesn't happen   Jn 5:14
and is w than an unbeliever.   1Tm 5:8
last state is w for them than   2Pt 2:20

WORSHIP (n)

w {consists of} man-made rules   Is 29:13
this is your spiritual w.   Rm 12:1
practices and the w of angels,   Col 2:18

WORSHIP (v)

altar to the LORD and w-ed Him.   Gn 12:8
and I will go over there to w;   Gn 22:5
not bow down to them or w them;   Ex 20:5
Fear the LORD your God, w Him,   Dt 6:13
gods your fathers w-ed beyond   Jos 24:15
W the LORD in the splendor of   1Ch 16:29
in confession and w of the LORD   Neh 9:3
He fell to the ground and w-ed,   Jb 1:20
All the earth will w You   Ps 66:4
Come, let us w and bow down;   Ps 95:6
All the gods must w Him.   Ps 97:7
even makes it into a god and w-s it;   Is 44:15
All mankind will come to w Me,   Is 66:23
fall down and w the gold statue   Dn 3:5
in the east and have come to w Him.   Mt 2:2
if You will fall down and w me.   Mt 4:9
those in the boat w-ed Him   Mt 14:33
They w Me in vain, teaching as   Mt 15:9

saw Him, they w-ed, but some　　Mt 28:17
those who w Him must w in spirit　Jn 4:24
fell at His feet, and w-ed him.　Ac 10:25
what you w in ignorance,　　Ac 17:23
w-ed ... something created instead　Rm 1:25
And all God's angels must w Him.　Heb 1:6
w the One who lives forever　　Rv 4:10
the elders fell down and w-ed.　Rv 5:14
and (count) those who w there.　Rv 11:1
W the Maker of heaven and earth,　Rv 14:7
If anyone w-s the beast and his　Rv 14:9
fell down and w-ed God,　　Rv 19:4

WORSHIPERS
when the true w will worship　　Jn 4:23

WORST
to save sinners"—and I am the w　1Tm 1:15

WORTH
Aren't you w more than they?　Mt 6:26
you are w more than many　　Mt 10:31
man is w far more than a sheep,　Mt 12:12
are not w comparing with the glory　Rm 8:18

WORTHLESS
enraged Me with their w idols.　Dt 32:21
or deliver you; they are w.　1Sm 12:21
pursued w idols and became w　2Kg 17:15
you are all w doctors.　　Jb 13:4
who are devoted to w idols,　Ps 31:6
for human help is w.　　Ps 60:11
eyes from looking at what is w;　Ps 119:37
A w man digs up evil,　　Pr 16:27
"It's w, it's w!" the buyer says,　Pr 20:14
who cling to w idols forsake　Jnh 2:8
to the w shepherd who deserts　Zch 11:17
turn from these w things to the　Ac 14:15
them over to a w mind to do what　Rm 1:28
not been raised, your faith is w;　1Co 15:17

WORTHWHILE
did not think it w to have God　Rm 1:28

WORTHY
to the LORD, who is w of praise,　2Sm 22:4
I am not w to have You come　Mt 8:8
and follow Me is not w of Me.　Mt 10:38
who were invited were not w.　Mt 22:8
I am not w to untie the strap of　Lk 3:16
the worker is w of his wages.　Lk 10:7
no longer w to be called your　Lk 15:19

were counted w to be dishonored　Ac 5:41
and I am not w to untie the　Ac 13:25
and do works w of repentance.　Ac 26:20
you to walk w of the calling　Eph 4:1
life in a manner w of the gospel　Php 1:27
that you may walk w of the Lord,　Col 1:10
one of you to walk w of God,　1Th 2:12
be counted w of God's kingdom,　2Th 1:5
consider you w of His calling,　2Th 1:11
The laborer is w of his wages.　1Tm 5:18
is considered w of more glory　Heb 3:3
The world was not w of them.　Heb 11:38
journey in a manner w of God,　3Jn 6
You are w to receive glory and　Rv 4:11
Who is w to open the scroll and　Rv 5:2
Lamb who was slaughtered is w　Rv 5:12

WOUND (n)
bruise for bruise, w for w.　Ex 21:25
My w is incurable,　　Jb 34:6
and binds up their w-s.　Ps 147:3
Who has w-s for no reason?　Pr 23:29
The w-s of a friend are trustworthy,　Pr 27:6
and heals the w-s He inflicted.　Is 30:26
and we are healed by His w-s.　Is 53:5
pain ... unending, my w incurable,　Jr 15:18
and will heal you of your w-s　Jr 30:17
For her w is incurable and has　Mc 1:9
What are these w-s on your chest?　Zch 13:6
bandaged his w-s, pouring oil　Lk 10:34
the night and washed their w-s.　Ac 16:33
but his fatal w was healed.　Rv 13:3

WOUND (v)
For I killed a man for w-ing me,　Gn 4:23
I give life; I w and I heal.　Dt 32:39
my heart is w-ed within me.　Ps 109:22
They beat and w-ed me;　　Sg 5:7
He has w-ed (us), and He will bind　Hs 6:1
and w their weak conscience,　1Co 8:12

WOUNDING (n)
by His w you have been healed.　1Pt 2:24

WOVEN (adj)
w in one piece from the top.　Jn 19:23

WRAP
his life is w-ped up with the boy's　Gn 44:30
he w-ped his face in his mantle　1Kg 19:13
of death were w-ped around me;　Ps 18:4

He w-s Himself in light as if it | Ps 104:2
like a robe he w-s around himself, | Ps 109:19
and He w-ped Himself in zeal as in | Is 59:17
seaweed was w-ped around my head | Jnh 2:5
body, w-ped it in clean, fine linen, | Mt 27:59
and she w-ped Him snugly in cloth | Lk 2:7

WRAPPING (n)
w that had been on His head was not | Jn 20:7

WRATH
w has come from the LORD; | Nm 16:46
the w of the LORD was on Judah | 2Ch 29:8
the LORD's w was so stirred | 2Ch 36:16
rescued from the day of w. | Jb 21:30
and terrifies them in His w: | Ps 2:5
do not discipline me in Your w. | Ps 6:1
Even human w will praise You; | Ps 76:10
Pour out Your w on the nations | Ps 79:6
Your w sweeps over me; | Ps 88:16
is not profitable on a day of w, | Pr 11:4
but a harsh word stirs up w. | Pr 15:1
Although I struck you in My w, | Is 60:10
and My w assisted Me. | Is 63:5
Take this cup of the wine of w | Jr 25:15
The LORD has exhausted His w, | Lm 4:11
after I have spent My w on them, | Ezk 5:13
In {Your} w remember mercy! | Hab 3:2
That day is a day of w, | Zph 1:15
you to flee from the coming w? | Mt 3:7
turn Your w from me—a sinner! | Lk 18:13
the w of God remains on him. | Jn 3:36
For God's w is revealed from | Rm 1:18
storing up w for yourself in the day | Rm 2:5
For the law produces w; | Rm 4:15
be saved through Him from w. | Rm 5:9
with much patience objects of w | Rm 9:22
instead, leave room for His w. | Rm 12:19
submit, not only because of w, | Rm 13:5
by nature we were children
    under w, | Eph 2:3
because of these things God's w is | Eph 5:6
Because of these, God's w comes | Col 3:6
rescues us from the coming w. | 1Th 1:10
For God did not appoint us to w, | 1Th 5:9
and from the w of the Lamb, | Rv 6:16
also drink the wine of God's w, | Rv 14:10
the great winepress of God's w. | Rv 14:19
pour out the seven bowls of God's w | Rv 16:1

WRECKED
the ships were w and were not | 2Ch 20:37

WRESTLED
man w with him until daybreak. | Gn 32:24
and as an adult he w with God. | Hs 12:3

WRETCHED
and we detest this w food! | Nm 21:5
What a w man I am! Who will | Rm 7:24
you don't know that you are w, | Rv 3:17

WRETCHEDNESS
ruin and w are in their paths. | Is 59:7
ruin and w are in their paths, | Rm 3:16

WRINKLE
without spot or w or any such | Eph 5:27

WRITE
Moses wrote down all the words | Ex 24:4
said to Moses, "W down these | Ex 34:27
W them on the doorposts of your | Dt 6:9
When Moses had finished w-ing | Dt 31:24
observe everything w-ten in it. | Jos 1:8
are w-ten about in the Historical | 1Kg 14:19
I have come; it is w-ten about me | Ps 40:7
all {my} days were w-ten in Your | Ps 139:16
w them on the tablet of your | Pr 3:3; 7:3
within them and w it on their
    hearts. | Jr 31:33
watched the hand that was w-ing, | Dn 5:5
w-ten in the book will escape. | Dn 12:1
rejoice that your names are w-ten | Lk 10:20
what is w-ten must be fulfilled | Lk 22:37
because he wrote about Me. | Jn 5:46
and started w-ing on the ground | Jn 8:6
What I have w-ten, I have w-ten. | Jn 19:22
are w-ten so that you may believe | Jn 20:31
if they were w-ten one by one, | Jn 21:25
the law is w-ten on their hearts. | Rm 2:15
w-ten before was w-ten for our | Rm 15:4
Nothing beyond what is w-ten. | 1Co 4:6
I wrote to you in a letter not to | 1Co 5:9
About the things you wrote: | 1Co 7:1
were w-ten as a warning to us, | 1Co 10:11
I w ... is the Lord's command. | 1Co 14:37
I wrote to you with many tears | 2Co 2:4
are our letter, w-ten on our hearts, | 2Co 3:2
So even though I wrote to you, | 2Co 7:12
why I am w-ing ... while absent, | 2Co 13:10

what large letters I have w-ten	Gl 6:11
To w to you again about this is	Php 3:1
every letter; this is how I w.	2Th 3:17
Paul, w this with my own hand;	Phm 19
I will w them on their hearts,	Heb 8:10
I will w them on their minds,	Heb 10:16
names have been w-ten in heaven	Heb 12:23
the second letter I've w-ten you;	2Pt 3:1
I am not w-ing you a new command,	1Jn 2:7
Yet I am w-ing you a new command,	1Jn 2:8
I have many things to w	2Jn 12; 3Jn 13
W on a scroll what you see	Rv 1:11
I will w on him the name of My	Rv 3:12
do not w it down!	Rv 10:4
whose name was not w-ten	Rv 13:8
name w-ten on their foreheads.	Rv 14:1
on her ... a cryptic name was w-ten:	Rv 17:5
only those w-ten in the Lamb's	Rv 21:27

WRITING (n)

and the w was God's w,	Ex 32:16
the charge against Him in w:	Mt 27:37
But if you don't believe his w-s,	Jn 5:47

WRITTEN (adj)

must give her a w-ten notice of	Mt 5:31

WRONG (n)

I am the one who has done w.	2Sm 24:17
We have sinned and done w;	1Kg 8:47
Yet no one proved Job w;	Jb 32:12
is impossible for God {to do} w,	Jb 34:10
do not envy those who do w.	Ps 37:1
They do nothing w; they follow	Ps 119:3
who distorts right and w	Pr 28:6,18
and says, "I've done nothing w."	Pr 30:20
too is futile and a great w.	Ec 2:21
wear themselves out doing w.	Jr 9:5
forgive all the w-s they have	Jr 33:8
sinned, done w, acted wickedly,	Dn 9:5
Friend, I'm doing you no w.	Mt 20:13
this man has done nothing w.	Lk 23:41
But if you do w, be afraid,	Rm 13:4
Love does no w to a neighbor.	Rm 13:10
does not keep a record of w-s;	1Co 13:5
burden you? Forgive me this w!	2Co 12:13

WRONGED

to the individual he has w.	Nm 5:7

have w no one, corrupted no	2Co 7:2
if he has w you in any way,	Phm 18

WRONGDOER

For the w will be paid back for	Col 3:25

WRONGDOING

must not follow a crowd in w.	Ex 23:2
forgiving w, rebellion, and sin.	Ex 34:7
each will die for his own w.	Jr 31:30
I will forgive their w and sin.	Jr 36:3
if you forgive people their w,	Mt 6:14
state what w they found in me	Ac 24:20
if someone is caught in any w,	Gl 6:1
I will be merciful to their w,	Heb 8:12

WRONGLY

don't receive because you ask w,	Jms 4:3

WRUNG

the fleece and w dew out of it,	Jdg 6:38

Y

YAH

Because Y, the LORD, is my	Is 12:2
because in Y, the LORD, is	Is 26:4

YAHWEH

Divine name by which God revealed Himself to Moses (Ex 3:15-16; 6:2-8; 15:3; 34:5-6). Usually translated LORD.

Y, the God of your fathers,	Ex 3:15
I did not make My name Y known	Ex 6:3
I am Y, and I will deliver you	Ex 6:6
LORD is a warrior; Y is His name.	Ex 15:3
proclaim the name Y before you.	Ex 33:19
and proclaimed {His} name Y.	Ex 34:5
Y—Y is a compassionate and	Ex 34:6
Know that Y your God is God,	Dt 7:9
awesome name—Y, your God—	Dt 28:58
there and called it Y Shalom.	Jdg 6:24
If Y is God, follow Him.	1Kg 18:21
and said, "Y, He is God!	1Kg 18:39
a prophet of Y here any more?	1Kg 22:7
call on the name of Y his God,	2Kg 5:11
rides on the clouds—His name is Y	Ps 68:4
I am Y your God, who brought you	Ps 81:10

sake of Your name, **Y**, let me live. Ps 143:11
Y is great and is highly praised; Ps 145:3
heard? **Y** is the everlasting God, Is 40:28
I am **Y**, that is My name; Is 42:8
His name is **Y** of Hosts Is 48:2; 51:15; 54:5
they will know that My name is **Y**. Jr 16:21
they will know that I am **Y**. Ezk 6:14
know that I, **Y**, have spoken. Ezk 17:21
nations will know that I am **Y** Ezk 36:23
city ... will be: **Y** Is There. Ezk 48:35
Y is ... God of Hosts; **Y** is His name. Hs 12:5
of the earth—**Y** is His name. Am 5:8
Y-'s name must not be invoked. Am 6:10
I worship **Y**, the God of the Jnh 1:9
in the majestic name of **Y** His God. Mc 5:4
they will trust in the name of **Y**. Zph 3:12
On that day **Y** will become king Zch 14:9
feared **Y** and had high regard for Mal 3:16

YARN

blue, purple, and scarlet **y**; Ex 25:4
cedar wood, scarlet **y**, and hyssop Lv 14:4
cedar wood, hyssop,
  and crimson **y**, Nm 19:6
skilled in ... crimson, and blue **y**. 2Ch 2:7

YEAR

festivals and for days and **y**-s. Gn 1:14
Methuselah's life lasted 969 **y**-s; Gn 5:27
it is the first month of your **y**. Ex 12:2
lived in Egypt was 430 **y**-s. Ex 12:40
in My honor three times a **y**. Ex 23:14
make atonement ... once a **y** Lv 16:34
rest for the land in the seventh, Lv 25:4
The fiftieth **y** will be your Jubilee; Lv 25:11
in the wilderness for 40 **y**-s Nm 14:33
seven **y**-s you must cancel debts. Dt 15:1
until 70 **y**-s were fulfilled. 2Ch 36:21
crown the **y** with Your goodness; Ps 65:11
a thousand **y**-s are like yesterday Ps 90:4
Our lives last seventy **y**-s or, if Ps 90:10
and Your **y**-s will never end. Ps 102:27
y-s will be added to your life. Pr 9:11
he lives a thousand **y**-s twice, Ec 6:6
In the **y** that King Uzziah died, Is 6:1
to proclaim the **y** of the LORD's favor, Is 61:2
When the 70 **y**-s are completed, Jr 25:12
number of **y**-s ... would be 70. Dn 9:2
When He was 12 **y**-s old, Lk 2:42
Jesus was about 30 **y**-s old and Lk 3:23

to proclaim the **y** of the Lord's favor. Lk 4:19
You aren't 50 **y**-s old yet, Jn 8:57
days, months, seasons, and **y**-s. Gl 4:10
and Your **y**-s will never end. Heb 1:12
second room ... only once a **y**, Heb 9:7
continually offer **y** after **y**. Heb 10:1
city and spend a **y** there and do Jms 4:13
the Lord one day is like 1,000 **y**-s, 2Pt 3:8
for 1,000 **y**-s. Rv 20:2,4,6

YEARLY

the sanctuary **y** with the blood Heb 9:25

YEARN

I long and **y** for the courts of Ps 84:2
My inner being **y**-s for him; Jr 31:20
caused to live in us **y**-s jealously? Jms 4:5

YEAR-OLD

an unblemished animal, a **y** male; Ex 12:5

YEAST

must remove **y** from your houses. Ex 12:15
of heaven is like **y** that a woman Mt 13:33
beware of the **y** of the Pharisees Mt 16:6
know that a little **y** permeates 1Co 5:6
little **y** leavens the whole lump Gl 5:9

YES

let your word 'y' be 'y,' Mt 5:37
that I say "Y, y" and "No, no" 2Co 1:17
God's promises is "Y" in Him. 2Co 1:20
Your "y" must be "y," and your Jms 5:12

YESTERDAY

were {born only} **y** and know nothing Jb 8:9
years are like **y** that passes Ps 90:4
Jesus Christ is the same **y**, today, Heb 13:8

YET

y He did not open His mouth. Is 53:7
y you did not return to Me Am 4:6
but the end is not **y**. Mt 24:6

YIELD

will never again give you its **y**. Gn 4:12
Then the land will **y** its fruit, Lv 25:19
vineyards that **y** a fruitful harvest. Ps 107:37
and the land will **y** its produce; Ezk 34:27
bear fruit and **y**-s: some 100, Mt 13:23
But we did not **y** in submission Gl 2:5
it **y**-s the fruit of peace and Heb 12:11

YOKE

will break his **y** from your neck.	Gn 27:40
place an iron **y** on your neck	Dt 28:48
Your father made our **y** harsh.	1Kg 12:4
have shattered their burdensome **y**	Is 9:4
broke a wooden **y** bar, but in its	Jr 28:13
I will break his **y** from your neck	Jr 30:8
to bear the **y** while he is still young.	Lm 3:27
when I break the bars of their **y**	Ezk 34:27
I will place a **y** on her fine neck.	Hs 10:11
take up My **y** and learn from Me,	Mt 11:29
For My **y** is easy and My burden	Mt 11:30
a **y** that neither our forefathers nor	Ac 15:10
submit again to a **y** of slavery.	Gl 5:1
are under the **y** as slaves must	1Tm 6:1

YOUNG

two turtledoves or two **y** pigeons	Lv 5:7
Though the boy was {still} **y**,	1Sm 1:24
I am **y** in years, while you are	Jb 32:6
I have been **y** and now I am old,	Ps 37:25
herself where she places her **y**	Ps 84:3
How can a **y** man keep his way	Ps 119:9
as well as **y** women, old and **y**	Ps 148:12
Even a **y** man is known by his	Pr 20:11
The glory of **y** men is their	Pr 20:29
Rejoice, **y** man, while you are **y**,	Ec 11:9
and **y** men stumble and fall,	Is 40:30
and your **y** men will see visions.	Jl 2:28
your **y** men will see visions,	Ac 2:17
encourage the **y** women to	Ti 2:4

YOUNGER

and the older will serve the **y**.	Gn 25:23
you have not pursued **y** men,	Ru 3:10
and your **y** sister was Sodom,	Ezk 16:46
of James the **y** and of Joses,	Mk 15:40
The older will serve the **y**.	Rm 9:12
y men as brothers,	1Tm 5:1
But refuse to enroll **y** widows;	1Tm 5:11
I want **y** women to marry,	1Tm 5:14
Likewise, you **y** men, be subject	1Pt 5:5

YOUNGEST

Bring your **y** brother to me so	Gn 42:20
and I am the **y** in my father's	Jdg 6:15
and David was the **y**.	1Sm 17:14
Benjamin, the **y**, leading them,	Ps 68:27
you must become like the **y**,	Lk 22:26

YOURS

I am **y**, along with all that I	1Kg 20:4
the battle is not **y**, but God's.	2Ch 20:15
I am **Y**; save me, for I have	Ps 119:94
For **Y** is the kingdom and the	Mt 6:13
were **Y**, You gave them to Me,	Jn 17:6

YOUTH

inclination is evil from his **y**.	Gn 8:21
You're just a **y**, and he's been a	1Sm 17:33
Yet I am just a **y** with no	1Kg 3:7
have feared the LORD from my **y**.	1Kg 18:12
Do not remember the sins of my **y**	Ps 25:7
GOD, my confidence from my **y**.	Ps 71:5
y is renewed like the eagle.	Ps 103:5
are the sons born in one's **y**.	Ps 127:4
abandons the companion of her **y**	Pr 2:17
take pleasure in the wife of your **y**.	Pr 5:18
Teach a **y** about the way he should	Pr 22:6
Don't withhold correction from a **y**;	Pr 23:13
but a **y** left to himself is a disgrace	Pr 29:15
be glad in the days of your **y**.	Ec 11:9
your Creator in the days of your **y**:	Ec 12:1
Y-s may faint and grow weary,	Is 40:30
you will forget the shame of your **y**,	Is 54:4
the **y** will die at a hundred	Is 65:20
to speak since I am {only} a **y**.	Jr 1:6
I bore the disgrace of my **y**.	Jr 31:19
against the wife of your **y**.	Mal 2:15
have kept all these from my **y**.	Mk 10:20
No one should despise your **y**;	1Tm 4:12

YOUTHFUL

Flee from **y** passions,	2Tm 2:22

Z

ZACCHAEUS

Tax collector who hosted Jesus and was converted (Lk 19:2-9).

ZADOK

Priest at the time of David and Solomon; descendant of Aaron (2Sm 8:17). Loyal to David against Absalom (2Sm 15:24-29) and Adonijah (1Kg 1).

ZALMUNNA

Midianite king killed by Gideon (Jdg 8:5-21; Ps 83:11).

ZAREPHATH

Sidonian city where Elijah stayed with a widow (1Kg 17:9-24; Lk 4:26).

ZEAL

Saul had tried to kill them in his z	2Sm 21:2
and see my z for the LORD!	2Kg 10:16
The z of the LORD of Hosts will	2Kg 19:31
z for Your house has consumed me,	Ps 69:9
z is not good without knowledge,	Pr 19:2
The z of the LORD of Hosts will	Is 9:7; 37:32
He stirs up His z like a soldier.	Is 42:13
Z for Your house will consume Me.	Jn 2:17
that they have z for God, but	Rm 10:2
deep longing, what z, what justice!	2Co 7:11
your z has stirred up most of them.	2Co 9:2
as to z, persecuting the church;	Php 3:6

ZEALOT

Jewish extremist (Mt 10:4; Ac 1:13).

ZEALOUS

because he was z for his God	Nm 25:13
I have been very z for the LORD	1Kg 19:10
and they are all z for the law.	Ac 21:20
since you are z in matters of	1Co 14:12
I was extremely z for the	Gl 1:14

ZEBAH

Midianite king killed by Gideon (Jdg 8:5-21; Ps 83:11).

ZEBEDEE

Father of James and John (Mt 4:21).

ZEBULUN

Son of Jacob and Leah (Gn 30:20). Tribe with territory between the Sea of Galilee and Mount Carmel (Jos 19:10-16).

ZECHARIAH

1. Son of Jeroboam II; king of Israel (2Kg 15:8-12).

2. Prophet after the exile; son of Berechiah; descendant of Iddo (Ezr 5:1; Zch 1:1).

3. Priest and prophet killed by Joash (2Ch 24:20-22).

4. Gatekeeper (1Ch 9:21).

5. Gibeonite (1Ch 9:37).

6. Temple musician (1Ch 15:20).

7. Teacher of the law under Jehoshaphat (2Ch 17:7).

8. Son of King Jehoshaphat; killed by his brother Jehoram (2Ch 21:2-4).

9. Advisor to Uzziah (2Ch 26:5).

10. One of Josiah's overseers (2Ch 34:12).

11. Witness used by Isaiah (Is 8:2).

12. Name of two who returned with Ezra (Ezr 8:3,11).

13. Ezra's messenger (Ezr 8:16).

14. Israelite who married a foreigner (Ezr 10:26).

15. Helped Ezra teach the law (Neh 8:4).

16. Priest under High Priest Jehoiakim (Neh 12:16).

17. Name of two musicians (Neh 12:35,41).

18. Descendant of Reuben (1Ch 5:7).

19. Name of several Levites (1Ch 15:18,24; 24:25; 26:2,11,14; 2Ch 20:14; 29:13; 35:8).

20. Father of John the Baptist (Lk 1:5-23, 59-79).

ZEDEKIAH

1. False prophet to Ahab (1Kg 22).

2. Son of Josiah; last king of Judah; originally called Mattaniah; sons blinded; exiled (2Kg 24:17–25:7).

3. False prophet who promised quick return from Babylon (Jr 29:21).

4. Official in Jeremiah's time (Jr 36:12).

5. Signer of Nehemiah's covenant (Neh 10:1).

ZELOPHEHAD

Manassite who had only daughters (Nm 26:33; 27:1-7; 36:2-11; Jos 17:3-4).

ZEPHANIAH

1. Levite (1Ch 6:36).

2. Prophet to Josiah; descendant of Hezekiah (Zch 1:1).

3. Priest and messenger at the time of Zedekiah and Jeremiah (Jr 21:1; 37:3).

ZERUBBABEL
Leader of those returning from exile to rebuild the temple (Ezr 2:2; 4:2; 5:2; Hg 1:1). Descendant of David and Jehoiachin; ancestor of Jesus (1Ch 3:9-19; Mt 1:13; Lk 3:27).

ZERUIAH
Mother of three of David's generals: Joab, Abishai, and Asahel (2Sm 2:18); David's relative (1Ch 2:15-16; 2Sm 17:25).

ZEUS
call Barnabas, Z,   Ac 14:12

ZIBA
Servant of Mephibosheth (2Sm 9); claimed that Mephibosheth was not loyal to David (16:1-4; 19:17,24-30).

ZIKLAG
City in Judah given to David (1Sm 27:6); plundered by Amalekites (1Sm 30).

ZILPAH
Leah's slave; mother of Gad and Asher (Gn 30:9-13).

ZIMRI
1. Son of Zerah; grandson of Judah (1Ch 2:6).

2. Simeonite slain for bringing a Midianite woman to the camp (Nm 25).

3. Chariot commander; killed Elah king of Israel; reigned seven days (1Kg 16:8-20).

4. Descendant of Saul (1Ch 8:36; 9:42).

ZIN
Wilderness region in the negev of Judah (Nm 13:21; 20:1; 33:36; 34:3; Jos 15:1).

ZION
Specifically, the stronghold in Jerusalem; also refers to the temple, hill, city, people, and heavenly city.

did capture the stronghold of Z,	2Sm 5:7
from Z, the city of David.	1Kg 8:1
and survivors from Mount Z.	2Kg 19:31
I have consecrated My King on Z,	Ps 2:6
Sing to the LORD, who dwells in Z;	Ps 9:11
Mount Z on the slopes of the north	Ps 48:2
pleasure, cause Z to prosper;	Ps 51:18
for God will save Z	Ps 69:35
Mount Z where You dwell	Ps 74:2

Salem, His dwelling place in Z.	Ps 76:2
Judah, Mount Z, which He loved.	Ps 78:68
The LORD is great in Z;	Ps 99:2
for the LORD will rebuild Z;	Ps 102:16
LORD restored the fortunes of Z,	Ps 126:1
For the LORD has chosen Z;	Ps 132:13
wept when we remembered Z.	Ps 137:1
Sing us one of the songs of Z.	Ps 137:3
Daughter Z is abandoned	Is 1:8
instruction will go out of Z	Is 2:3
My people who dwell in Z,	Is 10:24
king on Mount Z in Jerusalem,	Is 24:23
laid a stone in Z, a tested stone	Is 28:16
and come to Z with singing,	Is 35:10
Z, herald of good news,	Is 40:9
I will put salvation in Z,	Is 46:13
For the LORD will comfort Z;	Is 51:3
says to Z, "Your God reigns!"	Is 52:7
The Redeemer will come to Z,	Is 59:20
Z of the Holy One of Israel.	Is 60:14
Get up, let's go up to Z, to the LORD	Jr 31:6
Blow the horn in Z; sound the alarm	Jl 2:1
for the LORD dwells in Z.	Jl 3:21
The LORD roars from Z	Am 1:2
Woe to those ... at ease in Z	Am 6:1
be a deliverance on Mount Z,	Ob 17
instruction will go out of Z	Mc 4:2
Sing for joy, Daughter Z;	Zph 3:14
I am extremely jealous for Z;	Zch 8:2
Rejoice greatly, Daughter Z!	Zch 9:9
Tell Daughter Z, "See, your King	Mt 21:5
Fear no more, Daughter Z,	Jn 12:15
a stone in Z to stumble over,	Rm 9:33
The Liberator will come from Z;	Rm 11:26
I lay a stone in Z, a chosen and	1Pt 2:6
there on Mount Z stood the Lamb,	Rv 14:1

ZIPPORAH
Daughter of Reuel; wife of Moses; mother of Gershom and Eliezer (Ex 2:21-22; 18:4). Circumcised Gershom (4:24-25).

ZITHER
the horn, flute, z, lyre, harp,   Dn 3:5

ZOAR
City in the Jordan Valley near Sodom (Gn 13:10; 14:2,8; 19:22,30; Dt 34:3; Is 15:5)

ZOPHAR
One of Job's friends (Jb 2:11).

NUMBERS

〜∞〜

10

Suppose 10 are found there?	Gn 18:32
and changed my wages 10 times.	Gn 31:7
better to you than 10 sons?	1Sm 1:8
We have 10 shares in the king,	2Sm 19:43
I will give you 10 tribes,	1Kg 11:31
the shadow go back 10 steps.	2Kg 20:10
test your servants for 10 days.	Dn 1:12
The 10 horns are 10 kings who will	Dn 7:24
Bring the full 10 percent into	Mal 3:10
will be like 10 virgins who took	Mt 25:1
to the one who has 10 talents.	Mt 25:28
woman who has 10 silver coins,	Lk 15:8
Were not 10 cleansed?	Lk 17:17
mina has earned 10 more minas.	Lk 19:16
have tribulation for 10 days.	Rv 2:10
He had 10 horns and seven heads	Rv 13:1
The 10 horns you saw are 10 kings	Rv 17:12

11

and 11 stars were bowing down to	Gn 37:9
make 11 of these curtains.	Ex 26:7
The 11 disciples traveled to	Mt 28:16
numbered with the 11 apostles.	Ac 1:26

12

He will father 12 tribal leaders	Gn 17:20
Jacob had 12 sons:	Gn 35:22
altar and 12 pillars for the 12 tribes	Ex 24:4
The 12 stones are to correspond	Ex 28:21
Take 12 stones from this place	Jos 4:3
cloak ... tore it into 12 pieces,	1Kg 11:30
Elijah took 12 stones	1Kg 18:31
12 male goats as a sin offering	Ezr 6:17
the names of the 12 apostles:	Mt 10:2
they picked up 12 baskets full	Mt 14:20
on 12 thrones, judging	
the 12 tribes	Mt 19:28
(She was 12 years old.)	Mk 5:42
When He was 12 years old, they	Lk 2:42
Aren't there 12 hours in a day	Jn 11:9
there were about 12 men in all.	Ac 19:7
To the 12 tribes in the	Jms 1:1
and a crown of 12 stars on her	Rv 12:1

12 foundations, and ... the	
12 names of the Lamb's	
12 apostles.	Rv 21:14
The 12 gates are 12 pearls;	Rv 21:21
life bearing 12 kinds of fruit	Rv 22:2

13

Ishmael was 13 years old when	Gn 17:25
Levites ... received 13 cities by lot	Jos 21:4
after 13 years of construction.	1Kg 7:1

14

until the Messiah, 14 generations.	Mt 1:17
Then after 14 years I went up	Gl 2:1

15

of his spear weighed 15 pounds.	1Sm 17:7
two cherubim 15 feet high	1Kg 6:23
wingspan was 15 feet from tip to	1Kg 6:24
I will add 15 years to your life	2Kg 20:6
I bought her for 15 shekels	Hs 3:2

17

At 17 years of age, Joseph	Gn 37:2

18

disabled by a spirit for over 18	Lk 13:11

20

For 20 years I have worked in	Gn 31:41
sold him for 20 pieces of silver	Gn 37:28
registered, 20 years old or more,	Ex 30:14
those who are 20 years old or more	Nm 1:3
the nails was 20 ounces of gold	2Ch 3:9
Each contained 20 or 30 gallons	Jn 2:6

24

toes on each foot—24 in all.	2Sm 21:20
on the thrones sat 24 elders	Rv 4:4
and the 24 elders fell down	Rv 5:8
24 elders ... worshiped God,	Rv 11:16; 19:4

25

Levites: From 25 years old	Nm 8:24
there were about 25 men at the	Ezk 8:16

30

Joseph was 30 years old when he	Gn 41:46
He had 30 sons who rode on 30	Jdg 10:4
Saul was 30 years old when he	1Sm 13:1
David was 30 years old when he	2Sm 5:4
The Levites 30 years old and	1Ch 23:3
my wages, 30 pieces of silver	Zch 11:12
weighed out 30 pieces of silver	Mt 26:15

They took the 30 pieces of	Mt 27:9
30, 60, and 100 times	Mk 4:20
Jesus was about 30 years old and	Lk 3:23
contained 20 or 30 gallons.	Jn 2:6

33

Hebron and 33 years in Jerusalem.	1Kg 2:11

37

There were 37 in all.	2Sm 23:39

40

rain fell ... 40 days and 40 nights.	Gn 7:12
Isaac was 40 years old when he	Gn 25:20
on the mountain 40 days and 40	Ex 24:18
in the wilderness for 40 years	Nm 14:33
may be flogged with 40 lashes,	Dt 25:3
I was 40 years old when Moses	Jos 14:7
was peaceful 40 years,	Jdg 3:11; 5:31; 8:28
he reigned 40 years.	2Sm 5:4
he walked 40 days and 40 nights	1Kg 19:8
For 40 years I was disgusted with	Ps 95:10
I have assigned you 40 days,	Ezk 4:6
be uninhabited for 40 years.	Ezk 29:11
presented to Me during the 40 years	Am 5:25
In 40 days Nineveh will be	Jnh 3:4
40 days to be tempted by the Devil.	Lk 4:2
appearing to them during 40 days	Ac 1:3
the man was over 40 years old	Ac 4:22
sacrifices for 40 years in the desert,	Ac 7:42
from the Jews 40 lashes minus	2Co 11:24
was He "provoked for 40 years"?	Heb 3:17

42

and mauled 42 of the youths.	2Kg 2:24
trample the holy city for 42 months.	Rv 11:2
authority to act for 42 months.	Rv 13:5

46

This sanctuary took 46 years to build	Jn 2:20

48

cities ... Levites will be 48,	Nm 35:7

49

sabbatic years amounts to 49.	Lv 25:8

50

What if there are 50 righteous	Gn 18:24
You are to count 50 days until	Lv 23:16
But at 50 years old he is to retire	Nm 8:25
sent a captain of 50 with his 50	2Kg 1:9
in groups of about 50 each.	Lk 9:14
You aren't 50 years old yet,	Jn 8:57

52

wall was completed in 52 days,	Neh 6:15

60

if the person is 60 years or more,	Lv 27:7
increased 30, 60, and 100 times	Mk 4:8
she is at least 60 years old,	1Tm 5:9

62

be seven weeks and 62 weeks.	Dn 9:25

66

persons ... who came to Egypt: 66.	Gn 46:26

70

had come to Egypt: 70 persons.	Gn 46:27
water and 70 date palms,	Ex 15:27
and 70 of Israel's elders,	Ex 24:1,9
{the Spirit} on the 70 elders.	Nm 11:25
Gideon had 70 sons, his own	Jdg 8:30
All 70 of the king's sons were	2Kg 10:6
until 70 years were fulfilled.	2Ch 36:21
Tyre will be forgotten for 70 years	Is 23:15
Babylon for 70 years.	Jr 25:11
When 70 years for Babylon	Jr 29:10
number of years ... would be 70.	Dn 9:2
but 70 times seven.	Mt 18:22
the Lord appointed 70 others,	Lk 10:1

75

450 feet long, 75 feet wide,	Gn 6:15
Abram was 75 years old when he	Gn 12:4
crown weighed 75 pounds ... gold	2Sm 12:30
of about 75 pounds of myrrh	Jn 19:39
all his relatives, 75 people in all,	Ac 7:14

80

Moses was 80 years old and Aaron	Ex 7:7
the land was peaceful 80 years.	Jdg 3:30

84

and was a widow for 84 years.	Lk 2:37

99

When Abram was 99 years old,	Gn 17:1
Abraham was 99 years old when	Gn 17:24
leave the 99 in the open field	Lk 15:4
than over 99 righteous people	Lk 15:7

100

Abraham was 100 years old when	Gn 21:5

except **100** Philistine foreskins, 1Sm 18:25
took **100** prophets and hid them, 1Kg 18:4
will receive **100** times more Mt 19:29
crop: 30, 60, and **100** times Mk 4:20
who has **100** sheep and loses one Lk 15:4

110
Joseph died at the age of **110**. Gn 50:26

120
Their days will be **120** years. Gn 6:3
Moses was **120** years old when he Dt 34:7

123
Aaron was **123** years old when he Nm 33:39

127
Now Sarah lived **127** years; Gn 23:1
who ruled **127** provinces from Est 1:1

137
length of Ishmael's life: **137** years. Gn 25:17

144
144 cubits according to human Rv 21:17

147
Jacob ... life span was **147** years. Gn 47:28

150
waters surged on the earth **150** days. Gn 7:24

153
large fish—**153** of them. Jn 21:11

175
Abraham's life: **175** years. Gn 25:7

180
Isaac lived **180** years. Gn 35:28
bridles for about **180** miles. Rv 14:20

250
and the fire consumed **250** men. Nm 26:10

276
all there were **276** of us on the Ac 27:37

300
I will deliver you with the **300** men Jdg 7:7
He raised his spear against **300** 2Sm 23:18
and **300** concubines, 1Kg 11:3
been sold for more than **300** denarii Mk 14:5

390
you lie on your side, **390** days. Ezk 4:9

400
will be ... oppressed **400** years. Gn 15:13

and the **400** prophets of Ahserah 1Kg 18:19
and oppress them for **400** years. Ac 7:6

430
lived in Egypt was **430** years. Ex 12:40
which came **430** years later, Gl 3:17

450
The ark will be **450** feet long, Gn 6:15
with the **450** prophets of Baal 1Kg 18:19
This all took about **450** years. Ac 13:20

500
one out of {every} **500** humans, Nm 31:28
One owed **500** denarii, and the Lk 7:41
to over **500** brothers at one 1Co 15:6

600
Noah was **600** years old when the Gn 7:6
David and the **600** men 1Sm 30:9

666
of a man. His number is **666**. Rv 13:18

700
He had **700** wives who were 1Kg 11:3

777
Lamech's life lasted **777** years; Gn 5:31

800
He wielded his spear against **800** 2Sm 23:8

895
Mahalalel's life lasted **895** years; Gn 5:17

900
Jabin had **900** iron chariots, Jdg 4:3

905
Enosh's life lasted **905** years; Gn 5:11

910
Kenan's life lasted **910** years; Gn 5:14

912
Seth's life lasted **912** years; Gn 5:8

930
Adam's life lasted **930** years; Gn 5:5

950
Noah's life lasted **950** years; Gn 9:29

962
Jared's life lasted **962** years; Gn 5:20

969
Methuselah's life lasted **969** years; Gn 5:27

1,000

1,000 yards between ... and the ark	Jos 3:4
a donkey I have killed 1,000 men.	Jdg 15:16
one day is like 1,000 years,	2Pt 3:8
and bound him for 1,000 years.	Rv 20:2
reign with Him for 1,000 years.	Rv 20:6

1,005

and his songs numbered 1,005.	1Kg 4:32

1,100

give you 1,100 pieces of silver.	Jdg 16:5
He returned the 1,100 pieces of	Jdg 17:3

1,260

they will prophesy for 1,260 days,	Rv 11:3
to be fed there for 1,260 days.	Rv 12:6

1,290

there will be 1,290 days.	Dn 12:11

1,335

for and reaches 1,335 days.	Dn 12:12

2,000

herd of about 2,000 rushed down	Mk 5:13

2,300

For 2,300 evenings and mornings	Dn 8:14

3,000

Solomon composed 3,000 proverbs	1Kg 4:32
that day about 3,000 people were	Ac 2:41

4,000

those who ate were 4,000 men,	Mt 15:38

5,000

who ate were about 5,000 men,	Mt 14:21
the five loaves for the 5,000	Mt 16:9
of the men came to about 5,000.	Ac 4:4

7,000

But I will leave 7,000 in Israel	1Kg 19:18
I have left 7,000 men for Myself	Rm 11:4
and 7,000 people were killed in	Rv 11:13

10,000

100 of you will pursue 10,000;	Lv 26:8
turned back, but 10,000 remained.	Jdg 7:3
you are worth 10,000 of us.	2Sm 18:3
one who owed 10,000 talents was	Mt 18:24
if he is able with 10,000 to oppose	Lk 14:31
you can have 10,000 instructors	1Co 4:15
than 10,000 words in {another	1Co 14:19

12,000

12,000 sealed from the tribe of	Rv 7:5
with the rod at 12,000 stadia.	Rv 21:16

20,000

comes against him with 20,000?	Lk 14:31

24,000

in the plague numbered 24,000.	Nm 25:9
were 24,000 in each division	1Ch 27:1

40,000

Solomon had 40,000 stalls	1Kg 4:26

50,000

value, and found it to be 50,000	Ac 19:19

75,000

gave Pul 75,000 pounds of silver	2Kg 15:19
They killed 75,000 of those who	Est 9:16

80,000

porters and 80,000 stonecutters	1Kg 5:15

100,000

to pay king of Israel 100,000 lambs	2Kg 3:4

120,000

22,000 cattle and 120,000 sheep.	1Kg 8:63
has more than 120,000 people who	Jnh 4:11

144,000

144,000 sealed from every tribe	Rv 7:4
with Him were 144,000 who had	Rv 14:1

185,000

angel ... struck down 185,000	2Kg 19:35

400,000

400,000 armed foot-soldiers.	Jdg 20:2

500,000

and 500,000 men from Judah.	2Sm 24:9

600,000

about 600,000 soldiers on foot,	Ex 12:37
middle of a people with 600,000	Nm 11:21

603,550

registered group, 603,550 men.	Ex 38:26
registered numbered 603,550.	Nm 1:46

800,000

800,000 fighting men from Israel	2Sm 24:9

1,100,000

there were 1,100,000 swordsmen	1Ch 21:5

OWN THE ENTIRE SERIES!

Perfect in Content. Convenient in Price.